Commonly Used Notation

b	Retention or plowback ratio
C	Call option value
CF	Cash flow
D	Duration
E	Exchange rate
$E(x)$	Expected value of random variable x
F	Futures price
e	2.718, the base for the natural logarithm, used for continuous compounding
e_{it}	The firm-specific return, also called the residual return, of security i in period t
f	Forward rate of interest
g	Growth rate of dividends
H	Hedge ratio for an option, sometimes called the option's delta
i	Inflation rate
k	Market capitalization rate, the required rate of return on a firm's stock
ln	Natural logarithm function
M	The market portfolio
$N(d)$	Cumulative normal function, the probability that a standard normal random variable will have value less than d
p	Probability
P	Put value
PV	Present value
P/E	Price-to-earnings multiple
r	Rate of return on a security; for fixed-income securities, r may denote the rate of interest for a particular period

r_f	The risk-free rate of interest
r_M	The rate of return on the market portfolio
ROE	Return on equity, incremental economic earnings per dollar reinvested in the firm
S_p	Reward-to-volatility ratio of a portfolio, also called Sharpe's measure; the excess expected return divided by the standard deviation
t	Time
T_p	Treynor's measure for a portfolio, excess expected return divided by beta
V	Intrinsic value of a firm, the present value of future dividends per share
X	Exercise price of an option
y	Yield to maturity
α	Rate of return beyond the value that would be forecast from the market's return and the systematic risk of the security
β	Systematic or market risk of a security
ρ_{ij}	Correlation coefficient between returns on securities i and j
σ	Standard deviation
σ^2	Variance
$\text{Cov}(r_i, r_j)$	Covariance between returns on securities i and j

Welcome to the Educational Version of Market Insight!

www.mhhe.com/edumarketinsight

Check out your textbook's website for details on how this special offer enhances the value of your purchase!

1. To get started, use your web browser to go to **www.mhhe.com/edumarketinsight**

2. Enter your site ID exactly as it appears below.

3. You may be prompted to enter the site ID for future use—please keep this card.

Your site ID is:

> zk194a15

STANDARD &POOR'S

ISBN 978-0-07-336772-9
MHID 0-07-336772-9

 McGraw-Hill Irwin

*If you purchased a used book, this site ID may have expired.

ESSENTIALS *of* INVESTMENTS

The McGraw-Hill/Irwin Series in Finance, Insurance and Real Estate

Stephen A. Ross
Franco Modigliani Professor of Finance and Economics
Sloan School of Management
Massachusetts Institute of Technology
Consulting Editor

FINANCIAL MANAGEMENT

Adair
Excel Applications for Corporate Finance
First Edition
Block and Hirt
Foundations of Financial Management
Twelfth Edition
Brealey, Myers, and Allen
Principles of Corporate Finance
Ninth Edition
Brealey, Myers, and Allen
Principles of Corporate Finance, Concise Edition
First Edition
Brealey, Myers, and Marcus
Fundamentals of Corporate Finance
Fifth Edition
Brooks
FinGame Online 5.0
Bruner
Case Studies in Finance: Managing for Corporate Value Creation
Fifth Edition
Chew
The New Corporate Finance: Where Theory Meets Practice
Third Edition
DeMello
Cases in Finance
Second Edition
Grinblatt (editor)
Stephen A. Ross, Mentor: Influence through Generations
Grinblatt and Titman
Financial Markets and Corporate Strategy
Second Edition
Helfert
Techniques of Financial Analysis: A Guide to Value Creation
Eleventh Edition
Higgins
Analysis for Financial Management
Eighth Edition
Kester, Ruback, and Tufano
Case Problems in Finance
Twelfth Edition

Ross, Westerfield and Jaffe
Corporate Finance
Eighth Edition
Ross, Westerfield, Jaffe, and Jordan
Corporate Finance: Core Principles and Applications
First Edition
Ross, Westerfield, and Jordan
Essentials of Corporate Finance
Sixth Edition
Ross, Westerfield and Jordan
Fundamentals of Corporate Finance
Eighth Edition
Shefrin
Behavioral Corporate Finance: Decisions that Create Value
First Edition
White
Financial Analysis with an Electronic Calculator
Sixth Edition

INVESTMENTS

Adair
Excel Applications for investments
First Edition
Bodie, Kane, and Marcus
Essentials of Investments
Seventh Edition
Bodie, Kane, and Marcus
Investments
Eighth Edition
Hirt and Block
Fundamentals of Investment Management
Ninth Edition
Hirschey and Nofsinger
Investments: Analysis and Behavior
First Edition
Jordan and Miller
Fundamentals of Investments: Valuation and Management
Fourth Edition

FINANCIAL INSTITUTIONS AND MARKETS

Rose and Hudgins
Bank Management and Financial Services
Seventh Edition
Rose and Marquis
Money and Capital Markets: Financial Institutions and Instruments in a Global Marketplace
Tenth Edition

Saunders and Cornett
Financial Institutions Management: A Risk Management Approach
Sixth Edition
Saunders and Cornett
Financial Markets and Institutions: An Introduction to the Risk Management Approach
Third Edition

INTERNATIONAL FINANCE

Eun and Resnick
International Financial Management
Fourth Edition
Kuemmerle
Case Studies in International Entrepreneurship: Managing and Financing Ventures in the Global Economy
First Edition

REAL ESTATE

Brueggeman and Fisher
Real Estate Finance and Investments
Thirteenth Edition
Corgel, Ling and Smith
Real Estate Perspectives: An Introduction to Real Estate
Fourth Edition
Ling and Archer
Real Estate Principles: A Value Approach
Second Edition

FINANCIAL PLANNING AND INSURANCE

Allen, Melone, Rosenbloom, and Mahoney
Retirement Plans: 401(k)s, IRAs, and Other Deferred Compensation Approaches
Tenth Edition
Altfest
Personal Financial Planning
First Edition
Harrington and Niehaus
Risk Management and Insurance
Second Edition
Kapoor, Dlabay, and Hughes
Focus on Personal Finance: An Active Approach to Help You Develop Successful Financial Skills
Second Edition
Kapoor, Dlabay, and Hughes
Personal Finance
Eighth Edition

ESSENTIALS *of* INVESTMENTS

Seventh Edition

ZVI BODIE

Boston University

ALEX KANE

University of California, San Diego

ALAN J. MARCUS

Boston College

McGraw-Hill
Irwin

Boston   Burr Ridge, IL   Dubuque, IA   New York   San Francisco   St. Louis
Bangkok   Bogotá   Caracas   Kuala Lumpur   Lisbon   London   Madrid   Mexico City
Milan   Montreal   New Delhi   Santiago   Seoul   Singapore   Sydney   Taipei   Toronto

ESSENTIALS OF INVESTMENTS

Published by McGraw-Hill/Irwin, a business unit of The McGraw-Hill Companies, Inc., 1221 Avenue of the Americas, New York, NY, 10020. Copyright © 2008, 2007, 2004, 2001, 1998, 1995, 1992 by The McGraw-Hill Companies, Inc. All rights reserved. No part of this publication may be reproduced or distributed in any form or by any means, or stored in a database or retrieval system, without the prior written consent of The McGraw-Hill Companies, Inc., including, but not limited to, in any network or other electronic storage or transmission, or broadcast for distance learning.

Some ancillaries, including electronic and print components, may not be available to customers outside the United States.

This book is printed on acid-free paper.

1 2 3 4 5 6 7 8 9 0 WCK/WCK 0 9 8 7

ISBN 978-0-07-340517-9
MHID 0-07-340517-5

Executive editor: *Michele Janicek*
Developmental editor II: *Christina Kouvelis*
Marketing manager: *Ashley Smith*
Managing editor: *Lori Koetters*
Lead production supervisor: *Michael R. McCormick*
Senior designer: *Cara David*
Lead media project manager: *Cathy L. Tepper*
Cover design: *Eric Kass, funnel.tv*
Interior design: *Jenny El-Shamy*
Typeface: *10/12 Times Roman*
Compositor: *Laserwords Private Limited*
Printer: *Quebecor World Versailles Inc.*

Library of Congress Cataloging-in-Publication Data

Bodie, Zvi.
    Essentials of investments / Zvi Bodie, Alex Kane, Alan J. Marcus. —7th ed.
       p. cm. — (The McGraw-Hill/Irwin series in finance, insurance, and real estate)
    Includes index.
    ISBN-13: 978-0-07-340517-9 (alk. paper)
    ISBN-10: 0-07-340517-5 (alk. paper)
    1. Investments. I. Kane, Alex. II. Marcus, Alan J. III. Title.
HG4521.B563 2008
332.6—dc22   2007027273

www.mhhe.com

To our wives and eight wonderful daughters.

ABOUT THE AUTHORS

Zvi Bodie
Boston University

Zvi Bodie is Professor of Finance and Economics at Boston University School of Management. He holds a PhD from the Massachusetts Institute of Technology and has served on the finance faculty at Harvard Business School and MIT's Sloan School of Management. Professor Bodie has published widely on pension finance and investment strategy in leading professional journals. His books include *Foundations of Pension Finance, Pensions in the U.S. Economy, Issues in Pension Economics,* and *Financial Aspects of the U.S. Pension System.* His textbook *Investments,* co-authored with Alex Kane and Alan Marcus, is the market leader and is used in certification programs of the Financial Planning Association and the Society of Actuaries. His textbook *Finance* is co-authored by Nobel Prize–winning economist Robert C. Merton. Professor Bodie is a member of the Pension Research Council of the Wharton School, University of Pennsylvania. His latest book is *Worry-Free Investing: A Safe Approach to Achieving Your Lifetime Financial Goals.*

Alex Kane
University of California, San Diego

Alex Kane is Professor of Finance and Economics at the Graduate School of International Relations and Pacific Studies at the University of California, San Diego. He has been Visiting Professor at the Faculty of Economics, University of Tokyo; Graduate School of Business, Harvard; Kennedy School of Government, Harvard; and Research Associate, National Bureau of Economic Research. An author of many articles in finance and management journals, Professor Kane's research is mainly in corporate finance, portfolio management, and capital markets.

Alan J. Marcus
Boston College

Alan Marcus is Professor of Finance in the Wallace E. Carroll School of Management at Boston College. He received his PhD from MIT, has been a Visiting Professor at MIT's Sloan School of Management and Athens Laboratory of Business Administration, and has served as a Research Fellow at the National Bureau of Economic Research, where he participated in both the Pension Economics and the Financial Markets and Monetary Economics Groups. Professor Marcus also spent two years at the Federal Home Loan Mortgage Corporation (Freddie Mac), where he helped to develop mortgage pricing and credit risk models. Professor Marcus has published widely in the fields of capital markets and portfolio theory. He currently serves on the Research Foundation Advisory Board of the CFA Institute.

BRIEF CONTENTS

CONTENTS

The last two decades have brought rapid, profound, and ongoing change to the investments industry. This is due in part to an abundance of newly designed securities, in part to the creation of new trading strategies that would have been impossible without concurrent advances in computer and communications technology, and in part to continuing advances in the theory of investments. Of necessity, our text has evolved along with the financial markets. In this edition, we address many of the changes in the investment environment.

At the same time, many basic *principles* remain important. We continue to organize our book around one basic theme—that *security markets are nearly efficient,* meaning that most securities are usually priced appropriately given their risk and return attributes. There are few free lunches found in markets as competitive as the financial market. This simple observation is, nevertheless, remarkably powerful in its implications for the design of investment strategies, and our discussions of strategy are always guided by the implications of the efficient markets hypothesis. While the degree of market efficiency is, and will always be, a matter of debate, we hope our discussions throughout the book convey a good dose of healthy skepticism concerning much conventional wisdom.

This text also continues to emphasize *asset allocation* more than most other books. We prefer this emphasis for two important reasons. First, it corresponds to the procedure that most individuals actually follow when building an investment portfolio. Typically, you start with all of your money in a bank account, only then considering how much to invest in something riskier that might offer a higher expected return. The logical step at this point is to consider other risky asset classes, such as stock, bonds, or real estate. This is an asset allocation decision.

Second, in most cases the asset allocation choice is far more important than specific security-selection decisions in determining overall investment performance. Asset allocation is the primary determinant of the risk-return profile of the investment portfolio, and so it deserves primary attention in a study of investment policy.

Our book also focuses on investment analysis, which allows us to present the practical applications of investment theory, and to convey insights of practical value. In this edition of the text, we have continued to expand a systematic collection of Excel spreadsheets that give you tools to explore concepts more deeply than was previously possible. These spreadsheets are available on the text's Web site (**www.mhhe.com/bkm**), and provide a taste of the sophisticated analytic tools available to professional investors.

In our efforts to link theory to practice, we also have attempted to make our approach consistent with that of the CFA Institute. The Institute administers an education and certification program to candidates for the title of Chartered Financial Analyst (CFA). The CFA curriculum represents the consensus of a committee of distinguished scholars and practitioners regarding the core of knowledge required by the investment professional.

This text will introduce you to the major issues of concern to all investors. It can give you the skills to conduct a sophisticated assessment of current issues and debates covered by both the popular media and more specialized finance journals. Whether you plan to become an investment professional, or simply a sophisticated individual investor, you will find these skills essential.

Zvi Bodie
Alex Kane
Alan J. Marcus

ORGANIZATION of the Seventh Edition

Essentials of Investments, Seventh Edition, is intended as a textbook on investment analysis most applicable for a student's first course in investments. The chapters are written in a modular format to give instructors the flexibility to either omit certain chapters or rearrange their order. The highlights in the margins describe updates for this edition.

This part lays out the general framework for the investment process in a nontechnical manner. We discuss the major players in the financial markets and provide an overview of security types and trading mechanisms. These chapters make it possible for instructors to assign term projects analyzing securities early in the course.

Updated to reflect changes in financial markets such as electronic communication networks (ECNs) and market consolidation—the most current textbook available!

Includes excerpts from the "Code of Ethics and Standards of Professional Conduct" of the CFA Institute.

Contains the core of modern portfolio theory.For courses emphasizing security analysis, this part may be skipped without loss of continuity.

All data are updated in this edition and are available on the Web through our Online Learning Center.

This chapter introduces simple in-chapter spreadsheets that can be used to compute investment opportunity sets and the index model. The spreadsheet material is modular; it can be integrated with class material, but also may be skipped without problem.

This chapter has greater focus on the use of factor and index models as a means to understand and measure various risk exposures.

Updated discussion on evidence concerning market efficiency.

Extensive new material on behavioral finance. This new material also provides a foundation for the study of technical analysis.

First of three parts on security valuation

Includes spreadsheets for analyzing bond prices and yields, for example, pricing in-between coupon dates.

Contains spreadsheet material on duration and convexity.

Presented in a "top-down" manner, starting with the broad macroeconomic environment before moving to more specific analysis.

Current coverage of how international political developments have had major impacts on economic prospects.

Contains free cash flow equity valuation models as well as a discussion of corporate earnings management strategies.

Contains section on quality of earnings and the veracity of financial reports as well as a section on economic value added.

These markets have become crucial and integral to the financial universe and are major sources of innovation.

Thorough introduction to option payoffs, strategies, and securities with embedded options.

In-chapter spreadsheet material on the Black-Scholes model and estimation of implied volatility.

Material on active management has been unified in one part. Ideal for closing-semester unit on applying theory to actual portfolio management.

Evidence on international correlation and the benefits of diversification.

Extensive spreadsheet analysis of the interaction of taxes and inflation on long-term financial strategies.

Modeled after the CFA Institute curriculum, this chapter also includes guidelines on "How to Become a Chartered Financial Analyst."

Pedagogical Features

Chapter Objectives
Each chapter begins with a summary of the chapter objectives, providing students with an overview of the concepts they should understand after reading the chapter. A chapter overview follows.

AFTER STUDYING THIS CHAPTER YOU SHOULD BE ABLE TO:

- Define an investment.
- Distinguish between real assets and financial assets.
- Describe the major steps in the construction of an investment portfolio.
- Identify major participants in financial markets.
- Identify types of financial markets and recent trends in those markets.

What constitutes a satisfactory investment portfolio? Until the early 1970s, a reasonable answer would have been a bank savings account (a risk-free asset) plus a risky portfolio of U.S. stocks. Nowadays, investors have access to a vastly wider array of assets and may contemplate complex portfolio strategies that may include foreign stocks and bonds, real estate, precious metals, and collectibles. Even more complex strategies may include futures, options and other derivatives to insure portfolios against unacceptable losses. How might such portfolios be constructed?

Clearly every individual security must be judged on its contributions to both

Chapter Overview
Each chapter begins with a brief narrative to explain the concepts that will be covered in more depth. Relevant Web sites related to chapter material can be found on the book Web site at **www.mhhe.com/bkm**.

With decimal pricing, spread can be... The average... bid-ask... in the NYSE is less than 5 cents.

Stop orders are similar to limit orders in that the trade is not to be executed unless the stock hits a price limit. For *stop-loss orders*, the stock is to be *sold* if its price falls *below* a stipulated level. As the name suggests, the order lets the stock be sold to stop further losses from accumulating. Similarly, *stop-buy orders* specify that a stock should be bought when its price rises above a limit. These trades often accompany *short sales* (sales of securities you don't own but have borrowed from your broker) and are used to limit potential losses from the short position. Short sales are discussed in greater detail later in this chapter. Figure 3.6 organizes these types of trades in a convenient matrix.

stop order
Trade is not to be executed unless stock hits a price limit.

FIGURE 3.5
The limit order book for Intel on the Archipelago market, January 19, 2007.

Source: Archipelago Holdings, Inc.'s Archipelago Exchange®.
www.tradearca.com

Key Terms in the Margin
Key terms are indicated in color and defined in the margin the first time the term is used. A glossary is available on the book Web site at **www.mhhe.com/bkm**.

Numbered Equations
Key equations are called out in the text and identified by equation numbers. Equations that are frequently used are also featured on the text's end sheets for convenient reference.

we set after-tax yields equal and solve for the *equivalent taxable yield* of the tax-exempt bond. This is the rate a taxable bond would need to offer in order to match the after-tax yield on the tax-free municipal.

$$r(1 - t) = r_m \qquad \text{(2.1)}$$

or

$$r = \frac{r_m}{1 - t} \qquad \text{(2.2)}$$

Thus, the equivalent taxable yield is simply the tax-free rate divided by $1 - t$. Table 2.3 presents equivalent taxable yields for several municipal yields and tax rates.

This... frequently... appears in... market... literature... for tax-exempt municipal bond funds

On the **MARKET FRONT**

GOOGLING FOR GOLD

With the news that shares of online search giant Google Inc. (**GOOG**) had crossed the lofty $400-per-share mark in November 2005, the world may have witnessed something akin to the birth of a new financial planetary system. Given its market cap of $120 billion, double that of its nearest competitor, Yahoo!, Google now has the gravitational pull to draw in a host of institutions and company matchmakers unable to resist the potential profit opportunities. Google stock, with a price-earnings ratio of 70, represents one of the richest deal-making currencies anywhere. That heft has attracted a growing galaxy of entrepreneurs, venture capitalists, and investment bankers, all of whom are orbiting Google in the hopes of selling it anything

start-up companies. Instead of nurturing the most promising start-ups with an eye toward taking the fledgling businesses public, a growing number of VCs (venture capitalists) now scour the landscape for anyone with a technology or service that might fill a gap in Google's portfolio. Google itself and not the larger market has become the exit strategy as VCs plan for the day they can take their money out of their start-ups. Business founders have felt the tug as well. "You're hearing about a lot of entrepreneurs pitching VCs with their end goal to be acquired by Google," says Daniel Primack, editor of *PE Week Wire*, a deal-making digest popular in VC circles. "It's a complete 180 [degree turn] from the IPO craze of five years ago; now Google is looked at like NASDAQ ... then." Other entrepreneurs, meanwhile, are skip-

On the Market Front Boxes
Current articles from financial publications such as *The Wall Street Journal* are featured as boxed readings. Each box is referred to within the narrative of the text, and its real-world relevance to the chapter material is clearly defined for the students.

WebMaster Exercises
A great way to allow students to test their skills on the Internet. Each exercise consists of an activity related to practical problems and real-world scenarios. One exercise is featured within the body of the chapter and another at the end of the chapter.

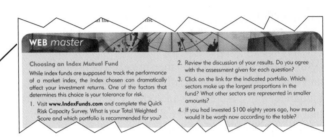

WEB *master*

Choosing an Index Mutual Fund

While index funds are supposed to track the performance of a market index, the index chosen can dramatically affect your investment returns. One of the factors that determines this choice is your tolerance for risk.

1. Visit **www.IndexFunds.com** and complete the Quick Risk Capacity Survey. What is your Total Weighted Score and which portfolio is recommended for you?

2. Review the discussion of your results. Do you agree with the assessment given for each question?

3. Click on the link for the indicated portfolio. Which sectors make up the largest proportions in the fund? What other sectors are represented in smaller amounts?

4. If you had invested $100 eighty years ago, how much would it be worth now according to the table?

Concept Checks
These self-test questions in the body of the chapter enable students to determine whether the preceding material has been understood and then reinforce understanding before students read further. Detailed solutions to the Concept Checks are found at the end of each chapter.

CONCEPT *check* **1.2** Computer networks have made it much cheaper and easier for small investors to trade for their own accounts and perform their own security analysis. What will be the likely effect on financial intermediation?

Numbered Examples
Numbered and titled examples are integrated in each chapter. Using the worked-out solutions to these examples as models, students can learn how to solve specific problems step-by-step as well as gain insight into general principles by seeing how they are applied to answer concrete questions.

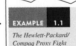

EXAMPLE 1.1

The Hewlett-Packard/ Compaq Proxy Fight

When Carly Fiorina, then the CEO of Hewlett-Packard, proposed a merger with Compaq Computer in 2001, Walter Hewlett, son of the company's founder and member of the HP board of directors, dissented. The merger had to be approved by shareholders, and Hewlett engaged in a proxy fight to block the deal. One estimate is that HP spent $150 million to lobby shareholders to support the merger; even small shareholders of HP reported receiving 20 or more phone calls from the company in support of the deal.[4] The merger ultimately was approved in an uncharacteristically close vote. No surprise that less than 1% of public companies face proxy contests in any particular year.

Excel Integration

Excel Applications

Since many courses now require students to perform analyses in spreadsheet format, Excel has been integrated throughout the book once again. It is used in examples as well as in this chapter feature which shows students how to create and manipulate spreadsheets to solve specific problems. This feature starts with an example presented in the chapter, briefly discusses how a spreadsheet can be valuable for investigating the topic, shows a sample spreadsheet, and then directs the student to the Web to work with an interactive version of the spreadsheet. The student can obtain the actual spreadsheet from the book's Web site (**www.mhhe.com/bkm**); available spreadsheets are denoted by an icon. At this site, there is a more detailed discussion on how the spreadsheet is built, and how it can be used to solve problems. As extra guidance, the spreadsheets include a comment feature that documents both inputs and outputs. Solutions for these exercises are located on the password-protected instructor site only, so instructors can assign these exercises either for homework or just for practice.

Excel application spreadsheets are available for the following:

Chapter 3: Buying on Margin; Short Sales
Chapter 6: Efficient Frontier for Many Stocks
Chapter 7: Estimating the Index Model
Chapter 11: Immunization; Convexity
Chapter 15: Options, Stock, and Lending; Straddles and Spreads
Chapter 17: Parity and Spreads
Chapter 18: Performance Attribution; Performance Measures
Chapter 19: International Portfolios

Spreadsheet exhibit templates are also available for the following:
Chapter 6: Spreadsheets 6.1–6.6
Chapter 10: Spreadsheets 10.1 & 10.2
Chapter 11: Spreadsheets 11.1 & 11.2
Chapter 13: Spreadsheets 13.1 & 13.2
Chapter 16: Spreadsheet 16.1
Chapter 20: Spreadsheets 20.1–20.10

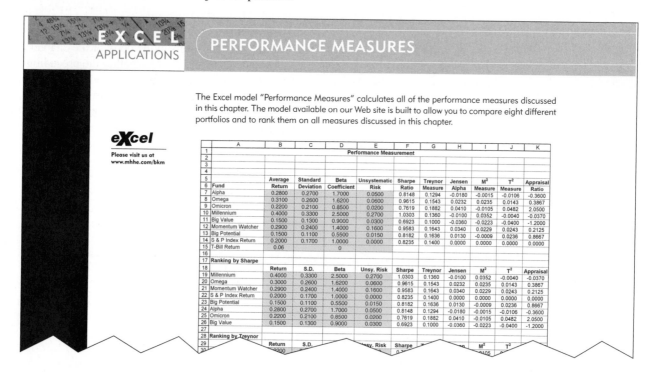

EXCEL APPLICATIONS — PERFORMANCE MEASURES

The Excel model "Performance Measures" calculates all of the performance measures discussed in this chapter. The model available on our Web site is built to allow you to compare eight different portfolios and to rank them on all measures discussed in this chapter.

eXcel
Please visit us at
www.mhhe.com/bkm

	A	B	C	D	E	F	G	H	I	J	K
1					Performance Measurement						
2											
3											
4											
5		Average	Standard	Beta	Unsystematic	Sharpe	Treynor	Jensen	M²	T²	Appraisal
6	Fund	Return	Deviation	Coefficient	Risk	Ratio	Measure	Alpha	Measure	Measure	Ratio
7	Alpha	0.2800	0.2700	1.7000	0.0500	0.8148	0.1294	-0.0180	-0.0015	-0.0106	-0.3600
8	Omega	0.3100	0.2600	1.6200	0.0600	0.9615	0.1543	0.0232	0.0235	0.0143	0.3867
9	Omicron	0.2200	0.2100	0.8500	0.0200	0.7619	0.1882	0.0410	-0.0105	0.0482	2.0500
10	Millennium	0.4000	0.3300	2.5000	0.2700	1.0303	0.1360	-0.0100	0.0352	-0.0040	-0.0370
11	Big Value	0.1500	0.1300	0.9000	0.0300	0.6923	0.1000	-0.0360	-0.0223	-0.0400	-1.2000
12	Momentum Watcher	0.2900	0.2400	1.4000	0.1600	0.9583	0.1643	0.0340	0.0229	0.0243	0.2125
13	Big Potential	0.1500	0.1100	0.5500	0.0150	0.8182	0.1636	0.0130	-0.0009	0.0236	0.8667
14	S & P Index Return	0.2000	0.1700	1.0000	0.0000	0.8235	0.1400	0.0000	0.0000	0.0000	0.0000
15	T-Bill Return	0.06		0							
16											
17	Ranking by Sharpe										
18		Return	S.D.	Beta	Unsy. Risk	Sharpe	Treynor	Jensen	M²	T²	Appraisal
19	Millennium	0.4000	0.3300	2.5000	0.2700	1.0303	0.1360	-0.0100	0.0352	-0.0040	-0.0370
20	Omega	0.3000	0.2600	1.6200	0.0600	0.9615	0.1543	0.0232	0.0235	0.0143	0.3867
21	Momentum Watcher	0.2900	0.2400	1.4000	0.1600	0.9583	0.1643	0.0340	0.0229	0.0243	0.2125
22	S & P Index Return	0.2000	0.1700	1.0000	0.0000	0.8235	0.1400	0.0000	0.0000	0.0000	0.0000
23	Big Potential	0.1500	0.1100	0.5500	0.0150	0.8182	0.1636	0.0130	-0.0009	0.0236	0.8667
24	Alpha	0.2800	0.2700	1.7000	0.0500	0.8148	0.1294	-0.0180	-0.0015	-0.0106	-0.3600
25	Omicron	0.2200	0.2100	0.8500	0.0200	0.7619	0.1882	0.0410	-0.0105	0.0482	2.0500
26	Big Value	0.1500	0.1300	0.9000	0.0300	0.6923	0.1000	-0.0360	-0.0223	-0.0400	-1.2000
27											
28	Ranking by Treynor										
29		Return	S.D.		Unsy. Risk	Sharpe			M²	T²	
30		0.2200				0.7			-0.0105		

End-of-Chapter Features

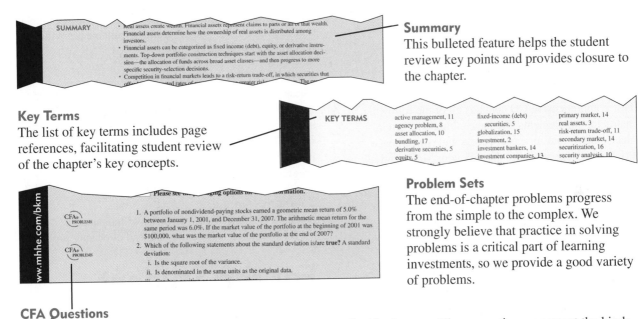

Summary

This bulleted feature helps the student review key points and provides closure to the chapter.

Key Terms

The list of key terms includes page references, facilitating student review of the chapter's key concepts.

Problem Sets

The end-of-chapter problems progress from the simple to the complex. We strongly believe that practice in solving problems is a critical part of learning investments, so we provide a good variety of problems.

CFA Questions

We provide several questions from recent CFA exams in applicable chapters. These questions represent the kinds of questions that professionals in the field believe are relevant to the practicing money manager. These problems are identified by an icon in the text margin. Appendix B, at the back of the book, lists each CFA question and the level and year of the CFA Exam it was included in, for easy reference when studying for the exam.

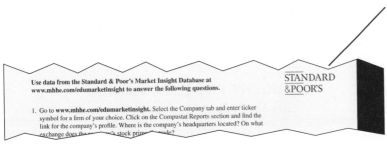

S&P Problems

Relevant chapters contain several new problems directly related to Standard & Poor's Educational Version of Market Insight. Because of our unique relationship with S&P, students have access to this remarkable database. Problems are based on market data provided by 1,000 real companies to gain better understanding of practical business situations. The site is updated daily to ensure the most current information is available.

Excel Problems

Selected end-of-chapter questions have been included that require the use of Excel. These problems are denoted with an icon. A template is available at the book Web site **www.mhhe.com/bkm**.

Supplements

For the Instructor

INSTRUCTOR'S RESOURCE CD
ISBN-13: 9780073308920 ISBN-10: 0073308927

This comprehensive CD contains all of the following instructor supplements. We have compiled them in electronic format for easier access and convenience. Print copies are available through your McGraw-Hill representative.

Instructor's Manual
Prepared by Sue Hine, Colorado State University, this instructional tool provides an integrated learning approach revised for this edition. Each chapter includes a Chapter Overview, Learning Objectives, and Presentation of Material—which outlines and organizes the material around the PowerPoint Presentation.

Test Bank
Prepared by Tim Manuel, University of Montana, contains more than 1,200 questions and will include over 300 new questions. Each question is ranked by level of difficulty (easy, medium, hard), which allows greater flexibility in creating a test. A computerized format for Windows is also available.

Computerized Test Bank
McGraw-Hill's EZ Test is a flexible and easy-to-use electronic testing program. The program allows instructors to create tests from book-specific items. It accommodates a wide range of question types, and instructors may add their own questions. Multiple versions of the test can be created, and any test can be exported for use with course management systems such as WebCT, BlackBoard, or PageOut. EZ Test Online is a new service and gives you a place to easily administer your EZ Test–created exams and quizzes online. The program is available for Windows and Macintosh environments.

PowerPoint Presentation System
These presentation slides, also developed by Sue Hine, contain Figures and Tables from the text, key points, and summaries in a visually stimulating collection of slides. These slides follow the order of the chapters, but if you have PowerPoint software, you may customize the program to fit your lecture.

Solutions Manual
Prepared by Matt Will, University of Indianapolis, provides detailed solutions to the end of chapter problems.

For the Student

SOLUTIONS MANUAL
ISBN-13: 9780073308944 ISBN-10: 0073308943

Revised by Matt Will, University of Indianapolis, provides detailed solutions to the end-of-chapter problems. The authors' involvement in the completion of the Solutions Manual ensures consistency between the solution approaches in the examples featured within the text and those presented in the manual.

STUDENT PROBLEM MANUAL
ISBN-13: 9780073308951 ISBN-10: 0073308951

Prepared by Maryellen Epplin, University of Central Oklahoma, this useful supplement contains problems created to specifically relate to the concepts discussed in each chapter. Solutions are provided at the end of each chapter in the manual. Perfect for additional practice in working through problems!

ONLINE LEARNING CENTER

www.mhhe.com/bkm
Find a wealth of information online! At this book's Web site instructors will have access to teaching supports such as electronic files of the ancillary materials. Students will have access to study materials created specifically for this text and much more. Links to additional support material will also be included. See below for a description of some of the exciting assets available to you.

Related Web Sites
A list of suggested Web sites is provided for each chapter. In order to keep Web addresses up to date, the suggested sites as well as their links are now provided online. Each chapter opener contains a reference to its related sites.

Excel Templates
There are templates for selected spreadsheets featured within the text, as well as the ones featured among the Excel Applications boxes. Selected end-of-chapter problems have also been designated as Excel problems, in which there is a template available for students to solve the problem and gain experience using spreadsheets. These templates were created by Peter R. Crabb of

Northwest Nazarene University. Each template can also be found at the book Web site **www.mhhe.com/bkm** and are denoted by an icon.

Online Quizzes
These multiple-choice questions are provided as an additional testing and reinforcement tool for students. Each quiz is organized by chapter to test the specific concepts presented in that particular chapter. Immediate scoring of the quiz will occur upon submission and the correct answers will be provided.

Standard & Poor's Educational Version of Market Insight
www.mhhe.com/edumarketinsight
McGraw-Hill/Irwin has partnered exclusively with Standard and Poor's to bring you the Educational Version of Market Insight. This rich online resource provides six years of financial data for 1,000 companies in the renowned COMPUSTAT ® database. S&P problems can be found at the end of relevant chapters of the text.

Packaging Options

Please contact your McGraw-Hill/Irwin sales representative to find out more about these exciting packaging options now available for your class.

BusinessWeek Package

Your students can subscribe to *BusinessWeek* for a special rate of $8.25 in addition to the price of the text. Students will receive a pass code card shrink-wrapped with their new text that will refer them to a registration site to receive their subscription. Subscriptions are available in print copy or digital format.

Financial Times Package

Your students can subscribe to the *Financial Times* for 15 weeks at a specially priced rate of $10 in addition to the price of the text. Students will receive a subscription card shrink-wrapped with their new text that will activate their subscriptions once they complete and submit the card. The subscription also provides access to FT.com.

Excel Applications for Investments 0073205575

by Troy Adair, University of North Carolina at Chapel Hill, can be packaged with *Essentials of Investments* at a discounted price. This supplement teaches students how to build financial models in Excel, and shows students how to use these models to solve a variety of common corporate investment problems

McGraw-Hill's Homework Manager®

Are you looking for a way to spend less time grading and to have more flexibility with the problems you assign as homework and tests? McGraw-Hill's Homework Manager is an exciting new package option developed for this text! Homework manager is a Web-based tool for instructors and students for delivering, answering, and grading end-of-chapter problems and tests, and providing a limitless supply of self-graded practice for students.

Select end-of-chapter problems are loaded into McGraw-Hill's Homework Manager, and instructors can choose to assign the exact problems as stated in the book, or algorithmic versions of them so each student has a unique set of variables for the problems. You create the assignments and control parameters such as: Do you want your students to receive hints? Is this a graded assignment or practice? and so on. The test bank is also available in McGraw-Hill's Homework Manager, giving you the ability to use those questions for online tests. Both the problems and the tests are automatically graded and the results are stored in a private grade book, which is created when you set up your class. Detailed results let you see at a glance how each student does on an assignment or an individual problem—you can even see how many tries it took them to solve it. If you order this special package, students will receive a McGraw-Hill's Homework Manager User's Guide and an access code packaged with their text.

McGraw-Hill's Homework Manager Plus™

There is also an enhanced version of McGraw-Hill's Homework Manager® through the McGraw-Hill's Homework Manager Plus package option. If you order the text packaged with McGraw-Hill's Homework Manager Plus, your students will receive McGraw-Hill's Homework Manager as described above, but with an integrated online text included. When students are in Homework Manager and need more help to solve a problem, there will be a link that takes them to the section of the text online that explains the concept they are struggling with. All of McGraw-Hill's media assets, such as videos, PowerPoint lectures, and additional online quizzing, are also integrated at the appropriate places of the online text to provide students with a full learning experience. If you order this special package, students will receive the McGraw-Hill's Homework Manager Plus card packaged with their text, which gives them access to all of these products, as well as an online homework manager User's Guide.

McGraw-Hill's Homework Manager is powered by Brownstone.

ACKNOWLEDGMENTS

We received help from many people as we prepared this book. An insightful group of reviewers commented on this and previous editions of this text. Their comments and suggestions improved the exposition of the material considerably. These reviewers all deserve special thanks for their contributions.

Sandro C. Andrade   *University of Miami*

Bala Arshanapalli   *Indiana University Northwest*

Randall S. Billingsley   *Virginia Polytechnic Institute and State University*

Howard Bohnen   *St. Cloud State University*

Paul Bolster   *Northeastern University*

Lyle Bowlin   *University of Northern Iowa*

Thor W. Bruce   *University of Miami*

Alyce R. Campbell   *University of Oregon*

Mark Castelino   *Rutgers University*

Greg Chaudoin   *Loyola University*

Ji Chen   *University of Colorado, Denver*

Mustafa Chowdhury   *Louisiana State University*

Ron Christner   *Loyola University, New Orleans*

Shane Corwin   *University of Notre Dame*

Brent Dalrymple   *University of Central Florida*

Diane Del Guercio   *University of Oregon*

David C. Distad   *University of California at Berkeley*

Gary R. Dokes   *University of San Diego*

Jeff Edwards   *Portland Community College*

Peter D. Ekman   *Kansas State University*

James Falter   *Franklin University*

James F. Feller   *Middle Tennessee State University*

Beverly Frickel   *University of Nebraska, Kearney*

Ken Froewiss   *New York University*

Phillip Ghazanfari   *California State University, Pomona*

Richard A. Grayson   *University of Georgia*

Richard D. Gritta   *University of Portland*

Deborah Gunthorpe   *University of Tennessee*

Weiyu Guo   *University of Nebraska, Omaha*

Pamela Hall   *Western Washington University*

Thomas Hamilton   *St. Mary's University*

Bing Han   *Ohio State University*

Yvette Harman   *Miami University of Ohio*

Gay Hatfield   *University of Mississippi*

Larry C. Holland   *Oklahoma State University*

Harris Hordon   *New Jersey City University*

Ron E. Hutchins   *Eastern Michigan University*

A. Can (John) Inci   *Florida State University*

Richard Johnson   *Colorado State University*

Douglas Kahl   *University of Akron*

Richard J. Kish   *Lehigh University*

Tom Krueger   *University of Wisconsin, La Crosse*

Donald Kummer   *University of Missouri, St. Louis*

Merouane Lakehal-Ayat   *St. John Fisher College*

Reinhold P. Lamb   *University of North Florida*

Angeline Lavin   *University of South Dakota*

Jim Locke   *Northern Virginia Community College*

John Loughlin   *St. Louis University*

David Louton   *Bryant College*

David Loy   *Illinois State University*

Christian Lundblad   *Indiana University*

Robert A. Lutz   *University of Utah*

Laurian Casson Lytle   *University of Wisconsin, Whitewater*

Leo Mahoney   *Bryant College*

Herman Manakyan   *Salisbury State University*

Steven V. Mann   *University of South Carolina*

Jeffrey A. Manzi   *Ohio University*

James Marchand   *Westminster College*

Robert J. Martel   *Bentley College*

Linda J. Martin   *Arizona State University*

Stanley A. Martin   *University of Colorado, Boulder*

Edward Miller   *University of New Orleans*

Walter Morales   *Louisiana State University*

Mbodja Mougoue   *Wayne State University*

Majed Muhtaseb   *California State Polytechnic University*

Deborah Murphy   *University of Tennessee, Knoxville*

Mike Murray   *Winona State University*

C. R. Narayanaswamy   *Georgia Institute of Technology*

Mike Nugent   *SUNY Stonybrook*

Raj Padmaraj   *Bowling Green University*

John C. Park   *Frostburg State University*

Percy Poon   *University of Nevada, Las Vegas*
Robert B. Porter   *University of Florida*
Dev Prasad   *University of Massachusetts, Lowell*
Rose Prasad   *Central Michigan University*
Elias A. Raad   *Ithaca College*
Murli Rajan   *University of Scranton*
Cecilia Ricci   *Montclair University*
Craig Ruff   *Georgia State University*
Tom Sanders   *University of Miami*
David Schirm   *John Carroll University*
Ravi Shukla   *Syracuse University*
Andrew Spieler   *Hofstra University*
Edwin Stuart   *Southeastern Oklahoma State University*
George S. Swales   *Southwest Missouri State University*
Paul Swanson   *University of Cincinnati*
Bruce Swensen   *Adelphi University*
Glenn Tanner   *University of Hawaii*
John L. Teall   *Pace University*
Anne Macy Terry   *West Texas A&M University*
Donald J. Thompson   *Georgia State University*
Steven Thorley   *Brigham Young University*
Steven Todd   *DePaul University*
William Trainor   *Western Kentucky University*
Cevdet Uruk   *University of Memphis*
Joseph Vu   *DePaul University*
Jessica Wachter   *New York University*
Richard Warr   *North Carolina State University*
Joe Walker   *University of Alabama at Birmingham*

William Welch   *Florida International University*
Andrew L. Whitaker   *North Central College*
Howard Whitney   *Franklin University*
Michael E. Williams   *University of Texas at Austin*
Michael Willoughby   *University of California, San Diego*
Tony Wingler   *University of North Carolina*
Annie Wong   *Western Connecticut State University*
Richard H. Yanow   *North Adams State College*
Allan Zebedee   *San Diego State University*
Zhong-guo Zhou   *California State University, Northridge*
Thomas J. Zwirlein   *University of Colorado, Colorado Springs*

For granting us permission to include many of their examination questions in the text, we are grateful to the CFA Institute.

Much credit is also due to the development and production team of McGraw-Hill/Irwin: Michele Janicek, Executive Editor; Christina Kouvelis, Developmental Editor II; Lori Koetters, Managing Editor; Ashley Smith, Marketing Manager; Michael McCormick, Lead Production Supervisor; Cara David, Senior Designer; and Cathy Tepper, Lead Media Project Manager.

Finally, once again, our most important debts are to Judy, Have, and Sheryl for their unflagging support.

Zvi Bodie
Alex Kane
Alan J. Marcus

PART ONE

ELEMENTS OF INVESTMENTS

Even a cursory glance at *The Wall Street Journal* reveals a bewildering collection of securities, markets, and financial institutions. But although it may appear so, the financial environment is not chaotic: There is rhyme and reason behind the vast array of financial instruments and the markets in which they trade.

These introductory chapters provide a bird's-eye view of the investing environment. We will give you a tour of the major types of markets in which securities trade, the trading process, and the major players in these arenas. You will see that both markets and securities have evolved to meet the changing and complex needs of different participants in the financial system.

Markets innovate and compete with each other for traders' business just as vigorously as competitors in other industries. The competition between the National Association of Securities Dealers Automatic Quotation System (Nasdaq), the New York Stock Exchange (NYSE), and a number of electronic and non-U.S. exchanges is fierce and public.

Trading practices can mean big money to investors. The explosive growth of online trading has saved them many millions of dollars in trading costs. Even more dramatically, new electronic communication networks promise to allow investors to trade directly without a broker. These advances will change the face of the investments industry, and Wall Street firms are scrambling to formulate strategies that respond to these changes.

These chapters will give you a good foundation with which to understand the basic types of securities and financial markets as well as how trading in those markets is conducted.

CHAPTERS IN THIS PART:

1 Investments: Background and Issues

2 Asset Classes and Financial Instruments

3 Securities Markets

4 Mutual Funds and Other Investment Companies

www.mhhe.com/bkm

CHAPTER
1

Investments: Background and Issues

AFTER STUDYING THIS CHAPTER
YOU SHOULD BE ABLE TO:

- Define an investment.

- Distinguish between real assets and financial assets.

- Describe the major steps in the construction of an investment portfolio.

- Identify major participants in financial markets.

- Identify types of financial markets and recent trends in those markets.

investment

Commitment of current resources in the expectation of deriving greater resources in the future.

An investment **is the _current_ commitment of money or other resources** in the expectation of reaping _future_ benefits. For example, an individual might purchase shares of stock anticipating that the future proceeds from the shares will justify both the time that her money is tied up as well as the risk of the investment. The time you will spend studying this text (not to mention its cost) also is an investment. You are forgoing either current leisure or the income you could be earning at a job in the expectation that your future career will be sufficiently enhanced to justify this commitment of time and effort. While these two investments differ in many ways, they share one key attribute that is central to all investments: You sacrifice something of value now, expecting to benefit from that sacrifice later.

This text can help you become an informed practitioner of investments. We will focus on investments in securities such as stocks, bonds, or options and futures contracts, but much of what we discuss will be useful in the analysis of any type of investment. The text will provide you with background in the organization of various securities markets, will survey the valuation and risk-management principles useful in particular markets, such as those for bonds or stocks, and will introduce you to the principles of portfolio construction.

Broadly speaking, this chapter addresses three topics that will provide a useful perspective for the material that is to come later. First, before delving into the topic of "investments," we consider the role of financial assets in the economy. We discuss the relationship between securities and the "real" assets that actually produce goods and services for consumers, and we consider why financial assets are important to the functioning of a developed economy. Given this background, we then take a first look at the types of decisions that confront investors as they assemble a portfolio of assets. These investment decisions are made in an environment where higher returns usually can be obtained only at the price of greater risk and in which it is rare to find assets that are so mispriced as to be obvious bargains. These themes—the risk-return trade-off and the efficient pricing of financial assets—are central to the investment process, so it is worth pausing for a brief discussion of their implications as we begin the text. These implications will be fleshed out in much greater detail in later chapters.

Finally, we conclude the chapter with an introduction to the organization of security markets, the various players that participate in those markets, and a brief overview of some of the more important changes in those markets in recent years. Together, these various topics should give you a feel for who the major participants are in the securities markets as well as the setting in which they act. We close the chapter with an overview of the remainder of the text.

Related Web sites for this chapter are available at www.mhhe.com/bkm.

1.1 REAL ASSETS VERSUS FINANCIAL ASSETS

The material wealth of a society is ultimately determined by the productive capacity of its economy, that is, the goods and services its members can create. This capacity is a function of the **real assets** of the economy: the land, buildings, equipment, and knowledge that can be used to produce goods and services.

In contrast to such real assets are **financial assets** such as stocks and bonds. Such securities are no more than sheets of paper or, more likely, computer entries and do not contribute directly to the productive capacity of the economy. Instead, these assets are the means by which individuals in well-developed economies hold their claims on real assets. Financial assets are claims to the income generated by real assets (or claims on income from the government). If we cannot own our own auto plant (a real asset), we can still buy shares in General Motors or Toyota (financial assets) and, thereby, share in the income derived from the production of automobiles.

While real assets generate net income to the economy, financial assets simply define the allocation of income or wealth among investors. Individuals can choose between consuming their wealth today or investing for the future. If they choose to invest, they may place their wealth in financial assets by purchasing various securities. When investors buy these securities from companies, the firms use the money so raised to pay for real assets, such as plant, equipment, technology, or inventory. So investors' returns on securities ultimately come from the income produced by the real assets that were financed by the issuance of those securities.

The distinction between real and financial assets is apparent when we compare the balance sheet of U.S. households, shown in Table 1.1, with the composition of national wealth in the United States, shown in Table 1.2. Household wealth includes financial assets such as bank accounts, corporate stock, or bonds. However, these securities, which are financial

real assets

Assets used to produce goods and services.

financial assets

Claims on real assets or the income generated by them.

3

TABLE 1.1

Balance sheet U.S. households, 2006

Assets	$ Billion	% Total	Liabilities and Net Worth	$ Billion	% Total
Real assets					
Real estate	$22,177	33.6%	Mortgages	$ 9,161	13.9%
Consumer durables	3,822	5.8	Consumer credit	2,150	3.3
Other	224	0.3	Bank & other loans	237	0.4
Total real assets	$26,223	39.7%	Security Credit	249	0.4
			Other	401	0.6
			Total liabilities	$12,199	18.5%
Financial assets					
Deposits	$ 6,251	9.5%			
Life insurance reserves	1,097	1.7			
Pension reserves	11,109	16.8			
Corporate equity	5,685	8.6			
Equity in noncorp. business	6,786	10.3			
Mutual fund shares	4,537	6.9			
Debt securities	3,216	4.9			
Other	1,126	1.7			
Total financial assets	39,807	60.3	Net worth	53,831	81.5
Total	$66,030	100.0%		$66,030	100.0%

Note: Column sums may differ from totals because of rounding error.

Source: *Flow of Funds Accounts of the United States,* Board of Governors of the Federal Reserve System, June 2006.

assets of households, are *liabilities* of the issuers of the securities. For example, a bond that you treat as an asset because it gives you a claim on interest income and repayment of principal from General Motors is a liability of General Motors, which is obligated to make these payments to you. Your asset is GM's liability. Therefore, when we aggregate over all balance sheets, these claims cancel out, leaving only real assets as the net wealth of the economy. National wealth consists of structures, equipment, inventories of goods, and land.[1]

TABLE 1.2	Assets	$ Billion
Domestic net worth	Nonresidential real estate	$13,713
	Residential real estate	22,198
	Equipment and software	3,811
	Inventories	1,634
	Consumer durables	3,843
	Total	$45,199

Note: Column sum may differ from total because of rounding error.

Source: *Flow of Funds Accounts of the United States,* Board of Governors of the Federal Reserve System, September 2006.

[1]You might wonder why real assets held by households in Table 1.1 amount to $26,223 billion, while total real assets in the domestic economy (Table 1.2) are far larger, at $45,199 billion. One major reason is that real assets held by firms, for example, property, plant, and equipment, are included as *financial* assets of the household sector, specifically through the value of corporate equity and other stock market investments. Another reason is that equity and stock investments in Table 1.1 are measured by market value, whereas the value of plant and equipment in Table 1.2 is valued at replacement cost.

We will focus almost exclusively on financial assets. But you shouldn't lose sight of the fact that the successes or failures of the financial assets we choose to purchase ultimately depend on the performance of the underlying real assets.

Are the following assets real or financial?
a. Patents
b. Lease obligations
c. Customer goodwill
d. A college education
e. A $5 bill

1.2 A TAXONOMY OF FINANCIAL ASSETS

It is common to distinguish among three broad types of financial assets: debt, equity, and derivatives. **Fixed-income** or **debt securities** promise either a fixed stream of income or a stream of income that is determined according to a specified formula. For example, a corporate bond typically would promise that the bondholder will receive a fixed amount of interest each year. Other so-called floating-rate bonds promise payments that depend on current interest rates. For example, a bond may pay an interest rate that is fixed at two percentage points above the rate paid on U.S. Treasury bills. Unless the borrower is declared bankrupt, the payments on these securities are either fixed or determined by formula. For this reason, the investment performance of debt securities typically is least closely tied to the financial condition of the issuer.

Nevertheless, debt securities come in a tremendous variety of maturities and payment provisions. At one extreme, the *money market* refers to fixed-income securities that are short term, highly marketable, and generally of very low risk. Examples of money market securities are U.S. Treasury bills or bank certificates of deposit (CDs). In contrast, the fixed-income *capital market* includes long-term securities such as Treasury bonds, as well as bonds issued by federal agencies, state and local municipalities, and corporations. These bonds range from very safe in terms of default risk (for example, Treasury securities) to relatively risky (for example, high yield or "junk" bonds). They also are designed with extremely diverse provisions regarding payments provided to the investor and protection against the bankruptcy of the issuer. We will take a first look at these securities in Chapter 2 and undertake a more detailed analysis of the fixed-income market in Part Three.

Unlike debt securities, common stock, or **equity,** in a firm represents an ownership share in the corporation. Equity holders are not promised any particular payment. They receive any dividends the firm may pay and have prorated ownership in the real assets of the firm. If the firm is successful, the value of equity will increase; if not, it will decrease. The performance of equity investments, therefore, is tied directly to the success of the firm and its real assets. For this reason, equity investments tend to be riskier than investments in debt securities. Equity markets and equity valuation are the topics of Part Four.

Finally, **derivative securities** such as options and futures contracts provide payoffs that are determined by the prices of *other* assets such as bond or stock prices. For example, a call option on a share of Intel stock might turn out to be worthless if Intel's share price remains below a threshold or "exercise" price such as $30 a share, but it can be quite valuable if the stock price rises above that level.[2] Derivative securities are so named because their values derive from the prices of other assets. For example, the value of the call option will depend on

fixed-income (debt) securities

Pay a specified cash flow over a specific period.

equity

An ownership share in a corporation.

derivative securities

Securities providing payoffs that depend on the values of other assets.

[2]A call option is the right to buy a share of stock at a given exercise price on or before the option's expiration date. If the market price of Intel remains below $30 a share, the right to buy for $30 will turn out to be valueless. If the share price rises above $30 before the option expires, however, the option can be exercised to obtain the share for only $30.

the price of Intel stock. Other important derivative securities are futures and swap contracts. We will treat these in Part Five.

Derivatives have become an integral part of the investment environment. One use of derivatives, perhaps the primary use, is to hedge risks or transfer them to other parties. This is done successfully every day, and the use of these securities for risk management is so commonplace that the multitrillion-dollar market in derivative assets is routinely taken for granted. Derivatives also can be used to take highly speculative positions, however. Every so often, one of these positions blows up, resulting in well-publicized losses of hundreds of millions of dollars. While these losses attract considerable attention, they are in fact the exception to the more common use of such securities as risk management tools. Derivatives will continue to play an important role in portfolio construction and the financial system. We will return to this topic later in the text.

In addition to these financial assets, individuals might invest directly in some real assets. For example, real estate or commodities such as precious metals or agricultural products are real assets that might form part of an investment portfolio.

1.3   FINANCIAL MARKETS AND THE ECONOMY

We stated earlier that real assets determine the wealth of an economy, while financial assets merely represent claims on real assets. Nevertheless, financial assets and the markets in which they trade play several crucial roles in developed economies. Financial assets allow us to make the most of the economy's real assets.

The Informational Role of Financial Markets

In a capitalist system, financial markets play a central role in the allocation of capital resources. Investors in the stock market ultimately decide which companies will live and which will die. If a corporation seems to have good prospects for future profitability, investors will bid up its stock price. The company's management will find it easy to issue new shares or borrow funds to finance research and development, build new production facilities, and expand its operations. The nearby box provides an illustration of this process. As Google's stock price surpassed $400 a share in 2005, it was able to expand and initiate many new business prospects. If, on the other hand, a company's prospects seem poor, investors will bid down its stock price. The company will have to downsize and may eventually disappear.

The process by which capital is allocated through the stock market sometimes seems wasteful. Some companies can be "hot" for a short period of time, attract a large flow of investor capital, and then fail after only a few years. But that is an unavoidable aspect of economic progress. It is impossible to accurately predict in advance which ventures will succeed and which will fail. But the stock market encourages allocation of capital to those firms that appear *at the time* to have the best prospects. Many smart, well-trained, and well-paid professionals analyze the prospects of firms whose shares trade on the stock market. Stock prices reflect their collective judgment.

Consumption Timing

Some individuals in an economy are earning more than they currently wish to spend. Others, for example, retirees, spend more than they currently earn. How can you shift your purchasing power from high-earnings periods to low-earnings periods of life? One way is to "store" your wealth in financial assets. In high-earnings periods, you can invest your savings in financial assets such as stocks and bonds. In low-earnings periods, you can sell these assets to provide funds for your consumption needs. By so doing, you can "shift" your consumption over the course of your lifetime, thereby allocating your consumption to periods that provide the greatest satisfaction. Thus, financial markets allow individuals to separate decisions concerning current consumption from constraints that otherwise would be imposed by current earnings.

GOOGLING FOR GOLD

With the news that shares of online search giant Google Inc. (**GOOG**) had crossed the lofty $400-per-share mark in November 2005, the world may have witnessed something akin to the birth of a new financial planetary system. Given its market cap of $120 billion, double that of its nearest competitor, Yahoo!, Google now has the gravitational pull to draw in a host of institutions and company matchmakers unable to resist the potential profit opportunities. Google stock, with a price–earnings ratio of 70, represents one of the richest deal-making currencies anywhere. That heft has attracted a growing galaxy of entrepreneurs, venture capitalists, and investment bankers, all of whom are orbiting Google in the hopes of selling it something—a new service, a start-up company, even a new strategy—anything to get their hands on a little of the Google gold.

The Google effect is already changing the delicate balance in Silicon Valley between venture capitalists and start-up companies. Instead of nurturing the most promising start-ups with an eye toward taking the fledgling businesses public, a growing number of VCs [venture capitalists] now scour the landscape for anyone with a technology or service that might fill a gap in Google's portfolio. Google itself and not the larger market has become the exit strategy as VCs plan for the day they can take their money out of their start-ups. Business founders have felt the tug as well. "You're hearing about a lot of entrepreneurs pitching VCs with their end goal to be acquired by Google," says Daniel Primack, editor of *PE Week Wire*, a deal-making digest popular in VC circles. "It's a complete 180 [degree turn] from the IPO craze of five years ago; now Google is looked at like NASDAQ was then." Other entrepreneurs, meanwhile, are skipping the VC stage altogether, hoping to sell directly to Google.

SOURCE: Excerpted from *BusinessWeek*, **http://businessweek.com/ magazine/content/05_49/b3962001.htm**, December 5, 2005.

Allocation of Risk

Virtually all real assets involve some risk. When GM builds its auto plants, for example, it cannot know for sure what cash flows those plants will generate. Financial markets and the diverse financial instruments traded in those markets allow investors with the greatest taste for risk to bear that risk, while other, less risk-tolerant individuals can, to a greater extent, stay on the sidelines. For example, if GM raises the funds to build its auto plant by selling both stocks and bonds to the public, the more optimistic or risk-tolerant investors can buy shares of stock in GM, while the more conservative ones can buy GM bonds. Because the bonds promise to provide a fixed payment, the stockholders bear most of the business risk but reap potentially higher rewards. Thus, capital markets allow the risk that is inherent to all investments to be borne by the investors most willing to bear that risk.

This allocation of risk also benefits the firms that need to raise capital to finance their investments. When investors are able to select security types with the risk-return characteristics that best suit their preferences, each security can be sold for the best possible price. This facilitates the process of building the economy's stock of real assets.

Separation of Ownership and Management

Many businesses are owned and managed by the same individual. This simple organization is well suited to small businesses and, in fact, was the most common form of business organization before the Industrial Revolution. Today, however, with global markets and large-scale production, the size and capital requirements of firms have skyrocketed. For example, in 2006 General Electric listed on its balance sheet about $71 billion of property, plant, and equipment, and total assets in excess of $660 billion. Corporations of such size simply cannot exist as owner-operated firms. GE actually has about 650,000 stockholders with an ownership stake in the firm proportional to their holdings of shares.

Such a large group of individuals obviously cannot actively participate in the day-to-day management of the firm. Instead, they elect a board of directors which in turn hires and supervises the management of the firm. This structure means that the owners and managers of the firm are different parties. This gives the firm a stability that the owner-managed firm cannot achieve. For example, if some stockholders decide they no longer wish to hold shares in the firm, they can sell their shares to other investors, with no impact on the management of the firm. Thus, financial assets and the ability to buy and sell those assets in the financial markets allow for easy separation of ownership and management.

How can all of the disparate owners of the firm, ranging from large pension funds holding hundreds of thousands of shares to small investors who may hold only a single share, agree on the objectives of the firm? Again, the financial markets provide some guidance. All may agree that the firm's management should pursue strategies that enhance the value of their shares. Such policies will make all shareholders wealthier and allow them all to better pursue their personal goals, whatever those goals might be.

Do managers really attempt to maximize firm value? It is easy to see how they might be tempted to engage in activities not in the best interest of shareholders. For example, they might engage in empire building or avoid risky projects to protect their own jobs or overconsume luxuries such as corporate jets, reasoning that the cost of such perquisites is largely borne by the shareholders. These potential conflicts of interest are called **agency problems** because managers, who are hired as agents of the shareholders, may pursue their own interests instead.

Several mechanisms have evolved to mitigate potential agency problems. First, compensation plans tie the income of managers to the success of the firm. A major part of the total compensation of top executives is typically in the form of stock options, which means that the managers will not do well unless the stock price increases, benefiting shareholders. (Of course, we've learned more recently that overuse of options can create its own agency problem. Options can create an incentive for managers to manipulate information to prop up a stock price temporarily, giving them a chance to cash out before the price returns to a level reflective of the firm's true prospects. More on this shortly.) Second, while boards of directors are sometimes portrayed as defenders of top management, they can, and in recent years increasingly do, force out management teams that are underperforming. The chief executives of Viacom, Boeing, Fannie Mae,[3] Hewlett-Packard, and Bristol-Myers Squibb all have been replaced in recent years. Even boards in Europe, which traditionally have been viewed as more management-friendly, have become more willing to force out underperforming managers: for example, senior management at Deutsche Telekom, Shell, and Vivendi Universal have recently been replaced. Third, outsiders such as security analysts and large institutional investors such as pension funds monitor the firm closely and make the life of poor performers at the least uncomfortable.

Finally, bad performers are subject to the threat of takeover. If the board of directors is lax in monitoring management, unhappy shareholders in principle can elect a different board. They can do this by launching a *proxy contest* in which they seek to obtain enough proxies (i.e., rights to vote the shares of other shareholders) to take control of the firm and vote in another board. However, this threat is usually minimal. Shareholders who attempt such a fight have to use their own funds, while management can defend itself using corporate coffers. Most proxy fights fail. The real takeover threat is from other firms. If one firm observes another underperforming, it can acquire the underperforming business and replace management with its own team. The stock price should rise to reflect the prospects of improved performance, which provides incentive for firms to engage in such takeover activity.

agency problem

Conflicts of interest between managers and stockholders.

EXAMPLE 1.1	When Carly Fiorina, then the CEO of Hewlett-Packard, proposed a merger with Compaq Computer in 2001, Walter Hewlett, son of the company's founder and member of the HP board of directors, dissented. The merger had to be approved by shareholders, and Hewlett engaged in a proxy fight to block the deal. One estimate is that HP spent $150 million to lobby shareholders to support the merger; even small shareholders of HP reported receiving 20 or more phone calls from the company in support of the deal.[4] The merger ultimately was approved in an uncharacteristically close vote. No surprise that less than 1% of public companies face proxy contests in any particular year.
The Hewlett-Packard/ Compaq Proxy Fight	

[3]The Federal National Mortgage Association (FNMA).
[4]See "Designed by Committee," *The Economist*, June 13, 2002.

Corporate Governance and Corporate Ethics

We've argued that securities markets can play an important role in facilitating the deployment of capital resources to their most productive uses. But for markets to effectively serve this purpose, there must be enough transparency for investors to make well-informed decisions. If firms can mislead the public about their prospects, then much can go wrong.

Despite the many mechanisms to align incentives of shareholders and managers, the three years between 2000 and 2002 were filled with a seemingly unending series of scandals that collectively signaled a crisis in corporate governance and ethics. For example, the telecom firm WorldCom overstated its profits by at least $3.8 billion by improperly classifying expenses as investments. When the true picture emerged, it resulted in the largest bankruptcy in U.S. history. The second-largest U.S. bankruptcy was Enron, which used its now notorious "special purpose entities" to move debt off its own books and similarly present a misleading picture of its financial status. Unfortunately, these firms had plenty of company. Other firms such as Rite Aid, HealthSouth, Global Crossing, and Qwest Communications also manipulated and misstated their accounts to the tune of billions of dollars. And the scandals were hardly limited to the U.S. Parmalat, the Italian dairy firm, claimed to have a $4.8 billion account at Bank of America that turned out not to exist, and in the end the size of its bankruptcy will likely rival those of World-Com or Enron. These episodes suggest that agency and incentive problems are far from solved.

Other scandals of that period included systematically misleading and overly optimistic research reports put out by stock market analysts (their favorable analysis was traded for the promise of future investment banking business, and analysts were commonly compensated not for their accuracy or insight, but for their role in garnering investment banking business for their firms) and allocations of initial public offerings to corporate executives as a quid pro quo for personal favors or the promise to direct future business back to the manager of the IPO.

What about the auditors who were supposed to be the watchdogs of the firms? Here too, incentives were skewed. Recent changes in business practice made the consulting businesses of these firms more lucrative than the auditing function. For example, Enron's (now defunct) auditor Arthur Andersen earned more money consulting for Enron than auditing it; given its incentive to protect its consulting profits, it should not be surprising that it, and other auditors, were overly lenient in their auditing work.

In 2002, in response to the spate of ethics scandals, Congress passed the Sarbanes-Oxley Act, which attempts to tighten the rules of corporate governance. For example, the Act requires corporations to have more independent directors, that is, more directors who are not themselves managers (or affiliated with managers). The Act also requires each CFO to personally vouch for the corporation's accounting statements, creates a new oversight board to oversee the auditing of public companies, and prohibits auditors from providing various other services to clients.

Wall Street and its regulators are seeking ways to restore credibility. There is (admittedly belated) recognition that markets require trust to function. In the wake of the scandals, the value of reputation and straightforward incentive structures has increased. As one Wall Street insider put it, "This is an industry of trust; it's one of its key assets. . . . [Wall Street] is going to have to invest in getting [that trust] back . . . without that trust, there's nothing."[5] Ultimately, a firm's reputation for integrity is key to building long-term relationships with its customers and is therefore one of its most valuable assets. Indeed, the motto of the London Stock Exchange is "My word is my bond." Every so often firms forget this lesson, but in the end, investments in reputation are in fact good business practice.

1.4 THE INVESTMENT PROCESS

An investor's *portfolio* is simply his collection of investment assets. Once the portfolio is established, it is updated or "rebalanced" by selling existing securities and using the proceeds to buy new securities, by investing additional funds to increase the overall size of the portfolio, or by selling securities to decrease the size of the portfolio.

---

[5]*BusinessWeek,* "How Corrupt Is Wall Street?" May 13, 2002.

asset allocation

Allocation of an investment portfolio across broad asset classes.

security selection

Choice of specific securities within each asset class.

Investment assets can be categorized into broad asset classes, such as stocks, bonds, real estate, commodities, and so on. Investors make two types of decisions in constructing their portfolios. The **asset allocation** decision is the choice among these broad asset classes, while the **security selection** decision is the choice of which particular securities to hold *within* each asset class.

"Top-down" portfolio construction starts with asset allocation. For example, an individual who currently holds all of his money in a bank account would first decide what proportion of the overall portfolio ought to be moved into stocks, bonds, and so on. In this way, the broad features of the portfolio are established. For example, while the average annual return on the common stock of large firms since 1926 has been about 12% per year, the average return on U.S. Treasury bills has been only 3.8%. On the other hand, stocks are far riskier, with annual returns (as measured by the Standard & Poor's 500 Index) that have ranged as low as −46% and as high as 55%. In contrast, T-bill returns are effectively risk-free: you know what interest rate you will earn when you buy the bills. Therefore, the decision to allocate your investments to the stock market or to the money market where Treasury bills are traded will have great ramifications for both the risk and the return of your portfolio. A top-down investor first makes this and other crucial asset allocation decisions before turning to the decision of the particular securities to be held in each asset class.

security analysis

Analysis of the value of securities.

Security analysis involves the valuation of particular securities that might be included in the portfolio. For example, an investor might ask whether Merck or Pfizer is more attractively priced. Both bonds and stocks must be evaluated for investment attractiveness, but valuation is far more difficult for stocks because a stock's performance usually is far more sensitive to the condition of the issuing firm.

In contrast to top-down portfolio management is the "bottom-up" strategy. In this process, the portfolio is constructed from the securities that seem attractively priced without as much concern for the resultant asset allocation. Such a technique can result in unintended bets on one or another sector of the economy. For example, it might turn out that the portfolio ends up with a very heavy representation of firms in one industry, from one part of the country, or with exposure to one source of uncertainty. However, a bottom-up strategy does focus the portfolio on the assets that seem to offer the most attractive investment opportunities.

1.5 MARKETS ARE COMPETITIVE

Financial markets are highly competitive. Thousands of intelligent and well-backed analysts constantly scour securities markets searching for the best buys. This competition means that we should expect to find few, if any, "free lunches," securities that are so underpriced that they represent obvious bargains. There are several implications of this no-free-lunch proposition. Let's examine two.

The Risk-Return Trade-Off

Investors invest for anticipated future returns, but those returns rarely can be predicted precisely. There will almost always be risk associated with investments. Actual or realized returns will almost always deviate from the expected return anticipated at the start of the investment period. For example, in 1931 (the worst calendar year for the market since 1926), the stock market lost 46% of its value. In 1933 (the best year), the stock market gained 55%. You can be sure that investors did not anticipate such extreme performance at the start of either of these years.

Naturally, if all else could be held equal, investors would prefer investments with the highest expected return.[6] However, the no-free-lunch rule tells us that all else cannot be held equal.

---

[6]The "expected" return is not the return investors believe they necessarily will earn, or even their most likely return. It is instead the result of averaging across all possible outcomes, recognizing that some outcomes are more likely than others. It is the average rate of return across possible economic scenarios.

If you want higher expected returns, you will have to pay a price in terms of accepting higher investment risk. If higher expected return can be achieved without bearing extra risk, there will be a rush to buy the high-return assets, with the result that their prices will be driven up. Individuals considering investing in the asset at the now-higher price will find the investment less attractive: If you buy at a higher price, your expected rate of return (that is, profit per dollar invested) is lower. The asset will be considered attractive and its price will continue to rise until its expected return is no more than commensurate with risk. At this point, investors can anticipate a "fair" return relative to the asset's risk, but no more. Similarly, if returns were independent of risk, there would be a rush to sell high-risk assets. Their prices would fall (and their expected future rates of return rise) until they eventually were attractive enough to be included again in investor portfolios. We conclude that there should be a **risk-return trade-off** in the securities markets, with higher-risk assets priced to offer higher expected returns than lower-risk assets.

risk-return trade-off
Assets with higher expected returns entail greater risk.

Of course, this discussion leaves several important questions unanswered. How should one measure the risk of an asset? What should be the quantitative trade-off between risk (properly measured) and expected return? One would think that risk would have something to do with the volatility of an asset's returns, but this guess turns out to be only partly correct. When we mix assets into diversified portfolios, we need to consider the interplay among assets and the effect of diversification on the risk of the entire portfolio. *Diversification* means that many assets are held in the portfolio so that the exposure to any particular asset is limited. The effect of diversification on portfolio risk, the implications for the proper measurement of risk, and the risk-return relationship are the topics of Part Two. These topics are the subject of what has come to be known as *modern portfolio theory*. The development of this theory brought two of its pioneers, Harry Markowitz and William Sharpe, Nobel Prizes.

Efficient Markets

Another implication of the no-free-lunch proposition is that we should rarely expect to find bargains in the security markets. We will spend all of Chapter 8 examining the theory and evidence concerning the hypothesis that financial markets process all relevant information about securities quickly and efficiently, that is, that the security price usually reflects all the information available to investors concerning the value of the security. According to this hypothesis, as new information about a security becomes available, the price of the security quickly adjusts so that at any time, the security price equals the market consensus estimate of the value of the security. If this were so, there would be neither underpriced nor overpriced securities.

One interesting implication of this "efficient market hypothesis" concerns the choice between active and passive investment-management strategies. **Passive management** calls for holding highly diversified portfolios without spending effort or other resources attempting to improve investment performance through security analysis. **Active management** is the attempt to improve performance either by identifying mispriced securities or by timing the performance of broad asset classes—for example, increasing one's commitment to stocks when one is bullish on the stock market. If markets are efficient and prices reflect all relevant information, perhaps it is better to follow passive strategies instead of spending resources in a futile attempt to outguess your competitors in the financial markets.

passive management
Buying and holding a diversified portfolio without attempting to identify mispriced securities.

active management
Attempting to identify mispriced securities or to forecast broad market trends.

If the efficient market hypothesis were taken to the extreme, there would be no point in active security analysis; only fools would commit resources to actively analyze securities. Without ongoing security analysis, however, prices eventually would depart from "correct" values, creating new incentives for experts to move in. Therefore, in Chapter 9, we examine challenges to the efficient market hypothesis. Even in environments as competitive as the financial markets, we may observe only *near*-efficiency, and profit opportunities may exist for especially diligent and creative investors. This motivates our discussion of active portfolio management in Part Six. More importantly, our discussions of security analysis and portfolio construction generally must account for the likelihood of nearly efficient markets.

1.6 | THE PLAYERS

From a bird's-eye view, there would appear to be three major players in the financial markets:

1. Firms are net borrowers. They raise capital now to pay for investments in plant and equipment. The income generated by those real assets provides the returns to investors who purchase the securities issued by the firm.
2. Households typically are net savers. They purchase the securities issued by firms that need to raise funds.
3. Governments can be borrowers or lenders, depending on the relationship between tax revenue and government expenditures. Since World War II, the U.S. government typically has run budget deficits, meaning that its tax receipts have been less than its expenditures. The government, therefore, has had to borrow funds to cover its budget deficit. Issuance of Treasury bills, notes, and bonds is the major way that the government borrows funds from the public. In contrast, in the latter part of the 1990s, the government enjoyed a budget surplus and was able to retire some outstanding debt.

Corporations and governments do not sell all or even most of their securities directly to individuals. For example, about half of all stock is held by large financial institutions such as pension funds, mutual funds, insurance companies, and banks. These financial institutions stand between the security issuer (the firm) and the ultimate owner of the security (the individual investor). For this reason, they are called *financial intermediaries*. Similarly, corporations do not directly market their securities to the public. Instead, they hire agents, called investment bankers, to represent them to the investing public. Let's examine the roles of these intermediaries.

Financial Intermediaries

Households want desirable investments for their savings, yet the small (financial) size of most households makes direct investment difficult. A small investor seeking to lend money to businesses that need to finance investments doesn't advertise in the local newspaper to find a willing and desirable borrower. Moreover, an individual lender would not be able to diversify across borrowers to reduce risk. Finally, an individual lender is not equipped to assess and monitor the credit risk of borrowers.

financial intermediaries

Institutions that "connect" borrowers and lenders by accepting funds from lenders and loaning funds to borrowers.

For these reasons, **financial intermediaries** have evolved to bring lenders and borrowers together. These financial intermediaries include banks, investment companies, insurance companies, and credit unions. Financial intermediaries issue their own securities to raise funds to purchase the securities of other corporations.

For example, a bank raises funds by borrowing (taking deposits) and lending that money to other borrowers. The spread between the interest rates paid to depositors and the rates charged to borrowers is the source of the bank's profit. In this way, lenders and borrowers do not need to contact each other directly. Instead, each goes to the bank, which acts as an intermediary

WEB *master*

Market Regulators

1. Visit the Web site of the Securities Exchange Commission, **www.sec.gov**. What is the mission of the SEC? What information and advice does the SEC offer to beginning investors?

2. Now visit the Web site of the NASD **www.nasd.com**. What is its mission? What information and advice does it offer to beginners?

3. Now visit the Web site of the IOSCO **www.iosco.org**. What is its mission? What information and advice does it offer to beginners?

between the two. The problem of matching lenders with borrowers is solved when each comes independently to the common intermediary.

Financial intermediaries are distinguished from other businesses in that both their assets and their liabilities are overwhelmingly financial. Table 1.3 presents the aggregated balance sheet of commercial banks, one of the largest sectors of financial intermediaries. Notice that the balance sheet includes only very small amounts of real assets. Compare Table 1.3 to the aggregated balance sheet of the nonfinancial corporate sector in Table 1.4 for which real assets are about half of all assets. The contrast arises because intermediaries simply move funds from one sector to another. In fact, the primary social function of such intermediaries is to channel household savings to the business sector.

Other examples of financial intermediaries are investment companies, insurance companies, and credit unions. All these firms offer similar advantages in their intermediary role. First, by pooling the resources of many small investors, they are able to lend considerable sums to large borrowers. Second, by lending to many borrowers, intermediaries achieve significant diversification, so they can accept loans that individually might be too risky. Third, intermediaries build expertise through the volume of business they do and can use economies of scale and scope to assess and monitor risk.

Investment companies, which pool and manage the money of many investors, also arise out of economies of scale. Here, the problem is that most household portfolios are not large enough to be spread among a wide variety of securities. It is very expensive in terms of brokerage fees and research costs to purchase one or two shares of many different firms. Mutual funds have the advantage of large-scale trading and portfolio management, while participating investors are assigned a prorated share of the total funds according to the size of

investment companies

Firms managing funds for investors. An investment company may manage several mutual funds.

TABLE 1.3					
Balance sheet of commercial banks					
Assets	**$ Billion**	**% Total**	**Liabilities and Net Worth**	**$ Billion**	**% Total**
Real assets			Liabilities		
Equipment and premises	$ 93.9	1.0%	Deposits	$6,383.0	66.5%
Other real estate	4.9	0.1	Borrowed funds	798.0	8.3
Total real assets	$ 98.8	1.0%	Subordinated debt	132.7	1.4
			Federal funds and		
			repurchase agreements	750.0	7.8
			Other	566.8	5.9
			Total liabilities	$8,630.5	89.9%
Financial assets					
Cash	$ 397.6	4.1%			
Investment securities	1,648.7	17.2			
Loans and Leases	5,589.3	58.2			
Other financial assets	1,082.4	11.3			
Total financial assets	$8,718.0	90.8			
Other assets					
Intangible assets	$ 345.6	3.6			
Other	440.0	4.6			
Total other assets	785.5	8.2	Net worth	971.7	10.1
Total	$9,602.3	100.0%		$9,602.3	100.0%

Note: Column sums may differ from totals because of rounding error.

Source: Federal Deposit Insurance Corporation, **www.fdic.gov,** September 2005.

TABLE 1.4

Balance sheet of nonfinancial U.S. business

Assets	$ Billion	% Total	Liabilities and Net Worth	$ Billion	% Total
Real assets			Liabilities		
Equipment and software	$ 3,642	15.8%	Bonds and mortgages	$ 4,034	17.5%
Real estate	6,769	29.4	Bank loans	651	2.8
Inventories	1,593	6.9	Other loans	772	3.4
Total real assets	$12,004	52.2%	Trade debt	1,658	7.2
			Other	3,256	14.1
			Total liabilities	$10,372	45.1%
Financial assets					
Deposits and cash	$ 973	4.2%			
Marketable securities	438	1.9			
Trade and consumer credit	2,077	9.0			
Other	7,525	32.7			
Total financial assets	11,014	47.8	Net worth	12,646	54.9
Total	$23,018	100.0%		$23,018	100.0%

Note: Column sums may differ from totals because of rounding error.

Source: *Flow of Funds Accounts of the United States,* Board of Governors of the Federal Reserve System, June 2006.

their investment. This system gives small investors advantages they are willing to pay for via a management fee to the mutual fund operator.

Investment companies also can design portfolios specifically for large investors with particular goals. In contrast, mutual funds are sold in the retail market, and their investment philosophies are differentiated mainly by strategies that are likely to attract a large number of clients.

Economies of scale also explain the proliferation of analytic services available to investors. Newsletters, databases, and brokerage house research services all engage in research to be sold to a large client base. This setup arises naturally. Investors clearly want information, but with small portfolios to manage, they do not find it economical to personally gather all of it. Hence, a profit opportunity emerges: A firm can perform this service for many clients and charge for it.

CONCEPT
check   **1.2**   Computer networks have made it much cheaper and easier for small investors to trade for their own accounts and perform their own security analysis. What will be the likely effect on financial intermediation?

investment bankers

Firms specializing in the sale of new securities to the public, typically by underwriting the issue.

primary market

A market in which new issues of securities are offered to the public.

secondary market

Previously issued securities are traded among investors.

Investment Bankers

Just as economies of scale and specialization create profit opportunities for financial intermediaries, so too do these economies create niches for firms that perform specialized services for businesses. Firms raise much of their capital by selling securities such as stocks and bonds to the public. Because these firms do not do so frequently, however, investment banking firms that specialize in such activities can offer their services at a cost below that of maintaining an in-house security issuance division.

Investment bankers such as Goldman, Sachs, or Merrill Lynch, or Citigroup advise the issuing corporation on the prices it can charge for the securities issued, appropriate interest rates, and so forth. Ultimately, the investment banking firm handles the marketing of the security in the **primary market,** where new issues of securities are offered to the public. Later, investors can trade previously issued securities among themselves in the so-called **secondary market.**

Investment bankers can provide more than just expertise to security issuers. Because investment bankers are constantly in the market, assisting one firm or another in issuing securities, it is in the banker's own interest to protect and maintain its reputation for honesty. Its investment in reputation is another type of scale economy that arises from frequent participation in the capital markets. The investment banker will suffer along with investors if the securities it underwrites are marketed to the public with overly optimistic or exaggerated claims; the public will not be so trusting the next time that investment banker participates in a security sale. As we have seen, this lesson was relearned with considerable pain in the boom years of the late 1990s and the subsequent high-tech crash of 2000–2002. Too many investment bankers seemed to get caught up in the flood of money that could be made by pushing stock issues to an overly eager public. The failure of many of these offerings soured the public on both the stock market and the firms managing the IPOs. At least some on Wall Street belatedly recognize that they squandered a valuable asset—reputational capital—and there are signs that they recognize as well that the conflicts of interest that engendered these deals are not only wrong but bad for business as well. The investment banker's effectiveness and ability to command future business depend on the reputation it has established over time.

1.7   RECENT TRENDS

Four important trends have changed the contemporary investment environment: (1) globalization, (2) securitization, (3) financial engineering, and (4) information and computer networks.

Globalization

If a wider range of investment choices can benefit investors, why should we limit ourselves to purely domestic assets? Increasingly efficient communication technology and the dismantling of regulatory constraints have encouraged **globalization** in recent years.

U.S. investors commonly can participate in foreign investment opportunities in several ways: (1) purchase foreign securities using American Depository Receipts (ADRs), which are domestically traded securities that represent claims to shares of foreign stocks; (2) purchase foreign securities that are offered in dollars; (3) buy mutual funds that invest internationally; and (4) buy derivative securities with payoffs that depend on prices in foreign security markets.

Brokers who act as intermediaries for American Depository Receipts purchase an inventory of stock from some foreign issuer. The broker then issues an American Depository Receipt that represents a claim to some number of those foreign shares held in inventory. The ADR is denominated in dollars and can be traded on U.S. stock exchanges but is in essence no more than a claim on a foreign stock. Thus, from the investor's point of view, there is no more difference between buying a British versus a U.S. stock than there is in holding a Massachusetts-based company compared with a California-based one. Of course, the investment implications may differ: ADRs still expose investors to exchange-rate risk.

World Equity Benchmark Shares (WEBS) are a variation on ADRs. WEBS use the same depository structure to allow investors to trade *portfolios* of foreign stocks in a selected country. Each WEBS security tracks the performance of an index of share returns for a particular country. WEBS can be traded by investors just like any other security and thus enable U.S. investors to obtain diversified portfolios of foreign stocks in one fell swoop.

A giant step toward globalization took place in 1999 when 11 European countries replaced their existing currencies with a new currency called the *euro*.[7] The idea behind the euro is that a common currency will facilitate trade and encourage integration of markets across national boundaries. Figure 1.1 is an announcement of a debt offering in the amount of 500 million euros. (In June 2007, the euro was worth about $1.35; the symbol for the euro is €.)

globalization

Tendency toward a worldwide investment environment, and the integration of international capital markets.

---

[7]The 11 countries are Belgium, Germany, Spain, France, Ireland, Italy, Luxembourg, The Netherlands, Austria, Portugal, and Finland. Greece became the 12th country to participate in the common currency in 2001. Several other countries, primarily in middle and eastern Europe, have joined the European Union and are slated to adopt the euro in 2007–2009.

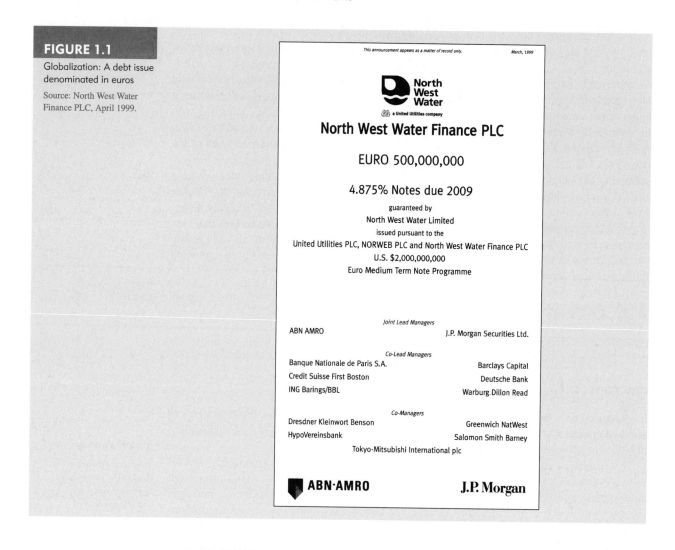

Securitization

**pass-through
securities**

Pools of loans (such as
home mortgage loans)
sold in one package.
Owners of pass-throughs
receive all of the principal
and interest payments
made by the borrowers.

securitization

Pooling loans into
standardized securities
backed by those loans,
which can then be traded
like any other security.

In 1970, mortgage **pass-through securities** were introduced by the Government National
Mortgage Association (GNMA, or Ginnie Mae). These securities aggregate individual home
mortgages into relatively homogeneous pools. Each pool acts as backing for a GNMA pass-
through security. Investors who buy GNMA securities receive prorated shares of all the principal and interest payments made on the underlying mortgage pool.

For example, the pool might total $100 million of 8%, 30-year conventional mortgages.
The banks that originated the mortgages continue to service them (receiving fee-for-service),
but they no longer own the mortgage investment; they pass the cash flows from the underlying
mortgages through to the GNMA security holders.

Pass-through securities represent a tremendous innovation in mortgage markets. The **securitization** of mortgages means mortgages can be traded just like other securities. Availability
of funds to homebuyers no longer depends on local credit conditions and is no longer subject
to local banks' potential monopoly powers; with mortgage pass-throughs trading in national
markets, mortgage funds can flow from any region (literally worldwide) to wherever demand
is greatest.

Securitization also expands the menu of choices for the investor. Whereas it would have
been impossible before 1970 for investors to invest in mortgages directly, they now can purchase mortgage pass-through securities or invest in mutual funds that offer portfolios of such
securities.

Today, the majority of home mortgages are pooled into mortgage-backed securities. The
two biggest players in the market are the Federal National Mortgage Association (FNMA, or

Fannie Mae) and the Federal Home Loan Mortgage Corporation (FHLMC, or Freddie Mac). Over $3.8 trillion of mortgage-backed securities are outstanding, making this market larger than the market for corporate bonds.

Other loans that have been securitized into pass-through arrangements include car loans, student loans, home equity loans, credit card loans, and debts of firms. Figure 1.2 documents the rapid growth of nonmortgage asset–backed securities since 1995.

Securitization also has been used to allow U.S. banks to unload their portfolios of shaky loans to developing nations. So-called *Brady bonds* (named after former Secretary of Treasury Nicholas Brady) were formed by securitizing bank loans to several countries in shaky fiscal condition. The U.S. banks exchanged their loans to developing nations for bonds backed by those loans. The payments that the borrowing nation would otherwise make to the lending-bank were directed instead to the holder of the bond. These bonds could be traded in capital markets. Therefore, if they chose to, banks could remove these loans from their portfolios simply by selling the bonds.

CONCEPT *check* **1.3**

When mortgages are pooled into securities, the pass-through agencies (Freddie Mac and Fannie Mae) typically guarantee the underlying mortgage loans. If the home-owner defaults on the loan, the pass-through agency makes good on the loan; the investor in the mortgage-backed security does not bear the credit risk.

a. Why does the allocation of risk to the pass-through agency rather than the security holder make economic sense?

b. Why was the allocation of credit risk less of an issue for Brady bonds?

Financial Engineering

Financial engineering refers to the creation of new securities by **unbundling**—breaking up and allocating the cash flows from one security to create several new securities—or by **bundling**—combining more than one security into a composite security. Such creative engineering of new investment products allows one to design securities with custom-tailored risk attributes. An example of bundling appears in Figure 1.3.

Boise Cascade, with the assistance of Goldman, Sachs and other underwriters, has issued a hybrid security with features of preferred stock combined with various call and put option

bundling, unbundling

Creation of new securities either by combining primitive and derivative securities into one composite hybrid or by separating returns on an asset into classes.

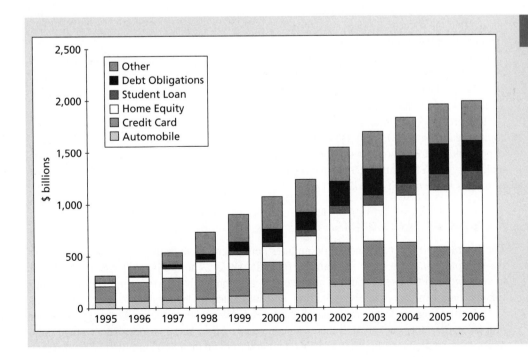

FIGURE 1.2

Asset-backed securities outstanding

Source: Securities Industry and Financial Markets Association, **www.sifma.org.**

FIGURE 1.3

Bundling creates a complex security

Source: *The Wall Street Journal*, December 19, 2001.

$172,500,000

Boise Cascade Corporation

7.50% Adjustable Conversion-rate Equity Security Unit

Price $50 Per Unit

Upon request, a copy of the Prospectus Supplement and the related Prospectus describing these securities and the business of the Company may be obtained within any State from any Underwriter who may legally distribute it within such State. The securities are offered only by means of the Prospectus Supplement and the related Prospectus and this announcement is neither an offer to sell nor a solicitation of any offer to buy.

Goldman, Sachs & Co.

ABN AMRO Rothschild LLC

Banc of America Securities LLC

JPMorgan

Wachovia Securities

December 19, 2001

contracts. The security is structured as preferred stock for four years, at which time it is converted into common stock of the company. However, the number of shares of common stock into which the security can be converted depends on the price of the stock in four years, which means that the security holders are exposed to risk similar to the risk they would bear if they held option positions on the firm.

Often, creating a security that appears to be attractive requires the unbundling of an asset. An example is given in Figure 1.4. There, a mortgage pass-through certificate is unbundled into classes. Class 1 receives only principal payments from the mortgage pool, whereas Class 2 receives only interest payments.

financial engineering

The process of creating and designing securities with custom-tailored characteristics.

The process of bundling and unbundling is called **financial engineering,** which refers to the creation and design of securities with custom-tailored characteristics, often regarding exposures to various sources of risk. Financial engineers view securities as bundles of (possible risky) cash flows that may be carved up and rearranged according to the needs or desires of traders in the security markets.

Computer Networks

The Internet and other advances in computer networking have transformed many sectors of the economy, and few more so than the financial sector. These advances will be treated in greater detail in Chapter 3, but for now we can mention a few important innovations: online trading, online information dissemination, and automated trade crossing.

Online trading connects a customer directly to a brokerage firm. Online brokerage firms can process trades more cheaply and therefore can charge lower commissions. The average commission for an online trade is below $20, compared to more than $100 at full-service brokers.

FIGURE 1.4

Unbundling of mortgages into principal- and interest-only securities

Source: Goldman, Sachs & Co., July 1987.

This announcement appears as a matter of record only.

$200,000,000*

Federal National Mortgage Association

FannieMae

Stripped Mortgage-Backed Securities

Principal and Interest payable on the 25th day of
each month, commencing August 25, 1987

SMBS Trust 20-CL—Fixed-Rate Residential Mortgage Loans

SMBS Class 1: 100% of Principal Payments on Underlying
9½% Fannie Mae Guaranteed Mortgage Pass-Through Certificates

SMBS Class 2: 100% of Interest Payments on Underlying
9½% Fannie Mae Guaranteed Mortgage Pass-Through Certificates

The obligations of Fannie Mae under its guaranty of the SMBS Certificates are obligations of Fannie Mae and are not backed by the full faith and credit of the United States. The SMBS Certificates are exempt from the registration requirements of the Securities Act of 1933 and are "Exempted Securities" within the meaning of the Securities Exchange Act of 1934.

Class 1 $200,000,000 Principal Amount*
Class 2 $200,000,000 Notional Principal Amount*

Goldman, Sachs & Co.

July 9, 1987   *Approximate

The Internet has also allowed vast amounts of information to be made cheaply and widely available to the public. Individual investors today can obtain data, investment tools, and even analyst reports that just a decade ago would have been available only to professionals.

Electronic communication networks that allow direct trading among investors have exploded in recent years. These networks allow members to post buy or sell orders and to have those orders automatically matched up or "crossed" with orders of other traders in the system without benefit of an intermediary such as a securities dealer.

1.8 OUTLINE OF THE TEXT

The text has six parts, which are fairly independent and may be studied in a variety of sequences, Part One is an introduction to financial markets, instruments, and trading of securities. This part also describes the mutual fund industry.

Part Two is a fairly detailed presentation of "modern portfolio theory." This part of the text treats the effect of diversification on portfolio risk, the efficient diversification of investor portfolios, the choice of portfolios that strike an attractive balance between risk and return, and the trade-off between risk and expected return. This part also treats the efficient market hypothesis as well as behavioral critiques of theories based on investor rationality.

Parts Three through Five cover security analysis and valuation. Part Three is devoted to debt markets and Part Four to equity markets. Part Five covers derivative assets, such as options and futures contracts.

Part Six is an introduction to active investment management. It shows how different investors' objectives and constraints can lead to a variety of investment policies. This part discusses the role of active management in nearly efficient markets and considers how one should evaluate the performance of managers who pursue active strategies. It also shows how the principles of portfolio construction can be extended to the international setting.

SUMMARY

- Real assets create wealth. Financial assets represent claims to parts or all of that wealth. Financial assets determine how the ownership of real assets is distributed among investors.

- Financial assets can be categorized as fixed income (debt), equity, or derivative instruments. Top-down portfolio construction techniques start with the asset allocation decision—the allocation of funds across broad asset classes—and then progress to more specific security-selection decisions.

- Competition in financial markets leads to a risk-return trade-off, in which securities that offer higher expected rates of return also impose greater risks on investors. The presence of risk, however, implies that actual returns can differ considerably from expected returns at the beginning of the investment period. Competition among security analysts also results in financial markets that are nearly informationally efficient, meaning that prices reflect all available information concerning the value of the security. Passive investment strategies may make sense in nearly efficient markets.

- Financial intermediaries pool investor funds and invest them. Their services are in demand because small investors cannot efficiently gather information, diversify, and monitor portfolios. The financial intermediary, in contrast, is a large investor that can take advantage of scale economies.

- Investment banking brings efficiency to corporate fund raising. Investment bankers develop expertise in pricing new issues and in marketing them to investors.

- Recent trends in financial markets include globalization, securitization, financial engineering of assets, and growth of information and computer networks.

KEY TERMS

active management, 11
agency problem, 8
asset allocation, 10
bundling, 17
derivative securities, 5
equity, 5
financial assets, 3
financial engineering, 18
financial intermediaries, 12

fixed-income (debt) securities, 5
globalization, 15
investment, 2
investment bankers, 14
investment companies, 13
passive management, 11
pass-through securities, 16

primary market, 14
real assets, 3
risk-return trade-off, 11
secondary market, 14
securitization, 16
security analysis, 10
security selection, 10
unbundling, 17

PROBLEM SETS

 Select problems are available in McGraw-Hill's Homework Manager®. Please see the packaging options of the preface for more information.

1. Suppose you discover a treasure chest of $10 billion in cash.
   a. Is this a real or financial asset?
   b. Is society any richer for the discovery?
   c. Are you wealthier?
   d. Can you reconcile your answers to (b) and (c)? Is anyone worse off as a result of the discovery?

2. Lanni Products is a start-up computer software development firm. It currently owns computer equipment worth $30,000 and has cash on hand of $20,000 contributed by Lanni's owners. For each of the following transactions, identify the real and/or financial assets that trade hands. Are any financial assets created or destroyed in the transaction?
   a. Lanni takes out a bank loan. It receives $50,000 in cash and signs a note promising to pay back the loan over three years.
   b. Lanni uses the cash from the bank plus $20,000 of its own funds to finance the development of new financial planning software.

   c. Lanni sells the software product to Microsoft, which will market it to the public under the Microsoft name. Lanni accepts payment in the form of 1,500 shares of Microsoft stock.

   d. Lanni sells the shares of stock for $80 per share and uses part of the proceeds to pay off the bank loan.

3. Reconsider Lanni Products from Problem 2.

   a. Prepare its balance sheet just after it gets the bank loan. What is the ratio of real assets to total assets?

   b. Prepare the balance sheet after Lanni spends the $70,000 to develop its software product. What is the ratio of real assets to total assets?

   c. Prepare the balance sheet after Lanni accepts the payment of shares from Microsoft. What is the ratio of real assets to total assets?

4. Financial engineering has been disparaged as nothing more than paper shuffling. Critics argue that resources used for *rearranging* wealth (that is, bundling and unbundling financial assets) might be better spent on *creating* wealth (that is, creating real assets). Evaluate this criticism. Are any benefits realized by creating an array of derivative securities from various primary securities?

5. Examine the balance sheet of commercial banks in Table 1.3. What is the ratio of tangible assets to total assets? What is that ratio for nonfinancial firms (Table 1.4)? Why should this difference be expected?

6. Consider Figure 1.5, which describes an issue of American gold certificates.

   a. Is this issue a primary or secondary market transaction?

   b. Are the certificates primitive or derivative assets?

   c. What market niche is filled by this offering?

7. Discuss the advantages and disadvantages of the following forms of managerial compensation in terms of mitigating agency problems, that is, potential conflicts of interest between managers and shareholders.

   a. A fixed salary.

   b. Stock in the firm.

   c. Call options on shares of the firm.

8. We noted that oversight by large institutional investors or creditors is one mechanism to reduce agency problems. Why don't individual investors in the firm have the same incentive to keep an eye on management?

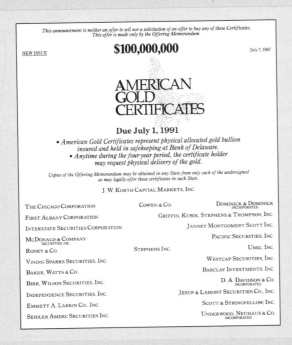

FIGURE 1.5

A gold-backed security

9. Why would you expect securitization to take place only in highly developed capital markets?

10. What is the relationship between securitization and the role of financial intermediaries in the economy? What happens to financial intermediaries as securitization progresses?

11. Although we stated that real assets comprise the true productive capacity of an economy, it is hard to conceive of a modern economy without well-developed financial markets and security types. How would the productive capacity of the U.S. economy be affected if there were no markets in which one could trade financial assets?

12. Give an example of three financial intermediaries and explain how they act as a bridge between small investors and large capital markets or corporations.

13. Firms raise capital from investors by issuing shares in the primary markets. Does this imply that corporate financial managers can ignore trading of previously issued shares in the secondary market?

14. The average rate of return on investments in large stocks has outpaced that on investments in Treasury bills by over 8% since 1926. Why, then, does anyone invest in Treasury bills?

15. What are some advantages and disadvantages of top-down versus bottom-up investing styles?

16. You see an advertisement for a book that claims to show how you can make $1 million with no risk and with no money down. Will you buy the book?

STANDARD &POOR'S

Use data from the Standard & Poor's Market Insight Database at www.mhhe.com/edumarketinsight to answer the following questions.

1. Select the Company tab and enter ticker symbol RRD. Click on the Company Profile in the Compustat Reports section. What kind of firm is Donnelley & Sons?

2. Open the S&P Stock Report for Donnelley. How many shares of the company's stock are outstanding? How many stockholders are there? Is Insider Activity rated as unfavorable, neutral, or favorable?

3. Open the most recently available Proxy Statement for Donnelley (under the EDGAR heading). Locate the section that describes the stock ownership. How many total shares are held by directors and officers? Approximately what percentage is this of the total number of shares outstanding?

4. Look at the Executive Compensation section, which lists data for executives' salaries and other benefits. How much of each executive's compensation is in the form of stock awards? How much is in the form of option awards? Compare these numbers with the executives' salaries.

5. Scroll down further in the Proxy Statement to see what other kinds of benefits executives received. What types of benefits are listed in this section?

6. How might stock awards, option awards, and other benefits affect Donnelley's agency costs?

WEB *master*

Globalization

World Equity Benchmark Shares (WEBS) offer a way for investors to diversify their portfolios by adding international investments. WEBS are one specific type of exchange traded funds (ETFs). Go to **www.amex.com** and click on the link for *Education*. What are some of the advantages of using ETFs as investment tools? Click on the link in the "What are ETFs?" section to get a complete list of American Stock Exchange–listed ETFs.

Locate the link for the iShares MSCI Malaysia Index Fund (symbol EWM). When the page opens, select the

Chart tab and choose a period of three months. Click on the link at the bottom of the chart to see the underlying data. Use the closing prices listed to calculate the three-month return on EWM: (Return = Current Price/Beginning Price − 1).

Repeat the process for the iShares MSCI Mexico Index Fund (EWW), the iShares MSCI Brazil Index Fund (EWZ), the iShares MSCI South Korea Index Fund (EWY), and the iShares MSCI Italy Index Fund (EWI). How did the funds perform relative to each other over the last three months? Which of the funds might appeal to you as an investor?

SOLUTIONS TO CONCEPT *checks*

1.1. *a.* Real
 b. Financial
 c. Real
 d. Real
 e. Financial

1.2. If the new technology enables investors to trade and perform research for themselves, the need for financial intermediaries will decline. Part of the service intermediaries now offer is a lower-cost method for individuals to participate in securities markets. This part of the intermediaries' service would be less sought after.

1.3. *a.* The pass-through agencies are far better equipped to evaluate the credit risk associated with the pool of mortgages. They are constantly in the market, have ongoing relationships with the originators of the loans, and find it economical to set up "quality control" departments to monitor the credit risk of the mortgage pools. Therefore, the pass-through agencies are better able to incur the risk; they charge for this "service" via a "guarantee fee." Investors might not find it worthwhile to purchase these securities if they must assess the credit risk of these loans for themselves. It is far cheaper for them to allow the agencies to collect the guarantee fee.

 b. In contrast to mortgage-backed securities, which are backed by large numbers of mortgages, Brady bonds are backed by a small number of large government loans. It is more feasible for the investor to evaluate the credit quality of a few governments than it is to evaluate dozens or hundreds of individual mortgages.

www.mhhe.com/bkm

Asset Classes and Financial Instruments

 Distinguish among the major assets that trade in money markets and in capital markets.

 Describe the construction of stock market indexes.

 Calculate the profit or loss on investments in options and futures contracts.

You learned in Chapter 1 that the process of building an investment portfolio usually begins by deciding how much money to allocate to broad classes of assets, such as safe money-market securities or bank accounts, longer-term bonds, stocks, or even asset classes such as real estate or precious metals. This process is called *asset allocation*. Within each class the investor then selects specific assets from a more detailed menu. This is called *security selection*.

Each broad asset class contains many specific security types, and the many variations on a theme can be overwhelming. Our goal in this chapter is to introduce you to the important features of broad classes of securities. Toward this end, we organize our tour of financial instruments according to asset class.

Financial markets are traditionally segmented into money markets and capital markets. Money market instruments include short-term, marketable, liquid, low-risk debt securities. Money market instruments sometimes are called *cash equivalents*, or just *cash* for short. Capital markets, in contrast, include longer-term and riskier securities. Securities in the capital market are much more diverse than those found within the money market. For this reason, we will subdivide the capital market into three segments: longer-term debt markets, equity markets, and derivative markets in which options and futures trade.

We first describe money market instruments. We then move on to debt and equity securities. We explain the structure of various stock market indexes in this chapter because market benchmark portfolios play an important role in portfolio construction and evaluation. Finally, we survey the derivative security markets for options and futures contracts. A selection of the markets, instruments, and indexes covered in this chapter appears in Table 2.1.

Related Web sites for this chapter are available at www.mhhe.com/bkm.

2.1 THE MONEY MARKET

The **money market** is a subsector of the debt market. It consists of very short-term debt securities that are highly marketable. Many of these securities trade in large denominations and so are out of the reach of individual investors. Money market mutual funds, however, are easily accessible to small investors. These mutual funds pool the resources of many investors and purchase a wide variety of money market securities on their behalf.

Figure 2.1 is an excerpt of a money rates listing from *The Wall Street Journal.* It includes the various instruments of the money market that we describe in detail below. Table 2.2 lists outstanding volume of the major instruments of the money market.

money markets

Include short-term, highly liquid, and relatively low-risk debt instruments.

Treasury Bills

U.S. **Treasury bills** (T-bills, or just bills, for short) are the most marketable of all money market instruments. T-bills represent the simplest form of borrowing. The government raises money by selling bills to the public. Investors buy the bills at a discount from the stated maturity value. At the bill's maturity, the holder receives from the government a payment equal to the face value of the bill. The difference between the purchase price and the ultimate maturity value represents the investor's earnings.

T-bills with initial maturities of 28, 91, and 182 days are issued weekly. Individuals can purchase T-bills directly from the Treasury or on the secondary market from a government securities dealer. T-bills are highly liquid; that is, they are easily converted to cash and sold at low transaction cost and with little price risk. Unlike most other money market instruments, which sell in minimum denominations of $100,000, T-bills sell in minimum denominations of only $1,000. While the income earned on T-bills is taxable at the federal level, it is exempt from all state and local taxes, another characteristic distinguishing T-bills from other money market instruments.

Treasury bills

Short-term government securities issued at a discount from face value and returning the face amount at maturity.

any body can get [handwritten annotation]

TABLE 2.1 Financial markets and indexes	**The money market** Treasury bills Certificates of deposit Commercial paper Bankers' acceptances Eurodollars Repos and reverses Federal funds Brokers' calls **Indexes** Dow Jones averages Standard & Poor's indexes Bond market indicators International indexes	**The bond market** Treasury bonds and notes Federal agency debt Municipal bonds Corporate bonds Mortgage-backed securities **Equity markets** Common stocks Preferred stocks **Derivative markets** Options Futures and forwards Swaps

FIGURE 2.1

Rates on money market securities

Source: From *The Wall Street Journal,* January 5, 2007. Reprinted by permission of Dow Jones & Company, Inc. via Copyright Clearance Center, Inc. © 2007 Dow Jones & Company, Inc. All Rights Reserved Worldwide.

Money Rates

January 4, 2007

International rates

	Latest	Week ago	52-WEEK High	52-WEEK Low
Prime rates				
U.S.	**8.25**	8.25	8.25	7.25
Canada	**6.00**	6.00	6.00	5.00
Euro zone	**3.50**	3.50	3.50	2.25
Japan	**1.625**	1.625	1.625	1.375
Britain	**5.00**	5.00	5.00	4.50
Overnight repurchase				
U.S.	**5.22**	5.19	5.28	4.13
U.K. (BBA)	**5.080**	5.047	5.150	4.100
Euro zone	**3.60**	3.77	3.77	2.26

U.S. government rates

	Latest	Week ago	52-WEEK High	52-WEEK Low
Federal funds				
Effective rate	**5.24**	5.25	5.37	4.21
Treasury bill auction				
4 weeks	**4.760**	4.660	5.170	3.950
13 weeks	**4.930**	4.875	4.990	4.070
26 weeks	**4.900**	4.900	5.110	4.250

Secondary market

	Latest	Week ago	52-WEEK High	52-WEEK Low
Freddie Mac				
30-year mortgage yields				
30 days	**5.92**	6.06	6.71	5.81
60 days	**5.93**	6.07	6.75	5.82
One-year ARM	**3.375**	3.375	3.375	3.375
Fannie Mae				
30-year mortgage yields				
30 days	**6.066**	6.107	6.792	5.913
60 days	**6.089**	6.125	6.821	5.924
Bankers acceptances				
30 days	**5.29**	5.31	5.38	4.35
60 days	**5.30**	5.31	5.43	4.44
90 days	**5.31**	5.31	5.49	4.49

Other short-term rates

	Latest	Week ago	52-WEEK High	52-WEEK Low
Commercial paper				
30 to 60 days	**5.23**	...	...	...
61 to 90 days	**5.22**	...	...	...
91 to 120 days	**5.20**	...	...	...
Dealer commercial paper				
30 days	**5.26**	5.27	5.36	4.32
60 days	**5.26**	5.28	5.41	4.42
90 days	**5.25**	5.30	5.46	4.46
Euro commercial paper				
30 day	**3.58**	3.58	3.62	2.00
Two month	**3.62**	3.62	3.63	2.39
Three month	**3.69**	3.68	3.69	2.45
London interbank offered rate, or Libor				
One month	**5.32000**	5.3256	5.4200	4.4188
Three month	**5.36000**	5.3600	5.5200	4.5500
Euro Libor				
One month	**3.628**	3.634	3.713	2.386
Three month	**3.733**	3.724	3.733	2.488
Euro interbank offered rate (Euribor)				
One month	**3.625**	3.634	3.672	2.384
Three month	**3.734**	3.723	3.734	2.490
Asian dollars				
One month	**5.335**	5.337	5.425	4.418
Three month	**5.363**	5.370	5.525	3.570

	LATEST Offer	Bid	Week ago	52-WEEK High	Low
Eurodollars (mid rates)					
One month	**5.28**	5.30	5.32	5.39	4.36
Two month	**5.29**	5.31	5.32	5.44	4.45
Three month	**5.30**	5.32	5.34	5.51	4.51

TABLE 2.2

Major components of the money market

	$ Billion
Repurchase agreements	$ 563.0
Small-denomination time deposits*	973.7
Large-denomination time deposits	1,359.4
Eurodollars	430.2
Treasury bills	963.9
Commercial paper	1,829.8
Savings deposits	3,620.5
Money market mutual funds	1,853.6

*Small denominations are less than $100,000

Source: *Economic Report of the President,* U.S. Government Printing Office, 2006; *Flow of Funds Accounts of the United States,* Board of Governors of the Federal Reserve System, September 2006.

Figure 2.2 is a listing of T-bills from *The Wall Street Journal* online (look for Market Data Center). Rather than providing prices of each bill, the financial press reports yields based on those prices. You will see yields corresponding to both bid and asked prices. The *asked price* is the price you would have to pay to buy a T-bill from a securities dealer. The *bid price* is the

Treasury Bills

MATURITY	DAYS TO MAT	BID	ASKED	CHG	ASK YLD
Jan 11 07	6	4.50	4.49	−0.11	4.56
Jan 18 07	13	4.57	4.56	−0.09	4.63
Jan 25 07	20	4.61	4.60	−0.01	4.68
Feb 01 07	27	4.70	4.69	−0.06	4.77
Feb 08 07	34	4.70	4.69	+0.01	4.78
Feb 15 07	41	4.73	4.72	−0.08	4.81
Feb 22 07	48	4.79	4.78	−0.04	4.88
Mar 01 07	55	4.83	4.82	−0.02	4.92
Mar 08 07	62	4.86	4.85	+0.01	4.96
Mar 15 07	69	4.85	4.84	−0.01	4.95
Mar 22 07	76	4.88	4.87	−0.02	4.99
Mar 29 07	83	4.88	4.87	−0.02	4.99
Apr 05 07	90	4.91	4.90	−0.01	5.03
Apr 12 07	97	4.90	4.89	−0.01	5.02
Apr 19 07	104	4.90	4.89	−0.01	5.03
Apr 26 07	111	4.90	4.89	−0.01	5.03

FIGURE 2.2

Treasury bill listings

Source: *The Wall Street Journal Online*, January 4, 2007.

slightly lower price you would receive if you wanted to sell a bill to a dealer. The *bid–asked spread* is the difference in these prices, which is the dealer's source of profit.

The first two yields in Figure 2.2 are reported using the *bank-discount method*. This means that the bill's discount from par value is "annualized" based on a 360-day year, and then reported as a percentage of par value. For example, for the highlighted bill maturing on April 5, days to maturity are 90 and the yield under the column labeled ASKED is given as 4.90%. This means that a dealer was willing to sell the bill at a discount from par value of 4.90% $\times$ (90/360) = 1.225%. So a bill with \$10,000 par value could be purchased for \$10,000 $\times$ (1 − .01225) = \$9,877.50. Similarly, on the basis of the bid yield of 4.91%, a dealer would be willing to *purchase* the bill for \$10,000 $\times$ [1 − .0491 $\times$ (90/360)] = \$9,877.25. Notice that prices and yields are inversely related, so the higher bid *yield* reported in Figure 2.2 implies a lower bid *price*.

The bank discount method for computing yields has a long tradition, but it is flawed for at least two reasons. First, it assumes that the year has only 360 days. Second, it computes the yield as a fraction of par value rather than of the price the investor paid to acquire the bill.[1] An investor who buys the bill for the asked price and holds it until maturity will see her investment grow over 90 days by a multiple of \$10,000/\$9,877.50 = 1.01240, or 1.240%. Annualizing this return using a 365-day year results in a yield of 1.240% $\times$ 365/90 = 5.03%, which is the value reported in the last column under "asked yield." This last value is called the Treasury bill's *bond-equivalent yield*.

Certificates of Deposit

A **certificate of deposit** (CD) is a time deposit with a bank. Time deposits may not be withdrawn on demand. The bank pays interest and principal to the depositor only at the end of the fixed term of the CD. CDs issued in denominations larger than \$100,000 are usually negotiable, however; that is, they can be sold to another investor if the owner needs to cash in the certificate before its maturity date. Short-term CDs are highly marketable, although the market significantly thins out for maturities of three months or more. CDs are treated as bank deposits by the Federal Deposit Insurance Corporation, so they are insured for up to \$100,000 in the event of a bank insolvency.

certificate of deposit

A bank time deposit.

[1] Both of these "errors" were dictated by computational simplicity in the days before computers. It is easier to compute percentage discounts from a round number such as par value rather than from purchase price. It is also easier to annualize using a 360-day year, since 360 is an even multiple of so many numbers.

Commercial Paper

commercial paper

Short-term unsecured debt issued by large corporations.

The typical corporation is a net borrower of both long-term funds (for capital investments) and short-term funds (for working capital). Large, well-known companies often issue their own short-term unsecured debt notes directly to the public, rather than borrowing from banks. These notes are called **commercial paper** (CP). Sometimes, CP is backed by a bank line of credit, which gives the borrower access to cash that can be used if needed to pay off the paper at maturity.

CP maturities range up to 270 days; longer maturities require registration with the Securities and Exchange Commission and so are almost never issued. CP most commonly is issued with maturities of less than one or two months in denominations of multiples of $100,000. Therefore, small investors can invest in commercial paper only indirectly, through money market mutual funds.

CP is considered to be a fairly safe asset, given that a firm's condition presumably can be monitored and predicted over a term as short as one month. CP trades in secondary markets and so is quite liquid. Most issues are rated by at least one agency such as Standard & Poor's. The yield on CP depends on its time to maturity and credit rating.

Bankers' Acceptances

bankers' acceptance

An order to a bank by a customer to pay a sum of money at a future date.

A **bankers' acceptance** starts as an order to a bank by a bank's customer to pay a sum of money at a future date, typically within six months. At this stage, it is like a postdated check. When the bank endorses the order for payment as "accepted," it assumes responsibility for ultimate payment to the holder of the acceptance. At this point, the acceptance may be traded in secondary markets much like any other claim on the bank. Bankers' acceptances are considered very safe assets, as they allow traders to substitute the bank's credit standing for their own. They are used widely in foreign trade where the creditworthiness of one trader is unknown to the trading partner. Acceptances sell at a discount from the face value of the payment order, just as T-bills sell at a discount from par value.

Eurodollars

Eurodollars

Dollar-denominated deposits at foreign banks or foreign branches of American banks.

Eurodollars are dollar-denominated deposits at foreign banks or foreign branches of American banks. By locating outside the United States, these banks escape regulation by the Federal Reserve Board. Despite the tag "Euro," these accounts need not be in European banks, although that is where the practice of accepting dollar-denominated deposits outside the United States began.

Most Eurodollar deposits are for large sums, and most are time deposits of less than six months' maturity. A variation on the Eurodollar time deposit is the Eurodollar certificate of deposit. A Eurodollar CD resembles a domestic bank CD except it is the liability of a non-U.S. branch of a bank, typically a London branch. The advantage of Eurodollar CDs over Eurodollar time deposits is that the holder can sell the asset to realize its cash value before maturity. Eurodollar CDs are considered less liquid and riskier than domestic CDs, however, and so offer higher yields. Firms also issue Eurodollar bonds, that is, dollar-denominated bonds outside the U.S., although such bonds are not a money market investment by virtue of their long maturities.

Repos and Reverses

repurchase agreements (repos)

Short-term sales of government securities with an agreement to repurchase the securities at a higher price.

Dealers in government securities use **repurchase agreements,** also called repos, or RPs, as a form of short-term, usually overnight, borrowing. The dealer sells securities to an investor on an overnight basis, with an agreement to buy back those securities the next day at a slightly higher price. The increase in the price is the overnight interest. The dealer thus takes out a one-day loan from the investor. The securities serve as collateral for the loan.

A *term repo* is essentially an identical transaction, except the term of the implicit loan can be 30 days or more. Repos are considered very safe in terms of credit risk because the loans are backed by the government securities. A *reverse repo* is the mirror image of a repo. Here, the dealer finds an investor holding government securities and buys them with an agreement to resell them at a specified higher price on a future date.

Brokers' Calls

Individuals who buy stocks on margin borrow part of the funds to pay for the stocks from their broker. The broker in turn may borrow the funds from a bank, agreeing to repay the bank immediately (on call) if the bank requests it. The rate paid on such loans is usually about one percentage point higher than the rate on short-term T-bills.

Federal Funds

Just as most of us maintain deposits at banks, banks maintain deposits of their own at the Federal Reserve Bank, or the Fed. Each member bank of the Federal Reserve System is required to maintain a minimum balance in a reserve account with the Fed. The required balance depends on the total deposits of the bank's customers. Funds in the bank's reserve account are called **Federal funds** or *Fed funds*. At any time, some banks have more funds than required at the Fed. Other banks, primarily big New York and other financial center banks, tend to have a shortage of Federal funds. In the Federal funds market, banks with excess funds lend to those with a shortage. These loans, which are usually overnight transactions, are arranged at a rate of interest called the Federal funds rate.

Federal funds

Funds in the accounts of commercial banks at the Federal Reserve Bank.

While the Fed funds rate is not directly relevant to most investors, it is used as one of the barometers of the money market and so is widely watched by them.

The LIBOR Market

The **London Interbank Offer Rate (LIBOR)** is the rate at which large banks in London are willing to lend money among themselves. This rate has become the premier short-term interest rate quoted in the European money market and serves as a reference rate for a wide range of transactions. A corporation might borrow at a rate equal to LIBOR plus two percentage points, for example. Like the Fed funds rate, LIBOR is a statistic widely followed by investors.

LIBOR

Lending rate among banks in the London market.

LIBOR interest rates may be tied to currencies other than the U.S. dollar. For example, LIBOR rates are widely quoted for transactions denominated in British pounds, yen, euros, and so on. There is also a similar rate called EURIBOR (European Interbank Offer Rate) at which banks in the euro zone are willing to lend euros among themselves.

Yields on Money Market Instruments

Although most money market securities are of low risk, they are not risk-free. The securities of the money market promise yields greater than those on default-free T-bills, at least in part because of their greater relative risk. Investors who require more liquidity also will accept lower yields on securities, such as T-bills, that can be more quickly and cheaply sold for cash. Figure 2.3 shows that bank CDs, for example, consistently have paid a risk premium over T-bills. Moreover, as Figure 2.3 shows, that premium increases with economic crises such as the energy price shocks associated with the Organization of Petroleum Exporting Countries (OPEC) disturbances, the failure of Penn Square Bank, the stock market crash in 1987, or the collapse of Long Term Capital Management in 1998.

FIGURE 2.3

Spread between three-month CD and T-bill rates

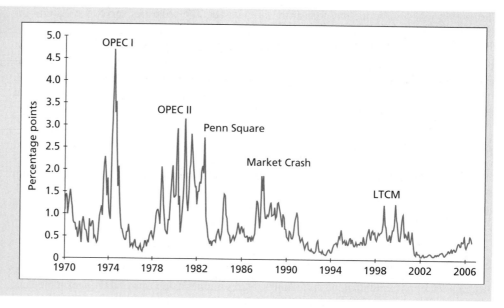

2.2 | THE BOND MARKET

The bond market is composed of longer-term borrowing or debt instruments than those that trade in the money market. This market includes Treasury notes and bonds, corporate bonds, municipal bonds, mortgage securities, and federal agency debt.

These instruments are sometimes said to comprise the *fixed-income capital market,* because most of them promise either a fixed stream of income or stream of income that is determined according to a specified formula. In practice, these formulas can result in a flow of income that is far from fixed. Therefore, the term "fixed income" is probably not fully appropriate. It is simpler and more straightforward to call these securities either debt instruments or bonds.

Treasury Notes and Bonds

Treasury notes or bonds

Debt obligations of the federal government with original maturities of one year or more.

The U.S. government borrows funds in large part by selling **Treasury notes** and **bonds.** T-note maturities range up to 10 years, while T-bonds are issued with maturities ranging from 10 to 30 years. Both bonds and notes are issued in denominations of $1,000 or more. Both bonds and notes make semiannual interest payments called *coupon payments,* so named because in precomputer days, investors would literally clip a coupon attached to the bond and present it to an agent of the issuing firm to receive the interest payment.

Figure 2.4 is an excerpt from a listing of Treasury issues in *The Wall Street Journal.* The highlighted bond matures in February 2014. The coupon income or interest paid by the bond is 4% of par value, meaning that for a $1,000 face value bond, $40 in annual interest payments will be made in two semiannual installments of $20 each. The numbers to the right of the colon in the bid and ask prices represent units of ½₂ of a point.

The bid price of the highlighted bond is 96⅞₂, or 96.281. The ask price is 96 ¹⁰⁄₃₂, or 96.3125. Although bonds are sold in denominations of $1,000 par value, the prices are quoted as a percentage of par value. Thus, the ask price of 96.3125 should be interpreted as 96.3125% of par or $963.125 for the $1,000 par value bond. Similarly, the bond could be sold to a dealer for $962.81. The +10 change means the closing price on this day rose ¹⁰⁄₃₂ (as a percentage of par value) from the previous day's closing price. Finally, the yield to maturity on the bond based on the ask price is 4.61%.

The yield to maturity reported in the last column is a measure of the annualized rate of return to an investor who buys the bond and holds it until maturity. It accounts for both coupon

FIGURE 2.4

Listing of Treasury issues

Source: From *The Wall Street Journal*, January 5, 2007. Reprinted by permission of Dow Jones & Company, Inc. via Copyright Clearance Center, Inc. © 2007 Dow Jones & Company, Inc. All Rights Reserved Worldwide.

U.S. Government Bonds and Notes

Representative Over-the-Counter quotation based on transactions of $1 million or more. Treasury bond, note and bill quotes are from midafternoon. Colons in bond and note bid-and-asked quotes represent 32nds; 101:01 means $101\frac{1}{32}$. Net change in 32nds. n-Treasury Note. i-Inflation-indexed issue. Treasury bill quotes in hundredths, quoted in terms of a rate of discount. Days to maturity calculated from settlement date. All yields are to maturity and based on the asked quote. For bonds callable prior to maturity, yields are computed to the earliest call date for issues quoted above par and to the maturity date for issues quoted below par.
*-When issued. Daily change expressed in basis points.

RATE	MATURITY MO/YR	BID	ASKED	CHG	ASK YLD	RATE	MATURITY MO/YR	BID	ASKED	CHG	ASK YLD
3.375	Jan 07i	99:28	99:29	.....	6.72	4.250	Nov 13n	97:29	97:30	+10	4.60
3.125	Jan 07n	99:27	99:28	.....	4.62	2.000	Jan 14i	97:16	97:17	+1	2.38
2.250	Feb 07n	99:21	99:22	.....	4.89	4.000	Feb 14n	96:09	96:10	+10	4.61
6.250	Feb 07n	100:04	100:05	.....	4.73	4.750	May 14n	100:26	100:27	+9	4.61
3.375	Feb 07n	99:23	99:24	.....	4.90	13.250	May 14	119:02	119:03	+4	4.61
3.750	Mar 07n	99:21	99:22	.....	4.99	2.000	Jul 14i	97:14	97:15	.....	2.37
3.875	Feb 13n	96:06	96:07	+8	4.59	4.250	Aug 14n	97:21	97:22	+10	4.61
3.625	May 13n	94:23	94:24	+8	4.58	12.500	Aug 14	119:04	119:05	+4	4.62
1.875	Jul 13i	97:00	97:01	+1	2.37	11.750	Nov 14	118:30	118:31	+6	4.59
4.250	Aug 13n	98:00	98:01	+9	4.60	4.250	Nov 14n	97:19	97:20	+9	4.61
12.000	Aug 13	111:04	111:05	+2	4.71	1.625	Jan 15i	94:18	94:19	+1	2.37

income as well as the difference between the purchase price of the bond and its final value of $1,000 at maturity. We discuss the yield to maturity in detail in Chapter 10.

What were the bid price, ask price, and yield to maturity of the 4¾% May 2014 Treasury note displayed in Figure 2.4? What was its ask price the previous day?

Inflation-Protected Treasury Bonds

The best place to start building an investment portfolio is at the least risky end of the spectrum. Around the world, governments of many countries, including the U.S., have issued bonds that are linked to an index of the cost of living in order to provide their citizens with an effective way to hedge inflation risk. See the nearby Web master box on inflation-protected bonds around the world.

In the United States, inflation-protected Treasury bonds are called TIPS (Treasury Inflation Protected Securities). The principal amount on these bonds is adjusted in proportion to increases in the Consumer Price Index. Therefore, they provide a constant stream of income in real (inflation-adjusted) dollars, and the real interest rates you earn on these securities are risk-free if you hold them to maturity. An *i* following the bond's maturity date in Figure 2.4

WEB *master*

Stock Market Index

Not all stock market indexes are created equal. Different methods are used to calculate various indexes, and different indexes will yield different assessments of "market performance." Using one of the following data sources, retrieve the stock price for 5 different firms on the first and last trading days of the previous month.

www.nasdaq.com—Get a quote, then select Charts and specify 1 month. When the chart appears, click on a data point to display the underlying data.

www.bloomberg.com—Get a quote, then plot the chart; next, use the moving line to see the closing price today and one month ago.

finance.yahoo.com—Get a quote, then click on Historical Data and specify a date range.

1. Compute the monthly return on a price-weighted index of the 5 stocks.
2. Compute the monthly return on a value-weighted index of the 5 stocks.
3. Compare the two returns and explain their differences. Explain how you would interpret each measure.

denotes that the bond is an inflation-indexed TIPS bond, and you will see that the reported yields on these bonds are lower than those on surrounding conventional Treasuries. Compare, for example, the reported yield on the July 14*i* bond, 2.37%, to the 4.61% yield on the August bond that follows it. The yields on TIPS bonds should be interpreted as real or inflation-adjusted interest rates. We return to TIPS bonds in more detail in Chapter 10.

Federal Agency Debt

Some government agencies issue their own securities to finance their activities. These agencies usually are formed for public policy reasons to channel credit to a particular sector of the economy that Congress believes is not receiving adequate credit through normal private sources.

The major mortgage-related agencies are the Federal Home Loan Bank (FHLB), the Federal National Mortgage Association (FNMA, or Fannie Mae), the Government National Mortgage Association (GNMA, or Ginnie Mae), and the Federal Home Loan Mortgage Corporation (FHLMC, or Freddie Mac).

Freddie Mac, Fannie Mae, and Ginnie Mae were organized to provide liquidity to the mortgage market. Until establishment of the pass-through securities sponsored by these government agencies, the lack of a secondary market in mortgages hampered the flow of investment funds into mortgages and made mortgage markets dependent on local, rather than national, credit availability. The pass-through financing initiated by these agencies represents one of the most important financial innovations of the 1980s.

Although the debt of federal agencies is not explicitly insured by the federal government, it is widely assumed the government will assist an agency nearing default. Thus, these securities are considered extremely safe assets, and their yield spread over Treasury securities is usually small.

International Bonds

Many firms borrow abroad and many investors buy bonds from foreign issuers. In addition to national capital markets, there is a thriving international capital market, largely centered in London, where banks of over 70 countries have offices.

A *Eurobond* is a bond denominated in a currency other than that of the country in which it is issued. For example, a dollar-denominated bond sold in Britain would be called a Euro-dollar bond. Similarly, investors might speak of Euroyen bonds, yen-denominated bonds sold outside Japan. Since the new European currency is called the euro, the term Eurobond may be confusing. It is best to think of them simply as international bonds.

In contrast to bonds that are issued in foreign currencies, many firms issue bonds in foreign countries but in the currency of the investor. For example, a Yankee bond is a dollar-denominated bond sold in the U.S. by a non-U.S. issuer. Similarly, Samurai bonds are yen-denominated bonds sold in Japan by non-Japanese issuers.

Municipal Bonds

municipal bonds

Tax-exempt bonds issued by state and local governments.

Municipal bonds ("munis") are issued by state and local governments. They are similar to Treasury and corporate bonds, except their interest income is exempt from federal income taxation. The interest income also is exempt from state and local taxation in the issuing state. Capital gains taxes, however, must be paid on munis if the bonds mature or are sold for more than the investor's purchase price.

There are basically two types of municipal bonds. *General obligation bonds* are backed by the "full faith and credit" (i.e., the taxing power) of the issuer, while *revenue bonds* are issued to finance particular projects and are backed either by the revenues from that project or by the municipal agency operating the project. Typical issuers of revenue bonds are airports, hospitals, and turnpike or port authorities. Revenue bonds are riskier in terms of default than general obligation bonds. Figure 2.5 plots outstanding amounts of both types of municipal securities.[2]

---

[2]A warning, however. Although interest on industrial development bonds usually is exempt from federal tax, it can be subject to the alternative minimum tax if the bonds are used to finance projects of for-profit companies.

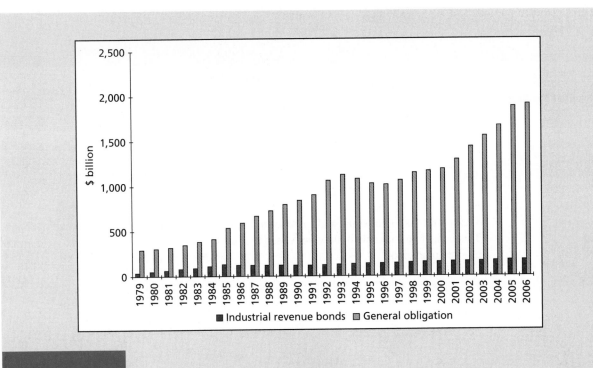

FIGURE 2.5

Outstanding tax-exempt debt

Source: *Flow of Funds Accounts of the U.S.*, Board of Governors of the Federal Reserve System, 2007.

An *industrial development bond* is a revenue bond that is issued to finance commercial enterprises, such as the construction of a factory that can be operated by a private firm. In effect, this device gives the firm access to the municipality's ability to borrow at tax-exempt rates, and the federal government limits the amount of these bonds that may be issued.

Like Treasury bonds, municipal bonds vary widely in maturity. A good deal of the debt issued is in the form of short-term tax anticipation notes that raise funds to pay for expenses before actual collection of taxes. Other municipal debt may be long term and used to fund large capital investments. Maturities range up to 30 years.

The key feature of municipal bonds is their tax-exempt status. Because investors pay neither federal nor state taxes on the interest proceeds, they are willing to accept lower yields on these securities.

An investor choosing between taxable and tax-exempt bonds needs to compare after-tax returns on each bond. An exact comparison requires the computation of after-tax rates of return with explicit recognition of taxes on income and realized capital gains. In practice, there is a simpler rule of thumb. If we let t denote the investor's combined federal plus local marginal tax rate and r denote the total before-tax rate of return available on taxable bonds, then $r(1 - t)$ is the after-tax rate available on those securities.[3] If this value exceeds the rate on municipal bonds, r_m, the investor does better holding the taxable bonds. Otherwise, the tax-exempt municipals provide higher after-tax returns.

One way of comparing bonds is to determine the interest rate on taxable bonds that would be necessary to provide an after-tax return equal to that of municipals. To derive this value,

[3]An approximation to the combined federal plus local tax rate is just the sum of the two rates. For example, if your federal tax rate is 28% and your state rate is 5%, your combined tax rate would be approximately 33%. A more precise approach would recognize that state taxes are deductible at the federal level. You owe federal taxes only on income net of state taxes. Therefore, for every dollar of income, your after-tax proceeds would be $(1 - t_{federal}) \times (1 - t_{state})$. In our example, your after-tax proceeds on each dollar earned would be $(1 - .28) \times (1 - .05) = .684$, which implies a combined tax rate of $1 - .684 = .316$ or 31.6%.

TABLE 2.3

Equivalent taxable yields corresponding to various tax-exempt yields

Marginal Tax Rate	Tax-Exempt Yield				
	1%	2%	3%	4%	5%
20%	1.25%	2.50%	3.75%	5.00%	6.25%
30	1.43	2.86	4.29	5.71	7.14
40	1.67	3.33	5.00	6.67	8.33
50	2.00	4.00	6.00	8.00	10.00

we set after-tax yields equal and solve for the *equivalent taxable yield* of the tax-exempt bond. This is the rate a taxable bond would need to offer in order to match the after-tax yield on the tax-free municipal.

$$r(1 - t) = r_m \tag{2.1}$$

or

$$r = \frac{r_m}{1 - t} \tag{2.2}$$

Thus, the equivalent taxable yield is simply the tax-free rate divided by $1 - t$. Table 2.3 presents equivalent taxable yields for several municipal yields and tax rates.

This table frequently appears in the marketing literature for tax-exempt mutual bond funds because it demonstrates to high tax-bracket investors that municipal bonds offer highly attractive equivalent taxable yields. Each entry is calculated from Equation 2.2. If the equivalent taxable yield exceeds the actual yields offered on taxable bonds, after taxes the investor is better off holding municipal bonds. The equivalent taxable interest rate increases with the investor's tax bracket; the higher the bracket, the more valuable the tax-exempt feature of municipals. Thus, high-bracket individuals tend to hold municipals.

We also can use Equation 2.1 or 2.2 to find the tax bracket at which investors are indifferent between taxable and tax-exempt bonds. The cutoff tax bracket is given by solving Equation 2.1 for the tax bracket at which after-tax yields are equal. Doing so, we find

$$t = 1 - \frac{r_m}{r} \tag{2.3}$$

Thus, the yield ratio r_m/r is a key determinant of the attractiveness of municipal bonds. The higher the yield ratio, the lower the cutoff tax bracket, and the more individuals will prefer to hold municipal debt. Figure 2.6 graphs the yield ratio since 1955.

EXAMPLE   2.1

Taxable versus Tax-Exempt Yields

Figure 2.6 shows that for most of the last 20 years, the ratio of tax-exempt to taxable yields fluctuated around .75. What does this imply about the cutoff tax bracket above which tax-exempt bonds provide higher after-tax yields? Equation 2.3 shows that an investor whose combined tax bracket (federal plus local) exceeds $1 - .75 = .25$, or 25%, will derive a greater after-tax yield from municipals. Note, however, that it is difficult to control precisely for differences in the risks of these bonds, so the cutoff tax bracket must be taken as approximate.

CONCEPT
check   2.2

Suppose your tax bracket is 28%. Would you prefer to earn a 6% taxable return or a 4% tax-free yield? What is the equivalent taxable yield of the 4% tax-free yield?

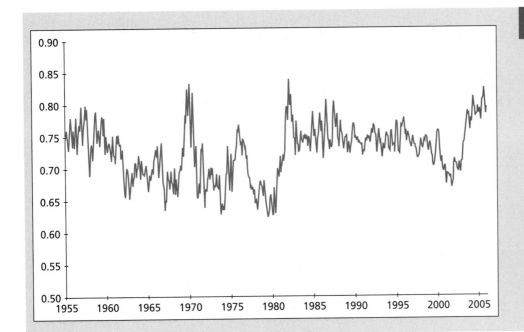

FIGURE 2.6

Ratio of yields on tax-exempt to taxable bonds

Corporate Bonds

Corporate bonds are the means by which private firms borrow money directly from the public. These bonds are structured much like Treasury issues in that they typically pay semiannual coupons over their lives and return the face value to the bondholder at maturity. Where they differ most importantly from Treasury bonds is in risk.

Default risk is a real consideration in the purchase of corporate bonds. We treat this issue in considerable detail in Chapter 10. For now, we distinguish only among secured bonds, which have specific collateral backing them in the event of firm bankruptcy; unsecured bonds, called *debentures,* which have no collateral; and subordinated debentures, which have a lower priority claim to the firm's assets in the event of bankruptcy.

Corporate bonds sometimes come with options attached. *Callable bonds* give the firm the option to repurchase the bond from the holder at a stipulated call price. *Convertible bonds* give the bondholder the option to convert each bond into a stipulated number of shares of stock. These options are treated in more detail in Part Three.

Figure 2.7 is a partial listing of corporate bond prices from the online edition of *The Wall Street Journal.* The listings provide the ticker symbol of each issue, the coupon rate, maturity date, daily high, low, and closing price, and yield to maturity. The Rating column provides the bond safety grade assigned by each of the three major bond-rating agencies: Moody's, Standard & Poor's, and Fitch. Bonds with ratings above Baa (Moody's or Fitch) or BBB (S&P) are considered low in terms of default or "credit" risk and are deemed "investment grade." Lower-rated bonds are called high-yield or junk bonds. We will discuss bond ratings and credit risk in more detail in Chapter 10.

corporate bonds

Long-term debt issued by private corporations typically paying semi-annual coupons and returning the face value of the bond at maturity.

Mortgages and Mortgage-Backed Securities

Forty years ago, your investments text probably would not have included a section on mortgage loans, for investors could not invest in these loans. Now, because of the explosion in mortgage-backed securities, almost anyone can invest in a portfolio of mortgage loans, and these securities have become a major component of the fixed-income market.

Until the 1970s, almost all home mortgages were written for a long term (15- to 30-year maturity), with a fixed interest rate over the life of the loan, and with equal, fixed monthly

ISSUER NAME	SYMBOL	COUPON	MATURITY	RATING MOODY'S/S&P/ FITCH	HIGH	LOW	LAST	CHANGE	YIELD %
Alltel	AT.GO	7.875%	Jul 2032	A2/A–/A	109.079	100.744	103.523	−5.617	7.561
Home Depot	HD.GH	5.400%	Mar 2016	Aa3/A+/A+	100.188	97.375	97.598	−0.232	5.740
Home Depot	HD.GK	5.875%	Dec 2036	Aa3/A+/A+	99.522	98.720	99.355	0.387	5.921
Goldman Sachs GP	GS.WB	5.750%	Oct 2016	Aa3/AA–/AA–	103.184	101.671	101.989	0.166	5.482
Walt Disney	DIS.HX	5.700%	Jul 2011	A3/A–/BBB+	102.131	101.865	102.058	0.158	5.183
R.R.Donnelley & Sons	DNY.GU	4.950%	Apr 2014	Baa2/BBB+/——	92.916	92.196	92.235	−1.115	6.302

FIGURE 2.7

Investment Grade Bond Listings

Source: From *The Wall Street Journal Online*, January 4, 2007. Reprinted by permission of Dow Jones & Company, Inc. via Copyright Clearance Center, Inc. © 2007 Dow Jones & Company, Inc. All Rights Reserved Worldwide.

payments. These so-called conventional mortgages are still the most popular, but a diverse set of alternative mortgage designs have appeared.

Fixed-rate mortgages can create considerable difficulties for banks in years of increasing interest rates. Because banks commonly issue short-term liabilities (the deposits of their customers) and hold long-term assets, such as fixed-rate mortgages, they suffer losses when interest rates increase. The rates they pay on deposits increase, while their mortgage income remains fixed.

The adjustable-rate mortgage was a response to this problem. These mortgages require the borrower to pay an interest rate that varies with some measure of the current market interest rate. The interest rate, for example, might be set at two points above the current rate on one-year Treasury bills and might be adjusted once a year. Often, the maximum interest rate change within a year and over the life of the loan is limited. The adjustable-rate contract shifts the risk of fluctuations in interest rates from the bank to the borrower. Because of the shifting of interest rate risk to their customers, lenders are willing to offer lower rates on adjustable-rate mortgages than on conventional fixed-rate mortgages.

A *mortgage-backed security* is either an ownership claim in a pool of mortgages or an obligation that is secured by such a pool. These claims represent securitization of mortgage loans. Mortgage lenders originate loans and then sell packages of these loans in the secondary market. Specifically, they sell their claim to the cash inflows from the mortgages as those loans are paid off. The mortgage originator continues to service the loan, collecting principal and interest payments, and passes these payments along to the purchaser of the mortgage. For this reason, these mortgage-backed securities are called *pass-throughs.*

Mortgage-backed pass-through securities were introduced by the Government National Mortgage Association (GNMA, or Ginnie Mae) in 1970. GNMA pass-throughs carry a guarantee from the U.S. government that ensures timely payment of principal and interest, even if the borrower defaults on the mortgage. This guarantee increases the marketability of the pass-through. Thus, investors can buy and sell GNMA securities like any other bond.

Other mortgage pass-throughs have since become popular. These are sponsored by FNMA (Fannie Mae) and FHLMC (Freddie Mac). By 2006, about $3.8 trillion of outstanding mortgages were securitized into mortgage-backed securities, making the mortgage-backed securities market larger than the $3.1 trillion corporate bond market and nearly the size of the $4.6 trillion market in Treasury securities. Figure 2.8 illustrates the explosive growth of these securities since 1979.

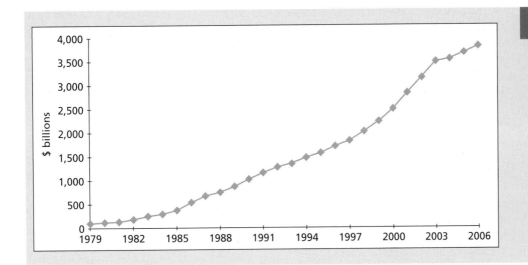

FIGURE 2.8

Mortgage-backed securities outstanding

Source: *Flow of Funds Accounts of the U.S.*, Board of Governors of the Federal Reserve System, September 2006.

The success of mortgage-backed pass-throughs has encouraged the introduction of pass-through securities backed by other assets. These "asset-backed" securities have grown rapidly, from a level of about $316 billion in 1995 to $1,986 billion in 2006.

2.3 EQUITY SECURITIES

Common Stock as Ownership Shares

Common stocks, also known as equity securities, or equities, represent ownership shares in a corporation. Each share of common stock entitles its owners to one vote on any matters of corporate governance put to a vote at the corporation's annual meeting and to a share in the financial benefits of ownership (e.g., the right to any dividends that the corporation may choose to distribute).[4]

> **common stocks**
>
> **Ownership shares in a publicly held corporation. Shareholders have voting rights and may receive dividends.**

A corporation is controlled by a board of directors elected by the shareholders.[5] The board, which meets only a few times each year, selects managers who run the corporation on a day-to-day basis. Managers have the authority to make most business decisions without the board's approval. The board's mandate is to oversee management to ensure that it acts in the best interests of shareholders.

The members of the board are elected at the annual meeting. Shareholders who do not attend the annual meeting can vote by proxy, empowering another party to vote in their name. Management usually solicits the proxies of shareholders and normally gets a vast majority of these proxy votes. Thus, management usually has considerable discretion to run the firm as it sees fit, without daily oversight from the equityholders who actually own the firm.

We noted in Chapter 1 that such separation of ownership and control can give rise to "agency problems," in which managers pursue goals not in the best interests of shareholders. However, there are several mechanisms designed to alleviate these agency problems. Among these are compensation schemes that link the success of the manager to that of the firm; oversight by the board of directors as well as outsiders such as security analysts, creditors, or large institutional investors; the threat of a proxy contest in which unhappy shareholders attempt to replace the current management team; or the threat of a takeover by another firm.

---

[4]Sometimes a corporation issues two classes of common stock, one bearing the right to vote, the other not. Because of their restricted rights, the nonvoting stocks sell for a lower price, reflecting the value of control.

[5]The voting system specified in the corporate articles determines the chances of affecting the elections to specific directorship seats. In a majority voting system, each shareholder can cast one vote per share for each seat. A cumulative voting system allows shareholders to concentrate all their votes in one seat, enabling minority shareholders to gain representation.

The common stock of most large corporations can be bought or sold freely on one or more of the stock markets. A corporation whose stock is not publicly traded is said to be *closely held.* In most closely held corporations, the owners of the firm also take an active role in its management. Takeovers generally are not an issue.

Characteristics of Common Stock

The two most important characteristics of common stock as an investment are its residual claim and its limited liability features.

Residual claim means stockholders are the last in line of all those who have a claim on the assets and income of the corporation. In a liquidation of the firm's assets, the shareholders have claim to what is left after paying all other claimants, such as the tax authorities, employees, suppliers, bondholders, and other creditors. In a going concern, shareholders have claim to the part of operating income left after interest and income taxes have been paid. Management either can pay this residual as cash dividends to shareholders or reinvest it in the business to increase the value of the shares.

Limited liability means that the most shareholders can lose in event of the failure of the corporation is their original investment. Shareholders are not like owners of unincorporated businesses, whose creditors can lay claim to the personal assets of the owner—such as houses, cars, and furniture. In the event of the firm's bankruptcy, corporate stockholders at worst have worthless stock. They are not personally liable for the firm's obligations: Their liability is limited.

CONCEPT *check* **2.3**

a. If you buy 100 shares of IBM common stock, to what are you entitled?
b. What is the most money you can make over the next year?
c. If you pay $95 per share, what is the most money you could lose over the year?

2.9 Stock Market Listings

Figure 2.9 is a partial listing from the online edition of *The Wall Street Journal* of stocks traded on the New York Stock Exchange. The NYSE is one of several markets in which investors may buy or sell shares of stock. We will examine issues of trading in these markets in the next chapter.

To interpret Figure 2.9, consider the highlighted listing for General Electric. The table provides the ticker symbol (GE), the closing price of the stock ($37.56), and its change (−$.19) from the previous trading day. Almost 27 million shares of GE traded on this day. The table also provides the highest and lowest price at which GE has traded in the last 52

FIGURE 2.9

Listing of stocks traded on the New York Stock Exchange

Source: From *The Wall Street Journal Online,* January 9, 2007. Reprinted by permission of Dow Jones & Company, Inc. © 2007 Dow Jones & Company, Inc. via Copyright Clearance Center, Inc. All Rights Reserved Worldwide.

NAME	SYMBOL	CLOSE	NET CHG	VOLUME	52 WK HIGH	52 WK LOW	DIV	YIELD	P/E	YTD% CHG
Gencorp	GY	13.59	−0.29	491,300	20.75	12.02	....	....	dd	−3.1
Genentech	DNA	83.68	−0.35	3,986,300	94.46	75.58	....	....	49	3.1
General Cable	BGC	42.67	−1.11	679,700	45.41	20.3	....	....	23	−2.4
General Dynamics	GD	74.59	0.17	1,497,300	77.98	56.68	0.92	1.2	16	0.3
General Electric	GE	37.56	−0.19	26,907,700	38.49	32.06	1.12	3	23	0.9
General Gwth Prop	GGP	51.51	−0.8	1,308,200	56.14	41.92	1.8	3.5	215	−1.4
General Maritime	GMR	34.56	−0.83	597,400	40.64	30.34	4.8	13.9	5	−1.8
General Mills	GIS	56.97	−0.42	1,355,600	59.23	47.05	1.48	2.6	18	−1.1
General Motors	GM	30.24	0.6	10,477,600	36.56	19	1	3.3	dd	−1.6
Genesco Inc	GCO	36.75	−0.9	127,900	43.72	25.5	....	....	15	−1.5
Genesee & Wyoming	GWR	25.86	−0.5	364,500	36.75	21	....	....	9	−1.4
Genesis Lease	GLS	23.6	0.1	298,500	24.4	23	....	....		0.4
Genuine Parts co.	GPC	46.86	−0.51	384,400	48.34	40	1.35	2.9	17	−1.2
Genworth Financial	GNW	33.79	−0.32	1,414,900	36.47	31	0.36	1.1	13	−1.2
Geo Group Inc	GEO	37.57	−1.53	157,500	40.3	14.69	....	....	35	0.1
Georgia Gulf	GGC	18.69	−0.38	479,000	34.65	18.36	0.32	1.7	6	−3.2
Gerber Scientific	GRB	12.32	−0.07	243,200	16.8	9	....	....	27	−1.9
Gerdau Ameristeel	GNA	8.59	−0.04	446,200	11.02	5.85	0.08	0.9	7	−3.7
Gerdau S.A. Ads	GGB	15.57	−0.56	1,729,100	18.16	11.27	0.58	3.7	....	−2.7

weeks. The 1.12 value in the Dividend column means that the last quarterly dividend payment was \$.28 per share, which is consistent with annual dividend payments of \$.28 $\times$ 4 = \$1.12. This corresponds to a dividend yield (i.e., annual dividend per dollar paid for the stock) of 1.12/37.56 = .030 or 3.0%.

The dividend yield is only part of the return on a stock investment. It ignores prospective *capital gains* (i.e., price increases) or losses. Shares in low dividend firms presumably offer greater prospects for capital gains, or investors would not be willing to hold these stocks in their portfolios. If you scan Figure 2.9, you will see that dividend yields vary widely across companies.

The P/E ratio, or price-to-earnings ratio, is the ratio of the current stock price to last year's earnings. The P/E ratio tells us how much stock purchasers must pay per dollar of earnings the firm generates for each share. For GE, the ratio of price to earnings is 23. The P/E ratio also varies widely across firms. Where the dividend yield and P/E ratio are not reported in Figure 2.9, the firms have zero dividends, or zero or negative earnings. We shall have much to say about P/E ratios in Part Four. Finally, we see that GE's stock price has increased by 0.9% since the beginning of the year.

Preferred Stock

Preferred stock has features similar to both equity and debt. Like a bond, it promises to pay to its holder a fixed stream of income each year. In this sense, preferred stock is similar to an infinite-maturity bond, that is, a perpetuity. It also resembles a bond in that it does not give the holder voting power regarding the firm's management.

preferred stock

Nonvoting shares in a corporation, usually paying a fixed stream of dividends.

Preferred stock is an equity investment, however. The firm retains discretion to make the dividend payments to the preferred stockholders: It has no contractual obligation to pay those dividends. Instead, preferred dividends are usually *cumulative;* that is, unpaid dividends cumulate and must be paid in full before any dividends may be paid to holders of common stock. In contrast, the firm does have a contractual obligation to make timely interest payments on the debt. Failure to make these payments sets off corporate bankruptcy proceedings.

Preferred stock also differs from bonds in terms of its tax treatment for the firm. Because preferred stock payments are treated as dividends rather than as interest on debt, they are not tax-deductible expenses for the firm. This disadvantage is largely offset by the fact that corporations may exclude 70% of dividends received from domestic corporations in the computation of their taxable income. Preferred stocks, therefore, make desirable fixed-income investments for some corporations.

Even though preferred stock ranks after bonds in terms of the priority of its claim to the assets of the firm in the event of corporate bankruptcy, preferred stock often sells at lower yields than corporate bonds. Presumably this reflects the value of the dividend exclusion, because the higher risk of preferred stock would tend to result in higher yields than those offered by bonds. Individual investors, who cannot use the 70% exclusion, generally will find preferred stock yields unattractive relative to those on other available assets.

Corporations issue preferred stock in variations similar to those of corporate bonds. Preferred stock can be callable by the issuing firm, in which case it is said to be *redeemable*. It also can be convertible into common stock at some specified conversion ratio. A relatively recent innovation is adjustable-rate preferred stock, which, like adjustable-rate bonds, ties the dividend rate to current market interest rates.

Depository Receipts

American Depository Receipts, or ADRs, are certificates traded in U.S. markets that represent ownership in shares of a foreign company. Each ADR may correspond to ownership of a fraction of a foreign share, one share, or several shares of the foreign corporation. ADRs were created to make it easier for foreign firms to satisfy U.S. security registration requirements. They are the most common way for U.S. investors to invest in and trade the shares of foreign corporations.

STOCK AND BOND MARKET INDEXES

Stock Market Indexes

The daily performance of the Dow Jones Industrial Average is a staple portion of the evening news report. While the Dow is the best-known measure of the performance of the stock market, it is only one of several indicators. Other more broadly based indexes are computed and published daily. In addition, several indexes of bond market performance are widely available.

The ever-increasing role of international trade and investments has made indexes of foreign financial markets part of the general news. Thus, foreign stock exchange indexes such as the Nikkei Average of Tokyo or the *Financial Times* index of London have become household names.

Dow Jones Averages

The Dow Jones Industrial Average (DJIA) of 30 large, "blue-chip" corporations has been computed since 1896. Its long history probably accounts for its preeminence in the public mind. (The average covered only 20 stocks until 1928.)

Originally, the DJIA was calculated as the simple average of the stocks included in the index. So, if there were 30 stocks in the index, one would add up the value of the 30 stocks and divide by 30. The percentage change in the DJIA would then be the percentage change in the average price of the 30 shares.

This procedure means that the percentage change in the DJIA measures the return (excluding any dividends paid) on a portfolio that invests one share in each of the 30 stocks in the index. The value of such a portfolio (holding one share of each stock in the index) is the sum of the 30 prices. Because the percentage change in the *average* of the 30 prices is the same as the percentage change in the *sum* of the 30 prices, the index and the portfolio have the same percentage change each day.

price-weighted average

An average computed by adding the prices of the stocks and dividing by a "divisor."

The Dow measures the return (excluding dividends) on a portfolio that holds one share of each stock. The amount of money invested in each company represented in the portfolio is proportional to that company's share price, so the Dow is called a **price-weighted average.**

EXAMPLE   2.2
Price-Weighted Average

Consider the data in Table 2.4 for a hypothetical two-stock version of the Dow Jones Average. Let's compare the changes in the value of the portfolio holding one share of each firm and the price-weighted index. Stock ABC starts at $25 a share and increases to $30. Stock XYZ starts at $100, but falls to $90.

Portfolio:	Initial value = $25 + $100 = $125
	Final value = $30 + $90 = $120
	Percentage change in portfolio value = −5/125 = −.04 = −4%
Index:	Initial index value = (25 + 100)/2 = 62.5
	Final index value = (30 + 90)/2 = 60
	Percentage change in index = −2.5/62.5 = −.04 = −4%

The portfolio and the index have identical 4% declines in value.

Notice that price-weighted averages give higher-priced shares more weight in determining the performance of the index. For example, although ABC increased by 20% while XYZ fell by only 10%, the index dropped in value. This is because the 20% increase in ABC represented a smaller dollar price gain ($5 per share) than the 10% decrease in XYZ ($10 per share). The "Dow portfolio" has four times as much invested in XYZ as in ABC because XYZ's price is four times that of ABC. Therefore, XYZ dominates the average. We conclude that a high-price stock can dominate a price-weighted average.

You might wonder why the DJIA is now (in mid-2007) at a level of about 13,000 if it is supposed to be the average price of the 30 stocks in the index. The DJIA no longer equals the

Stock	Initial Price	Final Price	Shares (millions)	Initial Value of Outstanding Stock ($ million)	Final Value of Outstanding Stock ($ million)
ABC	$ 25	$30	20	$500	$600
XYZ	100	90	1	100	90
Total				$600	$690

average price of the 30 stocks because the averaging procedure is adjusted whenever a stock splits, pays a stock dividend of more than 10%, or when one company in the group of 30 industrial firms is replaced by another. When these events occur, the divisor used to compute the "average price" is adjusted so as to leave the index unaffected by the event.

Suppose firm XYZ from Example 2.2 were to split two for one so that its share price fell to $50. We would not want the average to fall, as that would incorrectly indicate a fall in the general level of market prices. Following a split, the divisor must be reduced to a value that leaves the average unaffected. Table 2.5 illustrates this point. The initial share price of XYZ, which was $100 in Table 2.4, falls to $50 if the stock splits at the beginning of the period. Notice that the number of shares outstanding doubles, leaving the market value of the total shares unaffected.

We find the new divisor as follows. The index value before the stock split was 125/2 = 62.5. We must find a new divisor, d, that leaves the index unchanged after XYZ splits and its price falls to $50. Therefore we solve for d in the following equation:

$$\frac{\text{Price of ABC} + \text{Price of XYZ}}{d} = \frac{25 + 50}{d} = 62.5$$

which implies that the divisor must fall from its original value of 2.0 to a new value of 1.20.

Because the split changes the price of stock XYZ, it also changes the relative weights of the two stocks in the price-weighted average. Therefore, the return of the index is affected by the split.

At period-end, ABC will sell for $30, while XYZ will sell for $45, representing the same negative 10% return it was assumed to earn in Table 2.4. The new value of the price-weighted average is (30 + 45)/1.20 = 62.5. The index is unchanged, so the rate of return is zero, greater than the −4% return that would have resulted in the absence of a split. The relative weight of XYZ, which is the poorer-performing stock, is reduced by a split because its price is lower; so the performance of the average is higher. This example illustrates that the implicit weighting scheme of a price-weighted average is somewhat arbitrary, being determined by the prices rather than by the outstanding market values (price per share times number of shares) of the shares in the average.

Stock	Initial Price	Final Price	Shares (millions)	Initial Value of Outstanding Stock ($ million)	Final Value of Outstanding Stock ($ million)
ABC	$25	$30	20	$500	$600
XYZ	50	45	2	100	90
Total				$600	$690

On the MARKET FRONT

HOW THE 30 STOCKS IN THE DOW JONES INDUSTRIAL AVERAGE HAVE CHANGED SINCE OCT. 1, 1928

Oct. 1, 1928	1929	1930s	1940s 1950s
Wright Aeronautical	Curtiss-Wright ('29)	Hudson Motor ('30) Coca-Cola ('32) National Steel ('35)	Aluminum Co. of America ('59)
Allied Chemical & Dye			
North American		Johns-Manville ('30)	
Victor Talking Machine	Natl Cash Register ('29)	IBM ('32) AT&T ('39)	
International Nickel			
International Harvester			
Westinghouse Electric			
Texas Gulf Sulphur		Intl. Shoe ('32) United Aircraft ('33) National Distillers ('34)	Owens-Illinois ('59)
American Sugar		Borden ('30) DuPont ('35)	
American Tobacco (B)		Eastman Kodak ('30)	
Standard Oil (N.J.)			
General Electric			
General Motors			
Texas Corp.			Texaco* ('59)
Sears Roebuck			
Chrysler			
Atlantic Refining		Goodyear ('30)	
Paramount Publix		Loew's ('32)	Intl. Paper ('56)
Bethlehem Steel			
General Railway Signal		Liggett & Myers ('30) Amer. Tobacco ('32)	
Mack Trucks		Drug Inc. ('32) Corn Products ('33)	Swift & Co. ('59)
Union Carbide			
American Smelting			Anaconda ('59)
American Can			
Postum Inc.	General Foods* ('29)		
Nash Motors		United Air Trans. ('30) Procter & Gamble ('32)	
Goodrich		Standard Oil (Calif) ('30)	
Radio Corp.		Nash Motors ('32) United Aircraft ('39)	
Woolworth			
U.S. Steel			

Note: Year of change shown in (); *denotes name change, in some cases following a takeover or merger. To track changes in the components, begin in the column for 1928 and work across. For instance, American Sugar was replaced by Borden in 1930, which in turn was replaced by DuPont in 1935. Each of the new stocks added in 2004 doesn't specifically replace any of the departing stocks; it was simply a four-for-four switch.

Source: From *The Wall Street Journal*, October 27, 1999. Reprinted by permission of Dow Jones & Company, Inc. via Copyright Clearance Center, Inc. © 1999. Dow Jones & Company, Inc. All Rights Reserved Worldwide. Updated by authors.

1960s 1970s	1980s	1990s	April 8, 2004
		Alcoa*	Alcoa
	Allied Signal* ('85)	Honeywell*	Honeywell
	Amer. Express ('82)		American Express
			AIG Group
Inco Ltd.* ('76)	Boeing ('87)		Boeing
	Navistar* ('86)	Caterpillar ('91)	Caterpillar
		Travelers Group ('97)	Citigroup*
	Coca-Cola ('87)		Coca-Cola
			DuPont
			Pfizer
	Exxon* ('72)	ExxonMobil*	ExxonMobil
			General Electric
			General Motors
		Hewlett-Packard ('97)	Hewlett-Packard
		Home Depot	Home Depot
IBM ('79)			IBM
		Intel	Intel
			Verizon
		Johnson & Johnson ('97)	Johnson & Johnson
	McDonald's ('85)		McDonald's
Esmark* ('73) Merck ('79)			Merck
		Microsoft	Microsoft
Minn. Mining ('76)			Minn. Mining (3M)
	Primerica* ('87)	J.P. Morgan ('91)	J.P. Morgan
	Philip Morris ('85)		Philip Morris
			Procter & Gamble
	Chevron* ('84)	SBC Communications	SBC Communications
United Tech.* ('75)			United Technologies
		Wal-Mart Stores ('97)	Wal-Mart
	USX Corp.* ('86)	Walt Disney ('91)	Walt Disney

Because the Dow Jones averages are based on small numbers of firms, care must be taken to ensure that they are representative of the broad market. As a result, the composition of the average is changed every so often to reflect changes in the economy. The last change took place on April 8, 2004, when AIG Group, Pfizer, and Verizon replaced AT&T, Eastman Kodak, and International Paper in the index. The nearby box presents the history of the firms in the index since 1928. The fate of many companies once considered "the bluest of the blue chips" is striking evidence of the changes in the U.S. economy in the last 80 years.

In the same way that the divisor is updated for stock splits, if one firm is dropped from the average and another firm with a different price is added, the divisor has to be updated to leave the average unchanged by the substitution. By early 2007, the divisor for the Dow Jones Industrial Average had fallen to a value of about .125.

CONCEPT
c h e c k   **2.4**

Suppose XYZ's final price in Table 2.4 increases in price to $110, while ABC falls to $20. Find the percentage change in the price-weighted average of these two stocks. Compare that to the percentage return of a portfolio that holds one share in each company.

Dow Jones & Company also computes a Transportation Average of 20 airline, trucking, and railroad stocks; a Public Utility Average of 15 electric and natural gas utilities; and a Composite Average combining the 65 firms of the three separate averages. Each is a price-weighted average and thus overweights the performance of high-priced stocks.

Standard & Poor's Indexes

**market value–
weighted index**

**Computed by calculating
a weighted average
of the returns of each
security in the index, with
weights proportional to
outstanding market value.**

The Standard & Poor's Composite 500 (S&P 500) stock index represents an improvement over the Dow Jones averages in two ways. First, it is a more broadly based index of 500 firms. Second, it is a **market value–weighted index.** In the case of the firms XYZ and ABC in Example 2.2, the S&P 500 would give ABC five times the weight given to XYZ because the market value of its outstanding equity is five times larger, $500 million versus $100 million.

The S&P 500 is computed by calculating the total market value of the 500 firms in the index and the total market value of those firms on the previous day of trading.[6] The percentage increase in the total market value from one day to the next represents the increase in the index. The rate of return of the index equals the rate of return that would be earned by an investor holding a portfolio of all 500 firms in the index in proportion to their market value, except that the index does not reflect cash dividends paid by those firms.

EXAMPLE   2.4

*Value-Weighted
Indexes*

To illustrate how value-weighted indexes are computed, look again at Table 2.4. The final value of all outstanding stock in our two-stock universe is $690 million. The initial value was $600 million. Therefore, if the initial level of a market value-weighted index of stocks ABC and XYZ were set equal to an arbitrarily chosen starting value such as 100, the index value at year-end would be 100 × (690/600) = 115. The increase in the index would reflect the 15% return earned on a portfolio consisting of those two stocks held in proportion to outstanding market values.

Unlike the price-weighted index, the value-weighted index gives more weight to ABC. Whereas the price-weighted index fell because it was dominated by higher-price XYZ, the value-weighted index rose because it gave more weight to ABC, the stock with the higher total market value.

Note also from Tables 2.4 and 2.5 that market value–weighted indexes are unaffected by stock splits. The total market value of the outstanding XYZ stock increases from $100 million to $110 million regardless of the stock split, thereby rendering the split irrelevant to the performance of the index.

---

[6]Actually, most indexes today use a modified version of market-value weights. Rather than weighting by total market value, they weight by the market value of "free float," that is, by the value of shares that are freely tradable among investors. For example, this procedure does not count shares held by founding families or governments which are effectively not available for investors to purchase. The distinction is more important in Japan and Europe, where a higher fraction of shares are held in such nontraded portfolios.

n q s p c

1330.61
-21.46 /-1.59

A nice feature of both market value–weighted and price-weighted indexes is that they reflect the returns to straightforward portfolio strategies. If one were to buy each share in the index in proportion to its outstanding market value, the value-weighted index would perfectly track capital gains on the underlying portfolio. Similarly, a price-weighted index tracks the returns on a portfolio comprised of equal shares of each firm.

Investors today can easily buy market indexes for their portfolios. One way is to purchase shares in mutual funds that hold shares in proportion to their representation in the S&P 500 as well as other stock indexes. These *index funds* yield a return equal to that of the particular index and so provide a low-cost passive investment strategy for equity investors. Another approach is to purchase an *exchange-traded fund* or ETF, which is a portfolio of shares that can be bought or sold as a unit, just as a single share would be traded. Available ETFs range from portfolios that track extremely broad global market indexes all the way to narrow industry indexes. We discuss both mutual funds and ETFs in detail in Chapter 4.

Standard & Poor's also publishes a 400-stock Industrial Index, a 20-stock Transportation Index, a 40-stock Utility Index, and a 40-stock Financial Index.

Reconsider companies XYZ and ABC from Concept Check Question 2.4. Calculate the percentage change in the market value–weighted index. Compare that to the rate of return of a portfolio that holds $500 of ABC stock for every $100 of XYZ stock (i.e., an index portfolio).

CONCEPT *check* **2.5**

Other U.S. Market Value Indexes

The New York Stock Exchange publishes a market value–weighted composite index of all NYSE-listed stocks, in addition to subindexes for industrial, utility, transportation, and financial stocks. These indexes are even more broadly based than the S&P 500. The National Association of Securities Dealers publishes valued-weighted indexes of Nasdaq firms, including the Nasdaq Composite index and the Nasdaq 100 of the larger Nasdaq firms.

The ultimate U.S. equity index so far computed is the Wilshire 5000 Index of the market value of all NYSE and American Stock Exchange (Amex) stocks plus actively traded Nasdaq stocks. Despite its name, the index actually includes about 6,000 stocks. The performance of many of these indexes appears daily in *The Wall Street Journal*.

Figure 2.10 shows the performance of the S&P 500, Dow Jones Industrial Average, and Nasdaq composite over the six-year period ending in late 2006. Usually, the indexes move closely together. Occasionally though, they diverge. For example, during the Internet boom and bust of 1999–2002, the Nasdaq index, which is dominated by the technology sector, first greatly outperformed, and then underperformed, the S&P 500.

FIGURE 2.10

Comparative performance of several stock market indexes, 2001–2006

Equally Weighted Indexes

equally weighted index

An index computed from a simple average of returns.

Market performance is sometimes measured by an equally weighted average of the returns of each stock in an index. Such an averaging technique, by placing equal weight on each return, corresponds to a portfolio strategy that places equal dollar values in each stock. This is in contrast to both price weighting, which requires equal numbers of shares of each stock, and market value weighting, which requires investments in proportion to outstanding value.

Unlike price- or market value–weighted indexes, equally weighted indexes do not correspond to buy-and-hold portfolio strategies. Suppose you start with equal dollar investments in the two stocks of Table 2.4, ABC and XYZ. Because ABC increases in value by 20% over the year, while XYZ decreases by 10%, your portfolio is no longer equally weighted but is now more heavily invested in ABC. To reset the portfolio to equal weights, you would need to rebalance: Either sell some ABC stock and/or purchase more XYZ stock. Such rebalancing would be necessary to align the return on your portfolio with that on the equally weighted index.

Foreign and International Stock Market Indexes

Development in financial markets worldwide includes the construction of indexes for these markets. The most important are the Nikkei (Japan), FTSE (U.K., pronounced "footsie"), DAX (Germany), Hang Seng (Hong Kong), and TSX (Toronto). A leader in the construction of international indexes has been MSCI (Morgan Stanley Capital International), which computes over 50 country indexes and several regional indexes. Table 2.6 presents many of the indexes computed by MCSI.

Bond Market Indicators

Just as stock market indexes provide guidance concerning the performance of the overall stock market, several bond market indicators measure the performance of various categories of bonds. The three most well-known groups of indexes are those of Merrill Lynch, Lehman Brothers, and Salomon Smith Barney (now part of Citigroup). Table 2.7 lists the components of the bond market in 2006.

The major problem with these indexes is that true rates of return on many bonds are difficult to compute because bonds trade infrequently, which makes it hard to get reliable, up-to-date prices. In practice, some prices must be estimated from bond valuation models. These so-called matrix prices may differ from true market values.

2.5 DERIVATIVE MARKETS

derivative asset or contingent claim

A security with a payoff that depends on the prices of other securities.

A significant development in financial markets in recent years has been the growth of futures and options markets. Futures and options provide payoffs that depend on the values of other assets, such as commodity prices, bond and stock prices, or market index values. For this reason, these instruments sometimes are called derivative assets or contingent claims. Their values derive from or are contingent on the values of other assets. We discuss derivative assets in detail in Part Five, but the nearby box serves as a brief primer.

Options

call option

The right to buy an asset at a specified price on or before a specified expiration date.

A call option gives its holder the right to purchase an asset for a specified price, called the *exercise or strike price,* on or before some specified expiration date. An October call option on IBM stock with exercise price $85, for example, entitles its owner to purchase IBM stock for a price of $85 at any time up to and including the option's expiration date in October. Each option contract is for the purchase of 100 shares, with quotations made on a per share basis. The holder of the call need not exercise the option; it will make sense to exercise only if the market value of the asset that may be purchased exceeds the exercise price.

TABLE 2.6

Sample of MSCI stock indexes

Regional Indexes		Countries	
Developed Markets	**Emerging Markets**	**Developed Markets**	**Emerging Markets**
EAFE (Europe, Australia, Far East)	Emerging Markets (EM)	Australia	Argentina
EASEA (EAFE excluding Japan)	EM Asia	Austria	Brazil
Europe	EM Far East	Belgium	Chile
EMU	EM Latin America	Canada	China
Far East	Emerging Markets Free (EMF)	Denmark	Colombia
Kokusai (World excluding Japan)	EMF Asia	Finland	Czech Republic
Nordic Countries	EMF Eastern Europe	France	Egypt
North America	EMF Europe	Germany	Hungary
Pacific	EMF Europe & Middle East	Greece	India
The World Index	EMF Far East	Hong Kong	Indonesia
G7 countries	EMF Latin America	Ireland	Israel
World excluding U.S.		Italy	Jordan
		Japan	Korea
		Netherlands	Malaysia
		New Zealand	Mexico
		Norway	Morocco
		Portugal	Pakistan
		Singapore	Peru
		Spain	Philippines
		Sweden	Poland
		Switzerland	Russia
		U.K.	South Africa
		U.S.	Sri Lanka
			Taiwan
			Thailand
			Turkey
			Venezuela

Source: MSCI, **www.mscibarra.com**. Reprinted by permission.

TABLE 2.7

The U.S. bond market

Sector	Size ($ billion)	% of Market
Treasury	$ 4,554.4	25.0%
Gov't-sponsored enterprise	2,686.1	14.7
Corporate	3,111.4	17.1
Tax-exempt*	2,090.4	11.5
Mortgage-backed	3,818.3	20.9
Asset-backed	1,985.8	10.9
Total	$18,246.4	100.0%

*Includes private purpose tax-exempt debt.

Source: *Flow of Funds Accounts of the United States: Flows and Outstandings,* Board of Governors of the Federal Reserve System, September 2006.

When the market price exceeds the exercise price, the option holder may "call away" the asset for the exercise price and reap a benefit equal to the difference between the stock price and the exercise price. Otherwise, the option will be left unexercised. If not exercised before the expiration date, the option expires and no longer has value. Calls, therefore, provide greater profits when stock prices increase and so represent bullish investment vehicles.

A **put option** gives its holder the right to sell an asset for a specified exercise price on or before a specified expiration date. An October put on IBM with exercise price $85 entitles its owner to sell IBM stock to the put writer at a price of $85 at any time before expiration in October even if the market price of IBM is lower than $85. Whereas profits on call options increase when the asset increases in value, profits on put options increase when the asset value falls. The put is exercised only if its holder can deliver an asset worth less than the exercise price in return for the exercise price.

Figure 2.11 is an excerpt of the option quotations for IBM from the online edition of *The Wall Street Journal*. The current price of IBM shares is $98.31. The first two columns give the expiration month and exercise (equivalently, strike) price of each option. Thus, we see listings for call and put options on IBM with exercise prices ranging from $90 to $105, and with expiration dates from January to July.

The next columns provide the closing prices, trading volume, and open interest (outstanding contracts) of each option. For example, 6,895 contracts traded on the January 2007 expiration call with an exercise price of $95. The last trade was at $4.30, meaning that an option to purchase one share of IBM at an exercise price of $95 sold for $4.30. Each option *contract* (on 100 shares of stock), therefore, costs $4.30 × 100 = $430.

Notice that the prices of call options decrease as the exercise price increases. For example, the January 2007 expiration call with exercise price $100 costs only $1.26. This makes sense, as the right to purchase a share at a higher exercise price is less valuable. Conversely, put prices increase with the exercise price. The right to sell a share of IBM in January at a price of $95 costs $.63 while the right to sell at $100 costs $2.70.

Option prices also increase with time until expiration. Clearly, one would rather have the right to buy IBM for $95 at any time until July than at any time until January. Not surprisingly,

put option

The right to sell an asset at a specified exercise price on or before a specified expiration date.

FIGURE 2.11

Stock options on IBM

Source: From online edition of *The Wall Street Journal Online*, January 5, 2007. Reprinted by permission of Dow Jones & Company, Inc. via Copyright Clearance Center, Inc. © 2007 Dow Jones & Company, Inc. All Rights Reserved Worldwide.

Prices at close January 04, 2007

IBM (IBM) — Underlying stock price: 98.31

Expiration	Strike	Call			Put		
		Last	Volume	Open Interest	Last	Volume	Open Interest
Jan	90	8.60	305	39159	0.15	630	36837
Feb	90	9.10	22	167	0.30	47	914
Apr	90	10.60	49	6216	0.90	1314	8296
Jul	90	12.00	1	951	1.70	6	1074
Jan	95	4.30	6895	48822	0.63	1710	31335
Feb	95	4.90	4800	1579	1.10	723	6058
Apr	95	6.50	885	9230	1.90	1299	5367
Jul	95	8.10	44	1770	...	...	1641
Jan	100	1.26	3654	36888	2.70	3191	6420
Feb	100	1.90	1354	4339	3.07	4318	991
Apr	100	3.40	1569	10529	4.30	304	1139
Jul	100	5.30	41	5426	...	...	581
Jan	105	0.25	686	2406	6.60	174	151
Feb	105	0.55	860	1291	7.00	181	300
Apr	105	1.75	299	4532	7.60	2	519
Jul	105	3.10	197	1523	8.00	1	622

UNDERSTANDING THE WORLD OF DERIVATIVES

What are derivatives anyway, and why are people saying such terrible things about them?

Some critics see the derivatives market as a multitrillion-dollar house of cards composed of interlocking, highly leveraged transactions. They fear that the default of a single large player could stun the world financial system.

But others, including [former] Federal Reserve Chairman Alan Greenspan, say the risk of such a meltdown is negligible. Proponents stress that the market's hazards are more than outweighed by the benefits derivatives provide in helping banks, corporations, and investors manage their risks.

Because the science of derivatives is relatively new, there's no easy way to gauge the ultimate impact these instruments will have. There are now more than 1,200 different kinds of derivatives on the market, most of which require a computer program to figure out. Surveying this complex subject, dozens of derivatives experts offered these insights:

Q: What is the broadest definition of derivatives?

A: Derivatives are financial arrangements between two parties whose payments are based on, or "derived" from, the performance of some agreed-upon benchmark. Derivatives can be issued based on currencies, commodities, government or corporate debt, home mortgages, stocks, interest rates, or any combination of these.

Company stock options, for instance, allow employees and executives to profit from changes in a company's stock price without actually owning shares. Without knowing it, homeowners frequently use a type of privately traded "forward" contract when they apply for a mortgage and lock in a borrowing rate for their house closing, typically for as many as 60 days in the future.

Q: What are the most common forms of derivatives?

A: Derivatives come in two basic categories—option-type contracts and forward-type contracts. These may be exchange-listed, such as futures and stock options, or they may be privately traded.

Options give buyers the right, but not the obligation, to buy or sell an asset at a preset price over a specific period. The option's price is usually a small percentage of the underlying asset's value.

Forward-type contracts, which include forwards, futures, and swaps, commit the buyer and the seller to trade a given asset at a set price on a future date. These are "price-fixing" agreements that saddle the buyer with the same price risks as actually owning the asset. But normally, no money changes hands until the delivery date, when the contract is often settled in cash rather than by exchanging the asset.

Q: In business, what are they used for?

A: While derivatives can be powerful speculative instruments, businesses most often use them to hedge. For instance, companies often use forwards and exchange-listed futures to protect against fluctuations in currency or commodity prices, thereby helping to manage import and raw-materials costs. Options can serve a similar purpose; interest-rate options such as caps and floors help companies control financing costs in much the same way that caps on adjustable-rate mortgages do for homeowners.

Q: Why are derivatives potentially dangerous?

A: Because these contracts expose the two parties to market moves with little or no money actually changing hands, they involve leverage. And that leverage may be vastly increased by the terms of a particular contract. In the derivatives that hurt P&G, for instance, a given move in U.S. or German interest rates was multiplied 10 times or more.

When things go well, that leverage provides a big return, compared with the amount of capital at risk. But it also causes equally big losses when markets move the wrong way. Even companies that use derivatives to hedge, rather than speculate, may be at risk, since their operation would rarely produce perfectly offsetting gains.

Q: If they are so dangerous, why are so many businesses using derivatives?

A: They are among the cheapest and most readily available means at companies' disposal to buffer themselves against shocks in currency values, commodity prices, and interest rates. Donald Nicoliasen, a Price Waterhouse expert on derivatives, says derivatives "are a new tool in everybody's bag to better manage business returns and risks."

this shows up in a higher price for the July expiration options. For example, the call with exercise price $95 expiring in July sells for $8.10, compared to only $4.30 for the January call.

What would be the profit or loss per share of stock to an investor who bought the January 2007 expiration IBM call option with exercise price $100, if the stock price at the expiration of the option is $105? What about a purchaser of the put option with the same exercise price and expiration?

CONCEPT *check* **2.6**

Futures Contracts

futures contract

Obliges traders to purchase or sell an asset at an agreed-upon price at a specified future date.

A **futures contract** calls for delivery of an asset (or in some cases, its cash value) at a specified delivery or maturity date, for an agreed-upon price, called the *futures price,* to be paid at contract maturity. The long position is held by the trader who commits to purchasing the commodity on the delivery date. The trader who takes the short position commits to delivering the commodity at contract maturity.

Figure 2.12 illustrates the listing of several futures contracts for trading on January 4, 2007. The top line in boldface type gives the contract name, the exchange on which the futures contract is traded (in parentheses), and the contract size. Thus, the first contract listed is for corn traded on the Chicago Board of Trade (CBT). Each contract calls for delivery of 5,000 bushels of corn.

The next several rows detail prices for contracts expiring on various dates. The March maturity contract opened during the day at a futures price of $3.71 per bushel. The highest futures price during the day was $3.725, the lowest was $3.605, and the settlement price (a representative trading price during the last few minutes of trading) was $3.6225. The settlement price decreased by $.0825 from the previous trading day. Finally, open interest, or the number of outstanding contracts, was 591,430. Corresponding information is given for each maturity date.

The trader holding the long position profits from price increases. Suppose that at expiration, corn is selling for $3.8225 per bushel. The long position trader who entered the contract at the futures price of $3.6225 on January 4 would pay the previously agreed-upon $3.6225 for each unit of the index, which at contract maturity would be worth $3.8225.

Because each contract calls for delivery of 5,000 bushels, the profit to the long position, ignoring brokerage fees, would equal 5,000 × ($3.8225 − $3.6225) = $1,000. Conversely, the short position must deliver 5,000 bushels for the previously agreed-upon futures price. The short position's loss equals the long position's profit.

The distinction between the *right* to purchase and the *obligation* to purchase the asset is the difference between a call option and a long position in a futures contract. A futures contract *obliges* the long position to purchase the asset at the futures price; the call option merely *conveys the right* to purchase the asset at the exercise price. The purchase will be made only if it yields a profit.

Agriculture Futures

	OPEN	HIGH	LOW	SETTLE	CHG	OPEN INT
Corn (CBT)-5,000 bu.; cents per bu.						
March	371.00	372.50	360.50	**362.25**	−8.25	591,430
Dec	361.75	366.00	357.00	**359.00**	−3.00	311,690
Oats (CBT)-5,000 bu.; cents per bu.						
March	261.75	265.75	258.25	**261.25**	−.75	8,823
Dec	233.00	234.25	232.50	**233.75**	.75	3,907
Soybeans (CBT)-5,000 bu.; cents per bu.						
Jan	667.00	675.00	659.75	**662.75**	−6.50	9,947
March	681.00	687.75	672.50	**675.50**	−6.50	220,362

Currency Futures

	OPEN	HIGH	LOW	SETTLE	CHG	OPEN INT
Japanese Yen (CME)-¥12,500,000; $ per 100¥						
March	.8456	.8485	.8447	**.8479**	.0016	275,282
June	.8561	.8579	.8545	**.8577**	.0016	5,119
British Pound (CME)-£62,500; $ per £						
March	1.9516	1.9537	1.9403	**1.9448**	−.0063	136,995
June	1.9446	1.9531	1.9402	**1.9443**	−.0063	191

Index Futures

	OPEN	HIGH	LOW	SETTLE	CHG	OPEN INT
DJ Industrial Average (CBT)-$10 x index						
March	12543	12575	12470	**12549**	19	64,555
June	12629	12647	12601	**12647**	18	44
S&P 500 Index (CME)-$250 x index						
March	1425.20	1431.50	1417.00	**1427.50**	2.70	601,655
June	1432.00	1444.50	1430.50	**1440.10**	2.60	13,287

FIGURE 2.12

Listing of selected futures contracts

Source: From *The Wall Street Journal,* January 5, 2007. Reprinted by permission of Dow Jones & Company, Inc. via Copyright Clearance Center, Inc. © 2007 Dow Jones & Company, Inc. All Rights Reserved Worldwide.

Clearly, the holder of a call has a better position than the holder of a long position on a futures contract with a futures price equal to the option's exercise price. This advantage, of course, comes only at a price. Call options must be purchased; futures investments are contracts only. The purchase price of an option is called the *premium*. It represents the compensation the purchaser of the call must pay for the ability to exercise the option only when it is profitable to do so. Similarly, the difference between a put option and a short futures position is the right, as opposed to the obligation, to sell an asset at an agreed-upon price.

SUMMARY

- Money market securities are very short-term debt obligations. They are usually highly marketable and have relatively low credit risk. Their low maturities and low credit risk ensure minimal capital gains or losses. These securities trade in large denominations, but they may be purchased indirectly through money market funds.
- Much of U.S. government borrowing is in the form of Treasury bonds and notes. These are coupon-paying bonds usually issued at or near par value. Treasury bonds are similar in design to coupon-paying corporate bonds.
- Municipal bonds are distinguished largely by their tax-exempt status. Interest payments (but not capital gains) on these securities are exempt from income taxes.
- Mortgage pass-through securities are pools of mortgages sold in one package. Owners of pass-throughs receive all principal and interest payments made by the borrower. The firm that originally issued the mortgage merely services the mortgage, simply "passing through" the payments to the purchasers of the mortgage. The pass-through agency usually guarantees the payment of interest and principal on mortgages pooled into these pass-through securities.
- Common stock is an ownership share in a corporation. Each share entitles its owner to one vote on matters of corporate governance and to a prorated share of the dividends paid to shareholders. Stock, or equity, owners are the residual claimants on the income earned by the firm.
- Preferred stock usually pays a fixed stream of dividends for the life of the firm: It is a perpetuity. A firm's failure to pay the dividend due on preferred stock, however, does not set off corporate bankruptcy. Instead, unpaid dividends simply cumulate. New varieties of preferred stock include convertible and adjustable-rate issues.
- Many stock market indexes measure the performance of the overall market. The Dow Jones averages, the oldest and best-known indicators, are price-weighted indexes. Today, many broad-based, market value–weighted indexes are computed daily. These include the Standard & Poor's composite 500 stock index, the NYSE, the Nasdaq index, the Wilshire 5000 Index, and several international indexes, including the Nikkei, FTSE, and DAX.
- A call option is a right to purchase an asset at a stipulated exercise price on or before an expiration date. A put option is the right to sell an asset at some exercise price. Calls increase in value, while puts decrease in value as the value of the underlying asset increases.
- A futures contract is an obligation to buy or sell an asset at a stipulated futures price on a maturity date. The long position, which commits to purchasing, gains if the asset value increases, while the short position, which commits to delivering the asset, loses.

KEY TERMS

bankers' acceptance, 28
call option, 46
certificate of deposit, 27
commercial paper, 28
common stocks, 37
corporate bonds, 35
derivative asset/contingent claim, 46

equally weighted index, 46
Eurodollars, 28
Federal funds, 29
futures contract, 50
LIBOR, 29
market value–weighted index, 44
money markets, 25

municipal bonds, 32
preferred stock, 39
price-weighted average, 40
put option, 48
repurchase agreements, 28
Treasury bills, 25
Treasury bonds, 30
Treasury notes, 30

PROBLEM SETS

 Select problems are available in McGraw-Hill's Homework Manager®. Please see the packaging options of the preface for more information.

CFA®
PROBLEMS

1. A municipal bond carries a coupon rate of 6¾% and is trading at par. What would be the equivalent taxable yield of this bond to a taxpayer in a 35% tax bracket?

2. Straight preferred stock yields often are lower than yields on straight bonds of the same quality because of
   a. Marketability
   b. Risk
   c. Taxation
   d. Call protection

3. Turn back to Figure 2.4 and look at the first Treasury bond maturing in November 2014.
   a. How much would you have to pay to purchase one of these bonds?
   b. What is its coupon rate?
   c. What is the current yield of the bond?

4. In what ways is preferred stock like long-term debt? In what ways is it like equity?

5. Why are money market securities sometimes referred to as "cash equivalents"?

6. Find the after-tax return to a corporation that buys a share of preferred stock at $40, sells it at year-end at $40, and receives a $4 year-end dividend. The firm is in the 30% tax bracket.

7. Turn to Figure 2.9 and look at the listing for General Dynamics.
   a. What was the firm's closing price yesterday?
   b. How many shares could you buy for $5,000?
   c. What would be your annual dividend income from those shares?
   d. What must be its earnings per share?

8. Consider the three stocks in the following table. P_t represents price at time t, and Q_t represents shares outstanding at time t. Stock C splits two-for-one in the last period.

	P_0	Q_0	P_1	Q_1	P_2	Q_2
A	90	100	95	100	95	100
B	50	200	45	200	45	200
C	100	200	110	200	55	400

   a. Calculate the rate of return on a price-weighted index of the three stocks for the first period ($t = 0$ to $t = 1$).
   b. What must happen to the divisor for the price-weighted index in year 2?
   c. Calculate the rate of return of the price-weighted index for the second period ($t = 1$ to $t = 2$).

9. Using the data in Problem 8, calculate the first period rates of return on the following indexes of the three stocks:
   a. a market value-weighted index.
   b. an equally weighted index.

10. An investor is in a 30% combined federal plus state tax bracket. If corporate bonds offer 9% yields, what must municipals offer for the investor to prefer them to corporate bonds?

11. Suppose that short-term municipal bonds currently offer yields of 4%, while comparable taxable bonds pay 5%. Which gives you the higher after-tax yield if your tax bracket is:
   a. Zero
   b. 10%
   c. 20%
   d. 30%

www.mhhe.com/bkm

12. Find the equivalent taxable yield of the municipal bond in the previous problem for tax brackets of zero, 10%, 20%, and 30%.

13. Which security should sell at a greater price?
    a. A 10-year Treasury bond with a 9% coupon rate or a 10-year T-bond with a 10% coupon.
    b. A three-month maturity call option with an exercise price of $40 or a three-month call on the same stock with an exercise price of $35.
    c. A put option on a stock selling at $50 or a put option on another stock selling at $60. (All other relevant features of the stocks and options are assumed to be identical.)

14. Look at the futures listings for oats in Figure 2.12.
    a. Suppose you buy one contract for December 2007 delivery. If the contract closes in December at a price of $2.15 per bushel, what will be your profit or loss?
    b. How many December 2007 maturity contracts are outstanding? How many bushels of oats do they represent?

15. Turn back to Figure 2.11 and look at the IBM options. Suppose you buy an April expiration call option with exercise price 95.
    a. If the stock price in April is $101, will you exercise your call? What are the profit and rate of return on your position?
    b. What if you had bought the April call with exercise price 90?
    c. What if you had bought an April put with exercise price 95?

16. Why do call options with exercise prices higher than the price of the underlying stock sell for positive prices?

17. Both a call and a put currently are traded on stock XYZ; both have strike prices of $50 and maturities of six months. What will be the profit to an investor who buys the call for $4 in the following scenarios for stock prices in six months? (a) $40; (b) $45; (c) $50; (d) $55; (e) $60. What will be the profit in each scenario to an investor who buys the put for $6?

18. Explain the difference between a put option and a short position in a futures contract.

19. Explain the difference between a call option and a long position in a futures contract.

20. What would you expect to happen to the spread between yields on commercial paper and Treasury bills if the economy were to enter a steep recession?

21. Examine the stocks listed in Figure 2.9. For how many of these stocks is the 52-week high price at least 50% greater than the 52-week low price? What do you conclude about the volatility of prices on individual stocks?

Use data from the Standard & Poor's Market Insight Database at www.mhhe.com/edumarketinsight to answer the following questions.

STANDARD &POOR'S

Select the Company tab and enter ticket symbol DIS. Click on the EDGAR section and find the link for Disney's most recent annual report (10-K).

Locate the company's Consolidated Financial Statements and answer these questions:

1. How much preferred stock is Disney authorized to issue? How much has been issued?

2. How much common stock is Disney authorized to issue? How many shares are currently outstanding?

Search for the term "Financing Activities."

3. What is the total amount of borrowing listed for Disney? How much of this is medium-term notes?

4. What other types of debt does Disney have outstanding?

WEB *master*

Yield Spreads and Risk

The yield spreads among various fixed-income securities are indicators of their relative risks. Risk originates from a number of factors, ranging from macroeconomic conditions to unique firm circumstances. Use the bond Web links provided below to review the yields on Treasury bonds, investment grade corporate bonds, non-investment grade corporate bonds, and mortgage-backed securities.

www.bondsonline.com/Todays_Market/Composite_Bond_Yields.php (Click on the link below the charts to see the data.)

finance.yahoo.com/bonds/composite_bond_rates

1. Calculate the yield spread between a 10-year AAA grade corporate bond and a 10-year A grade corporate bond.

2. Calculate the yield spread between a 10-year AAA grade corporate bond and a 10-year Treasury bond.

3. Calculate the yield spread between a 10-year AAA grade corporate bond and a 20-year AAA grade corporate bond.

4. Calculate the yield spread between a 10-year Treasury bond and a 20-year Treasury bond.

5. How would you explain the difference in yields in each case?

6. Repeat the calculations based on the yields that existed one month ago and compare them with today's yield spreads. What factors might explain the differences?

SOLUTIONS TO CONCEPT *checks*

2.1. The bond sells for 100:26 bid which is a price of 100.813% of par or $1,008.13 and 100:27 ask, or $1,008.438. This ask price corresponds to a yield of 4.61%. The ask price rose 9/32 from its level yesterday, so the ask price then must have been 100:18 or $1,005.625.

2.2. A 6% taxable return is equivalent to an after-tax return of 6(1 − .28) = 4.32%. Therefore, you would be better off in the taxable bond. The equivalent taxable yield of the tax-free bond is 4/(1 − .28) = 5.55%. So a taxable bond would have to pay a 5.55% yield to provide the same after-tax return as a tax-free bond offering a 4% yield.

2.3. *a.* You are entitled to a prorated share of IBM's dividend payments and to vote in any of IBM's stockholder meetings.

b. Your potential gain is unlimited because IBM's stock price has no upper bound.

c. Your outlay was $95 × 100 = $9,500. Because of limited liability, this is the most you can lose.

2.4. The price-weighted index increases from 62.50[=(100 + 25)/2] to 65[=(110 + 20)/2], a gain of 4%. An investment of one share in each company requires an outlay of $125 that would increase in value to $130, for a return of 4% (5/125), which equals the return to the price-weighted index.

2.5. The market value–weighted index return is calculated by computing the increase in value of the stock portfolio. The portfolio of the two stocks starts with an initial value of $100 million + $500 million = $600 million and falls in value to $110 million + $400 million = $510 million, a loss of 90/600 = .15, or 15%. The index portfolio return is a weighted average of the returns on each stock with weights of ⅙ on XYZ and ⅚ on ABC (weights proportional to relative investments). Because the return on XYZ is 10%, while that on ABC is −20%, the index portfolio return is (⅙)10 + (⅚)(−20) = −15%, equal to the return on the market value–weighted index.

2.6. The payoff to the call option is $105 − $100 = $5. The call cost $1.26. The profit is $5 − $1.26 = $3.74 per share. The put will pay off zero—it expires worthless since the stock price exceeds the exercise price. The loss is the cost of the put, $2.70.

Securities Markets

AFTER STUDYING THIS CHAPTER
YOU SHOULD BE ABLE TO:

Describe the role of investment bankers in primary issues.

Identify the various security markets.

Compare trading practices in stock exchanges with those in dealer markets.

Describe the role of brokers.

Compare the mechanics and investment implications of buying on margin and short selling.

This chapter will provide you with a broad introduction to the many venues and procedures available for trading securities in the United States and international markets. We will see that trading mechanisms range from direct negotiation among market participants to fully automated computer crossing of trade orders.

The first time a security trades is when it is issued to the public. Therefore, we begin with a look at how securities are first marketed to the public by investment bankers, the midwives of securities. We turn next to a broad survey of how already-issued securities may be traded among investors, focusing on the differences between dealer markets, electronic markets, and specialist markets. With this background, we then turn to specific trading arenas such as the New York Stock Exchange, Nasdaq, and several foreign security markets, examining the competition among these markets for the patronage of security traders. We consider the costs of trading in these markets, the quality of trade execution, and the ongoing quest for cross-market integration of trading.

(continued)

We then turn to the essentials of some specific types of transactions, such as buying on margin and short-selling stocks. We close the chapter with a look at some important aspects of the regulations governing security trading, including insider trading laws, circuit breakers, and the role of security markets as self-regulating organizations.

3.1 HOW FIRMS ISSUE SECURITIES

primary market

Market for new issues of securities.

secondary market

Market for already-existing securities.

When firms need to raise capital they may choose to sell or *float* securities. These new issues of stocks, bonds, or other securities typically are marketed to the public by investment bankers in what is called the **primary market.** Trading of already-issued securities among investors occurs in the **secondary market.** Trading in secondary markets does not affect the outstanding amount of securities; ownership is simply transferred from one investor to another.

There are two types of primary market issues of common stock. **Initial public offerings,** or **IPOs,** are stocks issued by a formerly privately owned company that is going public, that is, selling stock to the public for the first time. *Seasoned equity offerings* are offered by companies that already have floated equity. For example, a sale by IBM of new shares of stock would constitute a seasoned new issue.

initial public offering (IPO)

First sale of stock by a formerly private company.

In the case of bonds, we also distinguish between two types of primary market issues, a *public offering* and a *private placement.* The former refers to an issue of bonds sold to the general investing public that can then be traded on the secondary market. The latter refers to an issue that usually is sold to one or a few institutional investors and is generally held to maturity.

Investment Banking

underwriters

Underwriters purchase securities from the issuing company and resell them.

Public offerings of both stocks and bonds typically are marketed by investment bankers who in this role are called **underwriters.** More than one investment banker usually markets the securities. A lead firm forms an underwriting syndicate of other investment bankers to share the responsibility for the stock issue.

Investment bankers advise the firm regarding the terms on which it should attempt to sell the securities. A preliminary registration statement must be filed with the Securities and Exchange Commission (SEC), describing the issue and the prospects of the company. This preliminary prospectus is known as a *red herring* because it includes a statement printed in red, stating that the company is not attempting to sell the security before the registration is approved. When the statement is in final form, and approved by the SEC, it is called the **prospectus.** At this point, the price at which the securities will be offered to the public is announced.

prospectus

A description of the firm and the security it is issuing.

In a typical underwriting arrangement, the investment bankers purchase the securities from the issuing company and then resell them to the public. The issuing firm sells the securities to the underwriting syndicate for the public offering price less a spread that serves as compensation to the underwriters. This procedure is called a *firm commitment.* In addition to the spread, the investment banker also may receive shares of common stock or other securities of the firm. Figure 3.1 depicts the relationships among the firm issuing the security, the lead underwriter, the underwriting syndicate, and the public.

As part of its marketing of the firm's securities, the underwriting syndicate often takes out advertisements in the financial press to announce the prospective sale. An example of these so-called *tombstone* advertisements is given in Figure 3.2. The underwriters plan to sell 115 million shares of stock at a price of $18.50 each, to raise $2,127.5 million for the Principal Financial Group. The four lead underwriters are presented in larger type; the firms taking a smaller role in marketing the securities are presented below in smaller type. Most of the shares will be sold in the U.S., but 15% of the issue will be sold abroad. Notice that the underwriters for the non-U.S. portion of the issue have far greater international representation.

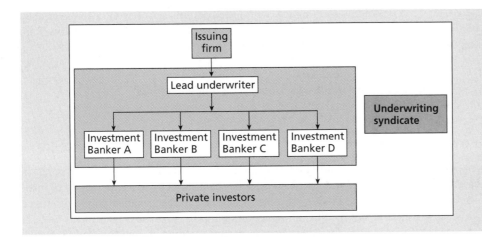

FIGURE 3.1

Relationship among a firm issuing securities, the underwriters, and the public

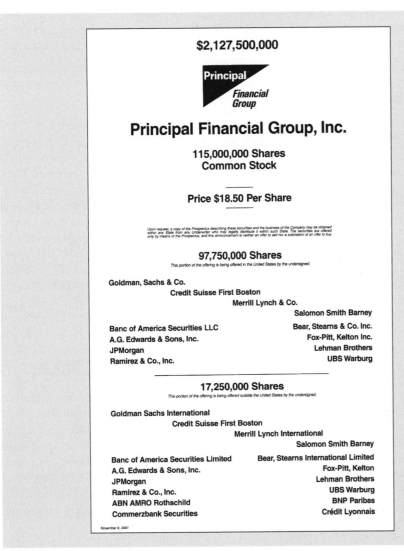

FIGURE 3.2

A tombstone advertisement

Shelf Registration

An important innovation in the issuing of securities was introduced in 1982 when the SEC approved Rule 415, which allows firms to register securities and gradually sell them to the public for two years following the initial registration. Because the securities are already registered, they can be sold on short notice, with little additional paperwork. Moreover, they can be sold in small amounts without incurring substantial flotation costs. The securities are "on the shelf," ready to be issued, which has given rise to the term *shelf registration.*

3.1   Why does it make sense for shelf registration to be limited in time?

Private Placements

private placement

Primary offerings in which shares are sold directly to a small group of institutional or wealthy investors.

Primary offerings also can be sold in a **private placement** rather than a public offering. In this case, the firm (using an investment banker) sells shares directly to a small group of institutional or wealthy investors. Private placements can be far cheaper than public offerings. This is because Rule 144A of the SEC allows corporations to make these placements without preparing the extensive and costly registration statements required of a public offering. On the other hand, because private placements are not made available to the general public, they generally will be less suited for very large offerings. Moreover, private placements do not trade in secondary markets like stock exchanges. This greatly reduces their liquidity and presumably reduces the prices that investors will pay for the issue.

Initial Public Offerings

Investment bankers manage the issuance of new securities to the public. Once the SEC has commented on the registration statement and a preliminary prospectus has been distributed to interested investors, the investment bankers organize *road shows* in which they travel around the country to publicize the imminent offering. These road shows serve two purposes. First, they generate interest among potential investors and provide information about the offering. Second, they provide information to the issuing firm and its underwriters about the price at which they will be able to market the securities. Large investors communicate their interest in purchasing shares of the IPO to the underwriters; these indications of interest are called a *book* and the process of polling potential investors is called *bookbuilding*. These indications of interest provide valuable information to the issuing firm because institutional investors often will have useful insights about both the market demand for the security as well as the prospects of the firm and its competitors. It is common for investment bankers to revise both their initial estimates of the offering price of a security and the number of shares offered based on feedback from the investing community.

Why do investors truthfully reveal their interest in an offering to the investment banker? Might they be better off expressing little interest, in the hope that this will drive down the offering price? Truth is the better policy in this case because truth telling is rewarded. Shares of IPOs are allocated across investors in part based on the strength of each investor's expressed interest in the offering. If a firm wishes to get a large allocation when it is optimistic about the security, it needs to reveal its optimism. In turn, the underwriter needs to offer the security at a bargain price to these investors to induce them to participate in bookbuilding and share their information. Thus, IPOs commonly are underpriced compared to the price at which they could be marketed. Such underpricing is reflected in price jumps that occur on the date when the shares are first traded in public security markets. The most dramatic case of underpricing occurred in December 1999 when shares in VA Linux were sold in an IPO at $30 a share and closed on the first day of trading at $239.25, a 698% one-day return.[1]

While the explicit costs of an IPO tend to be around 7% of the funds raised, such underpricing should be viewed as another cost of the issue. For example, if VA Linux had sold its shares for the $239 that investors obviously were willing to pay for them, its IPO would have raised

---

[1] It is worth noting, however, that by December 2000, shares in VA Linux (now renamed VA Software) were selling for less than $9 a share, and by 2002, for less than $1. This example is extreme, but consistent with the generally poor long-term investment performance of IPOs.

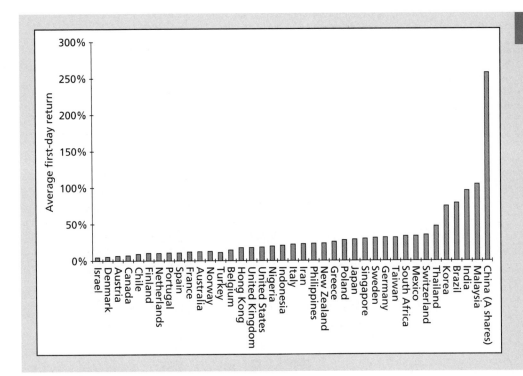

FIGURE 3.3

Average initial returns for IPOs in various countries

Source: Provided by Professor J. Ritter of the University of Florida, 2006. This is an updated version of the information contained in T. Loughran, J. Ritter, and K. Rydqvist, "Initial Public Offerings," *Pacific-Basin Finance Journal* 2 (1994), pp. 165–199. Copyright 1994 with permission from Elsevier Science.

8 times as much as it actually did. The money "left on the table" in this case far exceeded the explicit cost of the stock issue. This degree of underpricing is far more dramatic than is common, but underpricing seems to be a universal phenomenon.

Figure 3.3 presents average first-day returns on IPOs of stocks across the world. The results consistently indicate that IPOs are marketed to investors at attractive prices. Underpricing of IPOs makes them appealing to all investors, yet institutional investors are allocated the bulk of a typical new issue. Some view this as unfair discrimination against small investors. However, our analysis suggests that the apparent discounts on IPOs may be in part payments for a valuable service, specifically, the information contributed by the institutional investors. The right to allocate shares in this way may contribute to efficiency by promoting the collection and dissemination of such information.[2]

Both views of IPO allocations probably contain some truth. IPO allocations to institutions do serve a valid economic purpose as an information-gathering tool. Nevertheless, the system can be—and has been—abused. Part of the Wall Street scandals of 2000–2002 centered on the allocation of shares in IPOs. In a practice known as "spinning," some investment bankers used IPO allocations to corporate insiders to curry favors, in effect as implicit kickback schemes. These underwriters would award generous IPO allocations to executives of particular firms in return for the firm's future investment banking business.

Pricing of IPOs is not trivial and not all IPOs turn out to be underpriced. Some do poorly after issue. The 2006 IPO of Vonage was a notable disappointment. The stock lost about 30% of its value in its first seven days of trading. Other IPOs cannot even be fully sold to the market. Underwriters left with unmarketable securities are forced to sell them at a loss on the secondary market. Therefore, the investment banker bears the price risk of an underwritten issue.

Interestingly, despite their dramatic initial investment performance, IPOs have been poor long-term investments. Figure 3.4 compares the stock price performance of IPOs with shares of other firms of the same size for each of the five years after issue of the IPO. The year-by-year underperformance of the IPOs is dramatic, suggesting that, on average, the investing

[2]Benveniste and Wilhelm (1997) provide an elaboration of this point and a more complete discussion of the book-building process.

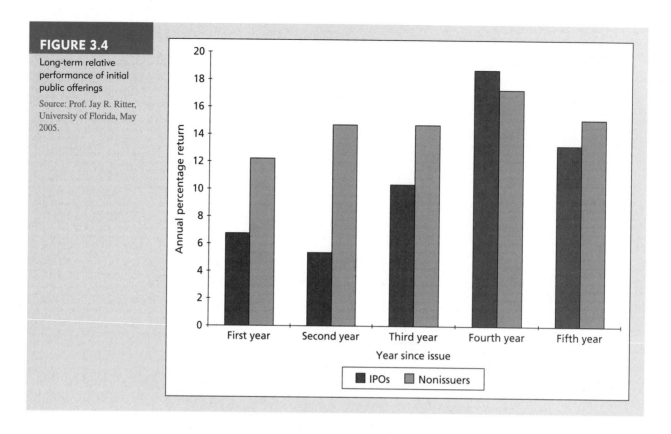

FIGURE 3.4

Long-term relative performance of initial public offerings

Source: Prof. Jay R. Ritter, University of Florida, May 2005.

public may be too optimistic about the prospects of these firms. Such long-lived systematic errors on the part of investors would be surprising. An interesting study by Brav, Geczy, and Gompers (2000), however, suggests that apparent IPO underperformance may be illusory. When they carefully match firms based on size and ratios of book values to market values, they find that IPO returns are actually similar to those of comparison firms.

IPOs can be expensive, especially for small firms. In an attempt to gain their business, W. R. Hambrecht & Co. conducts IPOs on the Internet geared toward smaller, retail investors. Unlike typical investment bankers that tend to favor institutional investors in the allocation of shares and that determine an offer price through the bookbuilding process, Hambrecht conducts a "Dutch auction." In this procedure, which Hambrecht has dubbed Open IPO, investors submit a price for a given number of shares. The bids are ranked in order of bid price, and shares are allocated to the highest bidders until the entire issue is absorbed.

To date, upstarts like Hambrecht have captured only a tiny share of the underwriting market. Their long-term prospects are still unclear. In fact, by 2004, most observers had written off the IPO auction model, when Google surprised the financial world by announcing that it would use such an auction in its multibillion dollar IPO, assisted in part by Hambrecht. The mutual fund research company Morningstar also used Hambrecht to manage an IPO auction in 2005. The nearby box discusses the Google IPO, but notes that it is too early to predict its long-term consequences for future IPOs.

3.2   HOW SECURITIES ARE TRADED

Financial markets develop to meet the needs of particular traders. Consider what would happen if organized markets did not exist. Any household wishing to invest in some type of financial asset would have to find others wishing to sell. Soon, venues where interested traders could meet would become popular. Eventually, financial markets would emerge from these meeting places. Thus, a pub in old London called Lloyd's launched the maritime insurance industry. A Manhattan curb on Wall Street became synonymous with the financial world.

GOOGLE AUCTION PROMISES TO BID ADIEU TO TRADITION

The initial public offering of Google Inc. threatens Wall Street's carefully controlled process of distributing new-stock issues, which often has greased the palms of big institutional investors and wealthy individuals.

The classic Wall Street underwriting model is an exquisitely choreographed series of events over a two- to three-month period. It starts with the kind of high-profile feature articles on the company Google has just enjoyed, followed by the release of a document formally describing the company's business to investors.

The underwriters next escort company executives on a series of roadshow meetings and one-on-one sit-downs with big mutual funds, hedge funds, and other institutional investors, who then convey their interest, or lack thereof, to highly paid salespeople at Wall Street firms. The underwriters then set a price that they hope will stay buoyed once trading begins, with investors who won't head for the exits at once. It is a judgment call that gives a clear preference to the underwriters' biggest and best customers.

The Google plan doesn't scrap that system altogether. But Google does aim to base its price, at least partly, on the results of an auction that it claims may give some preference to smaller orders from individual investors. In a pure so-called Dutch auction, the price is set at the highest level that will result in all the shares being sold.

"The Google auction process addresses two big complaints—the price surges on a stock's first trading day, which means that money has been left on the table by an issuer, and the freezing out of retail investors from a deal," said Brad Hintz, who follows securities firms at Sanford C. Bernstein & Co.

There have been just a handful of Dutch auction IPOs in recent years, and WR Hambrecht & Co., which is handling the process for Google, has the most experience.

The strength of the Google precedent is also a question mark. Most companies that go public don't have the kind of powerful market franchise—and thus leverage over Wall Street—that Google enjoys. Such companies must concentrate on survival, and the last thing most are inclined to do is thumb their noses at an entrenched group of top financial institutions, to which even in a best-case scenario they will have to return repeatedly for additional financing.

SOURCE: Adapted from Randall Smith and Susanne Craig, "Auction Promises to Bid Adieu to Tradition," *The Wall Street Journal Online*, April 30, 2004.

Types of Markets

We can differentiate four types of markets: direct search markets, brokered markets, dealer markets, and auction markets.

Direct search markets   A *direct search market* is the least organized market. Buyers and sellers must seek each other out directly. An example of a transaction in such a market is the sale of a used refrigerator where the seller advertises for buyers in a local newspaper. Such markets are characterized by sporadic participation and low-priced and nonstandard goods. It does not pay most people or firms to seek profits by specializing in such an environment.

Brokered markets   The next level of organization is a *brokered market*. In markets where trading in a good is active, brokers find it profitable to offer search services to buyers and sellers. A good example is the real estate market, where economies of scale in searches for available homes and for prospective buyers make it worthwhile for participants to pay brokers to conduct the searches. Brokers in particular markets develop specialized knowledge on valuing assets traded in that market.

An important brokered investment market is the so-called *primary market*, where new issues of securities are offered to the public. In the primary market, investment bankers who market a firm's securities to the public act as brokers; they seek investors to purchase securities directly from the issuing corporation.

Another brokered market is that for large block transactions, in which very large blocks of stock are bought or sold. These blocks are so large (technically more than 10,000 shares but usually much larger) that brokers or "block houses" often are engaged to search directly for other large traders, rather than bring the trade directly to the markets where relatively smaller investors trade.

dealer markets

Markets in which traders specializing in particular assets buy and sell for their own accounts.

Dealer markets   When trading activity in a particular type of asset increases, **dealer markets** arise. Dealers specialize in various assets, purchase these assets for their own accounts, and later sell them for a profit from their inventory. The spreads between dealers' buy (or "bid") prices and sell (or "ask") prices are a source of profit. Dealer markets save traders on search costs because market participants can easily look up the prices at which they can buy from or sell to dealers. A fair amount of market activity is required before dealing in a market is an attractive source of income. The over-the-counter (OTC) securities market is one example of a dealer market.

auction market

A market where all traders meet at one place to buy or sell an asset.

Auction markets   The most integrated market is an **auction market,** in which all traders converge at one place to buy or sell an asset. The New York Stock Exchange (NYSE) is an example of an auction market. An advantage of auction markets over dealer markets is that one need not search across dealers to find the best price for a good. If all participants converge, they can arrive at mutually agreeable prices and save the bid–ask spread.

Continuous auction markets (as opposed to periodic auctions, such as in the art world) require very heavy and frequent trading to cover the expense of maintaining the market. For this reason, the NYSE and other exchanges set up listing requirements, which limit the stocks traded on the exchange to those of firms in which sufficient trading interest is likely to exist.

The organized stock exchanges are also secondary markets. They are organized for investors to trade existing securities among themselves.

CONCEPT check 3.2

Many assets trade in more than one type of market. What types of markets do the following trade in?
   a.   Used cars
   b.   Paintings
   c.   Rare coins

Types of Orders

Before comparing alternative trading practices and competing security markets, it is helpful to begin with an overview of the types of trades an investor might wish to have executed in these markets. Broadly speaking, there are two types of orders: market orders and orders contingent on price.

bid price

The price at which a dealer or other trader is willing to purchase a security.

ask price

The price at which a dealer or other trader will sell a security.

bid–ask spread

The difference between a dealer's bid and asked price.

Market orders   Market orders are buy or sell orders that are to be executed immediately at current market prices. For example, our investor might call her broker and ask for the market price of IBM. The broker might report back that the best **bid price** is $90 and the best **ask price** is $90.05, meaning that the investor would need to pay $90.05 to purchase a share, and could receive $90 a share if she wished to sell some of her own holdings of IBM. The **bid–ask spread** in this case is $.05. So an order to buy 100 shares "at market" would result in purchase at $90.05, and an order to "sell at market" would be executed at $90.

This simple scenario is subject to a few potential complications. First, the posted price quotes actually represent commitments to trade up to a specified number of shares. If the market order is for more than this number of shares, the order may be filled at multiple prices. For example if the asked price is good for orders up to 1,000 shares, and the investor wishes to purchase 1,500 shares, it may be necessary to pay a slightly higher price for the last 500 shares. Second, another trader may beat our investor to the quote, meaning that her order would then be executed at a worse price. Finally, the best price quote may change before her order arrives, again causing execution at a different price than the one at the moment of the order.

limit buy (sell) order

An order specifying a price at which an investor is willing to buy or sell a security.

Price-contingent orders   Investors also may place orders specifying prices at which they are willing to buy or sell a security. A **limit buy order** may instruct the broker to buy some number of shares if and when IBM may be obtained at or below a stipulated price. Conversely, a **limit sell** instructs the broker to sell if and when the stock price rises *above* a specified limit. A collection of limit orders waiting to be executed is called a *limit order book.*

Figure 3.5 is a portion of the limit order book for shares in Intel taken from the Archipelago exchange (one of several electronic exchanges; more on these shortly) on one day in 2007. Notice that the best orders are at the top of the list: the offers to buy at the highest price and to sell at the lowest price. The buy and sell orders at the top of the list—$20.77 and $20.78—are called the *inside quotes;* they are the highest buy and lowest sell orders. For Intel, the inside spread is only 1 cent. Note, however, that order sizes at the inside quotes are often fairly small. Therefore, investors interested in larger trades face an *effective* spread greater than the nominal one since they cannot execute their entire trades at the inside price quotes.

Until 2001, when U.S. markets adopted decimal pricing, the minimum possible spread was "one tick," which on the New York Stock Exchange was $⅛ until 1997 and $1⁄16 thereafter. With decimal pricing, the spread can be far lower. The average quoted bid–ask spread on the NYSE is less than 5 cents.

Stop orders are similar to limit orders in that the trade is not to be executed unless the stock hits a price limit. For *stop-loss orders,* the stock is to be *sold* if its price falls *below* a stipulated level. As the name suggests, the order lets the stock be sold to stop further losses from accumulating. Similarly, *stop-buy orders* specify that a stock should be bought when its price rises above a limit. These trades often accompany *short sales* (sales of securities you don't own but have borrowed from your broker) and are used to limit potential losses from the short position. Short sales are discussed in greater detail later in this chapter. Figure 3.6 organizes these types of trades in a convenient matrix.

stop order

Trade is not to be executed unless stock hits a price limit.

FIGURE 3.5

The limit order book for Intel on the Archipelago market, January 19, 2007.

Source: New York Stock Exchange, **www.nyse.com**

INTC Intel Corp — NYSE Arca. [INTC] Go>>							
Bid				**Ask**			
ID	Price	Size	Time	ID	Price	Size	Time
ARCA	20.77	23100	14:08:23	ARCA	20.78	27200	14:08:23
ARCA	20.76	35725	14:08:22	ARCA	20.79	31800	14:08:23
ARCA	20.75	37391	14:08:21	ARCA	20.80	32000	14:08:22
ARCA	20.74	24275	14:08:23	ARCA	20.81	30500	14:08:22
ARCA	20.73	20524	14:08:23	ARCA	20.82	17090	14:08:21
ARCA	20.72	6890	14:08:21	ARCA	20.83	19650	14:08:01

FIGURE 3.6

Price-contingent orders

Action	Condition	
	Price falls below the limit	Price rises above the limit
Buy	Limit buy order	Stop-buy order
Sell	Stop-loss order	Limit sell order

CONCEPT **3.3**
check

What type of trading order might you give to your broker in each of the following circumstances?

a. You want to buy shares of Intel to diversify your portfolio. You believe the share price is approximately at the "fair" value, and you want the trade done quickly and cheaply.

b. You want to buy shares of Intel, but believe that the current stock price is too high given the firm's prospects. If the shares could be obtained at a price 5% lower than the current value, you would like to purchase shares for your portfolio.

c. You plan to purchase a condominium sometime in the next month or so and will sell your shares of Intel to provide the funds for your down payment. While you believe that Intel share price is going to rise over the next few weeks, if you are wrong and the share price drops suddenly, you will not be able to afford the purchase. Therefore, you want to hold on to the shares for as long as possible, but still protect yourself against the risk of a big loss.

Trading Mechanisms

Broadly speaking, there are three trading systems employed in the United States: over-the-counter dealer markets, electronic communication networks, and formal exchanges. The best-known markets such as Nasdaq or the New York Stock Exchange actually use a variety of trading procedures, so before delving into these markets, it is useful to understand the basic operation of each type of trading system.

over-the-counter (OTC) market

An informal network of brokers and dealers who negotiate sales of securities.

Dealer markets   Roughly 35,000 securities trade on the **over-the-counter** or **OTC market.** Thousands of brokers register with the SEC as security dealers. Dealers quote prices at which they are willing to buy or sell securities. A broker then executes a trade by contacting a dealer listing an attractive quote.

Before 1971, all OTC quotations were recorded manually and published daily on so-called pink sheets. In 1971, the National Association of Securities Dealers Automatic Quotations System, or Nasdaq, was developed to link brokers and dealers in a computer network where price quotes could be displayed and revised. Dealers can use the network to display the bid price at which they are willing to purchase a security and the ask price at which they are willing to sell. The difference in these prices, the bid–ask spread, is the source of the dealer's profit. Brokers representing clients may examine quotes over the computer network, contact the dealer with the best quote, and execute a trade.

As originally organized, Nasdaq was more of a price quotation system than a trading system. While brokers could survey bid and ask prices across the network of dealers in the search for the best trading opportunity, actual trades required direct negotiation (often over the phone) between the investor's broker and the dealer in the security. However, as we will see shortly, Nasdaq has progressed far beyond a pure price quotation system. While dealers still post bid and ask prices over the network, Nasdaq now allows for electronic execution of trades at quoted prices without the need for direct negotiation, and the bulk of trades are executed electronically.

ECNs

Computer networks that allow direct trading without the need for market makers.

Electronic communication networks (ECNs)   **Electronic communication networks** allow participants to post market and limit orders over computer networks. The limit order book is available to all participants. An example of such an order book from Archipelago, one of the leading ECNs, appeared in Figure 3.5. Orders that can be "crossed," that is, matched against another order, are done so automatically without requiring the intervention of a broker. For example, an order to buy a share at a price of $50 or lower will be immediately executed if there is an outstanding asked price of $50. Therefore, ECNs are true trading systems, not merely price quotation systems.

ECNs offer several attractions. Direct crossing of trades without using a broker-dealer system eliminates the bid–ask spread that otherwise would be incurred. Instead, trades are automatically crossed at a modest cost, typically less than a penny per share. ECNs are attractive as well because of the speed with which a trade can be executed. Finally, these systems offer investors considerable anonymity in their trades.

Specialist markets

In formal exchanges such as the New York Stock Exchange, trading in each security is managed by a **specialist** assigned responsibility for that security. Brokers who wish to buy or sell shares on behalf of their clients must direct the trade to the specialist's post on the floor of the exchange.

Each security is assigned to one specialist, but each specialist firm—currently there are fewer than 10 on the NYSE—makes a market in many securities. This task may require the specialist to act as either a broker or a dealer. The specialist's role as a broker is simply to execute the orders of other brokers. Specialists also may buy or sell shares of stock for their own portfolios, in this role acting as a dealer in the stock. When no other trader can be found to take the other side of a trade, specialists will do so even if it means they must buy for or sell from their own accounts. Specialist firms earn income both from commissions for managing orders (as implicit brokers) and from the spreads at which they buy and sell securities (as implicit dealers).

Part of the specialist's job as a broker is simply clerical. The specialist maintains a limit order book of all outstanding unexecuted limit orders entered by brokers on behalf of clients. When limit orders can be executed at market prices, the specialist executes, or "crosses," the trade.

The specialist is required to use the highest outstanding offered purchase price and the lowest outstanding offered selling price when matching trades. Therefore, the specialist system results in an auction market, meaning all buy and all sell orders come to one location, and the best orders "win" the trades. In this role, the specialist acts merely as a facilitator.

The more interesting function of the specialist is to maintain a "fair and orderly market" by acting as a dealer in the stock. In return for the exclusive right to make the market in a specific stock on the exchange, the specialist is required by the exchange to maintain an orderly market by buying and selling shares from inventory. Specialists maintain their own portfolios of stock and quoted bid and ask prices at which they are obligated to meet at least a limited amount of market orders.

Ordinarily, in an active market, specialists can match buy and sell orders without using their own accounts. That is, the specialist's own inventory of securities need not be the primary means of order execution. Sometimes, however, the specialist's bid and ask prices are better than those offered by any other market participant. Therefore, at any point, the effective ask price in the

specialist

A trader who makes a market in the shares of one or more firms and who maintains a "fair and orderly market" by dealing personally in the market.

WEB master

Choosing a Broker

There are several factors that should be considered when you are choosing which brokerage firm(s) to use to execute your trades. Go to the Web site **www.fool.com/dbc/dbc.htm** and read the information provided about choosing a broker. Then follow the link for the "Broker Comparison Table." Suppose that you have $3,000 to invest and want to put it in a non-IRA account.

1. Are all of the brokerage firms suitable if you want to open a cash account? Are they all suitable if you want a margin account?

2. Choose two of the firms listed. Assume that you want to buy 200 shares of Wax Works stock using a market order. If the order is filled at $12 per share, how much will the commission be for each firm if

you place an online order? How much will it be if you place it with broker assistance? (Be sure to read the footnotes and follow appropriate links if more information is necessary.)

3. Are there any maintenance fees associated with the account at either brokerage firm?

4. Now assume that you have a margin account and the balance is $3,000. Click on the link for "More Info" for one of the brokerage firms you chose. Find the information about margin rates. Calculate the interest rate would you pay if you borrowed money to buy stock. (You might have to follow links or search for a base rate by doing an Internet search for the firm's name and "margin rates." Alternatively, you can call the firm at the number listed on the Web page to ask what their margin rate is for your account level.)

market is the lower of either the specialist's ask price or the lowest of the unfilled limit-sell orders. Similarly, the effective bid price is the highest of the unfilled limit buy orders or the specialist's bid. These procedures ensure that the specialist provides liquidity to the market. In practice, specialists participate in approximately one-quarter of the transactions on the NYSE.

Specialists strive to maintain a narrow bid–ask spread for at least two reasons. First, one source of the specialist's income is frequent trading at the bid and ask prices, with the spread as a trading profit. A too-large spread would make the specialist's quotes uncompetitive with the limit orders placed by other traders. If the specialist's bid and asked quotes are consistently worse than those of public traders, the specialist will not participate in any trades and will lose the ability to profit from the bid–ask spread.

An equally important reason for narrow specialist spreads is that they are obligated to provide *price continuity* to the market. To illustrate price continuity, suppose the highest limit buy order for a stock is $30, while the lowest limit sell order is $32. When a market buy order comes in, it is matched to the best limit sell at $32. A market sell order would be matched to the best limit buy at $30. As market buys and sells come to the floor randomly, the stock price would fluctuate between $30 and $32. The exchange authorities would consider this excessive volatility, and the specialist would be expected to step in with bid and/or ask prices between these values to reduce the bid–ask spread to an acceptable level, typically below $.05 for large firms. When a firm is newly listed on an exchange, specialist firms vigorously compete to be awarded the rights to maintain the market in those shares. Since specialists are evaluated in part on their past performance in maintaining price continuity, they have considerable incentive to maintain tight spreads.

3.3 U.S. SECURITIES MARKETS

We have briefly sketched the three major trading mechanisms used in the United States: over-the-counter dealer markets, exchange trading managed by specialists, and direct trading among brokers or investors over electronic networks. The Nasdaq market is the most important dealer market in the United States, and the New York Stock Exchange is the most important formal equity exchange. As we will see, however, these markets have evolved in response to new information technology and both have dramatically increased their commitment to automated electronic trading.

Nasdaq

Nasdaq stock market

The computer-linked priced quotation system for the OTC market.

While any security can be traded in the over-the-counter network of security brokers and dealers, not all securities are included in the National Association of Security Dealers Automated Quotations System. That system, now called the **Nasdaq Stock Market,** lists about 3,200 firms and offers three listing options. The Nasdaq Global Select Market is for the largest, most actively traded firms, the Nasdaq Global Market is for the next tier of firms, and the Nasdaq Capital Market is the third tier of listed firms. Some of the requirements for initial listing are presented in Table 3.1. For even smaller firms that may not be eligible for listing or that wish to avoid disclosure requirements associated with listing on regulated markets, Pink

TABLE 3.1		**Nasdaq Global Market**	**Nasdaq Capital Market**
Partial requirements for initial listing on Nasdaq markets	Shareholders' equity	$15 million	$5 million
	Shares in public hands	1.1 million	1 million
	Market value of publicly traded shares	$8 million	$5 million
	Minimum price of stock	$5	$4
	Pretax income	$1 million	$750,000
	Shareholders	400	300

Source: The Nasdaq Stock Market, **www.nasdaq.com**, December 2006.

Sheets LLC offers real-time stock quotes on **www.pinksheets.com,** as well as Pink Link, an electronic messaging and trade negotiation service.

Because the Nasdaq system does not use a specialist, OTC trades do not require a centralized trading floor as do exchange-listed stocks. Dealers can be located anywhere they can communicate effectively with other buyers and sellers.

Nasdaq has three levels of subscribers. The highest, level 3 subscribers, are for firms dealing, or "making markets," in OTC securities. These market makers maintain inventories of a security and constantly stand ready to buy or sell these shares from or to the public at the quoted bid and ask prices. They earn profits from the spread between the bid and ask prices. Level 3 subscribers may enter the bid and ask prices at which they are willing to buy or sell stocks into the computer network and may update these quotes as desired.

Level 2 subscribers receive all bid and ask quotes, but they cannot enter their own quotes. These subscribers tend to be brokerage firms that execute trades for clients but do not actively deal in the stocks on their own account. Brokers buying or selling shares trade with the market maker (a level 3 subscriber) displaying the best price quote.

Level 1 subscribers receive only the inside quotes (i.e., the highest bid and lowest ask prices on each stock). Level 1 subscribers tend to be investors who are not actively buying and selling securities but want information on current prices.

As noted, Nasdaq was originally more a price quotation system than a trading system. But that has changed. Investors on Nasdaq today (through their brokers) typically access bids and offers electronically without human interaction. Nasdaq has steadily introduced ever-more sophisticated electronic trading platforms, which today handle the great majority of its trades. The latest version, called the Nasdaq Market Center, was introduced in 2004 and consolidates all of Nasdaq's previous electronic markets into one integrated system.

Market Center is Nasdaq's competitive response to the growing popularity of ECNs, which have captured a large share of order flow. By enabling automatic trade execution, Market Center allows Nasdaq to function much like an ECN. In addition, Nasdaq purchased Instinet, which operates the major electronic communications network INET in order to capture a greater share of the electronic trading market. Nevertheless, larger orders may still be negotiated among brokers and dealers, so Nasdaq retains some features of a pure dealer market.

The New York Stock Exchange

The New York Stock Exchange is by far the largest **stock exchange** in the United States. Shares of about 2,800 firms trade there, with a combined market capitalization in 2006 of around $15 trillion. Daily trading on the NYSE averaged 1.8 billion shares in 2006, with a dollar value of approximately $75 billion.

stock exchanges
Secondary markets where already-issued securities are bought and sold by members.

An investor who wishes to trade shares on the NYSE places an order with a brokerage firm, which either sends the order to the floor of the exchange via computer network or contacts its broker on the floor of the exchange to "work" the order. Smaller orders are almost always sent electronically for automatic execution, while larger orders that may require negotiation or judgment are more prone to be sent to a floor broker. A floor broker sent a trade order takes the order to the specialist's post. At the post is a monitor called the Display Book that presents current offers from interested traders to buy or sell given numbers of shares at various prices. The specialist can cross the trade with that of another broker if that is feasible, or match the trade using its own inventory of shares. Brokers might also seek out traders willing to take the other side of a trade at a price better than those currently appearing in the Display Book. If they can do so, they will bring the agreed-upon trade to the specialist for final execution.

Brokers must purchase the right to trade on the floor of the NYSE. Originally, the NYSE was organized as a not-for-profit company owned by its members or "seat holders." For example, in 2005 there were 1,366 seat-holding members of the NYSE. Each seat entitled its owner to place a broker on the floor of the exchange, where he or she could execute trades. Member firms could charge investors for executing trades on their behalf, which made a seat a valuable asset. The commissions that members might earn by trading on behalf of clients determined the market value of seat, which were bought and sold like any other asset. Seat prices fluctuated widely, ranging from as low as $4,000 (in 1878) to as high as $4 million (in 2005).

More recently, most exchanges have switched from a mutual form of organization, in which seat-holders are joint owners, to publicly traded corporations owned by shareholders. In 2006, the NYSE completed a merger with the Archipelago Exchange to form a publicly held company called the NYSE Group. (In 2007, the NYSE Group merged with Euronext to form NYSE-Euronext.) As a publicly traded corporation, its share price rather than the price of a seat on the exchange has become the best indicator of its financial health. Each seat on the exchange has been replaced by an annual license permitting traders to conduct business on the exchange floor.

The move toward public listing of exchanges is widespread. Other exchanges that have recently gone public include the Chicago Mercantile Exchange (derivatives trading, 2002), the International Securities Exchange (options, 2005), and the Chicago Board of Trade (derivatives, 2005). The Chicago Board Options Exchange reportedly also is considering going public.

Table 3.2 gives some of the initial listing requirements for the NYSE. These requirements ensure that a firm is of significant trading interest before the NYSE will allocate facilities for it to be traded on the floor of the exchange. If a listed company suffers a decline and fails to meet the criteria in Table 3.2, it may be delisted.

The American Stock Exchange, or Amex, focuses on listing smaller and younger firms than the NYSE. It was a leader in the development of exchange-traded funds, which are securities that represent claims to entire portfolios of stock, and which today account for a large share of total trading on the exchange. These products are described in greater detail in the following chapter.

Regional exchanges also sponsor trading of some firms that are traded on national exchanges. This dual listing enables local brokerage firms to trade in shares of large firms without purchasing a membership on the NYSE.

About 75 percent of the share volume transacted in NYSE-listed securities actually is executed on the NYSE. The NYSE's market share measured by trades rather than share volume is considerably lower, as smaller retail orders are far more likely to be executed off the exchange. Nevertheless, the NYSE remains the venue of choice for large trades.

block transactions

Large transactions in which at least 10,000 shares of stock are bought or sold.

Block sales   Institutional investors frequently trade blocks of tens of thousands of shares of stock. Table 3.3 shows that **block transactions** of over 10,000 shares account for about one-third of all trading on the NYSE. The larger block transactions are often too large for specialists to handle, as they do not wish to hold such large blocks of stock in their inventory. For example, the largest block transaction in 2006 was for $972 million worth of shares in DirecTV.

"Block houses" have evolved to aid in the placement of larger block trades. Block houses are brokerage firms that specialize in matching block buyers and sellers. Once a buyer and a seller have been matched, the block is sent to the exchange floor where specialists execute the trade. If a buyer cannot be found, the block house might purchase all or part of a block sale for its own account. The block house then can resell the shares to the public.

You can observe in Table 3.3 that the volume of block trading has declined considerably in the last decade. This reflects changing trading practices since the advent of electronic markets. Large trades are now much more likely to be split up into multiple small trades and executed electronically. The lack of depth on the electronic exchanges reinforces this pattern: Because

TABLE 3.2	Minimum annual pretax income in previous two years	$ 2,000,000
Some initial listing requirements for the NYSE	Revenue	$ 75,000,000
	Market value of publicly held stock	$100,000,000
	Shares publicly held	1,100,000
	Number of holders of 100 shares or more	2,200

Source: Data from the New York Stock Exchange, **www.nyse.com**, January 2007.

TABLE 3.3	Year	Shares (millions)	% Reported Volume	Average Number of Block Transactions per Day
Block transactions on the New York Stock Exchange	1965	48	03.1%	9
	1970	451	15.4	68
	1975	779	16.6	136
	1980	3,311	29.2	528
	1985	14,222	51.7	2,139
	1990	19,682	49.6	3,333
	1995	49,737	57.0	7,793
	2000	135,772	51.7	21,941
	2002	161,075	44.4	25,300
	2004	116,926	31.9	17,000
	2005	112,027	27.7	17,445
	2006	97,576	21.3	14,360

Source: Data from the New York Stock Exchange, **www.nyse.com,** January 2007.

the inside quote on these exchanges is valid only for small trades, it generally is preferable to buy or sell a large stock position in a series of smaller transactions.

SuperDot and electronic trading on the NYSE

SuperDot is an electronic order-routing system that enables NYSE member firms to send market and limit orders directly to the specialist over computer lines. In 2006, it processed more about 13 million trades per day, which were executed in a matter of seconds. The vast majority of all orders are submitted electronically through SuperDot, but these tend to be smaller orders and account for about 70% of NYSE trading volume.

SuperDot is especially useful to program traders. A **program trade** is a coordinated purchase or sale of an entire portfolio of stocks. Many trading strategies (such as index arbitrage, a topic we will study in Chapter 17) require that an entire portfolio of stocks be purchased or sold simultaneously in a coordinated program. SuperDot is the tool that enables many trading orders to be sent out at once and executed almost simultaneously.

program trade

Coordinated sale or purchase of a portfolio of stocks.

The NYSE has recently stepped up its commitment to electronic trading, instituting a fully automated trade-execution system called DirectPlus or Direct+ . It matches orders against the inside bid or ask price with execution times of less than one-half second. In 2006, Direct+ handled about 17% of NYSE trade volume, largely because the system would accept only smaller trades (up to 1,099 shares). However, the NYSE is in the process of eliminating the size limitation on Direct+ orders, so the fraction of shares cleared electronically should shortly rise. In stocks for which the size limitation was eliminated in the latter part of 2006, electronic trades rose to 80% of share volume within four months.

Settlement

Since June 1995, an order executed on the exchange must be settled within three working days. This requirement is often called T + 3, for trade date plus three days. The purchaser must deliver the cash, and the seller must deliver the stock to the broker, who in turn delivers it to the buyer's broker. Frequently, a firm's clients keep their securities in *street name*, which means the broker holds the shares registered in the firm's own name on behalf of the client. This convention can speed security transfer. T + 3 settlement has made such arrangements more important: It can be quite difficult for a seller of a security to complete delivery to the purchaser within the three-day period if the stock is kept in a safe deposit box.

Settlement is simplified further by the existence of a clearinghouse. The trades of all exchange members are recorded each day, with members' transactions netted out, so that each member need transfer or receive only the net number of shares sold or bought that day. An exchange member then settles with the clearinghouse instead of individually with every firm with which it made trades.

Electronic Communication Networks

ECNs are private computer networks that directly link buyers with sellers. As an order is received, the system determines whether there is a matching order, and if so, the trade is executed immediately. Brokers that have an affiliation with an ECN have computer access and can enter orders in the limit order book. Moreover, these brokers may make their terminals (or Internet access) available directly to individual traders who then can enter their own orders into the system.

ECNs have been highly successful, and have captured more than half of the trading volume in Nasdaq-listed stocks. They must be certified by the SEC and registered with the National Association of Security Dealers to participate in the Nasdaq market. The two biggest ECNs by far are INET, formed by a merger of Island and Instinet, and Archipelago.

As noted, the NYSE and Archipelago merged in 2006. In principle, the merged firm can fill simple orders quickly without human interaction through ArcaEx (the Archipelago Exchange), and large complex orders using human traders on the floor of the NYSE. At the same time, Nasdaq purchased the other leading ECN, Instinet, which operates INET. Thus, the securities markets appear to be consolidating and it seems that each market will, at least for a time, offer multiple trading platforms.

The National Market System

The Securities Act Amendments of 1975 directed the Securities and Exchange Commission to implement a national competitive securities market. Such a market would entail centralized reporting of transactions and a centralized quotation system, with the aim of enhanced competition among market makers.

In 1975, Consolidated Tape began reporting trades on the NYSE, Amex, and major regional exchanges, as well as trades of Nasdaq-listed stocks. In 1977, the Consolidated Quotations Service began providing online bid and ask quotes for NYSE securities also traded on various other exchanges. This has enhanced competition by allowing market participants, including brokers or dealers at different locations, to interact and for orders to be directed to the market in which the best price can be obtained.

In 1978, the Intermarket Trading System (ITS) was implemented. ITS currently links nine exchanges by computer: NYSE, Amex, Boston, National (formerly Cincinnati), Pacific, Philadelphia, Chicago, Nasdaq, and the Chicago Board Options Exchange. About 4,500 issues are eligible for trading on the ITS; these account for most of the securities that are traded on more than one exchange. The system allows brokers and market makers to display and view quotes for all markets and to execute cross-market trades when the Consolidated Quotation System shows better prices in other markets. For example, suppose a specialist firm on the Boston Exchange is currently offering to buy a security for $20, but a broker in Boston who is attempting to sell shares for a client observes a superior bid price on the NYSE, say, $20.05. The broker should route the order to the specialist's post on the NYSE, where it can be executed at the higher price. The transaction is then reported on the Consolidated Tape. Moreover, a specialist who observes a better price on another exchange is also expected either to match that price or route the trade to that market.

The ITS was only a limited success. Most trading took place in specialist markets, and orders needed to be directed to alternative markets by participants who might find it inconvenient or unprofitable to do so. However, the growth of automated electronic trading has made market integration more feasible. The SEC reaffirmed its so-called trade-through rule in 2005. Its Regulation NMS requires that investors' orders be filled at the best price that can be executed immediately, even if that price is available in a different market.

The trade-through rule is meant to improve speed of execution and enhance integration of competing stock markets. Linking these markets electronically through a unified book displaying all limit orders would be a logical extension of the ITS, enabling trade execution across markets. But this degree of integration has not yet been realized. Regulation NMS requires only that the inside quotes of each market be publicly shared. Because the inside or best quote is typically available only for a specified number of shares, there is still no guarantee that an investor will receive the best available prices for an entire trade, especially for larger trades.

Bond Trading

The New York Stock Exchange also operates a bond exchange where U.S. government, corporate, municipal, and foreign bonds may be traded. The centerpiece of the NYSE bond market is the Automated Bond System (ABS), which is an automated trading system that allows trading firms to obtain market information, to enter and execute trades over a computer network, and to receive immediate confirmations of trade execution.

However, the vast majority of bond trading occurs in the OTC market among bond dealers, even for bonds that are actually listed on the NYSE. This market is a network of bond dealers such as Merrill Lynch, Salomon Smith Barney (a division of Citigroup), or Goldman, Sachs that is linked by a computer quotation system. However, because these dealers do not carry extensive inventories of the wide range of bonds that have been issued to the public, they cannot necessarily offer to sell bonds from their inventory to clients or even buy bonds for their own inventory. They may instead work to locate an investor who wishes to take the opposite side of a trade. In practice, however, the corporate bond market often is quite "thin," in that there may be few investors interested in trading a bond at any particular time. As a result, the bond market is subject to a type of liquidity risk, for it can be difficult to sell one's holdings quickly if the need arises.

In 2006, the NYSE obtained regulatory approval to expand its bond trading system to include the debt issues of any NYSE-listed firm. In the past, each bond needed to be registered before listing; such a requirement was too onerous to justify listing most bonds. With the change, the NYSE may list up to 6,000 bond issues, an enormous increase from the roughly 1,000 bonds listed in 2006. The NYSE also plans an enhancement to its bond-trading platform, which will be called NYSE Bonds. If the experiment is successful, the new trading system will provide an alternative to the over-the-counter dealer market in bonds and improve the transparency of bond pricing for the public.

3.4 MARKET STRUCTURE IN OTHER COUNTRIES

The structure of security markets varies considerably from one country to another. A full cross-country comparison is far beyond the scope of this text. Therefore, we will instead briefly review three of the biggest non-U.S. stock markets: the London, Euronext, and Tokyo exchanges. Figure 3.7 shows the market capitalization of firms trading in the major stock markets.

London

Until 1997, trading arrangements in London were similar to those on Nasdaq. Competing dealers who wished to make a market in a stock would enter bid and ask prices into the Stock Exchange Automated Quotations (SEAQ) system. As in the U.S., London security firms acted as both dealers and brokerage firms, that is, both making a market in securities and executing trades for their clients.

In 1997, the London Stock Exchange introduced an electronic trading system dubbed SETS (Stock Exchange Electronic Trading Service). This is an electronic clearing system similar to ECNs in which buy and sell orders are submitted via computer networks and any buy and sell orders that can be crossed are executed automatically.

Most trading in London equities is now conducted using SETS, particularly for shares in larger firms. However, SEAQ continues to operate and may be more likely to be used for large block transactions or other less liquid transactions.

FIGURE 3.7

Market capitalization of listed firms, 2005

Source: New York Stock Exchange, **www.nyse.com,** January 20, 2007.

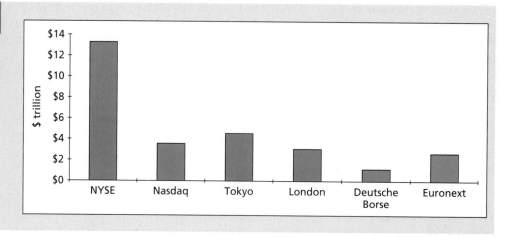

Euronext

Euronext was formed in 2000 by a merger of the Paris, Amsterdam, and Brussels exchanges. In 2007, Euronext merged with the NYSE Group. Euronext, like most European exchanges, uses an electronic trading system. Its system, called NSC (for Nouveau Système de Cotation, or New Quotation System), has fully automated order routing and execution. In fact, investors can enter their orders directly without contacting their brokers. An order submitted to the system is executed immediately if it can be crossed against an order in the public limit order book; if it cannot be executed, it is entered into the limit order book.

Euronext has established cross-trading agreements with several other European exchanges such as Helsinki or Luxembourg. In 2002, it also purchased LIFFE, the London International Financial Futures and Options Exchange.

Tokyo

The Tokyo Stock Exchange (TSE) is the largest stock exchange in Japan, accounting for about 80% of total trading. There is no specialist system on the TSE. Instead, a *saitori* maintains a public limit order book, matches market and limit orders, and is obliged to follow certain actions to slow down price movements when simple matching of orders would result in price changes greater than exchange-prescribed minimums. In their clerical role of matching orders, saitoris are somewhat similar to specialists on the NYSE. However, saitoris do not trade for their own accounts, and therefore they are quite different from either dealers or specialists in the United States.

Because the saitori performs an essentially clerical role, there are no market making services or liquidity provided to the market by dealers or specialists. The limit order book is the primary provider of liquidity. On the TSE, however, if order imbalances result in price movements across sequential trades that are considered too extreme by the exchange, the saitori may temporarily halt trading and advertise the imbalance in the hope of attracting additional trading interest to the "weak" side of the market.

Globalization and Consolidation of Stock Markets

All stock markets have come under increasing pressure in recent years to make international alliances or mergers. Much of this pressure is due to the impact of electronic trading. To a growing extent, traders view stock markets as networks that link them to other traders, and there are increasingly fewer limits on the securities around the world that they can trade. Against this background, it becomes more important for exchanges to provide the cheapest and most efficient mechanism by which trades can be executed and cleared. This argues for global alliances that can facilitate the nuts and bolts of cross-border trading and can benefit from economies of scale. Moreover, in the face of competition from electronic networks, established exchanges feel that they eventually need to offer 24-hour global markets. Finally, companies want to be able to go beyond national borders when they wish to raise capital.

These pressures have resulted in a broad trend toward market consolidation. In the last decade, most of the mergers were "local," that is, involving exchanges operating in the same continent. In the U.S., the NYSE merged with the Archipelago ECN, Nasdaq acquired Instinet (which operated the other major ECN, INET), and in the derivatives market, the Chicago Mercantile Exchange acquired the Chicago Board of Trade. In Europe, Euronext was formed by the merger of the Paris, Brussels, Lisbon, and Amsterdam exchanges and shortly thereafter purchased Liffe, the derivatives exchange based in London. Now a new wave of intercontinental mergers seems to be brewing. The NYSE Group and Euronext have already merged. The NYSE has purchased 5% of India's National Stock Exchange and in the longer term is discussing a strategic alliance with the Tokyo Stock Exchange. In March 2006, Nasdaq made an offer to acquire the London Stock Exchange, but the LSE rejected that proposal.

3.5 TRADING COSTS

Part of the cost of trading a security is obvious and explicit. Your broker must be paid a commission. Individuals may choose from two kinds of brokers: full-service or discount brokers. Full-service brokers who provide a variety of services often are referred to as account executives or financial consultants.

Besides carrying out the basic services of executing orders, holding securities for safekeeping, extending margin loans, and facilitating short sales, brokers routinely provide information and advice relating to investment alternatives.

Full-service brokers usually depend on a research staff that prepares analyses and forecasts of general economic as well as industry and company conditions and often makes specific buy or sell recommendations. Some customers take the ultimate leap of faith and allow a full-service broker to make buy and sell decisions for them by establishing a *discretionary account*. In this account, the broker can buy and sell prespecified securities whenever deemed fit. (The broker cannot withdraw any funds, though.) This action requires an unusual degree of trust on the part of the customer, for an unscrupulous broker can "churn" an account, that is, trade securities excessively with the sole purpose of generating commissions.

Discount brokers, on the other hand, provide "no-frills" services. They buy and sell securities, hold them for safekeeping, offer margin loans, facilitate short sales, and that is all. The only information they provide about the securities they handle is price quotations. Discount brokerage services have become increasingly available in recent years. Many banks, thrift institutions, and mutual fund management companies now offer such services to the investing public as part of a general trend toward the creation of one-stop "financial supermarkets." Stock trading fees have fallen steadily over the last decade, and discount brokerage firms such as Schwab, E*Trade, or Ameritrade now offer commissions below $15, or even below $10 for preferred customers.

In addition to the explicit part of trading costs—the broker's commission—there is an implicit part—the dealer's bid–ask spread. Sometimes the broker is a dealer in the security being traded and charges no commission but instead collects the fee entirely in the form of the bid–ask spread. Another implicit cost of trading that some observers would distinguish is the price concession an investor may be forced to make for trading in any quantity that exceeds the quantity the dealer is willing to trade at the posted bid or asked price.

An ongoing controversy between the NYSE and its competitors is the extent to which better execution on the NYSE offsets the generally lower explicit costs of trading in other markets. Execution refers to the size of the effective bid–ask spread and the possibility of "price improvement" in a market. The NYSE believes that many investors focus too intently on the costs they can see, despite the fact that quality of execution can be a far more important determinant of total costs. Many NYSE trades are executed at a price inside the quoted spread. This can happen because floor brokers at the specialist's post can bid above or sell below the specialist's quote. In this way, two public orders can cross without incurring the specialist's spread.

In particular, the NYSE touts the possibility of trades being crossed "inside the quoted spread." To illustrate, suppose IBM is trading at $98.03 bid, $98.07 asked. A broker who has received a market buy order can meet a broker with a market sell order, and agree to a price of $98.05. By meeting in the middle of the quoted spread, both buyer and seller obtain "price improvement," that is, transaction prices better than the best quoted prices. Such "meetings" of brokers are more than accidental. Because all trading takes place at the specialist's post, floor brokers know where to look for counterparties to a trade.

In contrast, in dealer markets, all trades go through the dealer, and all trades, therefore, are subject to a bid–ask spread. The client never sees the spread as an explicit cost, however. The price at which the trade is executed incorporates the dealer's spread, but this part of the price is never reported to the investor.

A controversial practice related to the bid–ask spread and the quality of trade execution is "paying for order flow." This entails paying a broker a rebate for directing the trade to a particular dealer rather than to the NYSE. By bringing the trade to a dealer instead of to the exchange, however, the broker eliminates the possibility that the trade could have been executed without incurring a spread. In fact, the opportunity to profit from the bid–ask spread is the major reason that the dealer is willing to pay the broker for the order flow. Moreover, a broker that is paid for order flow might direct a trade to a dealer that does not even offer the most competitive price. (Indeed, the fact that dealers can afford to pay for order flow suggests that they are able to lay off the trade at better prices elsewhere and, possibly, that the broker also could have found a better price with some additional effort.) Many of the online brokerage firms rely heavily on payment for order flow, since their explicit commissions are so minimal. They typically do not actually execute orders, instead sending an order either to a market maker or to a stock exchange for listed stocks.

Such practices raise serious ethical questions, because the broker's primary obligation is to obtain the best deal for the client. Payment for order flow might be justified if the rebate is passed along to the client either directly or through lower commissions, but it is not clear that such rebates are passed through.

3.6   BUYING ON MARGIN

When purchasing securities, investors have easy access to a source of debt financing called *broker's call loans*. The act of taking advantage of broker's call loans is called *buying on margin*.

Purchasing stocks on margin means the investor borrows part of the purchase price of the stock from a broker. The **margin** in the account is the portion of the purchase price contributed by the investor; the remainder is borrowed from the broker. The brokers in turn borrow money from banks at the call money rate to finance these purchases; they then charge their clients that rate (defined in Chapter 2), plus a service charge for the loan. All securities purchased on margin must be maintained with the brokerage firm in street name, for the securities are collateral for the loan.

The Board of Governors of the Federal Reserve System limits the extent to which stock purchases can be financed using margin loans. The current initial margin requirement is 50%, meaning that at least 50% of the purchase price must be paid for in cash, with the rest borrowed.

margin

Describes securities purchased with money borrowed in part from a broker. The margin is the net worth of the investor's account.

The percentage margin is defined as the ratio of the net worth, or the "equity value," of the account to the market value of the securities. To demonstrate, suppose an investor initially pays $6,000 toward the purchase of $10,000 worth of stock (100 shares at $100 per share), borrowing the remaining $4,000 from a broker. The initial balance sheet looks like this:

EXAMPLE 3.1

Margin

Assets		Liabilities and Owners' Equity	
Value of stock	$10,000	Loan from broker	$4,000
		Equity	$6,000

The initial percentage margin is

$$\text{Margin} = \frac{\text{Equity in account}}{\text{Value of stock}} = \frac{\$6,000}{\$10,000} = .60, \text{ or } 60\%$$

If the price declines to $70 per share, the account balance becomes:

Assets		Liabilities and Owners' Equity	
Value of stock	$7,000	Loan from broker	$4,000
		Equity	$3,000

The assets in the account fall by the full decrease in the stock value, as does the equity. The percentage margin is now

$$\text{Margin} = \frac{\text{Equity in account}}{\text{Value of stock}} = \frac{\$3,000}{\$7,000} = .43, \text{ or } 43\%$$

If the stock value in Example 3.1 were to fall below $4,000, owners' equity would become negative, meaning the value of the stock is no longer sufficient collateral to cover the loan from the broker. To guard against this possibility, the broker sets a *maintenance margin*. If the percentage margin falls below the maintenance level, the broker will issue a *margin call*, which requires the investor to add new cash or securities to the margin account. If the investor does not act, the broker may sell securities from the account to pay off enough of the loan to restore the percentage margin to an acceptable level.

Suppose the maintenance margin is 30%. How far could the stock price fall before the investor would get a margin call?

Let P be the price of the stock. The value of the investor's 100 shares is then $100P$, and the equity in the account is $100P - \$4,000$. The percentage margin is $(100P - \$4,000)/100P$. The price at which the percentage margin equals the maintenance margin of .3 is found by solving the equation

EXAMPLE 3.2

Maintenance Margin

$$\frac{100P - 4,000}{100P} = .3$$

Handout #4

$$V_t^* = \frac{(1-m)}{(1-x)} \, 100$$
$$\frac{1 - .6}{1 - .3} \, 100$$
$$= \$57.14$$

which implies that $P = \$57.14$. If the price of the stock were to fall below $57.14 per share, the investor would get a margin call.

Suppose the maintenance margin in Example 3.2 is 40%. How far can the stock price fall before the investor gets a margin call?

Concept check 3.4

$$\frac{1 - .60}{.60} = .40 \times 10,000$$

The Excel spreadsheet model below makes it easy to analyze the impacts of different margin levels and the volatility of stock prices. It also allows you to compare return on investment for a margin trade with a trade using no borrowed funds.

Please visit us at www.mhhe.com/bkm

	A	B	C	D	E	F	G	H
1								
2			Action or Formula	Ending	Return on		Ending	Return with
3			for Column B	St Price	Investment		St Price	No Margin
4	Initial Equity Investment	$10,000.00	Enter data		−42.00%			−19.00%
5	Amount Borrowed	$10,000.00	(B4/B10)−B4	$20.00	−122.00%		$20.00	−59.00%
6	Initial Stock Price	$50.00	Enter data	25.00	−102.00%		25.00	−49.00%
7	Shares Purchased	400	(B4/B10)/B6	30.00	−82.00%		30.00	−39.00%
8	Ending Stock Price	$40.00	Enter data	35.00	−62.00%		35.00	−29.00%
9	Cash Dividends During Hold Per.	$0.60	Enter data	40.00	−42.00%		40.00	−19.00%
10	Initial Margin Percentage	50.00%	Enter data	45.00	−22.00%		45.00	−9.00%
11	Maintenance Margin Percentage	30.00%	Enter data	50.00	−2.00%		50.00	1.00%
12				55.00	18.00%		55.00	11.00%
13	Rate on Margin Loan	8.00%	Enter data	60.00	38.00%		60.00	21.00%
14	Holding Period in Months	6	Enter data	65.00	58.00%		65.00	31.00%
15				70.00	78.00%		70.00	41.00%
16	**Return on Investment**			75.00	98.00%		75.00	51.00%
17	Capital Gain on Stock	−$4,000.00	B7*(B8−B6)	80.00	118.00%		80.00	61.00%
18	Dividends	$200.00	B7*B9					
19	Interest on Margin Loan	$400.00	B5*(B14/12)*B13					
20	Net Income	−$4,200.00	B17+B18−B19				LEGEND:	
21	Initial Investment	$10,000.00	B4				Enter data	
22	Return on Investment	−42.00%	B20/B21				Value calculated	

Why do investors buy securities on margin? They do so when they wish to invest an amount greater than their own money allows. Thus, they can achieve greater upside potential, but they also expose themselves to greater downside risk.

To see how, let's suppose an investor is bullish on IBM stock, which is selling for $100 per share. An investor with $10,000 to invest expects IBM to go up in price by 30% during the next year. Ignoring any dividends, the expected rate of return would be 30% if the investor invested $10,000 to buy 100 shares.

But now assume the investor borrows another $10,000 from the broker and invests it in IBM, too. The total investment in IBM would be $20,000 (for 200 shares). Assuming an interest rate on the margin loan of 9% per year, what will the investor's rate of return be now (again ignoring dividends) if IBM stock goes up 30% by year's end?

The 200 shares will be worth $26,000. Paying off $10,900 of principal and interest on the margin loan leaves $15,100 (i.e., $26,000 − $10,900). The rate of return in this case will be

$$\frac{\$15,100 - \$10,000}{\$10,000} = 51\%$$

The investor has parlayed a 30% rise in the stock's price into a 51% rate of return on the $10,000 investment.

Doing so, however, magnifies the downside risk. Suppose that, instead of going up by 30%, the price of IBM stock goes down by 30% to $70 per share. In that case, the 200 shares will be worth $14,000, and the investor is left with $3,100 after paying off the $10,900 of principal and interest on the loan. The result is a disastrous return of

$$\frac{\$3,100 - \$10,000}{\$10,000} = -69\%$$

Table 3.4 summarizes the possible results of these hypothetical transactions. If there is no change in IBM's stock price, the investor loses 9%, the cost of the loan.

EXCERPTS FROM CFA INSTITUTE STANDARDS OF PROFESSIONAL CONDUCT

I. Professionalism
- Knowledge of law. Members must understand knowledge of and comply with all applicable laws, rules, and regulations including the Code of Ethics and Standards of Professional Conduct.
- Independence and objectivity. Members shall maintain independence and objectivity in their professional activities.
- Misrepresentation. Members must not knowingly misrepresent investment analysis, recommendations, or other professional activities.

II. Integrity of Capital Markets
- Non-public information. Members must not exploit material non-public information.
- Market manipulation. Members shall not attempt to distort prices or trading volume with the intent to mislead market participants.

III. Duties to Clients
- Loyalty, prudence, and care. Members must place their clients' interests before their own and act with reasonable care on their behalf.
- Fair dealing. Members shall deal fairly and objectively with clients when making investment recommendations or taking actions.
- Suitability. Members shall make a reasonable inquiry into a client's financial situation, investment experience, and investment objectives prior to making appropriate investment recommendations.
- Performance presentation. Members shall attempt to ensure that investment performance is presented fairly, accurately, and completely.

- Confidentiality. Members must keep information about clients confidential unless the client permits disclosure.

IV. Duties to Employers
- Loyalty. Members must act for the benefit of their employer.
- Compensation. Members must not accept compensation from sources that would create a conflict of interest with their employer's interests without written consent from all involved parties.
- Supervisors. Members must make reasonable efforts to detect and prevent violation of applicable laws and regulations by anyone subject to their supervision.

V. Investment Analysis and Recommendations
- Diligence. Members must exercise diligence and have reasonable basis for investment analysis, recommendations, or actions.
- Communication. Members must distinguish fact from opinion in their presentation of analysis and disclose general principles of investment processes used in analysis.

VI. Conflicts of Interest
- Disclosure of conflicts. Members must disclose all matters that reasonably could be expected to impair their objectivity or interfere with their other duties.
- Priority of transactions. Transactions for clients and employers must have priority over transactions for the benefit of a member.

VII. Responsibilities as Member of CFA institute
- Conduct. Members must not engage in conduct that compromises the reputation or integrity of the CFA Institute or CFA designation.

SOURCE: Excerpts from the CFA Institute Standards of Professional Conduct, **www.cfainstitute.org/centre/ethics/code/pdf**, 2005.

- CEOs and CFOs must now personally certify that their firms' financial reports "fairly represent, in all material respects, the operations and financial condition of the company," and are subject to personal penalties if those reports turn out to be misleading. Following the letter of GAAP rules may still be necessary, but it is no longer sufficient accounting practice.
- Auditors may no longer provide several other services to their clients. This is intended to prevent potential profits on consulting work from influencing the quality of their audit.
- Requirements that the Board of Directors be composed of independent directors and hold regular meetings of Directors in which company management is not present (and therefore cannot impede or influence the discussion).

The SEC's Regulation FD (for Fair Disclosure), introduced in 2000, prohibits firms from divulging material information to one outside group (e.g., stock analysts) before making it available to the entire market. In addition, to settle charges brought by then New York Attorney General Eliot Spitzer concerning their publication of biased stock research as a quid pro quo for IPO allocations and investment banking contracts, major investment banks agreed in late 2002 to fence off stock research from the investment banking side of the firm.

Circuit Breakers

The market collapse of October 19, 1987, prompted several suggestions for regulatory change. Among these was a call for "circuit breakers" to slow or stop trading during periods of extreme volatility. Some of the current circuit breakers being used are as follows:

- *Trading halts.* If the Dow Jones Industrial Average falls by 10%, trading will be halted for one hour if the drop occurs before 2:00 P.M. (Eastern Standard Time), for one-half hour if the drop occurs between 2:00 and 2:30, but not at all if the drop occurs after 2:30. If the Dow falls by 20%, trading will be halted for two hours if the drop occurs before 1:00 P.M., for one hour if the drop occurs between 1:00 and 2:00, and for the rest of the day if the drop occurs after 2:00. A 30% drop in the Dow would close the market for the rest of the day, regardless of the time.
- *Collars.* When the Dow moves about two percentage points in either direction from the previous day's close, Rule 80A of the NYSE requires that index arbitrage orders pass a "tick test."[4] In a falling market, sell orders may be executed only at a plus tick or zero-plus tick, meaning that the trade may be done at a higher price than the last trade (a plus tick) or at the last price if the last recorded change in the stock price is positive (a zero-plus tick). The rule remains in effect for the rest of the day unless the Dow returns to within one percentage point of the previous day's close.

The idea behind circuit breakers is that a temporary halt in trading during periods of very high volatility can help mitigate informational problems that might contribute to excessive price swings. For example, even if a trader is unaware of any specific adverse economic news, if he sees the market plummeting, he will suspect that there might be a good reason for the price drop and will become unwilling to buy shares. In fact, he might decide to sell shares to avoid losses. Thus, feedback from price swings to trading behavior can exacerbate market movements. Circuit breakers give participants a chance to assess market fundamentals while prices are temporarily frozen. In this way, they have a chance to decide whether price movements are warranted while the market is closed.

Of course, circuit breakers have no bearing on trading in non-U.S. markets. It is quite possible that they simply have induced those who engage in program trading to move their operations into foreign exchanges.

Insider Trading

Regulations also prohibit insider trading. It is illegal for anyone to transact in securities to profit from **inside information,** that is, private information held by officers, directors, or major stockholders that has not yet been divulged to the public. But the definition of insiders can be ambiguous. While it is obvious that the chief financial officer of a firm is an insider, it is less clear whether the firm's biggest supplier can be considered an insider. Yet a supplier may deduce the firm's near-term prospects from significant changes in orders. This gives the supplier a unique form of private information, yet the supplier is not technically an insider. These ambiguities plague security analysts, whose job is to uncover as much information as possible concerning the firm's expected prospects. The distinction between legal private information and illegal inside information can be fuzzy.

The SEC requires officers, directors, and major stockholders to report all transactions in their firm's stock. A compendium of insider trades is published monthly in the SEC's *Official*

---

[4]The exact threshold is computed as 2% of the value of the Dow, updated quarterly, rounded down to the nearest 10 points.

Summary of Securities Transactions and Holdings. The idea is to inform the public of any implicit vote of confidence or no confidence made by insiders.

Insiders *do* exploit their knowledge. Three forms of evidence support this conclusion. First, there have been well-publicized convictions of principals in insider trading schemes.

Second, there is considerable evidence of "leakage" of useful information to some traders before any public announcement of that information. For example, share prices of firms announcing dividend increases (which the market interprets as good news concerning the firm's prospects) commonly increase in value a few days *before* the public announcement of the increase. Clearly, some investors are acting on the good news before it is released to the public. Share prices still rise substantially on the day of the public release of good news, however, indicating that insiders, or their associates, have not fully bid up the price of the stock to the level commensurate with the news.

A third form of evidence on insider trading has to do with returns earned on trades by insiders. Researchers have examined the SEC's summary of insider trading to measure the performance of insiders. In one of the best known of these studies, Jaffe (1974) examined the abnormal return of stocks over the months following purchases or sales by insiders. For months in which insider purchasers of a stock exceeded insider sellers of the stock by three or more, the stock had an abnormal return in the following eight months of about 5%. Moreover, when insider sellers exceeded insider buyers, the stock tended to perform poorly.

SUMMARY

- Firms issue securities to raise the capital necessary to finance their investments. Investment bankers market these securities to the public on the primary market. Investment bankers generally act as underwriters who purchase the securities from the firm and resell them to the public at a markup. Before the securities may be sold to the public, the firm must publish an SEC-approved prospectus that provides information on the firm's prospects.

- Already-issued securities are traded on the secondary market, that is, on organized stock exchanges; the over-the-counter market; and for large trades, through direct negotiation. Only license holders of exchanges may trade on the exchange. Brokerage firms holding licenses on the exchange sell their services to individuals, charging commissions for executing trades on their behalf.

- Trading may take place in dealer markets, via electronic communication networks, or in specialist markets. In dealer markets, security dealers post bid and ask prices at which they are willing to trade. Brokers for individuals execute trades at the best available prices. In electronic markets, the existing book of limit orders provides the terms at which trades can be executed. Mutually agreeable offers to buy or sell securities are automatically crossed by the computer system operating the market. In specialist markets, the specialist acts to maintain an orderly market with price continuity. Specialists maintain a limit order book, but also sell from or buy for their own inventories of stock. Thus, liquidity in specialist markets comes from both the limit order book and the specialist's inventory.

- Nasdaq was traditionally a dealer market in which a network of dealers negotiated directly over sales of securities. The NYSE was traditionally a specialist market. In recent years, as ECNs have commanded a greater share of trading activity, both exchanges have increased their commitment to electronic and automated trading. Most trades on Nasdaq today are electronic, and the NYSE has increased its electronic capabilities, including an expansion of Direct+.

- Trading costs include explicit commissions as well as the bid–ask spread. An ongoing controversy among markets concerns overall trading costs including the effect of spreads. The NYSE argues that it is often the cheapest trading venue when quality of execution (including the possibility of price improvement) is recognized.

- Buying on margin means borrowing money from a broker in order to buy more securities than can be purchased with one's own money alone. By buying securities on a margin, an investor magnifies both the upside potential and the downside risk. If the equity in a margin account falls below the required maintenance level, the investor will get a margin call from the broker.

- Short-selling is the practice of selling securities that the seller does not own. The short-seller borrows the securities sold through a broker and may be required to cover the short position at any time on demand. The cash proceeds of a short sale are kept in escrow by the broker, and the broker usually requires that the short-seller deposit additional cash or securities to serve as margin (collateral) for the short sale.

- Securities trading is regulated by the Securities and Exchange Commission, by other government agencies, and through self-regulation of the exchanges. Many of the important regulations have to do with full disclosure of relevant information concerning the securities in question. Insider trading rules also prohibit traders from attempting to profit from inside information.

KEY TERMS

ask price, 62
auction market, 62
bid–ask spread, 62
bid price, 62
block transactions, 68
dealer markets, 62
electronic communication
   networks (ECNs), 64
initial public offerings
   (IPOs), 56

inside information, 82
limit buy (sell) order, 62
margin, 74
Nasdaq, 66
over-the-counter (OTC)
   market, 64
primary market, 56
private placement, 58
program trade, 69
prospectus, 56

secondary market, 56
short sale, 77
specialist, 65
stock exchanges, 67
stop order 63
underwriters, 56

PROBLEM SETS

 Select problems are available in McGraw-Hill's Homework Manager®. Please see the packaging options of the preface for more information.

1. FBN, Inc., has just sold 100,000 shares in an initial public offering. The underwriter's explicit fees were $70,000. The offering price for the shares was $50, but immediately upon issue, the share price jumped to $53.
   a. What is your best guess as to the total cost to FBN of the equity issue?
   b. Is the entire cost of the underwriting a source of profit to the underwriters?

2. Suppose you short sell 100 shares of IBM, now selling at $120 per share.
   a. What is your maximum possible loss?
   b. What happens to the maximum loss if you simultaneously place a stop-buy order at $128?

3. Dée Trader opens a brokerage account, and purchases 300 shares of Internet Dreams at $40 per share. She borrows $4,000 from her broker to help pay for the purchase. The interest rate on the loan is 8%.
   a. What is the margin in Dée's account when she first purchases the stock?
   b. If the share price falls to $30 per share by the end of the year, what is the remaining margin in her account? If the maintenance margin requirement is 30%, will she receive a margin call?
   c. What is the rate of return on her investment?

4. Old Economy Traders opened an account to short sell 1,000 shares of Internet Dreams from the previous question. The initial margin requirement was 50%. (The margin account pays no interest.) A year later, the price of Internet Dreams has risen from $40 to $50, and the stock has paid a dividend of $2 per share.

    a. What is the remaining margin in the account?

    b. If the maintenance margin requirement is 30%, will Old Economy receive a margin call?

    c. What is the rate of return on the investment?

5. Do you think it is possible to completely replace market-making specialists with a fully automated, computerized trade-matching system?

6. Consider the following limit order book of a specialist. The last trade in the stock occurred at a price of $50.

Limit Buy Orders		Limit Sell Orders	
Price	**Shares**	**Price**	**Shares**
$49.75	500	$50.25	100
49.50	800	51.50	100
49.25	500	54.75	300
49.00	200	58.25	100
48.50	600		

    a. If a market buy order for 100 shares comes in, at what price will it be filled?

    b. At what price would the next market buy order be filled?

    c. If you were the specialist, would you want to increase or decrease your inventory of this stock?

7. You are bullish on Telecom stock. The current market price is $50 per share, and you have $5,000 of your own to invest. You borrow an additional $5,000 from your broker at an interest rate of 8% per year and invest $10,000 in the stock.

Please visit us at www.mhhe.com/bkm

    a. What will be your rate of return if the price of Telecom stock goes up by 10% during the next year? (Ignore the expected dividend.)

    b. How far does the price of Telecom stock have to fall for you to get a margin call if the maintenance margin is 30%? Assume the price fall happens immediately.

8. You are bearish on Telecom and decide to sell short 100 shares at the current market price of $50 per share.

Please visit us at www.mhhe.com/bkm

    a. How much in cash or securities must you put into your brokerage account if the broker's initial margin requirement is 50% of the value of the short position?

    b. How high can the price of the stock go before you get a margin call if the maintenance margin is 30% of the value of the short position?

9. Suppose that Intel currently is selling at $40 per share. You buy 500 shares using $15,000 of your own money, borrowing the remainder of the purchase price from your broker. The rate on the margin loan is 8%.

Please visit us at www.mhhe.com/bkm

    a. What is the percentage increase in the net worth of your brokerage account if the price of Intel *immediately* changes to: (i) $44; (ii) $40; (iii) $36? What is the relationship between your percentage return and the percentage change in the price of Intel?

    b. If the maintenance margin is 25%, how low can Intel's price fall before you get a margin call?

    c. How would your answer to (*b*) change if you had financed the initial purchase with only $10,000 of your own money?

    d. What is the rate of return on your margined position (assuming again that you invest $15,000 of your own money) if Intel is selling *after one year* at: (i) $44; (ii) $40;

(iii) $36? What is the relationship between your percentage return and the percentage change in the price of Intel? Assume that Intel pays no dividends.

 e. Continue to assume that a year has passed. How low can Intel's price fall before you get a margin call?

10. Suppose that you sell short 500 shares of Intel, currently selling for $40 per share, and give your broker $15,000 to establish your margin account.

 a. If you earn no interest on the funds in your margin account, what will be your rate of return after one year if Intel stock is selling at: (i) $44; (ii) $40; (iii) $36? Assume that Intel pays no dividends.

 b. If the maintenance margin is 25%, how high can Intel's price rise before you get a margin call?

 c. Redo parts (a) and (b), but now assume that Intel also has paid a year-end dividend of $1 per share. The prices in part (a) should be interpreted as ex-dividend, that is, prices after the dividend has been paid.

11. Call one full-service broker and one discount broker and find out the transaction costs of implementing the following strategies:

 a. Buying 100 shares of IBM now and selling them six months from now.

 b. Investing an equivalent amount in six-month at-the-money call options on IBM stock now and selling them six months from now.

12. Here is some price information on Marriott:

	Bid	Asked
Marriott	37.95	38.05

You have placed a stop-loss order to sell at $38. What are you telling your broker? Given market prices, will your order be executed?

13. Here is some price information on Fincorp stock. Suppose first that Fincorp trades in a dealer market.

Bid	Asked
55.25	55.50

 a. Suppose you have submitted an order to your broker to buy at market. At what price will your trade be executed?

 b. Suppose you have submitted an order to sell at market. At what price will your trade be executed?

 c. Suppose you have submitted a limit order to sell at $55.62. What will happen?

 d. Suppose you have submitted a limit order to buy at $55.37. What will happen?

14. Now reconsider Problem 13 assuming that Fincorp sells in an exchange market like the NYSE.

 a. Is there any chance for price improvement in the market orders considered in parts (a) and (b)?

 b. Is there any chance of an immediate trade at $55.37 for the limit buy order in part (d)?

15. What purpose does the SuperDot system serve on the New York Stock Exchange?

16. Who sets the bid and asked price for a stock traded over the counter? Would you expect the spread to be higher on actively or inactively traded stocks?

17. You've borrowed $20,000 on margin to buy shares in Disney, which is now selling at $40 per share. Your account starts at the initial margin requirement of 50%. The mainte-nance margin is 35%. Two days later, the stock price falls to $35 per share.

 a. Will you receive a margin call?

 b. How low can the price of Disney shares fall before you receive a margin call?

18. On January 1, you sold short one round lot (that is, 100 shares) of Zenith stock at $14 per share. On March 1, a dividend of $2 per share was paid. On April 1, you covered the short sale by buying the stock at a price of $9 per share. You paid 50 cents per share in commissions for each transaction. What is the value of your account on April 1?

19. If you place a stop-loss order to sell 100 shares of stock at $55 when the current price is $62, how much will you receive for each share if the price drops to $50?

   a. $50.
   b. $55.
   c. $54.87.
   d. Cannot tell from the information given.

20. You wish to sell short 100 shares of XYZ Corporation stock. If the last two transactions were at $34.12 followed by $34.25, you can sell short on the next transaction only at a price of

   a. 34.12 or higher
   b. 34.25 or higher
   c. 34.25 or lower
   d. 34.12 or lower

21. Specialists on the New York Stock Exchange do all of the following *except:*

   a. Act as dealers for their own accounts.
   b. Execute limit orders.
   c. Help provide liquidity to the marketplace.
   d. Act as odd-lot dealers.

Use data from the Standard & Poor's Market Insight Database at www.mhhe.com/edumarketinsight to answer the following questions.

1. Select the Company tab and enter ticker symbol for a firm of your choice. Click on the Compustat Reports section and find the link for the company's profile. Where is the company's headquarters located? On what exchange does the company's stock primarily trade?

2. Now link to the Corporate Actions section of the Compustat Reports. Briefly summarize what you find out about the company's history with regard to its name and its ticker symbol.

3. Link to the Financial Highlights section of the Compustat Reports. What firm is the primary auditor of Quebecor's financial statements? Is the auditor's opinion qualified in any way?

WEB *master*

IPOs

Go to the IPO Central Web site at **www.hoovers.com/global/ipoc/index.xhtml** to see a list of currently proposed initial public offerings and those that have recently started trading.

1. Click on the "IPO Scorecard" link, then the "Best/Worst Returns" link. How many firms had returns above 30% for the most recent quarter? How many had returns lower than −30%?

2. Under the "IPO Scorecard" menu, click on the "Biggest First Days" link. Which firms had the best and the worst first-day returns for the last quarter?

3. Follow the "Money Left on the Table" link in the "IPO Scorecard" section. Assume that explicit costs for each underwriting were 7.5% of the issue's value based on the offer price. Calculate the amount of the explicit costs for the first firm listed. How does this number compare to the money left on the table? Repeat the calculation for the next two firms listed.

4. For the first firm listed, calculate the number of shares offered in the IPO. What offer price would have made the explicit costs of the offering equal to the implicit costs?

SOLUTIONS TO CONCEPT *checks*

3.1. Limited time shelf registration was introduced because of its favorable trade-off of saving issue cost against mandated disclosure. Allowing unlimited shelf registration would circumvent "blue sky" laws that ensure proper disclosure as the financial circumstances of the firm change over time.

3.2. *a.* Used cars trade in dealer markets (used-car lots or auto dealerships) and in direct search markets when individuals advertise in local newspapers or Internet listings.

   b. Paintings trade in broker markets when clients commission brokers to buy or sell art for them, in dealer markets at art galleries, and in auction markets.

   c. Rare coins trade in dealer markets, for example, in coin shops or shows, but they also trade in auctions and in direct search markets when individuals advertise they want to buy or sell coins.

3.3. *a.* You should give your broker a market order. It will be executed immediately and is the cheapest type of order in terms of brokerage fees.

   b. You should give your broker a limit buy order, which will be executed only if the shares can be obtained at a price about 5% below the current price.

   c. You should give your broker a stop-loss order, which will be executed if the share price starts falling. The limit or stop price should be close to the current price to avoid the possibility of large losses.

3.4. Solving

$$\frac{100P - \$4,000}{100P} = .4$$

   yields $P = \$66.67$ per share.

3.5. The investor will purchase 150 shares, with a rate of return as follows:

Year-End Change in Price	Year-End Value of Shares	Repayment of Principal and Interest	Investor's Rate of Return
30%	$19,500	$5,450	40.5%
No change	15,000	5,450	−4.5
−30%	10,500	5,450	−49.5

3.6. *a.* Once Dot Bomb stock goes up to $110, your balance sheet will be:

Assets		Liabilities and Owner's Equity	
Cash	$100,000	Short position in Dot Bomb	$110,000
T-bills	50,000	Equity	40,000

   b. Solving

$$\frac{\$150,000 - 1,000P}{1,000P} = .4$$

   yields $P = \$107.14$ per share.

Mutual Funds and Other Investment Companies

 Cite advantages and disadvantages of investing with an investment company rather than buying securities directly.

 Contrast open-end mutual funds with closed-end funds and unit investment trusts.

 Define net asset value and measure the rate of return on a mutual fund.

 Classify mutual funds according to investment style.

 Demonstrate the impact of expenses and turnover on mutual fund investment performance.

The previous chapter provided an introduction to the mechanics of trading securities and the structure of the markets in which securities trade. Increasingly, however, individual investors are choosing not to trade securities directly for their own accounts. Instead, they direct their funds to investment companies that purchase securities on their behalf. The most important of these financial intermediaries are mutual funds, which are currently owned by about one-half of U.S. households. Other types of investment companies, such as unit investment trusts and closed-end funds, also merit distinction.

We begin the chapter by describing and comparing the various types of investment companies available to investors—unit investment trusts, closed-end investment companies, and open-end investment companies, more commonly known as mutual funds. We devote most of our attention to mutual funds, examining the functions of such funds, their investment styles and policies, and the costs of investing in these funds.

(continued)

Next, we take a first look at the investment performance of these funds. We consider the impact of expenses and turnover on net performance and examine the extent to which performance is consistent from one period to the next. In other words, will the mutual funds that were the best past performers be the best *future* performers? Finally, we discuss sources of information on mutual funds and consider in detail the information provided in the most comprehensive guide, Morningstar's *Mutual Fund Sourcebook*.

Related Web sites for this chapter are available at www.mhhe.com/bkm.

4.1 | INVESTMENT COMPANIES

investment companies

Financial intermediaries that invest the funds of individual investors in securities or other assets.

Investment companies are financial intermediaries that collect funds from individual investors and invest those funds in a potentially wide range of securities or other assets. Pooling of assets is the key idea behind investment companies. Each investor has a claim to the portfolio established by the investment company in proportion to the amount invested. These companies thus provide a mechanism for small investors to "team up" to obtain the benefits of large-scale investing.

Investment companies perform several important functions for their investors:

1. *Record keeping and administration.* Investment companies issue periodic status reports, keeping track of capital gains distributions, dividends, investments, and redemptions, and they may reinvest dividend and interest income for shareholders.

2. *Diversification and divisibility.* By pooling their money, investment companies enable investors to hold fractional shares of many different securities. They can act as large investors even if any individual shareholder cannot.

3. *Professional management.* Most, but not all, investment companies have full-time staffs of security analysts and portfolio managers who attempt to achieve superior investment results for their investors.

4. *Lower transaction costs.* Because they trade large blocks of securities, investment companies can achieve substantial savings on brokerage fees and commissions.

While all investment companies pool the assets of individual investors, they also need to divide claims to those assets among those investors. Investors buy shares in investment companies, and ownership is proportional to the number of shares purchased. The value of each share is called the **net asset value,** or **NAV.** Net asset value equals assets minus liabilities expressed on a per-share basis:

net asset value (NAV)

Assets minus liabilities expressed on a per-share basis.

$$\text{Net asset value} = \frac{\text{Market value of assets minus liabilities}}{\text{Shares outstanding}}$$

Consider a mutual fund that manages a portfolio of securities worth $120 million. Suppose the fund owes $4 million to its investment advisers and owes another $1 million for rent, wages due, and miscellaneous expenses. The fund has 5 million shareholders. Then

$$\text{Net asset value} = \frac{\$120 \text{ million} - \$5 \text{ million}}{5 \text{ million shares}} = \$23 \text{ per share}$$

Consider these data from the September 2006 balance sheet of the Growth and Income mutual fund sponsored by the Vanguard Group. (All values are in millions.) What was the net asset value of the portfolio?

Assets:	$5,092.2 *000,000*
Liabilities:	$ 4.6
Shares:	150.6

4.2 TYPES OF INVESTMENT COMPANIES

In the United States, investment companies are classified by the Investment Company Act of 1940 as either unit investment trusts or managed investment companies. The portfolios of unit investment trusts are essentially fixed and thus are called "unmanaged." In contrast, managed companies are so named because securities in their investment portfolios continually are bought and sold: The portfolios are managed. Managed companies are further classified as either closed-end or open-end. Open-end companies are what we commonly call mutual funds.

Unit Investment Trusts

Unit investment trusts are pools of money invested in a portfolio that is fixed for the life of the fund. To form a unit investment trust, a sponsor, typically a brokerage firm, buys a portfolio of securities which are deposited into a trust. It then sells to the public shares, or "units," in the trust, called *redeemable trust certificates*. All income and payments of principal from the portfolio are paid out by the fund's trustees (a bank or trust company) to the shareholders.

There is little active management of a unit investment trust because once established, the portfolio composition is fixed; hence these trusts are referred to as *unmanaged*. Trusts tend to invest in relatively uniform types of assets; for example, one trust may invest in municipal bonds, another in corporate bonds. The uniformity of the portfolio is consistent with the lack of active management. The trusts provide investors a vehicle to purchase a pool of one particular type of asset, which can be included in an overall portfolio as desired. The lack of active management of the portfolio implies that management fees can be lower than those of managed funds.

Sponsors of unit investment trusts earn their profit by selling shares in the trust at a premium to the cost of acquiring the underlying assets. For example, a trust that has purchased $5 million of assets may sell 5,000 shares to the public at a price of $1,030 per share, which (assuming the trust has no liabilities) represents a 3% premium over the net asset value of the securities held by the trust. The 3% premium is the trustee's fee for establishing the trust.

Investors who wish to liquidate their holdings of a unit investment trust may sell the shares back to the trustee for net asset value. The trustees can either sell enough securities from the asset portfolio to obtain the cash necessary to pay the investor, or they may instead sell the shares to a new investor (again at a slight premium to net asset value).

Unit investment trusts have steadily lost market share to mutual funds in recent years. Assets in such trusts declined from $105 billion in 1990 to only $41 billion in 2005.

unit investment trusts

Money pooled from many investors that is invested in a portfolio fixed for the life of the fund.

Managed Investment Companies

There are two types of managed companies: closed-end and open-end. In both cases, the fund's board of directors, which is elected by shareholders, hires a management company to manage the portfolio for an annual fee that typically ranges from .2% to 1.5% of assets.

In many cases the management company is the firm that organized the fund. For example, Fidelity Management and Research Corporation sponsors many Fidelity mutual funds and is responsible for managing the portfolios. It assesses a management fee on each Fidelity fund. In other cases, a mutual fund will hire an outside portfolio manager. For example, Vanguard has hired Wellington Management as the investment adviser for its Wellington Fund. Most management companies have contracts to manage several funds.

Open-end funds stand ready to redeem or issue shares at their net asset value (although both purchases and redemptions may involve sales charges). When investors in open-end funds wish to "cash out" their shares, they sell them back to the fund at NAV. In contrast, **closed-end funds** do not redeem or issue shares. Investors in closed-end funds who wish to cash out must sell their shares to other investors. Shares of closed-end funds are traded on organized exchanges and can be purchased through brokers just like other common stock; their prices therefore can differ from NAV.

Figure 4.1 is a listing of closed-end funds from the online edition of *The Wall Street Journal*. The first column gives the fund's name and ticker symbol. The next two columns give the fund's most recent net asset value and closing share price. The premium or discount is the percentage difference between price and NAV: (Price − NAV)/NAV. Notice that there are more funds selling at discounts to NAV (indicated by negative differences) than premiums. Finally, the 52-week return based on the percentage change in share price plus dividend income is presented in the last column.

The common divergence of price from net asset value, often by wide margins, is a puzzle that has yet to be fully explained. To see why this is a puzzle, consider a closed-end fund that is selling at a discount from net asset value. If the fund were to sell all the assets in the portfolio, it would realize proceeds equal to net asset value. The difference between the market price of the fund and the fund's NAV would represent the per-share increase in the wealth of the fund's investors. Despite this apparent profit opportunity, sizable discounts seem to persist for long periods of time.

Moreover, several studies (e.g., Thompson, 1978) have shown that on average, fund premia or discounts tend to dissipate over time, so funds selling at a discount receive a boost to their rate of return as the discount shrinks. Pontiff (1995) estimates that a fund selling at a 20% discount would have an expected 12-month return more than 6% greater than funds selling at net asset value.

Interestingly, while many closed-end funds sell at a discount from net asset value, the prices of these funds when originally issued are often above NAV. This is a further puzzle, as it is hard to explain why investors would purchase these newly issued funds at a premium to NAV when the shares tend to fall to a discount shortly after issue.

Many investors consider closed-end funds selling at a discount to NAV to be a bargain. Even if the market price never rises to the level of NAV, the dividend yield on an investment in the fund at this price would exceed the dividend yield on the same securities held outside the fund. To see this, imagine a fund with an NAV of $10 per share holding a portfolio that pays an annual dividend of $1 per share; that is, the dividend yield to investors that hold this portfolio directly is 10%. Now suppose that the market price of a share of this closed-end fund

open-end fund

A fund that issues or redeems its shares at net asset value.

closed-end fund

Shares may not be redeemed, but instead are traded at prices that can differ from net asset value.

FIGURE 4.1

Closed-end mutual funds

Source: *The Wall Street Journal Online*, January 16, 2007.

CLOSED-END FUNDS

FUND	NAV	MKT PRICE	PREM/DISC	52 WEEK RETURN %	FUND	NAV	MKT PRICE	PREM/DISC	52 WEEK RETURN %
Adams Express Company (ADX)	15.96	13.85	−13.22	13.84	First Tr Val Line 100 (FVL)	16.43	15.25	−7.18	4.79
Advent/Clay Enhcd G & I (LCM)	19.54	19.81	1.38	23.47	Gabelli Div & Inc Tr (GDV)	23.31	20.95	−10.12	23.57
Alliance All-Mkt Advantg (AMO)	13.51	14.50	7.33	3.92	Gabelli Equity Trust (GAB)	9.51	9.79	2.94	27.84
BlackRock Div Achvrs (BDV)	16.25	15.16	−6.71	19.34	General Amer Investors (GAM)	40.78	37.00	−9.27	11.37
BlackRock S & P 500 Pr Eq (PEFX)	10.08	9.77	−3.08	6.50	Source Capital (SOR)	65.48	66.07	0.90	−5.40
BlackRock Str Div Achvr (BDT)	16.55	15.05	−9.06	17.39	SunAmerica Foc Alpha Gr (FGF)	22.90	20.17	−11.92	20.52
Blue Chip Value Fund (BLU)	5.80	6.03	3.97	4.31	Tri-Continental Corp (TY)	25.91	22.75	−12.20	15.68
Eaton Vance Tax Div Inc (EVT)	28.91	27.11	−6.23	23.82	Zweig Fund (ZF)	5.97	5.82	−2.51	21.76
Equus II Incorporated (EQS)	11.32	8.41	−25.71	23.24					

is $9. If management pays out dividends received from the shares as they come in, then the dividend yield to those that hold the same portfolio through the closed-end fund will be $1/$9, or 11.1%.

In contrast to closed-end funds, the price of open-end funds cannot fall below NAV, because these funds stand ready to redeem shares at NAV. The offering price will exceed NAV, however, if the fund carries a **load.** A load is, in effect, a sales charge, which is paid to the seller. Load funds are sold by securities brokers and directly by mutual fund groups.

Unlike closed-end funds, open-end mutual funds do not trade on organized exchanges. Instead, investors simply buy shares from and liquidate through the investment company at net asset value. Thus, the number of outstanding shares of these funds changes daily. At the end of 2006, about $300 billion of assets were held in closed-end funds.

load

A sales commission charged on a mutual fund.

Other Investment Organizations

There are intermediaries not formally organized or regulated as investment companies that nevertheless serve functions similar to investment companies. Among the more important are commingled funds, real estate investment trusts, and hedge funds.

Commingled funds   Commingled funds are partnerships of investors that pool their funds. The management firm that organizes the partnership, for example, a bank or insurance company, manages the funds for a fee. Typical partners in a commingled fund might be trust or retirement accounts that have portfolios much larger than those of most individual investors but are still too small to warrant managing on a separate basis.

Commingled funds are similar in form to open-end mutual funds. Instead of shares, though, the fund offers *units,* which are bought and sold at net asset value. A bank or insurance company may offer an array of different commingled funds, for example, a money market fund, a bond fund, and a common stock fund.

Real Estate Investment Trusts (REITs)   A REIT is similar to a closed-end fund. REITs invest in real estate or loans secured by real estate. Besides issuing shares, they raise capital by borrowing from banks and issuing bonds or mortgages. Most of them are highly leveraged, with a typical debt ratio of 70%.

There are two principal kinds of REITs. *Equity trusts* invest in real estate directly, whereas *mortgage trusts* invest primarily in mortgage and construction loans. REITs generally are established by banks, insurance companies, or mortgage companies, which then serve as investment managers to earn a fee.

REITs are exempt from taxes as long as at least 95% of their taxable income is distributed to shareholders. For shareholders, however, the dividends are taxable as personal income.

Hedge funds   Like mutual funds, **hedge funds** are vehicles that allow private investors to pool assets to be invested by a fund manager. Unlike mutual funds, however, hedge funds are commonly structured as private partnerships and thus are not subject to many SEC regulations. Typically they are open only to wealthy or institutional investors. Many require investors to agree to initial "lock-ups," that is, periods as long as several years in which investments cannot be withdrawn. Lock-ups allow hedge funds to invest in illiquid assets without worrying about meeting demands for redemption of funds. Moreover, since hedge funds are only lightly regulated, their managers can pursue other investment strategies that are not open to mutual fund managers, for example, heavy use of derivatives, short sales, and leverage.

Hedge funds also differ from mutual funds in the compensation structure used for managers. Whereas mutual funds assess management fees equal to a fixed percentage of assets, for example between 1 to 1.5% annually for typical equity funds, hedge funds charge comparable fees *plus* a substantial fraction of any investment profits, typically 20%, but often more. Indeed, some observers characterize hedge funds only half-jokingly as "a compensation scheme masquerading as an asset class." In any case, it would be a mistake to view hedge funds as anything remotely like a uniform asset class. Hedge funds by design are empowered to invest in a wide

hedge fund

A private investment pool, open to wealthy or institutional investors, that is exempt from SEC regulation and can therefore pursue more speculative policies than mutual funds.

range of investments, with various funds focusing on derivatives, distressed firms, currency speculation, convertible bonds, emerging markets, merger arbitrage, and so on. Other funds may jump from one asset class to another as perceived investment opportunities shift.

Hedge funds commonly attempt to exploit temporary misalignments in security valuations. For example, if the yield on mortgage-backed securities seems abnormally high compared to that on Treasury bonds, the hedge fund would buy mortgage-backed and short sell Treasury securities. Notice that the fund is *not* betting on broad movement in the entire bond market; it buys one type of bond and sells another. By taking a long mortgage/short Treasury position, the fund "hedges" its interest rate exposure, while making a bet on the *relative* valuation across the two sectors. The idea is that when yield spreads converge back to their "normal" relationship, the fund will profit from the realignment regardless of the general trend in the level of interest rates. In this respect, it strives to be "market neutral," which gives rise to the term "hedge fund."

Of course even if the fund's position is market neutral, this does not mean that it is low risk. The fund is still speculating on valuation differences across the two sectors, often taking a very large position, and this decision can turn out to be right or wrong. Because the funds often operate with considerable leverage, returns can be quite volatile.

One of the major financial stories of 1998 was the collapse of Long-Term Capital Management (LTCM), probably the best-known hedge fund at the time. Among its many investments were several "convergence bets," such as the mortgage-backed/Treasury spread we have described. When Russia defaulted on some of its debts in August 1998, risk and liquidity premiums increased, so that instead of converging, the yield spread between safe Treasuries and almost all other bonds widened. LTCM lost billions of dollars in August and September of 1998; the fear was that given its extreme leverage, continued losses might more than wipe out the firm's capital and force it to default on its positions. Eventually, several Wall Street firms contributed a total of about $3.5 billion to bail out the fund, in return receiving a 90% ownership stake in the firm.

Despite these past problems, hedge funds have grown enormously in the past few years, from perhaps $50 billion in 1990 to well over $1 trillion under management in 2006. One of the fastest growing sectors has been in "funds of funds." These are funds that invest in several other hedge funds. The idea is to spread the risk across several different funds. Investors, however, need to be aware that these funds of funds operate with considerable leverage, on top of the leverage of the primary funds in which they invest, which can make returns highly volatile. Moreover, if the various hedge funds in which these funds of funds invest have similar investment styles, the diversification benefits of spreading investments across several funds may be illusory—but the extra layer of steep management fees paid to the manager of the fund of funds certainly is not.

4.3   MUTUAL FUNDS

Mutual fund is the common name for an open-end investment company. This is the dominant investment company in the U.S. today, accounting for more than 90% of investment company assets. Assets under management in the U.S. mutual fund industry were over $10 trillion in early 2007. Approximately another $9 trillion were invested in mutual funds of non-U.S. sponsors.

Investment Policies

Each mutual fund has a specified investment policy, which is described in the fund's prospectus. For example, money market mutual funds hold the short-term, low-risk instruments of the money market (see Chapter 2 for a review of these securities), while bond funds hold fixed-income securities. Some funds have even more narrowly defined mandates. For example, some bond funds will hold primarily Treasury bonds, others primarily mortgage-backed securities.

Management companies manage a family, or "complex," of mutual funds. They organize an entire collection of funds and then collect a management fee for operating them. By managing a collection of funds under one umbrella, these companies make it easy for investors to allocate assets across market sectors and to switch assets across funds while still benefiting from centralized record keeping. Some of the most well-known management companies are Fidelity, Vanguard, Putnam, and Dreyfus. Each offers an array of open-end mutual funds with different investment policies. In early 2007, there were over 8,000 mutual funds in the United States, which were offered by fewer than 500 fund complexes.

Some of the more important fund types, classified by investment policy, are discussed next.

Money market funds   These funds invest in money market securities such as commercial paper, repurchase agreements, or certificates of deposit. The average maturity of these assets tends to be a bit more than one month. They usually offer check-writing features, and net asset value is fixed at $1 per share, so that there are no tax implications such as capital gains or losses associated with redemption of shares.

Equity funds   Equity funds invest primarily in stock, although they may, at the portfolio manager's discretion, also hold fixed-income or other types of securities. Funds commonly will hold about 5% of total assets in money market securities to provide the liquidity necessary to meet potential redemption of shares.

It is traditional to classify stock funds according to their emphasis on capital appreciation versus current income. Thus *income funds* tend to hold shares of firms with high dividend yields that provide high current income. *Growth funds* are willing to forgo current income, focusing instead on prospects for capital gains. While the classification of these funds is couched in terms of income versus capital gains, it is worth noting that in practice the more relevant distinction concerns the level of risk these funds assume. Growth stocks—and therefore growth funds—are typically riskier and respond far more dramatically to changes in economic conditions than do income funds.

Specialized sector funds   Some equity funds, called *sector funds,* concentrate on a particular industry. For example, Fidelity markets dozens of "select funds," each of which invests in a specific industry such as biotechnology, utilities, precious metals, or telecommunications. Other funds specialize in securities of particular countries.

Bond funds   As the name suggests, these funds specialize in the fixed-income sector. Within that sector, however, there is considerable room for specialization. For example, various funds will concentrate on corporate bonds, Treasury bonds, mortgage-backed securities, or municipal (tax-free) bonds. Indeed, some of the municipal bond funds will invest only in bonds of a particular state (or even city!) in order to satisfy the investment desires of residents of that state who wish to avoid local as well as federal taxes on the interest paid on the bonds. Many funds also will specialize by the maturity of the securities, ranging from short-term to intermediate to long-term, or by the credit risk of the issuer, ranging from very safe to high-yield or "junk" bonds.

International funds   Many funds have international focus. *Global funds* invest in securities worldwide, including the United States. In contrast, *international funds* invest in securities of firms located outside the U.S. *Regional funds* concentrate on a particular part of the world, and *emerging market funds* invest in companies of developing nations.

Balanced funds   Some funds are designed to be candidates for an individual's entire investment portfolio. These *balanced funds* hold both equities and fixed-income securities in relatively stable proportions. *Life-cycle funds* are balanced funds in which the asset mix can range from aggressive (primarily marketed to younger investors) to conservative (directed at older investors). Static allocation life-cycle funds maintain a stable mix across stocks and bonds, while *targeted-maturity funds* gradually become more conservative as the investor ages.

Asset allocation and flexible funds   These funds are similar to balanced funds in that they hold both stocks and bonds. However, asset allocation funds may dramatically vary the proportions allocated to each market in accord with the portfolio manager's forecast of the relative performance of each sector. Hence, these funds are engaged in market timing and are not designed to be low-risk investment vehicles.

Index funds   An index fund tries to match the performance of a broad market index. The fund buys shares in securities included in a particular index in proportion to the security's representation in that index. For example, the Vanguard 500 Index Fund is a mutual fund that replicates the composition of the Standard & Poor's 500 stock price index. Because the S&P 500 is a value-weighted index, the fund buys shares in each S&P 500 company in proportion to the market value of that company's outstanding equity. Investment in an index fund is a low-cost way for small investors to pursue a passive investment strategy—that is, to invest without engaging in security analysis. Of course, index funds can be tied to nonequity indexes as well. For example, Vanguard offers a bond index fund and a real estate index fund.

Table 4.1 breaks down the number of mutual funds by investment orientation. Often the fund name describes its investment policy. For example, Vanguard's GNMA fund invests in mortgage-backed securities, the Municipal Intermediate fund invests in intermediate-term municipal bonds, and the High-Yield Corporate bond fund invests in large part in speculative grade, or "junk," bonds with high yields. However, names of common stock funds frequently reflect little or nothing about their investment policies. Examples are Vanguard's Windsor and Wellington funds.

How Funds Are Sold

Most mutual funds have an underwriter that has exclusive rights to distribute shares to investors. Mutual funds are generally marketed to the public either directly by the fund underwriter or indirectly through brokers acting on behalf of the underwriter. Direct-marketed funds are

TABLE 4.1

U.S. mutual funds by investment classification

	Assets ($ billion)	Percent of Total Assets	Number of Funds
Equity funds			
Capital appreciation focus	$ 2,701.0	25.9%	3,070
World/international	1314.1	12.6	915
Total return	1896.5	18.2	785
Total equity funds	$ 5,911.6	56.8%	4,770
Bond funds			
Corporate	$ 272.2	2.6%	289
High yield	156.2	1.5	207
World	59.4	0.6	113
Government	193.0	1.9	309
Strategic income	448.6	4.3	364
Single-state municipal	154.9	1.5	481
National municipal	210.0	2.0	230
Total bond funds	$ 1,494.4	14.4%	1,993
Hybrid (bond/stock) funds	$ 653.1	6.3%	508
Money market funds			
Taxable	$ 1,988.1	19.1%	576
Tax-exempt	366.4	3.5	273
Total money market fund	$ 2354.5	22.6%	849
Total	$10,413.6	100.0%	8,120

Note: Column sums subject to rounding error.

Source: Investment Company Institute, *2007 Investment Company Fact Book.* Copyright © 2007 by the Investment Company Institute.

sold through the mail, various offices of the fund, over the phone, and, increasingly, over the Internet. Investors contact the fund directly to purchase shares. For example, if you look at the financial pages of your local newspaper, you will see several advertisements for funds, along with toll-free phone numbers that you can call to receive a fund's prospectus and an application to open an account.

About half of fund sales today are distributed through a sales force. Brokers or financial advisers receive a commission for selling shares to investors. (Ultimately, the commission is paid by the investor. More on this shortly.) In some cases, funds use a "captive" sales force that sells only shares in funds of the mutual fund group they represent.

Investors who rely on their broker's advice to select their mutual funds should be aware that brokers may have a conflict of interest with regard to fund selection. This arises from a practice called *revenue sharing,* in which fund companies pay the brokerage firm for preferential treatment when making investment recommendations. The payment sometimes comes in the form of direct payments, computed either as a one-time payment based on sales of the mutual fund or as an ongoing payment based on fund assets held by the brokerage's clients.

Revenue-sharing arrangements pose potential conflicts of interest if they induce brokers to recommend mutual funds based on criteria other than the best interests of their clients. In addition, the mutual fund may be violating its obligation to its investors if it uses fund assets to obtain favored status in new sales.

Revenue sharing is not illegal as long as the investor is informed about the arrangement and the potential conflict of interest. Disclosure in practice, however, typically has been oblique at best. The SEC has proposed new rules that would require brokerage firms to explicitly reveal any compensation or other incentives they receive to sell a particular fund. This disclosure would be required both at the time of sale and in the trade confirmation.

Many funds also are sold through "financial supermarkets" that can sell shares in funds of many complexes. This approach was made popular by the OneSource program of Charles Schwab & Co. These programs allow customers to buy funds from many different fund groups. Instead of charging customers a sales commission, the supermarket splits management fees with the mutual fund company. Another advantage is unified record keeping for all funds purchased from the supermarket, even if the funds are offered by different complexes. On the other hand, many contend that these supermarkets result in higher expense ratios because mutual funds pass along the costs of participating in these programs in the form of higher management fees.

4.4   COSTS OF INVESTING IN MUTUAL FUNDS

Fee Structure

An individual investor choosing a mutual fund should consider not only the fund's stated investment policy and past performance, but also its management fees and other expenses. Comparative data on virtually all important aspects of mutual funds are available in the annual reports prepared by CDA/Wiesenberger or in Morningstar's *Mutual Fund Sourcebook,* which can be found in many academic and public libraries. You should be aware of four general classes of fees.

Operating expenses   Operating expenses are the costs incurred by the mutual fund in operating the portfolio, including administrative expenses and advisory fees paid to the investment manager. These expenses, usually expressed as a percentage of total assets under management, may range from 0.2% to 2%. Shareholders do not receive an explicit bill for these operating expenses; however, the expenses periodically are deducted from the assets of the fund. Shareholders pay for these expenses through the reduced value of the portfolio.

In addition to operating expenses, most funds assess fees to pay for marketing and distribution costs. These charges are used primarily to pay the brokers or financial advisors who sell the funds to the public. Investors can avoid these expenses by buying shares directly from the fund sponsor, but many investors are willing to incur these distribution fees in return for the advice they may receive from their broker.

Front-end load

A front-end load is a commission or sales charge paid when you purchase the shares. These charges, which are used primarily to pay the brokers who sell the funds, may not exceed 8.5%, but in practice they are rarely higher than 6%. *Low-load funds* have loads that range up to 3% of invested funds. *No-load funds* have no front-end sales charges. About half of all funds today (measured by assets) are no load. Loads effectively reduce the amount of money invested. For example, each $1,000 paid for a fund with a 6% load results in a sales charge of $60 and fund investment of only $940. You need cumulative returns of 6.4% of your net investment (60/940 = .064) just to break even.

Back-end load

A back-end load is a redemption, or "exit," fee incurred when you sell your shares. Typically, funds that impose back-end loads start them at 5% or 6% and reduce them by one percentage point for every year the funds are left invested. Thus, an exit fee that starts at 6% would fall to 4% by the start of your third year. These charges are known more formally as "contingent deferred sales charges."

12b-1 charges

The Securities and Exchange Commission allows the managers of so-called 12b-1 funds to use fund assets to pay for distribution costs such as advertising, promotional literature including annual reports and prospectuses, and, most important, commissions paid to brokers who sell the fund to investors. These 12b-1 fees are named after the SEC rule that permits use of these plans. Funds may use annual 12b-1 charges instead of, or in addition to, front-end loads to generate the fees with which to pay brokers. As with operating expenses, investors are not explicitly billed for 12b-1 charges. Instead, the fees are deducted from the assets of the fund. Therefore, 12b-1 fees (if any) must be added to operating expenses to obtain the true annual expense ratio of the fund. The SEC now requires that all funds include in the prospectus a consolidated expense table that summarizes all relevant fees. The 12b-1 fees are limited to 1% of a fund's average net assets per year.[1]

Many funds offer "classes" which represent ownership in the same portfolio of securities, but with different combinations of fees. Typical Class A shares have front-end loads and a small 12b-1 fee, often around .25%. Class B shares rely on larger 12b-1 fees, commonly 1%, and often charge a modest back-end load. If an investor holds Class B shares for a long enough duration, typically 6–8 years, the shares often will convert into Class A shares which have lower 12b-1 fees. Class C shares generally rely on 12b-1 fees and back-end loads. These shares usually will not convert to Class A shares.

12b-1 fees

Annual fees charged by a mutual fund to pay for marketing and distribution costs.

EXAMPLE 4.1	Here are fees for different classes of the Dreyfus Founders Growth Fund as of early 2007. Notice the trade-off between the front-end loads versus 12b-1 charges.

Fees for Various Classes (Dreyfus Founders Growth and Income Fund)

	Class A	Class B	Class C	Class T
Front-end load	0–5.75%[a]	0	0	0–4.50%[a]
Back-end load	0	0–4%[b]	0–1%[b]	0
12b-1 fees[c]	.25%	1.0	1.0	.50%
Expense ratio	1.16%	1.35%	1.17%	1.27%

Notes:

[a]Depending on size of investment

[b]Depending on years until holdings are sold

[c]Including service fee of .25%

[1]The maximum 12b-1 charge for the sale of the fund is .75%. However, an additional service fee of .25% of the fund's assets also is allowed for personal service and/or maintenance of shareholder accounts.

Each investor must choose the best combination of fees. Obviously, pure no-load no-fee funds distributed directly by the mutual fund group are the cheapest alternative, and these will often make the most sense for knowledgeable investors. But as we noted earlier, many investors are willing to pay for financial advice, and the commissions paid to advisers who sell these funds are the most common form of payment. Alternatively, investors may choose to hire a fee-only financial manager who charges directly for services and does not accept commissions. These advisers can help investors select portfolios of low- or no-load funds (as well as provide other financial advice). Independent financial planners have become increasingly important distribution channels for funds in recent years.

If you do buy a fund through a broker, the choice between paying a load and paying 12b-1 fees will depend primarily on your expected time horizon. Loads are paid only once for each purchase, whereas 12b-1 fees are paid annually. Thus, if you plan to hold your fund for a long time, a one-time load may be preferable to recurring 12b-1 charges.

Fees and Mutual Fund Returns

The rate of return on an investment in a mutual fund is measured as the increase or decrease in net asset value plus income distributions such as dividends or distributions of capital gains expressed as a fraction of net asset value at the beginning of the investment period. If we denote the net asset value at the start and end of the period as NAV_0 and NAV_1, respectively, then

$$\text{Rate of return} = \frac{NAV_1 - NAV_0 + \text{Income and capital gain distributions}}{NAV_0}$$

For example, if a fund has an initial NAV of $20 at the start of the month, makes income distributions of $.15 and capital gain distributions of $.05, and ends the month with NAV of $20.10, the monthly rate of return is computed as

$$\text{Rate of return} = \frac{\$20.10 - \$20.00 + \$.15 + \$.05}{\$20.00} = .015, \text{ or } 1.5\%$$

Notice that this measure of the rate of return ignores any commissions such as front-end loads paid to purchase the fund.

On the other hand, the rate of return is affected by the fund's expenses and 12b-1 fees. This is because such charges are periodically deducted from the portfolio, which reduces net asset value. Thus the rate of return on the fund equals the gross return on the underlying portfolio minus the total expense ratio.

To see how expenses can affect rate of return, consider a fund with $100 million in assets at the start of the year and with 10 million shares outstanding. The fund invests in a portfolio of stocks that provides no income but increases in value by 10%. The expense ratio, including 12b-1 fees, is 1%. What is the rate of return for an investor in the fund? The initial NAV equals $100 million/10 million shares = $10 per share. In the absence of expenses, fund assets would grow to $110 million and NAV would grow to $11 per share, for a 10% rate of return. However, the expense ratio of the fund is 1%. Therefore, $1 million will be deducted from the fund to pay these fees, leaving the portfolio worth only $109 million, and NAV equal to $10.90. The rate of return on the fund is only 9%, which equals the gross return on the underlying portfolio minus the total expense ratio.

EXAMPLE 4.2

Expenses and Rates of Return

Fees can have a big effect on performance. Table 4.2 considers an investor who starts with $10,000 and can choose between three funds that all earn an annual 12% return on investment before fees but have different fee structures. The table shows the cumulative amount in each fund after several investment horizons. Fund A has total operating expenses of .5%, no load, and no 12b-1 charges. This might represent a low-cost producer like Vanguard. Fund B has no load but has 1% management expenses and .5% in 12b-1 fees. This level of charges is fairly

TABLE 4.2 Impact of costs on investment performance		Cumulative Proceeds (all dividends reinvested)		
		Fund A	**Fund B**	**Fund C**
	Initial investment*	$10,000	$10,000	$ 9,200
	5 years	17,234	16,474	15,502
	10 years	29,699	27,141	26,123
	15 years	51,183	44,713	44,018
	20 years	88,206	73,662	74,173

*After front-end load, if any.

Notes:

1. Fund A is no-load with .5% expense ratio.

2. Fund B is no-load with 1.5% total expense ratio.

3. Fund C has an 8% load on purchases and a 1% expense ratio.

4. Gross return on all funds is 12% per year before expenses.

typical of actively managed equity funds. Finally, Fund C has 1% in management expenses, no 12b-1 charges, but assesses an 8% front-end load on purchases.

Note the substantial return advantage of low-cost Fund A. Moreover, that differential is greater for longer investment horizons.

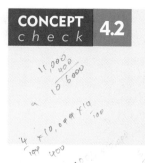

CONCEPT *check* **4.2**

The Equity Fund sells Class A shares with a front-end load of 4% and Class B shares with 12b-1 fees of .5% annually as well as back-end load fees that start at 5% and fall by 1% for each full year the investor holds the portfolio (until the fifth year). Assume the rate of return on the fund portfolio net of operating expenses is 10% annually. What will be the value of a $10,000 investment in Class A and Class B shares if the shares are sold after (a) 1 year, (b) 4 years, (c) 10 years? Which fee structure provides higher net proceeds at the end of each investment horizon?

soft dollars

The value of research services brokerage houses provide "free of charge" in exchange for the investment manager's business.

Although expenses can have a big impact on net investment performance, it is sometimes difficult for the investor in a mutual fund to measure true expenses accurately. This is because of the common practice of paying for some expenses in **soft dollars.** A portfolio manager earns soft-dollar credits with a brokerage firm by directing the fund's trades to that broker. Based on those credits, the broker will pay for some of the mutual fund's expenses, such as databases, computer hardware, or stock-quotation systems. The soft-dollar arrangement means that the stockbroker effectively returns part of the trading commission to the fund. Purchases made with soft dollars are not included in the fund's expenses, so funds with extensive soft-dollar arrangements may report artificially low expense ratios to the public. However, the fund will have paid its brokers needlessly high commissions to obtain its soft-dollar "rebates." The impact of the higher trading commissions shows up in net investment performance rather than the reported expense ratio.

WEB *master*

Choosing an Index Mutual Fund

While index funds are supposed to track the performance of a market index, the index chosen can dramatically affect your investment returns. One of the factors that determines this choice is your tolerance for risk.

1. Visit **www.IndexFunds.com** and complete the Quick Risk Capacity Survey. What is your Total Weighted Score and which portfolio is recommended for you?

2. Review the discussion of your results. Do you agree with the assessment given for each question?

3. Click on the link for the indicated portfolio. Which sectors make up the largest proportions in the fund? What sectors are represented in smaller amounts?

4. If you had invested $100 eighty years ago, what would your portfolio be worth today?

The SEC allows soft-dollar arrangements as long as the proceeds are used for research that may ultimately benefit the mutual fund shareholder. About half of such funds have been used to purchase stock research reports. There have certainly been cases in which soft dollars were used for purposes other than the welfare of shareholders, however, and the Investment Company Institute, the mutual fund industry trade group, has proposed that their use be curtailed. Moreover, amid the growing consensus that these arrangements make it difficult for investors to compare fund expenses, the SEC is currently considering requirements for more prominent disclosure of all brokerage commissions paid by the fund.

Late Trading and Market Timing

Mutual funds calculate net asset value (NAV) at the end of each trading day. All buy or sell orders arriving during the day are executed at that NAV following the market close at 4:00 P.M. New York time. Allowing some favored investors to buy shares below NAV or sell above NAV would impose costs on all other investors. Yet, that is precisely what many mutual funds did until these practices were exposed in 2003.

Late trading refers to the practice of accepting buy or sell orders after the market closes and NAV is determined. Suppose that based on market closing prices at 4:00, a fund's NAV equals $100, but at 4:30, some positive economic news is announced. While NAV already has been fixed, it is clear that the fair market value of each share now exceeds $100. If they are able to submit a late order, investors can buy shares at the now-stale NAV and redeem them the next day after prices and NAV have adjusted to reflect the news.[2] Late traders therefore can buy shares in the fund at a price below what NAV would be if it reflected up-to-date information. This transfers value from the other shareholders to the privileged traders and shows up as a reduction in the rate of return of the mutual fund.

Market timing also exploits stale prices. Consider the hypothetical "Pacific Basin Mutual Fund," which specializes in Japanese stocks. Because of time-zone differences, the Japanese market closes several hours before trading ends in New York. NAV is set based on the closing price of the Japanese shares. If the U.S. market jumps significantly while the Japanese market is closed, however, it is likely that Japanese prices will rise when the market opens in Japan the next day. A market timer will buy the Pacific Basin fund in the U.S. today at its now-stale NAV, planning to redeem those shares the next day for a likely profit. While such activity often is characterized as rapid in-and-out trading, the more salient issue is that the market timer is allowed to transact at a stale price.

While late trading clearly violates securities laws, market timing does not. However, many funds that claimed to prohibit or discourage such trading actually allowed it, at least for some customers. And some funds even had illicit arrangements with privileged customers to allow late trading. Why did they engage in practices that reduced the rate of return to most shareholders? The answer is the management fee. Market timers and late traders in essence paid for their access to such practices by investing large amounts in the funds on which the fund manager charged its management fee. Of course, the traders possibly earned far more than those fees through their trading activity, but those costs were borne by the other shareholders, not the fund sponsor.

By mid-2004, mutual fund sponsors had paid more than $1.65 billion in penalties to settle allegations of improper trading. In addition, new rules have been implemented and others proposed to eliminate these illicit practices. These include:

- *4:00 P.M. hard cutoff.* Strict policies that a trade order must arrive at the mutual fund (not merely an intermediary such as a broker) by 4:00 to be executed. Orders arriving after 4:00 are deferred until the close of the next trading day.

---

[2]Late trading can be difficult to monitor. Intermediaries such as brokerage firms or administrators of retirement plans that receive trade orders before 4:00 may legitimately send them on to the fund after 4:00 for execution at that day's NAV. This practice makes it difficult to trace late trading if a cooperative intermediary is willing to batch orders received after 4:00 with legitimate orders received before 4:00.

- *Fair value pricing.* When computing fund NAV, prices of securities in closed markets are adjusted to reflect the likely impact of big price changes in open markets.
- *Redemption fees.* A redemption fee of 2% or more to be charged on mutual funds shares sold within five days of purchase. These fees would be paid not to the management company, but directly into the fund to compensate other investors for potential losses due to the rapid trading.

Other Potential Reforms

In the wake of these scandals, other mutual fund practices have come under increased scrutiny. 12b-l fees, which are used primarily to compensate financial advisors or brokers for selling funds to the public, are under attack. The criticism is that these marketing expenses either should be paid directly by the management company or at least made explicit to the investor as a deduction from his account. Under currently policies, in which 12b-l charges are deducted from the assets of the fund, investors may not realize that their investment returns have been reduced by these fees, which can range up to 1% of assets annually.

Soft-dollar arrangements are also under attack. The Investment Company Institute, the mutual fund trade group, has called for substantial restrictions in the use of soft dollars, and it appears that they are in fact being applied to a more narrow range of expenses.

4.5 | TAXATION OF MUTUAL FUND INCOME

Investment returns of mutual funds are granted "pass-through status" under the U.S. tax code, meaning that taxes are paid only by the investor in the mutual fund, not by the fund itself. The income is treated as passed through to the investor as long as the fund meets several requirements, most notably that the fund be sufficiently diversified and that virtually all income is distributed to shareholders.

A fund's short-term capital gains, long-term capital gains, and dividends are passed through to investors as though the investor earned the income directly.[3] The pass-through of investment income has one important disadvantage for individual investors. If you manage your own portfolio, you decide when to realize capital gains and losses on any security; therefore, you can time those realizations to efficiently manage your tax liabilities. When you invest through a mutual fund, however, the timing of the sale of securities from the portfolio is out of your control, which reduces your ability to engage in tax management. Of course, if the mutual fund is held in a tax-deferred retirement account such as an IRA or 401(k) account, these tax management issues are irrelevant.

turnover

The ratio of the trading activity of a portfolio to the assets of the portfolio.

A fund with a high portfolio turnover rate can be particularly "tax inefficient." **Turnover** is the ratio of the trading activity of a portfolio to the assets of the portfolio. It measures the fraction of the portfolio that is "replaced" each year. For example, a $100 million portfolio with $50 million in sales of some securities with purchases of other securities would have a turnover rate of 50%. High turnover means that capital gains or losses are being realized constantly, and therefore that the investor cannot time the realizations to manage his or her overall tax obligation. Turnover rates in equity funds in the last decade have typically been around 60% when weighted by assets under management. By contrast, a low-turnover fund such as an index fund may have turnover as low as 2%, which is both tax efficient and economical with respect to trading costs.

In 2000, the SEC instituted new rules requiring funds to disclose the tax impact of portfolio turnover. Funds must include in their prospectus after-tax returns for the past 1-, 5-,

---

[3]An interesting problem that an investor needs to be aware of derives from the fact that capital gains and dividends on mutual funds are typically paid out to shareholders once or twice a year. This means that an investor who has just purchased shares in a mutual fund can receive a capital gain distribution (and be taxed on that distribution) on transactions that occurred long before he or she purchased shares in the fund. This is particularly a concern late in the year when such distributions typically are made.

and 10-year periods. Marketing literature that includes performance data also must include after-tax results. The after-tax returns are computed accounting for the impact of the taxable distributions of income and capital gains passed through to the investor, assuming the investor is in the maximum federal tax bracket.

An investor's portfolio currently is worth $1 million. During the year, the investor sells 1,000 shares of Microsoft at a price of $80 per share and 2,000 shares of Ford at a price of $40 per share. The proceeds are used to buy 1,600 shares of IBM at $100 per share.

   a.   What was the portfolio turnover rate?
   b.   If the shares in Microsoft originally were purchased for $70 each and those in Ford were purchased for $35, and if the investor's tax rate on capital gains income is 20%, how much extra will the investor owe on this year's taxes as a result of these transactions?

CONCEPT *c h e c k* **4.3**

4.6 EXCHANGE-TRADED FUNDS

Exchange-traded funds (ETFs) are offshoots of mutual funds first introduced in 1993 that allow investors to trade index portfolios just as they do shares of stock. The first ETF was the "Spider," a nickname for SPDR or Standard & Poor's Depository Receipt, which is a unit investment trust holding a portfolio matching the S&P 500 index. Unlike mutual funds, which can be bought or sold only at the end of the day when NAV is calculated, investors could trade Spiders throughout the day, just like any other share of stock. Spiders gave rise to many similar products such as "Diamonds" (based on the Dow Jones Industrial Average, ticker DIA), Qubes (pronounced cubes, based on the Nasdaq 100 Index, ticker QQQ), and WEBS (World Equity Benchmark Shares, which are shares in portfolios of foreign stock market indexes). By early 2007, over $400 billion was invested in over 300 ETFs in three general classes: broad U.S. market indexes, narrow industry or "sector" portfolios, and international indexes. Table 4.3, Panel A, presents some of the sponsors of ETFs; Panel B is a small sample of ETFs.

ETFs offer several advantages over conventional mutual funds. First, as we just noted, a mutual fund's net asset value is quoted—and therefore, investors can buy or sell their shares in the fund—only once a day. In contrast, ETFs trade continuously. ETFs account for a high percentage of total trading on Amex. Moreover, like other shares, but unlike mutual funds, ETFs can be sold short or purchased on margin.

ETFs also offer a potential tax advantage over mutual funds. When large numbers of mutual fund investors redeem their shares, the fund must sell securities to meet the redemptions. This can trigger capital gains taxes, which are passed through to and must be paid by the remaining shareholders. In contrast, when small investors wish to redeem their position in an ETF they simply sell their shares to other traders, with no need for the fund to sell any of the underlying portfolio. Moreover, when large traders wish to redeem their position in the ETF, redemptions are satisfied with shares of stock in the underlying portfolio. Again, a redemption does not trigger a stock sale by the fund sponsor.

The ability of large investors to redeem ETFs for a portfolio of stocks comprising the index, or to exchange a portfolio of stocks for shares in the corresponding ETF, ensures that the price of an ETF cannot depart significantly from the NAV of that portfolio. Any meaningful discrepancy would offer arbitrage trading opportunities for these large traders, which would quickly eliminate the disparity.

ETFs are also cheaper than mutual funds. Investors who buy ETFs do so through brokers, rather than buying directly from the fund. Therefore, the fund saves the cost of marketing itself directly to small investors. This reduction in expenses translates into lower management fees.

exchange-traded funds

Offshoots of mutual funds that allow investors to trade index portfolios.

TABLE 4.3

ETF sponsors and products

A. ETF Sponsors

Sponsor	Product Name
Barclays Global Investors	i-Shares
Merrill Lynch	HOLDRS (Holding Company Depository Receipts: "Holders")
StateStreet/Merrill Lynch	Select Sector SPDRs (S&P Depository Receipts: "Spiders")
Vanguard	VIPER (Vanguard Index Participation Equity Receipts: "VIPERS")

B. Sample of ETF Products

Name	Ticker	Index Tracked
Broad U.S. Indexes		
Spiders	SPY	S&P 500
Diamonds	DIA	Dow Jones Industrials
Qubes	QQQ	Nasdaq 100
iShares Russell 2000	IWM	Russell 2000
Total Stock Market VIPER	VTI	Wilshire 5000
Industry Indexes		
Energy Select Spider	XLE	S&P 500 energy companies
iShares Energy Sector	IYE	Dow Jones energy companies
Oil Service HOLDRS	OIH	Portfolio of oil service firms
Financial Sector Spider	XLF	S&P 500 financial companies
iShares Financial Sector	IYF	Dow Jones financial companies
Vanguard Financial VIPERS	VFH	MSCI financials index
International Indexes		
WEBS United Kingdom	EWU	MCSI U.K. Index
WEBS France	EWQ	MCSI France Index
WEBS Japan	EWJ	MCSI Japan Index

There are some disadvantages to ETFs, however. Because they trade as securities, there is the possibility that their prices can depart by small amounts from NAV. As noted, this discrepancy cannot be too large without giving rise to arbitrage opportunities for large traders, but even small discrepancies can easily swamp the cost advantage of ETFs over mutual funds. Second, while mutual funds can be bought for NAV with no expense from no-load funds, ETFs must be purchased from brokers for a fee. Investors also incur a bid–ask spread when purchasing an ETF.

4.7 | MUTUAL FUND INVESTMENT PERFORMANCE: A FIRST LOOK

We noted earlier that one of the benefits of mutual funds for the individual investor is the ability to delegate management of the portfolio to investment professionals. The investor retains control over the broad features of the overall portfolio through the asset allocation decision: Each individual chooses the percentages of the portfolio to invest in bond funds versus equity funds versus money market funds, and so forth, but can leave the specific security selection decisions within each investment class to the managers of each fund. Shareholders hope that these portfolio managers can achieve better investment performance than they could obtain on their own.

What is the investment record of the mutual fund industry? This seemingly straightforward question is deceptively difficult to answer because we need a standard against which

FIGURE 4.3

Morningstar report

On the MARKET FRONT

MUTUAL-FUND RATINGS COME UNDER FIRE

Two methods for rating mutual funds, including the widely used Morningstar system, have come under fire.

A new study concludes that mutual funds given high ratings by Morningstar and Value Line—both used by investors to choose among funds—don't necessarily perform better than those with middling ratings.

The ratings are widely trumpeted in mutual funds' advertisements, and many people rely on them to make key investment decisions, such as where to put their retirement savings. Last year, for example, stock funds with coveted four- and five-star ratings from Morningstar took in nearly $80 billion, compared with the more than $108 billion that was withdrawn from lower-rated funds, according to Nov. 30 [2002] data from Financial Research Corp.

"Mutual-fund ratings services can't really predict winners," says the study's author, finance professor Matthew R. Morey of New York's Pace University.

To test ratings' predictive abilities, Prof. Morey sifted the fund market for diversified stock funds that had at least three years of history at the end of 1994. He then tracked the performance of these funds over the next six years to see how funds with high ratings from Morningstar and Value Line compared with those with lower ratings.

Prof. Morey found that, from 1995 through 2000, lower-rated funds kept slumping to some extent. But highly rated funds, which draw heavy promotion and sales, didn't tend to perform any better than funds with middle-of-the-pack ratings.

Morningstar previously compared funds in four categories: U.S. stock, foreign stock, taxable bond and municipal bond. But this past summer the firm began comparing funds in 48 narrower stock- and bond-fund categories. The narrower categories keep one group from ending up with a disproportionate percentage of the top ratings, such as when 90% of rated tech funds had five stars at the end of 1999.

So, how should investors use fund ratings? Cautiously.

The best approach is to research how a rating is derived and, if you're comfortable with its criteria, only use it as a first cut to winnow the vast field of options. A ratings screen will leave you with a more manageable pack of funds to study closely and shoe-horn into a well-diversified portfolio.

SOURCE: Abridged from Ian McDonald, "Mutual-Fund Ratings Come under Fire," *The Wall Street Journal*, January 15, 2003.

from 1 to 10 years are calculated with all loads and back-end fees applicable to that investment period subtracted from total income. The return is then compared to the average return for the comparison group of funds to obtain the Morningstar Return vs. Category. Similarly, risk measures compared to category are computed and reported in the next column.

The last column presents Morningstar's risk-adjusted rating, ranging from one to five stars. The rating is based on the fund's return score minus risk score compared to other funds with similar investment styles. To allow funds to be compared to other funds with similar investment styles, Morningstar recently increased the number of categories; there are now 48 separate stock and bond fund categories. Of course, we are accustomed to the disclaimer that "past performance is not a reliable measure of future results," and this is true as well of the coveted Morningstar 5-star rating. The nearby box discusses the predictive value of the Morningstar ranking.

The tax analysis box shown on the left in Figure 4.3 provides some evidence on the tax efficiency of the fund. The after-tax return, given in the first column, is computed based on the dividends paid to the portfolio as well as realized capital gains, assuming the investor is in the maximum federal tax bracket at the time of the distribution. State and local taxes are ignored. The tax efficiency of the fund is measured by the "Tax-Cost Ratio," which is an estimate of the impact of taxes on the investor's after-tax return. Morningstar ranks each fund compared to its category for both tax-adjusted return and tax-cost ratio.

The bottom of the page in Figure 4.3 provides information on the expenses and loads associated with investments in the fund, as well as information on the fund's investment adviser. Thus, Morningstar provides a considerable amount of the information you would need to decide among several competing funds.

SUMMARY

- Unit investment trusts, closed-end management companies, and open-end management companies are all classified and regulated as investment companies. Unit investment trusts are essentially unmanaged in the sense that the portfolio, once established, is fixed. Managed investment companies, in contrast, may change the composition of the portfolio as deemed fit by the portfolio manager. Closed-end funds are traded like other securities; they do not redeem shares for their investors. Open-end funds will redeem shares for net asset value at the request of the investor.

- Net asset value equals the market value of assets held by a fund minus the liabilities of the fund divided by the shares outstanding.

- Mutual funds free the individual from many of the administrative burdens of owning individual securities and offer professional management of the portfolio. They also offer advantages that are available only to large-scale investors, such as lower trading costs. On the other hand, funds are assessed management fees and incur other expenses, which reduce the investor's rate of return. Funds also eliminate some of the individual's control over the timing of capital gains realizations.

- Mutual funds often are categorized by investment policy. Major policy groups include money market funds; equity funds, which are further grouped according to emphasis on income versus growth; fixed-income funds; balanced and income funds; asset allocation funds; index funds; and specialized sector funds.

- Costs of investing in mutual funds include front-end loads, which are sales charges; back-end loads, which are redemption fees or, more formally, contingent-deferred sales charges; fund operating expenses; and 12b-1 charges, which are recurring fees used to pay for the expenses of marketing the fund to the public.

- Income earned on mutual fund portfolios is not taxed at the level of the fund. Instead, as long as the fund meets certain requirements for pass-through status, the income is treated as being earned by the investors in the fund.

- The average rate of return of the average equity mutual fund in the last 25 years has been below that of a passive index fund holding a portfolio to replicate a broad-based index like the S&P 500 or Wilshire 5000. Some of the reasons for this disappointing record are the costs incurred by actively managed funds, such as the expense of conducting the research to guide stock-picking activities, and trading costs due to higher portfolio turnover. The record on the consistency of fund performance is mixed. In some sample periods, the better-performing funds continue to perform well in the following periods; in other sample periods they do not.

KEY TERMS

closed-end fund, 92
exchange-traded funds, 103
hedge fund, 93
investment company, 90

load, 93
net asset value (NAV), 90
open-end fund, 92
soft dollars, 100

12b-1 fees, 98
turnover, 102
unit investment trust, 91

PROBLEM SETS

 Select problems are available in McGraw-Hill's Homework Manager®.
Please see the packaging options section of the preface for more information.

1. Would you expect a typical open-end fixed-income mutual fund to have higher or lower operating expenses than a fixed-income unit investment trust? Why?

2. An open-end fund has a net asset value of $10.70 per share. It is sold with a front-end load of 6%. What is the offering price?

www.mhhe.com/bkm

3. If the offering price of an open-end fund is $12.30 per share and the fund is sold with a front-end load of 5%, what is its net asset value?

4. The composition of the Fingroup Fund portfolio is as follows:

Stock	Shares	Price
A	200,000	$35
B	300,000	40
C	400,000	20
D	600,000	25

The fund has not borrowed any funds, but its accrued management fee with the portfolio manager currently totals $30,000. There are 4 million shares outstanding. What is the net asset value of the fund?

5. Reconsider the Fingroup Fund in the previous problem. If during the year the portfolio manager sells all of the holdings of stock D and replaces it with 200,000 shares of stock E at $50 per share and 200,000 shares of stock F at $25 per share, what is the portfolio turnover rate?

6. The Closed Fund is a closed-end investment company with a portfolio currently worth $200 million. It has liabilities of $3 million and 5 million shares outstanding.
   a. What is the NAV of the fund?
   b. If the fund sells for $36 per share, what is its premium or discount as a percent of NAV?

7. Corporate Fund started the year with a net asset value of $12.50. By year-end, its NAV equaled $12.10. The fund paid year-end distributions of income and capital gains of $1.50. What was the rate of return to an investor in the fund?

8. A closed-end fund starts the year with a net asset value of $12.00. By year-end, NAV equals $12.10. At the beginning of the year, the fund is selling at a 2% premium to NAV. By the end of the year, the fund is selling at a 7% discount to NAV. The fund paid year-end distributions of income and capital gains of $1.50.
   a. What is the rate of return to an investor in the fund during the year?
   b. What would have been the rate of return to an investor who held the same securities as the fund manager during the year?

9. What are some comparative advantages of investing your assets in the following:
   a. Unit investment trusts.
   b. Open-end mutual funds.
   c. Individual stocks and bonds that you choose for yourself.

10. Open-end equity mutual funds find it necessary to keep a significant percentage of total investments, typically around 5% of the portfolio, in very liquid money market assets. Closed-end funds do not have to maintain such a position in "cash-equivalent" securities. What difference between open-end and closed-end funds might account for their differing policies?

11. Balanced funds and asset allocation funds invest in both the stock and bond markets. What is the difference between these types of funds?

12. a. Impressive Fund had excellent investment performance last year, with portfolio returns that placed it in the top 10% of all funds with the same investment policy. Do you expect it to be a top performer next year? Why or why not?
    b. Suppose instead that the fund was among the poorest performers in its comparison group. Would you be more or less likely to believe its relative performance will persist into the following year? Why?

13. Consider a mutual fund with $200 million in assets at the start of the year and with 10 million shares outstanding. The fund invests in a portfolio of stocks that provides

dividend income at the end of the year of $2 million. The stocks included in the fund's portfolio increase in price by 8%, but no securities are sold, and there are no capital gains distributions. The fund charges 12b-1 fees of 1%, which are deducted from portfolio assets at year-end. What is net asset value at the start and end of the year? What is the rate of return for an investor in the fund?

14. The New Fund had average daily assets of $2.2 billion in the past year. The fund sold $400 million and purchased $500 million worth of stock during the year. What was its turnover ratio?

15. If New Fund's expense ratio was 1.1% and the management fee was .7%, what were the total fees paid to the fund's investment managers during the year? What were the other administrative expenses?

16. You purchased 1,000 shares of the New Fund at a price of $20 per share at the beginning of the year. You paid a front-end load of 4%. The securities in which the fund invests increase in value by 12% during the year. The fund's expense ratio is 1.2%. What is your rate of return on the fund if you sell your shares at the end of the year?

17. The Investments Fund sells Class A shares with a front-end load of 6% and Class B shares with 12b-1 fees of .5% annually as well as back-end load fees that start at 5% and fall by 1% for each full year the investor holds the portfolio (until the fifth year). Assume the portfolio rate of return net of operating expenses is 10% annually. If you plan to sell the fund after four years, are Class A or Class B shares the better choice for you? What if you plan to sell after 15 years?

18. Suppose you observe the investment performance of 350 portfolio managers for five years and rank them by investment returns during each year. After five years, you find that 11 of the funds have investment returns that place the fund in the top half of the sample in each and every year of your sample. Such consistency of performance indicates to you that these must be the funds whose managers are in fact skilled, and you invest your money in these funds. Is your conclusion warranted?

19. You are considering an investment in a mutual fund with a 4% load and an expense ratio of .5%. You can invest instead in a bank CD paying 6% interest.
    a. If you plan to invest for two years, what annual rate of return must the fund portfolio earn for you to be better off in the fund than in the CD? Assume annual compounding of returns.
    b. How does your answer change if you plan to invest for six years? Why does your answer change?
    c. Now suppose that instead of a front-end load the fund assesses a 12b-1 fee of .75% per year. What annual rate of return must the fund portfolio earn for you to be better off in the fund than in the CD? Does your answer in this case depend on your time horizon?

20. Suppose that every time a fund manager trades stock, transaction costs such as commissions and bid–ask spreads amount to .4% of the value of the trade. If the portfolio turnover rate is 50%, by how much is the total return of the portfolio reduced by trading costs?

21. You expect a tax-free municipal bond portfolio to provide a rate of return of 4%. Management fees of the fund are .6%. What fraction of portfolio income is given up to fees? If the management fees for an equity fund also are .6%, but you expect a portfolio return of 12%, what fraction of portfolio income is given up to fees? Why might management fees be a bigger factor in your investment decision for bond funds than for stock funds? Can your conclusion help explain why unmanaged unit investment trusts tend to focus on the fixed-income market?

WEB *master*

Mutual Fund Report

Go to **www.morningstar.com**. In the Morningstar Tools section, click on the link for the Mutual Fund Screener. Set the criteria you desire, then click on the Show Results tab. If you get no funds that meet all of your criteria, choose the criterion that is least important to you and relax that constraint. Continue the process until you have several funds to compare.

1. Examine all of the views available in the drop-down box menu (Snapshot, Performance, Portfolio, and Nuts and Bolts) to answer the following questions:

   • Which fund has the best expense ratio?

   • Which funds have the lowest Morningstar Risk rating?

   • Which fund has the best 3-year return? Which has the best 10-year return?

   • Which fund has the lowest turnover ratio? Which has the highest?

   • Which fund has the longest manager tenure? Which has the shortest?

   • Do you need to eliminate any of the funds from consideration due to a minimum initial investment that is higher than you are capable of making?

2. Based on what you know about the funds, which one do you think would be the best one for your investment?

3. Select up to five funds that are of the most interest to you. Click on the button that says Score These Results. Customize the criteria listed by indicating their importance to you. Examine the Score Results. Does the fund with the highest score match the choice you made in Part 2?

SOLUTIONS TO CONCEPT *checks*

4.1. NAV = ($5,092.2 − $4.6)/150.6 = $33.78

4.2. The net investment in the Class A shares after the 4% commission is $9,600. If the fund earns a 10% return, the investment will grow after n years to $9,600 × $(1.10)^n$. The Class B shares have no front-end load. However, the net return to the investor after 12b-1 fees will be only 9.5%. In addition, there is a back-end load that reduces the sales proceeds by a percentage equal to (5 − years until sale) until the fifth year, when the back-end load expires.

Horizon	Class A Shares $9,600 × $(1.10)^n$	Class B Shares $10,000 × $(1.095)^n$ × (1 − percentage exit fee)
1 year	$10,560.00	$10,000 × (1.095) × (1 − .04) = $10,512.00
4 years	$14,055.36	$10,000 × $(1.095)^4$ × (1 − .01) = $14,232.89
10 years	$24,899.93	$10,000 × $(1.095)^{10}$ = $24,782.28

For a very short horizon such as one year, the Class A shares are the better choice. The front-end and back-end loads are equal, but the Class A shares don't have to pay the 12b-1 fees. For moderate horizons such as four years, the Class B shares dominate because the front-end load of the Class A shares is more costly than the 12b-1 fees and the now-smaller exit fee. For long horizons of 10 years or more, Class A again dominates. In this case, the one-time front-end load is less expensive than the continuing 12b-1 fees.

4.3. *a.* Turnover = $160,000 in trades per $1 million of portfolio value = 16%.

   b. Realized capital gains are $10 × 1,000 = $10,000 on Microsoft and $5 × 2,000 = $10,000 on Ford. The tax owed on the capital gains is therefore .20 × $20,000 = $4,000.

4.4. Twenty percent of the managers are skilled, which accounts for .2 × 400 = 80 of those managers who appear in the top half. There are 120 slots left in the top half, and 320 other managers, so the probability of an unskilled manager "lucking into" the top half in any year is 120/320, or .375. Therefore, of the 120 lucky managers in the first year, we would expect .375 × 120 = 45 to repeat as top-half performers next year. Thus, we should expect a total of 80 + 45 = 125, or 62.5%, of the better initial performers to repeat their top-half performance.

PART TWO

PORTFOLIO THEORY

Suppose you believe that investments in stocks offer an expected rate of return of 10% while the expected rate of return on bonds is only 6%. Would you invest all of your money in stocks? Probably not: Putting all of your eggs in one basket in such a manner would violate even the most basic notion of diversification. But what is the optimal combination of the entire universe of stocks and bonds? And how will the opportunity to invest in other asset classes—for example, real estate, foreign stocks, precious metals, and so on—affect your decision? In short, is there a "best" solution to your asset allocation problem?

These questions are the focus of the first chapters of Part Two, which address what has come to be known as Modern Portfolio Theory, or MPT. In large part, MPT addresses the question of "efficient diversification," how to achieve the best trade-off between portfolio risk and reward.

This analysis quickly leads to other questions. For example, how should one measure the risk of an individual asset held as part of a diversified portfolio? You will probably be surprised at the answer. Once we have an acceptable measure of risk, what precisely should be the relation between risk and return? And what is the minimally acceptable rate of return for an investment to be considered attractive? These questions also are addressed in this part of the text.

Finally, we come to one of the most controversial topics in investment management, the question of whether portfolio managers—amateur or professional—can outperform simple investment strategies such as "buy a market index fund." The evidence will at least make you pause before pursuing active strategies. You will come to appreciate how good active managers must be to outperform their passive counterparts.

CHAPTERS IN THIS PART:

www.mhhe.com/bkm

CHAPTER
5

Risk and Return: Past and Prologue

AFTER STUDYING THIS CHAPTER
YOU SHOULD BE ABLE TO:

 Use data on the past performance of stocks and bonds to characterize the risk and return features of these investments.

 Determine the expected return and risk of portfolios that are constructed by combining risky assets with risk-free investments in Treasury bills.

 Evaluate the performance of a passive strategy.

What constitutes a satisfactory investment portfolio? Until the early 1970s, a reasonable answer would have been a bank savings account (a risk-free asset) plus a risky portfolio of U.S. stocks. Nowadays, investors have access to a vastly wider array of assets and may contemplate complex portfolio strategies that may include foreign stocks and bonds, real estate, precious metals, and collectibles. Even more complex strategies may include futures, options, and other derivatives to insure portfolios against unacceptable losses. How might such portfolios be constructed?

Clearly every individual security must be judged on its contributions to both the expected return and the risk of the entire portfolio. To guide us in forming reasonable expectations for portfolio performance, we will start this chapter with an examination of various conventions for measuring and reporting rates of return. Given these measures, we turn to the historical performance of several broadly diversified investment portfolios. In doing so, we use a risk-free portfolio of Treasury bills as a benchmark to evaluate the historical performance of diversified stock and bond portfolios.

We then proceed to consider the trade-offs investors face when they practice the simplest form of risk control: choosing the fraction of the portfolio invested in virtually risk-free money market securities versus risky securities such as stocks.

We show how to calculate the performance one may reasonably expect from various allocations between a risk-free asset and a risky portfolio and discuss the considerations that determine the mix that would best suit different investors. With this background, we can evaluate a passive strategy that will serve as a benchmark for the active strategies considered in the next chapter.

Related Web sites for this chapter are available at www.mhhe.com/bkm.

5.1 RATES OF RETURN

A key measure of investors' success is the rate at which their funds have grown during the investment period. The total **holding-period return (HPR)** of a share of stock depends on the increase (or decrease) in the price of the share over the investment period as well as on any dividend income the share has provided. The rate of return is defined as dollars earned over the investment period (price appreciation as well as dividends) per dollar invested

holding-period return

Rate of return over a given investment period.

$$\text{HPR} = \frac{\text{Ending price} - \text{Beginning price} + \text{Cash dividend}}{\text{Beginning price } P_0} \qquad \textbf{(5.1)}$$

Handwritten annotations: P_1, P_1, D_1, P_0

This definition of the HPR assumes that the dividend is paid at the end of the holding period. To the extent that dividends are received earlier, the definition ignores reinvestment income between the receipt of the dividend and the end of the holding period. Recall also that the percentage return from dividends is called the dividend yield, and so the dividend yield plus the capital gains yield equals the HPR.

This definition of holding return is easy to modify for other types of investments. For example, the HPR on a bond would be calculated using the same formula, except that the bond's interest or coupon payments would take the place of the stock's dividend payments.

Handwritten annotations in right margin:
$$R_A = \frac{P_1 - P_0 + D_1}{P_0}$$
$$= \left[\frac{P_1 - P_0}{P_0}\right] + \left[\frac{D_1}{P_0}\right)$$
CAP. GAIN + DIVIDEND
YIELD   YIELD
g

> Suppose you are considering investing some of your money, now all invested in a bank account, in a stock market index fund. The price of a share in the fund is currently $100, and your time horizon is one year. You expect the cash dividend during the year to be $4, so your expected dividend yield is 4%.
>
> Your HPR will depend on the price one year from now. Suppose your best guess is that it will be $110 per share. Then your *capital gain* will be $10, so your capital gains yield is $10/$100 = .10, or 10%. The total holding period rate of return is the sum of the dividend yield plus the capital gain yield, 4% + 10% = 14%.
>
> $$\text{HPR} = \frac{\$110 - \$100 + \$4}{\$100} = .14, \text{ or } 14\%$$

EXAMPLE 5.1

Holding-Period Return

Handwritten annotation: 4 + 10 = 14

Measuring Investment Returns over Multiple Periods

The holding period return is a simple and unambiguous measure of investment return over a single period. But often you will be interested in average returns over longer periods of time. For example, you might want to measure how well a mutual fund has performed over the preceding five-year period. In this case, return measurement is more ambiguous.

Consider, for example, a fund that starts with $1 million under management at the beginning of the year. The fund receives additional funds to invest from new and existing shareholders, and also receives requests for redemptions from existing shareholders. Its net cash inflow can be positive or negative. Suppose its quarterly results are as given in Table 5.1 with negative numbers reported in parentheses.

The story behind these numbers is that when the firm does well (i.e., reports a good HPR), it attracts new funds; otherwise it may suffer a net outflow. For example, the 10% return in the

TABLE 5.1		1st Quarter	2nd Quarter	3rd Quarter	4th Quarter
Quarterly cash flows and rates of return of a mutual fund	Assets under management at start of quarter ($ million)	1.0	1.2	2.0	0.8
	Holding-period return (%)	10.0	25.0	(20.0)	25.0
	Total assets before net inflows	1.1	1.5	1.6	1.0
	Net inflow ($ million)*	0.1	0.5	(0.8)	0.0
	Assets under management at end of quarter ($ million)	1.2	2.0	0.8	1.0

*New investment less redemptions and distributions, all assumed to occur at the end of each quarter.

first quarter by itself increased assets under management by $0.10 \times \$1$ million = \$100,000; it also elicited new investments of \$100,000, thus bringing assets under management to \$1.2 million by the end of the quarter. An even better HPR in the second quarter elicited a larger net inflow, and the second quarter ended with \$2 million under management. However, HPR in the third quarter was negative, and net inflows were negative.

How would we characterize fund performance over the year, given that the fund experienced both cash inflows and outflows? There are several candidate measures of performance, each with its own advantages and shortcomings. These are the *arithmetic average*, the *geometric average*, and the *dollar-weighted return*. These measures may vary considerably, so it is important to understand their differences.

arithmetic average

The sum of returns in each period divided by the number of periods.

Arithmetic average   The **arithmetic average** of the quarterly returns is just the sum of the quarterly returns divided by the number of quarters; in the above example: $(10 + 25 - 20 + 25)/4 = 10\%$. Since this statistic ignores compounding, it does not represent an equivalent, single quarterly rate for the year. The arithmetic average is useful, though, because it is the best forecast of performance in future quarters, using this particular sample of historic returns. (Whether the sample is large enough or representative enough to make accurate forecasts is, of course, another question.)

geometric average

The single per-period return that gives the same cumulative performance as the sequence of actual returns.

Geometric average   The **geometric average** of the quarterly returns is equal to the single per-period return that would give the same cumulative performance as the sequence of actual returns. We calculate the geometric average by compounding the actual period-by-period returns and then finding the equivalent single per-period return. In this case, the geometric average quarterly return, r_G, is defined by:

$$(1 + 0.10) \times (1 + 0.25) \times (1 - 0.20) \times (1 + 0.25) = (1 + r_G)^4$$

The left-hand side of this equation is the compounded year-end value of a \$1 investment earning the four quarterly returns used in our example. The right-hand side is the compounded value of a \$1 investment earning r_G *each* quarter. We solve for r_G as:

$$r_G = [(1 + 0.10) \times (1 + 0.25) \times (1 - 0.20) \times (1 + 0.25)]^{1/4} - 1 = .0829, \text{ or } 8.29\% \qquad \textbf{(5.2)}$$

The geometric return is also called a *time-weighted average return* because it ignores the quarter-to-quarter variation in funds under management. In fact, an investor will obtain a larger cumulative return if high returns are earned in those periods when additional sums have been invested, while lower returns are realized when less money is at risk. In Table 5.1, the highest returns (25%) were achieved in quarters 2 and 4, when the fund managed \$1,200,000 and \$800,000, respectively. The worst returns (-20% and 10%) occurred when the fund managed \$2,000,000 and \$1,000,000, respectively. In this case, better returns were earned when *less* money was under management—an unfavorable combination.

The appeal of the time-weighted return is that in some cases we *wish* to ignore variation in money under management. For example, published data on past returns earned by mutual funds actually are *required* to be time-weighted returns. The rationale for this practice is that since

more relevant & more important
average compound return

the fund manager does not have full control over the amount of assets under management, we should not weight returns in one period more heavily than those in other periods when assessing "typical" past performance. Another reason to use the time-weighted average is that over time individual investors will add to or subtract from the amounts they have invested in the mutual fund. The total assets under management will not track the investment positions of any particular investor, and so we prefer a return measure that abstracts from funds under management.

Dollar-weighted return   When we wish to account for the varying amounts under management, we treat the fund cash flows to investors as we would a capital budgeting problem in corporate finance. The initial value of $1 million and the net cash inflows are treated as the cash flows associated with an investment "project." The final "liquidation value" of the project is the ending value of the portfolio. In this case, therefore, investor net cash flows are as follows:

	Time				
	0	**1**	**2**	**3**	**4**
Net cash flow ($ million)	−1.0	−0.1	−0.5	0.8	1.0

The entry for time 0 reflects the starting contribution of $1 million, while the entries for times 1, 2, and 3 represent net inflows at the end of the first three quarters. Finally, the entry for time 4 represents the value of the portfolio at the end of the fourth quarter. This is the value for which the portfolio could have been liquidated by year-end based on the initial investment and net additional investments earlier in the year.

The <u>dollar-weighted average return</u> is the internal rate of return (IRR) of the project, which is 4.17%. The IRR is the interest rate that sets the present value of the cash flows realized on the portfolio (including the $1 million for which the portfolio can be liquidated at the end of the year) equal to the initial cost of establishing the portfolio. It therefore is the interest rate that satisfies the following equation:

dollar-weighted average return

The internal rate of return on an investment.

$$1.0 = \frac{-0.1}{1 + IRR} + \frac{-0.5}{(1 + IRR)^2} + \frac{0.8}{(1 + IRR)^3} + \frac{1.0}{(1 + IRR)^4} \qquad \textbf{(5.3)}$$

The dollar-weighted return in this example is less than the time-weighted return of 8.29% because, as we noted, the portfolio returns were higher when less money was under management. The difference between the dollar- and time-weighted average return in this case is quite large.

> **CONCEPT check 5.1**
>
> A fund begins with $10 million and reports the following three-month results (with negative figures in parentheses):
>
> | | **Month** | | |
> |---|---|---|---|
> | | **1** | **2** | **3** |
> | Net inflows (end of month, $ million) | 3 | 5 | 0 |
> | HPR (%) | 2 | 8 | (4) |
>
> Compute the arithmetic, time-weighted, and dollar-weighted average returns.

Conventions for Quoting Rates of Return

We've seen that there are several ways to compute average rates of return. There also is some variation in how the mutual fund in our example might annualize its quarterly returns.

Returns on assets with regular cash flows, such as mortgages (with monthly payments) and bonds (with semiannual coupons), usually are quoted as annual percentage rates, or APRs, which annualize per-period rates using a simple interest approach, ignoring compound interest. The APR can be translated to an effective annual rate (EAR) by remembering that

$$\text{APR} = \text{Per-period rate} \times \text{Periods per year}$$

Therefore, to obtain the EAR if there are n compounding periods in the year, we first recover the rate per period as APR/n and then compound that rate for the number of periods in a year. (For example, $n = 12$ for mortgages and $n = 2$ for bonds making payments semiannually.)

$$1 + \text{EAR} = (1 + \text{Rate per period})^n = \left(1 + \frac{\text{APR}}{n}\right)^n$$

Rearranging,

$$\text{APR} = [(1 + \text{EAR})^{1/n} - 1] \times n \tag{5.4}$$

The formula assumes that you can earn the APR each period. Therefore, after one year (when n periods have passed), your cumulative return would be $(1 + \text{APR}/n)^n$. Note that one needs to know the holding period when given an APR in order to convert it to an effective rate.

The EAR diverges by greater amounts from the APR as n becomes larger (that is, as we compound cash flows more frequently). In the limit, we can envision continuous compounding when n becomes extremely large in Equation 5.4. With continuous compounding, the relationship between the APR and EAR becomes

$$1 + \text{EAR} = e^{\text{APR}}$$

or equivalently,

$$\text{APR} = \ln(1 + \text{EAR}) \tag{5.5}$$

EXAMPLE   5.2

Annualizing Treasury-Bill Returns

Suppose you buy a $10,000 face value Treasury bill maturing in one month for $9,900. On the bill's maturity date, you collect the face value. Since there are no other interest payments, the holding period return for this one-month investment is:

$$\text{HPR} = \frac{\text{Cash income} + \text{Price change}}{\text{Initial price}} = \frac{\$100}{\$9,900} = 0.0101 = 1.01\%$$

The APR on this investment is therefore $1.01\% \times 12 = 12.12\%$. The effective annual rate is higher:

$$1 + \text{EAR} = (1.0101)^{12} = 1.1282$$

which implies that EAR $= .1282 = 12.82\%$

A warning: terminology can be loose. Occasionally, "annual percentage yield" or APY (but not APR!) may be used interchangeably with effective annual rate, and this can lead to confusion. To avoid error, you must be alert to context.

The difficulties in interpreting rates of return over time do not end here. Two thorny issues remain: the uncertainty surrounding the investment in question and the effect of inflation.

5.2   RISK AND RISK PREMIUMS

Any investment involves some degree of uncertainty about future holding period returns, and in many cases that uncertainty is considerable. Sources of investment risk range from macroeconomic fluctuations, to the changing fortunes of various industries, to asset-specific unexpected developments. Analysis of these multiple sources of risk is presented in Part Four on Security Analysis.

WEB *master*

Scenario Analysis and Probability Distributions

When we attempt to quantify risk, we begin with the question: What HPRs are possible, and how likely are they? A good way to approach this question is to devise a list of possible economic outcomes, or *scenarios,* and specify both the likelihood (i.e., the probability) of each scenario and the HPR the asset will realize in that scenario. Therefore, this approach is called **scenario analysis.** The list of possible HPRs with associated probabilities is called the **probability distribution** of HPRs. Consider an investment in a broad portfolio of stocks, say, an index fund, which we will refer to as the "stock market." A very simple scenario analysis for the stock market (assuming only three possible scenarios) is illustrated in Table 5.2.

The probability distribution lets us derive measurements for both the reward and the risk of the investment. The reward from the investment is its **expected return,** which you can think of as the average HPR you would earn if you were to repeat an investment in the asset many times. The expected return also is called the mean of the distribution of HPRs and often is referred to as the *mean return.*

To compute the expected return from the data provided, we label scenarios by *s* and denote the HPR in each scenario as *r(s)*, with probability *p(s)*. The expected return, denoted *E(r)*, is then the weighted average of returns in all possible scenarios, *s* = 1, . . . , *S,* with weights equal to the probability of that particular scenario.

$$E(r) = \sum_{s=1}^{S} p(s)r(s)$$ *See instructor's version of this formula ? H 2 page 2 ? version or* **(5.6)**

We show in Example 5.3, which follows shortly, that the data in Table 5.2 imply *E(r)* = 14%.

Of course, there is risk to the investment, and the actual return may be more or less than 14%. If a "boom" materializes, the return will be better, 44%, but in a recession, the return will be a disappointing −16%. How can we quantify the uncertainty of the investment?

The "surprise" return on the investment in any scenario is the difference between the actual return and the expected return. For example, in a boom (scenario 1) the surprise is 30%: *r(1)* − *E(r)* = 44% − 14% = 30%. In a recession (scenario 3), the surprise is −30%: *r(3)* − *E(r)* = −16% − 14% = −30%.

Uncertainty surrounding the investment is a function of the magnitudes of the possible surprises. To summarize risk with a single number we first define the **variance** as the expected value of the *squared* deviation from the mean (i.e., the expected value of the squared "surprise" across scenarios).

scenario analysis

Process of devising a list of possible economic scenarios and specifying the likelihood of each one, as well as the HPR that will be realized in each case.

probability distribution

List of possible outcomes with associated probabilities.

expected return

The mean value of the distribution of HPR.

variance

The expected value of the squared deviation from the mean.

TABLE 5.2	**State of the Economy**	**Scenario, s**	**Probability, p(s)**	**HPR**
Probability distribution of HPR on the stock market	Boom	1	0.25	44%
	Normal growth	2	0.50	14
	Recession	3	0.25	−16

$$\text{Var}(r) \equiv \sigma^2 = \sum_{s=1}^{S} p(s)[r(s) - E(r)]^2 \tag{5.7}$$

We square the deviations because otherwise, negative deviations would offset positive deviations, with the result that the expected deviation from the mean return would necessarily be zero. Squared deviations are necessarily positive. Squaring (a nonlinear transformation) exaggerates large (positive or negative) deviations and relatively deemphasizes small deviations.

Another result of squaring deviations is that the variance has a dimension of percent squared. To give the measure of risk the same dimension as expected return (%), we use the **standard deviation**, defined as the square root of the variance:

standard deviation

The square root of the variance.

$$SD(r) \equiv \sigma = \sqrt{\text{Var}(r)} \tag{5.8}$$

A potential drawback to the use of variance and standard deviation as measures of risk is that they treat positive deviations and negative deviations from the expected return symmetrically. In practice investors welcome positive surprises, and a natural measure of risk would focus only on bad outcomes. However, if the distribution of returns is symmetric (meaning that the likelihood and magnitude of negative surprises are roughly equal to those of positive surprises), then standard deviation will approximate risk measures that concentrate solely on negative deviations. In the special case that the distribution of returns is approximately normal—represented by the well-known bell-shaped curve—the standard deviation will be perfectly adequate to measure risk. The evidence shows that for fairly short holding periods, the returns of most diversified portfolios are well described by a normal distribution.

EXAMPLE 5.3

Expected Return and Standard Deviation

Applying Equation 5.6 to the data in Table 5.2, we find that the expected rate of return on the stock index fund is

$$E(r) = 0.25 \times 44\% + 0.50 \times 14\% + 0.25 \times (-16\%) = 14\%$$

We use Equation 5.7 to find the variance. First we take the difference between the holding-period return in each scenario and the mean return, then we square that difference, and finally we multiply by the probability of each scenario. The sum of the probability-weighted squared deviations is the variance.

$$\sigma^2 = 0.25(44 - 14)^2 + 0.50(14 - 14)^2 + 0.25(-16 - 14)^2 = 450$$

and so the standard deviation is

$$\sigma = \sqrt{450} = 21.21\%$$

CONCEPT check 5.2

A share of stock of A-Star Inc. is now selling for $23.50. A financial analyst summarizes the uncertainty about next year's holding-period return on the stock by specifying three possible scenarios:

Business Conditions	Scenario, s	Probability, p	End-of-Year Price	Annual Dividend
High growth	1	0.35	$35	$4.40
Normal growth	2	0.30	27	4.00
No growth	3	0.35	15	4.00

What are the annual holding-period returns of A-Star stock for each of the three scenarios? Calculate the expected HPR and the standard deviation of the HPR.

Risk Premiums and Risk Aversion

How much, if anything, should you invest in an index stock fund such as the one described in Table 5.2? First, you must ask how much of an expected reward is offered to compensate for the risk involved in investing money in stocks.

We measure the "reward" as the difference between the expected HPR on the index stock fund and the **risk-free rate,** that is, the rate you can earn by leaving money in risk-free assets such as Treasury bills, money market funds, or the bank. We call this difference the **risk premium** on common stocks. For example, if the risk-free rate in the example is 6% per year, and the expected index fund return is 14%, then the risk premium on stocks is 8% per year.

The rate of return on Treasury bills also varies over time. However, we know the rate of return we will earn on T-bills *at the beginning* of the holding period, while we can't know the return we will earn on risky assets until the end of the holding period. Therefore, to study the risk premium available on risky assets we compile a series of **excess returns,** that is, returns in excess of the T-bill rate in each period. One possible forecast of the risk premium of any asset is the average of its historical excess returns.

The degree to which investors are willing to commit funds to stocks depends on **risk aversion.** It seems obvious that investors are risk averse in the sense that, if the risk premium were zero, people would not be willing to invest any money in stocks. In theory then, there must always be a positive risk premium on stocks in order to induce risk-averse investors to hold the existing supply of stocks instead of placing all their money in risk-free assets.

In fact, the risk premium is what distinguishes gambling from speculation. Investors who are willing to take on risk because they expect to earn a risk premium are speculating. Speculation is undertaken *despite* the risk because the speculator sees a favorable risk-return trade-off. In contrast, gambling is the assumption of risk for no purpose beyond the enjoyment of the risk itself. Gamblers take on risk even without the prospect of a risk premium.[1]

It occasionally will be useful to quantify an investor's degree of risk aversion. To do so, suppose that investors choose portfolios based on both expected return, $E(r_P)$, and the volatility of returns as measured by the variance. If we denote the risk-free rate on Treasury bills as r_f, then the risk premium of a portfolio is $E(r_P) - r_f$. Risk-averse investors will demand higher risk premiums to place their wealth in portfolios with higher volatility; that risk premium will be greater the greater their risk aversion. Therefore, if we quantify the degree of risk aversion with the parameter A, it makes sense to assert that the risk premium an investor demands of a portfolio will be dependent on both risk aversion A and the risk of the portfolio.

Therefore, we will assume that the risk premium that an investor demands to hold a risky portfolio rather than placing all of her funds in safe T-bills offering the risk-free rate is proportional to the product of her risk aversion, A, and the variance of the risky portfolio's rate of return:

$$E(r_P) - r_f = \tfrac{1}{2} A \sigma_P^2 \qquad \textbf{(5.9)}$$

(The factor of ½ on the right-hand side of Equation 5.9 is merely a scale factor. It is widely used by convention, but has no bearing on the analysis. Note also that to use this equation, all rates of return must be expressed as decimals rather than percentages.)

As a benchmark, notice that Equation 5.9 implies that investors would not demand a risk premium to hold a risk-free portfolio (for which $\sigma_P^2 = 0$). But for any positive variance, the required risk premium is positive and is greater for more risk-averse investors (who have higher values of A). Not surprisingly, when a risky portfolio offers a greater risk premium relative to risk, investors will place a higher fraction of their overall portfolios in it, and place a correspondingly lower fraction in the risk-free asset. Conversely, if a portfolio is riskier, investors will shy away from it.

Now consider the total market portfolio, which is the aggregation of the holdings of all investors and therefore may be viewed as representative of a "typical" investor's portfolio.[2]

risk-free rate

The rate of return that can be earned with certainty.

risk premium

An expected return in excess of that on risk-free securities.

excess return

Rate of return in excess of the Treasury-bill rate.

risk aversion

Reluctance to accept risk.

---

[1]Sometimes a gamble might *seem* like speculation to the participants. If two investors differ in their forecasts of the future, they might take opposite positions on a security, and both may have an expectation of earning a positive risk premium. In such cases, only one party can, in fact, be correct.
[2]In practice, a broad market index such as the S&P 500 is taken as representative of the entire market.

By examining the risk-return trade-off offered by this representative portfolio (and willingly held by the representative investor) we should be able to infer something about the typical investor's risk aversion. It turns out that if investors trade off risk against return in the manner specified by Equation 5.9, then we can infer the average degree of risk aversion from the characteristics of the market portfolio, M, as:

$$A = \frac{E(r_M) - r_f}{\sigma_M^2} \qquad (5.10)$$

Equation 5.10 quantifies the reasonable proposition that investors' risk aversion will be reflected in the risk premium they demand per unit of portfolio risk. A higher market risk premium (per unit of risk) must indicate that investors are more risk averse. For example, if the risk premium is 8%, and the standard deviation is 20%, then we would infer risk aversion as $A = .08/.20^2 = 2$. Notice that we must express returns as decimals to use Equation 5.10.

In practice, of course, we cannot observe the risk premium investors *expect* to earn. We can observe only actual returns after the fact. Moreover, different investors may have different expectations about the risk and return of various assets. Finally, Equations 5.9 and 5.10 apply only to the variance of an investor's overall portfolio, not to individual assets held in that portfolio. We usually cannot observe every element of an investor's total portfolio of assets. While the exact relationship between risk and return in capital markets therefore cannot be known exactly, many studies conclude that investors' risk aversion is likely in the range of 2–4. This implies that to accept an increase of .01 in portfolio variance, investors would require an increase in the risk premium of between .01 and .02 (i.e., 1%–2%).

The Sharpe (Reward-to-Volatility) Measure

Sharpe (or reward-to-volatility) measure

Ratio of portfolio risk premium to standard deviation.

Risk aversion implies that investors will accept a lower reward (as measured by their portfolio expected return) in exchange for a sufficient reduction in risk (as measured by the standard deviation of their portfolio return). A statistic commonly used to rank portfolios in terms of this risk-return trade-off is the **Sharpe (or reward-to-volatility) measure**, defined as:

$$S = \frac{\text{Portfolio risk premium}}{\text{Standard deviation of portfolio excess return}} = \frac{E(r_P) - r_f}{\sigma_P} \qquad (5.11)$$

A risk-free asset would have a risk premium of zero and a standard deviation of zero. Therefore, the reward-to-volatility measure of a risky portfolio quantifies the incremental reward (in terms of the increase in expected excess return compared to the risk-free position) for each increase of 1% in the standard deviation of that portfolio. For example, the Sharpe measure of a portfolio with an annual risk premium of 8% and standard deviation of 20% is $8/20 = 0.4$. A higher Sharpe measure indicates a better reward per unit of volatility, in other words, a more efficient portfolio. Portfolio analysis in terms of mean and standard deviation (or variance) of excess returns is called **mean-variance analysis**.

mean-variance analysis

Ranking portfolios by their Sharpe measures.

A warning: We will see in the next chapter that while standard deviation of returns is a useful risk measure for diversified portfolios, it is not a useful way to think about the risk of individual securities. Therefore, the Sharpe measure is a valid statistic only for ranking portfolios; it is *not* valid for individual assets. For now, therefore, let's examine the historical reward-to-volatility ratios of broadly diversified portfolios that reflect the performance of some important asset classes.

CONCEPT check 5.3

a. A respected analyst forecasts that the return of the S&P 500 Index portfolio over the coming year will be 10%. The one-year T-bill rate is 5%. Examination of recent returns of the S&P 500 Index suggest that the standard deviation of returns will be 18%. What does this information suggest about the degree of risk aversion of the average investor, assuming that the average portfolio resembles the S&P 500?

b. What is the Sharpe measure of the portfolio in (a)?

THE HISTORICAL RECORD

Bills, Bonds, and Stocks, 1926–2006

The record of past rates of return is one possible source of information about risk premiums and standard deviations. We can estimate the historical risk premium by taking an average of the past differences between the HPRs on an asset class and the risk-free rate. Table 5.3 presents statistics derived from the rates of return on a number of asset-class portfolios, as well as for Treasury bills and the rate of inflation over the period 1926–2006. The year-by-year rates of return are available at our Online Learning Center at **www.mhhe.com/bkm**. (Look for the link to Chapter 5 material.)

The "World Portfolio" of stocks is diversified across large capitalization stocks of 16 developed countries (including the U.S., Europe, and Japan). Until 1968, country portfolio shares in this index were determined by the relative size of gross domestic product, measured in U.S. dollars. Since 1967, shares were determined by the relative capitalization of each market, again measured in U.S. dollars. "Large Stocks" in Table 5.3 refers to Standard & Poor's market value–weighted portfolio of 500 U.S. common stocks selected from the largest market capitalization stocks. "Small U.S. Stocks" are the smallest 20% of the stocks trading on the NYSE.

The World Portfolio of bonds was constructed from the same set of countries as the world portfolio of stocks, using long-term bonds from each of the 16 countries. Until 1996, "Long-Term T-Bonds" were represented by U.S. government bonds with at least a 20-year maturity and approximately current-level coupon rate.[3] Since 1996, this bond series has been measured by the Lehman Brothers Long-Term Treasury Bond Index.

"T-Bills" in Table 5.3 are of approximately 30-day maturity, and the one-year HPR represents a policy of "rolling over" the bills as they mature. Because T-bill rates can change from month to month, the total rate of return on these T-bills is riskless only for 30-day holding periods.[4] The last column provides the annual inflation rate as measured by the rate of change in the Consumer Price Index.

Table 5.3A focuses on the total or "raw" annual returns of each asset class for the full period 1926–2006 as well as for several subperiods. The first two rows for each investment period present the arithmetic average of the historical rates of return as well as the geometric average return (i.e., the compound rate of return that would have provided the same total growth in value as the actual investment in the asset). The third row provides an estimate of the standard deviation of those returns. The higher the standard deviation, the more volatile the holding-period return.

The standard deviations reported in Table 5.3, however, are based on historical data rather than forecasts of future scenarios, as in Equations 5.7 and 5.8. To calculate a standard deviation from historical data, we treat each year's outcome as one possible scenario in a scenario analysis. Each historical outcome is taken as equally likely and given a "probability" of $1/n$.

The formula for historical variance is thus similar to Equation 5.7, but instead of using deviations of returns around *mean* returns based on the scenario analysis, we use deviations from *average* returns during the sample period. This procedure results in one minor complication. When we use the sample average return $\bar{r}$ in place of the mean return, $E(r)$, we must modify the average of the squared deviations for what statisticians call a "lost degree of freedom." The modification is easy: Multiply the average value of the squared deviations by $\frac{n}{n-1}$. The formula for variance based on historical data is thus:

$$\sigma^2 = \frac{n}{n-1} \times \text{Sample average of squared deviations from average return}$$

$$= \frac{n}{n-1} \times \sum_{i=1}^{n} \frac{(r_i - \bar{r})^2}{n} = \frac{1}{n-1} \sum_{i=1}^{n} (r_i - \bar{r})^2 \qquad (5.12)$$

---

[3]The importance of the coupon rate when comparing returns on bonds is discussed in Part Three.
[4]The few negative returns in this column in the year-by-year table (available on our Web site) at **www.mhhe.com/bkm**, all dating from before World War II, reflect periods where, in the absence of T-bills, returns on government securities with about 30-day maturity are reported. However, these securities included options to be exchanged for other securities, thus increasing their price and reducing their yield relative to what a simple T-bill would have offered.

TABLE 5.3

Rates of return statistics for 1926–2006 and various subperiods*

	World Portfolio		U.S. Market				
	Equity Return in U.S. Dollars	Bond Return in U.S. Dollars	Small Stocks	Large Stocks	Long-Term T-Bonds	T-Bills	Inflation
A. Raw Returns							
1926–2006							
Geometric average	9.80	5.80	12.43	10.23	5.35	3.72	3.04
Arithmetic average	11.32	6.17	18.14	12.19	5.64	3.77	3.13
Standard deviation	18.05	9.05	36.93	20.14	8.06	3.11	4.27
Minimum	−39.94	−13.29	−54.83	−45.56	−8.74	−0.04	−10.27
Maximum	70.81	34.21	151.83	54.56	32.68	14.72	18.13
1926–1965							
Geometric average	9.04	2.63	12.13	10.03	3.09	1.52	1.45
Arithmetic average	10.79	2.87	19.96	12.65	3.19	1.53	1.56
Standard deviation	19.60	7.32	43.56	23.30	4.51	1.34	4.81
Minimum	−39.94	−13.29	−54.83	−45.56	−5.31	−0.04	−10.27
Maximum	70.81	29.28	151.83	54.56	13.78	4.74	18.13
1966–2006							
Geometric average	10.55	8.99	12.73	10.43	7.61	5.92	4.62
Arithmetic average	11.84	9.38	16.37	11.74	8.04	5.95	4.66
Standard deviation	16.64	9.49	29.51	16.77	9.90	2.77	3.00
Minimum	−24.01	−5.60	−38.22	−26.40	−8.74	1.02	1.10
Maximum	40.37	34.21	103.64	37.71	32.68	14.72	13.29
1997–2006 (recent ten years)							
Geometric average	8.58	7.86	15.31	8.38	7.75	3.60	2.48
Arithmetic average	10.14	8.17	17.72	9.97	8.07	3.62	2.48
Standard deviation	18.95	8.71	26.16	19.10	8.68	1.79	0.81
Minimum	−17.02	−5.60	−11.72	−22.10	−8.74	1.02	1.55
Maximum	37.76	22.64	74.54	33.17	20.27	5.88	3.84
B. Excess Returns over the Risk-Free Rate							
1926–2006							
Risk premium	7.56	2.40	14.37	8.42	1.88		
Standard deviation	18.37	8.92	37.53	20.42	7.87		
Sharpe Measure	0.41	0.27	0.38	0.41	0.24		
1926–1965							
Risk premium	9.27	1.35	18.43	11.12	1.66		
Standard deviation	19.68	7.29	43.93	23.41	4.81		
Sharpe Measure	0.47	0.18	0.42	0.48	0.35		
1966–2006							
Risk premium	5.89	3.43	10.42	5.79	2.09		
Standard deviation	17.07	10.26	30.04	16.89	10.07		
Sharpe Measure	0.34	0.33	0.35	0.34	0.21		
1997–2006 (recent ten years)							
Risk premium	6.53	4.56	14.10	6.35	4.45		
Standard deviation	19.32	9.61	26.72	18.91	8.65		
Sharpe Measure	0.34	0.47	0.53	0.34	0.51		

*This table is available as a spreadsheet on the book's Web site at **www.mhhe.com/bkm**

Sources: Inflation data: Bureau of Labor Statistics. U.S. large stocks: S&P 500. U.S. small stocks: Fama & French 1st quantile (**http://mba.tuck.dartmouth.edu/pages/faculty/ken.french/data_library.html**). Long-term U.S. Government bonds: 1926–2003, return on 20-year T-bond; 2004–2006 Lehman Bros long-term Treasury index. World portfolio of large stocks: Datastream. World bonds: 1926–2003, Dimson, Marsh, and Staunton (2000); 2004–2006, Datastream.

e**X**cel

Please visit us at www.mhhe.com/bkm

When you are using large samples and n is large, the modification is unimportant, since $n/(n - 1)$ is close to 1.0 and $1/(n - 1)$ is close to $1/n$.

EXAMPLE **5.4**

Historical Means and Standard Deviations

To illustrate how to calculate average returns and standard deviations from historical data, let's compute these statistics for the returns on the S&P 500 portfolio using five years of data from the following table. The average return over this period is 16.7%, computed by dividing the sum of column (1) below, by the number of observations. In column (2), we take the deviation of each year's return from the 16.7% average return. In column (3), we calculate the squared deviation. The variance is, from Equation 5.12, the sum of the five squared deviations divided by (5 − 1). The standard deviation is the square root of the variance. If you input the column of rates into a spreadsheet, the "Average" and "StdDev" functions will give you the statistics directly.

Year	(1) Rate of Return	(2) Deviation from Average Return	(3) Squared Deviation
1	16.9%	0.2%	0.0
2	31.3	14.6	213.2
3	−3.2	−19.9	396.0
4	30.7	14.0	196.0
5	7.7	−9.0	81.0
Total	83.4%		886.2

$$\text{Average rate of return} = 83.4/5 = 16.7$$

$$\text{Variance} = \frac{1}{5-1} \times 886.2 = 221.6$$

$$\text{Standard deviation} = \sqrt{221.6} = 14.9\%$$

Figure 5.1 presents histograms of the annual rates of return of several U.S. asset classes. All four histograms are drawn to the same scale and centered on zero arithmetic average return. The associated averages and standard deviations appear next to each plot. The histograms are consistent with the risk-return trade-off: Riskier assets have provided higher average returns. The histograms vividly show that a higher standard deviation is associated with a greater dispersion of rates of return.

While Figure 5.1 and Table 5.3A focus on raw returns, Table 5.3B provides statistics for "excess" returns, that is, raw return in each period minus the return on T-bills. The risk premium over bills in Panel B is the arithmetic average of the difference between raw returns and T-bill returns over each subperiod. Because T-bill returns are not constant, the standard deviations of the excess returns in Panel B are slightly different from those of the raw returns in Panel A of Table 5.3. Given the historical risk premium and standard deviation of each asset class, we can evaluate the risk-return trade-off each has offered by examining its Sharpe measure (the reward-to-volatility ratio), provided in the last line of results for each subperiod.

As noted earlier, however, the Sharpe measure is applicable only to diversified portfolios that might be candidates for an investor's entire risky portfolio. Such portfolios would be constructed from combinations of the asset-class portfolios in Table 5.3, with possible additions of more exotic investments such as real estate or precious metals. Nevertheless, large stocks make up a large proportion of most investors' portfolios, and hence the Sharpe measures of the World and U.S. large-stock portfolios provide reasonable benchmarks to assess the risk-return trade-off available to many investors.

For the 81-year period 1926–2006, the Sharpe measure of both the World and U.S. large-stock portfolios was 0.41. What would this have meant for an investor contemplating an asset allocation decision? As funds are transferred from a risk-free portfolio of T-bills to a risky portfolio of large stocks, both risk and expected return will increase. The Sharpe ratio of .41

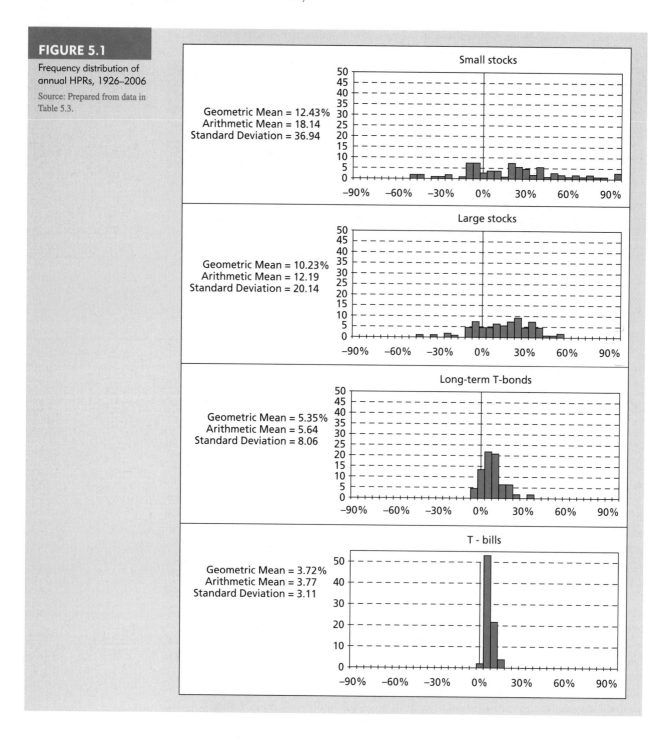

FIGURE 5.1

Frequency distribution of annual HPRs, 1926–2006

Source: Prepared from data in Table 5.3.

implies that over this period, each increase in portfolio standard deviation of 1% was rewarded by an increased risk premium of 0.41% (41 basis points). Notice that the Sharpe measure of all other asset classes was less than 0.41, as we would expect from less effectively diversified portfolios. We shall examine this issue in detail in the next chapter.

Looking at the subperiod results, we find that the Sharpe ratios for the large-stock portfolios over the 40 years from 1926 through 1965 (0.47 and 0.48 for World and U.S. large stocks, respectively) were higher than over the most recent 41 years from 1966 through 2006 (.34 for both the World and the U.S.). Performance over the most recent 10 years was similar, as the bear market of the early 2000s offset the end of the roaring 1990s and the recent recovery.

The potential import of the risk premium can be illustrated with a simple example. Consider two investors with $1 million as of December 31, 2000. One invests in the small-stock portfolio, and the other in T-bills. Suppose both investors reinvest all income from their portfolios and liquidate their investments five years later, on December 31, 2005. We can find the annual rates of return for this period from the spreadsheet of returns at the Online Learning Center. (Go to **www.mhhe.com/bkm**. Look for the link to Chapter 5 material.) We compute a "wealth index" for each investment by compounding wealth at the end of each year by the return earned in the following year. For example, we calculate the value of the wealth index for small stocks as of 2003 by multiplying the value as of 2002 (1.1372) by one plus the rate of return earned in 2003 (measured in decimals), that is, by 1 + 0.7454, to obtain 1.9849.

EXAMPLE 5.5

The Risk Premium and Growth of Wealth

	Small Stocks		T-Bills	
	Return	**Wealth Index**	**Return**	**Wealth Index**
2000		1.0		1.0
2001	28.82%	1.2882	3.72%	1.0372
2002	−11.72	1.1372	1.66	1.0544
2003	74.54	1.9849	1.01	1.0651
2004	14.34	2.2695	1.37	1.0797
2005	3.20	2.3422	3.13	1.1135

The final value of each portfolio as of December 31, 2005, equals its initial value ($1 million) multiplied by the wealth index at the end of the period:

	Small Stocks	T-Bills
December 31, 2000	$1,000,000	$1,000,000
December 31, 2005	2,342,200	1,113,500

The difference in total return is dramatic. The value of the small-stock portfolio after five years is more than double that of the T-bill portfolio.

We can also calculate the geometric average return of each portfolio over this period. For T-bills, the geometric average over the five-year period is computed from:

$$(1 + r_G)^5 = 1.1135$$
$$1 + r_G = 1.1135^{1/5} = 1.0217$$
$$r_G = 2.17\%$$

Similarly, the geometric average for small stocks is 18.56%. The large difference in geometric average reflects the large difference in cumulative wealth provided by the small-stock portfolio over this period.

Figure 5.2 provides another view of historical returns for three different asset classes. Here we plot the year-by-year returns for each investment on the same set of axes. The volatility of returns on large U.S. stocks (with a standard deviation of 20.14%) is far greater than that on long-term Treasury bonds (standard deviation 8.06%) or T-bills (3.11%), which shows up in far wider swings in annual holding-period returns.

An all-stock portfolio with a standard deviation of around 20% would represent a very volatile investment. For example, if stock returns are normally distributed with a standard deviation of 20% and an expected rate of return of 12% (near the historical average), then in roughly one year out of three, returns will be less than 12 − 20 = −8%, or greater than 12 + 20 = 32%.

Figure 5.3 is a graph of the normal curve with mean 12% and standard deviation 20%. The graph shows the theoretical probability of rates of return within various ranges given these parameters. Now observe the actual historical frequency distributions in Figure 5.1. The variation in

FIGURE 5.2

Rates of return on stocks, bonds and T-bills, 1926–2006

Source: Prepared from Table 5.3.

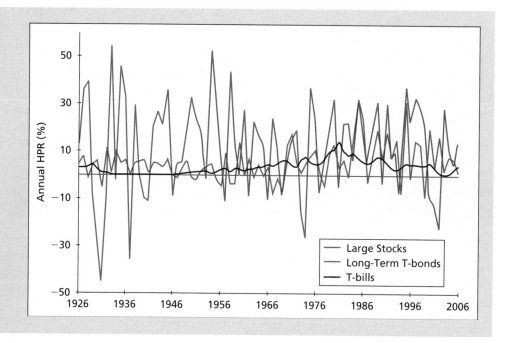

FIGURE 5.3

The normal distribution with mean return 12% and standard deviation 20%

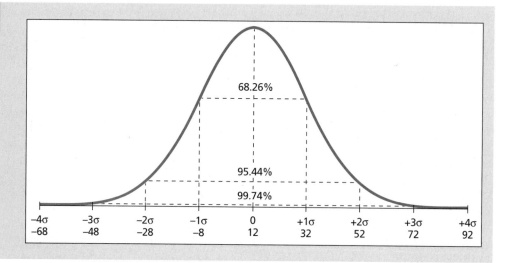

the dispersion of the frequency distributions across the different asset classes vividly illustrates the differences in standard deviation and their implication for risk.

The rough similarity of historical returns to a normal distribution allows us to use the historical average and standard deviation to estimate probabilities of various outcomes. For example, we estimate the probability that the return on the large-stock portfolio will be below zero in the next year at .27. This is so because a rate of zero is 12 percentage points, or .6 standard deviations (=12/20) below the mean. Using a table of the normal distribution, we find that the probability of a normal variable falling .6 or more standard deviations below its mean is .27.

Both the average return and standard deviation of the small-stock portfolio documented in Table 5.3 are striking. Table 5.4 shows average returns and standard deviations for NYSE portfolios arranged by firm size. Firms are ranked by size, as measured by the market value of outstanding equity, and are then assigned to one of 10 deciles, from the largest 10% of all firms (decile 1) to the smallest 10% (decile 10). Average returns generally are higher as firm size declines. The data clearly suggest that small firms have earned a substantial risk premium and therefore that firm size seems to be an important proxy for risk. In later chapters we will

TABLE 5.4	Decile	Geometric Average	Arithmetic Average	Standard Deviation
Size-decile portfolios of the NYSE/AMEX/NAS-DAQ Summary Statistics of Annual Returns, 1927–2006	1 Largest	9.6%	11.4%	19.1%
	2	10.9	13.2	21.6
	3	11.4	13.8	22.9
	4	11.9	14.8	25.2
	5	12.0	15.2	26.6
	6	12.1	15.6	27.6
	7	12.4	16.3	30.0
	8	12.5	17.0	32.5
	9	12.2	17.5	35.3
	10 Smallest	13.8	20.4	40.9
	Total Value Weighted Index	10.1%	12.1%	20.2%

Source: Web site of Professor Kenneth R. French, **http://mba.tuck.dartmouth.edu/pages/faculty/ken.french/data_library.html**.

further explore this phenomenon and will see that the size effect can be further related to other attributes of the firm.

Investing internationally is no longer considered exotic, and Table 5.3 also provides some information on the historical results from international investments. Over the 1926–2006 period, the world stock portfolio offered lower average returns, but also lower volatility, than large U.S. stocks. On the other hand, world bonds provided higher average returns but more volatility than long-term U.S. bonds. These patterns also are consistent with a risk-return trade-off. Foreign stocks offer U.S. investors opportunities for diversification, however, and we therefore devote Chapter 19 to international investing.

CONCEPT check 5.4

Compute the average excess return on large company stocks (over the T-bill rate) and the standard deviation for the years 1926–1934. You will need to obtain data from the spreadsheet available at the Online Learning Center at **www.mhhe.com/bkm**. Look for Chapter 5 material.

5.4 INFLATION AND REAL RATES OF RETURN

The historical rates of return we reviewed in the previous section were measured in nominal dollars. A 10% annual rate of return, for example, means that your investment was worth 10% more at the end of the year than it was at the beginning of the year. This does not necessarily mean, however, that you could have bought 10% more goods and services with that money, for it is possible that in the course of the year prices of goods also increased. If prices have changed, the increase in your purchasing power will not equal the increase in your dollar wealth.

At any time, the prices of some goods may rise while the prices of other goods may fall; the *general* trend in prices is measured by examining changes in the consumer price index, or CPI. The CPI measures the cost of purchasing a bundle of goods that is considered representative of the "consumption basket" of a typical urban family of four. Increases in the cost of this standardized consumption basket are indicative of a general trend toward higher prices. The **inflation rate,** or the rate at which prices are rising, is measured as the rate of increase of the CPI.

Suppose the rate of inflation (the percentage change in the CPI, denoted by i) for the last year amounted to $i = 6\%$. This tells you the purchasing power of money is reduced by 6% a year. The value of each dollar depreciates by 6% a year in terms of the goods it can buy. Therefore, part of your investment earnings are offset by the reduction in the purchasing power

inflation rate

The rate at which prices are rising, measured as the rate of increase of the CPI.

of the dollars you will receive at the end of the year. With a 10% interest rate, for example, after you net out the 6% reduction in the purchasing power of money, you are left with a net increase in purchasing power of about 4%. Thus, we need to distinguish between a **nominal interest rate**—the growth rate of your money—and a **real interest rate**—the growth rate of your purchasing power. If we call R the nominal rate, r the real rate, and i the inflation rate, then we conclude

nominal interest rate

The interest rate in terms of nominal (not adjusted for purchasing power) dollars.

real interest rate

The excess of the interest rate over the inflation rate. The growth rate of purchasing power derived from an investment.

$$r \approx R - i \tag{5.13}$$

In words, the real rate of interest is the nominal rate reduced by the loss of purchasing power resulting from inflation.

In fact, the exact relationship between the real and nominal interest rate is given by

$$1 + r = \frac{1 + R}{1 + i} \tag{5.14}$$

In words, the growth factor of your purchasing power, $1 + r$, equals the growth factor of your money, $1 + R$, divided by the new price level that is $1 + i$ times its value in the previous period. The exact relationship can be rearranged to

$$r = \frac{R - i}{1 + i} \tag{5.15}$$

which shows that the approximate rule overstates the real rate by the factor $1 + i$.

EXAMPLE 5.6 *Real versus Nominal Rates*	If the interest rate on a one-year CD is 8%, and you expect inflation to be 5% over the coming year, then using the approximation given in Equation 5.13, you expect the real rate to be $r = 8\% - 5\% = 3\%$. Using the exact formula given in Equation 5.15, the real rate is $r = \dfrac{.08 - .05}{1 + .05} = .0286$, or 2.86%. Therefore, the approximation rule overstates the expected real rate by only 0.14 percentage points. The approximation rule is more accurate for small inflation rates and is perfectly exact for continuously compounded rates.

To summarize, in interpreting the historical returns on various asset classes presented in Table 5.3, we must recognize that to obtain the real returns on these assets, we must reduce the nominal returns by the inflation rate presented in the last column of the table. In fact, while the return on a U.S. Treasury bill usually is considered to be riskless, this is true only with regard to its nominal return. To infer the expected real rate of return on a Treasury bill, you must subtract your estimate of the inflation rate over the coming period.

It is always possible to calculate the real rate after the fact. The inflation rate is published by the Bureau of Labor Statistics. The *future* real rate, however, is unknown, and one has to rely on expectations. In other words, because future inflation is risky, the real rate of return is risky even if the nominal rate is risk-free.

The Equilibrium Nominal Rate of Interest

We've seen that the real rate of return on an asset is approximately equal to the nominal rate minus the inflation rate. Because investors should be concerned with their real returns—the increase in their purchasing power—we would expect that as inflation increases, investors will demand higher nominal rates of return on their investments. This higher rate is necessary to maintain the expected real return offered by an investment.

Irving Fisher (1930) argued that the nominal rate ought to increase one-for-one with increases in the expected inflation rate. If we use the notation $E(i)$ to denote the current

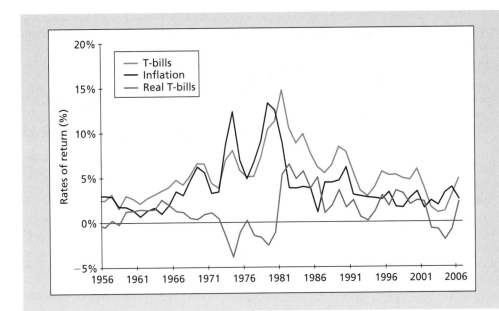

FIGURE 5.4

Interest, inflation, and real rates, 1956–2006

Source: Prepared from data in Table 5.3.

expectation of the inflation rate that will prevail over the coming period, then we can state the so-called Fisher equation formally as

$$R = r + E(i) \qquad (5.16)$$

Suppose the real rate of interest is 2%, and the inflation rate is 4%, so that the nominal interest rate is about 6%. If the expected inflation rate rises to 5%, the nominal interest rate should climb to roughly 7%. The increase in the nominal rate offsets the increase in expected inflation, giving investors an unchanged growth of purchasing power at a 2% real rate. The evidence for the Fisher equation is that periods of high inflation and high nominal rates generally coincide. Figure 5.4 illustrates this fact.

CONCEPT check 5.5

a. Suppose the real interest rate is 3% per year, and the expected inflation rate is 8%. What is the nominal interest rate?

b. Suppose the expected inflation rate rises to 10%, but the real rate is unchanged. What happens to the nominal interest rate?

5.5 ASSET ALLOCATION ACROSS RISKY AND RISK-FREE PORTFOLIOS

History shows us that long-term bonds have been riskier investments than investments in Treasury bills and that stock investments have been riskier still. On the other hand, the riskier investments have offered higher average returns. Investors, of course, do not make all-or-nothing choices from these investment classes. They can and do construct their portfolios using securities from all asset classes. Some of the portfolio may be in risk-free Treasury bills and some in high-risk stocks.

The most straightforward way to control the risk of a portfolio is through the fraction of the portfolio invested in Treasury bills and other safe money market securities versus risky assets. This is an example of an **asset allocation** choice—a choice among broad investment classes, rather than among the specific securities within each asset class. Most investment professionals

asset allocation

Portfolio choice among broad investment classes.

consider asset allocation the most important part of portfolio construction. Consider this statement by John Bogle, made when he was the chairman of the Vanguard Group of Investment Companies:

> The most fundamental decision of investing is the allocation of your assets: How much should you own in stock? How much should you own in bonds? How much should you own in cash reserves? . . . That decision [has been shown to account] for an astonishing 94% of the differences in total returns achieved by institutionally managed pension funds. . . . There is no reason to believe that the same relationship does not also hold true for individual investors.[5]

Therefore, we start our discussion of the risk-return trade-off available to investors by examining the most basic asset allocation choice: the choice of how much of the portfolio to place in risk-free money market securities versus other risky asset classes.

We will denote the investor's portfolio of risky assets as P, and the risk-free asset as F. We will assume for the sake of illustration that the risky component of the investor's overall portfolio comprises two mutual funds: one invested in stocks and the other invested in long-term bonds. For now, we take the composition of the risky portfolio as given and focus only on the allocation between it and risk-free securities. In the next chapter, we turn to security selection for the risky portfolio.

The Risky Asset

When we shift wealth from the risky portfolio (P) to the risk-free asset, we do not change the relative proportions of the various securities within the risky portfolio. Rather, we reduce the relative weight of the risky portfolio as a whole in favor of risk-free assets.

A simple example demonstrates the procedure. Assume the total market value of an investor's portfolio is $300,000. Of that, $90,000 is invested in shares of the Ready Assets money market fund, a risk-free asset. The remaining $210,000 is in risky securities, say, $113,400 in shares of Vanguard's S&P 500 index fund and $96,600 in shares of Fidelity's Investment Grade Bond Fund.

The Vanguard fund (V) is a passive equity fund that replicates the S&P 500 portfolio. The Fidelity Investment Grade Bond Fund (IG) invests primarily in corporate bonds with high safety ratings and also in Treasury bonds. We choose these two funds for the risky portfolio in the spirit of a low-cost, well-diversified portfolio. While in the next chapter we discuss portfolio optimization, here we simply assume the investor considers the given weighting of V and IG to be optimal.

The holdings of the Vanguard and Fidelity shares make up the risky portfolio, with 54% in V and 46% in IG.

$$w_V = 113,400/210,000 = 0.54 \text{ (Vanguard)}$$
$$w_{IG} = 96,600/210,000 = 0.46 \text{ (Fidelity)}$$

assumed

complete portfolio

The entire portfolio including risky and risk-free assets.

The weight of the risky portfolio, P, in the **complete portfolio,** *including* risk-free as well as risky investments, is denoted by y, and so the weight of the money market fund is $1 - y$.

$$y = 210,000/300,000 = 0.7 \text{ (risky assets, portfolio } P\text{)}$$
$$1 - y = 90,000/300,000 = 0.3 \text{ (risk-free assets)}$$

The weights of the individual assets in the *complete* portfolio (C) are:

Vanguard	113,400/300,000	=	0.378
Fidelity	96,600/300,000	=	0.322
Portfolio P	210,000/300,000	=	0.700
Ready Assets F	90,000/300,000	=	0.300
Portfolio C	300,000/300,000	=	1.000

[5] John C. Bogle, *Bogle on Mutual Funds* (Burr Ridge, IL: Irwin Professional Publishing, 1994), p. 235.

Suppose the investor decides to decrease risk by reducing the exposure to the risky portfolio from $y = 0.7$ to $y = 0.56$. The risky portfolio would total only $0.56 \times 300,000 = \$168,000$, requiring the sale of \$42,000 of the original \$210,000 risky holdings, with the proceeds used to purchase more shares in Ready Assets. Total holdings in the risk-free asset will increase to $300,000(1 - 0.56) = \$132,000$ (the original holdings plus the new contribution to the money market fund: $90,000 + 42,000 = \$132,000$).

The key point is that we leave the proportion of each asset in the risky portfolio unchanged. Because the weights of Vanguard and Fidelity in the risky portfolio are 0.54 and 0.46, respectively, we sell $0.54 \times 42,000 = \$22,680$ of Vanguard shares and $0.46 \times 42,000 = \$19,320$ of Fidelity shares. After the sale, the proportions of each fund in the risky portfolio are unchanged.

$$w_V = \frac{113,400 - 22,680}{210,000 - 42,000} = 0.54 \text{ (Vanguard)}$$

$$w_{IG} = \frac{96,600 - 19,320}{210,000 - 42,000} = 0.46 \text{ (Fidelity)}$$

This procedure shows that rather than thinking of our risky holdings as Vanguard and Fidelity separately, we may view our holdings as if they are in a single fund holding Vanguard and Fidelity in fixed proportions. In this sense, we may treat the collection of securities in our risky fund as a single risky asset. As we shift in and out of safe assets, we simply alter our holdings of that risky fund commensurately.

With this simplification, we now can turn to the desirability of reducing risk by changing the risky/risk-free asset mix, that is, reducing risk by decreasing the proportion y. Because we do not alter the weights of each asset within the risky portfolio, the probability distribution of the rate of return on the *risky portfolio* remains unchanged by the asset reallocation. What will change is the probability distribution of the rate of return on the *complete portfolio* of both risky and risk-free assets.

What will be the dollar value of your position in Vanguard and its proportion in your complete portfolio if you decide to hold 50% of your investment budget in Ready Assets?

The Risk-Free Asset

The power to tax and to control the money supply lets the government, and only the government, issue default-free (Treasury) bonds. The default-free guarantee by itself is not sufficient to make the bonds risk-free in real terms, since inflation affects the purchasing power of the proceeds from the bonds. The only risk-free asset in real terms would be a price-indexed government bond. Even then, a default-free, perfectly indexed bond offers a guaranteed real rate to an investor only if the maturity of the bond is identical to the investor's desired holding period.

These qualifications notwithstanding, it is common to view Treasury bills as *the* risk-free asset. Because they are short-term investments, their prices are relatively insensitive to interest rate fluctuations. An investor can lock in a short-term nominal return by buying a bill and holding it to maturity. Any inflation uncertainty over the course of a few weeks, or even months, is negligible compared to the uncertainty of stock market returns.

In practice, most investors treat a broader range of money market instruments as effectively risk-free assets. All the money market instruments are virtually immune to interest rate risk (unexpected fluctuations in the price of a bond due to changes in market interest rates) because of their short maturities, and all are fairly safe in terms of default or credit risk.

Money market mutual funds hold, for the most part, three types of securities: Treasury bills, bank certificates of deposit (CDs), and commercial paper. The instruments differ slightly in their default risk. The yields to maturity on CDs and commercial paper, for identical maturities, are always slightly higher than those of T-bills. A history of this yield spread for 90-day CDs is shown in Figure 2.3 in Chapter 2.

Money market funds have changed their relative holdings of these securities over time, but by and large, T-bills make up only about 15% of their portfolios. Nevertheless, the risk of such blue-chip, short-term investments as CDs and commercial paper is minuscule compared to that of most other assets, such as long-term corporate bonds, common stocks, or real estate. Hence, we treat money market funds as representing the most easily accessible risk-free asset for most investors.

Portfolio Expected Return and Risk

Now that we have specified the risky portfolio and the risk-free asset, we can examine the risk-return combinations that result from various investment allocations between these two assets. Finding the available combinations of risk and return is the "technical" part of asset allocation; it deals only with the opportunities available to investors given the features of the asset markets in which they can invest. In the next section, we address the "personal" part of the problem, the specific individual's choice of the best risk-return combination from the set of feasible combinations, given his or her level of risk aversion.

Since we assume the composition of the optimal risky portfolio (P) already has been determined, the concern here is with the proportion of the investment budget (y) to be allocated to it. The remaining proportion ($1 - y$) is to be invested in the risk-free asset (F).

We denote the *actual* risky rate of return by r_P, the *expected* rate of return on P by $E(r_P)$, and its standard deviation by σ_P. The rate of return on the risk-free asset is denoted as r_f. In the numerical example, we assume $E(r_P) = 15\%$, $\sigma_P = 22\%$, and $r_f = 7\%$. Thus, the risk premium on the risky asset is $E(r_P) - r_f = 8\%$.

Let's start with two extreme cases. If you invest all of your funds in the risky asset, that is, if you choose $y = 1.0$, the expected return on your complete portfolio will be 15% and the standard deviation will be 22%. This combination of risk and return is plotted as point P in Figure 5.5. At the other extreme, you might put all of your funds into the risk-free asset, that is, you choose $y = 0$. In this case, your portfolio would behave just as the risk-free asset, and you would earn a riskless return of 7%. (This choice is plotted as point F in Figure 5.5.)

Now consider more moderate choices. For example, if you allocate equal amounts of your overall or *complete portfolio, C,* to the risky and risk-free assets, that is, if you choose $y = 0.5$, the expected return on the complete portfolio will be an average of the expected return on portfolios F and P. Therefore, $E(r_C) = 0.5 \times 7\% + 0.5 \times 15\% = 11\%$. The risk premium of the complete portfolio is therefore $11\% - 7\% = 4\%$, which is half of the risk premium of P. The standard deviation of the portfolio also is one-half of P's, that is, 11%. When you reduce

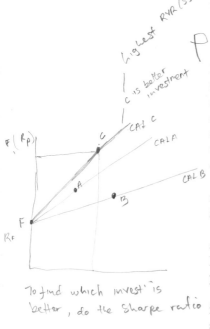

FIGURE 5.5

The investment opportunity set with a risky asset and a risk-free asset

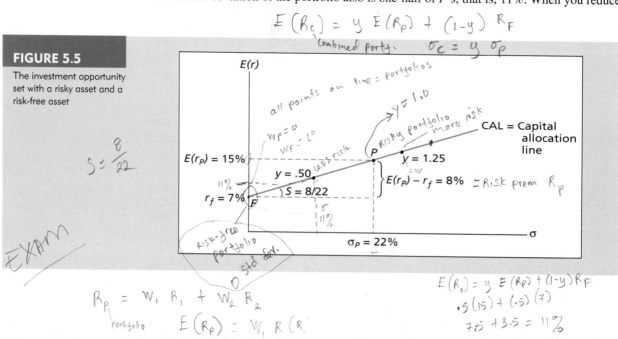

the fraction of the complete portfolio allocated to the risky asset by half, you reduce both the risk and risk premium by half.

To generalize, the risk premium of the complete portfolio, C, will equal the risk premium of the risky asset times the fraction of the portfolio invested in the risky asset.

$$E(r_C) - r_f = y[E(r_P) - r_f]$$ (5.17)

The standard deviation of the complete portfolio will equal the standard deviation of the risky asset times the fraction of the portfolio invested in the risky asset.

$$\sigma_C = y\sigma_P$$ (5.18)

In sum, both the risk premium and the standard deviation of the complete portfolio increase in proportion to the investment in the risky portfolio. Therefore, the points that describe the risk and return of the complete portfolio for various asset allocations, that is, for various choices of y, all plot on the straight line connecting F and P, as shown in Figure 5.5, with an intercept of r_f and slope (rise/run) of

$$S = \frac{E(r_P) - r_f}{\sigma_P} = \frac{15 - 7}{22} = 0.36$$ (5.19)

CONCEPT check 5.7

What are the expected return, risk premium, standard deviation, and ratio of risk premium to standard deviation for a complete portfolio with $y = 0.75$?

The Capital Allocation Line

The line plotted in Figure 5.5 depicts the risk-return combinations available by varying asset allocation, that is, by choosing different values of y. For this reason, it is called the **capital allocation line**, or **CAL**. The slope, S, of the CAL equals the increase in expected return that an investor can obtain per unit of additional standard deviation. In other words, it shows extra return per extra risk. For this reason, as we noted above, the slope also is called the reward-to-volatility ratio, or Sharpe measure, after William Sharpe who first suggested its use.

capital allocation line
Plot of risk-return combinations available by varying portfolio allocation between a risk-free asset and a risky portfolio.

Notice that the reward-to-volatility ratio is the same for risky portfolio P and the complete portfolio that was formed by mixing P and the risk-free asset in equal proportions.

	Expected Return	Risk Premium	Standard Deviation	Reward-to-Volatility Ratio
Portfolio P:	15%	8%	22%	$\frac{8}{22} = 0.36$
Portfolio C:	11%	4%	11%	$\frac{4}{11} = 0.36$

In fact, the reward-to-volatility ratio is the same for all complete portfolios that plot on the capital allocation line. While the risk-return combinations differ, the *ratio* of reward to risk is constant.

What about points on the line to the right of portfolio P in the investment opportunity set? If investors can borrow at the (risk-free) rate of $r_f = 7\%$, they can construct complete portfolios that plot on the CAL to the right of P. They simply choose values of y greater than 1.0.

Suppose the investment budget is $300,000, and our investor borrows an additional $120,000, investing the $420,000 in the risky asset. This is a levered position in the risky asset, which is financed in part by borrowing. In that case

EXAMPLE   5.7

Levered Complete Portfolios

$$y = \frac{420,000}{300,000} = 1.4$$

and $1 - y = 1 - 1.4 = -0.4$, reflecting a short position in the risk-free asset, or a borrowing position. Rather than lending at a 7% interest rate, the investor borrows at 7%. The portfolio rate of return is

$$E(r_C) = 7 + (1.4 \times 8) = 18.2$$

Another way to find this portfolio rate of return is as follows. Your income statement will show that you expect to earn $63,000 (15% of $420,000) and pay $8,400 (7% of $120,000) in interest on the loan. Simple subtraction yields an expected profit of $54,600, which is 18.2% of your investment budget of $300,000.

Your portfolio still exhibits the same reward-to-volatility ratio:

$$\sigma_C = 1.4 \times 22 = 30.8$$
$$S = \frac{E(r_C) - r_f}{\sigma_C} = \frac{11.2}{30.8} = 0.36$$

As you might have expected, the levered portfolio has both a higher expected return and a higher standard deviation than an unlevered position in the risky asset.

Risk Tolerance and Asset Allocation

We have developed the CAL, the graph of all feasible risk-return combinations available from allocating the complete portfolio between a risky portfolio and a risk-free asset. The investor confronting the CAL now must choose one optimal combination from the set of feasible choices. This choice entails a trade-off between risk and return. Individual investors with different levels of risk aversion, given an identical capital allocation line, will choose different positions in the risky asset. Specifically, the more risk-averse investors will choose to hold *less* of the risky asset and *more* of the risk-free asset.

Graphically, more risk-averse investors will choose portfolios near point *F* on the capital allocation line plotted in Figure 5.5. More risk-tolerant investors will choose points closer to *P*, with higher expected return and higher risk. The most risk-tolerant investors will choose portfolios to the right of point *P*. These levered portfolios provide even higher expected returns, but even greater risk.

The nearby box contains a further discussion of this risk-return trade-off, which sometimes is characterized as a decision to "eat well," versus "sleep well." You will eat well if you earn a high expected rate of return on your portfolio. However, this requires that you accept a large risk premium and, therefore, a large amount of risk. Unfortunately, this risk may make it difficult to sleep well.

The investor's asset allocation choice also will depend on the trade-off between risk and return. If the reward-to-volatility ratio increases, then investors might well decide to take on riskier positions. For example, suppose an investor reevaluates the probability distribution of the risky portfolio and now perceives a greater expected return without an accompanying increase in the standard deviation. This amounts to an increase in the reward-to-volatility ratio or, equivalently, an increase in the slope of the CAL. As a result, this investor will choose a higher *y*, that is, a greater position in the risky portfolio.

One role of a professional financial adviser is to present investment opportunity alternatives to clients, obtain an assessment of the client's risk tolerance, and help determine the appropriate complete portfolio.[6]

---

[6] "Risk tolerance" is simply the flip side of "risk aversion." Either term is a reasonable way to describe attitudes toward risk. We generally find it easier to talk about risk *aversion*, but practitioners often use the term risk *tolerance*.

THE RIGHT MIX: MAKE MONEY VERSUS SLEEP SOUNDLY

Plunged into doubt?

Amid the recent market turmoil, maybe you are wondering whether you really have the right mix of investments. Here are a few thoughts to keep in mind:

TAKING STOCK

If you are a bond investor who is petrified of stocks, the wild price swings of the past few weeks have probably confirmed all of your worst suspicions. But the truth is, adding stocks to your bond portfolio could bolster your returns, without boosting your portfolio's overall gyrations.

How can that be? While stocks and bonds often move up and down in tandem, this isn't always the case, and sometimes stocks rise when bonds are tumbling.

Indeed, Chicago researchers Ibbotson Associates figure a portfolio that's 100% in longer-term government bonds has the same risk profile as a mix that includes 83% in longer-term government bonds and 17% in the blue-chip stocks that constitute Standard & Poor's 500 stock index.

The bottom line? Everybody should own some stocks. Even cowards.

PADDING THE MATTRESS

On the other hand, maybe you're a committed stock market investor, but you would like to add a calming influence to your portfolio. What's your best bet?

When investors look to mellow their stock portfolios, they usually turn to bonds. Indeed, the traditional balanced portfolio, which typically includes 60% stocks and 40% bonds, remains a firm favorite with many investment experts.

A balanced portfolio isn't a bad bet. But if you want to calm your stock portfolio, I would skip bonds and instead add cash investments such as Treasury bills and money market funds. Ibbotson calculates that, over the past 25 years, a mix of 75% stocks and 25% Treasury bills would have performed about as well as a mix of 60% stocks and 40% longer-term government bonds, and with a similar level of portfolio price gyrations.

Moreover, the stock–cash mix offers more certainty, because you know that even if your stocks fall in value, your cash never will. By contrast, both the stocks and bonds in a balanced portfolio can get hammered at the same time.

PATIENCE HAS ITS REWARDS, SOMETIMES

Stocks are capable of generating miserable short-run results. During the past 50 years, the worst five-calendar-year stretch for stocks left investors with an annualized loss of 2.4%.

But while any investment can disappoint in the short run, stocks do at least sparkle over the long haul. As a long-term investor, your goal is to fend off the dual threats of inflation and taxes and make your money grow. And on that score, stocks have been supreme.

5.6 PASSIVE STRATEGIES AND THE CAPITAL MARKET LINE

The capital allocation line shows the risk-return trade-offs available by mixing risk-free assets with the investor's risky portfolio. Investors can choose the assets included in the risky portfolio using either passive or active strategies. A **passive strategy** is based on the premise that securities are fairly priced and it avoids the costs involved in undertaking security analysis. Such a strategy might at first blush appear to be naive. However, we will see in Chapter 8 that intense competition among professional money managers might indeed force security prices to levels at which further security analysis is unlikely to turn up significant profit opportunities. Passive investment strategies may make sense for many investors.

passive strategy

Investment policy that avoids security analysis.

To avoid the costs of acquiring information on any individual stock or group of stocks, we may follow a "neutral" diversification approach. A natural strategy is to select a diversified portfolio of common stocks that mirrors the corporate sector of the broad economy. This results in a value-weighted portfolio, which, for example, invests a proportion in GM stock that equals the ratio of GM's market value to the market value of all listed stocks.

Such strategies are called *indexing*. The investor chooses a portfolio with all the stocks in a broad market index such as the Standard & Poor's 500 index. The rate of return on the

EX POST

TABLE 5.5		Excess Return (%)		
		Average	**SD**	**Sharpe Ratio**
Average excess rate of return, standard deviations and the reward-to-volatility ratio of large common stocks over one-month bills over 1926–2006 and various subperiods	1926–1946	8.36	27.98	0.30
	1947–1966	12.72	18.05	0.70
	1967–1986	4.14	17.44	0.24
	1987–2006	8.47	16.22	0.52
	1926–2006	8.42	20.42	0.41

Source: Data in Table 5.3.

capital market line

The capital allocation line using the market index portfolio as the risky asset.

portfolio then replicates the return on the index. Indexing has become an extremely popular strategy for passive investors. We call the capital allocation line provided by one-month T-bills and a broad index of common stocks the **capital market line** (CML). That is, a passive strategy based on stocks and bills generates an investment opportunity set that is represented by the CML.

EXP OST _EX ANTE_

Historical Evidence on the Capital Market Line

Can we use past data to help forecast the risk-return trade-off offered by the CML? The notion that one can use historical returns to forecast the future seems straightforward but actually is somewhat problematic. On one hand, you wish to use all available data to obtain a large sample. But when using long time series, old data may no longer be representative of future circumstances. Another reason for weeding out subperiods is that some past events simply may be too improbable to be given equal weight with results from other periods. Do the data we have pose this problem?

Table 5.5 breaks the 81-year period 1926–2006 into four subperiods and shows the risk premium, standard deviation, and reward-to-volatility ratio for large U.S. stocks in each subperiod. That ratio is the slope of the CML based on the subperiod data. Indeed, the differences across subperiods are quite striking.

The most plausible explanation for the variation in subperiod returns is based on the observation that the standard deviation of returns is quite large in all subperiods. If we take the 81-year standard deviation of 20.4% as representative and assume that returns in one year are nearly uncorrelated with those in other years (the evidence suggests that any correlation across years is small), then the standard deviation of our estimate of the mean return in any of our 20-year subperiods will be $20.4/\sqrt{20} = 4.6\%$, which is fairly large. This means that in approximately one out of three cases, a 20-year average will deviate by 4.6% or more from the true mean. Applying this insight to the data in Table 5.5 tells us that we cannot reject with any confidence the possibility that the true mean is similar in all subperiods! In other words, the "noise" in the data is so large that we simply cannot make reliable inferences from average returns in any subperiod. The differences in returns across subperiods may simply reflect statistical variation, and we have to reconcile ourselves to the fact that the market return and the reward-to-volatility ratio for passive (as well as active!) strategies is simply very hard to predict.

The instability of average excess return on stocks over the 20-year subperiods in Table 5.5 also calls into question the precision of the 81-year average excess return (8.4%) as an estimate of the risk premium on stocks looking into the future. In fact, there has been considerable recent debate among financial economists about the "true" equity risk premium, with an emerging consensus that the historical average may be an unrealistically high estimate of the future risk premium. This argument is based on several factors: the use of longer time periods in which equity returns are examined; a broad range of countries rather than just the U.S. in which excess returns are computed (Dimson, Marsh, and Staunton, 2001); direct surveys of financial executives about their expectations for stock market returns (Graham and Harvey,

TRIUMPH OF THE OPTIMISTS

As a whole, the last 7 decades have been very kind to U.S. equity investors. Stock investments have outperformed investments in safe Treasury bills by more than 8% per year. The real rate of return averaged more than 9%, implying an expected doubling of the real value of the investment portfolio about every 8 years!

Is this experience representative? A book by three professors at the London Business School, Elroy Dimson, Paul Marsh, and Mike Staunton, extends the U.S. evidence to other countries and to longer time periods. Their conclusion is given in the book's title, *Triumph of the Optimists*[*]: in every country in their study (which included markets in North America, Europe, Asia, and Africa), the investment optimists—those who bet on the economy by investing in stocks rather than bonds or bills—were vindicated. Over the long haul, stocks beat bonds everywhere.

On the other hand, the equity risk premium is probably not as large as the post-1926 evidence from Table 5.3 would seem to indicate. First, results from the first 25 years of the last century (which included the first World War) were less favorable to stocks. Second, U.S. returns have been better than that of most other countries, and so a more representative value for the historical risk premium may be lower than the U.S. experience. Finally, the sample that is amenable to historical analysis suffers from a self-selection problem. Only those markets that have survived to be studied can be included in the analysis. This leaves out countries such as Russia or China, whose markets were shut down during communist rule, and whose results if included would surely bring down the average historical performance of equity investments. Nevertheless, there is powerful evidence of a risk premium that shows its force everywhere the authors looked.

SOURCE: *Elroy Dimson, Paul Marsh, Mike Staunton, *Triumph of the Optimists: 101 Years of Global Investment Returns* (Princeton, NJ: Princeton University Press, 2002). Reprinted by permission of Princeton University Press.

2001); and inferences from stock market data about investor expectations (Jagannathan, McGrattan, and Scherbina, 2000; Fama and French, 2002). The nearby box discusses some of this evidence.

Costs and Benefits of Passive Investing

How reasonable is it for an investor to pursue a passive strategy? We cannot answer such a question definitively without comparing passive strategy results to the costs and benefits accruing to an active portfolio strategy. Some issues are worth considering, however.

First, the alternative active strategy entails costs. Whether you choose to invest your own valuable time to acquire the information needed to generate an optimal active portfolio of risky assets or whether you delegate the task to a professional who will charge a fee, constructing an active portfolio is more expensive than constructing a passive one. The passive portfolio requires only small commissions on purchases of U.S. T-bills (or zero commissions if you purchase bills directly from the government) and management fees to a mutual fund company that offers a market index fund to the public. An index fund has the lowest operating expenses of all mutual stock funds because it requires the least effort.

A second argument supporting a passive strategy is the free-rider benefit. If you assume there are many active, knowledgeable investors who quickly bid up prices of undervalued assets and offer down overvalued assets (by selling), you have to conclude that most of the time most assets will be fairly priced. Therefore, a well-diversified portfolio of common stock will be a reasonably fair buy, and the passive strategy may not be inferior to that of the average active investor. We will expand on this insight and provide a more comprehensive analysis of the relative success of passive strategies in Chapter 8.

To summarize, a passive strategy involves investment in two passive portfolios: virtually risk-free short-term T-bills (or a money market fund) and a fund of common stocks that mimics a broad market index. Recall that the capital allocation line representing such a strategy is called the *capital market line*. Using Table 5.5, we see that using 1926 to 2006 data, the passive risky portfolio has offered an average excess return of 8.4% with a standard deviation of 20.4%, resulting in a reward-to-volatility ratio of 0.41.

SUMMARY

- Investors face a trade-off between risk and expected return. Historical data confirm our intuition that assets with low degrees of risk provide lower returns on average than do those of higher risk.

- Shifting funds from the risky portfolio to the risk-free asset is the simplest way to reduce risk. Another method involves diversification of the risky portfolio. We take up diversification in later chapters.

- U.S. T-bills provide a perfectly risk-free asset in nominal terms only. Nevertheless, the standard deviation of real rates on short-term T-bills is small compared to that of assets such as long-term bonds and common stocks, so for the purpose of our analysis, we consider T-bills the risk-free asset. Besides T-bills, money market funds hold short-term, safe obligations such as commercial paper and CDs. These entail some default risk but relatively little compared to most other risky assets. For convenience, we often refer to money market funds as risk-free assets.

- A risky investment portfolio (referred to here as the risky asset) can be characterized by its reward-to-volatility ratio. This ratio is the slope of the capital allocation line (CAL), the line connecting the risk-free asset to the risky asset. All combinations of the risky and risk-free asset lie on this line. Investors would prefer a steeper sloping CAL, because that means higher expected returns for any level of risk.

- An investor's preferred choice among the portfolios on the capital allocation line will depend on risk aversion. Risk-averse investors will weight their complete portfolios more heavily toward Treasury bills. Risk-tolerant investors will hold higher proportions of their complete portfolios in the risky asset.

- The capital market line is the capital allocation line that results from using a passive investment strategy that treats a market index portfolio, such as the Standard & Poor's 500, as the risky asset. Passive strategies are low-cost ways of obtaining well-diversified portfolios with performance that will reflect that of the broad stock market.

KEY TERMS

arithmetic average, 118
asset allocation, 133
capital allocation line, 137
capital market line, 140
complete portfolio, 134
dollar-weighted average
   return, 119
excess return, 123
expected return, 121

geometric average, 118
holding-period return, 117
inflation rate, 131
mean-variance analysis, 124
nominal interest rate, 132
passive strategy, 139
probability distribution, 121
real interest rate, 132
risk aversion, 123

risk-free rate, 123
risk premium, 123
Sharpe (or reward-to-
   volatility) measure, 124
scenario analysis, 121
standard deviation, 122
variance, 121

PROBLEM SETS

 Select problems are available in McGraw-Hill's Homework Manager®. Please see the packaging options section of the preface for more information.

CFA®
PROBLEMS

1. A portfolio of nondividend-paying stocks earned a geometric mean return of 5.0% between January 1, 2001, and December 31, 2007. The arithmetic mean return for the same period was 6.0%. If the market value of the portfolio at the beginning of 2001 was $100,000, what was the market value of the portfolio at the end of 2007?

CFA®
PROBLEMS

2. Which of the following statements about the standard deviation is/are *true*? A standard deviation:
    i. Is the square root of the variance.
    ii. Is denominated in the same units as the original data.
    iii. Can be a positive or a negative number.

3. Which of the following statements reflects the importance of the asset allocation decision to the investment process? The asset allocation decision:
   a. Helps the investor decide on realistic investment goals.
   b. Identifies the specific securities to include in a portfolio.
   c. Determines most of the portfolio's returns and volatility over time.
   d. Creates a standard by which to establish an appropriate investment time horizon.

4. Look at Table 5.2 in the text. Suppose you now revise your expectations regarding the stock market as follows:

State of the Economy	Probability	HPR
Boom	0.3	44%
Normal growth	0.4	14
Recession	0.3	−16

   Use Equations 5.6–5.8 to compute the mean and standard deviation of the HPR on stocks. Compare your revised parameters with the ones in the text.

5. The stock of Business Adventures sells for $40 a share. Its likely dividend payout and end-of-year price depend on the state of the economy by the end of the year as follows:

	Dividend	Stock Price
Boom	$2.00	$50
Normal economy	1.00	43
Recession	.50	34

   a. Calculate the expected holding-period return and standard deviation of the holding-period return. All three scenarios are equally likely.
   b. Calculate the expected return and standard deviation of a portfolio invested half in Business Adventures and half in Treasury bills. The return on bills is 4%.

Use the following data in answering Questions 6, 7, and 8.

Utility Formula Data		
Investment	Expected Return E(r)	Standard Deviation σ
1	.12	.30
2	.15	.50
3	.21	.16
4	.24	.21

$$U = E(r) - \tfrac{1}{2} A\sigma^2 \qquad \text{where } A = 4$$

6. Based on the utility formula above, which investment would you select if you were risk averse with $A = 4$?

7. Based on the utility formula above, which investment would you select if you were risk neutral?

8. The variable (A) in the utility formula represents the:
   a. investor's return requirement.
   b. investor's aversion to risk.
   c. certainty equivalent rate of the portfolio.
   d. preference for one unit of return per four units of risk.

Use the following scenario analysis for Stocks X and Y to answer Questions 9 through 11.

	Bear Market	Normal Market	Bull Market
Probability	0.2	0.5	0.3
Stock X	−20%	18%	50%
Stock Y	−15%	20%	10%

9. What are the expected returns for Stocks X and Y?

10. What are the standard deviations of returns on Stocks X and Y?

11. Assume that of your $10,000 portfolio, you invest $9,000 in Stock X and $1,000 in Stock Y. What is the expected return on your portfolio?

12. Probabilities for three states of the economy and probabilities for the returns on a particular stock in each state are shown in the table below.

State of Economy	Probability of Economic State	Stock Performance	Probability of Stock Performance in Given Economic State
Good	.3	Good	.6
		Neutral	.3
		Poor	.1
Neutral	.5	Good	.4
		Neutral	.3
		Poor	.3
Poor	.2	Good	.2
		Neutral	.3
		Poor	.5

What is the probability that the economy will be neutral *and* the stock will experience poor performance?

13. An analyst estimates that a stock has the following probabilities of return depending on the state of the economy. What is the expected return of the stock?

State of Economy	Probability	Return
Good	.1	15%
Normal	.6	13
Poor	.3	7

14. XYZ stock price and dividend history are as follows:

Year	Beginning-of-Year Price	Dividend Paid at Year-End
2005	$100	$4
2006	$110	$4
2007	$ 90	$4
2008	$ 95	$4

An investor buys three shares of XYZ at the beginning of 2005, buys another two shares at the beginning of 2006, sells one share at the beginning of 2007, and sells all four remaining shares at the beginning of 2008.

a. What are the arithmetic and geometric average time-weighted rates of return for the investor?

b. What is the dollar-weighted rate of return? *Hint:* Carefully prepare a chart of cash flows for the *four* dates corresponding to the turns of the year for January 1, 2005, to January 1, 2008. If your calculator cannot calculate internal rate of return, you will have to use a spreadsheet or trial and error.

15. a. Suppose you forecast that the standard deviation of the market return will be 20% in the coming year. If the measure of risk aversion in Equation 5.9 is $A = 4$, what would be a reasonable guess for the expected market risk premium?

b. What value of A is consistent with a risk premium of 9%?

c. What will happen to the risk premium if investors become more risk tolerant?

16. Using the historical risk premiums as your guide, what is your estimate of the expected annual HPR on the S&P 500 stock portfolio if the current risk-free interest rate is 5%?

17. What has been the historical average *real* rate of return on stocks, Treasury bonds, and Treasury bills?

18. Consider a risky portfolio. The end-of-year cash flow derived from the portfolio will be either $50,000 or $150,000, with equal probabilities of 0.5. The alternative riskless investment in T-bills pays 5%.

    a. If you require a risk premium of 10%, how much will you be willing to pay for the portfolio?

    b. Suppose the portfolio can be purchased for the amount you found in (a). What will the expected rate of return on the portfolio be?

    c. Now suppose you require a risk premium of 15%. What is the price you will be willing to pay now?

    d. Comparing your answers to (a) and (c), what do you conclude about the relationship between the required risk premium on a portfolio and the price at which the portfolio will sell?

For Problems 19–23, assume that you manage a risky portfolio with an expected rate of return of 17% and a standard deviation of 27%. The T-bill rate is 7%.

19. a. Your client chooses to invest 70% of a portfolio in your fund and 30% in a T-bill money market fund. What is the expected return and standard deviation of your client's portfolio?

    b. Suppose your risky portfolio includes the following investments in the given proportions:

Stock A	27%
Stock B	33%
Stock C	40%

    What are the investment proportions of your client's overall portfolio, including the position in T-bills?

    c. What is the reward-to-volatility ratio (S) of your risky portfolio and your client's overall portfolio?

    d. Draw the CAL of your portfolio on an expected return/standard deviation diagram. What is the slope of the CAL? Show the position of your client on your fund's CAL.

20. Suppose the same client in Problem 19 decides to invest in your risky portfolio a proportion (y) of his total investment budget so that his overall portfolio will have an expected rate of return of 15%.

    a. What is the proportion y?

    b. What are your client's investment proportions in your three stocks and the T-bill fund?

    c. What is the standard deviation of the rate of return on your client's portfolio?

21. Suppose the same client in Problem 19 prefers to invest in your portfolio a proportion (y) that maximizes the expected return on the overall portfolio subject to the constraint that the overall portfolio's standard deviation will not exceed 20%.

    a. What is the investment proportion, y?

    b. What is the expected rate of return on the overall portfolio?

22. You estimate that a passive portfolio invested to mimic the S&P 500 stock index yields an expected rate of return of 13% with a standard deviation of 25%. Draw the CML and your fund's CAL on an expected return/standard deviation diagram.

    a. What is the slope of the CML?

    b. Characterize in one short paragraph the advantage of your fund over the passive fund.

23. Your client (see Problem 19) wonders whether to switch the 70% that is invested in your fund to the passive portfolio.

    a. Explain to your client the disadvantage of the switch.

    b. Show your client the maximum fee you could charge (as a percent of the investment in your fund deducted at the end of the year) that would still leave him at least as well off investing in your fund as in the passive one. (*Hint:* The fee will lower the slope of your client's CAL by reducing the expected return net of the fee.)

24. What do you think would happen to the expected return on stocks if investors perceived an increase in the volatility of stocks?

25. You manage an equity fund with an expected risk premium of 10% and an expected standard deviation of 14%. The rate on Treasury bills is 6%. Your client chooses to invest $60,000 of her portfolio in your equity fund and $40,000 in a T-bill money market fund. What is the expected return and standard deviation of return on your client's portfolio?

26. What is the reward-to-volatility ratio for the *equity fund* in Problem 25?

For Problems 27–29, download the Spreadsheet of Table 5.3: Rates of return, 1926–2006, from www.mhhe.com/bkm.

27. Calculate the same subperiod means and standard deviations for small stocks as Table 5.5 of the text provides for large stocks.

    a. Have small stocks provided better reward-to-volatility ratios than large stocks?

    b. Do small stocks show a similar declining trend in standard deviation as Table 5.5 documents for large stocks?

28. Convert the nominal returns on both large and small stocks to real rates. Reproduce Table 5.5 using real rates instead of excess returns. Compare the results to those of Table 5.5.

29. Repeat Problem 28 for small stocks and compare with the results for nominal rates.

**Please visit us at
www.mhhe.com/bkm**

**Please visit us at
www.mhhe.com/bkm**

**Please visit us at
www.mhhe.com/bkm**

STANDARD &POOR'S

Use data from the Standard & Poor's Market Insight Database at www.mhhe.com/edumarketinsight to answer the following questions.

1. Select the Company tab and enter the ticker symbol ADBE. Click on the Stock Report link in the S&P Stock Reports section to view the report for Adobe Systems.

2. What is the latest price reported in the "Key Stock Statistics" section? What is the 12-month target price? Calculate the expected holding period return based on these prices.

3. In the "Key Stock Statistics" section, find the answer to the question "How much would I have today if I invested $10,000 in ADBE five years ago?" Using this information, calculate the five-year Holding Period Return (HPR) on Adobe's stock

4. What is Adobe's volatility rating (high, average, low)? Look for this in the Quantitative Evaluations section of the report.

5. What is S&P's fair value calculation for the price of Adobe stock today? By how much, in dollars and as a percent, does the stock's S&P fair value differ from its current price?

WEB *master*

Inflation and Interest Rates

Calculating the real rate of return is an important part of evaluating an investment's performance. To do this, you need to know the nominal yield on your investment and the rate of inflation during the corresponding period. To estimate the expected real rate of return before you make an investment, you can use the promised yield and the expected inflation rate.

1. Go to **www.bankrate.com** and click on the CDs and Investments tab. Find today's nominal 1-year CD rate in the table.

2. Use the St. Louis Federal Reserve's Web site at **research.stlouisfed.org/fred2** as a source for data about expected inflation. Search for "inflation," then locate the University of Michigan Inflation Expectation data series (MICH). Click on the View Data link and find the latest available data point. What is the expected inflation rate for the next year?

3. Based on your answers to parts 1 and 2, calculate the expected real rate of return on a 1-year CD investment.

5.1. *a.* The arithmetic average is $(2 + 8 - 4)/3 = 2\%$ per month.

   b. The time-weighted (geometric) average is
   $[(1 + .02) \times (1 + .08) \times (1 - .04)]^{1/3} - 1 = .0188 = 1.88\%$ per month.

   c. We compute the dollar-weighted average (IRR) from the cash flow sequence (in $ millions):

	Month		
	1	**2**	**3**
Assets under management at beginning of month	10.0	13.2	19.256
Investment profits during month (HPR × Assets)	0.2	1.056	(0.77)
Net inflows during month	3.0	5.0	0.0
Assets under management at end of month	13.2	19.256	18.486

	Time			
	0	**1**	**2**	**3**
Net cash flow*	−10	−3.0	−5.0	+18.486

   *Time 0 is today. Time 1 is the end of the first month. Time 3 is the end of the third month, when net cash flow equals the ending value (potential liquidation value) of the portfolio.

   The IRR of the sequence of net cash flows is 1.17% per month.

   The dollar-weighted average is less than the time-weighted average because the negative return was realized when the fund had the most money under management.

5.2. Computing the HPR for each scenario, we convert the price and dividend data to rate of return data:

Business Conditions	Probability	HPR
High growth	0.35	$67.66\% = (4.40 + 35 - 23.50)/23.50$
Normal growth	0.30	$31.91\% = (4.00 + 27 - 23.50)/23.50$
No growth	0.35	$-19.15\% = (4.00 + 15 - 23.50)/23.50$

   Using Equations 5.6 and 5.7 we obtain

   $E(r) = 0.35 \times 67.66 + 0.30 \times 31.91 + 0.35 \times (-19.15) = 26.55\%$

   $\sigma^2 = 0.35 \times (67.66 - 26.55)^2 + 0.30 \times (31.91 - 26.55)^2 + 0.35 \times (-19.15 - 26.55)^2 = 1331$

   and from Equation 5.8,

   $$\sigma = \sqrt{1331} = 36.5\%$$

5.3. *a.* If the average investor chooses the S&P 500 portfolio, then the implied degree of risk aversion is given by Equation 5.10:

   $$A = \frac{.10 - .05}{\frac{1}{2} \times .18^2} = 3.09$$

   b.
   $$S = \frac{10 - 5}{18} = 0.28$$

5.4. The mean excess return for the period 1926–1934 is 3.56% (below the historical average), and the standard deviation (using $n - 1$ degrees of freedom) is 32.55% (above the historical average). These results reflect the severe downturn of the great crash and the unusually high volatility of stock returns in this period.

5.5. *a.* Solving
   $$1 + R = (1 + r)(1 + i) = (1.03)(1.08) = 1.1124$$
   $$R = 11.24\%$$

   b. Solving
   $$1 + R = (1.03)(1.10) = 1.133$$
   $$R = 13.3\%$$

5.6. Holding 50% of your invested capital in Ready Assets means your investment proportion in the risky portfolio is reduced from 70% to 50%.

Your risky portfolio is constructed to invest 54% in Vanguard and 46% in Fidelity. Thus, the proportion of Vanguard in your overall portfolio is $0.5 \times 54\% = 27\%$, and the dollar value of your position in Vanguard is $300,000 \times 0.27 = \$81,000$.

5.7.

$$E(r) = 7 + 0.75 \times 8\% = 13\%$$
$$\sigma = 0.75 \times 22\% = 16.5\%$$
$$\text{Risk premium} = 13 - 7 = 6\%$$
$$\frac{\text{Risk premium}}{\text{Standard deviation}} = \frac{13 - 7}{16.5} = .36$$

Efficient Diversification

 Show how covariance and correlation affect the power of diversification to reduce portfolio risk.

 Construct efficient portfolios.

 Calculate the composition of the optimal risky portfolio.

Use factor models to analyze the risk characteristics of securities and portfolios.

I n this chapter we describe how investors can construct the best possible risky portfolio. The key concept is efficient diversification.

The formal notion of diversification is age-old. The adage "don't put all your eggs in one basket" obviously predates economic theory. However, a rigorous model showing how to make the most of the power of diversification was not devised until 1952, a feat for which Harry Markowitz eventually won the Nobel Prize in economics. This chapter is largely developed from his work, as well as from later insights that built on his work.

We start with a bird's-eye view of how diversification reduces the variability of portfolio returns. We then turn to the construction of optimal risky portfolios. We follow a top-down approach, starting with asset allocation across a small set of broad asset classes, such as stocks, bonds, and money market securities. Then we show how the principles of optimal asset allocation can easily be generalized to solve the problem of security selection among many risky assets. We discuss the efficient set of risky portfolios and show how it leads us to the best attainable capital allocation. Finally, we show how factor models of security

(continued)

returns can simplify the search for efficient portfolios and the interpretation of the risk characteristics of individual securities.

Related Web sites for this chapter are available at www.mhhe.com/bkm.

The last section examines the common fallacy that long-term investment horizons mitigate the impact of asset risk. We argue that the common belief in "time diversification" is in fact an illusion and is not real diversification.

6.1 DIVERSIFICATION AND PORTFOLIO RISK

Suppose you have in your risky portfolio only one stock, say, Dell Computer Corporation. What are the sources of risk affecting this "portfolio"?

We can identify two broad sources of uncertainty. The first is the risk that has to do with general economic conditions, such as the business cycle, the inflation rate, interest rates, exchange rates, and so forth. None of these macroeconomic factors can be predicted with certainty, and all affect the rate of return Dell stock eventually will provide. Then you must add to these macro factors firm-specific influences, such as Dell's success in research and development, its management style and philosophy, and so on. Firm-specific factors are those that affect Dell without noticeably affecting other firms.

Now consider a naive diversification strategy, adding another security to the risky portfolio. If you invest half of your risky portfolio in ExxonMobil, leaving the other half in Dell, what happens to portfolio risk? Because the firm-specific influences on the two stocks differ (statistically speaking, the influences are independent), this strategy should reduce portfolio risk. For example, when oil prices fall, hurting ExxonMobil, computer prices might rise, helping Dell. The two effects are offsetting, which stabilizes portfolio return.

But why stop at only two stocks? Diversifying into many more securities continues to reduce exposure to firm-specific factors, so portfolio volatility should continue to fall. Ultimately, however, even with a large number of risky securities in a portfolio, there is no way to avoid all risk. To the extent that virtually all securities are affected by common (risky) macroeconomic factors, we cannot eliminate our exposure to general economic risk, no matter how many stocks we hold.

Figure 6.1 illustrates these concepts. When all risk is firm-specific, as in Figure 6.1A, diversification can reduce risk to low levels. With all risk sources independent, and with investment spread across many securities, exposure to any particular source of risk is negligible. This is just an application of the law of averages. The reduction of risk to very low levels because of independent risk sources is sometimes called the *insurance principle.*

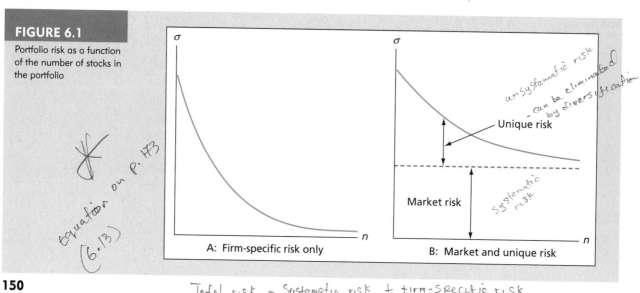

FIGURE 6.1

Portfolio risk as a function of the number of stocks in the portfolio

A: Firm-specific risk only

B: Market and unique risk

equation on p. 173 (6.13)

unsystematic risk - can be eliminated by diversification

systematic risk

$$\text{Total risk} = \text{Systematic risk} + \text{firm-specific risk}$$
$$= \beta_i^2 \sigma_m^2 + \sigma^2(e_i)$$

On the MARKET FRONT

DANGERS OF NOT DIVERSIFYING HIT INVESTORS

Mutual-fund firms and financial planners have droned on about the topic for years. But suddenly, it's at the epicenter of lawsuits, congressional hearings and presidential reform proposals.

Diversification—that most basic of investing principles—has returned with a vengeance. During the late 1990s, many people scoffed at being diversified, because the idea of investing in a mix of stocks, bonds and other financial assets meant missing out on some of the soaring gains of tech stocks.

But with the collapse of the tech bubble and then the fall of Enron Corp. wiping out the 401(k) holdings of many current and retired Enron employees, the dangers of overloading a portfolio with one stock—or even with a group of similar stocks—hit home for many investors.

While not immune from losses, mutual funds tend to weather storms better, because they spread their bets over dozens or hundreds of companies. "Most people think their company is safer than a stock mutual fund, when the data show that the opposite is true," says John Rekenthaler, president of Morningstar's online-advice unit.

But in picking an investing alternative to buying your employer's stock, some choices are more useful than others. For example, investors should take into account the type of company they work for when diversifying. Workers at small technology companies—the type of stock often held by growth funds—might find better diversification with a fund focusing on large undervalued companies. Conversely, an auto-company worker might want to put more money in funds that specialize in smaller companies that are less tied to economic cycles.

SOURCE: Abridged from Aaron Luccheth and Theo Francis, "Dangers of Not Diversifying Hit Investors," *The Wall Street Journal*, February 15, 2002.

When common sources of risk affect all firms, however, even extensive diversification cannot eliminate risk. In Figure 6.1B, portfolio standard deviation falls as the number of securities increases, but it is not reduced to zero. The risk that remains even after diversification is called **market risk**, risk that is attributable to marketwide risk sources. Other names are **systematic risk** or **nondiversifiable risk.** The risk that *can* be eliminated by diversification is called **unique risk, firm-specific risk, nonsystematic risk,** or **diversifiable risk.**

This analysis is borne out by empirical studies. Figure 6.2 shows the effect of portfolio diversification, using data on NYSE stocks. The figure shows the average standard deviations of equally weighted portfolios constructed by selecting stocks at random as a function of the number of stocks in the portfolio. On average, portfolio risk does fall with diversification, but the power of diversification to reduce risk is limited by common sources of risk. The nearby box "Dangers of Not Diversifying Hit Investors" highlights the dangers of neglecting diversification and points out that such neglect is widespread.

In light of this discussion, it is worth pointing out that general macroeconomic conditions in the U.S. do not move in lockstep with those in other countries. International diversification

market risk, systematic risk, nondiversifiable risk

Risk factors common to the whole economy.

unique risk, firm-specific risk, nonsystematic risk, diversifiable risk

Risk that can be eliminated by diversification.

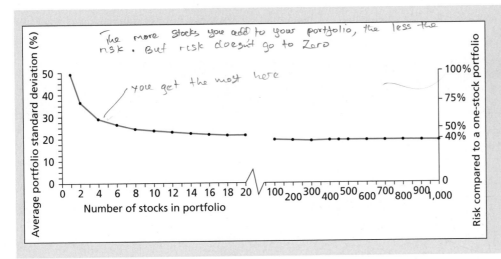

FIGURE 6.2

Portfolio risk decreases as diversification increases

Source: Meir Statman, "How Many Stocks Make a Diversified Portfolio?" *Journal of Financial and Quantitative Analysis* 22, September 1987.

may further reduce portfolio risk, but here too, global economic and political factors affecting all countries to various degrees will limit the extent of risk reduction.

6.2   ASSET ALLOCATION WITH TWO RISKY ASSETS

In the last chapter we examined the simplest asset allocation decision, that involving the choice of how much of the portfolio to place in risk-free money market securities versus in a risky portfolio. We simply assumed that the risky portfolio comprised a stock and a bond fund in given proportions. Of course, investors need to decide on the proportion of their portfolios to allocate to the stock versus the bond market. This, too, is an asset allocation decision. As the other nearby box "First Take Care of Asset Allocation Needs" emphasizes, most investment professionals recognize that the asset allocation decision must take precedence over the choice of particular stocks or mutual funds.

We examined capital allocation between risky and risk-free assets in the last chapter. We turn now to asset allocation between two risky assets, which we will continue to assume are two mutual funds, one a bond fund and the other a stock fund. After we understand the properties of portfolios formed by mixing two risky assets, we will reintroduce the choice of the third, risk-free portfolio. This will allow us to complete the basic problem of asset allocation across the three key asset classes: stocks, bonds, and risk-free money market securities. Once you understand this case, it will be easy to see how portfolios of many risky securities might best be constructed.

Covariance and Correlation

Because we now envision forming a risky portfolio from two risky assets, we need to understand how the uncertainties of asset returns interact. It turns out that the key determinant of portfolio risk is the extent to which the returns on the two assets tend to vary either in tandem or in opposition. Portfolio risk depends on the *correlation* between the returns of the assets in the portfolio. We can see why using a simple scenario analysis.

Suppose there are three possible scenarios for the economy: a recession, normal growth, and a boom. The performance of stock funds tends to follow the performance of the broad economy. So suppose that in a recession, the stock fund will have a rate of return of −11%, in a normal period it will have a rate of return of 13%, and in a boom period it will have a rate of return of 27%. In contrast, bond funds often do better when the economy is weak. This is because interest rates fall in a recession, which means that bond prices rise. Suppose that a bond fund will provide a rate of return of 16% in a recession, 6% in a normal period, and −4% in a boom. These assumptions and the probabilities of each scenario are summarized in Spreadsheet 6.1.

The expected return on each fund equals the probability-weighted average of the outcomes in the three scenarios. The last row of Spreadsheet 6.1 shows that the expected return of the stock fund is 10%, and that of the bond fund is 6%. As we discussed in the last chapter, the

---

SPREADSHEET 6.1

Capital market expectations for the stock and bond funds

e**X**cel

Please visit us at
www.mhhe.com/bkm

	A	B	C	D	E	F
1						
2			Stock Fund		Bond Fund	
3	Scenario	Probability	Rate of Return	Col B x Col C	Rate of Return	Col B x Col E
4	Recession	0.3	-11	-3.3	16	4.8
5	Normal	0.4	13	5.2	6	2.4
6	Boom	0.3	27	8.1	-4	-1.2
7	Expected or Mean Return:		SUM:	10.0	SUM:	6.0

FIRST TAKE CARE OF ASSET ALLOCATION NEEDS

If you want to build a top-performing mutual-fund portfolio, you should start by hunting for top-performing funds, right?

Wrong.

Too many investors gamely set out to find top-notch funds without first settling on an overall portfolio strategy. Result? These investors wind up with a mishmash of funds that don't add up to a decent portfolio. . . .

So what should you do? With thousands of stock, bond, and money-market funds to choose from, you couldn't possibly analyze all the funds available. Instead, to make sense of the bewildering array of funds available, you should start by deciding what basic mix of stock, bond, and money-market funds you want to hold. This is what experts call your "asset allocation."

This asset allocation has a major influence on your portfolio's performance. The more you have in stocks, the higher your likely long-run return.

But with the higher potential return from stocks come sharper short-term swings in a portfolio's value. As a result, you may want to include a healthy dose of bond and money-market funds, especially if you are a conservative investor or you will need to tap your portfolio for cash in the near future.

Once you have settled on your asset allocation mix, decide what sort of stock, bond, and money-market funds you want to own. This is particularly critical for the stock portion of your portfolio. One way to damp the price swings in your stock portfolio is to spread your money among large, small, and foreign stocks.

You could diversify even further by making sure that, when investing in U.S. large- and small-company stocks, you own both growth stocks with rapidly increasing sales or earnings and also beaten-down value stocks that are inexpensive compared with corporate assets or earnings.

Similarly, among foreign stocks, you could get additional diversification by investing in both developed foreign markets such as France, Germany, and Japan, and also emerging markets like Argentina, Brazil, and Malaysia.

SOURCE: Abridged from Jonathan Clements, "It Pays for You to Take Care of Asset-Allocation Needs Before Latching onto Fads," *The Wall Street Journal*, April 6, 1998. Reprinted by permission of Dow Jones & Company, Inc. via Copyright Clearance Center, Inc. © 1998 Dow Jones & Company, Inc. All Rights Reserved Worldwide.

variance is the probability-weighted average across all scenarios of the squared deviation between the actual return of the fund and its expected return; the standard deviation is the square root of the variance. These values are computed in Spreadsheet 6.2.

What about the risk and return characteristics of a portfolio made up from the stock and bond funds? The portfolio return is the weighted average of the returns on each fund with weights equal to the proportion of the portfolio invested in each fund. Suppose we form a portfolio with 60% invested in the stock fund and 40% in the bond fund. Then the portfolio return in each scenario is the weighted average of the returns on the two funds. For example

$$\text{Portfolio return in recession} = 0.60 \times (-11\%) + 0.40 \times 16\% = -0.20\%$$

which appears in cell C5 of Spreadsheet 6.3.

SPREADSHEET 6.2

Variance of returns

	A	B	C	D	E	F	G	H	I	J
1				Stock Fund				Bond Fund		
2				Deviation				Deviation		
3			Rate	from		Column B	Rate	from		Column B
4			of	Expected	Squared	x	of	Expected	Squared	x
5	Scenario	Prob.	Return	Return	Deviation	Column E	Return	Return	Deviation	Column I
6	Recession	0.3	-11	-21	441	132.3	16	10	100	30
7	Normal	0.4	13	3	9	3.6	6	0	0	0
8	Boom	0.3	27	17	289	86.7	-4	-10	100	30
9			expct 10		Variance = SUM	222.6			Variance:	60
10				Standard deviation = SQRT(Variance)		14.92			Std. Dev.:	7.75

eXcel

Please visit us at
www.mhhe.com/bkm

SPREADSHEET 6.3

Performance of the portfolio of stock and bond funds

Please visit us at www.mhhe.com/bkm

	A	B	C	D	E	F	G
1			Portfolio of 60% in stocks and 40% in bonds				
2			Rate	Column B	Deviation from		Column B
3			of	x	Expected	Squared	x
4	Scenario	Probability	Return	Column C	Return	Deviation	Column F
5	Recession	0.3	-0.2	-0.06	-8.60	73.96	22.188
6	Normal	0.4	10.2	4.08	1.80	3.24	1.296
7	Boom	0.3	14.6	4.38	6.20	38.44	11.532
8		Expected return:		8.40		Variance:	35.016
9						Standard deviation:	5.92

Spreadsheet 6.3 shows the rate of return of the portfolio in each scenario, as well as the portfolio's expected return, variance, and standard deviation. Notice that while the portfolio's expected return is just the weighted average of the expected return of the two assets, the standard deviation is actually less than that of *either* asset.

The low risk of the portfolio is due to the inverse relationship between the performance of the two funds. In a recession, stocks fare poorly, but this is offset by the good performance of the bond fund. Conversely, in a boom scenario, bonds fall, but stocks do well. Therefore, the portfolio of the two risky assets is less risky than either asset individually. Portfolio risk is reduced most when the returns of the two assets most reliably offset each other.

The natural question investors should ask, therefore, is how one can measure the tendency of the returns on two assets to vary either in tandem or in opposition to each other. The statistics that provide this measure are the covariance and the correlation coefficient.

The covariance is calculated in a manner similar to the variance. Instead of measuring the typical difference of an asset return from its expected value, however, we wish to measure the extent to which the variation in the returns on the two assets tend to reinforce or offset each other.

We start in Spreadsheet 6.4 with the deviation of the return on each fund from its expected or mean value. For each scenario, we multiply the deviation of the stock fund return from its mean by the deviation of the bond fund return from its mean. The product will be positive if both asset returns exceed their respective means in that scenario or if both fall short of their respective means. The product will be negative if one asset exceeds its mean return, while the other falls short of its mean return. For example, Spreadsheet 6.4 shows that the stock fund return in the recession falls short of its expected value by 21%, while the bond fund return exceeds its mean by 10%. Therefore, the product of the two deviations in the recession is $-21 \times 10 = -210$, as reported in column E. The product of deviations is negative if one asset performs well when the other is performing poorly. It is positive if both assets perform well or poorly in the same scenarios.

SPREADSHEET 6.4

Covariance between the returns of the stock and bond funds

Please visit us at www.mhhe.com/bkm

	A	B	C	D	E	F
1			Deviation from Mean Return		Covariance	
2	Scenario	Probability	Stock Fund	Bond Fund	Product of Dev	Col B x Col E
3	Recession	0.3	-21	10	-210	-63
4	Normal	0.4	3	0	0	0
5	Boom	0.3	17	-10	-170	-51
6				Covariance =	SUM:	-114
7	Correlation coefficient = Covariance/(StdDev(stocks)*StdDev(bonds)) =					-0.99

If we compute the probability-weighted average of the products across all scenarios, we obtain a measure of the *average* tendency of the asset returns to vary in tandem. Since this is a measure of the extent to which the returns tend to vary with each other, that is, to co-vary, it is called the *covariance.* Therefore, the formula for the covariance of the returns on the stock and bond portfolios is given in the following equation. Each particular scenario in this equation is labeled or "indexed" by i. In general, i ranges from scenario 1 to S (the total number of scenarios). In this example, $S = 3$, the three possible scenarios being recession, normal, and boom conditions. The probability of each scenario is denoted $p(i)$.

$$\text{Cov}(r_S, r_B) = \sum_{i=1}^{S} p(i)[r_S(i) - \bar{r}_S][r_B(i) - \bar{r}_B] \qquad \textbf{(6.1)}$$

The covariance of the stock and bond funds is computed in the next-to-last line of Spreadsheet 6.4 using Equation 6.1. The negative value for the covariance indicates that the two assets vary inversely, that is, when one asset performs well, the other tends to perform poorly.

Unfortunately, it is difficult to interpret the magnitude of the covariance. For instance, does the covariance of -114 in cell F6 indicate that the inverse relationship between the returns on stock and bond funds is strong or weak? It's hard to say. An easier statistic to interpret is the *correlation coefficient,* which is simply the covariance divided by the product of the standard deviations of the returns on each fund. We denote the correlation coefficient by the Greek letter rho, ρ.

$$\text{Correlation coefficient} = \rho_{SB} = \frac{\text{Cov}(r_S, r_B)}{\sigma_S \sigma_B} = \frac{-114}{14.92 \times 7.75} = -.99 \qquad \textbf{(6.2)}$$

Correlations can range from values of -1 to $+1$. Values of -1 indicate perfect negative correlation, that is, the strongest possible tendency for two returns to vary inversely. Values of $+1$ indicate perfect positive correlation. Correlations of zero indicate that the returns on the two assets are unrelated to each other. The correlation coefficient of -0.99 confirms the overwhelming tendency of the returns on the stock and bond funds to vary inversely in this particular scenario analysis.

Here is another reason that the correlation coefficient is a useful statistic. Like the variance, the dimension of covariance is percent square. However, a square root of the covariance is not available because the covariance can be negative. Instead, it is customary to refer to the correlation coefficient, which because it is a pure, scaled number between -1 and $+1$, is more telling. Equation 6.2 shows that whenever the covariance in called for in a calculation we can replace it with the following expression using the correlation coefficient:

$$\text{Cov}(r_S, r_B) = \rho_{SB}\sigma_S\sigma_B \qquad \textbf{(6.3)}$$

We are now in a position to derive the risk and return features of portfolios of risky assets.

> **CONCEPT check 6.1**
>
> Suppose the rates of return of the bond portfolio in the three scenarios of Spreadsheet 6.4 are 10% in a recession, 7% in a normal period, and 2% in a boom. The stock returns in the three scenarios are −12% (recession), 10% (normal), and 28% (boom). What are the covariance and correlation coefficient between the rates of return on the two portfolios?

Using Historical Data

We've seen that portfolio risk and return depend on the means and variances of the component securities, as well as on the covariance between their returns. One way to obtain these inputs is a scenario analysis as in Spreadsheets 6.1–6.4. As we noted in Chapter 5, however, a common alternative approach to produce these inputs is to make use of historical data.

In this approach, we use realized returns to estimate mean returns and volatility as well as the tendency for security returns to co-vary. The estimate of the mean return for each security is its average value in the sample period; the estimate of variance is the average value of the squared deviations around the sample average; the estimate of the covariance is the average value of the cross-product of deviations. As we noted in Chapter 5, Example 5.5, the averages used to compute variance and covariance are adjusted by the ratio $n/(n-1)$ to account for the "lost degree of freedom" when using the sample average in place of the true mean return, $E(r)$.

Notice that, as in scenario analysis, the focus for risk and return analysis is on average returns and the deviations of returns from their average value. Here, however, instead of using mean returns based on the scenario analysis, we use average returns during the sample period.

We can illustrate this approach with a simple example.

EXAMPLE   6.1

Using Historical Data to Estimate Means, Variances, and Covariances

More often than not, variances, covariances, and correlation coefficients are estimated from past data. The idea is that variability and covariability change slowly over time. Thus, if we estimate these statistics from a recent data sample, our estimates will provide useful predictions for the near future—perhaps next month or next quarter.

The computation of sample variances, covariances, and correlation coefficients is quite easy using a spreadsheet. Suppose you input 10 weekly, annualized returns for two NYSE stocks, ABC and XYZ, into columns B and C of the following Excel spreadsheet. The column averages in cells B15 and C15 provide estimates of the means, which are used in columns D and E to compute deviations of each return from the average return. These deviations are used in columns F and G to compute the squared deviations from means that are necessary to calculate variance and the cross-product of deviations to calculate covariance (column H). Row 15 of columns F, G, and H shows the averages of squared deviations and cross-product of deviations from the means.

As we noted above, to eliminate the bias in the estimate of the variance and covariance we need to multiply the average squared deviation by $n/(n-1)$, in this case, by 10/9, as we see in row 16.

Observe that the Excel commands from the Data Analysis menu provide a simple shortcut to these results. This feature of Excel can calculate a matrix of variances and covariances directly. The results from this procedure appear at the bottom of the spreadsheet.

	A	B	C	D	E	F	G	H
1		Rate of return		Deviations from		Squared Deviations		Product of
2		(annualized, %)		Average Return (%)		from Average Return		Deviations
3	Week	ABC	XYZ	ABC	XYZ	ABC	XYZ	ABC x XYZ
4	1	65.13	-22.55	45.51	-34.52	2071.34	1191.56	-1571.03
5	2	51.84	31.44	32.22	19.47	1038.26	379.12	627.39
6	3	-30.82	-6.45	-50.44	-18.42	2543.99	339.26	929.02
7	4	-15.13	-51.14	-34.75	-63.11	1207.42	3982.75	2192.91
8	5	70.63	33.78	51.01	21.81	2602.22	475.72	1112.62
9	6	107.82	32.95	88.20	20.98	7779.59	440.20	1850.57
10	7	-25.16	70.19	-44.78	58.22	2005.07	3389.68	-2607.02
11	8	50.48	27.63	30.86	15.66	952.46	245.27	483.33
12	9	-36.41	-48.79	-56.03	-60.76	3139.14	3691.66	3404.21
13	10	-42.20	52.63	-61.82	40.66	3821.47	1653.32	-2513.58
14								
15	Average	19.62	11.97			2716.10	1578.85	390.84
16	Average x 10/9					3017.89	1754.28	434.27
17								
18	Std. Deviation	54.94	41 88			Variances	Covariance	
19								
20	AVERAGE(B4:B13)		STDEV(C4:C13)				0.19	
21								
22					Correlation Coefficient =H16/(B18*C18)			
23		ABC return	XYZ return					
24	ABC return	3017.8851			Variances and Covariance			
25	XYZ return	434.26858	1754.2815		using "Covariance" from Data			
26					Analysis menu			
27		ABC return	XYZ return					
28	ABC return	1			"Correlation" from Data Analysis menu			
29	XYZ return	0.1887372	1					
30								

An important comment on Example 6.1 is in order. As mentioned in the example, estimates of variance and covariance constructed from past data are considered reliable forecasts of these statistics (at least for the short term). However, averages of past returns typically provide highly noisy (i.e., imprecise) forecasts of future expected returns. In this discussion we freely use past averages computed from small samples of data, because our objective here is to demonstrate the methodology. In practice, professional investors spend most of their resources on macroeconomic and security analysis to improve their estimates of mean returns.

The Three Rules of Two-Risky-Assets Portfolios

Suppose a proportion denoted by w_B is invested in the bond fund, and the remainder $1 - w_B$, denoted by w_S, is invested in the stock fund. The properties of the portfolio are determined by the following three rules, which apply the rules of statistics governing combinations of random variables:

Rule 1: The rate of return on the portfolio is a weighted average of the returns on the component securities, with the investment proportions as weights.

$$r_P = w_B r_B + w_S r_S \tag{6.4}$$

Rule 2: The expected rate of return on the portfolio is a weighted average of the expected returns on the component securities, with the same portfolio proportions as weights. In symbols, the expectation of Equation 6.4 is

$$E(r_P) = w_B E(r_B) + w_S E(r_S) \tag{6.5}$$

The first two rules are simple linear expressions. This is not so in the case of the portfolio variance, as the third rule shows.

Rule 3: The variance of the rate of return on the two-risky-asset portfolio is

$$\sigma_P^2 = (w_B \sigma_B)^2 + (w_S \sigma_S)^2 + 2(w_B \sigma_B)(w_S \sigma_S)\rho_{BS} \tag{6.6}$$

correlation coefficient

where ρ_{BS} is the correlation coefficient between the returns on the stock and bond funds. Notice that using Equation 6.3, we may replace the last term in Equation 6.6 with $2 w_B w_S \text{Cov}(r_B, r_S)$.

The variance of the portfolio is a *sum* of the contributions of the component security variances *plus* a term that involves the correlation coefficient (and hence, covariance) between the returns on the component securities. We know from the last section why this last term arises. If the correlation between the component securities is small or negative, then there will be a greater tendency for the variability in the returns on the two assets to offset each other. This will reduce portfolio risk. Notice in Equation 6.6 that portfolio variance is lower when the correlation coefficient is lower.

The formula describing portfolio variance is more complicated than that describing portfolio return. This complication has a virtue, however: namely, the tremendous potential for gains from diversification.

The Risk-Return Trade-Off with Two-Risky-Assets Portfolios

Suppose now that the standard deviation of bonds is 12% and that of stocks is 25%, and assume that there is zero correlation between the return on the bond fund and the return on the stock fund. A correlation coefficient of zero means that stock and bond returns vary independently of each other.

Say we start out with a position of 100% in bonds, and we now consider a shift: Invest 50% in bonds and 50% in stocks. We can compute the portfolio variance from Equation 6.6.

Input data:

$$E(r_B) = 6\%; E(r_S) = 10\%; \sigma_B = 12\%; \sigma_S = 25\%; \rho_{BS} = 0; w_B = 0.5; w_S = 0.5$$

Portfolio variance and standard deviation:

$$\sigma_P^2 = (0.5 \times 12)^2 + (0.5 \times 25)^2 + 2(0.5 \times 12) \times (0.5 \times 25) \times 0 = 192.25$$
$$\sigma_P = \sqrt{192.25} = 13.87\%$$

Had we mistakenly calculated portfolio risk by averaging the two standard deviations $[(25 + 12)/2 = 18.5\%]$, we would have incorrectly predicted an increase in the portfolio standard deviation by a full 6.50 percentage points. Instead, the addition of stocks to the formerly all-bond portfolio actually increases the portfolio standard deviation by only 1.87 percentage points. So the gain from diversification can be seen as a full $6.50 - 1.87 = 4.63\%$.

This gain is cost-free in the sense that diversification allows us to experience the full contribution of the stock's higher expected return, while keeping the portfolio standard deviation below the average of the component standard deviations. As Equation 6.5 shows, the portfolio's expected return is the weighted average of expected returns of the component securities. If the expected return on bonds is 6% and the expected return on stocks is 10%, then shifting from 0% to 50% investment in stocks will increase our expected return from 6% to 8%.

EXAMPLE 6.2	Suppose we invest 75% in bonds and only 25% in stocks. We can construct a portfolio with an expected return higher than bonds $(0.75 \times 6) + (0.25 \times 10) = 7\%$ and, at the same time, a standard deviation less than bonds. Using Equation 6.6 again, we find that the portfolio variance is
Benefits from Diversification	$$(0.75 \times 12)^2 + (0.25 \times 25)^2 + 2(0.75 \times 12)(0.25 \times 25) \times 0 = 120$$

and, accordingly, the portfolio standard deviation is $\sqrt{120} = 10.96\%$, which is less than the standard deviation of either bonds or stocks alone. Taking on a more volatile asset (stocks) actually reduces portfolio risk! Such is the power of diversification.

We can find investment proportions that will reduce portfolio risk even further. The risk-minimizing proportions will be 81.27% in bonds and 18.73% in stocks.[1] With these proportions, the portfolio standard deviation will be 10.82%, and the portfolio's expected return will be 6.75%.

Is this portfolio preferable to the one considered in Example 6.2, with 25% in the stock fund? That depends on investor preferences, because the portfolio with the lower variance also has a lower expected return.

investment opportunity set

Set of available portfolio risk-return combinations.

What the analyst can and must do, however, is to show investors the entire **investment opportunity set** as we do in Figure 6.3. This is the set of all attainable combinations of risk and return offered by portfolios formed using the available assets in differing proportions.

Points on the investment opportunity set of Figure 6.3 can be found by varying the investment proportions and computing the resulting expected returns and standard deviations from

---

[1]The minimum-variance portfolio is constructed to minimize the variance (and hence standard deviation) of returns, regardless of the expected return. With a zero correlation coefficient, the variance-minimizing proportion in the bond fund is given by the expression: $\sigma_S^2/(\sigma_B^2 + \sigma_S^2)$.

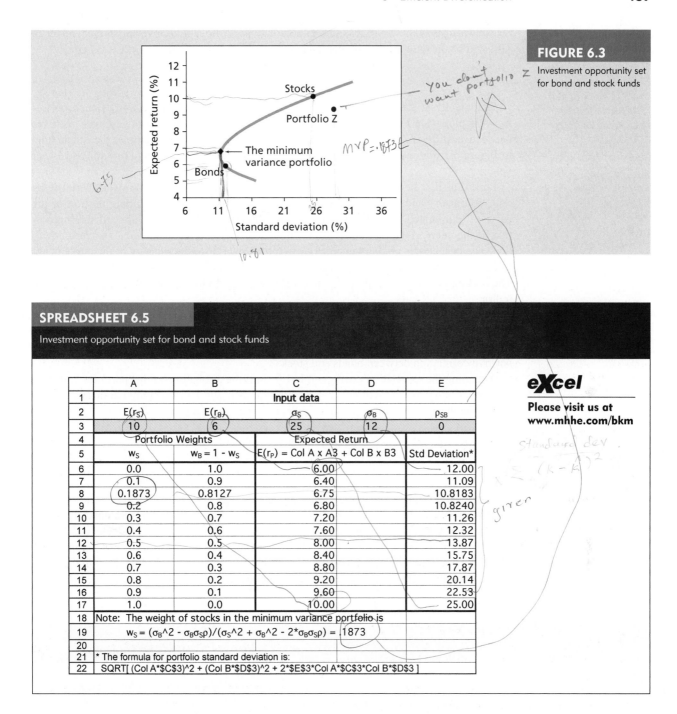

FIGURE 6.3
Investment opportunity set for bond and stock funds

SPREADSHEET 6.5

Investment opportunity set for bond and stock funds

	A	B	C	D	E
1			**Input data**		
2	$E(r_S)$	$E(r_B)$	σ_S	σ_B	ρ_{SB}
3	10	6	25	12	0
4	Portfolio Weights		Expected Return		
5	w_S	$w_B = 1 - w_S$	$E(r_P) = $ Col A x A3 + Col B x B3		Std Deviation*
6	0.0	1.0	6.00		12.00
7	0.1	0.9	6.40		11.09
8	0.1873	0.8127	6.75		10.8183
9	0.2	0.8	6.80		10.8240
10	0.3	0.7	7.20		11.26
11	0.4	0.6	7.60		12.32
12	0.5	0.5	8.00		13.87
13	0.6	0.4	8.40		15.75
14	0.7	0.3	8.80		17.87
15	0.8	0.2	9.20		20.14
16	0.9	0.1	9.60		22.53
17	1.0	0.0	10.00		25.00
18	Note: The weight of stocks in the minimum variance portfolio is				
19	$w_S = (\sigma_B^2 - \sigma_B\sigma_S\rho)/(\sigma_S^2 + \sigma_B^2 - 2*\sigma_B\sigma_S\rho) = .1873$				
20					
21	* The formula for portfolio standard deviation is:				
22	SQRT[(Col A*$C$3)^2 + (Col B*$D$3)^2 + 2*$E$3*Col A*$C$3*Col B*$D$3]				

*e**X**cel*

**Please visit us at
www.mhhe.com/bkm**

Equations 6.5 and 6.6. We can feed the input data and the two equations into a computer and let it draw the graph. With the aid of the computer, we can easily find the portfolio composition corresponding to any point on the opportunity set. Spreadsheet 6.5 shows the investment proportions and the mean and standard deviation for a few portfolios.

The Mean-Variance Criterion

Investors desire portfolios that lie to the "northwest" in Figure 6.3. These are portfolios with high expected returns (toward the "north" of the figure) and low volatility (to the "west"). These preferences mean that we can compare portfolios using a *mean-variance criterion* in the following way. Portfolio A is said to dominate portfolio B if all investors prefer A over B. This will be the case if it has higher mean return and lower variance:

$$E(r_A) \geq E(r_B) \qquad \text{and} \qquad \sigma_A \leq \sigma_B$$

Graphically, if the expected return and standard deviation combination of each portfolio were plotted in Figure 6.3, portfolio A would lie to the northwest of B. Given a choice between portfolios A and B, *all* investors would choose A. For example, the stock fund in Figure 6.3 dominates portfolio Z; the stock fund has higher expected return and lower volatility.

Portfolios that lie below the minimum-variance portfolio in the figure can therefore be rejected out of hand as inefficient. Any portfolio on the downward sloping portion of the curve is "dominated" by the portfolio that lies directly above it on the upward sloping portion of the curve since that portfolio has higher expected return and equal standard deviation. The best choice among the portfolios on the upward sloping portion of the curve is not as obvious, because in this region higher expected return is accompanied by greater risk. The best choice will depend on the investor's willingness to trade off risk against expected return.

So far we have assumed a correlation of zero between stock and bond returns. We know that low correlations aid diversification and that a higher correlation coefficient between stocks and bonds results in a reduced effect of diversification. What are the implications of perfect positive correlation between bonds and stocks?

Assuming the correlation coefficient is 1.0 simplifies Equation 6.6 for portfolio variance. Looking at it again, you will see that substitution of $\rho_{BS} = 1$ in Equation 6.6 means we can "complete the square" of the quantities $w_B \sigma_B$ and $w_S \sigma_S$ to obtain

$$\sigma_P^2 = w_B^2 \sigma_B^2 + w_S^2 \sigma_S^2 + 2 w_B \sigma_B w_S \sigma_S = (w_B \sigma_B + w_S \sigma_S)^2$$
$$\sigma_P = w_B \sigma_B + w_S \sigma_S$$

The portfolio standard deviation is a weighted average of the component security standard deviations only in the special case of perfect positive correlation. In this circumstance, there are no gains to be had from diversification. Whatever the proportions of stocks and bonds, both the portfolio mean and the standard deviation are simple weighted averages. Figure 6.4 shows the opportunity set with perfect positive correlation—a straight line through the component securities. No portfolio can be discarded as inefficient in this case, and the choice

WEB master

Return and Risk Parameters

Go to **http://moneycentral.msn.com** and click on the "Investing" tab. Look for "Stocks" on the left side menu, and click on the submenu "Quotes, Charts, News." Enter the symbol FRNT and select Chart from the drop-down menu. When you click "Go" you'll see a chart of Frontier Airlines' stock price.

Scroll down to where you can enter a custom date range and enter the dates that span the most recent year. Specify weekly data, then click the link to get the price history table. Download the file using the button provided and open it in Excel. Repeat the process for LUV, DELL, and TGT.

1. Calculate the weekly returns for all of the stocks using closing prices. Merge the returns for the four firms into a single Excel workbook. Be sure that the companies' returns are properly aligned according to date.

2. Using the Excel functions, calculate the average return and standard deviation for each of the firms.

3. Using the Correlation function or the Data Analysis Tool, construct the correlation matrix for the stocks using the weekly returns for the entire period.

4. Which pair of firms has the highest correlation coefficient? Which pair has the lowest? Do these results make sense?

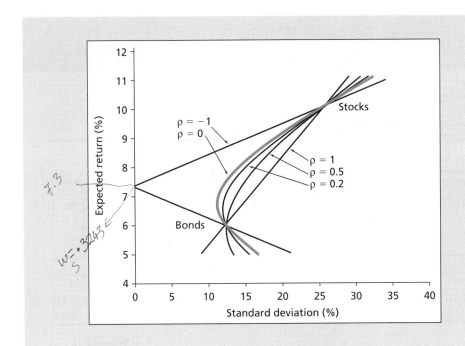

FIGURE 6.4

Investment opportunity sets for bonds and stocks with various correlation coefficients

among portfolios depends only on risk aversion. Diversification in the case of perfect positive correlation is not effective.

Perfect positive correlation is the *only* case in which there is no benefit from diversification. Whenever $\rho < 1$, the portfolio standard deviation is less than the weighted average of the standard deviations of the component securities. Therefore, *there are benefits to diversification whenever asset returns are less than perfectly correlated.*

Our analysis has ranged from very attractive diversification benefits ($\rho_{BS} < 0$) to no benefits at all ($\rho_{BS} = 1.0$). For ρ_{BS} within this range, the benefits will be somewhere in between. As Figure 6.4 illustrates, $\rho_{BS} = 0.5$ is a lot better for diversification than perfect positive correlation and quite a bit worse than zero correlation.

A realistic correlation coefficient between stocks and bonds based on historical experience is actually around 0.20. The expected returns and standard deviations that we have so far assumed also reflect historical experience, which is why we include a graph for $\rho_{BS} = 0.2$ in Figure 6.4. Spreadsheet 6.6 enumerates some of the points on the various opportunity sets in Figure 6.4.

Negative correlation between a pair of assets is also possible. Where negative correlation is present, there will be even greater diversification benefits. Again, let us start with an extreme. With perfect negative correlation, we substitute $\rho_{BS} = -1.0$ in Equation 6.6 and simplify it in the same way as with positive perfect correlation. Here, too, we can complete the square, this time, however, with different results

$$\sigma_P^2 = (w_B\sigma_B - w_S\sigma_S)^2$$

and, therefore,

$$\sigma_P = ABS[w_B\sigma_B - w_S\sigma_S] \tag{6.7}$$

The right-hand side of Equation 6.7 denotes the absolute value of $w_B\sigma_B - w_S\sigma_S$. The solution involves the absolute value because standard deviation is never negative.

With perfect negative correlation, the benefits from diversification stretch to the limit. Equation 6.7 points to the proportions that will reduce the portfolio standard deviation all the

SPREADSHEET 6.6

Investment opportunity set for bonds and stocks with various correlation coefficients

	A	B	C	D	E	F	G
1			**Input Data**				
2	$E(r_S)$	$E(r_B)$	σ_S	σ_B			
3	10	6	25	12			
4							
5	Weight in stocks	Portfolio expected return	Portfolio Standard Deviation[1] for Given Correlation, ρ				
6	w_S	$E(r_P)$ = Col A*A3 + (1-Col A)*B3	-1	0	0.2	0.5	1
7	0.0	6.0	12.0	12.0	12.0	12.0	12.0
8	0.2	6.8	4.6	10.8	11.7	12.9	14.6
9	0.4	7.6	2.8	12.3	13.4	15.0	17.2
10	0.6	8.4	10.2	15.7	16.6	17.9	19.8
11	0.8	9.2	17.6	20.1	20.6	21.3	22.4
12	1.0	10.0	25.0	25.0	25.0	25.0	25.0
13				Minimum Variance Portfolio[2,3,4,5]			
14	w_S(min) = (σ_B^2 - $\sigma_B\sigma_S\rho$) / (σ_S^2 + σ_B^2 - 2*$\sigma_B\sigma_S\rho$) =		0.3243	0.1873	0.1294	-0.0128	-0.9231
15	$E(r_P)$ = w_S(min)*A3+(1-w_S(min))*B3 =		7.30	6.75	6.52	5.95	2.31
16	σ_P =		0.00	10.82	11.54	11.997	0.00

Notes:

1. σ_P = SQRT[(Col A*C3)^2 + ((1 − Col A)*D3)^2 + 2*Col A*C3*(1 − Col A)*D3*ρ]

2. The standard deviation is calculated from Equation 6.6 using the weights of the miniumum-variance portfolio:

$$\sigma_P = \text{SQRT}[(w_S(\text{min})*\text{C3})^2 + ((1\text{-}w_S(\text{min}))*\text{D3})^2 + 2*w_S(\text{min})*\text{C3}*(1\text{-}w_S(\text{min}))*\text{D3}*\rho]$$

3. As the correlation coefficient grows, the minimum variance portfolio requires a smaller position in stocks (even a negative position for higher correlations), and the performance of this portfolio becomes less attractive.

4. Notice that with correlation of .5 or higher, minimum variance is achieved with a short position in stocks. The standard deviation is then slightly lower than that of bonds, but with a slightly lower mean as well.

5. With perfect positive correlation (column G), you can drive the standard deviation to zero by taking a large, short position in stocks. The mean return is then as low as 2.31%.

eXcel

**Please visit us at
www.mhhe.com/bkm**

way to zero.[2] With our data, this will happen when $w_B = 67.57\%$. While exposing us to zero risk, investing 32.43% in stocks (rather than placing all funds in bonds) will still increase the portfolio expected return from 6% to 7.30%. Of course, we can hardly expect results this attractive in reality.

CONCEPT check 6.2

Suppose that for some reason you are *required* to invest 50% of your portfolio in bonds and 50% in stocks.

a. If the standard deviation of your portfolio is 15%, what must be the correlation coefficient between stock and bond returns?

b. What is the expected rate of return on your portfolio?

c. Now suppose that the correlation between stock and bond returns is 0.22 but that you are free to choose whatever portfolio proportions you desire. Are you likely to be better or worse off than you were in part (a)?

[2] The proportion in bonds that will drive the standard deviation to zero when $\rho = -1$ is:

$$w_B = \frac{\sigma_S}{\sigma_B + \sigma_S}$$

Compare this formula to the formula in footnote 1 for the variance-minimizing proportions when $\rho = 0$.

EXAMPLE 6.3

Using Historical Data to Estimate the Investment Opportunity Set

Let's return to the data for ABC and XYZ in Example 6.1. Using the spreadsheet estimates of the means and standard deviations obtained from the AVERAGE and STDEV functions, and the estimate of the correlation coefficient we obtained in that example, we can compute the risk-return trade-off for various portfolios formed from ABC and XYZ.

Columns E and F in the lower half of the spreadsheet on the following page are calculated from Equations 6.5 and 6.6, respectively, and show the risk-return opportunities. These calculations use the estimates of the stocks' means in cells B16 and C16, the standard deviations in cells B17 and C17, and the correlation coefficient in cell F10.

Examination of column E shows that the portfolio mean starts at XYZ's mean of 11.97% and moves toward ABC's mean as we increase the weight of ABC and correspondingly reduce that of XYZ. Examination of the standard deviation in column F shows that diversification reduces the standard deviation until the proportion in ABC increases above 30%; thereafter, standard deviation increases. Hence, the minimum-variance portfolio uses weights of approximately 30% in ABC and 70% in XYZ.

The exact proportion in ABC in the minimum-variance portfolio can be computed from the formula shown in Spreadsheet 6.6. Note, however, that achieving a minimum-variance portfolio is not a compelling goal. Investors may well be willing to take on more risk in order to increase expected return. The investment opportunity set offered by stocks ABC and XYZ may be found by graphing the expected return–standard deviation pairs in columns E and F.

	A	B	C	D	E	F	G	H
1		Here are the data on ABC and XYZ from Example 6.1, shown below with the computed						
2		statistics of average, standard deviation and correlation.						
3								
4	Week		Anualized	%				
5		ABC return	XYZ return					
6	1	65.13	-22.55					
7	2	51.84	31.44					
8	3	-30.82	-6.45			ABC return	XYZ return	
9	4	-15.13	-51.14	ABC return	1			
10	5	70.63	33.78	XYZ return	0.18873716	1		
11	6	107.82	32.95					
12	7	-25.16	70.19					
13	8	50.48	27.63					
14	9	-36.41	-48.79	AVERAGE(C6:C15)			Correlation from	
15	10	-42.20	52.63				Data Analysis menu	
16	Average:	19.62	11.97	STDEV(C6:C15)				
17	Std deviation:	54.94	41.88					
20	CALCULATION OF INVESTMENT OPPORTUNITY SET:							
22			Portfolio	Proportions		Portfolio		
23			ABC	XYZ	Mean	Std. Dev.		
24	=C27*$B$16+D27*$C$16		0.00	1.00	11.97	41.88		
25			0.10	0.90	12.73	39.11		
26			0.20	0.80	13.50	37.18		
27			0.30	0.70	14.26	36.24		
28			0.40	0.60	15.03	36.37		
29			0.50	0.50	15.79	37.55		
30			0.60	0.40	16.56	39.69		
31			0.70	0.30	17.32	42.65		
32			0.80	0.20	18.09	46.27		
33			0.90	0.10	18.85	50.40		
34			1.00	0.00	19.62	54.94		
35	Minimum Variance Portfolio	0.3382	0.6618	14.56	36.17			
37					=(C32^2*$B$17^2+D32^2*$C$17^2			
38	(C17^2-B17*C17*F10)/				+2*C32*D32*$B$17*$C$17*$F$10)^.5			
39	(B17^2+C17^2-2*B17*C17*F10)							

CONCEPT **6.3**
check

The following tables present returns on various pairs of stocks in several periods. In part A, we show you a scatter diagram of the returns on the first pair of stocks. Draw (or prepare in Excel) similar scatter diagrams for cases B through E. Match up the diagrams (A–E) to the following list of correlation coefficients by choosing the correlation that best describes the relationship between the returns on the two stocks: $\rho = -1, 0, 0.2, 0.5, 1.0$.

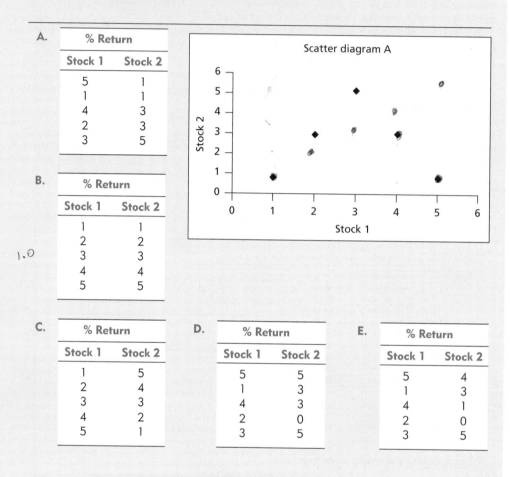

A.

% Return	
Stock 1	Stock 2
5	1
1	1
4	3
2	3
3	5

B.

% Return	
Stock 1	Stock 2
1	1
2	2
3	3
4	4
5	5

C.

% Return	
Stock 1	Stock 2
1	5
2	4
3	3
4	2
5	1

D.

% Return	
Stock 1	Stock 2
5	5
1	3
4	3
2	0
3	5

E.

% Return	
Stock 1	Stock 2
5	4
1	3
4	1
2	0
3	5

6.3 THE OPTIMAL RISKY PORTFOLIO WITH A RISK-FREE ASSET

Now we can expand the asset allocation problem to include a risk-free asset. Let us continue to use the input data from the bottom of Spreadsheet 6.5, but now assume a realistic correlation coefficient between stocks and bonds of 0.20. Suppose then that we are still confined to the risky bond and stock funds, but now can also invest in risk-free T-bills yielding 5%. Figure 6.5 shows the opportunity set generated from the bond and stock funds. This is the same opportunity set as graphed in Figure 6.4 with $\rho_{BS} = 0.20$.

Two possible capital allocation lines (CALs) are drawn from the risk-free rate ($r_f = 5\%$) to two feasible portfolios. The first possible CAL is drawn through the minimum-variance portfolio (A), which invests 87.06% in bonds and 12.94% in stocks. Portfolio A's expected return is 6.52% and its standard deviation is 11.54%. With a T-bill rate (r_f) of 5%, the reward-to-volatility ratio of portfolio A (which is also the slope of the CAL that combines T-bills with portfolio A) is

$$S_A = \frac{E(r_A) - r_f}{\sigma_A} = \frac{6.52 - 5}{11.54} = 0.13 \qquad \text{(6.8)}$$

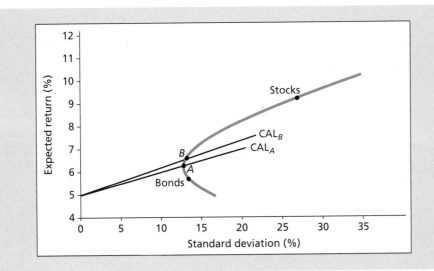

FIGURE 6.5

The opportunity set using
bonds and stocks and two
capital allocation lines

Now consider the CAL that uses portfolio B instead of A. Portfolio B invests 80% in bonds and 20% in stocks, providing an expected return of 6.80% with a standard deviation of 11.68%. Thus, the reward-to-volatility ratio of any portfolio on the CAL of B is

$$S_B = \frac{6.80 - 5}{11.68} = .15 \qquad \textbf{(6.9)}$$

This is higher than the reward-to-volatility ratio of the CAL of the minimum-variance portfolio A.

The difference in the reward-to-volatility ratios is $S_B - S_A = 0.02$. This implies that portfolio B provides 2 extra basis points (0.02%) of expected return for every percentage point increase in standard deviation.

The higher reward-to-volatility ratio of portfolio B means that its capital allocation line is steeper than that of A. Therefore, CAL_B plots above CAL_A in Figure 6.5. In other words, combinations of portfolio B and the risk-free asset provide a higher expected return for any level of risk (standard deviation) than combinations of portfolio A and the risk-free asset. Therefore, all risk-averse investors would prefer to form their complete portfolio using the risk-free asset with portfolio B rather than with portfolio A. In this sense, portfolio B dominates A.

But why stop at portfolio B? We can continue to ratchet the CAL upward until it reaches the ultimate point of tangency with the investment opportunity set. This must yield the CAL with the highest feasible reward-to-volatility ratio. Therefore, the tangency portfolio (O) in Figure 6.6 is the **optimal risky portfolio** to mix with T-bills, which may be defined as the risky portfolio resulting in the highest possible CAL. We can read the expected return and standard deviation of portfolio O (for "optimal") off the graph in Figure 6.6 as

$$E(r_O) = 8.68\%$$
$$\sigma_O = 17.97\%$$

optimal risky portfolio

The best combination of risky assets to be mixed with safe assets to form the complete portfolio.

which can be identified as the portfolio that invests 32.99% in bonds and 67.01% in stocks. These weights may be obtained algebraically from the following formula, which is the solution to the maximization of the reward-to-volatility ratio.

$$w_B = \frac{[E(r_B) - r_f]\sigma_S^2 - [E(r_S) - r_f]\sigma_B\sigma_S\rho_{BS}}{[E(r_B) - r_f]\sigma_S^2 + [E(r_S) - r_f]\sigma_B^2 - [E(r_B) - r_f + E(r_S) - r_f]\sigma_B\sigma_S\rho_{BS}}$$
$$w_S = 1 - w_B \qquad \textbf{(6.10)}$$

FIGURE 6.6

The optimal capital allocation line with bonds, stocks, and T-bills

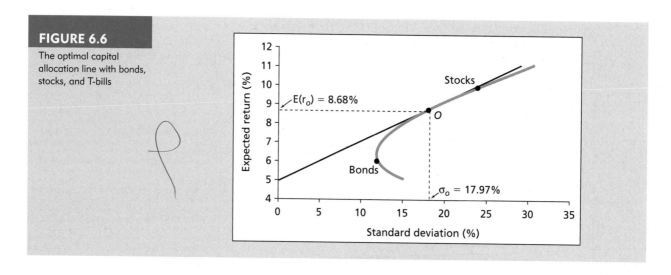

The CAL with our optimal portfolio has a slope of

$$S_O = \frac{8.68 - 5}{17.97} = .20$$

which is the reward-to-variability ratio of portfolio O. This slope exceeds the slope of any other feasible portfolio, as it must if it is to be the slope of the best feasible CAL.

In the last chapter we saw that the preferred *complete* portfolio formed from a risky portfolio and a risk-free asset depends on the investor's risk aversion. More risk-averse investors will prefer low-risk portfolios despite the lower expected return, while more risk-tolerant investors will choose higher-risk, higher-return portfolios. Both investors, however, will choose portfolio O as their risky portfolio since that portfolio results in the highest return per unit of risk, that is, the steepest capital allocation line. Investors will differ only in their allocation of investment funds between portfolio O and the risk-free asset.

Figure 6.7 shows one possible choice for the preferred complete portfolio, C. The investor places 55% of wealth in portfolio O and 45% in Treasury bills. The rate of return and volatility of the portfolio are

$$E(r_C) = 5 + 0.55 \times (8.68 - 5) = 7.02\%$$
$$\sigma_C = 0.55 \times 17.97 = 9.88\%$$

FIGURE 6.7

The complete portfolio

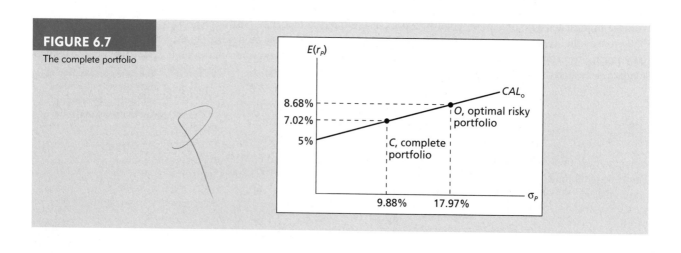

In turn, we found above that portfolio O is formed by mixing the bond fund and stock fund with weights of 32.99% and 67.01%. Therefore, the overall asset allocation of the complete portfolio is as follows:

Weight in risk-free asset		45.00%
Weight in bond fund	$0.3299 \times 55\% =$	18.14
Weight in stock fund	$0.6701 \times 55\% =$	36.86
Total		100.00%

Figure 6.8 depicts the overall asset allocation. The allocation reflects considerations of both efficient diversification (the construction of the optimal risky portfolio, O) and risk aversion (the allocation of funds between the risk-free asset and the risky portfolio O to form the complete portfolio, C).

CONCEPT check 6.4

A universe of securities includes a risky stock (X), a stock index fund (M), and T-bills. The data for the universe are:

	Expected Return	Standard Deviation
X	15%	50%
M	10	20
T-bills	5	0

The correlation coefficient between X and M is -0.2.
  a. Draw the opportunity set of securities X and M.
  b. Find the optimal risky portfolio (O) and its expected return and standard deviation.
  c. Find the slope of the CAL generated by T-bills and portfolio O.
  d. Suppose an investor places 2/9 (i.e., 22.22%) of the complete portfolio in the risky portfolio O and the remainder in T-bills. Calculate the composition of the complete portfolio.

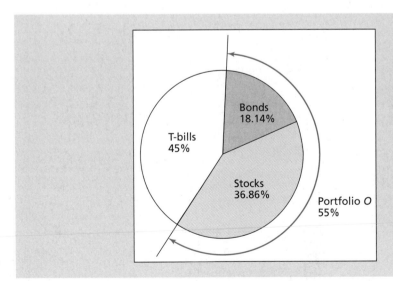

FIGURE 6.8

The composition of the complete portfolio: The solution to the asset allocation problem

6.4 | EFFICIENT DIVERSIFICATION WITH MANY RISKY ASSETS

We can extend the two-risky-assets portfolio construction methodology to cover the case of many risky assets and a risk-free asset. First, we offer an overview. As in the two-risky-assets example, the problem has three separate steps. To begin, we identify the best possible or most *efficient* risk-return combinations available from the universe of risky assets. Next we determine the optimal portfolio of risky assets by finding the portfolio that supports the steepest CAL. Finally, we choose an appropriate complete portfolio based on the investor's risk aversion by mixing the risk-free asset with the optimal risky portfolio.

The Efficient Frontier of Risky Assets

To get a sense of how additional risky assets can improve the investor's investment opportunities, look at Figure 6.9. Points *A, B,* and *C* represent the expected returns and standard deviations of three stocks. The curve passing through *A* and *B* shows the risk-return combinations of all the portfolios that can be formed by combining those two stocks. Similarly, the curve passing through *B* and *C* shows all the portfolios that can be formed from those two stocks. Now observe point *E* on the *AB* curve and point *F* on the *BC* curve. These points represent two portfolios chosen from the set of *AB* combinations and *BC* combinations. The curve that passes through *E* and *F* in turn represents all the portfolios that can be constructed from portfolios *E* and *F*. Since *E* and *F* are themselves constructed from *A, B,* and *C,* this curve also may be viewed as depicting some of the portfolios that can be constructed from these *three* securities. Notice that curve *EF* extends the investment opportunity set to the northwest, which is the desired direction.

Now we can continue to take other points (each representing portfolios) from these three curves and further combine them into new portfolios, thus shifting the opportunity set even farther to the northwest. You can see that this process would work even better with more stocks. Moreover, the efficient frontier, the boundary or "envelope" of all the curves thus developed, will lie quite away from the individual stocks in the northwesterly direction, as shown in Figure 6.10.

FIGURE 6.9

Portfolios constructed with three stocks (*A, B,* and *C*)

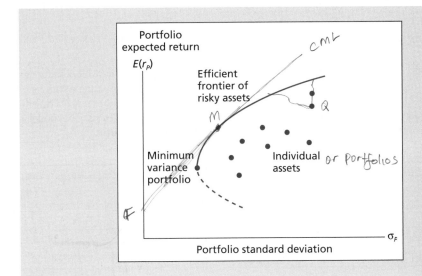

FIGURE 6.10

The efficient frontier of risky assets and individual assets

The analytical technique to derive the efficient frontier of risky assets was developed by Harry Markowitz at the University of Chicago in 1951 and ultimately earned him the Nobel Prize in economics. We will sketch his approach here.

First, we determine the risk-return opportunity set. The aim is to construct the northwestern-most portfolios in terms of expected return and standard deviation from the universe of securities. The inputs are the expected returns and standard deviations of each asset in the universe, along with the correlation coefficients between each pair of assets. These data come from security analysis, to be discussed in Part Four. The graph that connects all the northwesternmost portfolios is called the **efficient frontier** of risky assets. It represents the set of portfolios that offers the highest possible expected rate of return for each level of portfolio standard deviation. These portfolios may be viewed as efficiently diversified. One such frontier is shown in Figure 6.10.

Expected return–standard deviation combinations for any *individual* asset end up inside the efficient frontier, because single-asset portfolios are inefficient—they are not efficiently diversified.

When we choose among portfolios on the efficient frontier, we can immediately discard portfolios below the minimum-variance portfolio. These are dominated by portfolios on the upper half of the frontier with equal risk but higher expected returns. Therefore, the real choice is among portfolios on the efficient frontier above the minimum-variance portfolio.

Various constraints may preclude a particular investor from choosing portfolios on the efficient frontier, however. If an institution is prohibited by law from taking short positions in any asset, for example, the portfolio manager must add constraints to the computer-optimization program that rule out negative (short) positions.

Short sale restrictions are only one possible constraint. Some clients may want to assure a minimum level of expected dividend yield. In this case, data input must include a set of expected dividend yields. The optimization program is made to include a constraint to ensure that the expected *portfolio* dividend yield will equal or exceed the desired level. Another common constraint forbids investments in companies engaged in "undesirable social activity."

In principle, portfolio managers can tailor an efficient frontier to meet any particular objective. Of course, satisfying constraints carries a price tag. An efficient frontier subject to a number of constraints will offer a lower reward-to-variability ratio than a less constrained one. Clients should be aware of this cost and may want to think twice about constraints that are not mandated by law.

Deriving the efficient frontier may be quite difficult conceptually, but computing and graphing it with any number of assets and any set of constraints is quite straightforward. For a not too large number of assets, the efficient frontier can be computed and graphed even with a spreadsheet program.

efficient frontier

Graph representing a set of portfolios that maximizes expected return at each level of portfolio risk.

**Please visit us at
www.mhhe.com/bkm**

Excel spreadsheets can be used to construct an efficient frontier for a group of individual securities or a group of portfolios of securities. The Excel model "Efficient Portfolio" is built using a sample of actual returns on stocks that make up a part of the Dow Jones Industrial Average Index. The efficient frontier is graphed, similar to Figure 6.10, using various possible target returns. The model is built for eight securities and can be easily modified for any group of eight assets.

	A	B	C	D	E	F	G	H	I
3	TKR SYM	Return	S.D.						
4	C	46.6	34.8						
5	GE	37.3	25.0						
6	HD	41.8	31.4						
7	INTC	46.0	45.9						
8	JNJ	24.6	26.2						
9	MRK	32.6	31.0						
10	SBC	19.0	28.1						
11	WMT	41.2	31.4						
12									
13				Correlation Matrix					
14									
15		C	GE	HD	INTC	JNJ	MRK	SBC	WMT
16	C	1.00	0.54	0.26	0.26	0.35	0.29	0.25	0.40
17	GE	0.54	1.00	0.58	0.26	0.29	0.20	0.34	0.52
18	HD	0.26	0.58	1.00	-0.09	-0.02	-0.12	0.15	0.58
19	INTC	0.26	0.26	-0.09	1.00	0.09	0.11	-0.05	-0.02
20	JNJ	0.35	0.29	-0.02	0.09	1.00	0.58	0.28	0.28
21	MRK	0.29	0.20	-0.12	0.11	0.58	1.00	0.37	0.12
22	SBC	0.25	0.34	0.15	-0.05	0.28	0.37	1.00	0.16
23	WMT	0.40	0.52	0.58	-0.02	0.28	0.12	0.16	1.00
24									
25				Covariance Matrix					
26		C	GE	HD	INTC	JNJ	MRK	SBC	WMT
27	C	1211.55	468.81	282.30	419.81	320.52	308.52	239.86	440.95
28	GE	468.81	627.47	451.99	299.86	189.64	158.28	240.96	409.29
29	HD	282.30	451.99	983.39	-133.54	-17.19	-117.25	133.28	566.72
30	INTC	419.81	299.86	-133.54	2106.34	113.73	151.78	-63.77	-34.46
31	JNJ	320.52	189.64	-17.19	113.73	686.88	473.15	203.37	229.77
32	MRK	308.52	158.28	-117.25	151.78	473.15	961.63	324.53	119.16
33	SBC	239.86	240.96	133.28	-63.77	203.37	324.53	790.22	140.90
34	WMT	440.95	409.29	566.72	-34.46	229.77	119.16	140.90	987.13

The spreadsheet program available at **www.mhhe.com/bkm** can easily incorporate restrictions against short sales. We mention this because many investment managers are prohibited from engaging in short sales. To impose this restriction, the program simply requires that each weight in the optimal portfolio be greater than or equal to zero. One way to see whether the short-sale constraint actually matters is to find the efficient portfolio without it. If one or more of the weights in the optimal portfolio turn out negative, we know the short-sale restrictions will result in a different efficient frontier with a less attractive risk-return trade-off.

Choosing the Optimal Risky Portfolio

The second step of the optimization plan involves the risk-free asset. Using the current risk-free rate, we search for the capital allocation line with the highest reward-to-variability ratio (the steepest slope), as shown in Figures 6.5 and 6.6.

The CAL formed from the optimal risky portfolio (*O*) will be tangent to the efficient frontier of risky assets discussed above. This CAL dominates all alternative feasible lines (the dashed lines that are drawn through the frontier). Portfolio *O,* therefore, is the optimal risky portfolio. This step is also within the capability of a spreadsheet program.

The Preferred Complete Portfolio and the Separation Property

Finally, in the third step, the investor chooses the appropriate mix between the optimal risky portfolio (*O*) and T-bills, exactly as in Figure 6.7.

A portfolio manager will offer the same risky portfolio (*O*) to all clients, no matter what their degrees of risk aversion. Risk aversion comes into play only when clients select their desired point on the CAL. More risk-averse clients will invest more in the risk-free asset and less in the optimal risky portfolio *O* than less risk-averse clients, but both will use portfolio *O* as the optimal risky investment vehicle.

This result is called a **separation property,** introduced by James Tobin (1958), the 1983 Nobel Laureate for economics: It implies that portfolio choice can be separated into two independent tasks. The first task, which includes steps one and two, determination of the optimal risky portfolio (*O*), is purely technical. Given the particular input data, the best risky portfolio is the same for all clients regardless of risk aversion. The second task, construction of the complete portfolio from bills and portfolio *O,* however, depends on personal preference. Here the client is the decision maker.

Of course, the optimal risky portfolio for different clients may vary because of portfolio constraints such as dividend yield requirements, tax considerations, or other client preferences. Our analysis, though, suggests that a few portfolios may be sufficient to serve the demands of a wide range of investors. We see here the theoretical basis of the mutual fund industry.

If the optimal portfolio is the same for all clients, professional management is more efficient and less costly. One management firm can serve a number of clients with relatively small incremental administrative costs.

The (computerized) optimization technique is the easiest part of portfolio construction. If different managers use different input data to develop different efficient frontiers, they will offer different "optimal" portfolios. Therefore, the real arena of the competition among portfolio managers is in the sophisticated security analysis that underlies their choices. The rule of GIGO (garbage in–garbage out) applies fully to portfolio selection. If the quality of the security analysis is poor, a passive portfolio such as a market index fund can yield better results than an active portfolio tilted toward *seemingly* favorable securities.

separation property

The property that implies portfolio choice can be separated into two independent tasks: (1) determination of the optimal risky portfolio, which is a purely technical problem, and (2) the personal choice of the best mix of the risky portfolio and the risk-free asset.

Two portfolio managers work for competing investment management houses. Each employs security analysts to prepare input data for the construction of the optimal portfolio. When all is completed, the efficient frontier obtained by manager A dominates that of manager B in that A's optimal risky portfolio lies northwest of B's. Is the more attractive efficient frontier asserted by manager A evidence that she really employs better security analysts?

CONCEPT *check* **6.5**

6.5 A SINGLE-FACTOR ASSET MARKET

We started this chapter with the distinction between systematic and firm-specific risk. Systematic risk is largely macroeconomic, affecting all securities, while firm-specific risk factors affect only one particular firm or, perhaps, its industry. **Factor models** are statistical models designed to estimate these two components of risk for a particular security or portfolio. The first to use a factor model to explain the benefits of diversification was another Nobel Prize winner, William F. Sharpe (1963). We will introduce his major work (the capital asset pricing model) in the next chapter.

The popularity of factor models is due to their practicality. To construct the efficient frontier from a universe of 100 securities, we would need to estimate 100 expected returns, 100

factor model

Statistical model to measure the firm-specific versus systematic risk of a stock's rate of return.

variances, and $100 \times 99/2 = 4{,}950$ covariances. And a universe of 100 securities is actually quite small. A universe of 1,000 securities would require estimates of $1{,}000 \times 999/2 = 499{,}500$ covariances, as well as 1,000 expected returns and variances. We will see shortly that the assumption that one common factor is responsible for all the covariability of stock returns, with all other variability due to firm-specific factors, dramatically simplifies the analysis.

excess return

Rate of return in excess of the risk-free rate.

Let us use R_i to denote the **excess return** on a security, that is, the rate of return in excess of the risk-free rate: $R_i = r_i - r_f$. Then we can express the distinction between macroeconomic and firm-specific factors by decomposing this excess return in some holding period into three components

$$R_i = E(R_i) + \beta_i M + e_i \qquad (6.11)$$

In Equation 6.11, $E(R_i)$ is the *expected excess* holding-period return (HPR) at the start of the holding period. The next two terms reflect the impact of two sources of uncertainty. M quantifies the market or macroeconomic surprises (with zero meaning that there is "no surprise") during the holding period. β_i is the sensitivity of the security to the macroeconomic factor. Finally, e_i is the impact of unanticipated firm-specific events.

beta

The sensitivity of a security's returns to the systematic or market factor.

Both M and e_i have zero expected values because each represents the impact of unanticipated events, which by definition must average out to zero. The **beta**, (β_i) denotes the responsiveness of security i to macroeconomic events; this sensitivity will be different for different securities.

As an example of a factor model, suppose that the excess return on Dell stock is *expected* to be 9% in the coming holding period. However, on average, for every unanticipated increase of 1% in the vitality of the general economy, which we take as the macroeconomic factor M, Dell's stock return will be enhanced by 1.2%. Dell's β is therefore 1.2. Finally, Dell is affected by firm-specific surprises as well. Therefore, we can write the realized excess return on Dell stock as follows

$$R_D = 9\% + 1.2M + e_i$$

If the economy outperforms expectations by 2%, then we would revise upward our expectations of Dell's excess return by $1.2 \times 2\%$, or 2.4%, resulting in a new expected excess return of 11.4%. Finally, the effects of Dell's firm-specific news during the holding period must be added to arrive at the actual holding-period return on Dell stock.

Equation 6.11 describes a factor model for stock returns. This is a simplification of reality; a more realistic decomposition of security returns would require more than one factor in Equation 6.11.[3] We treat this issue in the next chapter, but for now, let us examine the single-factor case.

Specification of a Single-Index Model of Security Returns

A factor model description of security returns is of little use if we cannot specify a way to measure the factor that we say affects security returns. One reasonable approach is to use the rate of return on a broad index of securities, such as the S&P 500, as a proxy for the common macro factor. With this assumption, we can use the excess return on the market index, R_M, to measure the direction of macro shocks in any period.

---

[3]Equation 6.11 is surprisingly simple and would appear to require very strong assumptions about security market equilibrium. But in fact, if rates of return are normally distributed, then returns will be linear in one or more factors. Statistics theory tells us that, when rates of return on a set of securities are *joint-normally* distributed, then the rate of return on each asset is linear in one identical factor as in Equation 6.11. When rates of return exhibit a multivariate normal distribution, we can use a multifactor generalization of Equation 6.11. Practitioners employ factor models such as 6.11 extensively because of the ease of use as we explained earlier, but they would not do so unless empirical evidence supported them. We emphasize that the usefulness of these factor models is independent of the particular models of risk and return discussed in the next chapter. Hence, it is logical to introduce factor models in this chapter prior to a discussion of equilibrating forces and their potential impact on expected returns of various securities.

The **index model** separates the realized rate of return on a security into macro (systematic) and micro (firm-specific) components much like Equation 6.11. The excess rate of return on each security is the sum of three components:

	Symbol
1. The stock's excess return if the market factor is neutral, that is, if the market's excess return is zero.	α_i
2. The component of return due to movements in the overall market (as represented by the index R_M); β_i is the security's responsiveness to the market.	$\beta_i R_M$
3. The component attributable to unexpected events that are relevant only to this security (firm-specific).	e_i

index model

A model of stock returns
using a market index
such as the S&P 500 to
represent common or
systematic risk factors.

The excess return on the stock now can be stated as

$$R_i = \alpha_i + \beta_i R_M + e_i \qquad \textbf{(6.12)}$$

Equation 6.12 specifies two sources of security risk: market or systematic risk ($\beta_i R_M$), attributable to the security's sensitivity (as measured by beta) to movements in the overall market, and firm-specific risk (e_i), which is the part of uncertainty independent of the market factor. Because the firm-specific component of the firm's return is uncorrelated with the market return, we can write the variance of the excess return of the stock as[4]

$$\begin{aligned}
\text{Variance } (R_i) &= \text{Variance } (\alpha_i + \beta_i R_M + e_i) \\
&= \text{Variance } (\beta_i R_M) + \text{Variance } (e_i) \\
&= \beta_i^2 \sigma_M^2 + \sigma^2(e_i) \\
\text{Total risk} \rightarrow &= \text{Systematic risk } + \text{Firm-specific risk} \qquad \textbf{(6.13)}
\end{aligned}$$

Therefore, the total variability of the rate of return of each security depends on two components:

1. The variance attributable to the uncertainty common to the entire market. This systematic risk is attributable to the uncertainty in R_M. Notice that the systematic risk of each stock depends on both the volatility in R_M (that is, σ_M^2) *and* the sensitivity of the stock to fluctuations in R_M. That sensitivity is measured by β_i.
2. The variance attributable to firm-specific risk factors, the effects of which are measured by e_i. This is the variance in the part of the stock's return that is independent of market performance.

This single-index model is convenient. It relates security returns to a market index that investors follow. Moreover, as we soon shall see, its usefulness goes beyond mere convenience.

Statistical and Graphical Representation of the Single-Index Model

Equation 6.12, $R_i = \alpha_i + \beta_i R_M + e_i$, may be interpreted as a single-variable *regression equation* of R_i on the market excess return R_M. The excess return on the security (R_i) is the dependent variable that is to be explained by the regression. On the right-hand side of the equation are the intercept α_i; the regression (or slope) coefficient beta, β_i, multiplying the independent (or explanatory) variable R_M; and the security residual (unexplained) return, e_i. We can plot this regression relationship as in Figure 6.11, which shows a possible scatter diagram for Dell's excess return against the excess return of the market index.

---

[4] Notice that because α_i is a constant, it has no bearing on the variance of R_i.

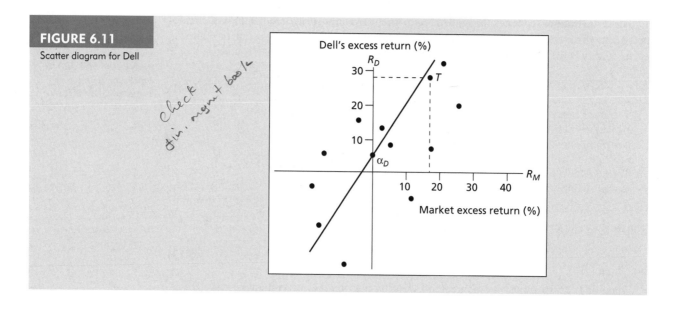

The horizontal axis of the scatter diagram measures the explanatory variable, here the market excess return, R_M. The vertical axis measures the dependent variable, here Dell's excess return, R_D. Each point on the scatter diagram represents a sample pair of returns (R_M, R_D) that might be observed for a particular holding period. Point T, for instance, describes a holding period when the excess return was 17% on the market index and 27% on Dell.

Regression analysis lets us use the sample of historical returns to estimate a relationship between the dependent variable and the explanatory variable. The regression line in Figure 6.11 is drawn so as to minimize the sum of all the squared deviations around it. Hence, we say the regression line "best fits" the data in the scatter diagram. The line is called the **security characteristic line**, or SCL.

security characteristic line

Plot of a security's excess return as a function of the excess return of the market.

The regression intercept (α_D) is measured from the origin to the intersection of the regression line with the vertical axis. Any point on the vertical axis represents zero market excess return, so the intercept gives us the *expected excess* return on Dell during the sample period when market performance was neutral. The intercept in Figure 6.11 is about 4.5%.

The slope of the regression line can be measured by dividing the rise of the line by its run. It also is expressed by the number multiplying the explanatory variable, which is called the regression coefficient or the slope coefficient or simply the beta. The regression beta is a natural measure of systematic risk since it measures the typical response of the security return to market fluctuations.

The regression line does not represent the *actual* returns: that is, the points on the scatter diagram almost never lie on the regression line, although the actual returns are used to calculate the regression coefficients. Rather, the line represents average tendencies; it shows the effect of the index return on our *expectation* of R_D. The algebraic representation of the regression line is

$$E(R_D | R_M) = \alpha_D + \beta_D R_M \tag{6.14}$$

which reads: The expectation of R_D *given* a value of R_M equals the intercept plus the slope coefficient times the given value of R_M.

Because the regression line represents expectations, and because these expectations may not be realized in any or all of the *actual* returns (as the scatter diagram shows), the *actual* security returns also include a residual, the firm-specific surprise, e_i. This surprise (at point T, for example) is measured by the vertical distance between the point of the scatter diagram and the regression line. For example, the expected return on Dell, given a market return of 17%, would have been $4.5\% + 1.4 \times 17\% = 28.3\%$. The actual return was only 27%, so point T falls below the regression line by 1.3%.

Equation 6.13 shows that the greater the beta of the security, that is, the greater the slope of the regression, the greater the security's systematic risk, as well as its total variance. The *average security* has a slope coefficient (beta) of 1.0: Because the market is composed of all securities, the typical response to a market movement must be one for one. An "aggressive" investment will have a beta higher than 1.0; that is, the security has above-average market risk.[5] In Figure 6.11, Dell's beta is 1.4. Conversely, securities with betas lower than 1.0 are called defensive.

A security may have a negative beta. Its regression line will then slope downward, meaning that, for more favorable macro events (higher R_M), we would expect a *lower* return, and vice versa. The latter means that when the macro economy goes bad (negative R_M) and securities with positive beta are expected to have negative excess returns, the negative-beta security will shine. The result is that a negative-beta security has *negative* systematic risk, that is, it provides a hedge against systematic risk.

The dispersion of the scatter of actual returns about the regression line is determined by the residual variance $\alpha^2(e_D)$, which measures the effects of firm-specific events. The magnitude of firm-specific risk varies across securities. One way to measure the relative importance of systematic risk is to measure the ratio of systematic variance to total variance.

$$\rho^2 = \frac{\text{Systematic (or explained) variance}}{\text{Total variance}}$$
$$= \frac{\beta_D^2 \sigma_M^2}{\sigma_D^2} = \frac{\beta_D^2 \sigma_M^2}{\beta_D^2 \sigma_M^2 + \sigma^2(e_D)} \qquad (6.15)$$

where ρ is the correlation coefficient between R_D and R_M. Its square measures the ratio of explained variance to total variance, that is, the proportion of total variance that can be attributed to market fluctuations. But if beta is negative, so is the correlation coefficient, an indication that the explanatory and dependent variables are expected to move in opposite directions.

At the extreme, when the correlation coefficient is either 1.0 or −1.0, the security return is fully explained by the market return, that is, there are no firm-specific effects. All the points of the scatter diagram will lie exactly on the line. This is called perfect correlation (either positive or negative); the return on the security is perfectly predictable from the market return. A large correlation coefficient (in absolute value terms) means systematic variance dominates the total variance; that is, firm-specific variance is relatively unimportant. When the correlation coefficient is small (in absolute value terms), the market factor plays a relatively unimportant part in explaining the variance of the asset, and firm-specific factors dominate.

Interpret the eight scatter diagrams of Figure 6.12 in terms of systematic risk, diversifiable risk, and the intercept.

CONCEPT **6.6**
check

---

[5]Note that the average beta of all securities will be 1.0 only when we compute a *weighted* average of betas (using market values as weights), since the stock market index is value weighted. We know from Chapter 5 that the distribution of securities by market value is not symmetric: There are relatively few large corporations and many more smaller ones. Thus, if you were to take a randomly selected sample of stocks, you should expect smaller companies to dominate. As a result, the simple average of the betas of individual securities, when computed against a value-weighted index such as the S&P 500, will be greater than 1.0, pushed up by the tendency for stocks of low-capitalization companies to have betas greater than 1.0.

EXAMPLE 6.4

Estimating the Index Model Using Historical Data

The direct way to calculate the slope and intercept of the characteristic lines for ABC and XYZ is from the variances and covariances. Here, we use the Data Analysis menu of Excel to obtain the covariance matrix in the following spreadsheet.

The slope coefficient for ABC is given by the formula

$$\beta_{ABC} = \frac{Cov(R_{ABC}, R_{Market})}{Var(R_{Market})} = \frac{773.31}{684.01} = 1.156$$

The intercept for ABC is

$$\alpha_{ABC} = Average(R_{ABC}) - \beta_{ABC} \times Average(R_{Market})$$
$$= 15.20 - 1.156 \times 9.40 = 4.33$$

Therefore, the security characteristic line of ABC is given by

$$R_{ABC} = 4.33 + 1.156\, R_{Market}$$

This result also can be obtained by using the "Regression" command from Excel's Data Analysis menu, as we show at the bottom of the spreadsheet. The minor differences between the direct regression output and our calculations above are due to rounding error.

	A	B	C	D	E	F	G	H	I
2			Annualized rates of return					Excess Returns	
3	Week	ABC	XYZ	Mkt. Index	Risk free		ABC	XYZ	Market
4	1	65.13	-22.55	64.40	5.23		59.90	-27.78	59.17
5	2	51.84	31.44	24.00	4.76		47.08	26.68	19.24
6	3	-30.82	-6.45	9.15	6.22		-37.04	-12.67	2.93
7	4	-15.13	-51.14	-35.57	3.78		-18.91	-54.92	-39.35
8	5	70.63	33.78	11.59	4.43		66.20	29.35	7.16
9	6	107.82	32.95	23.13	3.78		104.04	29.17	19.35
10	7	-25.16	70.19	8.54	3.87		-29.03	66.32	4.67
11	8	50.48	27.63	25.87	4.15		46.33	23.48	21.72
12	9	-36.41	-48.79	-13.15	3.99		-40.40	-52.78	-17.14
13	10	-42.20	52.63	20.21	4.01		-46.21	48.62	16.20
14	Average:						15.20	7.55	9.40
15									
16	COVARIANCE MATRIX:								
17		ABC	XYZ	Market					
18	ABC	3020.933							
19	XYZ	442.114	1766.923						
20	Market	773.306	396.789	669.010					
21									
22	SUMMARY OUTPUT OF EXCEL REGRESSION:								
23									
24	*Regression Statistics*								
25	Multiple R	0.544							
26	R Square	0.296							
27	Adj. R Square	0.208							
28	Standard Error	48.918							
29	Observations	10.000							
30									
31									
32		Coefficients	Std. Error	t Stat	P-value				
33	Intercept	4.336	16.564	0.262	0.800				
34	Market return	1.156	0.630	1.834	0.104				
35									

Note: This is the output provided by the Data Analysis tool in Excel. As a technical aside, we should point out that the covariance matrix produced by Excel does not adjust for degrees of freedom. In other words, it divides total squared deviations from mean (for variance) or total cross product of deviations from means (for covariance) by total observations, despite the fact that sample averages are estimated parameters. This procedure does not affect regression coefficients, however, because in the formula for beta, both the numerator (i.e., the covariance) and denominator (i.e., the variance) are affected equally.

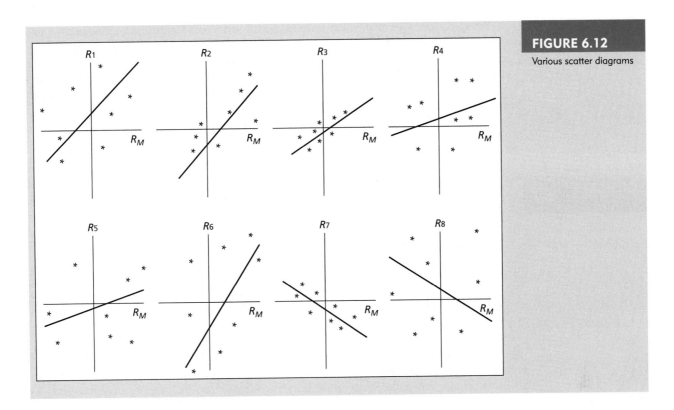

FIGURE 6.12

Various scatter diagrams

Diversification in a Single-Factor Security Market

Imagine a portfolio that is divided equally among securities whose returns are given by the single-index model in Equation 6.12. What are the systematic and nonsystematic (firm-specific) variances of this portfolio?

The beta of the portfolio is the simple average of the individual security betas, which we denote β. Hence, the systematic variance equals $\beta_P^2 \sigma_M^2$. This is the level of market risk in Figure 6.1B. The market variance (σ_M^2) and the market sensitivity of the portfolio (β_P) determine the market risk of the portfolio.

The systematic component of each security return, $\beta_i R_M$, is fully determined by the market factor and therefore is perfectly correlated with the systematic part of any other security's return. Hence, there are no diversification effects on systematic risk no matter how many securities are involved. As far as *market risk* goes, a single-security portfolio with a small beta will result in a low market-risk portfolio. The number of securities makes no difference.

It is quite different with firm-specific or unique risk. If you choose securities with small residual variances for a portfolio, it, too, will have low unique risk. But you can do even better simply by holding more securities, even if each has a large residual variance. Because the firm-specific effects are independent of each other, their risk effects are offsetting. This is the insurance principle applied to the firm-specific component of risk. The portfolio ends up with a negligible level of nonsystematic risk.

In sum, when we control the systematic risk of the portfolio by manipulating the average beta of the component securities, the number of securities is of no consequence. But in the case of *nonsystematic* risk, the number of securities involved is more important than the firm-specific variance of the securities. Sufficient diversification can virtually eliminate firm-specific risk. Understanding this distinction is essential to understanding the role of diversification in portfolio construction.

We have just seen that when forming highly diversified portfolios, firm-specific risk becomes *irrelevant*. Only systematic risk remains. We conclude that in measuring security risk for diversified investors, we should focus our attention on the security's systematic risk. This means that for diversified investors, the relevant risk measure for a security will be the security's beta, β, since firms with higher β have greater sensitivity to broad market disturbances. As Equation 6.13 makes clear, systematic risk will be determined both by market volatility, σ_M^2, and the firm's sensitivity to the market, β.

CONCEPT
c h e c k **6.7**

   a. What is the characteristic line of XYZ in Example 6.4?
   b. Does ABC or XYZ have greater systematic risk?
   c. What percent of the variance of XYZ is firm-specific risk?

6.6   RISK OF LONG-TERM INVESTMENTS

So far we have envisioned portfolio investment for one period. We have not made any explicit assumptions about the duration of that period, so one might take it to be of any length, and thus our analysis would seem to apply as well to long-term investments. Yet investors are frequently advised that stock investments for the long run are not as risky as it might appear from the statistics presented in this chapter and the previous one. To understand this widespread misconception, we must first understand how the argument goes.

Are Stock Returns Less Risky in the Long Run?

Advocates of the notion that investment risk is lower over longer horizons apply the logic of diversification across many risky *assets* to an investment in a risky portfolio over many *years*. Because stock returns in successive years are almost uncorrelated, they conclude that (1) the annual standard deviation of an investment in stocks falls with the investment horizon, and hence, (2) investment risk in a stock portfolio declines with the investment horizon.

To be concrete, consider a 2-year investment for which the rate of return in each year is normally distributed with an identical standard deviation of σ, and for which the returns in different years are uncorrelated with each other, so that $\text{Cov}(r_1, r_2) = 0$. The total rate of return over the two years[6] is: $r(2 \text{ years}) = r_1 + r_2$. The variance of the total return over the two years equals

$$
\begin{aligned}
\text{Var(2-year total return)} &= \text{Var}(r_1 + r_2) \\
&= \text{Var}(r_1) + \text{Var}(r_2) + 2\,\text{Cov}(r_1, r_2) \\
&= \sigma^2 + \sigma^2 + 0 \\
&= 2\sigma^2
\end{aligned}
$$

(6.16)

The standard deviation is the square root of the variance, so

$$\text{Standard deviation(2-year total return)} = \sigma\sqrt{2}$$

---

[6] To account for compounding of rates over the years, these rates must be viewed as continuously compounded returns, as explained in Chapter 5.

Thus, the variance of the total 2-year return is double that of the one-year return, and the standard deviation is higher by a multiple of $\sqrt{2}$. Generalizing to an investment horizon of n years, the variance and standard deviatioxn of the total return over n years will grow to:

$$\text{Var}(n\text{-year total return}) = n\,\sigma^2$$

$$\text{Standard deviation}(n\text{-year total return}) = \sigma\sqrt{n} \qquad \textbf{(6.17)}$$

To put the standard deviation of *total* return on a per-year or annualized basis, we divide the standard deviation by the number of years, n, to obtain:

$$\sigma(\text{annualized for an } n\text{-year investment}) = \frac{1}{n}\sigma\sqrt{n} = \frac{\sigma}{\sqrt{n}} \qquad \textbf{(6.18)}$$

In fact, this result seems identical to the annual standard deviation of an equally weighted portfolio diversified across n uncorrelated stocks, all with a common standard deviation, σ. To illustrate, consider a portfolio of two identical, uncorrelated stocks. Since the stocks are identical, the efficient portfolio will be equally weighted. Applying Equation 6.6 with weights of $w_A = w_B = \frac{1}{2}$,

$$\sigma_P^2 = (\tfrac{1}{2})^2\,\sigma_A^2 + (\tfrac{1}{2})^2\,\sigma_B^2 + 2[\tfrac{1}{2}\,\sigma_A][\tfrac{1}{2}\,\sigma_B]\rho_{AB} \qquad \textbf{(6.19)}$$

If each stock has identical standard deviation, then $\sigma_A = \sigma_B = \sigma$, and if they are uncorrelated, then $\rho_{AB} = 0$. In this case, therefore,

$$\sigma_P^2 = 2 \times (\tfrac{1}{2})^2\,\sigma^2 = \tfrac{1}{2}\sigma^2$$

$$\sigma_P = \sigma\sqrt{\tfrac{1}{2}}$$

Similarly for n stocks, with portfolio weights of $1/n$ in each stock,

$$\sigma_P = \frac{\sigma}{\sqrt{n}} \qquad \textbf{(6.20)}$$

In fact, we used Equation 6.20 to draw Figure 6.1A illustrating diversification with uncorrelated stocks. Since the annual standard deviation of a portfolio diversified across n identical, uncorrelated stocks in Equation 6.20 is similar to the annualized standard deviation of a stock portfolio invested over n years (Equation 6.18), there is a temptation (to which many financial advisors have succumbed) to interpret the latter as evidence of "time diversification" and conclude that risk over the long haul declines with investment horizon. By this reasoning, Figure 6.1A would seem to apply to time diversification as well, if you replace the number of stocks on the horizontal axis with the number of years. If this were true, time diversification would be very comforting to the many long-term investors who should, by this logic, replace safe investments with risky investments in stocks. Unfortunately, however, the logic is flawed.

The Fly in the "Time Diversification" Ointment (or More Accurately, the Snake Oil)

The flaw in the logic is the use of the annualized standard deviation to gauge the risk of a long-term investment. Annualized standard deviation is an appropriate measure of risk *only* for short-term (annual horizon) portfolios! It cannot serve to measure risk when comparing investments of different horizons and different scales.

To illustrate with an example, suppose that investors can invest in safe bonds indexed to the price level, and, to simplify, that the real rate of return on all bonds is zero. The real value of a stock portfolio in any year will either double or fall by one half with equal probability. Our investor considers two strategies:

A. Short-term risky strategy:

Invest the entire budget in stocks for one year, then liquidate and invest the proceeds in a safe bond for the second year.

B. Long-term risky strategy:

Invest the entire budget in stocks for two years. The possible outcomes to this strategy are: quadrupling of value (doubling in each year), unchanged value (doubling in one year and halving in the other), or value falling by a factor of ¼ (halving in each year).

The following table compares the probability distributions of final outcomes of the two investments.

A. One Year in Stocks		B. Two Years in Stocks	
Possible Outcome	**Probability**	**Possible Outcome**	**Probability**
Value doubles	0.5	Value quadruples	0.25
Value falls by half	0.5	Value unchanged	0.5
		Value falls by 75%	0.25

Since risk aversion makes investors concerned with downside risk, you can see that the two strategies cannot be compared on the basis of standard deviation of annualized returns. Surely a risk-averse investor will consider the two-year investment (for which value can decline by 75%) riskier and will reject outright the notion that the two-year stock investment is less risky. Time diversification advocates will say: "But the probability of a loss is smaller, only 25%." This argument implies that, somehow, *probability* of loss is now a valid measure of risk. The fact of the matter is that probability of loss alone is not a legitimate measure of risk any more than is the size of the loss alone.

The correct comparison is based on risk of the total (end of horizon) return, which accounts for both magnitudes as well as probabilities of possible losses. The variance of the total rate of return, which accounts for both, grows linearly with the number of years, and the standard deviation grows in proportion to $\sqrt{n}$, as in Equation 6.17. While the average risk per year may be smaller with longer horizons as in Equation 6.18, that risk compounds for a greater number of years, which certainly makes your cumulative investment outcome riskier, as Equation 6.17 makes clear.

Empirical evidence on this debate is provided by the actual cost of portfolio insurance. Such insurance is common and we can observe the actual cost of insurance for various horizons and loss coverage. Suppose that for the two-year stock portfolio in our example, we purchase portfolio insurance against an investment loss that exceeds 50%. Such a policy will pay us 25¢ per dollar invested if the portfolio value falls by 75%, thereby equating the maximum possible loss of the two strategies. The expected loss to the insurer, per dollar of coverage, is: 0.25 × 25 = 6.25¢. But we observe that in capital markets, such insurance costs much more for longer horizons, which contradicts any notion that the long-term risky investment is safer than shorter-term one. Time diversification advocates consistently ignore this unshakable fact.

- The expected rate of return of a portfolio is the weighted average of the component asset expected returns with the investment proportions as weights.
- The variance of a portfolio is a sum of the contributions of the component-security variances *plus* terms involving the correlation among assets.
- Even if correlations are positive, the portfolio standard deviation will be less than the weighted average of the component standard deviations, as long as the assets are not *perfectly* positively correlated. Thus, portfolio diversification is of value as long as assets are less than perfectly correlated.
- The contribution of an asset to portfolio variance depends on its correlation with the other assets in the portfolio, as well as on its own variance. An asset that is perfectly negatively correlated with a portfolio can be used to reduce the portfolio variance to zero. Thus, it can serve as a perfect hedge.
- The efficient frontier of risky assets is the graphical representation of the set of portfolios that maximizes portfolio expected return for a given level of portfolio standard deviation. Rational investors will choose a portfolio on the efficient frontier.
- A portfolio manager identifies the efficient frontier by first establishing estimates for the expected returns and standard deviations and determining the correlations among them. The input data are then fed into an optimization program that produces the investment proportions, expected returns, and standard deviations of the portfolios on the efficient frontier.
- In general, portfolio managers will identify different efficient portfolios because of differences in the methods and quality of security analysis. Managers compete on the quality of their security analysis relative to their management fees.
- If a risk-free asset is available and input data are identical, all investors will choose the same portfolio on the efficient frontier, the one that is tangent to the CAL. All investors with identical input data will hold the identical risky portfolio, differing only in how much each allocates to this optimal portfolio and to the risk-free asset. This result is characterized as the separation principle of portfolio selection. *separation property*
- The single-index representation of a single-factor security market expresses the excess rate of return on a security as a function of the market excess return: $R_i = \alpha_i + \beta_i R_M + e_i$. This equation also can be interpreted as a regression of the security excess return on the market-index excess return. The regression line has intercept α_i and slope β_i and is called the security characteristic line.
- In a single-index model, the variance of the rate of return on a security or portfolio can be decomposed into systematic and firm-specific risk. The systematic component of variance equals β^2 times the variance of the market excess return. The firm-specific component is the variance of the residual term in the index model equation.
- The beta of a portfolio is the weighted average of the betas of the component securities. A security with negative beta reduces the portfolio beta, thereby reducing exposure to market volatility. The unique risk of a portfolio approaches zero as the portfolio becomes more highly diversified.

beta, 172
diversifiable risk, 151
efficient frontier, 169
excess return, 172
factor model, 171
firm-specific risk, 151

index model, 173
investment opportunity
   set, 158
market risk, 151
nondiversifiable risk, 151
nonsystematic risk, 151

optimal risky portfolio, 165
security characteristic
   line, 174
separation property, 171
systematic risk, 151
unique risk, 151

PROBLEM SETS

Select problems are available in McGraw-Hill's Homework Manager®.
Please see the packaging options section of the preface for more information.

1. A three-asset portfolio has the following characteristics:

Asset	Expected Return	Standard Deviation	Weight
X	15%	22%	0.50
Y	10	8	0.40
Z	6	3	0.10

$\cdot 50(\cdot 15) + \cdot 40(\cdot 10) + \cdot 10(\cdot 06)$

What is the expected return on this three-asset portfolio?

2. George Stephenson's current portfolio of $2.0 million is invested as follows:

Summary of Stephenson's Current Portfolio				
	Value	Percent of Total	Expected Annual Return	Annual Standard Deviation
Short-term bonds	$ 200,000	10%	4.6%	1.6%
Domestic large-cap equities	600,000	30	12.4	19.5
Domestic small-cap equities	1,200,000	60	16.0	29.9
Total portfolio	$2,000,000	100%	13.8%	23.1%

Stephenson soon expects to receive an additional $2.0 million and plans to invest the entire amount in an index fund that best complements the current portfolio. Stephanie Coppa, CFA, is evaluating the four index funds shown in the following table for their ability to produce a portfolio that will meet two criteria relative to the current portfolio: (1) maintain or enhance expected return and (2) maintain or reduce volatility.

Each fund is invested in an asset class that is not substantially represented in the current portfolio.

Index Fund Characteristics			
Index Fund	Expected Annual Return	Expected Annual Standard Deviation	Correlation of Returns with Current Portfolio
Fund A	15%	25%	+0.80
Fund B	11	22	+0.60
Fund C	16	25	+0.90
Fund D	14	22	+0.65

State which fund Coppa should recommend to Stephenson. Justify your choice by describing how your chosen fund *best* meets both of Stephenson's criteria. No calculations are required.

3. Suppose that the returns on the stock fund presented in Spreadsheet 6.1 were −14%, 13%, and +30% in the three scenarios.

   a. Would you expect the mean return and variance of the stock fund to be more than, less than, or equal to the values computed in Spreadsheet 6.2? Why?

   b. Calculate the new values of mean return and variance for the stock fund using a format similar to Spreadsheet 6.2. Confirm your intuition from part (a).

   c. Calculate the new value of the covariance between the stock and bond funds using a format similar to Spreadsheet 6.4. Explain intuitively why covariance has increased.

4. Use the rate of return data for the stock and bond funds presented in Spreadsheet 6.1, but now assume that the probability of each scenario is: Recession: 0.4; Normal: 0.2; Boom: 0.4.

a. Would you expect the mean return and variance of the stock fund to be more than, less than, or equal to the values computed in Spreadsheet 6.2? Why?

b. Calculate the new values of mean return and variance for the stock fund using a format similar to Spreadsheet 6.2. Confirm your intuition from part (a).

c. Calculate the new value of the covariance between the stock and bond funds using a format similar to Spreadsheet 6.4. Explain intuitively why the absolute value of the covariance has increased.

5. Abigail Grace has a $900,000 fully diversified portfolio. She subsequently inherits ABC Company common stock worth $100,000. Her financial advisor provided her with the following estimates:

Risk and Return Characteristics		
	Expected Monthly Returns	Standard Deviation of Monthly Returns
Original Portfolio	0.67%	2.37%
ABC Company	1.25	2.95

The correlation coefficient of ABC stock returns with the original portfolio returns is 0.40.

a. The inheritance changes Grace's overall portfolio and she is deciding whether to keep the ABC stock. Assuming Grace keeps the ABC stock, calculate the:

i. Expected return of her new portfolio which includes the ABC stock.

ii. Covariance of ABC stock returns with the original portfolio returns.

iii. Standard deviation of her new portfolio which includes the ABC stock.

b. If Grace sells the ABC stock, she will invest the proceeds in risk-free government securities yielding 0.42 percent monthly. Assuming Grace sells the ABC stock and replaces it with the government securities, calculate the:

i. Expected return of her new portfolio which includes the government securities.

ii. Covariance of the government security returns with the original portfolio returns.

iii. Standard deviation of her new portfolio which includes the government securities.

c. Determine whether the beta of her new portfolio, which includes the government securities, will be higher or lower than the beta of her original portfolio.

d. Based on conversations with her husband, Grace is considering selling the $100,000 of ABC stock and acquiring $100,000 of XYZ Company common stock instead. XYZ stock has the same expected return and standard deviation as ABC stock. Her husband comments, "It doesn't matter whether you keep all of the ABC stock or replace it with $100,000 of XYZ stock." State whether her husband's comment is correct or incorrect. Justify your response.

e. In a recent discussion with her financial adviser, Grace commented, "If I just don't lose money in my portfolio, I will be satisfied." She went on to say, "I am more afraid of losing money than I am concerned about achieving high returns." Describe *one* weakness of using standard deviation of returns as a risk measure for Grace.

The following data apply to Problems 6–10.

A pension fund manager is considering three mutual funds. The first is a stock fund, the second is a long-term government and corporate bond fund, and the third is a T-bill money market fund that yields a sure rate of 5.5%. The probability distributions of the risky funds are:

	Expected Return	Standard Deviation
Stock fund (S)	15%	32%
Bond fund (B)	9	23

The correlation between the fund returns is 0.15.

6. Tabulate and draw the investment opportunity set of the two risky funds. Use investment proportions for the stock fund of 0 to 100% in increments of 20%. What expected return and standard deviation does your graph show for the minimum variance portfolio?

7. Draw a tangent from the risk-free rate to the opportunity set. What does your graph show for the expected return and standard deviation of the optimal risky portfolio?

8. What is the reward-to-variability ratio of the best feasible CAL?

9. Suppose now that your portfolio must yield an expected return of 12% and be efficient, that is, on the best feasible CAL.

    a. What is the standard deviation of your portfolio?

    b. What is the proportion invested in the T-bill fund and each of the two risky funds?

10. If you were to use only the two risky funds and still require an expected return of 12%, what would be the investment proportions of your portfolio? Compare its standard deviation to that of the optimal portfolio in the previous problem. What do you conclude?

11. Stocks offer an expected rate of return of 10% with a standard deviation of 20%, and gold offers an expected return of 5% with a standard deviation of 25%.

    a. In light of the apparent inferiority of gold to stocks with respect to both mean return and volatility, would anyone hold gold? If so, demonstrate graphically why one would do so.

    b. How would you answer (a) if the correlation coefficient between gold and stocks were 1.0? Draw a graph illustrating why one would or would not hold gold. Could these expected returns, standard deviations, and correlation represent an equilibrium for the security market?

12. Suppose that many stocks are traded in the market and that it is possible to borrow at the risk-free rate, r_f. The characteristics of two of the stocks are as follows:

Stock	Expected Return	Standard Deviation
A	8%	40%
B	13	60
Correlation = −1		

Could the equilibrium r_f be greater than 10%? (Hint: Can a particular stock portfolio be substituted for the risk-free asset?)

13. You can find a spreadsheet containing the historic returns presented in Table 5.3 on the text Web site at **www.mhhe.com/bkm.** (Look for the link to Chapter 5 material.) Copy the data for the last 20 years into a new spreadsheet. Next turn to Example 6.3 and use it as a model to analyze the risk-return trade-off that would have characterized portfolios constructed from large stocks and long-term Treasury bonds over the last 20 years. What was the average rate of return and standard deviation of each asset? What was the correlation coefficient of their annual returns? What would have been the average return and standard deviation of portfolios with differing weights in the two assets? For example, as in Example 6.3, consider weights in stocks starting at zero and incrementing by .10 up to a weight of 1.0. What was the average return and standard deviation of the minimum-variance combination of stocks and bonds?

14. Assume expected returns and standard deviations for all securities, as well as the risk-free rate for lending and borrowing, are known. Will investors arrive at the same optimal risky portfolio? Explain.

15. Your assistant gives you the following diagram, see next page, as the efficient frontier of the group of stocks you asked him to analyze. The diagram looks a bit odd, but your assistant insists he double-checked his analysis. Would you trust him? Is it possible to get such a diagram?

Please visit us at www.mhhe.com/bkm

16. What is the relationship of the portfolio standard deviation to the weighted average of the standard deviations of the component assets?

17. A project has a 0.7 chance of doubling your investment in a year and a 0.3 chance of halving your investment in a year. What is the standard deviation of the rate of return on this investment?

18. Investors expect the market rate of return this year to be 10%. The expected rate of return on a stock with a beta of 1.2 is currently 12%. If the market return this year turns out to be 8%, how would you revise your expectation of the rate of return on the stock?

19. The following figure shows plots of monthly rates of return and the stock market for two stocks.
    a. Which stock is riskier to an investor currently holding her portfolio in a diversified portfolio of common stock?
    b. Which stock is riskier to an undiversified investor who puts all of his funds in only one of these stocks?

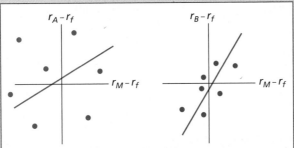

20. Go to **www.mhhe.com/bkm** and link to the material for Chapter 6, where you will find a spreadsheet containing monthly rates of return for GM, the S&P 500, and T-bills over a recent five-year period. Set up a spreadsheet just like that of Example 6.4 and find the beta of GM.

21. Here are rates of return for six months for Generic Risk, Inc. What is Generic's beta? (*Hint:* Find the answer by plotting the scatter diagram.)

Please visit us at www.mhhe.com/bkm

Month	Market Return	Generic Return
1	0%	+2%
2	0	0
3	−1	0
4	−1	−2
5	+1	+4
6	+1	+2

The following data apply to Problems 22–24:

Hennessy & Associates manages a $30 million equity portfolio for the multimanager Wilstead Pension Fund. Jason Jones, financial vice president of Wilstead, noted that Hennessy had rather consistently achieved the best record among the Wilstead's six equity managers. Performance of the Hennessy portfolio had been clearly superior to that of the S&P 500 in four of the past five years. In the one less favorable year, the shortfall was trivial.

Hennessy is a "bottom-up" manager. The firm largely avoids any attempt to "time the market." It also focuses on selection of individual stocks, rather than the weighting of favored industries.

There is no apparent conformity of style among the six equity managers. The five managers, other than Hennessy, manage portfolios aggregating $250 million, made up of more than 150 individual issues.

Jones is convinced that Hennessy is able to apply superior skill to stock selection, but the favorable results are limited by the high degree of diversification in the portfolio. Over the years, the portfolio generally held 40–50 stocks, with about 2% to 3% of total funds committed to each issue. The reason Hennessy seemed to do well most years was that the firm was able to identify each year 10 or 12 issues that registered particularly large gains.

Based on this overview, Jones outlined the following plan to the Wilstead pension committee:

Let's tell Hennessy to limit the portfolio to no more than 20 stocks. Hennessy will double the commitments to the stocks that it really favors and eliminate the remainder. Except for this one new restriction, Hennessy should be free to manage the portfolio exactly as before.

All the members of the pension committee generally supported Jones's proposal, because all agreed that Hennessy had seemed to demonstrate superior skill in selecting stocks. Yet, the proposal was a considerable departure from previous practice, and several committee members raised questions.

22. Answer the following:
    a. Will the limitation of 20 stocks likely increase or decrease the risk of the portfolio? Explain.
    b. Is there any way Hennessy could reduce the number of issues from 40 to 20 without significantly affecting risk? Explain.

23. One committee member was particularly enthusiastic concerning Jones's proposal. He suggested that Hennessy's performance might benefit further from reduction in the number of issues to 10. If the reduction to 20 could be expected to be advantageous, explain why reduction to 10 might be less likely to be advantageous. (Assume that Wilstead will evaluate the Hennessy portfolio independently of the other portfolios in the fund.)

24. Another committee member suggested that, rather than evaluate each managed portfolio independently of other portfolios, it might be better to consider the effects of a change in the Hennessy portfolio on the total fund. Explain how this broader point of view could affect the committee decision to limit the holdings in the Hennessy portfolio to either 10 or 20 issues.

25. What percent of the variance of stock ABC in Example 6.4 is systematic (market) risk?

26. Dudley Trudy, CFA, recently met with one of his clients. Trudy typically invests in a master list of 30 equities drawn from several industries. As the meeting concluded, the

client made the following statement: "I trust your stock-picking ability and believe that you should invest my funds in your five best ideas. Why invest in 30 companies when you obviously have stronger opinions on a few of them?" Trudy plans to respond to his client within the context of Modern Portfolio Theory.

a. Contrast the concepts of systematic risk and firm-specific risk, and give an example of each type of risk.

b. Critique the client's suggestion. Discuss how both systematic and firm-specific risk change as the number of securities in a portfolio is increased.

Use data from the Standard & Poor's Market Insight Database at www.mhhe.com/edumarketinsight to answer the following questions.

STANDARD &POOR'S

1. Use data from Market Insight to plot the characteristic lines for Alcoa and Sharper Image. First locate the Market Insight page for Alcoa by clicking on the "Company" tab. (If you don't know the stock symbol, use the "Lookup" feature to find it.) Find the 1-month total returns of Alcoa and the S&P 500 in the Monthly Adjusted Prices Report in the Excel Analytics, Market Data section. Download the data into Excel, and then plot the Alcoa returns vs. the S&P 500 returns. Use an XY Scatter Plot chart type, with no line joining the points. Select one of the data points, then right-click your mouse to get a shortcut menu which allows you to add a trend line. This is the characteristic line for Alcoa. Repeat the process for Sharper Image. What conclusions can you draw about Alcoa and Sharper Image based on their characteristic lines?

2. Use data from Market Insight to calculate the beta of Staples, Inc. Start by finding the monthly price changes of Staples and the S&P 500 in Monthly Adjusted Prices Report in the Excel Analytics, Market Data section. Copy the data into Excel and confirm the monthly rates of return (based on closing prices) for each series. Using the entire period for which data are available, estimate a regression with Staples' return as the dependent (Y) variable and the S&P 500 return as the independent (X) variable. Now repeat the procedure using only the most recent two years of data. Estimate a third regression using only the earliest two years of data. How stable is the beta estimate? Finally, compare your three results to the beta listed in Staples' S&P Stock Report (in the S&P Stock Reports section). Do any of your results match the S&P Report's beta? What factors might explain any differences?

3. The S&P Report gives information about the company's operations and opinions about its expected performance. Enter the symbol for Gap, Inc. and follow the link to S&P's Stock Report on the company. What companies does Gap operate? What is its weight in the S&P 500? What is the trend in Gap's earnings? What is the trend in its dividend payout ratio? Use the current price listed to calculate the holding period return on the stock assuming that you purchased it at the 52-week low price and that you received the specified dividends for the year. Repeat the calculation using the 52-week high price.

4. In the Excel Analytics section, find the monthly returns in the Monthly Adjusted Prices report for the following firms: Genzyme Corporation, Fujitsu LTD, Cardinal Health, Inc., Black and Decker Corporation, and Kellogg Company. Copy the returns from these five firms into a single Excel workbook, with the returns for each company properly aligned. Use the full range of available data. Then do the following:

a. Using the Excel functions for average (AVERAGE) and sample standard deviation (STDEV), calculate the average and the standard deviation of the returns for each of the firms.

b. Using Excel's correlation function (CORREL), construct the correlation matrix for the five stocks based on their monthly returns for the entire period. What are the lowest and the highest individual pairs of correlation coefficients? (*Alternative:* You may use Excel's Data Analysis Tool to generate the correlation matrix.)

www.mhhe.com/bkm

WEB *master*

Minimum Variance Portfolios

There are some free online tools that will calculate the optimal asset weights and draw the efficient frontier for the assets that you specify. One of the sites is **www. investorcraft.com/PortfolioTools/EfficientFrontier.aspx.**

Go to this site and enter at least 8 assets in the selection box. You can search for the companies by name or by symbol. Click on the "Next Step" button and select one of the time spans offered. Specify an appropriate risk-free rate, a minimum allowable asset weight of 0,

and a maximum allowable asset weight of 100. Click on "Calculate" to get your results.

1. What are the expected return and the standard deviation of the portfolio based on adjusted weights?

2. How do they compare to those for the optimal portfolio and the minimum variance portfolio?

3. Of the three portfolios shown, with which one would you feel most comfortable as an investor?

SOLUTIONS TO

CONCEPT *checks*

6.1. Recalculation of Spreadsheets 6.1, 6.2, and 6.4 shows that the correlation coefficient with the new rates of return is $-.98$.

	A	B	C	D	E	F
1			Stock Fund		Bond Fund	
2	Scenario	Probability	Rate of Return	Col. B × Col. C	Rate of Return	Col. B × Col. E
3	Recession	0.3	-12	-3.6	10	3
4	Normal	0.4	10	4	7	2.8
5	Boom	0.3	28	8.4	2	0.6
6	Expected or Mean Return		SUM:	8.8	SUM:	6.4
7						
8						
9			Stock Fund		Bond Fund	
10			Squared Deviations from Mean	Col. B × Col. C	Squared Deviations from Mean	Col. B × Col. E
11	Scenario	Probability				
12	Recession	0.3	432.64	129.792	12.96	3.888
13	Normal	0.4	1.44	0.576	0.36	0.144
14	Boom	0.3	368.64	110.592	19.36	5.808
15			Variance = SUM:	240.96	SUM:	9.84
16			Std Dev = √ Variance	15.52		3.14
17						
18			Deviation from Mean Return		Covariance	
19	Scenario	Probability	Stock Fund	Bond Fund	Product of Dev	Col. B × Col. E
20	Recession	0.3	-20.8	3.6	-74.88	-22.464
21	Normal	0.4	1.2	0.6	0.72	0.288
22	Boom	0.3	19.2	-4.4	-84.48	-25.344
23				Covariance:	SUM:	-47.52
24	Correlation coefficient = Covariance/(StdDev(stocks)*StdDev(bonds)):					-0.98

6.2. *a.* Using Equation 6.6 with the data: $\sigma_B = 12$; $\sigma_S = 25$; $w_B = 0.5$; and $w_S = 1 - w_B = 0.5$, we obtain the equation

$$\sigma_P^2 = 15^2 = (w_B\sigma_B)^2 + (w_S\sigma_S)^2 + 2(w_B\sigma_B)(w_S\sigma_S)\rho_{BS}$$
$$= (0.5 \times 12)^2 + (0.5 \times 25)^2 + 2(0.5 \times 12)(0.5 \times 25)\rho_{BS}$$

which yields $\rho = 0.2183$.

b. Using Equation 6.5 and the additional data: $E(r_B) = 6$; $E(r_S) = 10$, we obtain

$$E(r_P) = w_B E(r_B) + w_S E(r_S) = (0.5 \times 6) + (0.5 \times 10) = 8\%$$

c. On the one hand, you should be happier with a correlation of 0.2183 than with 0.22 since the lower correlation implies greater benefits from diversification and means that, for any level of expected return, there will be lower risk. On the other hand, the constraint that you must hold

Once you understand the intuition behind the CAPM, it becomes clear that the model may be improved by generalizing it to allow for multiple sources of risk. Therefore, we turn next to multifactor models of risk and return, and show how these result in richer descriptions of the risk-return relationship.

Finally, we consider an alternative derivation of the risk-return relationship known as Arbitrage Pricing Theory, or APT. Arbitrage is the exploitation of security mispricing to earn risk-free economic profits. The most basic principle of capital market theory is that prices ought to be sufficiently in alignment that risk-free profit opportunities should be eliminated. If actual prices allowed for such arbitrage, the resulting opportunities for profitable trading would lead to strong pressure on security prices that would persist until equilibrium was restored and the opportunities were eliminated. We will see that this no-arbitrage principle leads to a risk-return relationship like that of the CAPM. Like the generalized version of the CAPM, the simple APT is easily extended to accommodate multiple sources of systematic risk.

Related Web sites for this chapter are available at www.mhhe.com/bkm.

7.1 THE CAPITAL ASSET PRICING MODEL

The **capital asset pricing model**, or **CAPM**, was developed by Treynor, Sharpe, Lintner, and Mossin in the early 1960s, and further refined later. The model predicts the relationship between the risk and equilibrium expected returns on risky assets. We will approach the CAPM in a simplified setting. Thinking about an admittedly unrealistic world allows a relatively easy leap to the solution. With this accomplished, we can add complexity to the environment, one step at a time, and see how the theory must be amended. This process allows us to develop a reasonably realistic and comprehensible model.

A number of simplifying assumptions lead to the basic version of the CAPM. The fundamental idea is that individuals are as alike as possible, with the notable exceptions of initial wealth and risk aversion. The list of assumptions that describes the necessary conformity of investors follows:

capital asset pricing model (CAPM)

A model that relates the required rate of return for a security to its risk as measured by beta.

1. Investors cannot affect prices by their individual trades. This means that there are many investors, each with an endowment of wealth that is small compared with the total endowment of all investors. This assumption is analogous to the perfect competition assumption of microeconomics.

2. All investors plan for one identical holding period.

3. Investors form portfolios from a universe of publicly traded financial assets, such as stocks and bonds, and have access to unlimited risk-free borrowing or lending opportunities.

4. Investors pay neither taxes on returns nor transaction costs (commissions and service charges) on trades in securities. In such a simple world, investors will not care about the difference between returns from capital gains and those from dividends.

5. All investors attempt to construct efficient frontier portfolios; that is, they are rational mean-variance optimizers.

6. All investors analyze securities in the same way and share the same economic view of the world. Hence, they all end with identical estimates of the probability distribution of future cash flows from investing in the available securities. This means that, given a set of security prices and the risk-free interest rate, all investors use the same expected returns, standard deviations, and correlations to generate the efficient frontier and the unique optimal risky portfolio. This assumption is called *homogeneous expectations*.

Obviously, these assumptions ignore many real-world complexities. However, they lead to some powerful insights into the nature of equilibrium in security markets.

Given these assumptions, we summarize the equilibrium that will prevail in this hypothetical world of securities and investors. We elaborate on these implications in the following sections.

market portfolio

The portfolio for which each security is held in proportion to its market value.

1. All investors will choose to hold the **market portfolio (M),** which includes all assets of the security universe. For simplicity, we shall refer to all assets as stocks. The proportion of each stock in the market portfolio equals the market value of the stock (price per share times the number of shares outstanding) divided by the total market value of all stocks.

2. The market portfolio will be on the efficient frontier. Moreover, it will be the optimal risky portfolio, the tangency point of the capital allocation line (CAL) to the efficient frontier. As a result, the capital market line (CML), the line from the risk-free rate through the market portfolio, M, is also the best attainable capital allocation line. All investors hold M as their optimal risky portfolio, differing only in the amount invested in it as compared to investment in the risk-free asset.

3. The risk premium on the market portfolio will be proportional to the variance of the market portfolio and investors' typical degree of risk aversion. Mathematically

$$E(r_M) - r_f = A^* \sigma_M^2 \tag{7.1}$$

where σ_M is the standard deviation of the return on the market portfolio and A^* is a scale factor representing the degree of risk aversion of the average investor.

4. The risk premium on individual assets will be proportional to the risk premium on the market portfolio (M) and to the *beta coefficient* of the security on the market portfolio. This implies that the rate of return on the market portfolio is the single factor of the security market. The beta measures the extent to which returns on the stock respond to the returns of the market portfolio. Formally, beta is the regression (slope) coefficient of the security return on the market portfolio return, representing the sensitivity of the stock return to fluctuations in the overall security market.

Why All Investors Would Hold the Market Portfolio

Given all our assumptions, it is easy to see why all investors hold identical risky portfolios. If all investors use identical mean-variance analysis (assumption 5), apply it to the same universe of securities (assumption 3), with an identical time horizon (assumption 2), use the same security analysis (assumption 6), and experience identical tax consequences (assumption 4), they all must arrive at the same determination of the optimal risky portfolio. That is, they all derive identical efficient frontiers and find the same tangency portfolio for the capital allocation line (CAL) from T-bills (the risk-free rate, with zero standard deviation) to that frontier, as in Figure 7.1.

With everyone choosing to hold the same risky portfolio, stocks will be represented in the aggregate risky portfolio in the same proportion as they are in each investor's (common) risky portfolio. If GM represents 1% in each common risky portfolio, GM will be 1% of the aggregate risky portfolio. This in fact is the market portfolio since the market is no more than the aggregate of all individual portfolios. Because each investor uses the market portfolio for the optimal risky portfolio, the CAL in this case is called the capital market line, or CML, as in Figure 7.1.

Suppose the optimal portfolio of our investors does not include the stock of some company, say, Delta Air Lines. When no investor is willing to hold Delta stock, the demand is zero, and the stock price will take a free fall. As Delta stock gets progressively cheaper, it begins to look more attractive, while all other stocks look (relatively) less attractive. Ultimately, Delta will reach a price at which it is desirable to include it in the optimal stock portfolio, and investors will buy.

This price adjustment process guarantees that all stocks will be included in the optimal portfolio. The only issue is the price. At a given price level, investors will be willing to buy a stock; at another price, they will not. The bottom line is this: If all investors hold an *identical* risky portfolio, this portfolio must be the *market* portfolio.

FIGURE 7.1

The efficient frontier and
the capital market line

Handwritten annotations:
Like CAL!
$$E(r_c) = R_F + \left[\frac{(E(R)_m - R_F)}{\sigma_m} \right] \sigma_c$$
combined

The Passive Strategy Is Efficient

The CAPM implies that a passive strategy, using the CML as the optimal CAL, is a powerful alternative to an active strategy. The market portfolio proportions are a result of profit-oriented "buy" and "sell" orders that cease only when there is no more profit to be made. And in the simple world of the CAPM, all investors use precious resources in security analysis. A passive investor who takes a free ride by simply investing in the market portfolio benefits from the efficiency of that portfolio. In fact, an active investor who chooses any other portfolio will end on a CAL that is less efficient than the CML used by passive investors.

We sometimes call this result a **mutual fund theorem** because it implies that only one mutual fund of risky assets—the market portfolio—is sufficient to satisfy the investment demands of all investors. The mutual fund theorem is another incarnation of the separation property discussed in Chapter 6. Assuming all investors choose to hold a market index mutual fund, we can separate portfolio selection into two components: (1) a technical side, in which an efficient mutual fund is created by professional management; and (2) a personal side, in which an investor's risk aversion determines the allocation of the complete portfolio between the mutual fund and the risk-free asset. Here, all investors agree that the mutual fund they would like to hold is the market portfolio.

While different investment managers do create risky portfolios that differ from the market index, we attribute this in part to the use of different estimates of risk and expected return. Still, a passive investor may view the market index as a reasonable first approximation to an efficient risky portfolio.

The logical inconsistency of the CAPM is this: If a passive strategy is costless *and* efficient, why would anyone follow an active strategy? But if no one does any security analysis, what brings about the efficiency of the market portfolio?

We have acknowledged from the outset that the CAPM simplifies the real world in its search for a tractable solution. Its applicability to the real world depends on whether its predictions are accurate enough. The model's use is some indication that its predictions are reasonable. We discuss this issue in Section 7.3 and in greater depth in Chapter 8.

mutual fund theorem

States that all investors desire the same portfolio of risky assets and can be satisfied by a single mutual fund composed of that portfolio.

CONCEPT check 7.1

If only some investors perform security analysis while all others hold the market portfolio (M), would the CML still be the efficient CAL for investors who do not engage in security analysis? Explain.

The Risk Premium of the Market Portfolio

In Chapters 5 and 6 we showed how individual investors decide how much to invest in the risky portfolio when they can include a risk-free asset in the investment budget. Returning now to the decision of how much to invest in the market portfolio M and how much in the risk-free asset, what can we deduce about the equilibrium risk premium of portfolio M?

We asserted earlier that the equilibrium risk premium of the market portfolio, $E(r_M) - r_f$, will be proportional to the degree of risk aversion of the average investor and to the risk of the market portfolio, σ_M^2. Now we can explain this result.

When investors purchase stocks, their demand drives up prices, thereby lowering expected rates of return and risk premiums. But if risk premiums fall, then relatively more risk-averse investors will pull their funds out of the risky market portfolio, placing them instead in the risk-free asset. In equilibrium, of course, the risk premium on the market portfolio must be just high enough to induce investors to hold the available supply of stocks. If the risk premium is too high compared to the average degree of risk aversion, there will be excess demand for securities, and prices will rise; if it is too low, investors will not hold enough stock to absorb the supply, and prices will fall. The *equilibrium* risk premium of the market portfolio is therefore proportional to both the risk of the market, as measured by the variance of its returns, and to the degree of risk aversion of the average investor, denoted by A^* in Equation 7.1.

EXAMPLE   7.1

Market Risk, the Risk Premium, and Risk Aversion

Suppose the risk-free rate is 5%, the average investor has a risk-aversion coefficient of $A^* = 2$, and the standard deviation of the market portfolio is 20%. Then, from Equation 7.1, we estimate the equilibrium value of the market risk premium[1] as $2 \times 0.20^2 = 0.08$. So the expected rate of return on the market must be

$$E(r_M) = r_f + \text{Equilibrium risk premium}$$
$$= 0.05 + 0.08 = 0.13 = 13\%$$

If investors were more risk averse, it would take a higher risk premium to induce them to hold shares. For example, if the average degree of risk aversion were 3, the market risk premium would be $3 \times 0.20^2 = 0.12$, or 12%, and the expected return would be 17%.

CONCEPT
check   **7.2**

$RP = 8.5$
20

Historical data for the S&P 500 Index show an average excess return over Treasury bills of about 8.5% with standard deviation of about 20%. To the extent that these averages approximate investor expectations for the sample period, what must have been the coefficient of risk aversion of the average investor? If the coefficient of risk aversion were 3.5, what risk premium would have been consistent with the market's historical standard deviation?

Expected Returns on Individual Securities

The CAPM is built on the insight that the appropriate risk premium on an asset will be determined by its contribution to the risk of investors' overall portfolios. Portfolio risk is what matters to investors, and portfolio risk is what governs the risk premiums they demand.

We know that nonsystematic risk can be reduced to an arbitrarily low level through diversification (Chapter 6); therefore, investors do not require a risk premium as compensation for bearing nonsystematic risk. They need to be compensated only for bearing systematic risk, which cannot be diversified. We know also that the contribution of a single security to the risk of a large diversified portfolio depends only on the systematic risk of the security as measured by its beta, as we saw in Chapter 6, Section 6.5. Therefore, it should not be surprising that the

---

[1]To use Equation 7.1, we must express returns in decimal form rather than as percentages.

risk premium of an asset is proportional to its beta; for example, if you double a security's systematic risk, you must double its risk premium for investors still to be willing to hold the security. Thus, the ratio of risk premium to beta should be the same for any two securities or portfolios.

For example, if we were to compare the ratio of risk premium to systematic risk for the market portfolio, which has a beta of 1.0, with the corresponding ratio for Dell stock, we would conclude that

$$\frac{E(r_M) - r_f}{1} = \frac{E(r_D) - r_f}{\beta_D}$$

Rearranging this relationship results in the CAPM's **expected return–beta relationship**

$$E(r_D) = r_f + \beta_D[E(r_M) - r_f] \tag{7.2}$$

expected return–beta relationship

Implication of the CAPM that security risk premiums (expected excess returns) will be proportional to beta.

In words, the rate of return on any asset exceeds the risk-free rate by a risk premium equal to the asset's systematic risk measure (its beta) times the risk premium of the (benchmark) market portfolio. This expected return–beta relationship is the most familiar expression of the CAPM.

The expected return–beta relationship of the CAPM makes a powerful economic statement. It implies, for example, that a security with a high variance but a relatively low beta of 0.5 will carry one-third the risk premium of a low-variance security with a beta of 1.5. Thus, Equation 7.2 quantifies the conclusion we reached in Chapter 6 that only systematic risk matters to investors who can diversify and that systematic risk is measured by the beta of the security.

Suppose the risk premium of the market portfolio is 9%, and we estimate the beta of Dell as $\beta_D = 1.3$. The risk premium predicted for the stock is therefore 1.3 times the market risk premium, or $1.3 \times 9\% = 11.7\%$. The expected rate of return on Dell is the risk-free rate plus the risk premium. For example, if the T-bill rate were 5%, the expected rate of return would be $5\% + 11.7\% = 16.7\%$, or using Equation 7.2 directly, $$E(r_D) = r_f + \beta_D[\text{Market risk premium}]$$ $$= 5\% + 1.3 \times 9\% = 16.7\%$$ If the estimate of the beta of Dell were only 1.2, the required risk premium for Dell would fall to 10.8%. Similarly, if the market risk premium were only 8% and $\beta_D = 1.3$, Dell's risk premium would be only 10.4%.	**EXAMPLE 7.2** *Expected Returns and Risk Premiums*

The fact that few real-life investors actually hold the market portfolio does not necessarily invalidate the CAPM. Recall from Chapter 6 that reasonably well-diversified portfolios shed (for practical purposes) firm-specific risk and are subject only to systematic or market risk. Even if one does not hold the precise market portfolio, a well-diversified portfolio will be so highly correlated with the market that a stock's beta relative to the market still will be a useful risk measure.

In fact, several researchers have shown that modified versions of the CAPM will hold despite differences among individuals that may cause them to hold different portfolios. A study by Brennan (1970) examines the impact of differences in investors' personal tax rates on market equilibrium. Another study by Mayers (1972) looks at the impact of nontraded assets such as human capital (earning power). Both find that while the market portfolio is no longer each investor's optimal risky portfolio, a modified version of the expected return–beta relationship still holds.

If the expected return–beta relationship holds for any individual asset, it must hold for any combination of assets. The beta of a portfolio is simply the weighted average of the betas of the stocks in the portfolio, using as weights the portfolio proportions. Thus, beta also predicts the portfolio's risk premium in accordance with Equation 7.2.

Consider the following portfolio:

Asset	Beta	Risk Premium	Portfolio Weight
Microsoft	1.2	9.0%	0.5
Con Edison	0.8	6.0	0.3
Gold	0.0	0.0	0.2
Portfolio	0.84	?	1.0

If the market risk premium is 7.5%, the CAPM predicts that the risk premium on each stock is its beta times 7.5%, and the risk premium on the portfolio is 0.84 × 7.5% = 6.3%. This is the same result that is obtained by taking the weighted average of the risk premiums of the individual stocks. (Verify this for yourself.)

A word of caution: We often hear that well-managed firms will provide high rates of return. We agree this is true if one measures the *firm's* return on investments in plant and equipment. The CAPM, however, predicts returns on investments in the *securities* of the firm.

Say that everyone knows a firm is well run. Its stock price should, therefore, be bid up, and returns to stockholders who buy at those high prices will not be extreme. Security *prices* reflect public information about a firm's prospects, but only the risk of the company (as measured by beta in the context of the CAPM) should affect *expected returns*. In a rational market, investors receive high expected returns only if they are willing to bear risk.

Suppose the risk premium on the market portfolio is estimated at 8% with a standard deviation of 22%. What is the risk premium on a portfolio invested 25% in GM with a beta of 1.15 and 75% in Ford with a beta of 1.25?

The Security Market Line

We can view the expected return–beta relationship as a reward-risk equation. The beta of a security is the appropriate measure of its risk because beta is proportional to the risk the security contributes to the optimal risky portfolio.

Risk-averse investors measure the risk of the optimal risky portfolio by its standard deviation. In this world, we would expect the reward, or the risk premium on individual assets, to depend on the risk an individual asset contributes to the overall portfolio. Because the beta of a stock measures the stock's contribution to the standard deviation of the market portfolio, we expect the required risk premium to be a function of beta. The CAPM confirms this intuition, stating further that the security's risk premium is directly proportional to both the beta and the risk premium of the market portfolio; that is, the risk premium equals $\beta\ [E(r_M) - r_f]$.

security market line (SML)

Graphical representation of the expected return–beta relationship of the CAPM.

The expected return–beta relationship is graphed as the security market line (SML) in Figure 7.2. Its slope is the risk premium of the market portfolio. At the point where $\beta = 1.0$ (which is the beta of the market portfolio) on the horizontal axis, we can read off the vertical axis the expected return on the market portfolio.

It is useful to compare the security market line to the capital market line. The CML graphs the risk premiums of efficient portfolios (that is, complete portfolios made up of the risky market portfolio and the risk-free asset) as a function of portfolio standard deviation. This is appropriate because standard deviation is a valid measure of risk for portfolios that are candidates for an investor's complete (overall) portfolio.

The SML, in contrast, graphs *individual asset* risk premiums as a function of asset risk. The relevant measure of risk for individual assets (which are held as parts of a well-diversified portfolio) is not the asset's standard deviation; it is, instead, the contribution of the asset to the portfolio standard deviation as measured by the asset's beta. The SML is valid both for portfolios and individual assets.

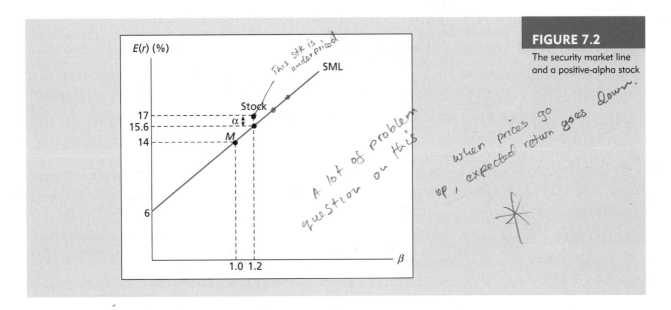

FIGURE 7.2

The security market line and a positive-alpha stock

The security market line provides a benchmark for evaluation of investment performance. Given the risk of an investment as measured by its beta, the SML provides the required rate of return that will compensate investors for the risk of that investment, as well as for the time value of money.

Because the security market line is the graphical representation of the expected return–beta relationship, "fairly priced" assets plot exactly on the SML. The expected returns of such assets are commensurate with their risk. Whenever the CAPM holds, all securities must lie on the SML in market equilibrium. Underpriced stocks plot above the SML: Given their betas, their expected returns are greater than is indicated by the CAPM. Overpriced stocks plot below the SML. The difference between the fair and actually expected rate of return on a stock is called the stock's **alpha,** denoted α.

alpha

The abnormal rate of return on a security in excess of what would be predicted by an equilibrium model such as the CAPM.

Suppose the return on the market is expected to be 14%, a stock has a beta of 1.2, and the T-bill rate is 6%. The SML would predict an expected return on the stock of

$$E(r) = r_f + \beta[E(r_M) - r_f]$$
$$= 6 + 1.2(14 - 6) = 15.6\%$$

If one believes the stock will provide instead a return of 17%, its implied alpha would be 1.4%, as shown in Figure 7.2.

EXAMPLE **7.4**

The Alpha of a Security

Applications of the CAPM

One place the CAPM may be used is in the investment management industry. Suppose the SML is taken as a benchmark to assess the *fair* expected return on a risky asset. Then an analyst calculates the return he or she actually expects. Notice that we depart here from the simple CAPM world in that some investors apply their own analysis to derive an "input list" that may differ from their competitors'. If a stock is perceived to be a good buy, or underpriced, it will provide a positive alpha, that is, an expected return in excess of the fair return stipulated by the SML.

The CAPM is also useful in capital budgeting decisions. If a firm is considering a new project, the CAPM can provide the return the project needs to yield to be acceptable to investors. Managers can use the CAPM to obtain this cutoff internal rate of return (IRR) or "hurdle rate" for the project.

Suppose Silverado Springs Inc. is considering a new spring-water bottling plant. The business plan forecasts an internal rate of return of 14% on the investment. Research shows the beta of similar products is 1.3. Thus, if the risk-free rate is 4%, and the market risk premium is estimated at 8%, the hurdle rate for the project should be $4 + 1.3 \times 8 = 14.4\%$. Because the IRR is less than the risk-adjusted discount or hurdle rate, the project has a negative net present value and ought to be rejected.

Yet another use of the CAPM is in utility rate-making cases. Here the issue is the rate of return a regulated utility should be allowed to earn on its investment in plant and equipment.

Suppose equityholders' investment in the firm is $100 million, and the beta of the equity is 0.6. If the T-bill rate is 6%, and the market risk premium is 8%, then a fair annual profit will be $6 + (0.6 \times 8) = 10.8\%$ of $100 million, or $10.8 million. Since regulators accept the CAPM, they will allow the utility to set prices at a level expected to generate these profits.

a. Stock XYZ has an expected return of 12% and risk of $\beta = 1.0$. Stock ABC is expected to return 13% with a beta of 1.5. The market's expected return is 11% and $r_f = 5\%$. According to the CAPM, which stock is a better buy? What is the alpha of each stock? Plot the SML and the two stocks and show the alphas of each on the graph.

b. The risk-free rate is 8% and the expected return on the market portfolio is 16%. A firm considers a project with an estimated beta of 1.3. What is the required rate of return on the project? If the IRR of the project is 19%, what is the project alpha?

7.2   THE CAPM AND INDEX MODELS

The CAPM has two limitations: It relies on the theoretical market portfolio, which includes *all* assets (such as real estate, foreign stocks, etc.), and it deals with *expected* as opposed to actual returns. To implement the CAPM, we cast it in the form of an *index model* and use realized, not expected, returns.

An index model uses actual portfolios, such as the S&P 500, rather than the theoretical market portfolio to represent the relevant systematic factors in the economy. The important advantage of index models is that the composition and rate of return of the index is easily measured and unambiguous.

In contrast to an index model, the CAPM revolves around the "market portfolio." However, because many assets are not traded, investors would not have full access to the market portfolio even if they could exactly identify it. Thus, the theory behind the CAPM rests on a shaky real-world foundation. But, as in all science, a theory may be viewed as legitimate if its predictions approximate real-world outcomes with a sufficient degree of accuracy. In particular, the reliance on the market portfolio shouldn't faze us if we can verify that the predictions of the CAPM are sufficiently accurate when the index portfolio is substituted for the market.

We can start with one central prediction of the CAPM: The market portfolio is mean-variance efficient. An index model can be used to test this hypothesis by verifying that an index chosen to be representative of the full market is a mean-variance efficient portfolio.

Another aspect of the CAPM is that it predicts relationships among *expected* returns, while all we can observe are realized (historical) holding-period returns; actual returns in a particular holding period seldom, if ever, match our initial expectations. To test the mean-variance

ALPHA BETTING

IT HAS never been easier to pay less to invest. No fewer than 136 exchange-traded funds (ETFs) were launched in the first half of 2006, more than in the whole of 2005.

For those who believe in efficient markets, this represents a triumph. ETFs are quoted securities that track a particular index, for a fee that is normally just a fraction of a percentage point. They enable investors to assemble a low-cost portfolio covering a wide range of assets from international equities, through government and corporate bonds, to commodities.

But as fast as the assets of ETFs and index-tracking mutual funds are growing, another section of the industry seems to be flourishing even faster. Watson Wyatt, a firm of actuaries, estimates that "alternative asset investment" (ranging from hedge funds through private equity to property) grew by around 20% in 2005, to $1.26 trillion. Investors who take this route pay much higher fees in the hope of better performance. One of the fastest-growing assets, funds of hedge funds, charge some of the highest fees of all.

Why are people paying up? In part, because investors have learned to distinguish between the market return, dubbed beta, and managers' outperformance, known as alpha. "Why wouldn't you buy beta and alpha separately?" asks Arno Kitts of Henderson Global Investors, a fund-management firm. "Beta is a commodity and alpha is about skill."

Clients have become convinced that no one firm can produce good performance in every asset class. That has led to a "core and satellite" model, in which part of the portfolio is invested in index trackers with the rest in the hands of specialists. But this creates its own problems. Relations with a single balanced manager are simple. It is much harder to research and monitor the performance of specialists. That has encouraged the middlemen—managers of managers (in the traditional institutional business) and funds-of-funds (in the hedge-fund world), which are usually even more expensive.

That their fees endure might suggest investors can identify outperforming fund managers in advance. However, studies suggest this is extremely hard. And even where you can spot talent, much of the extra performance may be siphoned off into higher fees. "A disproportionate amount of the benefits of alpha go to the manager, not the client," says Alan Brown at Schroders, an asset manager.

In any event, investors will probably keep pursuing alpha, even though the cheaper alternatives of ETFs and tracking funds are available. Craig Baker of Watson Wyatt says that, although above-market returns may not be available to all, clients who can identify them have a "first mover" advantage. As long as that belief exists, managers can charge high fees.

---

efficiency of an index portfolio, we would have to show that the reward-to-variability ratio of the index is not surpassed by any other portfolio. We will examine this question in the next chapter.

The Index Model, Realized Returns, and the Expected Return–Beta Relationship

To move from a model cast in expectations to a realized-return framework, we start with a form of the single-index equation in realized excess returns, similar to that of Equation 6.12 in Chapter 6. Notice this equation may be interpreted as a regression relationship

$$r_i - r_f = \alpha_i + \beta_i(r_M - r_f) + e_i \qquad \text{(7.3)}$$

where r_i is the holding-period return (HPR) on asset i, and α_i and β_i are the intercept and slope of the line that relates asset i's realized excess return to the realized excess return of the index. We denote the index return by r_M to emphasize that the index portfolio is proxying for the market. The e_i measures firm-specific effects during the holding period; it is the deviation of security i's realized HPR from the regression line, that is, the deviation from the forecast that accounts for the index's HPR. We set the relationship in terms of *excess* returns (over the risk-free rate, r_f), for consistency with the CAPM's logic of risk premiums.

Given that the CAPM is a statement about the expectation of asset returns, we look at the expected return of security i predicted by Equation 7.3. Recall that the expectation of e_i

is zero (the firm-specific surprise is expected to average zero over time), so the relationship expressed in terms of expectations is

$$E(r_i) - r_f = \alpha_i + \beta_i[E(r_M) - r_f] \tag{7.4}$$

Comparing this relationship to the expected return–beta relationship of the CAPM (Equation 7.2) reveals that the CAPM predicts $\alpha_i = 0$. Thus, we have converted the CAPM prediction about unobserved expectations of security returns relative to an unobserved market portfolio into a prediction about the intercept in a regression of observed variables: realized excess returns of a security relative to those of a specified index.

Operationalizing the CAPM in the form of an index model has a drawback, however. If intercepts of regressions of returns on an index differ substantially from zero, you will not be able to tell whether it is because you chose a bad index to proxy for the market or because the theory is not useful.

In actuality, few instances of persistent, positive significant alpha values have been identified; these will be discussed in Chapter 8. Among these are: (1) small versus large stocks; (2) stocks of companies that have recently announced unexpectedly good earnings; (3) stocks with high ratios of book value to market value; and (4) stocks that have experienced recent sharp price declines. In general, however, future alphas are practically impossible to predict from past values. The result is that index models are widely used to operationalize capital asset pricing theory (see the nearby box).

Estimating the Index Model

To illustrate how to estimate the index model, we will use actual data and apply the model to the stock of General Motors (GM), in a manner similar to that followed by practitioners. Let us rewrite Equation 7.3 for General Motors, denoting GM's excess return as R_{GM} (i.e., $R_{GM} = r_{GM} - r_f$) and denoting any particular month using the subscript t. Then the index model may be expressed as

$$R_{GMt} = \alpha_{GM} + \beta_{GM}R_{Mt} + e_{GMt}$$

As noted, this relationship may be viewed as a regression equation. The dependent variable in this case is GM's excess return in each month. It is a straight-line function of the excess return on the market index in that month, R_{Mt}, with intercept α_{GM} and slope β_{GM}.

In addition to the influence of the market, the excess return of GM is also affected by firm-specific factors, the net effect of which is captured by the last term in the equation, e_{GMt}. This term is called a residual, as it captures the variation in GM's monthly return that remains after taking account of the impact of the market. The residual is the difference between GM's actual return and the return that would be predicted from the regression line describing the usual relationship between the returns of GM and the market:

$$\text{Residual} = \text{Actual return} - \text{Predicted return for GM based on market return}$$
$$e_{GMt} = R_{GMt} - (\alpha_{GM} + \beta_{GM}R_{Mt})$$

We are interested in estimating the intercept α_{GM} and GM's systematic (i.e., market) risk as measured by the slope coefficient, β_{GM}. We would also like an estimate of the magnitude of GM's firm-specific risk. This can be measured by *residual standard deviation,* which is just the standard deviation of the residual terms, e. Because residuals are the part of excess returns not explained by the market index, that is, firm-specific effects, their standard deviation gives a guide as to the typical magnitude of those effects.

We conduct the analysis in three steps: Collect and process relevant data; feed the data into a statistical program (here we will use Excel) to estimate and interpret the regression Equation 7.3; and use the results to answer questions about GM's stock. For example, we will consider (*a*) what we have learned about the behavior of GM's returns, (*b*) what required rate of return is appropriate for investments with the same risk as GM's equity, and (c) how we might assess the performance of a portfolio manager who invested heavily in GM stock during this period.

Collecting and processing data We start with the monthly series of GM stock prices and the S&P 500 Index, adjusted for stock splits and dividends over the period January 1999–December 2003.[2] This is an interesting period in that it includes the last year of the dot-com boom, the subsequent meltdown, and then in 2003, the beginning of the recovery. From these series we computed 60 monthly holding-period returns on GM and the market index for this five-year period.

For the same period we download monthly rates of return on one-month T-bills, which will serve as the risk-free rate.[3] With these three series of returns we generate monthly excess return on GM's stock and the market index. Some statistics for these returns are shown in Table 7.1.

The negative average excess monthly return on the S&P 500 (−0.33%) resulted from the large negative returns in 2000–2002, when the technology bubble imploded. Clearly, market expectations of a positive risk premium for this five-year period were not realized. Despite this, GM's stock produced a modest, but positive, average excess return. The standard deviation of the monthly excess return on the market index is large (4.96%), but that of GM is much larger (11.24%), as we would expect of a single undiversified security. The geometric-average monthly returns of the securities, when compounded for 60 months, yield the total (cumulative) returns for the five-year period of 18.2%, −9.54%, and 9.10%, for bills, the S&P 500, and GM, respectively. Notice that the monthly variation in the T-bill return reported in Table 7.1 does not reflect risk, as investors knew the return on bills at the beginning of each month.

Figure 7.3 shows the evolution of the cumulative rates of return on the three securities over the period. It illustrates the positive index returns during the tail end of the boom of the 1990s that ended in mid-2000, the large negative returns during the downturn that followed, and the mild recovery since mid-2002. GM is seen to fluctuate more than the index, indicating greater volatility, and to move positively with the index, suggesting a positive beta, most likely greater than 1.0. Atypically, T-bills provided the highest return for the entire period, confirming that return realizations for both risky assets fell short of expectations.

Estimation results We regressed GM's excess returns against those of the index using the Regression command from the Data Analysis menu of Excel. The scatter diagram in Figure 7.4 shows the data points for each month as well as the regression line that best fits the data. As noted in the previous chapter, this is called the **security characteristic line** (SCL), because it can be used to describe the relevant characteristics of the stock. Figure 7.4 allows us to view the residuals, the deviation of GM's return each month from the prediction of the regression equation. By construction, these residuals *average* to zero, but in any particular month, the residual may be positive or negative.

security characteristic line (SCL)

A plot of a security's expected excess return over the risk-free rate as a function of the excess return on the market.

TABLE 7.1		**T-Bills**	**S&P 500**	**GM**
Monthly return statistics: T-bills, S&P 500, and General Motors, January 1999–December 2003	Average excess return (%)	0.28	−0.33	0.49
	Standard deviation (%)	0.16	4.96	11.24
	Geometric average (%)	0.28	−0.17	0.15
	Cumulative total 5-year return (%)	18.20	−9.54	9.10

[2] Returns are available from several Web sources. Market Insight (**www.mhhe.com/edumarketinsight**), which comes with this text, is a good source of returns. You can also find returns at sites such as **finance.yahoo.com**. We need to use the price series adjusted for dividends and splits in order to obtain holding period returns (HPRs). The unadjusted price series would tell us about capital gains alone rather than total returns.

[3] We downloaded these rates from Professor Kenneth French's Web site: **mba.tuck.dartmouth.edu/pages/faculty/ken.french/data_library.html.**

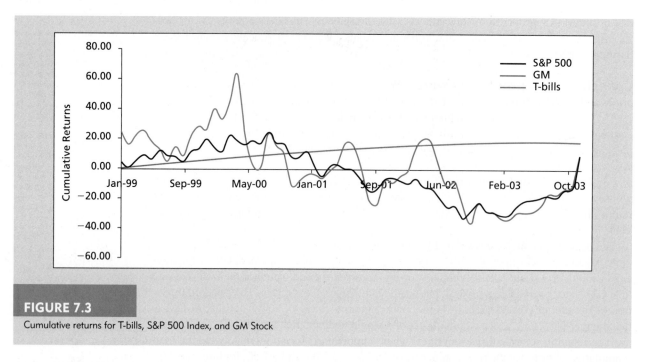

FIGURE 7.3

Cumulative returns for T-bills, S&P 500 Index, and GM Stock

FIGURE 7.4

Characteristic line for GM

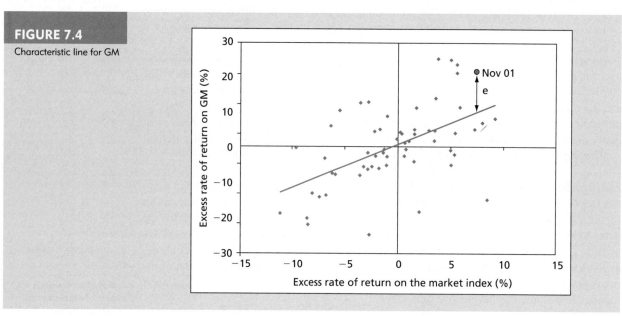

For example, the residual for November 2001 (10.09%) is labeled explicitly. The point lies above the regression line, indicating that in this month, GM's return was better than one would have predicted from knowledge of the market return. The spread between the point and the regression line is GM's firm-specific return, which is the residual for November.

The standard deviation of the residuals indicates the accuracy of predictions from the regression line. If there is a lot of firm-specific risk, for example, there will be a wide scatter of points around the line (a high residual standard deviation), indicating that knowledge of the market return will not enable a precise forecast of GM's return.

Table 7.2 is the regression output from Excel. The first line shows that the correlation coefficient between the excess returns of GM and the index was 0.546. The more relevant statistic, however, is the *adjusted R-square* (.287). It is the square of the correlation coefficient, adjusted downward for the number of coefficients or "degrees of freedom" used to estimate

7.3 THE CAPM AND THE REAL WORLD

In limited ways, portfolio theory and the CAPM have become accepted tools in the practitioner community. Many investment professionals think about the distinction between firm-specific and systematic risk and are comfortable with the use of beta to measure systematic risk. Still, the nuances of the CAPM are not nearly as well established in the community. For example, the compensation of portfolio managers is not based on appropriate performance measures (see Chapter 18). What can we make of this?

New ways of thinking about the world (that is, new models or theories) displace old ones when the old models become either intolerably inconsistent with data or when the new model is demonstrably more consistent with available data. For example, when Copernicus overthrew the age-old belief that the Earth is fixed in the center of the Universe and that the stars orbit about it in circular motions, it took many years before astronomers and navigators replaced old astronomical tables with superior ones based on his theory. The old tools fit the data available from astronomical observation with sufficient precision to suffice for the needs of the time. To some extent, the slowness with which the CAPM has permeated daily practice in the money management industry also has to do with its precision in fitting data, that is, in precisely explaining variation in rates of return across assets. Let's review some of the evidence on this score.

The CAPM was first published by Sharpe in the *Journal of Finance* (the journal of the American Finance Association) in 1964 and took the world of finance by storm. Early tests by Black, Jensen, and Scholes (1972) and Fama and MacBeth (1973) were only partially supportive of the CAPM: average returns were higher for higher-beta portfolios, but the reward for beta risk was less than the predictions of the simple theory.

While this sort of evidence against the CAPM remained largely within the ivory towers of academia, Roll's (1977) paper "A Critique of Capital Asset Pricing Tests" shook the practitioner world as well. Roll argued that since the true market portfolio can never be observed, the CAPM is *necessarily* untestable.

The publicity given the now classic "Roll's critique" resulted in popular articles such as "Is Beta Dead?" that effectively slowed the permeation of portfolio theory through the world of finance.[7] This is quite ironic since, although Roll is absolutely correct on theoretical grounds, some tests suggest that the error introduced by using a broad market index as proxy for the true, unobserved market portfolio is perhaps not the greatest of the problems involved in testing the CAPM.

Fama and French (1992) published a study that dealt the CAPM an even harsher blow. They claimed that once you control for a set of widely followed characteristics of the firm, such as the size of the firm and its ratio of market value to book value, the firm's beta (that is, its systematic risk) does not contribute anything to the prediction of future returns.

Fama and French and several others have published many follow-up studies of this topic. We will review some of this literature later in the chapter, and the nearby box discusses recent controversies about the risk-return relationship. However, it seems clear from these studies that beta does not tell the whole story of risk. There seem to be risk factors that affect security returns beyond beta's one-dimensional measurement of market sensitivity. In fact, in the next section of this chapter, we will introduce a theory of risk premiums that explicitly allows for multiple risk factors.

Liquidity, a different kind of risk factor, has been ignored for a long time. Although first analyzed by Amihud and Mendelson as early as 1986, it is yet to be accurately measured and incorporated in portfolio management. Measuring liquidity and the premium commensurate with illiquidity is part of a larger field in financial economics, namely, market structure. We now know that trading mechanisms on stock exchanges can affect the liquidity of assets traded on these exchanges and thus significantly affect their market value.

---

[7]A. Wallace, "Is Beta Dead?" *Institutional Investor* 14 (July 1980), pp. 22–30.

On the MARKET FRONT

TAKING STOCK

Since the stock market bubble of the late 1990s burst, investors have had ample time to ponder where to put the remains of their money. Economists and analysts too have been revisiting old ideas. None has been dearer to them than the capital asset pricing model (CAPM), a formula linking movements in a single share price to those of the market as a whole. The key statistic here is "beta."

Many investors and managers have given up on beta, however. Although it is useful for working out overall correlation with the market, it tells you little about share-price performance in absolute terms. In fact, the CAPM's obituary was already being written more than a decade ago when a paper by Eugene Fama and Kenneth French showed that the shares of small companies and "value stocks" (shares with low price–earnings ratios or high ratios of book value to market value) do much better over time than their betas would predict.

Another paper, by John Campbell and Tuomo Vuolteen-aho of Harvard University, tries to resuscitate beta by splitting it into two.* The authors start from first principles. In essence, the value of a company depends on two things: its expected profits and the interest rate used to discount these profits. Changes in share prices therefore stem from changes in one of these factors.

From this observation, these authors propose two types of beta: one to gauge shares' responses to changes in profits; the other to pick up the effects of changes in the interest rate. Allowing for separate cash flow versus interest rate betas helps better explain the performance of small and value companies. Shares of such companies are more sensitive than the average to news about profits, in part because they are bets on future growth. Shares with high price–earnings ratios vary more with the discount rate. In all cases, above-average returns compensate investors for above-average risks.

EQUITY'S ALLURE

Beta is a tool for comparing shares with each other. Recently, however, investors have been worried about equity as an asset class. The crash left investors asking what became of the fabled equity premium, the amount by which they can expect returns on shares to exceed those from government bonds.

History says that shareholders have a lot to be optimistic about. Over the past 100 years, investors in American shares have enjoyed a premium, relative to Treasury bonds, of around seven percentage points. Similar effects have been seen in other countries. Some studies have reached less optimistic conclusions, suggesting a premium of four or five points. But even this premium seems generous.

Many answers have been put forward to explain the premium. One is that workers cannot hedge against many risks, such as losing their jobs, which tend to hit at the same time as stock market crashes; this means that buying shares would increase the volatility of their income, so that investors require a premium to be persuaded to hold them. Another is that shares, especially in small companies, are much less liquid than government debt. It is also sometimes argued that in extreme times—in depression or war, or after bubbles—equities fare much worse than bonds, so that equity investors demand higher returns to compensate them for the risk of catastrophe.

Yes, over long periods equities have done better than bonds. But the equity "premium" is unpredictable. Searching for a consistent, God-given premium is a fool's errand.

*John Campbell and Tuomo Vuolteenaho, "Bad Beta, Good Beta," *American Economic Review* 94 (December 2004), pp. 1249–1275.

Despite all these issues, beta is not dead. Other research shows that when we use a more inclusive proxy for the market portfolio than the S&P 500 (specifically, an index that includes human capital) and allow for the fact that beta changes over time, the performance of beta in explaining security returns is considerably enhanced (Jagannathan and Wang, 1996). We know that the CAPM is not a perfect model and that ultimately it will be far from the last word on security pricing. Still, the logic of the model is compelling, and more sophisticated models of security pricing all rely on the key distinction between systematic versus diversifiable risk. The CAPM therefore provides a useful framework for thinking rigorously about the relationship between security risk and return. This is as much as Copernicus had when he was shown the prepublication version of his book just before he passed away.

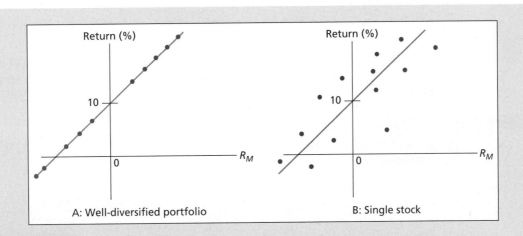

FIGURE 7.5

Security characteristic lines

return higher than the risk-free rate by the amount α_P. But this implies that α_P must equal zero, or else an immediate arbitrage opportunity opens up. For example, if α_P is greater than zero, you can borrow at the risk-free rate and use the proceeds to buy the well-diversified zero-beta portfolio. You borrow risklessly at rate r_f and invest risklessly at rate $r_f + \alpha_P$, clearing the riskless differential of α_P.

> Suppose that the risk-free rate is 6%, and a well-diversified zero-beta portfolio earns (a sure) rate of return of 7%, that is, an excess return of 1%. Then borrow at 6% and invest in the zero-beta portfolio to earn 7%. You will earn a sure profit of 1% of the invested funds without putting up any of your own money. If the zero-beta portfolio earns 5%, then you can sell it short and lend at 6% with the same result.

EXAMPLE 7.9

Arbitrage with a Zero-Beta Portfolio

In fact, we can go further and show that the alpha of *any* well-diversified portfolio in Equation 7.9 must be zero, even if the beta is not zero. The proof is similar to the easy zero-beta case. If the alphas were not zero, then we could combine two of these portfolios into a zero-beta riskless portfolio with a rate of return not equal to the risk-free rate. But this, as we have just seen, would be an arbitrage opportunity.

To see how the arbitrage strategy would work, suppose that portfolio V has a beta of β_v and an alpha of α_v. Similarly, suppose portfolio U has a beta of β_u and an alpha of α_u.

Taking advantage of any arbitrage opportunity involves buying and selling assets in proportions that create a risk-free profit on a costless position. To eliminate risk, we buy portfolio V and sell portfolio U in proportions chosen so that the combination portfolio $(V + U)$ will have a beta of zero. The portfolio weights that satisfy this condition are

$$w_v = \frac{-\beta_u}{\beta_v - \beta_u} \qquad w_u = \frac{\beta_v}{\beta_v - \beta_u}$$

Note that w_v plus w_u add up to 1.0 and that the beta of the combination is in fact zero:

$$\text{Beta}(V + U) = \beta_v \frac{-\beta_u}{\beta_v - \beta_u} + \beta_u \frac{\beta_v}{\beta_v - \beta_u} = 0$$

Therefore, the portfolio is riskless: It has no sensitivity to the factor. But the excess return of the portfolio is not zero unless α_v and α_u equal zero:

$$R(V + U) = \alpha_v \frac{-\beta_u}{\beta_v - \beta_u} + \alpha_u \frac{\beta_v}{\beta_v - \beta_u} \neq 0$$

Therefore, unless α_v and α_u equal zero, the zero-beta portfolio has a certain rate of return that differs from the risk-free rate (its excess return is different from zero). We have seen that this gives rise to an arbitrage opportunity.

EXAMPLE 7.10

Arbitrage with Mispriced Portfolios

Suppose that the risk-free rate is 7% and a well-diversified portfolio, V, with beta of 1.3 has an alpha of 2% and another well-diversified portfolio, U, with beta of 0.8 has an alpha of 1%. We go long on V and short on U with proportions

$$w_v = \frac{-0.8}{1.3 - 0.8} = -1.6 \qquad w_u = \frac{1.3}{1.3 - 0.8} = 2.6$$

These proportions add up to 1.0 and result in a portfolio with beta $= -1.6 \times 1.3 + 2.6 \times 0.8 = 0$. The alpha of the portfolio is: $-1.6 \times 2\% + 2.6 \times 1\% = -0.6\%$. This means that the riskless portfolio will earn a rate of return that is less than the risk-free rate by .6%. We now complete the arbitrage by selling (or going short on) the combination portfolio and investing the proceeds at 7%, risklessly profiting by the 60 basis point differential in returns.

We conclude that the only value for alpha that rules out arbitrage opportunities is zero. Therefore, rewrite Equation 7.9 setting alpha equal to zero

$$R_P = \beta_P R_M$$
$$r_P - r_f = \beta_P (r_M - r_f)$$
$$E(r_P) = r_f + \beta_P [E(r_M) - r_f]$$

Hence, we arrive at the same expected return–beta relationship as the CAPM without requiring assumptions about either investor preferences or access to the all-inclusive (and elusive) market portfolio.

The APT and the CAPM

Why did we need so many restrictive assumptions to derive the CAPM when the APT seems to arrive at the expected return–beta relationship with seemingly fewer and less objectionable assumptions? The answer is simple: The APT applies only to well-diversified portfolios. Absence of riskless arbitrage alone cannot guarantee that, in equilibrium, the expected return–beta relationship will hold for any and all assets.

With additional effort, however, one can use the APT to show that the relationship must hold approximately even for individual assets. The essence of the proof is that if the expected return–beta relationship were violated by many individual securities, it would be virtually impossible for all well-diversified portfolios to satisfy the relationship. So the relationship must *almost* surely hold true for individual securities.

We say "almost" because, according to the APT, there is no guarantee that all individual assets will lie on the SML. If only a few securities violated the SML, their effect on well-diversified portfolios could conceivably be negligible. In this sense, it is possible that the SML relationship is violated for some securities. If many securities violate the expected return–beta relationship, however, the relationship will no longer hold for well-diversified portfolios comprising these securities, and arbitrage opportunities will be available.

The APT serves many of the same functions as the CAPM. It gives us a benchmark for fair rates of return that can be used for capital budgeting, security evaluation, or investment performance evaluation. Moreover, the APT highlights the crucial distinction between nondiversifiable risk (systematic or factor risk) that requires a reward in the form of a risk premium and diversifiable risk that does not.

The bottom line is that neither of these theories dominates the other. The APT is more general in that it gets us to the expected return–beta relationship without requiring many of the unrealistic assumptions of the CAPM, particularly the reliance on the market portfolio. The latter improves the prospects for testing the APT. But the CAPM is more general in that it applies to all assets without reservation. The good news is that both theories agree on the expected return–beta relationship.

It is worth noting that because past tests of the expected return–beta relationship examined the rates of return on highly diversified portfolios, they actually came closer to testing the APT than the CAPM. Thus, it appears that econometric concerns, too, favor the APT.

Multifactor Generalization of the APT and CAPM

So far, we've examined the APT in a one-factor world. As we noted earlier in the chapter, this is too simplistic. In reality, there are several sources of systematic risk such as uncertainty in the business cycle, interest rates, energy prices, and so on. Presumably, exposure to any of these factors singly or together will affect a stock's perceived riskiness and appropriate expected rate of return. We can use a multifactor version of the APT to accommodate these multiple sources of risk.

Suppose we generalize the single-factor model expressed in Equation 7.8 to a two-factor model:

$$R_i = \alpha_i + \beta_{i1}R_{M1} + \beta_{i2}R_{M2} + e_i \qquad \textbf{(7.10)}$$

where R_{M1} and R_{M2} are the excess returns on portfolios that represent the two systematic factors. Factor 1 might be, for example, unanticipated changes in industrial production, while factor 2 might represent unanticipated changes in short-term interest rates. We assume again that there are many securities available with any combination of betas. This implies that we can form well-diversified **factor portfolios,** that is, portfolios that have a beta of 1.0 on one factor and a beta of zero on all others. Thus, a factor portfolio with a beta of 1.0 on the first factor will have a rate of return of R_{M1}; a factor portfolio with a beta of 1.0 on the second factor will have a rate of return of R_{M2}; and so on. Factor portfolios can serve as the benchmark portfolios for a multifactor generalization of the security market line relationship.

factor portfolio

A well-diversified portfolio constructed to have a beta of 1.0 on one factor and a beta of zero on any other factor.

Suppose the two-factor portfolios, here called portfolios 1 and 2, have expected returns $E(r_1) = 10\%$ and $E(r_2) = 12\%$. Suppose further that the risk-free rate is 4%. The risk premium on the first factor portfolio is therefore 6%, while that on the second factor portfolio is 8%.

Now consider an arbitrary well-diversified portfolio (A), with beta on the first factor, $\beta_{A1} = 0.5$, and on the second factor, $\beta_{A2} = 0.75$. The multifactor APT states that the portfolio risk premium must equal the sum of the risk premiums required as compensation to investors for each source of systematic risk. The risk premium attributable to risk factor 1 is the portfolio's exposure to factor 1, β_{A1}, times the risk premium earned on the first factor portfolio, $E(r_1) - r_f$. Therefore, the portion of portfolio A's risk premium that is compensation for its exposure to the first risk factor is $\beta_{A1}[E(r_1) - r_f] = 0.5(10\% - 4\%) = 3\%$, while the risk premium attributable to risk factor 2 is $\beta_{A2}[E(r_2) - r_f] = 0.75(12\% - 4\%) = 6\%$. The total risk premium on the portfolio, therefore, should be $3 + 6 = 9\%$, and the total return on the portfolio should be 13%.

EXAMPLE 7.11

Multifactor APT

4%	Risk-free rate
+ 3%	Risk premium for exposure to factor 1
+ 6%	Risk premium for exposure to factor 2
13%	Total expected return

To generalize the argument in Example 7.11, note that the factor exposure of any portfolio P is given by its betas, β_{P1} and β_{P2}. A competing portfolio, Q, can be formed from factor portfolios with the following weights: β_{P1} in the first factor portfolio; β_{P2} in the second factor

Please visit us at www.mhhe.com/bkm

The spreadsheet below also contains monthly returns for the stocks that comprise the Dow Jones Industrial Average. A related workbook (also available at **www.mhhe.com/bkm**) contains spreadsheets that show raw returns, risk premiums, correlation coefficients, and beta coefficients for the stocks in the DJIA. The security characteristic lines are estimated with five years of monthly returns.

Monthly Rates of Return: May 2000 - April 2005					
Month	GM	Ford	Toyota	T-Bills	S&P 500 Index
Apr-05	-12.15	-17.56	-3.33	0.24	-3.65
Mar-05	-17.56	-10.43	-4.37	0.23	-1.91
Feb-05	-3.15	-3.95	-0.52	0.22	1.89
Jan-05	-8.11	-10.04	-4.49	0.20	-2.53
Dec-04	3.81	3.24	9.58	0.19	3.25
Nov-04	0.10	8.83	-3.71	0.18	3.86
Oct-04	-9.25	-7.26	1.58	0.15	1.40

portfolio; and $1 - \beta_{P2} - \beta_{P2}$ in T-bills. By construction, Q will have betas equal to those of portfolio P and an expected return of

$$E(r_Q) = \beta_{P1}E(r_1) + \beta_{P2}E(r_2) + (1 - \beta_{P1} - \beta_{P2})r_f$$
$$= r_f + \beta_{P1}[E(r_1) - r_f] + \beta_{P2}[E(r_2) - r_f] \qquad (7.11)$$

Using the numbers in Example 7.11,

$$E(r_Q) = 4 + .5 \times (10 - 4) + .75 \times (12 - 4) = 13\%$$

Because portfolio Q has precisely the same exposures as portfolio A to the two sources of risk, their expected returns also ought to be equal. So portfolio A also ought to have an expected return of 13%.

Suppose, however, that the expected return on portfolio A is 12% rather than 13%. This return would give rise to an arbitrage opportunity. Form a portfolio from the factor portfolios with the same betas as portfolio A. This requires weights of 0.5 on the first factor portfolio, 0.75 on the second portfolio, and -0.25 on the risk-free asset. This portfolio has exactly the same factor betas as portfolio A: a beta of 0.5 on the first factor because of its 0.5 weight on the first factor portfolio and a beta of 0.75 on the second factor.

Now invest $1 in portfolio Q and sell (short) $1 in portfolio A. Your net investment is zero, but your expected dollar profit is positive and equal to

$$\$1 \times E(r_Q) - \$1 \times E(r_A) = \$1 \times .13 - \$1 \times .12 = \$.01.$$

Moreover, your net position is riskless. Your exposure to each risk factor cancels out because you are long $1 in portfolio Q and short $1 in portfolio A, and both of these well-diversified portfolios have exactly the same factor betas. Thus, if portfolio A's expected return differs from that of portfolio Q's, you can earn positive risk-free profits on a zero net investment position. This is an arbitrage opportunity.

Hence, any well-diversified portfolio with betas β_{P1} and β_{P2} must have the return given in Equation 7.11 if arbitrage opportunities are to be ruled out. A comparison of Equations 7.2

and 7.11 shows that 7.11 is simply a generalization of the one-factor SML. In fact, if you compare Equation 7.11 to Equation 7.6, you will see that they are nearly identical. Equation 7.6 is simply more specific about the identities of the relevant factor portfolios. We conclude that the multifactor generalizations of the security market line of the APT and the CAPM are effectively equivalent.

Finally, extension of the multifactor SML of Equation 7.11 to individual assets is precisely the same as for the one-factor APT. Equation 7.11 cannot be satisfied by every well-diversified portfolio unless it is satisfied by virtually every security taken individually. Equation 7.11 thus represents the multifactor SML for an economy with multiple sources of risk.

The generalized APT must be qualified with respect to individual assets just as in the single-factor case. A multifactor CAPM would, at the cost of additional assumptions, apply to any and all individual assets. As we have seen, the result will be a security market equation (a multidimensional SML) that is identical to that of the multifactor APT.

Using the factor portfolios of Example 7.11, find the fair rate of return on a security with $\beta_1 = 0.2$ and $\beta_2 = 1.4$.

CONCEPT check **7.6**

SUMMARY

- The CAPM assumes investors are rational, single-period planners who agree on a common input list from security analysis and seek mean-variance optimal portfolios.
- The CAPM assumes ideal security markets in the sense that: (*a*) markets are large and investors are price takers, (*b*) there are no taxes or transaction costs, (*c*) all risky assets are publicly traded, and (*d*) any amount can be borrowed and lent at a fixed, risk-free rate. These assumptions mean that all investors will hold identical risky portfolios. The CAPM implies that, in equilibrium, the market portfolio is the unique mean-variance efficient tangency portfolio, which indicates that a passive strategy is efficient.
- The market portfolio is a value-weighted portfolio. Each security is held in a proportion equal to its market value divided by the total market value of all securities. The risk premium on the market portfolio is proportional to its variance, σ_M^2, and to the risk aversion of the average investor.
- The CAPM implies that the risk premium on any individual asset or portfolio is the product of the risk premium of the market portfolio and the asset's beta. The security market line shows the return demanded by investors as a function of the beta of their investment. This expected return is a benchmark for evaluating investment performance.
- In a single-index security market, once an index is specified, a security beta can be estimated from a regression of the security's excess return on the index's excess return. This regression line is called the security characteristic line (SCL). The intercept of the SCL, called alpha, represents the average excess return on the security when the index excess return is zero. The CAPM implies that alphas should be zero.
- The CAPM and the security market line can be used to establish benchmarks for evaluation of investment performance or to determine appropriate discount rates for capital budgeting applications. They are also used in regulatory proceedings concerning the "fair" rate of return for regulated industries.
- The CAPM is usually implemented as a single-factor model, with all systematic risk summarized by the return on a broad market index. However, multifactor generalizations of the basic model may be specified to accommodate multiple sources of systematic risk. In such multifactor extensions of the CAPM, the risk premium of any security is determined by its sensitivity to each systematic risk factor as well as the risk premium associated with that source of risk.
- There are two general approaches to finding extra-market systematic risk factors. One is characteristics based and looks for factors that are empirically associated with high

www.mhhe.com/bkm

average returns and so may be proxies for relevant measures of systematic risk. The other focuses on factors that are plausibly important sources of risk to wide segments of investors and may thus command risk premiums.

- An arbitrage opportunity arises when the disparity between two or more security prices enables investors to construct a zero net investment portfolio that will yield a sure profit. The presence of arbitrage opportunities and the resulting volume of trades will create pressure on security prices that will persist until prices reach levels that preclude arbitrage. Only a few investors need to become aware of arbitrage opportunities to trigger this process because of the large volume of trades in which they will engage.
- When securities are priced so that there are no arbitrage opportunities, the market satisfies the no-arbitrage condition. Price relationships that satisfy the no-arbitrage condition are important because we expect them to hold in real-world markets.
- Portfolios are called *well diversified* if they include a large number of securities in such proportions that the residual or diversifiable risk of the portfolio is negligible.
- In a single-factor security market, all well-diversified portfolios must satisfy the expected return–beta relationship of the SML in order to satisfy the no-arbitrage condition. If all well-diversified portfolios satisfy the expected return–beta relationship, then all but a small number of securities also must satisfy this relationship.
- The APT implies the same expected return–beta relationship as the CAPM, yet does not require that all investors be mean-variance optimizers. The price of this generality is that the APT does not guarantee this relationship for all securities at all times.
- A multifactor APT generalizes the single-factor model to accommodate several sources of systematic risk.

KEY TERMS

alpha, 199	expected return–beta relationship, 197	security characteristic line (SCL), 203
arbitrage, 216	factor portfolio, 219	security market line (SML), 198
arbitrage pricing theory (APT), 216	market portfolio, 194	
capital asset pricing model (CAPM), 193	multifactor models, 211	well-diversified portfolio, 216
	mutual fund theorem, 195	

PROBLEM SETS

 Select problems are available in McGraw-Hill's Homework Manager®. Please see the packaging options section of the preface for more information.

1. Which of the following statements about the security market line (SML) are *true*?
   a. The SML provides a benchmark for evaluating expected investment performance.
   b. The SML leads all investors to invest in the same portfolio of risky assets.
   c. The SML is a graphic representation of the relationship between expected return and beta.
   d. Properly valued assets plot exactly on the SML.

2. Karen Kay, a portfolio manager at Collins Asset Management, is using the capital asset pricing model for making recommendations to her clients. Her research department has developed the information shown in the following exhibit.

Forecasted Returns, Standard Deviations, and Betas		
	Forecasted Return	Standard Deviation	Beta
Stock X	14.0%	36%	0.8
Stock Y	17.0	25	1.5
Market index	14.0	15	1.0
Risk-free rate	5.0		

a. Calculate expected return and alpha for each stock.
b. Identify and justify which stock would be more appropriate for an investor who wants to
  i. Add this stock to a well-diversified equity portfolio.
  ii. Hold this stock as a single-stock portfolio.

3. What must be the beta of a portfolio with $E(r_P) = 20\%$, if $r_f = 5\%$ and $E(r_M) = 15\%$?

4. The market price of a security is $40. Its expected rate of return is 13%. The risk-free rate is 7%, and the market risk premium is 8%. What will the market price of the security be if its beta doubles (and all other variables remain unchanged)? Assume the stock is expected to pay a constant dividend in perpetuity.

5. You are a consultant to a large manufacturing corporation considering a project with the following net after-tax cash flows (in millions of dollars)

Years from Now	After-Tax CF
0	−20
1–9	10
10	20

The project's beta is 1.7. Assuming $r_f = 9\%$ and $E(r_M) = 19\%$, what is the net present value of the project? What is the highest possible beta estimate for the project before its NPV becomes negative?

6. Are the following statements true or false? Explain.
a. Stocks with a beta of zero offer an expected rate of return of zero. False
b. The CAPM implies that investors require a higher return to hold highly volatile securities. False
c. You can construct a portfolio with a beta of 0.75 by investing 0.75 of the budget in T-bills and the remainder in the market portfolio. False

7. Consider the following table, which gives a security analyst's expected return on two stocks for two particular market returns:

Market Return	Aggressive Stock	Defensive Stock
5%	2%	3.5%
20	32	14

a. What are the betas of the two stocks?
b. What is the expected rate of return on each stock if the market return is equally likely to be 5% or 20%?
c. If the T-bill rate is 8%, and the market return is equally likely to be 5% or 20%, draw the SML for this economy.
d. Plot the two securities on the SML graph. What are the alphas of each?
e. What hurdle rate should be used by the management of the aggressive firm for a project with the risk characteristics of the defensive firm's stock?

If the simple CAPM is valid, which of the situations in Problems 8–14 below are possible? Explain. Consider each situation independently.

8.

Portfolio	Expected Return	Beta
A	20%	1.4
B	25	1.2

9.

Portfolio	Expected Return	Standard Deviation
A	30%	35%
B	40	25

10.

Portfolio	Expected Return	Standard Deviation
Risk-free	10%	0%
Market	18	24
A	16	12

11.

Portfolio	Expected Return	Standard Deviation
Risk-free	10%	0%
Market	18	24
A	20	22

12.

Portfolio	Expected Return	Beta
Risk-free	10%	0
Market	18	1.0
A	16	1.5

13.

Portfolio	Expected Return	Beta
Risk-free	10%	0
Market	18	1.0
A	16	.9

14.

Portfolio	Expected Return	Standard Deviation
Risk-free	10%	0%
Market	18	24
A	16	22

15. Go to **www.mhhe.com/bkm** and link to Chapter 7 materials, where you will find a spreadsheet with monthly returns for GM, Ford, and Toyota, the S&P 500, and Treasury bills.

    a. Estimate the index model for each firm over the full five-year period. Compare the betas of each firm.

    b. Now estimate the betas for each firm using only the first two years of the sample and then using only the last two years. How stable are the beta estimates obtained from these shorter subperiods?

In Problems 16–18 below, assume the risk-free rate is 8% and the expected rate of return on the market is 18%.

16. A share of stock is now selling for $100. It will pay a dividend of $9 per share at the end of the year. Its beta is 1.0. What do investors expect the stock to sell for at the end of the year?

17. I am buying a firm with an expected perpetual cash flow of $1,000 but am unsure of its risk. If I think the beta of the firm is zero, when the beta is really 1.0, how much *more* will I offer for the firm than it is truly worth?

18. A stock has an expected return of 6%. What is its beta?

19. Two investment advisers are comparing performance. One averaged a 19% return and the other a 16% return. However, the beta of the first adviser was 1.5, while that of the second was 1.0.

    a. Can you tell which adviser was a better selector of individual stocks (aside from the issue of general movements in the market)?

    b. If the T-bill rate were 6%, and the market return during the period were 14%, which adviser would be the superior stock selector?

    c. What if the T-bill rate were 3% and the market return 15%?

20. Suppose the yield on short-term government securities (perceived to be risk-free) is about 4%. Suppose also that the expected return required by the market for a portfolio with a beta of 1.0 is 12%. According to the capital asset pricing model:

    a. What is the expected return on the market portfolio?

    b. What would be the expected return on a zero-beta stock?

    c. Suppose you consider buying a share of stock at a price of $40. The stock is expected to pay a dividend of $3 next year and to sell then for $41. The stock risk has been evaluated at $\beta = -0.5$. Is the stock overpriced or underpriced?

21. Based on current dividend yields and expected capital gains, the expected rates of return on portfolios A and B are 11% and 14%, respectively. The beta of A is 0.8 while that of B is 1.5. The T-bill rate is currently 6%, while the expected rate of return of the S&P 500 Index is 12%. The standard deviation of portfolio A is 10% annually, while that of B is 31%, and that of the index is 20%.

    a. If you currently hold a market index portfolio, would you choose to add either of these portfolios to your holdings? Explain.

    b. If instead you could invest *only* in bills and one of these portfolios, which would you choose?

22. Joan McKay is a portfolio manager for a bank trust department. McKay meets with two clients, Kevin Murray and Lisa York, to review their investment objectives. Each client expresses an interest in changing his or her individual investment objectives. Both clients currently hold well-diversified portfolios of risky assets.

    a. Murray wants to increase the expected return of his portfolio. State what action McKay should take to achieve Murray's objective. Justify your response in the context of the capital market line.

    b. York wants to reduce the risk exposure of her portfolio, but does not want to engage in borrowing or lending activities to do so. State what action McKay should take to achieve York's objective. Justify your response in the context of the security market line.

CFA®
PROBLEMS

23. Consider the following data for a one-factor economy. All portfolios are well diversified.

Portfolio	E(r)	Beta
A	10%	1.0
F	4	0

Suppose another portfolio E is well diversified with a beta of 2/3 and expected return of 9%. Would an arbitrage opportunity exist? If so, what would the arbitrage strategy be?

24. Assume both portfolios A and B are well diversified, that $E(r_A) = 14\%$ and $E(r_B) = 14.8\%$. If the economy has only one factor, and $\beta_A = 1.0$ while $\beta_B = 1.1$, what must be the risk-free rate?

25. Assume a market index represents the common factor, and all stocks in the economy have a beta of 1.0. Firm-specific returns all have a standard deviation of 30%.

Suppose an analyst studies 20 stocks and finds that one-half have an alpha of 3%, and one-half have an alpha of −3%. The analyst then buys $1 million of an equally weighted portfolio of the positive alpha stocks and sells short $1 million of an equally weighted portfolio of the negative alpha stocks.

a. What is the expected profit (in dollars), and what is the standard deviation of the analyst's profit?

b. How does your answer change if the analyst examines 50 stocks instead of 20? 100 stocks?

26. If the APT is to be a useful theory, the number of systematic factors in the economy must be small. Why?

27. The APT itself does not provide information on the factors that one might expect to determine risk premiums. How should researchers decide which factors to investigate? Is industrial production a reasonable factor to test for a risk premium? Why or why not?

28. Suppose two factors are identified for the U.S. economy: the growth rate of industrial production, IP, and the inflation rate, IR. IP is expected to be 4% and IR 6%. A stock with a beta of 1.0 on IP and 0.4 on IR currently is expected to provide a rate of return of 14%. If industrial production actually grows by 5%, while the inflation rate turns out to be 7%, what is your best guess for the rate of return on the stock?

29. Suppose there are two independent economic factors, M_1 and M_2. The risk-free rate is 7%, and all stocks have independent firm-specific components with a standard deviation of 50%. Portfolios A and B are both well diversified.

Portfolio	Beta on M_1	Beta on M_2	Expected Return (%)
A	1.8	2.1	40
B	2.0	−0.5	10

What is the expected return–beta relationship in this economy?

30. Jeffrey Bruner, CFA, uses the capital asset pricing model (CAPM) to help identify mispriced securities. A consultant suggests Bruner use arbitrage pricing theory (APT) instead. In comparing CAPM and APT, the consultant made the following arguments:

a. Both the CAPM and APT require a mean-variance efficient market portfolio.

b. The CAPM assumes that one specific factor explains security returns but APT does not.

State whether each of the consultant's arguments is correct or incorrect. Indicate, for each incorrect argument, why the argument is incorrect.

31. As a finance intern at Pork Products, Jennifer Wainwright's assignment is to come up with fresh insights concerning the firm's cost of capital. She decides that this would be a good opportunity to try out the new material on the APT that she learned last semester. As such, she decides that three promising factors would be (i) the return on a broad-based index such as the S&P 500; (ii) the level of interest rates, as represented by the yield to maturity on 10-year Treasury bonds; and (iii) the price of hogs, which are particularly important to her firm. Her plan is to find the beta of Pork Products against each of these factors and to estimate the risk premium associated with exposure to each factor. Comment on Jennifer's choice of factors. Which are most promising with respect to the likely impact on her firm's cost of capital? Can you suggest improvements to her specification?

32. The security market line depicts:

a. A security's expected return as a function of its systematic risk.

b. The market portfolio as the optimal portfolio of risky securities.

c. The relationship between a security's return and the return on an index.

d. The complete portfolio as a combination of the market portfolio and the risk-free asset.

33. According to CAPM, the expected rate of return of a portfolio with a beta of 1.0 and an alpha of 0 is:
    a. Between r_M and r_f.
    b. The risk-free rate, r_f.
    c. $\beta\,(r_M - r_f)$.
    d. The expected return on the market, r_M.

The following table (for Problems 34 and 35) shows risk and return measures for two portfolios.

Portfolio	Average Annual Rate of Return	Standard Deviation	Beta
R	11%	10%	0.5
S&P 500	14%	12%	1.0

34. When plotting portfolio R on the preceding table relative to the SML, portfolio R lies:
    a. On the SML.
    b. Below the SML.
    c. Above the SML.
    d. Insufficient data given.

35. When plotting portfolio R relative to the capital market line, portfolio R lies:
    a. On the CML.
    b. Below the CML.
    c. Above the CML.
    d. Insufficient data given.

36. Briefly explain whether investors should expect a higher return from holding portfolio A versus portfolio B under capital asset pricing theory (CAPM). Assume that both portfolios are fully diversified.

	Portfolio A	Portfolio B
Systematic risk (beta)	1.0	1.0
Specific risk for each individual security	High	Low

37. Assume that both X and Y are well-diversified portfolios and the risk-free rate is 8%.

Portfolio	Expected Return	Beta
X	16%	1.00
Y	12%	0.25

In this situation you could conclude that portfolios X and Y:
    a. Are in equilibrium.
    b. Offer an arbitrage opportunity.
    c. Are both underpriced.
    d. Are both fairly priced.

38. According to the theory of arbitrage:
    a. High-beta stocks are consistently overpriced.
    b. Low-beta stocks are consistently overpriced.
    c. Positive alpha investment opportunities will quickly disappear.
    d. Rational investors will pursue arbitrage consistent with their risk tolerance.

39. A zero-investment portfolio with a positive alpha could arise if:
    a. The expected return of the portfolio equals zero.
    b. The capital market line is tangent to the opportunity set.
    c. The law of one price remains unviolated.
    d. A risk-free arbitrage opportunity exists.

40. An investor takes as large a position as possible when an equilibrium price relationship is violated. This is an example of:
    a. A dominance argument.
    b. The mean-variance efficient frontier.
    c. Arbitrage activity.
    d. The capital asset pricing model.

41. In contrast to the capital asset pricing model, arbitrage pricing theory:
    a. Requires that markets be in equilibrium.
    b. Uses risk premiums based on micro variables.
    c. Specifies the number and identifies specific factors that determine expected returns.
    d. Does not require the restrictive assumptions concerning the market portfolio.

STANDARD &POOR'S

1. In the previous chapter you used four years' data from Market Insight to calculate the beta of Alcoa. Now compute the alpha of the stock in two consecutive periods. Estimate the index model regression using the first two years of monthly data. (You can use 4-week T-bill rates to calculate excess returns from the Federal Reserve Web site at **www.federalreserve. gov/releases/h15/data.htm**). Now repeat the process using the last two years of monthly data. This will give you the alpha (intercept) and beta (slope) estimates for two consecutive time periods. How do the two alphas compare to the risk-free rate and to each other? Select 11 other firms and repeat the regressions to find the alphas for the first two-year period and the last two-year period.

2. Given your results for Question 1, investigate the extent to which beta in one period predicts beta in future periods and whether alpha in one period predicts alpha in future periods. Regress the beta of each firm in the second period (Y) against the beta in the first period (X). (If you estimated regressions for a dozen firms in Question 1, you will have 12 observations in this regression.) Do the same for the alphas of each firm. Use the coefficients you found to forecast the betas of the 12 firms for the next two-year period.

3. Our expectation is that beta in the first period predicts beta in the next period, but that alpha in the first period has no power to predict alpha in the next period. (In other words, the regression coefficient on first-period beta will be statistically significant in explaining second-period beta, but the coefficient on alpha will not be.) Why does this prediction make sense? Is it borne out by the data?

4. From Market Insight, enter ticker symbol BMY for Bristol Myers Squibb. In the Excel Analytics section, click on Monthly Valuation Data. The report summarizes seven months of data related to stock market activity and contains several comparison reports to market indexes. Then repeat the procedure to obtain data for CQB (Chiquita Brands Intl.), GE (General Electric), ET (E Trade Financial Corp.), and MLP (Maui Land and Pineapple Company). After reviewing the reports, answer the following questions:
    a. Which of the stocks would you classify as defensive? Which would be classified as aggressive?
    b. Do the beta coefficients for the low-beta firms make sense given the industries in which these firms operate? Briefly explain.
    c. Describe the variations in the reported beta coefficients over the seven months of data. (Check the "% change" worksheet to see the percentage changes.) Which firm has experienced the largest changes from month to month?

5. From Market Insight, enter the ticker symbol ALL for Allstate Corp. In the S&P Stock Reports section open the Wall Street Consensus Report. What is the Wall Street Consensus Opinion for Allstate? How do the analysts' expectations for earnings compare to the firm's performance to date this year? Now open the Industry Outlook Report. What other firms are in Allstate's peer group? What are the firms' beta coefficients? Why might the betas vary among firms? Repeat the process for Monsanto (MON) and the firms in its peer group. Is there more or less variation among the betas in this industry relative to Allstate and its peers?

WEB master

The Three-Factor Model

Calculate the expected return on a stock of your choice using the Fama/French three-factor model by following the directions below.

1. Go to Kenneth R. French's Web site **mba.tuck. dartmouth.edu/pages/faculty/ken.french/data_library. html** and locate the data for the daily Fama/French factors. After you download the file, copy the data for the most recent two years into an Excel spreadsheet. (You may have to use the Data, Text to Columns menu to get the data into a usable format.)

2. Download closing price data for a stock of your choice, with dates that correspond to the Fama/French data, from **finance.yahoo.com** or

moneycentral.msn.com/investor/research/ welcome.asp. Calculate the stock's daily returns.

3. Estimate the three-factor model for your stock:

$$r_S - r_f = \alpha_S + \beta_M(r_M - r_f) + \beta_{HML}r_{HML} + \beta_{SMB}r_{SMB} + e_S$$

To do this, line up the data in the order specified by the model, then use Excel's Tools, Data Analysis, Regression menu. (Use $r_S - r_f$ as the Y variable, $r_M - r_f$ as the first X variable, r_{HML} as the second X variable, and r_{SMB} as the third X variable.)

4. Use the resulting regression coefficients to estimate the expected return on your stock based on the most currently available Fama/French factors from the French Web site.

SOLUTIONS TO CONCEPT *checks*

7.1. The CML would still represent efficient investments. We can characterize the entire population by two representative investors. One is the "uninformed" investor, who does not engage in security analysis and holds the market portfolio, while the other optimizes using the Markowitz algorithm with input from security analysis. The uninformed investor does not know what input the informed investor uses to make portfolio purchases. The uninformed investor knows, however, that if the other investor is informed, the market portfolio proportions will be optimal. Therefore, to depart from these proportions would constitute an uninformed bet, which will, on average, reduce the efficiency of diversification with no compensating improvement in expected returns.

7.2. Substituting the historical mean and standard deviation in Equation 7.1 yields a coefficient of risk aversion of

$$A^* = \frac{E(r_M) - r_f}{\sigma_M^2} = \frac{.085}{0.20^2} = 2.1$$

This relationship also tells us that for the historical standard deviation and a coefficient of risk aversion of 3.5, the risk premium would be

$$E(r_M) - r_f = A^*\sigma_M^2 = 3.5 \times 0.20^2 = 0.14 = 14\%$$

7.3. $\beta_{Ford} = 1.25$, $\beta_{GM} = 1.15$. Therefore, given the investment proportions, the portfolio beta is

$$\beta_P = w_{Ford}\beta_{Ford} + w_{GM}\beta_{GM} = (0.75 \times 1.25) + (0.25 \times 1.15) = 1.225$$

and the risk premium of the portfolio will be

$$E(r_P) - r_f = \beta_P[E(r_M) - r_f] = 1.225 \times 8\% = 9.8\%$$

7.4. *a.* The alpha of a stock is its expected return in excess of that required by the CAPM.

$$\alpha = E(r) - \{r_f + \beta[E(r_M) - r_f]\}$$
$$\alpha_{XYZ} = 12 - [5 + 1.0(11 - 5)] = 1$$
$$\alpha_{ABC} = 13 - [5 + 1.5(11 - 5)] = -1\%$$

b. The project-specific required rate of return is determined by the project beta coupled with the market risk premium and the risk-free rate. The CAPM tells us that an acceptable expected rate of return for the project is

$$r_f + \beta[E(r_M) - r_f] = 8 + 1.3(16 - 8) = 18.4\%$$

which becomes the project's hurdle rate. If the IRR of the project is 19%, then it is desirable. Any project (of similar beta) with an IRR less than 18.4% should be rejected.

7.5. $E(r) = 4\% + 1.2 \times 4\% + .7 \times 2\% = 10.2\%$

7.6. Using Equation 7.11, the expected return is

$$4 + (0.2 \times 6) + (1.4 \times 8) = 16.4\%$$

The Efficient Market Hypothesis

Demonstrate why security price movements should be essentially unpredictable in an efficient market.

Cite evidence that supports and contradicts the efficient market hypothesis.

Provide interpretations of various stock market "anomalies."

Formulate investment strategies that make sense in informationally efficient markets.

One of the early applications of computers in economics in the 1950s was to analyze economic time series. Business cycle theorists felt that tracing the evolution of several economic variables over time would clarify and predict the progress of the economy through boom and bust periods. A natural candidate for analysis was the behavior of stock market prices over time. On the assumption that stock prices reflect the prospects of the firm, recurrent patterns of peaks and troughs in economic performance ought to show up in those prices.

When Maurice Kendall (1953) examined this proposition, however, he found to his great surprise that he could identify no predictable patterns in stock prices. Prices seemed to evolve randomly. They were as likely to go up as they were to go down on any particular day, regardless of past performance. The data provided no way to predict price movements.

At first blush, Kendall's results were disturbing to some financial economists. They seemed to imply that the stock market is dominated by erratic market psychology, or "animal spirits"—that it follows no logical rules. In short, the

(continued)

results appeared to confirm the irrationality of the market. On further reflection, however, economists came to reverse their interpretation of Kendall's study.

It soon became apparent that random price movements indicated a well-functioning or efficient market, not an irrational one. In this chapter we explore the reasoning behind what may seem a surprising conclusion. We show how competition among analysts leads naturally to market efficiency, and we examine the implications of the efficient market hypothesis for investment policy. We also consider empirical evidence that supports and contradicts the notion of market efficiency.

Related Web sites for this chapter are available at www.mhhe.com/bkm.

8.1 RANDOM WALKS AND THE EFFICIENT MARKET HYPOTHESIS

Suppose Kendall had discovered that stock prices are predictable. What a gold mine this would have been. If they could use Kendall's equations to predict stock prices, investors would reap unending profits simply by purchasing stocks that the computer model implied were about to increase in price and by selling those stocks about to fall in price.

A moment's reflection should be enough to convince yourself that this situation could not persist for long. For example, suppose that the model predicts with great confidence that XYZ stock price, currently at $100 per share, will rise dramatically in 3 days to $110. What would all investors with access to the model's prediction do today? Obviously, they would place a great wave of immediate buy orders to cash in on the forthcoming increase in stock price. No one holding XYZ, however, would be willing to sell. The net effect would be an *immediate* jump in the stock price to $110. The forecast of a future price increase will lead instead to an immediate price increase. In other words, the stock price will immediately reflect the "good news" implicit in the model's forecast.

This simple example illustrates why Kendall's attempt to find recurrent patterns in stock price movements was likely to fail. A forecast about favorable *future* performance leads instead to favorable *current* performance, as market participants all try to get in on the action before the price increase.

More generally, one might say that any information that could be used to predict stock performance should already be reflected in stock prices. As soon as there is any information indicating that a stock is underpriced and therefore offers a profit opportunity, investors flock to buy the stock and immediately bid up its price to a fair level, where only ordinary rates of return can be expected. These "ordinary rates" are simply rates of return commensurate with the risk of the stock.

However, if prices are bid immediately to fair levels, given all available information, it must be that they increase or decrease only in response to new information. New information, by definition, must be unpredictable; if it could be predicted, then the prediction would be part of today's information. Thus stock prices that change in response to new (unpredictable) information also must move unpredictably.

random walk

The notion that stock price changes are random and unpredictable.

This is the essence of the argument that stock prices should follow a random walk, that is, that price changes should be random and unpredictable. Far from a proof of market irrationality, randomly evolving stock prices would be the necessary consequence of intelligent investors competing to discover relevant information on which to buy or sell stocks before the rest of the market becomes aware of that information.

Don't confuse randomness in price *changes* with irrationality in the *level* of prices. If prices are determined rationally, then only new information will cause them to change. Therefore, a random walk would be the natural result of prices that always reflect all current knowledge. Indeed, if stock price movements were predictable, that would be damning evidence of stock

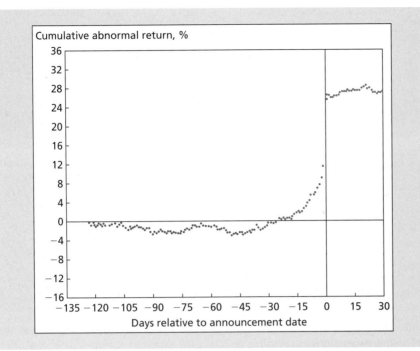

FIGURE 8.1

Cumulative abnormal returns before take-over attempts: Target companies

Source: Arthur Keown and John Pinkerton, "Merger Announcements and Insider Trading Activity," *Journal of Finance* 36 (September 1981). Reprinted by permission of the publisher, Blackwell Publishing, Inc.

market inefficiency, because the ability to predict prices would indicate that all available information was not already reflected in stock prices. Therefore, the notion that stocks already reflect all available information is referred to as the **efficient market hypothesis** (EMH).[1]

Figure 8.1 illustrates the response of stock prices to new information in an efficient market. The graph plots the price response of a sample of 194 firms that were targets of takeover attempts. In most takeovers, the acquiring firm pays a substantial premium over current market prices. Therefore, announcement of a takeover attempt should cause the stock price to jump. The figure shows that stock prices jump dramatically on the day the news becomes public. However, there is no further drift in prices *after* the announcement date, suggesting that prices reflect the new information, including the likely magnitude of the takeover premium, by the end of the trading day.

Even more dramatic evidence of rapid response to new information may be found in intraday prices. For example, Patel and Wolfson (1984) show that most of the stock price response to corporate dividend or earnings announcements occurs within 10 minutes of the announcement. A nice illustration of such rapid adjustment is provided in a study by Busse and Green (2002), who track minute-by-minute stock prices of firms that are featured on CNBC's "Morning" or "Midday Call" segments.[2] Minute 0 in Figure 8.2 is the time at which the stock is mentioned on the midday show. The top line is the average price movement of stocks that receive positive reports, while the bottom line reports returns on stocks with negative reports. Notice that the top line levels off, indicating that the market has fully digested the news, within 5 minutes of the report. The bottom line levels off within about 12 minutes.

efficient market hypothesis

The hypothesis that prices of securities fully reflect available information about securities.

Competition as the Source of Efficiency

Why should we expect stock prices to reflect "all available information"? After all, if you are willing to spend time and money on gathering information, it might seem reasonable that you could turn up something that has been overlooked by the rest of the investment community.

[1]Market efficiency should not be confused with the idea of efficient portfolios introduced in Chapter 6. An informationally efficient *market* is one in which information is rapidly disseminated and reflected in prices. An efficient *portfolio* is one with the highest expected return for a given level of risk.

[2]You can find a nice intraday movie version of this figure at **www.bus.emory.edu/cgreen/cnbc.html**.

FIGURE 8.2

Stock price reaction to CNBC reports. The figure shows the reaction of stock prices to on-air stock reports during the "Midday Call" segment on CNBC. The chart plots cumulative returns beginning 15 minutes before the stock report.

Source: Reprinted from J. A. Busse and T. C. Green, "Market Efficiency in Real Time," *Journal of Financial Economics* 65 (2002), p. 422. Copyright 2002 with permission from Elsevier Science.

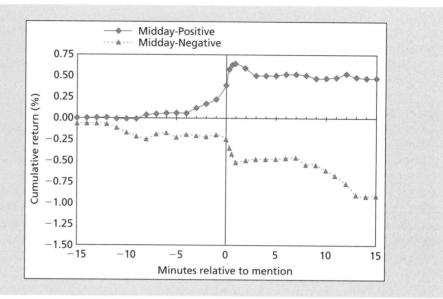

When information is costly to uncover and analyze, one would expect investment analysis calling for such expenditures to result in an increased expected return.

This point has been stressed by Grossman and Stiglitz (1980). They argued that investors will have an incentive to spend time and resources to analyze and uncover new information only if such activity is likely to generate higher investment returns. Thus, in market equilibrium, efficient information-gathering activity should be fruitful. Moreover, it would not be surprising to find that the degree of efficiency differs across various markets. For example, emerging markets that are less intensively analyzed than U.S. markets and in which accounting disclosure requirements are less rigorous may be less efficient than U.S. markets. Small stocks which receive relatively little coverage by Wall Street analysts may be less efficiently priced than large ones. Therefore, while we would not go so far as to say that you absolutely cannot come up with new information, it makes sense to consider and respect your competition.

EXAMPLE 8.1

Rewards for Incremental Performance

Consider an investment management fund currently managing a $5 billion portfolio. Suppose that the fund manager can devise a research program that could increase the portfolio rate of return by one-tenth of 1% per year, a seemingly modest amount. This program would increase the dollar return to the portfolio by $5 billion × .001, or $5 million. Therefore, the fund would be willing to spend up to $5 million per year on research to increase stock returns by a mere tenth of 1% per year. With such large rewards for such small increases in investment performance, it should not be surprising that professional portfolio managers are willing to spend large sums on industry analysts, computer support, and research effort, and therefore that price changes are, generally speaking, difficult to predict.

With so many well-backed analysts willing to spend considerable resources on research, easy pickings in the market will be rare. Moreover, the incremental rates of return on research activity may be so small that only managers of the largest portfolios will find them worth pursuing.

Although it may not literally be true that "all" relevant information will be uncovered, it is virtually certain that there are many investigators hot on the trail of most leads that seem likely to improve investment performance. Competition among these many well-backed, highly paid, aggressive analysts ensures that, as a general rule, stock prices ought to reflect available information regarding their proper levels.

A concrete illustration of this point appears in the nearby box, which reports on hedge funds paying lobbying firms up to $20,000 per *month* for tips on upcoming legislation that may affect the prospects of particular firms. These "investments in information" can easily pay for themselves when applied to very large portfolios. The article also notes that both Congress and the SEC are uneasy about the ethics and legalities of such arrangements.

Versions of the Efficient Market Hypothesis

It is common to distinguish among three versions of the EMH: the weak, semistrong, and strong forms of the hypothesis. These versions differ by their notions of what is meant by the term "all available information."

The **weak-form** hypothesis asserts that stock prices already reflect all information that can be derived by examining market trading data such as the history of past prices, trading volume, or short interest. This version of the hypothesis implies that trend analysis is fruitless. Past stock price data are publicly available and virtually costless to obtain. The weak-form hypothesis holds that if such data ever conveyed reliable signals about future performance, all investors already would have learned to exploit the signals. Ultimately, the signals lose their value as they become widely known because a buy signal, for instance, would result in an immediate price increase.

weak-form EMH

The assertion that stock prices already reflect all information contained in the history of past trading.

The **semistrong-form** hypothesis states that all publicly available information regarding the prospects of a firm already must be reflected in the stock price. Such information includes, in addition to past prices, fundamental data on the firm's product line, quality of management, balance sheet composition, patents held, earning forecasts, and accounting practices. Again, if investors have access to such information from publicly available sources, one would expect it to be reflected in stock prices.

semistrong-form EMH

The assertion that stock prices already reflect all publicly available information.

Finally, the **strong-form** version of the efficient market hypothesis states that stock prices reflect all information relevant to the firm, even including information available only to company insiders. This version of the hypothesis is quite extreme. Few would argue with the proposition that corporate officers have access to pertinent information long enough before public release to enable them to profit from trading on that information. Indeed, much of the activity of the Securities and Exchange Commission is directed toward preventing insiders from profiting by exploiting their privileged situation. Rule 10b-5 of the Security Exchange Act of 1934 sets limits on trading by corporate officers, directors, and substantial owners, requiring them to report trades to the SEC. These insiders, their relatives, and any associates who trade on information supplied by insiders are considered in violation of the law.

strong-form EMH

The assertion that stock prices reflect all relevant information, including inside information.

Defining insider trading is not always easy, however. After all, stock analysts are in the business of uncovering information not already widely known to market participants. As we saw in Chapter 3, the distinction between private and inside information is sometimes murky.

CONCEPT *check* **8.1**

a. Suppose you observed that high-level managers make superior returns on investments in their company's stock. Would this be a violation of weak-form market efficiency? Would it be a violation of strong-form market efficiency?

b. If the weak form of the efficient market hypothesis is valid, must the strong form also hold? Conversely, does strong-form efficiency imply weak-form efficiency?

8.2   IMPLICATIONS OF THE EMH

Technical Analysis

Technical analysis is essentially the search for recurrent and predictable patterns in stock prices. Although technicians recognize the value of information regarding future economic prospects of the firm, they believe that such information is not necessary for a successful trading strategy. This is because whatever the fundamental reason for a change in stock price, if the stock price responds slowly enough, the analyst will be able to identify a trend that can

technical analysis

Research on recurrent and predictable stock price patterns and on proxies for buy or sell pressure in the market.

On the MARKET FRONT

HEDGE FUNDS HIRE LOBBYISTS TO GATHER TIPS IN WASHINGTON

As federal authorities try to crack down on illegal trading using secrets leaked from companies, some hedge-fund managers are tapping another source of information: the corridors of the Capitol.

Hedge funds are finding that Washington can be a gold mine of market-moving information, easily gathered by the politically connected. The funds are hiring lobbyists—not to influence government, but to tell them what it's going to do. Several lobbying firms are ramping up their "political-intelligence" units and charging hedge funds between $5,000 and $20,000 a month for tips and predictions.

The Securities and Exchange Commission is looking into whether laws are being broken somewhere in the transfer of information between Congress and Wall Street. It's not illegal for lawmakers to disclose information that is not publicly known about the workings of Congress, even if it could affect stock prices. It breaks congressional ethics rules only if they or their aides profit directly. But one question the SEC is trying to resolve is whether the

passing of market-sensitive information by lobbyists to investors could violate insider-trading law.

The use of lobbyists as tipsters also is drawing attention from Congress. Democrats are considering requiring lobbyists to disclose their political-intelligence clients. Right now, lobbyists only have to disclose their work for clients seeking to influence government, while hedge funds and other clients seeking market-beating tips can stay in the shadows. Increasingly, lobbyists acting as advocates for a company on an issue may also have a client looking to trade on information about the same issue.

Employees of publicly traded companies are tightly bound by insider-trading laws, which also ban investors from trading public securities using material, nonpublic information that has been passed on improperly. But in most cases, members of Congress and their aides don't have a duty under the law to keep information private. They routinely exchange information about politics and policy with lobbyists—often not realizing that mere morsels are being sold to hedge funds who trade on the tidbits.

SOURCE: *The Wall Street Journal*, December 8, 2006, p. A1.

---

be exploited during the adjustment period. The key to successful technical analysis is a sluggish response of stock prices to fundamental supply-and-demand factors. This prerequisite, of course, is diametrically opposed to the notion of an efficient market.

resistance level

A price level above which it is supposedly unlikely for a stock or stock index to rise.

Technical analysts are sometimes called *chartists* because they study records or charts of past stock prices, hoping to find patterns they can exploit to make a profit. As an example of technical analysis, consider the *relative strength* approach. The chartist compares stock performance over a recent period to performance of the market or other stocks in the same industry. A simple version of relative strength takes the ratio of the stock price to a market indicator such as the S&P 500 index. If the ratio increases over time, the stock is said to exhibit relative strength because its price performance is better than that of the broad market. Such strength presumably may continue for a long enough period of time to offer profit opportunities.

support level

A price level below which it is supposedly unlikely for a stock or stock index to fall.

One of the most commonly heard components of technical analysis is the notion of **resistance levels** or **support levels.** These values are said to be price levels above which it is difficult for stock prices to rise, or below which it is unlikely for them to fall, and they are believed to be levels determined by market psychology.

EXAMPLE	8.2

Resistance Levels

Consider stock XYZ, which traded for several months at a price of $72, and then declined to $65. If the stock eventually begins to increase in price, $72 is considered a resistance level (according to this theory) because investors who bought originally at $72 will be eager to sell their shares as soon as they can break even on their investment. Therefore, at prices near $72 a wave of selling pressure would exist. Such activity imparts a type of "memory" to the market that allows past price history to influence current stock prospects.

The efficient market hypothesis implies that technical analysis is without merit. The past history of prices and trading volume is publicly available at minimal cost. Therefore, any information that was ever available from analyzing past prices has already been reflected in

236

stock prices. As investors compete to exploit their common knowledge of a stock's price history, they necessarily drive stock prices to levels where expected rates of return are exactly commensurate with risk. At those levels one cannot expect abnormal returns.

As an example of how this process works, consider what would happen if the market believed that a level of $72 truly were a resistance level for stock XYZ in Example 8.2. No one would be willing to purchase the stock at a price of $71.50, because it would have almost no room to increase in price, but ample room to fall. However, if no one would buy it at $71.50, then $71.50 would become a resistance level. But then, using a similar analysis, no one would buy it at $71, or $70, and so on. The notion of a resistance level is a logical conundrum. Its simple resolution is the recognition that if the stock is ever to sell at $71.50, investors *must* believe that the price can as easily increase as fall. The fact that investors are willing to purchase (or even hold) the stock at $71.50 is evidence of their belief that they can earn a fair expected rate of return at that price.

> **CONCEPT** **8.2**
> *check*
>
> If everyone in the market believes in resistance levels, why do these beliefs not become self-fulfilling prophecies?

An interesting question is whether a technical rule that seems to work will continue to work in the future once it becomes widely recognized. A clever analyst may occasionally uncover a profitable trading rule, but the real test of efficient markets is whether the rule itself becomes reflected in stock prices once its value is discovered. Once a useful technical rule (or price pattern) is discovered, it ought to be invalidated when the mass of traders attempts to exploit it. In this sense, price patterns ought to be *self-destructing*.

Thus the market dynamic is one of a continual search for profitable trading rules, followed by destruction by overuse of those rules found to be successful, followed by more search for yet-undiscovered rules. We return to the rationale for technical analysis as well as some of its methods in the next chapter.

Fundamental Analysis

Fundamental analysis uses earnings and dividend prospects of the firm, expectations of future interest rates, and risk evaluation of the firm to determine proper stock prices. Ultimately, it represents an attempt to determine the present discounted value of all the payments a stockholder will receive from each share of stock. If that value exceeds the stock price, the fundamental analyst would recommend purchasing the stock.

Fundamental analysts usually start with a study of past earnings and an examination of company balance sheets. They supplement this analysis with further detailed economic analysis, ordinarily including an evaluation of the quality of the firm's management, the firm's standing within its industry, and the prospects for the industry as a whole. The hope is to attain insight into future performance of the firm that is not yet recognized by the rest of the market. Chapters 12 through 14 provide a detailed discussion of the types of analyses that underlie fundamental analysis.

Once again, the efficient market hypothesis predicts that *most* fundamental analysis also is doomed to failure. If the analyst relies on publicly available earnings and industry information, his or her evaluation of the firm's prospects is not likely to be significantly more accurate than those of rival analysts. There are many well-informed, well-financed firms conducting such market research, and in the face of such competition it will be difficult to uncover data not also available to other analysts. Only analysts with a unique insight will be rewarded.

Fundamental analysis is much more difficult than merely identifying well-run firms with good prospects. Discovery of good firms does an investor no good in and of itself if the rest of the market also knows those firms are good. If the knowledge is already public, the investor will be forced to pay a high price for those firms and will not realize a superior rate of return.

fundamental analysis

Research on determinants of stock value, such as earnings and dividend prospects, expectations for future interest rates, and risk of the firm.

The trick is not to identify firms that are good, but to find firms that are *better* than everyone else's estimate. Similarly, poorly run firms can be great bargains if they are not quite as bad as their stock prices suggest.

This is why fundamental analysis is difficult. It is not enough to do a good analysis of a firm; you can make money only if your analysis is better than that of your competitors because the market price will already reflect all commonly available information.

Active versus Passive Portfolio Management

By now it is apparent that casual efforts to pick stocks are not likely to pay off. Competition among investors ensures that any easily implemented stock evaluation technique will be used widely enough so that any insights derived will be reflected in stock prices. Only serious analysis and uncommon techniques are likely to generate the *differential* insight necessary to yield trading profits.

Moreover, these techniques are economically feasible only for managers of large portfolios. If you have only $100,000 to invest, even a 1% per year improvement in performance generates only $1,000 per year, hardly enough to justify herculean efforts. The billion-dollar manager, however, reaps extra income of $10 million annually from the same 1% increment.

If small investors are not in a favored position to conduct active portfolio management, what are their choices? The small investor probably is better off investing in mutual funds. By pooling resources in this way, small investors can gain from economies of scale.

More difficult decisions remain, though. Can investors be sure that even large mutual funds have the ability or resources to uncover mispriced stocks? Furthermore, will any mispricing be sufficiently large to repay the costs entailed in active portfolio management?

passive investment strategy

Buying a well-diversified portfolio without attempting to search out mispriced securities.

Proponents of the efficient market hypothesis believe that active management is largely wasted effort and unlikely to justify the expenses incurred. Therefore, they advocate a **passive investment strategy** that makes no attempt to outsmart the market. A passive strategy aims only at establishing a well-diversified portfolio of securities without attempting to find under- or overvalued stocks. Passive management is usually characterized by a buy-and-hold strategy. Because the efficient market theory indicates that stock prices are at fair levels, given all available information, it makes no sense to buy and sell securities frequently, which generates large brokerage fees without increasing expected performance.

index fund

A mutual fund holding shares in proportion to their representation in a market index such as the S&P 500.

One common strategy for passive management is to create an **index fund,** which is a fund designed to replicate the performance of a broad-based index of stocks. For example, Vanguard's Index 500 Portfolio holds stocks in direct proportion to their weight in the Standard & Poor's 500 stock price index. The performance of the Index 500 fund therefore replicates the performance of the S&P 500. Investors in this fund obtain broad diversification with relatively low management fees. The fees can be kept to a minimum because Vanguard does not need to pay analysts to assess stock prospects and does not incur transaction costs from high portfolio turnover. Indeed, while the typical annual expense ratio for an actively managed equity fund is more than 1% of assets, Vanguard charges a bit less than .2% for the Index 500 Portfolio. Today, Vanguard's Index 500 Portfolio is among the largest equity mutual funds with over $100 billion of assets at the end of 2006, and about 10% of equity funds are indexed.

Indexing need not be limited to the S&P 500, however. For example, some of the funds offered by the Vanguard Group track the Wilshire 5000 index, the Salomon Brothers Broad Investment Grade Bond Index, the MSCI index of small-capitalization U.S. companies, the European equity market, and the Pacific Basin equity market. Several other mutual fund complexes offer indexed portfolios, but Vanguard dominates the retail market for indexed products.

Exchange traded funds, or ETFs, are a close (and usually lower-expense) alternative to indexed mutual funds. As noted in Chapter 4, these are shares in diversified portfolios that can be bought or sold just like shares of individual stock. ETFs matching several broad stock market indexes such as the S&P 500 or Wilshire 5000 indexes and dozens of international and industry stock indexes are available to investors who want to hold a diversified sector of a market without attempting active security selection.

A hybrid strategy also is fairly common, where the fund maintains a *passive core,* which is an indexed position, and augments that position with one or more actively managed portfolios.

CONCEPT check 8.3

What would happen to market efficiency if *all* investors attempted to follow a passive strategy?

The Role of Portfolio Management in an Efficient Market

If the market is efficient, why not throw darts at *The Wall Street Journal* instead of trying rationally to choose a stock portfolio? This is a tempting conclusion to draw from the notion that security prices are fairly set, but it is far too facile. There is a role for rational portfolio management, even in perfectly efficient markets.

You have learned that a basic principle in portfolio selection is diversification. Even if all stocks are priced fairly, each still poses firm-specific risk that can be eliminated through diversification. Therefore, rational security selection, even in an efficient market, calls for the selection of a well-diversified portfolio providing the systematic risk level that the investor wants.

Rational investment policy also requires that tax considerations be reflected in security choice. High-tax-bracket investors generally will not want the same securities that low-bracket investors find favorable. At an obvious level, high-bracket investors find it advantageous to buy tax-exempt municipal bonds despite their relatively low pretax yields, whereas those same bonds are unattractive to low-tax-bracket investors. At a more subtle level, high-bracket investors might want to tilt their portfolios in the direction of capital gains as opposed to interest income, because capital gains are taxed less heavily and because the option to defer the realization of capital gains income is more valuable the higher the current tax bracket. Hence these investors may prefer stocks that yield low dividends yet offer greater expected capital gain income. They also will be more attracted to investment opportunities for which returns are sensitive to tax benefits, such as real estate ventures.

A third argument for rational portfolio management relates to the particular risk profile of the investor. For example, a Toyota executive whose annual bonus depends on Toyota's profits generally should not invest additional amounts in auto stocks. To the extent that his or her compensation already depends on Toyota's well-being, the executive is already overinvested in Toyota and should not exacerbate the lack of diversification.

Investors of varying ages also might warrant different portfolio policies with regard to risk bearing. For example, older investors who are essentially living off savings might choose to avoid long-term bonds whose market values fluctuate dramatically with changes in interest rates (discussed in Part Four). Because these investors are living off accumulated savings, they require conservation of principal. In contrast, younger investors might be more inclined toward long-term inflation-indexed bonds. The steady flow of real income over long periods of time that is locked in with these bonds can be more important than preservation of principal to those with long life expectancies.

In conclusion, there is a role for portfolio management even in an efficient market. Investors' optimal positions will vary according to factors such as age, tax bracket, risk aversion, and employment. The role of the portfolio manager in an efficient market is to tailor the portfolio to these needs, rather than to beat the market.

Resource Allocation

We've focused so far on the investments implications of the efficient market hypothesis. Deviations from efficiency may offer profit opportunities to better-informed traders at the expense of less-informed traders.

However, deviations from informational efficiency would also result in a large cost that will be borne by all citizens, namely, inefficient resource allocation. Recall that in a capitalist economy, investments in *real* assets such as plant, equipment, and know-how are guided in large part by the prices of financial assets. For example, if the values of biotech assets as reflected in the stock market prices of biotech firms exceed the cost of acquiring those assets, the managers of such firms have a strong signal that further investments in the firm will be regarded by the market as a positive net present value venture. In this manner, capital market prices guide resource allocation. Security mispricing thus could entail severe social costs by fostering inappropriate investments on the real side of the economy.

Corporations with overpriced securities will be able to obtain capital too cheaply and corporations with undervalued securities might forgo investment opportunities because the cost of raising capital will be too high. Therefore, inefficient capital markets would diminish one of the most potent benefits of a market economy.

8.3   ARE MARKETS EFFICIENT?

The Issues

Not surprisingly, the efficient market hypothesis does not exactly arouse enthusiasm in the community of professional portfolio managers. It implies that a great deal of the activity of portfolio managers—the search for undervalued securities—is at best wasted effort, and quite probably harmful to clients because it costs money and leads to imperfectly diversified portfolios. Consequently, the EMH has never been widely accepted on Wall Street, and debate continues today on the degree to which security analysis can improve investment performance. Before discussing empirical tests of the hypothesis, we want to note three factors that together imply that the debate probably never will be settled: the *magnitude issue,* the *selection bias issue,* and the *lucky event issue.*

The magnitude issue   We noted that an investment manager overseeing a $5 billion portfolio who can improve performance by only 0.1% per year will increase investment earnings by .001 × $5 billion = $5 million annually. This manager clearly would be worth her salary! Yet can we, as observers, statistically measure her contribution? Probably not: A 0.1% contribution would be swamped by the yearly volatility of the market. Remember, the annual standard deviation of the well-diversified S&P 500 index has been around 20%. Against these fluctuations a small increase in performance would be hard to detect.

All might agree that stock prices are very close to fair values and that only managers of large portfolios can earn enough trading profits to make the exploitation of minor mispricing worth the effort. According to this view, the actions of intelligent investment managers are the driving force behind the constant evolution of market prices to fair levels. Rather than ask the qualitative question, Are markets efficient? we ought instead to ask a more quantitative question: How efficient are markets?

The selection bias issue   Suppose that you discover an investment scheme that could really make money. You have two choices: either publish your technique in *The Wall Street Journal* to win fleeting fame, or keep your technique secret and use it to earn millions of dollars. Most investors would choose the latter option, which presents us with a conundrum. Only investors who find that an investment scheme cannot generate abnormal returns will be willing to report their findings to the whole world. Hence opponents of the efficient markets view of the world always can use evidence that various techniques do not provide investment rewards as proof that the techniques that do work simply are not being reported to the public. This is a problem in *selection bias;* the outcomes we are able to observe have been preselected in favor of failed attempts. Therefore, we cannot fairly evaluate the true ability of portfolio managers to generate winning stock market strategies.

The lucky event issue   In virtually any month it seems we read an article about some investor or investment company with a fantastic investment performance over the recent past. Surely the superior records of such investors disprove the efficient market hypothesis.

On the MARKET FRONT

HOW TO GUARANTEE A SUCCESSFUL MARKET NEWSLETTER

Suppose you want to make your fortune publishing a market newsletter. You need first to convince potential subscribers that you have talent worth paying for. But what if you have no talent? The solution is simple: Start eight newsletters.

In year 1, let four of your newsletters predict an up-market and four a down-market. In year 2, let half of the originally optimistic group of newsletters continue to predict an up-market and the other half a down-market. Do the same for the originally pessimistic group. Continue in this manner to obtain the pattern of predictions in the table that follows (U = prediction of an up-market, D = prediction of a down-market).

After 3 years, no matter what has happened to the market, one of the newsletters would have had a perfect prediction record. This is because after 3 years there are $2^3 = 8$ outcomes for the market, and we have covered all eight possibilities with the eight newsletters. Now, we simply slough off the seven unsuccessful newsletters, and market the eighth newsletter based on its perfect track record.

If we want to establish a newsletter with a perfect track record over a 4-year period, we need $2^4 = 16$ newsletters. A 5-year period requires 32 newsletters, and so on.

After the fact, the one newsletter that was always right will attract attention for your uncanny foresight and investors will rush to pay large fees for its advice. Your fortune is made, and you have never even researched the market!

WARNING: This scheme is illegal! The point, however, is that with hundreds of market newsletters, you can find one that has stumbled onto an apparently remarkable string of successful predictions without any real degree of skill. After the fact, *someone's* prediction history can seem to imply great forecasting skill. This person is the one we will read about in *The Wall Street Journal*; the others will be forgotten.

Newsletter Predictions								
Year	1	2	3	4	5	6	7	8
1	U	U	U	U	D	D	D	D
2	U	U	D	D	U	U	D	D
3	U	D	U	D	U	D	U	D

Yet this conclusion is far from obvious. As an analogy to the investment game, consider a contest to flip the most number of heads out of 50 trials using a fair coin. The expected outcome for any person is, of course, 50% heads and 50% tails. If 10,000 people, however, compete in this contest, it would not be surprising if at least one or two contestants flipped more than 75% heads. In fact, elementary statistics tells us that the expected number of contestants flipping 75% or more heads would be two. It would be silly, though, to crown these people the "head-flipping champions of the world." Obviously, they are simply the contestants who happened to get lucky on the day of the event. (See the nearby box.)

The analogy to efficient markets is clear. Under the hypothesis that any stock is fairly priced given all available information, any bet on a stock is simply a coin toss. There is equal likelihood of winning or losing the bet. However, if many investors using a variety of schemes make fair bets, statistically speaking, *some* of those investors will be lucky and win a great majority of the bets. For every big winner, there may be many big losers, but we never hear of these managers. The winners, though, turn up in *The Wall Street Journal* as the latest stock market gurus; then they can make a fortune publishing market newsletters.

Our point is that after the fact there will have been at least one successful investment scheme. A doubter will call the results luck, the successful investor will call it skill. The proper test would be to see whether the successful investors can repeat their performance in another period, yet this approach is rarely taken.

With these caveats in mind, we turn now to some of the empirical tests of the efficient market hypothesis.

Legg Mason's Value Trust, managed by Bill Miller, outperformed the S&P 500 in each of the 15 years ending in 2005. Is Miller's performance sufficient to dissuade you from a belief in efficient markets? If not, would *any* performance record be sufficient to dissuade you?

CONCEPT *check* **8.4**

Weak-Form Tests: Patterns in Stock Returns

Returns over short horizons   Early tests of efficient markets were tests of the weak form. Could speculators find trends in past prices that would enable them to earn abnormal profits? This is essentially a test of the efficacy of technical analysis.

One way of discerning trends in stock prices is by measuring the *serial correlation* of stock market returns. Serial correlation refers to the tendency for stock returns to be related to past returns. Positive serial correlation means that positive returns tend to follow positive returns (a momentum type of property). Negative serial correlation means that positive returns tend to be followed by negative returns (a reversal or "correction" property). Both Conrad and Kaul (1988) and Lo and MacKinlay (1988) examine weekly returns of NYSE stocks and find positive serial correlation over short horizons. However, the correlation coefficients of weekly returns tend to be fairly small, at least for large stocks for which price data are the most reliably up-to-date. Thus, while these studies demonstrate weak price trends over short periods,[3] the evidence does not clearly suggest the existence of trading opportunities.

While broad market indexes demonstrate only weak serial correlation, there appears to be stronger momentum in performance across market sectors exhibiting the best and worst recent returns. In an investigation of intermediate-horizon stock price behavior (using 3- to 12-month holding periods), Jegadeesh and Titman (1993) found a **momentum effect** in which good or bad recent performance of particular stocks continues over time. They conclude that while the performance of individual stocks is highly unpredictable, *portfolios* of the best-performing stocks in the recent past appear to outperform other stocks with enough reliability to offer profit opportunities. Thus, it appears that there is evidence of short- to intermediate-horizon price momentum in both the aggregate market and cross-sectionally (i.e., across particular stocks).

Returns over long horizons   Although short- to intermediate-horizon returns suggest momentum in stock market prices, studies of long-horizon returns (i.e., returns over multiyear periods) by Fama and French (1988) and Poterba and Summers (1988) indicate pronounced *negative* long-term serial correlation in the performance of the aggregate market. The latter result has given rise to a "fads hypothesis," which asserts that the stock market might overreact to relevant news. Such overreaction leads to positive serial correlation (momentum) over short time horizons. Subsequent correction of the overreaction leads to poor performance following good performance and vice versa. The corrections mean that a run of positive returns eventually will tend to be followed by negative returns, leading to negative serial correlation over longer horizons. These episodes of apparent overshooting followed by correction give the stock market the appearance of fluctuating around its fair value.

These long-horizon results are dramatic, but the studies offer far from conclusive evidence regarding efficient markets. First, the study results need not be interpreted as evidence for stock market fads. An alternative interpretation of these results holds that they indicate only that the market risk premium varies over time. For example, when the risk premium and the required return on the market rises, stock prices will fall. When the market then rises (on average) at this higher rate of return, the data convey the impression of a stock price recovery. The apparent overshooting and correction is in fact no more than a rational response of market prices to changes in discount rates.

In addition to studies suggestive of overreaction in overall stock market returns over long horizons, many other studies suggest that over long horizons, extreme performance in particular securities also tends to reverse itself: The stocks that have performed best in the recent past seem to underperform the rest of the market in following periods, while the worst past performers tend to offer above-average future performance. De Bondt and Thaler (1985) and Chopra,

momentum effect

The tendency of poorly performing stocks and well-performing stocks in one period to continue that abnormal performance in following periods.

---

[3] On the other hand, there is evidence that share prices of individual securities (as opposed to broad market indexes) are more prone to reversals than continuations at very short horizons. See, for example, B. Lehmann, "Fads, Martingales and Market Efficiency," *Quarterly Journal of Economics* 105 (February 1990), pp. 1–28; and N. Jegadeesh, "Evidence of Predictable Behavior of Security Returns," *Journal of Finance* 45 (September 1990), pp. 881–98. However, as Lehmann notes, this is probably best interpreted as due to liquidity problems after big movements in stock prices as market makers adjust their positions in the stock.

Lakonishok, and Ritter (1992) find strong tendencies for poorly performing stocks in one period to experience sizable reversals over the subsequent period, while the best-performing stocks in a given period tend to follow with poor performance in the following period.

For example, the De Bondt and Thaler study found that if one were to rank-order the performance of stocks over a 5-year period and then group stocks into portfolios based on investment performance, the base-period "loser" portfolio (defined as the 35 stocks with the worst investment performance) outperformed the "winner" portfolio (the top 35 stocks) by an average of 25% (cumulative return) in the following 3-year period. This **reversal effect,** in which losers rebound and winners fade back, suggests that the stock market overreacts to relevant news. After the overreaction is recognized, extreme investment performance is reversed. This phenomenon would imply that a *contrarian* investment strategy—investing in recent losers and avoiding recent winners—should be profitable. Moreover, these returns seem pronounced enough to be exploited profitably.

Thus it appears that there may be short-run momentum but long-run reversal patterns in price behavior both for the market as a whole and across sectors of the market. One interpretation of this pattern is that short-run overreaction (which causes momentum in prices) may lead to long-term reversals (when the market recognizes its past error).

reversal effect

The tendency of poorly performing stocks and well-performing stocks in one period to experience reversals in the following period.

Predictors of Broad Market Returns

Several studies have documented the ability of easily observed variables to predict market returns. For example, Fama and French (1988) showed that the return on the aggregate stock market tends to be higher when the dividend/price ratio, the dividend yield, is high. Campbell and Shiller (1988) found that the earnings yield can predict market returns. Keim and Stambaugh (1986) showed that bond market data such as the spread between yields on high- and low-grade corporate bonds also help predict broad market returns.

Again, the interpretation of these results is difficult. On the one hand, they may imply that stock returns can be predicted, in violation of the efficient market hypothesis. More probably, however, these variables are proxying for variation in the market risk premium. For example, given a level of dividends or earnings, stock prices will be lower and dividend and earnings yields will be higher when the risk premium (and therefore the expected market return) is higher. Thus a high dividend or earnings yield will be associated with higher market returns. This does not indicate a violation of market efficiency. The predictability of market returns is due to predictability in the risk premium, not in risk-adjusted abnormal returns.

Fama and French (1989) showed that the yield spread between high- and low-grade bonds has greater predictive power for returns on low-grade bonds than for returns on high-grade bonds, and greater predictive power for stock returns than for bond returns, suggesting that the predictability in returns is in fact a risk premium rather than evidence of market inefficiency. Similarly, the fact that the dividend yield on stocks helps to predict bond market returns suggests that the yield captures a risk premium common to both markets rather than mispricing in the equity market.

Semistrong Tests: Market Anomalies

Fundamental analysis uses a much wider range of information to create portfolios than does technical analysis. Investigations of the efficacy of fundamental analysis ask whether publicly available information beyond the trading history of a security can be used to improve investment performance, and therefore are tests of semistrong-form market efficiency. Surprisingly, several easily accessible statistics, for example a stock's price–earnings ratio or its market capitalization, seem to predict abnormal risk-adjusted returns. Findings such as these, which we will review in the following pages, are difficult to reconcile with the efficient market hypothesis, and therefore are often referred to as efficient market **anomalies.**

A difficulty in interpreting these tests is that we usually need to adjust for portfolio risk before evaluating the success of an investment strategy. Many tests, for example, have used the CAPM to adjust for risk. However, we know that even if beta is a relevant descriptor of stock risk,

anomalies

Patterns of returns that seem to contradict the efficient market hypothesis.

the empirically measured quantitative trade-off between risk as measured by beta and expected return differs from the predictions of the CAPM. If we use the CAPM to adjust portfolio returns for risk, inappropriate adjustments may lead to the conclusion that various portfolio strategies can generate superior returns, when in fact it simply is the risk adjustment procedure that has failed.

Another way to put this is to note that tests of risk-adjusted returns are *joint tests* of the efficient market hypothesis *and* the risk adjustment procedure. If it appears that a portfolio strategy can generate superior returns, we must then choose between rejecting the EMH and rejecting the risk adjustment technique. Usually, the risk adjustment technique is based on more-questionable assumptions than is the EMH; by opting to reject the procedure, we are left with no conclusion about market efficiency.

An example of this issue is the discovery by Basu (1977, 1983) that portfolios of low price–earnings (P/E) ratio stocks have higher returns than do high P/E portfolios. The **P/E effect** holds up even if returns are adjusted for portfolio beta. Is this a confirmation that the market systematically misprices stocks according to P/E ratio? This would be an extremely surprising and, to us, disturbing conclusion, because analysis of P/E ratios is such a simple procedure. Although it may be possible to earn superior returns by using hard work and much insight, it hardly seems plausible that such a simplistic technique is enough to generate abnormal returns.

Another interpretation of these results is that returns are not properly adjusted for risk. If two firms have the same expected earnings, the riskier stock will sell at a lower price and lower P/E ratio. Because of its higher risk, the low P/E stock also will have higher expected returns. Therefore, unless the CAPM beta fully adjusts for risk, P/E will act as a useful additional descriptor of risk, and will be associated with abnormal returns if the CAPM is used to establish benchmark performance.

The small-firm-in-january effect
The so-called size or **small-firm effect**, originally documented by Banz (1981), is illustrated in Figure 8.3. It shows the historical performance of portfolios formed by dividing the NYSE stocks into 10 portfolios each year according to firm size (i.e., the total value of outstanding equity). Average annual returns between 1926 and 2005 are consistently higher on the small-firm portfolios. The difference in average annual return between portfolio 10 (with the largest firms) and portfolio 1 (with the smallest firms) is 10.30%. Of course, the smaller-firm portfolios tend to be riskier. But even when returns are adjusted for risk using the CAPM, there is still a consistent premium for the smaller-sized portfolios. Even on a risk-adjusted basis, the smallest-size portfolio outperforms the largest-firm portfolio by an average of 6.73% annually.

P/E effect

Portfolios of low P/E stocks have exhibited higher average risk-adjusted returns than high P/E stocks.

small-firm effect

Stocks of small firms have earned abnormal returns, primarily in the month of January.

FIGURE 8.3

Returns in excess of risk-free rate and in excess of the Security Market Line for 10 size-based portfolios, 1926–2005

Source: © 2007 Morningstar. All rights reserved. Used with permission.

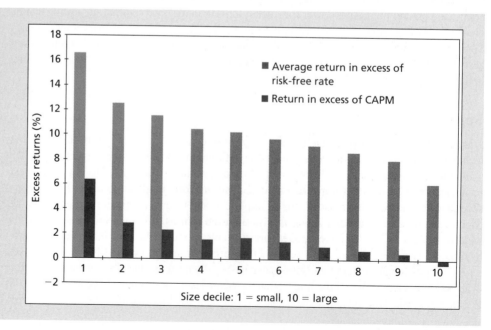

Imagine earning a premium of this size on a billion-dollar portfolio. Yet it is remarkable that following a simple (even simplistic) rule such as "invest in low-capitalization stocks" should enable an investor to earn excess returns. After all, any investor can measure firm size at little cost. One would not expect such minimal effort to yield such large rewards.

Later studies (Keim, 1983; Reinganum, 1983; and Blume and Stambaugh, 1983) showed that the small-firm effect occurs virtually entirely in January, in fact, in the first 2 weeks of January. The size effect is in fact a "small-firm-in-January" effect.

The neglected-firm and liquidity effects   Arbel and Strebel (1983) gave another interpretation of the small-firm-in-January effect. Because small firms tend to be neglected by large institutional traders, information about smaller firms is less available. This information deficiency makes smaller firms riskier investments that command higher returns. "Brand-name" firms, after all, are subject to considerable monitoring from institutional investors, which promises high-quality information, and presumably investors do not purchase "generic" stocks without the prospect of greater returns.

As evidence for the **neglected-firm effect,** Arbel (1985) divided firms into highly researched, moderately researched, and neglected groups based on the number of institutions holding the stock. The January effect was in fact largest for the neglected firms. An article by Merton (1987) shows that neglected firms might be expected to earn higher equilibrium returns as compensation for the risk associated with limited information. In this sense the neglected firm premium is not strictly a market inefficiency, but is a type of risk premium.

> **neglected-firm effect**
>
> **The tendency of investments in stock of less-well-known firms to generate abnormal returns.**

Work by Amihud and Mendelson (1986, 1991) on the effect of liquidity on stock returns might be related to both the small-firm and neglected-firm effects. They argue that investors will demand a rate-of-return premium to invest in less-liquid stocks that entail higher trading costs. Indeed, spreads for the least-liquid stocks easily can be more than 5% of stock value. In accord with their hypothesis, Amihud and Mendelson showed that these stocks show a strong tendency to exhibit abnormally high risk-adjusted rates of return. Because small and less-analyzed stocks as a rule are less liquid, the liquidity effect might be a partial explanation of their abnormal returns. However, this theory does not explain why the abnormal returns of small firms should be concentrated in January. In any case, exploiting these effects can be more difficult than it would appear. The high trading costs on small stocks can easily wipe out any apparent abnormal profit opportunity.

Book-to-market ratios   Fama and French (1992) showed that a powerful predictor of returns across securities is the ratio of the book value of the firm's equity to the market value of equity. Fama and French stratified firms into 10 groups according to book-to-market ratios and examined the average rate of return of each of the 10 groups. Figure 8.4 is an updated version

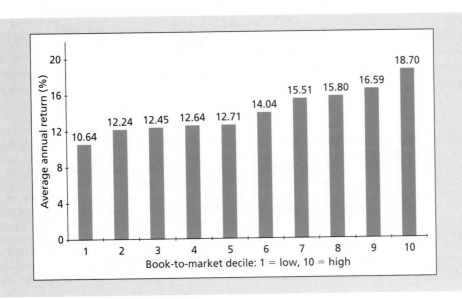

FIGURE 8.4

Average annual return as a function of the book-to-market ratio, 1963–2005.

Source: Web site of Prof. Kenneth French, **http://mba. tuck.dartmouth.edu/pages/ faculty/ken. french/data_ library.html.**

of their results. The decile with the highest book-to-market ratio had an average annual return of 18.70%, while the lowest-ratio decile averaged only 10.64%. The dramatic dependence of returns on book-to-market ratio is independent of beta, suggesting either that high book-to-market ratio firms are relatively underpriced, or that the book-to-market ratio is serving as a proxy for a risk factor that affects equilibrium expected returns.

In fact, Fama and French found that after controlling for the size and **book-to-market effects,** beta seemed to have no power to explain average security returns.[4] This finding is an important challenge to the notion of rational markets, since it seems to imply that a factor that should affect returns—systematic risk—seems not to matter, while a factor that should not matter—the book-to-market ratio—seems capable of predicting future returns. We will return to the interpretation of this anomaly.

book-to-market effect

The tendency for investments in shares of firms with high ratios of book value to market value to generate abnormal returns.

Post–earnings-announcement price drift

A fundamental principle of efficient markets is that any new information ought to be reflected in stock prices very rapidly. When good news is made public, for example, the stock price should jump immediately. A puzzling anomaly, therefore, is the apparently sluggish response of stock prices to firms' earnings announcements, as uncovered by Ball and Brown (1968). Their results were later confirmed and extended in many other papers.[5]

The "news content" of an earnings announcement can be evaluated by comparing the announcement of actual earnings to the value previously expected by market participants. The difference is the "earnings surprise." (Market expectations of earnings can be roughly measured by averaging the published earnings forecasts of Wall Street analysts or by applying trend analysis to past earnings.) Rendleman, Jones, and Latané (1982) provide an influential study of sluggish price response to earnings announcements. They calculate earnings surprises for a large sample of firms, rank the magnitude of the surprise, divide firms into 10 deciles based on the size of the surprise, and calculate abnormal returns for each decile. The abnormal return of each portfolio is the return adjusting for both the market return in that period and the portfolio beta. It measures return over and above what would be expected given market conditions in that period. Figure 8.5 plots cumulative abnormal returns by decile.

Their results are dramatic. The correlation between ranking by earnings surprise and abnormal returns across deciles is as predicted. There is a large abnormal return (a jump in cumulative abnormal return) on the earnings announcement day (time 0). The abnormal return is positive for positive-surprise firms and negative for negative-surprise firms.

The more remarkable, and interesting, result of the study concerns stock price movement *after* the announcement date. The cumulative abnormal returns of positive-surprise stocks continue to rise—in other words, exhibit momentum—even after the earnings information becomes public, while the negative-surprise firms continue to suffer negative abnormal returns. The market appears to adjust to the earnings information only gradually, resulting in a sustained period of abnormal returns.

Evidently, one could have earned abnormal profits simply by waiting for earnings announcements and purchasing a stock portfolio of positive-earnings-surprise companies. These are precisely the types of predictable continuing trends that ought to be impossible in an efficient market.

[4] However, a study by S. P. Kothari, Jay Shanken, and Richard G. Sloan (1995) finds that when betas are estimated using annual rather than monthly returns, securities with high beta values do in fact have higher average returns. Moreover, the authors find a book-to-market effect that is attenuated compared to the results in Fama and French and furthermore is inconsistent across different samples of securities. They conclude that the empirical case for the importance of the book-to-market ratio may be somewhat weaker than the Fama and French study would suggest.

[5] There is a voluminous literature on this phenomenon, often referred to as post–earnings-announcement price drift. For more recent papers that focus on why such drift may be observed, see V. Bernard and J. Thomas, "Evidence That Stock Prices Do Not Fully Reflect the Implications of Current Earnings for Future Earnings," *Journal of Accounting and Economics* 13 (1990), pp. 305–40, or R. H. Battalio and R. Mendenhall, "Earnings Expectation, Investor Trade Size, and Anomalous Returns around Earnings Announcements," *Journal of Financial Economics* 77 (2005). pp. 289–319.

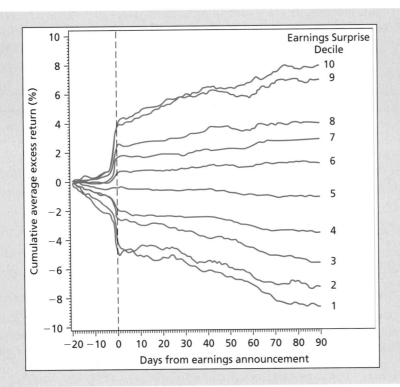

FIGURE 8.5

Cumulative abnormal returns in response to earnings announcements

Source: Reprinted from R.J. Rendleman Jr., C. P. Jones, and H. A. Latané, "Empirical Anomalies Based on Unexpected Earnings and the Importance of Risk Adjustments," *Journal of Financial Economics* 10 (1982), pp. 269–287. Copyright 1982 with permission from Elsevier Science.

Strong-Form Tests: Inside Information

It would not be surprising if insiders were able to make superior profits trading in their firm's stock. In other words, we do not expect markets to be strong-form efficient; we regulate and limit trades based on inside information. The ability of insiders to trade profitably in their own stock has been documented in studies by Jaffe (1974), Seyhun (1986), Givoly and Palmon (1985), and others. Jaffe's was one of the earlier studies that documented the tendency for stock prices to rise after insiders intensively bought shares and to fall after intensive insider sales.

WEB *master*

Earnings Surprises

Several Web sites list information on earnings surprises. Much of the information supplied is from Zacks.com. Each day the largest positive and negative surprises are listed. Go to **www.zacks.com/research/earnings/today_eps.php** and identify the top positive and the top negative earnings surprises for the day. The table will list the time and date of the announcement.

1. Do you notice any difference between the times of day that positive announcements tend to be made versus negative announcements?

2. Identify the tickers for the top three positive surprises. Once you have identified the top surprises, go to **finance.yahoo.com**. Enter the ticker symbols and obtain quotes for these securities. Examine the 5-day charts for each of the companies. Is the information incorporated into price quickly? Is there any evidence of prior knowledge or anticipation of the disclosure in advance of the trading?

3. Choose one of the stocks listed and click on its symbol to follow the link for more information. Click on the link for Interactive Java Charting that appears under the graph. In the Graph Control dialog box choose a period of 5 years and check the box that says "EPS Surprise." The resulting chart will show positive earnings surprises as green bars and negative surprises as red bars. You can move the cursor over various parts of the graph to investigate what happened to the price and trading volume of the stock around each of the surprise events. Do you notice any patterns?

Can other investors benefit by following insiders' trades? The Securities and Exchange Commission requires all insiders to register their trading activity and it publishes these trades in an *Official Summary of Security Transactions and Holdings.* Since 2002, insiders must report large trades to the SEC within 2 business days. Once the *Official Summary* is published, the trades become public information. At that point, if markets are efficient, fully and immediately processing the information released in the *Official Summary* of trading, an investor should no longer be able to profit from following the pattern of those trades. Several Internet sites contain information on insider trading.

The study by Seyhun, which carefully tracked the public release dates of the *Official Summary,* found that following insider transactions would be to no avail. Although there is some tendency for stock prices to increase even after the *Official Summary* reports insider buying, the abnormal returns are not of sufficient magnitude to overcome transaction costs.

Interpreting the Evidence

How should we interpret the ever-growing anomalies literature? Does it imply that markets are grossly inefficient, allowing for simplistic trading rules to offer large profit opportunities? Or are there other, more-subtle interpretations?

Risk premiums or inefficiencies?   The price-earnings, small-firm, market-to-book, momentum, and long-term reversal effects are currently among the most puzzling phenomena in empirical finance. There are several interpretations of these effects. First note that to some extent, some of these phenomena may be related. The feature that small firms, low-market-to-book firms, and recent "losers" seem to have in common is a stock price that has fallen considerably in recent months or years. Indeed, a firm can become a small firm or a low-market-to-book firm by suffering a sharp drop in price. These groups therefore may contain a relatively high proportion of distressed firms that have suffered recent difficulties.

Fama and French (1993) argue that these effects can be explained as manifestations of risk premiums. Using their 3-factor model, they show that stocks with higher "betas" (also known as factor loadings) on size or market-to-book factors have higher average returns; they interpret these returns as evidence of a risk premium associated with the factor. This model does a much better job than the 1-factor CAPM in explaining security returns. While size or book-to-market ratios per se are obviously not risk factors, they perhaps might act as proxies for more fundamental determinants of risk. Fama and French argue that these patterns of returns may therefore be consistent with an efficient market in which expected returns are consistent with risk. In this regard, it is worth noting that returns to "style factors," for example, the return on portfolios constructed based on the ratio of book-to-market value (specifically, the Fama-French high minus low book-to-market portfolio) or firm size (the return on the small-minus big-firm portfolio) do indeed seem to predict business cycles in many countries. Figure 8.6 shows that returns on these portfolios tend to have positive returns in years prior to rapid growth in gross domestic product.

The opposite interpretation is offered by Lakonishok, Shleifer, and Vishny (1995), who argue that these phenomena are evidence of inefficient markets, more specifically, of systematic errors in the forecasts of stock analysts. They believe that analysts extrapolate past performance too far into the future, and therefore overprice firms with recent good performance and underprice firms with recent poor performance. Ultimately, when market participants recognize their errors, prices reverse. This explanation is consistent with the reversal effect and also, to a degree, is consistent with the small-firm and book-to-market effects because firms with sharp price drops may tend to be small or have high book-to-market ratios.

If Lakonishok, Shleifer, and Vishney are correct, we ought to find that analysts systematically err when forecasting returns of recent "winner" versus "loser" firms. A study by La Porta (1996) is consistent with this pattern. He finds that equity of firms for which analysts predict low growth rates of earnings actually perform better than those with high expected earnings growth. Analysts seem overly pessimistic about firms with low growth prospects and overly optimistic about firms with high growth prospects. When these too-extreme expectations are "corrected," the low-expected-growth firms outperform high-expected-growth firms.

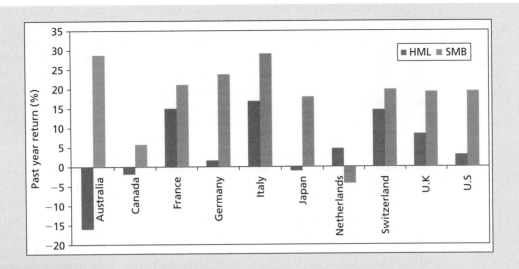

Return to style portfolio as a predictor of GDP growth. Average difference in the return on the style portfolio in years before good GDP growth versus in years before bad GDP growth. Positive value means the style portfolio does better in years prior to good macroeconomic performance. HML = high minus low portfolio, sorted on ratio of book-to-market value. SMB = small minus big portfolio, sorted on firm size.

Source: Reprinted from J. Liew and M. Vassalou, "Can Book-to-Market, Size, and Momentum Be Risk Factors That Predict Economic Growth?" *Journal of Financial Economics* 57 (2000), pp. 221–45. Copyright 2000 with permission from Elsevier Science.

Anomalies or data mining? We have covered many of the so-called anomalies cited in the literature, but our list could go on and on. Some wonder whether these anomalies are really unexplained puzzles in financial markets, or whether they instead are an artifact of data mining. After all, if one reruns the computer database of past returns over and over and examines stock returns along enough dimensions, simple chance will cause some criteria to *appear* to predict returns.

In this regard, it is noteworthy that some anomalies have not shown much staying power after being reported in the academic literature. For example, after the small-firm effect was published in the early 1980s, it promptly disappeared for much of the rest of the decade. Similarly, the book-to-market strategy, which commanded considerable attention in the early 1990s, was ineffective for the rest of that decade.

Still, even acknowledging the potential for data mining, a common thread seems to run through many of the anomalies we have considered, lending support to the notion that there is a real puzzle to explain. Value stocks—defined by low P/E ratio, high book-to-market ratio, or depressed prices relative to historic levels—seem to have provided higher average returns than "glamour" or growth stocks.

One way to address the problem of data mining is to find a data set that has not already been researched and see whether the relationship in question shows up in the new data. Such studies have revealed size, momentum, and book-to-market effects in other security markets around the world. While these phenomena may be a manifestation of a systematic risk premium, the precise nature of that risk is not fully understood.

The "Noisy Market Hypothesis" and Fundamental Indexing

The efficient market hypothesis argues in favor of capitalization-weighted indexed portfolios that provide broad diversification with minimal trading costs. But several researchers and practitioners (e.g., Arnott, 2006) have forcefully argued that such "cap-weighted" portfolios are necessarily inferior to a strategy they call fundamental indexing. The rationale for their argument goes by the name "noisy market hypothesis."

The hypothesis begins with the observation that market prices may well contain pricing errors or "noise" relative to the intrinsic or "true" value of a firm. Even if prices are correct on average, at any time some stocks will be overvalued and others undervalued. Overpriced stocks have inflated market values relative to intrinsic value, while the market values of underpriced stocks are too low. Because indexed portfolios invest in proportion to market capitalization, portfolio weights will track these pricing errors, with greater amounts invested in overpriced stocks (which have poor expected returns) and lesser amounts invested in underpriced stocks (which have high expected returns). The conclusion is that a capitalization-weighted strategy is destined to overweight precisely the firms with the worst return prospects. In contrast, a fundamental index that invests in proportion to intrinsic value would avoid the detrimental association between portfolio weights and the market's pricing errors, and would therefore outperform a capitalization-weighted index.

However, while this conclusion is correct, it begs the crucial question: how might one go about finding the intrinsic values necessary to form a fundamental index? The necessary inputs are in fact the holy grail of all active managers: true stock values or, equivalently, market pricing errors. Clearly, *given* the errors in market prices, one could outperform passive cap-weighted portfolios by tilting toward undervalued stocks and away from overpriced ones. This is hardly a surprise. The problem is finding a guide to these pricing errors. Unfortunately, market capitalization by itself tells you *nothing* about potential mispricing (indeed, this is the starting assumption of the noisy market hypothesis), and, therefore, gives you no guidance as to how to tilt your portfolio.[6]

Advocates of fundamental indexing propose that portfolio weights determined by indicators of intrinsic value such as dividends or earnings be used to construct an alternative to a cap-weighted index. These rules would result in allocations that are skewed (compared to cap weighting) toward firms with high-value indicators. But notice that these indicators are precisely the tools used in the value investing strategies that we discussed earlier in this section (e.g., dividend yield or price–earnings ratios). There may be good reasons to pursue value investing, chiefly the evidence reviewed earlier that value stocks have typically outperformed growth stocks over long periods in many countries. But we've also noted that there may be other, risk premium–based, explanations for that performance. Regardless of one's interpretation of the value premium, you should recognize that fundamental indexing is at heart nothing more than a value tilt, a point emphasized by Asness (2006). It is therefore, despite its name, *not* indexing, but rather a form of active investing, and it is hardly a radical new approach to either indexation or investment policy.

8.4   MUTUAL FUND AND ANALYST PERFORMANCE

We have documented some of the apparent chinks in the armor of efficient market proponents. For investors, the issue of market efficiency boils down to whether skilled investors can make consistent abnormal trading profits. The best test is to look at the performance of market professionals to see if they can generate performance superior to that of a passive index fund that buys and holds the market. We will look at two facets of professional performance: that of stock market analysts who recommend investment positions and that of mutual fund managers who actually manage portfolios.

Stock Market Analysts

Stock market analysts historically have worked for brokerage firms, which presents an immediate problem in interpreting the value of their advice: Analysts have tended to be overwhelmingly positive in their assessment of the prospects of firms.[7] For example, Barber, Lehavy,

---

[6] For a more rigorous demonstration of this point and an insightful discussion of fundamental indexing, see Perold (2007).

[7] This problem may be less severe in the future; as noted in Chapter 3, one recent reform intended to mitigate the conflict of interest in having brokerage firms that sell stocks also provide investment advice is to separate analyst coverage from the other activities of the firm.

McNichols, and Trueman (2001) find that on a scale of 1 (strong buy) to 5 (strong sell), the average recommendation for 5,628 covered firms in 1996 was 2.04. As a result, one cannot take positive recommendations (e.g., to buy) at face value. Instead, we must look at either the relative strength of analyst recommendations compared to those for other firms, or at the change in consensus recommendations.

Womack (1996) focuses on changes in analysts' recommendations and finds that positive changes are associated with increased stock prices of about 5%, and negative changes result in average price decreases of 11%. One might wonder whether these price changes reflect the market's recognition of analysts' superior information or insight about firms or, instead, simply result from new buy or sell pressure brought on by the recommendations themselves. Womack argues that price impact seems to be permanent, and therefore consistent with the hypothesis that analysts do in fact reveal new information. Jegadeesh, Kim, Krische, and Lee (2004) also find that changes in consensus recommendations are associated with price changes, but that the *level* of consensus recommendations is an inconsistent predictor of future stock performance.

Barber, Lehavy, McNichols, and Trueman (2001) focus on the level of consensus recommendations and show that firms with the most-favorable recommendations outperform those with the least-favorable recommendations. While their results seem impressive, the authors note that portfolio strategies based on analyst consensus recommendations would result in extremely heavy trading activity with associated costs that probably would wipe out the potential profits from the strategy.

In sum, the literature suggests some value added by analysts, but some ambiguity remains. Are superior returns following analyst upgrades due to revelation of new information or due to changes in investor demand in response to the changed outlook? Also, are these results exploitable by investors who necessarily incur trading costs?

Mutual Fund Managers

As we pointed out in Chapter 4, casual evidence does not support the claim that professionally managed portfolios can consistently beat the market. Figure 4.3 in that chapter demonstrated that between 1972 and 2005 the returns of a passive portfolio indexed to the Wilshire 5000 typically would have been better than those of the average equity fund. On the other hand, there was some (admittedly inconsistent) evidence of persistence in performance, meaning that the better managers in one period tended to be better managers in following periods. Such a pattern would suggest that the better managers can with some consistency outperform their competitors, and it would be inconsistent with the notion that market prices already reflect all relevant information.

The analyses cited in Chapter 4 were based on total returns; they did not properly adjust returns for exposure to systematic risk factors. In this section we revisit the question of mutual fund performance, paying more attention to the benchmark against which performance ought to be evaluated.

As a first pass, we can examine the risk-adjusted returns (i.e., the alpha, or return in excess of required return based on beta and the market return in each period) of a large sample of mutual funds. Malkiel (1995) computed these abnormal returns for a large sample of mutual funds between 1972 and 1991. The results, which appear in Figure 8.7, show that the distribution of alphas is roughly bell shaped, with a mean that is slightly negative but statistically indistinguishable from zero. On average, it does not appear that these funds outperform the market index (the S&P 500) on a risk-adjusted basis.

One problem in interpreting these alphas is that the S&P 500 may not be an adequate benchmark against which to evaluate mutual fund returns. Because mutual funds tend to maintain considerable holdings in equity of small firms, whereas the S&P 500 is exclusively comprised of large firms, mutual funds as a whole will tend to outperform the S&P when small firms outperform large ones and underperform when small firms fare worse. Thus a better benchmark for the performance of funds would be an index that incorporates the stock market performance of smaller firms.

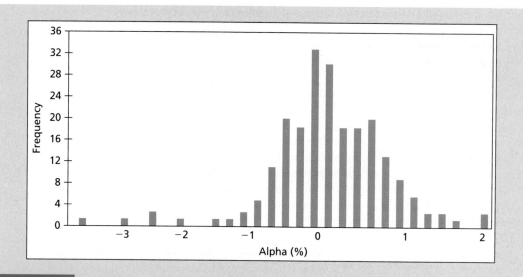

FIGURE 8.7

Estimates of individual mutual fund alphas, 1972–1991

Note: The frequency distribution of estimated alphas for all equity mutual funds with 10-year continuous records.

Source: Burton G. Malkiel, "Returns from Investing in Equity Mutual Funds 1971–1991," *Journal of Finance* 50 (June 1995), pp. 549–72. Reprinted by permission of the publisher, Blackwell Publishing, Inc.

The importance of the benchmark can be illustrated by examining the returns on small stocks in various subperiods.[8] In the 20-year period between 1945 and 1964, a small-stock index underperformed the S&P 500 by about 4% per year (i.e., the alpha of the small-stock index after adjusting for systematic risk was −4%). In the following 20-year period between 1965 and 1984, small stocks outperformed the S&P index by 10%. Thus if one were to examine mutual fund returns in the earlier period, they would tend to look poor, not necessarily because fund managers were poor stock pickers, but simply because mutual funds as a group tended to hold more small stocks than were represented in the S&P 500. In the later period, funds would look better on a risk-adjusted basis relative to the S&P 500 because small stocks performed better. The "style choice," that is, the exposure to small stocks (which is an asset allocation decision) would dominate the evaluation of performance even though it has little to do with managers' stock-picking ability.[9]

Elton, Gruber, Das, and Hlavka (1993) attempted to control for the impact of non–S&P assets on mutual fund performance. They used a multifactor version of the index model of security returns and calculated fund alphas by using regressions that include as explanatory variables the excess returns of three benchmark portfolios rather than just one proxy for the market index. Their three factors are the excess return on the S&P 500 index, the excess return on an equity index of non–S&P low capitalization (i.e., small) firms, and the excess return on a bond market index. Some of their results are presented in Table 8.1, which shows that average alphas are negative for each type of equity fund, although generally not of statistically significant magnitude. They concluded that after controlling for the relative performance of these three asset classes—large stocks, small stocks, and bonds—mutual fund managers as a group do not demonstrate an ability to beat passive index strategies that would simply mix

---

[8] This illustration and the statistics cited are based on E. J. Elton, M. J. Gruber, S. Das, and M. Hlavka, "Efficiency with Costly Information: A Reinterpretation of Evidence from Managed Portfolios," *Review of Financial Studies* 6 (1993), pp. 1–22, which is discussed shortly.

[9] Remember that the asset allocation decision is usually in the hands of the individual investor. Investors allocate their investment portfolios to funds in asset classes they desire to hold, and they can reasonably expect only that mutual fund portfolio managers will choose stocks advantageously *within* those asset classes.

**Select problems are available in McGraw-Hill's Homework Manager®.
Please see the packaging options section of the preface for more information.**

1. If markets are efficient, what should be the correlation coefficient between stock returns for two non-overlapping time periods?

2. Which of the following most appears to contradict the proposition that the stock market is *weakly* efficient? Explain.
   a. Over 25% of mutual funds outperform the market on average.
   b. Insiders earn abnormal trading profits.
   c. Every January, the stock market earns abnormal returns.

3. Suppose that, after conducting an analysis of past stock prices, you come up with the following observations. Which would appear to *contradict* the *weak form* of the efficient market hypothesis? Explain.
   a. The average rate of return is significantly greater than zero.
   b. The correlation between the return during a given week and the return during the following week is zero.
   c. One could have made superior returns by buying stock after a 10% rise in price and selling after a 10% fall.
   d. One could have made higher-than-average capital gains by holding stocks with low dividend yields.

4. Which of the following statements are *true* if the efficient market hypothesis holds?
   a. It implies that future events can be forecast with perfect accuracy.
   b. It implies that prices reflect all available information.
   c. It implies that security prices change for no discernible reason.
   d. It implies that prices do not fluctuate.

5. Which of the following observations would provide evidence *against* the *semistrong form* of the efficient market theory? Explain.
   a. Mutual fund managers do not on average make superior returns.
   b. You cannot make superior profits by buying (or selling) stocks after the announcement of an abnormal rise in dividends.
   c. Low P/E stocks tend to have positive abnormal returns.
   d. In any year approximately 50% of pension funds outperform the market.

Problems 6–13 are taken from past CFA exams.

6. The semistrong form of the efficient market hypothesis asserts that stock prices:
   a. Fully reflect all historical price information.
   b. Fully reflect all publicly available information.
   c. Fully reflect all relevant information including insider information.
   d. May be predictable.

7. Assume that a company announces an unexpectedly large cash dividend to its shareholders. In an efficient market *without* information leakage, one might expect:
   a. An abnormal price change at the announcement.
   b. An abnormal price increase before the announcement.
   c. An abnormal price decrease after the announcement.
   d. No abnormal price change before or after the announcement.

8. Which one of the following would provide evidence *against* the *semistrong form* of the efficient market theory?
   a. About 50% of pension funds outperform the market in any year.
   b. You cannot make abnormal profits by buying stocks after an announcement of strong earnings.
   c. Trend analysis is worthless in forecasting stock prices.
   d. Low P/E stocks tend to have positive abnormal returns over the long run.

CFA® PROBLEMS

9. According to the efficient market hypothesis:
   a. High-beta stocks are consistently overpriced.
   b. Low-beta stocks are consistently overpriced.
   c. Positive alphas on stocks will quickly disappear.
   d. Negative alpha stocks consistently yield low returns for arbitrageurs.

CFA® PROBLEMS

10. A "random walk" occurs when:
    a. Stock price changes are random but predictable.
    b. Stock prices respond slowly to both new and old information.
    c. Future price changes are uncorrelated with past price changes.
    d. Past information is useful in predicting future prices.

CFA® PROBLEMS

11. A market anomaly refers to:
    a. An exogenous shock to the market that is sharp but not persistent.
    b. A price or volume event that is inconsistent with historical price or volume trends.
    c. A trading or pricing structure that interferes with efficient buying and selling of securities.
    d. Price behavior that differs from the behavior predicted by the efficient market hypothesis.

CFA® PROBLEMS

12. Some scholars contend that professional managers are incapable of outperforming the market. Others come to an opposite conclusion. Compare and contrast the assumptions about the stock market that support (a) passive portfolio management and (b) active portfolio management.

CFA® PROBLEMS

13. You are a portfolio manager meeting a client. During the conversation that follows your formal review of her account, your client asks the following question:

    My grandson, who is studying investments, tells me that one of the best ways to make money in the stock market is to buy the stocks of small-capitalization firms late in December and to sell the stocks one month later. What is he talking about?

    a. Identify the apparent market anomalies that would justify the proposed strategy.
    b. Explain why you believe such a strategy might or might not work in the future.

14. A successful firm like Microsoft has consistently generated large profits for years. Is this a violation of the EMH?

15. Suppose you find that prices of stocks before large dividend increases show on average consistently positive abnormal returns. Is this a violation of the EMH?

16. "If the business cycle is predictable, and a stock has a positive beta, the stock's returns also must be predictable." Respond.

17. Which of the following phenomena would be either consistent with or a violation of the efficient market hypothesis? Explain briefly.
    a. Nearly half of all professionally managed mutual funds are able to outperform the S&P 500 in a typical year.
    b. Money managers that outperform the market (on a risk-adjusted basis) in one year are likely to outperform in the following year.
    c. Stock prices tend to be predictably more volatile in January than in other months.
    d. Stock prices of companies that announce increased earnings in January tend to outperform the market in February.
    e. Stocks that perform well in one week perform poorly in the following week.

18. "If all securities are fairly priced, all must offer equal expected rates of return." Comment.

CFA® PROBLEMS

19. a. Briefly explain the concept of the efficient market hypothesis (EMH) and each of its three forms—weak, semistrong, and strong—and briefly discuss the degree to which existing empirical evidence supports each of the three forms of the EMH.
    b. Briefly discuss the implications of the efficient market hypothesis for investment policy as it applies to:
       i. Technical analysis in the form of charting.
       ii. Fundamental analysis.
    c. Briefly explain the roles or responsibilities of portfolio managers in an efficient market environment.

20. Dollar-cost averaging means that you buy equal dollar amounts of a stock every period, for example, $500 per month. The strategy is based on the idea that when the stock price is low, your fixed monthly purchase will buy more shares, and when the price is high, fewer shares. Averaging over time, you will end up buying more shares when the stock is cheaper and fewer when it is relatively expensive. Therefore, by design, you will exhibit good market timing. Evaluate this strategy.

21. Steady Growth Industries has never missed a dividend payment in its 94-year history. Does this make it more attractive to you as a possible purchase for your stock portfolio?

22. We know that the market should respond positively to good news and that good-news events such as the coming end of a recession can be predicted with at least some accuracy. Why, then, can we not predict that the market will go up as the economy recovers?

23. If prices are as likely to increase as decrease, why do investors earn positive returns from the market on average?

24. You know that firm XYZ is very poorly run. On a scale of 1 (worst) to 10 (best), you would give it a score of 3. The market consensus evaluation is that the management score is only 2. Should you buy or sell the stock?

25. Examine the accompanying figure, which presents cumulative abnormal returns both before and after dates on which insiders buy or sell shares in their firms. How do you interpret this figure? What are we to make of the pattern of CARs before and after the event date?

Source: Reprinted from Nejat H. Seyhun, "Insiders, Profits, Costs of Trading and Market Efficiency," *Journal of Financial Economics* 16 (1986). Copyright 1986 with permission from Elsevier Science.

26. Good News, Inc., just announced an increase in its annual earnings, yet its stock price fell. Is there a rational explanation for this phenomenon?

27. Your investment client asks for information concerning the benefits of active portfolio management. She is particularly interested in the question of whether active managers

CFA®
PROBLEMS

www.mhhe.com/bkm

can be expected to consistently exploit inefficiencies in the capital markets to produce above-average returns without assuming higher risk.

The semistrong form of the efficient market hypothesis asserts that all publicly available information is rapidly and correctly reflected in securities prices. This implies that investors cannot expect to derive above-average profits from purchases made after information has become public because security prices already reflect the information's full effects.

    a. Identify and explain two examples of empirical evidence that tend to support the EMH implication stated above.

    b. Identify and explain two examples of empirical evidence that tend to refute the EMH implication stated above.

    c. Discuss reasons why an investor might choose not to index even if the markets were, in fact, semistrong-form efficient.

28. Growth and value can be defined in several ways. "Growth" usually conveys the idea of a portfolio emphasizing or including only companies believed to possess above-average future rates of per-share earnings growth. Low current yield, high price-to-book ratios, and high price-to-earnings ratios are typical characteristics of such portfolios. "Value" usually conveys the idea of portfolios emphasizing or including only issues currently showing low price-to-book ratios, low price-to-earnings ratios, above-average levels of dividend yield, and market prices believed to be below the issues' intrinsic values.

    a. Identify and provide reasons why, over an extended period of time, value-stock investing might outperform growth-stock investing.

    b. Explain why the outcome suggested in (*a*) should not be possible in a market widely regarded as being highly efficient.

STANDARD &POOR'S

Use data from the Standard & Poor's Market Insight Database at www.mhhe.com/edumarketinsight to answer the following questions.

1. Collect the following data for 25 firms from Market Insight.
   a. Book-to-market ratio.
   b. Price/EPS from Ops ratio.
   c. Market capitalization (size).
   d. Price/Cash Flow ratio
   e. Another criterion that interests you.

   You can find this information by choosing a company, then clicking on the *Financial Hlts.* link in the *Compustat Reports* section. Rank the firms based on each of the criteria separately and divide the firms into five groups based on their ranking for each criterion. Calculate the average rate of return for each group of firms.

   Do you confirm or reject any of the anomalies cited in this chapter? Can you uncover a new anomaly? Note: For your test to be valid, you must form your portfolios based on criteria observed at the *beginning* of the period when you form the stock groups. Why?

2. Use the price history from Market Insight to calculate the beta of each of the firms in the previous question. Use this beta, the T-bill rate, and the return on the S&P 500 to calculate the risk-adjusted abnormal return of each stock group. Does any anomaly uncovered in the previous question persist after controlling for risk?

3. Now form stock groups that use two criteria simultaneously. For example, form a portfolio of stocks that are both in the lowest quintile of price–earnings ratios and in the highest quintile of book-to-market ratio. Does selecting stocks based on more than one characteristic improve your ability to devise portfolios with abnormal returns? Repeat the analysis by forming groups that meet three criteria simultaneously. Does this yield any further improvement in abnormal returns?

WEB *master*

Efficient Markets and Insider Trading

Do restrictions on insider trading limit strong-form market efficiency? Go to **www.insider-Monitor.com** and click on the *Strategy* link. Read through the rules presented, paying special attention to the rules about purchases by company officers and clusters of inside buyers. On the left-side menu, click on the link to *Clusters This Week* and look for clusters of purchases by a company's officers (not directors or beneficial owners).

Once you have identified a company with this pattern, note the date(s) on which the trades occurred. Click on the stock's symbol, and then click on the link for *Basic Stock Information*. This will take you to the **Yahoo! Finance** site. Click on the link for *Historical Prices* on the left-side menu and enter a data range from 5 days before the earliest purchase date to the current date. Choose daily prices and determine what happened to the stock's price during this period. What do you conclude about the investment timing of the insiders?

SOLUTIONS TO **CONCEPT** *checks*

8.1. *a.* A high-level manager might well have private information about the firm. Her ability to trade profitably on that information is not surprising. This ability does not violate weak-form efficiency: The abnormal profits are not derived from an analysis of past price and trading data. If they were, this would indicate that there is valuable information that can be gleaned from such analysis. But this ability does violate strong-form efficiency. Apparently, there is some private information that is not already reflected in stock prices.

b. The information sets that pertain to the weak, semistrong, and strong form of the EMH can be described by the following illustration:

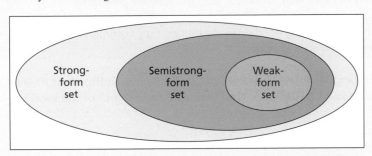

The weak-form information set includes only the history of prices and volumes. The semistrong-form set includes the weak form set *plus* all other publicly available information. In turn, the strong-form set includes the semistrong set *plus* insiders' information. It is illegal to act on this incremental information (insiders' private information). The direction of *valid* implication is

Strong-form EMH $\Rightarrow$ Semistrong-form EMH $\Rightarrow$ Weak-form EMH

The reverse direction implication is *not* valid. For example, stock prices may reflect all past price data (weak-form efficiency) but may not reflect relevant fundamental data (semistrong-form inefficiency).

8.2. The point we made in the preceding discussion is that the very fact that we observe stock prices near so-called resistance levels belies the assumption that the price can be a resistance level. If a stock is observed to sell *at any price,* then investors must believe that a fair rate of return can be earned if the stock is purchased at that price. It is logically impossible for a stock to have a resistance level *and* offer a fair rate of return at prices just below the resistance level. If we accept that prices are appropriate, we must reject any presumption concerning resistance levels.

8.3. If *everyone* follows a passive strategy, sooner or later prices will fail to reflect new information. At this point there are profit opportunities for active investors who uncover mispriced securities. As they buy and sell these assets, prices again will be driven to fair levels.

8.4. The answer depends on your prior beliefs about market efficiency. Miller's record has been incredibly strong. On the other hand, with so many funds in existence, it is less surprising that *some* fund would appear to be consistently superior after the fact. Exceptional past performance of a small number of managers is possible by chance even in an efficient market. A better test is provided in "continuation studies." Are better performers in one period more likely to repeat that performance in later periods?

CHAPTER 9

Behavioral Finance and Technical Analysis

AFTER STUDYING THIS CHAPTER YOU SHOULD BE ABLE TO:

 Demonstrate how the principles of behavioral finance can explain anomalies in stock market returns.

 Identify reasons why technical analysis may be profitable.

 Use the Dow theory to identify situations that technicians would characterize as buy or sell opportunities.

 Use indicators such as volume, put/call ratios, breadth, short interest, or confidence indexes to measure the "technical conditions" of the market.

The efficient market hypothesis makes two important predictions. First, it implies that security prices properly reflect whatever information is available to investors. A second implication follows immediately: Active traders will find it difficult to outperform passive strategies such as holding market indexes. To do so would require differential insight; this in a highly competitive market is very hard to come by.

Unfortunately, it is hard to devise measures of the "true" or intrinsic value of a security, and correspondingly difficult to test directly whether prices match those values. Therefore, most tests of market efficiency have focused on the performance of active trading strategies. These tests have been of two kinds. The anomalies literature has examined strategies that apparently *would* have provided superior risk-adjusted returns (e.g., investing in stocks with momentum or in value rather than glamour stocks). Other tests have looked at the results of *actual* investments by asking whether professional managers have been able to beat the market.

Neither class of tests has proven fully conclusive. The anomalies literature suggests that several strategies would have provided superior returns. But there are questions as to whether some of these apparent anomalies reflect risk premiums not captured by simple models of risk and return, or even if they merely reflect data mining. Moreover, the apparent inability of the typical money manager to turn these anomalies into superior returns on actual portfolios casts additional doubt on their "reality."

A relatively new school of thought dubbed *behavioral finance* argues that the sprawling literature on trading strategies has missed a larger and more important point by overlooking the first implication of efficient markets—the correctness of security prices. This may be the more important implication, since market economies rely on prices to allocate resources efficiently. The behavioral school argues that even if security prices are wrong, it still can be difficult to exploit them, and, therefore, that the failure to uncover obviously successful trading rules or traders cannot be taken as proof of market efficiency.

Whereas conventional theories presume that investors are rational, behavioral finance starts with the assumption that they might not be. We will examine some of the information-processing and behavioral irrationalities uncovered by psychologists in other contexts and show how these tendencies applied to financial markets might result in some of the anomalies discussed in the previous chapter. We then examine the limitations of strategies designed to take advantage of behaviorally induced mispricing. If the limits to such arbitrage activity are severe, mispricing can survive even if some rational investors attempt to exploit it. We turn next to technical analysis and show how behavioral models give some support to techniques that clearly would be useless in efficient markets. We close the chapter with a brief survey of some of these technical strategies.

Related Web sites for this chapter are available at www.mhhe.com/bkm.

9.1 THE BEHAVIORAL CRITIQUE

The premise of **behavioral finance** is that conventional financial theory ignores how real people make decisions and that people make a difference.[1] A growing number of economists have come to interpret the anomalies literature as consistent with several "irrationalities" that seem to characterize individuals making complicated decisions. These irrationalities fall into two broad categories: first, that investors do not always process information correctly and therefore infer incorrect probability distributions about future rates of return; and second, that even given a probability distribution of returns, they often make inconsistent or systematically suboptimal decisions.

behavioral finance

Models of financial markets that emphasize potential implications of psychological factors affecting investor behavior.

---

[1]The discussion in this section is based on two excellent survey articles: Nicholas Barberis and Richard Thaler, "A Survey of Behavioral Finance," in the *Handbook of the Economics of Finance,* eds. G. M. Constantinides, M. Harris, and R. Stulz (Amsterdam: Elsevier, 2003); and W. F. M. De Bondt and R. H. Thaler, "Financial Decision Making in Markets and Firms," in *Handbooks in Operations Research and Management Science, Volume 9: Finance,* eds. R. A. Jarrow, V. Maksimovic, and W. T. Ziemba (Amsterdam: Elsevier, 1995).

Of course, the existence of irrational investors would not by itself be sufficient to render capital markets inefficient. If such irrationalities did affect prices, then sharp-eyed arbitrageurs taking advantage of profit opportunities might be expected to push prices back to their proper values. Thus, the second leg of the behavioral critique is that in practice the actions of such arbitrageurs are limited and therefore insufficient to force prices to match intrinsic value.

This leg of the argument is important. Virtually everyone agrees that if prices are right (i.e., price = intrinsic value), then there are no easy profit opportunities. But the converse is not necessarily true. If behaviorists are correct about limits to arbitrage activity, then the absence of profit opportunities does not necessarily imply that markets are efficient. We've noted that most tests of the efficient market hypothesis have focused on the existence of profit opportunities, often as reflected in the performance of money managers. But their failure to systematically outperform passive investment strategies need not imply that markets are in fact efficient.

We will start our summary of the behavioral critique with the first leg of the argument, surveying a sample of the informational processing errors uncovered by psychologists in other areas. We next examine a few of the behavioral irrationalities that seem to characterize decision makers. Finally, we look at limits to arbitrage activity, and conclude with a tentative assessment of the import of the behavioral debate.

Information Processing

Errors in information processing can lead investors to misestimate the true probabilities of possible events or associated rates of return. Several such biases have been uncovered. Here are four of the more important ones.

Forecasting errors   A series of experiments by Kahneman and Tversky (1972, 1973) indicate that people give too much weight to recent experience compared to prior beliefs when making forecasts (sometimes dubbed a *memory bias*) and tend to make forecasts that are too extreme given the uncertainty inherent in their information. De Bondt and Thaler (1990) argue that the P/E effect can be explained by earnings expectations that are too extreme. In this view, when forecasts of a firm's future earnings are high, perhaps due to favorable recent performance, they tend to be *too* high relative to the objective prospects of the firm. This results in a high initial P/E (due to the optimism built into the stock price) and poor subsequent performance when investors recognize their error. Thus, high P/E firms tend to be poor investments.

Overconfidence   People tend to overestimate the precision of their beliefs or forecasts, and they tend to overestimate their abilities. In one famous survey, 90% of drivers in Sweden ranked themselves as better-than-average drivers. Such overconfidence may be responsible for the prevalence of active versus passive investment management—itself an anomaly to adherents of the efficient market hypothesis. Despite the growing popularity of indexing, only about 10% of the equity in the mutual fund industry is held in indexed accounts. The dominance of active management in the face of the typical underperformance of such strategies (consider the disappointing performance of actively managed mutual funds reviewed in Chapter 4 as well as in the previous chapter) is consistent with a tendency to overestimate ability.

An interesting example of overconfidence in financial markets is provided by Barber and Odean (2001), who compare trading activity and average returns in brokerage accounts of men and women. They find that men (in particular single men) trade far more actively than women, consistent with the greater overconfidence among men well-documented in the psychology literature. They also find that trading activity is highly predictive of poor investment performance. The top 20% of accounts ranked by portfolio turnover had average returns 7 percentage points lower than the 20% of the accounts with the lowest turnover rates. As they conclude, "trading [and by implication, overconfidence] is hazardous to your wealth."

conservatism

A conservatism bias means that investors are too slow (too conservative) in updating their beliefs in response to recent evidence.

Conservatism   A conservatism bias means that investors are too slow (too conservative) in updating their beliefs in response to new evidence. This means that they might initially underreact to news about a firm, so that prices will fully reflect new information only gradually. Such a bias would give rise to momentum in stock market returns.

Sample size neglect and representativeness   The notion of **representativeness** holds that people commonly do not take into account the size of a sample, apparently reasoning that a small sample is just as representative of a population as a large one. They may therefore infer a pattern too quickly based on a small sample and extrapolate apparent trends too far into the future. It is easy to see how such a pattern would be consistent with overreaction and correction anomalies. A short-lived run of good earnings reports or high stock returns would lead such investors to revise their assessments of likely future performance, and thus generate buying pressure that exaggerates the price run-up. Eventually, the gap between price and intrinsic value becomes glaring and the market corrects its initial error. Interestingly, stocks with the best recent performance suffer reversals precisely in the few days surrounding earnings announcements, suggesting that the correction occurs just as investors learn that their initial beliefs were too extreme (Chopra, Lakonishok, and Ritter, 1992).

representativeness bias

People are too prone to believe that a small sample is representative of a broad population and infer patterns too quickly.

We saw in the last chapter that stocks seem to exhibit a pattern of short- to middle-term momentum, along with long-term reversals. How might this pattern arise from an interplay between the conservatism and representativeness biases?

Behavioral Biases

Even if information processing were perfect, many studies conclude that individuals would tend to make less-than-fully rational decisions using that information. These behavioral biases largely affect how investors frame questions of risk versus return, and therefore make risk-return trade-offs.

Framing   Decisions seem to be affected by how choices are **framed.** For example, an individual may reject a bet when it is posed in terms of the risk surrounding possible gains but may accept that same bet when described in terms of the risk surrounding potential losses. In other words, individuals may act risk averse in terms of gains but risk seeking in terms of losses. But in many cases, the choice of how to frame a risky venture—as involving gains or losses—can be arbitrary.

framing

Decisions are affected by how choices are posed, for example, as gains relative to a low baseline level or losses relative to a higher baseline.

Consider a coin toss with a payoff of $50 for tails. Now consider a gift of $50 that is bundled with a bet that imposes a loss of $50 if that coin toss comes up heads. In both cases, you end up with zero for heads and $50 for tails. But the former description frames the coin toss as posing a risky gain while the latter frames the coin toss in terms of risky losses. The difference in framing can lead to different attitudes toward the bet.

Framing

Mental accounting   **Mental accounting** is a specific form of framing in which people segregate certain decisions. For example, an investor may take a lot of risk with one investment account, but establish a very conservative position with another account that is dedicated to her child's education. Rationally, it might be better to view both accounts as part of the investor's overall portfolio with the risk-return profiles of each integrated into a unified framework. Statman (1997) argues that mental accounting is consistent with some investors' irrational preference for stocks with high cash dividends (they feel free to spend dividend income, but would not "dip into capital" by selling a few shares of another stock with the same total rate of return) and with a tendency to ride losing stock positions for too long (since "behavioral investors" are reluctant to realize losses). In fact, investors are more likely to sell

mental accounting

Mental accounting is a specific form of framing in which people segregate certain decisions.

stocks with gains than those with losses, precisely contrary to a tax-minimization strategy (Shefrin and Statman, 1985; Odean, 1998).

Mental accounting effects also can help explain momentum in stock prices. The *house money effect* refers to gamblers' greater willingness to accept new bets if they currently are ahead. They think of (i.e., frame) the bet as being made with their "winnings account," that is, with the casino's and not with their own money, and thus are more willing to accept risk. Analogously, after a stock market run-up, individuals may view investments as largely funded out of a "capital gains account," become more tolerant of risk, discount future cash flows at a lower rate, and thus further push up prices.

Regret avoidance   Psychologists have found that individuals who make decisions that turn out badly have more regret (blame themselves more) when that decision was more unconventional. For example, buying a blue-chip portfolio that turns down is not as painful as experiencing the same losses on an unknown start-up firm. Any losses on the blue-chip stocks can be more easily attributed to bad luck rather than bad decision making and cause less regret. De Bondt and Thaler (1987) argue that such **regret avoidance** is consistent with both the size and book-to-market effect. Higher book-to-market firms tend to have depressed stock prices. These firms are "out of favor" and more likely to be in a financially precarious position. Similarly, smaller, less-well-known firms are also less conventional investments. Such firms require more "courage" on the part of the investor, which increases the required rate of return. Mental accounting can add to this effect. If investors focus on the gains or losses of individual stocks, rather than on broad portfolios, they can become more risk averse concerning stocks with recent poor performance, discount their cash flows at a higher rate, and thereby create a value-stock risk premium.

regret avoidance

People blame themselves more for unconventional choices that turn out badly so they avoid regret by making conventional decisions.

CONCEPT
c h e c k   **9.2**

How might the P/E effect (discussed in the previous chapter) also be explained as a consequence of regret avoidance?

prospect theory

Behavioral theory that investor utility depends on gains or losses from starting position, rather than on their levels of wealth.

Prospect theory   **Prospect theory** modifies the analytic description of rational risk-averse investors found in standard financial theory.[2] Figure 9.1, panel A, illustrates the conventional description of a risk-averse investor. Higher wealth provides higher satisfaction or "utility," but at a diminishing rate (the curve flattens as the individual becomes wealthier). This gives rise to risk aversion: A gain of $1,000 increases utility by less than a loss of $1,000 reduces it; therefore, investors will reject risky prospects that don't offer a risk premium.

Figure 9.1, panel B, shows a competing description of preferences characterized by "loss aversion." Utility depends not on the *level* of wealth as in panel A, but on *changes* in wealth from current levels. Moreover, to the left of zero (zero denotes no change from current wealth), the curve is convex rather than concave. This has several implications. Whereas many conventional utility functions imply that investors may become less risk averse as wealth increases, the function in panel B always recenters on current wealth, thereby ruling out such decreases in risk aversion and possibly helping to explain high average historical equity risk premiums. Moreover, the convex curvature to the left of the origin in panel B will induce investors to be risk seeking rather than risk averse when it comes to losses. Consistent with loss aversion, traders in the T-bond futures contract have been observed to assume significantly greater risk in afternoon sessions following morning sessions in which they have lost money (Coval and Shumway, 2005).

These are only a sample of many behavioral biases uncovered in the literature. Many have implications for investor behavior. The nearby box offers some good examples.

---

[2]Prospect theory originated with a highly influential paper about decision making under uncertainty by D. Kahneman and A. Tversky, "Prospect Theory: An Analysis of Decision under Risk," *Econometrica* 47 (1979), pp. 263–91.

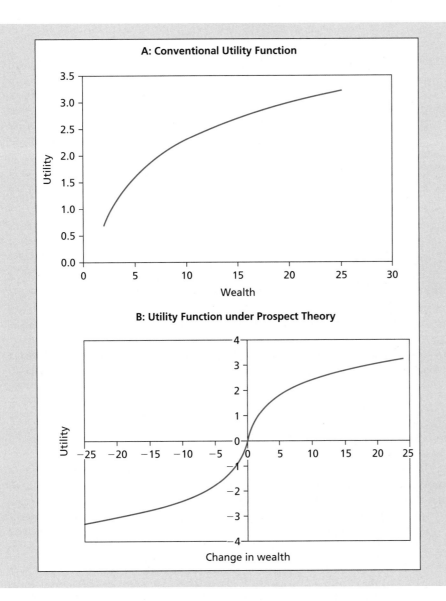

FIGURE 9.1
Prospect theory.
Panel A: A conventional utility function is defined in terms of wealth and is concave, resulting in risk aversion.
Panel B: Under loss aversion, the utility function is defined in terms of changes from current wealth. It is also convex to the left of the origin, giving rise to risk-seeking behavior in terms of losses.

Limits to Arbitrage

Behavioral biases would not matter for stock pricing if rational arbitrageurs could fully exploit the mistakes of behavioral investors. Trades of profit-seeking investors would correct any misalignment of prices. However, behavioral advocates argue that in practice, several factors limit the ability to profit from mispricing.[3]

Fundamental risk   Suppose that a share of IBM is underpriced. Buying it may present a profit opportunity, but it is hardly risk-free, since the presumed market underpricing can get worse. While price eventually should converge to intrinsic value, this may not happen until after the trader's investment horizon. For example, the investor may be a mutual fund manager who may lose clients (not to mention a job!) if short-term performance is poor, or a trader who may run through her capital if the market turns against her, even temporarily. The *fundamental risk* incurred in exploiting the apparent profit opportunity presumably will limit the activity of the traders.

---

[3] Some of the more influential references on limits to arbitrage are J. B. DeLong, A. Schleifer, L. Summers, and R. Waldmann, "Noise Trader Risk in Financial Markets," *Journal of Political Economy* 98 (August 1990), pp. 704–38; and A. Schleifer and R. Vishny, "The Limits of Arbitrage," *Journal of Finance* 52 (March 1997), pp. 35–55.

On the MARKET FRONT

WHY IT'S SO TOUGH TO FIX YOUR PORTFOLIO

If your portfolio is out of whack, you could ask an investment adviser for help. But you might have better luck with your therapist.

It's a common dilemma: You know you have the wrong mix of investments, but you cannot bring yourself to fix the mess. Why is it so difficult to change? At issue are three mental mistakes.

CHASING WINNERS

Looking to lighten up on bonds and get back into stocks? Sure, you know stocks are a long-term investment and, sure, you know they are best bought when cheap.

Yet it's a lot easier to pull the trigger and buy stocks if the market has lately been scoring gains. "People are influenced by what has happened most recently, and then they extrapolate from that," says Meir Statman, a finance professor at Santa Clara University in California. "But often, they end up being optimistic and pessimistic at just the wrong time."

Consider some results from the UBS Index of Investor Optimism, a monthly poll conducted by UBS and the Gallup Organization. Each month, the poll asks investors what gain they expect from their portfolio during the next 12 months. Result? You guessed it: The answers rise and fall with the stock market.

For instance, during the bruising bear market, investors grew increasingly pessimistic, and at the market bottom they were looking for median portfolio gains of just 5%. But true to form, last year's rally brightened investors' spirits and by January they were expecting 10% returns.

GETTING EVEN

This year's choppy stock market hasn't scared off just bond investors. It has also made it difficult for stock investors to rejigger their portfolios.

Blame it on the old "get even, then get out" syndrome. With stocks treading water, many investors are reluctant to sell, because they are a long way from recovering their bear-market losses. To be sure, investors who bought near the peak are underwater, whether they sell or not. But selling losers is still agonizing, because it means admitting you made a mistake.

"If you're rational and you have a loss, you sell, take the tax loss and move on," Prof. Statman says. "But if you're a normal person, selling at a loss tears your heart out."

MUSTERING COURAGE

Whether you need to buy stocks or buy bonds, it takes confidence to act. And right now, investors just aren't confident. "There's this status-quo bias," says John Nofsinger, a finance professor at Washington State University in Pullman, Washington. "We're afraid to do anything, because we're afraid we'll regret it."

Once again, it's driven by recent market action When markets are flying high, folks attribute their portfolio's gains to their own brilliance. That gives them the confidence to trade more and to take greater risks. Overreacting to short-term market results is, of course, a great way to lose a truckload of money. But with any luck, if you are aware of this pitfall, maybe you will avoid it.

Or maybe [this is] too optimistic. "You can tell somebody that investors have all these behavioral biases," says Terrance Odean, a finance professor at the University of California at Berkeley. "So what happens? The investor thinks, 'Oh, that sounds like my husband. I don't think many investors say, 'Oh, that sounds like me.'"

EXAMPLE 9.2

Fundamental Risk

In much of 2007, the Nasdaq index fluctuated at a level around 2,500. From that perspective, the value the index had reached 7 years earlier, around 5,000, seemed obviously crazy. Surely some investors living through the Internet "bubble" of the late 1990s must have identified the index as grossly overvalued, suggesting a good selling opportunity. But this hardly would have been a riskless arbitrage opportunity. Consider that Nasdaq may also have been overvalued in 1999 when it first crossed above 3,500 (40% higher than its value in 2007). An investor in 1999 who believed (as it turns out, quite correctly) that Nasdaq was overvalued at 3,500 and decided to sell it short would have suffered enormous losses as the index increased by another 1,500 points before finally peaking at 5,000. While the investor might have derived considerable satisfaction at eventually being proven right about the overpricing, by entering a year before the market "corrected," he might also have gone broke.

Implementation costs Exploiting overpricing can be particularly difficult. Short-selling a security entails costs; short-sellers may have to return the borrowed security on little notice, rendering the horizon of the short sale uncertain; other investors such as many pension or mutual fund managers face strict limits on their discretion to short securities. This can limit the ability of arbitrage activity to force prices to fair value.

Model risk One always has to worry that an apparent profit opportunity is more apparent than real. Perhaps you are using a faulty model to value the security, and the price actually is right. Mispricing may make a position a good bet, but it is still a risky one, which limits the extent to which it will be pursued.

Limits to Arbitrage and the Law of One Price

While one can debate the implications of much of the anomalies literature, surely the Law of One Price (positing that effectively identical assets should have identical prices) should be satisfied in rational markets. Yet there are several instances where the law seems to have been violated. These instances are good case studies of the limits to arbitrage.

"Siamese twin" companies [4] In 1907, Royal Dutch Petroleum and Shell Transport merged their operations into one firm. The two original companies, which continued to trade separately, agreed to split all profits from the joint company on a 60/40 basis. Shareholders of Royal Dutch receive 60% of the cash flow, and those of Shell receive 40%. One would therefore expect that Royal Dutch should sell for exactly 60/40 = 1.5 times the price of Shell. But this is not the case. Figure 9.2 shows that the relative value of the two firms has departed considerably from this "parity" ratio for extended periods of time.

FIGURE 9.2

Pricing of Royal Dutch relative to Shell (*deviation from parity*)

Source: O. A. Lamont and R. H. Thaler, "Anomalies: The Law of One Price in Financial Markets," *Journal of Economic Perspectives* 17 (Fall 2003), pp. 191–202.

[4]This discussion is based on K. A. Froot and E. M. Dabora, "How Are Stock Prices Affected by the Location of Trade?" *Journal of Financial Economics* 53 (1999), pp. 189–216.

Doesn't this mispricing give rise to an arbitrage opportunity? If Royal Dutch sells for more than 1.5 times Shell, why not buy relatively underpriced Shell and short-sell overpriced Royal? This seems like a reasonable strategy, but if you had followed it in February 1993 when Royal sold for about 10% more than its parity value, Figure 9.2 shows that you would have lost a lot of money as the premium widened to about 17% before finally reversing after 1999. As in Example 9.2, this opportunity posed fundamental risk.

Equity carve-outs   Several equity carve-outs also have violated the Law of One Price.[5] To illustrate, consider the case of 3Com, which in 1999 decided to spin off its Palm division. It first sold 5% of its stake in Palm in an IPO, announcing that it would distribute the remaining 95% of its Palm shares to 3Com shareholders 6 months later in a spinoff. Each 3Com shareholder would receive 1.5 shares of Palm in the spinoff.

Once Palm shares began trading, but prior to the spinoff, the share price of 3Com should have been *at least* 1.5 times that of Palm. After all, each share of 3Com entitled its owner to 1.5 shares of Palm *plus* an ownership stake in a profitable company. Instead, Palm shares at the IPO actually sold for *more* than the 3Com shares. The *stub value* of 3Com (i.e., the value of each 3Com share net of the value of the claim to Palm represented by that share) could be computed as the price of 3Com minus 1.5 times the price of Palm. This calculation, however, implies that 3Com's stub value was negative, this despite the fact that it was a profitable company with cash assets alone of about $10 per share.

Again, an arbitrage strategy seems obvious. Why not buy 3Com and sell Palm? The limit to arbitrage in this case was the inability of investors to sell Palm short. Virtually all available shares in Palm were already borrowed and sold short, and the negative stub values persisted for more than 2 months.

Closed-end funds   We noted in Chapter 4 that closed-end funds often sell for substantial discounts or premiums from net asset value. This is "nearly" a violation of the Law of One Price, since one would expect the value of the fund to equal the value of the shares it holds. We say nearly, because in practice, there are a few wedges between the value of the closed-end fund and its underlying assets. One is expenses. The fund incurs expenses that ultimately are paid for by investors, and these will reduce share price. On the other hand, if managers can invest fund assets to generate positive risk-adjusted returns, share price might exceed net asset value.

Lee, Shleifer, and Thaler (1991) argue that the patterns of discounts and premiums on closed-end funds are driven by changes in investor sentiment. They note that discounts on various funds move together and are correlated with the return on small stocks, suggesting that all are affected by common variation in sentiment. One might consider buying funds selling at a discount from net asset value and selling those trading at a premium, but discounts and premiums can widen, subjecting this strategy too to fundamental risk. Pontiff (1996) demonstrates that deviations of price from net asset value in closed-end funds tend to be higher in funds that are more difficult to arbitrage, for example, those with more idiosyncratic volatility.

CONCEPT   **9.3**
c h e c k

Fundamental risk may be limited by a "deadline" that forces a convergence between price and intrinsic value. What do you think would happen to a closed-end fund's discount if the fund announced that it plans to liquidate in 6 months, at which time it will distribute NAV to its shareholders?

Closed-end fund discounts are a good example of so-called anomalies that also may have rational explanations. Ross (2002) demonstrates that they can be reconciled with rational investors even if expenses or fund abnormal returns are modest. He shows that if a fund has a dividend yield of δ, an alpha (risk-adjusted abnormal return) of α, and expense ratio of ε, then using the constant-growth dividend discount model (see Chapter 13), the premium of the fund over its net asset value will be

---

[5] O. A. Lamont and R. H. Thaler, "Can the Market Add and Subtract? Mispricing in Tech Carve-outs," *Journal of Political Economy* 111 (2003), pp. 227–68.

$$\frac{\text{Price} - \text{NAV}}{\text{NAV}} = \frac{\alpha - \varepsilon}{\delta + \varepsilon - \alpha}$$

If the fund manager's performance more than compensates for expenses (i.e., if $\alpha > \varepsilon$), the fund will sell at a premium to NAV; otherwise it will sell at a discount. For example, suppose $\alpha = .015$, the expense ratio is $\varepsilon = .0125$, and the dividend yield is $\delta = .02$. Then the premium will be .14, or 14%. But if the market turns sour on the manager and revises its estimate of α downward to .005, that premium quickly turns into a discount of 43%.

This analysis might explain why closed-end funds often are issued to the public at a premium; if investors do not expect α to exceed ε, they won't purchase shares in the fund. But the fact that most premiums eventually turn into discounts indicates how difficult it is for management to fulfill these expectations.[6]

Bubbles and Behavioral Economics

In Example 9.2 above, we pointed out that the stock market run-up of the late 1990s, and even more spectacularly, the run-up of the technology-heavy Nasdaq market, seems in retrospect to have been an obvious bubble. In a 6-year period beginning in 1995, the Nasdaq index increased by a factor of more than 6. Former Fed Chairman Alan Greenspan famously characterized the dot-com boom as an example of "irrational exuberance," and his assessment turned out to be correct: By October 2002, the index fell to less than one-fourth the peak value it had reached only 2½ years earlier. This episode seems to be a case in point for advocates of the behavioral school, exemplifying a market moved by irrational investor sentiment. Moreover, in accord with behavioral patterns, as the dot-com boom developed, it seemed to feed on itself, with investors increasingly confident of their investment prowess (overconfidence bias) and apparently willing to extrapolate short-term patterns into the distant future (representativeness bias).

On the other hand, bubbles are a lot easier to identify as such once they are over. While they are going on, it is not as clear that prices are irrationally exuberant, and, indeed, many financial commentators at the time justified the boom as consistent with glowing forecasts for the "new economy." A simple example shows how hard it can be to tie down the fair value of stock investments.[7]

In 2000, the dividends paid by the firms included in the S&P 500 totaled $154.6 million. If the discount rate for the index was 9.2% and the expected dividend growth rate was 8%, the value of these shares according to the constant-growth dividend discount model (see Chapter 13 for more on this model) would be	**EXAMPLE 9.3** *A Stock Market Bubble?*

$$\text{Value} = \frac{\text{Dividend}}{\text{Discount rate} - \text{Growth rate}} = \frac{\$154.6}{.092 - .08} = \$12,883 \text{ million}$$

This was quite close to the actual total value of those firms at the time. But the estimate is highly sensitive to the input values, and even a small reassessment of their prospects would result in a big revision of price. Suppose the expected dividend growth rate fell to 7.4%. This would reduce the value of the index to

$$\text{Value} = \frac{\text{Dividend}}{\text{Discount rate} - \text{Growth rate}} = \frac{\$154.6}{.092 - .074} = \$8,589 \text{ million}$$

which was about the value to which the S&P 500 firms had fallen by October 2002. In light of this example, the run-up and crash of the 1990s seems easier to reconcile with rational behavior.

---

[6] We might ask why this logic of discounts and premiums does not apply to open-end mutual funds since they incur similar expense ratios. Because investors in these funds can redeem shares for NAV, the shares cannot sell at a discount to NAV. Expenses in open-end funds reduce returns in each period rather than being capitalized into price and inducing a discount.
[7] The following example is taken from R. A. Brealey, S. C. Myers, and F. Allen, *Principles of Corporate Finance,* 9th ed. (Burr Ridge, IL: McGraw-Hill/Irwin, 2008).

On the MARKET FRONT

AS TWO ECONOMISTS DEBATE MARKETS, THE TIDE SHIFTS

For forty years, economist Eugene Fama argued that financial markets were highly efficient in reflecting the underlying value of stocks. His longtime intellectual nemesis, Richard Thaler, a member of the "behaviorist" school of economic thought, contended that markets can veer off course when individuals make stupid decisions.

This long-running argument has big implications for real-life problems, ranging from the privatization of Social Security to the regulation of financial markets to the way corporate boards are run. Mr. Fama's ideas helped foster the free-market theories of the 1980s and spawned the $1 trillion index-fund industry. Mr. Thaler's theory suggests policymakers have an important role to play in guiding markets and individuals where they're prone to fail.

Behavioral economists argue that markets are imperfect because people often stray from rational decisions. They believe this behavior creates market breakdowns and also buying opportunities for savvy investors.

SMALL ANOMALIES

Even before the late 1990s, Mr. Thaler and a growing legion of behavioral finance experts were finding small anomalies that seemed to fly in the face of efficient-market theory. For example, researchers found that value stocks, companies that appear undervalued relative to their profits or assets, tended to outperform growth stocks, ones that are perceived as likely to increase profits rapidly. If the market was efficient and impossible to beat, why would one asset class outperform another? (Mr. Fama says there's a rational explanation: Value

stocks come with hidden risks and investors are rewarded for those risks with higher returns.)

Moreover, in a rational world, share prices should move only when new information hits the market. But with more than one billion shares a day changing hands on the New York Stock Exchange, the market appears overrun with traders making bets all the time.

Robert Shiller, a Yale University economist, has long argued that efficient-market theorists made one huge mistake: Just because markets are unpredictable doesn't mean they are efficient. The leap in logic, he wrote in the 1980s, was one of "the most remarkable errors in the history of economic thought." Mr. Fama says behavioral economists made the same mistake in reverse: The fact that some individuals might be irrational doesn't mean the market is inefficient.

Mr. Thaler's views have seeped into the mainstream through the support of a number of prominent economists who have devised similar theories about how markets operate. In 2002, Daniel Kahneman won a Nobel Prize for pioneering research in the field of behavioral economics. Even [former] Federal Reserve Chairman Alan Greenspan, a firm believer in the benefits of free markets, famously adopted the term "irrational exuberance" in 1996.

Defending efficient markets has gotten harder, but it's probably too soon for Mr. Thaler to declare victory. He concedes that most of his retirement assets are held in index funds, the very industry that Mr. Fama's research helped to launch. And despite his research on market inefficiencies, he also concedes that "it is not easy to beat the market, and most people don't."

SOURCE: Jon E. Hilsenrath, *The Wall Street Journal*, October 18, 2004, p. A1. © 2004 Dow Jones & Company, Inc. All rights reserved.

Still, other evidence seems to tag the dot-com boom as at least partially irrational. Consider, for example, the results of a study by Rau, Dimitrov, and Cooper (2001) documenting that firms adding ".com" to the end of their names during this period enjoyed a meaningful stock price increase. That doesn't sound like rational valuation to us.

Evaluating the Behavioral Critique

As investors, we are concerned with the existence of profit opportunities. The behavioral explanations of efficient market anomalies do not give guidance as to how to exploit any irrationality. For investors, the question is still whether there is money to be made from mispricing, and the behavioral literature is largely silent on this point.

However, as we have emphasized above, one of the important implications of the efficient market hypothesis is that security prices serve as reliable guides to the allocation of real capital. If prices are distorted, then capital markets will give misleading signals (and incentives) as to where the economy may best allocate resources. In this crucial dimension, the behavioral critique of the efficient market hypothesis is certainly important irrespective of any implication for investment strategies.

There is considerable debate among financial economists concerning the strength of the behavioral critique. Many believe that the behavioral approach is too unstructured, in effect allowing virtually any anomaly to be explained by some combination of irrationalities chosen from a laundry list of behavioral biases. While it is easy to "reverse engineer" a behavioral explanation for any particular anomaly, these critics would like to see a consistent or unified behavioral theory that can explain a *range* of anomalies.

More fundamentally, others are not convinced that the anomalies literature as a whole is a convincing indictment of the efficient market hypothesis. Fama (1998) reviews the anomalies literature and mounts a counterchallenge to the behavioral school. He notes that the anomalies are inconsistent in terms of their support for one type of irrationality versus another. For example, some papers document long-term corrections (consistent with overreaction) while others document long-term continuations of abnormal returns (consistent with underreaction). Moreover, the statistical significance of many of these results is less than meets the eye. Even small errors in choosing a benchmark against which to compare returns can cumulate to large apparent abnormalities in long-term returns. Therefore, many of the results in these studies are sensitive to small benchmarking errors, and Fama argues that seemingly minor changes in methodology can have big impacts on conclusions.

Behavioral finance is still in its infancy, however. Its critique of full rationality in investor decision making is well taken, but the extent to which limited rationality affects asset pricing is controversial. It is probably still too early to pass judgment on the behavioral approach, specifically, which behavioral models will "stick" and become part of the standard tool-kit of financial analysts. The nearby box discusses the ongoing debate between stock market "rationalists" and "behaviorists."

9.2   TECHNICAL ANALYSIS AND BEHAVIORAL FINANCE

Technical analysis attempts to exploit recurring and predictable patterns in stock prices to generate superior investment performance. Technicians do not deny the value of fundamental information, but believe that prices only gradually close in on intrinsic value. As fundamentals shift, astute traders can exploit the adjustment to a new equilibrium.

For example, one of the best-documented behavioral tendencies is the *disposition effect,* which refers to the tendency of investors to hold on to losing investments. Behavioral investors seem reluctant to realize losses. Grinblatt and Han (2005) show that the disposition effect can lead to momentum in stock prices even if fundamental values follow a random walk. The fact that the demand of "disposition investors" for a company's shares depends on the price history of those shares means that prices close in on fundamental values only over time, consistent with the central motivation of technical analysis.

Behavioral biases may also be consistent with technical analysts' use of volume data. An important behavioral trait noted above is overconfidence, a systematic tendency to overestimate one's abilities. As traders become overconfident, they may trade more, inducing an association between trading volume and market returns (Gervais and Odean, 2001). Technical analysis thus uses volume data as well as price history to direct trading strategy.

Finally, technicians believe that market fundamentals can be perturbed by irrational or behavioral factors, sometimes labeled sentiment variables. More or less random price fluctuations will accompany any underlying price trend, creating opportunities to exploit corrections as these fluctuations dissipate.

Trends and Corrections

Much of technical analysis seeks to uncover trends in market prices. This is in effect a search for momentum. Momentum can be absolute, in which case one searches for upward price trends, or relative, in which case the analyst looks to invest in one sector over another (or even take on a long-short position in the two sectors). Relative strength statistics (see page 279) are designed to uncover these potential opportunities.

Dow theory

A technique that attempts to discern long- and short-term trends in stock market prices.

Dow theory   The grandfather of trend analysis is the **Dow theory,** named after its creator, Charles Dow (who established *The Wall Street Journal*). Many of today's more technically sophisticated methods are essentially variants of Dow's approach.

The Dow theory posits three forces simultaneously affecting stock prices:

1. The *primary trend* is the long-term movement of prices, lasting from several months to several years.
2. *Secondary* or *intermediate trends* are caused by short-term deviations of prices from the underlying trend line. These deviations are eliminated via *corrections* when prices revert back to trend values.
3. *Tertiary* or *minor trends* are daily fluctuations of little importance.

Figure 9.3 represents these three components of stock price movements. In this figure, the primary trend is upward, but intermediate trends result in short-lived market declines lasting a few weeks. The intraday minor trends have no long-run impact on price.

Figure 9.4 depicts the course of the DJIA during 1988. The primary trend is upward, as evidenced by the fact that each market peak is higher than the previous peak (point *F*

FIGURE 9.3

Dow theory trends

Source: From Melanie F. Bowman and Thom Hartle, "Dow Theory," *Technical Analysis of Stocks and Commodities,* September 1990, p.690.

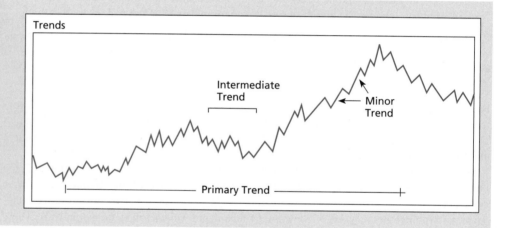

FIGURE 9.4

Dow Jones Industrial Average in 1988

Source: From Melanie F. Bowman and Thom Hartle, "Dow Theory" *Technical Analysis of Stocks and Commodities,* September 1990, p. 690.

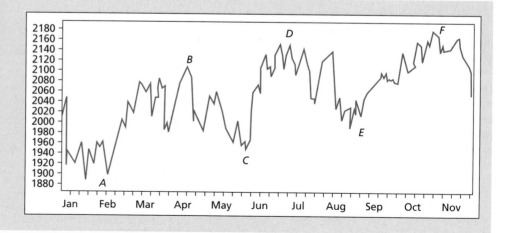

versus *D* versus *B*). Similarly, each low is higher than the previous low (*E* versus *C* versus *A*). This pattern of upward-moving "tops" and "bottoms" is one of the key ways to identify the underlying primary trend. Notice in Figure 9.4 that, despite the upward primary trend, intermediate trends still can lead to short periods of declining prices (points *B* through *C*, or *D* through *E*).

In evaluating the Dow theory, don't forget the lessons of the efficient market hypothesis. The Dow theory is based on a notion of predictably recurring price patterns. Yet the EMH holds that if any pattern is exploitable, many investors would attempt to profit from such predictability, which would ultimately move stock prices and cause the trading strategy to self-destruct. While Figure 9.4 certainly appears to describe a classic upward primary trend, one always must wonder whether we can see that trend only *after* the fact. Recognizing patterns as they emerge is far more difficult.

Recent variations on the Dow theory are the Elliott wave theory and the theory of Kondratieff waves. Like the Dow theory, the idea behind Elliott waves is that stock prices can be described by a set of wave patterns. Long-term and short-term wave cycles are superimposed and result in a complicated pattern of price movements, but by interpreting the cycles, one can, according to the theory, predict broad movements. Similarly, Kondratieff waves are named after a Russian economist who asserted that the macroeconomy (and therefore the stock market) moves in broad waves lasting between 48 and 60 years. The Kondratieff waves are therefore analogous to Dow's primary trend, although they are of far longer duration. Kondratieff's assertion is hard to evaluate empirically, however, because cycles that last about 50 years provide only two independent data points per century, which is hardly enough data to test the predictive power of the theory.

Point and figure charts A variant on pure trend analysis is the *point and figure chart* depicted in Figure 9.5. This figure has no time dimension. It simply traces significant upward or downward movements in stock prices without regard to their timing. The data for Figure 9.4 come from Table 9.1.

Suppose, as in Table 9.1, that a stock's price is currently $40. If the price rises by at least $2, you put an X in the first column at $42 in Figure 9.5. Another increase of at least $2 calls for placement of another X in the first column, this time at the $44 level. If the stock then falls by at least $2, you start a new column and put an O next to $42. Each subsequent $2 price fall results in another O in the second column. When prices reverse yet again and head upward, you begin the third column with an X denoting each consecutive $2 price increase.

WEB *master*

Charting and Technical Analysis

Yahoo! Finance (**finance.yahoo.com**) offers significant capabilities in charting and other technical indicators. Under the charting function, you can specify comparisons between companies by choosing the technical analysis tab. Short interest ratios are found under the *Company Profile* report. Prepare charts of moving averages and obtain short interest ratios for GE and SWY. Prepare a one-year chart of the 50- and 200-day average price of GE, SWY, and the S&P 500 Index.

1. Which if either of the companies is priced above its 50- and 200-day averages?

2. Would you consider their charts as bullish or bearish? Why?

3. What are the short interest ratios for the two companies?

4. Has short interest displayed any significant trend?

50				
48			X	
46			X	O
44		X	X	O
42		X	O	X	O
40			O	X	O
38			O	X	O
36			O	X	O
34				O

TABLE 9.1

Stock price history

Date	Price	Date	Price
January 2	$40	February 1	$40*
January 3	40.50	February 2	41
January 4	41	February 5	40.50
January 5	42*	February 6	42*
January 8	41.50	February 7	45*
January 9	42.50	February 8	44.50
January 10	43	February 9	46*
January 11	43.75	February 12	47
January 12	44*	February 13	48*
January 15	45	February 14	47.50
January 16	44	February 15	46†
January 17	41.50†	February 16	45
January 18	41	February 19	44*
January 19	40*	February 20	42*
January 22	39	February 21	41
January 23	39.50	February 22	40*
January 24	39.75	February 23	41
January 25	38*	February 26	40.50
January 26	35*	February 27	38*
January 29	36†	February 28	39
January 30	37	March 1	36*
January 31	39*	March 2	34*

*Indicates an event that has resulted in a stock price increase or decrease of at least $2.

†Denotes a price movement that has resulted in either an upward or a downward reversal in the stock price.

The single asterisks in Table 9.1 mark an event resulting in the placement of a new X or O in the chart. The daggers denote price movements that result in the start of a new column of Xs or Os.

Sell signals are generated when the stock price *penetrates* previous lows, and buy signals occur when previous high prices are penetrated. A *congestion area* is a horizontal band of Xs and Os created by several price reversals. These regions correspond to support and resistance levels and are indicated in Figure 9.6, which is an actual chart for Atlantic Richfield.

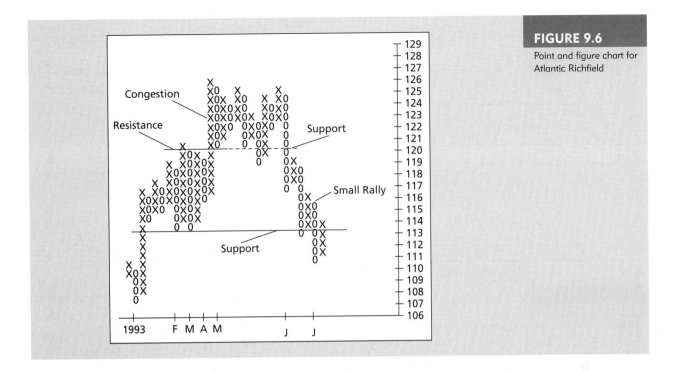

FIGURE 9.6

Point and figure chart for Atlantic Richfield

One can devise point and figure charts using price increments other than $2, but it is customary in setting up a chart to require reasonably substantial price changes before marking pluses or minuses.

Draw a point and figure chart using the history in Table 9.1 with price increments of $3.

CONCEPT *check* **9.4**

Moving averages   The moving average of a stock index is the average level of the index over a given interval of time. For example, a 52-week moving average tracks the average index value over the most recent 52 weeks. Each week, the moving average is recomputed by dropping the oldest observation and adding the latest. Figure 9.7 is a moving average chart for Apple Computer. Notice that the moving average plot (the colored curve) is a "smoothed" version of the original data series (dark curve).

After a period in which prices have generally been falling, the moving average will be above the current price (because the moving average "averages in" the older and higher prices). When prices have been rising, the moving average will be below the current price.

When the market price breaks through the moving average line from below, as at point A in Figure 9.7, it is taken as a bullish signal because it signifies a shift from a falling trend (with prices below the moving average) to a rising trend (with prices above the moving average). Conversely, when prices fall below the moving average as at point B, it's considered time to sell. (In this instance, however, the buy/sell signal turned out to be faulty.)

There is some variation in the length of the moving average considered most predictive of market movements. Two popular measures are 200-day and 53-week moving averages.

FIGURE 9.7

Share price and 50-day moving average for Apple Computer

Source: Copyright 2006 Yahoo! Inc., December 13, 2006, **http://finance.yahoo.com.** Reproduced with permission of Yahoo! Inc. © 2006 by Yahoo! Inc. Yahoo and the Yahoo! logo are trademarks of Yahoo! Inc.

EXAMPLE 9.4

Moving Averages

Consider the following price data. Each observation represents the closing level of the Dow Jones Industrial Average (DJIA) on the last trading day of the week. The 5-week moving average for each week is the average of the DJIA over the previous 5 weeks. For example, the first entry, for week 5, is the average of the index value between weeks 1 and 5: 12,290, 12,380, 12,399, 12,379, and 12,450. The next entry is the average of the index values between weeks 2 and 6, and so on.

Week	DJIA	5-Week Moving Average	Week	DJIA	5-Week Moving Average
1	12,290		11	12,590	12,555
2	12,380		12	12,652	12,586
3	12,399		13	12,625	12,598
4	12,379		14	12,657	12,624
5	12,450	12,380	15	12,699	12,645
6	12,513	12,424	16	12,647	12,656
7	12,500	12,448	17	12,610	12,648
8	12,565	12,481	18	12,595	12,642
9	12,524	12,510	19	12,499	12,610
10	12,597	12,540	20	12,466	12,563

Figure 9.8 plots the level of the index and the 5-week moving average. Notice that while the index itself moves up and down rather abruptly, the moving average is a relatively smooth series, since the impact of each week's price movement is averaged with that of the previous weeks. Week 16 is a bearish point according to the moving average rule. The price series crosses from above the moving average to below it, signifying the beginning of a downward trend in stock prices.

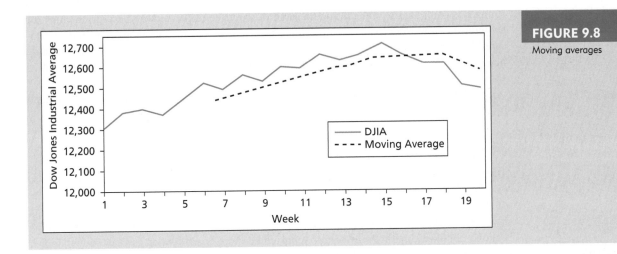

FIGURE 9.8

Moving averages

Breadth The **breadth** of the market is a measure of the extent to which movement in a market index is reflected widely in the price movements of all the stocks in the market. The most common measure of breadth is the spread between the number of stocks that advance and decline in price. If advances outnumber declines by a wide margin, then the market is viewed as being stronger because the rally is widespread. These breadth numbers are reported daily in *The Wall Street Journal* (see Figure 9.9).

Some analysts cumulate breadth data each day as in Table 9.2. The cumulative breadth for each day is obtained by adding that day's net advances (or declines) to the previous day's total. The direction of the cumulated series is then used to discern broad market trends. Analysts might use a moving average of cumulative breadth to gauge broad trends.

Relative strength **Relative strength** measures the extent to which a security has out-performed or underperformed either the market as a whole or its particular industry. Relative

breadth

The extent to which movements in broad market indexes are reflected widely in movements of individual stock prices.

relative strength

Recent performance of a given stock or industry compared to that of a broader market index.

Diaries

	NYSE	NASDAQ	AMEX
Issues traded	3,440	3,177	1,044
Advances	2,352	2,107	642
Declines	950	955	319
Unchanged	138	115	83
New highs	179	170	45
New lows	24	29	15
zAdv vol (000s)	1,256,091	1,766,819	52,821
zDecl vol (000s)	354,280	387,049	11,715
zTotal vol (000s)	1,628,930	2,170,216	68,357
Closing Tick	+1149	+793	+224
Closing Arms[1] (trin)	.70	.48	.45
zBlock trades	22,254	p13,895	p1,169

FIGURE 9.9

Market diary

Source: *The Wall Street Journal*, March 2, 2006. Reprinted by permission of Dow Jones & Company, Inc. via Copyright Clearance Center, Inc. © 2006 Dow Jones & Company, Inc. All Rights Reserved Worldwide.

TABLE 9.2	**Day**	**Advances**	**Declines**	**Net Advances**	**Cumulative Breadth**
Breadth	1	802	748	54	54
	2	917	640	277	331
	3	703	772	−69	262
	4	512	1122	−610	−348
	5	633	1004	−371	−719

Note: The sum of advances plus declines varies across days because some stock prices are unchanged.

strength is computed by calculating the ratio of the price of the security to a price index for the industry. For example, the relative strength of Ford versus the auto industry would be measured by movements in the ratio of the price of Ford divided by the level of an auto industry index. A rising ratio implies Ford has been outperforming the rest of the industry. If relative strength can be assumed to persist over time, then this would be a signal to buy Ford.

Similarly, the relative strength of an industry relative to the whole market can be computed by tracking the ratio of the industry price index to the market price index.

Sentiment Indicators

trin statistic

The ratio of average volume in declining issues to average volume in advancing issues.

Trin statistic   Market volume is sometimes used to measure the strength of a market rise or fall. Increased investor participation in a market advance or retreat is viewed as a measure of the significance of the movement. Technicians consider market advances to be a more favorable omen of continued price increases when they are associated with increased trading volume. Similarly, market reversals are considered more bearish when associated with higher volume. The **trin statistic** is defined as

$$\text{Trin} = \frac{\text{Volume declining/Number declining}}{\text{Volume advancing/Number advancing}}$$

Therefore, trin is the ratio of average trading volume in declining issues to average volume in advancing issues. Ratios above 1.0 are considered bearish because the falling stocks would then have higher average volume than the advancing stocks, indicating net selling pressure. *The Wall Street Journal* reports trin every day in the market diary section, as in Figure 9.9.

Note, however, that for every buyer, there must be a seller of stock. Rising volume in a rising market should not necessarily indicate a larger imbalance of buyers versus sellers. For example, a trin statistic above 1.0, which is considered bearish, could equally well be interpreted as indicating that there is more *buying* activity in declining issues.

Confidence index   *Barron's* computes a confidence index using data from the bond market. The presumption is that actions of bond traders reveal trends that will emerge soon in the stock market.

confidence index

Ratio of the yield of top-rated corporate bonds to the yield on intermediate-grade bonds.

The **confidence index** is the ratio of the average yield on 10 top-rated corporate bonds divided by the average yield on 10 intermediate-grade corporate bonds. The ratio will always be below 100% because higher rated bonds will offer lower promised yields to maturity. When bond traders are optimistic about the economy, however, they might require smaller default premiums on lower rated debt. Hence, the yield spread will narrow, and the confidence index will approach 100%. Therefore, higher values of the confidence index are bullish signals.

CONCEPT
check **9.5**

Yields on lower rated debt will rise after fears of recession have spread through the economy. This will reduce the confidence index. Should the stock market now be expected to fall or will it already have fallen?

short interest

The total number of shares currently sold-short in the market.

Short interest   **Short interest** is the total number of shares of stock currently sold-short in the market. Some technicians interpret high levels of short interest as bullish, some as bearish. The bullish perspective is that, because all short sales must be covered (i.e., short-sellers eventually must purchase shares to return the ones they have borrowed), short interest represents latent future demand for the stocks. As short sales are covered, the demand created by the share purchase will force prices up.

The bearish interpretation of short interest is based on the fact that short-sellers tend to be larger, more sophisticated investors. Accordingly, increased short interest reflects bearish sentiment by those investors "in the know," which would be a negative signal of the market's prospects.

Put/call ratio Call options give investors the right to buy a stock at a fixed "exercise" price and therefore are a way of betting on stock price increases. Put options give the right to sell a stock at a fixed price and therefore are a way of betting on stock price decreases.[8] The ratio of outstanding put options to outstanding call options is called the **put/call ratio.** Because put options do well in falling markets while call options do well in rising markets, deviations of the ratio from historical norms are considered to be a signal of market sentiment and therefore predictive of market movements.

Interestingly, however, a change in the ratio can be given a bullish or a bearish interpretation. Many technicians see an increase in the ratio as bearish, as it indicates growing interest in put options as a hedge against market declines. Thus, a rising ratio is taken as a sign of broad investor pessimism and a coming market decline. Contrarian investors, however, believe that a good time to buy is when the rest of the market is bearish because stock prices are then unduly depressed. Therefore, they would take an increase in the put/call ratio as a signal of a buy opportunity.

put/call ratio

Ratio of put options to call options outstanding on a stock.

A Warning

The search for patterns in stock market prices is nearly irresistible, and the ability of the human eye to discern apparent patterns is remarkable. Unfortunately, it is possible to perceive patterns that really don't exist. Consider Figure 9.10, which presents simulated and actual values of the Dow Jones Industrial Average during 1956 taken from a famous study by Harry Roberts (1959). In Figure 9.10B, it appears as though the market presents a classic head-and-shoulders pattern where the middle hump (the head) is flanked by two shoulders. When the price index "pierces the right shoulder"—a technical trigger point—it is believed to be heading lower, and it is time to sell your stocks. Figure 9.10A also looks like a "typical" stock market pattern.

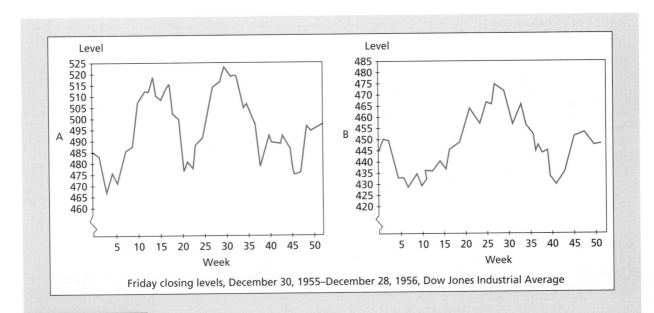

Friday closing levels, December 30, 1955–December 28, 1956, Dow Jones Industrial Average

FIGURE 9.10

Actual and simulated levels for stock market prices of 52 weeks

Note: Friday closing levels, December 30, 1955–December 28, 1956, Dow Jones Industrial Average.

Source: Harry Roberts, "Stock Market 'Patterns' and Financial Analysis: Methodological Suggestions," *Journal of Finance*, March 1959, pp. 11–25. Reprinted by permission of the publisher, Blackwell Publishing, Inc.

[8]Puts and calls were defined in Chapter 2, Section 2.5. They are discussed more fully in Chapter 15.

Can you tell which of the two graphs is constructed from the real value of the Dow and which from the simulated data? Figure 9.10A is based on the real data. The graph in panel B was generated using "returns" created by a random-number generator. These returns *by construction* were patternless, but the simulated price path that is plotted appears to follow a pattern much like that of panel A.

Figure 9.11 shows the weekly price *changes* behind the two panels in Figure 9.10. Here the randomness in both series—the stock price as well as the simulated sequence—is obvious.

A problem related to the tendency to perceive patterns where they don't exist is data mining. After the fact, you can always find patterns and trading rules that would have generated enormous profits. If you test enough rules, some will have worked in the past. Unfortunately, picking a theory that would have worked after the fact carries no guarantee of future success.

In evaluating trading rules, you should always ask whether the rule would have seemed reasonable *before* you looked at the data. If not, you might be buying into the one arbitrary rule among many that happened to have worked in the recent past. The hard but crucial question is whether there is reason to believe that what worked in the past should continue to work in the future.

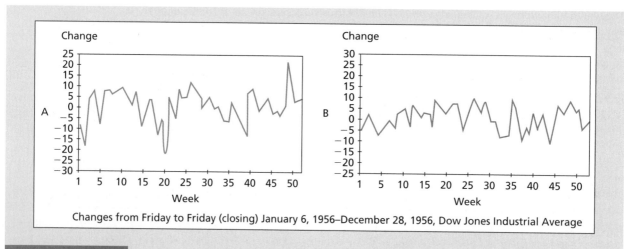

Changes from Friday to Friday (closing) January 6, 1956–December 28, 1956, Dow Jones Industrial Average

FIGURE 9.11

Actual and simulated changes in weekly stock prices for 52 weeks

Note: Changes from Friday to Friday (closing) January 6, 1956–December 28, 1956, Dow Jones Industrial Average.

Source: Harry Roberts, "Stock Market 'Patterns' and Financial Analysis: Methodological Suggestions," *Journal of Finance*, March 1959, pp. 11–25. Reprinted by permission of the publisher, Blackwell Publishing, Inc.

SUMMARY

- Behavioral finance focuses on systematic irrationalities that characterize investor decision making. These "behavioral shortcomings" may be consistent with several efficient market anomalies.
- Among the information processing errors uncovered in the psychology literature are memory bias, overconfidence, conservatism, and representativeness. Behavioral tendencies include framing, mental accounting, regret avoidance, and loss aversion.
- Limits to arbitrage activity impede the ability of rational investors to exploit pricing errors induced by behavioral investors. For example, fundamental risk means that even if a security is mispriced, it still can be risky to attempt to exploit the mispricing. This limits the actions of arbitrageurs who take positions in mispriced securities. Other limits to arbitrage are implementation costs, model risk, and costs to short-selling. Occasional failures of the Law of One Price suggest that limits to arbitrage are sometimes severe.

- The various limits to arbitrage mean that even if prices do not equal intrinsic value, it still may be difficult to exploit the mispricing. As a result, the failure of traders to beat the market may not be proof that markets are in fact efficient, with prices equal to intrinsic value.
- Technical analysis is the search for recurring and predictable patterns in stock prices. It is based on the premise that prices only gradually close in on intrinsic value. As fundamentals shift, astute traders can exploit the adjustment to a new equilibrium.
- Technical analysis also uses volume data and sentiment indicators. These are broadly consistent with several behavioral models of investor activity.
- The Dow theory attempts to identify underlying trends in stock indexes. Moving averages, relative strength, and breadth are used in other trend-based strategies.
- Some sentiment indicators are the trin statistic, the confidence index, and the put/call ratio.

PROBLEMS

 Select problems are available in McGraw-Hill's Homework Manager®. Please see the packaging options section of the preface for more information.

1. Don Sampson begins a meeting with his financial advisor by outlining his investment philosophy as shown below:

CFA® PROBLEMS

Statement Number	Statement
1	Investments should offer strong return potential but with very limited risk. I prefer to be conservative and to minimize losses, even if I miss out on substantial growth opportunities.
2	All nongovernmental investments should be in industry-leading and financially strong companies.
3	Income needs should be met entirely through interest income and cash dividends. All equity securities held should pay cash dividends.
4	Investment decisions should be based primarily on consensus forecasts of general economic conditions and company-specific growth.
5	If an investment falls below the purchase price, that security should be retained until it returns to its original cost. Conversely, I prefer to take quick profits on successful investments.
6	I will direct the purchase of investments, including derivative securities, periodically. These aggressive investments result from personal research and may not prove consistent with my investment policy. I have not kept records on the performance of similar past investments, but I have had some "big winners."

Select the statement from the table above that best illustrates each of the following behavioral finance concepts. Justify your selection.

    i. Mental accounting.

    ii. Overconfidence (illusion of control).

    iii. Reference dependence (framing).

2. Monty Frost's tax-deferred retirement account is invested entirely in equity securities. Because the international portion of his portfolio has performed poorly in the past, he

CFA® PROBLEMS

has reduced his international equity exposure to 2%. Frost's investment adviser has recommended an increased international equity exposure. Frost responds with the following comments:

a. Based on past poor performance, I want to sell all my remaining international equity securities once their market prices rise to equal their original cost.

b. Most diversified international portfolios have had disappointing results over the past 5 years. During that time, however, the market in Country XYZ has outperformed all other markets, even our own. If I do increase my international equity exposure, I would prefer that the entire exposure consist of securities from Country XYZ.

c. International investments are inherently more risky. Therefore, I prefer to purchase any international equity securities in my "speculative" account, my best chance at becoming rich. I do not want them in my retirement account, which has to protect me from poverty in my old age.

Frost's adviser is familiar with behavioral finance concepts but prefers a traditional or standard finance approach (modern portfolio theory) to investments.

Indicate the behavioral finance concept that Frost most directly exhibits in each of his three comments. Explain how each of Frost's comments can be countered by using an argument from standard finance.

3. Louise and Christopher Maclin live in London, United Kingdom, and currently rent an apartment in the metropolitan area. During an initial discussion of the Maclins' financial plans, Christopher Maclin makes the following statements to the Maclins' financial adviser, Grant Webb:

a. "I have used the Internet extensively to research the outlook for the housing market over the next 5 years, and I believe now is the best time to buy a house."

b. "I do not want to sell any bond in my portfolio for a lower price than I paid for the bond."

c. "I will not sell any of my company stock because I know my company and I believe it has excellent prospects for the future."

For each statement (a)–(c) identify the behavioral finance concept most directly exhibited. Explain how each behavioral finance concept is affecting the Maclins' investment decision making.

4. During an interview with her investment adviser, a retired investor made the following two statements:

a. "I have been very pleased with the returns I've earned on Petrie stock over the past 2 years and I am certain that it will be a superior performer in the future."

b. "I am pleased with the returns from the Petrie stock because I have specific uses for that money. For that reason, I certainly want my retirement fund to continue owning the Petrie stock."

Identify which principle of behavioral finance is most consistent with each of the investor's two statements.

5. Claire Pierce comments on her life circumstances and investment outlook:

I must support my parents who live overseas on Pogo Island. The Pogo Island economy has grown rapidly over the past 2 years with minimal inflation, and consensus forecasts call for a continuation of these favorable trends for the foreseeable future. Economic growth has resulted from the export of a natural resource used in an exciting new technology application.

I want to invest 10 percent of my portfolio in Pogo Island government bonds. I plan to purchase long-term bonds because my parents are likely to live more than 10 years. Experts uniformly do not foresee a resurgence of inflation on Pogo Island, so I am certain that the total returns produced by the bonds will cover my parents' spending needs for many years to come. There should be no exchange rate risk because the bonds are denominated in local currency. I want to buy the Pogo Island bonds, but am not willing to distort my portfolio's long-term asset allocation to do so. The overall mix of stocks, bonds, and other investments should not change. Therefore, I am considering selling one of my U.S. bond funds to raise cash to buy the Pogo Island bonds. One possibility is my High Yield Bond Fund, which has declined 5% in value year to date. I am not excited about this Fund's prospects; in fact I think it is likely to decline more, but there is a small probability that it could recover very quickly. So I have decided instead to sell my Core Bond Fund that has appreciated 5% this year. I expect this investment to continue to deliver attractive returns, but there is a small chance this year's gains might disappear quickly.

Once that shift is accomplished, my investments will be in great shape. The sole exception is my Small Company Fund, which has performed poorly. I plan to sell this investment as soon as the price increases to my original cost.

Identify three behavioral finance concepts illustrated in Pierce's comments and describe each of the three concepts. Discuss how an investor practicing standard or traditional finance would challenge each of the three concepts.

6. Use the data from *The Wall Street Journal* in Figure 9.9 to verify the trin ratio for the NYSE. Is the trin ratio bullish or bearish?

7. Calculate breadth for the NYSE using the data in Figure 9.9. Is the signal bullish or bearish?

8. Collect data on the DJIA for a period covering a few months. Try to identify primary trends. Can you tell whether the market currently is in an upward or downward trend?

9. Baa-rated bonds currently yield 9%, while Aa-rated bonds yield 8%. Suppose that due to an increase in the expected inflation rate, the yields on both bonds increase by 1%. What would happen to the confidence index? Would this be interpreted as bullish or bearish by a technical analyst? Does this make sense to you?

10. Table 10A presents price data for Computers, Inc., and a computer industry index. Does Computers, Inc., show relative strength over this period?

11. Use again the data in Table 10A to compute a 5-day moving average for Computers, Inc. Can you identify any buy or sell signals?

12. Construct a point and figure chart for Computers, Inc., using again the data in Table 10A. Use $2 increments for your chart. Do the buy or sell signals derived from your chart correspond to those derived from the moving average rule (see the previous problem)?

TABLE 10A

Computers, Inc., stock price history

Trading Day	Computers, Inc.	Industry Index	Trading Day	Computers, Inc.	Industry Index
1	19.63	50.0	21	19.63	54.1
2	20	50.1	22	21.50	54.0
3	20.50	50.5	23	22	53.9
4	22	50.4	24	23.13	53.7
5	21.13	51.0	25	24	54.8
6	22	50.7	26	25.25	54.5
7	21.88	50.5	27	26.25	54.6
8	22.50	51.1	28	27	54.1
9	23.13	51.5	29	27.50	54.2
10	23.88	51.7	30	28	54.8
11	24.50	51.4	31	28.50	54.2
12	23.25	51.7	32	28	54.8
13	22.13	52.2	33	27.50	54.9
14	22	52.0	34	29	55.2
15	20.63	53.1	35	29.25	55.7
16	20.25	53.5	36	29.50	56.1
17	19.75	53.9	37	30	56.7
18	18.75	53.6	38	28.50	56.7
19	17.50	52.9	39	27.75	56.5
20	19	53.4	40	28	56.1

TABLE 14A

Market advances and declines

Day	Advances	Declines	Day	Advances	Declines
1	906	704	6	970	702
2	653	986	7	1002	609
3	721	789	8	903	722
4	503	968	9	850	748
5	497	1095	10	766	766

13. Yesterday, the Dow Jones industrials gained 54 points. However, 1,704 issues declined in price while 1,367 advanced. Why might a technical analyst be concerned even though the market index rose on this day?

14. Table 14A contains data on market advances and declines. Calculate cumulative breadth and decide whether this technical signal is bullish or bearish.

15. If the trading volume in advancing shares on day 1 in the previous problem was 330 million shares, while the volume in declining issues was 240 million shares, what was the trin statistic for that day? Was trin bullish or bearish?

16. Given the following data, is the confidence index rising or falling? What might explain the pattern of yield changes?

	This Year	Last Year
Yield on top-rated corporate bonds	8%	8.5%
Yield on intermediate-grade corporate bonds	10.5	10

Please visit us at www.mhhe.com/bkm

17. Go to **www.mhhe.com/bkm** and link to the material for Chapter 9, where you will find 5 years of weekly returns for the S&P 500.
    a. Set up a spreadsheet to calculate the 26-week moving average of the index. Set the value of the index at the beginning of the sample period equal to 100. The index value in each week is then updated by multiplying the previous week's level by (1 + rate of return over previous week).
    b. Identify every instance in which the index crosses through its moving average from below. In how many of the weeks following a cross-through does the index increase? Decrease?
    c. Identify every instance in which the index crosses through its moving average from above. In how many of the weeks following a cross-through does the index increase? Decrease?
    d. How well does the moving average rule perform in identifying buy or sell opportunities?

Please visit us at www.mhhe.com/bkm

18. Go to **www.mhhe.com/bkm** and link to the material for Chapter 9, where you will find 5 years of weekly returns for the S&P 500 and Fidelity's Select Banking Fund (ticker FSRBX).
    a. Set up a spreadsheet to calculate the relative strength of the banking sector compared to the broad market. (*Hint:* as in the previous problem, set the initial value of the sector index and the S&P 500 index equal to 100, and use each week's rate of return to update the level of each index.)
    b. Identify every instance in which the relative strength ratio increases by at least 5% from its value 5 weeks earlier. In how many of the weeks following a substantial

increase in relative strength does the banking sector outperform the S&P 500? In how many of those weeks does the banking sector underperform the S&P 500?

c. Identify every instance in which the relative strength ratio decreases by at least 5% from its value 5 weeks earlier. In how many of the weeks following a substantial decrease in relative strength does the banking sector underperform the S&P 500? In how many of those weeks does the banking sector outperform the S&P 500?

d. How well does the relative strength rule perform in identifying buy or sell opportunities?

Use data from the Standard & Poor's Market Insight Database at www.mhhe.com/edumarketinsight to answer the following questions.

STANDARD &POOR'S

1. Find the monthly closing prices for the most recent 4 years for Abercrombie & Fitch (ANF) from the Excel Analytics section of Market Insight. Also collect the closing level of the S&P 500 Index over the same period.

   a. Calculate the 4-month moving average of both the stock and the S&P 500 over time. For each series, use Excel to plot the moving average against the actual level of the stock price or index. Examine the instances where the moving average and price series cross. Is the stock more or less likely to increase when the price crosses through the moving average? Does it matter whether the price crosses the moving average from above or below? How reliable would an investment rule based on moving averages be? Perform your analysis for both the stock price and the S&P 500.

   b. Calculate and plot the relative strength of the stock compared to the S&P 500 over the sample period. Find all instances in which relative strength of the stock increases by more than 10 percentage points (e.g., an increase in the relative strength index from .93 to 1.03) and all those instances in which relative strength of the stock decreases by more than 10 percentage points. Is the stock more or less likely to outperform the S&P in the following 2 months when relative strength has increased or to underperform when relative strength has decreased? In other words, does relative strength continue? How reliable would an investment rule based on relative strength be?

2. Go to the Market Insight database and click on the *Company* tab. Enter ticker symbol WMT for Wal-Mart Stores and click on *Go*.

   a. Select the *Charting by Profit* link on the menu. When the chart first appears you will need to reenter the WMT symbol in the box at the top left corner and click on *Go*. Click on the plus sign next to *Technical Studies,* then click on the plus sign next to *Moving Averages.* Double click on *Simple Moving Average* to see the Wal-Mart chart with a simple moving average. Do you see any patterns that might lead to a successful trading rule?

   b. Click on the plus sign next to *Support & Resistance*. Next, double click on *Projection Bands*. What observations do you have about how often the price has passed outside of these bands and what tends to happen after the price crosses the band line?

   c. At the top of the graph locate the selection box next to the stock symbol. The default setting is Bar. Change this to Candle to see a Candle chart for Wal-Mart. Change the frequency (three boxes to the right of the stock symbol) from "D" (daily) to "W" (weekly) to get a better view of the candles. As you move the cursor along the plotted data look at the price information on top of the chart to see how the Candle chart was plotted.

   d. Explore some of the other graphs in the *Technical Studies* section. Do you have any favorites that you think might be particularly useful for making investment decisions?

WEB *master*

Technical Analysis versus Market Efficiency
Go to **bigcharts.marketwatch.com** and search the Internet for other charting and technical analysis sites.
1. Is there a consensus among technical analysts concerning a specific technique that works best to generate excess returns?

2. Is there verifiable evidence to suggest that this method works in practice? If you can identify a rule that seems to work, try it out on real historical data that can be found at many sites such as **finance.yahoo.com.**

SOLUTIONS TO

CONCEPT *c h e c k s*

9.1. Conservatism implies that investors will at first respond too slowly to new information, leading to trends in prices. Representativeness can lead them to extrapolate trends too far into the future and overshoot intrinsic value. Eventually, when the pricing error is corrected, we observe a reversal.

9.2. Out-of-favor stocks will exhibit low prices relative to various proxies for intrinsic value such as earnings. Because of regret avoidance, these stocks will need to offer a more attractive rate of return to induce investors to hold them. Thus, low P/E stocks might on average offer higher rates of return.

9.3. At liquidation, price will equal NAV. This puts a limit on fundamental risk. Investors need only carry the position for a few months to profit from the elimination of the discount. Moreover, as the liquidation date approaches, the discount should dissipate. This greatly limits the risk that the discount can move against the investor. At the announcement of impending liquidation, the discount should immediately disappear, or at least shrink considerably.

9.4.

9.5. By the time the news of the recession affects bond yields, it also ought to affect stock prices. The market should fall *before* the confidence index signals that the time is ripe to sell.

PART THREE

DEBT SECURITIES

Bond markets used to be a sedate arena for risk-averse investors who wanted worry-free investments with modest but stable returns. They are no longer so quiet. Annual trading in U.S. government bonds alone is about 10 times the total amount of national debt. The market in mortgage-backed securities alone is now about $3.8 trillion.

Higher trading activity is not the only reason these markets are more interesting than they once were. These markets are no longer free of risk. Interest rates in the last two decades have become more volatile than anyone in 1965 would have dreamed possible. Volatility means that investors have great opportunities for gain, but also for losses, and we have seen dramatic examples of both in recent years.

Procter & Gamble lost about $100 million in interest rate swaps in 1994. Long-Term Capital Management lost more than $1 billion on its interest-rate positions in 1998. Two Bear Stearns hedge funds lost well over $1 billion on mortgage bonds in only a few months in 2007. Of course, there were traders on the other side of these transactions who did quite well in these instances.

The chapters in Part Three provide an introduction to debt markets and securities. We will show you how to value such securities and why their values change with interest rates. We will see what features determine the sensitivity of bond prices to interest rates, and how investors measure and manage interest rate risk.

CHAPTERS IN THIS PART

www.mhhe.com/bkm

10 Bond Prices and Yields

In the previous chapters on risk and return relationships, we have treated securities at a high level of abstraction. We have assumed implicitly that a prior, detailed analysis of each security already has been performed and that its risk and return features have been assessed.

We turn now to specific analyses of particular security markets. We examine valuation principles, determinants of risk and return, and portfolio strategies commonly used within and across the various markets.

We begin by analyzing debt securities. A debt security is a claim on a specified periodic stream of income. Debt securities are often called *fixed-income securities*, because they promise either a fixed stream of income or a stream of income that is determined according to a specified formula. These securities have the advantage of being relatively easy to understand because the payment formulas are specified in advance. Uncertainty surrounding cash flows paid to the security holder is minimal as long as the issuer of the security is sufficiently creditworthy. That makes these securities a convenient starting point for our analysis of the universe of potential investment vehicles.

The bond is the basic debt security, and this chapter starts with an overview of bond markets, including Treasury, corporate, and international bonds. We turn next to bond pricing, showing how bond prices are set in accordance with market interest rates and why bond prices change with those rates. Given this background, we can compare the myriad measures of bond returns such as yield to maturity, yield to call, holding-period return, or realized compound rate of return. We show how bond prices evolve over time, discuss certain tax rules that apply to debt securities, and show how to calculate after-tax returns. Next, we consider the impact of default or credit risk on bond pricing and look at the determinants of credit risk and the default premium built into bond yields. Finally, we turn to the term structure of interest rates, the relationship between yield to maturity and time to maturity.

Related Web sites for this chapter are available at www.mhhe.com/bkm.

10.1 | BOND CHARACTERISTICS

A **bond** is a security that is issued in connection with a borrowing arrangement. The borrower issues (i.e., sells) a bond to the lender for some amount of cash; the bond is in essence the "IOU" of the borrower. The arrangement obligates the issuer to make specified payments to the bondholder on specified dates. A typical coupon bond obligates the issuer to make semiannual payments of interest, called *coupon payments*, to the bondholder for the life of the bond. These are called coupon payments because, in precomputer days, most bonds had coupons that investors would clip off and mail to the issuer of the bond to claim the interest payment. When the bond matures, the issuer repays the debt by paying the bondholder the bond's **par value** (or equivalently, its **face value**). The **coupon rate** of the bond serves to determine the interest payment: The annual payment equals the coupon rate times the bond's par value. The coupon rate, maturity date, and par value of the bond are part of the *bond indenture,* which is the contract between the issuer and the bondholder.

To illustrate, a bond with a par value of $1,000 and a coupon rate of 8% might be sold to a buyer for $1,000. The issuer then pays the bondholder 8% of $1,000, or $80 per year, for the stated life of the bond, say, 30 years. The $80 payment typically comes in two semiannual installments of $40 each. At the end of the 30-year life of the bond, the issuer also pays the $1,000 par value to the bondholder.

Bonds usually are issued with coupon rates set just high enough to induce investors to pay par value to buy the bond. Sometimes, however, **zero-coupon bonds** are issued that make no coupon payments. In this case, investors receive par value at the maturity date, but receive no interest payments until then: The bond has a coupon rate of zero. These bonds are issued at prices considerably below par value, and the investor's return comes solely from the difference between issue price and the payment of par value at maturity. We will return to these bonds below.

bond

A security that obligates the issuer to make specified payments to the holder over a period of time.

face value, par value

The payment to the bondholder at the maturity of the bond.

coupon rate

A bond's annual interest payment per dollar of par value.

zero-coupon bond

A bond paying no coupons that sells at a discount and provides only a payment of par value at maturity.

Treasury Bonds and Notes

Figure 10.1 is an excerpt from the listing of Treasury issues from the *The Wall Street Journal Online.* Treasury note maturities range up to 10 years, while Treasury bonds with maturities ranging from 10 to 30 years appear in the figure. Both bonds and notes are issued in denominations of $1,000 or more. Both make semiannual coupon payments.

FIGURE 10.1

Listing of Treasury issues

Source: *The Wall Street Journal Online*, January 16, 2007. Reprinted by permission of Dow Jones & Company, Inc. via Copyright Clearance Center, Inc. © 2007 Dow Jones & Company. All Rights Reserved Worldwide.

U.S. Government Bonds and Notes

Representative Over-the-Counter quotation based on transactions of $1 million or more.
Treasury bond, note and bill quotes are from midafternoon. Colons in bond and note bid-and-asked quotes represent 32nds; 101:01 means 101 1/32. Net change in 32nds. n-Treasury Note. i-inflation-indexed issue. Treasury bill quotes in hundredths, quoted in terms of a rate of discount. Days to maturity calculated from settlement date. All yields are to maturity and based on the asked quote. For bonds callable prior to maturity, yields are computed to the earliest call date for issues quoted above par and to the maturity date for issues quoted below par.
*-When issued. Daily change expressed in basis points.

RATE	MATURITY MO/YR	BID	ASKED	CHG	ASK YLD
5.250	Feb 29	104:14	104:15	+9	4.92
3.875	Apr 29i	124:17	124:18	+16	2.44
6.125	Aug 29	116:12	116:13	+9	4.91
6.250	May 30	118:19	118:20	+10	4.90
5.375	Feb 31	106:20	106:21	+8	4.90
3.375	Apr 32i	119:09	119:10	+16	2.35
4.500	Feb 36	94:19	94:20	+9	4.84

RATE	MATURITY MO/YR	BID	ASKED	CHG	ASK YLD	RATE	MATURITY MO/YR	BID	ASKED	CHG	ASK YLD
3.125	Jan 07n	99:29	99:30	....	4.83	2.375	Apr 11i	99:11	99:12	+2	2.53
2.250	Feb 07n	99:24	99:25	....	4.88	4.875	Apr 11n	100:16	100:17	+3	4.73
6.250	Feb 07n	100:02	100:03	....	4.88	4.875	May 11n	100:17	100:18	+3	4.73
3.375	Feb 07n	99:25	99:26	....	4.97	5.125	Jun 11n	101:17	101:18	+4	4.73
3.750	Mar 07n	99:23	99:24	+1	4.97	4.875	Jul 11n	100:18	100:19	+4	4.73
3.625	Apr 07n	99:18	99:19	....	4.99	4.625	Dec 11n	99:15	99:16	+4	4.74
5.750	Aug 10n	103:09	103:10	+2	4.73	3.375	Jan 12i	104:01	104:02	+3	2.50
4.125	Aug 10n	98:00	98:01	+3	4.73	4.875	Feb 12n	100:24	100:25	+4	4.70
3.875	Sep 10n	97:03	97:04	+3	4.73	3.000	Jul 12i	102:17	102:18	+2	2.49
4.250	Oct 10n	98:10	98:11	+3	4.73	4.375	Aug 12n	98:13	98:14	+4	4.69
4.500	Nov 10n	99:05	99:06	+3	4.73	4.000	Nov 12n	96:13	96:14	+4	4.71
4.375	Dec 10n	98:22	98:23	+3	4.74	10.375	Nov 12	104:11	104:12	+2	4.87
4.250	Jan 11n	98:07	98:08	+3	4.74	3.375	Feb 13n	95:17	95:18	+4	4.72
3.500	Jan 11i	103:26	103:27	+3	2.48	3.625	May 13n	94:02	94:03	+5	4.71
5.000	Feb 11n	101:03	101:04	+3	4.69	1.375	Jul 13i	96:09	96:10	+4	2.49
4.500	Feb 11n	99:04	99:05	+3	4.73	4.250	Aug 13n	97:10	97:11	+6	4.72
4.750	Mar 11n	100:01	100:02	+3	4.73	5.250	Nov 28	104:12	104:13	+8	4.92

Treasury Bills

MATURITY	DAYS TO MAT	BID	ASKED	CHG	ASK YLD
Mar 22 07	64	4.96	4.95	+0.02	5.06
Mar 29 07	71	4.96	4.95	+0.01	5.07
Apr 05 07	78	4.96	4.95	+0.01	5.07
Apr 12 07	85	4.96	4.95	....	5.08
Apr 19 07	92	4.98	4.97	+0.02	5.10
Apr 26 07	99	4.96	4.95	....	5.09
May 03 07	106	4.96	4.95	+0.01	5.09
May 10 07	113	4.96	4.95	....	5.10
May 17 07	120	4.97	4.96	+0.01	5.11
May 24 07	127	4.97	4.96	+0.01	5.12
May 31 07	134	4.95	4.94	+0.01	5.10
Jun 07 07	141	4.94	4.93	+0.01	5.10
Jun 14 07	148	4.94	4.93	....	5.10
Jun 21 07	155	4.94	4.93	....	5.11
Jun 28 07	162	4.94	4.93	....	5.11
Jul 05 07	169	4.95	4.94	....	5.13
Jul 12 07	176	4.95	4.94	....	5.13

The highlighted issue in Figure 10.1 matures in January 2011. The *n* after 2011 denotes that this is a Treasury note, as opposed to a bond. Its coupon rate is 4.25%. Par value is $1,000; thus, the bond pays interest of $42.50 per year in two semiannual payments of $21.25. Payments are made in January and July of each year. The bid and ask prices[1] are quoted in points plus fractions of $\frac{1}{32}$ of a point (the numbers after the colons are the fractions of a point). Although bonds are sold in denominations of $1,000 par value, the prices are quoted as a percentage of par value. Therefore, the bid price of the bond is 98:07 = 98.219% of par value or $982.19, while the ask price is 98:08 = 98.25% of par, or $982.50.

The last column, labeled Ask Yld, is the bond's yield to maturity based on the ask price. The yield to maturity is often interpreted as a measure of the average rate of return to an investor who purchases the bond for the ask price and holds it until its maturity date. We will have much to say about yield to maturity below.[2]

Accrued interest and quoted bond prices

The bond prices that you see quoted in the financial pages are not actually the prices that investors pay for the bond. This is because the quoted price does not include the interest that accrues between coupon payment dates.

If a bond is purchased between coupon payments, the buyer must pay the seller for accrued interest, the prorated share of the upcoming semiannual coupon. For example, if 30 days have passed since the last coupon payment, and there are 182 days in the semiannual coupon period, the seller is entitled to a payment of accrued interest of $\frac{30}{182}$ of the semiannual coupon. The sale, or *invoice price* of the bond, which is the amount the buyer actually pays, would equal the stated price plus the accrued interest.

In general, the formula for the amount of accrued interest between two dates is

$$\text{Accrued interest} = \frac{\text{Annual coupon payment}}{2} \times \frac{\text{Days since last coupon payment}}{\text{Days separating coupon payments}}$$

[1] Recall that the bid price is the price at which you can sell the bond to a dealer. The ask price, which is slightly higher, is the price at which you can buy the bond from a dealer.

[2] Notice that some of the bonds in Figure 10.1 have the letter *i* after the maturity year and that these bonds have lower reported yields to maturity. These are inflation-indexed bonds, and their yields should be interpreted as after-inflation or real returns. We discuss these bonds in detail later in the chapter.

EXAMPLE   10.1

Accrued Interest

Suppose that the coupon rate is 8%. Then the semiannual coupon payment is $40. Because 30 days have passed since the last coupon payment, the accrued interest on the bond is $40 \times \left(\frac{30}{182} \right) = \$6.59$. If the quoted price of the bond is $990, then the invoice price will be $990 + \$6.59 = \$996.59$.

The practice of quoting bond prices net of accrued interest explains why the price of a maturing bond is listed at $1,000 rather than $1,000 plus one coupon payment. A purchaser of an 8% coupon bond one day before the bond's maturity would receive $1,040 on the following day and so should be willing to pay a total price of $1,040 for the bond. In fact, $40 of that total payment constitutes the accrued interest for the preceding half-year period. The bond price is quoted net of accrued interest in the financial pages and thus appears as $1,000.[3]

Corporate Bonds

Like the government, corporations borrow money by issuing bonds. Figure 10.2 is a sample of corporate bond listings from *The Wall Street Journal Online,* which reports only the most actively traded corporate bonds. Although some bonds trade on an electronic exchange operated by the New York Stock Exchange called the Automated Bond System, most bonds are traded over the counter in a network of bond dealers linked by a computer quotation system. In practice, the bond market can be quite "thin," in that there are few investors interested in trading a particular issue at any particular time.

The bond listings in Figure 10.2 include the coupon, maturity, price, and yield to maturity of each bond. The "rating" column is the estimation of bond safety given by the three major bond rating agencies, Moody's, Standard & Poor's, and Fitch. Bonds with A ratings are safer than those rated B or below. Notice that as a general rule, safer bonds with the higher ratings promise lower yields to maturity. We will return to this topic toward the end of the chapter.

Bonds issued in the United States today are *registered,* meaning that the issuing firm keeps records of the owner of the bond and can mail interest checks to the owner. Registration of

ISSUER NAME	SYMBOL	COUPON	MATURITY	RATING MOODY'S/S&P/ FITCH	HIGH	LOW	LAST	CHANGE	YIELD %
Gatx	GMT.IK	8.875%	Jun 2009	Baa1/BBB/BBB–	107.545	107.538	107.545	–0.100	5.433
Marshall & Ilsley	MI.YL	3.800%	Feb 2008	Aa3/A+/A+	98.514	98.470	98.514	0.064	5.263
Capital One	COF.HK	7.686%	Aug 2036	Baa2/BBB–/BBB–	113.895	113.390	113.733	0.257	6.621
Entergy Gulf States	ETR.KC	6.180%	Mar 2035	Baa3/BBB+/BBB	99.950	94.616	99.469	0.219	6.220
AOL Time Warner	AOL.HG	6.875%	May 2012	Baa2/BBB+/BBB	107.205	105.402	106.565	0.720	5.427
Household Intl	HI.HJG	8.875%	Feb 2008	Aa3/AA–/AA–	100.504	100.504	100.504	–0.109	5.348
SBC Comm	SBC.IF	5.875%	Feb 2012	A2/A/A	102.116	102.001	102.001	–0.156	5.415
American General Finance	AIG.GOU	5.750%	Sep 2016	A1/A+/A+	101.229	101.135	101.135	–0.530	5.595

FIGURE 10.2

Listing of corporate bonds

Source: *The Wall Street Journal Online,* January 12, 2007. Reprinted by permission of Dow Jones & Company, Inc. via Copyright Clearance Center, Inc. © 2007 Dow Jones & Company, Inc. All Rights Reserved Worldwide.

---

[3] In contrast to bonds, stocks do not trade at flat prices with adjustments for "accrued dividends." Whoever owns the stock when it goes "ex-dividend" receives the entire dividend payment, and the stock price reflects the value of the upcoming dividend. The price therefore typically falls by about the amount of the dividend on the "ex day." There is no need to differentiate between reported and invoice prices for stocks.

bonds is helpful to tax authorities in the enforcement of tax collection. *Bearer bonds* are those traded without any record of ownership. The investor's physical possession of the bond certificate is the only evidence of ownership. These are now rare in the United States, but more common in the Eurobond market, where anonymity is valued.

callable bonds

Bonds that may be repurchased by the issuer at a specified call price during the call period.

Call provisions on corporate bonds   While the Treasury no longer issues callable bonds, some corporate bonds are issued with call provisions, allowing the issuer to repurchase the bond at a specified *call price* before the maturity date. For example, if a company issues a bond with a high coupon rate when market interest rates are high, and interest rates later fall, the firm might like to retire the high-coupon debt and issue new bonds at a lower coupon rate to reduce interest payments. The proceeds from the new bond issue are used to pay for the repurchase of the existing higher coupon bonds at the call price. This is called *refunding*. Callable bonds typically come with a period of call protection, an initial time during which the bonds are not callable. Such bonds are referred to as *deferred* callable bonds.

The option to call the bond is valuable to the firm, allowing it to buy back the bonds and refinance at lower interest rates when market rates fall. Of course, the firm's benefit is the bondholder's burden. Holders of called bonds forfeit their bonds for the call price, thereby giving up the prospect of an attractive rate of interest on their original investment. To compensate investors for this risk, callable bonds are issued with higher coupons and promised yields to maturity than noncallable bonds.

CONCEPT check 10.1   Suppose that General Motors issues two bonds with identical coupon rates and maturity dates. One bond is callable, however, while the other is not. Which bond will sell at a higher price?

convertible bond

A bond with an option allowing the bondholder to exchange the bond for a specified number of shares of common stock in the firm.

Convertible bonds   Convertible bonds give bondholders an option to exchange each bond for a specified number of shares of common stock of the firm. The *conversion ratio* gives the number of shares for which each bond may be exchanged. Suppose a convertible bond is issued at par value of $1,000 and is convertible into 40 shares of a firm's stock. The current stock price is $20 per share, so the option to convert is not profitable now. Should the stock price later rise to $30, however, each bond may be converted profitably into $1,200 worth of stock. The *market conversion value* is the current value of the shares for which the bonds may be exchanged. At the $20 stock price, for example, the bond's conversion value is $800. The *conversion premium* is the excess of the bond price over its conversion value. If the bond were selling currently for $950, its premium would be $150.

Convertible bondholders benefit from price appreciation of the company's stock. Not surprisingly, this benefit comes at a price; convertible bonds offer lower coupon rates and stated or promised yields to maturity than nonconvertible bonds. At the same time, the actual return on the convertible bond may exceed the stated yield to maturity if the option to convert becomes profitable.

We discuss convertible and callable bonds further in Chapter 15.

put bond

A bond that the holder may choose either to exchange for par value at some date or to extend for a given number of years.

Puttable bonds   While the callable bond gives the issuer the option to extend or retire the bond at the call date, the *extendable* or **put bond** gives this option to the bondholder. If the bond's coupon rate exceeds current market yields, for instance, the bondholder will choose to extend the bond's life. If the bond's coupon rate is too low, it will be optimal not to extend; the bondholder instead reclaims principal, which can be invested at current yields.

floating-rate bonds

Bonds with coupon rates periodically reset according to a specified market rate.

Floating-rate bonds   Floating-rate bonds make interest payments that are tied to some measure of current market rates. For example, the rate might be adjusted annually to the current T-bill rate plus 2%. If the one-year T-bill rate at the adjustment date is 4%, the bond's coupon rate over the next year would then be 6%. This arrangement means that the bond always pays approximately current market rates.

The major risk involved in floaters has to do with changing credit conditions. The yield spread is fixed over the life of the security, which may be many years. If the financial health of the firm deteriorates, then investors will demand a greater yield premium than is offered by the security. In this case, the price of the bond will fall. While the coupon rate on floaters adjusts to changes in the general level of market interest rates, it does not adjust to changes in the financial condition of the firm.

Preferred Stock

Although preferred stock strictly speaking is considered to be equity, it often is included in the fixed-income universe. This is because, like bonds, preferred stock promises to pay a specified stream of dividends. However, unlike bonds, the failure to pay the promised dividend does not result in corporate bankruptcy. Instead, the dividends owed simply cumulate, and the common stockholders may not receive any dividends until the preferred stockholders have been paid in full. In the event of bankruptcy, the claim of preferred stockholders to the firm's assets has lower priority than that of bondholders, but higher priority than that of common stockholders.

Preferred stock commonly pays a fixed dividend. Therefore, it is in effect a perpetuity, providing a level cash flow indefinitely. More recently, however, adjustable or floating-rate preferred stock has become popular, in some years accounting for about half of new issues. Floating-rate preferred stock is much like floating-rate bonds. The dividend rate is linked to a measure of current market interest rates and is adjusted at regular intervals.

Unlike interest payments on bonds, dividends on preferred stock are not considered tax-deductible expenses to the firm. This reduces their attractiveness as a source of capital to issuing firms. On the other hand, there is an offsetting tax advantage to preferred stock. When one corporation buys the preferred stock of another corporation, it pays taxes on only 30% of the dividends received. For example, if the firm's tax bracket is 35%, and it receives $10,000 in preferred dividend payments, it will pay taxes on only $3,000 of that income: Total taxes owed on the income will be $0.35 \times \$3,000 = \$1,050$. The firm's effective tax rate on preferred dividends is therefore only $0.30 \times 35\% = 10.5\%$. Given this tax rule, it is not surprising that most preferred stock is held by corporations.

Preferred stock rarely gives its holders full voting privileges in the firm. However, if the preferred dividend is skipped, the preferred stockholders will then be provided some voting power.

Other Domestic Issuers

There are, of course, several issuers of bonds in addition to the Treasury and private corporations. For example, state and local governments issue municipal bonds. The outstanding feature of these is that interest payments are tax-free. We examined municipal bonds and the value of the tax exemption in Chapter 2.

Government agencies, such as the Federal Home Loan Bank Board, the Farm Credit agencies, and the mortgage pass-through agencies Ginnie Mae, Fannie Mae, and Freddie Mac also issue considerable amounts of bonds. These too were reviewed in Chapter 2.

International Bonds

International bonds are commonly divided into two categories: *foreign bonds* and *Eurobonds*. Foreign bonds are issued by a borrower from a country other than the one in which the bond is sold. The bond is denominated in the currency of the country in which it is marketed. For example, if a German firm sells a dollar-denominated bond in the U.S., the bond is considered a foreign bond. These bonds are given colorful names based on the countries in which they are marketed. For example, foreign bonds sold in the U.S. are called *Yankee bonds*. Like other bonds sold in the U.S., they are registered with the Securities and Exchange Commission. Yen-denominated bonds sold in Japan by non-Japanese issuers are called *Samurai bonds*. British pound-denominated foreign bonds sold in the U.K. are called *bulldog bonds*.

In contrast to foreign bonds, Eurobonds are bonds issued in the currency of one country but sold in other national markets. For example, the Eurodollar market refers to dollar-denominated bonds sold outside the U.S. (not just in Europe), although London is the largest market for Eurodollar bonds. Because the Eurodollar market falls outside of U.S. jurisdiction, these bonds are not regulated by U.S. federal agencies. Similarly, Euroyen bonds are yen-denominated bonds selling outside Japan, Eurosterling bonds are pound-denominated Eurobonds selling outside the U.K., and so on.

Innovation in the Bond Market

Issuers constantly develop innovative bonds with unusual features; these issues illustrate that bond design can be extremely flexible. Here are examples of some novel bonds. They should give you a sense of the potential variety in security design.

Inverse floaters   These are similar to the floating-rate bonds we described earlier, except that the coupon rate on these bonds *falls* when the general level of interest rates rises. Investors in these bonds suffer doubly when rates rise. Not only does the present value of each dollar of cash flow from the bond fall as the discount rate rises but the level of those cash flows falls as well. (Of course investors in these bonds benefit doubly when rates fall.)

Asset-backed bonds   Walt Disney has issued bonds with coupon rates tied to the financial performance of several of its films. Similarly, "David Bowie bonds" have been issued with payments that will be tied to royalties on some of his albums. These are examples of asset-backed securities. The income from a specified group of assets is used to service the debt. More conventional asset-backed securities are mortgage-backed securities or securities backed by auto or credit card loans, as we discussed in Chapter 2.

Pay-in-kind bonds   Issuers of pay-in-kind bonds may choose to pay interest either in cash or in additional bonds. If the issuer is short on cash, it will likely choose to pay with new bonds rather than scarce cash.

Catastrophe bonds   Oriental Land Co., which manages Tokyo Disneyland, issued a bond in 1999 with a final payment that depended on whether there had been an earthquake near the park. The Swiss firm Winterthur once issued a bond whose payments will be cut if a severe hailstorm in Switzerland results in extensive payouts on Winterthur policies. These bonds are a way to transfer "catastrophe risk" from insurance companies to the capital markets. Investors in these bonds receive compensation in the form of higher coupon rates for taking on the risk. But in the event of a catastrophe, the bondholders will give up all or part of their investments. "Disaster" can be defined either by total insured losses or by criteria such as wind speed in a hurricane or Richter level in an earthquake. Issuance of catastrophe bonds has surged in recent years, rising from about $1 billion in 2000 to $9 billion in 2006, as insurers have sought ways to spread their risks across a wider spectrum of the capital market. The nearby box discusses such "cat bonds" in greater detail.

Indexed bonds   Indexed bonds make payments that are tied to a general price index or the price of a particular commodity. For example, Mexico has issued bonds with payments that depend on the price of oil. Some bonds are indexed to the general price level. The United States Treasury started issuing such inflation-indexed bonds in January 1997. They are called Treasury Inflation Protected Securities (TIPS). By tying the par value of the bond to the general level of prices, coupon payments, as well as the final repayment of par value, on these bonds increase in direct proportion to the consumer price index. Therefore, the interest rate on these bonds is a risk-free real rate.

To illustrate how TIPS work, consider a newly issued bond with a three-year maturity, par value of $1,000, and a coupon rate of 4%. For simplicity, we will assume the bond makes annual coupon payments. Assume that inflation turns out to be 2%, 3%, and 1% in the next three years. Table 10.1 shows how the bond cash flows will be calculated. The first payment

KATRINA CLAIMS COULD LEAVE HOLDERS OF A "CAT BOND" WITH MAJOR LOSSES

As Hurricane Katrina approached the Gulf Coast, those anxiously following the storm included big investors around the globe. They are owners of $5.3 billion of "catastrophe bonds" that insurers issued in recent years to help pay claims from natural disasters.

Now, it appears holders of one such "cat bond" may be out of pocket by almost $200 million, while most of the other investors have avoided such losses. The bond in question: a special-purpose vehicle called Kamp Re. Under the terms of the $190 million bond, investors lose their money if Zurich Financial Services, the big Swiss insurance company, pays insurance claims of more than $1 billion on any hurricane or earthquake in the U.S. within five years.

Here is how cat bonds generally work: Insurance companies sell bonds to investors and agree to pay them an annual interest rate, typically three to five percentage points above the benchmark London Interbank Offered Rate, or LIBOR. However, if a natural catastrophe strikes of sufficient magnitude—measured by wind speed, earthquake force, or insured losses—the issuer gets to keep the cash to help pay its policyholders' claims.

Katrina, to be sure, was a big deal. U.S. risk-management firm ISO estimated that total private-sector insurance claims would amount to $34.4 billion, making it the costliest natural disaster in history. Other estimates have put insured losses as high as $60 billion.

But the triggers for most catastrophe bonds weren't met. That is because they are set so high as to be triggered only by a once-a-century storm. Christian Mumenthaler, Swiss Re's chief risk officer, said in an interview, "We set an extreme event at insured losses of $80 billion or $90 billion" in industrywide damage.

About half of the $5.3 billion in catastrophe bonds outstanding have trigger criteria based on objective parameters such as wind speed or earthquake force. In the event of a major storm like Katrina, Swiss Re's cat bonds take readouts from 3,600 weather stations around the U.S. Eastern and Southern coastline. The wind speed at each station is weighted according to the amount of insurance the company has underwritten in each location.

The other approximately half of the total bonds outstanding, such as the Kamp Re bonds, belongs to a second category known as indemnity bonds. They pay out according to actual insurance losses.

SOURCE: Charles Fleming, *The Wall Street Journal*, October 6, 2005, p. C1.

---

comes at the end of the first year, at $t = 1$. Because inflation over the year was 2%, the par value of the bond increases from $1,000 to $1,020; since the coupon rate is 4%, the coupon payment is 4% of this amount, or $40.80. Notice that principal value increases by the inflation rate, and because the coupon payments are 4% of principal, they too increase in proportion to the general price level. Therefore, the cash flows paid by the bond are fixed in *real* terms. When the bond matures, the investor receives a final coupon payment of $42.44 plus the (price-level-indexed) repayment of principal, $1,061.11.[4]

The *nominal* rate of return on the bond in the first year is

$$\text{Nominal return} = \frac{\text{Interest} + \text{Price appreciation}}{\text{Initial price}} = \frac{40.80 + 20}{1000} = 6.08\%$$

$$m_t = m_{t-1}(1 + i_t) = m_{t-1}\left(\frac{CPI_t}{CPI_{t-1}}\right)$$

TABLE 10.1

Principal and interest payments for a Treasury Inflation Protected Security

Time	Inflation in Year Just Ended	Par Value	Coupon Payment	+	Principal Repayment	=	Total Payment
0		$1,000.00					
1	2%	1,020.00	$40.80		0		$40.80
2	3	1,050.60	42.02		0		42.02
3	1	1,061.11	42.44		$1,061.11		1,103.55

[4] By the way, total nominal income (i.e., coupon plus that year's increase in principal) is treated as taxable income in each year.

The real rate of return is precisely the 4% real yield on the bond:

$$\text{Real return} = \frac{1 + \text{Nominal return}}{1 + \text{Inflation}} - 1 = \frac{1.0608}{1.02} = .04, \text{ or } 4\%$$

One can show in a similar manner (see Problem 12 in the end-of-chapter questions) that the rate of return in each of the three years is 4% as long as the real yield on the bond remains constant. If real yields do change, then there will be capital gains or losses on the bond. In mid-2007, the real yield on TIPS bonds was about 2.6%.

10.2   BOND PRICING

Because a bond's coupon and principal repayments all occur months or years in the future, the price an investor would be willing to pay for a claim to those payments depends on the value of dollars to be received in the future compared to dollars in hand today. This "present value" calculation depends in turn on market interest rates. As we saw in Chapter 5, the nominal risk-free interest rate equals the sum of (1) a real risk-free rate of return and (2) a premium above the real rate to compensate for expected inflation. In addition, because most bonds are not riskless, the discount rate will embody an additional premium that reflects bond-specific characteristics such as default risk, liquidity, tax attributes, call risk, and so on.

We simplify for now by assuming there is one interest rate that is appropriate for discounting cash flows of any maturity, but we can relax this assumption easily. In practice, there may be different discount rates for cash flows accruing in different periods. For the time being, however, we ignore this refinement.

To value a security, we discount its expected cash flows by the appropriate discount rate. The cash flows from a bond consist of coupon payments until the maturity date plus the final payment of par value. Therefore

$$\text{Bond value} = \text{Present value of coupons} + \text{Present value of par value}$$

If we call the maturity date T and call the discount rate r, the bond value can be written as

$$\text{Bond value} = \sum_{t=1}^{T} \frac{\text{Coupon}}{(1 + r)^t} + \frac{\text{Par value}}{(1 + r)^T} \tag{10.1}$$

The summation sign in Equation 10.1 directs us to add the present value of each coupon payment; each coupon is discounted based on the time until it will be paid. The first term on the right-hand side of Equation 10.1 is the present value of an annuity. The second term is the present value of a single amount, the final payment of the bond's par value.

You may recall from an introductory finance class that the present value of a $1 annuity that lasts for T periods when the interest rate equals r is $\frac{1}{r}\left[1 - \frac{1}{(1 + r)^T}\right]$. We call this expression the T-period *annuity factor* for an interest rate of r.[5] Similarly, we call $\frac{1}{(1 + r)^T}$ the

[5]Here is a quick derivation of the formula for the present value of an annuity. An annuity lasting T periods can be viewed as an equivalent to a perpetuity whose first payment comes at the end of the current period *less* another perpetuity whose first payment doesn't come until the end of period $T + 1$. The immediate perpetuity net of the delayed perpetuity provides exactly T payments. We know that the value of a $1 per period perpetuity is $1/r$. Therefore, the present value of the delayed perpetuity is $1/r$ discounted for T additional periods, or $\frac{1}{r} \times \frac{1}{(1 + r)^T}$. The present value of the annuity is the present value of the first perpetuity minus the present value of the delayed perpetuity, or $\frac{1}{r}\left[1 - \frac{1}{(1 + r)^T}\right]$.

PV factor, i.e., the present value of a single payment of $1 to be received in T periods. Therefore, we can write the price of the bond as

$$\text{Price} = \text{Coupon} \times \frac{1}{r}\left[1 - \frac{1}{(1+r)^T}\right] + \text{Par value} \times \frac{1}{(1+r)^T} \qquad \textbf{(10.2)}$$

$$= \text{Coupon} \times \text{Annuity factor}(r, T) + \text{Par value} \times \text{PV factor}(r, T)$$

EXAMPLE   10.2

Bond Pricing

We discussed earlier an 8% coupon, 30-year maturity bond with par value of $1,000 paying 60 semiannual coupon payments of $40 each. Suppose that the interest rate is 8% annually, or $r = 4\%$ per six-month period. Then the value of the bond can be written as

$$\text{Price} = \sum_{t=1}^{60} \frac{\$40}{(1.04)^t} + \frac{\$1,000}{(1.04)^{60}}$$

$$= \$40 \times \text{Annuity factor}(4\%, 60) + \$1,000 \times \text{PV factor}(4\%, 60)$$

It is easy to confirm that the present value of the bond's 60 semiannual coupon payments of $40 each is $904.94, and that the $1,000 final payment of par value has a present value of $95.06, for a total bond value of $1,000. You can calculate the value directly from Equation 10.2, perform these calculations on any financial calculator,[6] use a spreadsheet (see Spreadsheet 10.1 below), or a set of present value tables.

In this example, the coupon rate equals the market interest rate, and the bond price equals par value. If the interest rate were not equal to the bond's coupon rate, the bond would not sell at par value. For example, if the interest rate were to rise to 10% (5% per six months), the bond's price would fall by $189.29, to $810.71, as follows

$$\$40 \times \text{Annuity factor}(5\%, 60) + \$1,000 \times \text{PV factor}(5\%, 60)$$

$$= \$757.17 + \$53.54 = \$810.71$$

(handwritten notes in margin: .09506, $\frac{1}{.04}\left[1 - \frac{1}{(1.04)^{60}}\right]$, 25 X, 22, 1000, 10.51962741, 22.62)

At a higher interest rate, the present value of the payments to be received by the bond-holder is lower. Therefore, the bond price will fall as market interest rates rise. This illustrates a crucial general rule in bond valuation. When interest rates rise, bond prices must fall because the present value of the bond's payments is obtained by discounting at a higher interest rate.

Figure 10.3 shows the price of the 30-year, 8% coupon bond for a range of interest rates including 8%, at which the bond sells at par, and 10%, at which it sells for $810.71. The negative slope illustrates the inverse relationship between prices and yields. Note also from the figure (and from Table 10.2) that the shape of the curve implies that an increase in the interest rate results in a price decline that is smaller than the price gain resulting from a decrease of equal magnitude in the interest rate. This property of bond prices is called *convexity* because of the convex shape of the bond price curve. This curvature reflects the fact that progressive increases in the interest rate result in progressively smaller reductions in the bond price.[7] Therefore, the price curve becomes flatter at higher interest rates. We will return to the issue of convexity in the next chapter.

(handwritten note in margin: −.015)

CONCEPT *check* **10.2**

Calculate the price of the bond for a market interest rate of 3% per half year. Compare the capital gains for the interest rate decline to the losses incurred when the rate increases to 5%.

---

[6]On your financial calculator, you would enter the following inputs: *n* (number of periods) = 60; FV (face or future value) = 1000; PMT (payment each period) = 40; *i* (per period interest rate) = 4%; then you would compute the price of the bond (COMP PV or CPT PV). You should find that the price is $1,000. Actually, most calculators will display the result as *minus* $1,000. This is because most (but not all) calculators treat the initial purchase price of the bond as a cash *outflow*. We will discuss financial calculators and spreadsheets more fully in a few pages.

[7]The progressively smaller impact of interest rate increases results from the fact that at higher rates the bond is worth less. Therefore, an additional increase in rates operates on a smaller initial base, resulting in a smaller price reduction.

FIGURE 10.3

The inverse relationship between bond prices and yields. Price of an 8% coupon bond with 30-year maturity making semiannual coupon payments.

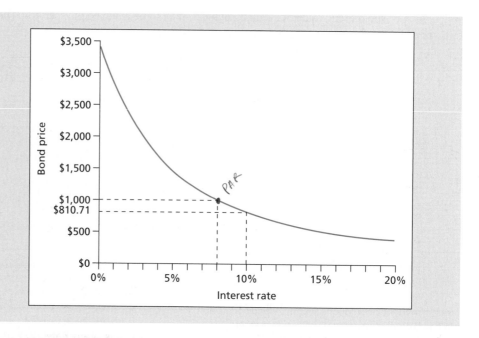

TABLE 10.2	**Time to Maturity**	**Bond Price at Given Market Interest Rate**				
Bond prices at different interest rates (8% coupon bond, coupons paid semiannually)		**4%**	**6%**	**8%**	**10%**	**12%**
	1 year	$1,038.83	$1,019.13	$1,000.00	$981.41	$963.33
	10 years	1,327.03	1,148.77	1,000.00	875.38	770.60
	20 years	1,547.11	1,231.15	1,000.00	828.41	699.07
	30 years	1,695.22	1,276.76	1,000.00	810.71	676.77

Corporate bonds typically are issued at par value. This means the underwriters of the bond issue (the firms that market the bonds to the public for the issuing corporation) must choose a coupon rate that very closely approximates market yields. In a primary issue of bonds, the underwriters attempt to sell the newly issued bonds directly to their customers. If the coupon rate is inadequate, investors will not pay par value for the bonds.

After the bonds are issued, bondholders may buy or sell bonds in secondary markets, such as the one operated by the New York Stock Exchange or the over-the-counter market, where most bonds trade. In these secondary markets, bond prices move in accordance with market forces. The bond prices fluctuate inversely with the market interest rate.

The inverse relationship between price and yield is a central feature of fixed-income securities. Interest rate fluctuations represent the main source of risk in the bond market, and we devote considerable attention in the next chapter to assessing the sensitivity of bond prices to market yields. For now, however, it is sufficient to highlight one key factor that determines that sensitivity, namely, the maturity of the bond.

A general rule in evaluating bond price risk is that, keeping all other factors the same, the longer the maturity of the bond, the greater the sensitivity of its price to fluctuations in the interest rate. For example, consider Table 10.2, which presents the price of an 8% coupon bond at different market yields and times to maturity. For any departure of the interest rate from 8% (the rate at which the bond sells at par value), the change in the bond price is greater for longer times to maturity.

This makes sense. If you buy the bond at par with an 8% coupon rate, and market rates subsequently rise, then you suffer a loss: You have tied up your money earning 8% when alternative investments offer higher returns. This is reflected in a capital loss on the bond—a fall in its market price. The longer the period for which your money is tied up, the greater the

SPREADSHEET 10.2

Finding yield to maturity using a spreadsheet (30-year maturity bond, coupon rate = 8%, price = 127.676% of par)

eXcel

**Please visit us at
www.mhhe.com/bkm**

	A	B	C	D	E	F	G
1					Semiannual		Annual
2					coupons		coupons
3							
4	Settlement date				1/1/2000		1/1/2000
5	Maturity date				1/1/2030		1/1/2030
6	Annual coupon rate				0.08		0.08
7	Bond price (flat)				127.676		127.676
8	Redemption value (% of face value)				100		100
9	Coupon payments per year				2		1
10							
11	Yield to maturity (decimal)				0.0600		0.0599
12							
13							
14		The formula entered here is: =YIELD(B4,B5,B6,B7,B8,B9)					

($1,000) rather than by the bond price ($1,276). In turn, the current yield exceeds yield to maturity because the yield to maturity accounts for the built-in capital loss on the bond; the bond bought today for $1,276 will eventually fall in value to $1,000 at maturity.

This example illustrates a general rule: For **premium bonds** (bonds selling above par value), coupon rate is greater than current yield, which in turn is greater than yield to maturity. For **discount bonds** (bonds selling below par value), these relationships are reversed (see Concept Check 10.3).

It is common to hear people talking loosely about the yield on a bond. In these cases, they almost always are referring to the yield to maturity.

premium bonds

Bonds selling above par value.

discount bonds

Bonds selling below par value.

CONCEPT **10.3**
check

What will be the relationship among coupon rate, current yield, and yield to maturity for bonds selling at discounts from par? Illustrate using the 8% (semiannual payment) coupon bond assuming it is selling at a yield to maturity of 10%.

Yield to Call

Yield to maturity is calculated on the assumption that the bond will be held until maturity. What if the bond is callable, however, and may be retired prior to the maturity date? How should we measure average rate of return for bonds subject to a call provision?

Figure 10.4 illustrates the risk of call to the bondholder. The colored line is the value at various market interest rates of a "straight" (that is, noncallable) bond with par value of $1,000, an 8% coupon rate, and a 30-year time to maturity. If interest rates fall, the bond price, which

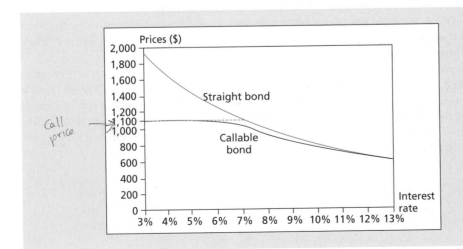

FIGURE 10.4

Bond prices: Callable and straight debt. Coupon = 8%; maturity = 30 years; semiannual payments equals the present value of the promised payments, can rise substantially. Now consider a bond that has the same coupon rate and maturity date but is callable at 110% of par value, or $1,100. When interest rates fall, the present value of the bond's *scheduled* payments rises, but the call provision allows the issuer to repurchase the bond at the call price. If the call price is less than the present value of the scheduled payments, the issuer can call the bond at the expense of the bondholder.

The dark line in Figure 10.4 is the value of the callable bond. At high market interest rates, the risk of call is negligible because the present value of scheduled payments is less than the call price; therefore, the values of the straight and callable bonds converge. At lower rates, however, the values of the bonds begin to diverge, with the difference reflecting the value of the firm's option to reclaim the callable bond at the call price. At very low market rates the present value of schedule payments significantly exceeds the call price, so the bond is called. Its value at this point is simply the call price, $1,100.

This analysis suggests that bond market analysts might be more interested in a bond's yield to call rather than its yield to maturity, especially if the bond is likely to be called. The yield to call is calculated just like the yield to maturity, except that the time until call replaces time until maturity and the call price replaces the par value. This computation is sometimes called "yield to first call," as it assumes the issuer will call the bond as soon as it may do so.

EXAMPLE 10.4
Yield to Call

Suppose the 8% coupon, 30-year maturity bond sells for $1,150 and is callable in 10 years at a call price of $1,100. Its yield to maturity and yield to call would be calculated using the following inputs:

	Yield to Call	Yield to Maturity
Coupon payment	$40	$40
Number of semiannual periods	20 periods	60 periods
Final payment	$1,100	$1,000
Price	$1,150	$1,150

Yield to call is then 6.64%. To confirm this on your calculator, input $n = 20$; PV $= (-)1150$; FV $= 1100$; PMT $= 40$; compute i as 3.32%, or 6.64% bond equivalent yield. In contrast, yield to maturity is 6.82%. To confirm, input $n = 60$; PV $= (-)1150$; FV $= 1000$; PMT $= 40$; compute i as 3.41%, or 6.82% bond equivalent yield. In Excel, you can calculate yield to call as =YIELD(DATE(2000,01,01), DATE(2010,01,01), .08, 115, 110, 2). Notice that redemption value is 110, i.e., 110% of par value.

We have noted that most callable bonds are issued with an initial period of call protection. In addition, an implicit form of call protection operates for bonds selling at deep discounts from their call prices. Even if interest rates fall a bit, deep-discount bonds still will sell below the call price and thus will not be subject to a call.

Premium bonds that might be selling near their call prices, however, are especially apt to be called if rates fall further. If interest rates fall, a callable premium bond is likely to provide a lower return than could be earned on a discount bond whose potential price appreciation is not limited by the likelihood of a call. Investors in premium bonds often are more interested in the bond's yield to call rather than yield to maturity as a consequence, because it may appear to them that the bond will be retired at the call date.

CONCEPT check 10.4

A 20-year maturity 9% coupon bond paying coupons semiannually is callable in five years at a call price of $1,050. The bond currently sells at a yield to maturity of 8% (bond equivalent yield). What is the yield to call?

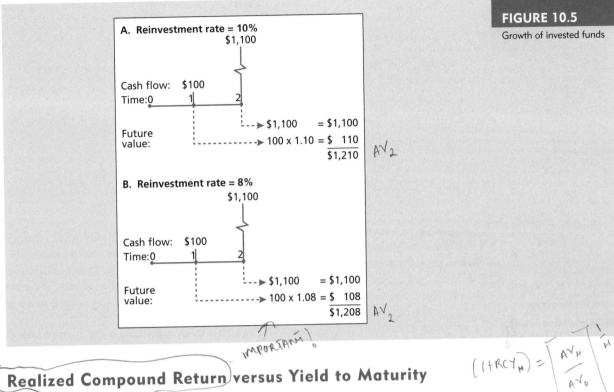

FIGURE 10.5

Growth of invested funds

$(1 + RCY_H) = \left[\dfrac{AV_H}{AV_0}\right]^{\frac{1}{H}}$

Realized Compound Return versus Yield to Maturity

IMPORTANT

We have noted that yield to maturity will equal the rate of return realized over the life of the bond if all coupons are reinvested at an interest rate equal to the bond's yield to maturity. Consider for example, a two-year bond selling at par value paying a 10% coupon once a year. The yield to maturity is 10%. If the $100 coupon payment is reinvested at an interest rate of 10%, the $1,000 investment in the bond will grow after two years to $1,210, as illustrated in Figure 10.5, Panel A. The coupon paid in the first year is reinvested and grows with interest to a second-year value of $110, which, together with the second coupon payment and payment of par value in the second year, results in a total value of $1,210. To summarize, the initial value of the investment is $V_0 = \$1,000$. The final value in two years is $V_2 = \$1,210$. The compound rate of return, therefore, is calculated as follows.

$$V_0 (1 + r)^2 = V_2$$
$$\$1,000 (1 + r)^2 = \$1,210$$
$$r = .10 = 10\%$$

With a reinvestment rate equal to the 10% yield to maturity, the **realized compound return** equals yield to maturity.

But what if the reinvestment rate is not 10%? If the coupon can be invested at more than 10%, funds will grow to more than $1,210, and the realized compound return will exceed 10%. If the reinvestment rate is less than 10%, so will be the realized compound return. Consider the following example.

realized compound return

Compound rate of return on a bond with all coupons reinvested until maturity.

If the interest rate earned on the first coupon is less than 10%, the final value of the investment will be less than $1,210, and the realized compound yield will be less than 10%. Suppose the interest rate at which the coupon can be invested equals 8%. The following calculations are illustrated in Panel B of Figure 10.5.

EXAMPLE 10.5

Realized Compound Return

(continued)

EXAMPLE   10.5

Realized Compound Return (concluded)

Future value of first coupon payment with interest earnings	$100 × 1.08 = $ 108
Cash payment in second year (final coupon plus par value)	1,100
Total value of investment with reinvested coupons	$1,208

The realized compound return is the compound rate of growth of invested funds, assuming that all coupon payments are reinvested. The investor purchased the bond for par at $1,000, and this investment grew to $1,208.

$$\$1,000(1 + r)^2 = \$1,208$$
$$r = 0.0991 = 9.91\%$$

Example 10.5 highlights the problem with conventional yield to maturity when reinvestment rates can change over time. However, in an economy with future interest rate uncertainty, the rates at which interim coupons will be reinvested are not yet known. Therefore, while realized compound return can be computed *after* the investment period ends, it cannot be computed in advance without a forecast of future reinvestment rates. This reduces much of the attraction of the realized return measure.

horizon analysis

Analysis of bond returns over multiyear horizon, based on forecasts of bond's yield to maturity and reinvestment rate of coupons.

We also can calculate realized compound yield over holding periods greater than one period. This is called **horizon analysis** and is similar to the procedure in Example 10.5. The forecast of total return will depend on your forecasts of *both* the yield to maturity of the bond when you sell it *and* the rate at which you are able to reinvest coupon income. With a longer investment horizon, however, reinvested coupons will be a larger component of your final proceeds.

EXAMPLE   10.6

Horizon Analysis

Suppose you buy a 30-year, 7.5% (annual payment) coupon bond for $980 (when its yield to maturity is 7.67%) and plan to hold it for 20 years. Your forecast is that the bond's yield to maturity will be 8% when it is sold and that the reinvestment rate on the coupons will be 6%. At the end of your investment horizon, the bond will have 10 years remaining until expiration, so the forecast sales price (using a yield to maturity of 8%) will be $966.45. The 20 coupon payments will grow with compound interest to $2,758.92. (This is the future value of a 20-year $75 annuity with an interest rate of 6%.)

Based on these forecasts, your $980 investment will grow in 20 years to $966.45 + $2,758.92 = $3,725.37. This corresponds to an annualized compound return of 6.90%:

$$\$980 (1 + r)^{20} = \$3,725.37$$
$$r = .0690 = 6.90\%$$

reinvestment rate risk

Uncertainty surrounding the cumulative future value of reinvested bond coupon payments.

Examples 10.5 and 10.6 demonstrate that as interest rates change, bond investors are actually subject to two sources of offsetting risk. On the one hand, when rates rise, bond prices fall, which reduces the value of the portfolio. On the other hand, reinvested coupon income will compound more rapidly at those higher rates. This **reinvestment rate risk** will offset the impact of price risk. In the next chapter, we will explore this trade-off in more detail and will discover that by carefully tailoring their bond portfolios, investors can precisely balance these two effects for any given investment horizon.

10.4   BOND PRICES OVER TIME

As we noted earlier, a bond will sell at par value when its coupon rate equals the market interest rate. In these circumstances, the investor receives fair compensation for the time value of money in the form of the recurring coupon payments. No further capital gain is necessary to provide fair compensation.

When the coupon rate is lower than the market interest rate, the coupon payments alone will not provide investors as high a return as they could earn elsewhere in the market. To receive a fair return on such an investment, investors also need to earn price appreciation on their bonds. The bonds, therefore, would have to sell below par value to provide a "built-in" capital gain on the investment.

EXAMPLE 10.7

Fair Holding-Period Return

To illustrate build-in capital gains or losses, suppose a bond was issued several years ago when the interest rate was 7%. The bond's annual coupon rate was thus set at 7%. (We will suppose for simplicity that the bond pays its coupon annually.) Now, with three years left in the bond's life, the interest rate is 8% per year. The bond's fair market price is the present value of the remaining annual coupons plus payment of par value. That present value is[10]

$$\$70 \times \text{Annuity factor (8\%, 3)} + \$1,000 \times \text{PV factor (8\%, 3)} = \$974.23$$

which is less than par value.
    In another year, after the next coupon is paid, the bond would sell at

$$\$70 \times \text{Annuity factor (8\%, 2)} + \$1,000 \times \text{PV factor (8\%, 2)} = \$982.17$$

thereby yielding a capital gain over the year of $7.94. If an investor had purchased the bond at $974.23, the total return over the year would equal the coupon payment plus capital gain, or $70 + $7.94 = $77.94. This represents a rate of return of $77.94/$974.23, or 8%, exactly the current rate of return available elsewhere in the market.

CONCEPT check 10.5

What will be the price of the bond in Example 10.7 in yet another year, when only one year remains until maturity? What is the rate of return to an investor who purchases the bond at $982.17 and sells it one year later?

When bond prices are set according to the present value formula, any discount from par value provides an anticipated capital gain that will augment a below-market coupon rate just sufficiently to provide a fair total rate of return. Conversely, if the coupon rate exceeds the market interest rate, the interest income by itself is greater than that available elsewhere in the market. Investors will bid up the price of these bonds above their par values. As the bonds approach maturity, they will fall in value because fewer of these above-market coupon payments remain. The resulting capital losses offset the large coupon payments so that the bondholder again receives only a fair rate of return.

Problem 9 at the end of the chapter asks you to work through the case of the high coupon bond. Figure 10.6 traces out the price paths of high and low coupon bonds (net of accrued interest) as time to maturity approaches, at least for the case in which the market interest rate is constant. The low coupon bond enjoys capital gains, while the high coupon bond suffers capital losses.[11]

We use these examples to show that each bond offers investors the same total rate of return. Although the capital gain versus income components differ, the price of each bond is set to provide competitive rates, as we should expect in well-functioning capital markets. Security returns all should be comparable on an after-tax risk-adjusted basis. If they are not, investors will try to sell low-return securities, thereby driving down the prices until the total return at the now-lower price is competitive with other securities. Prices should continue to adjust until all securities are fairly priced in that expected returns are comparable (given appropriate risk and tax adjustments).

[10]Using a calculator, enter $n = 3$, $i = 8$, PMT = 70, FV = 1000, and compute PV.
[11]If interest rates are volatile, the price path will be "jumpy," vibrating around the price path in Figure 10.6 and reflecting capital gains or losses as interest rates fluctuate. Ultimately, however, the price must reach par value at the maturity date, so on average, the price of the premium bond will fall over time while that of the discount bond will rise.

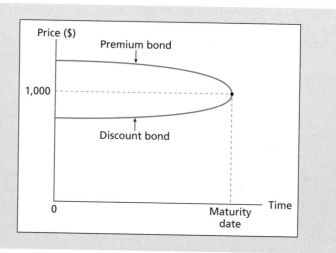

FIGURE 10.6

Price paths of coupon
bonds in the case
of constant market
interest rates

Yield to Maturity versus Holding-Period Return

In Example 10.7, the holding-period return and the yield to maturity were equal. The bond yield started and ended the year at 8%, and the bond's holding-period return also equaled 8%. This turns out to be a general result. When the yield to maturity is unchanged over the period, the rate of return on the bond will equal that yield. As we noted, this should not be surprising: The bond must offer a rate of return competitive with those available on other securities.

However, when yields fluctuate, so will a bond's rate of return. Unanticipated changes in market rates will result in unanticipated changes in bond returns, and after the fact, a bond's holding-period return can be better or worse than the yield at which it initially sells. An increase in the bond's yield to maturity acts to reduce its price, which means that the holding-period return will be less than the initial yield. Conversely, a decline in yield to maturity results in a holding-period return greater than the initial yield.

EXAMPLE   10.8

*Yield to Maturity
versus Holding-
Period Return*

Consider a 30-year bond paying an annual coupon of $80 and selling at par value of $1,000. The bond's initial yield to maturity is 8%. If the yield remains at 8% over the year, the bond price will remain at par, so the holding-period return also will be 8%. But if the yield falls below 8%, the bond price will increase. Suppose the yield falls and the price increases to $1,050. Then the holding-period return is greater than 8%:

$$\text{Holding-period return} = \frac{\$80 + (\$1,050 - \$1,000)}{\$1,000} = .13, \text{ or } 13\%$$

CONCEPT
check **10.6**

Show that if the yield to maturity increases, then holding-period return is *less* than that initial yield. For example, suppose in Example 10.8 that by the end of the first year, the bond's yield to maturity is 8.5%. Find the one-year holding-period return and compare it to the bond's initial 8% yield to maturity.

Here is another way to think about the difference between yield to maturity and holding-period return. Yield to maturity depends only on the bond's coupon, *current* price, and par value at maturity. All of these values are observable today, so yield to maturity can be easily calculated. Yield to maturity can be interpreted as a measure of the *average* rate of return if the investment in the bond is held until the bond matures. In contrast, holding-period return is the rate of return over a particular investment period and depends on the market price of the bond at the end of that holding period; of course this price is *not* known today. Since bond prices over the holding period will respond to unanticipated changes in interest rates, holding-period return can at most be forecast.

Zero-Coupon Bonds and Treasury STRIPS

Original issue discount bonds are less common than coupon bonds issued at par. These are bonds that are issued intentionally with low coupon rates that cause the bond to sell at a discount from par value. An extreme example of this type of bond is the *zero-coupon bond,* which carries no coupons and provides all its return in the form of price appreciation. Zeros provide only one cash flow to their owners, on the maturity date of the bond.

U.S. Treasury bills are examples of short-term zero-coupon instruments. If the bill has face value of $10,000, the Treasury issues or sells it for some amount less than $10,000, agreeing to repay $10,000 at maturity. All of the investor's return comes in the form of price appreciation.

Longer term zero-coupon bonds are commonly created from coupon-bearing notes and bonds with the help of the U.S. Treasury. A broker that purchases a Treasury coupon bond may ask the Treasury to break down the cash flows to be paid by the bond into a series of independent securities, where each security is a claim to one of the payments of the original bond. For example, a 10-year coupon bond would be "stripped" of its 20 semiannual coupons and each coupon payment would be treated as a stand-alone zero-coupon bond. The maturities of these bonds would thus range from six months to 10 years. The final payment of principal would be treated as another stand-alone zero-coupon security. Each of the payments would then be treated as an independent security and assigned its own CUSIP number, the security identifier that allows for electronic trading over the Fedwire system. The payments are still considered obligations of the U.S. Treasury. The Treasury program under which coupon stripping is performed is called STRIPS (Separate Trading of Registered Interest and Principal of Securities), and these zero-coupon securities are called *Treasury strips.*

What should happen to prices of zeros as time passes? On their maturity dates, zeros must sell for par value. Before maturity, however, they should sell at discounts from par, because of the time value of money. As time passes, price should approach par value. In fact, if the interest rate is constant, a zero's price will increase at exactly the rate of interest.

To illustrate this property, consider a zero with 30 years until maturity, and suppose the market interest rate is 10% per year. The price of the bond today will be $1,000/(1.10)^{30} = $57.31. Next year, with only 29 years until maturity, if the yield to maturity is still 10%, the price will be $1,000/(1.10)^{29} = $63.04, a 10% increase over its previous-year value. Because the par value of the bond is now discounted for one fewer year, its price has increased by the one-year discount factor.

Figure 10.7 presents the price path of a 30-year zero-coupon bond until its maturity date for an annual market interest rate of 10%. The bond's price rises exponentially, not linearly, until its maturity.

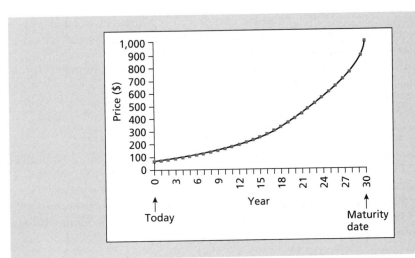

FIGURE 10.7

The price of a 30-year zero-coupon bond over time at a yield to maturity of 10%. Price equals $1000/(1.10)^T$ where T is time until maturity.

After-Tax Returns

The tax authorities recognize that the "built-in" price appreciation on original-issue discount (OID) bonds such as zero-coupon bonds represents an implicit interest payment to the holder of the security. The Internal Revenue Service (IRS), therefore, calculates a price appreciation schedule to impute taxable interest income for the built-in appreciation during a tax year, even if the asset is not sold or does not mature until a future year. Any additional gains or losses that arise from changes in market interest rates are treated as capital gains or losses if the OID bond is sold during the tax year.

EXAMPLE   10.9

Taxation of Original-Issue Discount Bonds

If the interest rate originally is 10%, the 30-year zero would be issued at a price of $1,000/(1.10)^{30}$ = \$57.31. The following year, the IRS calculates what the bond price would be if its yield were still 10%. This is $1,000/(1.10)^{29}$ = \$63.04. Therefore, the IRS imputes interest income of \$63.04 − \$57.31 = \$5.73. This amount is subject to tax. Notice that the imputed interest income is based on a "constant yield method" that ignores any changes in market interest rates.

If interest rates actually fall, let's say to 9.9%, the bond price will be $1,000/(1.099)^{29}$ = \$64.72. If the bond is sold, then the difference between \$64.72 and \$63.04 will be treated as capital gains income and taxed at the capital gains tax rate. If the bond is not sold, then the price difference is an unrealized capital gain and does not result in taxes in that year. In either case, the investor must pay taxes on the \$5.73 of imputed interest at the ordinary income tax rate.

The procedure illustrated in Example 10.9 applies as well to the taxation of other original issue discount bonds, even if they are not zero-coupon bonds. Consider, as another example, a 30-year maturity bond that is issued with a coupon rate of 4% and a yield to maturity of 8%. For simplicity, we will assume that the bond pays coupons once annually. Because of the low coupon rate, the bond will be issued at a price far below par value, specifically at a price of \$549.69. (Confirm this for yourself.) If the bond's yield to maturity is still 8%, then its price in one year will rise to \$553.66. (Confirm this also.) This would provide a pretax holding-period return of exactly 8%:

$$HPR = \frac{\$40 + (\$553.66 - \$549.69)}{\$549.69} = 0.08$$

The increase in the bond price based on a constant yield, however, is treated as interest income, so the investor is required to pay taxes on imputed interest income of \$553.66 − \$549.69 = \$3.97, as well as on the explicit coupon income of \$40. If the bond's yield actually changes during the year, the difference between the bond's price and the "constant yield value" of \$553.66 would be treated as capital gains income if the bond were sold at year-end.

CONCEPT check 10.7

Suppose that the yield to maturity of the 4% coupon, 30-year maturity bond falls to 7% by the end of the first year, and that the investor sells the bond after the first year. If the investor's federal plus state tax rate on interest income is 38% and the combined tax rate on capital gains is 20%, what is the investor's after-tax rate of return?

10.5 DEFAULT RISK AND BOND PRICING

Although bonds generally *promise* a fixed flow of income, that income stream is not risk-less unless the investor can be sure the issuer will not default on the obligation. While U.S. government bonds may be treated as free of default risk, this is not true of corporate bonds. If the company goes bankrupt, the bondholders will not receive all the payments they have been promised. Therefore, the actual payments on these bonds are uncertain, for they depend to some degree on the ultimate financial status of the firm.

Bond default risk is measured by Moody's Investor Services, Standard & Poor's Corporation, and Fitch Investors Service, all of which provide financial information on firms as well as the credit risk of large corporate and municipal bond issues. International sovereign bonds, which also entail default risk, especially in emerging markets, also are commonly rated for default risk. Each rating firm assigns letter grades to reflect its assessment of bond safety. The top rating is AAA or Aaa. Moody's modifies each rating class with a 1, 2, or 3 suffix (e.g., Aaa1, Aaa2, Aaa3) to provide a finer gradation of ratings. The other agencies use a + or − modification.

Those rated BBB or above (S&P, Fitch) or Baa and above (Moody's) are considered **investment grade bonds,** while lower-rated bonds are classified as **speculative grade** or **junk bonds.** Certain regulated institutional investors such as insurance companies have not always been allowed to invest in speculative grade bonds.

Figure 10.8 provides the definitions of each bond rating classification.

investment grade bond

A bond rated BBB and above by Standard & Poor's, or Baa and above by Moody's.

Junk Bonds

Junk bonds, also known as *high-yield bonds,* are nothing more than speculative grade (low-rated or unrated) bonds. Before 1977, almost all junk bonds were "fallen angels," that is, bonds issued by firms that originally had investment grade ratings but that had since been downgraded. In 1977, however, firms began to issue "original-issue junk."

Much of the credit for this innovation is given to Drexel Burnham Lambert, and especially its trader, Michael Milken. Drexel had long enjoyed a niche as a junk bond trader and had established a network of potential investors in junk bonds. Firms not able to muster an investment grade rating were happy to have Drexel (and other investment bankers) market their bonds directly to the public, as this opened up a new source of financing. Junk issues were a lower-cost financing alternative than borrowing from banks.

High-yield bonds gained considerable notoriety in the 1980s when they were used as financing vehicles in leveraged buyouts and hostile takeover attempts. Shortly thereafter, however, the legal difficulties of Drexel and Michael Milken in connection with Wall Street's insider trading scandals of the late 1980s tainted the junk bond market.

At the height of Drexel's difficulties, the high-yield bond market nearly dried up. Since then, the market has rebounded dramatically. However, it is worth noting that the average credit quality of high-yield debt issued today is higher than the average quality in the boom years of the 1980s.

speculative grade or junk bond

A bond rated BB or lower by Standard & Poor's, or Ba or lower by Moody's, or an unrated bond.

Determinants of Bond Safety

Bond rating agencies base their quality ratings largely on an analysis of the level and trend of some of the issuer's financial ratios. The key ratios used to evaluate safety are:

1. *Coverage ratios.* Ratios of company earnings to fixed costs. For example, the *times-interest-earned ratio* is the ratio of earnings before interest payments and taxes to interest obligations. The *fixed-charge coverage ratio* includes lease payments and sinking fund payments with interest obligations to arrive at the ratio of earnings to all fixed cash obligations. Low or falling coverage ratios signal possible cash flow difficulties.

2. *Leverage ratio.* Debt-to-equity ratio. A too-high leverage ratio indicates excessive indebtedness, signaling the possibility the firm will be unable to earn enough to satisfy the obligations on its bonds.

3. *Liquidity ratios.* The two common liquidity ratios are the *current ratio* (current assets/current liabilities) and the *quick ratio* (current assets excluding inventories/current liabilities). These ratios measure the firm's ability to pay bills coming due with its most liquid assets.

4. *Profitability ratios.* Measures of rates of return on assets or equity. Profitability ratios are indicators of a firm's overall performance. The *return on assets* (earnings before interest and taxes divided by total assets) or return on equity (net income/equity) are the most

FIGURE 10.8

Definitions of each bond rating class

Sources: From Stephen A. Ross, Randolph W. Westerfield, and Jeffrey F. Jaffe, *Corporate Finance,* McGraw-Hill Publishing. Data from various editions of *Standard & Poor's Bond Guide* and *Moody's Bond Guide.*

	Bond Ratings				
	Very High Quality	High Quality	Speculative		Very Poor
Standard & Poor's	AAA AA	A BBB	BB B		CCC D
Moody's	Aaa Aa	A Baa	Ba B		Caa C

At times both Moody's and Standard & Poor's use adjustments to these ratings. S&P uses plus and minus signs: A+ is the strongest A rating and A− the weakest. Moody's uses a 1, 2, or 3 designation, with 1 indicating the strongest.

Moody's	S&P	
Aaa	AAA	Debt rated Aaa and AAA has the highest rating. Capacity to pay interest and principal is extremely strong.
Aa	AA	Debt rated Aa and AA has a very strong capacity to pay interest and repay principal. Together with the highest rating, this group comprises the high-grade bond class.
A	A	Debt rated A has a strong capacity to pay interest and repay principal, although it is somewhat more susceptible to the adverse effects of changes in circumstances and economic conditions than debt in higher-rated categories.
Baa	BBB	Debt rated Baa and BBB is regarded as having an adequate capacity to pay interest and repay principal. Whereas it normally exhibits adequate protection parameters, adverse economic conditions or changing circumstances are more likely to lead to a weakened capacity to pay interest and repay principal for debt in this category than in higher-rated categories. These bonds are medium grade obligations.
Ba	BB	Debt rated in these categories is regarded, on balance, as predomi-
B	B	nantly speculative with respect to capacity to pay interest and repay
Caa	CCC	principal in accordance with the terms of the obligation. BB and Ba
Ca	CC	indicate the lowest degree of speculation, and CC and Ca the highest degree of speculation. Although such debt will likely have some quality and protective characteristics, these are outweighed by large uncertainties or major risk exposures to adverse conditions. Some issues may be in default.
C	C	This rating is reserved for income bonds on which no interest is being paid.
D	D	Debt rated D is in default, and payment of interest and/or repayment of principal is in arrears.

popular of these measures. Firms with higher return on assets or equity should be better able to raise money in security markets because they offer prospects for better returns on the firm's investments.

5. *Cash flow-to-debt ratio.* This is the ratio of total cash flow to outstanding debt.

Standard & Poor's periodically computes median values of selected ratios for firms in several rating classes, which we present in Table 10.3. Of course, ratios must be evaluated in the context of industry standards, and analysts differ in the weights they place on particular ratios. Nevertheless, Table 10.3 demonstrates the tendency of ratios to improve along with the firm's rating class. The last line of Table 10.3 provides cumulative five-year default rates of bonds with initial ratings in each category. Credit risk varies dramatically across rating classes.

TABLE 10.3							
Financial ratios and default risk by rating class, long-term debt							

	Three-Year (2002 to 2004) Medians						
	AAA	**AA**	**A**	**BBB**	**BB**	**B**	**CCC**
A. EBIT interest coverage multiple	23.8	19.5	8.0	4.7	2.5	1.2	0.4
EBITDA interest coverage multiple	25.5	24.6	10.2	6.5	3.5	1.9	0.9
Funds from operations/total debt (%)	203.3	79.9	48.0	35.9	22.4	11.5	5.0
Free operating cash flow/total debt (%)	127.6	44.5	25.0	17.3	8.3	2.8	(2.1)
Total debt/EBITDA multiple	0.4	0.9	1.6	2.2	3.5	5.3	7.9
Return on capital (%)	27.6	27.0	17.5	13.4	11.3	8.7	3.2
Total debt/total debt + equity (%)	12.4	28.3	37.5	42.5	53.7	75.9	113.5
B. Historical 5-year default rate (%)	0.2	0.6	0.6	2.3	5.9	12.9	28.0

Note: EBITDA is earnings before interest, taxes, depreciation, and amortization

Source: *Panel A—Corporate Rating Criteria*, Standard & Poor's, 2006. Reproduced by permission of Standard & Poor's, a division of The McGraw-Hill Companies, Inc. *Panel B*—Edward Altman, "The Importance and Subtlety of Credit Rating Migration," *Journal of Banking and Finance* 22 (1998), pp.1231–1247.

Bond Indentures

In addition to specifying a payment schedule, the bond **indenture,** which is the contract between the issuer and the bondholder, also specifies a set of restrictions that protect the rights of the bondholders. Such restrictions include provisions relating to collateral, sinking funds, dividend policy, and further borrowing. The issuing firm agrees to these so-called protective covenants in order to market its bonds to investors concerned about the safety of the bond issue.

indenture

The document defining the contract between the bond issuer and the bondholder.

Sinking funds   Bonds call for the payment of par value at the end of the bond's life. This payment constitutes a large cash commitment for the issuer. To help ensure that the commitment does not create a cash flow crisis, the firm may agree to establish a **sinking fund** to spread the payment burden over several years. The fund may operate in one of two ways:

sinking fund

A bond indenture that calls for the issuer to periodically repurchase some proportion of the outstanding bonds prior to maturity.

1. The firm may repurchase a fraction of the outstanding bonds in the open market each year.
2. The firm may purchase a fraction of outstanding bonds at a special call price associated with the sinking fund provision. The firm has an option to purchase the bonds at either the market price or the sinking fund price, whichever is lower. To allocate the burden of the sinking fund call fairly among bondholders, the bonds chosen for the call are selected at random based on serial number.[12]

The sinking fund call differs from a conventional call provision in two important ways. First, the firm can repurchase only a limited fraction of the bond issue at the sinking fund call price. At best, some indentures allow firms to use a *doubling option,* which allows repurchase of double the required number of bonds at the sinking fund call price. Second, while callable bonds generally have call prices above par value, the sinking fund call price usually is set at the bond's par value.

Although sinking funds ostensibly protect bondholders by making principal repayment more likely, they can hurt the investor. The firm will choose to buy back discount bonds (selling below par) at their market price, while exercising its option to buy back premium bonds (selling above par) at par. Therefore, if interest rates fall and bond prices rise, a firm will benefit

---

[12] While it is uncommon, the sinking fund provision also may call for periodic payments to a trustee, with the payments invested so that the accumulated sum can be used for retirement of the entire issue at maturity.

from the sinking fund provision that enables it to repurchase its bonds at below-market prices. In these circumstances, the firm's gain is the bondholder's loss.

One bond issue that does not require a sinking fund is a *serial bond* issue. In a serial bond issue, the firm sells bonds with staggered maturity dates. As bonds mature sequentially, the principal repayment burden for the firm is spread over time just as it is with a sinking fund. Serial bonds do not include call provisions. Unlike sinking fund bonds, serial bonds do not confront security holders with the risk that a particular bond may be called for the sinking fund. The disadvantage of serial bonds, however, is that the bonds of each maturity date are different bonds, which reduces the liquidity of the issue. Trading these bonds, therefore, is more expensive.

subordination clauses

Restrictions on additional borrowing that stipulate that senior bondholders will be paid first in the event of bankruptcy.

Subordination of further debt

One of the factors determining bond safety is the total outstanding debt of the issuer. If you bought a bond today, you would be understandably distressed to see the firm tripling its outstanding debt tomorrow. Your bond would be of lower quality than it appeared when you bought it. To prevent firms from harming bondholders in this manner, **subordination clauses** restrict the amount of their additional borrowing. Additional debt might be required to be subordinated in priority to existing debt; that is, in the event of bankruptcy, *subordinated* or *junior* debtholders will not be paid unless and until the prior senior debt is fully paid off. For this reason, subordination is sometimes called a "me-first rule," meaning the senior (earlier) bondholders are to be paid first in the event of bankruptcy.

Dividend restrictions

Covenants also limit the dividends firms may pay. These limitations protect the bondholders because they force the firm to retain assets rather than pay them out to stockholders. A typical restriction disallows payments of dividends if cumulative dividends paid since the firm's inception exceed cumulative retained earnings plus proceeds from sales of stock.

collateral

A specific asset pledged against possible default on a bond.

Collateral

Some bonds are issued with specific collateral behind them. **Collateral** can take several forms, but it represents a particular asset of the firm that the bondholders receive if the firm defaults on the bond. If the collateral is property, the bond is called a *mortgage bond*. If the collateral takes the form of other securities held by the firm, the bond is a *collateral trust bond*. In the case of equipment, the bond is known as an *equipment obligation bond*. This last form of collateral is used most commonly by firms such as railroads, where the equipment is fairly standard and can be easily sold to another firm should the firm default and the bondholders acquire the collateral.

debenture

A bond not backed by specific collateral.

Because of the specific collateral that backs them, collateralized bonds generally are considered the safest variety of corporate bonds. General **debenture** bonds by contrast do not provide for specific collateral; they are *unsecured* bonds. The bondholder relies solely on the general earning power of the firm for the bond's safety. If the firm defaults, debenture owners become general creditors of the firm. Because they are safer, collateralized bonds generally offer lower yields than general debentures.

Figure 10.9 shows the terms of a bond issued by Mobil as described in *Moody's Industrial Manual*. The terms of the bond are typical and illustrate many of the indenture provisions we have mentioned. The bond is registered and listed on the NYSE. Although it was issued in 1991, it was not callable until 2002. Although the call price started at 105.007% of par value, it falls gradually until it reaches par after 2020.

Yield to Maturity and Default Risk

Because corporate bonds are subject to default risk, we must distinguish between the bond's promised yield to maturity and its expected yield. The promised or stated yield will be realized only if the firm meets the obligations of the bond issue. Therefore, the stated yield is the *maximum possible* yield to maturity of the bond. The expected yield to maturity must take into account the possibility of a default.

FIGURE 10.9

Callable bond issued by Mobil

Source: *Moody's Industrial Manual*, Moody's Investor Services, 1997.

```
& Mobil Corp. debenture 8s, due 2032:
              Rating — Aa2
AUTH — $250,000,000.
OUTSTG — Dec. 31, 1993, $250,000,000.
DATED — Oct. 30, 1991.
INTEREST — F&A 12.
TRUSTEE — Chemical Bank.
DENOMINATION — Fully registered, $1,000 and
integral multiples thereof. Transferable and
exchangeable without service charge.
CALLABLE — As a whole or in part, at any time,
on or after Aug. 12, 2002, at the option of Co. on
at least 30 but not more than 60 days' notice to
each Aug. 11 as follows:
2003........105.007  2004.........104.756  2005.........104.506
2006........104.256  2007.........104.005  2008.........103.755
2009........103.505  2010.........103.254  2011.........103.004
2012........102.754  2013.........102.503  2014.........102.253
2015........102.003  2016.........101.752  2017.........101.502
2018........101.252  2019.........101.001  2020.........100.751
2021........100.501  2022.........100.250
and thereafter at 100 plus accrued interest.
SECURITY — Not secured. Ranks equally with all
other unsecured and unsubordinated indebtedness
of Co. Co. nor any Affiliate will not incurr any
indebtedness; provided that Co. will not create as
security for any indebtedness for borrowed money,
any mortgage, pledge, security interest or lien on
any stock or indebtedness is directly owned by
Co., without effectively providing that the debt
securities shall be secured equally and ratably with
such indebtedness, so long as such indebtedness
shall be so secured.
INDENTURE    MODIFICATION — Indenture
may be modified, except as provided with, consent
of 66⅔% of debs. outstg.
RIGHTS ON DEFAULT — Trustee, or 25% of
debs. outstg., may declare principal dua nad paya-
ble (30 days' grace for payment of interest).
LISTED — On New York Stock Exchange.
PURPOSE — Proceeds used for general corporate
purposes.
OFFERED — ($250,000,000) at 99.51 plus accrued
interest (proceeds to Co., 99.11) on Aug. 5, 1992
thru Merrill Lynch & Co., Donaldson, Lufkin &
Jenerette Securities Corp., PaineWebber Inc., Pru-
dential Securities Inc., Smith Barney, Harris
Upham & Co. Inc. and associates.
```

For example, in November 2001, as Enron Corp. approached bankruptcy, its 6.4% coupon bonds due in 2006 were selling at about 20% of par value, resulting in a yield to maturity of about 57%. Investors did not really expect these bonds to provide a 57% rate of return. They recognized that bondholders were very unlikely to receive all the payments promised in the bond contract and that the yield based on *expected* cash flows was far less than the yield based on *promised* cash flows.

EXAMPLE 10.10

Expected versus Promised Yield

Suppose a firm issued a 9% coupon bond 20 years ago. The bond now has 10 years left until its maturity date but the firm is having financial difficulties. Investors believe that the firm will be able to make good on the remaining interest payments but that at the maturity date, the firm will be forced into bankruptcy, and bondholders will receive only 70% of par value. The bond is selling at $750.

Yield to maturity (YTM) would then be calculated using the following inputs:

	Expected YTM	Stated YTM
Coupon payment	$45	$45
Number of semiannual periods	20 periods	20 periods
Final payment	$700	$1,000
Price	$750	$750

The yield to maturity based on promised payments is 13.7%. Based on the expected payment of $700 at maturity, however, the yield would be only 11.6%. The stated yield to maturity is greater than the yield to maturity investors actually expect to receive.

FIGURE 10.10

Yields on long-term bonds

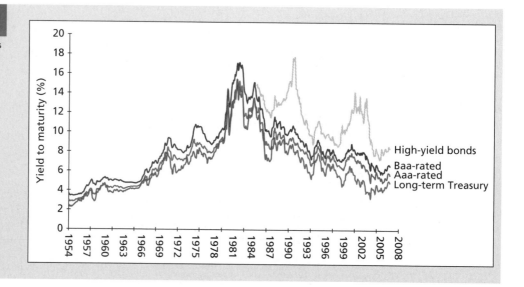

Example 10.10 suggests that when a bond becomes more subject to default risk, its price will fall, and therefore its promised yield to maturity will rise. Therefore, the default premium, the spread between the stated yield to maturity and that on otherwise-comparable Treasury bonds, will rise. However, its expected yield to maturity, which ultimately is tied to the systematic risk of the bond, will be far less affected. Let's continue the example.

EXAMPLE   10.11

Default Risk and the Default Premium

Suppose that the condition of the firm in Example 10.10 deteriorates further, and investors now believe that the bond will pay off only 55% of face value at maturity. Investors now demand an expected yield to maturity of 12% (i.e., 6% semiannually), which is 0.4% higher than in Example 10.10. But the price of the bond will fall from $750 to $688 [$n = 20$; $i = 6$; $FV = 550$; $PMT = 45]. At this price, the stated yield to maturity based on promised cash flows is 15.2%. While the expected yield to maturity has increased by 0.4%, the drop in price has caused the promised yield to maturity (and the default premium) to rise by 1.5%.

default premium

The increment to promised yield that compensates the investor for default risk.

To compensate for the possibility of default, corporate bonds must offer a **default premium.** The default premium is the difference between the promised yield on a corporate bond and the yield of an otherwise identical government bond that is riskless in terms of default. If the firm remains solvent and actually pays the investor all of the promised cash flows, the investor will realize a higher yield to maturity than would be realized from the government bond. If, however, the firm goes bankrupt, the corporate bond is likely to provide a lower return than the government bond. The corporate bond has the potential for both better and worse performance than the default-free Treasury bond. In other words, it is riskier.

The pattern of default premiums offered on risky bonds is sometimes called the *risk structure of interest rates.* The greater the default risk, the higher the default premium. Figure 10.10 shows the yield to maturity of bonds of different risk classes since 1954 and the yields on junk bonds since 1984. You can see here clear evidence of default-risk premiums on promised yields.

yield curve

A graph of yield to maturity as a function of term to maturity.

term structure of interest rates

The relationship between yields to maturity and terms to maturity across bonds.

10.6 THE YIELD CURVE

Return to Figure 10.1 again, and you will see that while yields to maturity on bonds of various maturities are reasonably similar, yields do differ. Bonds with shorter maturities generally offer lower yields to maturity than longer term bonds. The graphical relationship between the yield to maturity and the term to maturity is called the **yield curve.** The relationship also is called the **term structure of interest rates** because it relates yields to maturity to the term

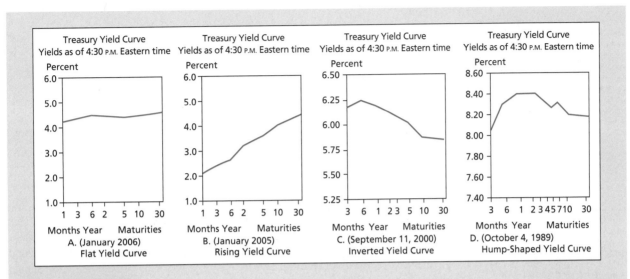

FIGURE 10.11

Treasury yield curves

Source: Various editions of *The Wall Street Journal*. Reprinted by permission of *The Wall Street Journal*, © 1989, 2000, 2006 Dow Jones & Company, Inc. All Rights Reserved Worldwide.

(maturity) of each bond. The yield curve is published regularly and may be found in *The Wall Street Journal* or on the Web at sites such as Yahoo! Finance. Four such sets of curves are reproduced in Figure 10.11. Figure 10.11 illustrates that a wide range of yield curves may be observed in practice. Panel A is an essentially flat yield curve. Panel B is an upward sloping curve, and Panel C is a downward sloping, or "inverted" yield curve. Finally the yield curve in Panel D is hump shaped, first rising and then falling. Rising yield curves are most commonly observed. We will see why momentarily.

Why should bonds of differing maturity offer different yields? The two most plausible possibilities have to do with expectations of future rates and risk premiums. We will consider each of these arguments in turn.

The Expectations Theory

Suppose everyone in the market believes firmly that while the current one-year interest rate is 8%, the interest rate on one-year bonds next year will rise to 10%. What would this belief imply about the proper yield to maturity on two-year bonds issued today?

WEB *master*

Data on Bond Issues

The NASD operates the TRACE (Trade Reporting and Compliance Engine) system, which reports over-the-counter secondary market trades of fixed income securities. Go to the NASD home page at **www.nasd.com/index.htm** and click on the link for "TRACE Information". Next, click the link for the TRACE Fact Book and link to the most recently available. Find the detailed data tables and locate the table with information on issues, excluding convertible bonds (typically Table 1). For each of the last three years, calculate the following:

1. The percentage of bonds that were publicly traded and the percentage that were privately traded.

2. The percentage of bonds that were investment grade and the percentage that were high-yield.

3. The percentage of bonds that had fixed coupon rates and the percentage that had floating rates.

4. Do any patterns emerge over time?

5. Repeat the calculations using the information for convertible bond issues (typically in Table 2).

FIGURE 10.12

Returns to two 2-year investment strategies

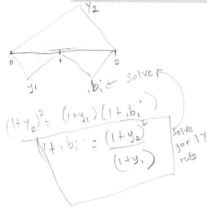

expectations hypothesis

The theory that yields to maturity are determined solely by expectations of future short-term interest rates.

It is easy to see that an investor who buys the one-year bond and rolls the proceeds into another one-year bond in the following year will earn, on average, about 9% per year. This value is just the average of the 8% earned this year and the 10% expected for next year. More precisely, the investment will grow by a factor of 1.08 in the first year and 1.10 in the second year, for a total two-year growth factor of $1.08 \times 1.10 = 1.188$. This corresponds to an annual growth rate of 8.995% (because $1.08995^2 = 1.188$).

For investments in two-year bonds to be competitive with the strategy of rolling over one-year bonds, these two-year bonds also must offer an average annual return of 8.995% over the two-year holding period. This is illustrated in Figure 10.12. The current short-term rate of 8% and the expected value of next year's short-term rate are depicted above the time line. The two-year rate that provides the same expected two-year total return is below the time line. In this example, therefore, the yield curve will be upward sloping; while one-year bonds offer an 8% yield to maturity, two-year bonds offer an 8.995% yield.

This notion is the essence of the **expectations hypothesis** of the yield curve, which asserts that the slope of the yield curve is attributable to expectations of changes in short-term rates. Relatively high yields on long-term bonds are attributed to expectations of future increases in rates, while relatively low yields on long-term bonds (a downward-sloping or inverted yield curve) are attributed to expectations of falling short-term rates.

One of the implications of the expectations hypothesis is that expected holding-period returns on bonds of all maturities ought to be about equal. Even if the yield curve is upward sloping (so that two-year bonds offer higher yields to maturity than one-year bonds), this does not necessarily mean investors expect higher rates of return on the two-year bonds. As we've seen, the higher initial yield to maturity on the two-year bond is necessary to compensate investors for the fact that interest rates the next year will be even higher. Over the two-year period, and indeed over any holding period, this theory predicts that holding-period returns will be equalized across bonds of all maturities.

EXAMPLE 10.12

Holding-Period Returns

Suppose we buy the one-year zero-coupon bond with a current yield to maturity of 8%. If its face value is $1,000, its price will be $925.93, providing an 8% rate of return over the coming year. Suppose instead that we buy the two-year zero-coupon bond at its yield of 8.995%. Its price today is $1,000/(1.08995)^2 = 841.76. After a year passes, the zero will have a remaining maturity of only one year; based on the forecast that the one-year yield next year will be 10%, it then will sell for $1,000/1.10 = 909.09. The expected rate of return over the year is thus ($909.09 − $841.76)/$841.76 = .08, or 8%, precisely the same return provided by the one-year bond. This makes sense: If risk considerations are ignored when pricing the two bonds, they ought to provide equal expected rates of return.

In fact, advocates of the expectations hypothesis commonly invert this analysis to *infer* the market's expectation of future short-term rates. They note that we do not directly observe the expectation of next year's rate, but we *can* observe yields on bonds of different maturities. Suppose, as in this example, we see that one-year bonds offer yields of 8% and two-year bonds offer yields of 8.995%. Each dollar invested in the two-year zero would grow after two years to $1 \times 1.08995^2 = \$1.188$. A dollar invested in the one-year zero would grow by a factor of 1.08 in the first year and, then, if reinvested or "rolled over" into another one-year zero in the second year, would grow by an additional factor of $1 + r_2$. Final proceeds would be $1 \times 1.08 \times (1 + r_2)$.

The final proceeds of the rollover strategy depend on the interest rate that actually transpires in year 2. However, we can solve for the second-year interest rate that makes the expected payoff of these two strategies equal. This "breakeven" value is called the **forward rate** for the second year, f_2, and is derived as follows:

$$1.08995^2 = 1.08 \times (1 + f_2)$$

which implies that $f_2 = .10$, or 10%. Notice that the forward rate equals the market's expectation of the year-2 short rate. Hence, we conclude that when the expected total return of a long-term bond equals that of a rolling over a short-term bond, the forward rate equals the expected short-term interest rate. This is why the theory is called the expectations hypothesis.

More generally, we obtain the forward rate by equating the return on an n-period zero-coupon bond with that of an $(n - 1)$-period zero-coupon bond rolled over into a one-year bond in year n:

$$(1 + y_n)^n = (1 + y_{n-1})^{n-1} (1 + f_n)$$

The actual total returns on the two n-year strategies will be equal if the short-term interest rate in year n turns out to equal f_n.

forward rate

The inferred short-term rate of interest for a future period that makes the expected total return of a long-term bond equal to that of rolling over short-term bonds.

EXAMPLE   10.13

Forward Rates

Suppose that two-year maturity bonds offer yields to maturity of 6%, and three-year bonds have yields of 7%. What is the forward rate for the third year? We could compare these two strategies as follows:

1. Buy a three-year bond. Total proceeds per dollar invested will be

$$\$1 \times (1.07)^3 = \$1.2250$$

2. Buy a two-year bond. Reinvest all proceeds in a one-year bond in the third year, which will provide a return in that year of r_3. Total proceeds per dollar invested will be the result of two years' growth of invested funds at 6% plus the final year's growth at rate r_3:

$$\$1 \times (1.06)^2 \times (1 + r_3) = \$1.1236 \times (1 + r_3)$$

The forward rate is the rate in year 3 that makes the total return on these strategies equal:

$$1.2250 = 1.1236 \times (1 + f_3)$$

We conclude that the forward rate for the third year satisfies $(1 + f_3) = 1.0902$, so that f_3 is 9.02%.

While the expectations hypothesis gives us a tool to infer expectations of future market interest rates from the yield curve, it tells us nothing of what underlying considerations generated those expectations. Ultimately, interest rates reflect investors' expectations of the state of the macroeconomy. Not surprisingly, then, forward rates and the yield curve have proven themselves to be useful inputs for economic forecasts. The slope of the yield curve is one of the more important components of the index of leading economic indicators used to predict the course of economic activity. Inverted yield curves in particular, which imply falling interest rates, turn out to be among the best indicators of a coming recession. The nearby box interprets the inverted yield curve in early 2007 in this light.

On the MARKET FRONT

GRADING BONDS ON INVERTED CURVE

The bond market is having relationship issues that are getting harder to ignore. Normally, yields on long-term government bonds are higher than yields on short-term ones. Investors demand a bigger return for the risk that comes with holding an investment that takes longer to repay. The relationship has been upside-down since July [2006], however, with yields on short-term U.S. Treasury bills exceeding those on long-term Treasury notes.

This unusual state of affairs—known as an inverted yield curve—has some economists wondering whether the bond market is signaling that the economy itself could turn upside-down. Yield inversions, many analysts say, are harbingers of hard times. When bond investors see a recession coming, they tend to buy long-term Treasury securities for two reasons. First, they are safer than stocks. Second, they are appealing when inflation is low, and recessions tend to beat down inflation. The buying that comes with recession fears drives down a long-term bond's yield, sometimes below the prevailing yield on short-term Treasury securities.

The market, in effect, is betting that the Federal Reserve, which dictates short-term rates, will have to cut its overnight fund rate to boost the economy, and investors are pushing long-term rates down in anticipation.

Some economists doubt the yield curve's effectiveness as a recession-forecasting tool. They think long-term rates are exceptionally low right now for other reasons, including lower long-term expectations about inflation and growing demand for U.S. government bonds from foreign investors needing somewhere to park their money.

But those who think highly of the yield curve's predictive power have history on their side. Seven times between 1965 and 2005, yields on the 10-year note have dropped below those on the three-month Treasury bill for an extended span. In six of those instances, the U.S. economy went into recession soon after.

SOURCE: Michael Hudson, *The Wall Street Journal Online*, January 8, 2007, p. C1.

The Liquidity Preference Theory

The expectations hypothesis starts from the assertion that bonds are priced so that "buy and hold" investments in long-term bonds provide the same returns as rolling over a series of short-term bonds. However, the risks of long- and short-term bonds are not equivalent.

We have seen that longer-term bonds are subject to greater interest rate risk than short-term bonds. As a result, investors in long-term bonds might require a risk premium to compensate them for this risk. In this case, the yield curve will be upward sloping even in the absence of any expectations of future increases in rates. The source of the upward slope in the yield curve is investor demand for higher expected returns on assets that are perceived as riskier.

This viewpoint is called the **liquidity preference theory** of the term structure. Its name derives from the fact that shorter term bonds have more "liquidity" than longer term bonds, in the sense that they offer greater price certainty and trade in more active markets with lower bid-ask spreads. The preference of investors for greater liquidity makes them willing to hold these shorter term bonds even if they do not offer expected returns as high as those of longer term bonds.

We can think of a **liquidity premium** as resulting from the extra compensation investors demand for holding longer term bonds with lower liquidity. We measure it as the spread between the forward rate of interest and the expected short rate:

$$f_n = E(r_n) + \text{Liquidity premium}$$

In the absence of a liquidity premium, the forward rate would equal the expectation of the future short rate. But generally, we expect the forward rate to exceed that expectation to compensate investors for the lower liquidity of longer term bonds.

Advocates of the liquidity preference theory also note that issuers of bonds seem to prefer to issue long-term bonds. This allows them to lock in an interest rate on their borrowing for long periods. If issuers do prefer to issue long-term bonds, they will be willing to pay higher yields on these issues as a way of eliminating interest rate risk. In sum, borrowers demand higher rates on longer term bonds, and issuers are willing to pay higher rates on longer term bonds. The conjunction of these two preferences means longer term bonds typically should offer higher expected rates of return to investors than shorter term bonds. These expectations will show up in an upward-sloping yield curve.

liquidity preference theory

The theory that investors demand a risk premium on long-term bonds.

liquidity premium

The extra expected return demanded by investors as compensation for the greater risk of longer term bonds.

If the liquidity preference theory is valid, forward rates of interest will exceed the market's expectations of future interest rates. Even if rates are expected to remain unchanged, for example, the yield curve will slope upward because of the liquidity premium. That upward slope would be mistakenly attributed to expectations of rising rates if one were to use the pure expectations hypothesis to interpret the yield curve.

Suppose that the short-term rate of interest is currently 8% and that investors expect it to remain at 8% next year. In the absence of a liquidity premium, with no expectation of a change in yields, the yield to maturity on two-year bonds also would be 8%, the yield curve would be flat, and the forward rate would be 8%. But what if investors demand a risk premium to invest in two-year rather than one-year bonds? If the liquidity premium is 1%, then the forward rate would be 8% + 1% = 9%, and the yield to maturity on the two-year bond would be determined by

$$(1 + y_2)^2 = 1.08 \times 1.09 = 1.1772$$

implying that $y_2 = .085 = 8.5\%$. Here, the yield curve is upward sloping due solely to the liquidity premium embedded in the price of the longer term bond.

EXAMPLE 10.14

Liquidity Premia and the Yield Curve

Suppose that the expected value of the interest rate for year 3 remains at 8% but that the liquidity premium for that year is also 1%. What would be the yield to maturity on three-year zeros? What would this imply about the slope of the yield curve?

CONCEPT **10.8**
check

A Synthesis

Of course, we do not need to make an either/or choice between expectations and risk premiums. Both of these factors influence the yield curve, and both should be considered in interpreting the curve.

Figure 10.13 shows two possible yield curves. In Figure 10.13A, rates are expected to rise over time. This fact, together with a liquidity premium, makes the yield curve steeply upward

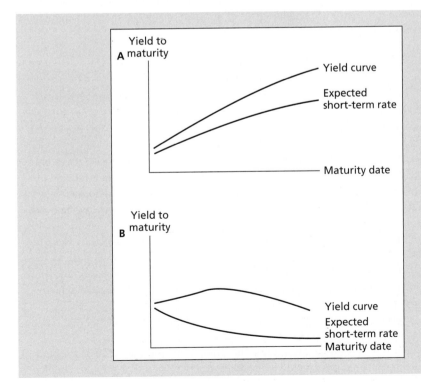

FIGURE 10.13

Illustrative yield curves

FIGURE 10.14

Term spread: Yields on
10-year versus 90-day
Treasury securities

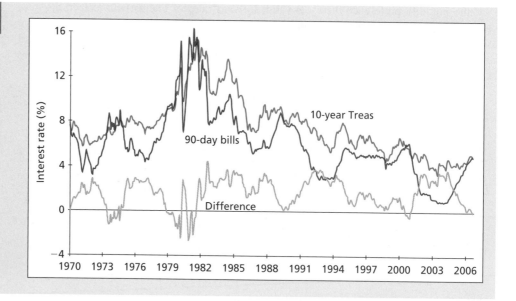

sloping. In Figure 10.13B, rates are expected to fall, which by itself would make the yield curve slope downward. However, the liquidity premium lends something of an upward slope. The net effect of these two opposing factors is a "hump-shaped" curve.

These two examples make it clear that the combination of varying expectations and liquidity premiums can result in a wide array of yield-curve profiles. For example, an upward-sloping curve does not in and of itself imply expectations of higher future interest rates, because the slope can result either from expectations or from risk premiums. A curve that is more steeply sloped than usual might signal expectations of higher rates, but even this inference is perilous.

Figure 10.14 presents yield spreads between 90-day T-bills and 10-year T-bonds since 1970. The figure shows that the yield curve is generally upward sloping in that the longer-term bonds usually offer higher yields to maturity, despite the fact that rates could not have been expected to increase throughout the entire period. This tendency is the empirical basis for the liquidity premium doctrine that at least part of the upward slope in the yield curve must be due to a risk premium.

SUMMARY

- Debt securities are distinguished by their promise to pay a fixed or specified stream of income to their holders. The coupon bond is a typical debt security.
- Treasury notes and bonds have original maturities greater than one year. They are issued at or near par value, with their prices quoted net of accrued interest.
- Callable bonds should offer higher promised yields to maturity to compensate investors for the fact that they will not realize full capital gains should the interest rate fall and the bonds be called away from them at the stipulated call price. Bonds often are issued with a period of call protection. In addition, discount bonds selling significantly below their call price offer implicit call protection.
- Put bonds give the bondholder rather than the issuer the choice to terminate or extend the life of the bond.
- Convertible bonds may be exchanged, at the bondholder's discretion, for a specified number of shares of stock. Convertible bondholders "pay" for this option by accepting a lower coupon rate on the security.
- Floating-rate bonds pay a fixed premium over a referenced short-term interest rate. Risk is limited because the rate paid is tied to current market conditions.
- The yield to maturity is the single interest rate that equates the present value of a security's cash flows to its price. Bond prices and yields are inversely related. For premium bonds,

the coupon rate is greater than the current yield, which is greater than the yield to maturity. The order of these inequalities is reversed for discount bonds.

- The yield to maturity often is interpreted as an estimate of the average rate of return to an investor who purchases a bond and holds it until maturity. This interpretation is subject to error, however. Related measures are yield to call, realized compound yield, and expected (versus promised) yield to maturity.

- Treasury bills are U.S. government-issued zero-coupon bonds with original maturities of up to one year. Treasury STRIPS are longer term default-free zero-coupon bonds. Prices of zero-coupon bonds rise exponentially over time, providing a rate of appreciation equal to the interest rate. The IRS treats this price appreciation as imputed taxable interest income to the investor.

- When bonds are subject to potential default, the stated yield to maturity is the maximum possible yield to maturity that can be realized by the bondholder. In the event of default, however, that promised yield will not be realized. To compensate bond investors for default risk, bonds must offer default premiums, that is, promised yields in excess of those offered by default-free government securities. If the firm remains healthy, its bonds will provide higher returns than government bonds. Otherwise, the returns may be lower.

- Bond safety often is measured using financial ratio analysis. Bond indentures offer safeguards to protect the claims of bondholders. Common indentures specify sinking fund requirements, collateralization, dividend restrictions, and subordination of future debt.

- The term structure of interest rates is the relationship between time to maturity and term to maturity. The yield curve is a graphical depiction of the term structure.

KEY TERMS

bond, 291
callable bonds, 294
collateral, 316
convertible bonds, 294
coupon rate, 291
current yield, 304
debenture, 316
default premium, 318
discount bonds, 305
expectations hypothesis, 320
face value, 291
floating-rate bonds, 294

forward rate, 321
horizon analysis, 308
indenture, 315
investment grade bonds, 313
liquidity preference
   theory, 322
liquidity premium, 322
par value, 291
premium bonds, 305
put bond, 294
realized compound
   return, 307

reinvestment rate
   risk, 308
sinking fund, 315
speculative grade or junk
   bonds, 313
subordination clauses, 316
term structure of interest
   rates, 318
yield curve, 318
yield to maturity, 303
zero-coupon bond, 291

PROBLEM SETS

 Select problems are available in McGraw-Hill's Homework Manager®. Please see the packaging options section of the preface for more information.

1. Which security has a higher *effective* annual interest rate?
   a. A three-month T-bill with face value of $100,000 currently selling at $97,645.
   b. A coupon bond selling at par and paying a 10% coupon semiannually.

2. Treasury bonds paying an 8% coupon rate with *semiannual* payments currently sell at par value. What coupon rate would they have to pay in order to sell at par if they paid their coupons *annually*?

3. Two bonds have identical times to maturity and coupon rates. One is callable at 105, the other at 110. Which should have the higher yield to maturity? Why?

4. Consider a bond with a 10% coupon and with yield to maturity = 8%. If the bond's YTM remains constant, then in one year, will the bond price be higher, lower, or unchanged? Why?

5. Under the expectations hypothesis, if the yield curve is upward sloping, the market must expect an increase in short-term interest rates. True/false/uncertain? Why?

6. A "fallen angel" bond is *best* defined as a bond issued:
   a. Below investment grade.
   b. At an original issue discount.
   c. As investment grade, but declined to speculative grade.
   d. As a secured bond, but the collateral value declined below par value.

7. Under the liquidity preference theory, if inflation is expected to be falling over the next few years, long-term interest rates will be higher than short-term rates. True/false/uncertain? Why?

8. The yield curve is upward sloping. Can you conclude that investors expect short-term interest rates to rise? Why or why not?

9. Consider a bond paying a coupon rate of 10% per year semiannually when the market interest rate is only 4% per half year. The bond has three years until maturity.
   a. Find the bond's price today and six months from now after the next coupon is paid.
   b. What is the total rate of return on the bond?

10. A 20-year maturity bond with par value $1,000 makes semiannual coupon payments at a coupon rate of 8%. Find the bond equivalent and effective annual yield to maturity of the bond if the bond price is:
   a. $950
   b. $1,000
   c. $1,050

11. Redo Problem 10 using the same data, but now assume that the bond makes its coupon payments annually. Why are the yields you compute lower in this case?

12. Return to Table 10.1 and calculate both the real and nominal rates of return on the TIPS bond in the second and third years.

13. Fill in the table below for the following zero-coupon bonds, all of which have par values of $1,000.

Price	Maturity (years)	Yield to Maturity
$400	20	?
$500	20	?
$500	10	?
?	10	10%
?	10	8%
$400	?	8%

14. Assume you have a one-year investment horizon and are trying to choose among three bonds. All have the same degree of default risk and mature in 10 years. The first is a zero-coupon bond that pays $1,000 at maturity. The second has an 8% coupon rate and pays the $80 coupon once per year. The third has a 10% coupon rate and pays the $100 coupon once per year.
   a. If all three bonds are now priced to yield 8% to maturity, what are their prices?
   b. If you expect their yields to maturity to be 8% at the beginning of next year, what will their prices be then? What is your rate of return on each bond during the one-year holding period?

15. A bond with a coupon rate of 7% makes semiannual coupon payments on January 15 and July 15 of each year. *The Wall Street Journal* reports the ask price for the bond on January 30 at 100:02. What is the invoice price of the bond? The coupon period has 182 days.

16. A bond has a current yield of 9% and a yield to maturity of 10%. Is the bond selling above or below par value? Explain.

17. Is the coupon rate of the bond in the previous problem more or less than 9%?

18. Consider a bond with a settlement date of February 22, 2008, and a maturity date of March 15, 2016. The coupon rate is 5.5%. If the yield to maturity of the bond is 5.34% (bond equivalent yield, semiannual compounding), what is the list price of the bond on the settlement date? What is the accrued interest on the bond? What is the invoice price of the bond?

19. Now suppose the bond in the previous question is selling for 102. What is the bond's yield to maturity? What would the yield to maturity be at a price of 102 if the bond paid its coupons only once per year?

20. On May 30, 2006, Janice Kerr is considering the newly issued 10-year AAA corporate bonds shown in the following exhibit:

Description	Coupon	Price	Callable	Call Price
Sentinal, due May 30, 2016	6.00%	100	Noncallable	NA
Colina, due May 30, 2016	6.20%	100	Currently callable	102

a. Suppose that market interest rates decline by 100 basis points (i.e., 1%). Contrast the effect of this decline on the price of each bond.
b. Should Kerr prefer the Colina over the Sentinal bond when rates are expected to rise or to fall?
c. What would be the effect, if any, of an increase in the *volatility* of interest rates on the prices of each bond?

21. A newly issued 20-year maturity, zero-coupon bond is issued with a yield to maturity of 8% and face value $1,000. Find the imputed interest income in the first, second, and last year of the bond's life.

22. A newly issued 10-year maturity, 4% coupon bond making *annual* coupon payments is sold to the public at a price of $800. What will be an investor's taxable income from the bond over the coming year? The bond will not be sold at the end of the year. The bond is treated as an original-issue discount bond.

23. A newly issued bond pays its coupons once a year. Its coupon rate is 5%, its maturity is 20 years, and its yield to maturity is 8%.
a. Find the holding-period return for a one-year investment period if the bond is selling at a yield to maturity of 7% by the end of the year.
b. If you sell the bond after one year when its yield is 7%, what taxes will you owe if the tax rate on interest income is 40% and the tax rate on capital gains income is 30%? The bond is subject to original-issue discount (OID) tax treatment.
c. What is the after-tax holding-period return on the bond?
d. Find the realized compound yield *before taxes* for a two-year holding period, assuming that (i) you sell the bond after two years, (ii) the bond yield is 7% at the end of the second year, and (iii) the coupon can be reinvested for one year at a 3% interest rate.
e. Use the tax rates in part (*b*) to compute the *after-tax* two-year realized compound yield. Remember to take account of OID tax rules.

24. A 30-year maturity, 8% coupon bond paying coupons semiannually is callable in five years at a call price of $1,100. The bond currently sells at a yield to maturity of 7% (3.5% per half year).
a. What is the yield to call?
b. What is the yield to call if the call price is only $1,050?
c. What is the yield to call if the call price is $1,100, but the bond can be called in two years instead of five years?

25. A 10-year bond of a firm in severe financial distress has a coupon rate of 14% and sells for $900. The firm is currently renegotiating the debt, and it appears that the lenders

will allow the firm to reduce coupon payments on the bond to one-half the originally contracted amount. The firm can handle these lower payments. What are the stated and expected yields to maturity of the bonds? The bond makes its coupon payments annually.

26. A two-year bond with par value $1,000 making annual coupon payments of $100 is priced at $1,000. What is the yield to maturity of the bond? What will be the realized compound yield to maturity if the one-year interest rate next year turns out to be (*a*) 8%, (*b*) 10%, (*c*) 12%?

27. The stated yield to maturity and realized compound yield to maturity of a (default-free) zero-coupon bond will always be equal. Why?

28. Suppose that today's date is April 15. A bond with a 10% coupon paid semiannually every January 15 and July 15 is listed in *The Wall Street Journal* as selling at an ask price of 101:04. If you buy the bond from a dealer today, what price will you pay for it?

29. Assume that two firms issue bonds with the following characteristics. Both bonds are issued at par.

	ABC Bonds	XYZ Bonds
Issue size	$1.2 billion	$150 million
Maturity	10 years*	20 years
Coupon	9%	10%
Collateral	First mortgage	General debenture
Callable	Not callable	In 10 years
Call price	None	110
Sinking fund	None	Starting in 5 years

*Bond is extendable at the discretion of the bondholder for an additional 10 years.

Ignoring credit quality, identify four features of these issues that might account for the lower coupon on the ABC debt. Explain.

30. A large corporation issued both fixed and floating-rate notes five years ago, with terms given in the following table:

	9% Coupon Notes	Floating-Rate Note
Issue size	$250 million	$280 million
Maturity	20 years	15 years
Current price (% of par)	93	98
Current coupon	9%	8%
Coupon adjusts	Fixed coupon	Every year
Coupon reset rule	—	1-year T-bill rate + 2%
Callable	10 years after issue	10 years after issue
Call price	106	102
Sinking fund	None	None
Yield to maturity	9.9%	—
Price range since issued	$85–$112	$97–$102

a. Why is the price range greater for the 9% coupon bond than the floating-rate note?

b. What factors could explain why the floating-rate note is not always sold at par value?

c. Why is the call price for the floating-rate note not of great importance to investors?

d. Is the probability of call for the fixed-rate note high or low?

e. If the firm were to issue a fixed-rate note with a 15-year maturity, callable after 5 years at 106, what coupon rate would it need to offer to issue the bond at par value?

f. Why is an entry for yield to maturity for the floating-rate note not appropriate?

31. Bonds of Zello Corporation with a par value of $1,000 sell for $960, mature in five years, and have a 7% annual coupon rate paid semiannually.

a. Calculate the:
   (1) Current yield.
   (2) Yield to maturity.
   (3) Horizon yield (also called realized compound return) for an investor with a three-year holding period and a reinvestment rate of 6% over the period. At the end of three years the 7% coupon bonds with two years remaining will sell to yield 7%.

b. Cite *one* major shortcoming for *each* of the following fixed-income yield measures:
   (1) Current yield.
   (2) Yield to maturity.
   (3) Horizon yield (also called realized compound return).

32. Masters Corp. issues two bonds with 20-year maturities. Both bonds are callable at $1,050. The first bond is issued at a deep discount with a coupon rate of 4% and a price of $580 to yield 8.4%. The second bond is issued at par value with a coupon rate of 8.75%.

a. What is the yield to maturity of the par bond? Why is it higher than the yield of the discount bond?

b. If you expect rates to fall substantially in the next two years, which bond would you prefer to hold?

c. In what sense does the discount bond offer "implicit call protection"?

33. A convertible bond has the following features:

Coupon	5.25%
Maturity	June 15, 2017
Market price of bond	$77.50
Market price of underlying common stock	$28.00
Annual dividend	$1.20
Conversion ratio	20.83 shares

Calculate the conversion premium for this bond.

34. a. Explain the impact on the offering yield of adding a call feature to a proposed bond issue.

b. Explain the impact on the bond's expected life of adding a call feature to a proposed bond issue.

c. Describe one advantage and one disadvantage of including callable bonds in a portfolio.

35. The yield to maturity on one-year zero-coupon bonds is 8%. The yield to maturity on two-year zero-coupon bonds is 9%.

a. What is the forward rate of interest for the second year?

b. If you believe in the expectations hypothesis, what is your best guess as to the expected value of the short-term interest rate next year?

c. If you believe in the liquidity preference theory, is your best guess as to next year's short-term interest rate higher or lower than in (b)?

36. The following table contains spot rates and forward rates for three years. However, the labels got mixed up. Can you identify which row of the interest rates represents spot rates and which one the forward rates?

Year:	1	2	3
Spot rates or Forward rates?	10%	12%	14%
Spot rates or Forward rates?	10%	14.0364%	18.1078%

37. The current yield curve for default-free zero-coupon bonds is as follows:

Maturity (Years)	YTM
1	10%
2	11
3	12

   a. What are the implied one-year forward rates?

   b. Assume that the pure expectations hypothesis of the term structure is correct. If market expectations are accurate, what will the pure yield curve (that is, the yields to maturity on one- and two-year zero coupon bonds) be next year?

   c. If you purchase a two-year zero-coupon bond now, what is the expected total rate of return over the next year? What if you purchase a three-year zero-coupon bond? (Hint: Compute the current and expected future prices.) Ignore taxes.

38. The term structure for zero-coupon bonds is currently:

Maturity (Years)	YTM
1	4%
2	5
3	6

Your forecasts for bond yields *next year* are:

Maturity (Years)	YTM
1	5%
2	6
3	7

   a. What do you expect the rate of return to be over the coming year on a three-year zero-coupon bond?

   b. Under the expectations theory, what yields to maturity does *the market* expect to observe on one- and two-year zeros next year? Is the market's expectation of the return on the three-year bond greater or less than yours?

39. The following multiple-choice problems are based on questions that appeared in past CFA examinations.

   a. A bond with a call feature:

     (1) Is attractive because the immediate receipt of principal plus premium produces a high return.

     (2) Is more apt to be called when interest rates are high because the interest saving will be greater.

     (3) Will usually have a higher yield to maturity than a similar noncallable bond.

     (4) None of the above.

   b. In which *one* of the following cases is the bond selling at a discount?

     (1) Coupon rate is greater than current yield, which is greater than yield to maturity.

     (2) Coupon rate, current yield, and yield to maturity are all the same.

     (3) Coupon rate is less than current yield, which is less than yield to maturity.

     (4) Coupon rate is less than current yield, which is greater than yield to maturity.

   c. Consider a five-year bond with a 10% coupon selling at a yield to maturity of 8%. If interest rates remain constant, one year from now the price of this bond will be:

     (1) Higher

     (2) Lower

     (3) The same

     (4) Par

   d. Which of the following statements is *true*?

(1) The expectations hypothesis indicates a flat yield curve if anticipated future short-term rates exceed current short-term rates.

(2) The basic conclusion of the expectations hypothesis is that the long-term rate is equal to the anticipated short-term rate.

(3) The liquidity hypothesis indicates that, all other things being equal, longer maturities will have higher yields.

(4) The liquidity preference theory states that a rising yield curve necessarily implies that the market anticipates increases in interest rates.

Use data from the Standard & Poor's Market Insight Database at www.mhhe.com/edumarketinsight to answer the following questions.

STANDARD
&POOR'S

1. Use the *Financial Highlights* section of Market Insight to obtain Standard & Poor's bond rating of at least 10 firms in the database. Try to choose a sample with a wide range of bond ratings. Next use Market Insight's Annual Ratio Report to obtain, for each firm, the financial ratios tabulated in Table 10.3. What is the relationship between bond rating and these ratios? Can you tell from your sample which of these ratios are the more important determinants of bond rating?

2. Use Altman's Z-score model for public firms, shown below, and the financial statements from Market Insight to calculate the Z-score for the firms in Problem 1. Based on the calculated Z-scores, assess the likelihood of bankruptcy for each firm. How well do the Z-scores match up with the bond ratings?

$$Z = 1.2 \frac{\text{Working Capital}}{\text{Total Assets}} + 1.4 \frac{\text{Retained Earnings}}{\text{Total Assets}} + 3.3 \frac{\text{EBIT}}{\text{Total Assets}} +$$

$$0.6 \frac{\text{Market Value of Equity}}{\text{Book Value of Liabilities}} + 0.99 \frac{\text{Sales}}{\text{Total Assets}}$$

Z-score	Likelihood of Bankruptcy
1.8 or less	likely
between 1.8 and 3.0	uncertain
3.0 or above	not likely

WEB *master*

Corporate Bond Yields

1. Go to **www.nasdbondinfo.com/asp/home.asp** and generate a list of zero-coupon bonds that are due to mature within three to five years. Restrict the list to bonds rated AAA that have been traded within the last 30 days. Sort the list in order of maturity. (If no bonds appear on the list, widen the trading range to the last 60 days.) Find the bond that has the latest maturity date. Set up a spreadsheet with the relevant data and use Excel's XIRR function to confirm the reported yield. (It is easiest to isolate the dates and the prices in contiguous cells before entering the XIRR function.)

2. Now relax the rating constraint by requesting bonds rated from AAA to C. At the same time, find bonds that have coupon rates between 10% and 12%. Choose the callable bond that has the latest maturity date. (Click on the "Descriptive Data" link for more details about the bond issue.) Use the information about the bond to calculate the amount of the coupon payment and the accrued interest for the purchase date listed. Set up a schedule of dates and cash flows, then use the XIRR function to calculate the bond's yield to maturity. Repeat the procedure to find the bond's yield to call, assuming the earliest listed call date and price.

www.mhhe.com/bkm

SOLUTIONS TO CONCEPT *checks*

10.1. The callable bond will sell at the *lower* price. Investors will not be willing to pay as much if they know that the firm retains a valuable option to reclaim the bond for the call price if interest rates fall.

10.2. At a semiannual interest rate of 3%, the bond is worth $40 × Annuity factor(3%, 60) + $1,000 × PV factor(3%, 60) = $1,276.76, which results in a capital gain of $276.76. This exceeds the capital loss of $189.29 ($1,000 − $810.71) when the interest rate increased to 5%.

10.3. Yield to maturity exceeds current yield, which exceeds coupon rate. Take as an example the 8% coupon bond with a yield to maturity of 10% per year (5% per half year). Its price is $810.71, and therefore its current yield is 80/810.77 = 0.0987, or 9.87%, which is higher than the coupon rate but lower than the yield to maturity.

10.4. The current price of the bond can be derived from the yield to maturity. Using your calculator, set: n = 40 (semiannual periods); PMT = $45 per period; FV = $1,000; i = 4% per semiannual period. Calculate present value as $1,098.96. Now we can calculate yield to call. The time to call is five years, or 10 semiannual periods. The price at which the bond will be called is $1,050. To find yield to call, we set: n = 10 (semiannual periods); PMT = $45 per period; FV = $1,050; PV = $1,098.96. Calculate the semiannual yield to call as 3.72%.

10.5. Price = $70 × Annuity factor(8%, 1) + $1,000 × PV factor(8%, 1) = $990.74

$$\text{Rate of return to investor} = \frac{\$70 + (\$990.74 - \$982.17)}{\$982.17} = 0.080 = 8\%$$

10.6. By year-end, remaining maturity is 29 years. If the yield to maturity were still 8%, the bond would still sell at par and the holding-period return would be 8%. At a higher yield, price and return will be lower. Suppose the yield to maturity is 8.5%. With annual payments of $80 and a face value of $1,000, the price of the bond is $946.70 ($n$ = 29; i = 8.5%; PMT = $80; FV = $1,000). The bond initially sold at $1,000 when issued at the start of the year. The holding-period return is

$$\text{HPR} = \frac{80 + (946.70 - 1,000)}{1,000} = .0267 = 2.67\%$$

which is less than the initial yield to maturity of 8%.

10.7. At the lower yield, the bond price will be $631.67 [$n$ = 29, i = 7%, FV = $1,000, PMT = $40]. Therefore, total after-tax income is

Coupon	$40 × (1 − 0.38) =	$24.80
Imputed interest	($553.66 − $549.69) × (1 − 0.38) =	2.46
Capital gains	($631.67 − $553.66) × (1 − 0.20) =	62.41
Total income after taxes:		$89.67

Rate of return = 89.67/549.69 = .163 = 16.3%

10.8. The yield to maturity on two-year bonds is 8.5%. The forward rate for the third year is f_3 = 8% + 1% = 9%. We obtain the yield to maturity on three-year zeros from:

$$(1 + y_3)^3 = (1 + y_2)^2 (1 + f_3) = 1.085^2 \times 1.09 = 1.2832$$

Therefore, y_3 = .0867 = 8.67%. We note that the yield on one-year bonds is 8%, on two-year bonds is 8.5%, and on three-year bonds is 8.67%. The yield curve is upward sloping due solely to the liquidity premium.

CHAPTER

11

Managing Bond Portfolios

AFTER STUDYING THIS CHAPTER
YOU SHOULD BE ABLE TO:

 Analyze the features of a bond that affect the sensitivity of its price to interest rates.

 Compute the duration of bonds.

 Formulate fixed-income immunization strategies for various investment horizons.

 Analyze the choices to be made in an actively managed bond portfolio.

In this chapter, we turn to various strategies that bond managers can pursue, making a distinction between passive and active strategies. A *passive investment strategy* takes market prices of securities as set fairly. Rather than attempting to beat the market by exploiting superior information or insight, passive managers act to maintain an appropriate risk-return balance given market opportunities. One special case of passive management is an immunization strategy that attempts to insulate the portfolio from interest rate risk.

An *active investment strategy* attempts to achieve returns that are more than commensurate with the risk borne. In the context of bond portfolios, this style of management can take two forms. Active managers either use interest rate forecasts to predict movements in the entire bond market, or they employ some form of intramarket analysis to identify particular sectors of the market (or particular securities) that are relatively mispriced.

Because interest rate risk is crucial to formulating both active and passive strategies, we begin our discussion with an analysis of the sensitivity of bond prices to interest rate fluctuations. This sensitivity is measured by the duration of the bond, and we devote considerable attention to what determines bond
(continued)

duration. We discuss several passive investment strategies, and show how duration-matching techniques can be used to immunize the holding-period return of a portfolio from interest rate risk. After examining the broad range of applications of the duration measure, we consider refinements in the way that interest rate sensitivity is measured, focusing on the concept of bond convexity. Duration is important in formulating active investment strategies as well, and we next explore several of these strategies. We consider strategies based on intramarket analysis as well as on interest rate forecasting.

Related Web sites for this chapter are available at www.mhhe.com/bkm.

11.1 INTEREST RATE RISK

You know already that there is an inverse relationship between bond prices and yields and that interest rates can fluctuate substantially. As interest rates rise and fall, bondholders experience capital losses and gains. It is these gains or losses that make fixed-income investments risky, even if the coupon and principal payments are guaranteed, as in the case of Treasury obligations.

Why do bond prices respond to interest rate fluctuations? In a competitive market, all securities must offer investors fair expected rates of return. If a bond is issued with an 8% coupon when competitive yields are 8%, then it will sell at par value. If the market rate rises to 9%, however, who would purchase an 8% coupon bond at par value? The bond price must fall until its expected return increases to the competitive level of 9%. Conversely, if the market rate falls to 7%, the 8% coupon on the bond is attractive compared to yields on alternative investments. Investors eager for that return will respond by bidding the bond price above its par value until the total rate of return falls to the market rate.

Interest Rate Sensitivity

The sensitivity of bond prices to changes in market interest rates is obviously of great concern to investors. To gain some insight into the determinants of interest rate risk, turn to Figure 11.1, which presents the percentage changes in price corresponding to changes in yield to maturity for four bonds that differ according to coupon rate, initial yield to maturity, and time to maturity. All four bonds illustrate that bond prices decrease when yields rise and that the price curve is convex, meaning that decreases in yields have bigger impacts on price than increases in yields of equal magnitude. We summarize these observations in the following two propositions:

1. *Bond prices and yields are inversely related: As yields increase, bond prices fall; as yields fall, bond prices rise.*
2. *An increase in a bond's yield to maturity results in a smaller price change than a decrease in yield of equal magnitude.*

Now compare the interest rate sensitivity of bonds *A* and *B*, which are identical except for maturity. Figure 11.1 shows that bond *B*, which has a longer maturity than bond *A*, exhibits greater sensitivity to interest rate changes. This illustrates another general property:

3. *Prices of long-term bonds tend to be more sensitive to interest rate changes than prices of short-term bonds.*

This is not surprising. If rates increase, for example, the bond is less valuable as its cash flows are discounted at a now-higher rate. The impact of the higher discount rate will be greater as that rate is applied to more-distant cash flows.

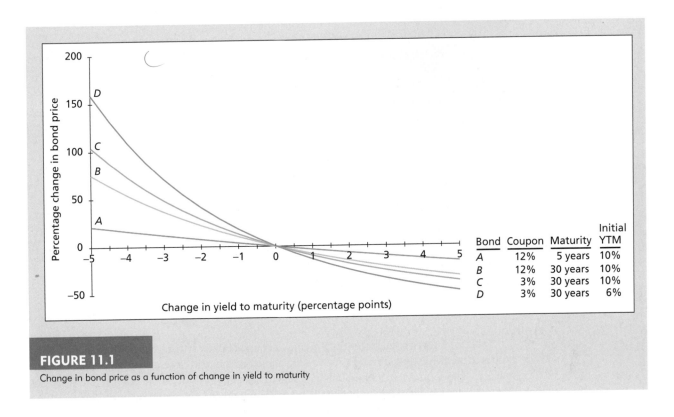

FIGURE 11.1

Change in bond price as a function of change in yield to maturity

Notice that while bond *B* has six times the maturity of bond *A,* it has less than six times the interest rate sensitivity. Although interest rate sensitivity seems to increase with maturity, it does so less than proportionally as bond maturity increases. Therefore, our fourth property is that:

4. *The sensitivity of bond prices to changes in yields increases at a decreasing rate as matu-rity increases. In other words, interest rate risk is less than proportional to bond maturity.*

Bonds *B* and *C,* which are alike in all respects except for coupon rate, illustrate another point. The lower-coupon bond exhibits greater sensitivity to changes in interest rates. This turns out to be a general property of bond prices:

5. *Interest rate risk is inversely related to the bond's coupon rate. Prices of low-coupon bonds are more sensitive to changes in interest rates than prices of high-coupon bonds.*

Finally, bonds *C* and *D* are identical except for the yield to maturity at which the bonds cur-rently sell. Yet bond *C,* with a higher yield to maturity, is less sensitive to changes in yields. This illustrates our final property:

6. *The sensitivity of a bond's price to a change in its yield is inversely related to the yield to maturity at which the bond currently is selling.*

The first five of these general properties were described by Malkiel (1962) and are some-times known as Malkiel's bond-pricing relationships. The last property was demonstrated by Homer and Liebowitz (1972).

These six propositions confirm that maturity is a major determinant of interest rate risk. However, they also show that maturity alone is not sufficient to measure interest rate sensitiv-ity. For example, bonds *B* and *C* in Figure 11.1 have the same maturity, but the higher coupon bond has less price sensitivity to interest rate changes. Obviously, we need to know more than a bond's maturity to quantify its interest rate risk.

To see why bond characteristics such as coupon rate or yield to maturity affect interest rate sensitivity, let's start with a simple numerical example.

TABLE 11.1	Bond's Yield to Maturity	T = 1 Year	T = 10 Years	T = 20 Years
Prices of 8% annual coupon bonds	8%	1,000	1,000	1,000
	9%	990.83	935.82	908.71
	Percent change in price*	−0.92%	−6.42%	−9.13%

*Equals value of bond at a 9% yield to maturity minus value of bond at (the original) 8% yield, divided by the value at 8% yield.

TABLE 11.2	Bond's Yield to Maturity	T = 1 Year	T = 10 Years	T = 20 Years
Prices of zero-coupon bonds	8%	925.93	463.19	214.55
	9%	917.43	422.41	178.43
	Percent change in price*	−0.92%	−8.80%	−16.84%

*Equals value of bond at a 9% yield to maturity minus value of bond at (the original) 8% yield, divided by the value at 8% yield.

Table 11.1 gives bond prices for 8% annual coupon bonds at different yields to maturity and times to maturity. (For simplicity, we assume coupons are paid once a year rather than semiannually.) The shortest term bond falls in value by less than 1% when the interest rate increases from 8% to 9%. The 10-year bond falls by 6.4% and the 20-year bond by more than 9%.

Let us now look at a similar computation using a zero-coupon bond rather than the 8% coupon bond. The results are shown in Table 11.2.

For maturities beyond one year, the price of the zero-coupon bond falls by a greater proportional amount than the price of the 8% coupon bond. The observation that long-term bonds are more sensitive to interest rate movements than short-term bonds suggests that in some sense a zero-coupon bond represents a longer term investment than an equal-time-to-maturity coupon bond.

In fact, this insight about the effective maturity of a bond is a useful one that we can make mathematically precise. To start, note that the times to maturity of the two bonds in this example are not perfect measures of the long- or short-term nature of the bonds. The 8% bond makes many coupon payments, most of which come years before the bond's maturity date. Each payment may be considered to have its own "maturity date." In this sense, it is often useful to view a coupon bond as a "portfolio" of coupon payments. The *effective* maturity of the bond should be measured as some sort of average of the maturities of all the cash flows paid out by the bond. The zero-coupon bond, by contrast, makes only one payment at maturity. Its time to maturity is a well-defined concept.

A high-coupon rate bond has a higher fraction of its value tied to coupons rather than payment of par value, and so the portfolio is more heavily weighted toward the earlier, short-maturity payments, which give it lower "effective maturity." This explains Malkiel's fifth rule, that price sensitivity falls with coupon rate.

Similar logic explains our sixth rule, that price sensitivity falls with yield to maturity. A higher yield reduces the present value of all of the bond's payments, but more so for more distant payments. Therefore, at a higher yield, a higher fraction of the bond's value is due to its earlier payments, which have lower effective maturity and interest rate sensitivity. The overall sensitivity of the bond price to changes in yields is thus lower.

Duration

To deal with the concept of the "maturity" of a bond that makes many payments, we need a measure of the average maturity of the bond's promised cash flows to serve as a summary statistic of the effective maturity of the bond. This measure should also give us some information on the sensitivity of a bond to interest rate changes because we have noted that price sensitivity tends to increase with time to maturity.

Frederick Macaulay (1938) called the effective maturity concept the duration of the bond. **Macaulay's duration** equals the weighted average of the times to each coupon or principal payment made by the bond. The weight applied to each time to payment clearly should be related to the "importance" of that payment to the value of the bond. In fact, the weight for each payment time is the proportion of the total value of the bond accounted for by that payment, the present value of the payment divided by the bond price.

Figure 11.2 can help us interpret Macaulay's duration by showing the cash flows made by an eight-year maturity bond with a coupon of 9%, selling at a yield to maturity of 10%. In the first seven years, cash flow is simply the $90 coupon payment; in the last year, cash flow is the sum of the coupon plus par value, or $1,090. The height of each bar is the size of the cash flow; the shaded part of each bar is the *present value* of that cash flow using a discount rate of 10%. If you view the cash flow diagram as a balancing scale, like a child's seesaw, the duration of the bond is the fulcrum point where the scale would be balanced using the present values of each cash flow as weights. The balancing point in Figure 11.2 is at 5.97 years, which is the weighted average of the times until each payment, with weights proportional to the present value of each cash flow. The coupon payments made prior to maturity make the effective (i.e., weighted average) maturity of the bond less than its actual time to maturity.

To calculate the weighted average directly, we define the weight, w_t, associated with the cash flow made at time t (denoted CF_t) as:

$$w_t = \frac{CF_t/(1 + y)^t}{\text{Bond price}}$$

where y is the bond's yield to maturity. The numerator on the right-hand side of this equation is the present value of the cash flow occurring at time t, while the denominator is the present value of all the payments forthcoming from the bond. These weights sum to 1.0 because the sum of the cash flows discounted at the yield to maturity equals the bond price.

Using these values to calculate the weighted average of the times until the receipt of each of the bond's payments, we obtain Macaulay's formula for duration, denoted D.

$$D = \sum_{t=1}^{T} t \times w_t \tag{11.1}$$

Macaulay's duration

A measure of the effective maturity of a bond, defined as the weighted average of the times until each payment, with weights proportional to the present value of the payment.

FIGURE 11.2

Cash flows paid by 9% coupon, annual payment bond with 8-year maturity and 10% yield to maturity. The height of each bar is the total of interest and principal. The shaded portion of each bar is the present value of that cash flow. The fulcrum point is Macaulay's duration, the weighted average of the time until each payment.

If we write out each term in the summation sign, we can express duration in the following equivalent equation

$$D = w_1 \quad + \quad 2w_2 \quad + \quad 3w_3 \quad + \quad 4w_4 \quad + \quad \cdots \quad + \quad Tw_T$$

time until   weight of   time until   weight of
2nd cash flow   2nd CF   4th CF   4th CF

An example of how to apply Equation 11.1 appears in Spreadsheet 11.1, where we derive the durations of an 8% coupon and zero-coupon bond each with three years to maturity. We assume that the yield to maturity on each bond is 10%. The present value of each payment is discounted at 10% for the number of years shown in column B. The weight associated with each payment time (column E) equals the present value of the payment (column D) divided by the bond price (the sum of the present values in column D).

The numbers in column F are the products of time to payment and payment weight. Each of these products corresponds to one of the terms in Equation 11.1. According to that equation, we can calculate the duration of each bond by adding the numbers in column F.

The duration of the zero-coupon bond is exactly equal to its time to maturity, three years. This makes sense for, with only one payment, the average time until payment must be the bond's maturity. The three-year coupon bond, in contrast, has a shorter duration of 2.7774 years.

While the top panel of the spreadsheet in Spreadsheet 11.1 presents numbers for our particular example, the bottom panel presents the formulas we actually entered in each cell. The inputs in the spreadsheet—specifying the cash flows the bond will pay—are given in columns

---

SPREADSHEET 11.1

Calculation of the duration of two bonds using Excel spreadsheet

Please visit us at www.mhhe.com/bkm

	A	B	C	D	E	F
1	Interest rate:	10%				
2						
3		Time until		Payment		Column (B)
4		Payment		Discounted		x
5		(Years)	Payment	at 10%	Weight*	Column (E)
6	A. 8% coupon bond	1	80	72.727	0.0765	0.0765
7		2	80	66.116	0.0696	0.1392
8		3	1080	811.420	0.8539	2.5617
9	Sum:			950.263	1.0000	2.7774
10						
11	B. Zero-coupon bond	1	0	0.000	0.0000	0.0000
12		2	0	0.000	0.0000	0.0000
13		3	1000	751.315	1.0000	3.0000
14	Sum:			751.315	1.0000	3.0000
15						
16	*Weight = Present value of each payment (column D) divided by bond price					

	A	B	C	D	E	F
1	Interest rate:	0.1				
2						
3		Time until		Payment		Column (B)
4		Payment		Discounted		times
5		(Years)	Payment	at 10%	Weight	Column (E)
6	A. 8% coupon bond	1	80	=C6/(1+$B$1)^B6	=D6/D$9	=E6*B6
7		2	80	=C7/(1+$B$1)^B7	=D7/D$9	=E7*B7
8		3	1080	=C8/(1+$B$1)^B8	=D8/D$9	=E8*B8
9	Sum:			=SUM(D6:D8)	=D9/D$9	=SUM(F6:F8)
10						
11	B. Zero-coupon	1	0	=C11/(1+$B$1)^B11	=D11/D$14	=E11*B11
12		2	0	=C12/(1+$B$1)^B12	=D12/D$14	=E12*B12
13		3	1000	=C13/(1+$B$1)^B13	=D13/D$14	=E13*B13
14	Sum:			=SUM(D11:D13)	=D14/D$14	=SUM(F11:F13)

B and C. In column D we calculate the present value of each cash flow using a discount rate of 10%, in column E we calculate the weights for Equation 11.1, and in column F we compute the product of time until payment and payment weight. Each of these terms corresponds to one of the terms in Equation 11.1. The sum of these terms, reported in cells F9 and F14, is therefore the duration of each bond. Using the spreadsheet, you can easily answer several "what if" questions such as the one in Concept Check 11.1.

CONCEPT check **11.1**

Suppose the interest rate decreases to 9%. What will happen to the price and duration of each bond in Spreadsheet 11.1?

Duration is a key concept in bond portfolio management for at least three reasons. First, it is a simple summary measure of the effective average maturity of the portfolio. Second, it turns out to be an essential tool in immunizing portfolios from interest rate risk. We will explore this application in the next section. Third, duration is a measure of the interest rate sensitivity of a bond portfolio, which we explore here.

We have already noted that long-term bonds are more sensitive to interest rate movements than short-term bonds. The duration measure enables us to quantify this relationship. It turns out that, when interest rates change, the percentage change in a bond's price is proportional to its duration. Specifically, the proportional change in a bond's price can be related to the change in its yield to maturity, y, according to the rule

$$\frac{\Delta P}{P} = -D \times \left[\frac{\Delta(1+y)}{1+y}\right] \qquad \text{(11.2)}$$

The proportional price change equals the proportional change in (1 plus the bond's yield) times the bond's duration. Therefore, bond price volatility is proportional to the bond's duration, and duration becomes a natural measure of interest rate exposure.[1] This relationship is key to interest rate risk management.

Practitioners commonly use Equation 11.2 in a slightly different form. They define **modified duration** as $D^* = D/(1+y)$ and rewrite Equation 11.2 as

$$\frac{\Delta P}{P} = -D^* \Delta y \qquad \text{(11.3)}$$

modified duration

Macaulay's duration divided by 1 + yield to maturity. Measures interest rate sensitivity of bond.

The percentage change in bond price is just the product of modified duration and the change in the bond's yield to maturity. Because the percentage change in the bond price is proportional to modified duration, modified duration is a natural measure of the bond's exposure to interest rate volatility.

A bond with maturity of 30 years has a coupon rate of 8% (paid annually) and a yield to maturity of 9%. Its price is $897.26, and its duration is 11.37 years. What will happen to the bond price if the bond's yield to maturity increases to 9.1%?

Equation 11.3 tells us that an increase of 0.1% in the bond's yield to maturity ($\Delta y = .001$ in decimal terms) will result in a price change of

$$\Delta P = -(D^* \Delta y) \times P$$
$$= -\frac{11.37}{1.09} \times 0.001 \times \$897.26 = -\$9.36$$

EXAMPLE **11.1**

Duration and Interest Rate Risk

[1]Actually, as we will see later, Equation 11.3 is only approximately valid for large changes in the bond's yield. The approximation becomes exact as one considers smaller, or localized, changes in yields.

To confirm the relationship between duration and the sensitivity of bond price to interest rate changes, let's compare the price sensitivity of the three-year coupon bond in Spreadsheet 11.1, which has a duration of 2.7774 years, to the sensitivity of a zero-coupon bond with maturity and duration of 2.7774 years. Both should have equal interest rate exposure if duration is a useful measure of price sensitivity.

The three-year bond sells for $950.263 at the initial interest rate of 10%. If the bond's yield increases by 1 basis point (1/100 of a percent) to 10.01%, its price will fall to $950.0231, a percentage decline of 0.0252%. The zero-coupon bond has a maturity of 2.7774 years. At the initial interest rate of 10%, it sells at a price of $1,000/1.10^{2.7774} = $767.425. When the interest rate increases, its price falls to $1,000/1.1001^{2.7774} = $767.2313, for an identical 0.0252% capital loss. We conclude that equal-duration assets are equally sensitive to interest rate movements.

Incidentally, this example confirms the validity of Equation 11.2. The equation predicts that the proportional price change of the two bonds should have been $-2.7774 \times 0.0001/1.10 = 0.000252$, or 0.0252%, just as we found from direct computation.

CONCEPT check 11.2

a. In Concept Check 11.1, you calculated the price and duration of a three-year maturity, 8% coupon bond for an interest rate of 9%. Now suppose the interest rate increases to 9.05%. What is the new value of the bond and the percentage change in the bond's price?

b. Calculate the percentage change in the bond's price predicted by the duration formula in Equation 11.2 or 11.3. Compare this value to your answer for (a).

The equations for the durations of coupon bonds are somewhat tedious, and spreadsheets like Spreadsheet 11.1 are cumbersome to modify for different maturities and coupon rates. Fortunately, spreadsheet programs such as Excel come with built-in functions for duration. Moreover, these functions easily accommodate bonds that are between coupon payment dates. Spreadsheet 11.2 illustrates how to use Excel to compute duration. The spreadsheets use many of the same conventions as the bond pricing spreadsheets described in Chapter 10.

We first use the spreadsheet to reconfirm the duration of the 8% coupon bond examined in Panel A of Spreadsheet 11.1. The settlement date (i.e., today's date) and maturity date are entered in cells B2 and B3 of Spreadsheet 11.2 using Excel's date function, DATE(year, month, day). For this three-year maturity bond, we don't have a specific settlement date. We arbitrarily set the settlement date to January 1, 2000, and use a maturity date precisely three years later. The coupon rate and yield to maturity are entered as decimals in cells B4 and B5, and the payment periods per year are entered in cell B6. Macaulay and modified duration

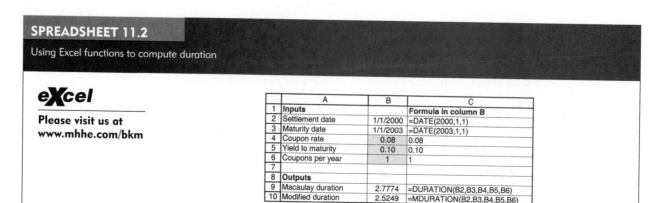

SPREADSHEET 11.2

Using Excel functions to compute duration

eXcel

Please visit us at
www.mhhe.com/bkm

	A	B	C
1	Inputs		Formula in column B
2	Settlement date	1/1/2000	=DATE(2000,1,1)
3	Maturity date	1/1/2003	=DATE(2003,1,1)
4	Coupon rate	0.08	0.08
5	Yield to maturity	0.10	0.10
6	Coupons per year	1	1
7			
8	Outputs		
9	Macaulay duration	2.7774	=DURATION(B2,B3,B4,B5,B6)
10	Modified duration	2.5249	=MDURATION(B2,B3,B4,B5,B6)

appear in cells B9 and B10. Cell B9 shows that the duration of the bond is indeed 2.7774 years. The modified duration of the bond is 2.5249, which equals 2.7774/1.10.

Figure 11.2 illustrates a 9% coupon, 8-year maturity bond with annual payments, selling at a yield to maturity of 10%. Confirm using Spreadsheet 11.2 that the bond's duration is 5.97 years. What would its duration be if the bond paid its coupon semiannually? Why intuitively does duration fall?

What Determines Duration?

Malkiel's bond price relations, which we laid out in the previous section, characterize the determinants of interest rate sensitivity. Duration allows us to quantify that sensitivity, which greatly enhances our ability to formulate investment strategies. For example, if we wish to speculate on interest rates, duration tells us how strong a bet we are making. Conversely, if we wish to remain "neutral" on rates, and simply match the interest rate sensitivity of a chosen bond market index, duration allows us to measure that sensitivity and mimic it in our own portfolio. For these reasons, it is crucial to understand the determinants of duration and convenient to have formulas to calculate the duration of some commonly encountered securities. Therefore, in this section, we present several "rules" that summarize most of the important properties of duration. These rules are also illustrated in Figure 11.3, which contains plots of durations of bonds of various coupon rates, yields to maturity, and times to maturity.

We have already established:

Rule 1: The duration of a zero-coupon bond equals its time to maturity.

We also have seen that the three-year coupon bond has a lower duration than the three-year zero because coupons early in the bond's life reduce the bond's weighted average time until payments. This illustrates another general property:

Rule 2: With time to maturity and yield to maturity held constant, a bond's duration and interest rate sensitivity are higher when the coupon rate is lower.

This property corresponds to Malkiel's fifth bond-pricing relationship and is attributable to the impact of early coupons on the average maturity of a bond's payments. The lower these coupons, the less weight these early payments have on the weighted average maturity of all the bond's payments. In other words, a lower fraction of the total value of the bond is tied up in the (earlier) coupon payments whose values are relatively insensitive to yields rather than the (later and more yield-sensitive) repayment of par value. Compare the plots in Figure 11.3 of the durations of the 3% coupon and 15% coupon bonds, each with identical yields of 15%. The plot of the duration of the 15% coupon bond lies below the corresponding plot for the 3% coupon bond.

Rule 3: With the coupon rate held constant, a bond's duration and interest rate sensitivity generally increase with time to maturity. Duration always increases with maturity for bonds selling at par or at a premium to par.

This property of duration corresponds to Malkiel's third relationship and is fairly intuitive. What is surprising is that duration need not always increase with time to maturity. For some deep discount bonds, such as the 3% coupon bond selling to yield 15% in Figure 11.3, duration may eventually fall with increases in maturity. For virtually all traded bonds, however, it is safe to assume that duration increases with maturity.

Notice in Figure 11.3 that for the zero-coupon bond, maturity and duration are equal. For all the coupon bonds, however, duration increases by less than a year for each year's increase in maturity. The slope of the duration graph is less than 1.0, and duration is always less than maturity for positive-coupon bonds.

FIGURE 11.3

Duration as a function of maturity

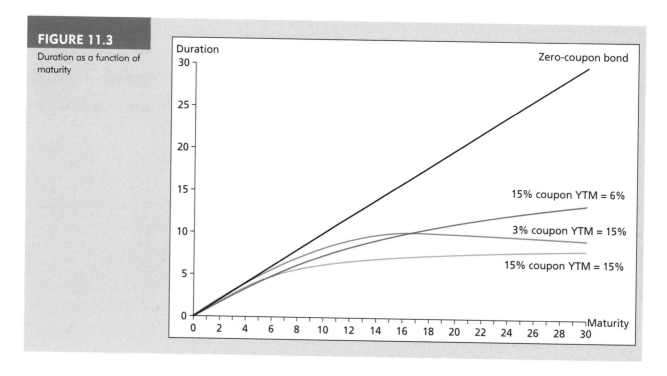

While long-maturity bonds generally will be high-duration bonds, duration is a better measure of the long-term nature of the bond because it also accounts for coupon payments. Only when the bond pays no coupons is time to maturity an adequate measure; then maturity and duration are equal.

Notice also in Figure 11.3 that the two 15% coupon bonds have different durations when they sell at different yields to maturity. The lower yield bond has longer duration. This makes sense, because at lower yields the more distant payments have relatively greater present values and thereby account for a greater share of the bond's total value. Thus, in the weighted-average calculation of duration, the distant payments receive greater weights, which results in a higher duration measure. This establishes

> *Rule 4: With other factors held constant, the duration and interest rate sensitivity of a coupon bond are higher when the bond's yield to maturity is lower.*

As we noted above, the intuition for this rule is that while a higher yield reduces the present value of all of the bond's payments, it reduces the value of more distant payments by a greater proportional amount. Therefore, at higher yields a higher fraction of the total value of the bond lies in its earlier payments, thereby reducing effective maturity. Rule 4, which is the sixth bond-pricing relationship noted above, applies to coupon bonds. For zeros, duration equals time to maturity, regardless of the yield to maturity.

Finally, we present an algebraic rule for the duration of a perpetuity. This rule is derived from and is consistent with the formula for duration given in Equation 11.1, but it is far easier to use for infinitely lived bonds.

> *Rule 5: The duration of a level perpetuity is*

$$\text{Duration of perpetuity} = \frac{1 + y}{y} \tag{11.4}$$

For example, at a 15% yield, the duration of a perpetuity that pays $100 once a year forever will equal 1.15/.15 = 7.67 years, while at an 8% yield, it will equal 1.08/.08 = 13.5 years.

Equation 11.4 makes it obvious that maturity and duration can differ substantially. The maturity of the perpetuity is infinite, while the duration of the instrument at a 15% yield is

TABLE 11.3		Coupon Rates (% per year)			
Durations of annual coupon bonds (initial bond yield = 8%)	**Years to Maturity**	**6**	**8**	**10**	**12**
	1	1.000	1.000	1.000	1.000
	5	4.439	4.312	4.204	4.110
	10	7.615	7.247	6.996	6.744
	20	11.231	10.604	10.182	9.880
	Infinite (perpetuity)	13.500	13.500	13.500	13.500

only 7.67 years. The present-value-weighted cash flows early on in the life of the perpetuity dominate the computation of duration. Notice from Figure 11.3 that as their maturities become ever longer, the durations of the two coupon bonds with yields of 15% both converge to the duration of the perpetuity with the same yield, 7.67 years.

CONCEPT check 11.4

Show that the duration of a perpetuity increases as the interest rate decreases, in accordance with Rule 4.

Durations can vary widely among traded bonds. Table 11.3 presents durations for several bonds all assumed to pay annual coupons and to yield 8% per year. Duration decreases as coupon rates increase and increases with time to maturity. According to Table 11.3 and Equation 11.2, if the interest rate were to increase from 8% to 8.1%, the 6% coupon, 20-year bond would fall in value by about 1.04% (= − 11.231 × 0.1%/1.08) while the 10% coupon, one-year bond would fall by only 0.093% (= − 1 × 0.1%/1.08). Notice also from Table 11.3 that duration is independent of coupon rate only for perpetuities.

[handwritten annotation:] $$\text{BOND DURATION} = \frac{1+y}{y} - \frac{(1+y) + T(c-y)}{c[(1+y)^T - 1] + y}$$

11.2 PASSIVE BOND MANAGEMENT

Passive managers take bond prices as fairly set and seek to control only the risk of their fixed-income portfolios. Generally, there are two ways of viewing this risk, depending on the investor's circumstances. Some institutions, such as banks, are concerned with protecting the portfolio's current net worth or net market value against interest rate fluctuations. Risk-based capital guidelines for commercial banks and thrift institutions require the setting aside of additional capital as a buffer against potential losses in market value incurred from interest rate fluctuations. The amount of capital required is directly related to the losses that may be incurred under various changes in market interest rates. Other investors, such as pension funds, may have an investment goal to be reached after a given number of years. These investors are more concerned with protecting the future values of their portfolios.

[handwritten annotation:] · ANNUITY DURATION $$D = \frac{1+y}{y} - \frac{T}{(1+y)^T - 1}$$

What is common to the bank and pension fund, however, is interest rate risk. The net worth of the firm and its ability to meet future obligations fluctuate with interest rates. If they adjust the maturity structure of their portfolios, these institutions can shed their interest rate risk. **Immunization** and dedication techniques refer to strategies that investors use to shield their net worth from exposure to interest rate fluctuations.

immunization

A strategy to shield net worth from interest rate movements.

Immunization

Many banks and thrift institutions have a natural mismatch between the maturities of assets and liabilities. For example, bank liabilities are primarily the deposits owed to customers; these liabilities are short-term in nature and consequently of low duration. Assets largely comprise commercial and consumer loans or mortgages. These assets are of longer duration than deposits, which means their values are correspondingly more sensitive than deposits to

On the MARKET FRONT

PENSION FUNDS LOSE GROUND DESPITE BROAD MARKET GAINS

The stock market had a banner year in 2003, with the S&P 500 providing a rate of return in excess of 25%. Not surprisingly, this performance showed up in the balance sheets of U.S. pension funds: Assets in these funds rose by more than $100 billion. Despite this apparent good news, pension funds actually *lost* ground in 2003, with the gap between assets and liabilities growing by about $45 billion.

How did this happen? Blame the decline in interest rates during the year that were in large part the force behind the stock market gains. As rates fell, the present value of pension obligations to retirees rose even faster than the value of the assets backing those promises. It turns out that the value of pension liabilities is more sensitive to interest rate changes than is the value of the typical assets held in those funds. So even though falling rates tend to pump up asset returns, they pump up liabilities even more so. In other words, the duration of fund investments tends to be shorter than the duration of its obligations. This duration mismatch makes funds vulnerable to interest rate declines.

Why don't funds better match asset and liability durations? One reason is that fund managers are often evaluated based on their performance relative to standard bond market indexes. Those indexes tend to have far shorter durations than pension fund liabilities. So to some extent, managers may be keeping their eyes on the wrong ball, one with the wrong interest rate sensitivity.

interest rate fluctuations. When interest rates increase unexpectedly, banks can suffer serious decreases in net worth—their assets fall in value by more than their liabilities.

Similarly, a pension fund may have a mismatch between the interest rate sensitivity of the assets held in the fund and the present value of its liabilities—the promise to make payments to retirees. The nearby box illustrates the dangers that pension funds face when they neglect the interest rate exposure of *both* assets and liabilities. The box "Pension Funds Lose Ground" points out that when interest rates change, the present value of the fund's liabilities change. For example, in some recent years pension funds lost ground despite the fact that they enjoyed excellent investment returns. As interest rates fell, the value of their liabilities grew even faster than the value of their assets. The conclusion: Funds should match the interest rate exposure of assets and liabilities so that the value of assets will track the value of liabilities whether rates rise or fall. In other words, the financial manager might want to *immunize* the fund against interest rate volatility.

Pension funds are not alone in this concern. Any institution with a future fixed obligation might consider immunization a reasonable risk management policy. Insurance companies, for example, also pursue immunization strategies. The notion of immunization was introduced by F. M. Redington (1952), an actuary for a life insurance company. The idea behind immunization is that duration-matched assets and liabilities let the asset portfolio meet the firm's obligations despite interest rate movements.

Consider, for example, an insurance company that issues a guaranteed investment contract, or GIC, for $10,000. (GICs are essentially zero-coupon bonds issued by the insurance company to its customers. They are popular products for individuals' retirement-savings accounts.) If the GIC has a five-year maturity and a guaranteed interest rate of 8%, the insurance company is obligated to pay $10,000 \times (1.08)^5 = \$14,693.28$ in five years.

Suppose that the insurance company chooses to fund its obligation with $10,000 of 8% *annual* coupon bonds, selling at par value, with six years to maturity. As long as the market interest rate stays at 8%, the company has fully funded the obligation, as the present value of the obligation exactly equals the value of the bonds.

Table 11.4A shows that if interest rates remain at 8%, the accumulated funds from the bond will grow to exactly the $14,693.28 obligation. Over the five-year period, the year-end coupon income of $800 is reinvested at the prevailing 8% market interest rate. At the end of the period, the bonds can be sold for $10,000; they still will sell at par value because the coupon rate still equals the market interest rate. Total income after five years from reinvested coupons and the sale of the bond is precisely $14,693.28.

TABLE 11.4	Payment Number	Years Remaining until Obligation	Accumulated Value of Invested Payment
Terminal value of a bond portfolio after five years (all proceeds reinvested)	**A. Rates remain at 8%**		
	1	4	$800 \times (1.08)^4 =$ 1,088.39
	2	3	$800 \times (1.08)^3 =$ 1,007.77
	3	2	$800 \times (1.08)^2 =$ 933.12
	4	1	$800 \times (1.08)^1 =$ 864.00
	5	0	$800 \times (1.08)^0 =$ 800.00
	Sale of bond	0	$10,800/1.08 =$ 10,000.00
			14,693.28
	B. Rates fall to 7%		
	1	4	$800 \times (1.07)^4 =$ 1,048.64
	2	3	$800 \times (1.07)^3 =$ 980.03
	3	2	$800 \times (1.07)^2 =$ 915.92
	4	1	$800 \times (1.07)^1 =$ 856.00
	5	0	$800 \times (1.07)^0 =$ 800.00
	Sale of bond	0	$10,800/1.07 =$ 10,093.46
			14,694.05
	C. Rates increase to 9%		
	1	4	$800 \times (1.09)^4 =$ 1,129.27
	2	3	$800 \times (1.09)^3 =$ 1,036.02
	3	2	$800 \times (1.09)^2 =$ 950.48
	4	1	$800 \times (1.09)^1 =$ 872.00
	5	0	$800 \times (1.09)^0 =$ 800.00
	Sale of bond	0	$10,800/1.09 =$ 9,908.26
			14,696.02

Note: The sale price of the bond portfolio equals the portfolio's final payment ($10,800) divided by $1 + r$, because the time to maturity of the bonds will be one year at the time of sale.

If interest rates change, however, two offsetting influences will affect the ability of the fund to grow to the targeted value of $14,693.28. If interest rates rise, the fund will suffer a capital loss, impairing its ability to satisfy the obligation. The bonds will be worth less in five years than if interest rates had remained at 8%. However, at a higher interest rate, reinvested coupons will grow at a faster rate, offsetting the capital loss. In other words, fixed-income investors face two offsetting types of interest rate risk: *price risk* and *reinvestment rate risk*. Increases in interest rates cause capital losses but at the same time increase the rate at which reinvested income will grow. If the portfolio duration is chosen appropriately, these two effects will cancel out exactly. When the portfolio duration is set equal to the investor's horizon date, the accumulated value of the investment fund at the horizon date will be unaffected by interest rate fluctuations. *For a horizon equal to the portfolio's duration, price risk and reinvestment risk exactly cancel out.* The obligation is immunized.

In the example we are discussing, the duration of the six-year maturity bonds used to fund the GIC is five years. You can confirm this using either Spreadsheets 11.1 or 11.2. The duration of the (zero-coupon) GIC is also five years. Because the fully funded plan has equal duration for its assets and liabilities, the insurance company should be immunized against interest rate fluctuations. To confirm that this is the case, let us now investigate whether the bond can generate enough income to pay off the obligation five years from now regardless of interest rate movements.

Tables 11.4B and C consider two possible interest rate scenarios: Rates either fall to 7% or increase to 9%. In both cases, the annual coupon payments from the bond are reinvested at the new interest rate, which is assumed to change before the first coupon payment, and the bond is sold in year 5 to help satisfy the obligation of the GIC.

Table 11.4B shows that if interest rates fall to 7%, the total funds will accumulate to $14,694.05, providing a small surplus of $0.77. If rates increase to 9% as in Table 11.4C, the fund accumulates to $14,696.02, providing a small surplus of $2.74.

Several points are worth highlighting. First, duration matching balances the difference between the accumulated value of the coupon payments (reinvestment rate risk) and the sale value of the bond (price risk). That is, when interest rates fall, the coupons grow less than in the base case, but the gain on the sale of the bond offsets this. When interest rates rise, the resale value of the bond falls, but the coupons more than make up for this loss because they are reinvested at the higher rate. Figure 11.4 illustrates this case. The solid curve traces out the accumulated value of the bonds if interest rates remain at 8%. The dashed curve shows that value if interest rates happen to increase. The initial impact is a capital loss, but this loss eventually is offset by the now-faster growth rate of reinvested funds. At the five-year horizon date, equal to the bond's duration, the two effects just cancel, leaving the company able to satisfy its obligation with the accumulated proceeds from the bond.

We can also analyze immunization in terms of present as opposed to future values. Table 11.5A shows the initial balance sheet for the insurance company's GIC account. Both assets and the obligation have market values of $10,000, so that the plan is just fully funded. Table 11.5B and C show that whether the interest rate increases or decreases, the value of the bonds funding the GIC and the present value of the company's obligation change by virtually identical amounts. Regardless of the interest rate change, the plan remains fully funded, with the surplus in Table 11.5B and C just about zero. The duration-matching strategy has ensured that both assets and liabilities react equally to interest rate fluctuations.

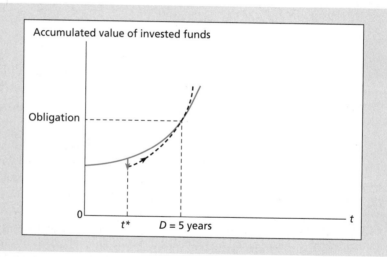

FIGURE 11.4

Growth of invested funds

Note: The solid curve represents the growth of portfolio value at the original interest rate. If interest rates increase at time t^* the portfolio value falls but increases thereafter at the faster rate represented by the broken curve. At time D (duration) the curves cross.

TABLE 11.5

Market value balance sheets

A. Interest rate = 8%

Assets		Liabilities	
Bonds	$10,000	Obligation	$10,000

B. Interest rate = 7%

Assets		Liabilities	
Bonds	$10,476.65	Obligation	$10,476.11

C. Interest rate = 9%

Assets		Liabilities	
Bonds	$9,551.41	Obligation	$9,549.62

Notes: Value of bonds = 800 × Annuity factor(r, 6) + 10,000 × PV factor(r, 6)

Value of obligation $= \dfrac{14,693.28}{(1 + r)^5} = 14,693.28 \times$ PV factor(r, 5)

Figure 11.5 is a graph of the present values of the bond and the single-payment obligation as a function of the interest rate. At the current rate of 8%, the values are equal, and the obligation is fully funded by the bond. Moreover, the two present value curves are tangent at $y = 8\%$. As interest rates change, the change in value of both the asset and the obligation are equal, so the obligation remains fully funded. For greater changes in the interest rate, however, the present value curves diverge. This reflects the fact that the fund actually shows a small surplus at market interest rates other than 8%.

Why is there any surplus in the fund? After all, we claimed that a duration-matched asset and liability mix would make the investor indifferent to interest rate shifts. Actually, such a claim is valid for only *small* changes in the interest rate, because as bond yields change, so too does duration. (Recall Rule 4 for duration.) In fact, while the duration of the bond in this example is equal to five years at a yield to maturity of 8%, the duration rises to 5.02 years when the bond yield falls to 7% and drops to 4.97 years at $y = 9\%$. That is, the bond and the obligation were not duration-matched *across* the interest rate shift, so the position was not fully immunized.

This example demonstrates the need for **rebalancing** immunized portfolios. As interest rates and asset durations continually change, managers must rebalance, that is, change the composition of, the portfolio of fixed-income assets to realign its duration with the duration of the obligation. Moreover, even if interest rates do not change, asset durations *will* change solely because of the passage of time. Recall from Figure 11.3 that duration generally decreases less rapidly than maturity as time passes, so even if an obligation is immunized at the outset, the durations of the asset and liability will fall at different rates. Without portfolio rebalancing, durations will become unmatched and the goals of immunization will not be realized. Therefore, immunization is a passive strategy only in the sense that it does not involve attempts to identify undervalued securities. Immunization managers still actively update and monitor their positions.

rebalancing

Realigning the proportions of assets in a portfolio as needed.

EXAMPLE 11.2

Constructing an Immunized Portfolio

An insurance company must make a payment of $19,487 in seven years. The market interest rate is 10%, so the present value of the obligation is $10,000. The company's portfolio manager wishes to fund the obligation using three-year zero-coupon bonds and perpetuities paying annual coupons. (We focus on zeros and perpetuities to keep the algebra simple.) How can the manager immunize the obligation?

Immunization requires that the duration of the portfolio of assets equal the duration of the liability. We can proceed in four steps:

Step 1. Calculate the duration of the liability. In this case, the liability duration is simple to compute. It is a single-payment obligation with duration of seven years.

Step 2. Calculate the duration of the asset portfolio. The portfolio duration is the weighted average of duration of each component asset, with weights proportional to the funds placed in each asset. The duration of the zero-coupon bond is simply its maturity, three years. The duration of the perpetuity is $1.10/.10 = 11$ years. Therefore, if the fraction of the portfolio invested in the zero is called w, and the fraction invested in the perpetuity is $(1 - w)$, the portfolio duration will be

$$\text{Asset duration} = w \times 3 \text{ years} + (1 - w) \times 11 \text{ years}$$

Step 3. Find the asset mix that sets the duration of assets equal to the seven-year duration of liabilities. This requires us to solve for w in the following equation

$$w \times 3 \text{ years} + (1 - w) \times 11 \text{ years} = 7 \text{ years}$$

This implies that $w = 1/2$. The manager should invest half the portfolio in the zero and half in the perpetuity. This will result in an asset duration of seven years.

Step 4. Fully fund the obligation. Since the obligation has a present value of $10,000, and the fund will be invested equally in the zero and the perpetuity, the manager must purchase $5,000 of the zero-coupon bond and $5,000 of the perpetuity. Note that the *face value* of the zero will be $5,000 \times (1.10)^3 = $6,655$.

FIGURE 11.5

Immunization. The coupon bond fully funds the obligation at an interest rate of 8%. Moreover, the present value curves are tangent at 8%, so the obligation will remain fully funded even if rates change by a small amount.

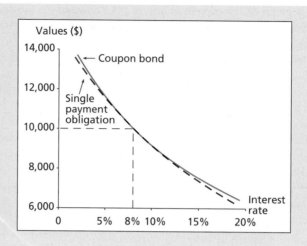

Even if a position is immunized, however, the portfolio manager still cannot rest. This is because of the need for rebalancing in response to changes in interest rates. Moreover, even if rates do not change, the passage of time also will affect duration and require rebalancing. Let us continue Example 11.2 and see how the portfolio manager can maintain an immunized position.

EXAMPLE   11.3

Rebalancing

Suppose that one year has passed, and the interest rate remains at 10%. The portfolio manager of Example 11.2 needs to reexamine her position. Is the position still fully funded? Is it still immunized? If not, what actions are required?

First, examine funding. The present value of the obligation will have grown to $11,000, as it is one year closer to maturity. The manager's funds also have grown to $11,000: The zero-coupon bonds have increased in value from $5,000 to $5,500 with the passage of time, while the perpetuity has paid its annual $500 coupons and remains worth $5,000. Therefore, the obligation is still fully funded.

The portfolio weights must be changed, however. The zero-coupon bond now will have a duration of two years, while the perpetuity duration remains at 11 years. The obligation is now due in six years. The weights must now satisfy the equation

$$w \times 2 + (1 - w) \times 11 = 6$$

which implies that $w = 5/9$. To rebalance the portfolio and maintain the duration match, the manager now must invest a total of $11,000 \times 5/9 = $6,111.11$ in the zero-coupon bond. This requires that the entire $500 coupon payment be invested in the zero, with an additional $111.11 of the perpetuity sold and invested in the zero-coupon bond.

Of course, rebalancing the portfolio entails transaction costs as assets are bought or sold, so continuous rebalancing is not feasible. In practice, managers strike a compromise between the desire for perfect immunization, which requires continual rebalancing, and the need to control trading costs, which dictates less frequent rebalancing.

CONCEPT
check **11.5**

Look again at Example 11.3. What would have been the immunizing weights in the second year if the interest rate had fallen to 8%?

The Excel immunization model allows you to analyze any number of time-period or holding-period immunization examples. The model is built using the Excel-supplied formulas for bond duration, which allow the investigation of any maturity bond without building a table of cash flows.

	A	B	C	D	E	F	G	H
1			Holding Period Immunization					
2								
3	YTM	0.0800	Mar Price	1000.00				
4	Coupon R	0.0800						
5	Maturity	6			Duration	#NAME?		
6	Par Value	1000.00						
7	Holding P	5						
8	Duration	4.9927						
9								
10								
11	If Rates Increase by 200 basis points				If Rates Increase by 100 basis points			
12	Rate	0.1000			Rate	0.0900		
13	FV of CPS	488.41			FV of CPS	478.78		
14	SalesP	981.82			SalesP	990.83		
15	Total	1470.23			Total	1469.60		
16	IRR	0.0801			IRR	0.0800		
17								
18								
19								
20	If Rates Decrease by 200 basis points				If Rates Decrease by 100 basis points			
21	Rate	0.0600			Rate	0.0700		
22	FV of CPS	450.97			FV of CPS	460.06		
23	SalesP	1018.87			SalesP	1009.35		
24	Total	1469.84			Total	1469.40		
25	IRR	0.0801			IRR	0.0800		

Cash Flow Matching and Dedication

The problems associated with immunization seem to have a simple solution. Why not simply buy a zero-coupon bond that provides a payment in an amount exactly sufficient to cover the projected cash outlay? This is **cash flow matching,** which automatically immunizes a portfolio from interest rate movements because the cash flow from the bond and the obligation exactly offset each other.

Cash flow matching on a multiperiod basis is referred to as a **dedication strategy.** In this case, the manager selects either zero-coupon or coupon bonds that provide total cash flows that match a series of obligations in each period. The advantage of dedication is that it is a once-and-for-all approach to eliminating interest rate risk. Once the cash flows are matched, there is no need for rebalancing. The dedicated portfolio provides the cash necessary to pay the firm's liabilities regardless of the eventual path of interest rates.

Cash flow matching is not widely pursued, however, probably because of the constraints it imposes on bond selection. Immunization/dedication strategies are appealing to firms that do not wish to bet on general movements in interest rates, yet these firms may want to immunize using bonds they believe are undervalued. Cash flow matching places enough constraints on bond selection that it can make it impossible to pursue a dedication strategy using only "underpriced" bonds. Firms looking for underpriced bonds exchange exact and easy dedication for the possibility of achieving superior returns from their bond portfolios.

Sometimes, cash flow matching is not even possible. To cash flow match for a pension fund that is obligated to pay out a perpetual flow of income to current and future retirees, the pension fund would need to purchase fixed-income securities with maturities ranging up to hundreds of years. Such securities do not exist, making exact dedication infeasible. Immunization is easy, however. If the interest rate is 8%, for example, the duration of the pension fund

cash flow matching

Matching cash flows from a fixed-income portfolio with those of an obligation.

dedication strategy

Refers to multiperiod cash flow matching.

obligation is 1.08/.08 = 13.5 years (see Rule 5 above). Therefore, the fund can immunize its obligation by purchasing zero-coupon bonds with maturity of 13.5 years and a market value equal to that of the pension liabilities.

a. Suppose that this pension fund is obligated to pay out $800,000 per year in perpetuity. What should be the maturity and face value of the zero-coupon bond it purchases to immunize its obligation?

b. Now suppose the interest rate immediately increases to 8.1%. How should the fund rebalance in order to remain immunized against further interest rate shocks? Ignore transaction costs.

How would an increase in trading costs affect the attractiveness of dedication versus immunization?

11.3 | CONVEXITY

Duration clearly is a key tool in bond portfolio management. Yet, the duration rule for the impact of interest rates on bond prices is only an approximation. Equation 11.3, which we repeat here, states that the percentage change in the value of a bond approximately equals the product of modified duration times the change in the bond's yield:

$$\frac{\Delta P}{P} = -D^* \Delta y$$

This equation asserts that the percentage price change is directly proportional to the change in the bond's yield. If this were *exactly* so, however, a graph of the percentage change in bond price as a function of the change in its yield would plot as a straight line, with slope equal to $-D^*$. Yet we know from Figure 11.1, and more generally from Malkiel's five bond-pricing relationships (specifically relationship 2), that the relationship between bond prices and yields is *not* linear. The duration rule is a good approximation for small changes in bond yield, but it is less accurate for larger changes.

Figure 11.6 illustrates this point. Like Figure 11.1, this figure presents the percentage change in bond price in response to a change in the bond's yield to maturity. The curved

FIGURE 11.6

Bond price convexity. The percentage change in bond price is a convex function of the change in yield to maturity.

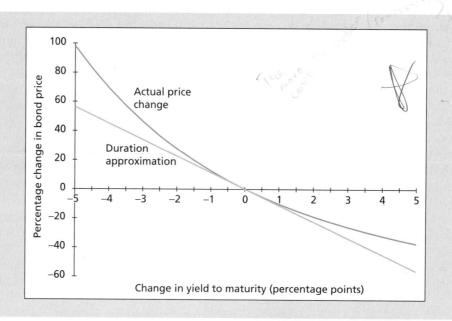

line is the percentage price change for a 30-year maturity, 8% coupon bond, selling at an initial yield to maturity of 8%. The straight line is the percentage price change predicted by the duration rule: The modified duration of the bond at its initial yield is 11.26 years, so the straight line is a plot of $-D^*\Delta y = -11.26 \times \Delta y$. Notice that the two plots are tangent at the initial yield. Thus, for small changes in the bond's yield to maturity, the duration rule is quite accurate. However, for larger changes in yield, there is progressively more "daylight" between the two plots, demonstrating that the duration rule becomes progressively less accurate.

Notice from Figure 11.6 that the duration approximation (the straight line) always understates the value of the bond; it underestimates the increase in bond price when the yield falls, and it overestimates the decline in price when the yield rises. This is due to the curvature of the true price-yield relationship. Curves with shapes such as that of the price-yield relationship are said to be convex, and the curvature of the price-yield curve is called the **convexity** of the bond.

We can quantify convexity as the rate of change of the slope of the price-yield curve, expressed as a fraction of the bond price.[2] As a practical rule, you can view bonds with higher convexity as exhibiting higher curvature in the price-yield relationship. The convexity of non-callable bonds, such as that in Figure 11.6, is positive: The slope increases (i.e., becomes less negative) at higher yields.

Convexity allows us to improve the duration approximation for bond price changes. Accounting for convexity, Equation 11.3 can be modified as follows:[3]

convexity

The curvature of the price-yield relationship of a bond.

$$\frac{\Delta P}{P} = -D^*\Delta y + \tfrac{1}{2} \times \text{Convexity} \times (\Delta y)^2 \qquad \textbf{(11.5)}$$

The first term on the right-hand side is the same as the duration rule, Equation 11.3. The second term is the modification for convexity. Notice that for a bond with positive convexity, the second term is positive, regardless of whether the yield rises or falls. This insight corresponds to the fact noted just above that the duration rule always underestimates the new value of a bond following a change in its yield. The more accurate Equation 11.5, which accounts for convexity, always predicts a higher bond price than Equation 11.3. Of course, if the change in yield is small, the convexity term, which is multiplied by $(\Delta y)^2$ in Equation 11.5, will be extremely small and will add little to the approximation. In this case, the linear approximation given by the duration rule will be sufficiently accurate. Thus, convexity is more important as a practical matter when potential interest rate changes are large.

Convexity is the reason that the immunization examples we considered above resulted in small errors. For example, if you turn back to Table 11.5 and Figure 11.5, you will see that the single payment obligation that was funded with a coupon bond of the same duration was well immunized for small changes in yields. However, for larger yield changes, the two pricing curves diverged a bit, implying that such changes in yields would result in small surpluses. This is due to the greater convexity of the coupon bond.

---

[2]If you have taken a calculus class, you will recognize that Equation 11.3 for modified duration can be written as $dP/P = -D^*dy$. Thus, $-D^* = 1/P \times dP/dy$ is the slope of the price-yield curve expressed as a fraction of the bond price. Similarly, the convexity of a bond equals the second derivative (the rate of change of the slope) of the price-yield curve divided by bond price: Convexity $= 1/P \times d^2P/dy^2$. The formula for the convexity of a bond with a maturity of n years making annual coupon payments is:

$$\text{Convexity} = \frac{1}{P \times (1 + y)^2} \sum_{t=1}^{n} \left[\frac{CF_t}{(1 + y)^t}(t^2 + t) \right] \qquad \text{\textit{too much}} \atop \text{\textit{not on exam}}$$

where CF_t is the cash flow paid to the bondholder at date t; CF_t represents either a coupon payment before maturity or final coupon plus par value at the maturity date.

[3]To use the convexity rule, you must express interest rates as decimals rather than percentages.

EXAMPLE   11.4

Convexity

The bond in Figure 11.6 has a 30-year maturity, an 8% coupon, and sells at an initial yield to maturity of 8%. Because the coupon rate equals yield to maturity, the bond sells at par value, or $1,000. The modified duration of the bond at its initial yield is 11.26 years, and its convexity is 212.4, which can be calculated using the formula in footnote 2. (You can find a spreadsheet to calculate the convexity of a 30-year bond at the book Web site at **www.mhhe.com/bkm.** See also the nearby Excel Application.) If the bond's yield increases from 8% to 10%, the bond price will fall to $811.46, a decline of 18.85%. The duration rule, Equation 11.3, would predict a price decline of

$$\frac{\Delta P}{P} = -D^* \Delta y = -11.26 \times 0.02 = -0.2252 = -22.52\%$$

which is considerably more than the bond price actually falls. The duration-with-convexity rule, Equation 11.5, is more accurate:

$$\frac{\Delta P}{P} = -D^* \Delta y + \frac{1}{2} \times \text{Convexity} \times (\Delta y)^2$$

$$= -11.26 \times 0.02 + \frac{1}{2} \times 212.4 \times (0.02)^2 = -0.1827 = -18.27\%$$

which is far closer to the exact change in bond price.

Notice that if the change in yield were smaller, say, 0.1%, convexity would matter less. The price of the bond actually would fall to $988.85, a decline of 1.115%. Without accounting for convexity, we would predict a price decline of

$$\frac{\Delta P}{P} = -D^* \Delta y = -11.26 \times 0.001 = 0.01126 = 1.126\%$$

Accounting for convexity, we get almost the precisely correct answer:

$$\frac{\Delta P}{P} = -11.26 \times 0.001 + \frac{1}{2} \times 212.4 \times (0.001)^2 = 0.01115 = 1.115\%$$

Nevertheless, the duration rule is quite accurate in this case, even without accounting for convexity.

Why Do Investors Like Convexity?

Convexity is generally considered a desirable trait. Bonds with greater curvature gain more in price when yields fall than they lose when yields rise. For example, in Figure 11.7 bonds *A* and *B* have the same duration at the initial yield. The plots of their proportional price changes as a function of interest rate changes are tangent, meaning that their sensitivities to changes in yields at that point are equal. However, bond *A* is more convex than bond *B*. It enjoys greater price increases and smaller price decreases when interest rates fluctuate by larger amounts. If interest rates are volatile, this is an attractive asymmetry that increases the expected return on the bond, since bond *A* will benefit more from rate decreases and suffer less from rate

WEB *master*

Duration and Convexity Calculators

Go to **www.derivativesmodels.com.** Choose the link for the classic page. You can also experiment with the enhanced page, which requires you first to establish a (free) user account. This site has a wealth of calculators. Scroll down to find *Bond Calculators*, and choose the link

for *calculator.* The calculator provides yield to maturity, modified duration, and bond convexity as the bond's price changes. Experiment by trying different inputs. What happens to duration and convexity as coupon increases? As maturity increases? As price increases (with coupon held fixed)?

The Convexity spreadsheet allows you to calculate bond convexity. You can specify yield to maturity and coupon and allow for short maturities by setting later cash flows equal to zero, setting the last cash flow equal to principal plus final coupon payment.

eXcel

Please visit us at
www.mhhe.com/bkm

	A	B	C	D	E	F	G	H
1					Chapter 11			
2					Convexity			
3								
4			Time (t)	Cash flow	PV(CF)	t + t^2	(t + t^2) x PV(CF)	
5								
6	Coupon	3	1	3	2.871	2	5.742	
7	YTM	0.045	2	3	2.747	6	16.483	
8	Maturity	10	3	3	2.629	12	31.547	
9	Price	$88.13	4	3	2.516	20	50.314	
10			5	3	2.407	30	72.221	
11			6	3	2.304	42	96.755	
12			7	3	2.204	56	123.451	
13			8	3	2.110	72	151.888	
14			9	3	2.019	90	181.684	
15			10	103	66.325	110	7295.701	
16								
17			Sum:		88.13092273		8025.785	
18								
19				Convexity:			83.392425	

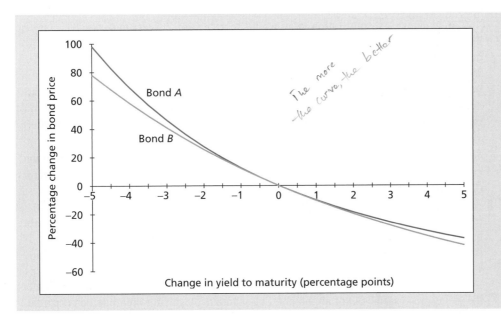

FIGURE 11.7

Convexity of two bonds. Bond A has greater convexity than bond B.

increases. Of course, if convexity is desirable, it will not be available for free: Investors will have to pay more and accept lower yields on bonds with greater convexity.

11.4 ACTIVE BOND MANAGEMENT

Sources of Potential Profit

Broadly speaking, there are two sources of potential value in active bond management. The first is interest rate forecasting; that is, anticipating movements across the entire spectrum of the fixed-income market. If interest rate declines are forecast, managers will increase portfolio duration; if increases seem likely, they will shorten duration. The second source of potential profit is identification of relative mispricing within the fixed-income market. An analyst might believe, for example, that the default premium on one bond is unnecessarily large and the bond is underpriced.

These techniques will generate abnormal returns only if the analyst's information or insight is superior to that of the market. There is no way of profiting from knowledge that rates are about to fall if everyone else in the market is onto this. In that case, the anticipated lower future rates are built into bond prices in the sense that long-duration bonds are already selling at higher prices that reflect the anticipated fall in future short rates. If the analyst does not have information before the market does, it will be too late to act on that information—prices will have responded already to the news. You know this from our discussion of market efficiency.

For now we simply repeat that valuable information is differential information. And it is worth noting that interest rate forecasters have a notoriously poor track record.

Homer and Leibowitz (1972) have developed a popular taxonomy of active bond portfolio strategies. They characterize portfolio rebalancing activities as one of four types of *bond swaps*. In the first two swaps, the investor typically believes the yield relationship between bonds or sectors is only temporarily out of alignment. Until the aberration is eliminated, gains can be realized on the underpriced bond during a period of realignment called the *workout period*.

substitution swap

Exchange of one bond for a bond with similar attributes but more attractively priced.

1. The substitution swap is an exchange of one bond for a nearly identical substitute. The substituted bonds should be of essentially equal coupon, maturity, quality, call features, sinking fund provisions, and so on. A substitution swap would be motivated by a belief that the market has temporarily mispriced the two bonds, with a discrepancy representing a profit opportunity.

   An example of a substitution swap would be a sale of a 20-year maturity, 8% coupon Toyota bond that is priced to provide a yield to maturity of 8.05% coupled with a purchase of an 8% coupon Honda bond with the same time to maturity that yields 8.15%. If the bonds have about the same credit risk, there is no apparent reason for the Honda bonds to provide a higher yield. Therefore, the higher yield actually available in the market makes the Honda bond seem relatively attractive. Of course, the equality of credit risk is an important condition. If the Honda bond is in fact riskier, then its higher promised yield does not represent a bargain.

intermarket spread swap

Switching from one segment of the bond market to another.

2. The intermarket spread swap is an exchange of two bonds from different sectors of the bond market. It is pursued when an investor believes the yield spread between two sectors of the bond market is temporarily out of line.

   For example, if the yield spread between 10-year Treasury bonds and 10-year Baa-rated corporate bonds is now 3%, and the historical spread has been only 2%, an investor might consider selling holdings of Treasury bonds and replacing them with corporates. If the yield spread eventually narrows, the Baa-rated corporate bonds will outperform the Treasury bonds.

   Of course, the investor must consider carefully whether there is a good reason that the yield spread seems out of alignment. For example, the default premium on corporate bonds might have increased because the market is expecting a severe recession. In this case, the wider spread would not represent attractive pricing of corporates relative to Treasuries, but would simply be an adjustment for a perceived increase in credit risk.

rate anticipation swap

A switch made in response to forecasts of interest rate changes.

3. The rate anticipation swap is an exchange of bonds with different maturities. It is pegged to interest rate forecasting. Investors who believe rates will fall will swap into bonds of longer duration. For example, the investor might sell a five-year maturity Treasury bond, replacing it with a 25-year maturity Treasury bond. The new bond has the same lack of credit risk as the old one, but it has longer duration.

pure yield pickup swap

Moving to higher yield bonds, usually with longer maturities.

4. The pure yield pickup swap is an exchange of a shorter duration bond for a longer duration bond. This swap is pursued not in response to perceived mispricing but as a means of increasing return by holding higher yielding, longer maturity bonds. The investor is willing to bear the interest rate risk this strategy entails.

A yield pickup swap can be illustrated using the Treasury bond listings in Figure 10.1 from the last chapter. You can see from that table that longer-term T-bonds offered higher yields to maturity than shorter ones. The investor who swaps the shorter term bond for the longer one will earn a higher rate of return as long as the yield curve does not shift upward during the holding period. Of course, if it does, the longer duration bond will suffer a greater capital loss.

We can add a fifth swap, called a **tax swap,** to this list. This simply refers to a swap to exploit some tax advantage. For example, an investor may swap from one bond that has decreased in price to another similar bond if realization of capital losses is advantageous for tax purposes.

tax swap

Swapping two similar bonds to receive a tax benefit.

Horizon Analysis

One form of interest rate forecasting, which we encountered in the last chapter, is called **horizon analysis.** The analyst selects a particular investment period and predicts bond yields at the end of that period. Given the predicted yield to maturity at the end of the investment period, the bond price can be calculated. The coupon income earned over the period is then added to the predicted capital gain or loss to obtain a forecast of the total return on the bond over the holding period.

horizon analysis

Forecast of bond returns based largely on a prediction of the yield curve at the end of the investment horizon.

A 20-year maturity bond with a 10% coupon rate (paid annually) currently sells at a yield to maturity of 9%. A portfolio manager with a two-year horizon needs to forecast the total return on the bond over the coming two years. In two years, the bond will have an 18-year maturity. The analyst forecasts that two years from now, 18-year bonds will sell at yields to maturity of 8%, and that coupon payments can be reinvested in short-term securities over the coming two years at a rate of 7%.

To calculate the two-year return on the bond, the analyst would perform the following calculations:

1. Current price = $100 × Annuity factor(9%, 20 years) + $1,000 × PV factor(9%, 20 years)
   = $1,091.29
2. Forecast price = $100 × Annuity factor(8%, 18 years) + $1,000 × PV factor(8%, 18 years)
   = $1,187.44
3. The future value of reinvested coupons will be ($100 × 1.07) + $100 = $207

4. The two-year return is $\dfrac{\$207 + (\$1,187.44 - \$1,091.29)}{\$1,091.29} = 0.278$, or 27.8%   *[handwritten: It RCY =]*

The annualized rate of return over the two-year period would then be $(1.278)^{1/2} - 1 = 0.13$, or 13%.

[handwritten: Realized Compound yield]

EXAMPLE   11.5

Horizon Analysis

What will be the rate of return in Example 11.5 if the manager forecasts that in two years the yield to maturity on 18-year maturity bonds will be 10% and that the reinvestment rate for coupons will be 8%?

CONCEPT **11.8**
check

Contingent Immunization

Some investment styles fall within the spectrum of active versus passive strategies. An example is a technique called **contingent immunization,** first suggested by Liebowitz and Weinberger (1982). The idea is to allow the fixed-income manager to manage the portfolio actively unless and until poor performance endangers the prospect of achieving a minimum acceptable

contingent immunization

A strategy that immunizes a portfolio if necessary to guarantee a minimum acceptable return but otherwise allows active management.

portfolio return. At that point, the portfolio is immunized, providing a guaranteed rate of return over the remaining portion of the investment period.

To illustrate, suppose a manager with a two-year horizon is responsible for a $10 million portfolio. The manager wishes to provide a two-year cumulative return of at least 10%, that is, the minimum acceptable final value of the portfolio is $11 million. If the interest rate currently is 10%, only $9.09 million would be necessary to guarantee a terminal value of $11 million, because $9.09 million invested in an immunized portfolio would grow after two years to $9.09 \times (1.10)^2 = $11 million. Since the manager starts with $10 million, she can afford to risk some losses at the outset and might therefore start out with an active strategy rather than immediately immunizing.

How much can the manager risk losing? If the interest rate at any time is r, and T is the time left until the horizon date, the amount needed to achieve a terminal value of $11 million is simply the present value of $11 million, or $11 million$/(1 + r)^T$. A portfolio of this size, if immunized, will grow risk-free to $11 million by the horizon date. This value becomes a trigger point: If and when the actual portfolio value dips to the trigger point, active management will cease. *Contingent* upon reaching the trigger point, an immunization strategy is initiated.

Figure 11.8 illustrates two possible outcomes in a contingent immunization strategy. In Figure 11.8A, the portfolio falls in value and hits the trigger at time t^*. At that point, immunization is pursued, and the portfolio rises smoothly to the $11 million value. In Figure 11.8B, the portfolio does well, never reaches the trigger point, and is worth more than $11 million at the horizon date.

FIGURE 11.8

Contingent immunization. In Panel A, the portfolio is immunized when its value falls to the trigger point time t^*. In Panel B, the portfolio value remains above the trigger point and can be managed actively for the whole period.

What is the trigger point if the manager has a three-year horizon, the interest rate is 8%, and the minimum acceptable terminal value is $10 million?

CONCEPT **11.9** *check*

An Example of a Fixed-Income Investment Strategy

To demonstrate a reasonable, active fixed-income portfolio strategy, we discuss here the policies of Sanford Bernstein & Co., as explained in a speech by its manager of fixed-income investments, Francis Trainer. The company believes big bets on general marketwide interest movements are unwise. Instead, it concentrates on exploiting numerous instances of perceived *relative* minor pricing misalignments *within* the fixed-income sector. The firm takes as a risk benchmark the Lehman Aggregate Bond Index, which includes the vast majority of publicly traded bonds with maturities greater than one year. Any deviation from this passive or neutral position must be justified by active analysis. Bernstein considers a neutral portfolio duration to be equal to that of the index.

The firm is willing to make only limited bets on interest rate movements. As Francis Trainer puts it in his speech:

> If we set duration of our portfolios at a level equal to the index and never allow them to vary, this would imply that we are perpetually neutral on the direction of interest rates. However, we believe the utilization of these forecasts will add value and, therefore, we incorporate our economic forecast into the bond management process by altering the durations of our portfolios.

> However, in order to prevent fixed-income performance from being dominated by the accuracy of just a single aspect of our research effort, we limit the degree to which we are willing to alter our interest rate exposure. Under the vast majority of circumstances, we will not permit the duration of our portfolios to differ from that of the [Lehman] Index by more than one year.

The company expends most of its effort in exploiting numerous but minor inefficiencies in bond prices that result from lack of attention by its competitors. Its analysts follow about 1,000 securities, attempting to "identify specific securities that are attractive or unattractive as well as identify trends in the richness or cheapness of industries and sectors." These two activities would be characterized as substitution swaps and intermarket spread swaps in the Homer–Leibowitz scheme.

Sanford Bernstein & Co. realizes that market opportunities will arise, if at all, only in sectors of the bond market that present the least competition from other analysts. For this reason, it tends to focus on relatively more complicated bond issues in the belief that extensive research efforts give the firm a comparative advantage in that sector. Finally, the company does not take unnecessary risks. If there do not appear to be enough seemingly attractive bonds, funds are placed in Treasury securities as a "neutral" parking space until new opportunities are identified.

To summarize the key features of this sort of strategy, we make the following observations:

1. A firm such as Bernstein has a respect for market prices. It believes that only minor mispricing usually can be detected. It works toward meaningful abnormal returns by combining numerous *small* profit opportunities, not by hoping for the success of one big bet.

2. To have value, information cannot already be reflected in market prices. A large research staff must focus on market niches that appear to be neglected by others.

3. Interest rate movements are extremely hard to predict, and attempts to time the market can wipe out all the profits of intramarket analysis.

SUMMARY

- Even default-free bonds such as Treasury issues are subject to interest rate risk. Longer term bonds generally are more sensitive to interest rate shifts than short-term bonds. A measure of the average life of a bond is Macaulay's duration, defined as the weighted average of the times until each payment made by the security, with weights proportional to the present value of the payment.

- Duration is a direct measure of the sensitivity of a bond's price to a change in its yield. The proportional change in a bond's price approximately equals the negative of duration times the proportional change in $1 + y$.

- Immunization strategies are characteristic of passive bond portfolio management. Such strategies attempt to render the individual or firm immune from movements in interest rates. This may take the form of immunizing net worth or, instead, immunizing the future accumulated value of a bond portfolio.

- Immunization of a fully funded plan is accomplished by matching the durations of assets and liabilities. To maintain an immunized position as time passes and interest rates change, the portfolio must be periodically rebalanced.

- Convexity refers to the curvature of a bond's price-yield relationship. Accounting for convexity can substantially improve on the accuracy of the duration approximation for bond-price sensitivity to changes in yields.

- A more direct form of immunization is dedication or cash flow matching. If a portfolio is perfectly matched in cash flow with projected liabilities, rebalancing will be unnecessary.

- Active bond management can be decomposed into interest rate forecasting techniques and intermarket spread analysis. One popular taxonomy classifies active strategies as substitution swaps, intermarket spread swaps, rate anticipation swaps, or pure yield pickup swaps.

KEY TERMS

cash flow matching, 349
contingent
    immunization, 355
convexity, 351
dedication strategy, 349
horizon analysis, 355

immunization, 343
intermarket spread
    swap, 354
Macaulay's duration, 337
modified duration, 339
pure yield pickup swap, 354

rate anticipation
    swap, 354
rebalancing, 347
substitution swap, 354
tax swap, 355

PROBLEM SETS

 Select problems are available in McGraw-Hill's Homework Manager®. Please see the packaging options section of the preface for more information.

1. A nine-year bond has a yield of 10% and a duration of 7.194 years. If the bond's yield changes by 50 basis points, what is the percentage change in the bond's price?

2. Find the duration of a 6% coupon bond making *annual* coupon payments if it has three years until maturity and a yield to maturity of 6%. What is the duration if the yield to maturity is 10%?

3. A pension plan is obligated to make disbursements of $1 million, $2 million, and $1 million at the end of each of the next three years, respectively. Find the duration of the plan's obligations if the interest rate is 10% annually.

4. If the plan in Problem 3 wants to fully fund and immunize its position, how much of its portfolio should it allocate to one-year zero-coupon bonds and perpetuities, respectively, if these are the only two assets funding the plan?

5. You own a fixed-income asset with a duration of five years. If the level of interest rates, which is currently 8%, goes down by 10 basis points, how much do you expect the price of the asset to go up (in percentage terms)?

6. Rank the interest rate sensitivity of the following pairs of bonds.
   a. Bond A is an 8% coupon bond, with 20-year time to maturity selling at par value. Bond B is an 8% coupon, 20-year maturity bond selling below par value.
   b. Bond A is a 20-year, noncallable coupon bond with a coupon rate of 8%, selling at par. Bond B is a 20-year, callable bond with a coupon rate of 9%, also selling at par.

7. Rank the following bonds in order of descending duration.

Bond	Coupon	Time to Maturity	Yield to Maturity
A	15%	20 years	10%
B	15	15	10
C	0	20	10
D	8	20	10
E	15	15	15

8. Philip Morris has issued bonds that pay annually with the following characteristics:

Coupon	Yield to Maturity	Maturity	Macaulay Duration
8%	8%	15 years	10 years

   a. Calculate modified duration using the information above.
   b. Explain why modified duration is a better measure than maturity when calculating the bond's sensitivity to changes in interest rates.
   c. Identify the direction of change in modified duration if:
      i. The coupon of the bond were 4%, not 8%.
      ii. The maturity of the bond were 7 years, not 15 years.

9. You will be paying $10,000 a year in tuition expenses at the end of the next two years. Bonds currently yield 8%.
   a. What is the present value and duration of your obligation?
   b. What maturity zero-coupon bond would immunize your obligation?
   c. Suppose you buy a zero-coupon bond with value and duration equal to your obligation. Now suppose that rates immediately increase to 9%. What happens to your net position, that is, to the difference between the value of the bond and that of your tuition obligation? What if rates fall to 7%?

10. Pension funds pay lifetime annuities to recipients. If a firm remains in business indefinitely, the pension obligation will resemble a perpetuity. Suppose, therefore, that you are managing a pension fund with obligations to make perpetual payments of $2 million per year to beneficiaries. The yield to maturity on all bonds is 16%.
    a. If the duration of five-year maturity bonds with coupon rates of 12% (paid annually) is 4 years and the duration of 20-year maturity bonds with coupon rates of 6% (paid annually) is 11 years, how much of each of these coupon bonds (in market value) will you want to hold to both fully fund and immunize your obligation?
    b. What will be the *par value* of your holdings in the 20-year coupon bond?

11. You are managing a portfolio of $1 million. Your target duration is 10 years, and you can choose from two bonds: a zero-coupon bond with maturity 5 years, and a perpetuity, each currently yielding 5%.
    a. How much of each bond will you hold in your portfolio?
    b. How will these fractions change *next year* if target duration is now nine years?

12. Find the duration of a bond with settlement date May 27, 2008, and maturity date November 15, 2017. The coupon rate of the bond is 7%, and the bond pays coupons semiannually. The bond is selling at a yield to maturity of 8%. You can use Spreadsheet 11.2, available at **www.mhhe.com/bkm**; link to Chapter 11 material.

Please visit us at
www.mhhe.com/bkm

13. What is the duration of the bond in the previous problem if coupons are paid annually? Explain why the duration changes in the direction it does.

Please visit us at
www.mhhe.com/bkm

14. You manage a pension fund that will provide retired workers with lifetime annuities. You determine that the payouts of the fund are essentially going to resemble level

perpetuities of $1 million per year. The interest rate is 10%. You plan to fully fund the obligation using 5-year and 20-year maturity zero-coupon bonds.

    a. How much *market value* of each of the zeros will be necessary to fund the plan if you desire an immunized position?

    b. What must be the *face value* of the two zeros to fund the plan?

15. Short-term interest rates are more volatile than long-term rates. Despite this, the rates of return of long-term bonds are more volatile than returns on short-term securities. How can these two empirical observations be reconciled?

16. As part of your analysis of debt issued by Monticello Corporation, you are asked to evaluate two specific bond issues, shown in the table below.

	Monticello Corporation Bond Information	
	Bond A (callable)	**Bond B (noncallable)**
Maturity	2013	2013
Coupon	11.50%	7.25%
Current price	125.75	100.00
Yield to maturity	7.70%	7.25%
Modified duration to maturity	6.20	6.80
Call date	2007	—
Call price	105	—
Yield to call	5.10%	—
Modified duration to call	3.10	—

    a. Using the duration and yield information in the table, compare the price and yield behavior of the two bonds under each of the following two scenarios:

      i. Strong economic recovery with rising inflation expectations.

      ii. Economic recession with reduced inflation expectations.

    b. Using the information in the table, calculate the projected price change for bond *B* if the yield-to-maturity for this bond falls by 75 basis points.

    c. Describe the shortcoming of analyzing bond *A* strictly to call or to maturity.

17. A 30-year maturity bond making annual coupon payments with a coupon rate of 12% has duration of 11.54 years and convexity of 192.4. The bond currently sells at a yield to maturity of 8%. Use a financial calculator or spreadsheet to find the price of the bond if its yield to maturity falls to 7% or rises to 9%. What prices for the bond at these new yields would be predicted by the duration rule and the duration-with-convexity rule? What is the percent error for each rule? What do you conclude about the accuracy of the two rules?

18. A 12.75-year maturity zero-coupon bond selling at a yield to maturity of 8% (effective annual yield) has convexity of 150.3 and modified duration of 11.81 years. A 30-year maturity 6% coupon bond making annual coupon payments also selling at a yield to maturity of 8% has nearly identical modified duration—11.79 years—but considerably higher convexity of 231.2.

    a. Suppose the yield to maturity on both bonds increases to 9%. What will be the actual percentage capital loss on each bond? What percentage capital loss would be predicted by the duration-with-convexity rule?

    b. Repeat part (*a*), but this time assume the yield to maturity decreases to 7%.

    c. Compare the performance of the two bonds in the two scenarios, one involving an increase in rates, the other a decrease. Based on their comparative investment performance, explain the attraction of convexity.

    d. In view of your answer to (*c*), do you think it would be possible for two bonds with equal duration, but different convexity, to be priced initially at the same yield to maturity if the yields on both bonds always increased or decreased by equal amounts, as in this example? Would anyone be willing to buy the bond with lower convexity under these circumstances?

19. Find the convexity of a 7-year maturity, 6% coupon bond selling at a yield to
    maturity of 8%. The bond pays its coupons annually. (Hint: You can use the
    spreadsheet from this chapter's Excel Application on Convexity, setting cash flows
    after year 7 equal to zero. The spreadsheet is available at **www.mhhe.com/bkm;** link to
    Chapter 11 material.)

eXcel

**Please visit us at
www.mhhe.com/bkm**

20. One common goal among fixed-income portfolio managers is to earn high incremental
    returns on corporate bonds versus government bonds of comparable durations. The
    approach of some corporate-bond portfolio managers is to find and purchase those
    corporate bonds having the largest initial spreads over comparable-duration govern-
    ment bonds. John Ames, HFS's fixed-income manager, believes that a more rigorous
    approach is required if incremental returns are to be maximized.

CFA®
PROBLEMS

    The following table presents data relating to one set of corporate/government spread
    relationships (in basis points, b.p.) present in the market at a given date:

	Current and Expected Spreads and Durations of High-Grade Corporate Bonds (One-Year Horizon)			
Bond Rating	Initial Spread over Governments	Expected Horizon Spread	Initial Duration	Expected Duration One Year from Now
Aaa	31 b.p.	31 b.p.	4 years	3.1 years
Aa	40 b.p.	50 b.p.	4 years	3.1 years

a. Recommend purchase of *either* Aaa *or* Aa bonds for a one-year investment horizon
    given a goal of maximizing incremental returns.
b. Ames chooses not to rely solely on initial spread relationships. His analytical frame-
    work considers a full range of other key variables likely to impact realized incremen-
    tal returns including: call provisions and potential changes in interest rates. Describe
    other variables that Ames should include in his analysis and explain how each of
    these could cause realized incremental returns to differ from those indicated by initial
    spread relationships.

21. Noah Kramer, a fixed-income portfolio manager based in the country of Sevista, is
    considering the purchase of a Sevista government bond. Kramer decides to evaluate
    two strategies for implementing his investment in Sevista bonds. Table 21A gives the
    details of the two strategies, and Table 21B contains the assumptions that apply to both
    strategies.

CFA®
PROBLEMS

TABLE 21A

Investment strategies (amounts are market value invested)

Strategy	5-Year Maturity (Modified Duration = 4.83 Years)	15-Year Maturity (Modified Duration = 14.35 Years)	25-Year Maturity (Modified Duration = 23.81 Years)
I	$5 million	0	$5 million
II	0	$10 million	0

TABLE 21B

Investment strategy assumptions

Market Value of Bonds	**$10 Million**
Bond maturities	5 and 25 years
	or
	15 years
Bond coupon rates	0.00%
Target modified duration	15 years

Before choosing one of the two bond investment strategies, Kramer wants to analyze how the market value of the bonds will change if an instantaneous interest rate shift occurs immediately after his investment. The details of the interest rate shift are shown in Table 21C. Calculate, for the instantaneous interest rate shift shown in Table 21C, the percent change in the market value of the bonds that will occur under each strategy.

TABLE 21C	Maturity	Interest Rate Change
Instantaneous interest rate shift immediately after investment	5 year	Down 75 basis points (bps)
	15 year	Up 25 bps
	25 year	Up 50 bps

22. *a.* Janet Meer is a fixed-income portfolio manager. Noting that the current shape of the yield curve is flat, she considers the purchase of a newly issued, option-free corporate bond priced at par; the bond is described in Table 22A. Calculate the duration of the bond.

TABLE 22A		Change in Yields	
7% Option-free bond, maturity = 10 years		**Up 10 Basis Points**	**Down 10 Basis Points**
	Price	99.29	100.71
	Convexity	35.00	

b. Meer is also considering the purchase of a second newly issued, option-free corporate bond, which is described in Table 22B. She wants to evaluate this second bond's price sensitivity to an instantaneous, downward parallel shift in the yield curve of 200 basis points. Estimate the total percentage price change for the bond if the yield curve experiences an instantaneous, downward parallel shift of 200 basis points.

TABLE 22B		
7.25% Option-free bond, maturity = 12 years	Original issue price	Par value, to yield 7.25%
	Modified duration (at original price)	7.90
	Convexity measure	41.55
	Convexity adjustment (yield change of 200 basis points)	1.66

23. Sandra Kapple presents Maria VanHusen with a description, given in the following exhibit, of the bond portfolio held by the Star Hospital Pension Plan. All securities in the bond portfolio are noncallable U.S. Treasury securities.

	STAR HOSPITAL PENSION PLAN BOND PORTFOLIO					
				Price if Yields Change		
Par Value (U.S. $)	Treasury Security	Market Value (U.S. $)	Current Price	Up 100 Basis Points	Down 100 Basis Points	Effective Duration
48,000,000	2.375% due 2006	48,667,680	101.391	99.245	103.595	2.15
50,000,000	4.75% due 2031	50,000,000	100.000	86.372	116.887	
98,000,000	Total bond portfolio	98,667,680	—	—	—	

a. Calculate the effective duration of each of the following:
   i. The 4.75% Treasury security due 2031
   ii. The total bond portfolio

b. VanHusen remarks to Kapple, "If you changed the maturity structure of the bond portfolio to result in a portfolio duration of 5.25, the price sensitivity of that portfolio would be identical to the price sensitivity of a single, noncallable Treasury security that has a duration of 5.25." In what circumstance would VanHusen's remark be correct?

24. The following questions appeared in past CFA examinations.
    a. Which set of conditions will result in a bond with the greatest price volatility?
       (1) A high coupon and a short maturity.
       (2) A high coupon and a long maturity.
       (3) A low coupon and a short maturity.
       (4) A low coupon and a long maturity.
    b. An investor who expects declining interest rates would be likely to purchase a bond that has a _____ coupon and a _____ term to maturity.
       (1) Low, long
       (2) High, short
       (3) High, long
       (4) Zero, long
    c. With a zero-coupon bond:
       (1) Duration equals the weighted average term to maturity.
       (2) Term to maturity equals duration.
       (3) Weighted average term to maturity equals the term to maturity.
       (4) All of the above.
    d. As compared with bonds selling at par, deep discount bonds will have:
       (1) Greater reinvestment risk.
       (2) Greater price volatility.
       (3) Less call protection.
       (4) None of the above.

25. The ability to *immunize* a bond portfolio is very desirable for bond portfolio managers in some instances.
    a. Discuss the components of interest rate risk—that is, assuming a change in interest rates over time, explain the two risks faced by the holder of a bond.
    b. Define immunization and discuss why a bond manager would immunize his or her portfolio.
    c. Explain why a duration-matching strategy is a superior technique to a maturity-matching strategy for the minimization of interest rate risk.
    d. Explain how contingent immunization, another bond portfolio management technique, differs from conventional immunization. Discuss why a bond portfolio manager would engage in contingent immunization.

26. You are the manager for the bond portfolio of a pension fund. The policies of the fund allow for the use of active strategies in managing the bond portfolio.

    It appears that the economic cycle is beginning to mature, inflation is expected to accelerate, and, in an effort to contain the economic expansion, central bank policy is moving toward constraint. For each of the situations below, state which one of the two bonds you would prefer. Briefly justify your answer in each case.
    a. Government of Canada (Canadian pay), 6% due in 2012, and priced at 98.75 to yield 6.50% to maturity;
       or
       Government of Canada (Canadian pay), 6% due in 2022, and priced at 91.75 to yield 7.19% to maturity.
    b. Texas Power and Light Co., 5½% due in 2016, rated AAA, and priced at 85 to yield 8.1% to maturity;
       or
       Arizona Public Service Co., 5.45% due in 2016, rated A − , and priced at 80 to yield 9.1% to maturity.

c. Commonwealth Edison, 2¾% due in 2016, rated Baa, and priced at 71 to yield 9.2% to maturity;

or

Commonwealth Edison, 11⅜% due in 2016, rated Baa, and priced at 114 to yield 9.2% to maturity.

d. Shell Oil Co., 8¾% sinking fund debentures due in 2023, rated AAA (sinking fund begins in 2010 at par), and priced at 79 to yield 9.91% to maturity;

or

Warner-Lambert, 8⅞% sinking fund debentures due in 2023, rated AAA (sinking fund begins in 2014 at par), and priced at 85 to yield 9.31% to maturity.

e. Bank of Montreal (Canadian pay), 6% certificates of deposit due in 2009, rated AAA, and priced at 100 to yield 6% to maturity;

or

Bank of Montreal (Canadian pay), floating-rate notes due in 2013, rated AAA. Coupon currently set at 5.65% and priced at 100 (coupon adjusted semiannually to 0.5% above the three-month Government of Canada Treasury bill rate).

27. The following bond swaps could have been made in recent years as investors attempted to increase the total return on their portfolio.

From the information presented below, identify possible reason(s) that investors may have made each swap.

	Action		Call	Price	YTM (%)
a.	Sell	Baa1 Electric Pwr. 1st mtg. 8⅜% due 2012	108.24	95	9.71
	Buy	Baa1 Electric Pwr. 1st mtg. 4⅜% due 2013	105.20	79	9.39
b.	Sell	Aaa Phone Co. notes 6½% due 2013	101.50	90	8.02
	Buy	U.S. Treasury notes 7½% due 2013	NC	97.15	7.78
c.	Sell	Aa1 Apex Bank zero coupon due 2015	NC	45	8.51
	Buy	Aa1 Apex Bank float rate notes due 2028	103.90	90	—
d.	Sell	A1 Commonwealth Oil & Gas 1st mtg. 6% due 2018	105.75	72	8.09
	Buy	U.S. Treasury bond 5½% due 2024	NC	80.60	7.40
e.	Sell	A1 Z mart convertible deb. 3% due 2018	103.90	62	6.92
	Buy	A2 Lucky Ducks deb. 7¾% due 2024	109.86	75	10.43

28. A member of a firm's investment committee is very interested in learning about the management of fixed-income portfolios. He would like to know how fixed-income managers position portfolios to capitalize on their expectations concerning three factors which influence interest rates. Assuming that no investment policy limitations apply, formulate and describe a fixed-income portfolio management strategy for each of the following interest rate factors that could be used to exploit a portfolio manager's expectations about that factor. (*Note:* Three strategies are required, one for each of the listed factors.)

a. Changes in the level of interest rates.

b. Changes in yield spreads across/between sectors.

c. Changes in yield spreads as to a particular instrument.

29. Long-term Treasury bonds currently are selling at yields to maturity of nearly 8%. You expect interest rates to fall. The rest of the market thinks that they will remain unchanged over the coming year. In each question, choose the bond that will provide the higher capital gain if you are correct. Briefly explain your answer.

a. (1) A Baa-rated bond with coupon rate 8% and time to maturity 20 years.

(2) An Aaa-rated bond with coupon rate 8% and time to maturity 20 years.

b. (1) An A-rated bond with coupon rate 4% and maturity 20 years, callable at 105.

(2) An A-rated bond with coupon rate 8% and maturity 20 years, callable at 105.

c. (1) A 6% coupon noncallable T-bond with maturity 20 years and YTM = 8%.

(2) A 9% coupon noncallable T-bond with maturity 20 years and YTM = 8%.

30. Currently, the term structure is as follows: one-year bonds yield 7%, two-year bonds yield 8%, three-year bonds and greater maturity bonds all yield 9%. You are choosing between one-, two-, and three-year maturity bonds all paying *annual* coupons of 8%, once a year. Which bond should you buy if you strongly believe that at year-end the yield curve will be flat at 9%?

31. A fixed-income portfolio manager is unwilling to realize a rate of return of less than 3% annually over a five-year investment period on a portfolio currently valued at $1 million. Three years later, the interest rate is 8%. What is the trigger point of the portfolio at this time, that is, how low can the value of the portfolio fall before the manager will be forced to immunize to be assured of achieving the minimum acceptable return?

32. A 30-year maturity bond has a 7% coupon rate, paid annually. It sells today for $867.42. A 20-year maturity bond has a 6.5% coupon rate, also paid annually. It sells today for $879.50. A bond market analyst forecasts that in five years, 25-year maturity bonds will sell at yields to maturity of 8% and that 15-year maturity bonds will sell at yields of 7.5%. Because the yield curve is upward sloping, the analyst believes that coupons will be invested in short-term securities at a rate of 6%. Which bond offers the higher expected rate of return over the five-year period?

33. *a.* Use a spreadsheet to calculate the durations of the two bonds in Spreadsheet 11.1 if the interest rate increases to 12%. Why does the duration of the coupon bond fall while that of the zero remains unchanged? (Hint: Examine what happens to the weights computed in column E.)

    b. Use the same spreadsheet to calculate the duration of the coupon bond if the coupon were 12% instead of 8%. Explain why the duration is lower. (Again, start by looking at column E.)

34. *a.* Footnote 2 in the chapter presents the formula for the convexity of a bond. Build a spreadsheet to calculate the convexity of the 8% coupon bond in Spreadsheet 11.1 at the initial yield to maturity of 10%.

    b. What is the convexity of the zero-coupon bond?

Use data from the Standard & Poor's Market Insight Database at www.mhhe.com/edumarketinsight to answer the following questions.

STANDARD
&POOR'S

1. At the Market Insight *Company* page enter the stock ticker symbol HLT for Hilton Hotels Corporation and do the following:

    a. Review the recent Industry Outlook (in the S&P Stock Reports section) for the Hotels, Resorts, and Cruise Lines subindustry. What is the outlook for hotels? How might the outlook affect outstanding debt and the issuance of new debt?

    b. Review the variety of Hilton bonds and notes outstanding that are listed in the latest EDGAR 10K report for Hilton. Use the Edit, Find on This Page menu and search for the term "bond" to find the list about halfway through the document. How does the company's debt structure in the current year compare with its debt structure in the previous year? Based on the types and maturities of bonds outstanding, how much interest rate risk do the bondholders face?

    c. What percentage of the debt issues outstanding represents current liabilities? How did the percentage change during the past year?

    d. Go to **http://bonds.yahoo.com,** and search for the Hilton bonds. What are the current ratings and yields to maturity for Hilton's debt securities? Use the prices and the coupon rates shown to perform calculations to confirm the Current Yield shown for each bond.

    e. What type of investor would be interested in these bonds? For what kinds of portfolios would they be inappropriate?

2. Enter the stock symbol S to locate information for Sprint Nextel Corp. on Market Insight. Find the company's most recent annual Balance Sheet in the Excel Analytics section.

a. Examine the company's assets and liabilities. What proportion of total assets are current assets? What proportion of total liabilities are current liabilities? Does it seem that there is a good match between the duration of the assets and the duration of the liabilities?

b. Look at the Annual Statement of Cash Flows for Sprint Nextel, which is also found in the Excel Analytics section. Check the Financing Activities section to see if the company has issued new debt or reduced its debt outstanding. How much interest did the firm pay during the period?

c. Repeat the exercise with several other companies of your choice. Try to pick companies in different industries. Do you notice any patterns that might be due to the industrial environments in which the firms operate?

WEB *master*

Bond Calculations

Many bond calculators are offered on the Web. You can retrieve information about a particular bond issue, then calculate duration and convexity with the click of a button.

1. Select a bond from the most actively traded corporate bond list at **www.investinginbonds.com.** Go to the "Bond Markets and Prices" link, then select "Corporate Market At-a-Glance" to link to the most active list. Select a bond that has a maturity date a few years away and click on its CUSIP number to find further information.

2. Choose the most recent trading date listed and click on the "run calculations" link. The bond's characteristics are entered for you.

3. Confirm the amount of the accrued interest and the cash flow schedule listed.

4. Confirm the bond's duration by either performing the calculations in a spreadsheet or using Excel's DURATION function.

5. Based on the bond's current price, by what percent would the price change if the yield were to change by .5%?

6. Repeat the calculations by entering assumed prices of 90, 100, and 110, then answer the following questions:

   a. What are the duration and the convexity for the bond at the each of the prices?

   b. Is the bond price more or less sensitive to interest rates at higher prices relative to lower ones? How does convexity change as the price changes? Is the change in convexity symmetrical? That is, as the price decreases by $10 (from 100 to 90), and increases by $10 (from 100 to 110), are the changes in convexity equal but opposite in sign?

SOLUTIONS TO CONCEPT *checks*

11.1. Interest rate: 0.09

	(B) Time until Payment (years)	(C) Payment	(D) Payment Discounted at 10%	(E) Weight	Column (B) times Column (E)
A. 8% coupon bond	1	80	73.394	0.0753	0.0753
	2	80	67.334	0.0691	0.1382
	3	1080	833.958	0.8556	2.5668
Sum:			974.687	1.0000	2.7803
B. Zero-coupon bond	1	0	0.000	0.0000	0.0000
	2	0	0.000	0.0000	0.0000
	3	1000	772.183	1.0000	3.0000
Sum:			772.183	1.0000	3.0000

The duration of the 8% coupon bond rises to 2.7803 years. Price increases to \$974.687. The duration of the zero-coupon bond is unchanged at 3 years, although its price also increases when the interest rate falls.

11.2. *a.* If the interest rate increases from 9% to 9.05%, the bond price falls from \$974.687 to \$973.445. The percentage change in price is −0.127%.

      b. The duration formula would predict a price change of

$$-\frac{2.7802}{1.09} \times .0005 = -.00127 = -.127\%$$

which is the same answer that we obtained from direct computation in part (*a*).

11.3. Use Excel to confirm that DURATION(DATE(2000,1,1), DATE(2008,1,1), .09, .10, 1) = 5.97 years. If you change the last argument of the duration function from 1 to 2 (to allow for semi-annual coupons), you will find that DURATION(DATE(2000,1,1), DATE(2008,1,1), .09, .10, 2) = 5.80 years. Duration is lower when coupons are paid semiannually rather than annually because, on average, payments come earlier. Instead of waiting until year-end to receive the annual coupon, investors receive half the coupon midway through the year.

11.4. The duration of a level perpetuity is $(1 + y)/y$ or $1 + 1/y$, which clearly falls as y increases. Tabulating duration as a function of y we get:

y	D
0.01 (i.e., 1%)	101 years
0.02	51
0.05	21
0.10	11
0.20	6
0.25	5
0.40	3.5

11.5. The perpetuity's duration now would be 1.08/0.08 = 13.5. We need to solve the following equation for w

$$w \times 2 + (1 - w) \times 13.5 = 6$$

Therefore, $w = 0.6522$.

11.6. *a.* The present value of the fund's obligation is \$800,000/0.08 = \$10 million. The duration is 13.5 years. Therefore, the fund should invest \$10 million in zeros with a 13.5 year maturity. The face value of the zeros will be \$10,000,000 × 1.08$^{13.5}$ = \$28,263,159.

      b. When the interest rate increases to 8.1%, the present value of the fund's obligation drops to 800,000/0.081 = \$9,876,543. The value of the zero-coupon bond falls by roughly the same amount, to \$28,263,159/1.081$^{13.5}$ = \$9,875,835. The duration of the perpetual obligation falls to 1.081/0.081 = 13.346 years. The fund should sell the zero it currently holds and purchase \$9,876,543 in zero-coupon bonds with maturity of 13.346 years.

11.7. Dedication would be more attractive. Cash flow matching eliminates the need for rebalancing and, thus, saves transaction costs.

11.8. Current price = \$1,091.29

Forecast price = \$100 × Annuity factor (10%,18 years) + \$1,000 × PV factor(10%,18 years) = \$1,000

The future value of reinvested coupons will be (\$100 × 1.08) + \$100 = \$208

The two-year return is $\dfrac{\$208 + (\$1,000 - \$1,091.29)}{\$1,091.29} = 0.107$, or 10.7%

The annualized rate of return over the two-year period would then be $(1.107)^{1/2} - 1 = .052$, or 5.2%.

11.9. The trigger point is the present value of the minimum acceptable terminal value:
\$10 million/(1.08)^3 = \$7.94 million.

SECURITY ANALYSIS

Tell your friends or relatives that you are studying investments and they will ask you, "What stocks should I buy?" This is the question at the heart of security analysis. How do analysts choose the stocks and other securities to hold in their portfolios?

Security analysis requires a wide mix of skills. You need to be a decent economist with a good grasp of both macroeconomics and microeconomics, the former to help you form forecasts of the general direction of the market and the latter to help you assess the relative position of particular industries or firms. You need a good sense of demographic and social trends to help identify industries with bright prospects. You need to be a quick study of the ins and outs of particular industries to choose the firms that will succeed within each industry. You need a good accounting background to analyze the financial statements that firms provide to the public. You also need to have mastered corporate finance, since security analysis at its core is the ability to value a firm. In short, a good security analyst will be a generalist, with a grasp of the widest range of financial issues. This is where there is the biggest premium on "putting it all together."

The chapters in Part Four are an introduction to security analysis. We will provide you with a "top-down" approach to the subject, starting with an overview of international, macroeconomic, and industry issues, and only then progressing to the analysis of particular firms. These topics form the core of fundamental analysis. After reading these chapters, you will have a good sense of the various techniques used to analyze stocks and the stock market.

CHAPTERS IN THIS PART

www.mhhe.com/bkm

AFTER STUDYING THIS CHAPTER YOU SHOULD BE ABLE TO:

 Predict the effect of monetary and fiscal policies on key macroeconomic variables such as gross domestic product, interest rates, and the inflation rate.

 Use leading, coincident, and lagging economic indicators to describe and predict the economy's path through the business cycle.

 Predict which industries will be more or less sensitive to business cycle fluctuations.

 Analyze the effect of industry life cycles and structure on industry earnings prospects over time.

fundamental analysis

The analysis of determinants of firm value, such as prospects for earnings and dividends.

To determine a proper price for a firm's stock, the security analyst must forecast the dividends and earnings that can be expected from the firm. This is the heart of **fundamental analysis,** that is, the analysis of determinants of value such as earnings prospects. Ultimately, the business success of the firm determines the dividends it can pay to shareholders and the price it will command in the stock market. Because the prospects of the firm are tied to those of the broader economy, however, valuation analyses must consider the business environment in which the firm operates. For some firms, macroeconomic and industry circumstances might have a greater influence on profits than the firm's relative performance within its industry. In other words, investors need to keep the big economic picture in mind.

Therefore, in analyzing a firm's prospects it often makes sense to start with the broad economic environment, examining the state of the aggregate economy and even the international economy. From there, one considers the implications of the outside environment on the industry in which the firm operates. Finally, the firm's position within the industry is examined.

This chapter examines the broad-based aspects of fundamental analysis—macroeconomic and industry analysis. The following two chapters cover firm-specific analysis. We begin with a discussion of international factors relevant to firm performance and move on to an overview of the significance of the key variables usually used to summarize the state of the economy. We then discuss government macroeconomic policy and the determination of interest rates. We conclude the analysis of the macroeconomic environment with a discussion of business cycles. Next, we move to industry analysis, treating issues concerning the sensitivity of the firm to the business cycle, the typical life cycle of an industry, and strategic issues that affect industry performance.

Related Web sites for this chapter are available at www.mhhe.com/bkm.

12.1 | THE GLOBAL ECONOMY

A top-down analysis of a firm's prospects must start with the global economy. The international economy might affect a firm's export prospects, the price competition it faces from foreign competitors, or the profits it makes on investments abroad. Certainly, despite the fact that the economies of most countries are linked in a global macroeconomy, there is considerable variation in economic performance across countries at any time. Consider, for example, Table 12.1, which presents data on several major economies. The table documents striking variation in growth rates of economic output. For example, while the Chinese economy grew by 10.4% in 2006 (see last column), output in Japan grew by only 1.6%. Similarly, there has been considerable variation in stock market returns in these countries in recent years, as documented in the first two columns of the table.

These data illustrate that the national economic environment can be a crucial determinant of industry performance. It is far harder for businesses to succeed in a contracting economy than in an expanding one. This observation highlights the role of a big-picture macroeconomic analysis as a fundamental part of the investment process.

TABLE 12.1		Stock Market Return (%)		Growth in GDP (%)
Economic performance, 2006		In Local Currency	In U.S. Dollars	
	Brazil	32.9	45.2	3.2
	Britain	12.5	27.3	2.7
	Canada	12.7	12.5	2.5
	China	130.6	138.4	10.4
	France	19.0	33.1	1.9
	Germany	23.7	38.4	2.8
	India	49.1	51.3	9.2
	Japan	6.9	5.7	1.6
	Mexico	49.5	47.8	4.6
	Russia	56.3	70.7	6.5
	Singapore	29.4	40.4	5.9
	Switzerland	17.6	26.7	2.4
	Thailand	20.9	22.5	4.7
	U.S.	13.5	13.5	3.0
	Venezuela	162.6	99.0	10.2

Source: *The Economist,* January 4, 2007. © 2007 The Economist Newspaper Group, Inc. Reprinted with permission. Further reproduction is prohibited. **www.economist.com**

In addition, the global environment presents political risks of far greater magnitude than are typically encountered in U.S.-based investments. In the last decade, we have seen several instances where political developments had major impacts on economic prospects. For example, the biggest international economic story in late 1997 and 1998 was the turmoil in several Asian economies, notably Thailand, Indonesia, and South Korea. These episodes also highlighted the close interplay between politics and economics, as both currency and stock values swung with enormous volatility in response to developments concerning the prospects for aid for these countries from the International Monetary Fund. In August 1998, the shock waves following Russia's devaluation of the ruble and default on some of its debt created havoc in world security markets, ultimately requiring a rescue of the giant hedge fund Long Term Capital Management to avoid further major disruptions. In the current environment, stock prices are highly sensitive to developments in Iraq and the security of energy supplies.

Other political issues that are less sensational but still extremely important to economic growth and investment returns include issues of protectionism and trade policy, the free flow of capital, and the status of a nation's workforce.

exchange rate

The rate at which domestic currency can be converted into foreign currency.

One obvious factor that affects the international competitiveness of a country's industries is the exchange rate between that country's currency and other currencies. The **exchange rate** is the rate at which domestic currency can be converted into foreign currency. For example, in early 2007, it took about 114 Japanese yen to purchase one U.S. dollar. We would say that the exchange rate is ¥114 per dollar, or equivalently, $0.0088 per yen.

As exchange rates fluctuate, the dollar value of goods priced in foreign currency similarly fluctuates. For example, in 1980, the dollar–yen exchange rate was about $0.0045 per yen. Since the exchange rate in 2007 was $0.0088 per yen, a U.S. citizen would have needed almost twice as many dollars in 2007 to buy a product selling for ¥10,000 as would have been required in 1980. If the Japanese producer were to maintain a fixed yen price for its product, the price expressed in U.S. dollars would have to double. This would make Japanese products more expensive to U.S. consumers, however, and result in lost sales. Obviously, appreciation of the yen creates a problem for Japanese producers such as automakers that must compete with U.S. producers.

Figure 12.1 shows the change in the purchasing power of the U.S. dollar relative to the purchasing power of several major currencies in the period between 1999 and 2006. The ratio of purchasing powers is called the "real" or inflation-adjusted exchange rate. The change in the real exchange rate measures how much more or less expensive foreign goods have become to U.S. citizens, accounting for both exchange rate fluctuations and inflation differentials across countries. A positive value in Figure 12.1 means that the dollar

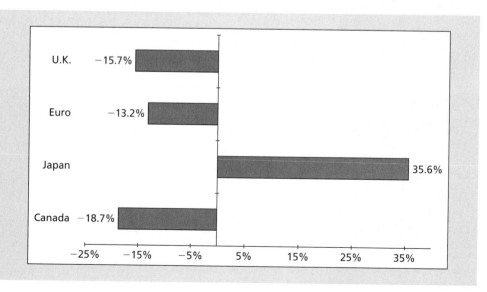

FIGURE 12.1

Change in real exchange rate: U.S. dollar versus major currencies, 1999–2006

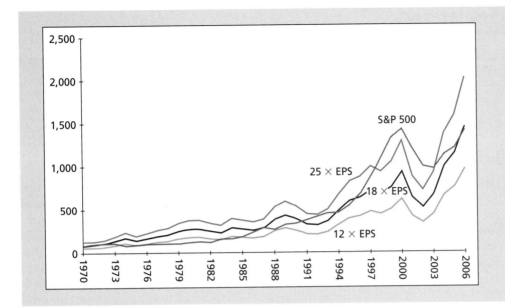

FIGURE 12.2

S&P 500 Index versus earnings per share

Source: Authors' calculations using data from *The Economic Report of the President*, 2007.

has gained purchasing power relative to another currency; a negative number indicates a depreciating dollar. Therefore, the figure shows that goods priced in terms of British pounds, euros, or Canadian dollars became more expensive to U.S. consumers in the last four years but that goods priced in yen became cheaper. Conversely, goods priced in U.S. dollars became more expensive to Japanese consumers, but more affordable to Canadian consumers.

12.2 THE DOMESTIC MACROECONOMY

The macroeconomy is the environment in which all firms operate. The importance of the macroeconomy in determining investment performance is illustrated in Figure 12.2, which compares the level of the S&P 500 stock price index to estimates of earnings per share of the S&P 500 companies. The graph shows that stock prices tend to rise along with earnings. While the exact ratio of stock price to earnings per share varies with factors such as interest rates, risk, inflation rates, and other variables, the graph does illustrate that, as a general rule, the ratio has tended to be in the range of 12 to 25. Given "normal" price-to-earnings ratios, we would expect the S&P 500 Index to fall within these boundaries. While the earnings-multiplier rule clearly is not perfect—note the dramatic increase in the P/E multiple in the 1990s—it also seems clear that the level of the broad market and aggregate earnings do trend together. Thus, the first step in forecasting the performance of the broad market is to assess the status of the economy as a whole.

The ability to forecast the macroeconomy can translate into spectacular investment performance. But it is not enough to forecast the macroeconomy well. One must forecast it *better* than one's competitors to earn abnormal profits.

In this section, we will review some of the key economic statistics used to describe the state of the macroeconomy.

Gross Domestic Product

Gross domestic product, or GDP, is the measure of the economy's total production of goods and services. Rapidly growing GDP indicates an expanding economy with ample opportunity for a firm to increase sales. Another popular measure of the economy's output is *industrial production*. This statistic provides a measure of economic activity more narrowly focused on the manufacturing side of the economy.

gross domestic product (GDP)

The market value of goods and services produced over a period of time.

Employment

unemployment rate

The ratio of the number of people classified as unemployed to the total labor force.

The **unemployment rate** is the percentage of the total labor force (i.e., those who are either working or actively seeking employment) yet to find work. The unemployment rate measures the extent to which the economy is operating at full capacity. The unemployment rate is a statistic related to workers only, but further insight into the strength of the economy can be gleaned from the employment rate of other factors of production. Analysts also look at the factory *capacity utilization rate,* which is the ratio of actual output from factories to potential output.

Inflation

inflation

The rate at which the general level of prices for goods and services is rising.

Inflation is the rate at which the general level of prices is rising. High rates of inflation often are associated with "overheated" economies, that is, economies where the demand for goods and services is outstripping productive capacity, which leads to upward pressure on prices. Most governments walk a fine line in their economic policies. They hope to stimulate their economies enough to maintain nearly full employment, but not so much as to bring on inflationary pressures. The perceived trade-off between inflation and unemployment is at the heart of many macroeconomic policy disputes. There is considerable room for disagreement as to the relative costs of these policies as well as the economy's relative vulnerability to these pressures at any particular time.

Interest Rates

High interest rates reduce the present value of future cash flows, thereby reducing the attractiveness of investment opportunities. For this reason, real interest rates are key determinants of business investment expenditures. Demand for housing and high-priced consumer durables such as automobiles, which are commonly financed, also is highly sensitive to interest rates because interest rates affect interest payments. In Section 12.3 we will examine the determinants of real interest rates.

Budget Deficit

budget deficit

The amount by which government spending exceeds government revenues.

The **budget deficit** of the federal government is the difference between government spending and revenues. Any budgetary shortfall must be offset by government borrowing. Large amounts of government borrowing can force up interest rates by increasing the total demand for credit in the economy. Economists generally believe excessive government borrowing will "crowd out" private borrowing and investing by forcing up interest rates and choking off business investment.

Sentiment

Consumers' and producers' optimism or pessimism concerning the economy are important determinants of economic performance. If consumers have confidence in their future income levels, for example, they will be more willing to spend on big-ticket items. Similarly, businesses will increase production and inventory levels if they anticipate higher demand for their products. In this way, beliefs influence how much consumption and investment will be pursued and affect the aggregate demand for goods and services.

CONCEPT *check* **12.1**

Consider an economy where the dominant industry is automobile production for domestic consumption as well as export. Now suppose the auto market is hurt by an increase in the length of time people use their cars before replacing them. Describe the probable effects of this change on (*a*) GDP, (*b*) unemployment, (*c*) the government budget deficit, and (*d*) interest rates.

12.3 INTEREST RATES

The level of interest rates is perhaps the most important macroeconomic factor to consider in one's investment analysis. Forecasts of interest rates directly affect the forecast of returns in the fixed-income market. If your expectation is that rates will increase by more than the consensus view, you will want to shy away from longer term fixed-income securities. Similarly, increases in interest rates tend to be bad news for the stock market. Unanticipated increases in rates generally are associated with stock market declines. Thus, a superior technique to forecast rates would be of immense value to an investor attempting to determine the best asset allocation for his or her portfolio.

Unfortunately, forecasting interest rates is one of the most notoriously difficult parts of applied macroeconomics. Nonetheless, we do have a good understanding of the fundamental factors that determine the level of interest rates:

1. The supply of funds from savers, primarily households.
2. The demand for funds from businesses to be used to finance physical investments in plant, equipment, and inventories.
3. The government's net supply and/or demand for funds as modified by actions of the Federal Reserve Bank.
4. The expected rate of inflation.

Although there are many different interest rates economywide (as many as there are types of securities), these rates tend to move together, so economists frequently talk as though there were a single representative rate. We can use this abstraction to gain some insights into determining the real rate of interest if we consider the supply and demand curves for funds.

Figure 12.3 shows a downward-sloping demand curve and an upward-sloping supply curve. On the horizontal axis, we measure the quantity of funds, and on the vertical axis, we measure the real rate of interest.

The supply curve slopes up from left to right because the higher the real interest rate, the greater the supply of household savings. The assumption is that at higher real interest rates, households will choose to postpone some current consumption and set aside or invest more of their disposable income for future use.

The demand curve slopes down from left to right because the lower the real interest rate, the more businesses will want to invest in physical capital. Assuming that businesses rank projects by the expected real return on invested capital, firms will undertake more projects the lower the real interest rate on the funds needed to finance those projects.

Equilibrium is at the point of intersection of the supply and demand curves, point E in Figure 12.3.

The government and the central bank (the Federal Reserve) can shift these supply and demand curves either to the right or to the left through fiscal and monetary policies. For example, consider an increase in the government's budget deficit. This increases the government's borrowing demand and shifts the demand curve to the right, which causes the equilibrium real interest rate to rise to point E'. That is, a forecast that indicates higher than previously expected government borrowing increases expectations of future interest rates. The Fed can offset such a rise through an increase in the money supply, which will increase the supply of loanable funds, and shift the supply curve to the right.

Thus, while the fundamental determinants of the real interest rate are the propensity of households to save and the expected productivity (or we could say profitability) of firms' investment in physical capital, the real rate can be affected as well by government fiscal and monetary policies.

The supply and demand framework illustrated in Figure 12.3 is a reasonable first approximation to the determination of the real interest rate. To obtain the *nominal* interest rate, one needs to add the expected inflation rate to the equilibrium real rate. As we discussed in Section 5.4, the inflation premium is necessary for investors to maintain a given real rate of return on their investments.

FIGURE 12.3

Determination of the equilibrium real rate of interest

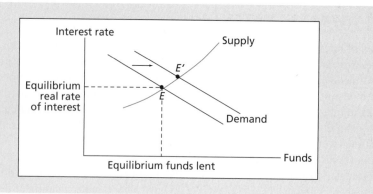

While monetary policy can clearly affect nominal interest rates, there is considerable controversy concerning its ability to affect real rates. There is widespread agreement that, in the long run, the ultimate impact of an increase in the money supply is an increase in prices with no permanent impact on real economic activity. A rapid rate of growth in the money supply, therefore, ultimately would result in a correspondingly high inflation rate and nominal interest rate, but it would have no sustained impact on the real interest rate. However, in the shorter run, changes in the money supply may well have an effect on the real interest rate.

12.4   DEMAND AND SUPPLY SHOCKS

demand shock

An event that affects the demand for goods and services in the economy.

supply shock

An event that influences production capacity and costs in the economy.

A useful way to organize your analysis of the factors that might influence the macroeconomy is to classify any impact as a supply or demand shock. A **demand shock** is an event that affects the demand for goods and services in the economy. Examples of positive demand shocks are reductions in tax rates, increases in the money supply, increases in government spending, or increases in foreign export demand. A **supply shock** is an event that influences production capacity and costs. Examples of supply shocks are changes in the price of imported oil; freezes, floods, or droughts that might destroy large quantities of agricultural crops; changes in the educational level of an economy's workforce; or changes in the wage rates at which the labor force is willing to work.

Demand shocks usually are characterized by aggregate output moving in the same direction as interest rates and inflation. For example, a big increase in government spending will tend to stimulate the economy and increase GDP. It also might increase interest rates by increasing the demand for borrowed funds by the government as well as by businesses that might desire to borrow to finance new ventures. Finally, it could increase the inflation rate if the demand for goods and services is raised to a level at or beyond the total productive capacity of the economy.

Supply shocks usually are characterized by aggregate output moving in the opposite direction as inflation and interest rates. For example, a big increase in the price of imported oil will be inflationary because costs of production will rise, which eventually will lead to increases in prices of finished goods. The increase in inflation rates over the near term can lead to higher nominal interest rates. Against this background, aggregate output will be falling. With raw materials more expensive, the productive capacity of the economy is reduced, as is the ability of individuals to purchase goods at now-higher prices. GDP, therefore, tends to fall.

How can we relate this framework to investment analysis? You want to identify the industries that will be most helped or hurt in any macroeconomic scenario you envision. For example, if you forecast a tightening of the money supply, you might want to avoid industries such as automobile producers that might be hurt by the likely increase in interest rates. We caution you again that these forecasts are no easy task. Macroeconomic predictions are notoriously unreliable. And again, you must be aware that in all likelihood your forecast will be made using only publicly available information. Any investment advantage you have will be a result only of better analysis—not better information.

12.5   FEDERAL GOVERNMENT POLICY

As the previous section would suggest, the government has two broad classes of macroeconomic tools—those that affect the demand for goods and services and those that affect their supply. For much of postwar history, demand-side policy has been of primary interest. The focus has been on government spending, tax levels, and monetary policy. Since the 1980s, however, increasing attention has also been focused on supply-side economics. Broadly interpreted, supply-side concerns have to do with enhancing the productive capacity of the economy, rather than increasing the demand for the goods and services the economy can produce. In practice, supply-side economists have focused on the appropriateness of the incentives to work, innovate, and take risks that result from our system of taxation. However, issues such as national policies on education, infrastructure (such as communication and transportation systems), and research and development also are properly regarded as part of supply-side macroeconomic policy.

Fiscal Policy

Fiscal policy refers to the government's spending and tax actions and is part of "demand-side management." Fiscal policy is probably the most direct way either to stimulate or to slow the economy. Decreases in government spending directly deflate the demand for goods and services. Similarly, increases in tax rates immediately siphon income from consumers and result in fairly rapid decreases in consumption.

Ironically, although fiscal policy has the most immediate impact on the economy, the formulation and implementation of such policy is usually painfully slow and involved. This is because fiscal policy requires enormous amounts of compromise between the executive and legislative branches. Tax and spending policy must be initiated and voted on by Congress, which requires considerable political negotiations, and any legislation passed must be signed by the president, requiring more negotiation. Thus, while the impact of fiscal policy is relatively immediate, its formulation is so cumbersome that fiscal policy cannot in practice be used to fine-tune the economy.

Moreover, much of government spending, such as that for Medicare or Social Security, is nondiscretionary, meaning that it is determined by formula rather than policy and cannot be changed in response to economic conditions. This places even more rigidity into the formulation of fiscal policy.

A common way to summarize the net impact of government fiscal policy is to look at the government's budget deficit or surplus, which is simply the difference between revenues and expenditures. A large deficit means the government is spending considerably more than it is taking in by way of taxes. The net effect is to increase the demand for goods (via spending) by more than it reduces the demand for goods (via taxes), therefore, stimulating the economy.

fiscal policy

The use of government spending and taxing for the specific purpose of stabilizing the economy.

Monetary Policy

Monetary policy refers to the manipulation of the money supply to affect the macroeconomy and is the other main leg of demand-side policy. Monetary policy works largely through its impact on interest rates. Increases in the money supply lower short-term interest rates, ultimately encouraging investment and consumption demand. Over longer periods, however, most economists believe a higher money supply leads only to a higher price level and does not have a permanent effect on economic activity. Thus, the monetary authorities face a difficult balancing act. Expansionary monetary policy probably will lower interest rates and thereby stimulate investment and some consumption demand in the short run, but these circumstances

monetary policy

Actions taken by the Board of Governors of the Federal Reserve System to influence the money supply or interest rates.

ultimately will lead only to higher prices. The stimulation/inflation trade-off is implicit in all debate over proper monetary policy.

Fiscal policy is cumbersome to implement but has a fairly direct impact on the economy, while monetary policy is easily formulated and implemented but has a less immediate impact. Monetary policy is determined by the Board of Governors of the Federal Reserve System. Board members are appointed by the president for 14-year terms and are reasonably insulated from political pressure. The board is small enough and often sufficiently dominated by its chairperson that policy can be formulated and modulated relatively easily.

Implementation of monetary policy also is quite direct. The most widely used tool is the open market operation, in which the Fed buys or sells Treasury bonds for its own account. When the Fed buys securities, it simply writes a check, thereby increasing the money supply. (Unlike us, the Fed can pay for the securities without drawing down funds at a bank account.) Conversely, when the Fed sells a security, the money paid for it leaves the money supply. Open market operations occur daily, allowing the Fed to fine-tune its monetary policy.

Other tools at the Fed's disposal are the *discount rate,* which is the interest rate it charges banks on short-term loans, and the *reserve requirement,* which is the fraction of deposits that banks must hold as cash on hand or as deposits with the Fed. Reductions in the discount rate signal a more expansionary monetary policy. Lowering reserve requirements allows banks to make more loans with each dollar of deposits and stimulates the economy by increasing the effective money supply.

While the discount rate is under the direct control of the Fed, it is changed relatively infrequently. The *federal funds rate* is by far the better guide to Federal Reserve policy. The federal funds rate is the interest rate at which banks make short-term, usually overnight, loans to each other. These loans occur because some banks need to borrow funds to meet reserve requirements, while other banks have excess funds. Unlike the discount rate, the fed funds rate is a market rate, meaning that it is determined by supply and demand rather than being set administratively. Nevertheless, the Federal Reserve Board targets the fed funds rate, expanding or contracting the money supply through open market operations as it nudges the fed funds to its targeted value. This is the benchmark short-term U.S. interest rate, and as such has considerable influence over other interest rates in the U.S. and the rest of the world.

Monetary policy affects the economy in a more roundabout way than fiscal policy. While fiscal policy directly stimulates or dampens the economy, monetary policy works largely through its impact on interest rates. Increases in the money supply lower interest rates, which stimulate investment demand. As the quantity of money in the economy increases, investors will find that their portfolios of assets include too much money. They will rebalance their portfolios by buying securities such as bonds, forcing bond prices up and interest rates down. In the longer run, individuals may increase their holdings of stocks as well and ultimately buy real assets, which stimulates consumption demand directly. The ultimate effect of monetary policy on investment and consumption demand, however, is less immediate than that of fiscal policy.

CONCEPT *check* **12.2**   Suppose the government wants to stimulate the economy without increasing interest rates. What combination of fiscal and monetary policy might accomplish this goal?

Supply-Side Policies

Fiscal and monetary policy are demand-oriented tools that affect the economy by stimulating the total demand for goods and services. The implicit belief is that the economy will not by itself arrive at a full employment equilibrium and that macroeconomic policy can push the economy toward this goal. In contrast, supply-side policies treat the issue of the productive capacity of the economy. The goal is to create an environment in which workers and owners of capital have the maximum incentive and ability to produce and develop goods.

Supply-side economists also pay considerable attention to tax policy. While demand-siders look at the effect of taxes on consumption demand, supply-siders focus on incentives and marginal tax rates. They argue that lowering tax rates will elicit more investment and improve incentives to work, thereby enhancing economic growth. Some go so far as to claim that reductions in tax rates can lead to increases in tax revenues because the lower tax rates will cause the economy and the revenue tax base to grow by more than the tax rate is reduced.

Large tax cuts in 2001 were followed by relatively rapid growth in GDP. How would demand-side and supply-side economists differ in their interpretations of this phenomenon?

CONCEPT *check* **12.3**

12.6   BUSINESS CYCLES

We've looked at the tools the government uses to fine-tune the economy, attempting to maintain low unemployment and low inflation. Despite these efforts, economies repeatedly seem to pass through good and bad times. One determinant of the broad asset allocation decision of many analysts is a forecast of whether the macroeconomy is improving or deteriorating. A forecast that differs from the market consensus can have a major impact on investment strategy.

The Business Cycle

The economy recurrently experiences periods of expansion and contraction, although the length and depth of these cycles can be irregular. These recurring patterns of recession and recovery are called **business cycles.** Figure 12.4 presents graphs of several measures of production and output. The production series all show clear variation around a generally rising trend. The bottom graph of capacity utilization also evidences a clear cyclical (although irregular) pattern.

The transition points across cycles are called peaks and troughs, identified by the boundaries of the shaded areas of the graph. A **peak** is the transition from the end of an expansion to the start of a contraction. A **trough** occurs at the bottom of a recession just as the economy enters a recovery. The shaded areas in Figure 12.4 all represent periods of recession.

As the economy passes through different stages of the business cycle, the relative profitability of different industry groups might be expected to vary. For example, at a trough, just before the economy begins to recover from a recession, one would expect that **cyclical industries,** those with above-average sensitivity to the state of the economy, would tend to outperform other industries. Examples of cyclical industries are producers of durable goods, such as automobiles or washing machines. Because purchases of these goods can be deferred during a recession, sales are particularly sensitive to macroeconomic conditions. Other cyclical industries are producers of capital goods, that is, goods used by other firms to produce their own products. When demand is slack, few companies will be expanding and purchasing capital goods. Therefore, the capital goods industry bears the brunt of a slowdown but does well in an expansion.

In contrast to cyclical firms, **defensive industries** have little sensitivity to the business cycle. These are industries that produce goods for which sales and profits are least sensitive to the state of the economy. Defensive industries include food producers and processors, pharmaceutical firms, and public utilities. These industries will outperform others when the economy enters a recession.

business cycles

Repetitive cycles of recession and recovery.

peak

The transition from the end of an expansion to the start of a contraction.

trough

The transition point between recession and recovery.

cyclical industries

Industries with above-average sensitivity to the state of the economy.

defensive industries

Industries with below-average sensitivity to the state of the economy.

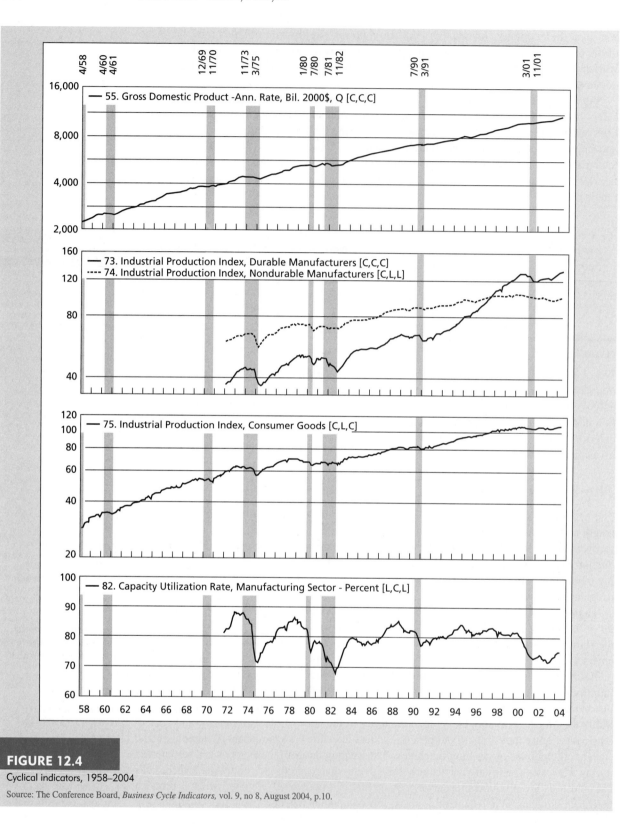

FIGURE 12.4

Cyclical indicators, 1958–2004

Source: The Conference Board, *Business Cycle Indicators*, vol. 9, no 8, August 2004, p.10.

The cyclical/defensive classification corresponds well to the notion of systematic or market risk introduced in our discussion of portfolio theory. When perceptions about the health of the economy become more optimistic, for example, the prices of most stocks will increase as forecasts of profitability rise. Because the cyclical firms are most sensitive to such developments, their stock prices will rise the most. Thus, firms in cyclical industries will tend to have high-beta stocks. In general, then, stocks of cyclical firms will show the best results when economic news is positive, but they will also show the worst results when that news is bad. Conversely, defensive firms will have low betas and performance that is comparatively unaffected by overall market conditions.

If your assessments of the state of the business cycle were reliably more accurate than those of other investors, choosing between cyclical and defensive industries would be easy. You would choose cyclical industries when you were relatively more optimistic about the economy, and you would choose defensive firms when you were relatively more pessimistic. As we know from our discussion of efficient markets, however, attractive investment choices will rarely be obvious. It is usually not apparent that a recession or expansion has started or ended until several months after the fact. With hindsight, the transitions from expansion to recession and back might seem obvious, but it is often quite difficult to say whether the economy is heating up or slowing down at any moment.

Economic Indicators

Given the cyclical nature of the business cycle, it is not surprising that to some extent the cycle can be predicted. The Conference Board publishes a set of cyclical indicators to help forecast, measure, and interpret short-term fluctuations in economic activity. **Leading economic indicators** are those economic series that tend to rise or fall in advance of the rest of the economy. Coincident and lagging indicators, as their names suggest, move in tandem with or somewhat after the broad economy.

Ten series are grouped into a widely followed composite index of leading economic indicators. Similarly, four coincident and seven lagging indicators form separate indexes. The composition of these indexes appears in Table 12.2.

Figure 12.5 graphs these three series. The numbers on the charts near the turning points of each series indicate the length of the lead time or lag time (in months) from the

leading economic indicators

Economic series that tend to rise or fall in advance of the rest of the economy.

TABLE 12.2	**A. Leading indicators**
Indexes of economic indicators	1. Average weekly hours of production workers (manufacturing). 2. Initial claims for unemployment insurance. 3. Manufacturers' new orders (consumer goods and materials industries). 4. Fraction of companies reporting slower deliveries. 5. New orders for nondefense capital goods. 6. New private housing units authorized by local building permits. 7. Yield curve: spread between 10-year T-bond yield and federal funds rate. 8. Stock prices, 500 common stocks. 9. Money supply (M2) growth rate. 10. Index of consumer expectations. **B. Coincident indicators** 1. Employees on nonagricultural payrolls. 2. Personal income less transfer payments. 3. Industrial production. 4. Manufacturing and trade sales. **C. Lagging indicators** 1. Average duration of unemployment. 2. Ratio of trade inventories to sales. 3. Change in index of labor cost per unit of output. 4. Average prime rate charged by banks. 5. Commercial and industrial loans outstanding. 6. Ratio of consumer installment credit outstanding to personal income. 7. Change in consumer price index for services.

Source: The Conference Board, *Business Cycle Indicators,* January 2007.

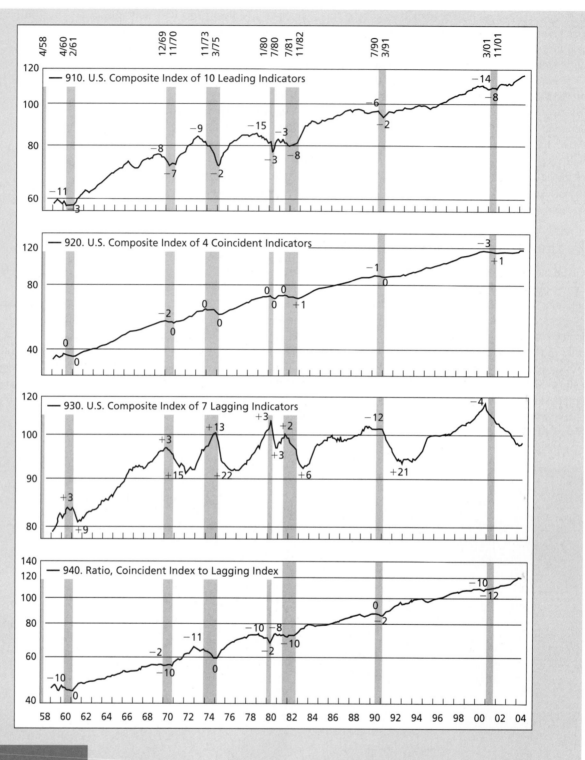

FIGURE 12.5

Indexes of leading, coincident, and lagging indicators

Source: The Conference Board, *Business Cycle Indicators*, August 2004, p. 3.

turning point to the designated peak or trough of the corresponding business cycle. While the index of leading indicators consistently turns before the rest of the economy, the lead time is somewhat erratic. Moreover, the lead time for peaks is consistently longer than that for troughs.

The stock market price index is a leading indicator. This is as it should be, as stock prices are forward-looking predictors of future profitability. Unfortunately, this makes the series of leading indicators much less useful for investment policy—by the time the series predicts an upturn, the market has already made its move. While the business cycle may be somewhat predictable, the stock market may not be. This is just one more manifestation of the efficient market hypothesis.

The money supply is another leading indicator. This makes sense in light of our earlier discussion concerning the lags surrounding the effects of monetary policy on the economy. An expansionary monetary policy can be observed fairly quickly, but it might not affect the economy for several months. Therefore, today's monetary policy might well predict future economic activity.

Other leading indicators focus directly on decisions made today that will affect production in the near future. For example, manufacturers' new orders for goods, contracts and orders for plant and equipment, and housing starts all signal a coming expansion in the economy.

A wide range of economic indicators are released to the public on a regular "economic calendar." Table 12.3 lists the public announcement dates and sources for about 20 statistics of interest. These announcements are reported in the financial press, for example, *The Wall Street Journal,* as they are released. They also are available at many sites on the Web, for

TABLE 12.3

Economic calendar

Statistic	Release Date*	Source	Web Site (www.)
Auto and truck sales	2nd of month	Commerce Department	commerce.gov
Business inventories	15th of month	Commerce Department	commerce.gov
Construction spending	1st business day of month	Commerce Department	commerce.gov
Consumer confidence	Last Tuesday of month	Conference Board	conference-board.org
Consumer credit	5th business day of month	Federal Reserve Board	federalreserve.gov
Consumer price index (CPI)	13th of month	Bureau of Labor Statistics	bls.gov
Durable goods orders	26th of month	Commerce Department	commerce.gov
Employment cost index	End of first month of quarter	Bureau of Labor Statistics	bls.gov
Employment record (unemployment, average workweek, nonfarm payrolls)	1st Friday of month	Bureau of Labor Statistics	bls.gov
Existing home sales	25th of month	National Association of Realtors	realtor.org
Factory orders	1st business day of month	Commerce Department	commerce.gov
Gross domestic product	3rd–4th week of month	Commerce Department	commerce.gov
Housing starts	16th of month	Commerce Department	commerce.gov
Industrial production	15th of month	Federal Reserve Board	federalreserve.gov
Initial claims for jobless benefits	Thursdays	Department of Labor	dol.gov
International trade balance	20th of month	Commerce Department	commerce.gov
Index of leading economic indicators	Beginning of month	Conference Board	conference-board.org
Money supply	Thursdays	Federal Reserve Board	federalreserve.gov
New home sales	Last business day of month	Commerce Department	commerce.gov
Producer price index	11th of month	Bureau of Labor Statistics	bls.gov
Productivity and costs	2nd month in quarter (approx. 7th day of month)	Bureau of Labor Statistics	bls.gov
Retail sales	13th of month	Commerce Department	commerce.gov
Survey of purchasing managers	1st business day of month	Institute for Supply Management	ism.ws

*Many of these release dates are approximate.

Last Week							Next Week	
Date	Time (ET)	Statistic	For	Actual	Briefing Forecast	Market Expects	Prior	Revised From
Feb 12	2:00 PM	Treasury Budget	Jan	$38.2B	$40.0B	$40.0B	$21.0B	–
Feb 13	8:30 AM	Trade Balance	Dec	–$61.2B	–$59.7B	–$59.5B	–$58.1B	–$58.2B
Feb 14	8:30 AM	Retail Sales	Jan	0.0%	0.5%	0.3%	1.2%	0.9%
Feb 14	10:00 AM	Business Inventories	Dec	0.0%	–0.1%	0.1%	0.2%	0.4%
Feb 14	10:30 AM	Crude Inventories	02/09	–589K	NA	NA	–449K	–

FIGURE 12.6

Economic calendar at Yahoo!

Source: Yahoo! Briefing Economic Calendar, **biz.yahoo.com/c/e.html,** February 14, 2007. Reproduced with permission of Yahoo! Inc. © 2007 by Yahoo! Inc. Yahoo! and the Yahoo! logo are trademarks of Yahoo! Inc.

example, at Yahoo!'s site. Figure 12.6 is an excerpt from a recent Economic Calendar page at Yahoo!. The page gives a list of the announcements released during the week of February 12, 2007. Notice that recent forecasts of each variable are provided along with the actual value of each statistic. This is useful, because in an efficient market, security prices will already reflect market expectations. The *new* information in the announcement will determine the market response.

Other Indicators

You can find lots of important information about the state of the economy from sources other than the official components of the economic calendar or the components of business cycle indicators. Table 12.4, which is derived from some suggestions in *Inc.* magazine, contains a few.[1]

TABLE 12.4

Useful economic indicators

CEO polls **www.brtable.org**	The business roundtable surveys CEOs about planned spending, a good measure of their optimism about the economy.
Temp jobs Search for "Temporary Help Services" at **www.bls.gov**	A useful leading indicator. Businesses often hire temporary workers as the economy first picks up, until it is clear that an upturn is going to be sustained. This series is available at the Bureau of Labor Statistics Web site.
Wal-Mart sales **www.walmartstores.com**	Wal-Mart sales are a good indicator of the retail sector. It publishes its same-store sales weekly.
Commercial and industrial loans **www.federalreserve.gov**	These loans are used by small and medium-sized firms. Information is published weekly by the Federal Reserve.
Semiconductors **www.semi.org**	The book-to-bill ratio (i.e., new sales versus actual shipments) indicates whether demand in the technology sector is increasing (ratio > 1) or falling. This ratio is published by Semiconductor Equipment and Materials International.
Commercial structures **www.bea.gov**	Investment in structures is an indicator of businesses' forecasts of demand for their products in the near future. This is one of the series compiled by the Bureau of Economic Analysis as part of its GDP series.

[1]Gene Sperling and Illustrations by Thomas Fuchs, "The Insider's Guide to Economic Forecasting," *Inc.,* August 2003, p. 96.

Leading Economic Indicators

This exercise will give you a chance to examine data on some of the leading economic indicators.

1. Download the data for new privately owned housing units authorized by building permits from **www.census. gov/const/www/C40/table1.html**. Choose the seasonally adjusted data for the United States in an Excel format. Graph the "Total" series.

2. Download the last five years of data for manufacturers' new orders of nondefense capital goods from the St. Louis Federal Reserve site at **research.stlouisfed. org/fred2/series/NEWORDER**. Graph the data.

3. Locate data for the average weekly hours of production workers in manufacturing, available at **www.bls.gov/lpc/lpcover.htm#Data**. Select

the historical time series link and then choose the Index data. Choose manufacturing as the sector and average weekly hours as the measure. Retrieve the report for the past five years. Use the options for a table format, non-HTML, and a space as a delimiter. This will give you both quarterly data and annual averages. When you copy the data into Excel you can use the Data, Text to Columns menu to put the data into a usable format. Create a graph of the data that shows the quarterly trend over the last five years.

4. The data series you retrieved are all leading economic indicators. Based on the tables and your graphs, what is your opinion of where the economy is heading in the near future?

12.7 INDUSTRY ANALYSIS

Industry analysis is important for the same reason that macroeconomic analysis is: Just as it is difficult for an industry to perform well when the macroeconomy is ailing, it is unusual for a firm in a troubled industry to perform well. Similarly, just as we have seen that economic performance can vary widely across countries, performance also can vary widely across industries. Figure 12.7 illustrates the dispersion of industry performance. It shows return on equity for several major industry groups. ROE ranged from 10.6% for electronic equipment to 29.2% for the cigarette industry.

Given this wide variation in profitability, it is not surprising that industry groups exhibit considerable dispersion in their stock market performance. Figure 12.8 illustrates the stock price performance of several industries in 2006. The market as a whole was up dramatically, but the spread in annual returns was remarkable, ranging from a −20.7% return for the home construction industry to a 61.7% return in the steel industry.

Even small investors can easily take positions in industry performance using mutual funds or exchange-traded funds with an industry focus. For example, Fidelity offers over 30 Select funds, each of which is invested in a particular industry, and there are dozens of industry-specific ETFs available to retail investors.

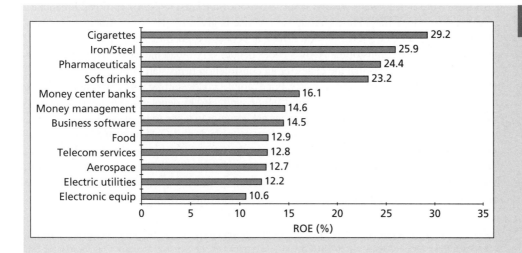

FIGURE 12.7

Return on equity

Source: Yahoo! Finance (**finance.yahoo.com**), February 6, 2007. Reproduced with permission of Yahoo! Inc. © 2000–2007 by Yahoo! Inc. Yahoo! and the Yahoo! logo are trademarks of Yahoo! Inc.

FIGURE 12.8

Industry stock price performance, 2006

Source: *The Wall Street Journal*, January 2, 2007.

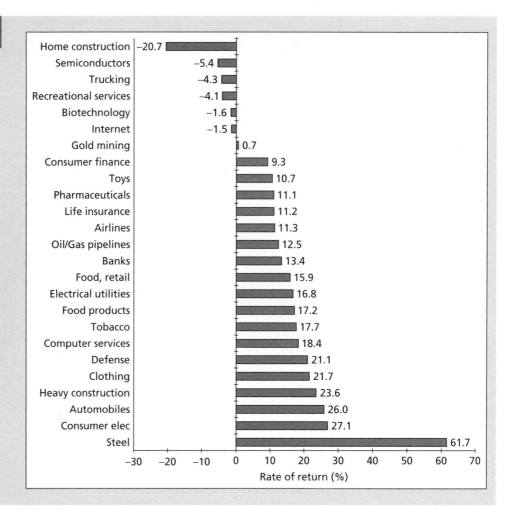

Defining an Industry

While we know what we mean by an industry, it can be difficult in practice to decide where to draw the line between one industry and another. Consider, for example, one of the industries depicted in Figure 12.7, money-center banks. There is substantial variation within this group by size, focus, and region, and one might well be justified in further dividing these banks into distinct subindustries. Their differences may result in considerable dispersion in financial performance. Figure 12.9 shows ROE for a sample of the banks included in this industry, and performance did indeed vary widely: from 12.3% for Sun Trust to 26.8% for PNC Financial.

A useful way to define industry groups in practice is given by the North American Industry Classification System, or **NAICS codes**.[2] These are codes assigned to group firms for statistical analysis. The first two digits of the NAICS codes denote very broad industry classifications. For example, Table 12.5 shows that the codes for all construction firms start with 23. The next digits define the industry grouping more narrowly. For example, codes starting with 236 denote *building* construction, 2361 denotes *residential* construction, and 236115 denotes *single-family* construction. Firms with the same 4-digit NAICS codes are commonly taken to be in the same industry.

Industry classifications are never perfect. For example, both J.C. Penney and Neiman Marcus might be classified as department stores. Yet the former is a high-volume "value" store, while the latter is a high-margin elite retailer. Are they really in the same industry? Still, these classifications are a tremendous aid in conducting industry analysis since they provide a means of focusing on very broadly or fairly narrowly defined groups of firms.

NAICS codes

Classification of firms into industry groups using numerical codes to identify industries.

---

[2] These codes are used for firms operating inside the NAFTA (North American Free Trade Agreement) region, which includes the U.S., Mexico, and Canada. NAICS codes have replaced the Standard Industry Classification or SIC codes previously used in the U.S.

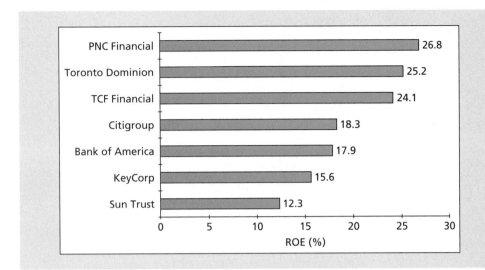

FIGURE 12.9
ROE of major banks
Source: Yahoo! Finance, February 6, 2007. Reproduced with permission of Yahoo! Inc. © 2007 by Yahoo! Inc. Yahoo! and the Yahoo! logo are trademarks of Yahoo! Inc.

Several other industry classifications are provided by other analysts, for example, Standard & Poor's reports on the performance of about 100 industry groups. S&P computes stock price indexes for each group, which is useful in assessing past investment performance. The *Value Line Investment Survey* reports on the conditions and prospects of about 1,700 firms, grouped into about 90 industries. Value Line's analysts prepare forecasts of the performance of industry groups as well as of each firm.

Sensitivity to the Business Cycle

Once the analyst forecasts the state of the macroeconomy, it is necessary to determine the implication of that forecast for specific industries. Not all industries are equally sensitive to the business cycle. For example, consider Figure 12.10, which plots changes in retail sales (year over year) in two industries: jewelry and grocery stores. Clearly, sales of jewelry, which is a luxury good, fluctuate more widely than those of grocery stores. The downturn in jewelry sales in 2001 when the economy was in a recession is notable. In contrast, sales growth in the grocery industry is relatively stable, with no years in which sales decline. These patterns reflect the fact that jewelry is a discretionary good, whereas most grocery products are staples for which demand will not fall significantly even in hard times.

Three factors will determine the sensitivity of a firm's earnings to the business cycle. First is the sensitivity of sales. Necessities will show little sensitivity to business conditions. Examples of industries in this group are food, drugs, and medical services. Other industries with

TABLE 12.5	NAICS Code	NAICS Title
Examples of NAICS industry codes	23	Construction
	236	Construction of Buildings
	2361	Residential Building Construction
	23611	Residential Building Construction
	236115	New Single-Family Housing Construction
	236116	New Multifamily Housing Construction
	236117	New Housing Operative Builders
	236118	Residential Remodelers
	2362	Nonresidential Building Construction
	23621	Industrial Building Construction
	236210	Industrial Building Construction
	23622	Commercial and Institutional Building Construction
	236220	Commercial and Institutional Building Construction

FIGURE 12.10

Industry cyclicality. Growth in sales, year over year, in two industries.

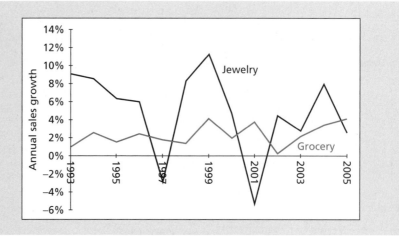

low sensitivity are those for which income is not a crucial determinant of demand. Tobacco products are examples of this type of industry. Another industry in this group is movies, because consumers tend to substitute movies for more expensive sources of entertainment when income levels are low. In contrast, firms in industries such as machine tools, steel, autos, and transportation are highly sensitive to the state of the economy.

The second factor determining business cycle sensitivity is operating leverage, which refers to the division between fixed and variable costs. (Fixed costs are those the firm incurs regardless of its production levels. Variable costs are those that rise or fall as the firm produces more or less product.) Firms with greater amounts of variable as opposed to fixed costs will be less sensitive to business conditions. This is because, in economic downturns, these firms can reduce costs as output falls in response to falling sales. Profits for firms with high fixed costs will swing more widely with sales because costs do not move to offset revenue variability. Firms with high fixed costs are said to have high operating leverage, as small swings in business conditions can have large impacts on profitability.

The third factor influencing business cycle sensitivity is financial leverage, which is the use of borrowing. Interest payments on debt must be paid regardless of sales. They are fixed costs that also increase the sensitivity of profits to business conditions. We will have more to say about financial leverage in Chapter 14.

Investors should not always prefer industries with lower sensitivity to the business cycle. Firms in sensitive industries will have high-beta stocks and are riskier. But while they swing lower in downturns, they also swing higher in upturns. As always, the issue you need to address is whether the expected return on the investment is fair compensation for the risks borne.

Sector Rotation

sector rotation

An investment strategy that entails shifting the portfolio into industry sectors that are expected to outperform others based on macroeconomic forecasts.

One way that many analysts think about the relationship between industry analysis and the business cycle is the notion of **sector rotation.** The idea is to shift the portfolio more heavily into industry or sector groups that are expected to outperform based on one's assessment of the state of the business cycle.

Figure 12.11 is a stylized depiction of the business cycle. Near the peak of the business cycle, the economy might be overheated with high inflation and interest rates and price pressures on basic commodities. This might be a good time to invest in firms engaged in natural resource extraction and processing such as minerals or petroleum.

Following a peak, when the economy enters a contraction or recession, one would expect defensive industries that are less sensitive to economic conditions, for example, pharmaceuticals, food, and other necessities, to be the best performers. At the height of the contraction, financial firms will be hurt by shrinking loan volume and higher default rates. Toward the end of the recession, however, contractions induce lower inflation and interest rates, which favor financial firms.

At the trough of a recession, the economy is poised for recovery and subsequent expansion. Firms might thus be spending on purchases of new equipment to meet anticipated increases in

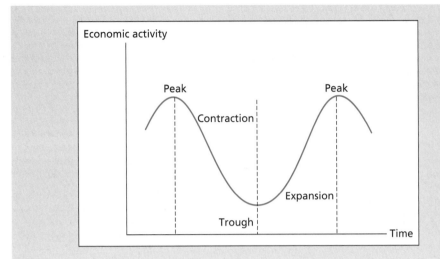

FIGURE 12.11

A stylized depiction of the business cycle

demand. This, then, would be a good time to invest in capital goods industries, such as equipment, transportation, or construction.

Finally, in an expansion, the economy is growing rapidly. Cyclical industries such as consumer durables and luxury items will be most profitable in this stage of the cycle. Banks might also do well in expansions, since loan volume will be high and default exposure low when the economy is growing rapidly.

The nearby box is an abridged sector rotation analysis from Standard & Poor's, which notes that the industries that performed best when investors were defensive concerning the economy were relative noncyclical industries such as consumer staples or health care. Given its forecast of an expansion, however, S&P recommends investments in more cyclical industries such as materials and technology.

Let us emphasize again that sector rotation, like any other form of market timing, will be successful only if one anticipates the next stage of the business cycle better than other investors. The business cycle depicted in Figure 12.11 is highly stylized. In real life, it is never as clear how long each phase of the cycle will last, nor how extreme it will be. These forecasts are where analysts need to earn their keep.

In which phase of the business cycle would you expect the following industries to enjoy their best performance?
(*a*) Newspapers; (*b*) Machine tools; (*c*) Beverages; (*d*) Timber.

Industry Life Cycles

Examine the biotechnology industry and you will find many firms with high rates of investment, high rates of return on investment, and very low dividends as a percentage of profits. Do the same for the electric utility industry and you will find lower rates of return, lower investment rates, and higher dividend payout rates. Why should this be?

The biotech industry is still new. Recently available technologies have created opportunities for the highly profitable investment of resources. New products are protected by patents, and profit margins are high. With such lucrative investment opportunities, firms find it advantageous to put all profits back into the firm. The companies grow rapidly on average.

Eventually, however, growth must slow. The high profit rates will induce new firms to enter the industry. Increasing competition will hold down prices and profit margins. New technologies become proven and more predictable, risk levels fall, and entry becomes even easier. As internal investment opportunities become less attractive, a lower fraction of profits is reinvested in the firm. Cash dividends increase.

On the MARKET FRONT

A CYCLICAL TAKE ON PERFORMANCE

Where are we in the current economic cycle, and which sectors, as a result, are poised to outperform? Those questions are at the heart of sector investing. Breaking expansions into early, middle, and late phases, and analyzing the performances of different industries during these periods, suggests a pattern of sector rotation, illustrated in the figure below.

This diagram offers a map to when sectors historically had their "day in the sun" during a typical economic cycle. But historical performances should always be viewed as a guide and not gospel. First, there's no guarantee that what worked in the past will work in the future. Moreover, economic cycles are rarely "typical." And finally, although investors frequently want to use the economic cycle as a guide to likely stock market performance, it might be more effective to look at things from the opposite perspective. Since the stock market is a leading indicator of future economic growth, wouldn't it be wiser to use the stock market as a guide to where the economic cycle may be headed?

That said, where does S&P think the U.S. is in the current cycle, and which sectors are expected to perform well in the coming months?

STILL GROWING

Through mid-May, S&P's consumer staples, energy, and health care sectors offered leadership. The market's embrace of these defensive sectors—consistent with the rotational wheel—was, in our view, the result of investor concern that the impending start of a rising interest rate environment, exacerbated by unrest in the Middle East and high oil prices, would ultimately throw the U.S. economy into the next recession.

But investors' concern about an economic recession may have been premature. S&P thinks the U.S. is midway into an expansion. First, we project GDP growth to last for two years. Second, the jobs picture has only recently improved, indicating that the current expansion has just finally taken hold. Third, even though we think the Federal Reserve will eventually raise the Fed funds rate, we believe it will be in an attempt to stop stimulating—rather than an effort to slow—the overall rate of growth of the U.S. economy. This analysis holds clues as to which sectors might be set to do well.

AREAS OF OPPORTUNITY

S&P analysts believe investment opportunities can still be found in economically sensitive (i.e., cyclical) sectors. Earnings leadership is projected to come from the materials, technology, and consumer discretionary sectors, while relative weakness is expected in telecommunications services, utilities, and consumer staples.

SOURCE: Sam Stovall, *BusinessWeek Online*, "A Cyclical Take on Performance." Reprinted with special permission from the July 8, 2004 issue of *BusinessWeek*. © 2004 McGraw-Hill Companies, Inc.

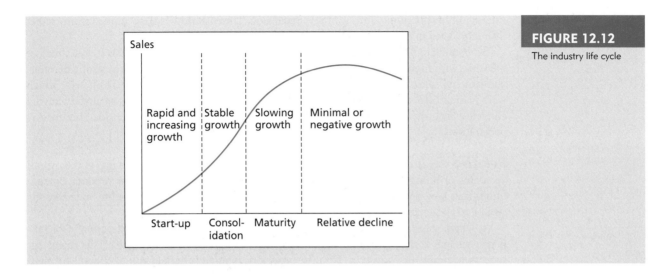

FIGURE 12.12

The industry life cycle

Ultimately, in a mature industry, we observe "cash cows," firms with stable dividends and cash flows and little risk. Their growth rates might be similar to that of the overall economy. Industries in early stages of their life cycles offer high-risk/high-potential-return investments. Mature industries offer lower risk, lower return combinations.

This analysis suggests that a typical **industry life cycle** might be described by four stages: a start-up stage characterized by extremely rapid growth; a consolidation stage characterized by growth that is less rapid but still faster than that of the general economy; a maturity stage characterized by growth no faster than the general economy; and a stage of relative decline, in which the industry grows less rapidly than the rest of the economy, or actually shrinks. This industry life cycle is illustrated in Figure 12.12. Let us turn to an elaboration of each of these stages.

industry life cycle

Stages through which firms typically pass as they mature.

Start-up stage   The early stages of an industry are often characterized by a new technology or product, such as VCRs or personal computers in the 1980s, cell phones in the 1990s, or flat-screen televisions today. At this stage, it is difficult to predict which firms will emerge as industry leaders. Some firms will turn out to be wildly successful, and others will fail altogether. Therefore, there is considerable risk in selecting one particular firm within the industry. For example, in the flat-screen television industry, there is still a battle among competing technologies, such as LCD versus plasma screens, and it is still difficult to predict which firms or technologies ultimately will dominate the market.

At the industry level, however, sales and earnings will grow at an extremely rapid rate since the new product has not yet saturated its market. For example, in 1990 very few households had cell phones. The potential market for the product therefore was huge. In contrast to this situation, consider the market for a mature product like refrigerators. Almost all households in the U.S. already have refrigerators, so the market for this good is primarily composed of households replacing old refrigerators. Obviously, the growth rate in this market in the next decade will be far lower than for flat-screen TVs.

Consolidation stage   After a product becomes established, industry leaders begin to emerge. The survivors from the start-up stage are more stable, and market share is easier to predict. Therefore, the performance of the surviving firms will more closely track the performance of the overall industry. The industry still grows faster than the rest of the economy as the product penetrates the marketplace and becomes more commonly used.

Maturity stage   At this point, the product has reached its potential for use by consumers. Further growth might merely track growth in the general economy. The product has become far more standardized, and producers are forced to compete to a greater extent on the basis of price. This leads to narrower profit margins and further pressure on profits. Firms at this stage sometimes are characterized as "cash cows," firms with reasonably stable cash flow but offering little opportunity for profitable expansion. The cash flow is best "milked from" rather than reinvested in the company.

We pointed to VCRs as a start-up industry in the 1980s. By the mid-1990s it was a mature industry, with high market penetration, considerable price competition, low profit margins, and slowing sales. By the late 1990s, VCR sales were giving way to DVD players, which were in their own start-up phase. By today, one would have to judge DVDs as already having entered a maturity stage, with standardization, price competition, and considerable market penetration.

Relative decline   In this stage, the industry might grow at less than the rate of the overall economy, or it might even shrink. This could be due to obsolescence of the product, competition from new products, or competition from new low-cost suppliers, as illustrated by the steady displacement of VCRs by DVDs.

At which stage in the life cycle are investments in an industry most attractive? Conventional wisdom is that investors should seek firms in high-growth industries. This recipe for success is simplistic, however. If the security prices already reflect the likelihood for high growth, then it is too late to make money from that knowledge. Moreover, high growth and fat profits encourage competition from other producers. The exploitation of profit opportunities brings about new sources of supply that eventually reduce prices, profits, investment returns, and finally, growth. This is the dynamic behind the progression from one stage of the industry life cycle to another. The famous portfolio manager Peter Lynch makes this point in *One Up on Wall Street*. He says:

> Many people prefer to invest in a high-growth industry, where there's a lot of sound and fury. Not me. I prefer to invest in a low-growth industry. . . . In a low-growth industry, especially one that's boring and upsets people [such as funeral homes or the oil-drum retrieval business], there's no problem with competition. You don't have to protect your flanks from potential rivals . . . and this gives [the individual firm] leeway to continue to grow. [page 131]

In fact, Lynch uses an industry classification system in a very similar spirit to the lifecycle approach we have described. He places firms in the following six groups:

1. *Slow Growers.* Large and aging companies that will grow only slightly faster than the broad economy. These firms have matured from their earlier fast-growth phase. They usually have steady cash flow and pay a generous dividend, indicating that the firm is generating more cash than can be profitably reinvested in the firm.

2. *Stalwarts.* Large, well-known firms like Coca-Cola or Colgate-Palmolive. They grow faster than the slow growers but are not in the very rapid growth start-up stage. They also tend to be in noncyclical industries that are relatively unaffected by recessions.

3. *Fast Growers.* Small and aggressive new firms with annual growth rates in the neighborhood of 20 to 25%. Company growth can be due to broad industry growth or to an increase in market share in a more mature industry.

4. *Cyclicals.* These are firms with sales and profits that regularly expand and contract along with the business cycle. Examples are auto companies, steel companies, or the construction industry.

5. *Turnarounds.* These are firms that are in bankruptcy or soon might be. If they can recover from what might appear to be imminent disaster, they can offer tremendous investment returns. A good example of this type of firm would be Chrysler in 1982, when it required a government guarantee on its debt to avoid bankruptcy. The stock price rose fifteenfold in the next five years.

6. *Asset Plays.* These are firms that have valuable assets not currently reflected in the stock price. For example, a company may own or be located on valuable real estate that is worth as much or more than the company's business enterprises. Sometimes the hidden asset can be tax-loss carryforwards. Other times the assets may be intangible. For example, a cable company might have a valuable list of cable subscribers. These assets do not immediately generate cash flow and so may be more easily overlooked by other analysts attempting to value the firm.

Industry Structure and Performance

The maturation of an industry involves regular changes in the firm's competitive environment. As a final topic, we examine the relationship between industry structure, competitive strategy, and profitability. Michael Porter (1980, 1985) has highlighted these five determinants of competition: threat of entry from new competitors, rivalry between existing competitors, price pressure from substitute products, the bargaining power of buyers, and the bargaining power of suppliers.

Threat of entry   New entrants to an industry put pressure on price and profits. Even if a firm has not yet entered an industry, the potential for it to do so places pressure on prices, since high prices and profit margins will encourage entry by new competitors. Therefore, barriers to entry can be a key determinant of industry profitability. Barriers can take many forms. For example, existing firms may already have secure distribution channels for their products based on long-standing relationships with customers or suppliers that would be costly for a new entrant to duplicate. Brand loyalty also makes it difficult for new entrants to penetrate a market and gives firms more pricing discretion. Proprietary knowledge or patent protection also may give firms advantages in serving a market. Finally, an existing firm's experience in a market may give it cost advantages due to the learning that takes place over time.

Rivalry between existing competitors   When there are several competitors in an industry, there will generally be more price competition and lower profit margins as competitors seek to expand their share of the market. Slow industry growth contributes to this competition since expansion must come at the expense of a rival's market share. High fixed costs also create pressure to reduce prices since fixed costs put greater pressure on firms to operate near full capacity. Industries producing relatively homogeneous goods also are subject to considerable price pressure since firms cannot compete on the basis of product differentiation.

Pressure from substitute products   Substitute products means that the industry faces competition from firms in related industries. For example, sugar producers compete with corn syrup producers. Wool producers compete with synthetic fiber producers. The availability of substitutes limits the prices that can be charged to customers.

Bargaining power of buyers   If a buyer purchases a large fraction of an industry's output, it will have considerable bargaining power and can demand price concessions. For example, auto producers can put pressure on suppliers of auto parts. This reduces the profitability of the auto parts industry.

Bargaining power of suppliers   If a supplier of a key input has monopolistic control over the product, it can demand higher prices for the good and squeeze profits out of the industry. One special case of this issue pertains to organized labor as a supplier of a key input to the production process. Labor unions engage in collective bargaining to increase the wages paid to workers. When the labor market is highly unionized, a significant share of the potential profits in the industry can be captured by the workforce.

The key factor determining the bargaining power of suppliers is the availability of substitute products. If substitutes are available, the supplier has little clout and cannot extract higher prices.

SUMMARY

- Macroeconomic policy aims to maintain the economy near full employment without aggravating inflationary pressures. The proper trade-off between these two goals is a source of ongoing debate.
- The traditional tools of macropolicy are government spending and tax collection, which comprise fiscal policy, and manipulation of the money supply via monetary policy. Expansionary fiscal policy can stimulate the economy and increase GDP but tends to increase interest rates. Expansionary monetary policy works by lowering interest rates.
- The business cycle is the economy's recurring pattern of expansions and recessions. Leading economic indicators can be used to anticipate the evolution of the business cycle because their values tend to change before those of other key economic variables.

www.mhhe.com/bkm

- Industries differ in their sensitivity to the business cycle. More sensitive industries tend to be those producing high-priced durable goods for which the consumer has considerable discretion as to the timing of purchase. Examples are automobiles or consumer durables. Other sensitive industries are those that produce capital equipment for other firms. Operating leverage and financial leverage increase sensitivity to the business cycle.

KEY TERMS

budget deficit, 374	fundamental analysis, 370	peak, 379
business cycles, 379	gross domestic product, 373	sector rotation, 388
cyclical industries, 379	industry life cycle, 391	NAICS codes, 386
defensive industries, 379	inflation, 374	supply shock, 376
demand shock, 376	leading economic	trough, 379
exchange rate, 372	indicators, 381	unemployment rate, 374
fiscal policy, 377	monetary policy, 377	

PROBLEM SETS

 Select problems are available in McGraw-Hill's Homework Manager®. Please see the packaging options section of the preface for more information.

1. What monetary and fiscal policies might be prescribed for an economy in a deep recession?

2. Unlike other investors, you believe the Fed is going to dramatically loosen monetary policy. What would be your recommendations about investments in the following industries?
   a. Gold mining
   b. Construction

3. If you believe the U.S. dollar is about to depreciate more dramatically than do other investors, what will be your stance on investments in U.S. auto producers?

4. According to supply-side economists, what will be the long-run impact on prices of a reduction in income tax rates?

5. Consider two firms producing DVDs. One uses a highly automated robotics process, while the other uses human workers on an assembly line and pays overtime when there is heavy production demand.
   a. Which firm will have higher profits in a recession? In a boom?
   b. Which firm's stock will have a higher beta?

6. Here are four industries and four forecasts for the macroeconomy. Choose the industry that you would expect to perform best in each scenario.

   Industries: Housing construction, health care, gold mining, steel production.

   Economic Forecasts:

   Deep recession: Falling inflation, falling interest rates, falling GDP.

   Superheated economy: Rapidly rising GDP, increasing inflation and interest rates.

   Healthy expansion: Rising GDP, mild inflation, low unemployment.

   Stagflation: Falling GDP, high inflation.

7. In which stage of the industry life cycle would you place the following industries? (Warning: There is often considerable room for disagreement concerning the "correct" answers to this question.)
   a. Oil well equipment.
   b. Computer hardware.
   c. Computer software.
   d. Genetic engineering.
   e. Railroads.

8. For each pair of firms, choose the one that you think would be more sensitive to the business cycle.
    a. General Autos or General Pharmaceuticals.
    b. Friendly Airlines or Happy Cinemas.

9. Choose an industry and identify the factors that will determine its performance in the next three years. What is your forecast for performance in that time period?

10. Why do you think the index of consumer expectations is a useful leading indicator of the macroeconomy? (See Table 12.2.)

11. Why do you think the change in the index of labor cost per unit of output is a useful lagging indicator of the macroeconomy? (See Table 12.2.)

12. You have $5,000 to invest for the next year and are considering three alternatives:
    a. A money market fund with an average maturity of 30 days offering a current yield of 6% per year.
    b. A one-year savings deposit at a bank offering an interest rate of 7.5%.
    c. A 20-year U.S. Treasury bond offering a yield to maturity of 9% per year.

    What role does your forecast of future interest rates play in your decisions?

13. As a securities analyst you have been asked to review a valuation of a closely held business, Wigwam Autoparts Heaven, Inc. (WAH), prepared by the Red Rocks Group (RRG). You are to give an opinion on the valuation and to support your opinion by analyzing each part of the valuation. WAH's sole business is automotive parts retailing. The RRG valuation includes a section called "Analysis of the

 CFA® PROBLEMS

TABLE 13A

Selected retail auto parts industry data

	2005	2004	2003	2002	2001	2000	1999	1998	1997	1996
Population 18–29 years old (percentage change)	−1.8%	−2.0%	−2.1%	−1.4%	−0.8%	−0.9%	−1.1%	−0.9%	−0.7%	−0.3%
Number of households with income more than $35,000 (percentage change)	6.0%	4.0%	8.0%	4.5%	2.7%	3.1%	1.6%	3.6%	4.2%	2.2%
Number of households with income less than $35,000 (percentage change)	3.0%	−1.0%	4.9%	2.3%	−1.4%	2.5%	1.4%	−1.3%	0.6%	0.1%
Number of cars 5–15 years old (percentage change)	0.9%	−1.3%	−6.0%	1.9%	3.3%	2.4%	−2.3%	−2.2%	−8.0%	1.6%
Automotive aftermarket industry retail sales (percentage change)	5.7%	1.9%	3.1%	3.7%	4.3%	2.6%	1.3%	0.2%	3.7%	2.4%
Consumer expenditures on automotive parts and accessories (percentage change)	2.4%	1.8%	2.1%	6.5%	3.6%	9.2%	1.3%	6.2%	6.7%	6.5%
Sales growth of retail auto parts companies with 100 or more stores	17.0%	16.0%	16.5%	14.0%	15.5%	16.8%	12.0%	15.7%	19.0%	16.0%
Market share of retail auto parts companies with 100 or more stores	19.0%	18.5%	18.3%	18.1%	17.0%	17.2%	17.0%	16.9%	15.0%	14.0%
Average operating margin of retail auto parts companies with 100 or more stores	12.0%	11.8%	11.2%	11.5%	10.6%	10.6%	10.0%	10.4%	9.8%	9.0%
Average operating margin of all retail auto parts companies	5.5%	5.7%	5.6%	5.8%	6.0%	6.5%	7.0%	7.2%	7.1%	7.2%

Retail Auto Parts Industry," based completely on the data in Table 13A and the following additional information:
- WAH and its principal competitors each operated more than 150 stores at year-end 2005.
- The average number of stores operated per company engaged in the retail auto parts industry is 5.3.
- The major customer base for auto parts sold in retail stores consists of young owners of old vehicles. These owners do their own automotive maintenance out of economic necessity.

    a. One of RRG's conclusions is that the retail auto parts industry as a whole is in the maturity stage of the industry life cycle. Discuss three relevant items of data from Table 13A that support this conclusion.

    b. Another RRG conclusion is that WAH and its principal competitors are in the consolidation stage of their life cycle. Cite three items from Table 13A that suggest this conclusion. How can WAH be in a consolidation stage while its industry is in a maturity stage?

14. Universal Auto is a large multinational corporation headquartered in the United States. For segment reporting purposes, the company is engaged in two businesses: production of motor vehicles and information processing services.

    The motor vehicle business is by far the larger of Universal's two segments. It consists mainly of domestic United States passenger car production, but it also includes small truck manufacturing operations in the United States and passenger car production in other countries. This segment of Universal has had weak operating results for the past several years, including a large loss in 2007. Although the company does not reveal the operating results of its domestic passenger car segments, that part of Universal's business is generally believed to be primarily responsible for the weak performance of its motor vehicle segment.

    Idata, the information processing services segment of Universal, was started by Universal about 15 years ago. This business has shown strong, steady growth that has been entirely internal: No acquisitions have been made.

    An excerpt from a research report on Universal prepared by Paul Adams, a CFA candidate, states: "Based on our assumption that Universal will be able to increase prices significantly on U.S. passenger cars in 2008, we project a multibillion dollar profit improvement . . ."

    a. Discuss the concept of an industrial life cycle by describing each of its four phases.

    b. Identify where each of Universal's two primary businesses—passenger cars and information processing—is in such a cycle.

    c. Discuss how product pricing should differ between Universal's two businesses, based on the location of each in the industrial life cycle.

15. Adams's research report (see Problem 14) continued as follows: "With a business expansion already under way, the expected profit surge should lead to a much higher price for Universal Auto stock. We strongly recommend purchase."

    a. Discuss the business cycle approach to investment timing. (Your answer should describe actions to be taken on both stocks and bonds at different points over a typical business cycle.)

    b. Assuming Adams's assertion is correct (that a business expansion is already under way), evaluate the timeliness of his recommendation to purchase Universal Auto, a cyclical stock, based on the business cycle approach to investment timing.

16. Janet Ludlow is preparing a report on U.S.-based manufacturers in the electric toothbrush industry and has gathered the information shown in Tables 16A and 16B on the next page. Ludlow's report concludes that the electric toothbrush industry is in the maturity (i.e., late) phase of its industry life cycle.

    a. Select and justify three factors from Table 16A that support Ludlow's conclusion.

    b. Select and justify three factors from Table 16B that refute Ludlow's conclusion.

TABLE 16A

Ratios for electric toothbrush industry index and broad stock market index

Year	2002	2003	2004	2005	2006	2007
Return on equity						
Electric toothbrush industry index	12.5%	12.0%	15.4%	19.6%	21.6%	21.6%
Market index	10.2	12.4	14.6	19.9	20.4	21.2
Average P/E						
Electric toothbrush industry index	28.5×	23.2×	19.6×	18.7×	18.5×	16.2×
Market index	10.2	12.4	14.6	19.9	18.1	19.1
Dividend payout ratio						
Electric toothbrush industry index	8.8%	8.0%	12.1%	12.1%	14.3%	17.1%
Market index	39.2	40.1	38.6	43.7	41.8	39.1
Average dividend yield						
Electric toothbrush industry index	0.3%	0.3%	0.6%	0.7%	0.8%	1.0%
Market index	3.8	3.2	2.6	2.2	2.3	2.1

TABLE 16B

Characteristics of the electric toothbrush manufacturing industry

- **Industry sales growth**—Industry sales have grown at 15–20% per year in recent years and are expected to grow at 10–15% per year over the next three years.
- **Non-U.S. markets**—Some U.S. manufacturers are attempting to enter fast-growing non-U.S. markets, which remain largely unexploited.
- **Mail order sales**—Some manufacturers have created a new niche in the industry by selling electric toothbrushes directly to customers through mail order. Sales for this industry segment are growing at 40% per year.
- **U.S. market penetration**—The current penetration rate in the United States is 60% of households and will be difficult to increase.
- **Price competition**—Manufacturers compete fiercely on the basis of price, and price wars within the industry are common.
- **Niche markets**—Some manufacturers are able to develop new, unexploited niche markets in the United States based on company reputation, quality, and service.
- **Industry consolidation**—Several manufacturers have recently merged, and it is expected that consolidation in the industry will increase.
- **New entrants**—New manufacturers continue to enter the market.

17. General Weedkillers dominates the chemical weed control market with its patented product Weed-ex. The patent is about to expire, however. What are your forecasts for changes in the industry? Specifically, what will happen to industry prices, sales, the profit prospects of General Weedkillers, and the profit prospects of its competitors? What stage of the industry life cycle do you think is relevant for the analysis of this market?

18. Dynamic Communication dominates a segment of the consumer electronics industry. A small competitor in that segment is Wade Goods & Co. Wade has just introduced a new product, the Carrycom, which will replace the existing Wade product line and could significantly affect the industry segment. Mike Brandreth is preparing an industry research update that focuses on Wade, including an analysis that makes extensive

CFA® PROBLEMS

www.mhhe.com/bkm

use of the five competitive forces identified by Michael Porter. Wade's president, Toby White, makes the following statements:

- "Wade has an exclusive three-year production license for Carrycom technology from the patent owners of the new technology. This will provide us a window of opportunity to establish a leading position with this new product before competitors enter the market with similar products."

- "A vital component in all existing competitive products is pari-copper, an enriched form of copper; production of pari-copper is limited and is effectively controlled by Dynamic. The Carrycom is manufactured with ordinary copper, thus overcoming the existing dependence on pari-copper. All other Carrycom components can be purchased from numerous sources."

- "Existing products based on pari-copper are designed to work in a single geographic region that is predetermined during the manufacturing process. The Carrycom will be the only product on the market that can be reset by the user for use in different regions. We expect other products within our industry segment to incorporate this functionality at the end of our exclusive license period."

- "The Carrycom and similar competitive products have recently added the function of automatic language conversion. This elevates these products to a superior position within the broader electronics market, ahead of personal digital assistants, personal computers, and other consumer electronics. We expect that the broader electronics market will not be able to integrate automatic language conversion for at least one year."

- "We intend to replace Dynamic as the market leader within the next three years. We expect ordinary copper-based products with automatic language conversion to be the industry standard in three years. This will result in a number of similar products and limited pricing power after the three-year license expires."

Brandreth has adequately researched two of Porter's competitive forces—the bargaining power of buyers and the bargaining power of suppliers—and now turns his attention to the remaining competitive forces needed to complete his analysis of Wade.

Identify the three remaining competitive forces. Determine, with respect to each of the remaining competitive forces, whether Wade's position in the industry is likely to be strong or weak, both one year from now and five years from now.

19. The following questions have appeared on CFA examinations.
   a. Which one of the following statements *best* expresses the central idea of countercyclical fiscal policy?
      (1) Planned government deficits are appropriate during economic booms, and planned surpluses are appropriate during economic recessions.
      (2) The balanced budget approach is the proper criterion for determining annual budget policy.
      (3) Actual deficits should equal actual surpluses during a period of deflation.
      (4) Government deficits are planned during economic recessions, and surpluses are utilized to restrain inflationary booms.
   b. Based on historical data and assuming less-than-full employment, periods of sharp acceleration in the growth rate of the money supply tend to be associated *initially* with:
      (1) Periods of economic recession.
      (2) An increase in the velocity of money.
      (3) A rapid growth of gross domestic product.
      (4) Reductions in real gross domestic product.
   c. Which *one* of the following propositions would a strong proponent of supply-side economics be *most* likely to stress?
      (1) Higher marginal tax rates will lead to a reduction in the size of the budget deficit and lower interest rates because they expand government revenues.
      (2) Higher marginal tax rates promote economic inefficiency and thereby retard aggregate output because they encourage investors to undertake low productivity projects with substantial tax-shelter benefits.

(3) Income redistribution payments will exert little impact on real aggregate supply because they do not consume resources directly.

(4) A tax reduction will increase the disposable income of households. Thus, the primary impact of a tax reduction on aggregate supply will stem from the influence of the tax change on the size of the budget deficit or surplus.

Use data from the Standard & Poor's Market Insight Database at www.mhhe.com/edumarketinsight to answer the following questions.

STANDARD &POOR'S

1. Find the Industry Profiles from Market Insight for the Photographic Products and Pharmaceuticals industries. Compare the industries' price/book ratios to each other and to the composite ratio for the S&P 500. Do the differences make sense in light of their different stages in the industry life cycle?

2. Compare the price/earnings ratios for the two industries to each other and to the S&P 500 composite ratio. How do the ratios reflect the life cycle stages of the industries? Look at the 1-year, 3-year, and 5-year industry total returns. Are the returns consistent with what you know about firm life cycles? To what extent do they reflect the general state of the economy during each period?

3. On the *Industry* tab of Market Insight, select the Publishing industry. Open the most recent S&P Industry Survey for Publishing, and then answer the following questions.

   a. What industries contribute the most advertising revenue to the publishing industry? How would the outlooks for these industries affect the performance of publishing companies?

   b. Look for the "Industry Trends" section of the report. What trends are noted? How might you expect these trends to affect the publishing industry's performance in the short term?

   c. Is this industry labor intensive? What demographic trends can you think of that might be important in this regard?

   d. Find the "Key Industry Statistics and Ratios" section of the report. Choose two of the features reported in this section and discuss how you think they will affect the industry.

   e. What suggestions does the Survey have for evaluating the financial health and the prospects of a firm that specializes in magazines?

WEB *master*

Identifying Trends in Economic Data

Economic data series are used by investors to search for trends that might predict the economy's direction or confirm a reversal of direction. Download the data series described below and use them to form an opinion about the state and direction of the economy.

The consumer price index (CPI), the producer price index (PPI), and the real earnings series show the percent change from the previous month. The unemployment rate is directly represented—it is not shown as a percent change. For each series, click on the dinosaur icon to download the most recent ten years of data.

1. Find the CPI data at **www.bls.gov/cpi.** Use the U.S. city average, all items. What has been the trend in the consumer price index over the last three years?

2. Get the data for the PPI at **www.bls.gov/ppi.** Select the finished goods series. What has been the trend in the producer price index for finished goods over the last three years?

3. Have there been any significant trends in real earnings **(www.bls.gov/ces)** over the last three years?

4. What have been the trends in the unemployment rate **(www.bls.gov/cps)** during the last three years?

www.mhhe.com/bkm

12.1.   The downturn in the auto industry will reduce the demand for the product in this economy. The economy will, at least in the short term, enter a recession. This would suggest that:

    a. GDP will fall.

    b. The unemployment rate will rise.

    c. The government deficit will increase. Income tax receipts will fall, and government expenditures on social welfare programs probably will increase.

    d. Interest rates should fall. The contraction in the economy will reduce the demand for credit. Moreover, the lower inflation rate will reduce nominal interest rates.

12.2.   Expansionary fiscal policy coupled with expansionary monetary policy will stimulate the economy, with the loose monetary policy keeping down interest rates.

12.3.   A traditional demand-side interpretation of the tax cuts is that the resulting increase in after-tax income increased consumption demand and stimulated the economy. A supply-side interpretation is that the reduction in marginal tax rates made it more attractive for businesses to invest and for individuals to work, thereby increasing economic output.

12.4.   *a.* Newspapers will do best in an expansion when advertising volume is increasing.

    b. Machine tools are a good investment at the trough of a recession, just as the economy is about to enter an expansion and firms may need to increase capacity.

    c. Beverages are defensive investments, with demand that is relatively insensitive to the business cycle. Therefore, they are good investments if a recession is forecast.

    d. Timber is a good investment at a peak period, when natural resource prices are high and the economy is operating at full capacity.

Whenever the intrinsic value, or the investor's own estimate of what the stock is really worth, exceeds the market price, the stock is considered undervalued and a good investment. In the case of ABC, using a one-year investment horizon and a forecast that the stock can be sold at the end of the year at price $P_1 = \$52$, the intrinsic value is

$$V_0 = \frac{E(D_1) + E(P_1)}{1 + k} = \frac{\$4 + \$52}{1.12} = \$50$$

Equivalently, at a price of $50, the investor would derive a 12% rate of return—just equal to the required rate of return—on an investment in the stock. However, at the current price of $48, the stock is underpriced compared to intrinsic value. At this price, it provides better than a fair rate of return relative to its risk. In other words, using the terminology of the CAPM, it is a positive-alpha stock, and investors will want to buy more of it than they would following a passive strategy.

In contrast, if the intrinsic value turns out to be lower than the current market price, investors should buy less of it than under the passive strategy. It might even pay to go short on ABC stock, as we discussed in Chapter 3.

In market equilibrium, the current market price will reflect the intrinsic value estimates of all market participants. This means the individual investor whose V_0 estimate differs from the market price, P_0, in effect must disagree with some or all of the market consensus estimates of $E(D_1)$, $E(P_1)$, or k. A common term for the market consensus value of the required rate of return, k, is the **market capitalization rate**, which we use often throughout this chapter.

market capitalization rate

The market-consensus estimate of the appropriate discount rate for a firm's cash flows.

CONCEPT *check* **13.1**

You expect the price of IBX stock to be $59.77 per share a year from now. Its current market price is $50, and you expect it to pay a dividend one year from now of $2.15 per share.
a. What is the stock's expected dividend yield, rate of price appreciation, and expected holding-period return?
b. If the stock has a beta of 1.15, the risk-free rate is 6% per year, and the expected rate of return on the market portfolio is 14% per year, what is the required rate of return on IBX stock?
c. What is the intrinsic value of IBX stock, and how does it compare to the current market price?

13.3 DIVIDEND DISCOUNT MODELS

Consider an investor who buys a share of Steady State Electronics stock, planning to hold it for one year. The intrinsic value of the share is the present value of the dividend to be received at the end of the first year, D_1, and the expected sales price, P_1. We will henceforth use the simpler notation P_1 instead of $E(P_1)$ to avoid clutter. Keep in mind, though, that future prices and dividends are unknown, and we are dealing with expected values, not certain values. We've already established that

$$V_0 = \frac{D_1 + P_1}{1 + k} \tag{13.1}$$

While this year's dividend is fairly predictable given a company's history, you might ask how we can estimate P_1, the year-end price. According to Equation 13.1, V_1 (the year-end value) will be

$$V_1 = \frac{D_2 + P_2}{1 + k}$$

If we assume the stock will be selling for its intrinsic value next year, then $V_1 = P_1$, and we can substitute this value for P_1 into Equation 13.1 to find

$$V_0 = \frac{D_1}{1 + k} + \frac{D_2 + P_2}{(1 + k)^2}$$

This equation may be interpreted as the present value of dividends plus sales price for a two-year holding period. Of course, now we need to come up with a forecast of P_2. Continuing in the same way, we can replace P_2 by $(D_3 + P_3)/(1 + k)$, which relates P_0 to the value of dividends plus the expected sales price for a three-year holding period.

More generally, for a holding period of H years, we can write the stock value as the present value of dividends over the H years, plus the ultimate sales price, P_H.

$$V_0 = \frac{D_1}{1 + k} + \frac{D_2}{(1 + k)^2} + \ldots + \frac{D_H + P_H}{(1 + k)^H} \tag{13.2}$$

Note the similarity between this formula and the bond valuation formula developed in Chapter 10. Each relates price to the present value of a stream of payments (coupons in the case of bonds, dividends in the case of stocks) and a final payment (the face value of the bond or the sales price of the stock). The key differences in the case of stocks are the uncertainty of dividends, the lack of a fixed maturity date, and the unknown sales price at the horizon date. Indeed, one can continue to substitute for price indefinitely to conclude

$$V_0 = \frac{D_1}{1 + k} + \frac{D_2}{(1 + k)^2} + \frac{D_3}{(1 + k)^3} + \ldots \tag{13.3}$$

dividend discount model (DDM)

A formula for the intrinsic value of a firm equal to the present value of all expected future dividends.

Equation 13.3 states the stock price should equal the present value of all expected future dividends into perpetuity. This formula is called the **dividend discount model (DDM)** of stock prices.

It is tempting, but incorrect, to conclude from Equation 13.3 that the DDM focuses exclusively on dividends and ignores capital gains as a motive for investing in stock. Indeed, we assume explicitly in Equation 13.1 that capital gains (as reflected in the expected sales price, P_1) are part of the stock's value. At the same time, the price at which you can sell a stock in the future depends on dividend forecasts at that time.

The reason only dividends appear in Equation 13.3 is not that investors ignore capital gains. It is instead that those capital gains will be determined by dividend forecasts at the time the stock is sold. That is why in Equation 13.2 we can write the stock price as the present value of dividends plus sales price for *any* horizon date. P_H is the present value at time H of all dividends expected to be paid after the horizon date. That value is then discounted back to today, time 0. The DDM asserts that stock prices are determined ultimately by the cash flows accruing to stockholders, and those are dividends.

The Constant Growth DDM

Equation 13.3 as it stands is still not very useful in valuing a stock because it requires dividend forecasts for every year into the indefinite future. To make the DDM practical, we need to introduce some simplifying assumptions. A useful and common first pass at the problem is to assume that dividends are trending upward at a stable growth rate that we will call g. Then if $g = 0.05$, and the most recently paid dividend was $D_0 = 3.81$, expected future dividends are

$$
\begin{aligned}
D_1 &= D_0(1 + g) &&= 3.81 \times 1.05 &&= 4.00 \\
D_2 &= D_0(1 + g)^2 &&= 3.81 \times (1.05)^2 &&= 4.20 \\
D_3 &= D_0(1 + g)^3 &&= 3.81 \times (1.05)^3 &&= 4.41 \text{ etc.}
\end{aligned}
$$

Using these dividend forecasts in Equation 13.3, we solve for intrinsic value as

$$V_0 = \frac{D_0(1 + g)}{1 + k} + \frac{D_0(1 + g)^2}{(1 + k)^2} + \frac{D_0(1 + g)^3}{(1 + k)^3} + \ldots$$

This equation can be simplified to

$$V_0 = \frac{D_0(1 + g)}{k - g} = \frac{D_1}{k - g} \qquad \textbf{(13.4)}$$

Note in Equation 13.4 that we divide D_1 (not D_0) by $k - g$ to calculate intrinsic value. If the market capitalization rate for Steady State is 12%, we can use Equation 13.4 to show that the intrinsic value of a share of Steady State stock is

$$\frac{\$4.00}{.12 - .05} = \$57.14$$

Equation 13.4 is called the **constant growth DDM** or the Gordon model, after Myron J. Gordon, who popularized the model. It should remind you of the formula for the present value of a perpetuity. If dividends were expected not to grow, then the dividend stream would be a simple perpetuity, and the valuation formula for such a nongrowth stock would be $P_0 = D_1/k$.[1] Equation 13.4 is a generalization of the perpetuity formula to cover the case of a *growing* perpetuity. As g increases, the stock price also rises.

constant growth DDM

A form of the dividend discount model that assumes dividends will grow at a constant rate.

Preferred stock that pays a fixed dividend can be valued using the constant growth dividend discount model. The constant growth rate of dividends is simply zero. For example, to value a preferred stock paying a fixed dividend of $2 per share when the discount rate is 8%, we compute

$$V_0 = \frac{\$2}{.08 - 0} = \$25$$

EXAMPLE 13.1

Preferred Stock and the DDM

High Flyer Industries has just paid its annual dividend of $3 per share. The dividend is expected to grow at a constant rate of 8% indefinitely. The beta of High Flyer stock is 1.0, the risk-free rate is 6%, and the market risk premium is 8%. What is the intrinsic value of the stock? What would be your estimate of intrinsic value if you believed that the stock was riskier, with a beta of 1.25?

Because a $3 dividend has just been paid and the growth rate of dividends is 8%, the forecast for the year-end dividend is $3 × 1.08 = $3.24. The market capitalization rate is 6% + 1.0 × 8% = 14%. Therefore, the value of the stock is

$$V_0 = \frac{D_1}{k - g} = \frac{\$3.24}{.14 - .08} = \$54$$

If the stock is perceived to be riskier, its value must be lower. At the higher beta, the market capitalization rate is 6% + 1.25 × 8% = 16%, and the stock is worth only

$$\frac{\$3.24}{.16 - .08} = \$40.50$$

EXAMPLE 13.2

The Constant Growth DDM

---

[1] Recall from introductory finance that the present value of a $1 per year perpetuity is $1/k$. For example, if $k = 10\%$, the value of the perpetuity is $1/.10 = $10. Notice that if $g = 0$ in Equation 13.4, the constant growth DDM formula is the same as the perpetuity formula.

The constant growth DDM is valid only when g is less than k. If dividends were expected to grow forever at a rate faster than k, the value of the stock would be infinite. If an analyst derives an estimate of g that is greater than k, that growth rate must be unsustainable in the long run. The appropriate valuation model to use in this case is a multistage DDM such as those discussed below.

The constant growth DDM is so widely used by stock market analysts that it is worth exploring some of its implications and limitations. The constant growth rate DDM implies that a stock's value will be greater:

1. The larger its expected dividend per share.
2. The lower the market capitalization rate, k.
3. The higher the expected growth rate of dividends.

Another implication of the constant growth model is that the stock price is expected to grow at the same rate as dividends. To see this, suppose Steady State stock is selling at its intrinsic value of $57.14, so that $V_0 = P_0$. Then

$$P_0 = \frac{D_1}{k - g}$$

Note that price is proportional to dividends. Therefore, next year, when the dividends paid to Steady State stockholders are expected to be higher by $g = 5\%$, price also should increase by 5%. To confirm this, note

$$D_2 = \$4(1.05) = \$4.20$$
$$P_1 = D_2/(k - g) = \$4.20/(.12 - .05) = \$60.00$$

which is 5% higher than the current price of $57.14. To generalize

$$P_1 = \frac{D_2}{k - g} = \frac{D_1(1 + g)}{k - g} = \frac{D_1}{k - g}(1 + g)$$
$$= P_0(1 + g)$$

Therefore, the DDM implies that, in the case of constant expected growth of dividends, the expected rate of price appreciation in any year will equal that constant growth rate, g. Note that for a stock whose market price equals its intrinsic value ($V_0 = P_0$) the expected holding-period return will be

$$E(r) = \text{Dividend yield} + \text{Capital gains yield}$$
$$= \frac{D_1}{P_0} + \frac{P_1 - P_0}{P_0} = \frac{D_1}{P_0} + g \qquad \textbf{(13.5)}$$

This formula offers a means to infer the market capitalization rate of a stock, for if the stock is selling at its intrinsic value, then $E(r) = k$, implying that $k = D_1/P_0 + g$. By observing the dividend yield, D_1/P_0, and estimating the growth rate of dividends, we can compute k. This equation is known also as the *discounted cash flow (DCF) formula*.

This is an approach often used in rate hearings for regulated public utilities. The regulatory agency responsible for approving utility pricing decisions is mandated to allow the firms to charge just enough to cover costs plus a "fair" profit, that is, one that allows a competitive return on the investment the firm has made in its productive capacity. In turn, that return is taken to be the expected return investors require on the stock of the firm. The $D_1/P_0 + g$ formula provides a means to infer that required return.

EXAMPLE **13.3**

The Constant Growth Model

Suppose that Steady State Electronics wins a major contract for its revolutionary computer chip. The very profitable contract will enable it to increase the growth rate of dividends from 5% to 6% without reducing the current dividend from the projected value of $4.00 per share. What will happen to the stock price? What will happen to future expected rates of return on the stock?

The stock price ought to increase in response to the good news about the contract, and indeed it does. The stock price jumps from its original value of $57.14 to a postannouncement price of

$$\frac{D_1}{k - g} = \frac{\$4.00}{.12 - .06} = \$66.67$$

Investors who are holding the stock when the good news about the contract is announced will receive a substantial windfall.

On the other hand, at the new price the expected rate of return on the stock is 12%, just as it was before the new contract was announced.

$$E(r) = \frac{D_1}{P_0} + g = \frac{\$4.00}{\$66.67} + .06 = .12, \text{ or } 12\%$$

This result makes sense, of course. Once the news about the contract is reflected in the stock price, the expected rate of return will be consistent with the risk of the stock. Since the risk of the stock has not changed, neither should the expected rate of return.

CONCEPT
check **13.2**

a. IBX's stock dividend at the end of this year is expected to be $2.15, and it is expected to grow at 11.2% per year forever. If the required rate of return on IBX stock is 15.2% per year, what is its intrinsic value?
b. If IBX's current market price is equal to this intrinsic value, what is next year's expected price?
c. If an investor were to buy IBX stock now and sell it after receiving the $2.15 dividend a year from now, what is the expected capital gain (i.e., price appreciation) in percentage terms? What is the dividend yield, and what would be the holding-period return?

Stock Prices and Investment Opportunities

Consider two companies, Cash Cow, Inc., and Growth Prospects, each with expected earnings in the coming year of $5 per share. Both companies could in principle pay out all of these earnings as dividends, maintaining a perpetual dividend flow of $5 per share. If the market capitalization rate were $k = 12.5\%$, both companies would then be valued at $D_1/k = \$5/.125 = \$40$ per share. Neither firm would grow in value, because with all earnings paid out as dividends, and no earnings reinvested in the firm, both companies' capital stock and earnings capacity would remain unchanged over time; earnings[2] and dividends would not grow.

Now suppose one of the firms, Growth Prospects, engages in projects that generate a return on investment of 15%, which is greater than the required rate of return, $k = 12.5\%$. It would be foolish for such a company to pay out all of its earnings as dividends. If Growth Prospects retains or plows back some of its earnings into its highly profitable projects, it can earn a 15% rate of return for its shareholders, whereas if it pays out all earnings as dividends, it forgoes

---

[2]Actually, we are referring here to earnings net of the funds necessary to maintain the productivity of the firm's capital, that is, earnings net of "economic depreciation." In other words, the earnings figure should be interpreted as the maximum amount of money the firm could pay out each year in perpetuity without depleting its productive capacity. For this reason, the net earnings number may be quite different from the accounting earnings figure that the firm reports in its financial statements. We will explore this further in the next chapter.

FIGURE 13.1

Dividend growth for two earnings reinvestment policies

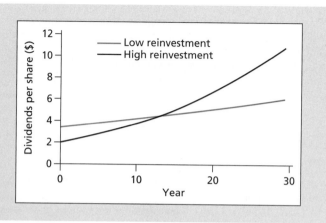

dividend payout ratio

Percentage of earnings paid out as dividends.

plowback ratio or earnings retention ratio

The proportion of the firm's earnings that is reinvested in the business (and not paid out as dividends).

the projects, leaving shareholders to invest the dividends in other opportunities at a fair market rate of only 12.5%. Suppose, therefore, Growth Prospects chooses a lower **dividend payout ratio** (the fraction of earnings paid out as dividends), reducing payout from 100% to 40%, and maintaining a **plowback ratio** (the fraction of earnings reinvested in the firm) of 60%. The plowback ratio also is referred to as the **earnings retention ratio.**

The dividend of the company, therefore, will be $2 (40% of $5 earnings) instead of $5. Will the share price fall? No, it will rise! Although dividends initially fall under the earnings reinvestment policy, subsequent growth in the assets of the firm because of reinvested profits will generate growth in future dividends, which will be reflected in today's share price.

Figure 13.1 illustrates the dividend streams generated by Growth Prospects under two dividend policies. A low reinvestment rate plan allows the firm to pay higher initial dividends but results in a lower dividend growth rate. Eventually, a high reinvestment rate plan will provide higher dividends. If the dividend growth generated by the reinvested earnings is high enough, the stock will be worth more under the high reinvestment strategy.

How much growth will be generated? Suppose Growth Prospects starts with plant and equipment of $100 million and is all-equity-financed. With a return on investment or equity (ROE) of 15%, total earnings are ROE × $100 million = 0.15 × $100 million = $15 million. There are 3 million shares of stock outstanding, so earnings per share are $5, as posited above. If 60% of the $15 million in this year's earnings is reinvested, then the value of the firm's capital stock will increase by 0.60 × $15 million = $9 million, or by 9%. The percentage increase in the capital stock is the rate at which income was generated (ROE) times the plowback ratio (the fraction of earnings reinvested in more capital), which we will denote as b.

Now endowed with 9% more capital, the company earns 9% more income and pays out 9% higher dividends. The growth rate of the dividends, therefore, is[3]

$$g = \text{ROE} \times b = 15\% \times 0.60 = 9\%$$

If the stock price equals its intrinsic value, and this growth rate can be sustained (i.e., if the ROE and payout ratios are consistent with the long-run capabilities of the firm), then the stock should sell at

$$P_0 = \frac{D_1}{k - g} = \frac{\$2}{.125 - .09} = \$57.14$$

---

[3]We can derive this relationship more generally by noting that with a fixed ROE, earnings (which equal ROE × Book value) will grow at the same rate as the book value of the firm. Abstracting from net new investment in the firm, the growth rate of book value equals reinvested earnings/book value. Therefore,

$$g = \frac{\text{Reinvested earnings}}{\text{Book value}} = \frac{\text{Reinvested earnings}}{\text{Total earnings}} \times \frac{\text{Total earnings}}{\text{Book value}} = b \times \text{ROE}$$

When Growth Prospects pursued a no-growth policy and paid out all earnings as dividends, the stock price was only $40. Therefore, you can think of $40 as the value per share of the assets the company already has in place.

When Growth Prospects decided to reduce current dividends and reinvest some of its earnings in new investments, its stock price increased. The increase in the stock price reflects the fact that planned investments provide an expected rate of return greater than the required rate. In other words, the investment opportunities have positive net present value. The value of the firm rises by the NPV of these investment opportunities. This net present value is also called the **present value of growth opportunities,** or **PVGO.**

Therefore, we can think of the value of the firm as the sum of the value of assets already in place, or the no-growth value of the firm, plus the net present value of the future investments the firm will make, which is the PVGO. For Growth Prospects, PVGO = $17.14 per share:

present value of growth opportunities (PVGO)

Net present value of a firm's future investments.

$$\text{Price} = \text{No-growth value per share} + \text{PVGO}$$

$$P_0 = \frac{E_1}{k} + \text{PVGO}$$

$$\$57.14 = \$40 + \$17.14 \tag{13.6}$$

We know that in reality, dividend cuts almost always are accompanied by steep drops in stock prices. Does this contradict our analysis? Not necessarily: Dividend cuts are usually taken as bad news about the future prospects of the firm, and it is the *new information* about the firm—not the reduced dividend yield per se—that is responsible for the stock price decline.

In one well-known case, Florida Power & Light announced a cut in its dividend, not because of financial distress, but because it wanted to better position itself for a period of deregulation. At first, the stock market did not believe this rationale—the stock price dropped 14% on the day of the announcement. But within a month, the market became convinced that the firm had in fact made a strategic decision that would improve growth prospects, and the share price actually rose *above* its preannouncement value. Even including the initial price drop, the share price outperformed both the S&P 500 and the S&P utility index in the year following the dividend cut.

It is important to recognize that growth per se is not what investors desire. Growth enhances company value only if it is achieved by investment in projects with attractive profit opportunities (i.e., with ROE > k). To see why, let's now consider Growth Prospects' unfortunate sister company, Cash Cow. Cash Cow's ROE is only 12.5%, just equal to the required rate of return, k. Therefore, the NPV of its investment opportunities is zero. We've seen that following a zero-growth strategy with $b = 0$ and $g = 0$, the value of Cash Cow will be $E_1/k = \$5/.125 = \$40$ per share. Now suppose Cash Cow chooses a plowback ratio of $b = 0.60$, the same as Growth Prospects' plowback. Then g would be

$$g = \text{ROE} \times b = .125 \times .60 = .075$$

but the stock price is still

$$P_0 = \frac{D_1}{k - g} = \frac{\$2}{.125 - .075} = \$40$$

no different from the no-growth strategy.

In the case of Cash Cow, the dividend reduction that frees funds for reinvestment in the firm generates only enough growth to maintain the stock price at the current level. This is as it should be: If the firm's projects yield only what investors can earn on their own, then NPV is zero, and shareholders cannot be made better off by a high reinvestment rate policy. This demonstrates that "growth" is not the same as growth opportunities. To justify reinvestment, the firm must engage in projects with better prospective returns than those shareholders can find elsewhere. Notice also that the PVGO of Cash Cow is zero: $\text{PVGO} = P_0 - E_1/k = 40 - 40 = 0$. With $\text{ROE} = k$, there is no advantage to plowing funds back into the firm; this shows up as PVGO of zero. In fact, this is why firms with considerable cash flow, but limited investment prospects, are called "cash cows." The cash these firms generate is best taken out of or "milked from" the firm.

EXAMPLE   13.4

Growth Opportunities

Takeover Target is run by entrenched management that insists on reinvesting 60% of its earnings in projects that provide an ROE of 10%, despite the fact that the firm's capitalization rate is $k = 15\%$. The firm's year-end dividend will be $2 per share, paid out of earnings of $5 per share. At what price will the stock sell? What is the present value of growth opportunities? Why would such a firm be a takeover target for another firm?

Given current management's investment policy, the dividend growth rate will be

$$g = \text{ROE} \times b = 10\% \times .6 = 6\%$$

and the stock price should be

$$P_0 = \frac{\$2}{.15 - .06} = \$22.22$$

The present value of growth opportunities is

$$\text{PVGO} = \text{Price per share} - \text{No-growth value per share}$$
$$= \$22.22 - E_1/k = \$22.22 - \$5/.15 = -\$11.11$$

PVGO is *negative*. This is because the net present value of the firm's projects is negative: The rate of return on those assets is less than the opportunity cost of capital.

Such a firm would be subject to takeover, because another firm could buy the firm for the market price of $22.22 per share and increase the value of the firm by changing its investment policy. For example, if the new management simply paid out all earnings as dividends, the value of the firm would increase to its no-growth value, $E_1/k = \$5/.15 = \$33.33$.

CONCEPT check 13.3

a. Calculate the price of a firm with a plowback ratio of .60 if its ROE is 20%. Current earnings, E_1, will be $5 per share, and $k = 12.5\%$.

b. What if ROE is 10%, which is less than the market capitalization rate? Compare the firm's price in this instance to that of a firm with the same ROE and E_1, but a plowback ratio of $b = 0$.

Life Cycles and Multistage Growth Models

As useful as the constant growth DDM formula is, you need to remember that it is based on a simplifying assumption, namely, that the dividend growth rate will be constant forever. In fact, firms typically pass through life cycles with very different dividend profiles in different phases. In early years, there are ample opportunities for profitable reinvestment in the company. Payout ratios are low, and growth is correspondingly rapid. In later years, the firm matures, production capacity is sufficient to meet market demand, competitors enter the market, and attractive opportunities for reinvestment may become harder to find. In this mature phase, the firm may choose to increase the dividend payout ratio, rather than retain earnings. The dividend level increases, but thereafter it grows at a slower rate because the company has fewer growth opportunities.

Table 13.2 illustrates this profile. It gives Value Line's forecasts of return on assets, dividend payout ratio, and three-year growth rate in earnings per share of a sample of the firms included in the computer software and services industry versus those of East Coast electric

TABLE 13.2			
Financial ratios in two industries			
	Return on Assets (%)	**Payout Ratio (%)**	**Growth Rate 2007–2009**
Computer Software			
Adobe Systems	14.5%	0.0%	16.8%
Cognizant	19.5	0.0	19.7
Compuware	10.5	0.0	11.2
Intuit	23.0	0.0	9.7
Microsoft	35.0	31.0	15.8
Novell	6.0	0.0	24.8
Oracle	28.5	0.0	17.7
Red Hat	9.5	0.0	28.9
Parametric Tech	17.0	0.0	19.1
SAP	22.5	25.0	11.4
Median	18.3%	0.0%	17.3%
Electric Utilities			
Central Hudson G&E	5.5%	71.0%	4.5%
Central Vermont	6.0	58.0	2.2
Consolidated Edison	6.0	78.0	1.7
Duquesne Light	8.0	68.0	7.7
Energy East	5.5	72.0	8.9
Northeast Utilities	5.5	56.0	5.4
Nstar	9.0	58.0	8.6
Pennsylvania Power	12.0	51.0	14.2
Public Services Enter.	8.5	49.0	2.1
United Illuminating	5.5	89.0	4.7
Median	6.0%	63.0%	5.1%

Source: From *Value Line Investment Survey,* November and December 2006. Reprinted with permission of Value Line Investment Survey © 2006 Value Line Publishing, Inc. All rights reserved.

utilities. (We compare return on assets rather than return on equity because the latter is affected by leverage, which tends to be far greater in the electric utility industry than in the software industry. Return on assets measures operating income per dollar of total assets, regardless of whether the source of the capital supplied is debt or equity. We will return to this issue in the next chapter.)

By and large, software firms have attractive investment opportunities. The median return on assets of these firms is forecast to be 18.3%, and the firms have responded with quite high plowback ratios. Most of these firms pay no dividends at all. The high returns on assets and high plowback ratios result in rapid growth. The median growth rate of earnings per share in this group is projected at 17.3%.

In contrast, the electric utilities are more representative of mature firms. Their median return on assets is lower, 6.0%; dividend payout is higher, 63%; and average growth rate is lower, 5.1%.

We conclude that the higher payouts of the electric utilities reflect their more limited opportunities to reinvest earnings at attractive rates of return. Consistent with this analysis, Microsoft's announcement in 2004 that it would sharply increase its dividend and initiate multibillion dollar stock buybacks was widely seen as an indication that the firm was maturing into a lower-growth stage. It was generating far more cash than it had the opportunity to invest attractively, and so was paying out that cash to its shareholders.

To value companies with temporarily high growth, analysts use a multistage version of the dividend discount model. Dividends in the early high-growth period are forecast and their combined present value is calculated. Then, once the firm is projected to settle down to a steady growth phase, the constant growth DDM is applied to value the remaining stream of dividends.

two-stage DDM

Dividend discount model in which dividend growth is assumed to level off only at some future date.

We can illustrate this with a real-life example using a **two-stage DDM.** Figure 13.2 is a *Value Line Investment Survey* report on Honda Motor Co. Some of Honda's relevant information in 2007 is highlighted.

Honda's beta appears at the circled A, its recent stock price at the B, the per-share dividend payments at the C, the ROE (referred to as "return on shareholder equity") at the D, and the dividend payout ratio (referred to as "all dividends to net profits") at the E.[4] The rows ending at C, D, and E are historical time series. The boldfaced italicized entries under 2007 are estimates for that year. Similarly, the entries in the far right column (labeled 09–11) are forecasts for some time between 2009 and 2011, which we will take to be 2010.

Value Line projects rapid growth in the near term, with dividends rising from $.59 in 2007 to $.85 in 2010. This rapid growth rate cannot be sustained indefinitely. We can obtain dividend inputs for this initial period by using the explicit forecasts for 2007 and 2010 and linear interpolation for the years between:

2007	$.59
2008	$.67
2009	$.76
2010	$.85

Now let us assume the dividend growth rate levels off in 2010. What is a good guess for that steady-state growth rate? Value Line forecasts a dividend payout ratio of 0.22 and an ROE of 12.5%, implying long-term growth will be

$$g = \text{ROE} \times b = 12.5\% \times (1 - 0.22) = 9.75\%$$

Our estimate of Honda's intrinsic value using an investment horizon of 2010 is therefore obtained from Equation 13.2, which we restate here

$$V_{2006} = \frac{D_{2007}}{(1 + k)} + \frac{D_{2008}}{(1 + k)^2} + \frac{D_{2009}}{(1 + k)^3} + \frac{D_{2010} + P_{2010}}{(1 + k)^4}$$

$$= \frac{.59}{(1 + k)} + \frac{.67}{(1 + k)^2} + \frac{.76}{(1 + k)^3} + \frac{.85 + P_{2010}}{(1 + k)^4}$$

Here, P_{2010} represents the forecast price at which we can sell our shares of Honda at the end of 2010, when dividends enter their constant growth phase. That price, according to the constant growth DDM, should be

$$P_{2010} = \frac{D_{2011}}{k - g} = \frac{D_{2010}(1 + g)}{k - g} = \frac{.85 \times 1.0975}{k - .0975}$$

The only variable remaining to be determined to calculate intrinsic value is the market capitalization rate, k.

One way to obtain k is from the CAPM. Observe from the Value Line data that Honda's beta is .80. The risk-free rate on longer term bonds in 2007 was about 5%. Suppose that the

---

[4]Because Honda is a Japanese firm, Americans would hold its shares via ADRs, or American Depository Receipts. ADRs are not shares of the firm, but are *claims* to shares of the underlying foreign stock that are then traded in U.S. security markets. Value Line notes that each Honda ADR is a claim on one common share, but in other cases, each ADR may represent a claim to either multiple shares, or even fractional shares.

FIGURE 13.2

Value Line Investment Survey report on Honda Motor Co.

Source: *From Value Line Investment Survey*, December 1, 2006. Reprinted with permission of Value Line Investment Survey. © 2006 Value Line Publishing, Inc. All rights reserved.

market risk premium were forecast at 8%, roughly in line with its historical average. This would imply that the forecast for the market return was

$$\text{Risk-free rate} + \text{Market risk premium} = 5\% + 8\% = 13\%$$

Therefore, we can solve for the market capitalization rate for Honda as

$$k = r_f + \beta[E(r_M) - r_f]$$
$$= 5\% + .80\,(13 - 5) = 11.4\%$$

Our forecast for the stock price in 2010 is thus

$$P_{2010} = \frac{\$.85 \times 1.0975}{.114 - .0975} = \$56.54$$

and today's estimate of intrinsic value is

$$V_{2006} = \frac{.59}{1.114} + \frac{.67}{(1.114)^2} + \frac{.76}{(1.114)^3} + \frac{.85 + 56.54}{(1.114)^4} = \$38.88$$

We know from the Value Line report that Honda's actual price was $35.08 (at the circled B). Our intrinsic value analysis indicates Honda was underpriced by about 9%. Should we increase our holdings of Honda stock?

Perhaps. But before betting the farm, stop to consider how much confidence you should place in this estimate. We've had to guess at dividends in the near future, the ultimate growth rate of those dividends, and the appropriate discount rate. Moreover, we've assumed Honda will follow a relatively simple two-stage growth process. In practice, the growth of dividends can follow more complicated patterns. Even small errors in these approximations could upset a conclusion.

For example, we saw in Chapter 7 that betas are typically estimated with considerable imprecision. Suppose that Honda's beta is actually .9 rather than .8. Then its risk premium will be larger, and its market capitalization rate will be 12.2%. At this higher capitalization rate, the intrinsic value of the firm based on the two-stage model falls to $26.16, which is considerably *less* than its recent stock price. Our conclusion regarding mispricing is reversed.

The exercise highlights the importance of assessing the sensitivity of your analysis to changes in underlying assumptions when you attempt to value stocks. Your estimates of stock values are no better than your assumptions. Sensitivity analysis will highlight the inputs that need to be most carefully examined. For example, we just found that changes in the estimated risk premium of the stock result in big changes in intrinsic value. Similarly, small changes in the assumed growth rate change intrinsic value substantially. On the other hand, reasonable changes in the dividends forecast between 2007 and 2010 have a small impact on intrinsic value.

CONCEPT check 13.4

Confirm that the intrinsic value of Honda using the same data as in our example, but assuming its beta is .9, is $26.16. (*Hint:* First calculate the discount rate and stock price in 2010. Then calculate the present value of all interim dividends plus the present value of the 2010 sales price.)

Multistage Growth Models

The two-stage growth model that we just considered for Honda is a good start toward realism, but clearly we could do even better if our valuation model allowed for more flexible patterns of growth. Multistage growth models allow dividends per share to grow at several different

SPREADSHEET 13.1

A three-stage growth model for Honda

	A	B	C	D	E	F	G	H	I
1	Inputs			Year	Dividend	Div growth	Term value	Investor CF	
2	beta	0.8		2007	0.59			0.59	
3	mkt_prem	0.08		2008	0.68			0.68	
4	rf	0.05		2009	0.76			0.76	
5	k_equity	0.114		2010	0.85			0.85	
6	plowback	0.78		2011	0.96	0.1300		0.96	
7	roe	0.125		2012	1.08	0.1268		1.08	
8	term_gwth	0.0975		2013	1.22	0.1235		1.22	
9				2014	1.36	0.1203		1.36	
10				2015	1.52	0.1170		1.52	
11				2016	1.69	0.1138		1.69	
12	Value line			2017	1.88	0.1105		1.88	
13	forecasts of			2018	2.08	0.1073		2.08	
14	annual dividends			2019	2.30	0.1040		2.30	
15				2020	2.53	0.1008		2.53	
16				2021	2.78	0.0975		2.78	
17	Transitional period			2022	3.05	0.0975	202.86	205.91	
18	with slowing dividend								
19	growth							45.02	= PV of CF
20		Beginning of constant			E17 * (1+ F17)/(B5 − F17)				
21		growth period						NPV(B5,H2:H17)	

eXcel

Please visit us at
www.mhhe.com/bkm

rates as the firm matures. Many analysts use three-stage growth models. They may assume an initial period of high dividend growth (or instead make year-by-year forecasts of dividends for the short term), a final period of sustainable growth, and a transition period in between, during which dividend growth rates taper off from the initial rapid rate to the ultimate sustainable rate. These models are conceptually no harder to work with than a two-stage model, but they require many more calculations and can be tedious to do by hand. It is easy, however, to build an Excel spreadsheet for such a model.

Spreadsheet 13.1 is an example of such a model. Column B contains the inputs we have used so far for Honda. Column E contains dividend forecasts. In cells E2 through E5 we present the Value Line estimates for the next four years. Dividend growth in this period is rapid, about 13% annually. Rather than assume a sudden transition to constant dividend growth starting in 2010, we assume instead that the dividend growth rate in 2010 will be 13%, and that it will decline linearly through 2021 (see column F), finally reaching the constant terminal growth rate of 9.75% in 2021. Each dividend in the transition period is the previous year's dividend times that year's growth rate. Terminal value once the firm enters a constant growth stage (cell G17) is computed from the constant-growth DDM. Finally, investor cash flow in each period (column H) equals dividends in each year plus the terminal value in 2022. The present value of these cash flows is computed in cell H19 as $45.02, well above the value we found in the two-stage model. We obtain a greater intrinsic value in this case because we assume that dividend growth only gradually declines to its steady-state value.

13.4 PRICE–EARNINGS RATIOS

The Price–Earnings Ratio and Growth Opportunities

Much of the real-world discussion of stock market valuation concentrates on the firm's **price–earnings multiple,** the ratio of price per share to earnings per share, commonly called the P/E ratio. In fact, one common approach to valuing a firm is to use an earnings multiplier. The value of the stock is obtained by multiplying projected earnings per share by a forecast of the P/E ratio. This procedure seems simple, but its apparent simplicity is deceptive. First, forecasting earnings is challenging. As we saw in the previous chapter, earnings will depend on international, macroeconomic, and industry as well as firm-specific factors, many of which

price–earnings multiple

The ratio of a stock's price to its earnings per share.

are highly unpredictable. Second, forecasting the P/E multiple is even more difficult. P/E ratios vary across industries and over time. Nevertheless, our discussion of stock valuation provides some insight into the factors that ought to determine a firm's P/E ratio.

Recall our discussion of growth opportunities, in which we compared two firms, Growth Prospects and Cash Cow, each of which had earnings per share of $5. Growth Prospects reinvested 60% of its earnings in prospects with an ROE of 15%, while Cash Cow paid out all of its earnings as dividends. Cash Cow had a price of $40, giving it a P/E multiple of 40/5 = 8.0, while Growth Prospects sold for $57.14, giving it a multiple of 57.14/5 = 11.4. This observation suggests the P/E ratio might serve as a useful indicator of expectations of growth opportunities. We can see this explicitly by rearranging Equation 13.6 to

$$\frac{P_0}{E_1} = \frac{1}{k}\left[1 + \frac{\text{PVGO}}{E_1/k}\right] \tag{13.7}$$

When PVGO = 0, Equation 13.7 shows that $P_0 = E_1/k$. The stock is valued like a nongrowing perpetuity of EPS$_1$. The P/E ratio is just $1/k$. However, as PVGO becomes an increasingly dominant contributor to price, the P/E ratio can rise dramatically. The ratio of PVGO to E/k has a simple interpretation. It is the ratio of the component of firm value reflecting growth opportunities to the component of value reflecting assets already in place (i.e., the no-growth value of the firm, E/k). When future growth opportunities dominate the estimate of total value, the firm will command a high price relative to current earnings. Thus, a high P/E multiple appears to indicate that a firm is endowed with ample growth opportunities.

EXAMPLE 13.5 *P/E Ratios and* *Growth Opportunities*	Return again to Takeover Target, the firm we first encountered in Example 13.4. Earnings are $5 per share, and the capitalization rate is 15%, implying that the no-growth value of the firm is $E_1/k = \$5/.15 = \$33.33$. The stock price actually is $22.22, implying that the present value of growth opportunities equals $-\$11.11$. This implies that the P/E ratio should be $$\frac{P_0}{E_1} = \frac{1}{k}\left[1 + \frac{\text{PVGO}}{E/k}\right] = \frac{1}{.15}\left[1 + \frac{-\$11.11}{\$33.3}\right] = 4.44$$ In fact, the stock price is $22.22 and earnings are $5 per share, so the P/E ratio is $22.22/\$5 = 4.44$.

Let's see if P/E multiples do vary with growth prospects. Between 1988 and 2006, for example, Limited Brands' P/E ratio averaged about 18.4 while Consolidated Edison's average P/E was only 12.3. These numbers do not necessarily imply that Limited was overpriced compared to Con Ed. If investors believed Limited would grow faster than Con Ed, the higher price per dollar would be justified. That is, investors might well pay a higher price per dollar of *current earnings* if they expect that earnings stream to grow more rapidly. In fact Limited's growth rate has been consistent with its higher P/E multiple. In this period, its earnings per share grew fivefold, while Con Ed's earnings grew by only 13%. Figure 13.4 (on page 424) shows the EPS history of the two companies.

Clearly, it is differences in expected growth opportunities that justify particular differentials in P/E ratios across firms. The P/E ratio is in large part a reflection of the market's optimism concerning a firm's growth prospects. In their use of a P/E ratio, analysts must decide whether they are more or less optimistic than the market. If they are more optimistic, they will recommend buying the stock.

There is a way to make these insights more precise. Look again at the constant growth DDM formula, $P_0 = D_1/(k - g)$. Now recall that dividends equal the earnings that are *not* reinvested in the firm: $D_1 = E_1(1 - b)$. Recall also that $g = \text{ROE} \times b$. Hence, substituting for D_1 and g, we find that

$$P_0 = \frac{E_1(1 - b)}{k - (\text{ROE} \times b)}$$

implying that the P/E ratio for a firm growing at a long-run sustainable pace is

$$\frac{P_0}{E_1} = \frac{1 - b}{k - (\text{ROE} \times b)} \tag{13.8}$$

It is easy to verify that the P/E ratio increases with ROE. This makes sense, because high ROE projects give the firm good opportunities for growth.[5] We also can verify that the P/E ratio increases for higher plowback, *b,* as long as ROE exceeds *k*. This too makes sense. When a firm has good investment opportunities, the market will reward it with a higher P/E multiple if it exploits those opportunities more aggressively by plowing back more earnings into those opportunities.

Remember, however, that growth is not desirable for its own sake. Examine Table 13.3, where we use Equation 13.8 to compute both growth rates and P/E ratios for different combinations of ROE and *b*. While growth always increases with the plowback ratio (move across the rows in Panel A of Table 13.3), the P/E ratio does not (move across the rows in Panel B). In the top row of Table 13.3B, the P/E falls as the plowback rate increases. In the middle row, it is unaffected by plowback. In the third row, it increases.

This pattern has a simple interpretation. When the expected ROE is less than the required return, *k,* investors prefer that the firm pay out earnings as dividends rather than reinvest earnings in the firm at an inadequate rate of return. That is, for ROE lower than *k,* the value of the firm falls as plowback increases. Conversely, when ROE exceeds *k,* the firm offers superior investment opportunities, so the value of the firm is enhanced as those opportunities are more fully exploited by increasing the plowback ratio.

Finally, where ROE just equals *k,* the firm offers "break-even" investment opportunities with a fair rate of return. In this case, investors are indifferent between reinvestment of earnings in the firm or elsewhere at the market capitalization rate, because the rate of return in either case is 12%. Therefore, the stock price is unaffected by the plowback ratio.

One way to summarize these relationships is to say the higher the plowback ratio, the higher the growth rate, but a higher plowback ratio does not necessarily mean a higher P/E ratio. A higher plowback ratio increases P/E only if investments undertaken by the firm offer an expected rate of return higher than the market capitalization rate. Otherwise, higher plowback hurts investors because it means more money is sunk into prospects with inadequate rates of return.

TABLE 13.3		Plowback Ratio (*b*)			
Effect of ROE and plowback on growth and the P/E ratio		0	0.25	0.50	0.75
		A. Growth Rate, *g*			
	ROE				
	10%	0%	2.5%	5.0%	7.5%
	12	0	3.0	6.0	9.0
	14	0	3.5	7.0	10.5
		B. P/E Ratio			
	ROE				
	10%	8.33	7.89	7.14	5.56
	12	8.33	8.33	8.33	8.33
	14	8.33	8.82	10.00	16.67

Note: Assumption: $k = 12\%$ per year.

[5]Note that Equation 13.8 is a simple rearrangement of the DDM formula, with $\text{ROE} \times b = g$. Because that formula requires that $g < k$, Equation 13.8 is valid only when $\text{ROE} \times b < k$.

Notwithstanding these fine points, P/E ratios commonly are taken as proxies for the expected growth in dividends or earnings. In fact, a common Wall Street rule of thumb is that the growth rate ought to be roughly equal to the P/E ratio. In other words, the ratio of P/E to g, often called the **PEG ratio,** should be about 1.0. Peter Lynch, the famous portfolio manager, puts it this way in his book *One Up on Wall Street:*

PEG ratio

Ratio of P/E multiple to earnings growth rate.

> The P/E ratio of any company that's fairly priced will equal its growth rate. I'm talking here about growth rate of earnings. . . . If the P/E ratio of Coca-Cola is 15, you'd expect the company to be growing at about 15% per year, etc. But if the P/E ratio is less than the growth rate, you may have found yourself a bargain.

Let's try his rule of thumb.

EXAMPLE 13.6

P/E Ratio versus Growth Rate

Assume:

$$r_f = 8\% \text{ (about the value when Peter Lynch was writing)}$$
$$r_M - r_f = 8\% \text{ (about the historical average market risk premium)}$$
$$b = 0.4 \text{ (a typical value for the plowback ratio in the U.S.)}$$

Therefore, $r_M = r_f +$ Market risk premium $= 8\% + 8\% = 16\%$, and $k = 16\%$ for an average ($\beta = 1$) company. If we also accept as reasonable that ROE $= 16\%$ (the same value as the expected return on the stock) we conclude that

$$g = \text{ROE} \times b = 16\% \times .4 = 6.4\%$$

and

$$P/E = \frac{1 - .4}{.16 - .064} = 6.26$$

Thus the P/E ratio and g are about equal using these assumptions, consistent with the rule of thumb. However, note that this rule of thumb, like almost all others, will not work in all circumstances. For example, the value of r_f today is more like 5%, so a comparable forecast of r_M today would be:

$$r_f + \text{Market risk premium} = 5\% + 8\% = 13\%$$

If we continue to focus on a firm with $\beta = 1$, and ROE still is about the same as k, then

$$g = 13\% \times .4 = 5.2\%$$

while

$$P/E = \frac{1 - .4}{.13 - .052} = 7.69$$

The P/E ratio and g now diverge and the PEG ratio is now 1.5. Nevertheless, lower-than-average PEG ratios are still widely seen as signalling potential underpricing.

Whatever its shortcomings, the PEG ratio is widely followed. The PEG ratio for the S&P over the last 20 years typically has fluctuated within the range between 1.0 and 1.5.

CONCEPT check 13.5

ABC stock has an expected ROE of 12% per year, expected earnings per share of $2, and expected dividends of $1.50 per share. Its market capitalization rate is 10% per year.

a. What are its expected growth rate, its price, and its P/E ratio?

b. If the plowback rate were 0.4, what would be the firm's expected dividend per share, growth rate, price, P/E, and PEG ratio?

On the MARKET FRONT

GURGLE

Google's share price peaked at $475, on January 11th. After slipping during the rest of the month, the price plunged to $343 on February 14th. In barely a month, some $38 billion has been wiped off the firm's market capitalization. Is there a good reason for this?

A serious debate about how to value Internet shares is long overdue. Since the disappointing months after Google's initial public offering in August 2004, when the shares appeared to have been overpriced at $85, they had risen inexorably. Yet some bulls think there remains plenty of upside: Mark Stahlman of Caris & Co, a brokerage firm, has $2,000 as a long-term target, on the assumption that Google eventually wins a 1% share of the global digital-services business.

Mary Meeker of Morgan Stanley is keen to be seen as prudent in her bullishness. Yet like most of her peers, she thinks the shares are worth more than $400. Discounting expected cash flow for the coming ten years, she calculates a fair price of $413. Using other valuation techniques, she gets as high as $597. But these valuations all rely on Google delivering the now expected future performance—which, as is clear from its current high ratio of share price to profits of 68 (compared with an average of 18 for the S&P 500), means spectacular growth. Whether it will achieve this growth is frankly anyone's guess, especially given how rapidly its market is evolving—a risk factor that surely argues for a far larger discount rate to be applied to future cash flow than the 11.5% in the Meeker model.

On the other hand, as Ms. Meeker points out, Google has so far consistently beaten her forecasts, both for revenues and for profit margins. Strikingly, just after Google went public, she predicted that it would generate revenues of $7 per user in 2005, up from $2 in 2002. In fact, it generated $10 per user—a number that, she plausibly argues, can be greatly improved on as ever more advertising dollars shift to new media from old.

SOURCE: *The Economist*, February 16, 2006.

The importance of growth opportunities is nowhere more evident than in the Internet boom of the late 1990s. Many companies that had yet to turn a profit were valued by the market at billions of dollars. The value of these companies was *exclusively* growth opportunities. For example, the online broker E-Trade, with *no* earnings in 1998, had a stock market value of $10 billion, while a traditional brokerage firm, Paine Webber, had 1998 earnings of $473 million but a market value of only $6.2 billion. Similarly, the online auction firm eBay had 1998 profits of $2.4 million, far less than the $45 million profit earned by the traditional auctioneer Sotheby's; yet eBay's market value was more than 10 times greater: $22 billion versus $1.9 billion. (As it turns out, the market was quite right to value eBay so much more aggressively than Sotheby's. By 2006, its net income was over $1 billion, more than 15 times that of Sotheby's, and still growing.)

Of course, when company valuation is determined primarily by growth opportunities, those values can be very sensitive to reassessments of such prospects. When the market became more skeptical of the business prospects of most Internet retailers at the close of the 1990s, that is, as it revised the estimates of growth opportunities downward, their stock prices plummeted.

The nearby box is an analysis of the fair price for Google. The box highlights the importance of growth prospects for the valuation analysis. As perceptions of Google's future prospects have waxed and waned, its share price has swung wildly. The box illustrates how hard it is to quantify growth prospects; ultimately however, those prospects drive the value of the most dynamic firms in the economy.

P/E Ratios and Stock Risk

One important implication of any stock valuation model is that (holding all else equal) riskier stocks will have lower P/E multiples. We can see this quite easily in the context of the constant growth model by examining the formula for the P/E ratio (Equation 13.8):

$$\frac{P}{E} = \frac{1 - b}{k - g}$$

Riskier firms will have higher required rates of return (i.e., higher values of k). Therefore, their P/E multiples will be lower. This is true even outside the context of the constant growth model. For *any* expected earnings and dividend stream, the present value of those cash flows will be lower when the stream is perceived to be riskier. Hence the stock price and the ratio of price to earnings will be lower.

Of course, if you scan *The Wall Street Journal,* you will observe many small, risky, start-up companies with very high P/E multiples. This does not contradict our claim that P/E multiples should fall with risk: Instead, it is evidence of the market's expectations of high growth rates for those companies. This is why we said that high risk firms will have lower P/E ratios *holding all else equal.* Given a growth projection, the P/E multiple will be lower when risk is perceived to be higher.

Pitfalls in P/E Analysis

No description of P/E analysis is complete without mentioning some of its pitfalls. First, consider that the denominator in the P/E ratio is accounting earnings, which are influenced by somewhat arbitrary accounting rules such as the use of historical cost in depreciation and inventory valuation. In times of high inflation, historic cost depreciation and inventory costs will tend to underrepresent true economic values because the replacement cost of both goods and capital equipment will rise with the general level of prices. As Figure 13.3 demonstrates, P/E ratios have tended to be lower when inflation has been higher. This reflects the market's assessment that earnings in these periods are of "lower quality," artificially distorted by inflation, and warranting lower P/E ratios.

earnings management

The practice of using flexibility in accounting rules to improve the apparent profitability of the firm.

Earnings management is the practice of using flexibility in accounting rules to improve the apparent profitability of the firm. We will have much to say on this topic in the next chapter on interpreting financial statements. A version of earnings management that became common in recent years was the reporting of "pro forma earnings" measures. These measures are sometimes called *operating earnings,* a term with no precise generally accepted definition.

Pro forma earnings are calculated ignoring certain expenses, for example, restructuring charges, stock-option expenses, or write-downs of assets from continuing operations. Firms argue that ignoring these expenses gives a clearer picture of the underlying profitability of the firm.

But when there is too much leeway for choosing what to exclude it becomes hard for investors or analysts to interpret the numbers or to compare them across firms. The lack of standards gives firms considerable leeway to manage earnings.

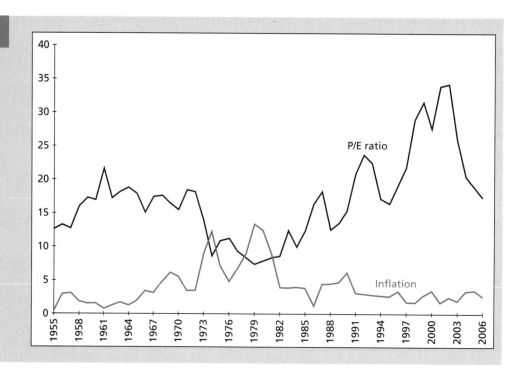

FIGURE 13.3

P/E ratio of the S&P 500 Index and inflation

Even GAAP allows firms considerable discretion to manage earnings. For example, in the late 1990s, Kellogg took restructuring charges, which are supposed to be one-time events, nine quarters in a row. Were these really one-time events, or were they more appropriately treated as ordinary expenses? Given the available leeway in reporting earnings, the justified P/E multiple becomes difficult to gauge.

In the wake of the accounting questions raised by the Enron, WorldCom, and Global Crossing bankruptcies, there is a new focus on transparency in accounting statements. In 2003, the SEC adopted Regulation G, which requires public companies that report non-GAAP financial measures to present with those measures both the most directly comparable GAAP measure as well as a reconciliation of those measures with the comparable GAAP figure. The motivation is to ensure that investors receive sufficient information to evaluate the true import of financial statistics even when those statistics are computed out of compliance with GAAP.

Another confounding factor in the use of P/E ratios is related to the business cycle. We were careful in deriving the DDM to define earnings as being net of *economic* depreciation, that is, the maximum flow of income that the firm could pay out without depleting its productive capacity. And reported earnings, as we note above, are computed in accordance with generally accepted accounting principles and need not correspond to economic earnings. Beyond this, however, notions of a normal or justified P/E ratio, as in Equation 13.7 or 13.8, assume implicitly that earnings rise at a constant rate, or, put another way, on a smooth trend line. In contrast, reported earnings can fluctuate dramatically around a trend line over the course of the business cycle.

Another way to make this point is to note that the "normal" P/E ratio predicted by Equation 13.8 is the ratio of today's price to the trend value of future earnings, E_1. The P/E ratio reported in the financial pages of the newspaper, by contrast, is the ratio of price to the most recent *past* accounting earnings. Current accounting earnings can differ considerably from future economic earnings. Because ownership of stock conveys the right to future as well as current earnings, the ratio of price to most recent earnings can vary substantially over the business cycle, as accounting earnings and the trend value of economic earnings diverge by greater and lesser amounts.

As an example, Figure 13.4 graphs the earnings per share of Limited Brands and Consolidated Edison since 1988. Note that Limited's EPS fluctuate around its trend line considerably. This reflects the company's higher sensitivity to macroeconomic conditions. Value Line

WEB *master*

Stock Valuation

The actually expected return on a stock based on estimates of future dividends and future price can be compared to the "required" or equilibrium return given its risk. If the expected return is greater than the required return, the stock may be an attractive investment.

1. First calculate the expected holding period return (HPR) on Target Corporation's stock based on its current price, its expected price, and its expected dividend.

   a. Go to **moneycentral.msn.com/investor/home.asp** and link to the Stock Research Wizard. Enter TGT to find information about Target Corporation. Find the average estimated target price for the next fiscal year.

   b. Click on the "Company Report" link and collect information about today's price and the dividend rate. Calculate the company's expected dividend in dollars for the next fiscal year.

   c. Use these inputs to calculate Target's expected HPR for the next year.

2. Calculate the required return based on the Capital Asset Pricing Model (CAPM).

   a. Use a risk-free rate from **moneycentral.msn. com/investor/market/treasuries.aspx**

   b. Use the beta coefficient shown in Target's Company Report.

   c. Calculate the historical return on a broad-based market index of your choice. You may use any time period that you deem appropriate. Your goal is to derive an estimate of the expected return on the market index for the coming year.

   d. Use the data you've collected as inputs for the CAPM to find the required rate of return for Target Corporation.

3. Compare the expected HPR you calculated in Part 1 to the required CAPM return you calculated in Part 2. What is your best judgment about the stock's current status—do you think it is selling at an appropriate price?

FIGURE 13.4

Earnings growth for two companies

FIGURE 13.5

Price–earnings ratios

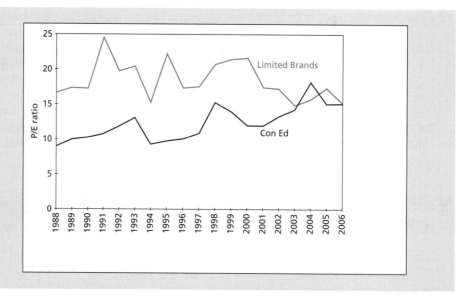

estimates its beta at 1.15. Con Ed, by contrast, shows much less variation in earnings per share around a smoother and flatter trend line. Its beta was only 0.75.

Because the market values the entire stream of future dividends generated by the company, when earnings are temporarily depressed, the P/E ratio should tend to be high—that is, the denominator of the ratio responds more sensitively to the business cycle than the numerator. This pattern is borne out well.

Figure 13.5 graphs the P/E ratios of the two firms. Limited, with the more volatile earnings profile, also has a more volatile P/E profile. For example, in 1995, when its earnings fell below the trend line (Figure 13.4), the P/E ratio correspondingly jumped (Figure 13.5). The market clearly recognized that earnings were depressed only temporarily. Similarly, the only year in which Con Ed's P/E ratio exceeded Limited's was in 2004, one of the rare years in which Con Ed's earnings fell below its trend line to a meaningful degree.

This example shows why analysts must be careful in using P/E ratios. There is no way to say a P/E ratio is overly high or low without referring to the company's long-run growth prospects, as well as to current earnings per share relative to the long-run trend line.

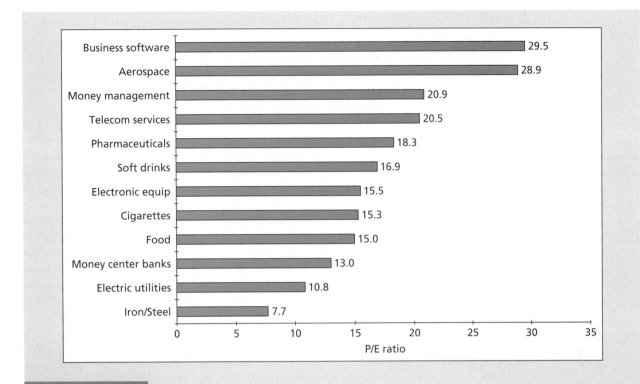

FIGURE 13.6

P/E ratios

Nevertheless, Figures 13.4 and 13.5 demonstrate a clear relationship between P/E ratios and growth. Despite considerable short-run fluctuations, Limited's EPS clearly trended upward over the period. Its compound rate of growth in the 1988–2006 period was 9.4%. Con Edison's earnings grew far less rapidly, with a compound growth rate of 0.7%. The growth prospects of Limited are reflected in its consistently higher P/E multiple.

This analysis suggests that P/E ratios should vary across industries and, in fact, they do. Figure 13.6 shows P/E ratios for a sample of industries. Notice that the industries with the highest multiples—business software and aerospace—have attractive investment opportunities and relatively high growth rates, whereas the industries with the lowest multiples— electric utilities and iron/steel manufacturers—are in more mature industries with limited growth prospects. The relationship between P/E and growth is not perfect, which is not surprising in light of the pitfalls discussed in this section, but it is clear that as a general rule, the P/E multiple tracks growth opportunities.

Combining P/E Analysis and the DDM

Some analysts use P/E ratios in conjunction with earnings forecasts to estimate the price of stock at an investor's horizon date. The Honda analysis in Figure 13.2 shows that Value Line forecasted a P/E ratio for 2010 of 15. EPS for 2010 were forecast at $3.90, implying a price in 2010 of 15 × $3.90 = $58.50. Given an estimate of $58.50 for the 2010 sales price, we would compute Honda's intrinsic value as

$$V_{2006} = \frac{.59}{(1.114)} + \frac{.67}{(1.114)^2} + \frac{.76}{(1.114)^3} + \frac{.85 + \$58.50}{(1.114)^4} = \$40.16$$

Other Comparative Valuation Ratios

The price–earnings ratio is an example of a comparative valuation ratio. Such ratios are used to assess the valuation of one firm versus another based on a fundamental indicator such as earnings. For example, an analyst might compare the P/E ratios of two firms in the same industry to test whether the market is valuing one firm "more aggressively" than the other. Other such comparative ratios are commonly used.

Price-to-book ratio   This is the ratio of price per share divided by book value per share. As we noted earlier in this chapter, some analysts view book as a useful measure of value and therefore treat the ratio of price-to-book value as an indicator of how aggressively the market values the firm.

Price-to-cash flow ratio   Earnings as reported on the income statement can be affected by the company's choice of accounting practices and thus are commonly viewed as subject to some imprecision and even manipulation. In contrast, cash flow—which tracks cash actually flowing into or out of the firm—is less affected by accounting decisions. As a result, some analysts prefer to use the ratio of price to cash flow per share rather than price to earnings per share. Some analysts use operating cash flow when calculating this ratio; others prefer free cash flow, that is, operating cash flow net of new investment.

Price-to-sales ratio   Many start-up firms have no earnings. As a result, the P/E ratio for these firms is meaningless. The price-to-sales ratio (the ratio of stock price to the annual sales per share) is sometimes taken as a valuation benchmark for these firms. Of course, price-to-sales ratios can vary markedly across industries, since profit margins vary widely.

Figure 13.7 presents the behavior of these valuation measures for the S&P 500. While the levels of these ratios differ considerably, for the most part they track each other fairly closely, with upturns and downturns at the same times.

Be creative   Sometimes a standard valuation ratio will simply not be available, and you will have to devise your own. In the 1990s, some analysts valued retail Internet firms based on the number of Web hits their sites received. In retrospect, they valued these firms using too generous "price-to-hits" ratios. Nevertheless, in a new investment environment, these analysts used the information available to them to devise the best valuation tools they could.

FIGURE 13.7

Valuation ratios for the S&P 500

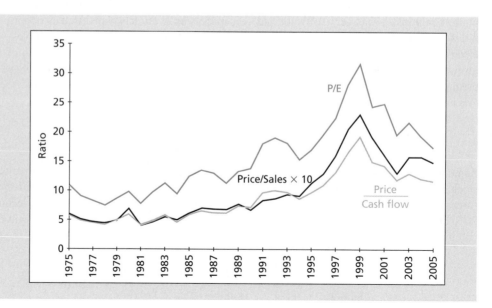

13.5 FREE CASH FLOW VALUATION APPROACHES

An alternative approach to the dividend discount model values the firm using free cash flow, that is, cash flow available to the firm or the equity holders net of capital expenditures. This approach is particularly useful for firms that pay no dividends, for which the dividend discount model would be difficult to implement. But free cash flow models are valid for any firm, and can provide useful insights about firm value beyond the DDM.

One approach is to discount the *free cash flow* for the *firm* (FCFF) at the weighted-average cost of capital to obtain the value of the firm, and then subtract the then-existing value of debt to find the value of equity. Another is to focus from the start on the free cash flow to *equity holders* (FCFE), discounting those directly at the cost of equity to obtain the market value of equity.

The free cash flow to the firm is given as follows:

$$FCFF = EBIT (1 - t_c) + \text{Depreciation} - \text{Capital expenditures} - \text{Increase in NWC} \quad \textbf{(13.9)}$$

where

$$EBIT = \text{earnings before interest and taxes}$$
$$t_c = \text{the corporate tax rate}$$
$$NWC = \text{net working capital}$$

This is the cash flow that accrues from the firm's operations, net of investments in capital and net working capital. It includes cash flows available to both debt and equity holders.[6]

Alternatively, we can focus on cash flow available to equity holders. This will differ from free cash flow to the firm by after-tax interest expenditures, as well as by cash flow associated with net issuance or repurchase of debt (i.e., principal repayments minus proceeds from issuance of new debt).

$$FCFE = FCFF - \text{Interest expense} \times (1 - t_c) + \text{Increases in net debt} \quad \textbf{(13.10)}$$

The free cash flow to the firm approach discounts year-by-year cash flows plus some estimate of terminal value, P_T. In Equation 13.11, we use the constant growth model to estimate terminal value. The appropriate discount rate is the weighted average cost of capital.

$$\text{Firm value} = \sum_{t=1}^{T} \frac{1 + FCFF_t}{(1 + WACC)^t} + \frac{P_T}{(1 + WACC)^T} \quad \textbf{(13.11)}$$

where

$$P_T = \frac{FCFF_{T+1}}{WACC - g}$$

To find equity value, we subtract the existing market value of debt from the derived value of the firm.

Alternatively, we can discount free cash flows to *equity* (FCFE) at the cost of *equity, k_E,*

$$\text{Market value of equity} = \sum_{t=1}^{T} \frac{FCFE_t}{(1 + k_E)^t} + \frac{P_T}{(1 + k_E)^T} \quad \textbf{(13.12)}$$

where

$$P_T = \frac{FCFE_{T+1}}{k_E - g}$$

---

[6]This is firm cash flow assuming all-equity financing. Any tax advantage to debt financing is recognized by using an after-tax cost of debt in the computation of weighted average cost of capital. This issue is discussed in any introductory corporate finance text.

SPREADSHEET 13.2

Free cash flow valuation of Honda

Please visit us at www.mhhe.com/bkm

	A	B	C	D	E	F	G	H	I	J	K	L	M
1			2006	2007	2008	2009	2010						
2	A. Value Line data												
3	P/E		9.80	11.10	12.40	13.70	15.00						
4	Cap spending/shr		2.80	2.90	2.97	3.03	3.10						
5	LT Debt		15000	13500	12333	11167	10000						
6	Shares		1825	1820	1813	1807	1800						
7	EPS		2.70	3.00	3.30	3.60	3.90						
8	Working Capital		5505	5660	6778	7897	9015						
9													
10	B. Cash flow calculations												
11	Profits (after tax)			4930.0	5460.0	5991.7	6523.3	7055.0					
12	Interest (after tax)			503.3	452.9	413.8	374.6	335.5	= r_debt × (1-tax) × LT Debt				
13	Chg Working Cap				155.0	1118.3	1118.3	1118.3					
14	Depreciation				2675.0	2750.0	2858.3	2950.0					
15	Cap Spending				5278.0	5378.7	5479.3	5580.0					
16								Terminal value					
17	FCFF				3154.9	2658.5	3158.6	3642.2	127451.8				
18	FCFE				1202.0	1078.0	1617.3	2140.0	116148.0		assumes fixed debt ratio after 2010		
19													
20	C. Discount rate calculations												
21	Current beta	0.8								from Value Line			
22	Unlevered beta	0.673								current beta /[1 + (1-tax)*debt/equity)]			
23	terminal growth	0.07											
24	tax_rate	0.39								from Value Line			
25	r_debt	0.055								YTM in 2007 on A rated LT debt			
26	risk-free rate	0.05											
27	market risk prem	0.08											
28	MV equity		48314	60606	74297	89370	105825			Row 3 × Row 11			
29	Debt/Value		0.24	0.18	0.14	0.11	0.09			Row 5 / (Row 5 + Row 28)			
30	Levered beta		0.800	0.764	0.741	0.724	0.711			unlevered beta × [1 + (1-tax)*debt/equity]			
31	k_equity		0.114	0.111	0.109	0.108	0.107	0.107		from CAPM and levered beta			
32	WACC		0.095	0.097	0.098	0.100	0.101	0.101		(1-t)*r_debt*D/V + k_equity*(1-D/V)			
33	PV factor for FCFF		1.000	0.912	0.830	0.755	0.686	0.686		Discount each year at WACC			
34	PV factor for FCFE		1.000	0.900	0.811	0.732	0.662	0.662		Discount each year at k_equity			
35													
36	D. Present values									Intrinsic val	Equity val	Intrin/share	
37	PV(FCFF)			2876	2206	2384	2497	87393		97356	82356	45.13	
38	PV(FCFE)			1082	875	1184	1416	76842		81399	81399	44.60	

As in the dividend discount model, free cash flow models use a terminal value to avoid adding the present values of an infinite sum of cash flows. That terminal value may simply be the present value of a constant-growth perpetuity (as in the formulas above) or it may be based on a multiple of EBIT, book value, earnings, or free cash flow. As a general rule, estimates of intrinsic value depend critically on terminal value.

Spreadsheet 13.2 presents a free cash flow valuation of Honda using the data supplied by Value Line in Figure 13.2. We start with the free cash flow to the firm approach given in Equation 13.9. Panel A of the spreadsheet lays out values supplied by Value Line. (Entries for middle years are interpolated from beginning and final values.) Panel B calculates free cash flow. The sum of after-tax profits in row 11 plus after-tax interest payments in row 12 [that is, interest expense × $(1 - t_c)$] equals EBIT$(1 - t_c)$. In row 13 we subtract the change in net working capital, in row 14 we add back depreciation, and in row 15 we subtract capital expenditures. The result in row 17 is the free cash flow to the firm, FCFF, for each year between 2007 and 2010.

To find the present value of these cash flows, we will discount at WACC, which is calculated in panel C. WACC is the weighted average of the after-tax cost of debt and the cost of equity in each year. When computing WACC, we must account for the change in leverage forecasted by Value Line. To compute the cost of equity, we will use the CAPM as in our earlier (dividend discount model) valuation exercise, but account for the fact that equity beta will decline each year as the firm reduces leverage.[7]

A reasonable approximation to Honda's cost of debt, which was rated A in 2006, is the yield to maturity on comparably rated long-term debt, approximately 5.5% (cell B25). Honda's debt-to-value ratio is computed in row 29 (assuming that its debt is selling near par value), and WACC is computed in row 32. WACC increases slightly over time as the debt-to-value ratio steadily declines between 2006 and 2010. The present value factor for cash flows accruing in each year is the previous year's factor divided by (1 + WACC) for that year. The present value of each cash flow (row 37) is the free cash flow times the cumulative discount factor.

The terminal value of the firm (cell H17) is computed from the constant-growth model as $FCFF_{2010} \times (1 + g)/(WACC_{2010} - g)$, where g (cell B23) is the assumed value for the steady growth rate.[8] We assume in the spreadsheet that $g = .07$, which is perhaps a bit higher than the long-run growth rate of the broad economy.[9] Terminal value is also discounted back to 2006 (cell H37), and the intrinsic value of the firm is thus found as the sum of discounted free cash flows between 2007 and 2010 plus the discounted terminal value. Finally, the value of debt in 2006 is subtracted from firm value to arrive at the intrinsic value of equity in 2006 (cell K37), and value per share is calculated in cell L37 as equity value divided by number of shares in 2006.

The free cash flow to equity approach yields a similar intrinsic value for the stock. FCFE (row 18) is obtained from FCFF by subtracting after-tax interest expense and net debt repurchases. The cash flows are then discounted at the equity rate. Like WACC, the cost of equity changes each period as leverage changes. The present value factor for equity cash flows is presented in row 34. Equity value is reported in cell J38, which is put on a per share basis in cell L38.

Spreadsheet 13.2 is available at the Online Learning Center, **www.mhhe.com/bkm.**

Comparing the Valuation Models

In principle, the free cash flow approach is fully consistent with the dividend discount model and should provide the same estimate of intrinsic value if one can extrapolate to a period in which the firm begins to pay dividends growing at a constant rate. This was demonstrated in two famous papers by Modigliani and Miller (1958, 1961). However, in practice, you will find that values from these models may differ, sometimes substantially. This is due to the fact

---

[7]Call β_L the firm's equity beta at the initial level of leverage as provided by Value Line. Equity betas reflect both business risk and financial risk. When a firm changes its capital structure (debt/equity mix), it changes financial risk, and therefore equity beta changes. How should we recognize the change in financial risk? As you may remember from an introductory corporate finance class, you must first unleverage beta. This leaves us a beta that reflects only business risk. We use the following formula to find unleveraged beta, β_U, (where D/E is the firm's current debt-equity ratio):

$$\beta_U = \frac{\beta_L}{1 + (D/E)(1 - t_c)}$$

Then, we re-leverage beta in any particular year using the forecast capital structure (which reintroduces the financial risk associated with that year's capital structure):

$$\beta_L = \beta_U[1 + (D/E)(1 - t_c)]$$

[8]Over the 2006–2010 period, Value Line predicts that Honda will retire a considerable fraction of its outstanding debt. The implied debt repurchases are a use of cash and reduce the cash flow available to equity. Such repurchases cannot be sustained indefinitely, however, for debt outstanding would soon be run down to zero. Therefore, in our estimate of terminal value, we compute the final cash flow assuming that by 2010 Honda will begin *issuing* enough debt to maintain its debt-to-value ratio unchanged. This approach is consistent with the assumption of constant growth and constant discount rates after 2010.

[9]In the long run a firm can't grow forever at a rate higher than the aggregate economy. So by the time we assert that growth is in a stable stage, it seems reasonable that the growth rate should not be significantly greater than that of the overall economy (although it can be less if the firm is in a declining industry).

that in practice, analysts are always forced to make simplifying assumptions. For example, how long will it take the firm to enter a constant-growth stage? How should depreciation best be treated? What is the best estimate of ROE? Answers to questions like these can have a big impact on value, and it is not always easy to maintain consistent assumptions across the models.

We have now valued Honda using several approaches, with estimates of intrinsic value as follows:

Model	Intrinsic Value
Two-stage dividend discount model	$38.88
DDM with earnings multiple terminal value	40.16
Three-stage DDM	45.02
Free cash flow to the firm	45.13
Free cash flow to equity	44.60
Market price in 2006	35.08

What should we make of these differences? The two-stage dividend discount model is the most conservative of the estimates, probably because it assumes that Honda's dividend growth rate will fall to its terminal value after only three years. In contrast, the 3-stage DDM allows growth to taper off over a longer period. The 3-stage model gives a value that is almost identical to those of both free cash flow models. But all three of these estimates are $10 higher than the actual stock price, a difference of 28%. The DDM with a terminal value provided by the earnings multiple is closer, but still $5 higher than the stock price. Perhaps the assumed terminal growth rate used in our valuation exercise is too high, or perhaps the stock is indeed underpriced compared to intrinsic value.

This valuation exercise shows that finding bargains is not as easy as it seems. While these models are easy to apply, establishing proper inputs is more of a challenge. This should not be surprising. In even a moderately efficient market, finding profit opportunities will be more involved than analyzing Value Line data for a few hours. The models are extremely useful to analysts, however. They provide ballpark estimates of intrinsic value. More than that, they force rigorous thought about underlying assumptions and highlight the variables with the greatest impact on value and the greatest payoff to further analysis.

13.6   THE AGGREGATE STOCK MARKET

The most popular approach to forecasting the overall stock market is the earnings multiplier approach applied at the aggregate level. The first step is to forecast corporate profits for the coming period. Then we derive an estimate of the earnings multiplier, the aggregate P/E ratio, based on a forecast of long-term interest rates. The product of the two forecasts is the estimate of the end-of-period level of the market.

The forecast of the P/E ratio of the market is sometimes derived from a graph similar to that in Figure 13.8, which plots the *earnings yield* (earnings per share divided by price per share, the reciprocal of the P/E ratio) of the S&P 500 and the yield to maturity on 10-year Treasury bonds. The figure shows that both yields rose dramatically in the 1970s. In the case of Treasury bonds, this was because of an increase in the inflationary expectations built into interest rates. The earnings yield on the S&P 500, however, probably rose because of inflationary distortions that artificially increased reported earnings. We have already seen that P/E ratios tend to fall when inflation rates increase. When inflation moderated in the 1980s, both Treasury and earnings yields fell. For most of the last 30 years, the earnings yield has been within about one percentage point of the T-bond rate.

One might use this relationship and the current yield on 10-year Treasury bonds to forecast the earnings yield on the S&P 500. Given that earnings yield, a forecast of earnings could be used to predict the level of the S&P in some future period. Let's consider a simple example of this procedure.

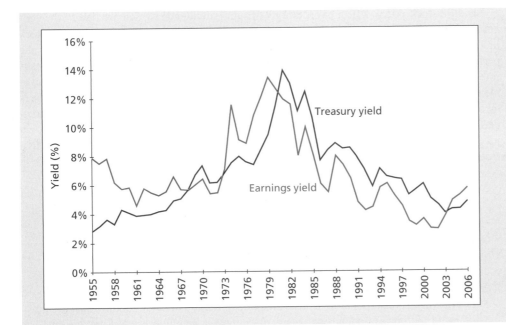

FIGURE 13.8

Earnings yield of S&P 500 versus 10-year Treasury bond yield

	Most Likely Scenario	Pessimistic Scenario	Optimistic Scenario
Treasury bond yield	4.8%	5.3%	4.3%
Earnings yield	5.8%	6.3%	5.3%
Resulting P/E ratio	17.2	15.9	18.9
EPS forecast	86	86	86
Forecast for S&P 500	1,483	1,365	1,623

TABLE 13.4

S&P 500 index forecasts under various scenarios

Note: The forecast for the earnings yield on the S&P 500 equals the Treasury bond yield plus 1%. The P/E ratio is the reciprocal of the forecasted earnings yield.

EXAMPLE   13.7

Forecasting the Aggregate Stock Market

The early 2007 forecast for 12-month forward earnings per share for the S&P 500 portfolio was about $86. The 10-year Treasury bond yield at this time was about 4.8%. Since the earnings yield on the S&P 500 is most recently about 1% above the 10-year Treasury yield, a first guess for the earnings yield on the S&P 500 might be 5.8%. This would imply a P/E ratio of 1/.058 = 17.24. Our forecast for the level of the S&P 500 index would then be 17.24 × 86 = 1483.

Of course, there is uncertainty regarding all three inputs into this analysis: the actual earnings on the S&P 500 stocks, the level of Treasury yields at year-end, and the spread between the Treasury yield and the earnings yield. One would wish to perform sensitivity or scenario analysis to examine the impact of changes in all of these variables. To illustrate, consider Table 13.4, which shows a simple scenario analysis treating possible effects of variation in the Treasury bond yield. The scenario analysis shows that the forecast level of the stock market varies inversely and with dramatic sensitivity to interest rate changes.

Some analysts use an aggregate version of the dividend discount model rather than an earnings multiplier approach. All of these models, however, rely heavily on forecasts of such macroeconomic variables as GDP, interest rates, and the rate of inflation, which are difficult to predict accurately.

Because stock prices reflect expectations of future dividends, which are tied to the economic fortunes of firms, it is not surprising that the performance of a broad-based stock index like the S&P 500 is taken as a leading economic indicator, that is, a predictor of the performance of the aggregate economy. Stock prices are viewed as embodying consensus forecasts of economic activity and are assumed to move up or down in anticipation of movements in the economy. The government's index of leading economic indicators, which is taken to predict the progress of the business cycle, is made up in part of recent stock market performance. However, the predictive value of the market is far from perfect. A well-known joke, often attributed to Paul Samuelson, is that the market has forecast eight of the last five recessions.

SUMMARY

- One approach to firm valuation is to focus on the firm's book value, either as it appears on the balance sheet or adjusted to reflect the current replacement cost of assets or the liquidation value. Another approach is to focus on the present value of expected future dividends.
- The dividend discount model holds that the price of a share of stock should equal the present value of all future dividends per share, discounted at an interest rate commensurate with the risk of the stock.
- The constant growth version of the DDM asserts that, if dividends are expected to grow at a constant rate forever, then the intrinsic value of the stock is determined by the formula

$$V_0 = \frac{D_1}{k - g}$$

This version of the DDM is simplistic in its assumption of a constant value of g. There are more sophisticated multistage versions of the model for more complex environments. When the constant growth assumption is reasonably satisfied, the formula can be inverted to infer the market capitalization rate for the stock:

$$k = \frac{D_1}{P_0} + g$$

- Stock market analysts devote considerable attention to a company's price–earnings ratio. The P/E ratio is a useful measure of the market's assessment of the firm's growth opportunities. Firms with no growth opportunities should have a P/E ratio that is just the reciprocal of the capitalization rate, k. As growth opportunities become a progressively more important component of the total value of the firm, the P/E ratio will increase.
- Many analysts form their estimates of a stock's value by multiplying their forecast of next year's EPS by a predicted P/E multiple. Some analysts mix the P/E approach with the dividend discount model. They use an earnings multiplier to forecast the terminal value of shares at a future date and add the present value of that terminal value with the present value of all interim dividend payments.
- The free cash flow approach is the one used most in corporate finance. The analyst first estimates the value of the firm as the present value of expected future free cash flows to the entire firm and then subtracts the value of all claims other than equity. Alternatively, the free cash flows to equity can be discounted at a discount rate appropriate to the risk of the stock.
- The models presented in this chapter can be used to explain or to forecast the behavior of the aggregate stock market. The key macroeconomic variables that determine the level of stock prices in the aggregate are interest rates and corporate profits.

**Select problems are available in McGraw-Hill's Homework Manager®.
Please see the packaging options section of the preface for more information.**

PROBLEM SETS

1. A common stock pays an annual dividend per share of $2.10. The risk-free rate is 7% and the risk premium for this stock is 4%. If the annual dividend is expected to remain at $2.10, what is the value of the stock?

2. Which of the following assumptions does the constant growth dividend discount model require?
   a. Dividends grow at a constant rate.
   b. The dividend growth rate continues indefinitely.
   c. The required rate of return is less than the dividend growth rate.

3. *a.* Computer stocks currently provide an expected rate of return of 16%. MBI, a large computer company, will pay a year-end dividend of $2 per share. If the stock is selling at $50 per share, what must be the market's expectation of the growth rate of MBI dividends?
   b. If dividend growth forecasts for MBI are revised downward to 5% per year, what will happen to the price of MBI stock? What (qualitatively) will happen to the company's price–earnings ratio?

4. Explain why the following statements are true/false/uncertain.
   a. With all else held constant, a firm will have a higher P/E if its beta is higher.
   b. P/E will tend to be higher when ROE is higher (assuming plowback is positive).
   c. P/E will tend to be higher when the plowback rate is higher.

5. Even Better Products has come out with a new and improved product. As a result, the firm projects an ROE of 20%, and it will maintain a plowback ratio of 0.30. Its earnings this year will be $2 per share. Investors expect a 12% rate of return on the stock.
   a. At what price and P/E ratio would you expect the firm to sell?
   b. What is the present value of growth opportunities?
   c. What would be the P/E ratio and the present value of growth opportunities if the firm planned to reinvest only 20% of its earnings?

6. *a.* MF Corp. has an ROE of 16% and a plowback ratio of 50%. If the coming year's earnings are expected to be $2 per share, at what price will the stock sell? The market capitalization rate is 12%.
   b. What price do you expect MF shares to sell for in three years?

7. At Litchfield Chemical Corp. (LCC), a director of the company said that the use of dividend discount models by investors is "proof" that the higher the dividend, the higher the stock price.
   a. Using a constant growth dividend discount model as a basis of reference, evaluate the director's statement.
   b. Explain how an increase in dividend payout would affect each of the following (holding all other factors constant):
      i. Sustainable growth rate.
      ii. Growth in book value.

8. The market consensus is that Analog Electronic Corporation has an ROE = 9% and a beta of 1.25. It plans to maintain indefinitely its traditional plowback ratio of 2/3. This year's earnings were $3 per share. The annual dividend was just paid. The consensus estimate of the coming year's market return is 14%, and T-bills currently offer a 6% return.

a. Find the price at which Analog stock should sell.

b. Calculate the P/E ratio.

c. Calculate the present value of growth opportunities.

d. Suppose your research convinces you Analog will announce momentarily that it will immediately reduce its plowback ratio to 1/3. Find the intrinsic value of the stock. The market is still unaware of this decision. Explain why V_0 no longer equals P_0 and why V_0 is greater or less than P_0.

9. The FI Corporation's dividends per share are expected to grow indefinitely by 5% per year.

a. If this year's year-end dividend is $8 and the market capitalization rate is 10% per year, what must the current stock price be according to the DDM?

b. If the expected earnings per share are $12, what is the implied value of the ROE on future investment opportunities?

c. How much is the market paying per share for growth opportunities (that is, for an ROE on future investments that exceeds the market capitalization rate)?

10. Chiptech, Inc., is an established computer chip firm with several profitable existing products as well as some promising new products in development. The company earned $1 a share last year, and just paid out a dividend of $.50 per share. Investors believe the company plans to maintain its dividend payout ratio at 50%. ROE equals 20%. Everyone in the market expects this situation to persist indefinitely.

a. What is the market price of Chiptech stock? The required return for the computer chip industry is 15%, and the company has just gone ex-dividend (i.e., the next dividend will be paid a year from now, at $t = 1$).

b. Suppose you discover that Chiptech's competitor has developed a new chip that will eliminate Chiptech's current technological advantage in this market. This new product, which will be ready to come to the market in 2 years, will force Chiptech to reduce the prices of its chips to remain competitive. This will decrease ROE to 15%, and, because of falling demand for its product, Chiptech will decrease the plowback ratio to .40. The plowback ratio will be decreased at the end of the second year, at $t = 2$: The annual year-end dividend for the second year (paid at $t = 2$) will be 60% of that year's earnings. What is your estimate of Chiptech's intrinsic value per share? (*Hint:* Carefully prepare a table of Chiptech's earnings and dividends for each of the next 3 years. Pay close attention to the change in the payout ratio in $t = 2$.)

c. No one else in the market perceives the threat to Chiptech's market. In fact, you are confident that no one else will become aware of the change in Chiptech's competitive status until the competitor firm publicly announces its discovery near the end of year 2. What will be the rate of return on Chiptech stock in the coming year (i.e., between $t = 0$ and $t = 1$)? In the second year (between $t = 1$ and $t = 2$)? The third year (between $t = 2$ and $t = 3$)? (*Hint:* Pay attention to when the *market* catches on to the new situation. A table of dividends and market prices over time might help.)

11. The risk-free rate of return is 10%, the required rate of return on the market is 15%, and High-Flyer stock has a beta coefficient of 1.5. If the dividend per share expected during the coming year, D_1, is $2.50 and $g = 5\%$, at what price should a share sell?

12. Phoebe Black's investment club wants to buy the stock of either NewSoft, Inc, or Capital Corp. In this connection, Black prepared the following table. You have been asked to help her interpret the data, based on your forecast for a healthy economy and a strong stock market over the next 12 months.

CFA®
PROBLEMS

	NewSoft, Inc.	Capital Corp.	S&P 500 Index
Current price	$30	$32	
Industry	Computer Software	Capital Goods	
P/E ratio (current)	25	14	16
P/E ratio (5-year average)	27	16	16
Price/book ratio (current)	10	3	3
Price/book ratio (5-year average)	12	4	2
Beta	1.5	1.1	1.0
Dividend yield	.3%	2.7%	2.8%

a. Newsoft's shares have higher price–earnings (P/E) and price–book value (P/B) ratios than those of Capital Corp. (The price–book ratio is the ratio of market value to book value.) Briefly discuss why the disparity in ratios may not indicate that NewSoft's shares are overvalued relative to the shares of Capital Corp. Answer the question in terms of the two ratios, and assume that there have been no extraordinary events affecting either company.

b. Using a constant growth dividend discount model, Black estimated the value of New-Soft to be $28 per share and the value of Capital Corp. to be $34 per share. Briefly discuss weaknesses of this dividend discount model and explain why this model may be less suitable for valuing NewSoft than for valuing Capital Corp.

c. Recommend and justify a more appropriate dividend discount model for valuing NewSoft's common stock.

13. Recalculate the intrinsic value of Honda using the three-stage growth model of Spread-sheet 13.1 (available at **www.mhhe.com/bkm;** link to Chapter 13 material). Treat each scenario independently.

a. ROE in the constant growth period will be 13%.

b. Honda's actual beta is .75.

c. The market risk premium is 8.5%.

Please visit us at
www.mhhe.com/bkm

14. Recalculate the intrinsic value of Honda shares using the free cash flow model of Spreadsheet 13.2 (available at **www.mhhe.com/bkm;** link to Chapter 13 material). Treat each scenario independently.

a. Honda's P/E ratio starting in 2010 will be 16.

b. Honda's unlevered beta is .9.

c. The market risk premium is 7.5%.

Please visit us at
www.mhhe.com/bkm

15. Peninsular Research is initiating coverage of a mature manufacturing industry. John Jones, CFA, head of the research department, gathered the following fundamental indus-try and market data to help in his analysis:

CFA®
PROBLEMS

Forecast industry earnings retention rate	40%
Forecast industry return on equity	25%
Industry beta	1.2
Government bond yield	6%
Equity risk premium	5%

a. Compute the price-to-earnings (P_0/E_1) ratio for the industry based on this fundamen-tal data.

b. Jones wants to analyze how fundamental P/E ratios might differ among countries. He gathered the following economic and market data:

Fundamental Factors	Country A	Country B
Forecast growth in real GDP	5%	2%
Government bond yield	10%	6%
Equity risk premium	5%	4%

Determine whether each of these fundamental factors would cause P/E ratios to be gen-erally higher for Country A or higher for Country B.

16. Janet Ludlow's firm requires all its analysts to use a two-stage DDM and the CAPM to value stocks. Using these measures, Ludlow has valued QuickBrush Company at $63 per share. She now must value SmileWhite Corporation.

    a. Calculate the required rate of return for SmileWhite using the information in the following table:

	December 2007	
	QuickBrush	**SmileWhite**
Beta	1.35	1.15
Market price	$45.00	$30.00
Intrinsic value	$63.00	?

    Note: Risk-free rate = 4.50%; expected market return = 14.50%.

    b. Ludlow estimates the following EPS and dividend growth rates for SmileWhite:

First three years:	12% per year
Years thereafter:	9% per year

    Estimate the intrinsic value of SmileWhite using the table above, and the two-stage DDM. Dividends per share in 2007 were $1.72.

    c. Recommend QuickBrush or SmileWhite stock for purchase by comparing each company's intrinsic value with its current market price.

    d. Describe *one* strength of the two-stage DDM in comparison with the constant growth DDM. Describe *one* weakness inherent in all DDMs.

17. The MoMi Corporation's cash flow from operations before interest and taxes was $2 million in the year just ended, and it expects that this will grow by 5% per year forever. To make this happen, the firm will have to invest an amount equal to 20% of pretax cash flow each year. The tax rate is 35%. Depreciation was $200,000 in the year just ended and is expected to grow at the same rate as the operating cash flow. The appropriate market capitalization rate for the unleveraged cash flow is 12% per year, and the firm currently has debt of $4 million outstanding. Use the free cash flow approach to value the firm's equity.

18. Rio National Corp. is a U.S.-based company and the largest competitor in its industry. Exhibits 18A–18D present financial statements and related information for the company. Exhibit 18E presents relevant industry and market data.

    The portfolio manager of a large mutual fund comments to one of the fund's analysts, Katrina Shaar: "We have been considering the purchase of Rio National Corp. equity shares, so I would like you to analyze the value of the company. To begin, based on Rio National's past performance, you can assume that the company will grow at the same rate as the industry."

    a. Calculate the value of a share of Rio National equity on December 31, 2002, using the Gordon growth model and the capital asset pricing model.

    b. Calculate the sustainable growth rate of Rio National on December 31, 2002. Use 2002 beginning-of-year balance sheet values.

19. While valuing the equity of Rio National Corp. (from the previous problem), Katrina Shaar is considering the use of either free cash flow to the firm (FCFF) or free cash flow to equity (FCFE) in her valuation process.

    a. State two adjustments that Shaar should make to FCFF to obtain free cash flow to equity.

    b. Shaar decides to calculate Rio National's FCFE for the year 2002, starting with net income. Determine for each of the five supplemental notes given in Exhibit 18C whether an adjustment should be made to net income to calculate Rio National's free cash flow to equity for the year 2002, and the dollar amount of any adjustment.

    c. Calculate Rio National's free cash flow to equity for the year 2002.

www.mhhe.com/bkm

EXHIBIT 18A		2002	2001
Rio National Corp. Summary year-end balance sheets (U.S. $ millions)	Cash	$ 13.00	$ 5.87
	Accounts receivable	30.00	27.00
	Inventory	209.06	189.06
	Current assets	$252.06	$221.93
	Gross fixed assets	474.47	409.47
	Accumulated depreciation	(154.17)	(90.00)
	Net fixed assets	320.30	319.47
	Total assets	$572.36	$541.40
	Accounts payable	$ 25.05	$ 26.05
	Notes payable	0.00	0.00
	Current portion of long-term debt	0.00	0.00
	Current liabilities	$ 25.05	$ 26.05
	Long-term debt	240.00	245.00
	Total liabilities	$265.05	$271.05
	Common stock	160.00	150.00
	Retained earnings	147.31	120.35
	Total shareholders' equity	$307.31	$270.35
	Total liabilities and shareholders' equity	$572.36	$541.40

EXHIBIT 18B		
Rio National Corp. Summary income statement for the year ended December 31, 2002 (U.S. $ millions)	Revenue	$300.80
	Total operating expenses	(173.74)
	Operating profit	127.06
	Gain on sale	4.00
	Earnings before interest, taxes, depreciation & amortization (EBITDA)	131.06
	Depreciation and amortization	(71.17)
	Earnings before interest & taxes (EBIT)	59.89
	Interest	(16.80)
	Income tax expense	(12.93)
	Net income	$ 30.16

EXHIBIT 18C

Rio National Corp. Supplemental notes for 2002

Note 1: Rio National had $75 million in capital expenditures during the year.

Note 2: A piece of equipment that was originally purchased for $10 million was sold for $7 million at year-end, when it had a net book value of $3 million. Equipment sales are unusual for Rio National.

Note 3: The decrease in long-term debt represents an unscheduled principal repayment; there was no new borrowing during the year.

Note 4: On 1 January 2002, the company received cash from issuing 400,000 shares of common equity at a price of $25.00 per share.

Note 5: A new appraisal during the year increased the estimated market value of land held for investment by $2 million, which was not recognized in 2002 income.

EXHIBIT 18D	Dividends paid (U.S. $ millions)	$3.20
Rio National Corp. Common equity data for 2002	Weighted average shares outstanding during 2002	16,000,000
	Dividend per share	$0.20
	Earnings per share	$1.89
	Beta	1.80

Note: The dividend payout ratio is expected to be constant.

EXHIBIT 18E	Risk-free rate of return	4.00%
Industry and market data December 31, 2002	Expected rate of return on market index	9.00%
	Median industry price/earnings (P/E) ratio	19.90
	Expected industry earnings growth-rate	12.00%

20. Shaar (from the previous problem) has revised slightly her estimated earnings growth rate for Rio National and, using normalized (underlying trend) EPS, which is adjusted for temporary impacts on earnings, now wants to compare the current value of Rio National's equity to that of the industry, on a growth-adjusted basis. Selected information about Rio National and the industry is given in Exhibit 20A.

EXHIBIT 20A	**Rio National**	
Rio National Corp. vs. industry	Estimated earnings growth rate	11.00%
	Current share price	$25.00
	Normalized (underlying trend) EPS for 2002	$ 1.71
	Weighted-average shares outstanding during 2002	16,000,000
	Industry	
	Estimated earnings growth rate	12.00%
	Median price/earnings (P/E) ratio	19.90

Compared to the industry, is Rio National's equity overvalued or undervalued on a P/E-to-growth (PEG) basis, using normalized (underlying) earnings per share. Assume that the risk of Rio National is similar to the risk of the industry.

21. The stock of Nogro Corporation is currently selling for $10 per share. Earnings per share in the coming year are expected to be $2. The company has a policy of paying out 50% of its earnings each year in dividends. The rest is retained and invested in projects that earn a 20% rate of return per year. This situation is expected to continue indefinitely.

   a. Assuming the current market price of the stock reflects its intrinsic value as computed using the constant growth rate DDM, what rate of return do Nogro's investors require?

   b. By how much does its value exceed what it would be if all earnings were paid as dividends and nothing were reinvested?

   c. If Nogro were to cut its dividend payout ratio to 25%, what would happen to its stock price? What if Nogro eliminated the dividend?

22. The risk-free rate of return is 8%, the expected rate of return on the market portfolio is 15%, and the stock of Xyrong Corporation has a beta coefficient of 1.2. Xyrong pays out 40% of its earnings in dividends, and the latest earnings announced were $10 per share. Dividends were just paid and are expected to be paid annually. You expect that Xyrong will earn an ROE of 20% per year on all reinvested earnings forever.

   a. What is the intrinsic value of a share of Xyrong stock?

   b. If the market price of a share is currently $100, and you expect the market price to be equal to the intrinsic value one year from now, what is your expected one-year holding-period return on Xyrong stock?

23. Helen Morgan, CFA, has been asked to use the DDM to determine the value of Sundanci, Inc. Morgan anticipates that Sundanci's earnings and dividends will grow at 32% for two years and 13% thereafter.

    Calculate the current value of a share of Sundanci stock by using a two-stage dividend discount model and the data from Tables 23A and 23B.

TABLE 23A	Income Statement	1999	2000
Sundanci actual 1999 and 2000 financial statements for fiscal years ending May 31 ($ million, except per-share data)	Revenue	$ 474	$ 598
	Depreciation	20	23
	Other operating costs	368	460
	Income before taxes	86	115
	Taxes	26	35
	Net income	60	80
	Dividends	18	24
	Earnings per share	$0.714	$0.952
	Dividend per share	$0.214	$0.286
	Common shares outstanding (millions)	84.0	84.0
	Balance Sheet	**1999**	**2000**
	Current assets	$ 201	$ 326
	Net property, plant and equipment	474	489
	Total assets	675	815
	Current liabilities	57	141
	Long-term debt	0	0
	Total liabilities	57	141
	Shareholders' equity	618	674
	Total liabilities and equity	675	815
	Capital expenditures	34	38

TABLE 23B		
Selected financial information	Required rate of return on equity	14%
	Growth rate of industry	13%
	Industry P/E ratio	26

24. To continue with Sundanci, Abbey Naylor, CFA, has been directed to determine the value of Sundanci's stock using the Free Cash Flow to Equity (FCFE) model. Naylor believes that Sundanci's FCFE will grow at 27% for two years and 13% thereafter. Capital expenditures, depreciation, and working capital are all expected to increase proportionately with FCFE.

    a. Calculate the amount of FCFE per share for the year 2000, using the data from Table 23A.

    b. Calculate the current value of a share of Sundanci stock based on the two-stage FCFE model.

    c. i. Describe one limitation of the two-stage DDM model that is addressed by using the two-stage FCFE model.

    ii. Describe one limitation of the two-stage DDM model that is *not* addressed by using the two-stage FCFE model.

25. Christie Johnson, CFA, has been assigned to analyze Sundanci using the constant dividend growth price/earnings (P/E) ratio model. Johnson assumes that Sundanci's earnings and dividends will grow at a constant rate of 13%.

    a. Calculate the P/E ratio based on information in Tables 23A and 23B and on Johnson's assumptions for Sundanci.

    b. Identify, within the context of the constant dividend growth model, how each of the following factors would affect the P/E ratio.

    • Risk (beta) of Sundanci.

    • Estimated growth rate of earnings and dividends.

    • Market risk premium.

Use data from the Standard & Poor's Market Insight Database at www.mhhe.com/edumarketinsight to answer the following questions.

1. Click on the Market Insight Company tab, then the Population tab, and scroll through the list to find 10 firms that interest you. Click on a firm's name and its symbol will automatically be entered. Click on Go, then on the Financial Highlights link in the Compustat Reports section.
   a. For each firm, find the return on equity (ROE), the number of shares outstanding, the dividends per share, and the net income. Record them in a spreadsheet.
   b. Calculate the total amount of dividends paid (dividends per share × number of shares outstanding), the dividend payout ratio (total dividends paid / net income), and the plowback ratio (1 – dividend payout ratio).
   c. Compute the sustainable growth rate, $g = b \times \text{ROE}$, where b equals the plowback ratio.
   d. Compare the growth rates (g) with the P/E ratios of the firms by plotting the P/Es against the growth rates in a scatter diagram. Is there a relationship between the two?
   e. Find the price-to-book, price-to-sales, and price-to-cash flow ratios for your sample of firms. Use a line chart to plot these three ratios on the same set of axes. What relationships do you see among the three series?
   f. For each firm, compare the 5-year growth rate of earnings per share with the growth rate you calculated above. Is the actual rate of earnings growth correlated with the sustainable growth rate you calculated?

2. Use the data from Market Insight to estimate the intrinsic values of three firms from your sample. Use the firms' betas from the S&P Stock Report section. Make reasonable judgments about the market risk premium and the risk-free rate or find estimates from the Internet.
   a. What is the required return on each firm based on the CAPM?
   b. Look in the Valuation Data section of the Excel Analytics menu. Find the forecasted price for next year. Use the forecasted price, information about dividends (collected in the previous problem), and the CAPM required return to calculate the intrinsic value of the stock today. How does this compare to the stock's current market price?
   c. Try using a two-stage growth model, making reasonable assumptions about how future growth rates will differ from current growth rates. Compare the intrinsic values derived from the two-stage model to the intrinsic values you found assuming a constant growth rate. Which estimate seems more reasonable for each firm?

3. On the Market Insight home page, click on the Industry tab and select the Restaurants category. In the Compustat Reports section, click on the Constituents link to get a list of companies in this industry. Choose 5 of the firms listed and follow the links to get to the Financial Highlights for each firm.
   a. Perform a "Valuation by Comparables" analysis by looking at the Price/Earnings, Price/Book Value, Price/Sales, and Price/Cash Flow ratios of the firms relative to each other and to the industry average. Which of the firms seem to be overvalued? Which seem to be undervalued? Can you think of reasons for any apparent mispricings?
   b. Calculate the firms' dividend payout ratios (total dividends paid/net income) and their sustainable growth rates ($g = b \times \text{ROE}$). What impact does the growth rate seem to have on firm value?

Computer a few years ago. (If the value of these acquisitions later falls, then they are deemed to be impaired, and the decline in value must then be charged off as an expense.)

The liability and shareholders' equity section is arranged similarly. Listed first are short-term or "current" liabilities, such as accounts payable, accrued taxes, and debts that are due within one year. Long-term debt and other liabilities due in more than a year follow. The difference between total assets and total liabilities is shareholders' equity. This is the net worth or book value of the firm. Shareholders' equity is divided into par value of stock, capital surplus (additional paid-in capital), and retained earnings, although this division is usually unimportant. Briefly, par value plus capital surplus represents the proceeds realized from the sale of stock to the public, while retained earnings represent the buildup of equity from profits plowed back into the firm. Even if the firm issues no new equity, book value will increase each year due to reinvested earnings.

The first column of numbers in the balance sheet in Table 14.2 presents the dollar value of each asset. To make it easier to compare firms of different sizes, analysts often present each item on the balance sheet as a percentage of total assets. This is called a *common-size balance sheet* and is presented in the last column of the table.

The Statement of Cash Flows

The income statement and balance sheets are based on accrual methods of accounting, which means revenues and expenses are recognized at the time of a sale even if no cash has yet been exchanged. In contrast, the statement of cash flows recognizes only transactions in which cash changes hands. For example, if goods are sold now, with payment due in 60 days, the income statement will treat the revenue as generated when the sale occurs, and the balance sheet will be immediately augmented by accounts receivable, but the statement of cash flows will not recognize the transaction until the bill is paid and the cash is in hand.

statement of cash flows

A financial statement showing a firm's cash receipts and cash payments during a specified period.

Table 14.3 is the 2006 statement of cash flows for HP. The first entry listed under cash flows from operations is net income. The following entries modify that figure for components of income that have been recognized but for which cash has not yet changed hands. Increases in accounts receivable, for example, mean income has been claimed on the income statement, but cash has not yet been collected. Hence, increases in accounts receivable reduce the cash flows realized from operations in this period. Similarly, increases in accounts payable mean expenses have been incurred, but cash has not yet left the firm. Any payment delay increases the company's net cash flows in this period.

Another major difference between the income statement and the statement of cash flows involves depreciation, which accounts for a substantial addition in the adjustment section of the statement of cash flows in Table 14.3. The income statement attempts to "smooth" large capital expenditures over time. The depreciation expense on the income statement is a way of doing this by recognizing capital expenditures over a period of many years rather than at the specific time of those expenditures. In contrast, the statement of cash flows recognizes the cash implication of a capital expenditure when it occurs. It will ignore the depreciation "expense" over time but will account for the full capital expenditure when it is paid.

Rather than smooth or allocate expenses over time, as in the income statement, the statement of cash flows reports cash flows separately for operations, investing, and financing activities. This way, any large cash flows such as those for big investments can be recognized as such without affecting the measure of cash flow generated by operating activities.

The second section of the statement of cash flows is the accounting of cash flows from investing activities. These entries are investments in the assets necessary for the firm to maintain or enhance its productive capacity.

Finally, the last section of the statement lists the cash flows realized from financing activities. Issuance of securities will contribute positive cash flows, while redemption of outstanding securities will use up cash. For example, HP repurchased $5,241 million of its shares of stock in 2006, which was a major use of cash. Its dividend payments, $894 million, also used cash. In total, HP's financing activities in 2006 absorbed $6,077 million.

To summarize, HP's operations generated a cash flow of $11,353 million. Some of that cash, $2,787 million, went to pay for new investments. Another part, $6,077 million, went to

TABLE 14.3		$ Million
Cash provided by operations		
Net income		$ 6,198
Adjustments to net income		
Depreciation		2,353
Changes in working capital		
Decrease (increase) in accounts receivable		(882)
Decrease (increase) in inventories		(1,109)
Increase (decrease) in taxes payable		(513)
Increase (decrease) in accounts payable		1,879
Other adjustments		3,427
Total adjustments		$ 5,155
Cash provided by operations		$11,353
Cash flows from investments		
Investments in tangible fixed assets		$ (1,980)
Investments in business acquisitions		(855)
Investment in other assets		48
Cash provided by (used for) investments		$ (2,787)
Cash provided by (used for) financing activities		
Additions to (reductions in) long-term debt		$ (138)
Net issues (repurchases of) shares		(5,241)
Dividends		(894)
Other		196
Cash provided by (used for) financing activities		$ (6,077)
Net increase in cash		$ 2,489

Statement of Cash Flows for Hewlett-Packard, 2006

Source: Hewlett-Packard Annual Report.

pay dividends and retire outstanding securities. HP's cash holdings therefore increased by $11,353 − $2,787 − $6,077 = $2,489 million. This is reported on the last line of Table 14.3.

The statement of cash flows provides important evidence on the well-being of a firm. If a company cannot pay its dividends and maintain the productivity of its capital stock out of cash flow from operations, for example, and it must resort to borrowing to meet these demands, this is a serious warning that the firm cannot maintain payout at its current level in the long run. The statement of cash flows will reveal this developing problem when it shows that cash flow from operations is inadequate and that borrowing is being used to maintain dividend payments at unsustainable levels.

14.2 ACCOUNTING VERSUS ECONOMIC EARNINGS

accounting earnings

Earnings of a firm as reported on its income statement.

We've seen that stock valuation models require a measure of economic earnings or sustainable cash flow that can be paid out to stockholders without impairing the productive capacity of the firm. In contrast, **accounting earnings** are affected by several conventions regarding the valuation of assets such as inventories (e.g., LIFO versus FIFO treatment) and by the way some expenditures such as capital investments are recognized over time (as depreciation expenses). We will discuss problems with some of these accounting conventions in greater detail later in the chapter. In addition to these accounting issues, as the firm makes its way through the business cycle, its earnings will rise above or fall below the trend line that might more accurately reflect sustainable **economic earnings.** This introduces an added complication in interpreting net income figures. One might wonder how closely accounting earnings approximate economic earnings and, correspondingly, how useful accounting data might be to investors attempting to value the firm.

economic earnings

The real flow of cash that a firm could pay out without impairing its productive capacity.

In fact, the net income figure on the firm's income statement does convey considerable information concerning a firm's products. We see this in the fact that stock prices tend to increase when firms announce earnings greater than market analysts or investors had anticipated.

14.3   PROFITABILITY MEASURES

Profitability measures focus on the firm's earnings. To facilitate comparisons across firms, total earnings are expressed on a per-dollar-invested basis. So return on equity (ROE), which measures profitability for contributors of equity capital, is defined as (after-tax) profits divided by the book value of equity. Similarly, return on assets (ROA), which measures profitability for all contributors of capital, is defined as earnings before interest and taxes divided by total assets. Not surprisingly, ROA and ROE are linked, but as we will see shortly, the relationship between them is affected by the firm's financial policies.

Past versus Future ROE

We noted in Chapter 13 that **return on equity (ROE)** is one of the two basic factors in determining a firm's growth rate of earnings. Sometimes it is reasonable to assume that future ROE will approximate its past value, but a high ROE in the past does not necessarily imply a firm's future ROE will be high. A declining ROE, on the other hand, is evidence that the firm's new investments have offered a lower ROE than its past investments. The vital point for a security analyst is not to accept historical values as indicators of future values. Data from the recent past may provide information regarding future performance, but the analyst should always keep an eye on the future. Expectations of *future* dividends and earnings determine the intrinsic value of the company's stock.

return on equity (ROE)

The ratio of net profits to common equity.

Financial Leverage and ROE

An analyst interpreting the past behavior of a firm's ROE or forecasting its future value must pay careful attention to the firm's debt–equity mix and to the interest rate on its debt. An example will show why. Suppose Nodett is a firm that is all-equity financed and has total assets of $100 million. Assume it pays corporate taxes at the rate of 40% of taxable earnings.

Table 14.4 shows the behavior of sales, earnings before interest and taxes, and net profits under three scenarios representing phases of the business cycle. It also shows the behavior of two of the most commonly used profitability measures: operating **return on assets (ROA)**, which equals EBIT/total assets, and ROE, which equals net profits/equity.

return on assets (ROA)

Earnings before interest and taxes divided by total assets.

Somdett is an otherwise identical firm to Nodett, but $40 million of its $100 million of assets are financed with debt bearing an interest rate of 8%. It pays annual interest expenses of $3.2 million. Table 14.5 shows how Somdett's ROE differs from Nodett's.

Note that annual sales, EBIT, and therefore ROA for both firms are the same in each of the three scenarios, that is, business risk for the two companies is identical. It is their financial risk that differs. Although Nodett and Somdett have the same ROA in each scenario, Somdett's ROE exceeds that of Nodett in normal and good years and is lower in bad years.

We can summarize the exact relationship among ROE, ROA, and leverage in the following equation[1]

$$\text{ROE} = (1 - \text{Tax rate})\left[\text{ROA} + (\text{ROA} - \text{Interest rate})\frac{\text{Debt}}{\text{Equity}}\right] \qquad \textbf{(14.1)}$$

The relationship has the following implications. If there is no debt or if the firm's ROA equals the interest rate on its debt, its ROE will simply equal (1 − tax rate) times ROA. If

---

[1]The derivation of Equation 14.1 is as follows:

$$\text{ROE} = \frac{\text{Net profit}}{\text{Equity}} = \frac{\text{EBIT} - \text{Interest} - \text{Taxes}}{\text{Equity}} = \frac{(1 - \text{Tax rate})(\text{EBIT} - \text{Interest})}{\text{Equity}}$$

$$= (1 - \text{Tax rate})\frac{(\text{ROA} \times \text{Assets} - \text{Interest rate} \times \text{Debt})}{\text{Equity}}$$

$$= (1 - \text{Tax rate})\left[\text{ROA} \times \frac{(\text{Equity} + \text{Debt})}{\text{Equity}} - \text{Interest rate} \times \frac{\text{Debt}}{\text{Equity}}\right]$$

$$= (1 - \text{Tax rate})\left[\text{ROA} + (\text{ROA} - \text{Interest rate})\frac{\text{Debt}}{\text{Equity}}\right]$$

TABLE 14.4

Nodett's profitability over the business cycle

Scenario	Sales ($ millions)	EBIT ($ millions)	ROA (% per year)	Net Profit ($ millions)	ROE (% per year)
Bad year	$ 80	$ 5	5%	$3	3%
Normal year	100	10	10	6	6
Good year	120	15	15	9	9

TABLE 14.5

Impact of financial leverage on ROE

Scenario	EBIT ($ millions)	Nodett		Somdett	
		Net Profit ($ millions)	ROE (%)	Net Profit* ($ millions)	ROE† (%)
Bad year	$ 5	$3	3%	$1.08	1.8%
Normal year	10	6	6	4.08	6.8
Good year	15	9	9	7.08	11.8

*Somdett's after-tax profits equal 0.6(EBIT − $3.2 million).

†Somdett's equity is only $60 million.

its ROA exceeds the interest rate, then its ROE will exceed (1 − tax rate) times ROA by an amount that will be greater the higher the debt/equity ratio.

This result makes intuitive sense: If ROA exceeds the borrowing rate, the firm earns more on its money than it pays out to creditors. The surplus earnings are available to the firm's owners, the equityholders, which raises ROE. If, on the other hand, ROA is less than the interest rate, then ROE will decline by an amount that depends on the debt/equity ratio.

EXAMPLE   14.1

Leverage and ROE

To illustrate the application of Equation 14.1, we can use the numerical example in Table 14.5. In a normal year, Nodett has an ROE of 6%, which is 0.6 (1 − tax rate) times its ROA of 10%. However, Somdett, which borrows at an interest rate of 8% and maintains a debt/equity ratio of ⅔, has an ROE of 6.8%. The calculation using Equation 14.1 is

$$ROE = 0.6[10\% + (10\% − 8\%)⅔]$$
$$= 0.6(10\% + \tfrac{4}{3}\%) = 6.8\%$$

The important point is that increased debt will make a positive contribution to a firm's ROE only if the firm's ROA exceeds the interest rate on the debt.

Notice that financial leverage increases the risk of the equityholder returns. Table 14.5 shows that ROE on Somdett is worse than that of Nodett in bad years. Conversely, in good years, Somdett outperforms Nodett because the excess of ROA over ROE provides additional funds for equityholders. The presence of debt makes Somdett's ROE more sensitive to the business cycle than Nodett's. Even though the two companies have equal business risk (reflected in their identical EBIT in all three scenarios), Somdett's stockholders carry greater financial risk than Nodett's because all of the firm's business risk is absorbed by a smaller base of equity investors.

Even if financial leverage increases the expected ROE of Somdett relative to Nodett (as it seems to in Table 14.5), this does not imply that Somdett's share price will be higher. Financial leverage increases the risk of the firm's equity as surely as it raises the expected ROE, and the higher discount rate will offset the higher expected earnings.

CONCEPT **14.1**
check

Mordett is a company with the same assets as Nodett and Somdett but a debt/equity ratio of 1.0 and an interest rate of 9%. What would its net profit and ROE be in a bad year, a normal year, and a good year?

14.4 RATIO ANALYSIS

Decomposition of ROE

To understand the factors affecting a firm's ROE, including its trend over time and its performance relative to competitors, analysts often "decompose" ROE into the product of a series of ratios. Each component ratio is in itself meaningful, and the process serves to focus the analyst's attention on the separate factors influencing performance. This kind of decomposition of ROE is often called the DuPont system.

One useful decomposition of ROE is

$$\text{ROE} = \underbrace{\frac{\text{Net profit}}{\text{Pretax profit}}}_{(1)} \times \underbrace{\frac{\text{Pretax profit}}{\text{EBIT}}}_{(2)} \times \underbrace{\frac{\text{EBIT}}{\text{Sales}}}_{(3)} \times \underbrace{\frac{\text{Sales}}{\text{Assets}}}_{(4)} \times \underbrace{\frac{\text{Assets}}{\text{Equity}}}_{(5)}$$

DuPont system

Decomposition of profitability measures into component ratios.

Table 14.6 shows all these ratios for Nodett and Somdett under the three different economic scenarios. Let us first focus on factors 3 and 4. Notice that their product gives us the firm's ROA = EBIT/Assets.

Factor 3 is known as the firm's operating profit margin, or return on sales, which equals operating profit per dollar of sales. In an average year, Nodett's margin is 0.10, or 10%; in a bad year, it is 0.0625, or 6.25%; and in a good year, it is 0.125, or 12.5%.

profit margin or return on sales

The ratio of operating profits per dollar of sales (EBIT divided by sales).

Factor 4, the ratio of sales to total assets, is known as total asset turnover (ATO). It indicates the efficiency of the firm's use of assets in the sense that it measures the annual sales generated by each dollar of assets. In a normal year, Nodett's ATO is 1.0 per year, meaning that sales of $1 per year were generated per dollar of assets. In a bad year, this ratio declines to 0.8 per year, and in a good year, it rises to 1.2 per year.

total asset turnover (ATO)

The annual sales generated by each dollar of assets (sales/assets).

Comparing Nodett and Somdett, we see that factors 3 and 4 do not depend on a firm's financial leverage. The firms' ratios are equal to each other in all three scenarios.

TABLE 14.6

Ratio decomposition analysis for Nodett and Somdett

	ROE	(1) Net Profit Pretax Profit	(2) Pretax Profit EBIT	(3) EBIT Sales (Margin)	(4) Sales Assets (Turnover)	(5) Assets Equity	(6) Compound Leverage Factor (2) × (5)
Bad year							
Nodett	0.030	0.6	1.000	0.0625	0.800	1.000	1.000
Somdett	0.018	0.6	0.360	0.0625	0.800	1.667	0.600
Normal year							
Nodett	0.060	0.6	1.000	0.100	1.000	1.000	1.000
Somdett	0.068	0.6	0.680	0.100	1.000	1.667	1.134
Good year							
Nodett	0.090	0.6	1.000	0.125	1.200	1.000	1.000
Somdett	0.118	0.6	0.787	0.125	1.200	1.667	1.311

Similarly, factor 1, the ratio of net income after taxes to pretax profit, is the same for both firms. We call this the tax-burden ratio. Its value reflects both the government's tax code and the policies pursued by the firm in trying to minimize its tax burden. In our example, it does not change over the business cycle, remaining a constant 0.6.

While factors 1, 3, and 4 are not affected by a firm's capital structure, factors 2 and 5 are. Factor 2 is the ratio of pretax profits to EBIT. The firm's pretax profits will be greatest when there are no interest payments to be made to debtholders. In fact, another way to express this ratio is

$$\frac{\text{Pretax profits}}{\text{EBIT}} = \frac{\text{EBIT} - \text{Interest expense}}{\text{EBIT}}$$

We will call this factor the *interest-burden (IB) ratio.* It takes on its highest possible value, 1, for Nodett, which has no financial leverage. The higher the degree of financial leverage, the lower the IB ratio. Nodett's IB ratio does not vary over the business cycle. It is fixed at 1.0, reflecting the total absence of interest payments. For Somdett, however, because interest expense is fixed in a dollar amount while EBIT varies, the IB ratio varies from a low of 0.36 in a bad year to a high of 0.787 in a good year.

A closely related statistic to the interest burden ratio is the interest coverage ratio, or times interest earned. The ratio is defined as

$$\text{Interest coverage} = \frac{\text{EBIT}}{\text{Interest expense}}$$

A high coverage ratio indicates that the likelihood of bankruptcy is low because annual earnings are significantly greater than annual interest obligations. It is widely used by both lenders and borrowers in determining the firm's debt capacity and is a major determinant of the firm's bond rating.

Factor 5, the ratio of assets to equity, is a measure of the firm's degree of financial leverage. It is called the leverage ratio and is equal to 1 plus the debt/equity ratio.[2] In our numerical example in Table 14.6, Nodett has a leverage ratio of 1, while Somdett's is 1.667.

From our discussion of Equation 14.1, we know that financial leverage helps boost ROE only if ROA is greater than the interest rate on the firm's debt. How is this fact reflected in the ratios of Table 14.6?

The answer is that to measure the full impact of leverage in this framework, the analyst must take the product of the IB and leverage ratios (that is, factors 2 and 5, shown in Table 14.6 as column 6). For Nodett, factor 6, which we call the compound leverage factor, remains a constant 1.0 under all three scenarios. But for Somdett, we see that the compound leverage factor is greater than 1 in normal years (1.134) and in good years (1.311), indicating the positive contribution of financial leverage to ROE. It is less than 1 in bad years, reflecting the fact that when ROA falls below the interest rate, ROE falls with increased use of debt.

We can summarize all of these relationships as follows:

$$\text{ROE} = \text{Tax burden} \times \text{Interest burden} \times \text{Margin} \times \text{Turnover} \times \text{Leverage}$$

Because

$$\text{ROA} = \text{Margin} \times \text{Turnover}$$

and

$$\text{Compound leverage factor} = \text{Interest burden} \times \text{Leverage}$$

we can decompose ROE equivalently as follows:

$$\text{ROE} = \text{Tax burden} \times \text{ROA} \times \text{Compound leverage factor}$$

---

[2] $\dfrac{\text{Assets}}{\text{Equity}} = \dfrac{\text{Equity} + \text{Debt}}{\text{Equity}} = 1 + \dfrac{\text{Debt}}{\text{Equity}}$

---

interest coverage ratio or times interest earned

A financial leverage measure arrived at by dividing earnings before interest and taxes by interest expense.

leverage ratio

Measure of debt to total capitalization of a firm.

TABLE 14.7		Margin	×	ATO	=	ROA
Differences between profit margin and asset turnover across industries	Supermarket chain	2%		5.0		10%
	Utility	20%		0.5		10%

Table 14.6 for Nodett and Somdett compares firms with the same profit margin and turnover but different degrees of financial leverage. Note, however, that comparison of profit margin and turnover usually is meaningful only in evaluating firms in the same industry. Cross-industry comparisons of these two ratios are often meaningless and can even be misleading.

Consider two firms with the same ROA of 10% per year. The first is a discount supermarket chain and the second is a gas and electric utility.

As Table 14.7 shows, the supermarket chain has a "low" profit margin of 2% and achieves a 10% ROA by "turning over" its assets five times per year. The capital-intensive utility, on the other hand, has a "low" asset turnover ratio (ATO) of only 0.5 times per year and achieves its 10% ROA through its higher, 20%, profit margin. The point here is that a "low" margin or ATO ratio need not indicate a troubled firm. Each ratio must be interpreted in light of industry norms.

Even within an industry, margin and ATO sometimes can differ markedly among firms pursuing different marketing strategies. In the retailing industry, for example, Neiman-Marcus pursues a high-margin, low-turnover policy compared to Wal-Mart, which pursues a low-margin, high-turnover policy.

EXAMPLE   14.2

Margin vs. Turnover

Do a ratio decomposition analysis for the Mordett corporation of Concept Check 1, preparing a table similar to Table 14.6.

CONCEPT **14.2**
check

Turnover and Other Asset Utilization Ratios

It is often helpful in understanding a firm's ratio of sales to assets to compute comparable efficiency-of-utilization, or turnover, ratios for subcategories of assets. For example, fixed-asset turnover would be

$$\frac{\text{Sales}}{\text{Fixed assets}}$$

This ratio measures sales per dollar of the firm's money tied up in fixed assets.

To illustrate how you can compute this and other ratios from a firm's financial statements, consider Growth Industries, Inc. (GI). GI's income statement and opening and closing balance sheets for the years 2006, 2007, and 2008 appear in Table 14.8.

GI's total asset turnover in 2008 was 0.303, which was below the industry average of 0.4. To understand better why GI underperformed, we compute asset utilization ratios separately for fixed assets, inventories, and accounts receivable.

GI's sales in 2008 were $144 million. Its only fixed assets were plant and equipment, which were $216 million at the beginning of the year and $259.2 million at year's end. Average fixed assets for the year were, therefore, $237.6 million [($216 million + $259.2 million)/2]. GI's fixed-asset turnover for 2008 was $144 million per year/$237.6 million = 0.606 per year. In other words, for every dollar of fixed assets, there was $0.606 in sales during the year 2006.

Comparable figures for the fixed-asset turnover ratio for 2006 and 2007 and the 2008 industry average are

2006	2007	2008	2008 Industry Average
0.606	0.606	0.606	0.700

TABLE 14.8

Growth Industries financial statements ($thousands)

	2005	2006	2007	2008
Income statements				
Sales revenue		$100,000	$120,000	$144,000
Cost of goods sold (including depreciation)		55,000	66,000	79,200
Depreciation		15,000	18,000	21,600
Selling and administrative expenses		15,000	18,000	21,600
Operating income		30,000	36,000	43,200
Interest expense		10,500	19,095	34,391
Taxable income		19,500	16,905	8,809
Income tax (40% rate)		7,800	6,762	3,524
Net income		11,700	10,143	5,285
Balance sheets (end of year)				
Cash and marketable securities	$ 50,000	$ 60,000	$ 72,000	$ 86,400
Accounts receivable	25,000	30,000	36,000	43,200
Inventories	75,000	90,000	108,000	129,600
Net plant and equipment	150,000	180,000	216,000	259,200
Total assets	$300,000	$360,000	$432,000	$518,400
Accounts payable	$ 30,000	$ 36,000	$ 43,200	$ 51,840
Short-term debt	45,000	87,300	141,957	214,432
Long-term debt (8% bonds maturing in 2020)	75,000	75,000	75,000	75,000
Total liabilities	$150,000	$198,300	$260,157	$341,272
Shareholders' equity (1 million shares outstanding)	$150,000	$161,700	$171,843	$177,128
Other data				
Market price per common share at year-end		$ 93.60	$ 61.00	$ 21.00

GI's fixed-asset turnover has been stable over time and below the industry average.

Notice that when a financial ratio includes one item from the income statement, which covers a period of time, and another from the balance sheet, which is a "snapshot" at a particular time, the practice is to take the average of the beginning and end-of-year balance sheet figures. Thus, in computing the fixed-asset turnover ratio you divide sales (from the income statement) by average fixed assets (from the balance sheet).

inventory turnover

Cost of goods sold divided by average inventory.

Another widely followed turnover ratio is the **inventory turnover ratio,** which is the ratio of cost of goods sold per dollar of inventory. It is usually expressed as cost of goods sold (instead of sales revenue) divided by average inventory. It measures the speed with which inventory is turned over.

WEB master

DuPont Analysis

DuPont analysis is a good way to analyze what fundamental factors drive changes in firm profitability.

1. Select five firms and retrieve their financial statements from **finance.yahoo.com** or another site that has financial information.

2. Perform a DuPont analysis of return on equity (ROE) for each of the selected firms by setting up a spreadsheet to calculate the relevant ratios. Multiply the ratios as appropriate to find ROE, then enter the ROE

formula directly (ROE = Net Profit/Equity) to confirm your work.

3. Calculate the compound leverage factor for each firm.

4. For each firm, identify areas of strength and areas of weakness. State two specific things the firm can do to improve its ROE.

5. A less detailed DuPont decomposition of ROE is available at **www.credit-to-cash-advisor.com/document_120. html**. You may explore this calculator by entering inputs directly from the financial statements.

In 2006, GI's cost of goods sold (less depreciation) was $40 million, and its average inventory was $82.5 million [($75 million + $90 million)/2]. Its inventory turnover was 0.485 per year ($40 million/$82.5 million). In 2007 and 2008, inventory turnover remained the same and continued below the industry average of 0.5 per year.

Another measure of efficiency is the ratio of accounts receivable to sales. The accounts receivable ratio usually is computed as average accounts receivable/sales × 365. The result is a number called the **average collection period,** or **days receivables,** which equals the total credit extended to customers per dollar of daily sales. It is the number of days' worth of sales tied up in accounts receivable. You can also think of it as the average lag between the date of sale and the date payment is received.

For GI in 2008, this number was 100.4 days:

$$\frac{(\$36 \text{ million} + \$43.2 \text{ million})/2}{\$144 \text{ million}} \times 365 = 100.4 \text{ days}$$

The industry average was 60 days.

In summary, use of these ratios lets us see that GI's poor total asset turnover relative to the industry is in part caused by lower than average fixed-asset turnover and inventory turnover, and higher than average days receivables. This suggests GI may be having problems with excess plant capacity along with poor inventory and receivables management procedures.

Liquidity Ratios

Liquidity and interest coverage ratios are of great importance in evaluating the riskiness of a firm's securities. They aid in assessing the financial strength of the firm.

Liquidity ratios include the current ratio, quick ratio, and cash ratio.

1. **Current ratio:** current assets/current liabilities. This ratio measures the ability of the firm to pay off its current liabilities by liquidating its current assets (that is, turning them into cash). It indicates the firm's ability to avoid insolvency in the short run. GI's current ratio in 2006, for example, was (60 + 30 + 90)/(36 + 87.3) = 1.46. In other years, it was

2006	2007	2008	2008 Industry Average
1.46	1.17	0.97	2.0

This represents an unfavorable time trend and poor standing relative to the industry.

2. **Quick ratio:** (cash + marketable securities + receivables)/current liabilities. This ratio is also called the **acid test ratio.** It has the same denominator as the current ratio, but its numerator includes only cash, cash equivalents such as marketable securities, and receivables. The quick ratio is a better measure of liquidity than the current ratio for firms whose inventory is not readily convertible into cash. GI's quick ratio shows the same disturbing trends as its current ratio:

2006	2007	2008	2008 Industry Average
0.73	0.58	0.49	1.0

3. **Cash ratio.** A company's receivables are less liquid than its holdings of cash and marketable securities. Therefore, in addition to the quick ratio, analysts also compute a firm's cash ratio, defined as

$$\text{Cash ratio} = \frac{\text{Cash} + \text{Marketable securities}}{\text{Current liabilities}}$$

average collection period, or days receivables

Accounts receivable per dollar of daily sales.

current ratio

Current assets/current liabilities.

quick ratio, or acid test ratio

A measure of liquidity similar to the current ratio except for exclusion of inventories.

cash ratio

Another liquidity measure. Ratio of cash and marketable securities to current liabilities.

GI's cash ratios are

2006	2007	2008	2008 Industry Average
.487	.389	.324	.70

GI's liquidity ratios have fallen dramatically over this three-year period, and by 2008, they are far below the industry average. The decline in the liquidity ratios combined with the decline in coverage ratio (you can confirm that times interest earned also has fallen over this period) suggest that its credit rating has been declining as well, and no doubt, GI is considered a relatively poor credit risk in 2008.

Market Price Ratios

There are two important market price ratios: the market-to-book-value ratio and the price–earnings ratio.

market-to-book-value ratio

Market price of a share divided by book value per share.

The **market-to-book-value ratio** (P/B) equals the market price of a share of the firm's common stock divided by its *book value,* that is, shareholders' equity per share. Analysts sometimes consider the stock of a firm with a low market-to-book value to be a "safer" investment, seeing the book value as a "floor" supporting the market price.

Analysts presumably view book value as the level below which market price will not fall because the firm always has the option to liquidate, or sell, its assets for their book values. However, this view is questionable. In fact, some firms do sometimes sell for less than book value. For example, in March 2006, shares in GM sold for only about 70% of book value per share. Nevertheless, a low market-to-book-value ratio is seen by some as providing a "margin of safety," and some analysts will screen out or reject high P/B firms in their stock selection process. Recall Chapter 8, where we saw that high book-to-market (or low P/B) firms seem to provide a "value premium."

The theory of equity valuation offers some insight into the significance of the P/B ratio. A high P/B ratio is an indication that investors think a firm has opportunities of earning a rate of return on their investment in excess of the market capitalization rate, k.

EXAMPLE 14.3

Price-to-Book Ratio and Investment Opportunities

Return to Table 13.3 in the previous chapter, which assumes the market capitalization rate is 12% per year. Now add the assumptions that the book value per share is $8.33 and that the coming year's expected EPS is $1, so that in the case for which the expected ROE on future investments also is 12%, the stock will sell at $1/.12 = $8.33, and the P/B ratio will be 1.

Table 14.9 shows the P/B ratio for alternative assumptions about future ROE and plowback ratio. Reading down any column, you can see how the P/B ratio changes with ROE. The numbers reveal that, for a given plowback ratio, the P/B ratio is higher, the higher the expected ROE. This makes sense, because the greater the expected profitability of the firm's future investment opportunities, the greater its market value as an ongoing enterprise compared with the cost of acquiring its assets.

TABLE 14.9		Plowback Ratio (b)			
Effect of ROE and plowback ratio on P/B	**ROE**	**0**	**25%**	**50%**	**75%**
	10%	1.00	0.95	0.86	0.67
	12	1.00	1.00	1.00	1.00
	14	1.00	1.06	1.20	2.00

Note: The assumptions and formulas underlying this table are: $E_1 = \$1$; book value per share = $8.33; $k = 12\%$ per year.

$$g = b \times \text{ROE}$$

$$P_0 = \frac{(1 - b)E}{k - g}$$

$$P/B = P_0 / \$8.33$$

We've noted that the **price–earnings ratio** that is based on the firm's financial statements and reported in newspaper stock listings is not the same as the price–earnings multiple that emerges from a discounted dividend model. The numerator is the same (the market price of the stock), but the denominator is different. The P/E ratio uses the most recent past accounting earnings, while the P/E multiple predicted by valuation models uses expected future economic earnings.

price–earnings ratio

The ratio of a stock's price to its earnings per share. Also referred to as the P/E multiple.

Many security analysts pay careful attention to the accounting P/E ratio in the belief that among low P/E stocks they are more likely to find bargains than with high P/E stocks. (Remember from Chapter 8 that low P/E stocks have in fact generally been positive-alpha investments using the CAPM as a benchmark.) The idea is that you can acquire a claim on a dollar of earnings more cheaply if the P/E ratio is low. For example, if the P/E ratio is 8, you pay $8 per share per $1 of *current* earnings, while if the P/E ratio is 12, you must pay $12 for a claim on $1 of current earnings.

Note, however, that current earnings may differ substantially from future earnings. The higher P/E stock still may be a bargain relative to the low P/E stock if its earnings and dividends are expected to grow at a faster rate. Our point is that ownership of the stock conveys the right to future earnings as well as to current earnings. An exclusive focus on the commonly reported accounting P/E ratio can be shortsighted because by its nature it ignores future growth in earnings.

An efficient markets adherent will be skeptical of the notion that a strategy of investing in low P/E stocks will result in an expected rate of return greater than that of investing in high or medium P/E stocks having the same risk. The empirical evidence on this question is mixed, but if the strategy has worked in the past, it surely should not work in the future because too many investors will be following it. This is the lesson of market efficiency.

Before leaving the P/B and P/E ratios, it is worth pointing out the relationship among these ratios and ROE.

$$\text{ROE} = \frac{\text{Earnings}}{\text{Book value}} = \frac{\text{Market price}}{\text{Book value}} \div \frac{\text{Market price}}{\text{Earnings}}$$

$$= \text{P/B ratio} \div \text{P/E ratio}$$

Rearranging terms, we find that a firm's **earnings yield,** the ratio of earnings to price, is equal to its ROE divided by the market-to-book-value ratio:

earnings yield

The ratio of earnings to price, E/P.

$$\frac{E}{P} = \frac{\text{ROE}}{\text{P/B}}$$

Thus, a company with a high ROE can have a relatively low earnings yield because its P/B ratio is high. This indicates that a high ROE does not in and of itself imply the stock is a good buy. The price of the stock already may be bid up to reflect an attractive ROE. If so, the P/B ratio will be above 1.0, and the earnings yield to stockholders will be below the ROE, as the equation demonstrates. The relationship shows that a strategy of investing in the stock of high ROE firms may produce a lower holding-period return than investing in the stock of firms with a low ROE.

For example, Clayman (1987) found that investing in the stocks of 29 "excellent" companies, with mean reported ROE of 19.05% during the period 1976 to 1980, produced results much inferior to investing in 39 "unexcellent" companies, those with a mean ROE of 7.09% during the period. An investor putting equal dollar amounts in the stock of the unexcellent companies would have earned a portfolio rate of return over the 1981 to 1985 period that was 11.3% higher per year than the rate of return on a comparable portfolio of excellent company stocks.

What were GI's ROE, P/E, and P/B ratios in the year 2008? How do they compare to the industry average ratios, which were:

ROE = 8.64%

P/E = 8

P/B = 0.69

How does GI's earnings yield in 2008 compare to the industry average?

Table 14.10 summarizes the ratios reviewed in this section.

TABLE 14.10

Summary of key financial ratios

Leverage ratios:

Interest burden
$$\frac{EBIT - \text{Interest expense}}{EBIT}$$

Interest coverage (Times interest earned)
$$\frac{EBIT}{\text{Interest expense}}$$

Leverage
$$\frac{\text{Assets}}{\text{Equity}} = 1 + \frac{\text{Debt}}{\text{Equity}}$$

Compound leverage factor
Interest burden $\times$ Leverage

Asset utilization:

Total asset turnover
$$\frac{\text{Sales}}{\text{Average total assets}}$$

Fixed asset turnover
$$\frac{\text{Sales}}{\text{Average fixed assets}}$$

Inventory turnover
$$\frac{\text{Cost of goods sold}}{\text{Average inventories}}$$

Days receivables
$$\frac{\text{Average accounts receivable}}{\text{Annual sales}} \times 365$$

Liquidity:

Current ratio
$$\frac{\text{Current assets}}{\text{Current liabilities}}$$

Quick ratio
$$\frac{\text{Cash} + \text{Marketable securities} + \text{Receivables}}{\text{Current liabilities}}$$

Cash ratio
$$\frac{\text{Cash} + \text{Marketable securities}}{\text{Current liabilities}}$$

Profitability ratios:

Return on assets
$$\frac{EBIT}{\text{Average total assets}}$$

Return on equity
$$\frac{\text{Net income}}{\text{Average stockholders' equity}}$$

Return on sales (Profit margin)
$$\frac{EBIT}{\text{Sales}}$$

Market price ratios:

Market-to-book
$$\frac{\text{Price per share}}{\text{Book value per share}}$$

Price–earnings ratio
$$\frac{\text{Price per share}}{\text{Earnings per share}}$$

Earnings yield
$$\frac{\text{Earnings per share}}{\text{Price per share}}$$

Choosing a Benchmark

We have discussed how to calculate the principal financial ratios. To evaluate the performance of a given firm, however, you need a benchmark to which you can compare its ratios. One obvious benchmark is the ratio for the same company in earlier years. For example, Figure 14.1 shows Hewlett-Packard's return on assets, profit margin, and asset turnover ratio for the last few years.

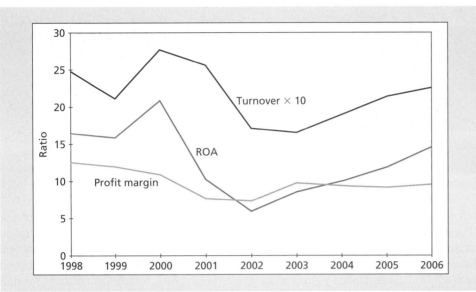

FIGURE 14.1

DuPont decomposition for Hewlett-Packard

TABLE 14.11

Financial Ratios for Major Industry Groups

	LT Debt Assets	Interest Coverage	Current Ratio	Quick Ratio	Asset Turnover	Profit Margin (%)	Return on Assets (%)	Return on Equity (%)	Payout Ratio
All manufacturing	0.18	4.06	1.29	0.92	0.97	6.57	6.35	17.18	0.43
Food products	0.25	3.71	1.22	0.71	1.33	6.43	8.54	17.93	0.41
Clothing	0.18	7.34	2.12	1.25	1.50	10.05	15.09	25.35	0.28
Printing/publishing	0.33	3.43	1.32	1.03	1.43	7.24	10.32	17.08	0.47
Chemicals	0.18	3.04	1.10	0.81	0.61	8.12	4.98	18.68	0.51
Drugs	0.14	6.05	1.19	0.94	0.50	10.27	5.09	22.50	0.45
Machinery	0.17	4.65	1.48	1.03	0.93	7.75	7.20	15.01	0.21
Electrical/electronic	0.11	5.46	1.49	1.17	0.66	6.61	4.34	12.04	0.27
Motor vehicles	0.18	−1.85	0.90	0.70	1.10	−4.10	−4.53	−11.70	−0.67

Source: U.S. Department of *Commerce, Quarterly Financial Report for Manufacturing, Mining and Trade Corporations,* third quarter 2005.

You can see there that most of the variation in HP's return on assets has been driven by the considerable variation in its asset turnover ratio. In contrast, its profit margin has been relatively stable.

It is also helpful to compare financial ratios to those of other firms in the same industry. Financial ratios for industries are published by the U.S. Department of Commerce, Dun & Bradstreet, the Risk Management Association, and others, and many ratios are available on the Web, for example, on the Yahoo! Finance site. Standard & Poor's Market Insight is a good source of ratios, and is available to users of this text at **www.mhhe.com/edumarketinsight**.

Table 14.11 presents ratios for a sample of major industry groups to give you a feel for some of the differences across industries. You should note that while some ratios such as asset turnover or total debt ratio tend to be relatively stable, others such as return on assets or equity are more sensitive to current business conditions. Notice for example the negative profitability measures for the motor vehicle industry.

14.5 ECONOMIC VALUE ADDED

One common use of financial ratios is to evaluate the performance of the firm. While it is common to use profitability to measure that performance, profitability is really not enough. A firm should be viewed as successful only if the return on its projects is better than the rate investors could expect to earn for themselves (on a risk-adjusted basis) in the capital market. Think back to Table 14.9, where we showed that plowing back funds into the firm increases share value

TABLE 14.12		EVA ($ billion)	Capital ($ billion)	ROA (%)	Cost of capital (%)
Economic Value Added, 2006	Royal Dutch Shell	$ 3.98	$121.15	12.2%	8.9%
	GlaxoSmithKline	3.26	29.41	18.2	7.2
	Wal-Mart	2.13	100.78	8.9	6.7
	Genentech	1.11	11.72	16.3	6.8
	Motorola	−0.80	21.43	6.9	10.6
	Intel	−1.35	38.59	9.8	13.3
	Hewlett-Packard	−2.35	41.39	6.2	11.9
	AT&T	−5.65	177.76	3.7	6.9

Source: Authors' calculations using data from Yahoo! Finance (**finance. yahoo.com**).

economic value added, or residual income

A measure of the dollar value of a firm's return in excess of its opportunity cost.

only if the firm earns a higher rate of return on the reinvested funds than the opportunity cost of capital, that is, the market capitalization rate. To account for this opportunity cost, we might measure the success of the firm using the difference between the return on assets, ROA, and the opportunity cost of capital. **Economic value added** (EVA) is the spread between ROA and the cost of capital multiplied by the capital invested in the firm. It therefore measures the dollar value of the firm's return in excess of its opportunity cost. Another term for EVA (the term coined by Stern Stewart, a consulting firm that has promoted the concept) is **residual income.**

EXAMPLE   14.4

Economic Value Added

In 2006, Wal-Mart had a weighted-average cost of capital of 6.7% (based on its cost of debt, its capital structure, its equity beta, and estimates derived from the CAPM for the cost of equity). Wal-Mart's return on assets was 8.9%, fully 2.2% greater than the opportunity cost of capital on its investments in plant, equipment, and know-how. In other words, each dollar invested by Wal-Mart earned about 2.2 cents more than the return that investors could have anticipated by investing in equivalent-risk stocks. Wal-Mart earned this superior rate of return on a capital base of $100.78 billion. Its economic value added, that is, its return in excess of opportunity cost was therefore (.089 − .067) × $100.78 = $2.13 billion.

Table 14.12 shows EVA for a small sample of firms.[3] The EVA leader in this sample was Royal Dutch Shell. Notice that its EVA was greater than GlaxoSmithKline's, despite a considerably smaller margin between ROA and the cost of capital. This is because Shell applied its margin to a much larger capital base. At the other extreme, AT&T earned less than its opportunity cost on a very large capital base, which resulted in a large negative EVA.

Notice that even the EVA "losers" in Table 14.12 had positive profits. For example, by conventional standards, Motorola was solidly profitable in 2006, with an ROA of 6.9%. But by virtue of its high business risk, its cost of capital was higher, at 10.6%. By this standard, Motorola did not cover its opportunity cost of capital, and its EVA in 2006 was negative. EVA treats the opportunity cost of capital as a real cost that, like other costs, should be deducted from revenues to arrive at a more meaningful "bottom line." A firm that is earning profits but is not covering its opportunity cost might be able to redeploy its capital to better uses. Therefore, a growing number of firms now calculate EVA and tie managers' compensation to it.

14.6   AN ILLUSTRATION OF FINANCIAL STATEMENT ANALYSIS

In her 2008 annual report to the shareholders of Growth Industries, Inc., the president wrote: "2008 was another successful year for Growth Industries. As in 2007, sales, assets, and operating income all continued to grow at a rate of 20%."

---

[3]Actual EVA estimates reported by Stern Stewart (a consulting firm that has done much to develop and promote the concept of EVA) differ from the values in Table 14.12 because of adjustments to the accounting data involving issues such as treatment of research and development expenses, taxes, advertising expenses, and depreciation. The estimates in Table 14.12 are designed to show the logic behind EVA but must be taken as imprecise.

TABLE 14.13
Key financial ratios of Growth Industries, Inc.

Year	ROE	(1) Net Profit Pretax Profit	(2) Pretax Profit EBIT	(3) EBIT Sales (Margin)	(4) Sales Assets (Turnover)	(5) Assets Equity	(6) Compound Leverage Factor (2) × (5)	(7) ROA (3) × (4)	P/E	P/B
2006	7.51%	0.6	0.650	30%	0.303	2.117	1.376	9.09%	8	0.58
2007	6.08	0.6	0.470	30	0.303	2.375	1.116	9.09	6	0.35
2008	3.03	0.6	0.204	30	0.303	2.723	0.556	9.09	4	0.12
Industry average	8.64	0.6	0.800	30	0.400	1.500	1.200	12.00	8	0.69

Is she right?

We can evaluate her statement by conducting a full-scale ratio analysis of Growth Industries. Our purpose is to assess GI's performance in the recent past, to evaluate its future prospects, and to determine whether its market price reflects its intrinsic value.

Table 14.13 shows some key financial ratios we can compute from GI's financial statements. The president is certainly right about the growth in sales, assets, and operating income. Inspection of GI's key financial ratios, however, contradicts her first sentence: 2008 was not another successful year for GI—it appears to have been another miserable one.

ROE has been declining steadily from 7.51% in 2006 to 3.03% in 2008. A comparison of GI's 2008 ROE to the 2008 industry average of 8.64% makes the deteriorating time trend especially alarming. The low and falling market-to-book-value ratio and the falling price–earnings ratio indicate that investors are less and less optimistic about the firm's future profitability.

The fact that ROA has not been declining, however, tells us that the source of the declining time trend in GI's ROE must be due to financial leverage. And in fact, as GI's leverage ratio climbed from 2.117 in 2006 to 2.723 in 2008, its interest-burden ratio worsened from 0.650 to 0.204—with the net result that the compound leverage factor fell from 1.376 to 0.556.

The rapid increase in short-term debt from year to year and the concurrent increase in interest expense make it clear that, to finance its 20% growth rate in sales, GI has incurred sizable amounts of short-term debt at high interest rates. The firm is paying rates of interest greater than the ROA it is earning on the investment financed with the new borrowing. As the firm has expanded, its situation has become ever more precarious.

In 2008, for example, the average interest rate on short-term debt was 20% versus an ROA of 9.09%. (We compute the average interest rate on short-term debt by taking the total interest expense of $34,391,000, subtracting the $6 million in interest on the long-term bonds, and dividing by the beginning-of-year short-term debt of $141,957,000.)

GI's problems become clear when we examine its statement of cash flows in Table 14.14. The statement is derived from the income statement and balance sheet in Table 14.8. GI's cash flow from operations is falling steadily, from $12,700,000 in 2006 to $6,725,000 in 2008. The firm's investment in plant and equipment, by contrast, has increased greatly. Net plant and equipment (i.e., net of depreciation) rose from $150,000,000 in 2005 to $259,200,000 in 2008. This near doubling of the capital assets makes the decrease in cash flow from operations all the more troubling.

The source of the difficulty is GI's enormous amount of short-term borrowing. In a sense, the company is being run as a pyramid scheme. It borrows more and more each year to maintain its 20% growth rate in assets and income. However, the new assets are not generating enough cash flow to support the extra interest burden of the debt, as the falling cash flow from operations indicates. Eventually, when the firm loses its ability to borrow further, its growth will be at an end.

At this point, GI stock might be an attractive investment. Its market price is only 12% of its book value, and with a P/E ratio of 4, its earnings yield is 25% per year. GI is a likely candidate for a takeover by another firm that might replace GI's management and build shareholder value through a radical change in policy.

TABLE 14.14		2006	2007	2008
Growth Industries statement of cash flows ($ thousands)	**Cash flow from operating activities**			
	Net income	$ 11,700	$ 10,143	$ 5,285
	+ Depreciation	15,000	18,000	21,600
	+ Decrease (increase) in accounts receivable	(5,000)	(6,000)	(7,200)
	+ Decrease (increase) in inventories	(15,000)	(18,000)	(21,600)
	+ Increase in accounts payable	6,000	7,200	8,640
		$ 12,700	$ 11,343	$ 6,725
	Cash flow from investing activities			
	Investment in plant and equipment*	$(45,000)	$(54,000)	$(64,800)
	Cash flow from financing activities			
	Dividends paid†	$ 0	$ 0	$ 0
	Short-term debt issued	42,300	54,657	72,475
	Change in cash and marketable securities‡	$ 10,000	$ 12,000	$ 14,400

*Gross investment equals increase in net plant and equipment plus depreciation.

†We can conclude that no dividends are paid because stockholders' equity increases each year by the full amount of net income, implying a plowback ratio of 1.0.

‡Equals cash flow from operations plus cash flow from investment activities plus cash flow from financing activities. Note that this equals the yearly change in cash and marketable securities on the balance sheet.

CONCEPT check 14.4

You have the following information for IBX Corporation for the years 2006 and 2009 (all figures are in $millions):

	2009	2006
Net income	$ 253.7	$ 239.0
Pretax income	411.9	375.6
EBIT	517.6	403.1
Average assets	4,857.9	3,459.7
Sales	6,679.3	4,537.0
Shareholders' equity	2,233.3	2,347.3

What is the trend in IBX's ROE, and how can you account for it in terms of tax burden, margin, turnover, and financial leverage?

14.7 COMPARABILITY PROBLEMS

Financial statement analysis gives us a good amount of ammunition for evaluating a company's performance and future prospects. But comparing financial results of different companies is not so simple. There is more than one acceptable way to represent various items of revenue and expense according to generally accepted accounting principles (GAAP). This means two firms may have exactly the same economic income yet very different accounting incomes.

Furthermore, interpreting a single firm's performance over time is complicated when inflation distorts the dollar measuring rod. Comparability problems are especially acute in this case because the impact of inflation on reported results often depends on the particular method the firm adopts to account for inventories and depreciation. The security analyst must adjust the earnings and the financial ratio figures to a uniform standard before attempting to compare financial results across firms and over time.

Comparability problems can arise out of the flexibility of GAAP guidelines in accounting for inventories and depreciation and in adjusting for the effects of inflation. Other important potential sources of noncomparability include the capitalization of leases and other expenses, the treatment of pension costs, and allowances for reserves, but they are beyond the scope of this book.

Inventory Valuation

There are two commonly used ways to value inventories: **LIFO** (last-in, first-out) and **FIFO** (first-in, first-out). We can explain the difference using a numerical example.

Suppose Generic Products, Inc. (GPI), has a constant inventory of 1 million units of generic goods. The inventory turns over once per year, meaning the ratio of cost of goods sold to inventory is 1.

The LIFO system calls for valuing the million units used up during the year at the current cost of production, so that the last goods produced are considered the first ones to be sold. They are valued at today's cost. The FIFO system assumes that the units used up or sold are the ones that were added to inventory first, and goods sold should be valued at original cost.

If the price of generic goods were constant, at the level of $1, say, the book value of inventory and the cost of goods sold would be the same, $1 million under both systems. But suppose the price of generic goods rises by 10 cents per unit during the year as a result of inflation.

LIFO accounting would result in a cost of goods sold of $1.1 million, while the end-of-year balance sheet value of the 1 million units in inventory remains $1 million. The balance sheet value of inventories is given as the cost of the goods still in inventory. Under LIFO, the last goods produced are assumed to be sold at the current cost of $1.10; the goods remaining are the previously produced goods, at a cost of only $1. You can see that, although LIFO accounting accurately measures the cost of goods sold today, it understates the current value of the remaining inventory in an inflationary environment.

In contrast, under FIFO accounting, the cost of goods sold would be $1 million, and the end-of-year balance sheet value of the inventory is $1.1 million. The result is that the LIFO firm has both a lower reported profit and a lower balance sheet value of inventories than the FIFO firm.

LIFO is preferred over FIFO in computing economics earnings (that is, real sustainable cash flow), because it uses up-to-date prices to evaluate the cost of goods sold. A disadvantage is that LIFO accounting induces balance sheet distortions when it values investment in inventories at original cost. This practice results in an upward bias in ROE because the investment base on which return is earned is undervalued.

Depreciation

Another source of problems is the measurement of depreciation, which is a key factor in computing true earnings. The accounting and economic measures of depreciation can differ markedly. According to the *economic* definition, depreciation is the amount of a firm's operating cash flow that must be reinvested in the firm to sustain its real cash flow at the current level.

The *accounting* measurement is quite different. Accounting depreciation is the amount of the original acquisition cost of an asset that is allocated to each accounting period over an arbitrarily specified life of the asset. This is the figure reported in financial statements.

LIFO

The last-in first-out accounting method of valuing inventories.

FIFO

The first-in first-out accounting method of valuing inventories.

Assume, for example, that a firm buys machines with a useful economic life of 20 years at $100,000 apiece. In its financial statements, however, the firm can depreciate the machines over 10 years using the straight-line method, for $10,000 per year in depreciation. Thus, after 10 years, a machine will be fully depreciated on the books, even though it remains a productive asset that will not need replacement for another 10 years.

In computing accounting earnings, this firm will overestimate depreciation in the first 10 years of the machine's economic life and underestimate it in the last 10 years. This will cause reported earnings to be understated compared with economic earnings in the first 10 years and overstated in the last 10 years.

Depreciation comparability problems add one more wrinkle. A firm can use different depreciation methods for tax purposes than for other reporting purposes. Most firms use accelerated depreciation methods for tax purposes and straight-line depreciation in published financial statements. There also are differences across firms in their estimates of the depreciable life of plant, equipment, and other depreciable assets.

The major problem related to depreciation, however, is caused by inflation. Because conventional depreciation is based on historical costs rather than on the current replacement cost of assets, measured depreciation in periods of inflation is understated relative to replacement cost, and *real* economic income (sustainable cash flow) is correspondingly overstated.

For example, suppose Generic Products, Inc., has a machine with a three-year useful life that originally cost $3 million. Annual straight-line depreciation is $1 million, regardless of what happens to the replacement cost of the machine. Suppose inflation in the first year turns out to be 10%. Then the true annual depreciation expense is $1.1 million in current terms, while conventionally measured depreciation remains fixed at $1 million per year. Accounting income therefore overstates *real* economic income.

Inflation and Interest Expense

While inflation can cause distortions in the measurement of a firm's inventory and depreciation costs, it has perhaps an even greater effect on the calculation of *real* interest expense. Nominal interest rates include an inflation premium that compensates the lender for inflation-induced erosion in the real value of principal. From the perspective of both lender and borrower, therefore, part of what is conventionally measured as interest expense should be treated more properly as repayment of principal.

EXAMPLE 14.5

Inflation and Real Income

Suppose Generic Products has debt outstanding with a face value of $10 million at an interest rate of 10% per year. Interest expense as conventionally measured is $1 million per year. However, suppose inflation during the year is 6%, so that the real interest rate is 4%. Then $0.6 million of what appears as interest expense on the income statement is really an inflation premium, or compensation for the anticipated reduction in the real value of the $10 million principal; only $0.4 million is *real* interest expense. The $0.6 million reduction in the purchasing power of the outstanding principal may be thought of as repayment of principal, rather than as an interest expense. Real income of the firm is, therefore, understated by $0.6 million.

This mismeasurement of real interest means that inflation results in an underestimate of real income. The effects of inflation on the reported values of inventories and depreciation that we have discussed work in the opposite direction.

CONCEPT
check **14.5**

In a period of rapid inflation, companies ABC and XYZ have the same *reported* earnings. ABC uses LIFO inventory accounting, has relatively fewer depreciable assets, and has more debt than XYZ. XYZ uses FIFO inventory accounting. Which company has the higher *real* income and why?

THE ONES THAT GET AWAY

It is corporate earnings season once again, and investors are poring over the numbers. Profits figures are meant to shed light on how a company—and its stock price—might fare in the future. But many experts worry that increasingly they don't. Past accounting scandals show that accounting numbers are malleable. And they are getting squishier as the use of estimates in company accounts increases.

Ever since accounting shifted from the simple tallying of cash in and cash out to "accrual accounting," where profits and expenses are booked when incurred, forward-looking estimates have played a critical role in measuring company profits. The biggest boost to estimation, however, has come from the gradual shift to "fair-value" accounting. Before, assets and liabilities were mostly carried at their historic, original cost; "fair value" is an attempt to show their current worth. Fair-value numbers are up-to-date and arguably more relevant than their static but verifiable precursors. But they also result in more volatile profits and a heavier reliance on estimates for the many items (bank loans, buildings) that may not have a ready market.

Baruch Lev of New York University's Stern School of Business and Siyi Li and Theodore Sougiannis from the University of Illinois at Urbana-Champaign harbor a deeper worry: that estimates, which are supposed to improve the relevance of financial information by giving managers a means to impart their forward-looking views, are not very useful at all. They found that while recent cash flows predicted future performance, adding estimates to them was of little help. Mr. Lev concludes that these results "point to the urgent need to enhance the reliability of accounting estimates—especially given the move to fair value."

On this point, even proponents of fair value agree. The Financial Accounting Standards Board (FASB) has devised a "hierarchy" of items according to how difficult they are to value. At the top are items that have an observable price in a deep, liquid market (e.g., listed corporate debt). In the middle are items where sophisticated valuation models are based on market inputs (e.g., employee stock options). At the bottom are items where valuations are based wholly on management projections (e.g., Enron's most esoteric financial instruments).

"Estimates are part of accounting. So the focus shouldn't be on the number of estimates," argues Neri Bukspan, chief accountant at Standard & Poor's, "but rather the objectivity and independence of those making the estimates and those tasked with verifying them." This puts a greater onus on auditors to weed out good estimates from hyped ones—making their independence even more critical than it seemed after Enron. The Public Accounting Oversight Board, recognizing this, also plans to expand its audit guidance on fair value.

Investors need to scrutinize the numbers harder, too. Both FASB and its international counterpart are drafting standards requiring increased disclosure of how fair values are derived and their impact on profits and balance sheets.

SOURCE: *The Economist*, July 28, 2005.

Fair Value Accounting

Many major assets and liabilities do not have easily observable values. For example, we cannot simply look up the values of employee stock options, health care benefits for retired employees, buildings and other real estate, or complex derivatives contracts. While the true financial status of a firm may depend critically on these values, which can swing widely over time, common practice has been to simply value them at historic cost. Proponents of **fair value accounting** argue that financial statements would give a truer picture of the firm if they better reflected the current market values of all assets and liabilities.

Opponents of this approach argue that fair value accounting relies too heavily on estimates. Such estimates potentially introduce considerable noise in firms' accounts and can induce great profit volatility as fluctuations in asset valuations are recognized. Even worse, subjective valuations may offer management a tempting tool to manipulate earnings or the apparent financial condition of the firm at opportune times. For example, Bergstresser, Desai, and Rauh (2006) find that firms make more aggressive assumptions about returns on defined benefit pension plans (which lowers the computed present value of pension obligations) during periods in which executives are actively exercising their stock options.

Despite these potential problems, regulators in both the U.S. and Europe are gradually moving toward greater use of fair value accounting. The nearby box reports on this trend.

fair value accounting

Use of current market values rather than historic cost in the firm's financial statements.

Quality of Earnings and Accounting Practices

Many firms make accounting choices that present their financial statements in the best possible light. The different choices that firms can make give rise to the comparability problems we have discussed. As a result, earnings statements for different companies may be more or less rosy presentations of true "economic earnings"—sustainable cash flow that can be paid to shareholders without impairing the firm's productive capacity. Analysts commonly evaluate the **quality of earnings** reported by a firm. This concept refers to the realism and conservatism of the earnings number, in other words, the extent to which we might expect the reported level of earnings to be sustained.

quality of earnings

The realism and sustainability of reported earnings.

Examples of the accounting choices that influence quality of earnings are:

- *Allowance for bad debt.* Most firms sell goods using trade credit and must make an allowance for bad debt. An unrealistically low allowance reduces the quality of reported earnings. Look for a rising average collection period on accounts receivable as evidence of potential problems with future collections.

- *Nonrecurring items.* Some items that affect earnings should not be expected to recur regularly. These include asset sales, effects of accounting changes, effects of exchange rate movements, or unusual investment income. For example, in 2003, which was a banner year for equity returns, some firms enjoyed large investment returns on securities held. These contributed to that year's earnings, but should not be expected to repeat regularly. They would be considered a "low-quality" component of earnings. Similarly gains in corporate pension plans can generate large, but one-time, contributions to reported earnings.

- *Earnings smoothing.* In 2003, Freddie Mac was the subject of a major accounting scandal, with the disclosure that it had improperly reclassified mortgages held in its portfolio in an attempt to *reduce* its current earnings. Similarly, in the 1990s, W. R. Grace chose to offset high earnings in one of its subsidiaries by setting aside extra reserves. Why would these firms take such actions? Because later, if earnings turned down, they could "release" earnings by reversing these transactions, and thereby create the appearance of steady earnings growth. Indeed, Freddie Mac's nickname on Wall Street was "Steady Freddie." Wall Street likes strong, steady earnings growth, but these firms planned to provide such growth only cosmetically, through earnings management.

- *Stock options.* Many firms, particularly start-ups, compensate employees in large part with stock options. To the extent that these options replace cash salary that otherwise would need to be paid, the value of the options should be considered as one component of the firm's labor expense. After more than a decade of debate, the Financial Accounting Standards Board decided to require firms to recognize stock option grants as an expense starting in 2005. However, the means to value employee options is far from standard, and thus is another source of variation in earnings quality.

- *Revenue recognition.* Under GAAP accounting, a firm is allowed to recognize a sale before it is paid. This is why firms have accounts receivable. But sometimes it can be hard to know when to recognize sales. For example, suppose a computer firm signs a contract to provide products and services over a five-year period. Should the revenue be booked immediately or spread out over five years? A more extreme version of this problem is called "channel stuffing," in which firms "sell" large quantities of goods to customers, but give them the right to later either refuse delivery or return the product. The revenue from the "sale" is booked now, but the likely returns are not recognized until they occur (in a future accounting period). According to the SEC, Sunbeam, which filed for bankruptcy in 2001, generated $60 million in fraudulent profits in 1999 using this technique. If you see accounts receivable increasing far faster than sales, or becoming a larger percentage of total assets, beware of these practices. Given the wide latitude firms have to manipulate revenue, many analysts choose instead to concentrate on cash flow, which is far harder for a company to manipulate.

- *Off-balance-sheet assets and liabilities.* Suppose that one firm guarantees the outstanding debt of another firm, perhaps a firm in which it has an ownership stake. That obligation

6. The information in the following table comes from the 1997 financial statements of QuickBrush Company and SmileWhite Corporation:

NOTES TO THE 1997 FINANCIAL STATEMENTS		
	QuickBrush	SmileWhite
Goodwill	The company amortizes goodwill over 20 years.	The company amortizes goodwill over 5 years.
Property, plant, and equipment	The company uses a straight-line depreciation method over the economic lives of the assets, which range from 5 to 20 years for buildings.	The company uses an accelerated depreciation method over the economic lives of the assets, which range from 5 to 20 years for buildings.
Accounts receivable	The company uses a bad debt allowance of 2% of accounts receivable.	The company uses a bad debt allowance of 5% of accounts receivable.

Determine which company has the higher quality of earnings by discussing *each* of the *three* notes.

7. An analyst applies the DuPont system of financial analysis to the following data for a company:
   - Leverage ratio   2.2
   - Total asset turnover   2.0
   - Net profit margin   5.5%
   - Dividend payout ratio   31.8%

   What is the company's return on equity?

8. An analyst gathers the following information about Meyer, Inc.:
   - Meyer has 1,000 shares of 8% cumulative preferred stock outstanding, with a par value of $100, and liquidation value of $110.
   - Meyer has 20,000 shares of common stock outstanding, with a par value of $20.
   - Meyer had retained earnings at the beginning of the year of $5,000,000.
   - Net income for the year was $70,000.
   - This year, for the first time in its history, Meyer paid no dividends on preferred or common stock.

   What is the book value per share of Meyer's common stock?

9. The cash flow data of Palomba Pizza Stores for the year ended December 31, 2007, are as follows:

Cash payment of dividends	$ 35,000
Purchase of land	14,000
Cash payments for interest	10,000
Cash payments for salaries	45,000
Sale of equipment	38,000
Retirement of common stock	25,000
Purchase of equipment	30,000
Cash payments to suppliers	85,000
Cash collections from customers	250,000
Cash at beginning of year	50,000

a. Prepare a statement of cash flows for Palomba showing:
  • Net cash provided by operating activities.
  • Net cash provided by or used in investing activities.
  • Net cash provided by or used in financing activities.
b. Discuss, from an analyst's viewpoint, the purpose of classifying cash flows into the three categories listed above.

CFA®
PROBLEMS

10. The financial statements for Chicago Refrigerator Inc. (see Tables 10A and 10B) are to be used to compute the ratios a through h for 2005.
  a. Quick ratio.
  b. Return on assets.
  c. Return on common shareholders' equity.
  d. Earnings per share of common stock.

TABLE 10A

Chicago Refrigerator Inc. balance sheet, as of December 31 ($ thousands)

	2004	2005
Assets		
Current assets		
Cash	$ 683	$ 325
Accounts receivable	1,490	3,599
Inventories	1,415	2,423
Prepaid expenses	15	13
Total current assets	$3,603	$6,360
Property, plant, equipment, net	1,066	1,541
Other	123	157
Total assets	$4,792	$8,058
Liabilities		
Current liabilities		
Notes payable to bank	$ —	$ 875
Current portion of long-term debt	38	115
Accounts payable	485	933
Estimated income tax	588	472
Accrued expenses	576	586
Customer advance payment	34	963
Total current liabilities	$1,721	$3,945
Long-term debt	122	179
Other liabilities	81	131
Total liabilities	$1,924	$4,255
Shareholders' equity		
Common stock, $1 par value 1,000,000 shares authorized; 550,000 and 829,000 outstanding, respectively	$ 550	$ 829
Preferred stock, Series A 10%; $25.00 par value; 25,000 authorized; 20,000 and 18,000 outstanding, respectively	500	450
Additional paid-in capital	450	575
Retained earnings	1,368	1,949
Total shareholders' equity	$2,868	$3,803
Total liabilities and shareholders' equity	$4,792	$8,058

TABLE 10B		2004	2005
Chicago Refrigerator Inc. income statement, years ending December 31 ($ thousands)	Net sales	$7,570	$12,065
	Other income, net	261	345
	Total revenues	$7,831	$12,410
	Cost of goods sold	$4,850	$ 8,048
	General administrative and marketing expenses	1,531	2,025
	Interest expense	22	78
	Total costs and expenses	$6,403	$10,151
	Net income before tax	$1,428	$ 2,259
	Income tax	628	994
	Net income	$ 800	$ 1,265

    e. Profit margin.
    f. Times interest earned.
    g. Inventory turnover.
    h. Leverage ratio.

11. In an inflationary period, the use of FIFO will make which *one* of the following more realistic than the use of LIFO?
    a. Balance sheet
    b. Income statement
    c. Cash flow statement
    d. None of the above

12. A company acquires a machine with an estimated 10-year service life. If the company uses the Accelerated Cost Recovery System depreciation method instead of the straight-line method:
    a. Income will be higher in the 10th year.
    b. Total depreciation expense for the 10 years will be lower.
    c. Depreciation expense will be lower in the first year.
    d. Scrapping the machine after eight years will result in a larger loss.

13. Why might a firm's ratio of long-term debt to long-term capital be lower than the industry average, but its ratio of income-before-interest-and-taxes to debt-interest charges be lower than the industry average?
    a. The firm has higher profitability than average.
    b. The firm has more short-term debt than average.
    c. The firm has a high ratio of current assets to current liabilities.
    d. The firm has a high ratio of total cash flow to total long-term debt.

14. During a period of falling price levels, the financial statements of a company using FIFO instead of LIFO for inventory accounting would show:
    a. Lower total assets and lower net income.
    b. Lower total assets and higher net income.
    c. Higher total assets and lower net income.
    d. Higher total assets and higher net income.

15. Scott Kelly is reviewing MasterToy's financial statements in order to estimate its sustainable growth rate. Using the information presented in Table 15A
    a. Identify and calculate the components of the DuPont formula.
    b. Calculate the ROE for 2005 using the components of the DuPont formula.
    c. Calculate the sustainable growth rate for 2005 from the firm's ROE and plowback ratios.

TABLE 15A		**2004**	**2005**
Mastertoy, Inc.: Actual 2004 and estimated 2005 financial statements for fiscal year ending December 31 ($ millions, except per-share data)	**Income Statement**		
	Revenue	$4,750	$5,140
	Cost of goods sold	2,400	2,540
	Selling, general, and administrative	1,400	1,550
	Depreciation	180	210
	Goodwill amortization	10	10
	Operating income	$ 760	$ 830
	Interest expense	20	25
	Income before taxes	$ 740	$ 805
	Income taxes	265	295
	Net income	$ 475	$ 510
	Earnings per share	$ 1.79	$ 1.96
	Average shares outstanding (millions)	265	260
	Balance Sheet		
	Cash	$ 400	$ 400
	Accounts receivable	680	700
	Inventories	570	600
	Net property, plant, and equipment	800	870
	Intangibles	500	530
	Total assets	$2,950	$3,100
	Current liabilities	$ 550	$ 600
	Long-term debt	300	300
	Total liabilities	$ 850	$ 900
	Stockholders' equity	2,100	2,200
	Total liabilities and equity	$2,950	$3,100
	Book value per share	$ 7.92	$ 8.46
	Annual dividend per share	0.55	0.60

16. Cash flow from investing activities *excludes:*
    a. Cash paid for acquisitions.
    b. Cash received from the sale of fixed assets.
    c. Inventory increases due to a new (internally developed) product line.
    d. All of the above.

17. Cash flow from operating activities *includes:*
    a. Inventory increases resulting from acquisitions.
    b. Inventory changes due to changing exchange rates.
    c. Interest paid to bondholders.
    d. Dividends paid to stockholders.

18. Janet Ludlow is a recently hired analyst. After describing the electric toothbrush industry, her first report focuses on two companies, QuickBrush Company and SmileWhite Corporation, and concludes:

    QuickBrush is a more profitable company than SmileWhite, as indicated by the 40% sales growth and substantially higher margins it has produced over the last few years. SmileWhite's sales and earnings are growing at a 10% rate and produce much lower margins. We do not think SmileWhite is capable of growing faster than its recent growth rate of 10% whereas QuickBrush can sustain a 30% long-term growth rate.

    a. Criticize Ludlow's analysis and conclusion that QuickBrush is more profitable, as defined by return on equity (ROE), than SmileWhite and that it has a higher sustainable growth rate. Use only the information provided in Tables 18A and 18B. Support your criticism by calculating and analyzing:
    • The five components that determine ROE.
    • The two ratios that determine sustainable growth: ROE and plowback.

14.2. Ratio decomposition analysis for Mordett Corporation:

Year	ROE	(1) Net Profit Pretax Profit	(2) Pretax Profit EBIT	(3) EBIT Sales (Margin)	(4) Sales Assets (Turnover)	(5) Assets Equity	(6) Compound Leverage Factor (2) × (5)
a. Bad year							
Nodett	0.030	0.6	1.000	0.0625	0.800	1.000	1.000
Somdett	0.018	0.6	0.360	0.0625	0.800	1.667	0.600
Mordett	0.006	0.6	0.100	0.0625	0.800	2.000	0.200
b. Normal year							
Nodett	0.060	0.6	1.000	0.100	1.000	1.000	1.000
Somdett	0.068	0.6	0.680	0.100	1.000	1.667	1.134
Mordett	0.066	0.6	0.550	0.100	1.000	2.000	1.100
c. Good year							
Nodett	0.090	0.6	1.000	0.125	1.200	1.000	1.000
Somdett	0.118	0.6	0.787	0.125	1.200	1.667	1.311
Mordett	0.126	0.6	0.700	0.125	1.200	2.000	1.400

14.3. GI's ROE in 2008 was 3.03%, computed as follows

$$\text{ROE} = \frac{\$5,285}{0.5(\$171,843 + \$177,128)} = 0.0303, \text{ or } 3.03\%$$

Its P/E ratio was $21/$5.285 = 4.0 and its P/B ratio was $21/$177 = .12. Its earnings yield was 25% compared with an industry average of 12.5%.

Note that in our calculations the earnings yield will not equal ROE/(P/B) because we have computed ROE with *average* shareholders' equity in the denominator and P/B with *end*-of-year shareholders' equity in the denominator.

14.4. IBX Ratio Analysis

Year	ROE	(1) Net Profit Pretax Profit	(2) Pretax Profit EBIT	(3) EBIT Sales (Margin)	(4) Sales Assets (Turnover)	(5) Assets Equity	(6) Compound Leverage Factor (2) × (5)	(7) ROA (3) × (4)
2009	11.4%	0.616	0.796	7.75%	1.375	2.175	1.731	10.65%
2006	10.2	0.636	0.932	8.88	1.311	1.474	1.374	11.65

ROE increased despite a decline in operating margin and a decline in the tax burden ratio because of increased leverage and turnover. Note that ROA declined from 11.65% in 2006 to 10.65% in 2009.

14.5. LIFO accounting results in lower reported earnings than does FIFO. Fewer assets to depreciate result in lower reported earnings because there is less bias associated with the use of historic cost. More debt results in lower reported earnings because the inflation premium in the interest rate is treated as part of interest.

PART FIVE

DERIVATIVE MARKETS

Horror stories about large losses incurred by high-flying traders in derivatives markets such as those for futures and options periodically become a staple of the evening news. Indeed, there were some amazing losses to report in the last decade: several totaling hundreds of millions of dollars, and a few amounting to more than a billion dollars. For example, in 2006, the hedge fund Amaranth Advisors lost about $6 billion on its energy derivatives positions in just a few days. In the wake of these debacles, some venerable institutions have gone under, notable among them, Barings Bank, which once helped the U.S. finance the Louisiana Purchase and the British Empire finance the Napoleonic Wars.

These stories, while important, fascinating, and even occasionally scandalous, often miss the point. Derivatives, when misused, can indeed provide a quick path to insolvency. Used properly, however, they are potent tools for risk management and control. In fact,

you will discover in these chapters that one firm was sued for *failing* to use derivatives to hedge price risk. One headline in *The Wall Street Journal* on hedging applications using derivatives was entitled "Index Options Touted as Providing Peace of Mind." Hardly material for bankruptcy court or the *National Enquirer*.

Derivatives provide a means to control risk that is qualitatively different from the techniques traditionally considered in portfolio theory. In contrast to the mean-variance analysis we discussed in Parts Two and Three, derivatives allow investors to change the *shape* of the probability distribution of investment returns. An entirely new approach to risk management follows from this insight.

The following chapters will explore how derivatives can be used as parts of a well-designed portfolio strategy. We will examine some popular portfolio strategies utilizing these securities and take a look at how derivatives are valued.

CHAPTERS IN THIS PART

www.mhhe.com/bkm

AFTER STUDYING THIS CHAPTER
YOU SHOULD BE ABLE TO:

Calculate the profit to various option positions as a function of ultimate security prices.

Formulate option strategies to modify portfolio risk-return attributes.

Identify embedded options in various securities and determine how option characteristics affect the prices of those securities.

Derivative securities, or simply *derivatives,* play a large and increasingly important role in financial markets. These are securities whose prices are determined by, or "derive from," the prices of other securities. These assets also are called *contingent claims* because their payoffs are contingent on the prices of other securities.

Options and futures contracts are both derivative securities. We will see that their payoffs depend on the value of other securities. Swap contracts, which we will discuss in Chapter 17, also are derivatives. Because the value of derivatives depends on the value of other securities, they can be powerful tools for both hedging and speculation. We will investigate these applications in the next three chapters, beginning in this chapter with options.

Trading of standardized options on a national exchange started in 1973 when the Chicago Board Options Exchange (CBOE) began listing call options. These contracts were almost immediately a great success, crowding out the previously existing over-the-counter trading in stock options.

Options contracts now are traded on several exchanges. They are written on common stock, stock indexes, foreign exchange, agricultural commodities, precious metals, and interest rates. In addition, the over-the-counter market also has enjoyed a tremendous resurgence in recent years as its trading in custom-tailored options has exploded. Popular and potent for modifying portfolio characteristics, options have become essential tools that every portfolio manager must understand.

This chapter is an introduction to options markets. It explains how puts and calls work and examines their investment characteristics. Popular option strategies are considered next. Finally, we will examine a range of securities with embedded options such as callable or convertible bonds.

Related Web sites for this chapter are available at www.mhhe.com/bkm.

15.1 THE OPTION CONTRACT

A **call option** gives its holder the right to purchase an asset for a specified price, called the **exercise** or **strike price,** on or before some specified expiration date. For example, an April call option on IBM stock with exercise price $95 entitles its owner to purchase IBM stock for a price of $95 at any time up to and including the expiration date in April. The holder of the call is not required to exercise the option. The holder will choose to exercise only if the market value of the asset to be purchased exceeds the exercise price. When the market price does exceed the exercise price, the option holder may "call away" the asset for the exercise price. Otherwise, the option may be left unexercised. If it is not exercised before the expiration date of the contract, a call option simply expires and no longer has value. Therefore, if the stock price is greater than the exercise price on the expiration date, the value of the call option will equal the difference between the stock price and the exercise price; but if the stock price is less than the exercise price at expiration, the call will be worthless. The *net profit* on the call is the value of the option minus the price originally paid to purchase it.

The purchase price of the option is called the **premium.** It represents the compensation the purchaser of the call must pay for the ability to exercise the option if exercise becomes profitable. Sellers of call options, who are said to *write* calls, receive premium income now as payment against the possibility they will be required at some later date to deliver the asset in return for an exercise price lower than the market value of the asset. If the option is left to expire worthless because the market price of the asset remains below the exercise price, then the writer of the call clears a profit equal to the premium income derived from the sale of the option. But if the call is exercised, the profit to the option writer is the premium income derived when the option was initially sold *minus* the difference between the value of the stock that must be delivered and the exercise price that is paid for those shares. If that difference is larger than the initial premium, the writer will incur a loss.

call option

The right to buy an asset at a specified exercise price on or before a specified expiration date.

exercise or strike price

Price set for calling (buying) an asset or putting (selling) an asset.

premium

Purchase price of an option.

Consider the April 2007 expiration call option on a share of IBM stock with an exercise price of $95 per share selling on March 2, 2007, for $1.35. Exchange-traded options expire on the third Friday of the expiration month, which for this option was April 20. Until the expiration day, the purchaser of the calls was entitled to buy shares of IBM for $95. On March 2, IBM sells for $90.90. Because the stock price is currently less than $95 a share, it clearly would not make sense at the moment to exercise the option to buy at $95. Indeed, if IBM stock remains below $95 by the expiration date, the call will be left to expire worthless. On the other hand, if IBM is selling above $95 at expiration, the call holder will find it optimal to exercise. For example, if IBM sells for $96 on April 20, the option will be exercised since it will give its holder the right to pay $95 for a stock worth $96. The value of the option on the expiration date would then be

$$\text{Value at expiration} = \text{Stock price} - \text{Exercise price} = \$96 - \$95 = \$1$$

EXAMPLE **15.1**

Profits and Losses on a Call Option

(continued)

EXAMPLE 15.1

Profits and Losses on a Call Option (Concluded)

Despite the $1 payoff at maturity, the call holder still realizes a loss of $.35 on his investment because the initial purchase price was $1.35:

$$\text{Profit} = \text{Final value} - \text{Original investment} = \$1 - \$1.35 = -\$.35$$

Nevertheless, exercise of the call is optimal at expiration if the stock price exceeds the exercise price because the exercise proceeds will offset at least part of the investment in the option. The investor in the call will clear a profit if IBM is selling above $96.35 at the maturity date. At that price, the proceeds from exercise will just cover the original cost of the call.

put option

The right to sell an asset at a specified exercise price on or before a specified expiration date.

A **put option** gives its holder the right to *sell* an asset for a specified exercise or strike price on or before some expiration date. An April put on IBM with exercise price $95 entitles its owner to sell IBM stock to the put writer at a price of $95 at any time before expiration in April, even if the market price of IBM is less than $95. While profits on call options increase when the asset increases in value, profits on put options increase when the asset value falls. A put will be exercised only if the exercise price is greater than the price of the underlying asset, that is, only if its holder can deliver for the exercise price an asset with market value less than the exercise price. (One doesn't need to own the shares of IBM to exercise the IBM put option. Upon exercise, the investor's broker purchases the necessary shares of IBM at the market price and immediately delivers or "puts them" to an option writer for the exercise price. The owner of the put profits by the difference between the exercise price and market price.)

EXAMPLE 15.2

Profits and Losses on a Put Option

Now consider the April 2007 expiration put option on IBM with an exercise price of $95, selling on March 2, 2007, for $4.90. It entitled its owner to sell a share of IBM for $95 at any time until April 20. If the holder of the put buys a share of IBM and immediately exercises the right to sell at $95, net proceeds will be $95 − $90.90 = $4.10. Obviously, an investor who pays $4.90 for the put has no intention of exercising it immediately. If, on the other hand, IBM sells for $88 at expiration, the put turns out to be a profitable investment. Its value at expiration would be

$$\text{Value at expiration} = \text{Exercise price} - \text{Stock price} = \$95 - \$88 = \$7$$

and the investor's profit would be $7 − $4.90 = $2.10. This is a holding-period return of $2.10/$4.90 = .429 or 42.9%—over only 49 days! Obviously, put option sellers on March 2 (who are on the other side of the transaction) did not consider this outcome very likely.

in the money

An option where exercise would be profitable.

out of the money

An option where exercise would not be profitable.

at the money

An option where the exercise price and asset price are equal.

An option is described as **in the money** when its exercise would produce a positive payoff for its holder. An option is **out of the money** when exercise would be unprofitable. Therefore, a call option is in the money when the exercise price is below the asset value. It is out of the money when the exercise price exceeds the asset value; no one would exercise the right to purchase for the exercise price an asset worth less than that price. Conversely, put options are in the money when the exercise price exceeds the asset's value, because delivery of the lower valued asset in exchange for the exercise price is profitable for the holder. Options are **at the money** when the exercise price and asset price are equal.

Options Trading

Some options trade on over-the-counter (OTC) markets. The OTC market offers the advantage that the terms of the option contract—the exercise price, maturity date, and number of shares committed—can be tailored to the needs of the traders. The costs of establishing an OTC option contract, however, are relatively high. Today, most option trading occurs on organized exchanges.

IBM (IBM)			Call		Underlying stock price: 90.90		Put	
Expiration	Strike	Last	Volume	Open Interest	Last	Volume	Open Interest
Mar 2007	85	7.50	172	1437	0.20	431	1487
Apr 2007	85	8.10	235	7167	0.70	455	10367
Jul 2007	85	9.40	27	1051	1.55	165	9914
Oct 2007	85	11.20	1	21	2.10	2	405
Mar 2007	90	2.20	3875	3088	1.05	8315	4649
Apr 2007	90	3.78	3779	7016	2.10	5499	11885
Jul 2007	90	5.50	108	1625	3.20	1067	2795
Oct 2007	90	7.70	114	159	...	...	1003
Mar 2007	95	0.35	1605	28920	4.00	2365	27969
Apr 2007	95	1.35	691	10348	4.90	3502	16796
Jul 2007	95	3.00	234	2805	5.20	3334	2780
Oct 2007	95	4.70	61	421	5.90	1	788

FIGURE 15.1

Options on IBM, March 2, 2007
Source: *The Wall Street Journal Online,* March 3, 2007

Options contracts traded on exchanges are standardized by allowable maturity dates and exercise prices for each listed option. Each stock option contract provides for the right to buy or sell 100 shares of stock (except when stock splits occur after the contract is listed and the contract is adjusted for the terms of the split).

Standardization of the terms of listed option contracts means all market participants trade in a limited and uniform set of securities. This increases the depth of trading in any particular option, which lowers trading costs and results in a more competitive market. Exchanges, therefore, offer two important benefits: ease of trading, which flows from a central marketplace where buyers and sellers or their representatives congregate, and a liquid secondary market where buyers and sellers of options can transact quickly and cheaply.

Until recently, most options trading in the U.S. took place on the Chicago Board Options Exchange. However, by 2003 the International Securities Exchange, an electronic exchange based in New York, had displaced the CBOE as the largest options market. Options trading in Europe is uniformly transacted in electronic exchanges.

Figure 15.1 is a reproduction of listed stock option quotations for IBM from the online edition of *The Wall Street Journal.* The last recorded price on the New York Stock Exchange for IBM stock was $90.90 per share.[1] Options are reported at exercise prices of $85 through $95, in $5 increments. These values also are called the *strike prices.*

The exercise or strike prices bracket the stock price. While exercise prices generally are set at five-point intervals for stocks, larger intervals may be set for stocks selling above $100, and intervals of $2.50 may be used for stocks selling below $30.[2] If the stock price moves outside the range of exercise prices of the existing set of options, new options with appropriate exercise prices may be offered. Therefore, at any time, both in-the-money and out-of-the-money options will be listed, as in this example.

Figure 15.1 shows both call and put options listed for each exercise price and expiration date. The three sets of columns for each option report closing price, trading volume in contracts (each contract is for 100 shares of stock), and open interest (number of outstanding contracts).

[1]Occasionally, this price may not match the closing price listed for the stock on the stock market page. This is because some NYSE stocks also trade on exchanges that close after the NYSE, and the stock pages may reflect the more recent closing price. The options exchanges, however, close with the NYSE, so the closing NYSE stock price is appropriate for comparison with the closing option price.

[2]If a stock splits, the terms of the option—such as the exercise price—are adjusted to offset the impact of the split. Therefore, stock splits will also result in exercise prices that are not multiples of $5.

When we compare the prices of call options with the same expiration date but different exercise prices in Figure 15.1, we see that the value of the call is lower when the exercise price is higher. This makes sense, for the right to purchase a share at a given exercise price is not as valuable when the purchase price is higher. Thus, the April expiration IBM call option with strike price $95 sells for only $1.35, while the $90 exercise price April call sells for $3.78. Conversely, put options are worth *more* when the exercise price is higher: You would rather have the right to sell IBM shares for $95 than for $90, and this is reflected in the prices of the puts. The April expiration put option with strike price $95 sells for $4.90, while the $90 exercise price April put sells for only $2.10.

Scanning Figure 15.1, you will see that some options may go an entire day without trading. A lack of trading is denoted by three dots in the volume and price columns. Because trading is infrequent, it is not unusual to find option prices that appear out of line with other prices. You might see, for example, two calls with different exercise prices that seem to sell for the same price. This discrepancy arises because the last trades for these options may have occurred at different times during the day. At any moment, the call with the lower exercise price must be worth more, and the put less, than an otherwise-identical call or put with a higher exercise price.

Expirations of most exchange-traded options tend to be fairly short, ranging up to only several months. For larger firms and several stock indexes, however, longer-term options are traded with expirations ranging up to three years. These options are called LEAPS (for Long-term Equity AnticiPation Securities).

a.   What will be the proceeds and net profits to an investor who purchases the April 2007 expiration IBM calls with exercise price $90 if the stock price at maturity is $80? What if the stock price at maturity is $100?

b.   Now answer part (a) for an investor who purchases an April expiration IBM put option with exercise price $90.

American and European Options

American option

Can be exercised on or before its expiration.

European option

Can be exercised only at expiration.

An **American option** allows its holder to exercise the right to purchase (if a call) or sell (if a put) the underlying asset on or *before* the expiration date. **European options** allow for exercise of the option only on the expiration date. American-style options, because they allow more leeway than their European-style counterparts, generally will be more valuable. Most traded options in the U.S. are American-style. Foreign currency options and some stock index options are notable exceptions to this rule, however.

The Option Clearing Corporation

The Option Clearing Corporation (OCC), the clearinghouse for options trading, is jointly owned by the exchanges on which stock options are traded. The OCC places itself between options traders, becoming the effective buyer of the option from the writer and the effective writer of the option to the buyer. All individuals, therefore, deal only with the OCC, which effectively guarantees contract performance.

When an option holder exercises an option, the OCC arranges for a member firm with clients who have written that option to make good on the option obligation. The member firm selects from among its clients who have written that option to fulfill the contract. The selected client must deliver 100 shares of stock at a price equal to the exercise price for each call option contract written or must purchase 100 shares at the exercise price for each put option contract written.

Because the OCC guarantees contract performance, option writers are required to post margin to guarantee that they can fulfill their contract obligations. The margin required is determined in part by the amount by which the option is in the money, because that value is an indicator of the potential obligation of the option writer upon exercise of the option. When the required margin exceeds the posted margin, the writer will receive a margin call. The *holder* of the option need not post margin because the holder will exercise the option only if it is profitable to do so. After purchasing the option, no further money is at risk.

Margin requirements also depend on whether the underlying asset is held in portfolio. For example, a call option writer owning the stock against which the option is written can satisfy the margin requirement simply by allowing a broker to hold that stock in the brokerage account. The stock is then guaranteed to be available for delivery should the call option be exercised. If the underlying security is not owned, however, the margin requirement is determined by the value of the underlying security as well as by the amount by which the option is in or out of the money. Out-of-the-money options require less margin from the writer, for expected payouts are lower.

Other Listed Options

Options on assets other than stocks also are widely traded. These include options on market indexes and industry indexes, on foreign currency, and even on the futures prices of agricultural products, gold, silver, fixed-income securities, and stock indexes. We will discuss these in turn.

Index options   An index option is a call or put based on a stock market index such as the S&P 500 or the New York Stock Exchange index. Index options are traded on several broad-based indexes as well as on several industry-specific indexes. We discussed many of these indexes in Chapter 2.

The construction of the indexes can vary across contracts or exchanges. For example, the S&P 100 index is a value-weighted average of the 100 stocks in the Standard & Poor's 100 stock group. The weights are proportional to the market value of outstanding equity for each stock. The Dow Jones Industrial Average, by contrast, is a price-weighted average of 30 stocks.

Options contracts on many foreign stock indexes also trade. For example, options on the Nikkei Stock Index of Japanese stocks trade on the Chicago Mercantile Exchange and options on the Japan Index trade on the American Stock Exchange. Options on European indexes such as the Financial Times Share Exchange (FTSE 100) and the Eurotrak index also trade. The Chicago Board Options Exchange as well as the American exchange list options on industry indexes such as the high-tech, pharmaceutical, or banking industries.

In contrast to stock options, index options do not require that the call writer actually "deliver the index" upon exercise or that the put writer "purchase the index." Instead, a cash settlement procedure is used. The payoff that would accrue upon exercise of the option is calculated, and the option writer simply pays that amount to the option holder. The payoff is equal to the difference between the exercise price of the option and the value of the index. For example, if the S&P index is at 1,280 when a call option on the index with exercise price 1,270 is exercised, the holder of the call receives a cash payment equal to the difference, 1,280 − 1,270, times the contract multiplier of $100, or $1,000 per contract.

Options on the major indices, that is, the S&P 100 contract, often called the OEX after its ticker symbol, the S&P 500 index (the SPX), and the Dow Jones Industrials (the DJX), are by far the most actively traded contracts on the CBOE. Together, these contracts dominate CBOE volume.

Futures options   Futures options give their holders the right to buy or sell a specified futures contract, using as a futures price the exercise price of the option. Although the delivery process is slightly complicated, the terms of futures options contracts are designed in effect to allow the option to be written on the futures price itself. The option holder receives upon exercise net proceeds equal to the difference between the current futures price on the specified asset and the exercise price of the option. Thus, if the futures price is, say, $37, and the call has an exercise price of $35, the holder who exercises the call option on the futures gets a payoff of $2.

Foreign currency options A currency option offers the right to buy or sell a quantity of foreign currency for a specified amount of domestic currency. Currency option contracts call for purchase or sale of the currency in exchange for a specified number of U.S. dollars. Contracts are quoted in cents or fractions of a cent per unit of foreign currency.

There is an important difference between currency options and currency *futures* options. The former provide payoffs that depend on the difference between the exercise price and the exchange rate at maturity. The latter are foreign exchange futures options that provide payoffs that depend on the difference between the exercise price and the exchange rate *futures price* at maturity. Because exchange rates and exchange rate futures prices generally are not equal, the options and futures-options contracts will have different values, even with identical expiration dates and exercise prices. Today, trading volume in currency futures options dominates by far trading in currency options.

Interest rate options Options also are traded on Treasury notes and bonds, Treasury bills, certificates of deposit, GNMA pass-through certificates, and yields on Treasury securities of various maturities. Options on several interest rate futures also are traded. Among them are contracts on Treasury bond, Treasury note, municipal bond, LIBOR, Eurodollar, and British and euro-denominated interest rates.

15.2   VALUES OF OPTIONS AT EXPIRATION

Call Options

Recall that a call option gives the right to purchase a security at the exercise price. If you hold a call option on Fin Corp stock with an exercise price of $80, and Fin Corp is now selling at $90, you can exercise your option to purchase the stock at $80 and simultaneously sell the shares at the market price of $90, clearing $10 per share. Yet if the shares sell below $80, you can sit on the option and do nothing, realizing no further gain or loss. The value of the call option at expiration equals

$$\text{Payoff to call holder at expiration} = \begin{matrix} S_T - X & \text{if } S_T > X \\ 0 & \text{if } S_T \leq X \end{matrix}$$

where S_T is the value of the stock at the expiration date, and X is the exercise price. This formula emphasizes the option property because the payoff cannot be negative. That is, the option is exercised only if S_T exceeds X. If S_T is less than X, exercise does not occur, and the option expires with zero value. The loss to the option holder in this case equals the price originally paid. More generally, the *profit* to the option holder is the payoff to the option minus the original purchase price.

The value at expiration of the call with exercise price $80 is given by the following schedule.

Stock price	$60	$70	$80	$90	$100
Option value	0	0	0	10	20

For stock prices at or below $80, the option expires worthless. Above $80, the option is worth the excess of the stock price over $80. The option's value increases by one dollar for each dollar increase in the stock price. This relationship can be depicted graphically, as in Figure 15.2.

The solid line in Figure 15.2 depicts the value of the call at expiration. The net *profit* to the holder of the call equals the gross payoff less the initial investment in the call. Suppose the

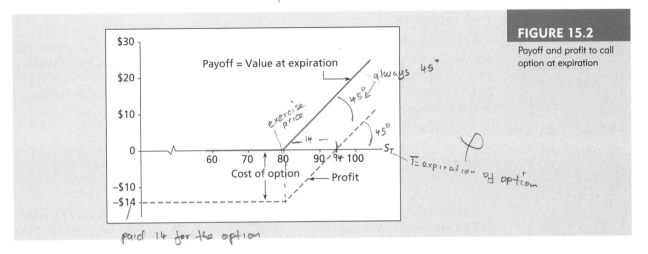

FIGURE 15.2

Payoff and profit to call option at expiration

call cost $14. Then the profit to the call holder would be as given in the dashed (bottom) line of Figure 15.2. At option expiration, the investor has suffered a loss of $14 if the stock price is less than or equal to $80.

Profits do not become positive unless the stock price at expiration exceeds $94. The break-even point is $94, because at that price the payoff to the call, $S_T - X = \$94 - \$80 = \$14$, equals the cost paid to acquire the call. Hence, the call holder shows a profit only if the stock price is higher.

Conversely, the writer of the call incurs losses if the stock price is high. In that scenario, the writer will receive a call and will be obligated to deliver a stock worth S_T for only X dollars.

$$\text{Payoff to call writer} = \begin{array}{l} -(S_T - X) \text{ if } S_T > X \\ 0 \text{ if } S_T \leq X \end{array}$$

The call writer, who is exposed to losses if the stock price increases, is willing to bear this risk in return for the option premium.

Figure 15.3 depicts the payoff and profit diagrams for the call writer. These are the mirror images of the corresponding diagrams for call holders. The break-even point for the option writer also is $94. The (negative) payoff at that point just offsets the premium originally received when the option was written.

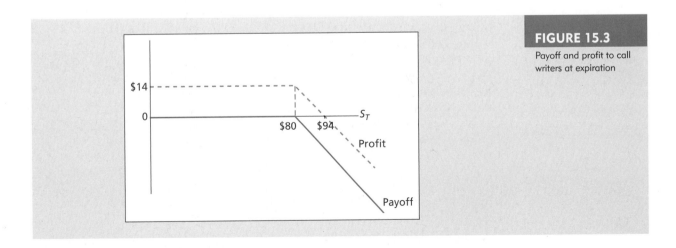

FIGURE 15.3

Payoff and profit to call writers at expiration

Put Options

A put option conveys the right to sell an asset at the exercise price. In this case, the holder will not exercise the option unless the asset price is *less* than the exercise price. For example, if Fin Corp shares were to fall to $70, a put option with exercise price $80 could be exercised to give a $10 payoff to its holder. The holder would purchase a share for $70 and simultaneously deliver it to the put option writer for the exercise price of $80.

The value of a put option at expiration is

$$\text{Payoff to put holder} = \begin{array}{ll} 0 & \text{if } S_T \geq X \\ X - S_T & \text{if } S_T < X \end{array}$$

The solid line in Figure 15.4 illustrates the payoff at expiration to the holder of a put option on Fin Corp stock with an exercise price of $80. If the stock price at option expiration is above $80, the put has no value, as the right to sell the shares at $80 would not be exercised. Below a price of $80, the put value at expiration increases by $1 for each dollar the stock price falls. The dashed line in Figure 15.4 is a graph of the put option owner's profit at expiration, net of the initial cost of the put.

Writing puts *naked* (i.e., writing a put without an offsetting short position in the stock for hedging purposes) exposes the writer to losses if the market falls. Writing naked out-of-the-money puts was once considered an attractive way to generate income, as it was believed that as long as the market did not fall sharply before the option expiration, the option premium could be collected without the put holder ever exercising the option against the writer. Because only sharp drops in the market could result in losses to the writer of the put, the strategy was not viewed as overly risky. However, the nearby box notes that in the wake of the market crash of October 1987, such put writers suffered huge losses. Participants now perceive much greater risk to this strategy.

CONCEPT check 15.2

Consider these four option strategies: (i) buy a call; (ii) write a call; (iii) buy a put; (iv) write a put.
a. For each strategy, plot both the payoff and profit diagrams as a function of the final stock price.
b. Why might one characterize both buying calls and writing puts as "bullish" strategies? What is the difference between them?
c. Why might one characterize both buying puts and writing calls as "bearish" strategies? What is the difference between them?

FIGURE 15.4

Payoff and profit to put option at expiration

THE BLACK HOLE: PUTS AND THE MARKET CRASH

THEIR SALES OF "NAKED PUTS" QUICKLY COME TO GRIEF, DAMAGE SUITS ARE FILED

When Robert O'Connor got involved in stock-index options, he hoped his trading profits would help put his children through college. His broker, Mr. O'Connor explains, "said we would make about $1,000 a month, and if our losses got to $2,000 to $3,000, he would close out the account."

Instead, Mr. O'Connor, the 46-year-old owner of a small medical X-ray printing concern in Grand Rapids, Michigan, got caught in one of the worst investor blow-outs in history. In a few minutes on October 19, he lost everything in his account plus an *additional* $91,000—a total loss of 175% of his original investment.

SCENE OF DISASTER

For Mr. O'Connor and hundreds of other investors, a little-known corner of the Chicago Board Options Exchange was the "black hole" of Black Monday's market crash. In a strategy marketed by brokers nationwide as a sure thing, these customers had sunk hundreds of millions of dollars into "naked puts"—unhedged, highly leveraged bets that the stock market was in no danger of plunging. Most of these naked puts seem to have been options on the Standard & Poor's 100 stock index, which are traded on the CBOE. When stocks crashed, many traders with unhedged positions got margin calls for several times their original investment.

THE "PUT" STRATEGY

The losses were especially sharp in "naked, out-of-the-money puts." A seller of puts agrees to buy stock or stock-index contracts at a set price before the put expires. These contracts are usually sold "out of the money"—priced at a level below current market prices that makes it unprofitable to exercise the option so long as the market rises or stays flat. The seller pockets a small amount per contract.

But if the market plunges, as it did October 19, the option swings into the money. The seller, in effect, has to pay pre-plunge stock prices to make good on his contract—and he takes a big loss.

"You have to recognize that there is unlimited potential for disaster" in selling naked options, says Peter Thayer, executive vice president of Gateway Investment Advisors Inc., a Cincinnati-based investment firm that trades options to hedge its stock portfolios. Last September, Gateway bought out-of-the-money put options on the S&P 100 stock index on the CBOE at $2 to $3 a contract as "insurance" against a plunging market. By October 20, the day after the crash, the value of those contracts had soared to $130. Although Gateway profited handsomely, the parties on the other side of the trade were clobbered.

FIRM SUED

Brokers who were pushing naked options assumed that the stock market wouldn't plunge into uncharted territory. Frank VanderHoff, one of the two main brokers who put 50 to 70 H.B. Shaine clients into stock-index options, says he told clients that the strategy's risk was "moderate barring a nuclear attack or a crash like 1929." It wasn't speculative. The market could go up or down, but not *substantially* up or down. If the crash had only been as bad as '29, he adds, "we would have made it."

SOURCE: Abridged from *The Wall Street Journal*, December 2, 1987. Reprinted by permission of *The Wall Street Journal*, © 1987 Dow Jones & Company, Inc. All Rights Reserved Worldwide.

Options versus Stock Investments

Purchasing call options is a bullish strategy; that is, the calls provide profits when stock prices increase. Purchasing puts, in contrast, is a bearish strategy. Symmetrically, writing calls is bearish, while writing puts is bullish. Because option values depend on the price of the underlying stock, the purchase of options may be viewed as a substitute for direct purchase or sale of a stock. Why might an option strategy be preferable to direct stock transactions? We can begin to answer this question by comparing the values of option versus stock positions in Fin Corp.

Suppose you believe the stock will increase in value from its current level, which we assume is $90. You know your analysis could be incorrect, however, and that the share price also could fall. Suppose a six-month maturity call option with exercise price of $90 sells for $10, and the semiannual interest rate is 2%. Consider the following three strategies for investing a sum of $9,000. Suppose the firm will not pay any dividends until after the options expire.

Strategy A: Invest entirely in stock. Buy 100 shares, each selling for $90.

Strategy B: Invest entirely in at-the-money call options. Buy 900 calls, each selling for $10. (This would require 9 contracts, each for 100 shares.)

Strategy C: Purchase 100 call options for $1,000. Invest the remaining $8,000 in six-month T-bills, to earn 2% interest.

Let us trace the possible values of these three portfolios when the options expire in six months as a function of the stock price at that time.

	Stock Price					
Portfolio	$85	$90	$95	$100	$105	$110
A: 100 shares stock	$8,500	$9,000	$9,500	$10,000	$10,500	$11,000
B: 900 call options	0	0	4,500	9,000	13,500	18,000
C: 100 calls plus $8,000 in T-bills	8,160	8,160	8,660	9,160	9,660	10,160

Portfolio A will be worth 100 times the share price. Portfolio B is worthless unless the shares sell for more than the exercise price of the call. Once that point is reached, the portfolio is worth 900 times the excess of the stock price over the exercise price. Finally, portfolio C is worth $8,160 from the investment in T-bills ($8,000 × 1.02 = $8,160) plus any profits from the 100 call options. Remember that each of these portfolios involves the same $9,000 initial investment. The rates of return on these three portfolios are as follows:

	Stock Price					
Portfolio	$85	$90	$95	$100	$105	$110
A: 100 shares stock	−5.56%	0.0%	5.56%	11.11%	16.67%	22.22%
B: 900 call options	−100.0	−100.0	−50.00	0.0	50.0	100.0
C: 100 calls plus $8,000 in T-bills	−9.33	−9.33	−3.78	1.78	7.33	12.89

These rates of return are graphed in Figure 15.5.

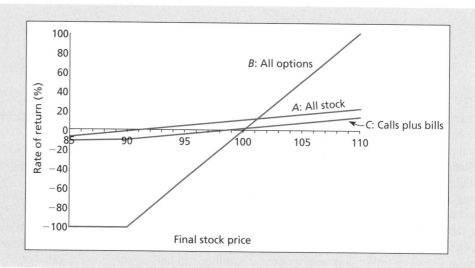

FIGURE 15.5

Rate of return to three strategies

An Excel model based on the Fin Corp example discussed in the text is shown below. The model allows you to use any variety of options, stock, and lending or borrowing with a set investment amount and demonstrates the investment flexibility of options.

eXcel

Please visit us at www.mhhe.com/bkm

	A	B	C	D	E	F	G	H
1	Current stock price	90						
2	Exercise price	90						
3	Interest rate	0.02						
4	Investment budget	9000						
5	Call price	10						
6								
7			Dollar value of portfolio as a function of Fin Corp price					
8	**Portfolio**		$85	$90	$95	$100	$105	$110
9	Portfolio A: All stock		$8,500	$9,000	$9,500	$10,000	$10,500	$11,000
10	Portfolio B: All call options		0	0	4,500	9,000	13,500	18,000
11	Portfolio A: Call plus bills		8,160	8,160	8,660	9,160	9,660	10,160
12								
13								
14			Rate of return as a function of Fin Corp price					
15	**Portfolio**		$85	$90	$95	$100	$105	$110
16	Portfolio A: All stock		-5.6%	0.00%	5.6%	11.1%	16.7%	22.2%
17	Portfolio B: All call options		-100.0%	-100.0%	-50.0%	0.0%	50.0%	100.0%
18	Portfolio A: Call plus bills		-9.33%	-9.33%	-3.78%	1.78%	7.33%	12.89%

Comparing the returns of portfolios *B* and *C* to those of the simple investment in stock represented by portfolio *A,* we see that options offer two interesting features. First, an option offers leverage. Compare the returns of portfolios *B* and *A*. When the stock fares poorly, ending anywhere below $90, the value of portfolio *B* falls precipitously to zero—a rate of return of negative 100%. Conversely, modest increases in the rate of return on the stock result in disproportionate increases in the option rate of return. For example, a 4.8% increase in the stock price from $105 to $110 would increase the rate of return on the call from 50% to 100%. In this sense, calls are a levered investment on the stock. Their values respond more than proportionately to changes in the stock value.

Figure 15.5 vividly illustrates this point. For stock prices above $90, the slope of the all-option portfolio is far steeper than that of the all-stock portfolio, reflecting its greater proportional sensitivity to the value of the underlying security. The leverage factor is the reason that investors (illegally) exploiting inside information commonly choose options as their investment vehicle.

The potential insurance value of options is the second interesting feature, as portfolio *C* shows. The T-bill plus option portfolio cannot be worth less than $8,160 after six months, as the option can always be left to expire worthless. The worst possible rate of return on portfolio *C* is −9.33%, compared to a (theoretically) worst possible rate of return on the stock of −100% if the company were to go bankrupt. Of course, this insurance comes at a price: When the share price increases, portfolio *C* does not perform as well as portfolio *A,* the all-stock portfolio. For stock prices above $90, portfolio *C* underperforms portfolio *A* by about 9.33 percentage points.

This simple example makes an important point. While options can be used by speculators as effectively leveraged stock positions, as in portfolio *B,* they also can be used by investors who desire to tailor their risk exposures in creative ways, as in portfolio *C*. For example, the call plus T-bills strategy of portfolio *C* provides a rate of return profile quite unlike that of the stock alone. The absolute limitation on downside risk is a novel and attractive feature of this strategy. In the next section we will discuss several option strategies that provide other novel risk profiles that might be attractive to hedgers and other investors.

Option Strategies

An unlimited variety of payoff patterns can be achieved by combining puts and calls with various exercise prices. Below we explain the motivation and structure of some of the more popular ones.

protective put

An asset combined with a put option that guarantees minimum proceeds equal to the put's exercise price.

Protective put Imagine you would like to invest in a stock, but you are unwilling to bear potential losses beyond some given level. Investing in the stock alone seems risky to you because in principle you could lose all the money you invest. You might consider instead investing in stock and purchasing a put option on the stock.

Table 15.1 shows the total value of your portfolio at option expiration. Whatever happens to the stock price, you are guaranteed a payoff equal to the put option's exercise price because the put gives you the right to sell the share for the exercise price even if the stock price is below that value.

Figure 15.6 illustrates the payoff and profit to this **protective put** strategy. The solid line in Figure 15.6C is the total payoff. The dashed line is displaced downward by the cost of establishing the position, $S_0 + P$. Notice that potential losses are limited.

EXAMPLE 15.3 *Protective Put*	Suppose the strike price is $X = \$90$ and the stock is selling for $87 at option expiration. Then the value of your total portfolio is $90: The stock is worth $87 and the value of the expiring put option is $$X - S_T = \$90 - \$87 = \$3$$ Another way to look at it is that you are holding the stock and a put contract giving you the right to sell the stock for $90. Even if $S < \$90$, you can still sell the stock for $90 by exercising the put. On the other hand, if the stock price is above $90, say, $94, then the right to sell a share at $90 is worthless. You allow the put to expire unexercised, ending up with a share of stock worth $S_T = \$94$.

It is instructive to compare the profit on the protective put strategy with that of the stock investment. For simplicity, consider an at-the-money protective put, so that $X = S_0$. Figure 15.7 compares the profits for the two strategies. The profit on the stock is zero if the stock price remains unchanged, and $S_T = S_0$. It rises or falls by $1 for every dollar swing in the ultimate stock price. The profit on the protective put is negative and equal to the cost of the put if S_T is below S_0. The profit on the protective put increases one for one with increases in the stock price once the stock price exceeds X.

Figure 15.7 makes it clear that the protective put offers some insurance against stock price declines in that it limits losses. As we shall see in the next chapter, protective put strategies are the conceptual basis for the portfolio insurance industry. The cost of the protection is that, in the case of stock price increases, your profit is reduced by the cost of the put, which turned out to be unneeded.

risk management

Strategies to limit the risk of a portfolio.

This example also shows that despite the common perception that "derivatives mean risk," derivative securities can be used effectively for **risk management.** In fact, such risk management is becoming accepted as part of the fiduciary responsibility of financial managers. Indeed, in a highly cited court case, *Brane* v. *Roth,* a company's board of directors was

TABLE 15.1		$S_T \leq X$	$S_T > X$
Payoff to protective put strategy	Stock	S_T	S_T
	Put	$X - S_T$	0
	Total	X	S_T

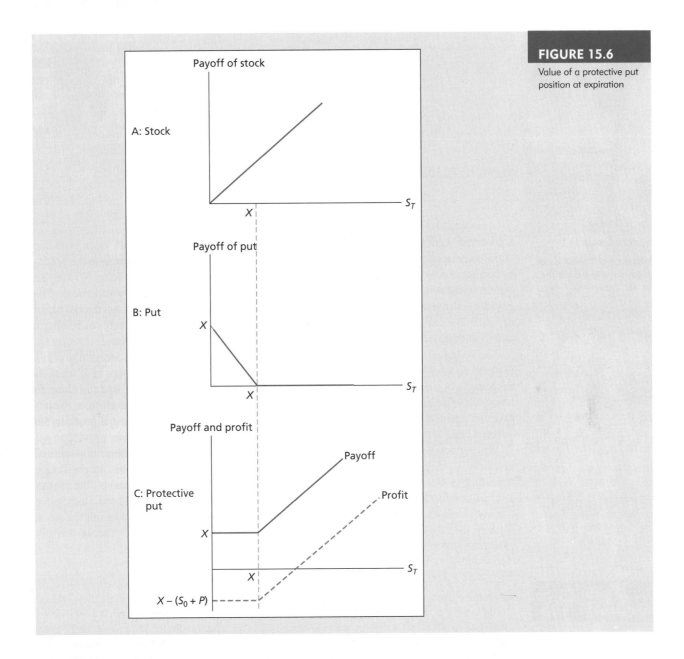

FIGURE 15.6

Value of a protective put position at expiration

successfully sued for failing to use derivatives to hedge the price risk of grain held in storage. Such hedging might have been accomplished using protective puts. Some observers believe that this case will ultimately lead to a broad legal obligation for firms to use derivatives and other techniques to manage risk.

FIGURE 15.7

Protective put versus stock investment (at-the-money put option)

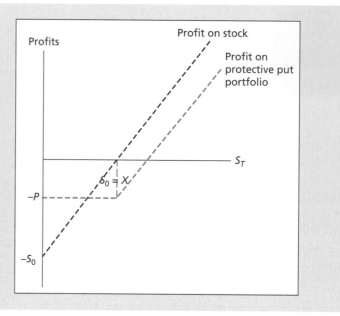

covered call

Writing a call on an asset together with buying the asset.

Covered calls   A **covered call** position is the purchase of a share of stock with the simultaneous sale of a call on that stock. The written option is "covered" because the potential obligation to deliver the stock is covered by the stock held in the portfolio. Writing an option without an offsetting stock position is called by contrast *naked option writing*. The payoff to a covered call, presented in Table 15.2, equals the stock value minus the payoff of the call. The call payoff is subtracted because the covered call position involves issuing a call to another investor who can choose to exercise it to profit at your expense.

The solid line in Figure 15.8C illustrates the payoff pattern. You see that the total position is worth S_T when the stock price at time T is below X and rises to a maximum of X when S_T exceeds X. In essence, the sale of the call option means the call writer has sold the claim to any stock value above X in return for the initial premium (the call price). Therefore, at expiration, the position is worth at most X. The dashed line of Figure 15.8C is the net profit to the covered call.

Writing covered call options has been a popular investment strategy among institutional investors. Consider the managers of a fund invested largely in stocks. They might find it appealing to write calls on some or all of the stock in order to boost income by the premiums collected. Although they thereby forfeit potential capital gains should the stock price rise above the exercise price, if they view X as the price at which they plan to sell the stock anyway, then the call may be viewed as enforcing a kind of "sell discipline." The written call guarantees the stock sale will occur as planned.

EXAMPLE   **15.4**

Covered Call

Assume a pension fund holds 1,000 shares of GXX stock, with a current price of $130 per share. Suppose the portfolio manager intends to sell all 1,000 shares if the share price hits $140, and a call expiring in 90 days with an exercise price of $140 currently sells for $5. By writing 10 GXX call contracts (100 shares each) the fund can pick up $5,000 in extra income. The fund would lose its share of profits from any movement of GXX stock above $140 per share, but given that it would have sold its shares at $140, it would not have realized those profits anyway.

straddle

A combination of a call and a put, each with the same exercise price and expiration date.

Straddle   A long **straddle** is established by buying both a call and a put on a stock, each with the same exercise price, X, and the same expiration date, T. Straddles are useful strategies for investors who believe a stock will move a lot in price but are uncertain about the

TABLE 15.2		$S_T \leq X$	$S_T > X$
Payoff to a covered call	Payoff of stock	S_T	S_T
	−Payoff of call	−0	$-(S_T - X)$
	Total	S_T	X

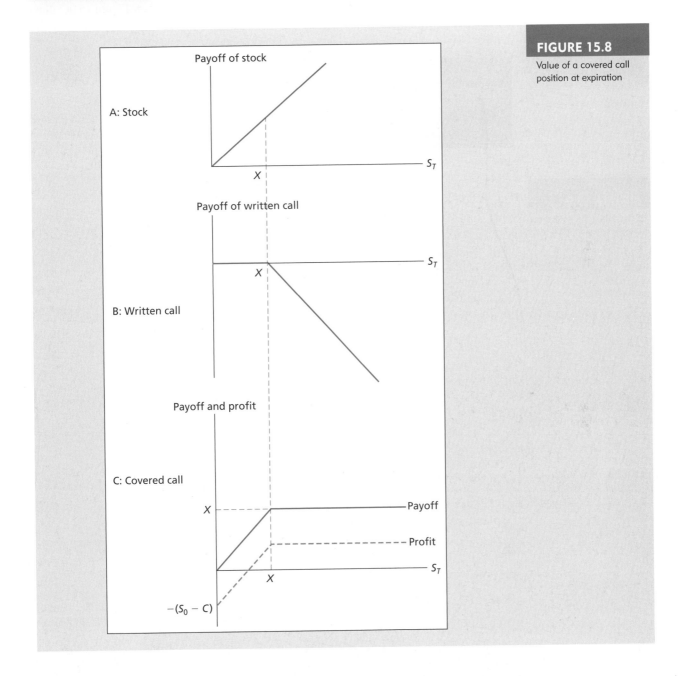

FIGURE 15.8

Value of a covered call position at expiration

direction of the move. For example, suppose you believe an important court case that will make or break a company is about to be settled, and the market is not yet aware of the situation. The stock will either double in value if the case is settled favorably or will drop by half if the settlement goes against the company. The straddle position will do well regardless of the outcome because its value is highest when the stock price makes extreme upward or downward moves from X.

The worst-case scenario for a straddle is no movement in the stock price. If S_T equals X, both the call and the put expire worthless, and the investor's outlay for the purchase of both options is lost. Straddle positions basically are bets on volatility. An investor who establishes a straddle must view the stock as more volatile than the market does. Conversely, investors who *write* straddles—selling both a call and a put—must believe the market is less volatile. They accept the option premiums now, hoping the stock price will not change much before option expiration.

The payoff to a straddle is presented in Table 15.3. The solid line of Figure 15.9C illustrates this payoff. Notice that the portfolio payoff is always positive, except at the one point

TABLE 15.3		$S_T \leq X$	$S_T > X$
Payoff to a straddle	Payoff of call	0	$S_T - X$
	+ Payoff of put	$+(X - S_T)$	$+0$
	Total	$X - S_T$	$S_T - X$

FIGURE 15.9

Payoff and profit to a straddle at expiration

Using spreadsheets to analyze combinations of options is very helpful. Once the basic models are built, it is easy to extend the analysis to different bundles of options. The Excel model "Spreads and Straddles" shown below can be used to evaluate the profitability of different strategies.

Please visit us at www.mhhe.com/bkm

	A	B	C	D	E	F	G	H	I	J	K	L
1					Spreads and Straddles							
2												
3	Stock Prices											
4	Beginning Market Price	116.5						X 110 Straddle			X 120 Straddle	
5	Ending Market Price	130										
6							Ending	Profit		Ending	Profit	
7	Buying Options:						Stock Price	-15.40		Stock Price	-24.00	
8	Call Options Strike	Price	Payoff	Profit	Return %		50	24.60		50	36.00	
9	110	22.80	20.00	-2.80	-12.28%		60	14.60		60	26.00	
10	120	16.80	10.00	-6.80	-40.48%		70	4.60		70	16.00	
11	130	13.60	0.00	-13.60	-100.00%		80	-5.40		80	6.00	
12	140	10.30	0.00	-10.30	-100.00%		90	-15.40		90	-4.00	
13							100	-25.40		100	-14.00	
14	Put Options Strike	Price	Payoff	Profit	Return %		110	-35.40		110	-24.00	
15	110	12.60	0.00	-12.60	-100.00%		120	-25.40		120	-34.00	
16	120	17.20	0.00	-17.20	-100.00%		130	-15.40		130	-24.00	
17	130	23.60	0.00	-23.60	-100.00%		140	-5.40		140	-14.00	
18	140	30.50	10.00	-20.50	-67.21%		150	4.60		150	-4.00	
19							160	14.60		160	6.00	
20	Straddle	Price	Payoff	Profit	Return %		170	24.60		170	16.00	
21	110	35.40	20.00	-15.40	-43.50%		180	34.60		180	26.00	
22	120	34.00	10.00	-24.00	-70.59%		190	44.60		190	36.00	
23	130	37.20	0.00	-37.20	-100.00%		200	54.60		200	46.00	
24	140	40.80	10.00	-30.80	-75.49%		210	64.60		210	56.00	
25												

where the portfolio has zero value, $S_T = X$. You might wonder why all investors don't pursue such a no-lose strategy. To see why, remember that the straddle requires that both the put and the call be purchased. The value of the portfolio at expiration, while never negative, still must exceed the initial cash outlay for a straddle investor to clear a profit.

The dashed line of Figure 15.9C is the profit to the straddle. The profit line lies below the payoff line by the cost of purchasing the straddle, $P + C$. It is clear from the diagram that the straddle position generates a loss unless the stock price deviates substantially from X. The stock price must depart from X by the total amount expended to purchase the call *and* the put in order for the purchaser of the straddle to clear a profit.

Strips and *straps* are variations of straddles. A strip is two puts and one call on a security with the same exercise price and expiration date. A strap is two calls and one put.

Graph the profit and payoff diagrams for strips and straps.

CONCEPT 15.3
check

Spreads   A **spread** is a combination of two or more call options (or two or more puts) on the same stock with differing exercise prices or times to maturity. Some options are bought, while others are sold, or written. A *money spread* involves the purchase of one option and the simultaneous sale of another with a different exercise price. A *time spread* refers to the sale and purchase of options with differing expiration dates.

Consider a money spread in which one call option is bought at an exercise price X_1, while another call with identical expiration date, but higher exercise price, X_2, is written. The payoff

spread

A combination of two or more call options or put options on the same asset with differing exercise prices or times to expiration.

to this position will be the difference in the value of the call held and the value of the call written, as in Table 15.4.

There are now three instead of two outcomes to distinguish: the lowest-price region, where S_T is below both exercise prices; a middle region, where S_T is between the two exercise prices; and a high-price region, where S_T exceeds both exercise prices. Figure 15.10 illustrates the payoff and profit to this strategy, which is called a *bullish spread* because the payoff either increases or is unaffected by stock price increases. Holders of bullish spreads benefit from stock price increases.

One motivation for a bullish spread might be that the investor thinks one option is overpriced relative to another. For example, an investor who believes an $X = \$50$ call is cheap compared to an $X = \$55$ call might establish the spread, even without a strong desire to take a bullish position in the stock.

Collars

collar

An options strategy that brackets the value of a portfolio between two bounds.

A **collar** is an options strategy that brackets the value of a portfolio between two bounds. Suppose that an investor currently is holding a large position in Eagle Corp., which is currently selling at $70 per share. A lower bound of $60 can be placed on the value of the portfolio by buying a protective put with exercise price $60. This protection, however, requires that the investor pay the put premium. To raise the money to pay for the put, the investor might write a call option, say, with exercise price $80. The call might sell for roughly the same price as the put, meaning that the net outlay for the two options positions is approximately zero. Writing the call limits the portfolio's upside potential. Even if the stock price moves above $80, the investor will do no better than $80, because at a higher price the stock will be called away. Thus the investor obtains the downside protection represented by the exercise price of the put by selling her claim to any upside potential beyond the exercise price of the call.

EXAMPLE 15.5

Collars

A collar would be appropriate for an investor who has a target wealth goal in mind but is unwilling to risk losses beyond a certain level. Suppose you are contemplating buying a house for $160,000, for example. You might set this figure as your goal. Your current wealth may be $140,000, and you are unwilling to risk losing more than $20,000. A collar established by (1) purchasing 2,000 shares of stock currently selling at $70 per share, (2) purchasing 2,000 put options (20 option contracts) with exercise price $60, and (3) writing 2,000 calls with exercise price $80 would give you a good chance to realize the $20,000 capital gain without risking a loss of more than $20,000.

CONCEPT check 15.4

Graph the payoff diagram for the collar described in Example 15.5.

WEB *master*

Collar

The CBOE regularly publishes strategies that show how options can be used. An archive of the published strategies can be found at:
www.cboe.com/Strategies/WeeklyArchive.aspx.

1. Select the "zero-cost equity collar" strategy published on April 10, 2006.
2. Explain the motivation behind the strategy.

TABLE 15.4		$S_T \leq X_1$	$X_1 < S_T \leq X_2$	$S_T > X_2$
Payoff to a bullish spread	Payoff of first call, exercise price $= X_1$	0	$S_T - X_1$	$S_T - X_1$
	$-$Payoff of second call; exercise price $= X_2$	-0	-0	$-(S_T - X_2)$
	Total	0	$S_T - X_1$	$X_2 - X_1$

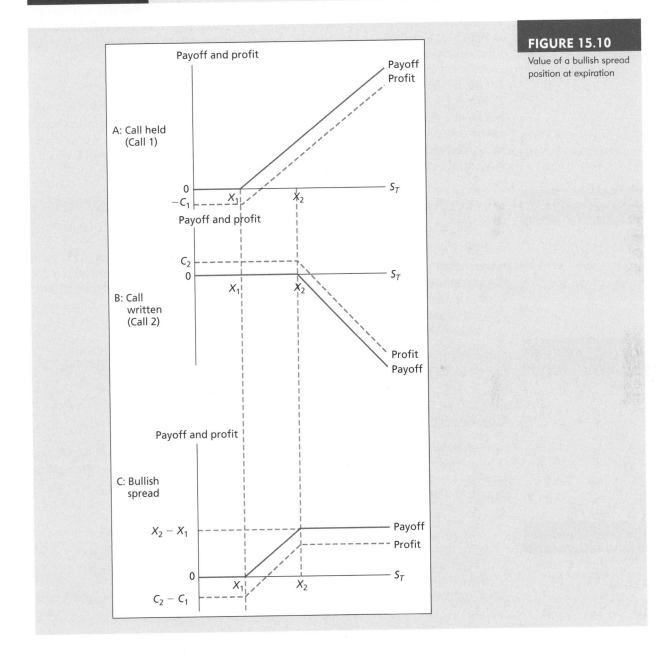

FIGURE 15.10

Value of a bullish spread position at expiration

15.3 OPTIONLIKE SECURITIES

Suppose you never intend to trade an option directly. Why do you need to appreciate the properties of options in formulating an investment plan? Many financial instruments and agreements have features that convey implicit or explicit options to one or more parties. If you are to value and use these securities correctly, you must understand these embedded option attributes.

Callable Bonds

You know from Chapter 10 that many corporate bonds are issued with call provisions entitling the issuer to buy bonds back from bondholders at some time in the future at a specified call price. A call provision conveys a call option to the issuer, where the exercise price is equal to the price at which the bond can be repurchased. A callable bond arrangement is essentially a sale of a *straight bond* (a bond with no option features such as callability or convertibility) to the investor and the concurrent sale of a call option by the investor to the bond-issuing firm.

Investors must receive some compensation for offering this implicit call option. If the callable bond were issued with the same coupon rate as a straight bond, we would expect it to sell at a discount to the straight bond equal to the value of the call. To sell callable bonds at par, firms must issue them with coupon rates higher than the coupons on straight debt. The higher coupons are the investor's compensation for the call option retained by the issuer. Coupon rates usually are selected so that the newly issued bond will sell at par value.

Figure 15.11 illustrates this optionlike property. The horizontal axis is the value of a straight bond with otherwise identical terms as the callable bond. The dashed 45-degree line represents the value of straight debt. The solid line is the value of the callable bond, and the dotted line is the value of the call option retained by the firm. A callable bond's potential for capital gains is limited by the firm's option to repurchase at the call price.

How is a callable bond similar to a covered call strategy on a straight bond?

The option inherent in callable bonds actually is more complex than an ordinary call option because usually it may be exercised only after some initial period of call protection. The price at which the bond is callable may change over time also. Unlike exchange-listed options, these features are defined in the initial bond covenants and will depend on the needs of the issuing firm and its perception of the market's tastes.

Suppose the period of call protection is extended. How will this affect the coupon rate the company needs to offer to enable it to sell the bonds at par value?

Convertible Securities

Convertible bonds and convertible preferred stock convey options to the holder of the security rather than to the issuing firm. A convertible security typically gives its holder the right to exchange each bond or share of preferred stock for a fixed number of shares of common stock, regardless of the market prices of the securities at the time.

FIGURE 15.11

Values of callable bonds compared with straight bonds

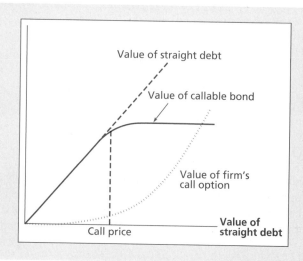

CONCEPT 15.7
check

Should a convertible bond issued at par value have a higher or lower coupon rate than a nonconvertible bond issued at par?

For example, a bond with a conversion ratio of 10 allows its holder to convert one bond of par value $1,000 into 10 shares of common stock. Alternatively, we say the conversion price in this case is $100: To receive 10 shares of stock, the investor sacrifices bonds with face value $1,000 or $100 of face value per share. If the present value of the bond's scheduled payments is less than 10 times the value of one share of stock, it may pay to convert; that is, the conversion option is in the money. A bond worth $950 with a conversion ratio of 10 could be converted profitably if the stock were selling above $95, as the value of the 10 shares received for each bond surrendered would exceed $950. Most convertible bonds are issued "deep out of the money." That is, the issuer sets the conversion ratio so that conversion will not be profitable unless there is a substantial increase in stock prices and/or decrease in bond prices from the time of issue.

A bond's conversion value equals the value it would have if you converted it into stock immediately. Clearly, a bond must sell for at least its conversion value. If it did not, you could purchase the bond, convert it immediately, and clear a riskless profit. This condition could never persist, for all investors would pursue such a strategy and quickly bid up the price of the bond.

The straight bond value or "bond floor" is the value the bond would have if it were not convertible into stock. The bond must sell for more than its straight bond value because a convertible bond has more value; it is in fact a straight bond plus a valuable call option. Therefore, the convertible bond has two lower bounds on its market price: the conversion value and the straight bond value.

Figure 15.12 illustrates the optionlike properties of the convertible bond. Figure 15.12A shows the value of the straight debt as a function of the stock price of the issuing firm. For healthy firms, the straight debt value is almost independent of the value of the stock because default risk is small. However, if the firm is close to bankruptcy (stock prices are low), default risk increases, and the straight bond value falls. Panel B shows the conversion value of the bond. Panel C compares the value of the convertible bond to these two lower bounds.

When stock prices are low, the straight bond value is the effective lower bound, and the conversion option is nearly irrelevant. The convertible will trade like straight debt. When stock prices are high, the bond's price is determined by its conversion value. With conversion all but guaranteed, the bond is essentially equity in disguise.

We can illustrate with two examples.

	Bond A	Bond B
Annual coupon	$80	$80
Maturity date	10 years	10 years
Quality rating	Baa	Baa
Conversion ratio	20	25
Stock price	$30	$50
Conversion value	$600	$1,250
Market yield on 10-year Baa-rated bonds	8.5%	8.5%
Value as straight debt	$967	$967
Actual bond price	$972	$1,255
Reported yield to maturity	8.42%	4.76%

Bond *A* has a conversion value of only $600. Its value as straight debt, in contrast, is $967. This is the present value of the coupon and principal payments at a market rate for straight debt of 8.5%. The bond's price is $972, so the premium over straight bond value is only $5, reflecting the low probability of conversion. Its reported yield to maturity based on scheduled coupon payments and the market price of $972 is 8.42%, close to that of straight debt.

FIGURE 15.12

Value of a convertible bond as a function of stock price

The conversion option on bond *B* is in the money. Conversion value is $1,250, and the bond's price, $1,255, reflects its value as equity (plus $5 for the protection the bond offers against stock price declines). The bond's reported yield is 4.76%, far below the comparable yield on straight debt. The big yield sacrifice is attributable to the far greater value of the conversion option.

In theory, we could value convertible bonds by treating them as straight debt plus call options. In practice, however, this approach is often impractical for several reasons:

1. The conversion price frequently increases over time, which means the exercise price for the option changes.

2. Stocks may pay several dividends over the life of the bond, further complicating the option value analysis.

3. Most convertibles also are callable at the discretion of the firm. In essence, both the investor and the issuer hold options on each other. If the issuer exercises its call option to repurchase the bond, the bondholders typically have a month during which they still can convert. When issuers use a call option, knowing that bondholders will choose to convert, the issuer is said to have *forced a conversion*. These conditions together mean the actual maturity of the bond is indeterminate.

Warrants

Warrants are essentially call options issued by a firm. One important difference between calls and warrants is that exercise of a warrant requires the firm to issue a new share of stock to satisfy its obligation—the total number of shares outstanding increases. Exercise of a call option requires only that the writer of the call deliver an already-issued share of stock to discharge the obligation. In this case, the number of shares outstanding remains fixed. Also unlike call options, warrants result in a cash flow to the firm when the warrant holder pays the exercise price. These differences mean warrant values will differ somewhat from the values of call options with identical terms.

warrant

An option issued by the firm to purchase shares of the firm's stock.

Like convertible debt, warrant terms may be tailored to meet the needs of the firm. Also like convertible debt, warrants generally are protected against stock splits and dividends in that the exercise price and the number of warrants held are adjusted to offset the effects of the split.

Warrants often are issued in conjunction with another security. Bonds, for example, may be packaged together with a warrant "sweetener," frequently a warrant that may be sold separately. This is called a *detachable warrant*.

Issues of warrants and convertible securities create the potential for an increase in outstanding shares of stock if exercise occurs. Exercise obviously would affect financial statistics that are computed on a per-share basis, so annual reports must provide earnings per share figures under the assumption that all convertible securities and warrants are exercised. These figures are called *fully diluted earnings per share.*[3]

Collateralized Loans

Many loan arrangements require that the borrower put up collateral to guarantee the loan will be paid back. In the event of default, the lender takes possession of the collateral. A nonrecourse loan gives the lender no recourse beyond the right to the collateral. That is, the lender may not sue the borrower for further payment if the collateral turns out not to be valuable enough to repay the loan.[4]

This arrangement gives an implicit call option to the borrower. Assume the borrower is obligated to pay back L dollars at the maturity of the loan. The collateral will be worth S_T dollars at maturity. (Its value today is S_0.) The borrower has the option to wait until loan maturity and repay the loan only if the collateral is worth more than the L dollars necessary to satisfy the loan. If the collateral is worth less than L, the borrower can default on the loan, discharging the obligation by forfeiting the collateral, which is worth only S_T.

Another way of describing such a loan is to view the borrower as turning over collateral to the lender but retaining the right to reclaim it by paying off the loan. The transfer of the collateral with the right to reclaim it is equivalent to a payment of S_0 dollars, less a simultaneous recovery of a sum that resembles a call option with exercise price L. In effect, the borrower turns over collateral, but keeps an option to "repurchase" it for L dollars at the maturity of the loan if L turns out to be less than S_T. This is a call option.

A third way to look at a collaterized loan is to assume the borrower will repay the L dollars with certainty but also retain the option to sell the collateral to the lender for L dollars, even if S_T is less than L. In this case, the sale of the collateral would generate the cash necessary to satisfy the loan. The ability to "sell" the collateral for a price of L dollars represents a put option, which guarantees the borrower can raise enough money to satisfy the loan simply by turning over the collateral.

---

[3]We should note that the exercise of a convertible bond need not reduce earnings per share (EPS). Diluted EPS will be less than undiluted EPS only if interest saved (per share) on the converted bonds is less than the prior EPS.

[4]In reality, of course, defaulting on a loan is not so simple. Losses of reputation are involved as well as considerations of ethical behavior. This is a description of a pure nonrecourse loan where both parties agree from the outset that only the collateral backs the loan and that default is not to be taken as a sign of bad faith if the collateral is insufficient to repay the loan.

Figure 15.13 illustrates these interpretations. Figure 15.13A is the value of the payment to be received by the lender, which equals the minimum of S_T or L. Panel B shows that this amount can be expressed as S_T minus the payoff of the call implicitly written by the lender and held by the borrower. Panel C shows it also can be viewed as a receipt of L dollars minus the proceeds of a put option.

Levered Equity and Risky Debt

Investors holding stock in incorporated firms are protected by limited liability, which means that if the firm cannot pay its debts, the firm's creditors may attach only the firm's assets and may not sue the corporation's equityholders for further payment. In effect, any time the corporation borrows money, the maximum possible collateral for the loan is the total of the firm's assets. If the firm declares bankruptcy, we can interpret this as an admission that the assets of the firm are insufficient to satisfy the claims against it. The corporation may discharge its obligations by transferring ownership of the firm's assets to the creditors.

FIGURE 15.13

Collateralized loan

(A) Payoff to collateralized loan.

(B) Lender can be viewed as collecting the collateral from the borrower, but issuing an option to the borrower to call back the collateral for the face value of the loan.

(C) Lender can be viewed as collecting a risk-free loan from the borrower, but issuing a put to the borrower to sell the collateral for the face value of the loan.

(A) When S_T exceeds L, the loan is repaid and the collateral is reclaimed. Otherwise, the collateral is forfeited and the total loan repayment is worth only S_T.

(B) Payoff to call with exercise price L / S_T dollars minus the payoff to the implicit call option

(C) Payoff to a put with exercise price L / L dollars minus the payoff to the implicit put option

Just as is true for nonrecourse collateralized loans, the required payment to the creditors represents the exercise price of the implicit option, while the value of the firm is the underlying asset. The equityholders have a put option to transfer their ownership claims on the firm to the creditors in return for the face value of the firm's debt.

Alternatively, we may view the equityholders as retaining a call option. They have, in effect, already transferred their ownership claim to the firm to the creditors but have retained the right to reacquire the ownership claim by paying off the loan. Hence, the equityholders have the option to "buy back" the firm for a specified price, or they have a call option.

The significance of this observation is that analysts can value corporate bonds using option-pricing techniques. The default premium required of risky debt in principle can be estimated using option valuation models. We will consider some of these models in the next chapter.

15.4   EXOTIC OPTIONS

Investors clearly value the portfolio strategies made possible by trading options; this is reflected in the heavy trading volume in these markets and their tremendous success. Success breeds imitation, and in recent years we have witnessed tremendous innovation in the range of option instruments available to investors. Part of this innovation has occurred in the market for customized options, which now trade in active over-the-counter markets. Many of these options have terms that would have been highly unusual even a few years ago; they therefore are called "exotic options." In this section, we will survey some of the more interesting variants of these new instruments.

Asian Options

You already have been introduced to American and European options. *Asian options* are options with payoffs that depend on the average (rather than final) price of the underlying asset during at least some portion of the life of the option. For example, an Asian call option may have a payoff equal to the average stock price over the last three months minus the exercise price, if that value is positive, or zero. These options may be of interest to firms that wish to hedge a profit stream that depends on the average price of a commodity over some period of time.

Barrier Options

Barrier options have payoffs that depend not only on some asset price at option expiration but also on whether the underlying asset price has crossed through some "barrier." For example, a *down-and-out option* is one type of barrier option that automatically expires worthless if and when the stock price falls below some barrier price. Similarly, *down-and-in options* will not provide a payoff unless the stock price *does* fall below some barrier at least once during the life of the option. These options also are referred to as knock-out and knock-in options.

Lookback Options

Lookback options have payoffs that depend in part on the minimum or maximum price of the underlying asset during the life of the option. For example, a lookback call option might provide a payoff equal to the maximum stock price during the life of the option minus the exercise price, as opposed to the *closing* stock price minus the exercise price. Such an option provides (at a price, of course) a form of perfect market timing, providing the call holder with a payoff equal to the one that would accrue if the asset were purchased for X dollars and later sold at what turns out to be its highest price.

Currency-Translated Options

Currency-translated options have either asset or exercise prices denominated in a foreign currency. A good example of such an option is the *quanto,* which allows an investor to fix in advance the exchange rate at which an investment in a foreign currency can be converted back into dollars. The right to translate a fixed amount of foreign currency into dollars at a given exchange

On the MARKET FRONT

ECONOMIC DERIVATIVES MARKETS

In 2005, the Chicago Mercantile Exchange initiated auction markets in several macroeconomic variables, including U.S. Gross Domestic Product, U.S. nonfarm payrolls, the European Consumer Price Index, and several other variables. Traders can buy or sell either digital or conventional options on these series.

Suppose a trader is optimistic about job growth, and therefore considers buying a call option on growth in nonfarm payrolls (NFP) with a strike (exercise) price of 125,000 jobs. The conventional or "vanilla" version of the option pays out $100 for every job created in excess of 125,000. The trader may also purchase a digital version of the call. For example, a $100,000 digital call option with strike price equal to 125,000 jobs will pay off $100,000 if job growth exceeds 125,000. Either call will expire worthless if job creation is below 125,000.

These new contracts offer traders the opportunity to take positions—either for hedging or speculation—on each traded macroeconomic variable. They also provide a new opportunity to gauge the expectations of other market participants.

Table 15.5 shows the prices on March 23, 2006, of digital calls on the change in initial jobless claims. For example, one would pay $.9550 for an option that will pay off $1 if jobless claims are above 280,000, or $.9124 for an option that will pay off $1 if jobless claims are above 285,000. If you were to *buy* the 280,000 strike option and *write* the 285,000 strike option, your net expenditure would be $.9550 − $.9124 = $.0426, and you would receive a net cash flow of $1 only if jobless claims are between 280,000 and 285,000. (If claims are below 280,000, both options expire out of the money; if claims are above 285,000, both options expire in the money, and the net cash flow from your long/short position is zero.) We conclude that the market views the probability that jobless claims will be in this interval as approximately .0426, or 4.26%.*

Using the full set of option prices in Table 15.5, we can create the entire probability distribution for future jobless claims shown in Figure 15.14. The frequency distribution implies that the expected value for claims is 305,000. Moreover, the dispersion of the distribution indicates the uncertainty surrounding these market forecasts. These markets thus give investors a good sense of (the market's assessment of) the distribution of possible outcomes for a range of macroeconomic variables.

TABLE 15.5

Prices of digital options on initial jobless claims

Strike (thousands of claims)	Call Option Price ($ per dollar payoff)	Strike (thousands of claims)	Call Option Price ($ per dollar payoff)
280	0.9550	310	0.3700
285	0.9124	315	0.2297
290	0.8544	320	0.1498
295	0.7870	325	0.0876
300	0.6801	330	0.0450
305	0.5295		

Note: Strike price is in thousands of claims. Call option pays off $1 if actual claims exceed strike price and zero otherwise.

Source: Chicago Mercantile Exchange: prices as of March 23, 2006.

*We say "approximately" because the probabilities may be affected by risk premia. However, early evidence on these contracts suggests that the impact of risk premia on these implied probabilities seems to be small. See R. S. Gürkaynak and J. Wolfers, "Macroeconomic Derivatives: An Initial Analysis of Market-Based Macro Forecasts, Uncertainty, and Risk," NBER Working Paper No. 11929 (January 2006).

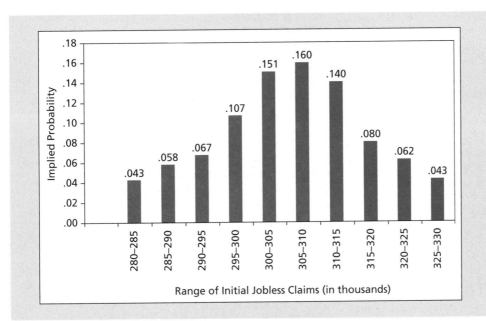

FIGURE 15.14

Implied probability of jobless claims derived from traded digital options

Source: Data collected from **auctions.cme.com.** Prices as of March 23, 2006.

rate is a simple foreign exchange option. Quantos are more interesting, however, because the amount of currency that will be translated into dollars depends on the investment performance of the foreign security. Therefore, a quanto in effect provides a *random number* of options.

Digital Options

Digital options, also called *binary* or "bet" options, have fixed payoffs that depend on whether a condition is satisfied by the price of the underlying asset. For example, a binary call option might pay off a fixed amount of $100 if the stock price at maturity exceeds the exercise price.

The Chicago Mercantile Exchange now offers opportunities to trade digital options on various macroeconomic indicators. This gives traders the opportunity to either hedge or tailor their exposure to a variety of economic variables. Digital options (as well as more conventional options) currently trade on variables including gross domestic product, the U.S. balance of trade, jobless claims, nonfarm payrolls, and inflation. See the nearby box for more discussion of these options.

SUMMARY

- A call option is the right to buy an asset at an agreed-upon exercise price. A put option is the right to sell an asset at a given exercise price.
- American-style options allow exercise on or before the exercise date. European-style options allow exercise only on the expiration date. Most traded options are American in nature.
- Options are traded on stocks, stock indexes, foreign currencies, fixed-income securities, and several futures contracts.
- Options can be used either to lever up an investor's exposure to an asset price or to provide insurance against volatility of asset prices. Popular option strategies include covered calls, protective puts, straddles, and spreads.
- Many commonly traded securities embody option characteristics. Examples of these securities are callable bonds, convertible bonds, and warrants. Other arrangements, such as collateralized loans and limited-liability borrowing, can be analyzed as conveying implicit options to one or more parties.

KEY TERMS

American option, 484
at the money, 482
call option, 481
collar, 498
covered call, 494
European option, 484

exercise price, 481
in the money, 482
out of the money, 482
premium, 481
protective put, 492
put option, 482

risk management, 492
spread, 497
straddle, 494
strike price, 481
warrant, 503

PROBLEM SETS

 **Select problems are available in McGraw-Hill's Homework Manager®.
Please see the packaging options section of the preface for more information.**

CFA®
PROBLEMS

1. Which one of the following statements about the value of a call option at expiration is *false*?
   a. A short position in a call option will result in a loss if the stock price exceeds the exercise price.
   b. The value of a long position equals zero or the stock price minus the exercise price, whichever is higher.
   c. The value of a long position equals zero or the exercise price minus the stock price, whichever is higher.
   d. A short position in a call option has a zero value for all stock prices equal to or less than the exercise price.

2. The following diagram shows the value of a put option at expiration:

Ignoring transaction costs, which of the following statements about the value of the put option at expiration is *true*?
   a. The value of the short position in the put is $4 if the stock price is $76.
   b. The value of the long position in the put is −$4 if the stock price is $76.
   c. The long put has value when the stock price is below the $80 exercise price.
   d. The value of the short position in the put is zero for stock prices equaling or exceeding $76.

3. The following price quotations are for exchange-listed options on Primo Corporation common stock.

Company	Strike	Expiration	Call	Put
Primo 61.12	55	Feb	7.25	.48

With transaction costs ignored, how much would a buyer have to pay for one call option contract?

4. Turn back to Figure 15.1, which lists the prices of various IBM options. Use the data in the figure to calculate the payoff and the profits for investments in each of the

following July maturity options, assuming that the stock price on the maturity date is $90.

a. Call option, $X = 85$

b. Put option, $X = 85$

c. Call option, $X = 90$

d. Put option, $X = 90$

e. Call option, $X = 95$

f. Put option, $X = 95$

5. Suppose you think Wal-Mart stock is going to appreciate substantially in value in the next year. Say the stock's current price, S_0, is $100, and the call option expiring in one year has an exercise price, X, of $100 and is selling at a price, C, of $10. With $10,000 to invest, you are considering three alternatives:

a. Invest all $10,000 in the stock, buying 100 shares.

b. Invest all $10,000 in 1,000 options (10 contracts).

c. Buy 100 options (one contract) for $1,000 and invest the remaining $9,000 in a money market fund paying 4% interest annually.

What is your rate of return for each alternative for four stock prices one year from now? Summarize your results in the table and diagram below.

RATE OF RETURN ON INVESTMENT			
	Price of Stock 1 Year from Now		
	$80	$100	$110	$120
a. All stocks (100 shares)				
b. All options (1,000 shares)				
c. Bills + 100 options				

6. The common stock of the P.U.T.T. Corporation has been trading in a narrow price range for the past month, and you are convinced it is going to break far out of that range in the next three months. You do not know whether it will go up or down, however. The current price of the stock is $100 per share, the price of a three-month call option with an exercise price of $100 is $10, and a put with the same expiration date and exercise price costs $7.

a. What would be a simple options strategy to exploit your conviction about the stock price's future movements?

b. How far would the price have to move in either direction for you to make a profit on your initial investment?

7. The common stock of the C.A.L.L. Corporation has been trading in a narrow range around $50 per share for months, and you believe it is going to stay in that range for the next three months. The price of a three-month put option with an exercise price of $50 is $4, and a call with the same expiration date and exercise price sells for $7.

a. What would be a simple options strategy using a put and a call to exploit your conviction about the stock price's future movement?

b. What is the most money you can make on this position? How far can the stock price move in either direction before you lose money?

c. How can you create a position involving a put, a call, and riskless lending that would have the same payoff structure as the stock at expiration? The stock will pay no dividends in the next three months. What is the net cost of establishing that position now?

8. Joseph Jones, a manager at Computer Science, Inc. (CSI), received 10,000 shares of company stock as part of his compensation package. The stock currently sells at $40 a share. Joseph would like to defer selling the stock until the next tax year. In January, however, he will need to sell all his holdings to provide for a down payment on his new house. Joseph is worried about the price risk involved in keeping his shares. At current prices, he would receive $40,000 for the stock. If the value of his stock holdings falls below $35,000, his ability to come up with the necessary down payment would be jeopardized. On the other hand, if the stock value rises to $45,000, he would be able to maintain a small cash reserve even after making the down payment. Joseph considers three investment strategies:

   a. Strategy A is to write January call options on the CSI shares with strike price $45. These calls are currently selling for $3 each.

   b. Strategy B is to buy January put options on CSI with strike price $35. These options also sell for $3 each.

   c. Strategy C is to establish a zero-cost collar by writing the January calls and buying the January puts.

   Evaluate each of these strategies with respect to Joseph's investment goals. What are the advantages and disadvantages of each? Which would you recommend?

9. a. A butterfly spread is the purchase of one call at exercise price X_1, the sale of two calls at exercise price X_2, and the purchase of one call at exercise price X_3. X_1 is less than X_2, and X_2 is less than X_3 by equal amounts, and all calls have the same expiration date. Graph the payoff diagram to this strategy.

   b. A vertical combination is the purchase of a call with exercise price X_2 and a put with exercise price X_1, with X_2 greater than X_1. Graph the payoff to this strategy.

10. A bearish spread is the purchase of a call with exercise price X_2 and the sale of a call with exercise price X_1, with X_2 greater than X_1. Graph the payoff to this strategy and compare it to Figure 15.10.

11. You are attempting to formulate an investment strategy. On the one hand, you think there is great upward potential in the stock market and would like to participate in the upward move if it materializes. However, you are not able to afford substantial stock market losses and so cannot run the risk of a stock market collapse, which you also think is a possibility. Your investment adviser suggests a protective put position: Buy shares in a market index stock fund *and* put options on those shares with three-months until expiration and exercise price of $1,040. The stock index is currently at $1,200. However, your uncle suggests you instead buy a three-month call option on the index fund with exercise price $1,120 and buy three-month T-bills with face value $1,120.

   a. On the same graph, draw the *payoffs* to each of these strategies as a function of the stock fund value in three months. (Hint: Think of the options as being on one "share" of the stock index fund, with the current price of each share of the index equal to $1,200.)

   b. Which portfolio must require a greater initial outlay to establish? (Hint: Does either portfolio provide a final payoff that is always at least as great as the payoff of the other portfolio?)

   c. Suppose the market prices of the securities are as follows.

Stock fund	$1,200
T-bill (face value $1,120)	1,080
Call (exercise price $1,120)	160
Put (exercise price $1,040)	8

   Make a table of profits realized for each portfolio for the following values of the stock price in three months: $S_T =$ $0, $1,040, $1,120, $1,200, and $1,280. Graph the profits to each portfolio as a function of S_T on a single graph.

   d. Which strategy is riskier? Which should have a higher beta?

Please visit us at
www.mhhe.com/bkm

12. Use the spreadsheet from the Excel Application boxes on spreads and straddles (available at **www.mhhe.com/bkm;** link to Chapter 15 material) to answer these questions.
    a. Plot the payoff and profit diagrams to a straddle position with an exercise (strike) price of $130. Assume the options are priced as they are in the Excel Application.
    b. Plot the payoff and profit diagrams to a spread position with exercise (strike) prices of $120 and $130. Assume the options are priced as they are in the Excel Application.

13. The agricultural price support system guarantees farmers a minimum price for their output. Describe the program provisions as an option. What is the asset? The exercise price?

14. In what ways is owning a corporate bond similar to writing a put option? A call option?

15. Donna Donie, CFA, has a client who believes the common stock price of TRT Materials (currently $58 per share) could move substantially in either direction in reaction to an expected court decision involving the company. The client currently owns no TRT shares, but asks Donie for advice about implementing a strangle strategy to capitalize on the possible stock price movement. A strangle is a portfolio of a put and a call with different exercise prices but the same expiration date. Donie gathers the following TRT option price data:

Characteristic	Call Option	Put Option
Price	$ 5	$ 4
Strike Price	$60	$55
Time to expiration	90 days from now	90 days from now

    a. Recommend whether Donie should choose a long strangle strategy or a short strangle strategy to achieve the client's objective.
    b. Calculate, at expiration for the appropriate strangle strategy in part (*a*), the:
        i. Maximum possible loss per share.
        ii. Maximum possible gain per share.
        iii. Break-even stock price(s).

16. An executive compensation scheme might provide a manager a bonus of $1,000 for every dollar by which the company's stock price exceeds some cutoff level. In what way is this arrangement equivalent to issuing the manager call options on the firm's stock?

17. Consider the following options portfolio. You write a July 2007 expiration call option on IBM with exercise price $90. You also write a July expiration IBM put option with exercise price $85.
    a. Graph the payoff of this portfolio at option expiration as a function of IBM's stock price at that time.
    b. What will be the profit/loss on this position if IBM is selling at $87 on the option maturity date? What if IBM is selling at $95? Use *The Wall Street Journal* listing from Figure 15.1 to answer this question.
    c. At what two stock prices will you just break even on your investment?
    d. What kind of "bet" is this investor making; that is, what must this investor believe about IBM's stock price in order to justify this position?

18. A member of an investment committee, interested in learning more about fixed-income investment procedures, recalls that a fixed-income manager recently stated that derivative instruments could be used to control portfolio duration, saying "a futures-like position can be created in a portfolio by using put and call options on Treasury bonds."
    a. Identify the options market exposure or exposures that create a "futures-like position" similar to being long Treasury bond futures. Explain why the position you created is similar to being long Treasury bond futures.
    b. Explain in which direction and why the exposure(s) you identified in part (*a*) would affect portfolio duration.
    c. Assume that a pension plan's investment policy requires the fixed-income manager to hold portfolio duration within a narrow range. Identify and briefly explain circumstances or transactions in which the use of Treasury bond futures would be helpful in managing a fixed-income portfolio when duration is constrained.

19. Consider the following portfolio. You *write* a put option with exercise price $90 and *buy* a put with the same maturity date with exercise price $95.
    a. Plot the value of the portfolio at the expiration date of the options.
    b. On the same graph, plot the profit of the portfolio. Which option must cost more?

20. A put option with strike price $60 trading on the Acme options exchange sells for $2. To your amazement, a put on the firm with the same expiration selling on the Apex options exchange but with strike price $62 also sells for $2. If you plan to hold the options position until expiration, devise a zero-net-investment arbitrage strategy to exploit the pricing anomaly. Draw the profit diagram at expiration for your position.

21. You buy a share of stock, write a one-year call option with $X = \$10$, and buy a one-year put option with $X = \$10$. Your net outlay to establish the entire portfolio is $9.50. What must be the risk-free interest rate? The stock pays no dividends.

22. Suresh Singh, CFA, is analyzing a convertible bond. The characteristics of the bond and the underlying common stock are given in the following exhibit:

Convertible Bond Characteristics	
Par value	$1,000
Annual coupon rate (annual pay)	6.5%
Conversion ratio	22
Market price	105% of par value
Straight value	99% of par value
Underlying Stock Characteristics	
Current market price	$40 per share
Annual cash dividend	$1.20 per share

Compute the bond's:
a. Conversion value.
b. Market conversion price.

23. Rich McDonald, CFA, is evaluating his investment alternatives in Ytel Incorporated by analyzing a Ytel convertible bond and Ytel common equity. Characteristics of the two securities are given in the following exhibit:

Characteristics	Convertible Bond	Common Equity
Par value	$1,000	—
Coupon (annual payment)	4%	—
Current market price	$980	$35 per share
Straight bond value	$925	—
Conversion ratio	25	—
Conversion option	At any time	—
Dividend	—	$0
Expected market price in 1 year	$1,125	$45 per share

a. Calculate, based on the exhibit, the:
    i. Current market conversion price for the Ytel convertible bond.
    ii. Expected one-year rate of return for the Ytel convertible bond.
    iii. Expected one-year rate of return for the Ytel common equity.

One year has passed and Ytel's common equity price has increased to $51 per share. Also, over the year, the yield to maturity on Ytel's nonconvertible bonds of the same maturity increased, while credit spreads remained unchanged.

b. Name the two components of the convertible bond's value. Indicate whether the value of each component should decrease, stay the same, or increase in response to the:
    i. Increase in Ytel's common equity price.
    ii. Increase in bond yield.

24. Joe Finance has just purchased a stock index fund, currently selling at $1,200 per share. To protect against losses, Joe plans to purchase an at-the-money European put option on the fund for $60, with exercise price $1,200, and three-month time to expiration. Sally Calm, Joe's financial adviser, points out that Joe is spending a lot of money on the put. She notes that three-month puts with strike prices of $1,170 cost only $45, and suggests that Joe use the cheaper put.

   a. Analyze Joe's and Sally's strategies by drawing the *profit* diagrams for the stock-plus-put positions for various values of the stock fund in three months.

   b. When does Sally's strategy do better? When does it do worse?

   c. Which strategy entails greater systematic risk?

25. You write a call option with $X = \$50$ and buy a call with $X = \$60$. The options are on the same stock and have the same expiration date. One of the calls sells for $3; the other sells for $9.

   a. Draw the *payoff* graph for this strategy at the option expiration date.

   b. Draw the *profit* graph for this strategy.

   c. What is the break-even point for this strategy? Is the investor bullish or bearish on the stock?

26. Devise a portfolio using only call options and shares of stock with the following value (payoff) at the option expiration date. If the stock price is currently $53, what kind of bet is the investor making?

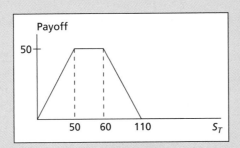

Use data from the Standard & Poor's Market Insight Database at www.mhhe.com/edumarketinsight to answer the following questions.

STANDARD & POOR'S

1. On the Company page, enter stock symbol GE for General Electric. Go to the S&P Stock Reports section for GE.

   a. Scroll down to Key Stock Statistics and locate the 52-week range for GE.

   b. Now go to Yahoo! Finance (**finance.yahoo.com**) and enter stock symbol GE. At what price did GE last trade?

   c. Click on the link to Options on the left side of the Yahoo! Finance screen. Choose an expiration date three months in the future, and then choose one of the call options listed by selecting an exercise (strike) price. What is the last price (premium) shown for the call option?

   d. Is the call option in the money?

   e. Draw a graph that shows the payoff and the profit to the holder of this call option over a range of prices, including the prices you found in the 52-week range of the S&P Stock Report.

   f. Repeat the steps for a put option on GE with the same expiration date and the same strike price.

2. Select ten firms that interest you from the Market Insight population. For each firm, open the S&P Recommendation. Based on this information, if you had to choose between buying a put option or a call option on the stock, which would you choose? Under the lower right corner of the Price Performance chart, check to see if there are options available on the stock and, if so, where they trade.

WEB *master*

Options and Straddles

Go to **www.nasdaq.com** and select IBM in the quote section. Once you have the information quote, request the information on options. You will be able to access the prices for the calls and puts that are closest to the money. For example, if the price of IBM is $86.40, you will use the options with the $85 exercise price. Use near-term options. For example, in February, you would select April and July expirations.

1. What are the prices for the put and call with the nearest expiration date?

2. What would be the cost of a straddle using these options?

3. At expiration, what would be the break-even stock prices for the straddle?

4. What would be the percentage increase or decrease in the stock price required to break even?

5. What are the prices for the put and call with a later expiration date?

6. What would be the cost of a straddle using the later expiration date? At expiration, what would be the break-even stock prices for the straddle?

7. What would be the percentage increase or decrease in the stock price required to break even?

SOLUTIONS TO
CONCEPT
c h e c k s

15.1. *a.* Proceeds $= S_T - X = S_T - \$90$ if this value is positive; otherwise, the call expires worthless.
Profit $=$ Proceeds $-$ Price of call option $=$ Proceeds $- \$3.78$.

	$S_T = \$80$	$S_T = \$100$
Proceeds	$0	$10
Profits	−3.78	6.22

b. Proceeds $= X - S_T = \$90 - S_T$ if this value is positive; otherwise, the put expires worthless.
Profit $=$ Proceeds $-$ Price of put option $=$ Proceeds $- \$2.10$.

	$S_T = \$80$	$S_T = \$100$
Proceeds	$10	$0
Profits	7.90	−2.10

15.2. *a.*

b. The payoffs and profits to both buying calls and writing puts generally are higher when the stock price is higher. In this sense, both positions are bullish. Both involve potentially taking delivery of the stock. However, the call holder will *choose* to take delivery when the stock price is high, while the put writer *is obligated* to take delivery when the stock price is low.

c. The payoffs and profits to both writing calls and buying puts generally are higher when the stock price is lower. In this sense, both positions are bearish. Both involve potentially making delivery of the stock. However, the put holder will *choose* to make delivery when the stock price is low, while the call writer *is obligated* to make delivery when the stock price is high.

PAYOFF TO A STRIP

	$S_T \leq X$	$S_T > X$
2 Puts	$2(X - S_T)$	0
1 Call	0	$S_T - X$

15.3.

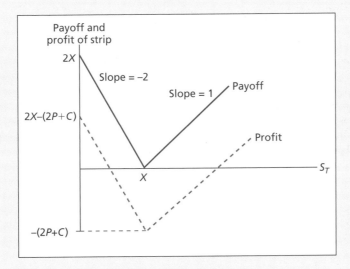

PAYOFF TO A STRAP

	$S_T \leq X$	$S_T > X$
1 Put	$X - S_T$	0
2 Calls	0	$2(S_T - X)$

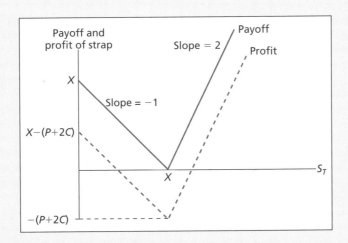

15.4. The payoff table on a per-share basis is as follows:

	$S_T < 60$	$60 < S_T < 80$	$S_T > 80$
Buy put ($X = 60$)	$60 - S_T$	0	0
Share	S_T	S_T	S_T
Write call ($X = 80$)	0	0	$-(S_T - 80)$
Total	60	S_T	80

The graph of the payoff follows. If you multiply the per-share values by 2,000, you will see that the collar provides a minimum payoff of $120,000 (representing a maximum loss of $20,000) and a maximum payoff of $160,000 (which is the cost of the house).

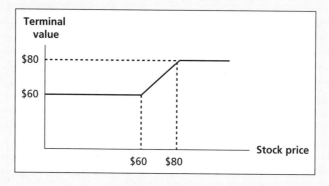

15.5. The covered call strategy would consist of a straight bond with a call written on the bond. The payoff value of the covered call position at option expiration as a function of the value of the straight bond is given in the following figure, and is virtually identical to the value of the callable bond in Figure 15.11.

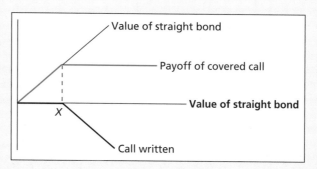

15.6. The call option is less valuable as call protection is expanded. Therefore, the coupon rate need not be as high.

15.7. Lower. Investors will accept a lower coupon rate in return for the conversion option.

Option Valuation

CHAPTER

16

AFTER STUDYING THIS CHAPTER YOU SHOULD BE ABLE TO:

Identify the features of an option that affect its market value.

Compute an option value in a two-scenario model of the economy.

Compute the Black-Scholes value and implied volatility of an option.

Compute the proper relationship between call and put prices.

Compute the hedge ratio of an option.

Formulate a portfolio insurance plan using option hedge ratios.

I n the previous chapter, we examined option markets and strategies. We ended by noting that many securities contain embedded options that affect both their values and their risk-return characteristics. In this chapter, we turn our attention to option valuation issues. Understanding most option valuation models requires considerable mathematical and statistical background. Still, many of the ideas and insights of these models can be demonstrated in simple examples, and we will concentrate on these.

We start with a discussion of the factors that ought to affect option prices. After this qualitative discussion, we present a simple "two-state" quantitative option valuation model and show how we can generalize it into a useful and accurate pricing tool. Next, we move on to one particular option valuation formula, the famous Black-Scholes model. Option pricing models allow us to "back out" market estimates of stock-price volatility, and we will examine these estimates of implied volatility. Next we turn to some of the more important applications of

(continued)

Related Web sites
for this chapter
are available at
www.mhhe.com/bkm.

option pricing theory in risk management. Finally, we take a brief look at some of the empirical evidence on option pricing, and the implications of that evidence concerning the limitations of the Black-Scholes model.

16.1 OPTION VALUATION: INTRODUCTION

Intrinsic and Time Values

Consider a call option that is out of the money at the moment, with the stock price below the exercise price. This does not mean the option is valueless. Even though immediate exercise would be unprofitable, the call retains a positive value because there is always a chance the stock price will increase sufficiently by the expiration date to allow for profitable exercise. If not, the worst that can happen is that the option will expire with zero value.

intrinsic value

Stock price minus exercise price, or the profit that could be attained by immediate exercise of an in-the-money call option.

time value

Difference between an option's price and its intrinsic value.

The value $S_0 - X$ is sometimes called the **intrinsic value** of an in-the-money call option because it gives the payoff that could be obtained by immediate exercise. Intrinsic value is set equal to zero for out-of-the-money or at-the-money options. The difference between the actual call price and the intrinsic value is commonly called the **time value** of the option.

Time value is an unfortunate choice of terminology because it may confuse the option's time value with the time value of money. Time value in the options context simply refers to the difference between the option's price and the value the option would have if it were expiring immediately. It is the part of the option's value that may be attributed to the fact that it still has positive time to expiration.

Most of an option's time value typically is a type of "volatility value." As long as the option holder can choose not to exercise, the payoff cannot be worse than zero. Even if a call option is out of the money now, it still will sell for a positive price because it offers the potential for a profit if the stock price increases, while imposing no risk of additional loss should the stock price fall. The volatility value lies in the right *not* to exercise the option if that action would be unprofitable. The option to exercise, as opposed to the obligation to exercise, provides insurance against poor stock price performance.

As the stock price increases substantially, it becomes more likely that the call option will be exercised by expiration. In this case, with exercise all but assured, the volatility value becomes minimal. As the stock price gets ever larger, the option value approaches the "adjusted" intrinsic value—the stock price minus the present value of the exercise price, $S_0 - PV(X)$.

Why should this be? If you *know* the option will be exercised and the stock purchased for X dollars, it is as though you own the stock already. The stock certificate might as well be sitting in your safe-deposit box now, as it will be there in only a few months. You just haven't paid for it yet. The present value of your obligation is the present value of X, so the present value of the net payoff of the call option is $S_0 - PV(X)$.[1]

Figure 16.1 illustrates the call option valuation function. The value curve shows that when the stock price is low, the option is nearly worthless because there is almost no chance that it will be exercised. When the stock price is very high, the option value approaches adjusted intrinsic value. In the midrange case, where the option is approximately at the money, the option curve diverges from the straight lines corresponding to adjusted intrinsic value. This is because, while exercise today would have a negligible (or negative) payoff,

---

[1]This discussion presumes the stock pays no dividends until after option expiration. If the stock does pay dividends before maturity, then there *is* a reason you would care about getting the stock now rather than at expiration—getting it now entitles you to the interim dividend payments. In this case, the adjusted intrinsic value of the option must subtract the value of the dividends the stock will pay out before the call is exercised. Adjusted intrinsic value would more generally be defined as $S_0 - PV(X) - PV(D)$, where D represents dividends to be paid before option expiration.

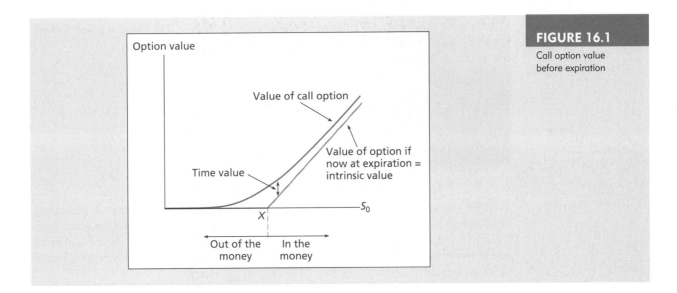

FIGURE 16.1

Call option value
before expiration

the volatility value of the option is quite high in this region. The option always increases in value with the stock price. The slope is greatest, however, when the option is deep in the money. In this case, exercise is all but assured, and the option increases in price one-for-one with the stock price.

Determinants of Option Values

We can identify at least six factors that should affect the value of a call option: the stock price, the exercise price, the volatility of the stock price, the time to expiration, the interest rate, and the dividend rate of the stock. The call option should increase in value with the stock price and decrease in value with the exercise price because the payoff to a call, if exercised, equals $S_T - X$. The magnitude of the expected payoff from the call increases with the difference $S_0 - X$.

Call option value also increases with the volatility of the underlying stock price. To see why, consider circumstances where possible stock prices at expiration may range from $10 to $50 compared to a situation where stock prices may range only from $20 to $40. In both cases, the expected, or average, stock price will be $30. Suppose the exercise price on a call option is also $30. What are the option payoffs?

High-Volatility Scenario					
Stock price	$10	$20	$30	$40	$50
Option payoff	0	0	0	10	20

Low-Volatility Scenario					
Stock price	$20	$25	$30	$35	$40
Option payoff	0	0	0	5	10

If each outcome is equally likely, with probability 0.2, the expected payoff to the option under high-volatility conditions will be $6, but under the low-volatility conditions, the expected payoff to the call option is half as much, only $3.

Despite the fact that the average stock price in each scenario is $30, the average option payoff is greater in the high-volatility scenario. The source of this extra value is the limited loss an option holder can suffer, or the volatility value of the call. No matter how far below $30 the stock price drops, the option holder will get zero. Obviously, extremely poor stock price performance is no worse for the call option holder than moderately poor performance.

TABLE 16.1	**If This Variable Increases**	**The Value of a Call Option**
Determinants of call option values	Stock price, S	Increases
	Exercise price, X	Decreases
	Volatility, σ	Increases
	Time to expiration, T	Increases
	Interest rate, r_f	Increases
	Dividend payouts	Decreases

In the case of good stock performance, however, the call option will expire in the money, and it will be more profitable the higher the stock price. Thus, extremely good stock outcomes can improve the option payoff without limit, but extremely poor outcomes cannot worsen the payoff below zero. This asymmetry means volatility in the underlying stock price increases the expected payoff to the option, thereby enhancing its value.[2]

CONCEPT **16.1**
c h e c k

Should a put option increase in value with the volatility of the stock?

Similarly, longer time to expiration increases the value of a call option. For more distant expiration dates, there is more time for unpredictable future events to affect prices, and the range of likely stock prices increases. This has an effect similar to that of increased volatility. Moreover, as time to expiration lengthens, the present value of the exercise price falls, thereby benefiting the call option holder and increasing the option value. As a corollary to this issue, call option values are higher when interest rates rise (holding the stock price constant), because higher interest rates also reduce the present value of the exercise price.

Finally, the dividend payout policy of the firm affects option values. A high dividend payout policy puts a drag on the rate of growth of the stock price. For any expected total rate of return on the stock, a higher dividend yield must imply a lower expected rate of capital gain. This drag on stock appreciation decreases the potential payoff from the call option, thereby lowering the call value. Table 16.1 summarizes these relationships.

CONCEPT **16.2**
c h e c k

Prepare a table like Table 16.1 for the determinants of put option values. How should put values respond to increases in S, X, T, σ, r_f, and dividend payout?

16.2 | BINOMIAL OPTION PRICING

Two-State Option Pricing

A complete understanding of commonly used option valuation formulas is difficult without a substantial mathematics background. Nevertheless, we can develop valuable insight into option valuation by considering a simple special case. Assume a stock price can take only two possible values at option expiration: The stock will either increase to a given higher price or

---

[2]You should be careful interpreting the relationship between volatility and option value. Neither the focus of this analysis on total (as opposed to systematic) volatility, nor the conclusion that options buyers seem to like volatility, contradicts modern portfolio theory. In conventional discounted cash flow analysis, we find the discount rate appropriate for a *given* distribution of future cash flows. Greater risk implies a higher discount rate and lower present value. Here, however, the cash flow from the *option* depends on the volatility of the *stock*. The option value increases not because traders like risk but because the expected cash flow to the option holder increases along with the volatility of the underlying asset.

Show that the initial value of the call option in Example 16.1 is $4.434.
a. Confirm that the spread in option values is $C_u - C_d = \$6.984$.
b. Confirm that the spread in stock values is $uS_0 - dS_0 = \$15$.
c. Confirm that the hedge ratio is .4656 shares purchased for each call written.
d. Demonstrate that the value in one period of a portfolio comprising .4656 shares and one call written is riskless.
e. Calculate the present value of this payoff.
f. Solve for the option value.

As we break the year into progressively finer subintervals, the range of possible year-end stock prices expands and, in fact, will ultimately take on a familiar bell-shaped distribution. This can be seen from an analysis of the event tree for the stock for a period with three subintervals.

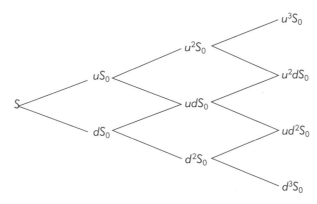

First, notice that as the number of subintervals increases, the number of possible stock prices also increases. Second, notice that extreme events such as u^3S_0 or d^3S_0 are relatively rare, as they require either three consecutive increases or decreases in the three subintervals. More moderate, or midrange, results such as u^2dS_0 can be arrived at by more than one path; any combination of two price increases and one decrease will result in stock price u^2dS_0. Thus, the midrange values will be more likely. The probability of each outcome is described by the binomial distribution, and this multiperiod approach to option pricing is called the **binomial model**.

For example, using an initial stock price of $100, equal probability of stock price increases or decreases, and three intervals for which the possible price increase is 5% and the decrease is 3%, we can obtain the probability distribution of stock prices from the following calculations. There are eight possible combinations for the stock price movement in the three periods: *uuu, uud, udu, duu, udd, dud, ddu, ddd.* Each has a probability of ⅛. Therefore, the probability distribution of stock prices at the end of the last interval would be as follows.

binomial model

An option valuation model predicated on the assumption that stock prices can move to only two values over any short time period.

Event	Probability	Final Stock Price	
3 up movements	⅛	$100 × 1.05³	= $115.76
2 up and 1 down	⅜	$100 × 1.05² × 0.97	= $106.94
1 up and 2 down	⅜	$100 × 1.05 × 0.97²	= $ 98.79
3 down movements	⅛	$100 × 0.97³	= $ 91.27

The midrange values are three times as likely to occur as the extreme values. Figure 16.2A is a graph of the frequency distribution for this example. The graph begins to exhibit the appearance of the familiar bell-shaped curve. In fact, as the number of intervals increases, as

FIGURE 16.2

Probability distributions

A. Possible outcomes and associated probabilities for stock prices after three periods. The stock price starts at $100, and in each period it can increase by 5% or decrease by 3%.

B. Each period is subdivided into two smaller subperiods. Now there are six periods, and in each of these the stock price can increase by 2.5% or fall by 1.5%. As the number of periods increases, the stock price distribution approaches the familiar bell-shaped curve.

in Figure 16.2B, the frequency distribution progressively approaches the lognormal distribution rather than the normal distribution.[3]

Suppose we were to continue subdividing the interval in which stock prices are posited to move up or down. Eventually, each node of the event tree would correspond to an infinitesimally small time interval. The possible stock price movement within that time interval would be correspondingly small. As those many intervals passed, the end-of-period stock price would more and more closely resemble a lognormal distribution. Thus, the apparent oversimplification of the two-state model can be overcome by progressively subdividing any period into many subperiods.

At any node, one still could set up a portfolio that would be perfectly hedged over the next tiny time interval. Then, at the end of that interval, on reaching the next node, a new hedge ratio could be computed and the portfolio composition could be revised to remain hedged over the coming small interval. By continuously revising the hedge position, the portfolio would remain hedged and would earn a riskless rate of return over each interval. This is called *dynamic hedging,* the continued updating of the hedge ratio as time passes. As the dynamic hedge becomes ever finer, the resulting option valuation procedure becomes more precise.

CONCEPT *check* **16.5**   Would you expect the hedge ratio to be higher or lower when the call option is more in the money?

16.3 BLACK-SCHOLES OPTION VALUATION

While the binomial model we have described is extremely flexible, it requires a computer to be useful in actual trading. An option-pricing *formula* would be far easier to use than the tedious algorithm involved in the binomial model. It turns out that such a formula can be

---

[3]Actually, more complex considerations enter here. The limit of this process is lognormal only if we assume also that stock prices move continuously, by which we mean that over small time intervals only small price movements can occur. This rules out rare events such as sudden, extreme price moves in response to dramatic information (like a takeover attempt). For a treatment of this type of "jump process," see John C. Cox and Stephen A. Ross, "The Valuation of Options for Alternative Stochastic Processes," *Journal of Financial Economics* 3 (January–March 1976), pp. 145–66; or Robert C. Merton, "Option Pricing When Underlying Stock Returns Are Discontinuous," *Journal of Financial Economics* 3 (January–March 1976), pp. 125–44.

derived if one is willing to make just two more assumptions: that both the risk-free interest rate and stock price volatility are constant over the life of the option. In this case, as the time to expiration is divided into ever more subperiods, the distribution of the stock price at expiration progressively approaches the lognormal distribution, as suggested by Figure 16.2. When the stock price distribution is actually lognormal, we can derive an exact option-pricing formula.

The Black-Scholes Formula

Financial economists searched for years for a workable option-pricing model before Black and Scholes (1973) and Merton (1973) derived a formula for the value of a call option. Now widely used by options market participants, the **Black-Scholes pricing formula** for a European-style call option is

$$C_0 = S_0 e^{-\delta T} N(d_1) - X e^{-rT} N(d_2)$$ **(16.1)**

where

$$d_1 = \frac{\ln(S_0/X) + (r - \delta + \sigma^2/2)T}{\sigma\sqrt{T}}$$

$$d_2 = d_1 - \sigma\sqrt{T}$$

and where

- C_0 = Current call option value.
- S_0 = Current stock price.
- $N(d)$ = The probability that a random draw from a standard normal distribution will be less than d. This equals the area under the normal curve up to d, as in the shaded area of Figure 16.3. In Excel, this function is called NORMSDIST( ).
- X = Exercise price.
- e = The base of the natural log function, approximately 2.71828. In Excel, e^x can be evaluated using the function EXP(x).
- δ = Annual dividend yield of underlying stock. (We assume for simplicity that the stock pays a continuous income flow, rather than discrete periodic payments, such as quarterly dividends.)

Black-Scholes pricing formula

A formula to value an option that uses the stock price, the risk-free interest rate, the time to maturity, and the standard deviation of the stock return.

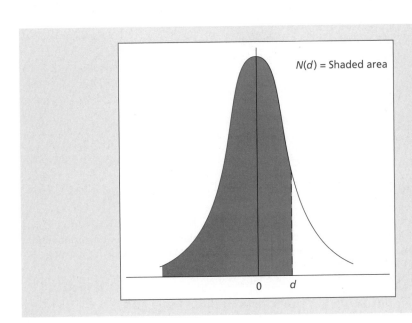

FIGURE 16.3

A standard normal curve

$N(d)$ = Shaded area

r = Risk-free interest rate, expressed as a decimal (the annualized continuously compounded rate[4] on a safe asset with the same maturity as the expiration date of the option, which is to be distinguished from r_f, the discrete period interest rate).

T = Time remaining until expiration of option (in years).

ln = Natural logarithm function. In Excel, $\ln(x)$ can be calculated as LN(x).

σ = Standard deviation of the annualized continuously compounded rate of return of the stock, expressed as a decimal, not a percent.

Notice a surprising feature of Equation 16.1: The option value does not depend on the expected rate of return on the stock. In a sense, this information is already built into the formula with inclusion of the stock price, which itself depends on the stock's risk and return characteristics. This version of the Black-Scholes formula is predicated on the assumption that the underlying asset has a constant dividend (or income) yield.

Although you may find the Black-Scholes formula intimidating, we can explain it at a somewhat intuitive level. Consider a nondividend paying stock, for which $\delta = 0$. Then $S_0 e^{-\delta T} = S_0$.

The trick is to view the $N(d)$ terms (loosely) as risk-adjusted probabilities that the call option will expire in the money. First, look at Equation 16.1 assuming both $N(d)$ terms are close to 1.0; that is, when there is a very high probability that the option will be exercised. Then the call option value is equal to $S_0 - Xe^{-rT}$, which is what we called earlier the adjusted intrinsic value, $S_0 - \text{PV}(X)$. This makes sense; if exercise is certain, we have a claim on a stock with current value S_0 and an obligation with present value $\text{PV}(X)$, or with continuous compounding, Xe^{-rT}.

Now look at Equation 16.1, assuming the $N(d)$ terms are close to zero, meaning the option almost certainly will not be exercised. Then the equation confirms that the call is worth nothing. For middle-range values of $N(d)$ between 0 and 1, Equation 16.1 tells us that the call value can be viewed as the present value of the call's potential payoff adjusting for the probability of in-the-money expiration.

How do the $N(d)$ terms serve as risk-adjusted probabilities? This question quickly leads us into advanced statistics. Notice, however, that d_1 and d_2 both increase as the stock price increases. Therefore, $N(d_1)$ and $N(d_2)$ also increase with higher stock prices. This is the property we would desire of our "probabilities." For higher stock prices relative to exercise prices, future exercise is more likely.

| EXAMPLE 16.2 | You can use the Black-Scholes formula fairly easily. Suppose you want to value a call option under the following circumstances: |

Black-Scholes Call Option Valuation

Stock price	$S_0 = 100$
Exercise price	$X = 95$
Interest rate	$r = 0.10$
Dividend yield	$\delta = 0$
Time to expiration	$T = 0.25$ (one-quarter year)
Standard deviation	$\sigma = 0.50$

First calculate

$$d_1 = \frac{\ln(100/95) + (0.10 - 0 + 0.5^2/2)0.25}{0.5\sqrt{0.25}} = 0.43$$

$$d_2 = 0.43 - 0.5\sqrt{0.25} = 0.18$$

Next find $N(d_1)$ and $N(d_2)$. The normal distribution function is tabulated and may be found in many statistics textbooks. A table of $N(d)$ is provided as Table 16.2. The normal distribution function $N(d)$ is also provided in any spreadsheet program. In Microsoft Excel, for example,

---

[4]See Chapter 5, Section 5.1, for a review of continuous compounding.

the function name is NORMSDIST. Using either Excel or Table 16.2 (using interpolation for 0.43), we find that

$$N(0.43) = 0.6664$$
$$N(0.18) = 0.5714$$

Finally, remember that with $\delta = 0$, $S_0 e^{-\delta T} = S_0$. Thus, the value of the call option is

$$C = 100 \times 0.6664 - 95e^{-0.10 \times 0.25} \times 0.5714$$
$$= 66.64 - 52.94 = \$13.70$$

Calculate the call option value if the standard deviation on the stock is 0.6 instead of 0.5. Confirm that the option is worth more using this higher volatility.

CONCEPT *check* **16.6**

What if the option price in Example 16.2 were $15 rather than $13.70? Is the option mispriced? Maybe, but before betting your career on that, you may want to reconsider the valuation analysis. First, like all models, the Black-Scholes formula is based on some simplifying abstractions that make the formula only approximately valid.

Some of the important assumptions underlying the formula are the following:

1. The stock will pay a constant, continuous dividend yield until the option expiration date.
2. Both the interest rate, r, and variance rate, σ^2, of the stock are constant (or in slightly more general versions of the formula, both are *known* functions of time—any changes are perfectly predictable).
3. Stock prices are continuous, meaning that sudden extreme jumps, such as those in the aftermath of an announcement of a takeover attempt, are ruled out.

Variants of the Black-Scholes formula have been developed to deal with many of these limitations.

Second, even within the context of the Black-Scholes model, you must be sure of the accuracy of the parameters used in the formula. Four of these—S_0, X, T, and r—are straightforward. The stock price, exercise price, and time to maturity are readily determined. The interest rate used is the money market rate for a maturity equal to that of the option, and the dividend yield is usually reasonably stable, at least over short horizons.

The last input, though, the standard deviation of the stock return, is not directly observable. It must be estimated from historical data, from scenario analysis, or from the prices of other options, as we will describe momentarily. Because the standard deviation must be estimated, it is always possible that discrepancies between an option price and its Black-Scholes value are simply artifacts of error in the estimation of the stock's volatility.

WEB *master*

Implied Volatility

Calculating implied volatility can be difficult if you don't have a spreadsheet handy. Fortunately, many tools are available to perform the calculation; **www.numa.com** contains an option calculator that also computes implied volatility.

Using daily price data, calculate the annualized standard deviation of the daily percentage change in a stock price. For the same stock, use **www.numa.com** to find the implied volatility. Option price data can be retrieved from **www.cboe.com**.

Recalculate the standard deviation using 3 months, 6 months, and 9 months of daily data. Which of the calculations most closely approximates implied volatility? What time frame does the market seem to use for assessing stock price volatility?

TABLE 16.2	d	N(d)	d	N(d)	d	N(d)
Cumulative normal distribution	−3.00	0.0013	−1.58	0.0571	−0.76	0.2236
	−2.95	0.0016	−1.56	0.0594	−0.74	0.2297
	−2.90	0.0019	−1.54	0.0618	−0.72	0.2358
	−2.85	0.0022	−1.52	0.0643	−0.70	0.2420
	−2.80	0.0026	−1.50	0.0668	−0.68	0.2483
	−2.75	0.0030	−1.48	0.0694	−0.66	0.2546
	−2.70	0.0035	−1.46	0.0721	−0.64	0.2611
	−2.65	0.0040	−1.44	0.0749	−0.62	0.2676
	−2.60	0.0047	−1.42	0.0778	−0.60	0.2743
	−2.55	0.0054	−1.40	0.0808	−0.58	0.2810
	−2.50	0.0062	−1.38	0.0838	−0.56	0.2877
	−2.45	0.0071	−1.36	0.0869	−0.54	0.2946
	−2.40	0.0082	−1.34	0.0901	−0.52	0.3015
	−2.35	0.0094	−1.32	0.0934	−0.50	0.3085
	−2.30	0.0107	−1.30	0.0968	−0.48	0.3156
	−2.25	0.0122	−1.28	0.1003	−0.46	0.3228
	−2.20	0.0139	−1.26	0.1038	−0.44	0.3300
	−2.15	0.0158	−1.24	0.1075	−0.42	0.3373
	−2.10	0.0179	−1.22	0.1112	−0.40	0.3446
	−2.05	0.0202	−1.20	0.1151	−0.38	0.3520
	−2.00	0.0228	−1.18	0.1190	−0.36	0.3594
	−1.98	0.0239	−1.16	0.1230	−0.34	0.3669
	−1.96	0.0250	−1.14	0.1271	−0.32	0.3745
	−1.94	0.0262	−1.12	0.1314	−0.30	0.3821
	−1.92	0.0274	−1.10	0.1357	−0.28	0.3897
	−1.90	0.0287	−1.08	0.1401	−0.26	0.3974
	−1.88	0.0301	−1.06	0.1446	−0.24	0.4052
	−1.86	0.0314	−1.04	0.1492	−0.22	0.4129
	−1.84	0.0329	−1.02	0.1539	−0.20	0.4207
	−1.82	0.0344	−1.00	0.1587	−0.18	0.4286
	−1.80	0.0359	−0.98	0.1635	−0.16	0.4365
	−1.78	0.0375	−0.96	0.1685	−0.14	0.4443
	−1.76	0.0392	−0.94	0.1736	−0.12	0.4523
	−1.74	0.0409	−0.92	0.1788	−0.10	0.4602
	−1.72	0.0427	−0.90	0.1841	−0.08	0.4681
	−1.70	0.0446	−0.88	0.1894	−0.06	0.4761
	−1.68	0.0465	−0.86	0.1949	−0.04	0.4841
	−1.66	0.0485	−0.84	0.2005	−0.02	0.4920
	−1.64	0.0505	−0.82	0.2061	0.00	0.5000
	−1.62	0.0526	−0.80	0.2119	0.02	0.5080
	−1.60	0.0548	−0.78	0.2177	0.04	0.5160

implied volatility

The standard deviation of stock returns that is consistent with an option's market value.

In fact, market participants often give the option valuation problem a different twist. Rather than calculating a Black-Scholes option value for a given stock standard deviation, they ask instead: What standard deviation would be necessary for the option price that I actually observe to be consistent with the Black-Scholes formula? This is called the **implied volatility** of the option, the volatility level for the stock that the option price implies. Investors can then judge whether they think the actual stock standard deviation exceeds the implied volatility. If it does, the option is considered a good buy; if actual volatility seems greater than the implied volatility, the option's fair price would exceed the observed price.

Another variation is to compare two options on the same stock with equal expiration dates but different exercise prices. The option with the higher implied volatility would be considered relatively expensive because a higher standard deviation is required to justify its price. The analyst might consider buying the option with the lower implied volatility and writing the option with the higher implied volatility.

TABLE 16.2	d	N(d)	d	N(d)	d	N(d)
(concluded)	0.06	0.5239	0.86	0.8051	1.66	0.9515
	0.08	0.5319	0.88	0.8106	1.68	0.9535
	0.10	0.5398	0.90	0.8159	1.70	0.9554
	0.12	0.5478	0.92	0.8212	1.72	0.9573
	0.14	0.5557	0.94	0.8264	1.74	0.9591
	0.16	0.5636	0.96	0.8315	1.76	0.9608
	0.18	0.5714	0.98	0.8365	1.78	0.9625
	0.20	0.5793	1.00	0.8414	1.80	0.9641
	0.22	0.5871	1.02	0.8461	1.82	0.9656
	0.24	0.5948	1.04	0.8508	1.84	0.9671
	0.26	0.6026	1.06	0.8554	1.86	0.9686
	0.28	0.6103	1.08	0.8599	1.88	0.9699
	0.30	0.6179	1.10	0.8643	1.90	0.9713
	0.32	0.6255	1.12	0.8686	1.92	0.9726
	0.34	0.6331	1.14	0.8729	1.94	0.9738
	0.36	0.6406	1.16	0.8770	1.96	0.9750
	0.38	0.6480	1.18	0.8810	1.98	0.9761
	0.40	0.6554	1.20	0.8849	2.00	0.9772
	0.42	0.6628	1.22	0.8888	2.05	0.9798
	0.44	0.6700	1.24	0.8925	2.10	0.9821
	0.46	0.6773	1.26	0.8962	2.15	0.9842
	0.48	0.6844	1.28	0.8997	2.20	0.9861
	0.50	0.6915	1.30	0.9032	2.25	0.9878
	0.52	0.6985	1.32	0.9066	2.30	0.9893
	0.54	0.7054	1.34	0.9099	2.35	0.9906
	0.56	0.7123	1.36	0.9131	2.40	0.9918
	0.58	0.7191	1.38	0.9162	2.45	0.9929
	0.60	0.7258	1.40	0.9192	2.50	0.9938
	0.62	0.7324	1.42	0.9222	2.55	0.9946
	0.64	0.7389	1.44	0.9251	2.60	0.9953
	0.66	0.7454	1.46	0.9279	2.65	0.9960
	0.68	0.7518	1.48	0.9306	2.70	0.9965
	0.70	0.7580	1.50	0.9332	2.75	0.9970
	0.72	0.7642	1.52	0.9357	2.80	0.9974
	0.74	0.7704	1.54	0.9382	2.85	0.9978
	0.76	0.7764	1.56	0.9406	2.90	0.9981
	0.78	0.7823	1.58	0.9429	2.95	0.9984
	0.80	0.7882	1.60	0.9452	3.00	0.9986
	0.82	0.7939	1.62	0.9474	3.05	0.9989
	0.84	0.7996	1.64	0.9495		

The Black-Scholes call-option valuation formula, as well as implied volatilities, are easily calculated using an Excel spreadsheet, as in Spreadsheet 16.1. The model inputs are provided in column B, and the outputs are given in column E. The formulas for d_1 and d_2 are provided in the spreadsheet, and the Excel formula NORMSDIST(d_1) is used to calculate $N(d_1)$. Cell E6 contains the Black-Scholes call option formula.

To compute an implied volatility, we can use the Goal Seek command from the Tools menu in Excel. (See Figure 16.4 for an illustration.) Goal Seek asks us to change the value of one cell to make the value of another cell (called the target cell) equal to a specific value. For example, if we observe a call option selling for $7 with other inputs as given in the spreadsheet, we can use Goal Seek to change the value in cell B2 (the standard deviation of the stock) to set the option value in cell E6 equal to $7. The target cell, E6, is the call price, and the spreadsheet manipulates cell B2. When you click "OK," the spreadsheet finds that a standard deviation equal to .2783 is consistent with a call price of $7; therefore, 27.83% would be the call's implied volatility if it were selling at $7.

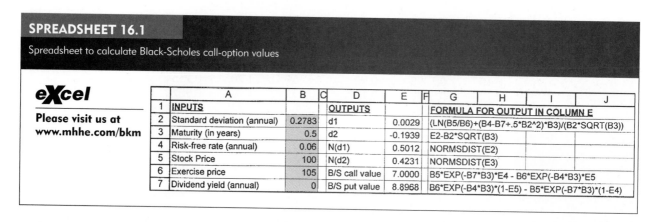

SPREADSHEET 16.1

Spreadsheet to calculate Black-Scholes call-option values

	A	B	C	D	E	F	G	H	I	J
1	INPUTS			OUTPUTS			FORMULA FOR OUTPUT IN COLUMN E			
2	Standard deviation (annual)	0.2783		d1	0.0029		(LN(B5/B6)+(B4-B7+.5*B2^2)*B3)/(B2*SQRT(B3))			
3	Maturity (in years)	0.5		d2	-0.1939		E2-B2*SQRT(B3)			
4	Risk-free rate (annual)	0.06		N(d1)	0.5012		NORMSDIST(E2)			
5	Stock Price	100		N(d2)	0.4231		NORMSDIST(E3)			
6	Exercise price	105		B/S call value	7.0000		B5*EXP(-B7*B3)*E4 - B6*EXP(-B4*B3)*E5			
7	Dividend yield (annual)	0		B/S put value	8.8968		B6*EXP(-B4*B3)*(1-E5) - B5*EXP(-B7*B3)*(1-E4)			

Please visit us at
www.mhhe.com/bkm

CONCEPT 16.7
check

Consider the call option in Example 16.2. If it sells for $15 rather than the value of $13.70 found in the example, is its implied volatility more or less than 0.5? Use Spreadsheet 16.1 (available at the Online Learning Center) to find its implied volatility at this price.

The Chicago Board Options Exchange regularly computes the implied volatility of major stock indexes. Figure 16.5 is a graph of the implied (30-day) volatility of the S&P 500. During periods of turmoil, implied volatility can spike quickly. Notice the peaks in January 1991 (Gulf War), in August 1998 (collapse of Long-Term Capital Management), on September 11, 2001, and in 2002 (buildup to invasion of Iraq). Because implied volatility correlates with crisis, it is sometimes called an "investor fear gauge."

In March 2004, a futures contract on the 30-day implied volatility of the S&P 500 began trading on the CBOE Futures Exchange. The payoff of the contract depends on market implied volatility at the expiration of the contract. The ticker symbol of the contract is VIX.

Figure 16.5 also reveals an awkward empirical fact. While the Black-Scholes formula is derived assuming that stock volatility is constant, the time series of implied volatilities

	A	B	C	D	E	F	G	H	I	J	K
1	INPUTS			OUTPUTS			FORMULA FOR OUTPUT IN COLUMN E				
2	Standard deviation (annual)	0.2783		d1	0.0029		(LN(B5/B6)+(B4-B7+.5*B2^2)*B3)/(B2*SQRT(B3))				
3	Maturity (in years)	0.5		d2	-0.1939		E2-B2*SQRT(B3)				
4	Risk-free rate (annual)	0.06		N(d1)	0.5012		NORMSDIST(E2)				
5	Stock price	100		N(d2)	0.4231		NORMSDIST(E3)				
6	Exercise price	105		B/S call value	7.0000		B5*EXP(-B7*B3)*E4-B6*EXP(-B4*B3)*E5				
7	Dividend yield (annual)	0		B/S Put value	8.8968		B6*EXP(-B4*B3)*(1-E5) - B5*EXP(-B7*B3)*(1-E4)				
8											
9											
10											
11											
12											
13											
14											
15											
16											
17											

Goal Seek

Set cell: $E$6

To value: 7

By changing cell: $B$2

OK   Cancel

FIGURE 16.4

Using Goal Seek to find implied volatility

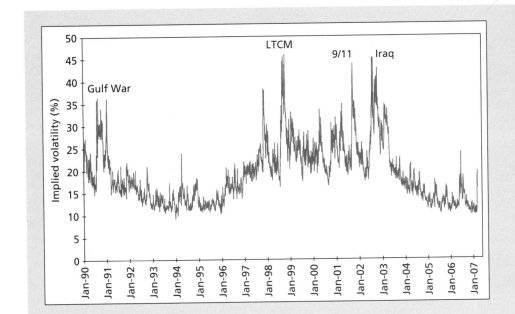

FIGURE 16.5

Implied volatility of the S&P 500 (VIX index)

Source: Chicago Board Options Exchange.

consistent with that formula is in fact far from constant. This contradiction reminds us that the Black-Scholes model (like all models) is a simplification that does not capture all aspects of real markets. In this particular context, extensions of the pricing model that allow stock volatility to evolve randomly over time would be desirable, and in fact, many extensions of the model along these lines have been suggested.[5]

The fact that volatility changes unpredictably means that it can be difficult to choose the proper volatility input to use in any option-pricing model. A considerable amount of recent research has been devoted to techniques to predict changes in volatility. These techniques, which go by the name ARCH and stochastic volatility models, posit that changes in volatility are partially predictable and that by analyzing recent levels and trends in volatility, one can improve predictions of future volatility.[6]

The Put-Call Parity Relationship

So far, we have focused on the pricing of call options. In many important cases, put prices can be derived simply from the prices of calls. This is because prices of European put and call options are linked together in an equation known as the put-call parity relationship. Therefore, once you know the value of a call, put pricing is easy.

To derive the parity relationship, suppose you buy a call option and write a put option, each with the same exercise price, X, and the same expiration date, T. At expiration, the payoff on your investment will equal the payoff to the call, minus the payoff that must be made on the put. The payoff for each option will depend on whether the ultimate stock price, S_T, exceeds the exercise price at contract expiration.

	$S_T \leq X$	$S_T > X$
Payoff of call held	0	$S_T - X$
− Payoff of put written	$-(X - S_T)$	0
Total	$S_T - X$	$S_T - X$

[5]Influential articles on this topic are Hull and White (1987), Wiggins (1987), and Heston (1993). For a more recent review, see Ghysels, Harvey, and Renault (1996).
[6]For an introduction to these models see Alexander (2001).

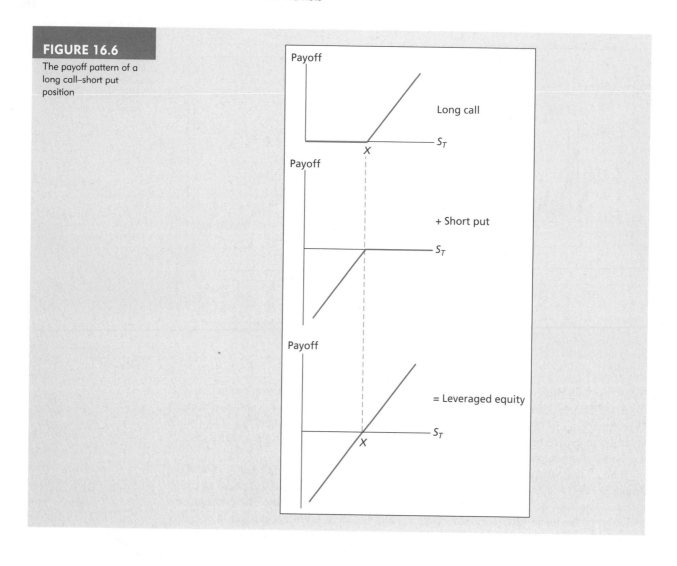

FIGURE 16.6

The payoff pattern of a long call–short put position

Figure 16.6 illustrates this payoff pattern. Compare the payoff to that of a portfolio made up of the stock plus a borrowing position, where the money to be paid back will grow, with interest, to X dollars at the maturity of the loan. Such a position is a *levered equity position* in which $PV(X) = Xe^{-rT}$ dollars is borrowed today (so that X will be repaid at maturity), and S_0 dollars is invested in the stock. The total payoff of the levered equity position is $S_T - X$, the same as that of the option strategy. Thus, the long call–short put position replicates the levered equity position. Again, we see that option trading provides leverage.

Because the option portfolio has a payoff identical to that of the levered equity position, the costs of establishing them must be equal. The net cash outlay necessary to establish the option position is $C - P$: The call is purchased for C, while the written put generates income of P. Likewise, the levered equity position requires a net cash outlay of $S_0 - Xe^{-rT}$, the cost of the stock less the proceeds from borrowing. Equating these costs, we conclude

put-call parity relationship

An equation representing the proper relationship between put and call prices.

$$C - P = S_0 - Xe^{-rT} \qquad (16.2)$$

Equation 16.2 is called the **put-call parity relationship** because it represents the proper relationship between put and call prices. If the parity relationship is ever violated, an arbitrage opportunity arises.

Suppose you observe the following data for a certain stock.

EXAMPLE 16.3

Put-Call Parity

Stock price	$110
Call price (six-month maturity, $X = \$105$)	14
Put price (six-month maturity, $X = \$105$)	5
Risk-free interest rate	5% continuously compounded rate

We use these data in the put-call parity relationship to see if parity is violated.

$$C - P \overset{?}{=} S_0 - Xe^{-rT}$$

$$14 - 5 \overset{?}{=} 110 - 105e^{-.05 \times 5}$$

$$9 \overset{?}{=} 7.59$$

This result, a violation of parity (9 does not equal 7.59) indicates mispricing and leads to an arbitrage opportunity. You can buy the relatively cheap portfolio (the stock plus borrowing position represented on the right-hand side of Equation 16.2) and sell the relatively expensive portfolio (the long call–short put position corresponding to the left-hand side, that is, write a call and buy a put).

Let's examine the payoff to this strategy. In six months, the stock will be worth S_T. You borrowed the present value of the exercise price, $105, and must pay back the loan with interest, resulting in a cash outflow of $105. The written call will result in a cash outflow of $S_T - \$105$ if S_T exceeds $105. The purchased put pays off $105 - S_T$ if the stock price is below $105.

Table 16.3 summarizes the outcome. The immediate cash inflow is $1.41, precisely equal to the mispricing of the option. In six months, the various positions provide exactly offsetting cash flows: The $1.41 inflow is realized risklessly without any offsetting outflows. This is an arbitrage opportunity that investors will pursue on a large scale until buying and selling pressure restores the parity condition expressed in Equation 16.2.

Equation 16.2 actually applies only to options on stocks that pay no dividends before the expiration date of the option. It also applies only to European options, as the cash flow streams from the two portfolios represented by the two sides of Equation 16.2 will match only if each position is held until expiration. If a call and a put may be optimally exercised at different times before their common expiration date, then the equality of payoffs cannot be assured, or even expected, and the portfolios will have different values.

The extension of the parity condition for European call options on dividend-paying stocks is, however, straightforward. Problem 23 at the end of the chapter leads you through the extension of the parity relationship. The more general formulation of the put-call parity condition is

$$P = C - S_0 + PV(X) + PV(\text{dividends}) \tag{16.3}$$

		Immediate	Cash Flow in Six Months	
TABLE 16.3			$S_T < 105$	$S_T \geq 105$
Arbitrage strategy	**Position**	**Cash Flow**		
	Buy stock	−110	S_T	S_T
	Borrow $Xe^{-rT} = \$102.41$	+102.41	−105	−105
	Sell call	+14	0	$-(S_T - 105)$
	Buy put	−5	$105 - S_T$	0
	Total	1.41	0	0

where PV(dividends) is the present value of the dividends that will be paid by the stock during the life of the option. If the stock does not pay dividends, Equation 16.3 becomes identical to Equation 16.2.

Notice that this generalization would apply as well to European options on assets other than stocks. Instead of using dividend income in Equation 16.3, we would let any income paid out by the underlying asset play the role of the stock dividends. For example, European put and call options on bonds would satisfy the same parity relationship, except that the bond's coupon income would replace the stock's dividend payments in the parity formula.

Let's see how well parity works using real data on the IBM options in Figure 15.1 from the previous chapter. The April expiration call with exercise price $95 and time to expiration of 49 days cost $1.35 while the corresponding put option cost $4.90. IBM was selling for $90.90, and the annualized short-term interest rate on this date was 4.9%. No dividends will be paid between the date of the listing, March 2, and the option expiration date. According to parity, we should find that

$$
\begin{aligned}
P &= C &+& \text{PV}(X) &-& S_0 &+& \text{PV(dividends)} \\
4.90 &= 1.35 &+& \frac{95}{(1.049)^{49/365}} &-& 90.90 &+& 0 \\
4.90 &= 1.35 &+& 94.39 &-& 90.90 \\
4.90 &= 4.84
\end{aligned}
$$

So, parity is violated by about $0.06 per share. Is this a big enough difference to exploit? Probably not. You have to weigh the potential profit against the trading costs of the call, put, and stock. More important, given the fact that options trade relatively infrequently, this deviation from parity might not be "real" but may instead be attributable to "stale" (i.e., out-of-date) price quotes at which you cannot actually trade.

Put Option Valuation

As we saw in Equation 16.3, we can use the put-call parity relationship to value put options once we know the call option value. Sometimes, however, it is easier to work with a put option valuation formula directly. The Black-Scholes formula for the value of a European put option[7]

$$ P = Xe^{-rT}[1 - N(d_2)] - S_0 e^{-\delta T}[1 - N(d_1)] \tag{16.4} $$

EXAMPLE 16.4

Black-Scholes Put Option Valuation

Using data from the Black-Scholes call option in Example 16.2 we find that a European put option on that stock with identical exercise price and time to maturity is worth

$$ \$95 e^{-.10 \times .25}(1 - .5714) - \$100(1 - .6664) = \$6.35 $$

Notice that this value is consistent with put-call parity:

$$ P = C + \text{PV}(X) - S_0 + \text{PV(Div)} = 13.70 + 95 e^{-.10 \times .25} - 100 + 0 = 6.35 $$

As we noted traders can do, we might then compare this formula value to the actual put price as one step in formulating a trading strategy.

Equation 16.4 is valid for European puts. Most listed put options are American-style, however, and offer the opportunity of early exercise. Because an American option allows its owner

---

[7]This formula is consistent with the put-call parity relationship, and in fact can be derived from it. If you want to try to do so, remember to take present values using continuous compounding, and note that when a stock pays a continuous flow of income in the form of a constant dividend yield, δ, the present value of that dividend flow is $S_0(1 - e^{-\delta T})$. (Notice that $e^{-\delta T}$ approximately equals $1 - \delta T$, so the value of the dividend flow is approximately $\delta T S_0$.)

to exercise at any time before the expiration date, it must be worth at least as much as the corresponding European option. However, while Equation 16.4 describes only the lower bound on the true value of the American put, in many applications the approximation is very accurate.

16.4 USING THE BLACK-SCHOLES FORMULA

Hedge Ratios and the Black-Scholes Formula

In the last chapter, we considered two investments in FinCorp stock: 100 shares or 900 call options. We saw that the call option position was more sensitive to swings in the stock price than the all-stock position. To analyze the overall exposure to a stock price more precisely, however, it is necessary to quantify these relative sensitivities. A tool that enables us to summarize the overall exposure of portfolios of options with various exercise prices and times to expiration is the hedge ratio. An option's **hedge ratio** is the change in the price of an option for a $1 increase in the stock price. A call option, therefore, has a positive hedge ratio, and a put option has a negative hedge ratio. The hedge ratio is commonly called the option's **delta.**

hedge ratio or delta

The number of shares of stock required to hedge the price risk of holding one option.

If you were to graph the option value as a function of the stock value as we have done for a call option in Figure 16.7, the hedge ratio is simply the slope of the value function evaluated at the current stock price. For example, suppose the slope of the curve at $S_0 = \$120$ equals 0.60. As the stock increases in value by $1, the option increases by approximately $0.60, as the figure shows.

For every call option written, 0.60 shares of stock would be needed to hedge the investor's portfolio. For example, if one writes 10 options and holds six shares of stock, according to the hedge ratio of 0.6, a $1 increase in stock price will result in a gain of $6 on the stock holdings, while the loss on the 10 options written will be $10 \times \$0.60$, an equivalent $6. The stock price movement leaves total wealth unaltered, which is what a hedged position is intended to do. The investor holding both the stock and options in proportions dictated by their relative price movements hedges the portfolio.

Black-Scholes hedge ratios are particularly easy to compute. The hedge ratio for a call is $N(d_1)$, while the hedge ratio for a put is $N(d_1) - 1$. We defined $N(d_1)$ as part of the Black-Scholes formula in Equation 16.1. Recall that $N(d)$ stands for the area under the standard normal curve up to d. Therefore, the call option hedge ratio must be positive and less than 1.0, while the put option hedge ratio is negative and of smaller absolute value than 1.0.

Figure 16.7 verifies the insight that the slope of the call option valuation function is less than 1.0, approaching 1.0 only as the stock price becomes extremely large. This tells us that option values change less than one-for-one with changes in stock prices. Why should this be? Suppose an option is so far in the money that you are absolutely certain it will be exercised. In that case, every $1 increase in the stock price would increase the option value by $1. But if there is a reasonable chance the call option will expire out of the money, even after a moderate stock

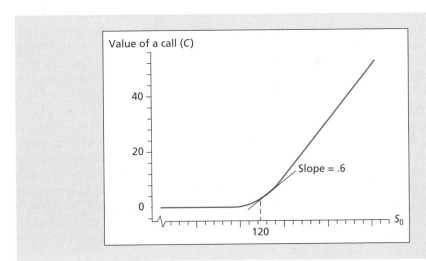

FIGURE 16.7

Call option value and hedge ratio

price gain, a $1 increase in the stock price will not necessarily increase the ultimate payoff to the call; therefore, the call price will not respond by a full $1.

The fact that hedge ratios are less than 1.0 does not contradict our earlier observation that options offer leverage and are sensitive to stock price movements. Although *dollar* movements in option prices are slighter than dollar movements in the stock price, the *rate of return* volatility of options remains greater than stock return volatility because options sell at lower prices. In our example, with the stock selling at $120, and a hedge ratio of 0.6, an option with exercise price $120 may sell for $5. If the stock price increases to $121, the call price would be expected to increase by only $0.60, to $5.60. The percentage increase in the option value is $0.60/$5.00 = 12%, however, while the percentage stock price increase is only $1/$120 = 0.83%. The ratio of the percent changes is 12%/0.83% = 14.4. For every 1% increase in the stock price, the option price increases by 14.4%. This ratio, the percent change in option price per percent change in stock price, is called the **option elasticity.**

option elasticity

The percentage increase in an option's value given a 1% increase in the value of the underlying secrity.

The hedge ratio is an essential tool in portfolio management and control. An example will show why.

EXAMPLE   16.5

Portfolio Hedge Ratios

Consider two portfolios, one holding 750 IBM calls and 200 shares of IBM and the other holding 800 shares of IBM. Which portfolio has greater dollar exposure to IBM price movements? You can answer this question easily using the hedge ratio.

Each option changes in value by H dollars for each dollar change in stock price, where H stands for the hedge ratio. Thus, if H equals 0.6, the 750 options are equivalent to 450 shares ($= 0.6 \times 750$) in terms of the response of their market value to IBM stock price movements. The first portfolio has less dollar sensitivity to stock price change because the 450 share-equivalents of the options plus the 200 shares actually held are less than the 800 shares held in the second portfolio.

This is not to say, however, that the first portfolio is less sensitive to the stock's rate of return. As we noted in discussing option elasticities, the first portfolio may be of lower total value than the second, so despite its lower sensitivity in terms of total market value, it might have greater rate of return sensitivity. Because a call option has a lower market value than the stock, its price changes more than proportionally with stock price changes, even though its hedge ratio is less than 1.0.

CONCEPT check   16.8

What is the elasticity of a put option currently selling for $4 with exercise price $120, and hedge ratio −0.4 if the stock price is currently $122?

Portfolio Insurance

In Chapter 15, we showed that protective put strategies offer a sort of insurance policy on an asset. The protective put has proven to be extremely popular with investors. Even if the asset price falls, the put conveys the right to sell the asset for the exercise price, which is a way to lock in a minimum portfolio value. With an at-the-money put ($X = S_0$), the maximum loss that can be realized is the cost of the put. The asset can be sold for X, which equals its original price, so even if the asset price falls, the investor's net loss over the period is just the cost of the put. If the asset value increases, however, upside potential is unlimited. Figure 16.8 graphs the profit or loss on a protective put position as a function of the change in the value of the underlying asset.

portfolio insurance

Portfolio strategies that limit investment losses while maintaining upside potential.

While the protective put is a simple and convenient way to achieve **portfolio insurance,** that is, to limit the worst-case portfolio rate of return, there are practical difficulties in trying to insure a portfolio of stocks. First, unless the investor's portfolio corresponds to a standard market index for which puts are traded, a put option on the portfolio will not be available for purchase. And if index puts are used to protect a nonindexed portfolio, tracking error can result. For example, if the portfolio falls in value while the market index rises, the put will fail to provide the intended protection. Tracking error limits the investor's freedom to pursue active stock selection because such error will be greater as the managed portfolio departs more substantially from the market index.

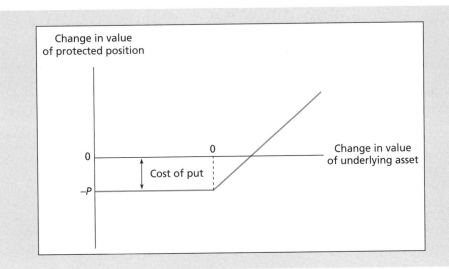

FIGURE 16.8

Profit on a protective put strategy

Moreover, the desired horizon of the insurance program must match the maturity of a traded put option in order to establish the appropriate protective put position. Today, long-term index options called LEAPS (for Long-Term Equity AnticiPation Securities) trade on the Chicago Board Options Exchange with maturities of several years. However, in the mid-1980s, while most investors pursuing insurance programs had horizons of several years, actively traded puts were limited to maturities of less than a year. Rolling over a sequence of short-term puts, which might be viewed as a response to this problem, introduces new risks because the prices at which successive puts will be available in the future are not known today.

Providers of portfolio insurance with horizons of several years, therefore, cannot rely on the simple expedient of purchasing protective puts for their clients' portfolios. Instead, they follow trading strategies that replicate the payoffs to the protective put position.

Here is the general idea. Even if a put option on the desired portfolio with the desired expiration date does not exist, a theoretical option-pricing model (such as the Black-Scholes model) can be used to determine how that option's price *would* respond to the portfolio's value if the option did trade. For example, if stock prices were to fall, the put option would increase in value. The option model could quantify this relationship. The net exposure of the (hypothetical) protective put portfolio to swings in stock prices is the sum of the exposures of the two components of the portfolio: the stock and the put. The net exposure of the portfolio equals the equity exposure less the (offsetting) put option exposure.

We can create "synthetic" protective put positions by holding a quantity of stocks with the same net exposure to market swings as the hypothetical protective put position. The key to this strategy is the option delta, or hedge ratio, that is, the change in the price of the protective put option per change in the value of the underlying stock portfolio.

Suppose a portfolio is currently valued at $100 million. An at-the-money put option on the portfolio might have a hedge ratio or delta of −0.6, meaning the option's value swings $0.60 for every dollar change in portfolio value, but in an opposite direction. Suppose the stock portfolio falls in value by 2%. The profit on a hypothetical protective put position (if the put existed) would be as follows (in millions of dollars):

EXAMPLE   16.6

Synthetic Protective Puts

Loss on stocks:	2% of $100 =	$2.00
+ Gain on put:	0.6 × $2.00 =	1.20
Net loss		$0.80

(Continued)

EXAMPLE   16.6

*Synthetic
Protective Puts
(Concluded)*

We create the synthetic option position by selling a proportion of shares equal to the put option's delta (i.e., selling 60% of the shares) and placing the proceeds in risk-free T-bills. The rationale is that the hypothetical put option would have offset 60% of any change in the stock portfolio's value, so one must reduce portfolio risk directly by selling 60% of the equity and putting the proceeds into a risk-free asset. Total return on a synthetic protective put position with $60 million in risk-free investments such as T-bills and $40 million in equity is

Loss on stocks:	2% of $40 = $0.80
+ Loss on bills:	0
Net loss	$0.80

The synthetic and actual protective put positions have equal returns. We conclude that if you sell a proportion of shares equal to the put option's delta and place the proceeds in cash equivalents, your exposure to the stock market will equal that of the desired protective put position.

The difficulty with synthetic positions is that deltas constantly change. Figure 16.9 shows that as the stock price falls, the absolute value of the appropriate hedge ratio increases. Therefore, market declines require extra hedging, that is, additional conversion of equity into cash. This constant updating of the hedge ratio is called **dynamic hedging,** as discussed in Section 16.2. Another term for such hedging is *delta hedging,* because the option delta is used to determine the number of shares that need to be bought or sold.

dynamic hedging

**Constant updating of
hedge positions as market
conditions change.**

Dynamic hedging is one reason portfolio insurance has been said to contribute to market volatility. Market declines trigger additional sales of stock as portfolio insurers strive to increase their hedging. These additional sales are seen as reinforcing or exaggerating market downturns.

In practice, portfolio insurers do not actually buy or sell stocks directly when they update their hedge positions. Instead, they minimize trading costs by buying or selling stock index futures as a substitute for sale of the stocks themselves. As you will see in the next chapter, stock prices and index future prices usually are very tightly linked by cross-market arbitrageurs so that futures transactions can be used as reliable proxies for stock transactions. Instead of selling equities based on the put option's delta, insurers will sell an equivalent number of futures contracts.[8]

FIGURE 16.9

Hedge ratios change as
the stock price fluctuates

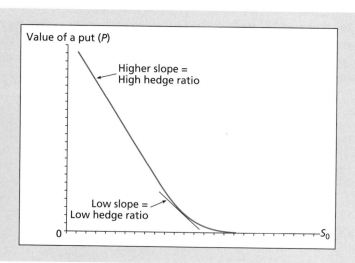

[8]Notice, however, that the use of index futures reintroduces the problem of tracking error between the portfolio and the market index.

J. P. MORGAN ROLLS DICE ON MICROSOFT OPTIONS

Microsoft, in a shift that could be copied throughout the technology business, said yesterday that it plans to stop issuing stock options to its employees, and instead will provide them with restricted stock.

The deal could portend a seismic shift for Microsoft's Silicon Valley rivals, and it could well have effects on Wall Street. Though details of the plan still aren't clear, J. P. Morgan effectively plans to buy the options from Microsoft employees who opt for restricted stock instead. Employee stock options are granted as a form of compensation and allow employees the right to exchange the options for shares of company stock.

The price offered to employees for the options presumably will be lower than the current value, giving J. P. Morgan a chance to make a profit on the deal. Rather than holding the options, and thus betting Microsoft's stock will rise, people familiar with the bank's strategy say J. P. Morgan probably will match each option it buys from the company's employees with a separate trade in the stock market that both hedges the bet and gives itself a margin of profit.

For Wall Street's so-called rocket scientists who do complicated financial transactions such as this one, the strategy behind J. P. Morgan's deal with Microsoft isn't particularly unique or sophisticated. They add that the bank has several ways to deal with the millions of Microsoft options that could come its way.

The bank, for instance, could hedge the options by shorting, or betting against, Microsoft stock. Microsoft has the largest market capitalization of any stock in the market, and its shares are among the most liquid, meaning it would be easy to hedge the risk of holding those options.

J. P. Morgan also could sell the options to investors, much as they would do with a syndicated loan, thereby spreading the risk. During a conference call with investors, [Microsoft Chief Exeutive Steve] Ballmer said employees could sell their options to "a third party or set of third parties," adding that the company was still working out the details with J. P. Morgan and the SEC.

SOURCE: Excerpt from *The Wall Street Journal*, July 9, 2003.

Several portfolio insurers suffered great setbacks during the market "crash" of October 19, 1987, when the Dow Jones Industrial Average fell more than 20%. A description of what happened then should help you appreciate the complexities of applying a seemingly straightforward hedging concept.

1. Market volatility at the crash was much greater than ever encountered before. Put option deltas computed from historical experience were too low; insurers underhedged, held too much equity, and suffered excessive losses.

2. Prices moved so fast that insurers could not keep up with the necessary rebalancing. They were "chasing deltas" that kept getting away from them. The futures market saw a "gap" opening, where the opening price was nearly 10% below the previous day's close. Prices dropped before insurers could update their hedge ratios.

3. Execution problems were severe. First, current market prices were unavailable, with trade execution and the price quotation system hours behind, which made computation of correct hedge ratios impossible. Moreover, trading in stocks and stock futures ceased during some periods. The continuous rebalancing capability that is essential for a viable insurance program vanished during the precipitous market collapse.

4. Futures prices traded at steep discounts to their proper levels compared to reported stock prices, thereby making the sale of futures (as a proxy for equity sales) to increase hedging seem expensive. While you will see in the next chapter that stock index futures prices normally exceed the value of the stock index, on October 19, futures sold far below the stock index level. When some insurers gambled that the futures price would recover to its usual premium over the stock index and chose to defer sales, they remained underhedged. As the market fell farther, their portfolios experienced substantial losses.

While most observers believe that the portfolio insurance industry will never recover from the market crash, dynamic hedges are still widely used by large firms to hedge potential losses from options positions. For example, the nearby box notes that when Microsoft ended its employee stock option program and J. P. Morgan purchased many already-issued options from Microsoft employees, it was widely expected that Morgan would protect its options position by selling shares in Microsoft in accord with a delta hedging strategy.

16.5 EMPIRICAL EVIDENCE

There have been an enormous number of empirical tests of the Black-Scholes option-pricing model. For the most part, the results of the studies have been positive in that the Black-Scholes model generates option values quite close to the actual prices at which options trade. At the same time, some smaller but regular empirical failures of the model have been noted.

Whaley (1982) examines the performance of the Black-Scholes formula relative to that of more complicated option formulas that allow for early exercise. His findings indicate that formulas that allow for the possibility of early exercise do better at pricing than the Black-Scholes formula. The Black-Scholes formula seems to perform worst for options on stocks with high dividend payouts. The true American call option formula, on the other hand, seems to fare equally well in the prediction of option prices on stocks with high or low dividend payouts.

Rubinstein (1994) has emphasized a more serious problem with the Black-Scholes model. If the model were accurate, the implied volatility of all options on a particular stock with the same expiration date would be equal—after all, the underlying asset and expiration date are the same for each option, so the volatility inferred from each also ought to be the same. But in fact, when one actually plots implied volatility as a function of exercise price, the typical results appear as in Figure 16.10, which treats S&P 500 index options as the underlying asset. Implied volatility steadily falls as the exercise price rises. Clearly, the Black-Scholes model is missing something.

Rubinstein suggests that the problem with the model has to do with fears of a market crash like that of October 1987. The idea is that deep out-of-the-money puts would be nearly worthless if stock prices evolve smoothly, since the probability of the stock falling by a large amount (and the put option thereby moving into the money) in a short time would be very small. But a possibility of a sudden large downward jump that could move

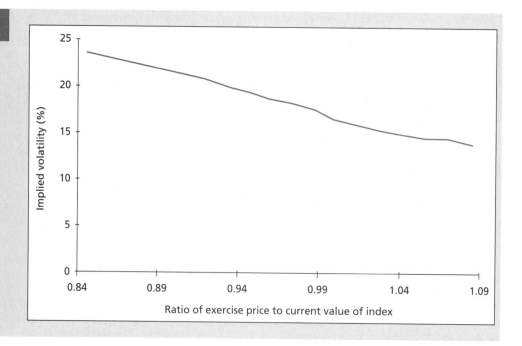

FIGURE 16.10

Implied volatility as a function of exercise price

Source: Mark Rubinstein, "Implied Binomial Trees," *Journal of Finance* (July 1994), pp. 771–818.

the puts into the money, as in a market crash, would impart greater value to these options. Thus, the market might price these options as though there is a bigger chance of a large drop in the stock price than would be suggested by the Black-Scholes assumptions. The result of the higher option price is a greater implied volatility derived from the Black-Scholes model.

Interestingly, Rubinstein points out that prior to the 1987 market crash, plots of implied volatility like the one in Figure 16.10 were relatively flat, consistent with the notion that the market was then less attuned to fears of a crash. However, post-crash plots have been consistently downward sloping, exhibiting a shape often called the *option smirk*. When we use option-pricing models that allow for more general stock price distributions, including jumps and random changes in volatility, they generate downward-sloping implied volatility curves similar to the one observed in Figure 16.10.[9]

SUMMARY

- Option values may be viewed as the sum of intrinsic value plus time or "volatility" value. The volatility value is the right to choose not to exercise if the stock price moves against the holder. Thus, option holders cannot lose more than the cost of the option regardless of stock price performance.
- Call options are more valuable when the exercise price is lower, when the stock price is higher, when the interest rate is higher, when the time to expiration is greater, when the stock's volatility is greater, and when dividends are lower.
- Options may be priced relative to the underlying stock price using a simple two-period, two-state pricing model. As the number of periods increases, the model can approximate more realistic stock price distributions. The Black-Scholes formula may be seen as a limiting case of the binomial option model, as the holding period is divided into progressively smaller subperiods.
- The put-call parity theorem relates the prices of put and call options. If the relationship is violated, arbitrage opportunities will result. Specifically, the relationship that must be satisfied is

$$P = C - S_0 + PV(X) + PV(\text{dividends})$$

where X is the exercise price of both the call and the put options, and $PV(X)$ is the present value of the claim to X dollars to be paid at the expiration date of the options.
- The implied volatility of an option is the standard deviation of stock returns consistent with an option's market price. It can be backed out of an option pricing model by finding the stock volatility that makes the option's value equal to its observed price.
- The hedge ratio is the number of shares of stock required to hedge the price risk involved in writing one option. Hedge ratios are near zero for deep out-of-the-money call options and approach 1.0 for deep in-the-money calls.
- Although hedge ratios are less than 1.0, call options have elasticities greater than 1.0. The rate of return on a call (as opposed to the dollar return) responds more than one-for-one with stock price movements.
- Portfolio insurance can be obtained by purchasing a protective put option on an equity position. When the appropriate put is not traded, portfolio insurance entails a dynamic hedge strategy where a fraction of the equity portfolio equal to the desired put option's delta is sold, with proceeds placed in risk-free securities.
- Empirically, implied volatilities derived from the Black-Scholes formula tend to be lower on options with higher exercise prices. This may be evidence that the option prices reflect the possibility of a sudden dramatic decline in stock prices. Such "crashes" are inconsistent with the Black-Scholes assumptions.

[9] For an extensive discussion of these more general models, see R. L. McDonald, *Derivatives Markets,* 2nd ed. (Boston: Pearson Education, Addison-Wesley, 2006).

www.mhhe.com/bkm

KEY TERMS

binomial model, 525
Black-Scholes pricing
    formula, 527
delta, 537
dynamic hedging, 540

hedge ratio, 537
implied volatility, 530
intrinsic value, 518
option elasticity, 538
portfolio insurance, 538

put-call parity
    relationship, 534
time value, 518

PROBLEM SETS

 Select problems are available in McGraw-Hill's Homework Manager®.
Please see the packaging options section of the preface for more information.

1. We showed in the text that the value of a call option increases with the volatility of the stock. Is this also true of put option values? Use the put-call parity relationship as well as a numerical example to prove your answer.

2. In each of the following questions, you are asked to compare two options with parameters as given. The risk-free interest rate for *all* cases should be assumed to be 6%. Assume the stocks on which these options are written pay no dividends.

   a.

Put	T	X	σ	Price of Option
A	0.5	50	0.20	10
B	0.5	50	0.25	10

   Which put option is written on the stock with the lower price?
   (1) A
   (2) B
   (3) Not enough information

   b.

Put	T	X	σ	Price of Option
A	0.5	50	0.2	10
B	0.5	50	0.2	12

   Which put option must be written on the stock with the lower price?
   (1) A
   (2) B
   (3) Not enough information

   c.

Call	S	X	σ	Price of Option
A	50	50	0.20	12
B	55	50	0.20	10

   Which call option must have the lower time to expiration?
   (1) A
   (2) B
   (3) Not enough information

d.

Call	T	X	S	Price of Option
A	0.5	50	55	10
B	0.5	50	55	12

Which call option is written on the stock with higher volatility?

(1) A

(2) B

(3) Not enough information

e.

Call	T	X	S	Price of Option
A	0.5	50	55	10
B	0.5	55	55	7

Which call option is written on the stock with higher volatility?

(1) A

(2) B

(3) Not enough information

3. Reconsider the determination of the hedge ratio in the two-state model, where we showed that one-third share of stock would hedge one option. What would be the hedge ratio for each of the following exercise prices: $120, $110, $100, $90? What do you conclude about the hedge ratio as the option becomes progressively more in the money?

4. Show that Black-Scholes call option hedge ratios increase as the stock price increases. Consider a one-year option with exercise price $50 on a stock with annual standard deviation 20%. The T-bill rate is 8% per year. Find $N(d_1)$ for stock prices $45, $50, and $55.

5. We will derive a two-state put option value in this problem. Data: $S_0 = 100$; $X = 110$; $1 + r = 1.10$. The two possibilities for S_T are 130 and 80.

a. Show that the range of S is 50 while that of P is 30 across the two states. What is the hedge ratio of the put?

b. Form a portfolio of three shares of stock and five puts. What is the (nonrandom) pay-off to this portfolio? What is the present value of the portfolio?

c. Given that the stock currently is selling at 100, show that the value of the put must be 10.91.

6. Calculate the value of a *call* option on the stock in Problem 5 with an exercise price of 110. Verify that the put-call parity relationship is satisfied by your answers to Problems 5 and 6. (Do not use continuous compounding to calculate the present value of X in this example, because the interest rate is quoted as an effective annual yield.)

7. Use the Black-Scholes formula to find the value of a call option on the following stock:

Time to expiration = 6 months

Standard deviation = 50% per year

Exercise price   = $50

Stock price   = $50

Interest rate   = 10%

8. Find the Black-Scholes value of a put option on the stock in the previous problem with the same exercise price and expiration as the call option.

Please visit us at
www.mhhe.com/bkm

Please visit us at
www.mhhe.com/bkm

www.mhhe.com/bkm

9. What would be the Excel formula in Spreadsheet 16.1 for the Black-Scholes value of a straddle position?

10. Recalculate the value of the option in Problem 7, successively substituting one of the changes below while keeping the other parameters as in Problem 7:
    a. Time to expiration = 3 months
    b. Standard deviation = 25% per year
    c. Exercise price   = $55
    d. Stock price   = $55
    e. Interest rate   = 15%

    Consider each scenario independently. Confirm that the option value changes in accordance with the prediction of Table 16.1.

11. Would you expect a $1 increase in a call option's exercise price to lead to a decrease in the option's value of more or less than $1?

12. All else being equal, is a put option on a high beta stock worth more than one on a low beta stock? The firms have identical firm-specific risk.

13. All else being equal, is a call option on a stock with a lot of firm-specific risk worth more than one on a stock with little firm-specific risk? The betas of the stocks are equal.

14. All else being equal, will a call option with a high exercise price have a higher or lower hedge ratio than one with a low exercise price?

15. Should the rate of return of a call option on a long-term Treasury bond be more or less sensitive to changes in interest rates than the rate of return of the underlying bond?

16. If the stock price falls and the call price rises, then what has happened to the call option's implied volatility?

17. If the time to expiration falls and the put price rises, then what has happened to the put option's implied volatility?

18. According to the Black-Scholes formula, what will be the value of the hedge ratio of a call option as the stock price becomes infinitely large? Explain briefly.

19. According to the Black-Scholes formula, what will be the value of the hedge ratio of a put option for a very small exercise price?

20. The hedge ratio of an at-the-money call option on IBM is 0.4. The hedge ratio of an at-the-money put option is −0.6. What is the hedge ratio of an at-the-money straddle position on IBM?

21. Consider a 6-month expiration European call option with exercise price $105. The underlying stock sells for $100 a share, and pays no dividends. The risk-free rate is 5%. What is the implied volatility of the option if the option currently sells for $8? Use Spreadsheet 16.1 (available at **www.mhhe.com/bkm;** link to Chapter 16 material) to answer this question.
    a. Go to the Tools menu of the spreadsheet and select Goal Seek. The dialog box will ask you for three pieces of information. In that dialog box, you should *set cell* E6 *to value* 8 *by changing cell* B2. In other words, you ask the spreadsheet to find the value of standard deviation (which appears in cell B2) that forces the value of the option (in cell E6) equal to $8. Then click OK, and you should find that the call is now worth $8, and the entry for standard deviation has been changed to a level consistent with this value. This is the call's implied standard deviation at a price of $8.
    b. What happens to implied volatility if the option is selling at $9? Why has implied volatility increased?
    c. What happens to implied volatility if the option price is unchanged at $8, but option expiration is lower, say, only four months? Why?
    d. What happens to implied volatility if the option price is unchanged at $8, but the exercise price is lower, say, only $100? Why?
    e. What happens to implied volatility if the option price is unchanged at $8, but the stock price is lower, say, only $98? Why?

22. These three put options all are written on the same stock. One has a delta of -0.9, one a delta of -0.5, and one a delta of -0.1. Assign deltas to the three puts by filling in the table below.

Put	X	Delta
A	10	
B	20	
C	30	

23. In this problem, we derive the put-call parity relationship for European options on stocks that pay dividends before option expiration. For simplicity, assume that the stock makes one dividend payment of $D per share at the expiration date of the option.
    a. What is the value of the stock-plus-put position on the expiration date of the option?
    b. Now consider a portfolio consisting of a call option and a zero-coupon bond with the same maturity date as the option and with face value $(X + D)$. What is the value of this portfolio on the option expiration date? You should find that its value equals that of the stock-plus-put portfolio, regardless of the stock price.
    c. What is the cost of establishing the two portfolios in parts (a) and (b)? Equate the cost of these portfolios, and you will derive the put-call parity relationship, Equation 16.3.

24. A collar is established by buying a share of stock for $50, buying a six-month put option with exercise price $45, and writing a six-month call option with exercise price $55. Based on the volatility of the stock, you calculate that for an exercise price of $45 and maturity of six months, $N(d_1) = .60$, whereas for the exercise price of $55, $N(d_1) = .35$.
    a. What will be the gain or loss on the collar if the stock price increases by $1?
    b. What happens to the delta of the portfolio if the stock price becomes very large? Very small?

25. Ken Webster manages a $200 million equity portfolio benchmarked to the S&P 500 index. Over the past two years, the S&P 500 Index has appreciated considerably. Webster believes the market is overvalued when measured by several traditional fundamental/economic indicators. He is concerned about maintaining the excellent gains the portfolio has experienced in the past two years but recognizes that the S&P 500 Index could still move above its current 1336 level.

    Webster is considering the following *option collar* strategy:
    • Protection for the portfolio can be attained by purchasing an S&P 500 Index put with a strike price of 1330 (just out of the money).
    • The put can be financed by selling two 1350 calls (further out-of-the-money) for every put purchased.
    • Because the combined delta of the two calls (see following table) is less than 1 (that is, $2 \times 0.36 = 0.72$) the options will not lose more than the underlying portfolio will gain if the market advances.

    The information in the following table describes the two options used to create the collar.

Characteristics	1350 Call	1330 Put
Option price	$ 8.60	$ 16.10
Option implied volatility	11.00%	14.00%
Option's delta	0.36	−0.44
Contracts needed for collar	602	301

Notes:

Ignore transaction costs.

S&P 500 historical 30-day volatility = 12.00%.

Time to option expiration 30 days.

a. Describe the potential returns of the combined portfolio (the underlying portfolio plus the option collar) if after 30 days the S&P 500 index has:
   i. risen approximately 5% to 1402.
   ii. remained at 1336 (no change).
   iii. declined by approximately 5% to 1270.
   (No calculations are necessary.)
b. Discuss the effect on the hedge ratio (delta) of *each* option as the S&P 500 approaches the level for *each* of the potential outcomes listed in part (*a*).
c. Evaluate the pricing of each of the following in relation to the volatility data provided:
   i. the put
   ii. the call

26. You are *very* bullish (optimistic) on stock EFG, much more so than the rest of the market. In each question, choose the portfolio strategy that will give you the biggest dollar profit if your bullish forecast turns out to be correct. Explain your answer.
    a. *Choice A:* $100,000 invested in calls with $X = 50$.
       Choice B: $100,000 invested in EFG stock.
    b. *Choice A:* 10 call options contracts (for 100 shares each), with $X = 50$.
       Choice B: 1,000 shares of EFG stock.

27. Michael Weber, CFA, is analyzing several aspects of option valuation, including the determinants of the value of an option, the characteristics of various models used to value options, and the potential for divergence of calculated option values from observed market prices.
    a. What is the expected effect on the value of a call option on common stock if (i) the volatility of the underlying stock price decreases; (ii) The time to expiration of the option increases.
    b. Using the Black-Scholes option-pricing model, Weber calculates the price of a three-month call option and notices the option's calculated value is different from its market price. With respect to Weber's use of the Black-Scholes option-pricing model (i) discuss why the calculated value of an out-of-the-money European option may differ from its market price; (ii) discuss why the calculated value of an American option may differ from that its market price.

28. Imagine you are a provider of portfolio insurance. You are establishing a four-year program. The portfolio you manage is currently worth $100 million, and you promise to provide a minimum return of 0%. The equity portfolio has a standard deviation of 25% per year, and T-bills pay 5% per year. Assume for simplicity that the portfolio pays no dividends (or that all dividends are reinvested).
    a. What fraction of the portfolio should be placed in bills? What fraction in equity?
    b. What should the manager do if the stock portfolio falls by 3% on the first day of trading?

29. You would like to be holding a protective put position on the stock of XYZ Co. to lock in a guaranteed minimum value of $100 at year-end. XYZ currently sells for $100. Over the next year, the stock price will either increase by 10% or decrease by 10%. The T-bill rate is 5%. Unfortunately, no put options are traded on XYZ Co.
    a. Suppose the desired put option were traded. How much would it cost to purchase?
    b. What would have been the cost of the protective put portfolio?
    c. What portfolio position in stock and T-bills will ensure you a payoff equal to the payoff that would be provided by a protective put with $X = $100? Show that the payoff to this portfolio and the cost of establishing the portfolio matches that of the desired protective put.

30. You are attempting to value a call option with an exercise price of $100 and one year to expiration. The underlying stock pays no dividends, its current price is $100, and you

believe it has a 50% chance of increasing to $120 and a 50% chance of decreasing to $80. The risk-free rate of interest is 10%. Calculate the call option's value using the two-state stock price model.

31. Consider an increase in the volatility of the stock in the previous problem. Suppose that if the stock increases in price, it will increase to $130, and that if it falls, it will fall to $70. Show that the value of the call option is higher than the value derived using the original assumptions.

32. A stock index is currently trading at 50. Paul Tripp, CFA, wants to value two-year index options using the binomial model. In any year, the stock will either increase in value by 20% or fall in value by 20%. The annual risk-free interest rate is 6%. No dividends are paid on any of the underlying securities in the index.

   a. Construct a two-period binomial tree for the value of the stock index.
   b. Calculate the value of a European call option on the index with an exercise price of 60.
   c. Calculate the value of a European put option on the index with an exercise price of 60.
   d. Confirm that your solutions for the values of the call and the put satisfy put-call parity.

33. Return to Example 16.1. Use the binomial model to value a one-year European put option with exercise price $110 on the stock in that example. Does your solution for the put price satisfy put-call parity?

Use data from the Standard & Poor's Market Insight Database at www.mhhe.com/edumarketinsight to answer the following questions.

Go to the Market Insight page.

   a. Click on the Company tab and enter BUD for Anheuser-Busch Cos, Inc. Find the company's report in the S&P Stock Reports section. What is Anheuser-Busch's current price? What is its 12-month target price? What is the S&P buy/hold/sell recommendation? Based on this information, would it make more sense to buy a call option or a put option on Anheuser-Busch?

   b. What is Anheuser-Busch's volatility rating? You can find this in the Quantitative Evaluations section. How would this affect the value of the company's options? Relate your answer to the Black-Scholes model.

   c. On the Market Insight main page enter stock symbol TAP for Molson Coors Brewing Co. Find the company's current price, 12-month target price, S&P buy/hold/sell recommendation, and volatility rating by looking at its S&P Stock Report. Based on this information, would it make more sense to buy a call option or a put option on Molson Coors?

   d. Now find similar information for Genzyme Corporation (GENZ) and Cephalon, Inc. (CEPH). Would you recommend the purchase of a call option or a put option on these stocks?

   e. Can you see a general pattern for the brewery industry, represented by BUD and TAP vs. the biotechnology industry, represented by GENZ and CEPH, with respect to
   • volatility
   • buy/hold/sell recommendation
   • expected price increases or decreases?

   f. Suppose you believe that the volatility of BUD is going to increase from currently anticipated levels. Would its call options be overpriced or underpriced? What about its put options?

   g. Could you take positions in both puts and calls on BUD in such a manner as to speculate on your volatility beliefs without taking a stance on whether the stock price is going to increase or decrease? Would you buy or write each type of option?

   h. How would your relative positions in puts and calls be related to the delta of each option?

WEB *master*

Option Price Differences

Select a stock for which options are listed on the CBOE Web site (**www.cboe.com**). The price data for captions can be found on the "delayed quotes" menu option of the CBOE Web site. Enter a sticker symbol for a stock of your choice and pull up its option price data.

Using daily price data from a Web site such as **finance.yahoo.com,** calculate the annualized standard deviation of the daily percentage change in the stock price. Create a Black-Scholes option pricing model in

a spreadsheet such as Spreadsheet 16.1, available at **www.mhhe.com/bkm** with Chapter 16 material. Using the standard deviation and a risk-free rate found at **www.bloomberg.com/markets/index.html**, calculate the value of the call options.

How do the calculated values compare to the market prices of the options? On the basis of the difference between the price you calculated based on historical volatility and the actual price of the option, what do you conclude about expected trends in market volatility?

SOLUTIONS TO

CONCEPT
c h e c k s

16.1. Yes. Consider the same scenarios as for the call.

Stock price	$10	$20	$30	$40	$50
Put payoff	20	10	0	0	0
Stock price	20	25	30	35	40
Put payoff	10	5	0	0	0

The low volatility scenario yields a lower expected payoff.

16.2.

If This Variable Increases . . .	The Value of a Put Option
S	Decreases
X	Increases
σ	Increases
T	Increases/Uncertain*
r_f	Decreases
Dividend payouts	Increases

*For American puts, increase in time to expiration *must* increase value. One can always choose to exercise early if this is optimal; the longer expiration date simply expands the range of alternatives open to the option holder, thereby making the option more valuable. For a European put, where early exercise is not allowed, longer time to expiration can have an indeterminate effect. Longer maturity increases volatility value since the final stock price is more uncertain, but it reduces the present value of the exercise price that will be received if the put is exercised. The net effect on put value is ambiguous.

16.3. Because the option now is underpriced, we want to reverse our previous strategy.

		Initial Cash Flow	Cash Flow in 1 Year for Each Possible Stock Price	
			S = $90	S = $120
Buy 3 options		$−16.50	$ 0	$ 30
Short-sell 1 share; re-pay in 1 year		100	−90	−120
Lend $83.50 at 10% interest rate		−83.50	91.85	91.85
Total		$ 0	$ 1.85	$ 1.85

The riskless cash flow in 1 year per option is $1.85/3 = \$.6167$, and the present value is $\$.6167/1.10 = \$.56$, precisely the amount by which the option is underpriced.

16.4. *a.* $C_u - C_d = \$6.984 - 0 = \$6.984$

   b. $uS_0 - dS_0 = \$110 - \$95 = \$15$

   c. $6.984/15 = .4656$

   d.

Action Today (time 0)	Value in Next Period as Function of Stock Price	
	$dS_0 = \$95$	$uS_0 = \$110$
Buy .4656 shares at price $S_0 = \$100$	\$44.232	\$51.216
Write 1 call at price C_0	0	−6.984
Total	\$44.232	\$44.232

The portfolio must have a market value equal to the present value of $44.232.

   e. $\$44.232/1.05 = \$42.126$

   f. $.4656 \times \$100 - C_0 = \$42.126$

   $C_0 = \$46.56 - \$42.126 = \$4.434$

16.5. Higher. For deep out-of-the-money options, an increase in the stock price still leaves the option unlikely to be exercised. Its value increases only fractionally. For deep in-the-money options, exercise is likely, and option holders benefit by a full dollar for each dollar increase in the stock, as though they already own the stock.

16.6. Because $\sigma = 0.6$, $\sigma^2 = 0.36$.

$$d_1 = \frac{\ln(100/95) + (0.10 + 0.36/2)0.25}{0.6\sqrt{0.25}} = 0.4043$$
$$d_2 = d_1 - 0.6\sqrt{0.25} = 0.1043$$

Using Table 16.2 and interpolation, or a spreadsheet function,

$$N(d_1) = 0.6570$$
$$N(d_2) = 0.5415$$
$$C = 100 \times 0.6570 - 95e^{-0.10 \times 0.25} \times 0.5415 = 15.53$$

16.7. Implied volatility exceeds 0.5. Given a standard deviation of 0.5, the option value is $13.70. A higher volatility is needed to justify the actual $15 price. Using Spreadsheet 16.1 and Goal Seek, we find the implied volatility is .5714, or 57.14%.

16.8. A $1 increase in stock price is a percentage increase of $1/122 = 0.82\%$. The put option will fall by $(0.4 \times \$1) = \$0.40$, a percentage decrease of $\$0.40/\$4 = 10\%$. Elasticity is $-10/0.82 = -12.2$.

Futures Markets and Risk Management

 Calculate the profit on futures positions as a function of current and eventual futures prices.

 Formulate futures market strategies for hedging or speculative purposes.

 Compute the futures price appropriate to a given price on the underlying asset.

 Design arbitrage strategies to exploit futures market mispricing.

 Determine how swaps can be used to mitigate interest rate risk.

Futures and forward contracts are like options in that they specify the purchase or sale of some underlying security at some future date. The key difference is that the holder of an option to buy is not compelled to buy and will not do so if the trade is unprofitable. A futures or forward contract, however, carries the obligation to go through with the agreed-upon transaction.

A forward contract is not an investment in the strict sense that funds are paid for an asset. It is only a commitment today to transact in the future. Forward arrangements are part of our study of investments, however, because they offer a powerful means to hedge other investments and generally modify portfolio characteristics.

Forward markets for future delivery of various commodities go back at least to ancient Greece. Organized *futures markets*, though, are a relatively modern development, dating only to the 19th century. Futures markets replace informal forward contracts with highly standardized, exchange-traded securities.

While futures markets have their roots in agricultural products and commodities, the markets today are dominated by trading in financial futures such as those on stock indices, interest-rate-dependent securities such as government bonds, and foreign exchange. The markets themselves also have changed. An ever-greater proportion of futures trading is conducted electronically, and this trend seems sure to continue.

This chapter describes the workings of futures markets and the mechanics of trading in these markets. We show how futures contracts are useful investment vehicles for both hedgers and speculators and how the futures price relates to the spot price of an asset. Next, we take a look at some specific financial futures contracts—those written on stock indexes, foreign exchange, and fixed-income securities. Finally, we show how swap contracts, an extension of forward contracts, may be used in portfolio management.

Related Web sites for this chapter are available at www.mhhe.com/bkm.

17.1 | THE FUTURES CONTRACT

To see how futures and forwards work and how they might be useful, consider the portfolio diversification problem facing a farmer growing a single crop, let us say wheat. The entire planting season's revenue depends critically on the highly volatile crop price. The farmer can't easily diversify his position because virtually his entire wealth is tied up in the crop.

The miller who must purchase wheat for processing faces a portfolio problem that is the mirror image of the farmer's. He is subject to profit uncertainty because of the unpredictable future cost of the wheat.

Both parties can reduce this source of risk if they enter into a **forward contract** calling for the farmer to deliver the wheat when harvested at a price agreed upon now, regardless of the market price at harvest time. No money need change hands at this time. A forward contract is simply a deferred-delivery sale of some asset with the sales price agreed upon now. All that is required is that each party be willing to lock in the ultimate price to be paid or received for delivery of the commodity. A forward contract protects each party from future price fluctuations.

forward contract

An arrangement calling for future delivery of an asset at an agreed-upon price.

Futures markets formalize and standardize forward contracting. Buyers and sellers do not have to rely on a chance matching of their interests; they can trade in a centralized futures market. The futures exchange also standardizes the types of contracts that may be traded: It establishes contract size, the acceptable grade of commodity, contract delivery dates, and so forth. While standardization eliminates much of the flexibility available in informal forward contracting, it has the offsetting advantage of liquidity because many traders will concentrate on the same small set of contracts. Futures contracts also differ from forward contracts in that they call for a daily settling up of any gains or losses on the contract. In contrast, in the case of forward contracts, no money changes hands until the delivery date.

In a centralized market, buyers and sellers can trade through brokers without personally searching for trading partners. The standardization of contracts and the depth of trading in each contract allows futures positions to be liquidated easily through a broker rather than personally renegotiated with the other party to the contract. Because the exchange guarantees the performance of each party to the contract, costly credit checks on other traders are not necessary. Instead, each trader simply posts a good faith deposit, called the *margin*, in order to guarantee contract performance.

The Basics of Futures Contracts

The futures contract calls for delivery of a commodity at a specified delivery or maturity date, for an agreed-upon price, called the **futures price,** to be paid at contract maturity. The contract specifies precise requirements for the commodity. For agricultural commodities, the exchange

futures price

The agreed-upon price to be paid on a futures contract at maturity.

sets allowable grades (e.g., No. 2 hard winter wheat or No. 1 soft red wheat). The place or means of delivery of the commodity is specified as well. Delivery of agricultural commodities is made by transfer of warehouse receipts issued by approved warehouses. In the case of financial futures, delivery may be made by wire transfer; in the case of index futures, delivery may be accomplished by a cash settlement procedure such as those used for index options. (Although the futures contract technically calls for delivery of an asset, delivery rarely occurs. Instead, parties to the contract much more commonly close out their positions before contract maturity, taking gains or losses in cash.)[1]

long position

The futures trader who commits to purchasing the asset.

Because the futures exchange specifies all the terms of the contract, the traders need bargain only over the futures price. The trader taking the **long position** commits to purchasing the commodity on the delivery date. The trader who takes the **short position** commits to delivering the commodity at contract maturity. The trader in the long position is said to "buy" a contract; the short-side trader "sells" a contract. The words *buy* and *sell* are figurative only, because a contract is not really bought or sold like a stock or bond; it is entered into by mutual agreement. At the time the contract is entered into, no money changes hands.

short position

The futures trader who commits to delivering the asset.

Figure 17.1 shows prices for a sample of futures contracts as they appear in *The Wall Street Journal.* The boldface heading lists in each case the commodity, the exchange where the futures contract is traded in parentheses, the contract size, and the pricing unit. For example, the first contract listed under "Agriculture Futures" is for corn, traded on the Chicago Board of Trade (CBT). Each contract calls for delivery of 5,000 bushels, and prices in the entry are quoted in cents per bushel.

The next several rows detail price data for contracts expiring on various dates. The May 2007 maturity corn contract, for example, opened during the day at a futures price of 423.75 cents per bushel. The highest futures price during the day was 436.50, the lowest was 421.75, and the settlement price (a representative trading price during the last few minutes of trading) was 435.50. The settlement price increased by 11.25 cents from the previous trading day. Finally, open interest, or the number of outstanding contracts, was 544,527. Similar information is given for each maturity date.

The trader holding the long position, that is, the person who will purchase the good, profits from price increases. Suppose that when the contract matures in May, the price of corn turns out to be 440.50 cents per bushel. The long position trader who entered the contract at the futures price of 435.50 cents on March 2 (the date of the *Wall Street Journal* listing) earns a profit of 5 cents per bushel: The eventual price is 5 cents higher than the originally agreed-upon futures price. As each contract calls for delivery of 5,000 bushels (ignoring brokerage fees), the profit to the long position equals $5,000 \times \$0.05 = \$250$ per contract. Conversely, the short position loses 5 cents per bushel. The short position's loss equals the long position's gain.

To summarize, at maturity

$$\text{Profit to long} = \text{Spot price at maturity} - \text{Original futures price}$$
$$\text{Profit to short} = \text{Original futures price} - \text{Spot price at maturity}$$

where the spot price is the actual market price of the commodity at the time of the delivery.

The futures contract is, therefore, a *zero sum game,* with losses and gains to all positions netting out to zero. Every long position is offset by a short position. The aggregate profits to futures trading, summing over all investors, also must be zero, as is the net exposure to changes in the commodity price.

Figure 17.2, panel A, is a plot of the profits realized by an investor who enters the long side of a futures contract as a function of the price of the asset on the maturity date. Notice that profit is zero when the ultimate spot price, P_T, equals the initial futures price, F_0. Profit per unit of the underlying asset rises or falls one-for-one with changes in the final spot price. Unlike the payoff of a call option, the payoff of the long futures position can be negative: This

[1] We will show you how this is done later in the chapter.

FIGURE 17.1

Futures listings for March 2, 2007

Source: From *The Wall Street Journal*, March 3, 2007. Reprinted by permission of Dow Jones & Company, Inc.

KEY TO EXCHANGES: **CBT:** Chicago Board of Trade; **CME:** Chicago Mercantile Exchange; **CMX:** Comex; **KC:** Kansas City Board of Trade; **MPLS:** Minneapolis Grain Exchange; **NYBOT:** New York Board of Trade; **NYM:** New York Mercantile Exchange, or Nymex

Metal & Petroleum Futures

	Open	High	Low	Settle	Chg	Open interest

Copper-High (CMX)-25,000 lbs.; cents per lb.

	Open	High	Low	Settle	Chg	Open interest
March	272.10	278.75	270.20	**273.30**	-7.20	7,272
May	274.30	281.50	271.90	**275.20**	-7.30	42,514

Gold (CMX)-100 troy oz.; $ per troy oz.

March	665.60	674.50	662.00	**669.40**	-14.50	67
April	669.40	680.50	664.00	**672.50**	-14.70	241,133
June	673.60	686.80	670.20	**678.80**	-14.90	46,460
Oct	688.90	691.00	686.10	**691.00**	-15.20	26,308
Dec	694.60	701.00	689.00	**697.00**	-15.40	54,287
Dec'08	733.00	733.00	730.00	**731.60**	-16.40	11,052

Platinum (NYM)-50 troy oz.; $ per troy oz.

April	1232.50	1269.90	1232.50	**1256.40**	3.10	11,624
July	1256.00	1280.00 ▲	1247.00	**1267.40**	4.40	633

Silver (CMX)-5,000 troy oz.; cnts per troy oz.

March	1416.5	1438.5	1398.0	**1410.0**	-44.5	4,936
May	1435.0	1456.0	1412.0	**1423.5**	-45.5	76,114

Crude Oil, Light Sweet (NYM)-1,000 bbls.; $ per bbl.

April	60.28	62.10	59.92	**61.79**	0.33	331,101
May	61.52	63.30	61.11	**63.06**	0.44	149,450
June	62.24	64.18	62.05	**63.97**	0.45	104,494
Dec	64.91	67.08	64.91	**66.89**	0.53	144,627
Dec'08	67.39	68.25	67.10	**68.25**	0.62	74,559
Dec'09	67.50	68.30	67.28	**68.25**	0.80	46,710

Heating Oil No. 2 (NYM)-42,000 gal.; $ per gal.

March	1.7405	1.7900	1.7390	**1.7804**	.0011	8,476
April	1.7345	1.7804	1.7300	**1.7781**	.0076	80,693

Gasoline-NY RBOB (NYM)-42,000 gal.; $ per gal.

March	1.7850	1.8700	1.7825	**1.8476**	.0315	4,709
April	1.8200	1.8800	1.8200	**1.8738**	.0247	54,591

Natural Gas (NYM)-10,000 MMBtu.; $ per MMBtu.

April	7.450	7.485	7.242	**7.300**	-.233	90,378
May	7.520	7.540	7.350	**7.405**	-.213	86,821
Oct	7.900	7.990	7.825	**7.860**	-.188	45,108
Dec	9.050	9.081	8.990	**9.015**	-.143	37,270
Jan'08	9.317	9.438	9.272	**9.320**	-.138	35,258
March	9.120	9.148	9.080	**9.095**	-.138	45,380

Agriculture Futures

Corn (CBT)-5,000 bu.; cents per bu.

March	411.00	426.00	409.25	**425.25**	14.25	51,030
May	423.75	436.50	421.75	**435.50**	11.25	544,527

Ethanol (CBT)-29,000 gal.; $ per gal.

March	...	...	...	**2.258**	-.002	67
April	2.180	2.200	2.180	**2.200**	.020	89
June	2.120	2.120	2.120	**2.120**	...	89

Oats (CBT)-5,000 bu.; cents per bu.

March	251.00	256.00	249.00	**253.00**	3.75	264
Dec	245.50	250.00	245.50	**250.00**	2.00	8,443

Soybeans (CBT)-5,000 bu.; cents per bu.

March	762.75	774.00	757.25	**773.25**	9.75	22,759
May	773.25	788.75	772.50	**787.50**	8.75	251,994

Soybean Meal (CBT)-100 tons; $ per ton.

March	223.30	224.90	221.00	**224.40**	.90	6,812
May	228.80	231.70	227.20	**230.70**	1.00	107,477

Soybean Oil (CBT)-60,000 lbs.; cents per lb.

March	30.10	30.52	29.96	**30.25**	.11	14,413
May	30.53	31.12	30.39	**30.76**	.07	167,011

Rough Rice (CBT)-2,000 cwt.; cents per cwt.

March	1005.00	1023.00	1004.00	**1022.00**	17.50	1,080
May	1035.00	1056.00	1035.00	**1052.00**	14.50	8,972

Wheat (CBT)-5,000 bu.; cents per bu.

March	469.75	475.00	465.00	**474.50**	4.25	12,118
May	477.75	489.00	477.75	**488.00**	4.50	216,114

Cattle-Live (CME)-40,000 lbs.; cents per lb.

Feb	94.800	95.175 ▲	94.050	**94.450**	-.300	2,714
April	97.300	97.800	96.900	**97.050**	-.400	154,953

Hogs-Lean (CME)-40,000 lbs.; cents per lb.

April	67.200	68.800	67.050	**67.750**	.325	89,729
June	77.350	78.550	77.200	**78.050**	.600	38,915

Coffee (NYBOT)-37,500 lbs.; cents per lb.

	Open	High	Low	Settle	Chg	Open interest
March	117.00	117.80	116.75	**117.70**	.40	1,463
May	118.30	119.10	117.40	**118.50**	.20	85,453

Sugar-World (NYBOT)-112,000 lbs.; cents per lb.

March	11.22	11.45	11.00	**11.31**	-.14	22,971
May	10.57	10.74	10.52	**10.56**	-.24	295,035

Cotton (NYBOT)-50,000 lbs.; cents per lb.

March	55.45	55.65	55.20	**55.55**	.50	2,758
May	53.40	53.83	52.83	**53.82**	.76	115,348

Orange Juice (NYBOT)-15,000 lbs.; cents per lb.

March	207.00	207.25	203.50	**205.00**	-2.90	780
May	201.50	202.40	198.40	**200.50**	-2.45	20,258

Interest Rate Futures

Treasury Bonds (CBT)-$100,000; pts 32nds of 100%

March	113-14	113-15	112-21	**113-00**	-13	369,798
June	113-13	113-14	112-19	**112-30**	-14	559,287

Treasury Notes (CBT)-$100,000; pts 32nds of 100%

March	108-265	108-270	108-125	**108-180**	-7.0	651,188
June	108-280	108-285	108-125	**108-190**	-8.0	1,618,573

5 Yr. Treasury Notes (CBT)-$100,000; pts 32nds of 100%

March	105-295	105-300	105-190	**105-250**	-4.0	388,604
June	106-035	106-040	105-245	**105-305**	-4.5	1,139,504

2 Yr. Treasury Notes (CBT)-$200,000; pts 32nds of 100%

March	102-107	102-110	102-057	**102-087**	-1.5	198,517
June	102-170	102-185	102-120	**102-152**	-2.0	648,003

30 Day Federal Funds (CBT)-$5,000,000; 100 - daily avg.

Feb	94.745	94.750	94.745	**94.750**	...	95,711
April	94.770	94.770	94.755	**94.760**	-.005	124,050

1 Month Libor (CME)-$3,000,000; pts of 100%

March	94.6850	94.6850	94.6800	**94.6850**	...	29,998
April	94.7050	94.7075	94.7025	**94.7025**	-.0025	9,288

Eurodollar (CME)-$1,000,000; pts of 100%

March	94.6875	94.6875	94.6500	**94.6625**	-.0125	1,325,356
June	94.8400	94.8450	94.7600	**94.8100**	-.0200	1,507,553
Sept	95.0300	95.0350	94.9300	**94.9950**	-.0350	1,439,476
Dec	95.1900	95.2050	95.0850	**95.1500**	-.0450	1,649,586

Currency Futures

Japanese Yen (CME)-¥12,500,000; $ per 100¥

March	.8486	.8499	.8436	**.8473**	-.0009	292,962
June	.8590	.8595	.8535	**.8571**	-.0009	27,392

Canadian Dollar (CME)-CAD 100,000; $ per CAD

March	.8573	.8583	.8523	**.8553**	-.0026	128,647
June	.8599	.8605	.8545	**.8575**	-.0027	7,304

British Pound (CME)-£62,500; $ per £

March	1.9637	1.9646	1.9516	**1.9637**	.0005	157,318
June	1.9620	1.9639	1.9512	**1.9629**	.0005	2,859

Swiss Franc (CME)-CHF 125,000; $ per CHF

March	.8227	.8232	.8181	**.8225**	-.0008	101,873
June	.8286	.8290	.8246	**.8288**	-.0008	1,393

Australian Dollar (CME)-AUD 100,000; $ per AUD

March	.7871	.7890	.7852	**.7875**	-.0029	137,709
June	.7850	.7870	.7836	**.7856**	-.0029	2,017

Mexican Peso (CME)-MXN 500,000; $ per 10MXN

March	.89200	.89700	.89175	**.89400**	.00200	69,449
Dec	.88100	.88100	.88100	**.87925**	.00200	21,512

Euro (CME)-€125,000; $ per €

March	1.3252	1.3252	1.3192	**1.3242**	-.0013	215,942
June	1.3297	1.3297	1.3239	**1.3289**	-.0013	5,000

Index Futures

DJ Industrial Average (CBT)-$10 x index

March	12178	12355	12155	**12274**	94	73,582
June	12261	12450	12261	**12369**	89	715

S&P 500 Index (CME)-$250 x index

March	1395.90	1418.20	1390.50	**1408.90**	13.60	569,126
June	1416.20	1430.50	1411.50	**1421.50**	13.80	73,657

Nasdaq 100 (CME)-$100 x index

March	1750.50	1783.00	1744.25	**1765.50**	15.00	54,888
June	1777.00	1797.00	1776.00	**1786.50**	15.00	872

FIGURE 17.2

Profits to buyers and sellers of futures and options contracts
A: Long futures position (buyer) **B:** Short futures position (seller) **C:** Buy call option

will be the case if the spot price falls below the original futures price. Unlike the holder of a call, who has an *option* to buy, the long futures position trader cannot simply walk away from the contract. Also unlike options, in the case of futures there is no need to distinguish gross payoffs from net profits. This is because the futures contract is not purchased; it is simply a contract that is agreed to by two parties. The futures price adjusts to make the present value of either side of the contract equal to zero.

The distinction between futures and options is highlighted by comparing panel A of Figure 17.2 to the payoff and profit diagrams for an investor in a call option with exercise price, X, chosen equal to the futures price F_0 (see panel C). The futures investor is exposed to considerable losses if the asset price falls. In contrast, the investor in the call cannot lose more than the cost of the option.

Figure 17.2, panel B, is a plot of the profits realized by an investor who enters the short side of a futures contract. It is the mirror image of the profit diagram for the long position.

a.   Compare the profit diagram in Figure 17.2B to the payoff diagram for a long position in a put option. Assume the exercise price of the option equals the initial futures price.

b.   Compare the profit diagram in Figure 17.2B to the payoff diagram for an investor who writes a call option.

Existing Contracts

single stock futures

A futures contract on the shares of an individual company.

Futures and forward contracts are traded on a wide variety of goods in four broad categories: agricultural commodities, metals and minerals (including energy commodities), foreign currencies, and financial futures (fixed-income securities and stock market indexes). In addition to indexes on broad stock indexes, one can now trade so-called single stock futures on individual stocks and narrowly based indexes. OneChicago (a joint venture of the Chicago Board Options Exchange, Chicago Mercantile Exchange, and Chicago Board of Trade) has operated an entirely electronic market in single stock futures since 2002. The exchange maintains futures markets in actively traded stocks with the most liquidity. However, trading volume in this market has to date been somewhat disappointing.

PRESIDENTIAL AND OTHER PREDICTION FUTURES

If you find S&P 500 or T-bond contracts a bit dry, perhaps you'd be interested in futures contacts with payoffs that depend on the winner of the next presidential election, or the severity of the next influenza season, or the host city of the 2012 Olympics. You can now find "futures markets" in these events and many others.

For example both Intrade (**www.intrade.com**) and Iowa Electronic Markets (**www.biz.uiowa.edu/iem**) maintain presidential futures markets. Contracts pay off $1 if the candidate you "purchase" wins the election. The contract price for each candidate therefore may be viewed as the probability of that candidate's success, at least according to the consensus view of the participants in the market.

The table below reproduces presidential futures prices from Intrade on March 6, 2007, a date still far in advance of the 2008 election. If you wished to bet on a Hillary Clinton victory, you could have purchased a Clinton contract for the ask price of $.26, which would pay off $1 if she were to win in November. Alternatively, if you wanted to bet against her, you could *sell* a Clinton contract for the bid price of $.233. You'd then be on the hook for $1 if she were to win the election. Based on these prices, the odds of a Clinton victory seemed to be around 25%. There were no clear favorites at this time, which was still 20 months in advance of the election—no one's futures prices were greater than $.26.

Notice that the sum of the bid prices for all of the candidates combined is $.93, a bit below $1.00. Can you explain why this makes sense? Notice also that the sum of the ask prices is $1.105, which is a bit above $1.00. Does this make sense? (The answers appear with the Concept Checks Solutions at the end of the chapter.)

Contract	Best to Sell		Best to Buy				
	BQty	Bid	Offer	AQty	Last	Vol	Chge
Trade 2008.PRES.McCAIN	9	16.6	19.0	50	17.0	11.1k	0
Trade 2008.PRES.OBAMA	1	15.2	19.9	72	19.9	8056	−0.1
Trade 2008.PRES.WARNER	7	0.1	1.0	100	1.0	1037	0
Trade 2008.PRES.CLINTON(H)	20	23.3	26.0	2	26.5	17.1k	0
Trade 2008.PRES.GIULIANI	30	17.0	19.8	4	19.0	8778	0
Trade 2008.PRES.ROMNEY	100	8.7	8.9	20	8.5	4887	0
Trade 2008.PRES.ALLEN	0	–	1.0	99	1.0	344	0
Trade 2008.PRES.EDWARDS	100	5.0	7.0	5	8.1	1574	0
Trade 2008.PRES.GORE	20	7.1	7.9	20	7.8	7280	−0.1

Innovation in financial futures has been rapid and is ongoing. Table 17.1 offers a sample of contracts trading in 2006. Contracts now trade on items that would not have been considered possible only a few years ago. For example, there are now electricity as well as weather futures and options contracts. Weather derivatives (which trade on the Chicago Mercantile Exchange) have payoffs that depend on average weather conditions, for example, the number of degree-days by which the temperature in a region exceeds or falls short of 65 degrees Fahrenheit. The potential use of these derivatives in managing the risk surrounding electricity or oil and natural gas use should be evident.

While Table 17.1 includes many contracts, the large and ever-growing array of markets makes this list necessarily incomplete. The nearby box discusses some comparatively fanciful futures markets in which payoffs may be tied to the winner of presidential elections, the box office receipts of a particular movie, or anything else in which participants are willing to take positions.

Outside the futures markets, a well-developed network of banks and brokers has established a forward market in foreign exchange. This forward market is not a formal exchange in the sense that the exchange specifies the terms of the traded contract. Instead, participants in a forward contract may negotiate for delivery of any quantity of goods at any time, whereas, in the formal futures markets, contract size and delivery dates are set by the exchange. In forward arrangements, banks and brokers simply negotiate contracts for clients (or themselves) as needed.

TABLE 17.1

Sample of futures contracts

Foreign Currencies	Agricultural	Metals and Energy	Interest Rate Futures	Equity Indexes
British pound	Corn	Copper	Eurodollars	Dow Jones Industrials
Canadian dollar	Oats	Aluminum	Euroyen	S&P Midcap 400
Japanese yen	Soybeans	Gold	Euro-denominated	Nasdaq 100
Euro	Soybean meal	Platinum	bond	NYSE index
Swiss franc	Soybean oil	Palladium	Euroswiss	Russell 2000 index
Australian dollar	Wheat	Silver	Sterling	Nikkei 225 (Japanese)
Mexican peso	Barley	Crude oil	British gov't bond	FTSE index (British)
Brazilian real	Flaxseed	Heating oil	German gov't bond	CAC index (French)
	Canola	Gas oil	Italian gov't bond	DAX index (German)
	Rye	Natural gas	Canadian gov't bond	All ordinary (Australian)
	Cattle	Gasoline	Treasury bonds	Toronto 35 (Canadian)
	Milk	Propane	Treasury notes	Titans 30 (Italian)
	Hogs	Commodity	Treasury bills	Dow Jones Euro STOXX 50
	Pork bellies	index	LIBOR	Industry indexes, e.g.,
	Cocoa	Electricity	EURIBOR	banking
	Coffee	Weather	Municipal bond index	natural resources
	Cotton		Federal funds rate	chemical
	Orange juice		Bankers' acceptance	health care
	Sugar		S&P 500 index	technology
	Lumber		Interest rate swaps	retail
	Rice			utilities
				telecom

17.2 MECHANICS OF TRADING IN FUTURES MARKETS

The Clearinghouse and Open Interest

Until recently, most futures trades in the United States occurred among floor traders in the "trading pit" for each contract. Participants there use voice or hand signals to signify their desire to buy or sell and locate a trader willing to accept the opposite side of a trade. Today, however, trading is increasingly done over electronic networks, particularly for financial futures.

The impetus for this shift originated in Europe, where electronic trading is the norm. Eurex, which is jointly owned by the Deutsche Börse and Swiss exchange, is currently the world's largest futures and options exchange. It operates a fully electronic trading and clearing platform, and in 2004, received clearance from regulators to list contracts in the U.S. In response, the Chicago Board of Trade adopted an electronic platform provided by Eurex's European rival Euronext.liffe,[2] and the great majority of the CBOT's Treasury contracts are now traded electronically. The Chicago Mercantile Exchange maintains another electronic trading system called Globex. These electronic exchanges enable trading around the clock. The CBOT and CME agreed in 2007 to merge into one combined company, to be named CME Group, intending to ultimately move all electronic trading from both exchanges onto CME Globex. It seems inevitable that electronic trading will continue to displace floor trading. The combined firm will be the world's largest derivatives exchange as well as a very strong competitor in the over-the-counter derivatives market.

---

[2]Euronext.liffe is the international derivatives market of Euronext. It resulted from Euronext's purchase of LIFFE (the London International Financial Futures and Options Exchange) and a merger with the Lisbon exchange in 2002. Euronext was itself the result of a 2000 merger of the exchanges of Amsterdam, Brussels, and Paris.

Once a trade is agreed to, the **clearinghouse** enters the picture. Rather than having the long and short traders hold contracts with each other, the clearinghouse becomes the seller of the contract for the long position and the buyer of the contract for the short position. The clearinghouse is obligated to deliver the commodity to the long position and to pay for delivery from the short; consequently, the clearinghouse's position nets to zero. This arrangement makes the clearinghouse the trading partner of each trader, both long and short. The clearinghouse, bound to perform on its side of each contract, is the only party that can be hurt by the failure of any trader to observe the obligations of the futures contract. This arrangement is necessary because a futures contract calls for future performance, which cannot be as easily guaranteed as an immediate stock transaction.

Figure 17.3 illustrates the role of the clearinghouse. Panel A shows what would happen in the absence of the clearinghouse. The trader in the long position would be obligated to pay the futures price to the short position trader, and the trader in the short position would be obligated to deliver the commodity. Panel B shows how the clearinghouse becomes an intermediary, acting as the trading partner for each side of the contract. The clearinghouse's position is neutral, as it takes a long and a short position for each transaction.

The clearinghouse makes it possible for traders to liquidate positions easily. If you are currently long in a contract and want to undo your position, you simply instruct your broker to enter the short side of a contract to close out your position. This is called a *reversing trade*. The exchange nets out your long and short positions, reducing your net position to zero. Your zero net position with the clearinghouse eliminates the need to fulfill at maturity either the original long or reversing short position.

The *open interest* on the contract is the number of contracts outstanding. (Long and short positions are not counted separately, meaning that open interest can be defined as either the number of long or short contracts outstanding.) The clearinghouse's position nets out to zero, and so it is not counted in the computation of open interest. When contracts begin trading, open interest is zero. As time passes, open interest increases as progressively more contracts are entered.

There are many apocryphal stories about futures traders who wake up to discover a small mountain of wheat or corn on their front lawn. But the truth is that futures contracts rarely result in actual delivery of the underlying asset. Traders establish long or short positions in contracts that will benefit from a rise or fall in the futures price and almost always close out those positions before the contract expires. The fraction of contracts that result in actual delivery is estimated to range from less than 1% to 3%, depending on the commodity and activity in the contract. In the unusual case of actual deliveries of commodities, they occur via regular channels of supply, usually via warehouse receipts.

clearinghouse

Established by exchanges to facilitate trading. The clearinghouse may interpose itself as an intermediary between two traders.

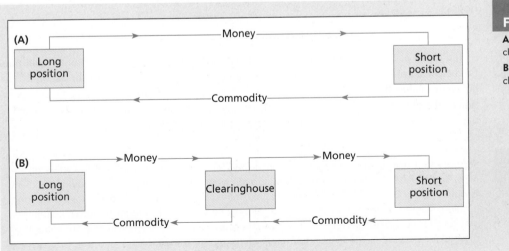

FIGURE 17.3

A. Trading without the clearinghouse

B. Trading with a clearinghouse

You can see the typical pattern of open interest in Figure 17.1. In the gold contract, for example, the March delivery contracts are close to maturity, and open interest is small; most contracts have been reversed already. The next few maturities have significantly greater open interest. Finally, the most distant maturity contracts have less open interest, as they have been available only recently, and few participants have yet traded. For other contracts such as crude oil, for which the nearest maturity is still more than a month away, open interest is highest in the nearest contract.

Marking to Market and the Margin Account

The total profit or loss realized by the long trader who buys a contract at time 0 and closes, or reverses, it at time t is just the change in the futures price over the period, $F_t - F_0$. Symmetrically, the short trader earns $F_0 - F_t$.

marking to market

The daily settlement of obligations on futures positions.

The process by which profits or losses accrue to traders is called **marking to market.** At initial execution of a trade, each trader establishes a margin account. The margin is a security account consisting of cash or near-cash securities, such as Treasury bills, that ensures the trader will be able to satisfy the obligations of the futures contract. Because both parties to the futures contract are exposed to losses, both must post margin. To illustrate, return to the May corn contract listed in Figure 17.1. If the initial required margin on corn, for example, is 10%, the trader must post $2,177.50 per contract for the margin account. This is 10% of the value of the contract ($4.355 per bushel $\times$ 5,000 bushels per contract).

Because the initial margin may be satisfied by posting interest-earning securities, the requirement does not impose a significant opportunity cost of funds on the trader. The initial margin is usually set between 5% and 15% of the total value of the contract. Contracts written on assets with more volatile prices require higher margins.

On any day that futures contracts trade, futures prices may rise or fall. Instead of waiting until the maturity date for traders to realize all gains and losses, the clearinghouse requires all positions to recognize profits as they accrue daily. If the futures price of corn rises from 435.5 to 437.5 cents per bushel, for example, the clearinghouse credits the margin account of the long position for 5,000 bushels times 2 cents per bushel, or $100 per contract. Conversely, for the short position, the clearinghouse takes this amount from the margin account for each contract held. Therefore, as futures prices change, proceeds accrue to the trader's account immediately.

Marking to market is the major way in which futures and forward contracts differ, besides contract standardization. Futures follow this pay- (or receive-) as-you-go method. Forward contracts are simply held until maturity, and no funds are transferred until that date, although the contracts may be traded.

> **CONCEPT check 17.2**
>
> What must be the net inflow or outlay from marking to market for the clearinghouse?

maintenance margin

An established value below which a trader's margin may not fall. Reaching the maintenance margin triggers a margin call.

If a trader accrues sustained losses from daily marking to market, the margin account may fall below a critical value called the **maintenance margin.** If the value of the account falls below this value, the trader receives a margin call. Margins and margin calls safeguard the position of the clearinghouse. Positions are closed out before the margin account is exhausted—the trader's losses are covered, and the clearinghouse is not put at risk.

> **EXAMPLE 17.1**
>
> *Maintenance Margin*
>
> Suppose the maintenance margin is 5% while the initial margin was 10% of the value of the corn, or $2,177.50. Then a margin call will go out when the original margin account has fallen about in half, or by $1,089. Each 1 cent decline in the corn price results in a $50 loss to the long position. Therefore, the futures price need fall only by 22 cents to trigger a margin call. Either new funds must be transferred into the margin account, or the broker will close out enough of the trader's account to reestablish the required margin for the position.

It is important to note that the futures price on the delivery date will equal the spot price of the commodity on that date. As a maturing contract calls for immediately delivery, the futures price on that day must equal the spot price—the cost of the commodity from the two competing sources is equalized in a competitive market.[3] You may obtain delivery of the commodity either by purchasing it directly in the spot market or by entering the long side of a maturing futures contract.

A commodity available from two sources (the spot and futures markets) must be priced identically, or else investors will rush to purchase it from the cheap source in order to sell it in the high-priced market. Such arbitrage activity could not persist without prices adjusting to eliminate the arbitrage opportunity. Therefore, the futures price and the spot price must converge at maturity. This is called the **convergence property.**

For an investor who establishes a long position in a contract now (time 0) and holds that position until maturity (time T), the sum of all daily settlements will equal $F_T - F_0$, where F_T stands for the futures price at contract maturity. Because of convergence, however, the futures price at maturity, F_T, equals the spot price, P_T, so total futures profits also may be expressed as $P_T - F_0$. Thus, we see that profits on a futures contract held to maturity perfectly track changes in the value of the underlying asset.

convergence property

The convergence of futures prices and spot prices at the maturity of the futures contract.

Assume the current futures price for silver for delivery five days from today is $12.10 per ounce. Suppose that over the next five days, the futures price evolves as follows:

Day	Futures Price
0 (today)	$12.10
1	12.20
2	12.25
3	12.18
4	12.18
5 (delivery)	12.21

EXAMPLE 17.2

Marking to Market and Futures Contract Profits

The spot price of silver on the delivery date is $12.21: The convergence property implies that the price of silver in the spot market must equal the futures price on the delivery day.

The daily mark-to-market settlements for each contract held by the long positions will be as follows:

Day	Profit (loss) per Ounce	× 5,000 Ounces/Contract = Daily Proceeds
1	$12.20 − $12.10 = $ 0.10	$500
2	12.25 − 12.20 = 0.05	250
3	12.18 − 12.25 = −0.07	−350
4	12.18 − 12.18 = 0	0
5	12.21 − 12.18 = 0.03	150
		Sum = $550

The profit on day 1 is the increase in the futures price from the previous day, or ($12.20 − $12.10) per ounce. Because each silver contract on the Commodity Exchange calls for purchase and delivery of 5,000 ounces, the profit per contract is 5,000 times $0.10, or $500. On day 3, when the futures price falls, the long position's margin account will be debited by $350. By day 5, the sum of all daily proceeds is $550. This is exactly equal to 5,000 times the difference between the final futures price of $12.21 and the original futures price of $12.10. Thus, the sum of all the daily proceeds (per ounce of silver held long) equals $P_T - F_0$.

---

[3]Small differences between the spot and futures prices at maturity may persist because of transportation costs, but this is a minor factor.

Cash versus Actual Delivery

Most futures markets call for delivery of an actual commodity, such as a particular grade of wheat or a specified amount of foreign currency, if the contract is not reversed before maturity. For agricultural commodities, where quality of the delivered good may vary, the exchange sets quality standards as part of the futures contract. In some cases, contracts may be settled with higher or lower grade commodities. In these cases, a premium or discount is applied to the delivered commodity to adjust for the quality differences.

cash settlement

The cash value of the underlying asset (rather than the asset itself) is delivered to satisfy the contract.

Some futures contracts call for **cash settlement.** An example is a stock index futures contract where the underlying asset is an index such as the Standard & Poor's 500 index. Delivery of every stock in the index clearly would be impractical. Hence, the contract calls for "delivery" of a cash amount equal to the value that the index attains on the maturity date of the contract. The sum of all the daily settlements from marking to market results in the long position realizing total profits or losses of $S_T - F_0$, where S_T is the value of the stock index on the maturity date T, and F_0 is the original futures price. Cash settlement closely mimics actual delivery, except the cash value of the asset rather than the asset itself is delivered by the short position in exchange for the futures price.

More concretely, the S&P 500 index contract calls for delivery of $250 times the value of the index. At maturity, the index might list at 1,300, a market value-weighted index of the prices of all 500 stocks in the index. The cash settlement contract would then call for delivery of $250 × 1,300, or $325,000 cash in return for $250 times the futures price. This yields exactly the same profit as would result from directly purchasing 250 units of the index for $325,000 and then delivering it for $250 times the original futures price.

Regulations

Futures markets are regulated by the Commodity Futures Trading Commission (CFTC), a federal agency. The CFTC sets capital requirements for member firms of the futures exchanges, authorizes trading in new contracts, and oversees maintenance of daily trading records.

The futures exchange may set limits on the amount by which futures prices may change from one day to the next. For example, if the price limit on silver contracts is $1, and silver futures close today at $12.10 per ounce, trades in silver tomorrow may vary only between $13.10 and $11.10 per ounce. The exchange may increase or reduce these price limits in response to perceived changes in the price volatility of the contract. Price limits often are eliminated as contracts approach maturity, usually in the last month of trading.

Price limits traditionally are viewed as a means to limit violent price fluctuations. This reasoning seems dubious. Suppose an international monetary crisis overnight drives up the spot price of silver to $17.00. No one would sell silver futures at prices for future delivery as low as $12.10. Instead, the futures price would rise each day by the $1 limit, although the quoted price would represent only an unfilled bid order—no contracts would trade at the low quoted price. After several days of limit moves of $1 per day, the futures price would finally reach its equilibrium level, and trading would occur again. This process means no one could unload a position until the price reached its equilibrium level. This example shows that price limits offer no real protection against fluctuations in equilibrium prices.

Taxation

Because of the mark-to-market procedure, investors do not have control over the tax year in which they realize gains or losses. Instead, price changes are realized gradually, with each daily settlement. Therefore, taxes are paid at year-end on cumulated profits or losses regardless of whether the position has been closed out.

17.3 | FUTURES MARKET STRATEGIES

Hedging and Speculation

Hedging and speculating are two polar uses of futures markets. A speculator uses a futures contract to profit from movements in futures prices, a hedger to protect against price movements.

If speculators believe prices will increase, they will take a long position for expected profits. Conversely, they exploit expected price declines by taking a short position.

Suppose you believe that crude oil prices are going to increase. You might purchase crude oil futures, the listings for which appear in Figure 17.1. Each contract calls for delivery of 1,000 barrels of oil. The current futures price for delivery in April (the first listed contract) is $61.79 per barrel. For every dollar increase in the price of crude, the long position gains $1,000 and the short position loses that amount. Conversely, suppose you think that prices are heading lower. If crude oil prices fall, then the short side gains $1,000 for every dollar that prices decline. If crude oil is selling for $63.79 at the contract maturity date, the long side will profit by $2,000 per contract purchased. The short side will lose an identical amount on each contract sold. On the other hand, if oil has fallen to $59.79, the long side will lose, and the short side will gain, $2,000 per contract.

EXAMPLE 17.3

Speculating with Oil Futures

Why would a speculator buy a futures contract? Why not buy the underlying asset directly? One reason lies in transaction costs, which are far smaller in futures markets.

Another reason is the leverage futures trading provides. Recall that futures contracts require traders to post margin considerably less than the value of the asset underlying the contract. Therefore, they allow speculators to achieve much greater leverage than is available from direct trading in a commodity.

Suppose the initial margin requirement for the oil contract is 10%. At a current futures price of $61.79, and contract size of 1,000 barrels, this would require margin of .10 × 61.79 × 1,000 = $6,179. A $2 jump in oil prices represents an increase of 3.237%, and results in a $2,000 gain on the contract for the long position. This is a percentage gain of 32.37% in the $6,179 posted as margin, precisely 10 times the percentage increase in the oil price. The 10-to-1 ratio of percentage changes reflects the leverage inherent in the futures position, since the contract was established with an initial margin of one-tenth the value of the underlying asset.

EXAMPLE 17.4

Futures and Leverage

Hedgers, by contrast, use futures to insulate themselves against price movements. A firm planning to sell oil, for example, might anticipate a period of market volatility and wish to protect its revenue against price fluctuations. To hedge the total revenue derived from the sale, the firm enters a short position in oil futures. As the following example illustrates, this locks in its total proceeds (i.e., revenue from the sale of the oil plus proceeds from its futures position).

Consider an oil distributor planning to sell 100,000 barrels of oil in April that wishes to hedge against a possible decline in oil prices. Because each contract calls for delivery of 1,000 barrels, it would sell 100 contracts. Any decrease in prices would then generate a profit on the contracts that would offset the lower sales revenue from the oil. **(Continued)**

EXAMPLE 17.5

Hedging with Oil Futures

EXAMPLE   17.5

Hedging with Oil Futures (Concluded)

To illustrate, continue to use the oil futures listing in Figure 17.1, and suppose that the only three possible prices for oil in April are $59.79, $61.79, and $63.79 per barrel. The revenue from the oil sale will be 100,000 times the price per barrel. The profit on each contract sold will be 1,000 times any decline in the futures price. At maturity, the convergence property ensures that the final futures price will equal the spot price of oil. Therefore, the profit on the 100 contracts sold will equal $100,000 \times (F_0 - P_T)$, where P_T is the oil price on the delivery date, and F_0 is the original futures price, $61.79.

Now consider the firm's overall position. The total revenue in April can be computed as follows:

	Oil Price in April, P_T		
	$59.79	**$61.79**	**$63.79**
Revenue from oil sale: $100,000 \times P_T$	$5,979,000	$6,179,000	$6,379,000
+ Profit on futures: $100,000 \times (F_0 - P_T)$	200,000	0	−200,000
Total Proceeds	$6,179,000	$6,179,000	$6,179,000

The revenue from the oil sale plus the proceeds from the contracts equals the current futures price, $61.79 per barrel. The variation in the price of the oil is precisely offset by the profits or losses on the futures position. For example, if oil falls to $59.79 a barrel, the short futures position generates $200,000 profit, just enough to bring total revenues to $6,179,000. The total is the same as if one were to arrange today to sell the oil in April at the futures price.

Figure 17.4 illustrates the nature of the hedge in Example 17.5. The upward-sloping line is the revenue from the sale of oil. The downward-sloping line is the profit on the futures contract. The horizontal line is the sum of sales revenue plus futures profits. This line is flat, as the hedged position is independent of oil prices.

To generalize Example 17.5, note that oil will sell for P_T per barrel at the maturity of the contract. The profit per barrel on the futures will be $F_0 - P_T$. Therefore, total revenue is $P_T + (F_0 - P_T) = F_0$, which is independent of the eventual oil price.

The utility in this example engaged in a *short hedge*, taking a short futures position to offset risk in the sales price of a particular asset. A *long hedge* is the analogous hedge for someone who wishes to eliminate the risk of an uncertain purchase price. For example, suppose a power

FIGURE 17.4

Hedging revenues using futures, Example 17.5 (Futures price = $61.79)

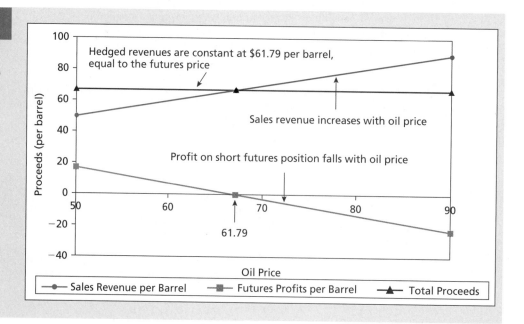

supplier planning to purchase oil is afraid that prices might rise by the time of the purchase. As the following Concept Check illustrates, the supplier might *buy* oil futures to lock in the net purchase price at the time of the transaction.

> Suppose as in Example 17.5 that oil will be selling in April for $59.79, $61.79, or $63.79 per barrel. Consider a firm that plans to buy 100,000 barrels of oil in April. Show that if the firm buys 100 oil contracts, its net expenditures will be hedged and equal to $6,179,000.
>
> **CONCEPT check 17.3**

Exact futures hedging may be impossible for some goods because the necessary futures contract is not traded. For example, a portfolio manager might want to hedge the value of a diversified, actively managed portfolio for a period of time. However, futures contracts are listed only on indexed portfolios. Nevertheless, because returns on the manager's diversified portfolio will have a high correlation with returns on broad-based indexed portfolios, an effective hedge may be established by selling index futures contracts. Hedging a position using futures on another asset is called *cross-hedging*.

> What are the sources of risk to an investor who uses stock index futures to hedge an actively managed stock portfolio?
>
> **CONCEPT check 17.4**

Basis Risk and Hedging

The **basis** is the difference between the futures price and the spot price.[4] As we have noted, on the maturity date of a contract, the basis must be zero: The convergence property implies that $F_T - P_T = 0$. Before maturity, however, the futures price for later delivery may differ substantially from the current spot price.

For example, in Example 17.5, we discussed the case of a short hedger who manages risk by entering a short position to deliver oil in the future. If the asset and futures contract are held until maturity, the hedger bears no risk. Risk is eliminated because the futures price and spot price at contract maturity must be equal: Gains and losses on the futures and the underlying asset will exactly cancel. If the contract and asset are to be liquidated early, before contract maturity, however, the hedger bears **basis risk,** because the futures price and spot price need not move in perfect lockstep at all times before the delivery date. In this case, gains and losses on the contract and the asset may not exactly offset each other.

basis

The difference between the futures price and the spot price.

basis risk

Risk attributable to uncertain movements in the spread between a futures price and a spot price.

WEB *master*

Hedging Commodities

Farmers can hedge crop-price fluctuations with futures contracts. Futures contract specifications can be found at **www.cbot.com.** Look at the contract details for corn futures. Assume that you are a corn farmer with a 20,000-bushel harvest expected in the fall. Answer the following questions about creating a hedge.

1. Which contract will you use to institute your hedge?
2. Based on the contract details, calculate the number of futures contracts to best hedge your position.
3. Describe the impact of both a rise and a decline in the spot price of corn at the time of harvest and when the contract expires.

---

[4]Usage of the word *basis* is somewhat loose. It sometimes is used to refer to the futures-spot difference, $F - P$, and other times it is used to refer to the spot-futures difference, $P - F$. We will consistently call the basis $F - P$.

Some speculators try to profit from movements in the basis. Rather than betting on the direction of the futures or spot prices per se, they bet on the changes in the difference between the two. A long spot–short futures position will profit when the basis narrows.

Consider an investor holding 100 ounces of gold, who is short one gold futures contract. Suppose that gold today sells for $691 an ounce, and the futures price for June delivery is $696 an ounce. Therefore, the basis is currently $5. Tomorrow, the spot price might increase to $694, while the futures price increases to $698.50, so the basis narrows to $4.50. The investor's gains and losses are as follows:

Gain on holdings of gold (per ounce): $694 − $691 = $3.00
Loss on gold futures position (per ounce): $698.50 − $696 = $2.50

The investor gains $3 per ounce on the gold holdings, but loses $2.50 an ounce on the short futures position. The net gain is the decrease in the basis, or $0.50 an ounce.

spread (futures)

Taking a long position in a futures contract of one maturity and a short position in a contract of a different maturity, both on the same commodity.

A related strategy is a **spread** position, where the investor takes a long position in a futures contract of one maturity and a short position in a contract on the same commodity, but with a different maturity. Profits accrue if the difference in futures prices between the two contracts changes in the hoped-for direction; that is, if the futures price on the contract held long increases by more (or decreases by less) than the futures price on the contract held short. Like basis strategies, spread positions aim to exploit movements in relative price structures rather than to profit from movements in the general level of prices.

Consider an investor who holds a September maturity contract long and a June contract short. If the September futures price increases by 5 cents while the June futures price increases by 4 cents, the net gain will be 5 cents − 4 cents, or 1 cent.

17.4 THE DETERMINATION OF FUTURES PRICES

Spot-Futures Parity

There are at least two ways to obtain an asset at some date in the future. One way is to purchase the asset now and store it until the targeted date. The other way is to take a long futures position that calls for purchase of the asset on the date in question. As each strategy leads to an equivalent result, namely, the ultimate acquisition of the asset, you would expect the market-determined cost of pursuing these strategies to be equal. There should be a predictable relationship between the current price of the asset, including the costs of holding and storing it, and the futures price.

To make the discussion more concrete, consider a futures contract on gold. This is a particularly simple case: Explicit storage costs for gold are minimal, gold provides no income flow for its owners (in contrast to stocks or bonds that make dividend or coupon payments), and gold is not subject to the seasonal price patterns that characterize most agricultural commodities. Instead, in market equilibrium, the price of gold will be at a level such that the expected rate of capital gains will equal the fair expected rate of return given gold's investment risk. Two strategies that will assure possession of the gold at some future date T are:

Strategy A: Buy the gold now, paying the current or "spot" price, S_0, and hold it until time T, when its spot price will be S_T.

Strategy B: Initiate a long futures position, and invest enough money now in order to pay the futures price when the contract matures.

Strategy B will require an immediate investment of the *present value* of the futures price in a riskless security such as Treasury bills, that is, an investment of $F_0/(1 + r_f)^T$ dollars, where r_f is the rate paid on T-bills. Examine the cash flow streams of the following two strategies.[5]

	Action	Initial Cash Flow	Cash Flow at Time T
Strategy A:	Buy gold	$-S_0$	S_T
Strategy B:	Enter long position	0	$S_T - F_0$
	Invest $F_0/(1 + r_f)^T$ in bills	$-F_0/(1 + r_f)^T$	F_0
	Total for strategy B	$-F_0/(1 + r_f)^T$	S_T

The initial cash flow of strategy A is negative, reflecting the cash outflow necessary to purchase the gold at the current spot price, S_0. At time T, the gold will be worth S_T.

Strategy B involves an initial investment equal to the present value of the futures price that will be paid at the maturity of the futures contract. By time T, the investment will grow to F_0. In addition, the profits to the long position at time T will be $S_T - F_0$. The sum of the two components of strategy B will be S_T dollars, exactly enough to purchase the gold at time T regardless of its price at that time.

Each strategy results in an identical value of S_T dollars at T. Therefore, the cost, or initial cash outflow, required by these strategies also must be equal; it follows that

$$F_0/(1 + r_f)^T = S_0$$

or

$$F_0 = S_0(1 + r_f)^T \tag{17.1}$$

This gives us a relationship between the current price and the futures price of the gold. The interest rate in this case may be viewed as the "cost of carrying" the gold from the present to time T. The cost in this case represents the time-value-of-money opportunity cost—instead of investing in the gold, you could have invested risklessly in Treasury bills to earn interest income.

EXAMPLE   17.8

Futures Pricing

Suppose that gold currently sells for $600 an ounce. If the risk-free interest rate is 0.5% per month, a six-month maturity futures contract should have a futures price of

$$F_0 = S_0(1 + r_f)^T = \$600(1.005)^6 = \$618.23$$

If the contract has a 12-month maturity, the futures price should be

$$F_0 = \$600(1.005)^{12} = \$637.01$$

---

[5]We ignore the margin requirement on the futures contract and treat the cash flow involved in establishing the futures position as zero for the two reasons mentioned above: First, the margin is small relative to the amount of gold controlled by one contract; and second, and more important, the margin requirement may be satisfied with interest-bearing securities. For example, the investor merely needs to transfer Treasury bills already owned into the brokerage account. There is no time-value-of-money cost.

If Equation 17.1 does not hold, investors can earn arbitrage profits. For example, suppose the six-month maturity futures price in Example 17.8 were $619 rather than the "appropriate" value of $618.23 that we just derived. An investor could realize arbitrage profits by pursuing a strategy involving a long position in strategy A (buy the gold) and a short position in strategy B (sell the futures contract and borrow enough to pay for the gold purchase).

Action	Initial Cash Flow	Cash Flow at Time T (6 months)
Borrow $600, repay with interest at time T	+$600	$-\$600(1.005)^6 = -\$618.23$
Buy gold for $600	−600	S_T
Enter short futures position ($F_0 = \$619$)	0	$619 - S_{T}$
Total	$ 0	$0.77

The net initial investment of this strategy is zero. Moreover, its cash flow at time T is positive and riskless: The total payoff at time T will be $0.77 regardless of the price of gold. (The profit is equal to the mispricing of the futures contract, $619 rather than $618.23.) Risk has been eliminated because profits and losses on the futures and gold positions exactly offset each other. The portfolio is perfectly hedged.

Such a strategy produces an arbitrage profit—a riskless profit requiring no initial net investment. If such an opportunity existed, all market participants would rush to take advantage of it. The results? The price of gold would be bid up, and/or the futures price offered down, until Equation 17.1 is satisfied. A similar analysis applies to the possibility that F_0 is less than $618.23. In this case, you simply reverse the above strategy to earn riskless profits. We conclude, therefore, that in a well-functioning market in which arbitrage opportunities are competed away, $F_0 = S_0(1 + r_f)^T$.

CONCEPT check 17.5

Return to the arbitrage strategy just laid out. What would be the three steps of the strategy if F_0 were too low, say, $617? Work out the cash flows of the strategy now and at time T in a table like the one above.

The arbitrage strategy can be represented more generally as follows:

Action	Initial Cash Flow	Cash Flow at Time T
1. Borrow S_0	$-S_0$	$-S_0(1 + r_f)^T$
2. Buy gold for S_0	$-S_0$	S_T
3. Enter short futures position	0	$F_0 - S_T$
Total	0	$F_0 - S_0(1 + r_f)^T$

spot-futures parity theorem, or cost-of-carry relationship

Describes the theoretically correct relationship between spot and futures prices. Violation of the parity relationship gives rise to arbitrage opportunities.

The initial cash flow is zero by construction: The money necessary to purchase the gold in step 2 is borrowed in step 1, and the futures position in step 3, which is used to hedge the value of the gold, does not require an initial outlay. Moreover, the total cash flow to the strategy at time T is riskless because it involves only terms that are already known when the contract is entered. This situation could not persist, as all investors would try to cash in on the arbitrage opportunity. Ultimately prices would change until the time T cash flow was reduced to zero, at which point F_0 would equal $S_0(1 + r_f)^T$. This result is called the **spot-futures parity**

The Parity spreadsheet allows you to calculate futures prices corresponding to a spot price for different maturities, interest rates, and income yields. You can use the spreadsheet to see how prices of more distant contracts will fluctuate with spot prices and the cost of carry.

You can learn more about this spreadsheet by using the version available on our Web site at **www.mhhe.com/bkm.**

eXcel

**Please visit us at
www.mhhe.com/bkm**

	A	B	C	D	E
1					
2		**Spot Futures Parity and Time Spreads**			
3					
4	Spot price	100			
5	Income yield (%)	2		Futures prices versus maturity	
6	Interest rate (%)	4.5			
7	Today's date	5/14/05		Spot price	100.00
8	Maturity date 1	11/17/05		Futures 1	101.26
9	Maturity date 2	1/2/06		Futures 2	101.58
10	Maturity date 3	6/7/06		Futures 3	102.66
11					
12	Time to maturity 1	0.51			
13	Time to maturity 2	0.63			
14	Time to maturity 3	1.06			

theorem or **cost-of-carry relationship**; it gives the normal or theoretically correct relationship between spot and futures prices.

We can easily extend the parity theorem to the case where the underlying asset provides a flow of income to its owner. For example, consider a futures contract on a stock index such as the S&P 500. In this case, the underlying asset (i.e., the stock portfolio indexed to the S&P 500 index), pays a dividend yield to the investor. If we denote the dividend yield as d, then the net cost of carry is only $r_f - d$; the forgone interest earnings on the wealth tied up in the stock is offset by the flow of dividends from the stock. The net opportunity cost of holding the stock is the forgone interest less the dividends received. Therefore, in the dividend-paying case, the spot-futures parity relationship is[6]

$$F_0 = S_0(1 + r_f - d)^T \qquad \textbf{(17.2)}$$

where d is the dividend yield on the stock. Problem 8 at the end of the chapter leads you through a derivation of this result.

Although dividends of individual securities may fluctuate unpredictably, the annualized dividend yield of a broad-based index such as the S&P 500 is fairly stable, recently in the neighborhood of about 2% per year. The yield is seasonal, however, with regular peaks and troughs, so the dividend yield for the relevant months must be the one used. Figure 17.5 illustrates the yield pattern for the S&P 500. Some months, such as January or April, have consistently low yields, while others, such as May, have consistently high ones.

The arbitrage strategy just described should convince you that these parity relationships are more than just theoretical results. Any violations of the parity relationship give rise to

[6]This relationship is only approximate in that it assumes the dividend is paid just before the maturity of the contract.

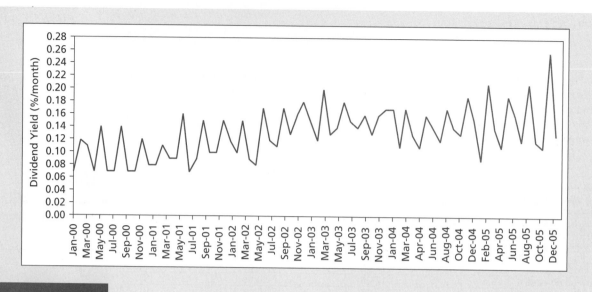

arbitrage opportunities that can provide large profits to traders. We will see shortly that index arbitrage in the stock market is a tool used to exploit violations of the parity relationship for stock index futures contracts.

EXAMPLE   17.9

Stock Index Futures Pricing

Suppose that the risk-free interest rate is 0.5% per month, the dividend yield on the stock index is 0.1% per month, and the stock index is currently at 1,200. The net cost of carry is therefore 0.5% − 0.1% = 0.4% per month. Given this, a three-month contract should have a futures price of $1,200(1.004)^3 = 1,214.46$, while a six-month contract should have a futures price of $1,200(1.004)^6 = 1,229.09$. If the index rises to 1,210, both futures prices will rise commensurately: The three-month futures price will rise to $1,210(1.004)^3 = 1,224.58$, while the six-month futures price will rise to $1,210(1.004)^6 = 1,239.33$.

Spreads

Just as we can predict the relationship between spot and futures prices, there are similar ways to determine the proper relationships among futures prices for contracts of different maturity dates. Equation 17.2 shows that the futures price is in part determined by time to maturity. If $r_f > d$, as is usually the case for stock index futures, then the futures price will be higher on longer-maturity contracts. You can easily verify this by examining Figure 17.1, which includes *Wall Street Journal* listings of several stock index futures contracts. For futures on assets like gold, which pay no "dividend yield," we can set $d = 0$ and conclude that F must increase as time to maturity increases.

Equation 17.2 shows that futures prices should all move together. It is not surprising that futures prices for different maturity dates move in unison, for all are linked to the same spot price through the parity relationship. Figure 17.6 plots futures prices on gold for three maturity

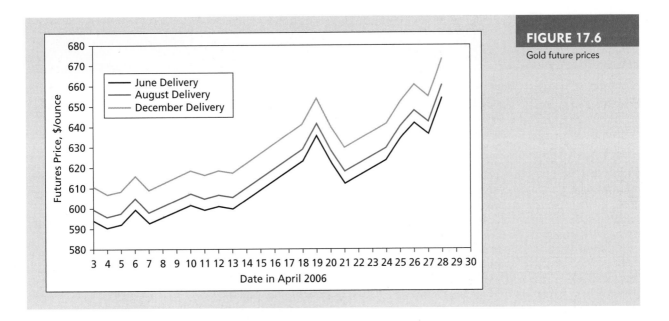

FIGURE 17.6

Gold future prices

dates. It is apparent that the prices move in virtual lockstep and that the more distant delivery dates command higher futures prices, as Equation 17.2 predicts.

17.5 FINANCIAL FUTURES

Although futures markets have their origins in agricultural commodities, today's market is dominated by contracts on financial assets. We review the most important of these contracts in this section: stock index contracts, foreign exchange contracts, and interest-rate contracts.

Stock Index Futures

Futures trade actively on stock market indexes such as the Standard & Poor's 500. In contrast to most futures contracts, which call for delivery of a specified asset, these contracts are settled by a cash amount equal to the value of the stock index in question on the contract maturity date times a multiplier that scales the size of the contract. This cash settlement duplicates the profits that would arise with actual delivery.

There are several stock index futures contracts currently traded. Table 17.2 lists some contracts on major indexes, showing under contract size the multiplier used to calculate contract settlements. An S&P 500 contract with an initial futures price of 1,400 and a final index value of 1,410, for example, would result in a profit for the long side of $250 \times (1,410 - 1,400) = \$2,500$. The S&P contract by far dominates the market in stock index futures.[7]

The broad-based U.S. stock market indexes are all highly correlated. Table 17.3 presents a correlation matrix for four U.S. indexes. Notice that the correlations among the Dow Jones Industrial Average, the New York Stock Exchange Index, and the S&P 500 are all well above .9. The Nasdaq Composite index, which is dominated by technology firms, and the Russell 2000 Index of smaller capitalization firms have smaller correlations with the large-cap indexes and with each other, but for the most part even these are above .8.

---

[7]We should point out that while the multipliers on these contracts may make the resulting positions too large for many small investors, there are effectively equivalent futures contracts with only one-half the multiplier called *E-Minis* that are traded on the Chicago Mercantile Exchange's Globex electronic exchange. The exchange offers E-Mini contracts in several stock indexes as well as foreign currencies.

TABLE 17.2

Stock index futures

Contract	Underlying Market Index	Contract Size	Exchange
S&P 500	Standard & Poor's 500 index. A value-weighted arithmetic average of 500 stocks.	$250 times the S&P 500 index.	Chicago Mercantile Exchange
Dow Jones Industrials (DJIA)	Price-weighted arithmetic average of 30 blue-chip stocks.	$10 times the Dow Jones Industrial Average	Chicago Board of Trade
S&P Midcap	Index of 400 firms of midrange market value.	$500 times index.	Chicago Mercantile Exchange
Nasdaq 100	Value-weighted arithmetic average of 100 of the largest over-the-counter stocks.	$100 times the OTC index.	Chicago Mercantile Exchange
Russell 2000	Index of 2,000 smaller firms.	$500 times the index.	Chicago Mercantile Exchange
Nikkei	Nikkei 225 stock average.	$5 times the Nikkei index.	Chicago Mercantile Exchange
FTSE 100	Financial Times-Stock Exchange Index of 100 U.K. firms.	£ 10 times the FTSE Index.	London International Financial Futures Exchange
CAC 40	Index of 40 of the largest French firms.	10 euros times the index.	Euronext Paris
DAX 30	Index of 30 of the largest German firms.	25 euros times the index.	Eurex
DJ Euro STOXX 50	Value-weighted index of 50 large stocks in Eurozone.	10 euros times the index.	Eurex

TABLE 17.3

Correlations among major U.S. stock market indexes

	DJIA	NYSE	Nasdaq	S&P 500	Russell 2000
DJIA	1.000				
NYSE	0.931	1.000			
Nasdaq	0.839	0.825	1.000		
S&P 500	0.957	0.973	0.899	1.000	
Russell 2000	0.758	0.837	0.855	0.822	1.000

Note: Correlations computed using monthly returns for 5 years ending in March 2006.

Creating Synthetic Stock Positions

One reason stock index futures are so popular is that they can substitute for holdings in the underlying stocks themselves. Index futures let investors participate in broad market movements without actually buying or selling large numbers of stocks.

Because of this, we say futures represent "synthetic" holdings of the market position. Instead of holding the market directly, the investor takes a long futures position in the index. Such a strategy is attractive because the transaction costs involved in establishing and liquidating futures positions are much lower than what would be required to take actual spot positions. Investors who wish to buy and sell market positions frequently find it much cheaper and easier to play the futures market. Market timers who speculate on broad market moves rather than individual securities are large players in stock index futures for this reason.

One way to market time is to shift between Treasury bills and broad-based stock market holdings. Timers attempt to shift from bills into the market before market upturns and to shift

3. A silver futures contract requires the seller to deliver 5,000 Troy ounces of silver. Jerry Harris sells one July silver futures contract at a price of $14 per ounce, posting a $4,000 initial margin. If the required maintenance margin is $2,500, what is the *first* price per ounce at which Harris would receive a maintenance margin call?

4. *a.* Turn to Figure 17.1, and locate the contract on the Standard & Poor's 500 index. If the margin requirement is 10% of the futures price times the multiplier of $250, how much must you deposit with your broker to trade the March contract?

   b. If the March futures price were to increase to 1450, what percentage return would you earn on your net investment if you entered the long side of the contract at the price shown in the figure?

   c. If the March futures price falls by 1%, what is the percentage gain or loss on your net investment?

5. Why is there no futures market in cement?

6. Why might individuals purchase futures contracts rather than the underlying asset?

7. What is the difference in cash flow between short-selling an asset and entering a short futures position?

8. Consider a stock that will pay a dividend of D dollars in one year, which is when a futures contract matures. Consider the following strategy: Buy the stock, short a futures contract on the stock, and borrow S_0 dollars, where S_0 is the current price of the stock.

   a. What are the cash flows now and in one year? (Remember the dividend the stock will pay.)

   b. Show that the equilibrium futures price must be $F_0 = S_0(1 + r) - D$ to avoid arbitrage.

   c. Call the dividend yield $d = D/S_0$, and conclude that $F_0 = S_0(1 + r - d)$.

9. *a.* A single-stock futures contract on a nondividend-paying stock with current price $150 has a maturity of one year. If the T-bill rate is 6%, what should the futures price be?

   b. What should the futures price be if the maturity of the contract is three years?

   c. What if the interest rate is 8% and the maturity of the contract is three years?

10. The Excel Application box in the chapter (available at **www.mhhe.com/bkm;** link to Chapter 17 material) shows how to use the spot-futures parity relationship to find a "term structure of futures prices," that is, futures prices for various maturity dates.

    a. Suppose that today is January 1, 2008. Assume the interest rate is 4% per year and a stock index currently at 1400 pays a dividend yield of 1.5%. Find the futures price for contract maturity dates of February 14, 2008, May 21, 2008, and November 18, 2008.

    b. What happens to the term structure of futures prices if the dividend yield is higher than the risk-free rate? For example, what if the dividend yield is 5%?

11. In each of the following cases, discuss how you, as a portfolio manager, could use financial futures to protect a portfolio.

    a. You own a large position in a relatively illiquid bond that you want to sell.

    b. You have a large gain on one of your long Treasuries and want to sell it, but you would like to defer the gain until the next accounting period, which begins in four weeks.

    c. You will receive a large contribution next month that you hope to invest in long-term corporate bonds on a yield basis as favorable as is now available.

12. Suppose the value of the S&P 500 stock index is currently $1,300. If the one-year T-bill rate is 5% and the expected dividend yield on the S&P 500 is 2%, what should the one-year maturity futures price be?

13. It is now January. The current interest rate is 5%. The June futures price for gold is $646.30, while the December futures price is $652. Is there an arbitrage opportunity here? If so, how would you exploit it?

Please visit us at
www.mhhe.com/bkm

14. One Chicago has just introduced a new single-stock futures contract on the stock of Brandex, a company that currently pays no dividends. Each contract calls for delivery of 1,000 shares of stock in one year. The T-bill rate is 6% per year.
    a. If Brandex stock now sells at $120 per share, what should the futures price be?
    b. If the Brandex stock price drops by 3%, what will be the change in the futures price and the change in the investor's margin account?
    c. If the margin on the contract is $12,000, what is the percentage return on the investor's position?

15. The multiplier for a futures contract on the stock market index is $250. The maturity of the contract is one year, the current level of the index is 1,200, and the risk-free interest rate is .5% per month. The dividend yield on the index is .2% per month. Suppose that after one month, the stock index is at 1,210.
    a. Find the cash flow from the mark-to-market proceeds on the contract. Assume that the parity condition always holds exactly.
    b. Find the one-month holding-period return if the initial margin on the contract is $15,000.

16. Maria VanHusen, CFA, suggests that forward contracts on fixed income securities can be used to protect the value of the Star Hospital Pension Plan's bond portfolio against the possibility of rising interest rates. VanHusen prepares the following example to illustrate how such protection would work:
    • A 10-year bond with a face value of $1,000 is issued today at par value. The bond pays an annual coupon.
    • An investor intends to buy this bond today and sell it in six months.
    • The six-month risk-free interest rate today is 5% (annualized).
    • A six-month forward contract on this bond is available, with a forward price of $1,024.70.
    • In six months, the price of the bond, including accrued interest, is forecast to fall to $978.40 as a result of a rise in interest rates.
    a. Should the investor buy or sell the forward contract to protect the value of the bond against rising interest rates during the holding period?
    b. Calculate the value of the forward contract for the investor at the maturity of the forward contract if VanHusen's bond-price forecast turns out to be accurate.
    c. Calculate the change in value of the combined portfolio (the underlying bond and the appropriate forward contract position) six months after contract initiation.

17. Futures contracts and options contracts can be used to modify risk. Identify the fundamental distinction between a futures contract and an option contract, and briefly explain the difference in the manner that futures and options modify portfolio risk.

18. Suppose the S&P 500 index portfolio pays a dividend yield of 2% annually. The index currently is 1,200. The T-bill rate is 5%, and the S&P futures price for delivery in one year is $1,243. Construct an arbitrage strategy to exploit the mispricing and show that your profits one year hence will equal the mispricing in the futures market.

19. a. How should the parity condition (Equation 17.2) for stocks be modified for futures contracts on Treasury bonds? What should play the role of the dividend yield in that equation?
    b. In an environment with an upward-sloping yield curve, should T-bond futures prices on more distant contracts be higher or lower than those on near-term contracts?
    c. Confirm your intuition by examining Figure 17.1.

20. Joan Tam, CFA, believes she has identified an arbitrage opportunity for a commodity as indicated by the information given in the following exhibit.

Commodity Price and Interest Rate Information	
Spot price for commodity	$120
Futures price for commodity expiring in 1 year	$125
Interest rate for one year	8%

    a. Describe the transactions necessary to take advantage of this specific arbitrage opportunity.
    b. Calculate the arbitrage profit.

21. The one-year futures price on a particular stock-index portfolio is 406, the stock index currently is 400, the one-year risk-free interest rate is 3%, and the year-end dividend that will be paid on a $400 investment in the index portfolio is $5.

    a. By how much is the contract mispriced?

    b. Formulate a zero-net-investment arbitrage portfolio and show that you can lock in riskless profits equal to the futures mispricing.

    c. Now assume (as is true for small investors) that if you short-sell the stocks in the market index, the proceeds of the short sale are kept with the broker, and you do not receive any interest income on the funds. Is there still an arbitrage opportunity (assuming you don't already own the shares in the index)? Explain.

    d. Given the short-sale rules, what is the no-arbitrage *band* for the stock-futures price relationship? That is, given a stock index of 400, how high and how low can the futures price be without giving rise to arbitrage opportunities?

22. The S&P 500 index is currently at 1,400. You manage a $7 million indexed equity portfolio. The S&P 500 futures contract has a multiplier of $250.

    a. If you are temporarily bearish on the stock market, how many contracts should you sell to fully eliminate your exposure over the next six months?

    b. If T-bills pay 2% per six months and the semiannual dividend yield is 1%, what is the parity value of the futures price? Show that if the contract is fairly priced, the total risk-free proceeds on the hedged strategy in part (*a*) provide a return equal to the T-bill rate.

    c. How would your hedging strategy change if, instead of holding an indexed portfolio, you hold a portfolio of only one stock with a beta of 0.6? How many contracts would you now choose to sell? Would your hedged position be riskless? What would be the beta of the hedged position?

23. The margin requirement on the S&P 500 futures contract is 10%, and the stock index is currently 1,200. Each contract has a multiplier of $250. How much margin must be put up for each contract sold? If the futures price falls by 1% to 1,188, what will happen to the margin account of an investor who holds one contract? What will be the investor's percentage return based on the amount put up as margin?

24. The multiplier for a futures contract on a certain stock market index is $250. The maturity of the contract is one year, the current level of the index is 1200, and the risk-free interest rate is 0.5% per *month*. The dividend yield on the index is 0.2% per month. Suppose that *after one month*, the stock index is at 1230.

    a. Find the cash flow from the mark-to-market proceeds on the contract. Assume that the parity condition always holds exactly.

    b. Find the holding-period return if the initial margin on the contract is $15,000.

25. You are a corporate treasurer who will purchase $1 million of bonds for the sinking fund in three months. You believe rates soon will fall and would like to repurchase the company's sinking fund bonds, which currently are selling below par, in advance of requirements. Unfortunately, you must obtain approval from the board of directors for such a purchase, and this can take up to two months. What action can you take in the futures market to hedge any adverse movements in bond yields and prices until you actually can buy the bonds? Will you be long or short? Why?

26. A manager is holding a $1 million bond portfolio with a modified duration of eight years. She would like to hedge the risk of the portfolio by short-selling Treasury bonds. The modified duration of T-bonds is 10 years. How many dollars' worth of T-bonds should she sell to minimize the risk of her position?

27. A corporation plans to issue $10 million of 10-year bonds in three months. At current yields the bonds would have modified duration of eight years. The T-note futures contract is selling at $F_0 = 100$ and has modified duration of six years. How can the firm use this futures contract to hedge the risk surrounding the yield at which it will be able to sell its bonds? Both the bond and the contract are at par value.

28. What type of interest rate swap would be appropriate for a speculator who believes interest rates soon will fall?

29. Several Investment Committee members have asked about interest rate swap agreements and how they are used in the management of domestic fixed-income portfolios.
   a. Define an interest rate swap and briefly describe the obligation of each party involved.
   b. Cite and explain two examples of how interest rate swaps could be used by a fixed-income portfolio manager to control risk or improve return.

30. A corporation has issued a $10 million issue of floating-rate bonds on which it pays an interest rate 1% over the LIBOR rate. The bonds are selling at par value. The firm is worried that rates are about to rise, and it would like to lock in a fixed interest rate on its borrowings. The firm sees that dealers in the swap market are offering swaps of LIBOR for 7%. What swap arrangement will convert the firm's borrowings to a synthetic fixed-rate loan? What interest rate will it pay on that synthetic fixed-rate loan?

31. Janice Delsing, a U.S.-based portfolio manager, manages an $800 million portfolio ($600 million in stocks and $200 million in bonds). In reaction to anticipated short-term market events, Delsing wishes to adjust the allocation to 50 percent stocks and 50 percent bonds through the use of futures. Her position will be held only until "the time is right to restore the original asset allocation." Delsing determines a financial futures-based asset allocation strategy is appropriate. The stock futures index multiplier is $250 and the denomination of the bond futures contract is $100,000. Other information relevant to a futures-based strategy is given in the following exhibit.

Information for Futures-Based Strategy	
Bond portfolio modified duration	5 years
Bond portfolio yield to maturity	7%
Price value of basis point (PVBP) of bond futures	$97.85
Stock index futures price	1378
Stock portfolio beta	1.0

   a. Describe the financial futures-based strategy needed and explain how the strategy allows Delsing to implement her allocation adjustment. No calculations are necessary.
   b. Compute the number of each of the following needed to implement Delsing's asset allocation strategy:
      i. Bond futures contracts
      ii. Stock index futures contracts

WEB *master*

Profit or Loss on a Spread Position

1. Suppose that you want to create a spread position using S&P 500 futures contracts. Go to **www.cme.com** and click on "Contract Specifications" in the menu. In the CME equities category, choose the S&P 500 futures contract and confirm the contract's specifications. Click on the "Current Listings" link to see the contracts that are available for trading. Note the code for one contract that expires in approximately 5–6 months and the code for another one that expires in approximately one year.

2. Assume that you bought a 5–6 month contract and sold a 1-year contract two months ago. Go to **www.futuresguide.com/historical-data.php,** where you will see a calendar with a link for each date. Choose a trading date that occurred two months ago and click on its link. In the list of settlement prices, find the closing prices for the two contracts that you selected.

3. Return to the calendar and click on the link to the most recent trading date. Find the closing prices of the two contracts on that date. Assume that you closed your positions in both contracts on that day.

4. Using the beginning and ending prices for the futures contracts that you bought and sold, calculate the return you earned on the spread position during the 2-month period, before commissions.

17.1. *a.* The payoff on the put looks like that on the short futures contract when the asset price falls below X or F_0, but when the asset price rises above F_0, the futures payoff turns negative whereas the value of the put cannot fall below zero. The put (which must be purchased) gives you upside potential if the asset price falls but limits downside risk, whereas the futures gives you both upside and downside exposure.

    b. The payoff on the written call looks like that on the short futures contract when the asset price rises above F_0, but when the asset price falls, the futures payoff is positive, whereas the payoff on the written call is never positive. The written call gives you downside exposure, but your upside potential is limited to the premium you received for the option.

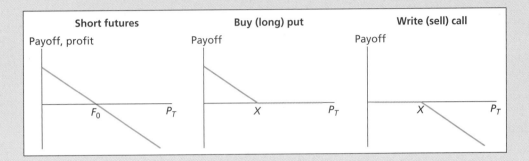

17.2. The clearinghouse has a zero net position in all contracts. Its long and short positions are offsetting, so that net cash flow from marking to market must be zero.

17.3.

	Oil Price in April, P_T		
	$59.79	**$61.79**	**$63.79**
Cash flow to purchase oil: $-100{,}000 \times P_T$	$-\$5{,}979{,}000$	$-\$6{,}179{,}000$	$-\$6{,}379{,}000$
$+$ Profit on long futures: $100{,}000 \times (P_T - F_0)$	$-200{,}000$	0	$+200{,}000$
Total cash flow	$-\$6{,}179{,}000$	$-\$6{,}179{,}000$	$-\$6{,}179{,}000$

17.4. The risk would be that the index and the portfolio do not move perfectly together. Thus, risk involving the spread between the futures price and the portfolio value could persist even if the index futures price were set perfectly relative to index itself.

17.5.

Action	Initial Cash Flow	Time-T Cash Flow
Lend $600	$-\$600$	$\$600(1.005)^6 = \$618.23$
Sell gold short	$+600$	$-S_T$
Long futures	0	$S_T - \$617$
Total	$\$0$	$\$1.23$ risklessly

17.6. The price value of a basis point is still $9,000, as a one-basis-point change in the interest rate reduces the value of the $20 million portfolio by $.01\% \times 4.5 = .045\%$. Therefore, the number of futures needed to hedge the interest rate risk is the same as for a portfolio half the size with double the modified duration.

17.7. The manager would like to hold on to the money market securities because of their attractive relative pricing compared to other short-term assets. However, there is an expectation that rates will fall. The manager can hold this *particular* portfolio of short-term assets and still benefit from the drop in interest rates by entering a swap to pay a short-term interest rate and receive a fixed interest rate. The resulting synthetic fixed-rate portfolio will increase in value if rates do fall.

Solution to question in On the Market Front box, "Presidential and Other Prediction Futures"

Suppose you sell a contract on every candidate. No matter which of these candidate wins, your obligation come November will be $1 (and if a yet-unknown candidate happens to enter the race and win, your obligation will be zero). Therefore, if the total proceeds from selling each contract (at the bid price) were more than $1, you would have an arbitrage opportunity: Your up-front proceeds would *necessarily* be greater than your future obligation. Such opportunities are not likely to be found in even mildly rational markets. We conclude that the sum of the bid prices *must* be less than $1.

The rationale for why the sum of ask prices is greater than $1 is not as strong. If you *buy* each contract (at the ask price), and if any of the candidates wins, you will receive a payoff of $1. Of course, if a previously unanticipated candidate enters and wins the race, you will end up with nothing. If the possibility of a dark-horse candidate is highly remote, then you should expect to pay approximately the present value of $1 for the portfolio of long positions on each candidate. In this case, we can view the excess of the sum of all ask prices above the present value of a dollar as reflecting bid–ask spreads, which are far higher here than in markets for conventional securities. But if the probability of a surprise candidate is not trivial, the expected payoff of the portfolio of long positions on each candidate will be less than $1, so the sum of the ask prices could in fact be less than $1.

ACTIVE INVESTMENT MANAGEMENT

Passive investment, or indexing, is the preferred strategy for those who believe markets are essentially efficient. While administration of passive portfolios requires an efficient organizational and trading structure, there is obviously less need for knowledge of security analysis or portfolio strategy if one is limited to managing index portfolios. In contrast, active managers take it on faith that markets are not always efficient and that, at least occasionally, bargains may be found in security markets. Active managers must apply asset valuation and portfolio theory to best establish their positions.

Chapter 18 begins this part of the text by discussing the theory of active portfolio management in imperfectly efficient markets. Effective exploitation of security mispricing calls for balancing investment in underpriced securities with diversification concerns. How should this balance be struck? The answer is inseparable from the quandary of how to assess the performance of an active portfolio. Accordingly, Chapter 18 begins with methods of performance evaluation and proceeds to suggest techniques to achieve the goal of superior performance.

Investing across borders is conceptually a simple extension of portfolio diversification. This pursuit confronts the effects of political risk and uncertain exchange rates on future performance, however. These issues, unique to international investing, are addressed in Chapter 19.

Investments originate with a savings plan that diverts funds from consumption to investment. Taxes and inflation complicate the relationship between how much you save and what you will be able to achieve with your accumulating investment fund. Chapter 20 introduces a framework and tools that can be used to formulate a comprehensive household savings/investment plan.

Professional management of active investment begins with a contractual relationship between a client and portfolio manager. The economic needs of clients must be articulated and their objectives translated into an operational financial plan. For this purpose, the CFA Institute has laid out a broad framework for active investment management. Chapter 21 familiarizes you with this framework.

CHAPTERS IN THIS PART:

www.mhhe.com/bkm

18

Performance Evaluation and Active Portfolio Management

AFTER STUDYING THIS CHAPTER YOU SHOULD BE ABLE TO:

 Compute risk-adjusted rates of return, and use these rates to evaluate investment performance.

 Decompose excess returns into components attributable to asset allocation choices versus security selection choices.

 Assess the risk-adjusted performance of portfolio managers.

 Assess the value of market timing ability.

 Use the Treynor-Black model of efficient security analysis.

In previous chapters, we derived predictions for expected return as a function of risk. In this chapter, we ask how we can evaluate the performance of a portfolio manager given the risk of his or her portfolio. Difficulties in adjusting average returns for risk present a host of issues, as the proper measure of risk may not be obvious, and risk levels may change along with portfolio composition.

We begin with conventional approaches to risk adjustment. These use the risk measures developed in Part Two of the text to compare investment results. We show the problems with these approaches when you try to apply them in a real and complex world. Finally, we examine evaluation procedures used in the field. We show how overall investment results are decomposed and attributed to the underlying asset allocation and security selection decisions of the portfolio manager.

Even if you largely accept the efficient market hypothesis, we will see that there are reasons to consider active portfolio management. We consider the objective of active management and analyze two forms: market timing based solely on macroeconomic factors, and security selection that includes microeconomic forecasting.

Related Web sites for this chapter are available at www.mhhe.com/bkm.

18.1 RISK-ADJUSTED RETURNS

Comparison Groups

The major difficulty in portfolio performance evaluation is that average portfolio returns must be adjusted for risk before we can compare them meaningfully.

The fact that common stocks have offered higher average returns than Treasury bonds or bills (as demonstrated in Table 18.1) does not prove that stocks are superior investment vehicles. One must consider the fact that stocks also have been more volatile investments. For the same reason, the fact that a mutual fund outperforms the S&P 500 over a long period is not necessarily evidence of superior stock selection ability. If the mutual fund has a higher beta than the index, it *should* outperform the index (on average) to compensate investors in the fund for the greater nondiversifiable risk they bear. Thus, performance evaluation must involve risk as well as return comparisons.

The simplest and most popular way to adjust returns for portfolio risk is to compare rates of return with those of other investment funds with similar risk characteristics. For example, high-yield bond portfolios are grouped into one "universe," growth stock equity funds are grouped into another universe, and so on. Then the average returns of each fund within the universe are ordered, and each portfolio manager receives a percentile ranking depending on relative performance within the **comparison universe,** the collection of funds to which performance is compared. For example, the manager with the ninth-best performance in a universe of 100 funds would be the 90th percentile manager: Her performance was better than 90% of all competing funds over the evaluation period.

These relative rankings usually are displayed in a chart like that shown in Figure 18.1. The chart summarizes performance rankings over four periods: one quarter, one year, three years, and five years. The top and bottom lines of each box are drawn at the rate of return of the 95th and 5th percentile managers. The three dotted lines correspond to the rates of return of the 75th, 50th (median), and 25th percentile managers. The diamond is drawn at the average return of a particular fund, the Markowill Group, and the square is drawn at the average return of a benchmark index such as the S&P 500. This format provides an easy-to-read representation of the performance of the fund relative to the comparison universe.

This comparison with other managers of similar investment groups is a useful first step in evaluating performance. Even so, such rankings can be misleading. Consider that within a particular universe some managers may concentrate on particular subgroups, so that portfolio characteristics are not truly comparable. For example, within the equity universe, one manager may concentrate on high-beta stocks. Similarly, within fixed-income universes, interest rate risk can vary across managers. These considerations suggest that we need a more precise means for risk adjustment.

comparison universe

The set of portfolio managers with similar investment styles that is used in assessing the relative performance of an individual portfolio manager.

Risk Adjustments

Methods of risk-adjusted performance using mean-variance criteria developed simultaneously with the capital asset pricing model (CAPM). Jack Treynor (1966), William Sharpe (1966), and Michael Jensen (1969) were quick to recognize the implications of the CAPM

TABLE 18.1		Arithmetic Average	Geometric Average	Standard Deviation
Average annual returns by investment class, 1926–2006	Common stocks of small firms*	18.14	12.43	36.93
	Common stocks of large firms	12.19	10.23	20.14
	Long-term Treasury bonds	5.64	5.35	8.06
	U.S. Treasury bills	3.77	3.72	3.11

*These are firms in the bottom 20% when ranked by market values of equity. Market capitalization is computed as price per share times shares outstanding.

Source: Prepared from data in Table 5.3.

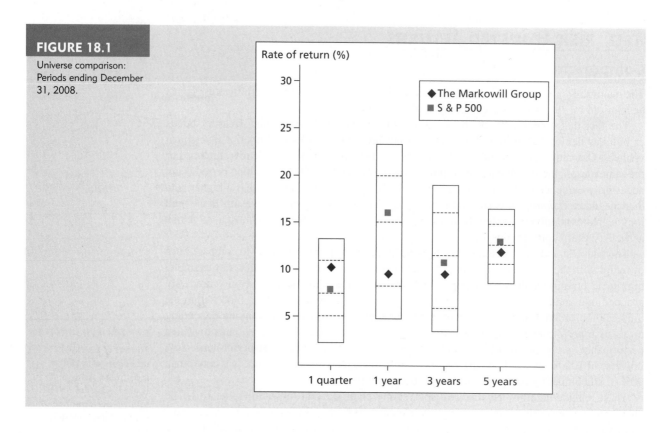

FIGURE 18.1

Universe comparison: Periods ending December 31, 2008.

for rating the performance of managers. Within a short time, academicians were in command of a battery of performance measures, and a bounty of scholarly investigation of mutual fund performance was pouring from the ivory tower. Soon after, agents emerged who were willing to supply rating services to portfolio managers eager for regular feedback. These days, risk-adjusted performance measures are accessible to all investors through the Internet. We will use these statistics in our analysis here.

We begin with a catalogue of the major risk-adjusted performance measures and examine the circumstances in which each measure might be most relevant. To illustrate these measures, we will use a hypothetical portfolio for which monthly returns in the past five years resulted in the following statistics. We also present comparable data for the market portfolio for the same period.

	Portfolio	Market
Average return	16%	14%
Standard deviation	20%	24%
Beta	0.8	1.0

Finally, suppose the average return on risk-free assets during the five-year period was 6%.

The Sharpe measure, the Treynor measure, and the Jensen measure are three risk-adjusted performance statistics. The Sharpe measure is calculated as follows:

$$\frac{\overline{r}_p - \overline{r}_f}{\sigma_p}$$

Sharpe measure

Reward-to-volatility ratio; ratio of portfolio excess return to standard deviation.

The **Sharpe measure** divides average portfolio excess return over the sample period by the standard deviation of returns over that period. The numerator is the incremental return the portfolio earned in comparison with an alternative investment in the risk-free asset, and the denominator is the increment in portfolio volatility compared with the risk-free alternative. Therefore, the ratio measures the reward to (total) volatility trade-off. (The bars over r_p as well as r_f denote the fact that, because the risk-free rate may not be constant over the measurement period, we are taking a sample average of each.) Using our numbers, the Sharpe measure for the portfolio is $(16 - 6)/20 = 0.5$, while for the market it is $(14 - 6)/24 = 0.33$.

In contrast, the Treynor measure is given as follows:

$$\frac{\overline{r}_p - \overline{r}_f}{\beta_p}$$

Like Sharpe's, the **Treynor measure** gives average excess return per unit of risk incurred, but it uses systematic risk instead of total risk. The Treynor measure for the portfolio over this period is $(16 - 6)/0.8 = 12.5$, while for the market portfolio it is $(14 - 6)/1.0 = 8$.

A third popular performance measure, the Jensen measure, is as follows:

$$\alpha_p = \overline{r}_p - [\overline{r}_f + \beta_p(\overline{r}_M - \overline{r}_f)]$$

The **Jensen measure** is the average return on the portfolio over and above that predicted by the CAPM, given the portfolio's beta and the average market return. The Jensen measure is the portfolio's alpha value. Using our numbers, the Jensen measure is $16 - [6 + 0.8(14 - 6)] = 3.6\%$.

Each measure has its own appeal. In this instance, all three measures are consistent in revealing that the portfolio outperformed the market benchmark on a risk-adjusted basis. However, this need not be the case. As the following Concept Check illustrates, the three measures do not necessarily provide consistent assessments of relative performance, as the approaches used to adjust returns for risk differ substantially.

Treynor measure

Ratio of portfolio excess return to beta.

Jensen measure

The alpha of an investment.

CONCEPT check 18.1

Consider the following data for a particular sample period:

	Portfolio P	Market M
Average return	35%	28%
Beta	1.2	1.0
Standard deviation	42%	30%

Calculate the following performance measures for portfolio P and the market: Sharpe, Jensen (alpha), and Treynor. The T-bill rate during the period was 6%. By which measures did portfolio P outperform the market?

The M² Measure of Performance

While the Sharpe ratio can be used to rank portfolio performance, its numerical value is not easy to interpret. Comparing the ratios for portfolios M and P in Concept Check 18.1, you should have found that $S_P = .69$ and $S_M = .73$. This suggests that portfolio P underperformed the market index. But is a difference of .04 in the Sharpe ratio economically meaningful? We are used to comparing rates of return, but these ratios are difficult to interpret.

A variant of Sharpe's measure was introduced by Graham and Harvey and by Leah Modigliani of Morgan Stanley and her grandfather Franco Modigliani, past winner of the Nobel Prize for economics.[1] Their approach has been dubbed the M^2 measure (for Modigliani-squared). Like the Sharpe ratio, the M^2 measure focuses on total volatility as a measure of risk, but its risk-adjusted measure of performance has the easy interpretation of a differential return relative to the benchmark index.

---

[1]John R. Graham and Campbell R. Harvey, "Grading the Performance of Market Timing Newsletter," *Financial Analysts Journal* 53 (November/December 1997), pp. 54–66; and Franco Modigliani and Leah Modigliani, "Risk-Adjusted Performance," *Journal of Portfolio Management,* Winter 1997, pp. 45–54.

To compute the M^2 measure, we imagine that a managed portfolio, P, is mixed with a position in T-bills so that the complete, or "adjusted," portfolio matches the volatility of a market index such as the S&P 500. For example, if the managed portfolio has 1.5 times the standard deviation of the index, the adjusted portfolio would be two-thirds invested in the managed portfolio and one-third invested in bills. The adjusted portfolio, which we call P^*, would then have the same standard deviation as the index. (If the managed portfolio had *lower* standard deviation than the index, it would be leveraged by borrowing money and investing the proceeds in the portfolio.) Because the market index and portfolio P^* have the same standard deviation, we may compare their performance simply by comparing returns. This is the M^2 measure:

$$M^2 = r_{P*} - r_M$$

In the example of Concept Check 18.1, P has a standard deviation of 42% versus a market standard deviation of 30%. Therefore, the adjusted portfolio P^* would be formed by mixing bills and portfolio P with weights 30/42 = .714 in P and 1 − .714 = .286 in bills. The average return on this portfolio would have been (.286 × 6%) + (.714 × 35%) = 26.7%, which is 1.3% less than the average market return. Thus portfolio P had an M^2 measure of −1.3%.

A graphical representation of the M^2 measure appears in Figure 18.2. We move down the capital allocation line corresponding to portfolio P (by mixing P with T-bills) until we reduce the standard deviation of the adjusted portfolio to match that of the market index. The M^2 measure is then the vertical distance (i.e., the difference in expected returns) between portfolios P^* and M. You can see from Figure 18.2 that P will have an M^2 measure below that of the market when its capital allocation line is less steep than the capital market line, that is, when its Sharpe ratio is less than that of the market index.

Choosing the Right Measure of Risk

Because different risk adjustment procedures can yield different implications for performance evaluation, it is essential that you choose the appropriate measure for the task. For example, suppose you are a pension fund manager who is selecting potential portfolio managers to oversee investment of the fund's assets. If you envision hiring one investment manager to manage all the fund's assets, then you must be concerned with the total variability of investment performance. Both the systematic and firm-specific risk remaining in the portfolio will affect total risk because the pension fund is not diversified across managers. The manager's

FIGURE 18.2

The M^2 of portfolio P

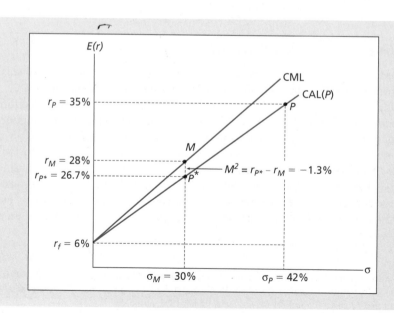

TABLE 18.2		Portfolio P	Portfolio Q	Market
Portfolio performance	Excess return, $r - r_f$	13%	20%	10%
	Beta	0.80	1.80	1.0
	Alpha*	5%	2%	0
	Treynor measure	16.25	11.11	10

*Alpha = Excess return − (Beta × Market excess return)
   $= (r - r_f) - \beta(r_M - r_f) = r - [r_f + \beta(r_M - r_f)]$

portfolio will be the fund's entire portfolio, with no further opportunities for diversification. In this case, the Sharpe measure or the portfolio's M^2 would be the appropriate basis on which to evaluate the manager. Because that manager is in charge of the entire portfolio, she must be attentive to diversification of firm-specific risk and should be judged on her achievement of excess return to *total* portfolio volatility.

In contrast, suppose your pension fund is large, and you envision hiring many managers, giving each a fraction of the total assets of the plan. You hope that hiring a set of managers, each with an investment specialty, will enhance returns. This means the pension plan effectively ends up with a portfolio of portfolio managers. Each manager can pursue his or her specialty without paying much attention to issues of diversification because the plan as a whole will have diversified returns across the several managed portfolios. With assets spread across many portfolio managers, the residual firm-specific risks of each portfolio become irrelevant because of diversification across portfolios. In this case, only nondiversifiable risk should matter. Such circumstances call for the use of a beta-based risk adjustment, and the Treynor measure would be appropriate.

We can use a variant of the Treynor measure to express the difference in portfolio performance in terms of rates of return. Consider a portfolio P, with the characteristics summarized in Table 18.2. To convert the difference between the Treynor measure of P and that of the market to an easier-to-interpret percentage return basis, we will consider a measure analogous to M^2 that we call Treynor-Square (T^2). To start, we will create a portfolio P^* by mixing P and T-bills to match the beta of the market, 1.0. (In contrast, to obtain the M^2 measure we mixed bills and P to match the *standard deviation* of the market.)

Recall that both the beta and the excess return of T-bills are zero. Therefore, if we construct portfolio P^* by investing w in portfolio P and $1 - w$ in T-bills, the excess return and beta of P^* will be:

$$R_{P*} = wR_P, \qquad \beta_{P*} = w\beta_P$$

We can construct P^* from portfolio P and T-bills with any desired beta. If you desire a beta equal to β_{P*}, simply set: $w = \beta_{P*}/\beta_P$; hence, $R_{P*} = wR_P = R_P \times \beta_{P*}/\beta_P$. Because the market beta is 1.0, P^* can be constructed to match the market beta by setting

$$w = \beta_M/\beta_P = 1/\beta_P = 1/.8$$

Therefore, $R_{P*} = wR_P = (1/\beta_P) \times R_P = 13\%/.8 = 16.25\%$. Notice that $w > 1$ implies that P^* is a leveraged version of P. Leverage is necessary to match the market beta since the beta of P is less than that of the market. Notice also that R_{P*} is in fact the Treynor measure of portfolio P—it equals the excess return of P divided by beta.

Portfolio P^* is constructed to have the same beta as the market, so the difference between the return of P^* and the market is a valid measure of relative performance when systematic risk is of concern to investors. Therefore, as an analogy to the M^2 measure of performance, we define the Treynor-square (or T^2) measure as

$$T_P^2 = R_{P*} - R_M = R_P/\beta_P - R_M = 13/.8 - 10 = 6.25\%.$$

Figure 18.3A shows a graphical representation of the T^2 measure for portfolio P. Portfolio P^* is a leveraged version of portfolio P with the same beta as the market, 1.0. The T^2 measure is simply the difference in expected returns at this common beta.

FIGURE 18.3

Treynor-Square measure

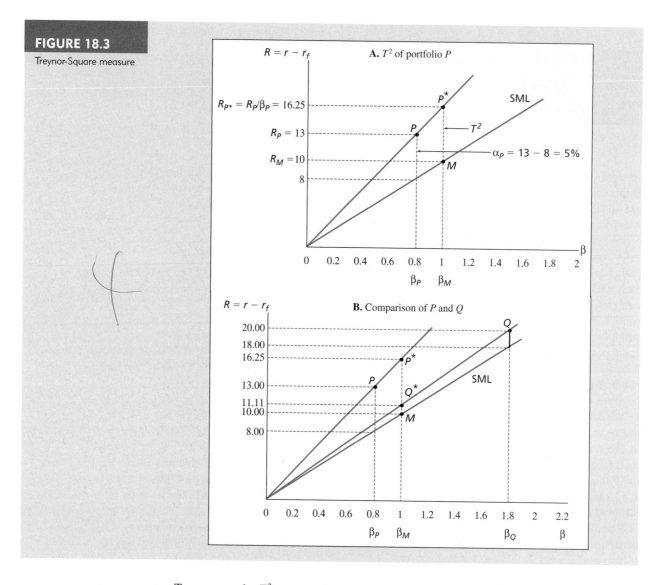

To compare the T^2 measure for the two portfolios, P and Q, described in Table 18.2, we compute for portfolio Q

$$T_Q^2 = 20/1.8 - 10 = 1.11\%$$

which is smaller than the T^2 measure of P by 5.14%. Figure 18.3B shows the positions of P and Q. Portfolios on a given line from the origin (notice that the vertical axis measures *excess* returns), all have the same Treynor measure. P is located on a steeper line because it has a higher Treynor measure. As a result, P^* is farther above the SML than Q^*, and the difference between the T^2 measures, the line segment P^*Q^*, measures the difference in the systematic risk-adjusted percent return.

Risk Adjustments with Changing Portfolio Composition

One potential problem with risk-adjustment techniques is that they all assume that portfolio risk, whether it is measured by standard deviation or beta, is constant over the relevant time period. This isn't necessarily so. If a manager attempts to increase portfolio beta when she thinks the market is about to go up and to decrease beta when she is pessimistic, both the standard deviation and the beta of the portfolio will change over time. This can wreak havoc with our performance measures.

FIGURE 18.4

Portfolio returns. In the first four quarters, the firm follows a low-risk, low-return policy. In the next four quarters, it shifts to a high-risk, high-return policy.

EXAMPLE   18.1

Risk Measurement with Changing Portfolio Composition

Suppose the Sharpe measure of the passive strategy (investing in a market index fund) is 0.4. A portfolio manager is in search of a better, active strategy. Over an initial period of, say, four quarters, he executes a low-risk or defensive strategy with an annualized mean excess return of 1% and a standard deviation of 2%. This makes for a Sharpe measure of 0.5, which beats the passive strategy.

Over the next period of another four quarters, this manager finds that a high-risk strategy is optimal, with an annual mean excess return of 9% and standard deviation of 18%. Here again the Sharpe measure is 0.5. Over the two years, our manager maintains a better-than-passive Sharpe measure.

Figure 18.4 shows a pattern of (annualized) quarterly returns that is consistent with our description of the manager's strategy over two years. In the first four quarters, the excess returns are −1%, 3%, −1%, and 3%, making for an average of 1% and standard deviation of 2%. In the next four quarters, the excess returns are −9%, 27%, −9%, and 27%, making for an average of 9% and standard deviation of 18%. Thus, *each* year exhibits a Sharpe measure of 0.5.

But if we take the eight-quarter sequence as a single measurement period, instead of two independent periods, and measure the portfolio's mean and standard deviation over that full period, we get an average excess return of 5% and standard deviation of 13.42%, resulting in a Sharpe measure of only 0.37, apparently inferior to the passive strategy!

What went wrong in Example 18.1? Sharpe's measure does not recognize the shift in the mean from the first four quarters to the next as a result of a strategy change. Instead, the difference in mean returns in the two years adds to the *appearance* of volatility in portfolio returns. The change in mean returns across time periods contributed to the variability of returns over the same period. But in this case, variability per se should not be interpreted as volatility or riskiness in returns. Part of the variability in returns is due to intentional choices that shift the expected or mean return. This part should not be ascribed to uncertainty in returns. Unfortunately, an outside observer might not realize that policy changes within the sample period are the source of some of the return variability. Therefore, the active strategy with shifting means appears riskier than it really is, which biases the estimate of the Sharpe measure downward.

When assessing the performance of actively managed portfolios, therefore, it is crucial to keep track of portfolio composition and changes in portfolio mean return and risk. We will see another example of this problem when we turn to market timing.

The Excel model "Performance Measures" calculates all of the performance measures discussed in this chapter. The model available on our Web site is built to allow you to compare eight different portfolios and to rank them on all measures discussed in this chapter.

eXcel

Please visit us at
www.mhhe.com/bkm

	A	B	C	D	E	F	G	H	I	J	K
1					Performance Measurement						
2											
3											
4											
5		Average	Standard	Beta	Unsystematic	Sharpe	Treynor	Jensen	M^2	T^2	Appraisal
6	Fund	Return	Deviation	Coefficient	Risk	Ratio	Measure	Alpha	Measure	Measure	Ratio
7	Alpha	0.2800	0.2700	1.7000	0.0500	0.8148	0.1294	-0.0180	-0.0015	-0.0106	-0.3600
8	Omega	0.3100	0.2600	1.6200	0.0600	0.9615	0.1543	0.0232	0.0235	0.0143	0.3867
9	Omicron	0.2200	0.2100	0.8500	0.0200	0.7619	0.1882	0.0410	-0.0105	0.0482	2.0500
10	Millennium	0.4000	0.3300	2.5000	0.2700	1.0303	0.1360	-0.0100	0.0352	-0.0040	-0.0370
11	Big Value	0.1500	0.1300	0.9000	0.0300	0.6923	0.1000	-0.0360	-0.0223	-0.0400	-1.2000
12	Momentum Watcher	0.2900	0.2400	1.4000	0.1600	0.9583	0.1643	0.0340	0.0229	0.0243	0.2125
13	Big Potential	0.1500	0.1100	0.5500	0.0150	0.8182	0.1636	0.0130	-0.0009	0.0236	0.8667
14	S & P Index Return	0.2000	0.1700	1.0000	0.0000	0.8235	0.1400	0.0000	0.0000	0.0000	0.0000
15	T-Bill Return	0.06		0							
16											
17	Ranking by Sharpe										
18		Return	S.D.	Beta	Unsy. Risk	Sharpe	Treynor	Jensen	M^2	T^2	Appraisal
19	Millennium	0.4000	0.3300	2.5000	0.2700	1.0303	0.1360	-0.0100	0.0352	-0.0040	-0.0370
20	Omega	0.3000	0.2600	1.6200	0.0600	0.9615	0.1543	0.0232	0.0235	0.0143	0.3867
21	Momentum Watcher	0.2900	0.2400	1.4000	0.1600	0.9583	0.1643	0.0340	0.0229	0.0243	0.2125
22	S & P Index Return	0.2000	0.1700	1.0000	0.0000	0.8235	0.1400	0.0000	0.0000	0.0000	0.0000
23	Big Potential	0.1500	0.1100	0.5500	0.0150	0.8182	0.1636	0.0130	-0.0009	0.0236	0.8667
24	Alpha	0.2800	0.2700	1.7000	0.0500	0.8148	0.1294	-0.0180	-0.0015	-0.0106	-0.3600
25	Omicron	0.2200	0.2100	0.8500	0.0200	0.7619	0.1882	0.0410	-0.0105	0.0482	2.0500
26	Big Value	0.1500	0.1300	0.9000	0.0300	0.6923	0.1000	-0.0360	-0.0223	-0.0400	-1.2000
27											
28	Ranking by Treynor										
29		Return	S.D.	Beta	Unsy. Risk	Sharpe	Treynor	Jensen	M^2	T^2	Appraisal
30	Omicron	0.2200	0.2100	0.8500	0.0200	0.7619	0.1882	0.0410	-0.0105	0.0482	2.0500
31	Momentum Watcher	0.2900	0.2400	1.4000	0.1600	0.9583	0.1643	0.0340	0.0229	0.0243	0.2125
32	Big Potential	0.1500	0.1100	0.5500	0.0150	0.8182	0.1636	0.0130	-0.0009	0.0236	0.8667
33	Omega	0.3100	0.2600	1.6200	0.0600	0.9615	0.1543	0.0232	0.0235	0.0143	0.3867
34	S & P Index Return	0.2000	0.1700	1.0000	0.0000	0.8235	0.1400	0.0000	0.0000	0.0000	0.0000
35	Millennium	0.4000	0.3300	2.5000	0.2700	1.0303	0.1360	-0.0100	0.0352	-0.0040	-0.0370
36	Alpha	0.2800	0.2700	1.7000	0.0500	0.8148	0.1294	-0.0180	-0.0015	-0.0106	-0.3600

Another warning: When we address the performance of mutual funds selected *because* they have been successful, we need to be highly cautious in evaluating their track records. In particular, we need to recognize that even if all managers were equally skilled, a few "winners" would emerge by sheer chance each period. With thousands of funds in operation, the best performing funds will have been wildly successful, even if these results reflect luck rather than skill. The nearby box addresses this issue.

WEB master

Analyzing Performance

Morningstar has an extensive ranking system for mutual funds, including a screening program that allows you to select funds based on a number of factors. Open the Morningstar Web site at **www.morningstar.com** and click on the Funds link. Select the Mutual Fund Quickrank link from the right-side menu. Use the Quickrank screener to find a list of the funds with the highest 5-year returns. Repeat the process to find the funds with the highest 10-year returns. How many funds appear on both lists?

Select three of the funds that appear on both lists. For each fund, click on the ticker symbol to get its Morningstar report and look in the Risk Measures section.

1. What is the fund's standard deviation?
2. What is the fund's Sharpe ratio?
3. What is the standard index? What is the best fit index?
4. What are the beta and alpha coefficients using both the standard index and the best fit index? How do these compare to the fund's parameters?

Look at the Management section of the report. Was the same manager in place for the entire 10-year period?

THE MAGELLAN FUND AND MARKET EFFICIENCY: ASSESSING THE PERFORMANCE OF MONEY MANAGERS

Fidelity's Magellan Fund outperformed the S&P 500 in eleven of the thirteen years ending in 1989. Is such performance consistent with the efficient market hypothesis? Casual statistical analysis would suggest not.

If outperforming the market were like flipping a fair coin, as would be the case if all securities were fairly priced, then the odds of an arbitrarily selected manager producing eleven out of thirteen winning years would be only about 0.95%, or 1 in 105. The Magellan Fund, however, is not a randomly selected fund. Instead, it is the fund that emerged after a thirteen-year "contest" as a clear winner. Given that we have chosen to focus on the winner of a money management contest, should we be surprised to find performance far above the mean? Clearly not.

Once we select a fund precisely because it has outperformed all other funds, the proper benchmark for predicted performance is no longer a standard index such as the S&P 500. The benchmark must be the expected performance of the best-performing fund out of a sample of randomly selected funds.

Consider as an analogy a coin flipping contest. If fifty contestants were to flip a coin thirteen times, and the winner were to flip eleven heads out of thirteen, we would not consider that evidence that the winner's coin was biased. Instead, we would recognize that with fifty contestants, the probability is greater than 40% that the individual who emerges as the winner would in fact flip heads eleven or more times. (In contrast, a coin chosen at random that resulted in eleven out of thirteen heads would be highly suspect!)

How then ought we evaluate the performance of those managers who show up in the financial press as (recently) superior performers. We know that after the fact some managers will have been lucky. When is the performance of a manager so good that even after accounting for selection bias—the selection of the ex post winner—we still cannot account for such performance by chance?

SELECTION BIAS AND PERFORMANCE BENCHMARKS

Consider this experiment. Allow fifty money managers to flip a coin thirteen times, and record the maximum number of heads realized by any of the contestants. (If markets are efficient, the coin will have the same probability of turning up heads as that of a money manager beating the market.) Now repeat the contest, and again record the winning number of heads. Repeat this experiment 10,000 times. When we are done, we can compute the frequency distribution of the winning number of heads over the 10,000 trials.

Table 1 (column 1) presents the results of such an experiment simulated on a computer. The table shows that in 9.2% of the contests, the winning number of

heads was nine; in 47.4% of the trials ten heads would be enough to emerge as the best manager. Interestingly, in 43.3% of the trials, the winning number of heads was eleven or better out of thirteen.

TABLE 1

PROBABILITY DISTRIBUTION OF NUMBER OF SUCCESSFUL YEARS OUT OF THIRTEEN FOR THE BEST-PERFORMING MONEY MANAGER

Winning Years	Managers in Contest			
	50	100	250	500
8	0.1%	0	0	0
9	9.2	0.9	0	0
10	47.4	31.9	5.7	0.2
11	34.8	51.3	59.7	42.3
12	7.7	14.6	31.8	51.5
13	0.8	1.2	2.8	5.9
Mean winning years of best performer	10.43	10.83	11.32	11.63

Viewed in this context, the performance of Magellan is still impressive but somewhat less surprising. The simulation shows that out of a large sample of managers, chance alone would provide a 43.3% probability that *someone* would beat the market at least eleven out of thirteen years. Averaging over all 10,000 trials, the mean number of winning years necessary to emerge as most reliable manager over the thirteen-year contest was 10.43.

Therefore, once we recognize that Magellan is not a fund chosen at random, but a fund that came to our attention precisely because it turned out to perform so well, the frequency with which it beat the market is no longer high enough to be considered a violation of market efficiency. Indeed, using the conventional 5% confidence level, we could not reject the hypothesis that the consistency of its performance was due to chance.

The other columns in Table 1 present the frequency distributions of the winning number of successful coin flips (analogously, the number of years in which the best-performing manager beats an efficient market) for other possible sample sizes. Not surprisingly, as the pool of managers increases, the predicted best performance steadily gets better. By providing as a benchmark the probability distribution of the best performance, rather than the average performance, the table tells us how many grains of salt to add to reports of the latest investment guru.

TABLE 18.3		Regression Coefficient*
Sharpe's style portfolios for the Magellan fund	Bills	0
	Intermediate bonds	0
	Long-term bonds	0
	Corporate bonds	0
	Mortgages	0
	Value stocks	0
	Growth stocks	47
	Medium-cap stocks	31
	Small stocks	18
	Foreign stocks	0
	European stocks	4
	Japanese stocks	0
	Total	100.00
	R-squared	97.3%

* Regressions are constrained to have nonnegative coefficients and to have coefficients that sum to 100%.

Source: William F. Sharpe, "Asset Allocation: Management Style and Performance Evaluation," *Journal of Portfolio Management,* Winter 1992, pp. 7–19. Copyrighted material is reprinted with permission from Institutional Investor.

18.2   STYLE ANALYSIS

Style analysis was introduced by Nobel Laureate William Sharpe.[2] The popularity of the concept was aided by a well-known study[3] concluding that 91.5% of the variation in returns of 82 mutual funds could be explained by the funds' asset allocation to bills, bonds, and stocks. Later studies that considered asset allocation across a broader range of asset classes found that as much as 97% of fund returns can be explained by asset allocation alone.

Sharpe considered 12 asset class (style) portfolios. His idea was to regress fund returns on indexes representing a range of asset classes. The regression coefficient on each index would then measure the implicit allocation to that "style." Because funds are barred from short positions, the regression coefficients are constrained to be either zero or positive and to sum to 100%, so as to represent a complete asset allocation. The R-square of the regression would then measure the percentage of return variability due to style choice rather than security selection.

To illustrate the approach, consider Sharpe's study of the monthly returns on Fidelity's Magellan Fund over the period January 1985 through December 1989, shown in Table 18.3. While there are 12 asset classes, each one represented by a stock index, the regression coefficients are positive for only four of them. We can conclude that the fund returns are well explained by only four style portfolios. Moreover, these three style portfolios alone explain 97.3% of returns.

The proportion of return variability *not* explained by asset allocation can be attributed to security selection within asset classes. For Magellan, this was $100 - 97.3 = 2.7\%$. To evaluate the average contribution of stock selection to fund performance we track the residuals from the regression, displayed in Figure 18.5. The figure plots the cumulative effect of these residuals; the steady upward trend confirms Magellan's success at stock selection in this period. Notice that the plot in Figure 18.5 is far smoother than the plot in Figure 18.6, which shows Magellan's performance compared to a standard benchmark, the S&P 500. This reflects the fact that the regression-weighted index portfolio tracks Magellan's overall style much better than the S&P 500. The performance spread is much noisier using the S&P as the benchmark.

Of course, Magellan's consistently positive residual returns (reflected in the steadily increasing plot of cumulative return difference) is hardly common. Figure 18.7 shows the frequency distribution of average residuals across 636 mutual funds. The distribution has the familiar bell shape with a slightly negative mean of $-.074\%$ per month.

[2]William F. Sharpe, "Asset Allocation: Management Style and Performance Evaluation," *Journal of Portfolio Management,* Winter 1992, pp. 7–19.
[3]Gary Brinson, Brian Singer, and Gilbert Beebower, "Determinants of Portfolio Performance," *Financial Analysts Journal,* May/June 1991.

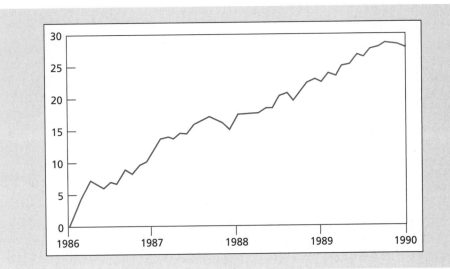

FIGURE 18.5
Fidelity Magellan Fund cumulative return difference: fund versus style benchmark
Source: William F. Sharpe, "Asset Allocation: Management Style and Performance Evaluation," *Journal of Portfolio Management*, Winter 1992, pp. 7–19. Copyrighted material is reprinted with permission from Institutional Investor.

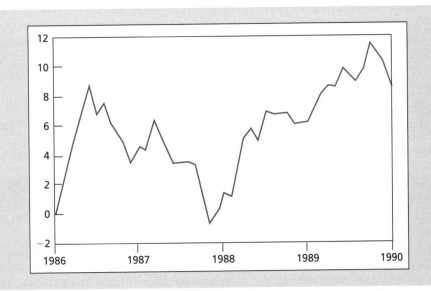

FIGURE 18.6
Fidelity Magellan Fund cumulative return difference: fund versus S&P 500
Source: William F. Sharpe, "Asset Allocation: Management Style and Performance Evaluation," *Journal of Portfolio Management*, Winter 1992, pp. 7–19. Copyrighted material is reprinted with permission from Institutional Investor.

Style analysis has become very popular in the investment management industry and has spawned quite a few variations on Sharpe's methodology. Many portfolio managers utilize Web sites that help investors identify their style and stock selection performance. The nearby box (page 601) shows that style analysis is at the heart of recent debates about the investment performance of hedge funds.

18.3   MORNINGSTAR'S RISK-ADJUSTED RATING

The commercial success of Morningstar, Inc., the premier source of information on mutual funds, has made its *Risk Adjusted Rating* (RAR) among the most widely used performance measures. The Morningstar five-star rating is coveted by the managers of the thousands of funds covered by the service.

Morningstar calculates a number of RAR performance measures that are similar, although not identical, to the standard mean-variance measures (see Chapter 4 for a more detailed discussion). The most distinct measure, the Morningstar Star Rating, is based on comparison of each fund to a peer group. The peer group for each fund is selected on the basis of the fund's investment universe (e.g., international, growth versus value, fixed-income, and so on) as well as portfolio characteristics such as average price-to-book value, price–earnings ratio, and market capitalization.

FIGURE 18.7

Average tracking error, 636 mutual funds, 1985–1989

Source: William F. Sharpe, "Asset Allocation: Management Style and Performance Evaluation," *Journal of Portfolio Management,* Winter 1992, pp. 7–19. Copyrighted material is reprinted with permission from Institutional Investor.

Morningstar computes fund returns (adjusted for loads) as well as a risk measure based on fund performance in its worst years. The risk-adjusted performance is ranked across funds in a style group and stars are awarded based on the following table:

Percentile	Stars
0–10	1
10–32.5	2
32.5–67.5	3
67.5–90	4
90–100	5

The Morningstar RAR method produces results that are similar but not identical to that of the mean/variance-based Sharpe ratios. Figure 18.8 demonstrates the fit between ranking by RAR and by Sharpe ratios from the performance of 1,286 diversified equity funds over the period 1994–1996. Sharpe notes that this period is characterized by high returns that contribute to a good fit.

FIGURE 18.8

Rankings based on Morningstar's category RARs and excess return Sharpe ratios

Source: William F. Sharpe, "Morningstar Performance Measures," **www.stanford. edu/~wfsharpe.**

On the MARKET FRONT

WHAT'S IT ALL ABOUT, ALPHA?

Too many notes. That's what Emperor Joseph II famously said to Mozart on seeing his opera "The Marriage of Figaro." But surely to think of a musical work as just a series of notes is to miss the magic.

Could the same be said about fund management? It is the fashion these days to separate beta (the systematic return delivered by the market) from alpha (the manager's skill). Investors are happy to pay high fees for the skill, but regard the market return as a commodity. Distinguishing the two is, however, sometimes difficult.

A fund manager might beat the market because of luck or recklessness, rather than skill, for example. Suppose he has packed his portfolio with oil stocks and then profits when the price of crude rises. More generally, alpha skeptics often attribute abnormal returns to "style bias," such as the manager who favors stocks with an energy focus. Popular style biases are often based on factors that seem to have predicted past alpha, such as firm size. But should the skeptics be biased against style bias? After all, the only portfolio utterly free of bias would be one that included the entire market.

Academics have entered this debate, trying to pin down the factors that drive a fund's performance. Bill Fung and Narayan Naik of London Business School have come up with a seven-factor model which, they say, can explain the bulk of hedge-fund performance. After allowing for these factors, the average fund of hedge funds has not produced any alpha in the past decade, except during the dot-com bubble. This approach suggests the whole idea of alpha might be an illusion.

However, it is also possible to take the opposite tack. This type of analysis gives managers no credit for choosing the systematic factors—the betas—that drive their portfolios. Yes, these betas could often have been bought for very low fees. But would an investor have been able to put them together in the right combination?

It is as if a diner in Gordon Ramsay's restaurants were brave enough to tell the irascible chef: "This meal was delicious. But chemical analysis shows it is 65% chicken, 20% carrot, 10% flour and 5% milk. I could have bought those ingredients for £1.50. Why should I pay £20?" The chef's reply, shorn of its expletives, might be: "The secret is in the mixing." This debate matters because people are now trying to replicate the performance of hedge funds with cloned portfolios.

There are two potential criticisms of the cloned approach. One is that it will simply reproduce all the systematic returns that hedge funds generate and none of their idiosyncratic magic. However, this "magic" is hard to pin down, and even if it does exist, it may be worth no more than the fees hedge funds charge.

The second criticism is that the clones will always be a step behind the smart money. You cannot clone a hedge fund until you know where it has been. But by then it may have moved on.

Mozart might have sympathized. His operas were more than the sum of his notes. But even if the great composer had no peers, he has had plenty of imitators.

SOURCE: *The Economist*, March 22, 2007.

18.4 PERFORMANCE ATTRIBUTION PROCEDURES

Rather than focus on risk-adjusted returns, practitioners often want simply to ascertain which decisions resulted in superior or inferior performance. Superior investment performance depends on an ability to be in the "right" securities at the right time. Such timing and selection ability may be considered broadly, such as being in equities as opposed to fixed-income securities when the stock market is performing well. Or it may be defined at a more detailed level, such as choosing the relatively better-performing stocks within a particular industry.

Portfolio managers constantly make both broad-brush asset market allocation decisions as well as more detailed sector and security allocation decisions within markets. Performance attribution studies attempt to decompose overall performance into discrete components that may be identified with a particular level of the portfolio selection process.

Attribution analysis starts from the broadest asset allocation choices and progressively focuses on ever-finer details of portfolio choice. The difference between a managed portfolio's performance and that of a benchmark portfolio then may be expressed as the sum of the contributions to performance of a series of decisions made at the various levels of the portfolio construction process. For example, one common attribution system decomposes performance into three components: (1) broad asset market allocation choices *across* equity, fixed-income, and money markets; (2) industry (sector) choice *within* each market; and (3) security choice within each sector.

TABLE 18.4

Performance of the managed portfolio

	Bogey Performance and Excess Return	
Component	**Benchmark Weight**	**Return of Index during Month (%)**
Equity (S&P 500)	0.60	5.81
Bonds (Lehman Bros. Index)	0.30	1.45
Cash (money market)	0.10	0.48
Bogey = (0.60 × 5.81) + (0.30 × 1.45) + (0.10 × 0.48) = 3.97%		
Return of managed portfolio		5.34%
−Return of bogey portfolio		3.97
Excess return of managed portfolio		1.37%

bogey

The rate of return an investment manager is compared to for performance evaluation.

To illustrate this method, consider the attribution results for a hypothetical portfolio. The portfolio invests in stocks, bonds, and money market securities. An attribution analysis appears in Tables 18.4 through 18.7. The portfolio return over the month is 5.34%.

The first step is to establish a benchmark level of performance against which performance ought to be compared. This benchmark is called the **bogey.** It is designed to measure the returns the portfolio manager would earn if she were to follow a completely passive strategy. "Passive" in this context has two attributes. First, it means the allocation of funds across broad asset classes is set in accord with a notion of "usual" or neutral allocation across sectors. This would be considered a passive asset market allocation. Second, it means that, within each asset class, the portfolio manager holds an indexed portfolio, for example, the S&P 500 index for the equity sector. The passive strategy used as a performance benchmark rules out both asset allocation and security selection decisions. Any departure of the manager's return from the passive benchmark must be due to either asset allocation bets (departures from the neutral allocation across markets) or security selection bets (departures from the passive index within asset classes).

While we've already discussed in earlier chapters the justification for indexing within sectors, it is worth briefly explaining the determination of the neutral allocation of funds across the broad asset classes. Weights that are designated as "neutral" will depend on the risk tolerance of the investor and must be determined in consultation with the client. For example, risk-tolerant clients may place a large fraction of their portfolio in the equity market, perhaps directing the fund manager to set neutral weights of 75% equity, 15% bonds, and 10% cash equivalents. Any deviation from these weights must be justified by a belief that one or another market will either over- or underperform its usual risk-return profile. In contrast, more risk-averse clients may set neutral weights of 45%/35%/20% for the three markets. Therefore, their portfolios in normal circumstances will be exposed to less risk than that of the risk-tolerant clients. Only intentional bets on market performance will result in departures from this profile.

In Table 18.4, the neutral weights have been set at 60% equity, 30% fixed-income, and 10% cash equivalents (money market securities). The bogey portfolio, comprising investments in each index with the 60/30/10 weights, returned 3.97%. The managed portfolio's measure of performance is positive and equal to its actual return less the return of the bogey: 5.34 − 3.97 = 1.37%. The next step is to allocate the 1.37% excess return to the separate decisions that contributed to it.

Asset Allocation Decisions

The managed portfolio is actually invested in the equity, fixed-income, and money markets with weights of 70%, 7%, and 23%, respectively. The portfolio's performance could be due to the departure of this weighting scheme from the benchmark 60/30/10 weights and/or to superior or inferior results *within* each of the three broad markets.

TABLE 18.5

Performance attribution

A. Contribution of Asset Allocation to Performance

Market	(1) Actual Weight in Market	(2) Benchmark Weight in Market	(3) Excess Weight	(4) Index Return (%)	(5) = (3) × (4) Contribution to Performance (%)
Equity	0.70	0.60	0.10	5.81	.5810
Fixed-income	0.07	0.30	−0.23	1.45	−.3335
Cash	0.23	0.10	0.13	0.48	.0624
Contribution of asset allocation					0.3099

B. Contribution of Selection to Total Performance

Market	(1) Portfolio Performance (%)	(2) Index Performance (%)	(3) Excess Performance (%)	(4) Portfolio Weight	(5) = (3) × (4) Contribution (%)
Equity	7.28	5.81	1.47	0.70	1.03
Fixed-income	1.89	1.45	0.44	0.07	0.03
Contribution of selection within markets					1.06

To isolate the effect of the manager's asset allocation choice, we measure the performance of a hypothetical portfolio that would have been invested in the *indexes* for each market with weights 70/7/23. This return measures the effect of the shift away from the benchmark 60/30/10 weights without allowing for any effects attributable to active management of the securities selected within each market.

Superior performance relative to the bogey is achieved by overweighting investments in markets that turn out to perform better than the bogey and by underweighting those in poorly performing markets. The contribution of asset allocation to superior performance equals the sum over all markets of the excess weight in each market times the return of the market index.

Table 18.5A demonstrates that asset allocation contributed 31 basis points to the portfolio's overall excess return of 137 basis points. The major factor contributing to superior performance in this month is the heavy weighting of the equity market in a month when the equity market has an excellent return of 5.81%.

Sector and Security Selection Decisions

If 0.31% of the excess performance can be attributed to advantageous asset allocation across markets, the remaining 1.06% then must be attributable to sector selection and security selection within each market. Table 18.5B details the contribution of the managed portfolio's sector and security selection to total performance.

Panel B shows that the equity component of the managed portfolio has a return of 7.28% versus a return of 5.81% for the S&P 500. The fixed-income return is 1.89% versus 1.45% for the Lehman Brothers Index. The superior performance in both equity and fixed-income markets weighted by the portfolio proportions invested in each market sums to the 1.06% contribution to performance attributable to sector and security selection.

Table 18.6 documents the sources of the equity market performance by each sector within the market. The first three columns detail the allocation of funds within the equity market

TABLE 18.6

Sector allocation within the equity market

Sector	(1) Beginning of Month Weights Portfolio	(2) S&P 500	(3) Difference in Weights	(4) Sector Return (%)	(5) = (3) × (4) Contribution of Sector Allocation (%)
Basic materials	0.0196	0.083	−0.0634	6.9	−0.437
Business services	0.0784	0.041	0.0374	7.0	0.262
Capital goods	0.0187	0.078	−0.0593	4.1	−0.243
Consumer cyclical	0.0847	0.125	−0.0403	8.8	−0.355
Consumer noncyclical	0.4037	0.204	0.1997	10.0	1.997
Credit sensitive	0.2401	0.218	0.0221	5.0	0.111
Energy	0.1353	0.142	−0.0067	2.6	−0.017
Technology	0.0195	0.109	−0.0895	0.3	−0.027
Total	1.0000	1.000	0.0000		1.290

compared to their representation in the S&P 500. Column (4) shows the rate of return of each sector, and column (5) equals the product of the difference in the sector weight and the sector's performance.

Note that good performance derives from overweighting well-performing sectors such as consumer noncyclicals, as well as underweighting poorly performing sectors such as technology. The excess return of the equity component of the portfolio attributable to sector allocation alone is 1.29%. As the equity component of the portfolio outperformed the S&P 500 by 1.47%, we conclude that the effect of security selection within sectors must have contributed an additional 1.47 − 1.29, or 0.18%, to the performance of the equity component of the portfolio.

A similar sector analysis can be applied to the fixed-income portion of the portfolio, but we do not show those results here.

Summing Up Component Contributions

In this particular month, all facets of the portfolio selection process were successful. Table 18.7 details the contribution of each aspect of performance. Asset allocation across the major security markets contributes 31 basis points. Sector and security allocation within those markets contributes 106 basis points, for total excess portfolio performance of 137 basis points.

The sector and security allocation of 106 basis points can be partitioned further. Sector allocation within the equity market results in excess performance of 129 basis points, and security selection within sectors contributes 18 basis points. (The total equity excess performance of 147 basis points is multiplied by the 70% weight in equity to obtain contribution to portfolio performance.) Similar partitioning could be done for the fixed-income sector.

CONCEPT *check* **18.2**

a.   Suppose the benchmark weights had been set at 70% equity, 25% fixed-income, and 5% cash equivalents. What then would be the contributions of the manager's asset allocation choices?

b.   Suppose the S&P 500 return had been 5%. Recompute the contribution of the manager's security selection choices.

plus a random number that is zero with a probability of 0.5 and 5% with a probability of 0.5. The results for each strategy are

	Strategy 1 (%)	Strategy 2 (%)
Expected return	5	7.5
Standard deviation	0	2.5
Highest return	5	10
Lowest return	5	5

Clearly, strategy 2 dominates strategy 1, as its rate of return is *at least* equal to that of strategy 1 and sometimes greater. No matter how risk averse you are, you will always prefer strategy 2 to strategy 1, even though strategy 2 has a significant standard deviation. Compared to strategy 1, strategy 2 provides only good surprises, so the standard deviation in this case cannot be a measure of risk.

You can look at these strategies as analogous to the case of the perfect timer compared with either an all-equity or all-bills strategy. In every period, the perfect timer obtains at least as good a return, in some cases better. Therefore, the timer's standard deviation is a misleading measure of risk when you compare perfect timing to an all-equity or all-bills strategy.

Valuing Market Timing as an Option

Merton (1981) shows that the key to analyzing the pattern of returns of a perfect market timer is to compare the returns of a perfect foresight investor with those of another investor who holds a call option on the equity portfolio. Investing 100% in bills plus holding a call option on the equity portfolio will yield returns identical to those of the portfolio of the perfect timer who invests 100% in either the safe asset or the equity portfolio, whichever will yield the higher return. The perfect timer's return is shown in Figure 18.9. The rate of return is bounded from below by the risk-free rate, r_f.

To see how the value of information can be treated as an option, suppose the market index currently is at S_0 and a call option on the index has exercise price of $X = S_0(1 + r_f)$. If the market outperforms bills over the coming period, S_T will exceed X; it will be less than X otherwise. Now look at the payoff to a portfolio consisting of this option and S_0 dollars invested in bills.

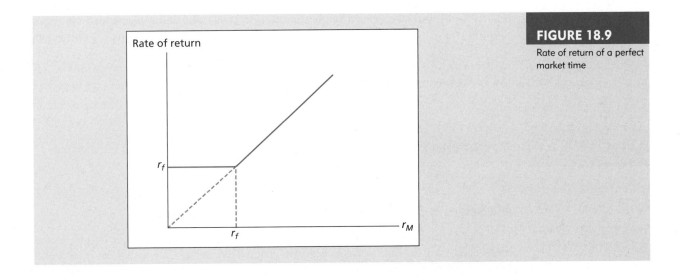

FIGURE 18.9

Rate of return of a perfect market time

	Payoff to Portfolio	
Outcome:	$S_T \leq X$	$S_T > X$
Bills	$S_0(1 + r_f)$	$S_0(1 + r_f)$
Option	0	$S_T - X$
Total	$S_0(1 + r_f)$	S_T

The portfolio returns the risk-free rate when the market is bearish (that is, when the market return is less than the risk-free rate) and pays the market return when the market is bullish and beats bills. This represents perfect market timing. Consequently, the value of perfect timing ability is equivalent to the value of the call option, for a call enables the investor to earn the market return only when it exceeds r_f.

Valuation of the call option embedded in market timing is relatively straightforward using the Black-Scholes formula. Set $S = \$1$ (to find the value of the call per dollar invested in the market), use an exercise price of $X = (1 + r_f)$ (the current risk-free rate is about 5%), and a volatility of $\sigma = 20\%$ (the historical volatility of the S&P 500). For a once-a-year timer, $T = 1$ year. According to the Black-Scholes formula, the call option conveyed by market timing ability is worth about 8% of assets, and this is the annual fee one could presumably charge for such services. More frequent timing would be worth more. If one could time the market on a monthly basis, then $T = \frac{1}{12}$ and the value of perfect timing would be 2.3% *per month*.

The Value of Imperfect Forecasting

But managers are not perfect forecasters. While managers who are right most of the time presumably do very well, "right most of the time" does not mean merely the *percentage* of the time a manager is right. For example, a Tucson, Arizona, weather forecaster who *always* predicts "no rain" may be right 90% of the time, but this "stopped clock" strategy does not require any forecasting ability.

Neither is the overall proportion of correct forecasts an appropriate measure of market forecasting ability. If the market is up two days out of three, and a forecaster always predicts a market advance, the two-thirds success rate is not a measure of forecasting ability. We need to examine the proportion of bull markets ($r_M > r_f$) correctly forecast *and* the proportion of bear markets ($r_M < r_f$) correctly forecast.

If we call P_1 the proportion of the correct forecasts of bull markets and P_2 the proportion for bear markets, then $P_1 + P_2 - 1$ is the correct measure of timing ability. For example, a forecaster who always guesses correctly will have $P_1 = P_2 = 1$ and will show ability of 1 (100%). An analyst who always bets on a bear market will mispredict all bull markets ($P_1 = 0$), will correctly "predict" all bear markets ($P_2 = 1$), and will end up with timing ability of $P_1 + P_2 - 1 = 0$. If C denotes the (call option) value of a perfect market timer, then $(P_1 + P_2 - 1)C$ measures the value of imperfect forecasting ability.

The incredible potential payoff to accurate timing versus the relative scarcity of billionaires should suggest to you that market timing is far from a trivial exercise and that very imperfect timing is the most that we can hope for.

CONCEPT check 18.4   What is the market timing score of someone who flips a fair coin to predict the market?

Measurement of Market Timing Performance

In its pure form, market timing involves shifting funds between a market index portfolio and a safe asset, such as T-bills or a money market fund, depending on whether the market as a whole is expected to outperform the safe asset. In practice, most managers do not shift fully

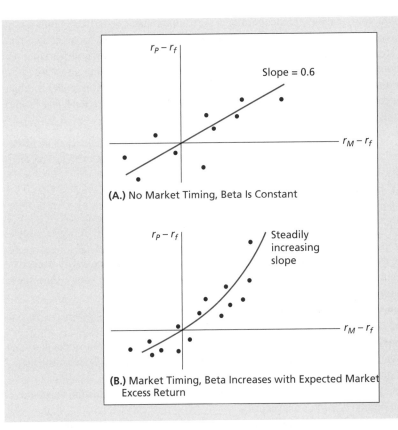

FIGURE 18.10

Characteristic lines **A:** No market timing, beta is constant **B:** Market timing, beta increases with expected market excess return

between bills and the market. How might we measure partial shifts into the market when it is expected to perform well?

To simplify, suppose the investor holds only the market index portfolio and T-bills. If the weight on the market were constant, say, 0.6, then the portfolio beta would also be constant, and the portfolio characteristic line would plot as a straight line with a slope 0.6, as in Figure 18.10A. If, however, the investor could correctly time the market and shift funds into it in periods when the market does well, the characteristic line would plot as in Figure 18.10B. The idea is that if the timer can predict bull and bear markets, more will be shifted into the market when the market is about to go up. The portfolio beta and the slope of the characteristic line will be higher when r_M is higher, resulting in the curved line that appears in Figure 18.10B.

Treynor and Mazuy (1966) tested to see whether portfolio betas did in fact increase prior to market advances, but they found little evidence of timing ability. A similar test was implemented by Henriksson (1984). His examination of market timing ability for 116 funds in 1968–1980 found that, on average, portfolio betas actually *fell* slightly during the market advances, although in most cases the response of portfolio betas to the market was not statistically significant. Eleven funds had statistically positive values of market timing, while eight had significantly negative values. Overall, 62% of the funds had negative point estimates of timing ability.

In sum, empirical tests to date show little evidence of market timing ability. Perhaps this should be expected; given the tremendous values to be reaped by a successful market timer, it would be surprising to uncover clear-cut evidence of such skills in nearly efficient markets.

18.7 SECURITY SELECTION: THE TREYNOR-BLACK MODEL

Overview of the Treynor-Black Model

Security analysis is the other dimension of active investment besides timing the overall market and asset allocation. Suppose you are an analyst studying individual securities. Quite likely, you will turn up several securities that appear to be mispriced and offer positive alphas. But how do you exploit your analysis? Concentrating a portfolio on these securities entails a cost, namely, the firm-specific risk you could shed by more fully diversifying. As an active manager, you must strike a balance between aggressive exploitation of security mispricing and diversification considerations that dictate against concentrating a portfolio in a few stocks.

Jack Treynor and Fischer Black (1973) developed a portfolio construction model for managers who use security analysis. It assumes security markets are nearly efficient. The essence of the model is this:

1. Security analysts in an active investment management organization can analyze in depth only a relatively small number of stocks out of the entire universe of securities. The securities not analyzed are assumed to be fairly priced.

2. For the purpose of efficient diversification, the market index portfolio is the baseline portfolio, which is treated as the passive portfolio.

3. The macro forecasting unit of the investment management firm provides forecasts of the expected rate of return and variance of the passive (market index) portfolio.

4. The objective of security analysis is to form an active portfolio of a necessarily limited number of securities. Perceived mispricing of the analyzed securities is what determines the composition of this active portfolio.

5. Analysts follow several steps to make up the active portfolio and forecast its performance:
   a. Estimate the characteristic line of each analyzed security and obtain its beta and residual variance. From the beta and the macro forecast, $E(r_M) - r_f$, determine the *required* rate of return of the security.
   b. Determine the expected return. Subtracting the required return yields the expected *abnormal* return (alpha) of the security.
   c. Use the estimates for the values of alpha, beta, and residual risk to determine the optimal weight of each security in the active portfolio.
   d. Estimate the alpha, beta, and residual variance for the active portfolio according to the weights of the securities in the portfolio.

6. The macroeconomic forecasts for the passive index portfolio and the composite forecast for the active portfolio are used to determine the optimal risky portfolio, which will be a combination of the passive and active portfolios.

Treynor-Black model

An optimizing model for portfolio managers who use security analysis in a nearly efficient market.

Although some sophisticated investment managers use the **Treynor-Black model**, it has not taken the industry by storm. This is unfortunate for several reasons:

1. Just as even imperfect market-timing ability has enormous value, security analysis of the sort Treynor and Black propose has similar potential value. Even with far-from-perfect security analysis, active management can add value.

2. The Treynor-Black model is easy to implement. Moreover, it is useful even relaxing some of its simplifying assumptions.

3. The model lends itself to use with decentralized decision making, which is essential to efficiency in complex organizations.

Portfolio Construction

With all securities assumed to be fairly priced and with the index model used as a guideline for the rate of return on securities, the rate of return on security i is given by

$$r_i = r_f + \beta_i(r_M - r_f) + e_i \tag{18.1}$$

where e_i is the zero mean, firm-specific (nonsystematic) component.

Absent security analysis, Treynor and Black take Equation 18.1 to represent the rate of return on all securities and assume the index portfolio (M) is efficient. For simplicity, they also assume the nonsystematic components of returns, e_i, are independent across securities. Market timing is incorporated in the terms r_M and σ_M, representing index portfolio forecasts.

The overall investment in the risky portfolio will be affected by the optimism or pessimism reflected in these numbers.

Assume a team of security analysts investigates a subset of the universe of available securities, with the objective of forming an active portfolio. That portfolio will then be mixed with the index portfolio to improve diversification. For each security, k, that is researched, we write the rate of return as

$$r_k = r_f + \beta_k(r_M - r_f) + e_k + \alpha_k \qquad \textbf{(18.2)}$$

where α_k represents the extra (abnormal) expected return attributable to perceived mispricing of the security. Thus, for each security analyzed, the research team estimates the parameters

$$\alpha_k, \; \beta_k, \; \sigma^2(e_k)$$

If all the α_k turn out to be zero, there would be no reason to depart from the passive strategy, and the index portfolio would remain the manager's choice. But this is a remote possibility. In general, there will be a significant number of nonzero α values, some positive and some negative.

Consider first how you would use the active portfolio once you found it. Suppose the **active portfolio** (A) has been constructed and has the parameters

$$\alpha_A, \; \beta_A, \; \sigma^2(e_A)$$

The total variance of the active portfolio is the sum of its systematic variance, $\beta_A^2 \sigma_M^2$, plus the nonsystematic variance, $\sigma^2(e_A)$. These three parameters, plus the mean and variance of the index portfolio, are sufficient to identify the opportunity set generated by the active and passive portfolios.

Figure 18.11 shows the optimization process with active and passive portfolios. The dashed efficient frontier line represents the universe of all securities, assuming they are all fairly priced, that is, that all alphas are zero. By definition, the market index (M) is on this efficient frontier and is tangent to the (dashed) capital market line (CML). In practice, our analysts do not need to (indeed cannot) know this frontier, but they need to forecast the index portfolio and construct the optimal risky portfolio using the index and active (A) portfolios. The optimal portfolio (P) will lie on the capital allocation line (CAL) that lies above the CML.

active portfolio

In the context of the Treynor-Black model, the portfolio formed by mixing analyzed stocks with perceived nonzero alpha values. This portfolio is ultimately mixed with the passive market index portfolio.

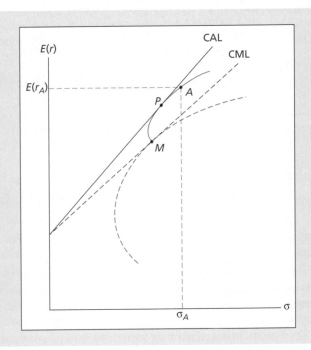

FIGURE 18.11

The optimization process with active and passive portfolios

From the viewpoint of an investor with superior analysis, the index portfolio will be inefficient; that is, the active portfolio (A) constructed from mispriced securities will lie above the CML.

The optimal combination of the active portfolio with the passive portfolio takes off from the construction of an optimal risky portfolio from two risky assets that we first encountered in Chapter 6. As the active portfolio is not perfectly correlated with the index, further diversification—that is, mixing it with the index—is likely to be beneficial.

We can judge the success of active management, and the contribution of the active portfolio (A), by the Sharpe measure (ratio of reward to variability) of the resultant risky portfolio (P), compared with that of the index portfolio (M).

The mathematics of the efficient frontier reveals that the Sharpe measure of the risky portfolio is

$$S(P) = [S^2(M) + \alpha_A^2/\sigma^2(e_A)]^{1/2} \tag{18.3}$$

Thus, the critical variable in determining the success of the active portfolio is its ratio of alpha to nonsystematic risk, $\alpha_A/\sigma(e_A)$.

The intuition here is straightforward. You mix the active portfolio with the index for the benefit of diversification. The position to take in the active portfolio relative to the market portfolio depends on the ratio of the active portfolio's abnormal return, α_A, relative to its weakness given by its diversifiable risk, $\sigma(e_A)$. This ratio is sometimes referred to as the *appraisal ratio*.

The contribution of individual securities (say, k) to the active portfolio (A) is analogous to that of the active portfolio to the risky portfolio (P). It is measured by the appraisal ratio, $\alpha_k/\sigma(e_k)$.

SUMMARY

- The appropriate performance measure depends on the investment context. The Sharpe measure is most appropriate when the portfolio represents the entire investment fund. The Treynor measure or Jensen measure is appropriate when the portfolio is to be mixed with several other assets, allowing for diversification of firm-specific risk outside of each portfolio.

- The shifting mean and variance of actively managed portfolios make it harder to assess performance. A typical example is the attempt of portfolio managers to time the market, resulting in ever-changing portfolio betas and standard deviations.

- Common attribution procedures partition performance improvements to asset allocation, sector selection, and security selection. Performance is assessed by calculating departures of portfolio composition from a benchmark or neutral portfolio.

- Active portfolio managers attempt to construct a risky portfolio that improves on the reward-to-variability (Sharpe) ratio of a passive strategy.

- Active management has two components: market timing (or, more generally, asset allocation) and security analysis.

- The value of perfect market-timing ability is enormous. The rate of return to a perfect market timer will be uncertain, but the risk cannot be measured by standard deviation, because perfect timing dominates a passive strategy, providing only "good" surprises.

- Perfect-timing ability is equivalent to having a call option on the market portfolio. The value of that option can be determined using valuation techniques such as the Black-Scholes formula.

- The value of *imperfect* market timing depends on the sum of the probabilities of the true outcome conditional on the forecast: $P_1 + P_2 - 1$. If perfect timing is equivalent to call option C, then imperfect timing can be valued by: $(P_1 + P_2 - 1)C$.

- The Treynor-Black model is based on an index model that takes market-timing forecasts as given. The investment manager uses security analysis to construct an active portfolio. The active portfolio is mixed with the index portfolio to maximize the Sharpe measure of the optimal risky portfolio.

- In the Treynor-Black model, the weight of each analyzed security is proportional to the ratio of its alpha to its residual variance.

**Select problems are available in McGraw-Hill's Homework Manager®.
Please see the packaging options section of the preface for more information.**

PROBLEM SETS

Problems 1–3 appeared in past CFA examinations.

1. A plan sponsor with a portfolio manager who invests in small-capitalization, high-growth stocks should have the plan sponsor's performance measured against which *one* of the following?

    a. S&P 500 index.

    b. Wilshire 5000 index.

    c. Dow Jones Industrial Average.

    d. Russell 2000 index.

2. Assume you purchased a rental property for $50,000 and sold it one year later for $55,000 (there was no mortgage on the property). At the time of the sale, you paid $2,000 in commissions and $600 in taxes. If you received $6,000 in rental income (all of it received at the end of the year), what annual rate of return did you earn?

3. A two-year investment of $2,000 results in a return of $150 at the end of the first year and a return of $150 at the end of the second year, in addition to the return of the original investment. What is the internal rate of return on the investment?

4. Based on current dividend yields and expected capital gains, the expected rates of return on portfolios *A* and *B* are 11% and 14%, respectively. The beta of *A* is 0.8 while that of *B* is 1.5. The T-bill rate is currently 6%, while the expected rate of return of the S&P 500 index is 12%. The standard deviation of portfolio *A* is 10% annually, while that of *B* is 31%, and that of the index is 20%.

    a. If you currently hold a market index portfolio, would you choose to add either of these portfolios to your holdings? Explain.

    b. If instead you could invest *only* in bills and *one* of these portfolios, which would you choose?

5. Evaluate the timing and selection abilities of four managers whose performances are plotted in the following four scatter diagrams.

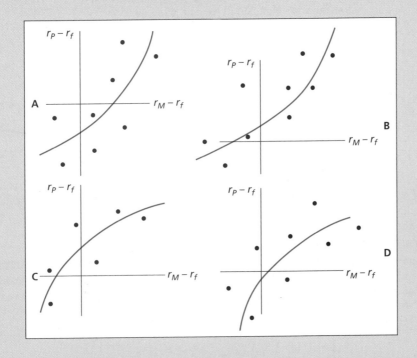

6. Consider the following information regarding the performance of a money manager in a recent month. The table presents the actual return of each sector of the manager's portfolio in column (1), the fraction of the portfolio allocated to each sector in column (2), the benchmark or neutral sector allocations in column (3), and the returns of sector indexes in column (4).

	(1) Actual Return	(2) Actual Weight	(3) Benchmark Weight	(4) Index Return
Equity	2.0%	0.70	0.60	2.5% (S&P 500)
Bonds	1.0	0.20	0.30	1.2 (Aggregate Bond index)
Cash	0.5	0.10	0.10	0.5

a. What was the manager's return in the month? What was her over- or underperformance?

b. What was the contribution of security selection to relative performance?

c. What was the contribution of asset allocation to relative performance? Confirm that the sum of selection and allocation contributions equals her total "excess" return relative to the bogey.

7. Conventional wisdom says one should measure a manager's investment performance over an entire market cycle. What arguments support this contention? What arguments contradict it?

8. Does the use of universes of managers with similar investment styles to evaluate relative investment performance overcome the statistical problems associated with instability of beta or total variability?

9. During a particular year, the T-bill rate was 6%, the market return was 14%, and a portfolio manager with beta of 0.5 realized a return of 10%. Evaluate the manager based on the portfolio alpha.

10. The chairman provides you with the following data, covering one year, concerning the portfolios of two of the fund's equity managers (manager *A* and manager *B*). Although the portfolios consist primarily of common stocks, cash reserves are included in the calculation of both portfolio betas and performance. By way of perspective, selected data for the financial markets are included in the following table.

	Total Return	Beta
Manager A	24.0%	1.0
Manager B	30.0	1.5
S&P 500	21.0	
Lehman Bond Index	31.0	
91-day Treasury bills	12.0	

a. Calculate and compare the risk-adjusted performance of the two managers relative to each other and to the S&P 500.

b. Explain *two* reasons the conclusions drawn from this calculation may be misleading.

11. Go to **www.mhhe.com/bkm** and link to the material for Chapter 18, where you will find five years of monthly returns for two mutual funds, Vanguard's U.S. Growth Fund and U.S. Value Fund, as well as corresponding returns for the S&P 500 and the Treasury bill rate.

Please visit us at www.mhhe.com/bkm

a. Set up a spreadsheet to calculate each fund's excess rate of return over T-bills in each month.

b. Calculate the standard deviation of each fund over the five-year period.

c. What was the beta of each fund over the five-year period? (You may wish to review the spreadsheets from Chapters 5 and 6 on the Index model.)

d. What were the Sharpe, Jensen, and Treynor measures for each fund?

12. Carl Karl, a portfolio manager for the Alpine Trust Company, has been responsible since 2010 for the City of Alpine's Employee Retirement Plan, a municipal pension fund. Alpine is a growing community, and city services and employee payrolls have expanded in each of the past 10 years. Contributions to the plan in fiscal 2015 exceeded benefit payments by a three-to-one ratio.

The plan's Board of Trustees directed Karl five years ago to invest for total return over the long term. However, as trustees of this highly visible public fund, they cautioned him that volatile or erratic results could cause them embarrassment. They also noted a state statute that mandated that not more than 25% of the plan's assets (at cost) be invested in common stocks.

At the annual meeting of the trustees in November 2015, Karl presented the folling portfolio and performance report to the Board.

Alpine Employee Retirement Plan				
Asset Mix as of 9/30/15	At Cost (millions)		At Market (millions)	
Fixed-income assets:				
Short-term securities	$ 4.5	11.0%	$ 4.5	11.4%
Long-term bonds and mortgages	26.5	64.7	23.5	59.5
Common stocks	10.0	24.3	11.5	29.1
	$41.0	100.0%	$39.5	100.0%

Investment Performance		
	Annual Rates of Return for Periods Ending 9/30/15	
	5 Years	1 Year
Total Alpine Fund:		
Time-weighted	8.2%	5.2%
Dollar-weighted (Internal)	7.7%	4.8%
Assumed actuarial return	6.0%	6.0%
U.S. Treasury bills	7.5%	11.3%
Large sample of pension funds	10.1%	14.3%
(average 60% equities, 40% fixed income)		
Common stocks—Alpine Fund	13.3%	14.3%
Average portfolio beta coefficient	0.90	0.89
Standard & Poor's 500 stock index	13.8%	21.1%
Fixed-income securities—Alpine Fund	6.7%	1.0%
Salomon Brothers' bond index	4.0%	−11.4%

Karl was proud of his performance and was chagrined when a trustee made the following critical observations:

a. "Our one-year results were terrible, and it's what you've done for us lately that counts most."

b. "Our total fund performance was clearly inferior compared to the large sample of other pension funds for the last five years. What else could this reflect except poor management judgment?"

c. "Our common stock performance was especially poor for the five-year period."

d. "Why bother to compare your returns to the return from Treasury bills and the actuarial assumption rate? What your competition could have earned for us or how we would have fared if invested in a passive index (which doesn't charge a fee) are the only relevant measures of performance."

e. "Who cares about time-weighted return? If it can't pay pensions, what good is it!"

Appraise the merits of each of these statements and give counterarguments that Mr. Karl can use.

13. Historical data suggest the standard deviation of an all-equity strategy is about 5.5% per month. Suppose the risk-free rate is now 1% per month and market volatility is at its historical level. What would be a fair monthly fee to a perfect market timer, according to the Black-Scholes formula?

14. A fund manager scrutinizing the record of two market timers comes up with this information:

Number of months that $r_M > r_f$	135
Correctly predicted by timer A 78	
Correctly predicted by timer B 86	
Number of months that $r_M < r_f$	92
Correctly predicted by timer A 57	
Correctly predicted by timer B 50	

a. What are the conditional probabilities, P_1 and P_2, and the total ability parameters for timers A and B?

b. Using the historical data of Problem 13, what is a fair monthly fee for the two timers?

15. A portfolio manager summarizes the input from the macro and micro forecasts in the following table:

Micro Forecasts			
Asset	Expected Return (%)	Beta	Residual Standard Deviation (%)
Stock A	20	1.3	58
Stock B	18	1.8	71
Stock C	17	0.7	60
Stock D	12	1.0	55

Macro Forecasts		
Asset	Expected Return (%)	Standard Deviation (%)
T-bills	8	0
Passive equity portfolio	16	23

a. Calculate expected excess returns, alpha values, and residual variances for these stocks.

b. Construct the optimal risky portfolio.

c. What is Sharpe's measure for the optimal portfolio and how much of it is contributed by the active portfolio? What is the M^2?

WEB *master*

Security Selection

There are several sites that offer advice on how to select securities that are expected to outperform the market. One tutorial is available on the Investopedia Web site at **www.investopedia.com/university/stockpicking.** Toward the bottom of the page are links that explain some of the better-known stock selection methods.

Some ready-made portfolios of stocks expected to outperform the market also are available. Open the fact sheet on Standard & Poor's Stock Appreciation Ranking System (STARS) at **www2.standardandpoors.com/spf/pdf/index/All_STARS_Factsheet.pdf.** Although the details are proprietary, the fact sheet gives general information about the characteristics of stocks chosen.

1. Which factors are considered when determining a STARS ranking?

2. How are weights determined for the stocks in a STARS basket?

3. How have the U.S. S&P All STARS performed relative to the S&P 500 index over the past 1, 3, and 5 years?

4. How do the 3- and 5-year standard deviations of the U.S. All STARS compare with those of the corresponding S&P 500 standard deviations?

5. How do the 3- and 5-year Sharpe measures of the U.S. All STARS compare with those of the corresponding S&P 500 Sharpe measures?

6. How many companies are in the U.S. S&P All STARS portfolio?

SOLUTIONS TO CONCEPT *checks*

18.1. Sharpe: $(\bar{r} - \bar{r}_f)/\sigma$

$S_P = (35 - 6)/42 = 0.69$

$S_M = (28 - 6)/30 = 0.733$

Jensen (or alpha): $\bar{r} - [\bar{r}_f + \beta(\bar{r}_M - \bar{r}_f)]$

$\alpha_P = 35 - [6 + 1.2(28 - 6)] = 2.6\%$

$\alpha_M = 0$

Treynor: $(\bar{r} - \bar{r}_f)/\beta$

$T_P = (35 - 6)/1.2 = 24.2$

$T_M = (28 - 6)/1.0 = 22$

18.2. Performance attribution

First compute the new bogey performance as

$(0.70 \times 5.81) + (0.25 \times 1.45) + (0.05 \times 0.48) = 4.45\%$

a. Contribution of asset allocation to performance

Market	(1) Actual Weight in Market	(2) Benchmark Weight in Market	(3) Excess Weight	(4) Index Return (%)	(5) = (3) × (4) Contribution to Performance (%)
Equity	0.70	0.70	0.00	5.81	0.000
Fixed-income	0.07	0.25	−0.18	1.45	−.261
Cash	0.23	0.05	0.18	0.48	.086
Contribution of asset allocation					−.175

b. Contribution of selection to total performance

Market	(1) Portfolio Performance (%)	(2) Index Performance (%)	(3) Excess Performance (%)	(4) Portfolio Weight	(5) = (3) × (4) Contribution (%)
Equity	7.28	5.00	2.28	0.70	1.60
Fixed-income	1.89	1.45	0.44	0.07	0.03
Contribution of selection within markets					1.63

18.3. Beginning-of-period fund: $F_0 = \$1$
End-of-period fund for each strategy:

$$F_1 = \begin{cases} 17.56 & \text{Strategy} = \text{Bills only} \\ 1{,}992.80 & \text{Strategy} = \text{Market only} \\ 148{,}472.83 & \text{Strategy} = \text{Perfect timing} \end{cases}$$

Number of periods: $N = 78$ years
Annual compounded rate:

$$(1 + r_A)^N = \frac{F_1}{F_0}$$

$$r_A = \left(\frac{F_1}{F_0}\right)^{1/N} - 1$$

$$r_A = \begin{cases} 3.74\% & \text{Strategy} = \text{Bills only} \\ 10.23\% & \text{Strategy} = \text{Market only} \\ 16.49\% & \text{Strategy} = \text{Perfect timing} \end{cases}$$

18.4. The timer will guess bear or bull markets randomly. One-half of all bull markets will be preceded by a correct forecast, and, similarly, one-half of all bear markets will be preceded by a correct forecast. Hence, $P_1 + P_2 - 1 = \frac{1}{2} + \frac{1}{2} - 1 = 0$.

Globalization and International Investing

Demonstrate the advantages of international diversification.

Formulate hedge strategies to offset the currency risk involved
in international investments.

Understand international investment strategies.

Decompose investment returns into contributing factors such as country,
currency, and stock selection.

Although we in the United States often treat the S&P 500 as the
market index portfolio, this practice is increasingly inappropriate. Equities represent less than 25% of total U.S. wealth and a much smaller
proportion than that of world wealth. In this chapter, we look beyond domestic
markets to survey issues of extended diversification.

In one sense, international investing may be viewed as no more than a
straightforward generalization of our earlier treatment of portfolio selection with
a larger menu of assets from which to construct a portfolio. One faces similar
issues of diversification, security analysis, security selection, and asset allocation.
On the other hand, international investments pose some problems not encountered in domestic markets. Among these are the presence of exchange rate risk,
restrictions on capital flows across national boundaries, an added dimension of
political risk and country-specific regulations, and differing accounting practices
in different countries.

We begin by looking at market capitalization of stock exchanges around
the world and its relation to the home country GDP. Next, we examine exchange
rate risk and how such risk can be mitigated by using foreign exchange futures

(continued)

and forward contracts. We also introduce political and country-specific risk that must be considered in the overall risk assessment of international investments. We then examine correlation across country portfolios with and without hedging foreign exchange risk.

Based on these insights, we assess the efficacy of investing globally in the context of equilibrium in international capital markets. Finally, we show how performance attribution procedures can be adapted to an international setting.

Related Web sites for this chapter are available at www.mhhe.com/bkm.

19.1 GLOBAL MARKETS FOR EQUITIES

Developed Countries

To appreciate the myopia of an exclusive investment focus on U.S. stocks and bonds, consider the data in Table 19.1, developed by the authors in a 2003 study. Developed (high-income) countries are defined as those with per capita income exceeding $9,386 (in 2003), and their broad stock indexes are generally less risky than those of emerging markets. The World Bank listed 54 developed countries in 2003, many of them with very small exchanges. Our list includes 25 countries with the largest equity capitalization, the smallest of which is New Zealand with a capitalization of $21 billion in 2003. These countries made up 79% of the World gross domestic product in 2003.

The first six columns of Table 19.1 show market capitalization over the years 1998–2003. The first line shows capitalization for all world exchanges, showing total capitalization of corporate equity in 2003 as $20.0 trillion, of which U.S. stock exchanges made up $9.2 trillion (45.8%). The year-to-year changes in the figures in these columns demonstrate the volatility of these markets.

The next three columns of Table 19.1 show country equity capitalization as a percentage of the world's in 2003 and 1998 and the growth in capitalization over those five years. The weights of the five largest countries behind the U.S. (Japan, U.K., France, Germany, and Switzerland) added up to 29.9% in 2003, so that in the universe of these six countries alone, the weight of the U.S. was only 61% [45.8/(45.8 + 29.9)]. Clearly, U.S. stocks may not comprise an adequately diversified portfolio of equities.

The last three columns of Table 19.1 show GDP, per capita GDP, and the equity capitalization as a percentage of GDP for the year 2003. As we would expect, per capital GDP in developed countries is not as variable across countries as total GDP, which is determined in part by total population. But market capitalization as a percentage of GDP is quite variable, suggesting widespread differences in economic structure even across developed countries. We return to this issue in the next section.

Emerging Markets

For a passive strategy, one could argue that a portfolio of equities of just the six countries with the largest capitalization would make up 75.7% (in 2003) of the world portfolio and may be sufficiently diversified. However, this argument will not hold for active portfolios that seek to tilt investments toward promising assets. Active portfolios will naturally include many stocks or indexes of emerging markets.

Table 19.2 makes the point. Surely, active portfolio managers must prudently scour stocks in markets such as China, Brazil, or Thailand. Table 19.2 shows data from the 20 largest emerging markets, the most notable of which is China, which grew by 230% between 1998

TABLE 19.1

Market capitalization of stock exchanges in developed countries

Market Capitalization

| | Billions of U.S. Dollars | | | | | | Percent of World | | Growth (%) | GDP | GDP per Capita | Market Capitalization as % of GDP |
	2003	2002	2001	2000	1999	1998	2003	1998	1998–2003	2003	2003	2003
World	**$20,026**	**$23,842**	**$27,473**	**$31,026**	**$23,313**	**$18,127**	**100%**	**100%**	**10.48%**	**36,356**	**5,797**	**55%**
United States	9,172	11,850	12,900	13,763	11,240	8,240	45.8	45.5	11.30	10,882	37,388	84
Japan	2,076	2,254	3,140	4,701	2,493	2,231	10.4	12.3	−6.92	4,326	34,010	48
United Kingdom	1,796	2,157	2,566	2,708	2,223	1,867	9.0	10.3	−3.82	1,795	30,278	100
France	911	1,068	1,278	1,312	888	601	4.6	3.3	51.62	1,748	29,267	52
Germany	633	831	1,061	1,262	1,075	744	3.2	4.1	−14.87	2,401	29,081	26
Switzerland	543	604	783	698	718	503	2.7	2.8	7.93	309	42,138	176
Canada	488	547	615	667	458	446	2.4	2.5	9.34	834	26,380	58
Italy	463	508	716	686	559	324	2.3	1.8	42.97	1,466	25,429	32
Netherlands	437	551	680	729	643	495	2.2	2.7	−11.72	512	31,548	85
Hong Kong	402	462	564	553	296	333	2.0	1.8	20.75	159	23,268	254
Australia	360	362	349	412	333	242	1.8	1.3	48.84	518	26,062	70
Spain	312	351	331	331	336	222	1.6	1.2	40.44	836	20,343	37
Korea	200	186	123	260	93	29	1.0	0.2	600.03	605	12,634	33
Sweden	170	218	274	338	216	198	0.8	1.1	−14.32	301	33,586	56
Finland	133	183	280	348	144	62	0.7	0.3	115.22	162	31,007	82
Belgium	127	146	159	177	187	114	0.6	0.6	11.04	302	29,205	42
Singapore	92	106	136	168	86	93	0.5	0.5	−0.50	91	21,492	101
Denmark	72	80	99	94	87	71	0.4	0.4	0.92	212	39,429	34
Norway	65	64	52	61	44	54	0.3	0.3	20.54	222	48,592	29
Ireland	53	69	82	65	65	44	0.3	0.2	19.76	149	37,637	35
Greece	52	63	72	117	66	27	0.3	0.2	92.64	173	16,203	30
Portugal	46	50	64	68	73	53	0.2	0.3	−12.10	149	14,665	31
Israel	33	42	46	41	23	25	0.2	0.1	31.99	104	15,504	32
Austria	31	22	28	31	33	30	0.2	0.2	5.98	251	31,202	12
New Zealand	21	19	20	27	27	30	0.1	0.2	−32.46	76	19,021	27
Other	1,337	1,050	1,056	1,409	908	1,048	6.7	5.8	27.50			

TABLE 19.2

Market capitalization of stock exchanges in emerging markets

| | Market Capitalization | | | | | | Percent of World | | Growth (%) | GDP | GDP per Capita | Market Capitalization as % of GDP |
| | Billions of U.S. Dollars | | | | | | | | | | | |
	2003	2002	2001	2000	1999	1998	2003	1998	1998–2003	2003	2003	2003
Taiwan	$190	$235	$177	$295	$171	$188	10.9%	1.0%	0.89%	143	2,309	133%
Brazil	111	157	180	212	138	140	0.6	0.8	−20.71	492	2,788	23
South Africa	102	71	104	142	106	122	0.5	0.7	−16.17	160	3,530	64
Russia	101	78	44	44	18	108	0.5	0.6	−6.43	433	3,022	23
India	101	85	107	144	74	92	0.5	0.5	10.33	599	563	17
Mexico	99	121	112	135	77	124	0.5	0.7	−20.16	626	6,121	16
Malaysia	94	90	83	102	47	67	0.5	0.4	40.45	103	4,164	91
Chile	43	49	44	51	37	54	0.2	0.3	−19.87	72	4,591	59
Thailand	33	27	23	44	32	17	0.2	0.1	94.35	143	2,309	23
Peru	29	21	17	23	18	26	0.1	0.1	12.10	61	2,247	48
Turkey	29	40	50	96	28	52	0.1	0.3	−44.78	238	3,365	12
Poland	27	25	27	25	18	9	0.1	0.0	208.39	210	5,487	13
Indonesia	24	18	21	42	19	23	0.1	0.1	2.89	208	971	12
China (excluding Hong Kong)	20	18	13	5	4	6	0.1	0.0	229.66	1,410	1,094	1
Philippines	16	17	20	35	30	26	0.1	0.1	−39.56	81	989	20
Hungary	13	10	12	16	14	15	0.1	0.1	−10.80	83	8,182	16
Czech Republic	12	11	12	13	11	11	0.1	0.1	8.87	85	8,375	14
Argentina	7	19	24	38	42	57	0.0	0.3	−87.24	130	3,381	6
Colombia	6	6	4	7	9	13	0.0	0.1	−51.78	78	1,747	8
Venezuela	3	4	6	4	4	8	0.0	0.0	−62.44	85	3,319	4

and 2003. But managers also would not want to have missed a market like Poland, with a growth of 208% over the same years.

These 20 emerging markets make up 5.3% of the world GDP and, together with the 25 developed markets in Table 19.1, make up 95% of the world GDP. Per capita GDP in these emerging markets was quite variable, ranging from $563 (India) to $8,375 (Czech Republic); still, no active manager would want to ignore India in an international portfolio. Market capitalization as a percent of GDP, which ranges from 1% (China) to 133% (Taiwan), suggests that these financial markets are expected to show significant growth over the coming years, even absent spectacular growth in GDP.

The growth of capitalization in emerging markets over this period was much more volatile than growth in developed countries (as disastrous as −87% for Argentina), suggesting that both risk and rewards in this segment of the globe may be substantial.

Market Capitalization and GDP

The contemporary view of economic development (rigorously stated in de Soto, 2000) holds that an important requirement for economic advancement is a developed code of business laws, institutions, and regulations that allows citizens to legally own, capitalize, and trade capital assets. As a corollary, we expect that development of equity markets will serve as catalysts for enrichment of the population, that is, that countries with larger relative capitalization of equities will tend to be richer.

Figure 19.1 is a simple (perhaps simplistic, since other relevant explanatory variables are omitted) rendition of the argument that a developed market for corporate equity contributes to the enrichment of the population. The R-square of the regression line shown in Figure 19.1 is 28% and the slope coefficient is .66, suggesting that an increase of 1% in the ratio of market capitalization to GDP is associated with an increase in per capita GDP of 0.66%. It is remarkable that of the 25 developed countries, only Hong Kong lies below the regression line; in contrast, most of the low-income emerging markets lie below the line. Countries like Venezuela and Norway that lie above the line, that is, exhibit higher per capita GDP than predicted by the regression, enjoy oil wealth that contributes to population income. Countries below the line, such as Indonesia, Philippines, Colombia, and Peru, suffered from deterioration of the business environment due to political strife and/or government policies that restricted the private sector.

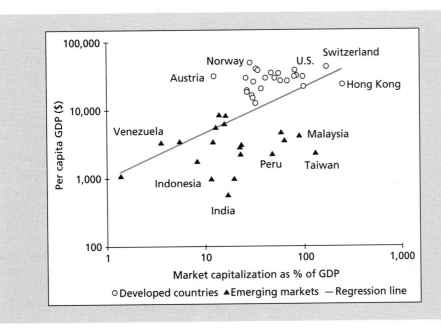

FIGURE 19.1

Per capita GDP and market capitalization as percent of GDP (log scale, 2003 data)

Home-Country Bias

One would expect that most investors, particularly institutional and professional investors, would be aware of the opportunities offered by international investing. Yet in practice, investor portfolios notoriously overweight home-country stocks compared to a neutral indexing strategy and underweight, or even completely ignore, foreign equities. This has come to be known as the *home-country bias*. Despite a continuous increase in cross-border investing, home-country bias still pervades investor portfolios. We return to this issue in Section 19.3.

19.2 RISK FACTORS IN INTERNATIONAL INVESTING

Opportunities in international investments do not come free of risk or of the cost of specialized analysis. The risk factors that are unique to international investments are exchange rate risk and country-specific risk, discussed in the next two sections.

Exchange Rate Risk

It is best to begin with a simple example.

EXAMPLE 19.1

Exchange Rate Risk

Consider an investment in risk-free British government bills paying 10% annual interest in British pounds. While these U.K. bills would be the risk-free asset to a British investor, this is not the case for a U.S. investor. Suppose, for example, the current exchange rate is $2 per pound, and the U.S. investor starts with $20,000. That amount can be exchanged for £10,000 and invested at a riskless 10% rate in the United Kingdom to provide £11,000 in one year.

What happens if the dollar–pound exchange rate varies over the year? Say that during the year, the pound depreciates relative to the dollar, so that by year-end only $1.80 is required to purchase £1. The £11,000 can be exchanged at the year-end exchange rate for only $19,800 (=£11,000 × $1.80/£), resulting in a loss of $200 relative to the initial $20,000 investment. Despite the positive 10% pound-denominated return, the dollar-denominated return is a negative 1%.

We can generalize from Example 19.1. The $20,000 is exchanged for $20,000/E_0$ pounds, where E_0 denotes the original exchange rate ($2/£). The U.K. investment grows to $(20,000/E_0)[1 + r_f(\text{UK})]$ British pounds, where $r_f(\text{UK})$ is the risk-free rate in the United Kingdom. The pound proceeds ultimately are converted back to dollars at the subsequent exchange rate E_1, for total dollar proceeds of $20,000(E_1/E_0)[1 + r_f(\text{UK})]$. The dollar-denominated return on the investment in British bills, therefore, is

$$1 + r(\text{US}) = [1 + r_f(\text{UK})]E_1/E_0 \qquad (19.1)$$

We see in Equation 19.1 that the dollar-denominated return for a U.S. investor equals the pound-denominated return times the exchange rate "return." For a U.S. investor, the investment in British bills is a combination of a safe investment in the United Kingdom and a risky investment in the performance of the pound relative to the dollar. Here, the pound fared poorly, falling from a value of $2.00 to only $1.80. The loss on the pound more than offsets the earnings on the British bill.

Figure 19.2 illustrates this point. It presents rates of returns on stock market indexes in several countries for the last year of our study, 2003. The dark boxes depict returns in local currencies, while the light boxes depict returns in dollars, adjusted for exchange rate movements. It's clear that exchange rate fluctuations over this period had large effects on dollar-denominated returns in several countries.

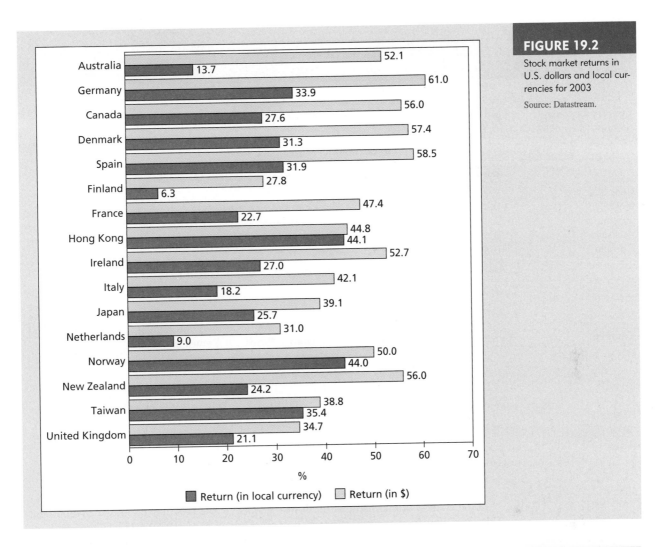

FIGURE 19.2

Stock market returns in U.S. dollars and local currencies for 2003

Source: Datastream.

CONCEPT check 19.1

Using the data in Example 19.1, calculate the rate of return in dollars to a U.S. investor holding the British bill if the year-end exchange rate is: (a) $E_1 = \$2.00/\pounds$; (b) $E_1 = \$2.20/\pounds$.

Pure **exchange rate risk** is the risk borne by investments in foreign safe assets. The investor in U.K. bills of Example 19.1 bears only the risk of the U.K./U.S. exchange rate. We can assess the magnitude of exchange rate risk by examination of historical rates of change in various exchange rates and their correlations.

Table 19.3A shows historical exchange rate risk measured by the standard deviation of monthly percent changes in the exchange rates of major currencies against the U.S. dollar over the period 1999–2003. The data show that currency risk is quite high. The annualized standard deviation of the percent changes in the exchange rate ranged from 6.34% (Canadian dollar) to 12.0% (Australian dollar). The standard deviation of returns on U.S. large stocks for the same period was 17.35%. Hence, exchange rate risk alone would amount to between 35% (6.34/17.35) and 69% (12.0/17.35) of the volatility on stocks. Clearly, an active investor who believes that Japanese stocks are underpriced, but has no information about any mispricing of the Japanese yen, should consider hedging the yen risk exposure when tilting the portfolio toward Japanese stocks. Exchange rate risk of the major currencies seems quite stable over time. For example, a study by Solnik (1999) for the period 1971–1998 finds similar standard deviations, ranging from 4.8% (Canadian dollar) to 12.0% (Japanese yen).

exchange rate risk

The uncertainty in asset returns due to movements in the exchange rates between the U.S. dollar and foreign currency.

TABLE 19.3

Rates of change in the U.S. dollar against major world currencies, 1999–2003 (monthly data)

A. Standard Deviation (annualized)

Country Currency	Euro (€)	U.K. (£)	Japan (¥)	Australia ($A)	Canada ($C)
Standard deviation	10.20	7.35	10.14	12.00	6.34

B. Correlation Matrix

	Euro	U.K.	Japan	Australia	Canada
Euro	1.00				
U.K.	0.73	1.00			
Japan	0.44	0.32	1.00		
Australia	0.48	0.32	0.37	1.00	
Canada	0.31	0.23	0.26	0.75	1.00

C. Average Annual Returns from Rolling Over One-Month LIBOR Rates

Country	Currency	Return in Local Currency	Gains from Exchange Rates	Average Annual Return in U.S. $	Standard Deviation of the Average Annual Return
U.S.		3.68		3.68	
Australia	A$	5.06	−2.74	2.33	5.36
Canada	C$	4.01	−3.14	0.87	2.84
U.K.	£	4.84	−0.45	4.40	3.29
Europe	€	3.41	0.14	3.55	4.56
Japan	¥	0.15	−0.10	0.06	4.54

Source: Exchange rates: Datastream: LIBOR rates: **www.economagic.com**.

In the context of international portfolios, exchange rate risk may be mostly diversifiable. This is evident from the low correlation coefficients in Table 19.3B. (This observation will be reinforced when we compare the risk of hedged and unhedged country portfolios in a later section.) Thus, passive investors with well-diversified international portfolios need not be concerned with hedging exposure to foreign currencies.

The effect of exchange rate fluctuations also shows up in Table 19.3C, which presents the returns on money market investments in different countries. While these investments are virtually risk-free in local currency, they are risky in dollar terms because of exchange rate risk. International investment flows by currency speculators should equalize the expected dollar returns in various currencies, adjusted for risk. Moreover, exchange risk is largely diversifiable, as Table 19.3B shows, and hence we would expect similar dollar returns from cash investments in major currencies.

The low yen LIBOR rate relative to the U.S. dollar LIBOR rate throughout the period suggests that investors expected the yen to appreciate against the dollar. But those expectations were not realized; the yen actually depreciated against the dollar at an annual rate of 10 basis points, leaving a meager annual dollar-denominated return of 6 basis points for the period. However, deviations of this magnitude of returns from prior expectations are not shocking. The standard deviation of the average annual return on a five-year investment (assuming no serial correlation in returns) equals the annual standard deviation divided by $\sqrt{5}$, which amounts to 4.54% for the yen. Thus, the shortfall of 3.59% (3.68% − 0.06%) is less than one standard deviation.

Investors can hedge exchange rate risk using a forward or futures contract in foreign exchange. Recall that such contracts entail delivery or acceptance of one currency for another at a stipulated exchange rate. To illustrate, recall Example 19.1. In this case, to hedge her exposure to the British pound, the U.S. investor would agree to deliver pounds for dollars at a fixed exchange rate, thereby eliminating the future risk involved with conversion of the pound investment back into dollars.

EXAMPLE   19.2

Hedging Exchange Rate Risk

If the futures exchange rate in Example 19.1 had been $F_0 = \$1.93/£$ when the investment was made, the U.S. investor could have assured a riskless dollar-denominated return by locking in the year-end exchange rate at $\$1.93/£$. In this case, the riskless U.S. return would have been 6.15%:

$$[1 + r_f(\text{UK})]F_0/E_0$$
$$= (1.10)\,1.93/2.00$$
$$= 1.0615$$

Here are the steps to lock in the dollar-denominated returns. The futures contract entered in the second step exactly offsets the exchange rate risk incurred in step 1.

Initial Transaction	End-of-Year Proceeds in Dollars
Exchange $20,000 for £10,000 and invest at 10% in the United Kingdom.	£11,000 × E_1
Enter a contract to deliver £11,000 for dollars at the (forward) exchange rate $1.93/£.	£11,000(1.93 − E1)
Total	£11,000 × $1.93/£ = $21,230

You may recall that the futures hedge in Example 19.2 is the same type of hedging strategy at the heart of the spot-futures parity relationship discussed in Chapter 17. In both instances, futures markets are used to eliminate the risk of holding another asset. The U.S. investor can lock in a riskless dollar-denominated return either by investing in the United Kingdom and hedging exchange rate risk or by investing in riskless U.S. assets. Because the returns on two riskless strategies must provide equal returns, we conclude that

$$[1 + r_f(\text{UK})]\,F_0/E_0 = 1 + r_f(\text{US})$$

or

$$\frac{F_0}{E_0} = \frac{1 + r_f(\text{US})}{1 + r_f(\text{UK})} \qquad\qquad \textbf{(19.2)}$$

This relationship is called the **interest rate parity relationship** or **covered interest arbitrage relationship.**

Consider the intuition behind this result. If $r_f(\text{US})$ is greater than $r_f(\text{UK})$, money invested in the United States will grow at a faster rate than money invested in the United Kingdom. If this is so, why wouldn't all investors decide to invest their money in the United States? One important reason is that the dollar may be depreciating relative to the pound. Although dollar investments in the United States grow faster than pound investments in the United Kingdom, each dollar is worth progressively fewer pounds as time passes. Such an effect will exactly offset the advantage of the higher U.S. interest rate.

To complete the argument, we need only determine how a depreciating dollar will be reflected in Equation 19.2. If the dollar is depreciating, meaning that progressively more dollars are required to purchase each pound, then the forward exchange rate, F_0 (which equals the dollars required to purchase one pound for delivery in the future), must exceed E_0, the current exchange rate.

interest rate parity relationship, or covered interest arbitrage relationship

The spot-futures exchange rate relationship that precludes arbitrage opportunities.

That is exactly what Equation 19.2 tells us: When r_f(US) exceeds r_f(UK), F_0 must exceed E_0. The depreciation of the dollar embodied in the ratio of F_0 to E_0 exactly compensates for the difference in interest rates available in the two countries. Of course, the argument also works in reverse: If r_f(US) is less than r_f(UK), then F_0 will be less than E_0.

<table>
<tr><td>EXAMPLE 19.3

Covered Interest Arbitrage</td><td colspan="3">What if the interest rate parity relationship were violated? Suppose r_f(US) is 6.15%, but the futures price is $1.90/£ instead of $1.93/£. You could adopt the following strategy to reap arbitrage profits. In this example, let E_1 denote the exchange rate that will prevail in one year. E_1 is, of course, a random variable from the perspective of today's investors.</td></tr>
<tr><td></td><td>Action</td><td>Initial Cash Flow
(in $)</td><td>Cash Flow in One Year
(in $)</td></tr>
<tr><td></td><td>1. Borrow 1 British pound in London. Repay in one year.</td><td>$ 2.00</td><td>$-E_1(1.10)$</td></tr>
<tr><td></td><td>2. Convert the pound to $2 and lend in the United States.</td><td>$-2.00</td><td>2.00(1.0615)</td></tr>
<tr><td></td><td>3. Enter a contract to purchase 1.10 pounds at a (futures) price of $F_0 = \$1.90/£$</td><td>0</td><td>$1.10(E_1 - 1.90)$</td></tr>
<tr><td></td><td>Total</td><td>$ 0</td><td>$0.033</td></tr>
</table>

In step 1, you borrow one pound in the United Kingdom (worth $2 at the current exchange rate) and, after one year, repay the pound borrowed with interest. Because the loan is made in the United Kingdom at the U.K. interest rate, you would repay 1.10 pounds, which would be worth $E_1(1.10)$ dollars. The U.S. loan in step 2 is made at the U.S. interest rate of 6.15%. The futures position in step 3 results in receipt of 1.10 pounds, for which you would first pay F_0 (i.e., 1.90) dollars each and then convert into dollars at exchange rate E_1.

The exchange rate risk here is exactly offset between the pound obligation in step 1 and the futures position in step 3. The profit from the strategy is, therefore, riskless and requires no net investment. This is an arbitrage opportunity.

CONCEPT check 19.2   What are the arbitrage strategy and associated profits if the initial future price is $F_0 = \$1.95/\text{pound}$?

Ample empirical evidence bears out this theoretical relationship. For example, on January 20, 2005, the interest rate on one-year U.S. LIBOR loans was 3.25%, while the LIBOR rate in the United Kingdom was 4.95%. The spot exchange rate was $1.870/£. Substituting these values into Equation 19.2, we find that interest rate parity implies that the forward exchange rate for delivery in one year should have been $1.870 \times 1.0325/1.0495 = \$1.840/£$. The actual forward rate was $1.841/£, which was so close to the parity value that transaction costs would have prevented arbitrageurs from profiting from the discrepancy.

Direct versus indirect quotes   The exchange rate in Example 19.1 is expressed as dollars per pound. This is an example of what is termed a *direct* exchange rate quote. The euro–dollar exchange rate is also typically expressed as a direct quote. In contrast, exchange rates for other currencies such as the Japanese yen or Swiss franc are typically expressed as *indirect* quotes, that is, as units of foreign currency per dollar, for example, 120 yen per dollar. For currencies expressed as indirect quotes, depreciation of the dollar would result in a *decrease* in the quoted exchange rate ($1 buys fewer yen); in contrast, dollar depreciation versus the pound would show up as a *higher* exchange rate (more dollars are required to buy £1). When the exchange rate is quoted as foreign currency per dollar, the domestic and foreign exchange rates in Equation 19.2 must be switched: in this case the equation becomes

$$F_0(\text{foreign currency/\$}) = \frac{1 + r_f(\text{foreign})}{1 + r_f(\text{U.S.})} \times E_0(\text{foreign currency/\$})$$

For example, if the interest rate in the U.S. is higher than in Japan, the dollar will sell in the forward market at a lower price than in the spot market.

Imperfect Exchange Rate Risk Hedging

Unfortunately, perfect exchange rate hedging usually is not so easy. In Example 19.2, we knew exactly how many pounds to sell in the forward or futures market because the pound-denominated proceeds in the United Kingdom were riskless. If the U.K. investment had not been in bills, but instead had been in risky U.K. equity, we would know neither the ultimate value in pounds of our U.K. investment nor how many pounds to sell forward. That is, the hedging opportunity offered by foreign exchange forward contracts would be imperfect.

To summarize, the generalization of Equation 19.1 is that

$$1 + r(\text{US}) = [1 + r(\text{foreign})]E_1/E_0 \qquad \textbf{(19.3)}$$

where $r(\text{foreign})$ is the possibly risky return earned in the currency of the foreign investment. You can set up a perfect hedge only in the special case that $r(\text{foreign})$ is itself a known number. In that case, you know you must sell in the forward or futures market an amount of foreign currency equal to $[1 + r(\text{foreign})]$ for each unit of that currency you purchase today.

CONCEPT *check* **19.3**

How many pounds would the investor in Example 19.2 need to sell forward to hedge exchange rate risk if: (*a*) $r(\text{UK}) = 20\%$; and (*b*) $r(\text{UK}) = 30\%$?

Country-Specific Risk

In principle, security analysis at the macroeconomic, industry, and firm-specific level is similar in all countries. Such analysis aims to provide estimates of expected returns and risk of individual assets and portfolios. However, to achieve the same quality of information about

---

WEB *master*

Interest Rate Parity

A common misconception is that investors can earn excess returns by investing in foreign bonds with higher interest rates than are available in the U.S. Interest rate parity implies that any such interest-rate differentials will be offset by premiums or discounts in the forward or futures market for foreign currency.

Interest rates on government bonds in the U.S., U.K., Japan, Germany, Brazil, and Australia can be found at **www.bloomberg.com/markets/rates/index.html**

Spot exchange rates on international currencies can be found at: **www.bloomberg.com/markets/currencies/fxc.html**

Forward exchange rates on currency futures contracts can be found at: **www.cme.com/trading/dta/del/globex.html**

1. Select one of these countries and record the yield on a short-term government security from the Bloomberg Web site. Also make note of the U.S. Treasury yield on an instrument with the same maturity.

2. Record the spot exchange rate from the Bloomberg site and the futures contract exchange rate from the CME Web site for the date closest to the maturity of the investment you chose in the previous step.

3. Calculate the rate of return available on the foreign government security, converting the foreign currency transactions into dollars at the current and forward exchange rates.

4. How well does interest-rate parity seem to hold? Are there bargains to be found in other currencies? What factors might account for interest-rate parity violation?

assets in a foreign country is by nature more difficult and hence more expensive. Moreover, the risk of coming by false or misleading information is greater.

Consider two investors: an American wishing to invest in Indonesian stocks and an Indonesian wishing to invest in U.S. stocks. While each would have to consider macroeconomic analysis of the foreign country, the task would be much more difficult for the American investor. The reason is not that investment in Indonesia is necessarily riskier than investment in the U.S. You can easily find many U.S. stocks that are, in the final analysis, riskier than a number of Indonesian stocks. The difference lies in the fact that U.S. financial markets are more transparent than those of Indonesia.

political risk

Possibility of expropriation of assets, changes in tax policy, restrictions on the exchange of foreign currency for domestic currency, or other changes in the business climate of a country.

In the past, when international investing was novel, the added risk was referred to as **political risk** and its assessment was an art. As cross-border investment has increased and more resources have been utilized, the quality of related analysis has improved. A leading organization in the field (which is quite competitive) is the PRS Group (Political Risk Services) and the presentation here follows the PRS methodology.[1]

PRS's country risk analysis results in a country composite risk rating on a scale of 0 (most risky) to 100 (least risky). Countries are then ranked by the composite risk measure and divided into five categories: very low risk (100–80), low risk (79.9–70), moderate risk (69.9–60), high risk (59.9–50), and very high risk (less than 50). To illustrate, Table 19.4 shows the placement of five countries in the October 2004 issue of the PRS *International Country Risk Guide.* It is not surprising to find Norway at the top of the very-low-risk list, and small emerging markets at the bottom, with Zimbabwe (ranked 140) closing the list. What may be surprising is the fairly mediocre ranking of the U.S. (rank 42) comparable to that of China (44) and India (67), all three appearing in the low-risk category.

TABLE 19.4					
Composite risk ratings for October 2004 and November 2003					
Rank October 2004	**Country**	**Composite Risk Rating October 2004**	**Composite Risk Rating November 2003**	**October 2004 Minus November 2003**	**Rank in November 2003**
	Very low risk				
1	Norway	**92.3**	90.5	1.75	2
14	Japan	**84.5**	86.3	−1.75	9
15	United Kingdom	**84.0**	84.0	0	17
	Low risk				
42	United States	**77.5**	75.8	1.75	48
44	China	**76.8**	77.3	−0.5	40
55	Mexico	**74.8**	70.5	4.25	65
67	India	**71.8**	69.0	2.75	72
	Moderate risk				
86	Argentina	**67.5**	64.0	3.5	92
109	Indonesia	**62.5**	60.8	1.75	108
	High risk				
119	Lebanon	**59.0**	55.5	3.5	124
125	Sierra Leone	**58.3**	50.8	7.5	133
	Very high risk				
139	Iraq	**38.0**	41.5	−3.5	138
140	Zimbabwe	**36.3**	34.3	2	140

Source: *International Country Risk Guide,* October 2004, Table 1.

[1] You can find more information on the Web site: **www.prsgroup.com**. We are grateful to the PRS Group for supplying us data and guidance.

The composite risk rating is a weighted average of three measures: political risk, financial risk, and economic risk. Political risk is measured on a scale of 100–0, while financial and economic risk are measured on a scale of 50–0. The three measures are added and divided by two to obtain the composite rating. The variables used by PRS to determine the composite risk rating from the three measures are shown in Table 19.5.

Table 19.6 shows the three risk measures for five of the countries in Table 19.4, in order of the October 2004 ranking of the composite risk ratings. The table shows that by political risk, the five countries ranked in the same order. But in the financial risk measure, the U.S. ranked *last* among these countries. The surprisingly poor performance of the U.S. in this dimension is probably due to its exceedingly large government and balance-of-trade deficits, which have put considerable pressure on its exchange rate. Exchange rate stability, foreign trade imbalance, and foreign indebtedness all enter PRS's computation of financial risk.

Country risk is captured in greater depth by scenario analysis for the composite measure and each of its components. Table 19.7 (A and B) shows one- and five-year worst case and best case scenarios for the composite ratings and for the political risk measure. Risk stability is based on the difference in the rating between the best and worst case scenarios and is quite large in most cases. The worst case scenario can move a country to a higher risk category. For example, Table 19.7B shows that in the worst-case five-year scenario, Indonesia was particularly vulnerable to deterioration in the political environment.

Finally, Table 19.8 shows ratings of political risk by each of its 12 components. Corruption (variable F) in China is rated worse than in India but better than in Indonesia. In democratic

TABLE 19.5

Variables used in PRS's political risk score

Political Risk Variables	Financial Risk Variables	Economic Risk Variables
Government stability	Foreign debt (% of GDP)	GDP per capita
Socioeconomic conditions	Foreign debt service (% of GDP)	Real annual GDP growth
Investment profile	Current account (% of exports)	Annual inflation rate
Internal conflicts	Net liquidity in months of imports	Budget balance (% of GDP)
External conflicts	Exchange rate stability	Current account balance (% GDP)
Corruption		
Military in politics		
Religious tensions		
Law and order		
Ethnic tensions		
Democratic accountability		
Bureaucracy quality		

TABLE 19.6

Current risk ratings and composite risk forecasts

Country	Composite Ratings		Current Ratings		
	Year Ago November 2003	Current October 2004	Political Risk October 2004	Financial Risk October 2004	Economic Risk October 2004
Japan	86.3	**84.5**	82	46.5	40.5
United States	75.8	**77.5**	82	33.5	39.5
China	77.3	**76.8**	70.5	44.5	38.5
India	69	**71.8**	63.5	44.5	35.5
Indonesia	60.8	**62.5**	50.5	37.5	37

Source: *International Country Risk Guide,* October 2004, Table 2B.

TABLE 19.7

Composite and political risk forecasts

A. Composite Risk Forecasts

Country	Current Rating October 2004	One Year Ahead			Five Years Ahead		
		Worst Case	Best Case	Risk Stability	Worst Case	Best Case	Risk Stability
Japan	84.5	81.8	86.5	4.8	76.5	90.0	13.5
United States	77.5	73.3	79.8	6.5	72.8	83.5	10.8
China	76.8	74.0	78.0	4.0	62.8	81.8	19.0
India	71.8	69.3	74.3	5.0	63.8	77.3	13.5
Indonesia	62.5	60.5	65.3	4.8	55.0	72.0	17.0

B. Political Risk Forecasts

Country	Current Rating October 2004	One Year Ahead			Five Years Ahead		
		Worst Case	Best Case	Risk Stability	Worst Case	Best Case	Risk Stability
Japan	82.0	80.5	84.0	12.0	76.0	94.0	18.0
United States	82.0	80.5	84.0	15.0	80.0	88.0	8.0
China	70.5	69.0	72.5	7.0	60.0	74.0	14.0
India	63.5	62.0	65.5	13.0	58.0	67.0	9.0
Indonesia	50.5	40.0	52.5	10.0	40.0	64.0	24.0

Sources: **A.** *International Country Risk Guide,* October 2004, Table 2C; **B.** *International Country Risk Guide,* October 2004, Table 3C.

TABLE 19.8

Political risk points by component, October 2004

This table lists the total points for each of the following political risk components out of the maximum points indicated. The final columns in the table show the overall political risk rating (the sum of the points awarded to each component) and the change from the preceding month.

A	Government Stability	12	
B	Socioeconomic Conditions	12	
C	Investment Profile	12	
D	Internal Conflict	12	
E	External Conflict	12	
F	Corruption	6	

G	Military in Politics	6
H	Religious Tensions	6
I	Law and Order	6
J	Ethnic Tensions	6
K	Democratic Accountability	6
L	Bureaucracy Quality	4

Country	A	B	C	D	E	F	G	H	I	J	K	L	Political Risk Rating October 2004	Change from September 2004
Japan	9.0	8.0	11.5	10.5	9.5	3.5	5.0	5.5	5.0	5.5	5.0	4.0	82.0	−1.5
United States	9.5	8.0	11.5	10.5	8.0	5.0	4.0	5.5	5.0	5.0	6.0	4.0	82.0	−0.5
China	11.0	7.0	7.5	11.5	11.0	2.0	3.0	5.0	4.5	5.0	1.0	2.0	70.5	0.0
India	8.0	3.5	9.0	8.5	10.0	2.5	4.0	2.5	4.0	2.5	6.0	3.0	63.5	0.0
Indonesia	5.5	3.5	6.5	7.5	11.0	1.0	2.5	1.0	3.0	2.0	5.0	2.0	50.5	−1.0

Source: *International Country Risk Guide,* October 2004, Table 3B.

accountability (variable K), China ranked worst and the United States and India best, while China ranked best in government stability (variable A).

Each monthly issue of the *International Country Risk Guide* of the PRS Group includes great detail and holds some 250 pages. Other organizations compete in supplying such evaluations. The result is that today's investor can become well equipped to properly assess the risk involved in international investing.

19.3 INTERNATIONAL INVESTING: RISK, RETURN, AND BENEFITS FROM DIVERSIFICATION

U.S. investors have several avenues through which they can invest internationally. The most obvious method, which is available in practice primarily to larger institutional investors, is to purchase securities directly in the capital markets of other countries. However, even small investors now can take advantage of several investment vehicles with an international focus.

Shares of several foreign firms are traded in U.S. markets in the form of American depository receipts, or ADRs. A U.S. financial institution such as a bank will purchase shares of a foreign firm in that firm's country, then issue claims to those shares in the United States. Each ADR is then a claim on a given number of the shares of stock held by the bank. In this way, the stock of foreign companies can be traded on U.S. stock exchanges. Trading foreign stocks with ADRs is therefore as easy as trading U.S. stocks.

There is also a wide array of mutual funds and exchange-traded funds with an international focus. Single-country funds invest in the shares of only one country. In addition to single-country funds, there are several open-end mutual and exchange-traded funds with an international focus. For example, Fidelity offers funds with investments concentrated overseas, generally in Europe, in the Pacific Basin, and in developing economies in its emerging opportunities fund. Vanguard, consistent with its indexing philosophy, offers separate index funds for Europe, the Pacific Basin, and emerging markets. The nearby box discusses a wide range of single-country index funds.

U.S. investors also can trade derivative securities based on prices in foreign security markets. For example, they can trade options and futures on the Nikkei stock index of 225 stocks traded on the Tokyo stock exchange, or on FTSE (Financial Times Share Exchange) indexes of U.K. and European stocks.

Risk and Return: Summary Statistics

Table 19.9 contains comprehensive statistics of the country portfolio results for 1999–2003, which we will use to develop insights into risk-return trade-offs in international investing. Both panels of Table 19.9 (A. Developed Countries, and B. Emerging Markets) are sorted by annual standard deviation, denoted SD, of returns denominated in U.S. dollars. This table is organized to serve the purpose of a would-be U.S. investor who is considering diversifying internationally. The table provides statistics for returns denominated in U.S. dollars as well as local-currency returns. In addition to average returns and standard deviations, the table also shows beta coefficients against the U.S. index and the correlation of each index with the U.S. index.

Are Investments in Emerging Markets Riskier?

In Figure 19.3, developed countries and emerging markets are separately ordered from lowest to highest standard deviation. The standard deviations of investments in emerging markets are charted with those in developed countries. The graphs clearly show that investment in emerging markets is generally riskier than in developed countries, at least as measured by total volatility of returns. Still, you can find emerging markets that appear safer than some developed countries.

TABLE 19.9

Risk and return across the globe, 1999–2003 (sorted by standard deviation of return in $U.S.)

Country	% Per Annum in U.S. Dollars				% Per Annum in Local Currency			
	Average	SD	Beta on U.S.	Corr. w/U.S.	Average	SD	Beta on U.S.	Corr. w/U.S.
A. Developed Countries								
Finland	12.99	41.52	1.57	0.66	12.32	43.43	1.60	0.64
Korea	18.94	38.78	1.55	0.70	17.73	36.57	1.46	0.69
Greece	2.54	31.27	0.54	0.30	0.80	30.53	0.58	0.33
Sweden	8.54	30.35	1.35	0.77	5.59	28.59	1.24	0.76
Israel	19.49	29.38	0.76	0.45	19.67	26.07	0.63	0.42
Denmark	21.60	27.73	0.83	0.70	18.12	26.68	0.87	0.75
Singapore	9.84	27.00	0.89	0.58	9.92	25.16	0.86	0.59
Hong Kong	10.99	24.82	1.01	0.70	11.04	24.84	1.01	0.70
Germany	1.35	24.11	1.08	0.78	0.00	24.36	1.11	0.79
Japan	4.21	22.76	0.71	0.54	2.45	19.19	0.61	0.55
Norway	11.56	22.61	0.89	0.68	8.36	20.37	0.87	0.74
France	6.39	22.21	0.97	0.75	4.92	22.00	1.00	0.79
Italy	2.26	21.62	0.68	0.55	0.68	20.85	0.72	0.60
New Zealand	15.54	21.56	0.66	0.53	9.62	12.56	0.41	0.56
Netherlands	−0.39	20.93	0.87	0.72	−1.81	20.99	0.91	0.75
Ireland	4.38	20.48	0.69	0.58	2.86	20.02	0.72	0.63
Spain	2.93	20.04	0.81	0.70	1.44	19.66	0.84	0.74
Portugal	−0.87	19.74	0.46	0.41	−2.92	16.25	0.50	0.53
Belgium	−1.78	19.72	0.50	0.44	−3.77	16.50	0.53	0.56
Canada	13.49	19.29	0.91	0.82	9.37	15.64	0.71	0.79
Australia	11.81	18.85	0.83	0.76	6.47	10.61	0.46	0.75
United States	0.78	17.35	1.00	1.00	0.78	17.35	1.00	1.00
Switzerland	1.24	16.82	0.61	0.62	−0.93	16.29	0.73	0.78
Austria	10.01	16.21	0.32	0.34	8.03	12.30	0.36	0.51
United Kingdom	1.94	15.87	0.77	0.84	0.56	16.27	0.79	0.84
B. Emerging Markets								
Turkey	33.42	70.80	2.30	0.56	59.70	65.88	1.77	0.47
Indonesia	13.33	57.11	0.74	0.22	6.50	32.75	0.71	0.37
Brazil	21.21	43.13	1.68	0.68	33.35	27.29	1.14	0.72
Venezuela	−2.97	42.26	0.50	0.21	25.23	32.22	0.38	0.21
Thailand	20.05	41.29	1.18	0.49	20.19	36.94	1.04	0.49
Malaysia	18.94	38.78	0.45	0.27	17.73	36.57	0.45	0.30
Argentina	3.16	38.29	0.82	0.37	25.78	44.13	0.64	0.25
China	36.57	36.07	0.38	0.18	36.57	36.07	0.38	0.18
Taiwan	4.89	35.59	0.99	0.48	5.47	34.09	0.93	0.48
Poland	11.40	35.25	1.04	0.51	11.51	31.87	0.90	0.49
India	23.95	33.89	0.72	0.37	25.15	33.21	0.70	0.37
Hungary	8.54	29.07	0.81	0.48	6.92	25.73	0.79	0.53
Philippines	−6.99	27.87	0.57	0.35	−0.86	24.29	0.55	0.39
Czech Republic	21.60	27.73	0.41	0.26	18.12	26.68	0.44	0.28
Colombia	1.19	27.40	0.40	0.25	11.56	22.31	0.12	0.09
Mexico	14.98	26.72	1.09	0.71	16.71	23.07	0.92	0.69
South Africa	19.16	26.18	0.87	0.58	20.66	21.79	0.82	0.66
Chile	13.67	20.22	0.67	0.57	17.23	14.58	0.43	0.51
Peru	15.02	15.96	0.15	0.16	16.71	14.66	0.15	0.18

NEW FUNDS THAT TRACK FOREIGN MARKETS

LOW-COST FOREIGN INDEX FUNDS CALLED WEBS ELIMINATE SOME OF THE GUESSWORK AND COSTS OF INVESTING ABROAD

With foreign markets generally stronger this year, a new way to invest abroad has appeared at a good time. WEBS, an acronym for World Equity Benchmark Shares, represents an investment in a portfolio of publicly traded foreign stocks in a selected country. Each WEBS Index Series seeks to generate investment results that generally correspond to the price and yield performance of a specific Morgan Stanley Capital International (MSCI) index.

You sell these shares rather than redeeming them, but there the similarity to closed-end country funds ends. WEBS are equity securities, not mutual funds. WEBS shares trade continuously on a secondary market, the Amex, during regular Amex trading hours, like any other publicly traded U.S. stock listed on the exchange. In contrast, mutual fund shares do not trade in the secondary market, and are normally bought and sold from the issuing mutual fund at prices determined only at the end of the day. The new funds create and redeem shares in large blocks as needed, thus preventing the big premiums or discounts to net asset value typical of closed-end country funds. As index portfolios, WEBS are passively managed, so their expenses run much lower than for current open- or closed-end country funds.

WEBS shares offer U.S. investors portfolio exposure to country-specific equity markets, in a single, listed security you can easily buy, sell, or short on the Amex. Unlike American Depository Receipts (ADRs) that give you an investment in just one company, WEBS shares enable you to gain exposure to a broad portfolio of a desired foreign country's stocks. You gain broad exposure in the country or countries of your choice without the complications usually associated with buying, owning, or monitoring direct investments in foreign countries. You also have the conveniences of trading on a major U.S. exchange and dealing in U.S. dollars.

Some investors may prefer the active management, diversity, and flexibility of open-end international equity index funds as a way to limit currency and political risks of investing in foreign markets. As conventional open-end funds, however, the international funds are sometimes forced by net redemptions to sell stocks at inopportune times, which can be a particular problem in foreign markets with highly volatile stocks.

You pay brokerage commissions on the purchase and sale of WEBS, but since their portfolios are passively managed, their management and administrative fees are relatively low and they eliminate most of the transaction charges typical of managed funds.

FOREIGN INDEX BASKETS

WEBS	Ticker Symbol	WEBS	Ticker Symbol
Australia	EWA	Malaysia	EWM
Austria	EWO	Mexico	EWW
Belgium	EWK	Netherlands	EWN
Canada	EWC	Singapore	EWS
France	EWQ	Spain	EWP
Germany	EWG	Sweden	EWD
Hong Kong	EWH	Switzerland	EWL
Italy	EWI	U.K.	EWU
Japan	EWJ		

SOURCES: Modified from *The Outlook*, May 22, 1996, published by Standard and Poor's; and Amex Web site, **www.amex.com**, February 2000. Reprinted by permission of Standard & Poor's, a division of The McGraw-Hill Companies, Inc.

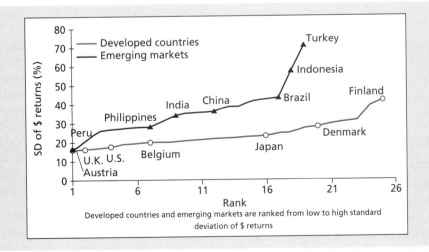

FIGURE 19.3

Annualized standard deviation of investments across the globe (dollar-denominated returns, 1999–2003)

It is evident that standard deviations of developed market portfolios are more uniform than those of emerging markets. With the exception of Finland, the difference between the lowest and highest SD among developed markets is about 10%. In contrast, even ignoring the most extreme countries (Indonesia and Turkey), emerging markets show a spread in SD between the lowest ranked (Peru) to the 17th ranked (Brazil) of more than 20%.

However, if one considers adding a country index to an indexed U.S. portfolio, the more relevant risk measure is the country's beta against the U.S. Figure 19.4 therefore ranks and charts the betas of country returns (in U.S. dollars) against the U.S. index. Here we see a more moderate picture. The most striking example is Indonesia. Although it had the second highest index in terms of SD, its beta of 0.74 is lower than that of the U.K. (0.77), which had the lowest SD among developed countries. Both countries' betas are slightly below average for the entire sample of 43 countries (0.84), and can be considered as appropriate diversification assets. Another example of the hazard of using SD as a risk measure is China's beta (0.37), the second lowest in the entire sample, despite its high SD of 36%. All in all, the spread of betas across emerging markets suggests that international diversification may reduce portfolio variance.

Are Average Returns Higher in Emerging Markets?

Figure 19.5 repeats the previous exercise for average returns. The graph shows that emerging markets generally provided higher average returns over the period 1999–2003 than developed markets. The fact that a number of markets averaged a lower rate than the risk-free alternative for the period (with some average returns even negative) is proof positive that realized returns may fall short of expectations even over fairly long periods. Beyond that, we see that countries with relatively low betas (e.g., China) earned higher returns than countries with relatively high betas, even the highest-beta country, Turkey.

We shouldn't be too surprised by these results. Remember again that the SD of an average estimated over five years (absent serial correlation, which indeed is absent from the data) is given by: SD(5-year average) = SD(1-year average)/$\sqrt{5}$. Thus, the SD of the five-year average for China would be about 16%, and that of Turkey about 32%. An outcome of one SD in the opposite direction for these two portfolios would cover a distance of 48%. The conclusion is one we've noted before: We cannot read too much into realized averages even over periods as long as five years.

Given this imprecision, the question to be asked is: "Can we learn anything from these data about the risk-return trade-off in international investing?" Here, the answer is more encouraging. Look at the correlation matrix in Table 19.10. Average returns are clearly positively correlated with both the SD of returns and the beta against the U.S. index. Average return is also negatively correlated with country-index market capitalization. We know from theory that

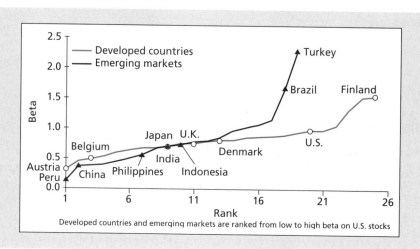

FIGURE 19.4

Beta on U.S. stocks across the globe 1999–2003

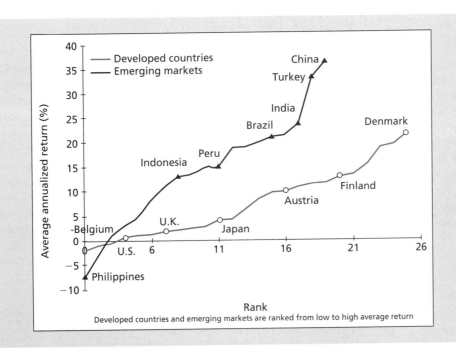

FIGURE 19.5

Annualized average dollar-denominated return of investments across the globe 1999–2003

TABLE 19.10		Average Return	SD	Beta on U.S.
Correlation matrix of relevant statistics	Standard deviation (SD)	0.48		
	Beta on U.S.	0.32	0.56	
	Capitalization	−0.24	−0.25	0.06

returns should be positively correlated with systematic risk as measured by beta, and this view is vindicated here in the international context.

Empirical studies on individual stocks clearly show average returns to be negatively correlated with market capitalization. This has come to be known as the "size effect." One explanation for the size effect is that more security analysts follow large corporate stocks and thus generate greater transparency, more accurate earnings forecasts, and greater liquidity, all of which reduce required rates of return. A similar effect might be expected in the international markets, where larger market capitalization also attracts more resources for research. In addition, these larger markets are generally better regulated and entail lower trading costs. Estimates from a regression of average returns on beta and capitalization over 1999–2003 are shown in Table 19.11. Average returns rise with beta and fall with market capitalization.

TABLE 19.11	**Regression Statistics**			
Regression of average returns on beta and market capitalization	Multiple R	0.41		
	R-Square	0.17		
	Adjusted R-Square	0.13		
	Standard error	8.91		
	Observations	44		
		Coefficients	**Standard Error**	**t-Stat**
	Intercept	4.47	3.19	1.40
	Beta on U.S.	8.10	3.44	2.36
	Market cap	−35.41	19.20	−1.84

Is Exchange Rate Risk Important in International Portfolios?

Table 19.3 revealed that changes in exchange rates are not highly correlated across countries. This suggests that when international portfolios are well diversified, the exchange rate component of overall risk will be effectively diminished. Another feature that would render exchange rate risk diversifiable is low correlation between changes in exchange rates and country stock returns in local currencies.

In Figures 19.6–19.8 we compare results for SD, beta coefficients, and correlation with U.S. stock returns using dollar and local-currency returns. These graphs show that local currency SDs (Figure 19.6) are slightly lower than SDs of dollar returns, indicating the presence of exchange rate risk. Beta coefficients (Figure 19.7) are also lower on average using local currency returns, in some cases significantly so, indicating that a portion of exchange rate risk may be systematic. However, the graph for correlations with U.S. stock returns suggests

FIGURE 19.6

Standard deviation of investments across the globe in U.S. dollars vs. local currency, 1999–2003

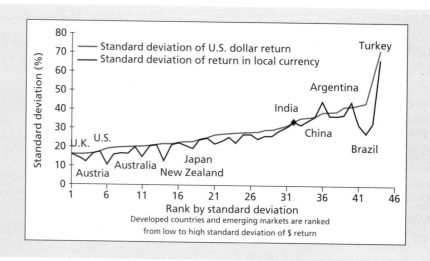

FIGURE 19.7

Beta against U.S. market, measuring returns in U.S. dollars and in local currency

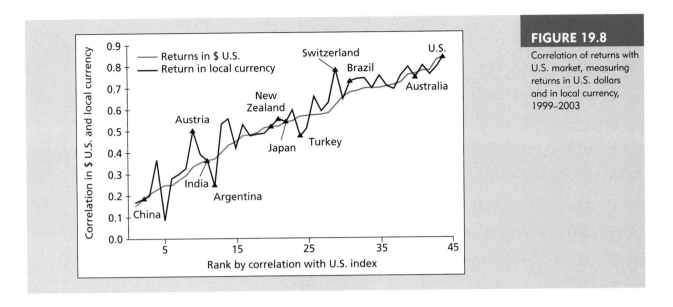

FIGURE 19.8

Correlation of returns with U.S. market, measuring returns in U.S. dollars and in local currency, 1999–2003

that we may just be seeing statistical noise. The correlations of local returns appear higher on average than those of dollar returns. On balance, exchange rate risk in diversified portfolios probably is a small fraction of overall risk.

Benefits from International Diversification

Table 19.12 presents correlations between returns on stock and long-term bond portfolios in various countries. Panel A shows correlation of returns in U.S. dollars, that is, returns to a U.S. investor when currency risk is not hedged. Panel B shows correlation of returns in local currencies, that is, returns to a U.S. investor when the exchange risk is hedged. As noted earlier, the correlation coefficients of the hedged (local currency) and unhedged (U.S. dollar) returns are very similar, suggesting that hedging currencies is not a significant issue in diversifying internationally.

The correlation coefficients between a stock index of one country and bond portfolios of another are very low, implying that income portfolios that are balanced between stocks and bonds would greatly benefit from international diversification. The correlation among unhedged stock portfolios of the countries in Table 19.12A is much higher, in the range of .40 (Japan–Germany) to .94 (France–Germany). These correlation coefficients are much higher than conventional wisdom; they suggest that cross-border correlation of stock indexes has been increasing. For another, independent example, Table 19.13 shows the correlation of various country indexes with U.S. stocks using monthly excess returns over the period 1970–1989, next to the same coefficients estimated over 1999–2003. The marked increase in correlation with 17 stock indexes and the world portfolio is uniform.

These results raise the question of whether the increase in correlation is an artifact of the sample period or a result of globalization and increased capital market integration that would be expected to increase cross-border correlation. While there is no question that a five-year sample period is quite short and limits precision, the fact that we find the increase in correlation across the board suggests that globalization and market integration are the more plausible cause, as discussed in the nearby box.

The observed high correlation across markets brings into question the conventional wisdom of large diversification benefits from international investing. This conventional wisdom is depicted in Figure 19.9, which is based on data for the period 1961–1975. Figure 19.9

TABLE 19.12

Correlations for asset returns; unhedged and hedged currencies

A. Correlation of Monthly Asset Return 1999–2003 in $U.S. (unhedged currencies)

	Stocks							Bonds						
	U.S.	Germany	U.K.	Japan	Australia	Canada	France	U.S.	Germany	U.K.	Japan	Australia	Canada	France
Stocks														
U.S.	1.00													
Germany	0.77	1.00												
U.K.	0.84	0.85	1.00											
Japan	0.54	0.40	0.52	1.00										
Australia	0.76	0.72	0.77	0.53	1.00									
Canada	0.82	0.77	0.77	0.55	0.75	1.00								
France	0.75	0.94	0.88	0.46	0.69	0.78	1.00							
Bonds														
U.S.	−0.10	−0.07	−0.12	0.07	−0.19	0.00	−0.03	1.00						
Germany	−0.27	−0.20	−0.29	−0.27	−0.26	−0.19	−0.20	0.66	1.00					
U.K.	−0.19	−0.09	−0.19	−0.09	−0.25	−0.10	−0.09	0.80	0.85	1.00				
Japan	−0.08	−0.13	−0.06	0.01	−0.11	−0.05	−0.07	0.75	0.40	0.56	1.00			
Australia	−0.22	−0.09	−0.19	−0.10	−0.29	0.00	−0.09	0.78	0.71	0.81	0.51	1.00		
Canada	−0.17	−0.13	−0.21	−0.10	−0.23	−0.05	−0.11	0.88	0.77	0.77	0.55	0.80	1.00	
France	−0.28	−0.20	−0.30	−0.28	−0.25	−0.18	−0.21	0.66	0.99	0.83	0.39	0.68	0.77	1.00

B. Correlation of Monthly Asset Return 1999–2003 in $U.S. (hedged currencies)

	Stocks							Bonds						
	U.S.	Germany	U.K.	Japan	Australia	Canada	France	U.S.	Germany	U.K.	Japan	Australia	Canada	France
Stocks														
U.S.	1.00													
Germany	0.79	1.00												
U.K.	0.84	0.82	1.00											
Japan	0.55	0.46	0.46	1.00										
Australia	0.74	0.74	0.75	0.48	1.00									
Canada	0.79	0.75	0.74	0.52	0.69	1.00								
France	0.79	0.95	0.86	0.51	0.71	0.78	1.00							
Bonds														
U.S.	−0.10	0.00	−0.08	0.00	−0.04	0.07	0.05	1.00						
Germany	−0.25	−0.17	−0.23	−0.31	−0.16	−0.11	−0.15	0.75	1.00					
U.K.	−0.18	−0.09	−0.16	−0.16	−0.14	−0.01	−0.06	0.87	0.89	1.00				
Japan	−0.06	0.00	0.02	0.01	0.04	0.04	0.07	0.76	0.47	0.61	1.00			
Australia	−0.16	−0.05	−0.14	−0.13	−0.13	0.08	−0.01	0.88	0.83	0.91	0.58	1.00		
Canada	−0.15	−0.07	−0.11	−0.14	−0.08	0.01	−0.02	0.91	0.87	0.86	0.59	0.87	1.00	
France	−0.25	−0.16	−0.22	−0.30	−0.14	−0.10	−0.15	0.74	0.99	0.87	0.47	0.80	0.87	1.00

On the MARKET FRONT

DANCING IN STEP

Individual stock markets are increasingly being driven by global rather than local factors. But why do national markets not have minds of their own? They did have once.

Traditionally, one way that investors sought to reduce risk was by diversifying overseas: when American shares slumped, the loss there would be offset by a gain in, say, European shares. That, at any rate, was the theory. In recent years, however, stock markets seem to have moved more closely in step with one another. The correlation between changes in American and European share prices has risen from 0.4 in the mid-1990s to 0.8 last year.

The health of a market's home economy may matter less than it used to for a number of reasons. First, the scrapping of controls on capital (combined with more efficient trading systems) has increased cross-border trading of shares, creating something closer to a global equity market. Second, it has become increasingly common for big companies to be listed on more than one market. Third, as a result of the wave of cross-border mergers and acquisitions, overseas profits account for a bigger slice of many companies' overall profits—high-tech firms are especially global in their reach. And finally, the Internet has made it easier for investors to get information on foreign firms. So firms in the same industry, but in different economies, are valued on a similar basis.

By breaking down movements in share prices into global effects, country-specific effects, and firm-specific effects, a new study by economists at the IMF tries to find out what percentage of a stock's performance is due to global rather than country factors. The model distinguishes between two kinds of global factors: the global business cycle and global-industry effects, which similarly influence firms in the same sector but in different countries.

The study finds that there has indeed been a big increase in the importance of global factors—of both kinds—in explaining movements in share prices since the mid-1990s.

SOURCE: Abridged from *The Economist*, March 22, 2001. Copyright © 2001 The Economist Newspaper Group, Inc. Reprinted with permission. Further reproduction prohibited. **www.economist.com.**

TABLE 19.13		Monthly Excess Return in U.S. Dollars	
Correlation of U.S. equity returns with country equity returns		**1999–2003***	**1970–1989****
	World	0.95	0.86
	United Kingdom	0.84	0.49
	Canada	0.82	0.72
	Sweden	0.77	0.38
	Germany	0.77	0.33
	Australia	0.76	0.47
	France	0.75	0.42
	Netherlands	0.72	0.56
	Hong Kong	0.70	0.29
	Denmark	0.70	0.33
	Spain	0.69	0.25
	Norway	0.68	0.44
	Switzerland	0.62	0.49
	Italy	0.54	0.22
	Japan	0.54	0.27
	Belgium	0.43	0.41
	Austria	0.33	0.12

Source: *Datastream; **Campbell R. Harvey, "The World Price of Covariance Risk," *Journal of Finance,* March 1991, Vol. 46, issue 1, pp. 111–158.

suggests that international diversification can reduce the standard deviation of a domestic portfolio by as much as half (from about 27% to about 12%). This improvement may well be exaggerated if correlation across markets has markedly increased as data from recent years suggest.

International diversification. Portfolio standard deviation as a percent of the average standard deviation of a one-stock portfolio.

Source: B. Solnik, "Why Not Diversify Internationally Rather Than Domestically," *Financial Analysts Journal*, January/February 1995. Reprinted by permission.

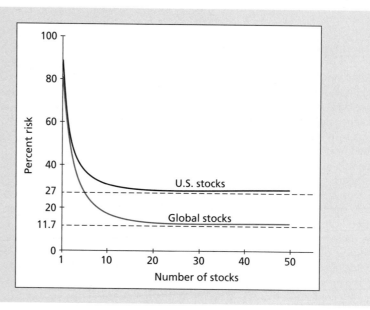

Misleading Representation of Diversification Benefits

The baseline technique for constructing efficient portfolios is the efficient frontier. A useful efficient frontier is constructed from *expected* returns and an estimate of the covariance matrix of returns. This frontier, combined with cash assets generates the capital allocation line, the set of efficient complete portfolios, as elaborated in Chapter 6 and the first section of Chapter 7. The benefit from this efficient diversification is reflected in the curvature of the efficient frontier. Other things equal, the lower the covariance across stocks, the greater the curvature of the efficient frontier and the greater the risk reduction for any desired *expected* return. So far, so good. But suppose we replace *expected* returns with *realized* average returns from a sample period to construct an efficient frontier; what is the possible use of this graph?

The ex post efficient frontier (derived from realized returns) describes the portfolio choices of only one investor—the clairvoyant who actually expected the precise averages of realized returns on all assets and estimated a covariance matrix that materialized, precisely, in the actual realizations of the sample period returns on all assets. Obviously, we are talking about a slim to empty set of investors. For all other, less than clairvoyant, investors such a frontier may have value only for purposes of performance evaluation.

In the world of volatile stocks, some stocks are bound to realize large, *unexpected* average returns. This will be reflected in ex post efficient frontiers of enormous "potential." They will, however, suggest exaggerated diversification benefits. Such (elusive) potential was enumerated in Chapter 18 on performance evaluation. It has no use as a tool to discuss the potential for future investments for real-life investors.

Realistic Benefits from International Diversification

While recent realized returns can be highly misleading estimates of expected future returns, they are more useful for measuring prospective risk. There are two compelling reasons for this. First, market efficiency (or even near efficiency) implies that stock price movements will be impossible to predict with any accuracy, but no such implication applies to risk measures. Second, it is a statistical fact that errors in estimates of standard deviation and correlation from realized data are of a lower order of magnitude than estimates of expected returns. For these reasons, using risk estimates from realized returns does not exaggerate as much the potential benefits from diversification.

Figure 19.10 shows the efficient frontier using realized average monthly returns on the stock indexes of the 25 developed countries, with and without short sales. Even when the

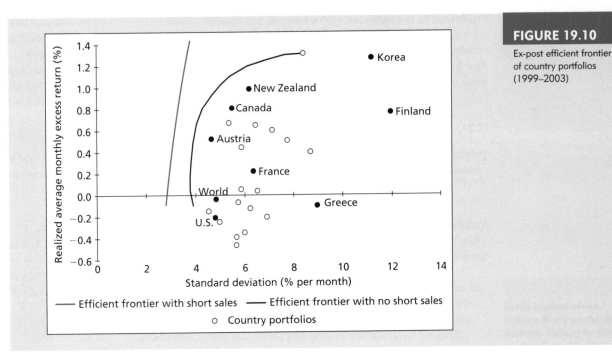

FIGURE 19.10

Ex-post efficient frontier of country portfolios (1999–2003)

(ex post) efficient frontier is constrained to preclude short sales, it greatly exaggerates the benefits from diversification. Unfortunately, such misleading efficient frontiers are presented in many articles and texts on the benefits of diversification.

A more reasonable description of diversification is achievable only when we input reasonable equilibrium expected returns. Absent superior information, such expected returns are best based on appropriate risk measures of the assets. The capital asset pricing model (CAPM) suggests using the beta of the stock against the world portfolio. To generate expected excess returns (over the risk-free rate) for all assets, we specify the expected excess return on the world portfolio. We obtain the expected excess return on each asset by multiplying the beta of the asset by the world portfolio expected excess return. This procedure presupposes that the world portfolio will lie on the efficient frontier, at the point of tangency with the world capital market line. The curvature of the efficient frontier will not be affected by the estimate of the world portfolio excess return. A higher estimate will shift the curve upward. The capital market line will have a steeper slope.

We perform this procedure with risk measures estimated from actual returns, and further impose the likely applicable constraint on short sales. We use the betas to compute the expected return on individual markets, assuming the expected excess return on the world portfolio is either .3% or .6% per month. These excess returns are in the range of averages realized over the period 1999–2003, and in line with the average return over the previous 50 years. Varying this estimate would not qualitatively affect the results shown in Figures 19.11a and 19.11b. The figures reveal modest benefits for U.S. investors from international diversification using only developed markets. Incorporating emerging markets would slightly increase these benefits.

Are Benefits from International Diversification Preserved in Bear Markets?

Some studies (e.g., Longin and Solnik, 1995, or Jacquier and Marcus, 2001) suggest that correlation in country portfolio returns increases during periods of turbulence in capital markets. If so, benefits from diversification would be lost exactly when they are needed the most. For example, a study by Roll (1988) of the crash of October 1987 shows that all 23 country indexes studied declined over the crash period of October 12–26. This correlation is reflected in the movements of regional indexes depicted in Figure 19.12. Roll found that the beta of

Efficient frontier of country portfolios (world expected excess return = .3% per month)

Efficient frontier of country portfolios (world expected excess return = .6% per month)

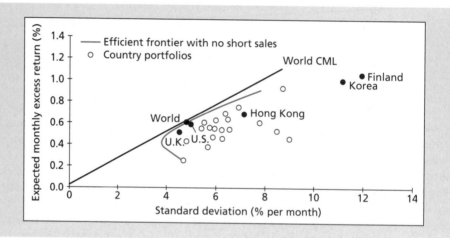

Regional indexes around the crash, October 14–October 26, 1987

Source: From Richard Roll, "The International Crash of October 1987," *Financial Analysts Journal*, September–October 1988. Copyright 1998, CFA Institute. Reproduced and republished from *Financial Analysts Journal* with permission from the CFA Institute. All Rights Reserved.

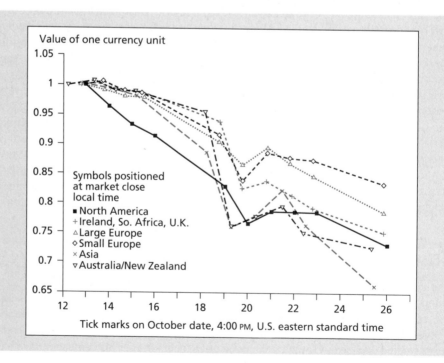

a country index on the world index (estimated prior to the crash) was the best predictor of that index's response to the October crash of the U.S. stock market. This suggests a common factor underlying the movement of stocks around the world. This model predicts that a macroeconomic shock would affect all countries and that diversification can only mitigate country-specific events. Our best guess is that the diversification benefits shown by the world CAPM model are real, but modest.

19.4 HOW TO GO ABOUT INTERNATIONAL DIVERSIFICATION AND THE BENEFIT WE CAN EXPECT

So far, we have dissected our sample of recent returns for 1999–2003 for clues about the benefits from international diversification. But all of this tells us little about how a U.S. investor might actually implement the idea. We begin with the case of a passive investor.

As noted earlier, scholars have indirectly questioned passive as well as active investors for their apparently home country–biased portfolios. A certain degree of home bias may be justified on theoretical grounds. Investor consumption consists in large part of goods and services produced in the home country, and prices of these goods and services are correlated with home-country stock prices. To illustrate, consider an investor who lives in Silicon Valley. Prices of homes and other big-ticket items will be correlated with the success of local corporations. These prices therefore can be partially hedged by investing in the equity of local firms.[2] Moreover, "keeping up with the Joneses" of Silicon Valley also calls for tilting your portfolio toward local investment opportunities to keep your wealth aligned with that of your neighbors.

On top of these considerations, moving from a U.S. to a world portfolio would reduce portfolio standard deviation from 17.40% to 16.74%. This surprisingly meager reduction in volatility of 0.66% is based on monthly data over 1999–2003, but given the persistent increase in correlation across country portfolios due to greater economic integration, we should not expect this picture to improve in the foreseeable future. At the same time, a reduction in portfolio standard deviation of this magnitude can be easily achieved just by diversifying into only three international indexes such as Vanguard's European, Pacific, and Emerging Market stock-index funds.

It is not easy to devise a feasible plan for a passive investor to implement more efficient international diversification than using indexed portfolios such as the Vanguard regional and emerging market indexes. Surely, a passive investor, often with a limited investment budget, would not be expected to invest in dozens of foreign country indexes in order to beat the easy diversification using regional funds such as Vanguard's.[3]

Suppose a modest plan to improve over the regional indexes calls for diversifying the U.S. stock portfolio into a subset of individual foreign countries, for example, three additional country indexes. Which indexes would be best? We consider three alternatives: (1) estimate the efficient frontier arising from all possible sets of three foreign indexes, (2) choose the three countries with the lowest beta with U.S. stocks, and (3) choose the three indexes with the largest market capitalization.

In implementing these alternatives we must remember that a passive investor would have no specifically informed forecasts of expected returns. One can easily form reasonable estimates of covariances from past data, but recent data reveals little, if anything, about expected future returns. Let us focus instead purely on risk reduction.

Choosing among Efficient Portfolios

This alternative sounds good in theory, but in fact is unworkable. Suppose we decide to add three indexes to the U.S. portfolio, chosen from only the 43 foreign countries in our sample. There are more than 12,000 combinations of three countries that you can select from a set of

---

[2] For a formal analysis of this idea, see DeMarzo (2005).
[3] While it is not explicitly designed to do so, Vanguard's Emerging Market Index gives the investor considerable exposure to Latin American economies, thus filling out much of the world diversification already achieved by adding the European and Pacific indexes to a broad U.S. index such as the Wilshire 5000.

43 countries! Clearly this is not a feasible task. Furthermore, the weights of various indexes in these portfolios may be undesirable, suggesting, for instance, that you invest only 10% of your funds in your home country portfolio, or 90% of it in Peru. You might avoid this problem by imposing a constraint on various weights, but deciding on these constraints will itself require complex optimization, or become fairly arbitrary.

Choosing Lowest Beta or Covariance Indexes

This is a reasonable alternative. Choosing the lowest-beta countries is easy. Of course, you must then decide on proportions to invest in these indexes. One way is to compute the efficient frontier portfolio of the four indexes you now have (including the U.S. index), perhaps imposing a constraint to avoid underinvestment in U.S. stocks. The downside here is that you will then need forecasts of country index returns and may find yourself investing a large proportion of your funds in very small markets with low beta. To avoid these complications, you may want to invest in the chosen indexes according to their market capitalization. This quickly leads us to the third alternative.

Choosing Largest Capitalization Indexes

This alternative is the easiest to implement. Although it appears to stray far afield from efficient diversification, the departure may be much smaller than one would think. By selecting indexes with the largest market capitalization, you will be investing predominantly in markets that are among the best in terms of transparency and regulation. Moreover, if a world CAPM were in force, a capitalization-weighted portfolio would be the efficient portfolio. Since a passive investor is not in a position to determine the worldwide efficient portfolio based on mean return and covariance forecasts, a capitalization-weighted world portfolio might well be the second-best alternative.

What We Can Expect from International Diversification

To get an idea of what we can expect from international diversification, we compare the second and third alternatives using the covariance data from our sample. For comparison, we also include the results of mixing Vanguard's three international indexes with the U.S. index portfolio.

The results appear in Figure 19.13, which shows the results of applying our three alternatives to any subset of country indexes. The plot labeled "index ordered by market capitalization" adds the three Vanguard indexes to the U.S. index (and to the U.S. plus Canadian indexes, which we label the North American, or NA, index) in order of market capitalization. The horizontal axis shows the cumulative percent of the world portfolio you obtain as additional foreign indexes are added to the portfolio. Notice that once the European, Pacific, and emerging market funds are added to North America, virtually 100% of world capitalization is accounted for. The vertical axis shows portfolio standard deviation computed from the covariance matrix of returns over the 1999–2003 sample period. It reveals a gradual decline in standard deviation with diversification, first as Europe and then the Pacific index is added to North America. However, when the high-volatility emerging markets fund is added, volatility increases despite the additional diversification, and the graph turns back upward.

The graph titled "ordered by beta" shows the portfolio configuration when countries are added on the basis of covariance (beta) with U.S. stocks, starting with the lowest-beta countries, and progressing in ascending order of beta. The weight applied to each country is proportional to its market capitalization.

A capitalization-weighted portfolio of all 44 countries of our sample accounts for over 98% of the entire world capitalization and reduces standard deviation by 0.66% compared to the U.S.-only portfolio, but in this plot too, the most inclusive portfolio is not the minimum-variance portfolio. Recall from our discussions of efficient diversification, however, that no investor would actually choose to hold the minimum-variance portfolio.

The plot ordered by beta reveals fairly good relative efficiency. With a subset of 27 indexes, investing in each according to its market capitalization, we achieve the lowest standard deviation of 15.8%, close to that of the minimum-variance portfolio that would be obtained by minimizing establish a new pension fund. Darwin asks Irish about international equities and whether the Investment Committee should consider them as an additional asset for the pension fund.

a. Explain the rationale for including international equities in General's equity portfolio. Identify and describe three relevant considerations in formulating your answer.

b. List three possible arguments against international equity investment and briefly discuss the significance of each.

c. To illustrate several aspects of the performance of international securities over time, Irish shows Darwin the accompanying graph of investment results experienced by a U.S. pension fund in the recent past. Compare the performance of the U.S. dollar and non-U.S. dollar equity and fixed-income asset categories, and explain the significance of the result of the account performance index relative to the results of the four individual asset class indexes.

12. You are a U.S. investor considering purchase of one of the following securities. Assume that the currency risk of the Canadian government bond will be hedged, and the 6-month discount on Canadian dollar forward contracts is −.75% versus the U.S. dollar.

Bond	Maturity	Coupon	Price
U.S. government	6 months	6.50%	100.00
Canadian government	6 months	7.50%	100.00

Calculate the expected price change required in the Canadian government bond which would result in the two bonds having equal total returns in U.S. dollars over a 6-month horizon. Assume that the yield on the U.S. bond is expected to remain unchanged.

13. After much research on the developing economy and capital markets of the country of Otunia, your firm, GAC, has decided to include an investment in the Otunia stock market in its Emerging Markets Commingled Fund. However, GAC has not yet decided whether to invest actively or by indexing. Your opinion on the active versus indexing decision has been solicited. The following is a summary of the research findings:

Otunia's economy is fairly well diversified across agricultural and natural resources, manufacturing (both consumer and durable goods), and a growing finance sector. Transaction costs in securities markets are relatively large in Otunia because of high commissions and government "stamp taxes" on securities trades. Accounting standards and disclosure regulations are quite detailed, resulting in wide public availability of reliable information about companies' financial performance.

Capital flows into and out of Otunia, and foreign ownership of Otunia securities is strictly regulated by an agency of the national government. The settlement procedures under these ownership rules often cause long delays in settling trades made by nonresidents. Senior finance officials in the government are working to deregulate capital flows and foreign ownership, but GAC's political consultant believes that isolationist sentiment may prevent much real progress in the short run.

a. Briefly discuss aspects of the Otunia environment that favor investing actively, and aspects that favor indexing.

b. Recommend whether GAC should invest in Otunia actively or by indexing. Justify your recommendation based on the factors identified in part (*a*).

WEB *master*

International Correlation

Go to the Yahoo! Finance Investing site at **http://finance. yahoo.com/marketupdate?u** and scroll down to the Market Statistics section. Click on the World Market Indices link, choose one index from each of the tabs (Americas, Asia/Pacific, Europe, and Africa/Middle East), and collect historical daily closing prices for the past year.

1. Download the data into Excel and calculate the daily returns for all of the indexes. Check

to be sure that the dates match up across the various indices.

2. Calculate the correlation between the returns for each pair of countries and construct a correlation matrix.

3. If you were to invest in mutual funds that tracked the indexes, which combination of countries would be most effective in terms of limiting portfolio risk? Which would be least effective?

SOLUTIONS TO CONCEPT checks

19.1. $1 + r(\text{US}) = [(1 + r_f(\text{UK}))] \times (E_1/E_0)$

a. $1 + r(\text{US}) = 1.1 \times 1.0 = 1.10$. Therefore, $r(\text{US}) = 10\%$.

b. $1 + r(\text{US}) = 1.1 \times 1.1 = 1.21$. Therefore, $r(\text{US}) = 21\%$.

19.2. According to interest rate parity, F_0 should be $1.93. As the futures price is too high, we should reverse the arbitrage strategy just considered.

Action	Cash Flow Now ($)	Cash Flow in One Year ($)
Borrow $2 in the United States.	$ 2.00	$-2.00(1.0615)
Convert the borrowed dollars to pounds, and lend in the United Kingdom at a 10% interest rate.	−2.00	$1.10E_1$
Enter a contract to sell 1.10 pounds at a futures price of $1.95/£.	0.00	$1.10(1.95 - E_1)$
Total	$ 0.00	$ 0.022

19.3. You must sell forward the number of pounds you will end up with at the end of the year. This value cannot be known with certainty, however, unless the rate of return of the pound-denominated investment is known.

a. $10,000 \times 1.20 = 12,000$ pounds

b. $10,000 \times 1.30 = 13,000$ pounds

19.4. *Country selection:*

$$(0.40 \times 10\%) + (0.20 \times 5\%) + (0.40 \times 15\%) = 11\%$$

This is a loss of 1.5% (11% versus 12.5%) relative to the EAFE passive benchmark.

Currency selection:

$$(0.40 \times 10\%) + (0.20 \times (-10\%)) + (0.40 \times 30\%) = 14\%$$

This is a loss of 6% (14% versus 20%) relative to the EAFE benchmark.

$2.5 million (E39) is worth only $873,631 in today's purchasing power (E39/C39). Such is the effect of inflation. If you wish to do better than that, you must save more.

In our initial plan (Spreadsheet 20.1), we envisioned consuming a level, nominal annuity for the retirement years. This is an inappropriate goal once we account for inflation, since it would imply a declining standard of living starting at age 65. Its purchasing power at age 65 in terms of current dollars would be $68,320 (i.e., $192,244/1.03^{35}$), and at age 90 only $32,630. (Check this!)

It is tempting to contemplate solving the problem of an inadequate retirement annuity by increasing the assumed rate of return on investments. However, this can only be accomplished by putting your savings at risk. Much of this text elaborates on how to do so efficiently; yet it also emphasizes that while taking on risk will give you an *expectation* for a better retirement, it implies as well a nonzero probability of doing a lot worse. At the age of 30, you should be able to tolerate some risk to the retirement annuity for the simple reason that if things go wrong, you can change course, increase your savings rate, and work harder. As you get older, this option progressively fades, and increasing risk becomes less of a viable option. If you do choose to increase risk, you can set a "safety-first target" (i.e., a minimum acceptable goal) for the retirement annuity and continuously monitor your risky portfolio. If the portfolio does poorly and approaches the safety-first target, you progressively shift into risk-free bonds—you may recognize this strategy as a version of dynamic hedging.

The difficulty with this strategy is twofold: First, it requires monitoring, which is time-consuming and may be nerve-racking as well. Second, when decision time comes, it may be psychologically hard to withdraw. By shifting out of the risky portfolio if and when your portfolio is hammered, you give up any hope of recovery. This is hard to do and many investors fail the test. For these investors, therefore, the right approach is to stick with the safe, lower ROR and make the effort to balance standard of living before and after retirement. Avoiding sleepless nights is ample reward.

Therefore, the only variable we leave under your control in this spreadsheet is the rate of saving. To improve retirement life style relative to the preretirement years, without jeopardizing its safety, you will have to lower consumption during the saving years—there is no free lunch.

If you project a rate of inflation of 4%, what nominal ROR on investments would you need to maintain the same real retirement annuity as in Spreadsheet 20.2?

CONCEPT *check* **20.2**

An Alternative Savings Plan

In Spreadsheet 20.2, we saved a constant fraction of income. But since real income grows over time (nominal income grows at 7% while inflation is only 3%), we might consider deferring our savings toward future years when our real income is higher. By applying a higher savings rate to our future (higher) real income, we can afford to reduce the current savings rate. In Spreadsheet 20.3, we use a base savings rate of 10% (lower than the savings rate in the previous spreadsheet), but we increase the savings target by 3% per year. Saving in each year therefore equals a fixed savings rate times annual income (column B), times 1.03^t. By saving a larger fraction of income in later years, when real income is larger, you create a smoother profile of real consumption.

Spreadsheet 20.3 shows that with an *initial* savings rate of 10%, compared with the unchanging 15% rate in the previous spreadsheet, you can achieve a retirement annuity of $59,918, larger than the $49,668 annuity in the previous plan.

Notice that real consumption in the early years is greater than with the previous plan. What you have done is to postpone saving until your income is much higher. At first blush, this plan is preferable: It allows for a more comfortable consumption of 90% of income at the outset, a consistent increase in standard of living during your earning years, all without significantly affecting the retirement annuity. But this program has one serious downside: By postponing the

SPREADSHEET 20.3

Backloading the real savings plan

eXcel

**Please visit us at
www.mhhe.com/bkm**

	A	B	C	D	E	F
1	Retirement Years	Income Growth	Rate of Inflation	Savings Rate	ROR	rROR
2	25	0.07	0.03	0.1	0.06	0.0291
3	Age	Income	Deflator	Savings	Cumulative Savings	rConsumption
4	30	50,000	1.00	5,000	5,000	45,000
5	31	53,500	1.03	5,511	10,811	46,592
9	35	70,128	1.16	8,130	44,351	53,480
19	45	137,952	1.56	21,492	260,927	74,751
29	55	271,372	2.09	56,819	947,114	102,471
39	65	533,829	2.81	150,212	2,964,669	136,331
40	Total	7,445,673		1,572,466	Real Annuity	59,918

	A	B	C	D	E	F
1	Retirement Years	Income Growth	Rate of Inflation	Savings Rate	ROR	rROR
2	25	0.07	0.03	0.1	0.06	=(E2-C2)/(1+C2)
3	Age	Income	Deflator	Savings	Cumulative Savings	rConsumption
4	30	50000	1	=B4*C4*$D$2	=D4	=(B4-D4)/C4
5	31	=B4*(1+$B$2)	=C4*(1+$C$2)	=B5*C5*$D$2	=E4*(1+$E$2)+D5	=(B5-D5)/C5
39	65	=B38*(1+$B$2)	=C38*(1+$C$2)	=B39*C39*$D$2	=E38*(1+$E$2)+D39	=(B39-D39)/C39
40	Total	=SUM(B4:B39)		=SUM(D4:D39)	Real Annuity	=PMT($F$2,$A$2,-$E$39/$C$39,0,0)

bulk of your savings to a later age, you come to depend on your health, longevity, and, more ominously (and without possibility of insurance), on a successful future career. Put differently, this plan achieves comfort by increasing risk, making this choice a matter of risk tolerance.

CONCEPT check 20.3

Suppose you like the plan of tilting savings toward later years, but worry about the increased risk of postponing the bulk of your savings to later years. Is there anything you can do to mitigate the risk?

20.3   ACCOUNTING FOR TAXES

flat tax

A tax code that taxes all income above some exemption at a fixed rate.

To initiate a discussion of taxes, let's assume that you are subject to a **flat tax** rate of 25% on taxable income less one exemption of $15,000. This is similar to several proposals for a simplified U.S. tax code that have been floated by one presidential candidate or another prior to elections—at least when you add state taxes to the proposed flat rate. An important feature of this (and the existing) tax code is that the tax rate is levied on nominal income and applies as well to investment income. (This is the concept of double taxation—you pay taxes when you earn income and then you pay taxes again when your savings earn interest.) Some relief from the effect of taxing nominal dollars both in this proposal and the current U.S. code is provided by raising the exemption, annually, by the rate of inflation. To adapt our spreadsheet to this simple tax code, we must add columns for taxes and after-tax income. The tax-adjusted plan is shown in Spreadsheet 20.4. It adapts the savings plan of Spreadsheet 20.2.

The top panel of the sheet deals with the earning years. Column D adjusts the exemption (D2) by the price level (column C). Column E applies the tax rate (cell E2) to taxable income (column B − column D). The savings rate (F2) is applied to after-tax income (column B − column E), allowing us to calculate cumulative savings (column G) and real consumption (column H). The formula view shows the detailed construction.

As you might have expected, real consumption is lower in the presence of taxes, as are savings and the retirement fund. The retirement fund provides for a real, before-tax annuity of only $37,882, compared with $49,668 absent taxes in Spreadsheet 20.2.

The bottom panel of the sheet shows the further reduction in real consumption due to taxes paid during the retirement years. While you do not pay taxes on the cumulative savings in the retirement plan (you did that already as the savings accrued interest), you do pay taxes on interest

SPREADSHEET 20.4

Saving with a simple tax code

	A	B	C	D	E	F	G	H
1	Retirement Years	Income Growth	Rate of Inflation	Exemption Now	Tax Rate	Savings Rate	ROR	rROR
2	25	0.07	0.03	15000	0.25	0.15	0.06	0.0291
3	Age	Income	Deflator	Exemption	Taxes	Savings	Cumulative Savings	rConsumption
4	30	50,000	1.00	15,000	8,750	6,188	6,188	35,063
5	31	53,500	1.03	15,450	9,605	6,584	13,143	36,224
9	35	70,128	1.16	17,389	13,775	8,453	50,188	41,319
19	45	137,952	1.56	23,370	31,892	15,909	245,334	57,864
29	55	271,372	2.09	31,407	69,943	30,214	733,467	81,773
39	65	533,829	2.81	42,208	148,611	57,783	1,874,346	116,365
40	Total				1,884,163	834,226	Real Annuity=	37,882
41	**RETIREMENT**							
42	Age	Nom Withdraw	Deflator	Exemption	Taxes		Funds Left	rConsumption
43	66	109,792	2.90	43,474	17,247		1,877,014	31,931
47	70	123,572	3.26	48,931	15,743		1,853,382	33,056
52	75	143,254	3.78	56,724	12,200		1,721,015	34,656
57	80	166,071	4.38	65,759	6,047		1,422,954	36,503
62	85	192,521	5.08	76,232	0		883,895	37,882
67	90	223,185	5.89	88,374	0		0	37,882
68	Total	4,002,944			203,199			

	A	B	C	D	E	F	G	H
1	Retirement Years	Income Growth	Rate of Inflation	Exemption Now	Tax Rate	Savings Rate	ROR	rROR
2	25	0.07	0.03	15000	0.25	0.15	0.06	=(G2-C2)/(1+C2)
3	Age	Income	Deflator	Exemption	Taxes	Savings	Cumulative Savings	rConsumption
4	30	50000	1	=$D$2*C4	=(B4-D4)*$E$2	=(B4-E4)*$F$2	=F4	=(B4-E4-F4)/C4
5	31	=B4*(1+$B$2)	=C4*(1+$C$2)	=$D$2*C5	=(B5-D5+G4*$G$2)*$E$2	=(B5-E5)*$F$2	=G4*(1+$G$2)+F5	=(B5-E5-F5)/C5
39	65	=B38*(1+$B$2)	=C38*(1+$C$2)	=$D$2*C39	=(B39-D39+G38*$G$2)*$E$2	=(B39-E39)*$F$2	=G38*(1+$G$2)+F39	=(B39-E39-F39)/C39
40	Total				=SUM(E4:E39)	=SUM(F4:F39)	Real Annuity=	=PMT($H$2,$A$2,-$G$39/$C$39,0,0)
41	**RETIREMENT**							
42	Age	Nom Withdraw	Deflator	Exemption	Taxes		Funds Left	rConsumption
43	66	=$H$40*C43	=C39*(1+$C$2)	=$D$2*C43	=MAX(0,(G39*$G$2-D43)*$E$2)		=G39*(1+$G$2)-B43	=(B43-E43)/C43
44	67	=$H$40*C44	=C43*(1+$C$2)	=$D$2*C44	=MAX(0,(G43*$G$2-D44)*$E$2)		=G43*(1+$G$2)-B44	=(B44-E44)/C44
67	90	=$H$40*C67	=C66*(1+$C$2)	=$D$2*C67	=MAX(0,(G66*$G$2-D67)*$E$2)		=G66*(1+$G$2)-B67	=(B67-E67)/C67
68	Total	=SUM(B43:B67)			=SUM(E43:E67)			

eXcel

Please visit us at www.mhhe.com/bkm

earned by the fund while you are drawing it down. These taxes are quite significant and further deplete the fund and its net-of-tax earning power. For this reason, your consumption annuity is lower in the early years when your fund has not yet been depleted and taxable interest income is higher.

In the end, despite a handsome income that grows at a real rate of almost 4%, an aggressive savings rate of 15%, a modest rate of inflation, and a modest tax, you will be able to achieve only a modest (but at least low-risk) real retirement income. This is a reality with which most people must struggle. Whether to sacrifice more of today's standard of living through an increased rate of saving, or take some risk in the form of saving a real annuity and/or invest in a risky portfolio with a higher expected return, is a question of preference and risk tolerance.

One often hears complaints about the double taxation resulting from taxing income earned on savings from dollars on which taxes were already paid. It is interesting to see what effective tax rate is imposed on your lifetime earnings by double taxation. To do so, we use Spreadsheet 20.4 to set up your lifetime earnings, exemptions, and taxes:

Income		
(1) Lifetime labor income		$7,445,673
Total exemptions during working years	949,139	
(2) Lifetime taxable labor income		6,496,534
Taxes		
During labor years	1,884,163	
During retirement	203,199	
(3) Lifetime taxes		2,087,362
Lifetime average tax rate = (3)/(1)		28%
Lifetime tax rate on taxable income = (3)/(2)		32%

Thus, double taxation is equivalent to raising the tax rate on taxable income to 32%. It creates a lifetime *average* tax rate (28%) that is higher than the prescribed *marginal* rate of 25%.

CONCEPT **20.4**   Would a 1% increase in the exemption compensate you for a 1% increase in the tax rate?
c h e c k

20.4 | THE ECONOMICS OF TAX SHELTERS

tax shelters

Means by which to postpone payment of tax liabilities for as long as possible.

Tax shelters range from the simple to the mind-bogglingly complex, yet they all have one common objective: to postpone payment of tax liabilities for as long as possible. We know already that this isn't small fry. Postponement implies a smaller present value of tax payment, and a tax paid with a long delay can have present value near zero. However, delay is necessarily beneficial only when the tax rate doesn't increase over time. If the tax rate on retirement income is higher than during earning years, the value of a tax deferral may be questionable; if the tax rate will decline, deferral is even more preferable.

A Benchmark Tax Shelter

Postponing tax payments is the only attainable (legal) objective since, whenever you have taxable income, a tax liability is created that can (almost) never be erased.[3] For this reason, a benchmark tax shelter *postpones all* taxes on savings and the income on those savings. In this case, your entire savings account is liable to taxation and will be paid upon retirement, as you draw down the retirement fund. This sort of shelter is actually equivalent to the tax treatment of Individual Retirement Accounts (IRAs) which we discuss later, so we will describe this structure as having an "IRA style."

To examine the impact of an IRA-style structure (assuming you could shelter all your savings) in a situation comparable to the nonsheltered flat-tax case, we maintain the same consumption level as in Spreadsheet 20.4 (flat tax with no shelter), but now input the new, sheltered savings plan in Spreadsheet 20.5. This focuses the entire effect of the tax shelter onto retirement consumption.

In this sheet, we input desired real consumption (column H, copied from Spreadsheet 20.4). Taxes (column E) are then calculated by applying the tax rate (E2) to nominal consumption less the exemption (H × C − D). Thus, savings are the residual from nominal income (B) minus taxes (E), minus nominal consumption (H × C). The retirement panel shows that you pay taxes on all withdrawals—all funds in the retirement account are subject to tax.

The results are interesting. Total lifetime taxes paid with the IRA tax shelter amount to $2.5 million, a lot more than $2.1 million absent the shelter. The reason is that the tax shelter allows for larger savings that increase lifetime income to $3.7 million compared with only $1.9 million absent the shelter. Since in this comparison income and consumption during the earnings years are the same, the entire net gain from the shelter is pushed to the retirement years. Thus, the real annuity (annual consumption) during retirement increases from $37,882 to $76,052.

CONCEPT **20.5**   With the IRA-style tax shelter, all your taxes are due during retirement. Is the trade-off
c h e c k   between exemption and tax rate different from the circumstance where you have no shelter?

The Effect of the Progressive Nature of the Tax Code

Because of the exemption, the flat tax is somewhat progressive: Taxes are an increasing fraction of income as income rises. For very high incomes, the marginal tax rate (25%) is only slightly higher than the average rate. For example, with income of $50,000 at the outset, the average tax rate is 17.5% (.25 × 35,000/50,000), and grows steadily over time. In general, with a flat tax, the ratio of the average to marginal rate equals the ratio of taxable to gross income. This ratio becomes .89 at age 45, at which point the average tax rate is

[3]Bankruptcy or death can erase some tax liabilities, though. We will avoid dealing with these unhappy outcomes.

SPREADSHEET 20.5

Saving with a flat tax and an IRA-style tax shelter

	A	B	C	D	E	F	G	H
1	Retirement Years	Income Growth	Rate of Inflation	Exemption Now	Tax Rate	Savings Rate	ROR	rROR
2	25	0.07	0.03	15000	0.25	0.15	0.06	0.0291
3	Age	Income	Deflator	Exemption	Taxes	Savings	Cumulative Savings	rConsumption
4	30	50,000	1.00	15,000	5,016	9,922	9,922	35,063
5	31	53,500	1.03	15,450	5,465	10,724	21,242	36,224
9	35	70,128	1.16	17,389	7,628	14,600	83,620	41,319
19	45	137,952	1.56	23,370	16,695	31,106	438,234	57,864
29	55	271,372	2.09	31,407	34,952	65,205	1,393,559	81,773
39	65	533,829	2.81	42,208	71,307	135,087	3,762,956	116,365
40	Total				944,536	1,773,854	Real Annuity	76,052
41	**RETIREMENT**							
42	Age	Nom Withdraw	Deflator	Exemption	Taxes		Funds Left	rConsumption
43	66	220,420	2.90	43,474	44,236		3,768,313	60,789
47	70	248,085	3.26	48,931	49,789		3,720,867	60,789
52	75	287,598	3.78	56,724	57,719		3,455,127	60,789
57	80	333,405	4.38	65,759	66,912		2,856,737	60,789
62	85	386,508	5.08	76,232	77,569		1,774,517	60,789
67	90	448,068	5.89	88,374	89,924		0	60,789
68	Total	8,036,350			1,612,828			

	A	B	C	D	E	F	G	H
1	Retirement Years	Income Growth	Rate of Inflation	Exemption Now	Tax Rate	Savings Rate	ROR	rROR
2	25	0.07	0.03	15000	0.25	0.15	0.06	=(G2-C2)/(1+C2)
3	Age	Income	Deflator	Exemption	Taxes	Savings	Cumulative Savings	rConsumption
4	30	50000	1	=$D$2*C4	=(H4*C4-D4)*$E$2	=B4-E4-H4*C4	=F4	35062.5
5	31	=B4*(1+$B$2)	=C4*(1+$C$2)	=$D$2*C5	=(H5*C5-D5)*$E$2	=B5-E5-H5*C5	=G4*(1+$G$2)+F5	36223.7712378641
39	65	=B38*(1+$B$2)	=C38*(1+$C$2)	=$D$2*C39	=(H39*C39-D39)*$E$2	=B39-E39-H39*C39	=G38*(1+$G$2)+F39	116364.980523664
40	Total				=SUM(E4:E39)	=SUM(F4:F39)	Real Annuity	=PMT($H$2,$A$2,-$G$39/$C$39,0,0)
41	**RETIREMENT**							
42	Age	Nom Withdraw	Deflator	Exemption	Taxes		Funds Left	rConsumption
43	66	=$H$40*C43	=C39*(1+$C$2)	=$D$2*C43	=MAX(0,(B43-D43)*$E$2)		=G39*(1+$G$2)-B43	=(B43-E43)/C43
44	67	=$H$40*C44	=C43*(1+$C$2)	=$D$2*C44	=MAX(0,(B44-D44)*$E$2)		=G43*(1+$G$2)-B44	=(B44-E44)/C44
67	90	=$H$40*C67	=C66*(1+$C$2)	=$D$2*C67	=MAX(0,(B67-D67)*$E$2)		=G66*(1+$G$2)-B67	=(B67-E67)/C67
68	Total	=SUM(B43:B67)			=SUM(E43:E67)			

above 22%. The current U.S. tax code, with multiple income brackets, is much more progressive than our assumed structure.

In Spreadsheet 20.6 we work with a more **progressive tax** structure that is closer to the U.S. Federal tax code augmented with an average state tax. Our hypothetical tax schedule is described in Table 20.1.

Spreadsheet 20.6 is almost identical to Spreadsheet 20.4, the only difference being the tax built into column E according to the schedule in Table 20.1.

progressive tax

Taxes are an increasing fraction of income.

SPREADSHEET 20.6

Saving with a progressive tax

	A	B	C	D	E	F	G	H
1	Retirement Years	Income Growth	Rate of Inflation	Exemption Now	Tax rates in	Savings Rate	ROR	rROR
2	25	0.07	0.03	10000	Table 20.1	0.15	0.06	0.0291
3	Age	Income	Deflator	Exemption	Taxes	Savings	Cumulative Savings	rConsumption
4	30	50,000	1.00	10,000	8,000	6,300	6,300	35,700
5	31	53,500	1.03	10,300	8,716	6,718	13,396	36,958
9	35	70,128	1.16	11,593	12,489	8,646	51,310	42,262
19	45	137,952	1.56	15,580	32,866	15,763	248,018	57,333
29	55	271,372	2.09	20,938	76,587	29,218	731,514	79,076
39	65	533,829	2.81	28,139	186,335	52,124	1,833,644	104,970
40	Total			Total	632,759	2,116,533	799,371	Real Annuity	37,059
41	**RETIREMENT**							
42	Age	Nom Withdraw	Deflator	Exemption	Taxes		Fund Left	rConsumption
43	66	107,408	2.90	28,983	16,207		1,836,254	31,467
47	70	120,889	3.26	32,620	15,371		1,813,134	32,347
52	75	140,143	3.78	37,816	13,083		1,683,643	33,599
57	80	162,464	4.38	43,839	8,831		1,392,054	35,045
62	85	188,341	5.08	50,821	1,757		864,701	36,714
67	90	218,338	5.89	58,916	0		0	37,059
68	Total	3,916,018			227,675			

TABLE 20.1	Taxable Income* Over	But Not Over	The Tax Is	of the Amount Over
Income tax schedule used for the progressive tax	$ 0	$ 50,000	$ 0 + 20%	$ 0
	50,000	150,000	10,000 + 30	50,000
	150,000	…	40,000 + 40	150,000

*Current exemption with this code is assumed to be $10,000. The exemption and tax brackets are adjusted for future inflation.

Despite the more progressive schedule of this tax code, at the income level we assume, you would end up with a similar standard of living. This is due to the large lower-rate bracket. The early increased savings offset some of the bite of the overall higher tax rate. Another important result of the nature of this code is the lower marginal tax rate upon retirement when taxable income is lower. This is the environment in which a tax shelter is most effective, as we shall soon see.

Spreadsheet 20.7 augments the progressive tax code with our benchmark (IRA-style) tax shelter that allows you to pay taxes on consumption (minus an exemption) and accumulate tax liability to be paid during your retirement years. The construction of this spreadsheet is identical to Spreadsheet 20.5, with the only difference being the tax structure built into column E. We copied the real preretirement consumption stream from Spreadsheet 20.6 to focus the effect of the tax shelter on the standard of living during the retirement years. Spreadsheet 20.7 shows that the lower tax bracket during the retirement years allows you to pay lower taxes over the life of the plan and significantly increases retirement consumption. The use of the IRA-style tax shelter increases the retirement annuity by an average of $32,000 a year, a better improvement than we obtained from the shelter with the flat tax.

SPREADSHEET 20.7

The benchmark (IRA) tax shelter with a progressive tax code

eXcel

Please visit us at
www.mhhe.com/bkm

	A	B	C	D	E	F	G	H
1	Retirement Years	Income Growth	Rate of Inflation	Exemption Now	Tax rates in	Savings Rate	ROR	rROR
2	25	0.07	0.03	10000	Table 20.1	0.15	0.06	0.0291
3	Age	Income	Deflator	Exemption	Taxes	Savings	Cumulative Savings	rConsumption
4	30	50,000	1.00	10,000	5,140	9,160	9,160	35,700
5	31	53,500	1.03	10,300	5,553	9,880	19,590	36,958
9	35	70,128	1.16	11,593	7,480	13,654	77,112	42,262
19	45	137,952	1.56	15,580	14,749	33,880	434,916	57,333
29	55	271,372	2.09	20,938	32,920	72,885	1,455,451	79,076
39	65	533,829	2.81	28,139	66,100	172,359	4,125,524	104,970
40	Total			632,759	879,430	2,036,474	Real Annuity	83,380
41	**RETIREMENT**							
42	Age	Nom Withdraw	Deflator	Exemption	Taxes		Funds Left	rConsumption
43	66	241,658	2.90	28,983	49,311		4,131,398	66,366
47	70	271,988	3.26	32,620	55,500		4,079,381	66,366
52	75	315,309	3.78	37,816	64,340		3,788,036	66,366
57	80	365,529	4.38	43,839	74,588		3,131,989	66,366
62	85	423,749	5.08	50,821	86,467		1,945,496	66,366
67	90	491,241	5.89	58,916	100,239		0	66,366
68	Total	8,810,670	Total		1,797,848			

The effectiveness of the shelter also has a sort of hedge quality. If you become fortunate and strike it rich, the tax shelter will be less effective, since your tax bracket will be higher at retirement. However, mediocre or worse outcomes will result in low marginal rates upon retirement, making the shelter more effective and the tax bite lower.

CONCEPT check 20.6

Are you indifferent between an increase in the low-income bracket tax rate versus an equal increase in the high bracket tax rates?

20.5 | A MENU OF TAX SHELTERS

Individual Retirement Accounts

Individual Retirement Accounts (IRAs) were set up by Congress to increase the incentives to save for retirement. The limited scope of these accounts is an important feature. Currently, annual contributions are limited to $5,000. Workers 50 years of age and up can increase annual contributions by up to another $1,000. IRAs are somewhat illiquid (as are most shelters), in that there is a 10% penalty on withdrawals prior to age 59½. However, allowances for early withdrawal with no penalty for qualified reasons such as (one-time) purchase of a home or higher education expenses substantially mitigate the problem.

There are two types of IRAs to choose from; the better alternative is not easy to determine.

Traditional IRA   Contributions to **traditional IRA** accounts are tax deductible, as are the earnings until retirement. In principle, if you were able to contribute all your savings to a traditional IRA, your savings plan would be identical to our benchmark tax shelter (Spreadsheets 20.5 and 20.7), with the effectiveness of tax mitigation depending on your marginal tax rate upon retirement.

Roth IRA   A **Roth IRA** is a variation on the traditional IRA tax shelter, with both a drawback and an advantage. Contributions to Roth IRAs are *not* tax deductible. However, earnings on the accumulating funds in the Roth account are tax-free, and unlike a traditional IRA, no taxes are paid upon withdrawals of savings during retirement. The trade-off is not easy to evaluate. To gain insight and illustrate how to analyze the trade-off, we contrast Roth with traditional IRAs under our two alternative tax codes.

Roth IRA with the Progressive Tax Code

As we have noted, a traditional IRA is identical to the benchmark tax shelter set up under two alternative tax codes in Spreadsheets 20.5 and 20.7. We saw that, as a general rule, the effectiveness of a tax shelter depends on the progressivity of the tax code: Lower tax rates during retirement favor the postponement of tax obligations until one's retirement years. However, with a Roth IRA, you pay no taxes at all on withdrawals during the retirement phase. In this case, therefore, the effectiveness of the shelter does not depend on the tax rates during the retirement years. The question for any investor is whether this advantage is sufficient to compensate for the nondeductibility of contributions, which is the primary advantage of the traditional IRA.

To evaluate the trade-off, Spreadsheet 20.8 modifies Spreadsheet 20.7 (progressive tax) to conform to the features of a Roth IRA, that is, we eliminate deductibility of contributions and

traditional IRA

Contributions to the account and investment earnings are tax sheltered until retirement.

Roth IRA

Contributions are not tax sheltered, but investment earnings are tax free.

SPREADSHEET 20.8

Roth IRA with a progressive tax

	A	B	C	D	E	F	G	H
3	Retirement Years	Income Growth	Rate of Inflation	Exemption Now	Tax Rates in	Savings Rate	ROR	rROR
4	25	0.07	0.03	10000	Table 20.1	0.15	0.06	0.0291
5	Age	Income	Deflator	Exemption	Taxes	Savings	Cumulative Savings	rConsumption
6	30	50,000	1.00	10,000	8,000	6,300	6,300	35,700
7	31	53,500	1.03	10,300	8,640	6,793	13,471	36,958
11	35	70,128	1.16	11,593	11,764	9,370	52,995	42,262
21	45	137,952	1.56	15,580	28,922	19,707	278,528	57,333
31	55	271,372	2.09	20,938	64,661	41,143	883,393	79,076
41	65	533,829	2.81	28,139	145,999	92,460	2,432,049	104,970
42	Total	7,445,673		632,759	1,752,425	1,163,478	Real Annuity	49,153
43	**RETIREMENT**							
44	Age	Nom Withdraw	Deflator	Exemption	Taxes		Funds Left	rConsumption
45	66	142,460	2.90	28,983	0		2,435,512	49,153
49	70	160,340	3.26	32,620	0		2,404,847	49,153
54	75	185,879	3.78	37,816	0		2,233,096	49,153
59	80	215,484	4.38	43,839	0		1,846,348	49,153
64	85	249,805	5.08	50,821	0		1,146,895	49,153
69	90	289,593	5.89	58,916	0		0	49,153
70	Total	5,194,003			0			

eXcel

Please visit us at www.mhhe.com/bkm

TABLE 20.2		**Traditional IRA**	**Roth IRA**
Traditional vs. Roth IRA tax shelters under a progressive tax code	Lifetime labor income	**$7,445,673**	**$7,445,673**
	Taxes ($)		
	Earning years	$ 879,430	$1,752,425
	Retirement years	1,797,848	0
	Total paid over lifetime	**2,677,278**	**1,752,425**
	Lifetime average tax rate (%)	35.96%	23.54%
	Retirement annuity:		
	Before-tax	$ 83,380	$ 49,153
	After-tax	66,366	49,153

taxes during the retirement phase. We keep consumption during the earning years the same as they were in the benchmark (traditional IRA) tax shelter to compare the standard of living in retirement afforded by a Roth IRA tax shelter.

Table 20.2 demonstrates the difference between the two types of shelters. In both cases, lifetime income and real consumption during the earning years, as well as the progressive tax scheme, are identical. The only difference is which IRA plan you choose, traditional or Roth. Hence the first line of Table 20.2, lifetime labor income, is fixed at $7.4 million. But the shelter works differently in each case. The traditional IRA shelters more income during the earning years, resulting in total taxes of only $879,430, compared with $1.75 million under the Roth IRA. In the retirement years, however, the Roth IRA plan entails no taxes, while the traditional IRA results in taxes of just under $1.8 million. Lifetime taxes are $2.7 million using the traditional IRA compared with only $1.75 million for the Roth IRA. Despite this, the larger accumulation in the traditional IRA saving account results in a larger retirement fund ($4.1 million compared with $2.4 million) and a larger real after-tax retirement annuity of $66,366. The bottom line is that the traditional IRA is more effective for the middle-income family we examine here.

The explanation of why the traditional IRA is better for a middle-income family also indicates when the Roth IRA may be preferred. If earnings are sharply back-loaded, that is, most of your earnings are close to retirement, then tax-free accumulation of investment income is less important, and the Roth IRA may dominate. This can happen if you start with fewer years to retirement and your income grows faster. Without changing the number of years to retirement, you would need to change nominal income growth in both spreadsheets from 7% to an extreme 40% for the Roth IRA to dominate. (The Web site **www.quicken.com** allows you to make the comparison for your own circumstances.)

Notice in Table 20.2 that the lifetime average tax rate for saving with traditional IRAs is 35.96%. This is a result of large accumulation of earnings on savings that are taxed on retirement and shows the importance of early accumulation. Despite the higher lifetime taxes, this tax shelter ends up with larger after-tax real consumption during retirement.

CONCEPT *check* **20.7**

Suppose all taxpayers were like you, and the IRS wished to raise a fixed tax revenue. Would it be wise to offer the Roth IRA option?

401k and 403b Plans

These days the majority of employees receive retirement benefits in the form of a defined contribution plan (see Chapter 21 for more discussion of these plans). These are named after the relevant sections of the U.S. tax code: 401k in the corporate sector and 403b in the public and tax-exempt sectors. These are quite similar and the discussion of 401k plans applies to 403b plans as well.

401k plans have two distinct features. First and foremost, your employer may match your contribution to various degrees, up to a certain level. This means that if you elect not to participate in the plan, you forgo part of your potential employment compensation. Needless to say, regardless of tax considerations, any employee should contribute to the plan at least as much as the employer will match, except for extreme circumstances of cash needs. While some employees may face cash constraints and think they would be better off skipping contributions, in many circumstances, they would be better off borrowing to bridge the liquidity shortfall while continuing to contribute up to the level matched by the employer.

The second feature of the plan is akin to a traditional IRA in tax treatment and similar in other restrictions. Contributions to 401k plans are restricted (details can be found on many Web sites, e.g., **www.morningstar.com**), but the limits on contributions generally exceed the level matched by the employer. Hence you must decide how much of your salary to contribute beyond the level matched by your employer. You can incorporate 401k plans, like the traditional IRA, in your savings-plan spreadsheet, review the trade-off, and make an informed decision on how much to save.

> **401k plans**
>
> **Defined employee contribution plans wherein the employer matches the employee's contribution up to a set percentage.**

Risky Investments and Capital Gains as Tax Shelters

So far we have limited our discussion to safe investments that yield a sure 6%. This number, coupled with the inflation assumption (3%), determined the results of various savings rules under the appropriate tax configuration. You must recognize, however, that the 6% return and 3% inflation are not hard numbers and consider the implications of other possible scenarios over the life of the savings plan. The spreadsheets we developed make scenario analysis quite easy. Once you set up a spreadsheet with a contemplated savings plan, you simply vary the inputs for ROR (the nominal rate of return) and inflation and record the implications for each scenario. The probabilities of possible deviations from the expected numbers and your risk tolerance will dictate which savings plan provides you with sufficient security of obtaining your goals. This sensitivity analysis will be even more important when you consider risky investments.

The tax shelters we have described allow you to invest in a broad array of securities and mutual funds and you can invest your nonsheltered savings in anything you please. Which portfolio to choose is a matter of risk versus return. That said, taxes lend importance to the otherwise largely irrelevant aspect of dividends versus capital gains.

According to current U.S. tax law, there are two applicable capital gains rates for most investments: 15% if your marginal tax rate is higher than 25%, and 5%[4] if you are in a lower tax bracket. More important, you pay the applicable rate only when you sell the security. Thus, investing in nondividend-paying securities is an automatic partial tax shelter with no restrictions on contributions or withdrawals. Because this investment is not tax deductible, it is similar to a Roth IRA, but somewhat inferior in that you do pay a tax on withdrawal, however low. Still, such investments can be more effective than traditional IRA and 401k plans, as we discussed earlier. Since annual contributions to all IRAs and 401k plans are quite limited, investment in a low- or no-dividend portfolio may be the efficient shelter for many investors who wish to exceed the contribution limit. Another advantage of such portfolios is that you can sell those securities that have lost value to realize capital losses and thereby reduce your tax bill in any given year. This virtue of risky securities is called the *tax-timing option*. Managing a portfolio with efficient utilization of the tax-timing option requires expert attention, however, and may not be appropriate for many savers.

The average dividend yield on the S&P 500 stocks is on the order of 2%, and other indexes (such as Nasdaq) bear an even lower yield. This means that you can easily construct a well-diversified portfolio with a very low dividend yield. Such a portfolio allows you to utilize the tax advantage of capital gains versus dividends. Spreadsheet 20.9 adapts Spreadsheet 20.6 (progressive tax with no shelter) to a no-dividend portfolio of stocks, maintaining the same

---

[4]The rate goes up to 10% if you hold the security for less than five years.

**Please visit us at
www.mhhe.com/bkm**

	A	B	C	D	E	F	G	H
3	Retirement Years	Income Growth	Rate of Inflation	Exemption Now	Tax rates in	Savings Rate	ROR	rROR
4	25	0.07	0.03	10000	Table 20.1	0.15	0.06	0.0291
5	Age	Income	Deflator	Exemption	Taxes	Savings	Cumulative Savings	rConsumption
6	30	50,000	1.00	10,000	8,000	6,300	6,300	35,700
7	31	53,500	1.03	10,300	8,640	6,793	13,471	36,958
11	35	70,128	1.16	11,593	11,764	9,370	52,995	42,262
21	45	137,952	1.56	15,580	28,922	19,707	278,528	57,333
31	55	271,372	2.09	20,938	64,661	41,143	883,393	79,076
41	65	533,829	2.81	28,139	145,999	92,460	2,432,049	104,970
42	Total				1,752,425	1,163,478	Real Annuity	49,153
43	**RETIREMENT**				Tax rate on	capital gains		0.15
44	Age	Nom Withdraw	Deflator	Cum cap gains	Exemption	Taxes	Funds Left	rConsumption
45	66	142,460	2.90	1,340,186	28,983	6,799	2,435,512	46,808
49	70	160,340	3.26	1,561,124	32,620	10,178	2,404,847	46,033
54	75	185,879	3.78	1,660,844	37,816	14,598	2,233,096	45,293
59	80	215,484	4.38	1,503,386	43,839	19,338	1,846,348	44,742
64	85	249,805	5.08	995,489	50,821	24,535	1,146,895	44,326
69	90	289,593	5.89	1,500	58,916	30,626	0	43,955
70	Total				1,056,691	445,850		

preretirement consumption stream, holding the ROR at 6% and assuming 15% capital gains tax. Real retirement consumption, averaging $45,105, is almost identical to that supported by a Roth IRA (Spreadsheet 20.8).[5]

Sheltered versus Unsheltered Savings

Suppose your desired level of savings is double the amount allowed in IRAs and 401k (or 403b) plans. At the same time you wish to invest equal amounts in stocks and bonds. Where should you keep the stocks and where the bonds? You will be surprised to know how many investors make the costly mistake of holding the stocks in a tax-protected account and the bonds in an unsheltered account. This is a mistake because most of the return from bonds is in the form of taxable interest payments, while stocks by their nature already provide some tax shelter.

Recall that tax shelters enhance the retirement annuity with two elements: (1) tax deferral on contributions and (2) tax deferral on income earned on savings. The effectiveness of each element depends on the tax rate on withdrawals. Of the two types of tax shelters we analyzed, traditional IRA and 401k (or 403b) plans contain both elements, while a Roth IRA provides only the second, but with the advantage that the tax rate on withdrawals is zero. Therefore, we need to analyze the stock–bond shelter question separately for each type of retirement plan. Table 20.3 shows the hierarchy of this analysis when a Roth IRA is used. The difference is apparent by comparing the taxes in each column. With stocks inside and bonds outside the shelter you pay taxes early and at the ordinary income rate. When you remove stocks from and move bonds into the shelter you pay taxes later at the lower capital gains rate.

TABLE 20.3	Phase	Asset	**Stocks Inside; Bonds Outside**	**Stocks Outside; Bonds Inside**
Investing Roth IRA contributions in stocks and bonds	Savings	Bonds	Taxed upon accrual	No taxes
		Stocks	No taxes	Taxes deferred
	Withdrawal	Bonds	No taxes	No taxes
		Stocks	No taxes	Taxed at capital gains rate

[5]In Spreadsheet 20.9 we did not take full advantage of the tax code. You can defer capital gains longer by specifying the particular shares you sell so that you sell first new shares with little capital gains and old shares last.

TABLE 20.4	Phase	Asset	Stocks Inside; Bonds Outside	Stocks Outside; Bonds Inside
Investing traditional IRA or 401k contributions in stocks and bonds	Savings	Bonds	Taxed on accrual	Taxes deferred
		Stocks	Tax deferred	Taxes deferred
	Withdrawal	Bonds	No taxes	Taxed at marginal rate
		Stocks	Taxed at marginal rate	Taxed at capital gains rate

When you use either a traditional IRA or 401k plan, contributions are tax deferred regardless of whether you purchase stocks or bonds, so we need to compare only taxes on income from savings and withdrawal. Table 20.4 shows the trade-off for a traditional IRA or 401k plan.

The advantage ends up being the same as with the Roth IRA. By removing stocks from and moving bonds into the shelter you gain the deferral on the bond interest during the savings phase. During the retirement phase you gain the difference between the ordinary income and the capital gains rate on the gains from the stocks.

Does the rationale of sheltering bonds rather than stocks apply to preferred stocks?

CONCEPT
check **20.8**

20.6 SOCIAL SECURITY

Social Security (SS) is a cross between a pension and an insurance plan. It is quite regressive in the way it is financed, in that employees pay a proportional (currently 7.65%) tax on gross wages, with no exemption but with an income cap ($90,000 in 2007). Employers match employees' contributions and pay SS directly.[6]

On the other hand, SS is progressive in the way it allocates benefits; low-income individuals receive a relatively larger share of preretirement income upon retirement. Of the SS tax of 7.65%, 6.2% goes toward the retirement benefit and 1.45% toward retirement healthcare services provided by Medicare. Thus, combining your payments with your employer's, the real retirement annuity is financed by $2 \times 6.2 = 12.4\%$ of your income (up to the aforementioned cap); we do not examine the Medicare component of SS in this chapter.

SS payments are made throughout one's entire working life; however, only 35 years of contributions count for the determination of benefits. Benefits are in the form of a lifetime real annuity based on a retirement age of 65, although you can retire earlier (as of age 62) or later (up to age 70) and draw a smaller or larger annuity, respectively. One reason SS is projected to face fiscal difficulties in future years is the increased longevity of the population. The current plan to mitigate this problem is to gradually increase the retirement age.

Calculation of benefits for individuals retiring in a given year is done in four steps:

1. The series of your taxed annual earnings (using the cap) is compiled. The status of this series is shown in your annual SS statement.
2. An indexing factor series is compiled for all past years. This series is used to account for the time value of your lifetime contributions.
3. The indexing factors are applied to your recorded earnings to arrive at the Average Indexed Monthly Earnings (AIME).

Social Security

Federally mandated pension plan established to provide minimum retirement benefits to all workers.

---

[6]Absent the SS tax, it is reasonable to assume that the amount contributed by employers would be added to your pretax income, hence your actual contribution is really 15.3%. For this reason, self-employed individuals are required to contribute 15.3% to SS.

4. Your AIME is used to determine the Primary Insurance Amount (PIA), which is your monthly retirement annuity.

All this sounds more difficult than it really is, so let's describe steps 2 through 4 in detail.

The Indexing Factor Series

Suppose your first wage on which you paid the SS tax was earned 40 years ago. To arrive at today's value of this wage, we must calculate its future value over the 40 years, that is, $FV = \text{wage} \times (1 + g)^{40}$. The SS administration refers to this as the indexed earnings for that year, and the FV factor, $(1 + g)^{40}$, is the index for that year. This calculation is made for each year, resulting in a series of indexed earnings which, when summed, is the value today of the entire stream of lifetime taxed earnings.

A major issue is what rate, g, to use in producing the index for each year. SS uses for each year the growth in the average wage of the U.S. working population in that year. Arbitrarily, the index for the most recent two years is set to 1.0 (implying a recent growth rate of zero) and then increased each year, going backward, by the growth rate of wages in that year. For example, in the year 2001 the index for 1967 (35 years earlier) was 6.16768. Thus the 1967 wage is assumed to have been invested for 35 years at 5.34% ($1.0534^{35} = 6.16768$). The actual average growth rate of wages in the U.S. over the years 1967–2001 was 5.48%;[7] the index is slightly lower because the growth rate in the two most recent years prior to retirement has been set to zero.

Wage growth was not constant over these years. For example, it was as high as 10.07% in 1980–1981, and as low as 0.86% in 1992–1993. By comparison, the (geometric) average T-bill rate over the years 1966–2006 was 5.92% and the rate of inflation 4.62%, implying a real interest rate of 1.30%. For recent retirees, the average *real* growth rate applied to their SS contributions was about 0.40% (depending on how much they contributed in each year), significantly lower than the real interest rate over their working years, but closer to the longer-term (1926–2006) real rate of 0.64%. (See Table 5.3.)

The Average Indexed Monthly Income

The series of a retiree's lifetime indexed contributions (there may be zeros in the series for periods when the retiree was unemployed) is used to determine the base for the retirement annuity. The 35 highest indexed contributions are identified, summed, and then divided by $35 \times 12 = 420$ to achieve your Average Indexed Monthly Income (AIME). If you worked less than 35 years, all your indexed earnings will be summed, but your AIME might be low since you still divide the sum by 420. If you worked more than 35 years, only the 35 highest indexed wages will be used to compute the average.

The Primary Insurance Amount

In this stage of the calculation of monthly SS benefits, low-income workers (with a low AIME) are favored in order to increase income equality. The exact formula may change from one year to the next, but the example of four representative individuals who retired in 2005 demonstrates the principle. The AIME of these individuals relative to the average in the population and their Primary Insurance Amount (PIA) are calculated in Table 20.5.

Table 20.5 presents the value of SS to U.S. employees who retired in 2005. The first part of the table shows how SS calculates the real annuity to be paid to retirees.[8] The results differ for the four representative individuals. One measure of this differential is the *income replacement rate* (i.e., retirement income as a percent of working income) provided to the four income

---

[7]We use a wage growth rate of 7% in our exercises, assuming our readers are well educated and can expect a higher than average growth. Special attention must be given to this input (and the others) if you advise other people.
[8]The annuity of special-circumstance low-income retirees is supplemented.

TABLE 20.5

Calculation of the retirement annuity of representative retirees of 2005

AIME Rank	Low	Average	High	Maximum
% of average wage	50	100	150	Max*
AIME ($ month)	1,400	2,800	4,200	5,800
PIA formula:				
90% of the first $592	533	533	533	533
32% of AIME over $592 through $3,567	259	707	952	952
15% of AIME over $3,567	0	0	95	335
Total = PIA ($/month)	791	1,239	1,580	1,820
Real retirement annuity = PIA × 12	9,496	14,872	18,957	21,837
Income replacement (%)	56.5%	44.3%	37.6%	NA*
IRR** assuming longevity = 81; Inflation = 3%	6.52	5.51	4.83	3.82
IRR** assuming longevity = 84; Inflation = 3%	7.02	6.06	5.41	4.51
Longevity implied by SS (years) for IRR = 6%	14	19	23	30

*Income is above the maximum taxable and income replacement cannot be calculated.

**Internal Rate of Return.

brackets in Table 20.5. Low-income retirees have a replacement rate of 56.5%, more than 1.5 times that of the high-wage employees (37.6%).

The net after-tax benefits may be reduced if the individual has other sources of income, because a portion of the retirement annuity is subject to income tax. Currently, retired households with combined taxable income over $32,000 pay taxes on a portion of the SS benefits. At income of $44,000, 50% of the SS annuity is subject to tax, but the proportion rises at higher income levels. You can find current numbers and some useful calculators at **www.ssa. gov.** This Web site also allows you to project Social Security benefits at various levels of sophistication.

When evaluating the attractiveness of SS as an investment for current retirees (the bottom part of Table 20.5), we must consider current **longevity** figures. For a male, current remaining life expectancy at age 65 is roughly an additional 15 years, and for a female 19 years. Using these figures, the current PIA provides male retirees an internal rate of return on SS contributions in the range of 6.52–3.82%, and female retirees 7.02–4.51%.[9] These IRRs are obtained by taking 12.4% (the combined SS tax) of the series of 35 annual earnings of the four employees as cash outflows. The series of annuity payments (16 years for males and 19 for females), assuming inflation at 3%, is used to compute cash inflows.

To examine SS performance another way, the last line in the table shows the longevity (number of payments) required to achieve an IRR of 6%. Except for the highest income bracket, all have life expectancy greater than this threshold. Why are these numbers so attractive, when SS is so often criticized for poor investment performance? The reason benefits are so generous is that the PIA formula sets a high replacement rate relative to the SS tax rate, the proportion of income taxed. Taking history as a guide, to achieve an IRR equal to the rate of inflation plus the historical average rate on a safe investment such as T-bills (with a historical real rate of 0.7%), the formula would need to incorporate a lower replacement rate. With a future rate of inflation of 3%, this would imply a nominal IRR of 3.7%. Is the ROR assumed in our spreadsheets (6%) the right one to use, or is the expected IRR based on past real rates the correct one to use? In short, we simply don't know. But averaging across the population, SS may well be a fair pension plan, taking into consideration its role in promoting equality of income.

longevity

Remaining life expectancy.

[9]However, income is correlated with longevity and with durability of marriage. This means that wealthy retirees and their spouses draw longer annuities than the poor do. It is suggested that this difference may as much as completely offset the progressivity built into the PIA schedule.

The solvency of SS is threatened by two factors: population longevity and a below-replacement growth of the U.S. population. Over the next 35 years, longevity is expected to increase by almost two years, increasing steady-state expenditures by more than 10%. To keep a level population (ignoring immigration) requires an average of 2.1 children per female, yet the current average of 1.9 is expected to decline further.[10] The projected large deficit, beginning in 2016, requires reform of SS. Increasing the retirement age to account for increased longevity does not constitute a reduction in the plan's IRR and therefore seems a reasonable solution to deficits arising from this factor. Eliminating the deficit resulting from population decline is more difficult. It is projected that doing so by increasing the SS tax may require an increase in the combined SS tax of as much as 10% within your working years. Such a simple solution is considered politically unacceptable, so you must expect changes in benefits.

The question of privatizing a portion of SS so that investors will be able to choose portfolios with risk levels according to their personal risk tolerance has become a hot public policy issue. Clearly, the current format that provides a guaranteed real rate is tailored to individuals with low risk tolerance. Although we advocate that at least a portion of SS be considered as a safety-first proposition (with a very low-risk profile), investors who are willing to monitor and rebalance risky portfolios cannot be faulted for investing in stocks. The main point with respect to this option is that the media and even some finance experts claim that a long-term investment in stocks is not all that risky. We cannot disagree more. We project that with appropriate risk adjustment, future retirees will find it difficult to beat the SS plan and should be made fully aware of this fact.[11]

> **CONCEPT check 20.9**   Part of your retirement expenditures will be paid for with your Social Security benefits. Part will come from your retirement savings. Compare the risks surrounding the income stream that will be generated from each of these sources.

20.7   CHILDREN'S EDUCATION AND LARGE PURCHASES

Sending a child to a private college can cost a family in excess of $40,000 a year, in current dollars, for four years. Even a state college can cost in excess of $25,000 a year. Many families will send two or more children to college within a few years, creating a need to finance large expenditures within a few years. Other large expenditures such as a second home (we deal with the primary residence in the next section) or an expensive vehicle present similar problems on a smaller scale.

The question is whether planned, large outflows during the working years require a major innovation to our planning tools. The answer is no. All you need to do is add a column to your spreadsheet for extra-consumption expenditures that come out of savings. As long as cumulative savings do not turn negative as the outflows take place, the only effect to consider is the reduction in the retirement annuity that results from these expenditures. To respond to a lower-than-desired retirement annuity you have four options: (1) increase the savings rate, (2) live with a smaller retirement annuity, (3) do away with or reduce the magnitude of the expenditure item, or (4) increase expected ROR by taking on more risk. Recall though, that in Section 20.2, we suggested option 4 isn't viable for many investors.

The situation is a little more complicated when the extra-consumption expenditures create negative cumulative savings in the retirement plan. In principle, one can simply borrow to

---

[10]Fertility rates in Europe, Japan, and (until recently) in China are even lower, exacerbating the problems of their Social Security systems.

[11]Here, again, we collide with those who consider stocks low-risk investments in the long run (some of them esteemed colleagues). One cannot overestimate the misleading nature of this assessment (see Chapter 6, Section 6.6).

SPREADSHEET 20.10

Financing children's education

	A	B	C	D	E	F	G
1	Retirement Years	Income Growth	Rate of Inflation	Savings Rate	ROR	rROR	Extra-Cons
2	25	0.07	0.03	0.15	0.06	0.0291	40,000
3	Age	Income	Deflator	Savings	Cumulative Savings	rConsumption	Expenditures
4	30	50,000	1.00	7,500	7,500	42,500	0
5	31	53,500	1.03	8,025	15,975	44,150	0
9	35	70,128	1.16	10,519	61,658	51,419	0
19	45	137,952	1.56	20,693	308,859	75,264	0
22	48	168,997	1.70	25,349	375,099	84,378	68,097
23	49	180,826	1.75	27,124	354,588	87,654	70,140
24	50	193,484	1.81	29,023	260,397	91,058	144,489
25	51	207,028	1.86	31,054	158,252	94,595	148,824
26	52	221,520	1.92	33,228	124,331	98,268	76,644
27	53	237,026	1.97	35,554	88,401	102,084	78,943
28	54	253,618	2.03	38,043	131,748	106,049	0
29	55	271,372	2.09	40,706	180,359	110,167	0
39	65	533,829	2.81	80,074	1,090,888	161,257	0
40	Total			1,116,851	Real Annuity	22,048	

eXcel

Please visit us at
www.mhhe.com/bkm

finance these expenditures with debt (as is common for large purchases such as automobiles). Again, the primary variable of interest is the retirement annuity. The problem, however, is that if you arrive at a negative savings level quite late in your savings plan, you will be betting the farm on the success of the plan in later years. Recalling, again, the discussion of Section 20.2, pushing risk into later years, other things being equal, is more dangerous since you will have little time to recover from any setbacks.

An illuminating example requires adding only one column to Spreadsheet 20.2, as shown in Spreadsheet 20.10. Column G adds the extra-consumption expenditures. We use as input (cell G2) the current cost of one college year per child—$40,000. We assume your first child will be college-bound when you are 48 years old and the second when you are 50. The expenditures in column G are inflated by the price level in column C and subtracted from cumulative savings in column E.

The real retirement annuity prior to this extra-consumption expenditure was $49,688, but "after-children" only $22,048, less than half. The expenditure of $320,000 in today's dollars costs you total lifetime real consumption of 25 × ($49,688 − $22,048) = $690,514 because of the loss of interest on the funds that would have been saved. If you change the input in G2 to $25,000 (reflecting the cost of a public college), the retirement annuity falls to $32,405, a loss of "only" 35% in the standard of living.

What if anything should you do about the risk of rapid increase in college tuition?	**CONCEPT** check **20.10**

20.8 HOME OWNERSHIP: THE RENT-VERSUS-BUY DECISION

Most people dream of owning a home and for good reason. In addition to the natural desire for roots that goes with owning your home, this investment is an important hedge for most families. Dwelling is the largest long-term consumption item and fluctuations in the cost of dwelling are responsible for the largest consumption risk they face. Dwelling costs, in turn, are subject to general price inflation, as well as to significant fluctuations specific to geographic location. This combination makes it difficult to hedge the risk with investments in securities. In addition, the law favors home ownership in a number of ways, chief of which is tax deductibility of mortgage interest.

Common (though not necessarily correct) belief is that the mortgage tax break is the major reason for investing in rather than renting a home. In competitive markets, though, rents will reflect the mortgage tax-deduction that applies to rental residence as well. Moreover, homes are illiquid assets and transaction costs in buying/selling a house are high. Therefore, purchasing a home that isn't expected to be a long-term residence for the owner may well be a speculative investment with inferior expected returns. The right time for investing in your home is when you are ready to settle someplace for the long haul. Speculative investments in real estate ought to be made in a portfolio context through instruments such as Real Estate Investment Trusts (REITs).

With all this in mind, it is evident that investment in a home enters the savings plan in two ways. First, during the working years the cash down payment should be treated just like any other large extra-consumption expenditure as discussed earlier. Second, home ownership affects your retirement plan because if you own your home free and clear by the time you retire, you will need a smaller annuity to get by; moreover, the value of the house is part of retirement wealth.

CONCEPT *check*	**20.11**	Should you have any preference for fixed versus variable rate mortgages?

20.9 UNCERTAIN LONGEVITY AND OTHER CONTINGENCIES

Perhaps the most daunting uncertainty in our life is the time it will end. Most people consider this uncertainty a blessing, yet, blessing or curse, this uncertainty has economic implications. Old age is hard enough without worrying about expenses. Yet the amount of money you may need is at least linear in longevity, if not exponential. Not knowing how much you will need, plus a healthy degree of risk aversion, would require us to save a lot more than necessary just to insure against the fortune of longevity.

life annuity

An annuity that pays you income until you die.

One solution to this problem is to invest in a life annuity to supplement Social Security benefits, your base life annuity. When you own a **life annuity** (an annuity that pays you income until you die), the provider takes on the risk of the time of death. To survive, the provider must be sure to earn a rate of return commensurate with the risk. Except for wars and natural disasters, however, an individual's time of death is a unique, nonsystematic risk.[12] It would appear, then, that the cost of a life annuity should be a simple calculation of interest rates applied to life expectancy from mortality tables. Unfortunately, adverse selection comes in the way.

adverse selection

The tendency for any proposed deal to attract the type of party who would make the deal a losing proposition to the offering party.

Adverse selection is the tendency for any proposed contract (deal) to attract the type of party who would make the contract (deal) a losing proposition to the offering party. A good example of adverse selection arises in health care. Suppose that Blue Cross offers health coverage where you choose your doctor and Blue Cross pays 80% of the costs. Suppose another HMO covers 100% of the cost and charges only a nominal fee per treatment. If HMOs were to price the services on the basis of a survey of the average health care needs in the population at large, they would be in for an unpleasant surprise. People who need frequent and expensive care would prefer the HMO over Blue Cross. The adverse selection in this case is that high-need individuals will choose the plan that provides more complete coverage. The individuals that the HMO most wants *not* to insure are most likely to sign up for coverage. Hence, to stay in business HMOs must expect their patients to have greater than average needs, and price the policy on this basis.

Providers of life annuities can expect a good dose of adverse selection as well, as people with the longest life expectancies will be their most enthusiastic customers. Therefore, it is advantageous to acquire these annuities at a younger age, before individuals are likely to know much about their personal life expectancies. The SS trust does not face adverse selection since virtually the entire population is forced into the purchase, allowing it to be a fair deal on both sides.

---

[12]For this reason, life insurance policies include fine print excluding payment in case of events such as wars, epidemics, and famine.

Unfortunately we also must consider untimely death or disability. These require an appropriate amount of life and disability insurance, particularly in the early stage of the lifecycle. The appropriate coverage should be thought of in the context of a retirement annuity. Coverage should replace at least the most essential part of the retirement annuity.

Finally, there is the need to hedge labor income. Since you cannot insure wages, the least you can do is maintain a portfolio that is uncorrelated with your labor income. As Enron and other recent bankruptcies have demonstrated, too many are unaware of the perils of having their pension income tied to their career, employment, and compensation. Investing a significant fraction of your portfolio in the industry you work in is akin to a "Texas hedge," betting on the horse you own.

Insurance companies offer life insurance on your children. Is this a good idea?   **CONCEPT** *check* **20.12**

20.10 MATRIMONY, BEQUEST, AND INTERGENERATIONAL TRANSFERS

In the context of a retirement plan we think of risk in terms of safety first. The imperative to avoid disastrous outcomes makes mean-variance analysis inadequate. We have already touched on this issue earlier, in the context of (1) raising the ROR with risky investments, (2) avoiding savings plans that rely too heavily on savings in later years, and (3) acquiring life insurance and including life annuities in the savings portfolio.

One sort of insurance the market cannot supply is wage insurance. If we could obtain wage insurance, a savings plan would be a lot easier to formulate. **Moral hazard** is the reason for this void in the marketplace. Moral hazard is the phenomenon whereby a party to a contract (deal) has an incentive to change behavior in a way that makes the deal less attractive to the other party.[13] For example, a person who buys wage insurance would then have an incentive to consume leisure at the expense of work effort. Moral hazard is also why insuring items for more than their market or intrinsic value is prohibited. If your warehouse were insured for lots more than its value, you might have less incentive to prevent fires, an obvious moral hazard.

In contrast, marriage provides a form of co-insurance that extends also to the issue of longevity. A married couple has a greater probability that at least one will survive to an older age, giving greater incentive to save for a longer life. Put differently, saving for a longer life has a smaller probability of going to waste. A study by Kotlikoff and Spivack (1981)[14] simulated reasonable individual preferences to show that a marriage contract increases the dollar value of lifetime savings by as much as 25%. Old sages who have been preaching the virtue of matrimony for millennia must have known more about economics than we give them credit for.

Bequest is another motive for saving. There is something special about bequest that differentiates it from other "expense" items. When you save for members of the next generation (or beyond), you double the planning horizon, and by considering later generations as well, you can make it effectively infinite. This has implications for the composition of the savings portfolio. For example, the conventional wisdom that as you grow older you should gradually shift out of stocks and into bonds is not as true when bequest is an important factor in the savings plan.

Having discussed marriage co-insurance and bequest, we cannot fail to mention that despite the virtues of saving for the longest term, many individuals overshoot the mark. When a person saves for old age and passes on before taking full advantage of the nest egg, the estate is called an "involuntary, intergenerational transfer." Data show that such transfers are widespread. Kotlikoff and Summers (1981)[15] estimate that about 75% of wealth left behind

moral hazard

The phenomenon whereby a party to a contract has an incentive to change behavior in a way that makes the contract less attractive to the other party.

---

[13] Moral hazard and adverse selection can reinforce each other. Restaurants that offer an all-you-can-eat meal attract big eaters (adverse selection) and induce "normal" eaters to overeat (moral hazard).

[14] Laurence J. Kotlikoff and Avia Spivack, "The Family as an Incomplete Annuities Market," *Journal of Political Economy* 89, no. 2 (April 1981), pp. 372–91.

[15] Laurence J. Kotlikoff and Lawrence H. Summers, "The Role of Intergenerational Transfers in Aggregate Capital Accumulation," *The Journal of Political Economy* 89, no. 4 (August 1981), pp. 706–32.

is actually involuntary transfer. This suggests that people make too little use of the market for life annuities. Hopefully you will not be one of them, both because you will live to a healthy old age and because you'll have a ball spending your never-expiring annuity.

 If matrimony is such a good deal, but you haven't yet found a soul mate, should you rush to surf the Web for a potential spouse?

SUMMARY

- The major objective of a savings plan is to provide for adequate retirement income.
- Even moderate inflation will affect the purchasing power of the retirement annuity. Therefore, the plan must be cast in terms of real consumption and retirement income.
- From a standpoint of smoothing consumption, it is advantageous to save a fixed or rising fraction of real income. However, postponement of savings to later years increases the risk of the retirement fund.
- The IRA-style tax shelter, akin to a consumption tax, defers taxes on both contributions and earnings on savings.
- The progressive tax code sharpens the importance of taxes during the retirement years. High tax rates during retirement reduce the effectiveness of the tax shelter.
- A Roth IRA tax shelter does not shield contributions but eliminates taxes during retirement. Savers who anticipate high retirement income (and taxes) must examine whether this shelter is more beneficial than a traditional IRA account.
- 401k plans are similar to traditional IRAs and allow matched contributions by employers. This benefit should not be forgone.
- Capital gains can be postponed and later taxed at a lower rate. Therefore, investment in low-dividend stocks is a natural tax shelter. Investments in interest-bearing securities should be sheltered first.
- Social Security benefits are an important component of retirement income.
- Savings plans should be augmented for large expenditures such as children's education.
- Home ownership should be viewed as a hedge against rental cost.
- Uncertain longevity and other contingencies should be handled via life annuities and appropriate insurance coverage.

KEY TERMS

401k plans, 669	moral hazard, 677	Social Security, 671
adverse selection, 676	progressive tax, 665	tax shelters, 664
flat tax, 662	real consumption, 660	traditional IRA, 667
life annuity, 676	retirement annuity, 659	
longevity, 673	Roth IRA, 667	

PROBLEM SETS

 Select problems are available in McGraw-Hill's Homework Manager®. Please see the packaging options section of the preface for more information.

1. With no taxes or inflation (Spreadsheet 20.1), what would be your retirement annuity if you increase the savings rate by 1%?

2. With a 3% inflation (Spreadsheet 20.2), by how much would your retirement annuity grow if you increase the savings rate by 1%? Is the benefit greater in the face of inflation?

eXcel

Please visit us at
www.mhhe.com/bkm

eXcel

Please visit us at
www.mhhe.com/bkm

www.mhhe.com/bkm

3. What savings rate from real income (Spreadsheet 20.3) will produce the same retirement annuity as a 15% savings rate from nominal income?

4. Under the flat tax (Spreadsheet 20.4), will a 1% increase in ROR offset a 1% increase in the tax rate?

5. With an IRA tax shelter (Spreadsheet 20.5), compare the effect on real consumption during retirement of a 1% increase in the rate of inflation to a 1% increase in the tax rate.

6. With a progressive tax (Spreadsheet 20.6), compare an increase of 1% in the lower tax bracket to an increase of 1% in the highest tax bracket.

7. Verify that the IRA tax shelter with a progressive tax (Spreadsheet 20.7) acts as a hedge. Compare the effect of a decline of 2% in the ROR to an increase of 2% in ROR.

8. What is the trade-off between ROR and the rate of inflation with a Roth IRA under a progressive tax (Spreadsheet 20.8)?

9. Suppose you could defer capital gains tax to the last year of your retirement (Spreadsheet 20.9). Would it be worthwhile given the progressivity of the tax code?

10. Project your Social Security benefits with the parameters of Section 20.6.

11. Using Spreadsheet 20.10, assess the present value of a 1% increase in college tuition as a fraction of the present value of labor income.

12. Give another example of adverse selection.

13. In addition to expected longevity, what traits might affect an individual's demand for a life annuity?

14. Give another example of a moral hazard problem.

WEB master

Retirement Planning

Visit the AARP's Financial Planning and Retirement Web site at **www.aarp.org/money/financial_planning.** Locate the Retirement Roadmap link in the Retirement Planning section. Click on the link and take the interactive survey to see how your expectations for retirement match your financial capacity.

Return to the Financial Planning and Retirement page and follow the link to the Retirement Planning Calculator. The calculator allows you to enter information about your retirement plans, your current level of assets, expected benefits from other sources, and your spouse's financial data and needs. Use the AARP Retirement Planning Calculator to enter your specific data and assumptions. Take advantage of the "Estimate" features offered to get a better idea of realistic inputs.

1. On the Results page, do you have a projected excess of funds or a shortfall of funds at the end of the retirement period? Can you meet your goals by following your current financial path? What suggestion(s) does the simulator make to help you achieve your goals?

2. Look at the list of parameters toward the bottom of the page. Which one would be the easiest for you to change to make your goals attainable? Some people might choose to work longer, some to leave a smaller estate, etc. Choose the combination of factors that would work best for you, then click on the Recalculate button to see the new results. Repeat if necessary. Can you come up with a plan that offers you a combination of factors that offers you an acceptable level of comfort?

SOLUTIONS TO CONCEPT checks

20.1. When ROR falls by 1% to 5%, the retirement annuity falls from $192,244 to $149,855 (i.e., by 22.45%). To restore this annuity, the savings rate must rise by 4.24 percentage points to 19.24%. With this savings rate, the entire loss of 1% in ROR falls on consumption during the earning years.

20.2. Intuition suggests you need to keep the real rate (2.91%) constant, that is, increase the nominal rate to 7% (confirm this). However, this will not be sufficient because the nominal income growth of 7% (Column B) has a lower real growth when inflation is higher. Result: You must increase the real ROR to compensate for a lower growth in real income, ending with a nominal rate of 7.67%.

20.3.   There are two components to the risk of relying on future labor income: disability/death and career failure/unemployment. You can insure the first component, but not the second.

20.4.   With before-tax income held constant, your after-tax income will remain unchanged if your average tax rate, and hence total tax liability, is unchanged:

$$\text{Total tax} = (\text{Income} - \text{Exemption}) \times \text{Tax rate, or } T = (I - E) \times t$$

A 1% increase in the tax rate will increase T by $.01(I - E)$. A 1% increase in the exemption will decrease T by $.01 \times E \times t$. Realistically, $I - E$ will be greater than $E \times t$ and hence you will be worse off with the increase in exemption and tax rate.

20.5.   The qualitative result is the same. However, with no shelter you are worse off early and hence lose also the earning power of the additional tax bills.

20.6.   No, an increase in the low-bracket tax rate applies to your entire taxable income, while an increase in the high-bracket tax rate applies only to a fraction of your taxable income.

20.7.   No, in your hypothetical case, the Roth IRA tax shelter produces less taxes yet a smaller real retirement annuity. The reason is the timing of the taxes. The timing issue does not affect the stream of tax revenues to the IRS because at any point in time, taxpayers are distributed over all ages. In this case, the IRS can replace all Roth IRAs with traditional IRAs and lower the tax rates. The IRS will collect similar revenue each year, and retirees will enjoy higher real retirement annuities.

20.8.   No, in terms of cash income, preferred stocks are more similar to bonds.

20.9.   Your projected retirement fund is risky because of uncertainty about future labor income and future real returns on savings. The projected Social Security real annuity is risky because of political uncertainty about future benefits. It's hard to judge which risk is greater.

20.10. You can invest in savings accounts that yield a floating rate tied to an index of college tuition.

20.11. A fixed-rate mortgage is the lower risk, higher expected cost option. Homeowners with greater risk tolerance might opt for a variable-rate mortgage which is expected to average a lower rate over the life of the mortgage.

20.12. In the old days, children were more than a bundle of joy; they also provided a hedge for old-age income. Under such circumstance, insuring children would make economic sense. These days, children may well be a financial net expenditure, ruling out insurance on economic grounds. Other nonfinancial considerations are a matter of individual preference.

20.13. Rushing into marriage for economic reasons is a very risky proposition. A bad marriage can be a financial, as well as an emotional, calamity.

Investors and the Investment Process

- Specify investment objectives of individual and institutional investors.

- Identify constraints on individual and institutional investors.

- Compare and contrast major types of investment policies.

Translating the aspirations and circumstances of diverse households into appropriate investment decisions is a daunting task. The task is equally difficult for institutions, most of which have many stakeholders and often are regulated by various authorities. The investment process is not easily reduced to a simple or mechanical algorithm.

While many principles of investments are quite general and apply to virtually all investors, some issues are peculiar to the specific investor. For example, tax bracket, age, risk tolerance, wealth, job prospects, and uncertainties make each investor's circumstances somewhat unique. In this chapter we focus on the process by which investors systematically review their particular objectives, constraints, and circumstances. Along the way, we survey some of the major classes of institutional investors and examine the special issues they must confront.

There is of course no unique "correct" investment process. However, some approaches are better than others, and it can be helpful to take one high-quality approach as a useful case study. For this reason, we will examine the systematic approach suggested by the CFA Institute. Among other things, the Institute administers examinations to certify investment professionals as CFAs, or Chartered Financial Analysts. Therefore, the approach we outline is also one that a highly respected professional group endorses through the curriculum that it requires investment practitioners to master. The nearby box describes how to become a Chartered Financial Analyst.

(continued)

The basic framework involves dividing the investment process into four stages: specifying objectives, specifying constraints, formulating policy, and monitoring and updating the portfolio as needed. We will treat each of these activities in turn. We start with a description of the major types of investors, both individual and institutional, as well as their special objectives. We turn next to the constraints or circumstances peculiar to each investor class, and we consider some of the investment policies that each can choose.

21.1 | INVESTORS AND OBJECTIVES

Most investors would agree with the notion that they want to earn as much money on their investments as possible. But while the concept "earn money" is simple enough *after the fact,* since you simply count the profits on your investments, it is vague when applied to an investment *before the fact,* since you rarely will know for sure what your earnings will be. Almost all investments entail uncertainty. Thus, while investors all wish to earn the highest rate of return possible, they also seek to avoid risk. It is not surprising that ultimately, then, investments that offer higher expected returns will impose greater risk. This is the risk-return trade-off.

Investors will differ in their choice of investments because they differ in their willingness to trade off expected return against risk. We describe the willingness to accept higher risk to attain higher expected returns as the investor's **risk tolerance;** equivalently, we can describe attitudes toward risk using the concept of the investor's **risk aversion,** or reluctance to accept risk. The box on page 684 explores these concepts and shows that while they seem straightforward, real-life behavior can be difficult to characterize so neatly.

These terms describe behavior: If we could observe an investor making many choices among assets whose return and risk were well understood, we could measure an investor's risk aversion (or risk tolerance) by observing his or her willingness to invest in various portfolios with differing risk and return attributes. With no access to such data, and without perfect insight into the risk-return characteristics of investments, we can only surmise an investor's risk aversion. Note that, explicitly or implicitly, many professional investors do exactly that (although, obviously they do more than just that); by choosing investments on behalf of their clients, they make the risk-return choices for their clients.

A natural place to begin a study of the investment process, therefore, is to specify the investor's objectives with two indicators: *return requirement* and *risk tolerance.* The investor then must reconcile these objectives with what is feasible, since any investor faces several constraints. This means that the objective cannot be set as a hard number, but rather as a set of guidelines as to the choice of assets.

Investor objectives arise from a number of factors. Understanding these factors helps investors determine appropriate objectives. It also makes it easier for professional investors to derive appropriate policies for their clients.

risk tolerance

The investor's willingness to accept higher risk to attain higher expected returns.

risk aversion

The investor's reluctance to accept risk.

Individual Investors

The basic factors affecting an individual investor usually arise from that investor's stage in the life cycle. The first significant investment decision for most individuals concerns education, which is an investment in "human capital." The major asset most people have during their early working years is the earning power derived from their skills. For these people, the financial risk due to illness or injury is far greater than that associated with the rate of return on their portfolios of financial assets. At this point in the life cycle, the most important financial decisions concern insurance against the possibility of disability or death.

On the MARKET FRONT

The first major economic asset many people acquire is their own house. One can view the purchase of a house as a hedge[1] against two types of risk. The first is the risk of increases in rental rates. If you "pay rent to yourself," you do not need to be concerned with increases in the cost of housing. The second kind of risk is that the particular house or apartment where you live may not always be available to you. By buying, you guarantee its availability.

As one ages and accumulates savings to provide for consumption during retirement, the composition of wealth shifts from human capital toward financial capital. At this point, portfolio choices become progressively more important. In middle age, most investors will be willing to take on a meaningful amount of portfolio risk in order to increase their expected rates of return. As retirement draws near, however, risk tolerance seems to diminish.

The evidence in Table 21.1 supports the life-cycle view of investment behavior. Questionnaire results suggest that attitudes shift away from risk tolerance and toward risk aversion as investors near retirement age. With age, individuals lose the potential to recover from a disastrous investment performance. When they are young, investors can respond to a loss by working harder and saving more of their income. But as retirement approaches, investors realize there will be less time to recover, hence, the shift to safe assets.

TABLE 21.1		**Under 25**	**35–54**	**55 and Over**
Amount of risk investors said they were willing to take by age	No risk	54%	55%	71%
	A little risk	30	28	21
	Some risk	14	16	8
	A lot of risk	2	1	1

Source: From Market Facts, Inc., Chicago, IL. Reprinted by permission of Market Facts, Inc.

[1]To hedge means to mitigate a financial risk, a possible loss from a decline in the value of an asset. The return on a hedging asset will be higher when losses from the risk in question are greater. In other words, the return on the hedge asset offsets the risk in question—its returns are inversely related to the exposure from that risk. The greater the negative correlation between the returns on the hedge asset and the risk, the better the hedge. For example, an insurance policy against a specified risk is a perfect hedge, since it is designed precisely to cover a potential loss; its correlation is perfectly negative, -1.

TIME FOR INVESTING'S FOUR-LETTER WORD

What four-letter word should pop into mind when the stock market takes a harrowing nose dive?

No, not those. R-I-S-K.

Risk is the potential for realizing low returns or even losing money, possibly preventing you from meeting important objectives, like sending your kids to the college of their choice or having the retirement lifestyle you crave.

Assessing your risk tolerance, however, can be tricky. You must consider not only how much risk you can *afford* to take but also how much risk you can *stand* to take. Determining how much risk you can stand—your temperamental tolerance for risk—is more difficult. It isn't quantifiable.

To that end, many financial advisers, brokerage firms, and mutual-fund companies have created risk quizzes to help people determine whether they are conservative, moderate, or aggressive investors. Some firms that offer such quizzes include Merrill Lynch, T. Rowe Price Associates Inc., Baltimore, Zurich Group Inc.'s Scudder Kemper Investments Inc., New York, and Vanguard Group in Malvern, Pa.

Typically, risk questionnaires include 7 to 10 questions about a person's investing experience, financial security, and tendency to make risky or conservative choices.

The benefit of the questionnaires is that they are an objective resource people can use to get at least a rough idea of their risk tolerance. "It's impossible for someone to assess their risk tolerance alone," says Mr. Bernstein. "I may say I don't like risk, yet will take more risk than the average person."

Many experts warn, however, that the questionnaires should be used simply as a first step to assessing risk tolerance. The second step, many experts agree, is to ask yourself some difficult questions, such as: How much can you stand to lose over the long term?

"Most people can stand to lose a heck of a lot temporarily," says Mr. Schatsky. The real acid test, he says, is how much of your portfolio's value you can stand to lose over months or years.

As it turns out, most people rank as middle-of-the-road risk-takers, say several advisers. "Only about 10% to 15% of my clients are aggressive," says Mr. Roge.

WHAT'S YOUR RISK TOLERANCE?

Circle the letter that corresponds to your answer.

1. Just 60 days after you put money into an investment, its price falls 20 percent. Assuming none of the fundamentals have changed, what would you do?
   a. Sell to avoid further worry and try something else
   b. Do nothing and wait for the investment to come back
   c. Buy more. It was a good investment before; now it's a cheap investment, too

2. Now look at the previous question another way. Your investment fell 20 percent, but it's part of a portfolio being used to meet investment goals with three different time horizons.

2A. What would you do if the goal were five years away?
   a. Sell
   b. Do nothing
   c. Buy more

2B. What would you do if the goal were 15 years away?
   a. Sell
   b. Do nothing
   c. Buy more

The task of life-cycle financial planning is a formidable one for most people. It is not surprising that a whole industry has sprung up to provide personal financial advice.

Professional Investors

Professional investors provide investment management services for a fee. Some are employed directly by wealthy individual investors. Most professional investors, however, either pool many individual investor funds and manage them or serve institutional investors.

personal trust

An interest in an asset held by a trustee for the benefit of another person.

Personal trusts A **personal trust** is established when an individual confers legal title to property to another person or institution, who then manages that property for one or more beneficiaries. The holder of the title is called the *trustee*. The trustee is usually a bank, a lawyer, or an investment professional. Investment of a trust is subject to state trust laws and *prudent investor rules* that limit the types of allowable trust investment.

The objectives of personal trusts normally are more limited in scope than those of the individual investor. Because of their fiduciary responsibility, personal trust managers typically are expected to invest with more risk aversion than individual investors. Certain asset classes, such as options and futures contracts, for example, and strategies, such as short-selling (betting the

2C. What would you do if the goal were 30 years away?

    a. Sell

    b. Do nothing

    c. Buy more

3. The price of your retirement investment jumps 25% a month after you buy it. Again, the fundamentals haven't changed. After you finish gloating, what do you do?

    a. Sell it and lock in your gains

    b. Stay put and hope for more gain

    c. Buy more: It could go higher

4. You're investing for retirement, which is 15 years away. Which would you rather do?

    a. Invest in a money-market fund or guaranteed investment contract, giving up the possibility of major gains, but virtually assuring the safety of your principal

    b. Invest in a 50-50 mix of bond funds and stock funds, in hopes of getting some growth, but also giving yourself some protection in the form of steady income

    c. Invest in aggressive growth mutual funds whose value will probably fluctuate significantly during the year, but have the potential for impressive gains over five or 10 years

5. You just won a big prize! But which one? It's up to you.

    a. $2,000 in cash

    b. A 50% chance to win $5,000

    c. A 20% chance to win $15,000

6. A good investment opportunity just came along. But you have to borrow money to get in. Would you take out a loan?

    a. Definitely not

    b. Perhaps

    c. Yes

7. Your company is selling stock to its employees. In three years, management plans to take the company public. Until then, you won't be able to sell your shares and you will get no dividends. But your investment could multiply as much as 10 times when the company goes public. How much money would you invest?

    a. None

    b. Two months' salary

    c. Four months' salary

SCORING YOUR RISK TOLERANCE

To score the quiz, add up the number of answers you gave in each category *a–c,* then multiply as shown to find your score:

(*a*) answers _____ × 1 = _____ points

(*b*) answers _____ × 2 = _____ points

(*c*) answers _____ × 3 = _____ points

YOUR SCORE _____ points

If you scored . . .	You may be a:
9–14 points	Conservative investor
15–21 points	Moderate investor
22–27 points	Aggressive investor

price of a security will fall) or buying on margin (borrowing up to 50% of the purchase price), are ruled out. Short sales and margin purchases were discussed in Chapter 3.

Mutual funds **Mutual funds** are firms that manage pools of individual investor money. They invest in accordance with their objectives and issue shares that entitle investors to a pro rata portion of the income generated by the funds.

A mutual fund's objectives are spelled out in its prospectus. We discussed mutual funds in detail in Chapter 4.

mutual fund

A firm pooling and managing funds of investors.

Pension funds There are two basic types of pension plans: *defined contribution* and *defined benefit.* Defined contribution plans are in effect savings accounts established by the firm for its employees. The employer contributes funds to the plan, but the employee bears all the risk of the fund's investment performance. These plans are called defined contribution because the firm's only obligation is to make the stipulated contributions to the employee's retirement account. The employee is responsible for directing the management of the assets, usually by selecting among several investment funds in which the assets can be placed. Investment earnings in these retirement plans are not taxed until the funds are withdrawn, usually after retirement.

In defined benefit plans, by contrast, the employer has an obligation to provide a specified annual retirement benefit. That benefit is defined by a formula that typically takes into account years of service and the level of salary or wages. For example, the employer may pay the retired employee a yearly amount equal to 2% of the employee's final annual salary for each year of service. A 30-year employee would then receive an annual benefit equal to 60% of his or her final salary. The payments are an obligation of the employer, and the assets in the pension fund provide collateral for the promised benefits. If the investment performance of the assets is poor, the firm is obligated to make up the shortfall by contributing additional assets to the fund. In contrast to defined contribution plans, the risk surrounding investment performance in defined benefit plans is borne by the firm.

A pension actuary makes an assumption about the rate of return that will be earned on the plan's assets and uses this assumed rate to compute the amount the firm must contribute regularly to fund the plan's liabilities. For example, if the actuary assumes a rate of return of 10%, then the firm must contribute $385.54 now to fund $1,000 of pension liabilities that will arise in 10 years, because $385.54 \times 1.10^{10} = $1,000$.

If a pension fund's *actual* rate of return exceeds the actuarial *assumed* rate, then the firm's shareholders reap an unanticipated gain, because the excess return can be used to reduce future contributions. If the plan's actual rate of return falls short of the assumed rate, however, the firm will have to increase future contributions. Because the sponsoring firm's shareholders bear the risk in a defined benefit pension plan, the objective of the plan will be consistent with the objective of the firm's shareholders.

Many pension plans view their assumed actuarial rate of return as their target rate of return and have little tolerance for earning less than that. Hence, they will take only as much risk as necessary to earn the actuarial rate.

Life Insurance Companies

Life insurance companies generally invest so as to hedge their liabilities, which are defined by the policies they write. The company can reduce its risk by investing in assets that will return more in the event the insurance policy coverage becomes more expensive.

For example, if the company writes a policy that pays a death benefit linked to the consumer price index, then the company is subject to inflation risk. It might search for assets expected to return more when the rate of inflation rises, thus hedging the price-index linkage of the policy.

There are as many objectives as there are distinct types of insurance policies. Until the 1970s, only two types of life insurance policies were available for individuals: whole-life and term.

A *whole-life insurance policy* combines a death benefit with a kind of savings plan that provides for a gradual buildup of cash value that the policyholder can withdraw later in life, usually at age 65. *Term insurance,* on the other hand, provides death benefits only, with no buildup of cash value.

The interest rate embedded in the schedule of cash value accumulation promised under the whole-life policy is a fixed rate. One way life insurance companies try to hedge this liability is by investing in long-term bonds. Often the insured individual has the right to borrow at a prespecified fixed interest rate against the cash value of the policy.

During the high-interest-rate years of the 1970s and early 1980s, many older whole-life policies allowed policyholders to borrow at rates as low as 4 or 5% per year; some holders borrowed heavily against the cash value to invest in assets paying double-digit yields. Other actual and potential policyholders abandoned whole-life policies and took out term insurance, which accounted for more than half the volume of new sales of individual life policies.

In response to these developments, the insurance industry came up with two new policy types: variable life and universal life. A *variable life policy* entitles the insured to a fixed death benefit plus a cash value that can be invested in the policyholder's choice of mutual funds. A *universal life policy* allows policyholders to increase or reduce either the insurance premium (the annual fee paid on the policy) or the death benefit (the cash amount paid to beneficiaries in the event of death) according to their changing needs. Furthermore, the interest rate on the cash value component changes with market interest rates.

21.5 MONITORING AND REVISING INVESTMENT PORTFOLIOS

Choosing the investment portfolio requires the investor to set objectives, acknowledge constraints, determine asset-class proportions, and perform security analysis. Is the process ever finished and behind us? By the time we have completed all of these steps, many of the inputs we have used will be out of date. Moreover, our circumstances as well as our objectives change over time. Therefore, the investment process requires that we continually monitor and update our portfolios.

Moreover, even if our circumstances do not change, our portfolios necessarily will. For example, suppose you currently hold 1,000 shares of ExxonMobil, selling at $65 a share, and 1,000 shares of Microsoft, selling at $80 a share. If the price of ExxonMobil falls to $50 a share, while that of Microsoft rises to $90 a share, the fractions of your portfolio allocated to each security change without your taking any direct action. The value of your investment in ExxonMobil is now lower, and the value of the Microsoft investment is higher. Unless you are happy with this reallocation of investment proportions, you will need to take some action to restore the portfolio weights to desired levels.

Asset allocation also will change over time, as the investment performance of different asset classes diverges. If the stock market outperforms the bond market, the proportion of your portfolio invested in stocks will increase, while the proportion invested in bonds will decrease. If you are uncomfortable with this shift in the asset mix, you must rebalance the portfolio by selling some of the stocks and purchasing bonds.

Therefore, investing is a *dynamic process,* meaning that you must continually update and reevaluate your decisions over time.

SUMMARY

- The CFA Institute has developed a systematic framework for the translation of investor goals to investment strategy. Its three main parts are: objectives, constraints, and policy. Investor objectives include the return requirement and risk tolerance, reflecting the overriding concern of investment with the risk-return trade-off. Investor constraints include liquidity requirements, investment horizon, regulatory concerns, tax obligations, and the unique needs of various investors. Investment policies specify the portfolio manager's asset allocation and security selection decisions.

- Major institutional investors include pension funds, mutual funds, life insurance companies, non-life-insurance companies, banks, and endowment funds. For individual investors, life-cycle concerns are the most important factor in setting objectives, constraints, and policies.

- Major asset classes include: cash (money market assets), fixed-income securities (bonds), stocks, real estate, precious metals, and collectibles. Asset allocation refers to the decision made as to the investment proportion to be allocated to each asset class. An active asset allocation strategy calls for the production of frequent market forecasts and the adjustment of asset allocation according to these forecasts.

- Active security selection requires security analysis and portfolio choice. Analysis of individual securities is required to choose securities that will make up a coherent portfolio and outperform a passive benchmark.

- Perhaps the most important feature of the investment process is that it is dynamic. Portfolios must be continually monitored and updated. The frequency and timing of various decisions are in themselves important decisions. Successful investment management requires management of these dynamic aspects.

KEY TERMS

asset universe, 692	liquidity, 688	prudent investor rule, 688
endowment funds, 687	mutual funds, 685	risk aversion, 682
investment horizon, 688	personal trust, 684	risk tolerance, 682

www.mhhe.com/bkm

PROBLEM SETS

**Select problems are available in McGraw-Hill's Homework Manager®.
Please see the packaging options section of the preface for more information.**

1. Your client says, "With the unrealized gains in my portfolio, I have almost saved enough money for my daughter to go to college in eight years, but educational costs keep going up." Based on this statement alone, which one of the following appears to be least important to your client's investment policy?

    a. Time horizon.

    b. Purchasing power risk.

    c. Liquidity.

    d. Taxes.

2. The aspect least likely to be included in the portfolio management process is

    a. Identifying an investor's objectives, constraints, and preferences.

    b. Organizing the management process itself.

    c. Implementing strategies regarding the choice of assets to be used.

    d. Monitoring market conditions, relative values, and investor circumstances.

3. A clearly written investment policy statement is critical for

    a. Mutual funds

    b. Individuals

    c. Pension funds

    d. All investors

4. The investment policy statement of an institution must be concerned with all of the following *except:*

    a. Its obligations to its clients.

    b. The level of the market.

    c. Legal regulations.

    d. Taxation.

5. Under the provisions of a typical corporate defined-benefit pension plan, the employer is responsible for:

    a. Paying benefits to retired employees.

    b. Investing in conservative fixed-income assets.

    c. Counseling employees in the selection of asset classes.

    d. Maintaining an actuarially determined, fully funded pension plan.

6. Which of the following statements reflects the importance of the asset allocation decision to the investment process? The asset allocation decision:

    a. Helps the investor decide on realistic investment goals.

    b. Identifies the specific securities to include in a portfolio.

    c. Determines most of the portfolio's returns and volatility over time.

    d. Creates a standard by which to establish an appropriate investment time horizon.

7. You are a portfolio manager and senior executive vice president of Advisory Securities Selection, Inc. Your firm has been invited to meet with the trustees of the Wood Museum Endowment Funds. Wood Museum is a privately endowed charitable institution that is dependent on the investment return from a $25 million endowment fund to balance the budget. The treasurer of the museum has recently completed the budget that indicates a need for cash flow of $3 million in 2009, $3.2 million in 2010, and $3.5 million in 2011 from the endowment fund to balance the budget in those years. Currently, the entire endowment portfolio is invested in Treasury bills and money market funds because the trustees fear a financial crisis. The trustees do not anticipate any further capital contributions to the fund.

    The trustees are all successful businesspeople, and they have been critical of the fund's previous investment advisers because they did not follow a logical decision-making process. In fact, several previous managers have been dismissed because of their inability to communicate with the trustees and their preoccupation with the fund's relative performance rather than the cash flow needs.

Advisory Securities Selection, Inc., has been contacted by the trustees because of its reputation for understanding and relating to the client's needs. The trustees have asked you, as a prospective portfolio manager for the Wood Museum Endowment Fund, to prepare a written report in response to the following questions. Your report will be circulated to the trustees before the initial interview on June 15, 2009.

Explain in detail how each of the following relates to the determination of either investor objectives or investor constraints that can be used to determine the portfolio policies for this three-year period for the Wood Museum Endowment Fund.

a. Liquidity requirements.

b. Return requirements.

c. Risk tolerance.

d. Time horizon.

e. Tax considerations.

f. Regulatory and legal considerations.

g. Unique needs and circumstances.

8. Mrs. Mary Atkins, age 66, has been your firm's client for five years, since the death of her husband, Dr. Charles Atkins. Dr. Atkins had built a successful newspaper business that he sold two years before his death to Merit Enterprises, a publishing and broadcasting conglomerate, in exchange for Merit common stock. The Atkinses have no children, and their wills provide that upon their deaths the remaining assets shall be used to create a fund for the benefit of Good Samaritan Hospital, to be called the Atkins Endowment Fund.

Good Samaritan is a 180-bed, not-for-profit hospital with an annual operating budget of $12.5 million. In the past, the hospital's operating revenues have often been sufficient to meet operating expenses and occasionally even generate a small surplus. In recent years, however, rising costs and declining occupancy rates have caused Good Samaritan to run a deficit. The operating deficit has averaged $300,000 to $400,000 annually over the last several years. Existing endowment assets (that is, excluding the Atkins's estate) of $7.5 million currently generate approximately $375,000 of annual income, up from less than $200,000 five years ago. This increased income has been the result of somewhat higher interest rates, as well as a shift in asset mix toward more bonds. To offset operating deficits, the Good Samaritan Board of Governors has determined that the endowment's current income should be increased to approximately 6% of total assets (up from 5% currently). The hospital has not received any significant additions to its endowment assets in the past five years.

Identify and describe an appropriate set of investment objectives and constraints for the Atkins Endowment Fund to be created after Mrs. Atkins's death.

9. Several discussion meetings have provided the following information about one of your firm's new advisory clients, a charitable endowment fund recently created by means of a one-time $10 million gift:

Objectives

Return requirement. Planning is based on a minimum total return of 8% per year, including an initial current income component of $500,000 (5% on beginning capital). Realizing this current income target is the endowment fund's primary return goal. (See "unique needs" below.)

Constraints

Time horizon. Perpetuity, except for requirement to make an $8,500,000 cash distribution on June 30, 2010. (See "unique needs.")

Liquidity needs. None of a day-to-day nature until 2010. Income is distributed annually after year-end. (See "unique needs.")

Tax considerations. None; this endowment fund is exempt from taxes.

Legal and regulatory considerations. Minimal, but the prudent investor rule applies to all investment actions.

Unique needs, circumstances, and preferences. The endowment fund must pay out to another tax-exempt entity the sum of $8,500,000 in cash on June 30, 2010. The assets remaining after this distribution will be retained by the fund in perpetuity. The endowment fund has adopted a "spending rule" requiring a first-year current income payout of $500,000; thereafter, the annual payout is to rise by 3% in real terms. Until 2010, annual income in excess of that required by the spending rule is to be reinvested. After 2010, the spending rate will be reset at 5% of the then-existing capital.

With this information and information found in this chapter, do the following:

a. Formulate an appropriate investment policy statement for the endowment fund.

b. Identify and briefly explain three major ways in which your firm's initial asset allocation decisions for the endowment fund will be affected by the circumstances of the account.

10. You have been named as investment adviser to a foundation established by Dr. Walter Jones with an original contribution consisting entirely of the common stock of Jomedco, Inc. Founded by Dr. Jones, Jomedco manufactures and markets medical devices invented by the doctor and collects royalties on other patented innovations.

    All of the shares that made up the initial contribution to the foundation were sold at a public offering of Jomedco common stock, and the $5 million proceeds will be delivered to the foundation within the next week. At the same time, Mrs. Jones will receive $5 million in proceeds from the sale of her stock in Jomedco.

    Dr. Jones's purpose in establishing the Jones Foundation was to "offset the effect of inflation on medical school tuition for the maximum number of worthy students."

    You are preparing for a meeting with the foundation trustees to discuss investment policy and asset allocation.

    a. Define and give examples that show the differences between an investment objective, an investment constraint, and investment policy.

    b. Identify and describe an appropriate set of investment objectives and investment constraints for the Jones Foundation.

    c. Based on the investment objectives and investment constraints identified in part *b,* prepare a comprehensive investment policy statement for the Jones Foundation to be recommended for adoption by the trustees.

11. You are P. J. Walter, CFA, a managing partner of a prestigious investment counseling firm that specializes in individual rather than institutional accounts. The firm has developed a national reputation for its ability to blend modern portfolio theory and traditional portfolio methods. You have written a number of articles on portfolio management. You are an authority on the subject of establishing investment policies and programs for individual clients, tailored to their particular circumstances and needs.

    Dr. and Mrs. A. J. Mason have been referred to your firm and to you in particular. At your first meeting on June 2, 2006, Dr. Mason explained that he is an electrical engineer and long-time professor at the Essex Institute. He is also an inventor, and, after 30 years of teaching, the rights to one of his patented inventions, the "inverse thermothrocle valve," have just been acquired by a new electronics company, ACS, Inc.

    In anticipation of the potential value of his invention, Dr. Mason had followed his accountant's advice and established a private corporation, wholly owned by the Masons, to hold the title to the inverse thermothrocle valve patent. It was this corporation that ACS acquired from the Masons for $1 million in cash, payable at the closing on June 7, 2006. In addition, ACS has agreed to pay royalties to Dr. Mason or his heirs based on its sales of systems that utilize the inverse thermothrocle valve.

    Since ACS has no operating record, it is difficult for either the company or Dr. Mason to forecast future sales and royalties. While all parties are optimistic about prospects for success, they are also mindful of the risks associated with any new firm, especially those exposed to the technological obsolescence of the electronics industry. The management of ACS has indicated to Dr. Mason that he might expect royalties of as much as $100,000 in the first year of production and maximum royalties of as much as $500,000 annually thereafter.

During your counseling meeting, Mrs. Mason expressed concern for the proper investment of the $1,000,000 initial payment. She pointed out that Dr. Mason has invested all of their savings in his inventions. Thus, they will have only their Social Security retirement benefits and a small pension from the Essex Institute to provide for their retirement. Dr. Mason will be 65 in 2010. His salary from the Essex Institute is $55,000 per year. Additionally, he expects to continue earning $10,000–$25,000 annually from consulting and speaking engagements.

The Masons have two daughters and a son, all of whom are married and have families of their own. Dr. and Mrs. Mason are interested in helping with the education of their grandchildren and have provided in their wills for their estate to be divided among their children and grandchildren.

In the event that the royalty payments from ACS meet the projections cited above, Mrs. Mason is interested in providing a scholarship fund in the name of Dr. Mason for the benefit of enterprising young engineers attending the Essex Institute. The scholarship fund ranks third behind the provision for the Masons' retirement and for the education of their grandchildren.

In your discussions with Dr. and Mrs. Mason, you have stressed the importance of identifying investment objectives and constraints and having an appropriate investment policy. Identify and describe an appropriate set of investment objectives and investment constraints for Dr. and Mrs. Mason, and prepare a comprehensive investment policy statement based on these investment objectives and constraints.

12. You are being interviewed for a job as a portfolio manager at an investment counseling partnership. As part of the interview, you are asked to demonstrate your ability to develop investment portfolio policy statements for the clients listed below:

   a. A pension fund that is described as a mature defined-benefit plan; with the workforce having an average age of 54; no unfunded pension liabilities; and wage cost increases forecast at 9% annually.

   b. A university endowment fund that is described as conservative; with investment returns being utilized along with gifts and donations received to meet current expenses, the spending rate is 5% per year; and inflation in costs is expected at 8% annually.

   c. A life insurance company that is described as specializing in annuities; policy premium rates are based on a minimum annual accumulation rate of 14% in the first year of the policy and a 10% minimum annual accumulation rate in the next five years.

   List and discuss separately for *each* client described above the objectives and constraints that will determine the portfolio policy you would recommend for that client.

WEB *master*

Personal Diversification

Go to **www.money.com/money/depts/retirement** and find the calculator for diversifying your portfolio. When you work in a given industry, investing in other industries may be effective in diversifying your overall economic well-being. This calculator shows good and bad choices for diversification for employees of different industries.

For each of the following industries, what are the 10 best and 10 worst industries for diversification: oil and gas (drilling and equipment); homebuilding; electronics (semiconductor).

1. Are the industries identified as best and worst diversifiers considerably different for these three industries?

2. Contrast the features that seem to characterize the diversification attributes of these industries.

21.1. A convenient and effective way to organize the answer to this question is to cast it in the context of the investment policy statement framework.

Risk: Endowment funds have no "safety nets" such as pension funds enjoy in the event of difficulty, either in the form of corporate assets to fall back on or a call on public assistance, such as from the Pension Benefit Guaranty Corporation. Moreover, endowment fund cash flows may be highly erratic due to the uncertain timing of income from gifts and/or bequests, while pension fund cash flows tend to be very predictable and steady. These differences suggest the typical endowment fund will adopt a more conservative risk-bearing posture than will the typical pension fund, both as to asset-class exposures and to the type of security content of such exposures.

Return: Because investment-related spending usually is limited to "income yield," endowment funds often focus their return goals on the matter of current spendable income; pension funds, on the other hand, tend to adopt total return approaches, at least until a plan matures. Although inflation protection should be of great importance to both types of funds, endowment funds appear to be less concerned with real return production than are pension funds, perhaps because of their common emphasis on "income now" in setting return goals.

Time horizon: Theoretically, an endowment fund is a perpetuity while a pension fund may well have a finite life span. Therefore, an endowment fund should operate with a very long-term view of investment. However, such funds in practice tend to adopt shorter horizons than are typical of pension funds (just as they typically assume less risk). Their tendency to emphasize income production in the near term is the probable reason for this common occurrence.

Liquidity: Endowment funds, particularly those that use gifts and bequests to supplement their investment income, often have fairly large liquidity reserves—both to protect against fluctuations in their cash flows and reflecting their generally conservative outlooks—while, except for very mature plans, pension funds tend to require minimum liquidity reserves. Endowment funds also frequently maintain substantial liquid holdings to provide for known future cash payout requirements, such as for new buildings.

Taxes: Here, although differing in detail, the situations of the two forms of institutions are very much the same. In the United States, tax considerations are normally of minimal importance in both cases.

Regulatory/Legal: Endowment fund investment is carried out under state governance, while pension fund investment, in the United States, is carried out under federal law, specifically under ERISA. The difference is significant. Endowment funds operate under the prudent investor rule, whereby each investment must be judged on its own merits apart from any other portfolio holdings, while pension plans operate under a broader context for investment—each security being judged in terms of the portfolio as a whole—and an ERISA-mandated diversification requirement that often leads to wider asset-class exposures.

Unique circumstances: Endowment funds often are faced with unique situations that sometimes affect pension fund management, including the scrutiny of such special-interest groups as trustees, alumni, faculty, student organizations, local community pressure groups, etc., each with separate and often incompatible constraints and goals that may need to be accommodated in policy setting and/or in investment content. Similarly, endowment funds may be subjected to severe "social pressures" that, as in the case of tobacco firm divestment, can have an important investment impact by restricting the available universe of investment securities, mandating participation or nonparticipation in certain industries, sectors, or countries, or otherwise changing investment action from what it would otherwise have been. In pension fund investment, ERISA requires that no other interests be put ahead of the interests of the beneficiaries in determining investment actions.

21.2. Identify the elements that are life-cycle driven in the two schemes of objectives and constraints.

21.3. *a.* Policy, asset allocation.

b. Constraint, regulation.

c. Objective, return requirement.

d. Constraint, horizon.

e. Policy, market timing.

f. Constraint, taxes.

g. Objectives, risk tolerance.

h. Constraint, liquidity.

REFERENCES

Affleck-Graves, John, and Richard R. Mendenhall. "The Relation between the Value Line Enigma and Post-Earnings-Announcement Drift." *Journal of Financial Economics* 31 (February 1992), pp. 75–96.

Alexander, C. *Market Models.* Chichester, England: Wiley, 2001.

Alexander, Sidney. "Price Movements in Speculative Markets: Trends or Random Walks, No. 2." In *The Random Character of Stock Market Prices,* ed. Paul Cootner. Cambridge, MA: MIT Press, 1964.

Amihud, Yakov, and Haim Mendelson. "Asset Pricing and the Bid-Ask Spread." *Journal of Financial Economics* 17 (December 1986), pp. 223–50.

———. "Liquidity, Asset Prices, and Financial Policy." *Financial Analysts Journal* 47 (November/ December 1991), pp. 56–66.

Arbel, Avner. "Generic Stocks: An Old Product in a New Package." *Journal of Portfolio Management,* Summer 1985, pp. 4–13.

Arbel, Avner, and Paul J. Strebel. "Pay Attention to Neglected Firms." *Journal of Portfolio Management,* Winter 1983, pp. 37–42.

Arnott, Robert. "Orthodoxy Overwrought." *Institutional Investor,* December 18, 2006.

Asness, Cliff. "The Value of Fundamental Indexing." *Institutional Investor,* October 16, 2006, pp. 94–99.

Ball, R., and P. Brown. "An Empirical Evaluation of Accounting Income Numbers." *Journal of Accounting Research* 9 (1968), pp. 159–78.

Banz, Rolf. "The Relationship between Return and Market Value of Common Stocks." *Journal of Financial Economics* 9 (March 1981), pp. 3–18.

Barber, B.; R. Lehavy; M. McNichols; and B. Trueman. "Can Investors Profit from the Prophets? Security Analysts Recommendations and Stock Returns." *Journal of Finance* 56 (April 2001), pp. 531–63.

Barber, Brad, and Terrance Odean. "Trading Is Hazardous to Your Wealth: The Common Stock Investment Performance of Individual Investors." *Journal of Finance* 55 (2000), pp. 773–806.

———. "Boys Will Be Boys: Gender, Overconfidence, and Common Stock Investment." *Quarterly Journal of Economics* 16 (2001), pp. 262–92.

Barberis, Nicholas, and Richard Thaler. "A Survey of Behavioral Finance." In *The Handbook of the Economics of Finance,* ed. G. M. Constantinides, M. Harris, and R. Stulz. Amsterdam: Elsevier, 2003.

Basu, Sanjoy. "The Investment Performance of Common Stocks in Relation to Their Price-Earnings Ratios: A Test of the Efficient Market Hypothesis." *Journal of Finance* 32 (June 1977), pp. 663–82.

———. "The Relationship between Earnings Yield, Market Value, and Return for NYSE Common Stocks: Further Evidence." *Journal of Financial Economics* 12 (June 1983), pp. 129–56.

Battalio, R. H., and R. Mendenhall. "Earnings Expectation, Investor Trade Size, and Anomalous Returns around Earnings Announcements." *Journal of Financial Economics* 77 (2005), pp. 289–319.

Benveniste, Lawrence, and William Wilhelm. "Initial Public Offerings: Going by the Book." *Journal of Applied Corporate Finance* 10 (March 1997), pp. 98–108.

Bergstresser, D.; M. Desai; and J. Rauh. "Earnings Manipulation, Pension Assumptions, and Managerial Investment Decisions." *Quarterly Journal of Economics* 121 (2006), pp. 157–95.

Bernard, Victor L., and Jacob K. Thomas. "Post-Earnings-Announcement Drift: Delayed Price Response or Risk Premium?" *Journal of Accounting Research* 27 (1989), pp. 1–36.

Bernard, V., and J. Thomas. "Evidence That Stock Prices Do Not Fully Reflect the Implications of Current Earnings for Future Earnings." *Journal of Accounting and Economics* 13 (1990), pp. 305–40.

Bernhard, Arnold. *Value Line Methods of Evaluating Common Stocks.* New York: Arnold Bernhard, 1979.

Black, Fischer. "Yes, Virginia, There Is Hope: Tests of the Value Line Ranking System." Graduate School of Business, University of Chicago, 1971.

Black, Fischer; Michael C. Jensen; and Myron Scholes. "The Capital Asset Pricing Model: Some Empirical Tests." *Studies in the Theory of Capital Markets,* ed. Michael C. Jensen. New York: Praeger, 1972.

Black, Fischer, and Myron Scholes. "The Pricing of Options and Corporate Liabilities." *Journal of Political Economy* 81 (May–June 1973), pp. 637–59.

From Black-Scholes to Black Holes: New Frontiers in Options. London: *RISK Magazine,* 1992.

Blake, Christopher; Edwin J. Elton; and Martin J. Gruber. "The Performance of Bond Mutual Funds." *Journal of Business* 66 (July 1993), pp. 371–404.

Blume, Marshall E., and Robert F. Stambaugh. "Biases in Computed Returns: An Application to the Size Effect." *Journal of Finance Economics,* 1983, pp. 387–404.

Bogle, John C. "Investing in the 1990s: Remembrance of Things Past, and Things Yet to Come." *Journal of Portfolio Management,* Spring 1991, pp. 5–14.

———. *Bogle on Mutual Funds.* Burr Ridge, IL: Irwin, 1994.

Brav, Alon; Christopher Geczy; and Paul A. Gompers. "Is the Abnormal Return Following Equity Issuances Anomalous?" *Journal of Financial Economics* 56 (2000), pp. 209–49.

Brennan, Michael. "Taxes, Market Valuation and Corporate Financial Policy." *National Tax Journal,* 1970.

Brinson, G.; C. R. Hood; and G. Beebower. "Determinants of Portfolio Performance." *Financial Analysts Journal,* July–August 1986.

Brock, William; Josef Lakonishok; and Blake LeBaron. "Simple Technical Trading Rules and the Stochastic Properties of Stock Returns." *Journal of Finance* 47 (December 1992), pp. 1731–64.

Brown, David, and Robert H. Jennings. "On Technical Analysis." *Review of Financial Studies* 2 (1989), pp. 527–52.

Brown, Lawrence D., and Michael Rozeff. "The Superiority of Analysts' Forecasts as Measures of Expectations: Evidence from Earnings." *Journal of Finance,* March 1978.

Brown. S. J.; W. Goetzmann; R. G. Ibbotson; and S. A. Ross. "Survivorship Bias in Performance Studies." *Review of Financial Studies* 5 (1992).

Busse, J. A., and T. C. Green. "Market Efficiency in Real Time." *Journal of Financial Economics* 65 (2002), pp. 415–37.

Campbell, John Y., and Robert Shiller. "Stock Prices, Earnings and Expected Dividends." *Journal of Finance* 43 (July 1988), pp. 661–76.

Carhart, Mark. "On Persistence in Mutual Fund Performance." *Journal of Finance* 52 (1997), pp. 57–82.

Chen, Nai-fu; Richard Roll; and Stephen Ross. "Economic Forces and the Stock Market." *Journal of Business* 59 (1986), pp. 383–403.

Chopra, Navin; Josef Lakonishok; and Jay R. Ritter. "Measuring Abnormal Performance: Do Stocks Overreact?" *Journal of Financial Economics* 31 (1992), pp. 235–68.

Clarke, Roger, and Mark P. Kritzman. *Currency Management: Concepts and Practices.* Charlottesville: Research Foundation of the Institute of Chartered Financial Analysts, 1996.

Clayman, Michelle. "In Search of Excellence: The Investor's Viewpoint." *Financial Analysts Journal,* May–June 1987.

Connolly, Robert. "An Examination of the Robustness of the Weekend Effect." *Journal of Financial and Quantitative Analysis* 24 (June 1989), pp. 133–69.

Conrad, Jennifer, and Gautam Kaul. "Time-Variation in Expected Returns." *Journal of Business* 61 (October 1988), pp. 409–25.

Copeland, Thomas E., and David Mayers. "The Value Line Enigma (1965–1978): A Case Study of Performance Evaluation Issues." *Journal of Financial Economics,* November 1982.

Coval, Joshua D., and Tyler Shumway. "Do Behavioral Biases Affect Prices?" *Journal of Finance* 60 (February 2005), pp. 1–34.

Davis, James L.; Eugene F. Fama; and Kenneth R. French. "Characteristics, Covariances, and Average Returns, 1929 to 1997." *Journal of Finance* 55 (2000), pp. 389–406.

De Bondt, W. F. M., and R. H. Thaler. "Does the Stock Market Overreact?" *Journal of Finance* 40 (1985), pp. 793–805.

———. "Further Evidence on Investor Overreaction and Stock Market Seasonality." *Journal of Finance* 42 (1987), pp. 557–81.

———. "Do Security Analysts Overreact?" *American Economic Review* 80 (1990), pp. 52–57.

———. "Financial Decision Making in Markets and Firms." In *Handbooks in Operations Research and Management Science, Vol. 9: Finance,* ed. R. A. Jarrow, V. Maksimovic, and W. T. Ziemba. Amsterdam: Elsevier, 1995.

DeLong, J. Bradford; Andrei Schleifer; Lawrence Summers; and Robert Waldmann. "Noise Trader Risk in Financial Markets." *Journal of Political Economy* 98 (August 1990), pp. 704–38.

DeMarzo, Peter M., Ron Kaniel, and Ilan Kremer, "Diversification as a Public Good: Community Effects in Portfolio Choice," *Journal of Finance* 59 (August 2004), pp. 1677–1716.

de Soto, Hernando. *The Mystery of Capital: Why Capitalism Triumphs in the West and Fails Everywhere Else.* New York: Basic Books, 2000.

Dimson, E.; P. R. Marsh; and M. Staunton. *Millennium Book II: 101 Years of Investment Returns.* London: ABN-Amro and London Business School, 2001.

Douglas, George W. "Risk in Equity Markets: An Empirical Appraisal of Market Efficiency." *Yale Economic Essays* IX (Spring 1969).

Dunn, Patricia, and Rolf D. Theisen. "How Consistently Do Active Managers Win?" *Journal of Portfolio Management* 9 (Summer 1983), pp. 47–53.

Elton, E. J.; M. J. Gruber; S. Das; and M. Hlavka. "Efficiency with Costly Information: A Reinterpretation of Evidence from Managed Portfolios." *Review of Financial Studies* 6 (1993), pp. 1–22.

Errunza, Vihang, and Etienne Losq. "International Asset Pricing under Mild Segmentation: Theory and Test." *Journal of Finance* 40 (March 1985), pp. 105–24.

Fama, Eugene. "The Behavior of Stock Market Prices." *Journal of Business* 38 (January 1965), pp. 34–105.

———. "Market Efficiencies, Long-Term Returns, and Behavioral Finance." *Journal of Financial Economics* 49 (September 1998), pp. 283–306.

Fama, Eugene, and Marshall Blume. "Filter Rules and Stock Market Trading Profits." *Journal of Business* 39 (Supplement, January 1966), pp. 226–41.

Fama, Eugene F., and Kenneth R. French. "Permanent and Temporary Components of Stock Prices." *Journal of Political Economy* 96 (1988), pp. 246–73.

————. "Dividend Yields and Expected Stock Returns." *Journal of Financial Economics* 22 (October 1988), pp. 3–25.

————. "Business Conditions and Expected Returns on Stocks and Bonds." *Journal of Financial Economics* 25 (November 1989), pp. 3–22.

————. "The Cross Section of Expected Stock Returns." *Journal of Finance* 47 (June 1992), pp. 427–65.

————. "Common Risk Factors in the Returns on Stocks and Bonds." *Journal of Financial Economics* 33 (1993), pp. 3–56.

————. "Multifactor Explanations of Asset Pricing Anomalies." *Journal of Finance* 51 (1996), pp. 55–84.

————. "The Equity Premium." *Journal of Finance* 57 (April 2002), pp. 637–60.

Fama, Eugene, and James MacBeth. "Risk, Return and Equilibrium: Empirical Tests." *Journal of Political Economy* 81 (March 1973).

Fisher, Irving. *The Theory of Interest: As Determined by Impatience to Spend Income and Opportunity to Invest It.* New York: Augustus M. Kelley, 1965, originally published in 1930.

Flannery, Mark J., and Christopher M. James. "The Effect of Interest Rate Changes on the Common Stock Returns of Financial Institutions." *Journal of Finance* 39 (September 1984), pp. 1141–54.

Foster, George; Chris Olsen; and Terry Shevlin. "Earnings Releases, Anomalies, and the Behavior of Security Returns." *The Accounting Review* 59 (October 1984).

French, Kenneth. "Stock Returns and the Weekend Effect." *Journal of Financial Economics* 8 (March 1980), pp. 55–69.

Froot, K. A., and E. M. Dabora. "How Are Stock Prices Affected by the Location of Trade?" *Journal of Financial Economics* 53 (1999), pp. 189–216.

Gervais, S., and T. Odean. "Learning to Be Overconfident." *Review of Financial Studies* 14 (2001), pp. 1–27.

Geske, Robert, and Richard Roll. "On Valuing American Call Options with the Black-Scholes European Formula." *Journal of Finance* 39 (June 1984), pp. 443–56.

Ghysels, E.; A. Harvey; and E. Renault. "Stochastic Volatility." In *Statistical Methods in Finance,* ed. C. Rao and G. Maddala. Amsterdam: Elsevier Science, North-Holland Series in Statistics and Probability, 1996.

Gibbons, Michael, and Patrick Hess. "Day of the Week Effects and Asset Returns." *Journal of Business* 54 (October 1981), pp. 579–98.

Givoly, Dan, and Dan Palmon. "Insider Trading and Exploitation of Inside Information: Some Empirical Evidence." *Journal of Business* 58 (1985), pp. 69–87.

Goetzmann, William N., and Roger G. Ibbotson. "Do Winners Repeat?" *Journal of Portfolio Management,* Winter 1994, pp. 9–18.

Graham, J. R., and C. R. Harvey. "Expectations of Equity Risk Premia, Volatility and Asymmetry from a Corporate Finance Perspective." Working Paper, Duke University, Fuqua School of Business, November 2001.

————. "Grading the Performance of Market Timing Newsletters." *Financial Analysts Journal* 53 (November/December 1997), pp. 54–66.

Grieves, Robin, and Alan J. Marcus. "Riding the Yield Curve: Reprise." *Journal of Portfolio Management,* Winter 1992.

Grinblatt, Mark, and Bing Han. "The Disposition Effect and Momentum." Working Paper, UCLA, 2001.

————. "Prospect Theory, Mental Accounting, and Momentum." *Journal of Financial Economics* 78 (November 2005), pp. 311–39.

Grinblatt, Mark, and Sheridan Titman. "Mutual Fund Performance: An Analysis of Quarterly Portfolio Holdings." *Journal of Business* 62 (1989), pp. 393–416.

Grossman, Sanford J., and Joseph E. Stiglitz. "On the Impossibility of Informationally Efficient Markets." *American Economic Review* 70 (June 1980), pp. 393–408.

Haugen, Robert A. *The New Finance: The Case Against Efficient Markets.* Englewood Cliffs, NJ: Prentice Hall, 1995.

Hendricks, Darryll; Jayendu Patel; and Richard Zeckhauser. "Hot Hands in Mutual Funds: Short-Run Persistence of Relative Performance, 1974–1988." *Journal of Finance* 43 (March 1993), pp. 93–130.

Henriksson, Roy D. "Market Timing and Mutual Fund Performance: An Empirical Investigation." *Journal of Business* 57 (January 1984).

Heston, S. L. "A Closed-Form Solution for Options with Stochastic Volatility with Applications to Bonds and Currency Options." *Review of Financial Studies* 6 (1993), pp. 327–43.

Hirshleifer, David. "Investor Psychology and Asset Pricing." *Journal of Finance* 56 (August 2001), pp. 1533–97.

Homer, Sidney, and Martin L. Leibowitz. *Inside the Yield Book: New Tools for Bond Market Strategy.* Englewood Cliffs, NJ: Prentice Hall, 1972.

Hull, J. C., and A. White. "The Pricing of Options on Assets with Stochastic Volatilities." *Journal of Finance* 42 (1987), pp. 281–300.

Ibbotson, Roger G. "Price Performance of Common Stock New Issues." *Journal of Financial Economics* 2 (September 1975).

Ibbotson, Roger; Richard C. Carr; and Anthony W. Robinson. "International Equity and Bond Returns." *Financial Analysts Journal,* July–August 1982.

Ibbotson, R. G., and L. B. Siegel. "The World Market Wealth Portfolio." *Journal of Portfolio Management,* Winter 1983.

Ibbotson, R. G.; L. B. Siegel; and K. Love. "World Wealth: Market Values and Returns." *Journal of Portfolio Management,* Fall 1985.

Jacquier, Eric, and Alan Marcus. "Asset Allocation Models and Market Volatility." *Financial Analysts Journal* 57 (March/April 2001), pp. 16–30.

Jaffe, Jeffrey F. "Special Information and Insider Trading." *Journal of Business* 47 (July 1974), pp. 410–28.

————. "Gold and Gold Stocks as Investments for Institutional Portfolios." *Financial Analysts Journal* 45 (March–April 1989), pp. 53–59.

Jagannathan, R.; E. R. McGrattan; and A. Scherbina. "The Declining U.S. Equity Premium." *Federal Reserve Bank of Minneapolis Quarterly Review* 24 (Fall 2000), pp. 3–19.

Jagannathan, Ravi, and Zhenyu Wang. "The Conditional CAPM and the Cross-Section of Expected Returns." *Staff Report 208,* Federal Reserve Bank of Minneapolis, 1996.

Jegadeesh, Narasimhan. "Evidence of Predictable Behavior of Security Returns." *Journal of Finance* 45 (September 1990), pp. 881–98.

Jegadeesh, N.; J. Kim; S. D. Krische; and C. M. Lee. "Analyzing the Analysts: When Do Recommendations Add Value?" *Journal of Finance* 59 (June 2004), pp. 1083–1124.

Jegadeesh, Narasimhan, and Sheridan Titman. "Returns to Buying Winners and Selling Losers: Implications for Stock Market Efficiency." *Journal of Finance* 48 (March 1993), pp. 65–91.

Jensen, Michael C. "The Performance of Mutual Funds in the Period 1945–1964." *Journal of Finance,* May 1968.

———. "Risk, the Pricing of Capital Assets, and the Evaluation of Investment Portfolios." *Journal of Business* 42 (April 1969), pp. 167–247.

Kahneman, D., and A. Tversky. "Subjective Probability: A Judgment of Representativeness." *Cognitive Psychology* 3 (1972), pp. 430–54.

———. "On the Psychology of Prediction." *Psychology Review* 80 (1973), pp. 237–51.

Keim, Donald B. "Size Related Anomalies and Stock Return Seasonality: Further Empirical Evidence." *Journal of Financial Economics* 12 (June 1983), pp. 13–32.

Keim, Donald B., and Robert F. Stambaugh. "Predicting Returns in the Stock and Bond Markets." *Journal of Financial Economics* 17 (1986), pp. 357–90.

Kendall, Maurice. "The Analysis of Economic Time Series, Part I: Prices." *Journal of the Royal Statistical Society* 96 (1953), pp. 11–25.

Kopcke, Richard W., and Geoffrey R. H. Woglom. "Regulation Q and Savings Bank Solvency—The Connecticut Experience." In *The Regulation of Financial Institutions,* Federal Reserve Bank of Boston Conference Series, No. 21, 1979.

Kosowski, R.; A. Timmermann; R. Wermers; and H. White. "Can Mutual Fund 'Stars' Really Pick Stocks? New Evidence from a Bootstrap Analysis." *Journal of Finance* 61 (December 2006), pp. 2551–95.

Kothari, S. P.; Jay Shanken; and Richard G. Sloan. "Another Look at the Cross-Section of Expected Stock Returns." *Journal of Finance* 50 (March 1995), pp. 185–224.

Lakonishok, Josef; Andrei Shleifer; and Robert W. Vishny. "Contrarian Investment, Extrapolation, and Risk." *Journal of Finance* 50 (1995), pp. 1541–78.

Lamont, O. A., and R. H. Thaler. "Can the Market Add and Subtract? Mispricing in Tech Carve-touts." *Journal of Political Economy* 111 (2003), pp. 227–68.

La Porta, Raphael. "Expectations and the Cross-Section of Stock Returns." *Journal of Finance* 51 (December 1996), pp. 1715–42.

Latane, H. A., and C. P. Jones. "Standardized Unexpected Earnings—1971–1977." *Journal of Finance,* June 1979.

Lease, R.; W. Lewellen; and G. Schlarbaum. "Market Segmentation: Evidence on the Individual Investor." *Financial Analysts Journal* 32 (1976), pp. 53–60.

Lee, C. M.; A. Shleifer; and R. H. Thaler. "Investor Sentiment and the Closed-End Fund Puzzle." *Journal of Finance* 46 (March 1991), pp. 75–109.

Lehmann, Bruce. "Fads, Martingales and Market Efficiency." *Quarterly Journal of Economics* 105 (February 1990), pp. 1–28.

Levy, Robert A. "The Predictive Significance of Five-Point Chart Patterns." *Journal of Business* 44 (July 1971), pp. 316–23.

Liebowitz, Martin L., and Alfred Weinberger. "Contingent Immunization—Part I: Risk Control Procedure." *Financial Analysts Journal* 38 (November–December 1982).

Lo, Andrew W., and Craig MacKinlay. "Stock Market Prices Do Not Follow Random Walks: Evidence from a Simple Specification Test." *Review of Financial Studies* 1 (Spring 1988), pp. 41–66.

Loeb, T. F. "Trading Cost: The Critical Link between Investment Information and Results." *Financial Analysts Journal,* May–June 1983.

Longin, F., and B. Solnik. "Is the Correlation in International Equity Returns Constant: 1960–1990?" *Journal of International Money and Finance* 14 (1995), pp. 3–26.

Lynch, Peter, with John Rothchild. *One Up on Wall Street.* New York: Penguin Books, 1989.

Macaulay, Frederick. *Some Theoretical Problems Suggested by the Movements of Interest Rates, Bond Yields, and Stock Prices in the United States since 1856.* New York: National Bureau of Economic Research, 1938.

Malkiel, Burton G. "Expectations, Bond Prices, and the Term Structure of Interest Rates." *Quarterly Journal of Economics* 76 (May 1962), pp. 197–218.

———. "Returns from Investing in Equity Mutual Funds: 1971–1991." *Journal of Finance* 50 (June 1995), pp. 549–72.

Marcus, Alan J. "The Magellan Fund and Market Efficiency." *Journal of Portfolio Management* 17 (Fall 1990), pp. 85–88.

Mayers, David. "Nonmarketable Assets and Capital Market Equilibrium under Uncertainty." In *Studies in the Theory of Capital Markets,* ed. M. C. Jensen. New York: Praeger, 1972.

McDonald, Robert L. *Derivative Markets,* 2nd ed. Boston: Addison-Wesley, 2005.

Merton, Robert C. "Theory of Rational Option Pricing." *Bell Journal of Economics and Management Science* 4 (Spring 1973), pp. 141–83.

———. "On Market Timing and Investment Performance: An Equilibrium Theory of Value for Market Forecasts." *Journal of Business* 54 (July 1981).

———. "A Simple Model of Capital Market Equilibrium with Incomplete Information." *Journal of Finance* 42 (1987), pp. 483–510.

Miller, Merton H., and Myron Scholes. "Rate of Return in Relation to Risk: A Re-examination of Some Recent Findings." In *Studies in the Theory of Capital Markets,* ed. Michael C. Jensen. New York: Praeger, 1972.

Modigliani, Franco, and M. Miller. "The Cost of Capital, Corporation Finance, and the Theory of Investment." *American Economic Review,* June 1958.

———. "Dividend Policy, Growth, and the Valuation of Shares." *Journal of Business,* October 1961.

Morrell, John A. "Introduction to International Equity Diversification." In *International Investing for U.S. Pension Funds,* Institute for Fiduciary Education, London/Venice, May 6–13, 1989.

Niederhoffer, Victor, and Patrick Regan. "Earnings Changes, Analysts' Forecasts, and Stock Prices." *Financial Analysts Journal,* May–June 1972.

Norby, W. C. "Applications of Inflation-Adjusted Accounting Data." *Financial Analysts Journal,* March–April 1983.

Odean, T. "Are Investors Reluctant to Realize Their Losses?" *Journal of Finance* 53 (1998), pp. 1775–98.

Patel, J. M., and M. A. Wolfson. "The Intraday Speed of Adjustment of Stock Prices to Earnings and Dividend Announcements." *Journal of Financial Economics* 13 (June 1984), pp. 223–52.

Perold, André. "Fundamentally Flawed Indexing." HBS mimeo, January 2007.

Perry, Kevin, and Robert A. Taggart. "The Growing Role of Junk Bonds in Corporate Finance." *Continental Bank Journal of Applied Corporate Finance* 1 (Spring 1988).

Pontiff, Jeffrey. "Closed-End Fund Premia and Returns Implications for Financial Market Equilibrium." *Journal of Financial Economics* 37 (1995), pp. 341–70.

———. "Costly Arbitrage: Evidence from Closed-End Funds." *Quarterly Journal of Economics* 111 (November 1996), pp. 1135–51.

Porter, Michael E. *Competitive Advantage: Creating and Sustaining Superior Performance.* New York: Free Press, 1985.

———. *Competitive Strategy: Techniques for Analyzing Industries and Competitors.* New York: Free Press, 1980.

Poterba, James M., and Lawrence Summers. "Mean Reversion in Stock Market Prices: Evidence and Implications." *Journal of Financial Economics* 22 (1988), pp. 27–59.

Rau, P. R.; O. Dimitrov; and M. Cooper. "A Rose.com by Any Other Name." *Journal of Finance* 56 (2001), pp. 2371–88.

Ready, Mark J. "Profits from Technical Trading Rules." *Financial Management* 31 (Autumn 2002), pp. 43–62.

Redington, F. M. "Review of the Principle of Life-Office Valuations." *Journal of the Institute of Actuaries* 78 (1952), pp. 286–340.

Reinganum, Marc R. "The Anatomy of a Stock Market Winner." *Financial Analysts Journal,* March–April 1988, pp. 272–84.

———. "The Anomalous Stock Market Behavior of Small Firms in January: Empirical Tests for Tax-Loss Effects." *Journal of Financial Economics* 12 (June 1983), pp. 89–104.

Rendleman, Richard J., Jr.; Charles P. Jones; and Henry A. Latané. "Empirical Anomalies Based on Unexpected Earnings and the Importance of Risk Adjustments." *Journal of Financial Economics* 10 (November 1982), pp. 269–87.

Ritter, Jay R. "The Buying and Selling Behavior of Individual Investors at the Turn of the Year." *Journal of Finance* 43 (July 1988), pp. 701–17.

Roberts, Harry. "Stock Market 'Patterns' and Financial Analysis: Methodological Suggestions." *Journal of Finance* 14 (March 1959), pp. 11–25.

Roll, Richard. "A Critique of the Capital Asset Theory Tests: Part I: On Past and Potential Testability of the Theory." *Journal of Financial Economics* 4 (1977).

———. "The International Crash of October 1987." *Financial Analysts Journal,* September–October 1988.

Ross, Stephen A. "Neoclassical Finance, Alternative Finance and the Closed End Fund Puzzle." *European Financial Management* 8 (2002), pp. 129–37, **ssrn.com/abstract = 313444.**

———. "Return, Risk and Arbitrage." In *Risk and Return in Finance,* ed. I. Friend and J. Bicksler. Cambridge, MA: Ballinger, 1976.

Rubinstein, Mark. "Implied Binomial Trees." *Journal of Finance* 49 (July 1994), pp. 771–818.

Samuelson, Paul. "The Judgment of Economic Science on Rational Portfolio Management." *Journal of Portfolio Management* 16 (Fall 1989), pp. 4–12.

Schleifer, Andrei. *Inefficient Markets.* New York: Oxford University Press, 2000.

Schleifer, Andrei, and Robert Vishny. "Equilibrium Short Horizons of Investors and Firms." *American Economic Review* 80 (May 1990), pp. 148–53.

———. "The Limits of Arbitrage." *Journal of Finance* 52 (March 1997), pp. 35–55.

Seyhun, H. Nejat. "Insiders' Profits, Costs of Trading and Market Efficiency." *Journal of Financial Economics* 16 (1986), pp. 189–212.

Sharpe, William F. "Mutual Fund Performance." *Journal of Business* 39 (January 1966).

———. "A Simplified Model for Portfolio Analysis." *Management Science* IX (January 1963), pp. 277–93.

Shefrin, Hersh. *Beyond Greed and Fear.* Boston: Harvard Business School Press, 2002.

Shefrin, Hersh, and Meir Statman. "The Disposition to Sell Winners Too Early and Ride Losers Too Long: Theory and Evidence." *Journal of Finance* 40 (July 1985), pp. 777–90.

Shiller, Robert. "Do Stock Prices Move Too Much to Be Justified by Subsequent Changes in Dividends?" *American Economic Review* 71 (June 1981).

Solnik, B. *International Investing,* 4th ed. Reading, MA: Addison-Wesley, 1999.

Solnik, Bruno, and A. De Freitas. "International Factors of Stock Price Behavior." CESA Working Paper, February 1986 (cited in Bruno Solnik, *International Investments.* Reading, MA: Addison-Wesley, 1988).

Speidell, Lawrence S., and Vinod Bavishi. "GAAP Arbitrage: Valuation Opportunities in International Accounting Standards." *Financial Analysts Journal,* November–December 1992, pp. 58–66.

Statman, Meir. "Behavioral Finance." *Contemporary Finance Digest* 1 (Winter 1997), pp. 5–22.

Stickel, Scott E. "The Effect of Value Line Investment Survey Rank Changes on Common Stock Prices." *Journal of Financial Economics* 14 (1986), pp. 121–44.

Thaler, Richard H. *The Winner's Curse.* Princeton, NJ: Princeton University Press, 1992.

———. *Advances in Behavioral Finance.* New York: Russell Sage Foundation, 1993.

Thompson, Rex. "The Information Content of Discounts and Premiums on Closed-End Fund Shares." *Journal of Financial Economics* 6 (1978), pp. 151–86.

Tobin, James. "Liquidity Preference as Behavior toward Risk." *Review of Economic Studies* XXVI (February 1958), pp. 65–86.

Treynor, Jack L. "How to Rate Management Investment Funds." *Harvard Business Review* 43 (January–February 1966).

Treynor, Jack L., and Kay Mazuy. "Can Mutual Funds Outguess the Market?" *Harvard Business Review* 43 (July–August 1966).

Treynor, Jack, and Fischer Black. "How to Use Security Analysis to Improve Portfolio Selection." *Journal of Business* 46 (January 1973).

Trippi, Robert R., and Duane Desieno. "Trading Equity Index Futures with Neural Networks." *Journal of Portfolio Management* 19 (Fall 1992).

Trippi, Robert R.; Duane Desieno; and Efraim Turban, eds. *Neural Networks in Finance and Investing.* Chicago: Probus, 1993.

Wallace, A. "Is Beta Dead?" *Institutional Investor* 14 (July 1980), pp. 22–30.

Whaley, Robert E. "Valuation of American Call Options on Dividend-Paying Stocks: Empirical Tests." *Journal of Financial Economics* 10 (1982), pp. 29–58.

Wiggins, J. B. "Option Values under Stochastic Volatilities." *Journal of Financial Economics* 19 (1987), pp. 351–72.

Womack, K. L. "Do Brokerage Analysts' Recommendations Have Investment Value?" *Journal of Finance* 51 (March 1996), pp. 137–67.

REFERENCES TO CFA QUESTIONS

Each end-of-chapter CFA question is reprinted with permission from the CFA Institute, Charlottesville, Virginia.[1] Following is a list of the CFA questions in the end-of-chapter material and the exams/study guides from which they were taken and updated.

Chapter 2

2. 1986 Level II CFA Study Guide, © 1986.

Chapter 3

1. 1986 Level I CFA Study Guide, © 1986.
19–21. 1986 Level I CFA Study Guide, © 1986.

Chapter 5

1–3. 1998 Level I CFA Study Guide, © 1998.
6–8. 1991 Level I CFA Study Guide, © 1991.
9–13. 1993 Level I CFA Study Guide, © 1993.
25. 1993 Level I CFA Study Guide, © 1993.

Chapter 6

1. 1998 Level I CFA Study Guide, © 1998.
2. 2001 Level III CFA Study Guide, © 2001.
5. 2001 Level II CFA Study Guide, © 2001.
22–24. 1982 Level III CFA Study Guide, © 1982.
26. 2000 Level II CFA Study Guide, © 2000.

Chapter 7

1. 1998 Level I CFA Study Guide, © 1998.
2. 2000 Level II CFA Study Guide, © 2000.
22. 2002 Level II CFA Study Guide, © 2002.
30. 2001 Level II CFA Study Guide, © 2001.
32–41. Various CFA exams.

Chapter 8

6–10. 1993 Level I CFA Study Guide, © 1993.
11. 1998 Level I CFA Study Guide, © 1998.
12. 1981 Level I CFA Study Guide, © 1981.
13. 1989 Level III CFA Study Guide, © 1989.
19. 1996 Level III CFA Study Guide, © 1996.

27. 1996 Level III CFA Study Guide, © 1996.
28. 1996 Level III CFA Study Guide, © 1996.

Chapter 9

1. 2000 Level III CFA Study Guide, © 2000.
2. 2001 Level III CFA Study Guide, © 2001.
3. 2004 Level III CFA Study Guide, © 2004.
4. 2003 Level III CFA Study Guide, © 2003.
5. 2002 Level III CFA Study Guide, © 2002.

Chapter 10

6. 1998 Level I CFA Study Guide, © 1998.
20. 1999 Level II CFA Study Guide, © 1999.
31. 1994 Level I CFA Study Guide, © 1994.
33. 1992 Level II CFA Study Guide, © 1992.
34. 1993 Level I CFA Study Guide, © 1993.
39. From various CFA exams.

Chapter 11

7. 1985 Level I CFA Study Guide, © 1985.
8. 1985 Level I CFA Study Guide, © 1985.
16. 1992 Level II CFA Study Guide, © 1992.
20. 1983 Level III CFA Study Guide, © 1983.
21. 2001 Level II CFA Study Guide, © 2001.
22. 2003 Level II CFA Study Guide, © 2003.
23. 2004 Level II CFA Study Guide, © 2004.
24. From various CFA exams.
25–28. 1983 Level III CFA Study Guide, © 1983.

Chapter 12

13. 1995 Level II CFA Study Guide, © 1995.
14. 1993 Level II CFA Study Guide, © 1993.
15. 1993 Level II CFA Study Guide, © 1993.
16. 1998 Level II CFA Study Guide, © 1998.
18. 2004 Level II CFA Study Guide, © 2004
19. From various CFA exams.

Chapter 13

2. 1998 Level I CFA Study Guide, © 1998.
7. 1995 Level II CFA Study Guide, © 1995.
12. 1987 Level I CFA Study Guide, © 1987.
15. 2001 Level II CFA Study Guide, © 2001.

[1]The CFA Institute does not endorse, promote, review, or warrant the accuracy of the product or services offered by The McGraw-Hill Companies.

16. 1994 Level II CFA Study Guide, © 1994.
18. 2003 Level I CFA Study Guide, © 2003.
19. 2003 Level I CFA Study Guide, © 2003.
20. 2003 Level II CFA Study Guide, © 2003.
23. 2001 Level II CFA Study Guide, © 2001.
24. 2001 Level II CFA Study Guide, © 2001.
25. 2001 Level II CFA Study Guide, © 2001.

Chapter 14

3. 2002 Level II CFA Study Guide, © 2002
4. 1988 Level I CFA Study Guide, © 1988.
7. 1998 Level II CFA Study Guide, © 1998.
9. 1992 Level I CFA Study Guide, © 1992.
10. 1987 Level I CFA Study Guide, © 1987.
11–14. From various CFA exams.
15. 1999 Level II CFA Study Guide, © 1999.
18. 1998 Level II CFA Study Guide, © 1998.
19. 1998 Level II CFA Study Guide, © 1998.

Chapter 15

1. 1984 Level III CFA Study Guide, © 1984.
15. 2000 Level II CFA Study Guide, © 2000.
18. 1984 Level III CFA Study Guide, © 1984.
22. 2001 Level II CFA Study Guide, © 2001.
23. 2002 Level II CFA Study Guide, © 2002.
25. 2002 Level II CFA Study Guide, © 2002

Chapter 16

25. 2000 Level I CFA Study Guide, © 2000.
31. 2000 Level II CFA Study Guide, © 2000.

Chapter 17

1–3. 1998 Level I CFA Study Guide, © 1998.
11. 1982 Level III CFA Study Guide, © 1982.
16. 2004 Level II CFA Study Guide, © 2004.
17. 1986 Level III CFA Study Guide, © 1986.
20. 2000 Level II CFA Study Guide, © 2000.
29. 1993 Level I CFA Study Guide, © 1993.
31. 2000 Level III Study Guide, © 2000

Chapter 18

1–3. From various CFA exams.
10. 1981 Level I Study Guide, © 1981.
12. 1981 Level I Study Guide, © 1981.
15. 2000 Level I Study Guide, © 2000.

Chapter 19

7. 1986 Level III Study Guide, © 1986.
11. 1986 Level III Study Guide, © 1986.
12. 1991 Level II Study Guide, © 1991.
13. 1998 Level II Study Guide, © 1998.

Chapter 21

1. 1988 Level I CFA Study Guide, © 1988.
2. 1988 Level I CFA Study Guide, © 1988.
3. From various CFA exams.
4. From various CFA exams.
5. 1981 Level II CFA Study Guide, © 1981.
6. 1985 Level III CFA Study Guide, © 1985.
7. 1988 Level I CFA Study Guide, © 1988.
8. 1982 Level III CFA Study Guide, © 1982.
9–12. From various CFA exams.

INDEX

Entries in **bold** indicate a definition on that page. Page numbers with n indicate material found in notes.

Useful Formulas

Measures of Risk

Variance of returns: $\sigma^2 = \sum_s p(s)[r(s) - E(r)]^2$

Standard deviation: $\sigma = \sqrt{\sigma^2}$

Covariance between returns:
$$\text{Cov}(r_i, r_j) = \sum_s p(s)[r_i(s) - E(r_i)]\,[r_j(s) - E(r_j)]$$

Beta of security i: $\beta_i = \dfrac{\text{Cov}(r_i, r_M)}{\text{Var}(r_M)}$

Portfolio Theory

Expected rate of return on a portfolio with weights w_i in each security:
$$E(r_p) = \sum_{i=1}^{n} w_i E(r_i)$$

Variance of portfolio rate of return:
$$\sigma_p^2 = \sum_{j=1}^{n} \sum_{i=1}^{n} w_j w_i \text{Cov}(r_i, r_j)$$

Market Equilibrium

The security market line: $E(r_i) = r_f + \beta_i[E(r_M) - r_f]$

Fixed-Income Analysis

Present value of $1:

Discrete period compounding: $\text{PV} = 1/(1 + r)^T$

Continuous compounding: $\text{PV} = e^{-rT}$

Forward rate of interest for period T: $f_T = \dfrac{(1 + y_T)^T}{(1 + y_{T-1})^{T-1}} - 1$

Real interest rate: $r = \dfrac{1 + R}{1 + i} - 1$

where R is the nominal interest rate and i is the inflation rate

Duration of a security: $D = \sum_{t=1}^{T} t \times \dfrac{CF_t}{(1 + y)^t} \big/ \text{Price}$

Modified duration: $D^* = D/(1 + y)$